De Gruyter Lexikon
Medieval Oral Literature

# Medieval Oral Literature

Edited by
Karl Reichl

De Gruyter

Cover illustration: Title-page of *Varie canzoni alla villotta in lingua pauana*, Misc. 2213.9 (16th c.) of the Biblioteca Nazionale Marciana (Venice). Reproduced with permission of the Ministerio dei Beni e delle Attività Culturali e del Turismo – Biblioteca Nazionale Marciana. Divieto di riproduzione / Unauthorized reproduction prohibited.

ISBN (Paperback): 978-3-11-044761-3
ISBN (Hardcover): 978-3-11-018934-6
e-ISBN: 978-3-11-024112-9

**Library of Congress Cataloging-in-Publication Data**
A CIP catalog record for this book has been applied for at the Library of Congress.

**Bibliographic information published by the Deutsche Nationalbibliothek**
The Deutsche Nationalbibliothek lists this publication in the Deutsche Nationalbibliografie; detailed bibliographic data are available on the Internet at http://dnb.dnb.de.

© 2016 Walter de Gruyter GmbH, Berlin/Boston
Typesetting: epline, Kirchheim unter Teck
Printing and binding: CPI books GmbH, Leck
♾ Printed on acid-free paper
Printed in Germany

www.degruyter.com

# Contents

List of Contributors. . . . . . . . . . . . . . . . . . . . . . . . . . . . . . . . . . . XV
Preface . . . . . . . . . . . . . . . . . . . . . . . . . . . . . . . . . . . . . . . . . . . . XVII
Abbreviations. . . . . . . . . . . . . . . . . . . . . . . . . . . . . . . . . . . . . . . XIX
Note on Transliteration . . . . . . . . . . . . . . . . . . . . . . . . . . . . . . . XXI

## INTRODUCTION

1  Plotting the Map of Medieval Oral Literature . . . . . . . . . . . . . . . . . . . . 3
   KARL REICHL

## PART I: CONCEPTS AND APPROACHES

2  Oral Theory and Medieval Literature . . . . . . . . . . . . . . . . . . . . . . . 71
   JOHN MILES FOLEY AND PETER RAMEY

3  The Written Word in Context: The Early Middle Ages . . . . . . . . . . . . . . 103
   MICHAEL RICHTER

4  Orality and Literacy: The Case of Anglo-Saxon England . . . . . . . . . . . . . 121
   KATHERINE O'BRIEN O'KEEFFE

5  Performance and Performers . . . . . . . . . . . . . . . . . . . . . . . . . . . 141
   JOSEPH HARRIS AND KARL REICHL

6  Oral Poetics: The Linguistics and Stylistics of Orality . . . . . . . . . . . . . . . 203
   THOMAS A. DUBOIS

7  Oral Literature, Ritual, and the Dialectics of Performance . . . . . . . . . . . . 225
   PANAGIOTIS ROILOS

## PART II: TRADITIONS AND GENRES

8  Older Germanic Poetry, with a Note on the Icelandic Sagas . . . . . . . . . . . 253
   JOSEPH HARRIS

9  Oral Tradition and Performance in Medieval Ireland . . . . . . . . . . . . . . . 279
   JOSEPH FALAKY NAGY

10  Medieval German Literature: Literacy, Orality and Semi-Orality ......... 295
    JAN-DIRK MÜLLER

11  Middle English Romances and the Oral Tradition .................. 335
    AD PUTTER

12  The *Chanson de geste* and Orality ............................. 353
    DOMINIQUE BOUTET

13  The Italian *Cantari* between Orality and Writing ................. 371
    RAFFAELE MORABITO

14  Court Poetry, Village Verse: Romanian Oral Epic in the Medieval World .... 387
    MARGARET H. BEISSINGER

15  Hispanic Epic and Ballad .................................... 411
    ROGER WRIGHT

16  The Late-Medieval Ballad .................................... 429
    THOMAS PETTITT

17  Medieval Greek Epic Poetry .................................. 459
    ELIZABETH JEFFREYS

18  The *Song of Igor* and its Medieval Context in Russian Oral Poetry ........ 485
    S. N. AZBELEV

19  Oral Traditions in a Literate Society:
    The Hebrew Literature of the Middle Ages ...................... 499
    ELI YASSIF

20  Woman's Song in Medieval Western Europe ..................... 521
    ANNE L. KLINCK

21  Popular Song and the Middle English Lyric ...................... 555
    KARIN BOKLUND-LAGOPOULOU

22  The Pastourelle as a Popular Genre ............................ 581
    LUCILLA SPETIA

23  Andalusī-Arabic Strophic Poetry as an Example of Literary Hybridization:
    Ibn Quzmān's 'Zajal 147' (The Poet's Reluctant Repentance) ........... 601
    JAMES T. MONROE

24 Orality and the Tradition of Arabic Epic Storytelling . . . . . . . . . . . . . . . . 629
   THOMAS HERZOG

25 Orality in Medieval Persian Literature . . . . . . . . . . . . . . . . . . . . . . . . . 653
   JULIA RUBANOVICH

26 Medieval Turkish Epic and Popular Narrative . . . . . . . . . . . . . . . . . . . . 681
   KARL REICHL

27 Dramatic Pastime, Custom and Entertainment . . . . . . . . . . . . . . . . . . . 701
   THOMAS PETTITT

Notes on the Illustrations . . . . . . . . . . . . . . . . . . . . . . . . . . . . . . . . . . . . . 725

Index . . . . . . . . . . . . . . . . . . . . . . . . . . . . . . . . . . . . . . . . . . . . . . . . . . 729

# Detailed Chapter Contents

## Introduction

1 Plotting the Map of Medieval Oral Literature . . . . . . . . . . . . . . . . . . . 3
  Karl Reichl
  1 Confines of Time and Place . . . . . . . . . . . . . . . . . . . . . . . . . . . . 4
    1.1 Confines of Time . . . . . . . . . . . . . . . . . . . . . . . . . . . . . . 5
    1.2 Confines of Place. . . . . . . . . . . . . . . . . . . . . . . . . . . . . . 6
  2 Orality and Literacy. . . . . . . . . . . . . . . . . . . . . . . . . . . . . . . . . 8
    2.1 Textualization . . . . . . . . . . . . . . . . . . . . . . . . . . . . . . . . 8
    2.2 Litteratus / illitteratus . . . . . . . . . . . . . . . . . . . . . . . . . . . 10
    2.3 Orality vs. Literacy . . . . . . . . . . . . . . . . . . . . . . . . . . . . . 11
    2.4 Beyond Verbal Art . . . . . . . . . . . . . . . . . . . . . . . . . . . . . 13
  3 Traces of Orality in the Written Text . . . . . . . . . . . . . . . . . . . . . 16
    3.1 Oral Theory and Neotraditionalism . . . . . . . . . . . . . . . . . . 16
    3.2 Aurality . . . . . . . . . . . . . . . . . . . . . . . . . . . . . . . . . . . . . 17
    3.3 Reading Aloud . . . . . . . . . . . . . . . . . . . . . . . . . . . . . . . . 18
    3.4 Fictitious Orality . . . . . . . . . . . . . . . . . . . . . . . . . . . . . . 20
    3.5 Variability. . . . . . . . . . . . . . . . . . . . . . . . . . . . . . . . . . . 21
  4 Oral Tradition . . . . . . . . . . . . . . . . . . . . . . . . . . . . . . . . . . . . 22
    4.1 Oral Tradition: Training . . . . . . . . . . . . . . . . . . . . . . . . . 23
    4.2 Remembering vs. Memorizing. . . . . . . . . . . . . . . . . . . . . . 25
    4.3 Oral Composition . . . . . . . . . . . . . . . . . . . . . . . . . . . . . 29
  5 Oral Literature and Genre. . . . . . . . . . . . . . . . . . . . . . . . . . . . . 31
    5.1 Smaller Genres and 'niedere Dichtung' . . . . . . . . . . . . . . . . 33
    5.2 The Case of Slavic Epic Poetry . . . . . . . . . . . . . . . . . . . . . 33
    5.3 Epic and Romance . . . . . . . . . . . . . . . . . . . . . . . . . . . . . 38
  6 Orality, Folksong and Medieval Lyrics . . . . . . . . . . . . . . . . . . . . 40
    6.1 Folksong . . . . . . . . . . . . . . . . . . . . . . . . . . . . . . . . . . . . 41
    6.2 Folksong Collecting and Medieval Lyrics . . . . . . . . . . . . . . 43
    6.3 Refrains. . . . . . . . . . . . . . . . . . . . . . . . . . . . . . . . . . . . . 45
    6.4 Popular Voices from the Iberian Peninsula . . . . . . . . . . . . . 46
  7 Conclusion . . . . . . . . . . . . . . . . . . . . . . . . . . . . . . . . . . . . . . 52

## Part I: Concepts and Approaches

2 Oral Theory and Medieval Literature . . . . . . . . . . . . . . . . . . . . . . . 71
  John Miles Foley and Peter Ramey

|  |  | 1 | Origins and Early History ............................... 72 |
|---|---|---|---|

      1   Origins and Early History ............................... 72
          1.1  The Homeric Question .............................. 72
          1.2  Philology ......................................... 73
          1.3  Anthropology...................................... 74
          1.4  Milman Parry and Albert Lord...................... 75
          1.5  A Third Stage of Development..................... 78
      2   Recent Contributions .................................. 79
          2.1  Expanding the Traditional Formula................. 80
          2.2  Comparative Approaches .......................... 83
          2.3  Middle English Literature ......................... 86
          2.4  Manuscript Transmission .......................... 89
          2.5  Performance and Reception........................ 90
      3   Opportunities for the Future............................ 94
          3.1  Comparative Studies and Diversity ................ 94
          3.2  Aesthetics and Verbal Art ......................... 95
          3.3  Digital and Web-Based Interventions............... 96

3   The Written Word in Context: The Early Middle Ages ............... 103
    Michael Richter
      1   The Medieval 'Latin Church' and its Implications ............ 105
      2   Latin Europe........................................... 107
      3   Beyond Latin Europe .................................. 109
          3.1  Ireland ............................................ 110
          3.2  Britain ............................................ 111
      4   The Carolingian Interlude .............................. 112
      5   Glimpses of Oral Culture............................... 114
          5.1  Ireland ............................................ 114
          5.2  Wales.............................................. 115
          5.3  The Carolingian World ........................... 116
          5.4  The Continental Saxons........................... 117

4   Orality and Literacy: The Case of Anglo-Saxon England ............. 121
    Katherine O'Brien O'Keeffe
      1   Bede and the Uses of Orality and Literacy .................. 122
      2   The Literacies of King Alfred ........................... 127
      3   Reading, Speaking, and Remembering
          in the Late Anglo-Saxon Classroom ..................... 134

5   Performance and Performers ................................. 141
    Joseph Harris and Karl Reichl
      1   Performance and Medieval Performance: General Model ............ 142
      2   Performance and Performers in the Early Middle Ages ............. 146
          2.1  The Performance of Skaldic Poetry ................. 150
          2.2  The Performance of Eddic Verse.................... 155
          2.3  West Germanic Oral Performance, with a Note on Celtic ........ 157

|  |  | 2.4 The Problem of Music ............................. | 163 |
|---|---|---|---|
|  | 3 | Performance and Performers in the High and Late Middle Ages....... | 166 |
|  |  | 3.1 The Medieval Entertainer: Functions, Sources, Terms .......... | 168 |
|  |  | 3.2 Repertoire ................................... | 176 |
|  |  | 3.3. Performer, Transmitter, Poet...................... | 180 |
|  |  | 3.4 Performance Modes and Audience Interaction .............. | 184 |

6 Oral Poetics: The Linguistics and Stylistics of Orality ................. 203
THOMAS A. DUBOIS

    1 Breakthrough into Performance ........................... 204
    2 The Formal Markers of Breakthrough ...................... 205
    3 Mnemonic Anchors and Poetic Form....................... 214
    4 Mnemonic Anchoring through Content...................... 219
    5 From Anchors to Attractors............................ 220
    6 Acts of Composition ................................ 221

7 Oral Literature, Ritual, and the Dialectics of Performance ............. 225
PANAGIOTIS ROILOS

    1 Oral Traditional Literature: Comparative Perspectives ............... 225
    2 Oral Literature in the Middle Ages:
       Beyond Polarizing Schemata and Scholarly Preconceptions .......... 229
    3 Performability in Medieval and Early Modern Literature............. 233
    4 Ritual Poetics and Performance ......................... 238

## PART II: TRADITIONS AND GENRES

8 Older Germanic Poetry, with a Note on the Icelandic Sagas ............. 253
JOSEPH HARRIS

    1 Oral Literature and Writing ........................... 254
    2 'New' Comparative Poetics ............................ 257
       2.1 Ordering Affinity............................. 257
       2.2 Renewing Poetics............................. 260
       2.3 The Role of Metrics............................ 261
    3 'Old' Comparative Literature........................... 263
       3.1 Heroic Legend and its Realizations..................... 263
       3.2 Old Germanic Genres........................... 268
    4 A Note on the Icelandic Sagas .......................... 272

9 Oral Tradition and Performance in Medieval Ireland ................. 279
JOSEPH FALAKY NAGY

10 Medieval German Literature: Literacy, Orality and Semi-Orality ......... 295
JAN-DIRK MÜLLER

    1 The Semi-Oral Culture of the German Middle Ages ............... 295

  1.1 Orality vs. Literacy, Latin vs. the Vernacular................ 295
  1.2 'Literature' under Oral Conditions:
    Verse – Rhyme – Strophe – Formula..................... 298
 2 Periods................................................ 302
  2.1 The Early Middle Ages................................ 302
  2.2 The High Middle Ages................................ 304
  2.3 The Late Middle Ages................................ 308
 3 Genres................................................. 310
  3.1 Heroic Epic......................................... 311
  3.2 Sangspruchdichtung.................................. 319
  3.3 Minnesang / Lied.................................... 321
  3.4 Religious and Secular Drama.......................... 325
 4 Conclusion............................................. 328

11 Middle English Romances and the Oral Tradition ............... 335
  AD PUTTER

12 The *Chanson de geste* and Orality ............................ 353
  DOMINIQUE BOUTET

 1 The Conditions of Oral Communication..................... 353
 2 The Style of the *Chansons de geste* and Orality ............. 355
 3 The Discussion of the Theory of Improvisation................ 359
 4 An Aesthetics of the Voice................................ 362
 5 Orality and the History of the Genre ....................... 366

13 The Italian *Cantari* between Orality and Writing ................ 371
  RAFFAELE MORABITO

14 Court Poetry, Village Verse: Romanian Oral Epic in the Medieval World .... 387
  MARGARET H. BEISSINGER

 1 Story in Song: The Imagined Past .......................... 389
 2 Early Epic: The Heroic Age ............................... 391
 3 Epic in Medieval Manuscripts: Travel Accounts and Chronicles........ 394
 4 Epic Songs Move to the Villages and Towns..................... 400
 5 Oral Epic: Transcribed Texts and Ethnographic Findings............ 402
 6 Conclusion............................................. 405
 7 Additional Commentary on the Music and Instruments
  of Romanian Epic ...................................... 406

15 Hispanic Epic and Ballad .................................... 411
  ROGER WRIGHT

 1 Ballads................................................ 411
 2 Epics.................................................. 416
 3 Scholarly Discussion of Ballads ............................ 424
 4 Scholarly Discussion of the Epic ........................... 425

*Detailed Chapter Contents* XIII

16 The Late-Medieval Ballad .................................. 429
   THOMAS PETTITT
   1 The Ballad as Narrative: Towards a Contextual Formalism .......... 430
   2 Oral Tradition: The Theories.................................. 433
   3 The Evidence................................................ 435
   4 The Oral Ballad in the Later Middle Ages....................... 449

17 Medieval Greek Epic Poetry .................................. 459
   ELIZABETH JEFFREYS
   1 Preamble.................................................... 459
   2 Medieval Greek ............................................. 460
   3 Twelfth-Century Background................................... 461
   4 *Digenis Akritis* ........................................... 463
   5 The Fourteenth Century and Oral Poetry....................... 468
   6 Epic........................................................ 476
   7 Conclusion ................................................. 476

18 The *Song of Igor* and its Medieval Context in Russian Oral Poetry ....... 485
   S. N. AZBELEV

19 Oral Traditions in a Literate Society:
   The Hebrew Literature of the Middle Ages .................... 499
   ELI YASSIF

20 Woman's Song in Medieval Western Europe .................... 521
   ANNE L. KLINCK
   1 What is Woman's Song?....................................... 521
   2 An Oral or Popular Mode?.................................... 522
   3 Defining the Parameters of Woman's Song..................... 524
   4 Medieval Terms for Woman's Songs ........................... 526
   5 Old English................................................. 527
   6 Early Celtic and Norse...................................... 528
   7 Hispano-Arabic ............................................. 529
   8 Woman's Song in a 'Latent State': Evidence from the Church ........ 531
   9 Occitan .................................................... 531
   10 Northern French............................................ 533
   11 Medieval Latin............................................. 535
   12 German .................................................... 537
   13 Italian ................................................... 540
   14 Galician-Portuguese and Castilian .......................... 541
   15 Middle English............................................. 544
   16 Mode and Gender: Markers of Author and Voice ............... 546

21 Popular Song and the Middle English Lyric .................... 555
   KARIN BOKLUND-LAGOPOULOU

   1  Orality and Literacy in England after the Norman Conquest ......... 555
   2  Types of Orality in Middle English Lyrics...................... 557
   3  Forms of Transmission: Records of Popular Song ............. 558
   4  Orality in Written Lyrics................................ 568

22 The Pastourelle as a Popular Genre............................ 581
   LUCILLA SPETIA

   Appendix: Marcabru's 'L'autrer jost' una sebissa' ................ 594

23 Andalusī-Arabic Strophic Poetry as an Example of Literary Hybridization:
   Ibn Quzmān's 'Zajal 147' (The Poet's Reluctant Repentance) .......... 601
   JAMES T. MONROE

   1  Preliminary Remarks..................................... 601
   2  The *zajal* and the Romance Tradition........................ 604
   3  Ibn Quzmān and his Literary Profile......................... 608
   4  Ibn Quzmān's 'Zajal 147'................................. 609
   5  The Chiastic Structure of 'Zajal 147' ....................... 612
   6  Concluding Remarks..................................... 620
   Appendix: Verse Passage from the *Táin Bó Cúalnge*............... 623

24 Orality and the Tradition of Arabic Epic Storytelling ............... 629
   THOMAS HERZOG

25 Orality in Medieval Persian Literature ......................... 653
   JULIA RUBANOVICH

   1  The *Shāh-nāma* and the Quest for Orality: Sources
      and their Provenance; Patterns of Composition and Transmission ...... 654
   2  The *dāstān* Genre in Medieval Persian Literature:
      Aspects of Production................................... 660
   3  Modalities of Communication.............................. 666
   4  Oral Traditional Aesthetics................................ 671

26 Medieval Turkish Epic and Popular Narrative ..................... 681
   KARL REICHL

   1  Popular 'Romance'...................................... 683
   2  *The Book of Dede Korkut* ................................. 687
   3  Epic Singers, Minstrels, Public Entertainers.................... 695

27 Dramatic Pastime, Custom and Entertainment ................... 701
   THOMAS PETTITT

   1  Textual Imperatives ..................................... 702
   2  The Role of Oral Tradition ................................ 706
   3  Elements of Improvisation ................................ 714
   4  Conclusion............................................ 719

# Contributors

S. N. AZBELEV, Institut Russkoy Literatury Rossiyskoy Akademii Nauk, Pushkinskiy Dom, St. Petersburg
MARGARET BEISSINGER, Princeton University
KARIN BOKLUND-LAGOPOULOU, Aristotle University of Thessaloniki
DOMINIQUE BOUTET, University of Paris, Sorbonne
THOMAS A. DUBOIS, University of Wisconsin, Madison
JOHN MILES FOLEY, University of Missouri, Columbia
JOSEPH HARRIS, Harvard University
THOMAS HERZOG, University of Bern
ELIZABETH JEFFREYS, University of Oxford
ANNE L. KLINCK, University of New Brunswick, Canada
JAMES T. MONROE, University of California, Berkeley
RAFFAELE MORABITO, University of L'Aquila
JAN-DIRK MÜLLER, University of Munich
JOSEPH FALAKY NAGY, University of California, Los Angeles
KATHERINE O'BRIEN O'KEEFFE, University of California, Berkeley
THOMAS PETTITT, University of Southern Denmark, Odense
AD PUTTER, University of Bristol
PETER RAMEY, University of Missouri, Columbia
KARL REICHL, University of Bonn
MICHAEL RICHTER, University of Konstanz
PANAGIOTIS ROILOS, Harvard University
JULIA RUBANOVICH, The Hebrew University, Jerusalem
LUCILLA SPETIA, University of L'Aquila
ROGER WRIGHT, University of Liverpool
ELI YASSIF, Tel-Aviv University

# Preface

In her book *Oral Poetry*, published by Cambridge University Press in 1977, Ruth Finnegan notes that oral poetry 'is not an odd or aberrant phenomenon in human culture', but 'is of common occurrence in human society, literate as well as non-literate' (p. 3). She explicitly mentions medieval European poetry in her list of oral poetry past and present. This is, of course, no surprising observation: from the days of Johann Gottfried Herder and Thomas Percy the oral background to a great deal of medieval literature has been stressed, perhaps unduly so, as later scholars have maintained in their criticism of the romantics' views on medieval poetry. With the appearance of Albert Lord's *The Singer of Tales* in 1960 a new chapter in the debate on the orality of medieval poetry, in particular epic poetry, was opened. In Lord's study of South Slavic oral epic poetry, three medieval epics were also included among those texts to which the methodology developed by Milman Parry was applied: *Beowulf*, the *Chanson de Roland*, and *Digenis Akritis*. Lord's analyses put the study of medieval oral literature on a new footing, and called forth a voluminous literature in which his suggestions were followed up and deepened, but also criticized and sometimes even rejected outright. Today, fifty years after the publication of Lord's seminal book, the scholarly debate on medieval oral literature has reached a stage in which the extremes of earlier views have been discarded and a synthesis that does justice to the many-facetted interplay of orality and literacy in the Middle Ages is possible.

The present book attempts such a synthesis. It is intended to reflect the current state of affairs in a comprehensive survey, written by an international group of twenty-five scholars, who are well-known specialists in their various fields. The comprehensive nature of this handbook is also underlined by the fact that in addition to chapters on the medieval literature of the Germanic and Romance peoples, there are also chapters on Celtic, Russian, Greek, Hispano-Arabic and Hebrew oral literature and three chapters in which medieval oral narrative poetry in Arabic, Persian and Turkish (with some modern continuations) is discussed. This will enable readers to appreciate parallels and similarities in medieval oral literature across linguistic, religious and cultural borders.

This book would not have been written had it not been for the initiative of Dr. Heiko Hartmann, who invited me to edit and write this volume in the series of the 'de Gruyter Lexikon'. I am very grateful for his suggestion and his continuing support of the project. My thanks go also to Mrs. Birgitta Zeller-Ebert, who competently steered the book through its last stages of publication. I am also indebted to all the contributors to this book; it was a great pleasure to receive their positive replies to my first inquiry and then their substantial chapters. Some of the chapters had to be translated. My thanks go to Ms. Emily Kneebone for translating chapter 10 by Jan-Dirk Müller (from German) and to Mr. Johannes von Vacano for translating chapter 13 by Raffaele Morabito (from

Italian). I acted as translator for chapters 12 by Dominique Boutet (from French), 18 by S. N. Azebelev (from Russian), 22 by Lucilla Spetia (from Italian), and 24 by Thomas Herzog (from German). All authors have read their chapters in the edited (and translated) form and are ultimately responsible for their contents. My special thanks go to Emily Kneebone, University of Cambridge. She has read and corrected all the chapters written by non-native speakers of English, including my own, and all translations. Her good judgement has helped to improve the quality of the texts greatly. I am also grateful to Ms. Astrid Schröder, M. A., who has proof-read the book not only while she was still one of my research assistants but also at a time when her work was done on an entirely voluntary basis. Finally, I would like to thank Boydell and Brewer for permission to print a poem by Marcabru in the appendix to chapter 22 from the edition by S. Gaunt, R. Harvey and L. Paterson 2000 and the various libraries, publishing houses and institutions for permission to reproduce the illustrations listed and acknowledged in the Notes on the Illustrations (pp. 725–727).

# Note on the Paperback Edition

As the editor of *Medieval Oral Literature* I am pleased and gratified with the publisher's decision to reprint the book in a paperback edition. This will make the book accessible to a wider readership and affordable to a greater number of students and scholars. I am most grateful to Ms. Maria Zucker, Project Editor of Medieval and Early Modern Studies at De Gruyter, for her encouragement and unflagging support. Sadly, two of the contributors have died since the publication of the hardback edition: Professor Michael Richter, an authority on the medieval history of the Celts and the cultural history of medieval vernaculars, and Professor John Miles Foley, the founder of the journal *Oral Tradition* and one of the most distinguished representatives of orality studies in the wake of Parry's and Lord's Oral Theory.

Bonn, November 2015                                                                                       Karl Reichl

# Abbreviations

Abbreviated titles of books are listed in the bibliography accompanying each chapter. General abbreviations (such as 'ch.' for 'chapter') and abbreviations for American States follow general scholarly practice as detailed in the *Chicago Manual of Style* and are not listed below. Remarks in square brackets (often references to other chapters in the book) are editorial. Among less familiar graphic conventions, the Tironian note '7' as an abbreviation for 'and' in Old English and Old Irish is used in some quotations.

| | |
|---|---|
| *ASE* | *Anglo-Saxon England* |
| AW | Akademie der Wissenschaften |
| AN | Akademiya Nauk |
| *BGDSL* | *Beiträge zur Geschichte der deutschen Sprache und Literatur* |
| BL | British Library |
| BnF | Bibliothèque Nationale de France |
| CCSL | Corpus Christianorum, Series Latina |
| CFMA | Classiques Français du Moyen Âge |
| CSASE | Cambridge Studies in Anglo-Saxon England |
| CSCO | Corpus Scriptorum Christianorum Orientalium |
| CNRS | Centre Nationale de la Recherche Scientifique |
| CSASE | Cambridge Studies in Anglo-Saxon England |
| CSML | Cambridge Studies in Medieval Literature |
| CUP | Cambridge University Press |
| EDAM | Early Drama, Art, and Music |
| EETS (ES) | Early English Text Society (Extra Series) |
| *GRM* | *Germanisch-romanische Monatsschrift* |
| Izd. | Izdatelstvo |
| *JAF* | *Journal of American Folklore* |
| *JAOS* | *Journal of the American Oriental Society* |
| *JEGP* | *Journal of English and Germanic Philology* |
| ME | Middle English |
| MGH | Monumenta Germaniae Historica |
| MHRA | Modern Humanities Research Association |
| MTU | Münchener Texte und Untersuchungen zur deutschen Literatur des Mittelalters |
| OE | Old English |
| ON | Old Norse |
| OS | Old Saxon |
| OUP | Oxford University Press |
| PG | Patrologia, Series Graeca |

| | |
|---|---|
| PL | Patrologia, Series Latina |
| *PMLA* | *Publications of the Modern Language Association* |
| SB | Sitzungsberichte |
| SATF | Société des Anciens Textes Français |
| WB | Wissenschaftliche Buchgesellschaft |
| *ZDMG* | *Zeitschrift der deutschen morgenländischen Gesellschaft* |
| Zs. | Zeitschrift |

# Note on Transliteration

Words and bibliographical references in languages that use non-Latin scripts have generally been transliterated For Russian the Anglicized system proposed by the U. S. Board on Geographic Names has been used, with slight modifications (-ый is transliterated as -y, -ий as -iy). For Hebrew the simplified general transliteration system advocated in the *Encyclopedia Judaica* has been chosen (adding, however, the symbol ''' for 'ayin'). Arabic, Persian and Ottoman Turkish are transliterated according to the System used in the *International Journal of Middle East Studies*. For Modern Turkish (and Uzbek), the current Latin alphabets are used. Words in Byzantine and Modern Greek are transliterated according to standard linguistic practices; in the bibliographies of chapters 7 (P. Roilos) and 17 (E. Jeffreys) the titles of books and articles are left in Greek.

# Introduction

# 1 Plotting the Map of Medieval Oral Literature

## Karl Reichl

> Come back past
> philology and kennings,
> re-enter memory ...

These lines come from Seamus Heaney's poem 'Bone Dreams'. In this poem, a 'White bone found/ on the grazing' sets in motion a train of thoughts which reach back into a distant, medieval past, 'to the scop's/ twang, the iron/ flash of consonants/ cleaving the line' (1990: 62–65). Philology is invoked to recreate this past, not in vain, it seems. Heaney, the Nobel Prize winner of 1995, set himself the philological task of making 'the scop's twang', the Anglo-Saxon singer's voice, heard again by translating the Old English epic of *Beowulf*. His translation was published in 1999 and has been hailed as a masterpiece of poetic translation. For Heaney, *Beowulf* is a poem to be heard, heard in its original Anglo-Saxon setting, but also heard when translated into Modern English. In the same year that his translation was published, a recording of Heaney's reading of his translation was also released. Heaney is right in considering *Beowulf* a poem that is firmly placed in a tradition of oral recitation. But 'the scop's twang' is only accessible to us via the written work on the manuscript leaf. This is not only true of *Beowulf*; medieval orality – in all its forms – can only be reconstructed (if at all) from the written record. Philology is indeed needed.

In medieval society many sectors of life were predominantly oral: politics, the legal system, the transmission of skills and knowledge, preaching, the art of disputation, music, and, of course, communication in general. Although some of these areas of orality will be touched upon, the focus of this book is on orality in works of verbal art. The main concern of this and the following chapters is medieval oral literature. 'Oral literature', it has been observed, is a contradiction in terms, at least if we understand 'literature' in its 'literal' sense, as something that has been written down in letters. How can something written down in letters be oral? Some scholars have therefore opted for other terms, such as 'oral poetry' or 'orature', where the objectionable term 'literature' has been removed. But how objectionable is this term? Is the literal understanding tenable? If we insist on the literal meaning of 'literature' we would have to exclude anything that has not been written down in *letters*. Chinese literature, for instance, cannot be called 'literature' in the strict, etymological sense of the word, as its writing system does not use letters but rather characters derived from pictograms.

It is a historical coincidence that English (like other European languages) uses the word 'literature' with its evident etymological connection to Latin *littera* 'letter'. It is understandable that some scholars balk at the use of the phrase 'oral literature' (e. g., Ong 1982: 10–16). In German the problem of a seemingly contradictory phrase can be avoided by using *Dichtung* instead of *Literatur*. *Dichtung* in its wider sense comprises all kinds of 'belles lettres', irrespective of their form (verse or prose) or of their medial presentation, and the expression *mündliche Dichtung* therefore raises no objections. In Turkish 'oral literature' is called *halk edebiyatı*, 'folk literature'. Turkish *edebiyat* is an Arabic loan-word (*adabīyāt*). The concept of *adabīyāt* is somewhat different from the European concept of literature; the word is a derivation from *adab*, a word with senses such as 'culture, refinement; good breeding; politeness; humaneness; belles lettres; literature'; in other words, it implies a certain level of civilized behaviour, of which literature is a part. Literature here is in fact primarily written literature. Orality and *adabīyāt* belong to different spheres of poetic activity, hence the qualification by *halk* 'folk' in *halk edebiyatı*.[1] In other languages the combination of 'oral' and 'literature', even if the latter is etymologically linked to writing, is no problem. Croatian and Serbian have the term *književnost* for 'literature', which is a derivation from *knjiga* 'book'; yet the large body of South Slavic oral poetry is quite naturally referred to as *usmena književnost* 'oral literature'. The question of the terms which are used in different languages for the kind of verbal art called 'literature' in English would make a fascinating topic for an onomasiological study. The examples given are not meant as a contribution to such a study; they are simply meant as an apology for the term 'oral literature' to those readers who find the combination of 'oral' and 'literature' somewhat contradictory.[2]

## 1 Confines of Time and Place

A book on medieval oral literature will doubtless raise certain expectations as to its contents. Taking English literature as an example, no one will expect to find information on Shakespeare's History Plays in this book, however medieval they are in their theme and in some cases also their style, nor on Chaucer's *Astrolabe*, which is medieval but neither oral (in any sense of the word) nor a work of literature. This is not to say that the concept of literature is clearly defined for the Middle Ages. As Horst Brunner has explained in his history of medieval German literature:

> While literary histories of the modern period are almost always restricted to the three central literary genres of lyric, epic and drama and leave out non-fictional literature (*Sachliteratur*) almost completely, for the history of medieval literature the so-called enlarged concept of literature is valid. This means that with the exception of charters, as far as these are restricted to the fixation of legal dealings, all preserved texts are considered; thus, in addition to the various poetic genres, also non-fictional texts (*Sachtexte*) of all kinds: religious literature ran-

---

[1] See Fähndrich 1990; compare also chapter 24 by T. Herzog in this volume.
[2] In this book the position advocated by H. M. Chadwick and Nora K. Chadwick has been adopted; they write (1932–40: I, 5, n. 1): 'Purists may perhaps object to this use of the word [literature applied to oral cultures] on the ground that etymologically it implies writing. But there is no other term available apart from cumbrous circumlocutions. Commonly we use the expression "poetry and saga"; but this is not entirely comprehensive. The reader will doubtless understand what we mean, and that is enough.' For a justification of the term 'oral literature', see also Harris 1991: 7–12.

ging from the Lord's Prayer to works of the mystics, historiographic literature, texts connected to law and medicine, even collections of glosses and vocabularies, i. e. dictionaries. (1997: 34)[3]

A number of these 'literary' forms of the wider concept of literature are of relevance to a discussion of orality: instruction was largely oral, legal matters were, at least in earlier periods, regulated orally and much of religious expression was also oral. Some of these forms will be mentioned or analysed in the following chapters. On the whole, however, it should be stressed that the three 'classic' literary genres are privileged – as they are in the majority of historical treatments of medieval literature (see further section 5 below). It is hoped that despite their vagueness, terms like 'oral' and 'literature', in conjunction with 'medieval', point to a field of enquiry that is clearly visible in its general outline, even if its borders are blurred and its internal structure in need of clarification.

## 1.1 Confines of Time

Let us first look at the time span covered by 'medieval' in this book. Textbooks on medieval European history generally begin sometime in Late Antiquity and end in the sixteenth century. The central period is presented as the time between the middle of the eighth and the middle of the fourteenth centuries, from the rise of the Carolingians to what historians call the 'crisis of the fourteenth century'. Less clearly defined are the beginning and end. The Christianization of the Roman Empire in the fourth century is described in many history books as the threshold of the Early Middle Ages (the 'Barbarian centuries'), while Humanism and the Renaissance, the invention of printing and the fall of Constantinople in 1453 are some of the catchwords for the end of our period. As with any classification, this periodization is both approximate and relative. Jacob Burckhardt begins his *Civilization of the Renaissance in Italy* in the fourteenth century (1990 [1860]), while the *Waning of the Middle Ages* is understood by Johan Huizinga as the fourteenth and fifteenth centuries in France and the Netherlands (1924 [1919]). 'Renaissance', of course, means something different north and south of the Alps, and the same consequently holds for the 'Middle Ages'.[4]

Notwithstanding such differences, there is general consensus on the confines of the Middle Ages in the 'Latin West', in the countries of western, northern, central and southern Europe which adopted Christianity in its Roman, Latin form. In eastern and south-eastern Europe, Christianity in its Greek Orthodox form predominated. The Byzantine period is by and large coterminous with the Western medieval period, extending as it does from the time of Constantine to the fall of Constantinople. In other areas of the Orthodox Church, however, the time frame of the Middle Ages is differently defined. This is particularly true of Russia, which was under Mongol-Tatar domination for centuries and which emerged into the post-medieval world only at the beginning of

---

[3] Unless indicated otherwise, all translations of quotations from primary and secondary sources are mine.
[4] On the problems of defining the period of the Middle Ages, see Goetz 1999: 39–46. 'Oral literature' continues in Western societies well beyond the medieval period; for a study of the oral and the literate in early modern England, see Fox 2000.

the seventeenth century. This is reflected in the period-division of Russian language and literature. Standard textbooks posit a dividing line between medieval and post-medieval forms of language and literature somewhere in the seventeenth century.[5]

As the sources on which the discussions in this book are based are primarily of a literary kind, the earliest documents might be as early as the seventh century for some traditions, and as late as the fourteenth century for others. Even earlier dates can, however, be proposed for some traditions. It can be argued, for instance, that for an understanding of orality and literacy in the Jewish world the starting point would have to be in about 200 CE (AD 200), the time of the writing down of the Mishnah, the Rabbinical interpretations of the laws of Scripture, conventionally seen as going back to an oral tradition (Neusner 1987). On the other hand it has been argued that many Russian *byliny*, orally transmitted narrative songs, are medieval in origin, and a case could be made for considering them here, even if the earliest collection of texts was made only as late as the second half of the eighteenth century (by Kirsha Danilov) (see further section 5.2 below). The same is true of other orally transmitted poetry that can be shown to have its roots in the Middle Ages but which was written down only much later, such as the English and Scottish ballads, the bulk of which come from the post-medieval period. A certain flexibility in including later (and occasionally earlier) material is called for, even if the emphasis in most chapters is on the central medieval period from the eighth to the fourteenth centuries.

## 1.2 Confines of Place

The term 'Middle Ages' refers to a certain period in the history of civilization, however fuzzy its temporal limits. When originally coined, the term 'Middle Ages' also referred to a geographical area, the area of Europe, both the Latin west and the Greek east. If we look at a historical map of Europe in the year 1000, it will agree in many details with a map of modern Europe, although some borders have shifted, new states (like Belgium or Holland) have emerged and others (like the kingdom of Burgundy) have disappeared.[6] The differences are most notable on the Iberian peninsula in the south-west, and in eastern and south-eastern Europe. In the year 1000 the greater part of the Iberian Peninsula was under the dominion of the Umayyad Caliphate of Cordova; it was only with the fall of Granada in 1492 that the Reconquista succeeded in reclaiming the whole of the peninsula. In the year 1000, the German Empire was bordered on its eastern frontier by the Principality of Poland and the Kingdom of Hungary, both of comparatively recent date. Further east the Principality of Russia (Kievan Rus') extended from the Carpathian Mountains to the region of Lake Ladoga, lying like a wedge between the pagan Finnish and Baltic tribes on the Baltic sea and the Turkic Volga Bulgars, Petchenegs (Patzinaks) and Khazars in the south-east. Anatolia in its entirety was still part of the Byzantine Empire; it was only after the battle of Manzikert (Manāzgird) in 1071 that the Seljuks gained control over most of Anatolia. The Mediterranean was, as today, bordered by

---

[5] See Rothe 2000; Janet Martin's textbook of medieval Russian history (1995) spans the period from 980 to 1584.

[6] See, for example, the map of AD 998 in McEvedy 1961: 53.

Islamic countries along its southern shore; in the year 1000 the coastal areas of northern Africa, Egypt and the Levant were almost exclusively under the dominion of the Fatimid Caliphate.

None of these areas remained stable in the course of medieval history, but some areas changed more than others. Four hundred years earlier, in the year 600, the Eastern Roman Empire embraced not only Anatolia and Greece, but also most of Italy, northern Africa and the Levant. Its neighbour in the east was the Persian Empire of the Sasanian dynasty. With the expansion of the Seljuks and the foundation of the Ottoman Sultanate, however, the Byzantine Empire had virtually disappeared by the end of the Middle Ages. In eastern Europe, in the year 600, we find Slavic and Baltic peoples and the nomadic Avars further south. By the thirteenth century the map of eastern Europe had changed completely. Various Russian principalities had to pay tribute to the Golden Horde; Russia had come under the 'Tatar yoke', which it only shook off in the fifteenth century. A similarly drastic transformation characterizes the Iberian Peninsula, which was a Visigothic kingdom in AD 600, in 1000 belonged in large part to the Ummayad Khalifate and in 1500 was divided between Spain and Portugal, ruled by the Catholic monarchs Isabella of Castille and Ferdinand of Aragon and the Portuguese king Manuel I.

In view of the ever-shifting map of medieval Europe, it is difficult to decide what belongs in a book on medieval oral literature and what does not. Should medieval orality be sought only in Christian Spain and Portugal? Should Anatolia as a cultural area be included only while it was part of the Byzantine Empire? How far east should we go? Should Russia under the 'Tatar yoke' be included? In some cases the answer will be a negative one: not because one border-region or the other of what is commonly understood to constitute Europe in a geographical sense lies beyond its confines, but simply because there are no texts from that region in medieval times. Sometimes we have later evidence of a medieval oral tradition, and it is this later material that can serve as a basis for further discussion (see section 5.2 below). In other cases there is plenty of documentation, but the concept of Europe as the 'Occident' that is differentiated from (and often opposed to) the 'Orient' makes an inclusion seem questionable. The oral literature of Muslim Spain, of Turkish Anatolia and its Persian neighbour, and of the Arabic Levant and northern Africa might at first sight seem out of place in this book. Some consideration of the 'Orient' has, however, been thought necessary. One of the reasons is that there was an intensive cultural exchange between the Latin West and Muslim and Jewish Spain; this included the realm of popular literature. It is a well-known fact that the very earliest specimens of Romance lyric poetry have been preserved in the *kharjas* in Arabic and Hebrew lyrics (see section 6.4 below). The popular narratives in the Turkish-, Arabic- and Persian-speaking world around the southern and eastern Mediterranean and in Iran share the same narrative pool as the 'Occident'; the medieval Alexander legend is a case in point. These oriental traditions are also of great interest, because they offer the possibility of studying the continuance of orality into more recent times.[7]

---

[7] See the chapters on the Hispano-Arabic lyric by J. Monroe (ch. 23) and on popular narrative in Arabic by T. Herzog (ch. 24), in Persian by J. Rubanovich (ch. 25) and in Turkish by myself (ch. 26) in this volume.

## 2 Orality and Literacy

When Raymond Firth wrote down the songs of the Tikopia on the Solomon Islands in 1928–1929, he could be sure that he was recording oral literature. Although the French explorer Jules Dumont d'Urville had compiled a small vocabulary of Tikopian during his expedition of 1826–1829, by the beginning of the twentieth century Tikopian was still a basically unwritten language, and a book of prayers printed by the Melanesian Mission sometime before 1920 was virtually the only written text in this language. The songs that Firth heard and noted down were doubtless not only orally performed, but also orally transmitted and orally composed. We might say that in such a case we are in the presence of a fully oral tradition ('primary orality').[8]

For the study of medieval oral literature, no direct investigation is possible. All we have is the reflection of oral tradition in writing. This reflection can be of various kinds. As in the Tikopian case, some of the medieval testimonies might be comparable to the ethnographer's field-notes: an attempt to render in written symbols what otherwise only exists as sounds produced, heard and remembered. Some of the vernacular poems written on the margins of medieval manuscripts seem to be of this kind. They look like folksongs, but were written down by literate scribes, and, as with all medieval texts, their relationship to oral tradition, to 'real' folksongs, is a matter of conjecture. Other texts might be closer to the publications of the Missionary Society, in which traditional ways of expression are adapted to new ideas. Early Germanic biblical poetry such as the Old English and Old Saxon *Genesis* exemplifies this type of transformation. An older oral tradition is still visible, palimpsest-like, in the style and patterning of these poems, but is overlaid by new concepts. The opposite is also found: rather than expressing new ideas in the forms of traditional poetry, old ideas might be expressed in new, or at any rate non-traditional forms. The re-telling of the Germanic legend of Walther of Aquitaine in Latin hexameters by a monk of St. Gall in the ninth or tenth century is a case in point. Clearly, this is not a work of oral poetry, and scholars have found numerous echoes from the *Aeneid* and the Bible. Even in its classical garb, however, *Waltharius* betrays its origin in an earlier tradition, not only through its content, but also through the composition of its scenes and the traces of formulaic diction. The hero's breastplate, for instance, is called *Wielandia fabrica*, 'the work of Weland [the legendary smith]', just as in the Old English epic Beowulf's armour is described as *Wēlandes weorc*.[9]

### 2.1 Textualization

The difference between the *transposition* from the medium of spoken language to the medium of writing on the one hand and the *transformation* of oral speech into a written text on the other can be captured by the German terms *Verschriftung* and *Verschriftlichung* as used and defined by Peter Koch and Wulf Oesterreicher. While the first

---

[8] See Firth 1990 for an account of this traditions; the songs are edited, translated and interpreted on pp. 127–292.
[9] See Olsen 1993; on the phrase in *Beowulf* (l. 455), see Klaeber 2008: 144.

denotes a mere change of medium, as in the transcription of a spoken text, the latter designates the re-orientation of spoken discourse according to the forms and, more importantly, the concepts of written texts.[10] By *Verschriftung* no more than a change of medium is ideally implied, but in practice much is left out when transposing speech into writing; the vocal, acoustic side of a spoken text – pitch, intonation, degrees of volume etc. – is only imperfectly captured in writing. Oral poetry is as a rule sung poetry, and yet few ethnographic transcriptions (and even fewer medieval texts) record the music. In *Verschriftlichung*, on the other hand, a colloquial register or a dialect form might be replaced by the forms appropriate to the written standard, or a native genre might be recast in the mould of written poetry. The degree of 'literariness' varies and ranges from the total re-writing of oral discourse on one end of the scale – as in *Waltharius* (assuming that there was an oral tradition behind the poem) – to a point where the oral utterance is left largely 'unedited' and *Verschriftlichung* and *Verschriftung* virtually merge.

The textualization of orally performed texts is a problem that also confronts folklorists and ethnologists. Methodologies have been developed and the theoretical implications of textualization discussed. Although modern technology, enabling the tape-recording and filming of oral performance, has opened up new possibilities of documentation, the problem of translating one medium into another has to be solved if the performance is to be analysed.[11]

For the textualization of medieval literature with an oral background, the term 'inscribed' has been proposed by Carol B. Pasternack: 'I would use the term "inscribed" to discuss these texts [e. g. the Old English elegies], since they inherit significant elements of vocality from their oral forebears and yet address the reader from the pages of manuscripts' (1995:2). Other terms are also used. The interplay of oral and literate forms in medieval German literature is characterized by Jan-Dirk Müller as 'semi-orality' (see ch. 10 below). John Miles Foley calls epics like the *Odyssey* or *Beowulf* oral-derived texts, which he defines as 'the manuscript or tablet works of finally uncertain provenance that nonetheless show oral traditional characteristics' (1990:5).

When speaking of *Verschriftung* and *Verschriftlichung* the opposite process should also be mentioned: the transition from writing to oral tradition. There are various aspects to this phenomenon. Ballad and folksong scholars have repeatedly drawn attention to the written origin of oral songs; in some cases this process has been seen as a descent from high to low forms of literature and the works have been accordingly termed 'sunk cultural goods' (*gesunkenes Kulturgut*). In other cases oral poetry that had entered the world of written literature was subsequently 're-oralized'.[12]

Most if not all medieval works discussed as oral literature in this book show some degree of 'literariness'; the exact degree, however, is a matter of interpretation. The Vir-

---

[10] See Oesterreicher 1993 and Koch 1997; compare Bakker 1999:29–33. The differences between language in its spoken and written forms have been studied by a number of linguists; see Akinnaso 1982; Tannen 1982b and the contributions in Tannen 1982a; Raible 1996.

[11] On the methodology of rendering oral performance in writing, see Fine 1984; on the problems encountered in many traditions when oral epics are to be textualized, see the contributions to Honko 2000. The observations in the chapter that I have contributed to this volume have been put into practice in Reichl 2007 (see the discussion on pp. 142–62).

[12] See Bäuml 1993 and the contributions in Tristram 1996.

gilian parallels in *Beowulf*, for example, can be seen as learned influence on the native tradition, an elaboration along the lines of written epic poetry. A more radical view, however, is to impute to the model of the *Aeneid* and other classical epics the cause of the very existence of the epic of *Beowulf*. Andreas Heusler was of the opinion that the Anglo-Saxon epics, both secular and religious, were 'book-epics' and in consequence far removed from oral tradition.[13] Clearly, one of the major tasks of scholarship interested in medieval oral literature is to disentangle oral and literary-written elements in the works analysed and to assess their role in the constitution and orientation of these works.

While there is plenty of evidence about the existence of oral literature in the Middle Ages, there is little certainty about the relationship between the written texts that have come down to us and the oral tradition that is presumed to lie behind them. Each period, each linguistic and cultural area, each genre poses its specific problems. We know from Einhard's *Vita Caroli Magni* that Charlemagne had the *antiquissima et barbara cantica* of his people collected and written down. We can be certain that these 'most ancient and barbarous songs' were orally performed, orally transmitted and orally composed. Unfortunately, the manuscript containing Charlemagne's collection has not been preserved, and we have no safe guide-line for the interpretation of the 'barbarous songs' that have survived, such as for instance the Old High German *Hildebrandslied* (*Lay of Hildebrand*), of which a version might very well have figured in Charlemagne's manuscript (see Illustration 10, p. 316). How does this and other poetry relate to the oral tradition that flourished in the Early Middle Ages? Has it been written down from the mouth of a singer or has a process of adaptation led to its written form? The same questions can be asked about any work suspected of having been orally performed and perhaps also created and transmitted in an oral mileu. Answers have been given, but they are based on assumptions that are not shared by all.

## 2.2 Litteratus / illitteratus

What makes it so difficult to understand the oral background to medieval literature is not only the fact that we have to reconstruct orality from written sources but also that orality and literacy are curiously interconnected in the medieval period. The degree of literacy at different times and in different medieval societies has been variously calculated. Although no definite numbers can be given, the general course seems uncontroversial.[14] Literacy is of course linked to writing and is a skill limited at first to the profes-

---

[13] On Virgilian echoes in *Beowulf*, see Andersson 1976; Heusler's position is expounded, for instance, in his *Altgermanische Dichtung* (1941: 192–200). See also the chapter on Older Germanic traditions by J. Harris in this volume (ch. 8).

[14] There is no space here for a comprehensive bibliography; for a survey, see Briggs 2000; for the literacy of the laity, see Parkes 1973, for pragmatic literacy, Arlinghaus et al. 2006. Among collections of studies, McKitterick 1995 deals with the Early Middle Ages, Pryce 1998 with Celtic traditions. On medieval literacy and illiteracy in connection with oral literature, see also Bäuml 1980. The distinction between *litteratus* and *illitteratus* has been much (and sometimes controversially) discussed; see Clanchy 1993: 224–52. See further the chapters on orality and literacy in the Early Middle Ages (ch. 3, M. Richter) and in Anglo-Saxon England (ch. 4, K. O'Brien O'Keeffe) in this volume; see also ch. 10 on medieval German literature (J.-D. Müller), section 1.1.

sional class of educated scribes and clerics. Reading and writing are not congruent; a person capable of reading might not have been able to write. What was read and written were first and foremost texts in the classical languages, Greek in the East and Latin in the West. As Herbert Grundmann has shown in a seminal article, the modern concepts of 'literate' and 'illiterate' do not tally with their Latin cognates. In the western half of the medieval world, by *litteratus* and *illitteratus* no simple contrast between 'educated' and 'non-educated' is implied:

> [...] in the Middle Ages, the terms *litteratus* and *illitteratus* do not distinguish different degrees of education, but different kinds, even worlds, of education, which co-exist just as, side by side with Latin writing and book-learning of Classical-Roman and Biblical-Patristic provenance, the vernacular languages with their non-written traditions in poetry, history, legend, law and customs continued to thrive and have their educational effects. These two forms and traditions of education are distributed over different estates (leaving aside certain overlaps and exceptions): *litterati* with a knowledge of Latin are in general only clerics and monks, men of the church and the monastery, who were charged by the nobility to do all the chancery work. *Illitterati*, persons without a knowledge of Latin and of writing, were in general the laymen of all social strata; only noble women and the sons of kings were expected to possess a certain amount of literary education and skill. For other laymen it is unusual and striking to be *litterati*, while it is a deficiency and a blemish for clerics or monks to be *illitterati*. (1958: 13–14)

That which has survived the ravages of time we owe to the activity of the *litterati*, and these were at first almost exclusively clerics. These same *litterati* were also responsible for the gradual alphabetization of the vernacular languages, a process that ultimately resulted in the accessibility of written texts to an ever-increasing circle of readers, also including the laity. The emergence of the vernaculars as written languages proceeded on a tortuous path; some languages were alphabetized early, as for instance Gothic in Ulfilas' translation of the Bible (fourth century), some late, such as Lithuanian (around 1500), some only in the modern period, and some never.[15]

## 2.3 Orality vs. Literacy

In a society in which both literacy and illiteracy exist the description and demarcation of orality poses a number of problems. When Milman Parry recorded South Slavic oral epics in the 1930s, he was careful to focus on singers who had acquired their repertoire orally and who performed from memory. Salih Ugljanin, for instance, the first singer in the published volumes of the Parry collection, stated that he learned ten heroic poems from Ćor Huso Husović of Kolašin in the course of one month. Actually, a printed edition of the *Song of Bagdad*, the first song published and translated in the *Serbocroation Heroic Songs*, exists, but we can be reasonably sure that Salih did not know it (*SCHS*: I, 11–14; 332). Illiteracy is, of course, no guarantee that a singer has not had access to a printed version of a song. There is always the possibility of someone reading

---

[15] The development of the writing of various vernacular languages has been studied extensively in the various linguistic disciplines concerned; for an introductory overview (limited to western Europe), see Wolff 1971.

the printed text to an illiterate bard. Hans Fromm gives the following amusing example of a Karelian singer from the end of the nineteenth century:

> The attempt by Lönnrot's friend, J. F. Cajan, to stimulate the Karelian singer to sing by reading to him from the Kalevala, appears to be extremely immediate [...]. An interesting case in this context is that of Vihtoora Lesoni from Vuokkiniemi, who sang verses to the collector in 1894; the latter – it was Karjalainen – was delighted at the coherence and quality of these verses, until he later discovered that they came from the Kalevala itself [...]. Vihtoora was illiterate and learned these verses aurally – and it is worth mentioning here that this is a good argument against the claim by orthodox followers of the oral tradition school that the singers built up their repertoire of songs solely on the basis of formulaic learning. (1990: 102–3)

Despite these complications, in ethnographic field-work singers can be asked and, provided they tell the truth, their dependence on literary models can be ascertained. This is not possible in the same way with medieval texts.

It is nevertheless important to know where a text is to be placed, in an oral or in a literate milieu. Parry wanted his South Slavic material to be unambiguously oral in order to analyse the characteristics of oral rather than written epics. Both Parry and Lord have insisted on the fundamental difference between oral and written literature, a difference that other scholars have also emphasized, contrasting orality and literacy not only as different media for the production and transmission of texts but also as different mentalities, different approaches to conceptualization and expression in language. Walter J. Ong (1982) distinguishes between thought and expression based on orality on the one hand and the restructuring of consciousness by writing on the other. Jack Goody and Ian P. Watt criticize the assumption of radically different mind-sets in oral and literate society, but nonetheless maintain a difference in conceptualization:

> Nevertheless, although we must reject any dichotomy based upon the assumption of radical differences between the mental attributes of literate and non-literate peoples, and accept the view that previous formulations of the distinction were based on faulty premises and inadequate evidence, there may still exist general differences between literate and non-literate societies somewhat along the lines suggested by Lévy-Bruhl. One reason for their existence, for instance, may be what has been described above: the fact that writing establishes a different kind of relationship between the word and its referent, a relationship that is more general and more abstract, and less closely connected with the particularities of person, place and time, than obtains in oral communication. (1963: 21)

Ruth Finnegan has similarly criticized a rigorous dichotomy into 'non-literate societies as small-scale and homogeneous, "oral", dominated by tradition at least and probably also by religion and ascribed kinship, unself-conscious, perhaps more organic and close to nature than ourselves, and certainly untouched by mechanization, advanced technology, and mass culture' and literate societies 'dominated by the tradition of the written word; secular and rationalistic; oriented towards achievement and individual development; at the same time, highly mechanized, perhaps bound together by artificial rather than natural links, and with a well-developed technology' (1974: 52). She advocates the concept of a continuum rather than a dichotomy, arguing that in most so-called oral societies as they are known today 'the relation between oral and written forms need not just be one of parallel and independent coexistence, far less of mutual exclusion, but can easily exhibit constant and positive interaction' (57).

It certainly holds true for medieval literature that in many periods and areas orality and literacy are found in close symbiosis. This is particularly true of the Jewish world. Judaism is the religion – and culture – of the book *par excellence*, and yet, as Eli Yassif shows in his chapter on medieval Hebrew literature in this volume (ch. 19), both the spoken word and oral tradition had an important place in medieval Jewish *literate* society. This interweaving of orality and literacy in medieval literature does not obviate the cognitive distinction between orality and literacy. Their difference continues, even if orality and literacy are intermingled and difficult to distinguish in reality. It has to be stressed that their respective identification in a work affects its interpretation. In *Beowulf*, for instance, the hero's fight with Grendel and his mother is described twice, once by the narrator and once in Beowulf's own words, when he reports to King Hygelac on his return home. In a number of details the two accounts are at odds with one another. While scholars persuaded of the written origin of the epic have maintained that the variations are minimal and heighten, if anything, the artistic effect of the epic, Francis P. Magoun has argued that the difference might very well stem from the stitching together of two different oral songs on Beowulf's adventures, respectively denoted as *A* and *A'*. As he somewhat mischievously observed, the assumption that an anthologizing scribe combined *A* and *A'* 'allows one to have a higher opinion of the work of both *A* and *A'* and relieves the critic of feeling obliged to try to convert inconsistencies into artistic triumphs'.[16] More importantly, the fact that a work belongs to an oral rather than a literate milieu entails a different kind of aesthetics, as chiefly anthropologists and folklorists have maintained.[17] Albert Lord has expressed this in no uncertain terms: 'There *is* a difference between oral traditional poetics and written poetics, and one must know with what kind of poetry one is dealing in order correctly to appreciate its aesthetics and to describe and edit its texts' (1995:202). From the perspective of medieval studies, the most eloquent proponent of an 'oral aesthetics' was doubtless Paul Zumthor, especially in his *Introduction à la poésie orale*.[18]

## 2.4 Beyond Verbal Art

The focus of this book is on oral *literature*, on the reflection of orality and oral poetic traditions in medieval *literary* texts. Oral literature is, of course, placed in wider contexts: the contexts of medieval society, political and intellectual history, culture, art, and religion. As we have seen, scholars like Ong and Goody have maintained that orality and literacy are not just two different manners of producing, transmitting and receiving information, but also encompass different ways of conceptualizing reality and of structuring knowledge. Although an overly dichotomous approach to orality and literacy has been criticized, with arguments for an orality-literacy continuum rather than an orality-literacy divide, the belief that the two poles of this continuum comprise more than the medial realization of speech is shared by a great number of cultural historians and med-

---

[16] Magoun 1958:100; for arguments against Magoun, see Brodeur 1970.
[17] See esp. Hymes 1981 and Tedlock 1983.
[18] Zumthor 1983; see also Niles 1999 and ch. 6 (T. DuBois) in this volume; compare also ch. 2 (J. M. Foley and P. Ramey), section 3.2.

ievalists. Koch and Oesterreicher (1985) also contrast orality and literacy as a 'culture of nearness' and a 'culture of distance', two concepts that imply distinctive modes of verbalization. In societies with limited literacy, forms of oral communication are essential and not restricted to verbal exchanges.

One area which has been intensively studied for a long time, is the use of pictorial art as an addition to or substitute for literary texts. This is a field which lies outside the scope of this book and this introductory chapter. Here attention can only be drawn to the relevance of art for a wider orality debate. Volker Schupp has coined the term 'pictorality' for the telling of stories in pictorial representation; pictorial narrative was the subject of an earlier study by the art historian Otto Pächt, who saw its rise in connection with the so-called Twelfth Century Renaissance in Anglo-Norman England.[19] Visible forms in art (and ritual) have also been studied in their interplay with literary forms of expression, both oral and written (Wenzel 1995). Ritual and symbolic acts have been in the foreground in the studies of a number of medieval historians and cultural historians, who have argued that gestures and rituals rich in meaning and enhanced by powerful symbols were used to regulate much of medieval politics and public life.[20]

With the growth of literacy in the High and Late Middle Ages, some of these symbolic acts were replaced by the writing and signing of documents. As an example from the thirteenth century, Michael Clanchy (1993: 35–38) mentions the story of the Earl Warenne, who, when asked to prove his title to his lands, showed a sword from the Norman Conquest instead of a charter. He is reported to have said: 'This is my warrant!' The truth of this story has been doubted by historians, but, as Clanchy observes, 'The story seems to be a desparate reassertion of the primacy of oral tradition over recorded history and of non-literate forms of proof over Edward I's lawyers and their demands for charters' (36). The 'primacy of oral tradition over recorded history' has many facets. One of these is genealogical knowledge, which was passed on orally in the Early Middle Ages from generation to generation.[21] Genealogical concerns inform also poetic works, most significantly heroic poetry. This has most persuasively been shown to be the case in a number of *chansons de geste*, but it can be argued that the transmission of knowledge about the ancestors of an ethnic group, about a group's roots and past, is perhaps the strongest motivating force for the cultivation of heroic song and epic in general (Reichl 2000: esp. 135 ff.). Closely related is the endeavour to preserve and enshrine cultural values in oral traditions. Eric Havelok has stressed the encyclopaedic nature of the Homeric epics and their educational function in ancient Greece; for older Germanic poetry the presence of maxims and gnomic sayings has similarly been seen as an indication of their culture-preserving character.[22]

The closest parallel to the transmission of oral literature is the handing-down of music from one generation to the next in the Middle Ages. The development of musical notation lagged far behind that of writing, with staffless neumes as a first approximation

---

[19] See Schupp 1993; Pächt 1962; see also Bäuml 1998.
[20] See Althoff 1997 and 2003; Witthöft 2004.
[21] See Moisl 1981; Spiegel 1997: 99–110.
[22] See Havelock 1963; on the traditional character of Old English maxims and gnomes, see Shippey 1977; on Old Norse and Old English wisdom poetry, see Larrington 1993; compare also the general discussion of wisdom literature in Bloomfield and Dunn 1989: 120–49.

to the contours of sound. Not all types of music were notated, and the notational systems that were developed become fully interpretable only with the rise of mensural notation in the thirteenth century.[23] A study of the way music was taught and transmitted reveals in its combination of oral/aural transmission and mnemonic techniques interesting parallels to the memorial transmission of literary works.[24] Indeed a literary genre like the sequence even owes its existence to a mnemonic device. As Notker Balbulus of St. Gall writes in the preface to his *Liber Hymnorum*:

> Cum adhuc juvenculus essem et melodiae longissimae, saepius memoriae commendatae, instabile corculum aufugerent, coepi tacitus mecum volvere, quonam modo eas potuerim colligare. (von den Steinen 1948: 8)
>
> When I was still a young man and the very long melodies commited to memory would flee from my unstable little memory, I began to ponder in which manner I might be able to keep them.

Notker is referring to the long melismas on the final *-a* of the *Alleluia*. The solution was presented to him when a monk from Jumiège came one day to St. Gall; in his antiphonary the *Alleluia* melismas were underlaid by a text. Notker composed his sequences in imitation (Crocker 1990: 256–64).

Cultural memory, as discussed and elaborated by Jan Assmann (1992), has been associated primarily with the development of writing in the ancient world, but it is no doubt also a main concern of oral traditions. 'Cultural memory' and 'collective memory' as understood by Maurice Halbwachs (1925) are powerful concepts for the analysis of cultural artefacts, independent of their medial representation. Historians have also focused on the endeavour to keep the memory of persons or events alive in medieval society, stressing the centrality of *memoria* in medieval culture, both oral and literate.[25]

Oral literature, like all cultural artefacts, does not exist in a vacuum; it has, to use a term coined by the biblical scholar Hermann Gunkel with reference to the Psalms, a 'seat in life' (*Sitz im Leben*). Some forms of oral literature are intimately connected to spiritual and religious movements, such as the popular lyric promulgated by the Franciscans in the thirteenth century or the songs of the flagellants in the fourteenth century. Especially in the High and Late Middle Ages, oral poetry flourished in the milieu of popular culture, in the public entertainments on feast days, in the rites and customs of carnival, or in the charms and incantations of the popular healer.[26]

It would certainly have been desirable to have separate chapters on topics like symbolic communication, the interplay of text and picture, cultural memory and memorial culture, popular culture or the relationship of orality and writing in teaching or in religious rites. This would have doubled the size of this volume, and it would have moved the centre of attention away from works of verbal art. In a number of chapters, however, some of the points just mentioned are touched upon; all that can be done in the context of this introductory chapter is to make the reader aware of these wider issues.

---

[23] For a survey of the development of medieval notation, see Bent et al. 2001: 84–140 (sections III.1–3).
[24] See Treitler 1974 and 1981. See also sections 4.1 and 4.2 below.
[25] See Oexle 1994 and the contributions in Geuenich and Oexle 1994. On the concept of cultural memory, see also the collection of articles edited by Erll, Nünning and Young 2008.
[26] See Gurevich 1988 and 1992; see also the chapter on drama by T. Pettitt (ch. 27).

## 3 Traces of Orality in the Written Text

For the discussion of oral literature, the central question is: how can we be sure where to place a text, in the world of oral tradition or of written literature? The methodology developed by Parry and Lord, which goes under the name of 'oral-formulaic theory' or simply 'Oral Theory', offers one possibility of finding the correct answer. As is well-known, the basic logics of this theory consists in first isolating a number of linguistic, stylistic or structural traits typical of oral poetry, then asking whether these traits are found in a given text transmitted in writing (but suspected of oral provenance) and finally classifying this text accordingly. Parry's and Lord's approach, it seems to me, is fundamentally sound: the only way we can get beyond the circularity of interpreting written texts as oral poetry on the evidence of other written texts is by studying unwritten oral poetry. Here empirical observations can be made about what it is for poetry to be oral, i. e. to be orally performed and transmitted. The impact of the Oral Theory on medieval studies has been enormous, with many stimulating and lasting results, as is shown in a separate chapter below (see ch. 2 by J. M. Foley and P. Ramey).

### 3.1 Oral Theory and Neotraditionalism

The enthusiasm which some scholars have displayed in applying the theory to medieval poetry has, however, sparked off a reserved, if not hostile reaction. Some of the debates have been acrimonious, as for instance the dispute between William Calin and Joseph J. Duggan with reference to the Old French *chansons de geste* in the 1981 issue of the journal *Olifant*.[27] This particular debate has several antecedents: Maurice Delbouille's opposition to Jean Rychner's study of the art of the jongleur in the late 1950s and, at the end of the nineteenth/beginning of the twentieth century, the famous dispute between the traditionalists and the individualists in the interpretations of the *chansons de geste* in general and the *Chanson de Roland* in particular.[28] In this connection the neotraditionalism of Ramón Menéndez Pidal should also be mentioned, a position which insists on the fundamental traditionality of Romance epics like the *Chanson de Roland* or the *Cantar de mio Cid*, a traditionality that rests on oral tradition and implies the interpretation of these works within an oral rather than a literary-written context.[29] Medievalists like Jean Rychner or Menéndez Pidal – just like Bowra and Kirk in the area of ancient Greek epic – worked outside the Parry-Lord paradigm, but

---

[27] See Calin 1980–81a and b and Duggan 1980–81a and b. Calin begins his attack by stating his belief that most of the members of the Société Rencesvals would rather read the Bible or Virgil or even Chrétien de Troyes than 'The Wedding of Smailagić Meho' (the showpiece of Parry's collection) (1980–81a: 227); with so much disdain for oral poetry it is not surprising that he is violently opposed to seeing any traces of orality in the *chansons de geste*.

[28] See Delbouille 1959 vs. Rychner 1955. See also the chapter by D. Boutet on the *chanson de geste* in this volume (ch. 12), esp. section 3.

[29] For an explication of his neotraditionalist stance, see Menéndez Pidal 1960: 451–517; compare also the useful overview by Faulhaber 1976–77 and the chapter by R. Wright on Spanish epic and ballad in this volume (ch. 15).

showed the same sympathy as Parry, Lord and their followers with a traditionalist-oralist point of view.[30]

Scholars have been quick to find flaws in Parry's and Lord's argumentation, and sceptics have remained unconvinced. Two vulnerable points in the Oral Theory are that what Parry and Lord identified as typical of oral tradition (formulaic style, composition in performance) is not in the same way characteristic of all oral traditions of which we have some knowledge; in a number of cases, 'memorizing' – in the sense of aiming at maximum fidelity to the model acquired by the singer – plays a more important role than Parry and Lord were ready to allow (see section 4.2 below). Secondly, even if a text shows all the signs of orality, there is no guarantee that it actually belongs to an oral milieu. In societies in transition from orality to literacy, literary productions, if not directly imitated from (foreign) written literature, may show the same stylistic traits as native oral works. The poetic idiom of one's own tradition is used for new forms of literary expression. This can be seen in the popular novel of the 1940s and 1950s among the Yakut, a Turkic-speaking Siberian people with a rich oral epic tradition, but also in the religious epics and poetry of the Anglo-Saxons. In both cases literature that originated in writing shows the signs of oral literature.[31] The criticism levelled at the Oral Theory does not invalidate the insights it provides, but does restrict its value as a mechanical heuristic device.

## 3.2 Aurality

More immediately accessible than formulas and other elements of a presumed oral style are other signs of orality. Oral performance, for instance, seems to be implied by appeals to the audience to be quiet and pay attention to the story about to be told. Three examples, from Middle English (*Havelok*), Middle High German (*Biterolf and Dietleib*) and French (*Chanson d'Aspremont*) epic poems will illustrate this:

> At the beginning of ure tale
> Fil me a cuppe of ful god ale,
> And wile drinken, her y spelle,
> That Crist us shilde alle fro helle!
> (*Havelok*, ll. 13–16) (Smithers 1987: 1)

At the beginning of our tale/ fill me a cup of very good ale/ and I will drink, before I narrate./ May Christ protect us from hell!

> nu ruochet hoeren mîne bete
> daz ir swîget dar zuo
> daz ich iu das kunt getuo.
> (*Biterolf and Dietleib*, ll. 16–18) (Jänicke 1866: 1)

Now be so kind as to hear my request,/ namely that you be silent,/ so that I may tell you (the story).

> Plaist vos oïr bone cançon vallant
> De Carlemainne, le rice roi poisçant,

---
[30] See, e. g., Kirk 1965: 1–32; Bowra 1972: 10–31.
[31] See Petrov 1982 (Yakut prose); Benson 1966 (Anglo-Saxon).

> Del duc Namlon que li rois ama tant? [...]
> Or escotés des ici en avant.
> S'ele vos plaist, bone cançon vos cant
>   (*Chanson d'Aspremont*, ll. 1–3, 18–19) (Brandin 1970: I,1)
>
> Would you like to hear a good brave song/ about Charlemagne, the magnificent powerful king,/ and about Duke Naimes, whom the king loved so much?/ [...] / Now listen from here on./ If you like, I will sing you a good song.

These lines seem innocent and clear enough, but doubts linger. Are they the transcript of words actually spoken (or possibly sung) by a minstrel? And if so, were they composed *by* the minstrel or were they composed *for* the minstrel? Or are they only meant to give the impression of an oral performance, to give the poems an oral ring by pretending that a narrator is addressing a group of listeners?

We can be sure of one thing: if certain types of narrative poetry – to which *Havelok, Biterolf and Dietleib* and the *Chanson d'Aspremont* obviously belong – were not meant to be orally performed then there would be little point in addressing listeners rather than readers. *Havelok* might not have been performed orally, but the kind of narrative poem to which *Havelok* belongs was. Of course, once a poem has been written down it can be read by anybody who is able to read, on their own and without an audience. The appeal to listeners is then no more than a reminder of what must have been the natural milieu for this kind of text: a public, oral delivery.

In the Middle Ages, a great deal of poetry, from all literary genres, was orally performed (Crosby 1936). Despite disagreement about the creation, transmission and precise form of oral delivery, medievalists generally concur that much medieval poetry came to life, as it were, only as spoken, recited or sung poetry. For a fuller appreciation and understanding of such works, their *vocalité*, as Paul Zumthor has insisted, has to be taken into account.[32] This 'vocality' leaves traces in the text:

> By 'sign of orality' I understand everything in a text that informs us about the intervention of the human voice in its *publication*: that is, in the change by which this passed, once or several times, from a virtual state into actuality and existed from then on in the attention and memory of a certain number of individuals. (Zumthor 1987:37)

One of these signs is the appeal to an audience of listeners.

## 3.3 Reading Aloud

From the point of view of the receiver, an oral communication is something heard, something listened to. Its oral/aural nature is independent of whether the speaker speaks freely or is reading from a written source. Reading aloud to a group of listeners is a practice which, before the advent of the radio, tape-recorder, television and the computer, was widespread globally and certainly very common in the Middle Ages. Given the importance of reading aloud, medieval texts have been interpreted as scripts for oral

---

[32] See esp. Zumthor 1987; see also ch. 12 below (D. Boutet), esp. section 4; for Anglo-Saxon, see Schaefer 1992 and for Medieval German ch. 10 (J.-D. Müller). On performance in general, see ch. 5 (J. Harris and K. Reichl).

1 – 'Or m'escoutés li grant e li menor / bone chanson de la geste francor' (Now listen to me, great and small, to a good song from the 'Deeds of the Franks'). Beginning of *La Prise de Cordres et de Sebille*, Paris, BnF MS fr. 1448, fol. 164r

performance, with indications about their oral recitation in the way they are structured or even placed on the manuscript page.[33] The practice of reading aloud does not only apply to the Early and High Middle Ages. As Joyce Coleman (1996) has argued, in late medieval England and France the prevaling mode for the reception of 'court-oriented' secular literature was that of listening to a public reading, irrespective of the spread of literacy. 'Professional readers' are of many kinds: authors like Chaucer or Froissart reading to their patrons or to court circles, valets and librarians employed in aristocratic households, monks performing the task of lector in monastic communities, and public entertainers like the English minstrel. In the Middle English popular romances we find repeated references to the reading of romances by a narrator or entertainer, as for instance at the beginning of the second part of *Guy of Warwick*:

> God graunt hem heven blis to mede
> Þat herken to mi romaunce rede
> Al of a gentil kniȝt. (Zupitza 1887: 384)

---

[33] For Anglo-Saxon, see O'Brien O'Keeffe 1990; Doane 1994. See also ch. 5 (section 2.3, pp. 160–61).

> May God grant heaven's bliss as a reward to those/ who listen to me reading a romance/ of a noble knight.

It is true that some of these passages are ambiguous since Middle English *reden* can besides 'read' also mean 'recite' or 'narrate', but there is no reason to exclude the possibility of a public entertainer using a manuscript for his performance.[34] As other traditions such as those discussed in the chapters on Arabic, Persian and Turkic popular narrative in the volume show, the 'public reader' is a common figure in these traditions and can be considered an analogue to the medieval entertainer, at least in some of his functions (see chapters 24, 25, and 26 below).

The predominance of oral delivery and aural reception of certain kinds of medieval literature is nicely underlined by the beginning of Chaucer's *Troilus and Criseyde*. Chaucer the narrator addresses his audience as listeners who are about to *hear* a story:

> Now herkneth with a good entencioun,
> For now wil I gon streght to my matere,
> In which ye may the double sorwes here
> Of Troilus in lovynge of Criseyde,
> And how that she forsook hym er she deyde. (bk. I, ll. 52–56)

> Now listen with good intention,/ for now I will go straight to my story,/ in which you will hear about the double sorrow/ of Troilus in his love to Criseyde,/ and how she forsook him before she died.

Indeed one of the manuscripts of *Troilus* has an illumination showing the poet reading to a courtly audience.[35] Here oral delivery means reading aloud. When we say that poetry is orally performed, we generally mean, however, that poetry is performed without the help of a book or manuscript. There is no reason to doubt that as a rule the medieval minstrel, jongleur or *spilman* recited or sang poems and narratives that were stored in his head rather than on a piece of paper or parchment. The narrator of an anonymous romance like *Havelok* or a *chanson de geste* like the *Chanson d'Aspremont* is cast in the role of such a popular entertainer. But how trustworthy is this suggestion of a minstrel or jongleur telling a story? Is it simply a conventional trait of certain types of narratives, a feint and make-believe? Is the orality implied by such appeals to an audience to listen 'real' or 'fictitious'?

## 3.4 Fictitious Orality

'Fictitious orality' is certainly a common factor in much medieval literature, and not only there.[36] Scholars sceptical of an oral background to works like the *chansons de geste* or the popular romances have used the notion of 'fictitious orality' to maintain that

---

[34] On the meaning of 'romance-reading', see ch. 11 on the Middle English romance (A. Putter) in this volume, esp. pp. 339–44. Compare also Reichl 2009: 134–36.

[35] Quoted from Benson 1987: 474 (*entencioun* in l. 52 might also be translated by 'attention') ; the illumination on fol. 1v of Cambridge, Corpus Christi College MS 61, has often been reproduced; it is also available at <http://parkerweb.stanford.edu/parker/actions/page.do?forward=page_turner&ms_no=61>.

[36] See Goetsch 1985, with examples from the nineteenth-century English novel.

vitually no signs of orality are what they seem to be, namely signs of orality. It is argued that literate authors and sometimes hack writers have composed these works, giving them a semblance of orality either to adapt them to the performance of popular entertainers or simply in imitation of oral literature. The idea of literary hacks producing Middle English romances in fourteenth-century London by translating and adapting French originals has been much in favour among medievalists ever since Laura Hibbard Loomis formulated her London bookshop theory for the romances of the so-called Auchinleck Manuscript in the 1940s.[37] While written transmission and in many cases composition as well has certainly played a significant part in the creation and transmission of Middle English popular romances, there is no reason to deny the popular entertainers (minstrels) an active role not only in performing but also in transmitting and – why not? – occasionally composing such narratives.[38] 'Hack writer' vs. 'minstrel', 'orality' vs. 'fictitious orality': as with formulaic diction, every case has to be analysed carefully before a verdict can be given about the correctness of one or the other of these dichotomies. In many cases, given the lack of conclusive evidence, the question must remain open. It has to be noted, however, that it seems strange that appeals to the audience and other markers of orality should *never* be meant literally, as the critics of an oralist position maintain. This is certainly counter-intuitive. For medieval German literature, D. H. Green has painstakingly studied the use of verbs like *hoeren* 'listen', *sprechen* 'speak', *sagen* 'say', *singen* 'sing', and *lesen* 'read' and has come to the conclusion that, depending on the genre, an aural reception must also be implied in cases of imputed 'fictitious orality'.[39]

Apart from appeals to the audience, other traits indicating oral performance have been proposed; these include clichés, parallelism, repetitions, and of course formulaic diction and thematic patterning. Renate Baader, for instance, has argued that some of the narrative characteristics found in the Old French *chantefable* of *Aucassin et Nicolette* indicate an oral background: 'Repetitions and parallel patterning, a string of identical building blocks, recurring formulas, also including those in distant sections of the narrative, flat, non-descriptive epithets, which reappear in identical form or as synonyms – this is the style of narration, a style that can be appreciated adequately only if it is understood as narration without writing.'[40] Some of these 'oral traits' are not restricted to poetic texts, such as, for instance, the eight types of orality discussed by Wulf Oesterreicher, which apply to oral speech in general.[41]

## 3.5 Variability

In this context, we must mention another peculiarity of medieval literature, in particular literature for which an oral background is proposed, namely the variations encountered

---

[37] See Loomis 1942; for corrections, see Shonk 1985.
[38] See Reichl 1991 and 2002; compare also A. Putter's apposite remark at the end of ch. 11 in this volume (p. 349).
[39] See Green 1994; Green sees oral/aural reception as the primary mode of reception for genres such as heroic poetry; see also Green 2002: 35–46.
[40] Baader 1974: 12. On the style of oral poetry, see ch. 6 (T. A. DuBois) in this volume.
[41] Oesterreicher 1997; for an analysis of signs of orality in Old and Middle English texts on the basis of both the Oral Theory and historical pragmatics, see Arnovick 2006.

in different versions of a medieval text. Textual variation occurs in many forms of literature and need not be connected to orality; it can be seen as the result of the vagaries of manuscript transmission and the activity of scribes. It is, however, also a sign of the fundamental 'fluidity' of an originally oral text and its various written realizations. Paul Zumthor has dubbed this phenomenon 'mouvance', which he defined as 'the characteristics of a work of literature which as such, before the age of the book, exists in a quasi-abstract state, while the concrete texts that embody it present, by the play of variants and adaptations, something like an incessant vibration and a fundamental instability' (Zumthor 1972: 507). Editors of medieval texts have been puzzled by the types of variation found in different manuscripts of a text, which often defy all attempts at constructing a manuscript stemma. Some of these variants are scribal, but editors have also found aural variants and variations manifestly due to transformations in the course of committing a text to memory. For one of the versions of the Middle English *Alexander* romance its editor notes that '[t]he kind and the degree of error contained in it are such as would arise in oral transmission of a text, and specifically in a copy based on (and perhaps designed as) the version of a minstrel'.[42] The editor of the Old French *chanson de geste* of *La Prise d'Orange* writes about one of the manuscripts transmitting the text (Paris, BnF MS fr. 1448 = D): 'As to D, this manuscript transmits an archaic version, which a jongleur has put together with the help of a written model and which he has completed with recourse to his professional repertoire. Unfortunately, due to lapses of memory, he has sometimes omitted essential indications, mixed up the order of episodes and the sequence of verses.'[43] To these we could add many examples which underline the possibility (according to some, the necessity) of an oral phase in the transmission of the manuscript texts of works presumably destined for oral recitation.

## 4 Oral Tradition

As we have seen, speaking of oral performance in the Middle Ages can mean many things; 'oral performance' can refer to reading aloud from a manuscript and might on closer inspection even turn out to be something quite different, namely 'fictitious orality'. There is nevertheless no reason to doubt that poetry was orally performed by medieval entertainers without the help of a manuscript, and it is this scenario which medievalists generally have in mind when they discuss oral poetry. Here the question arises of how the bards, minstrels, jongleurs etc. acquired their knowledge.[44] Although many possibilites can be imagined, two seem to be the most basic: the performers learned a poem or narrative from a written text or they acquired their repertoire by word of mouth, i. e. by oral transmission. In the modern world many people know some poems by heart because they have memorized them from a written text (often in their school-time) and

---

[42] Smithers 1952–57: II, 11–12. For an assessment of the oral factor in editing Middle English texts, especially romances, see Machan 1991.
[43] Régnier 1969: 12–13. See also ch. 12 (D. Boutet), p. 360.
[44] By and large the medieval performers of poetry, especially narrative poetry, seem to have been men; there are, of course, women poets as well as women dancers etc.; in post-medieval and modern oral poetry women performers of ballads, *byliny* or epics are fairly common in some traditions. On the various types of medieval performers, see further ch. 5 (J. Harris and K. Reichl).

some, as, for instance, the lyrics of a pop-song, because they have heard them often enough to remember them.

With longer poetry a good memory and some special training are necessary. Memorizing has been a central tool of education since ancient times. In medieval schools large portions of Virgil's *Aeneid* were learned by heart, and the Latin Psalter had to be memorized by members of a religious community.[45] In Islam, both medieval and modern, the Koran (Qurʾān) is mainly taught as a book to be committed to memory, and the title of a *ḥāfiẓ* is given to the person who can recite all the 114 suras by rote. George Makdisi remarks on the role of memorization in medieval Islamic education:

> The methodology of learning in medieval Islam relied heavily on memorization. The cultivation of memory and its aids, repetition (*iʿāda*), discussion (*mudhākara*), and notebooks, served both the Koran and *ḥadīth*. From the emphasis on memory and its aids, cultivated to ensure the correct transmission (*riwāya*) of the sacred Scripture, emphasis came to be placed also on understanding (*dirāya*). Besides the Koran and *ḥadīth*, a vast repertoire of poetry from pre-Islamic and early Islamic times was committed to memory for its lexical value in clarifying the sacred Scripture. (Makdisi 1988: 67)

A public performer who has memorized a fixed text is expected to give an accurate delivery and will be rated by the audience according to the closeness of his recital to the source. When poetry destined for oral performance has an author who is, however, not the performer, the performer is sometimes enjoined to keep to the words of the original. This is found, for instance, in troubadour poetry, as when Guiraut de Bornelh (second half of the 12th c.) warns the jongleur (or *joglar*) not to 'worsen his song' (Mölk 1982: 60–61).

## 4.1 Oral Tradition: Training

Matters become more complicated when an entertainer, a 'singer of tales', has acquired his repertoire by word of mouth. There is some medieval evidence for 'oral training', but much of it is unclear. At the end of the Anglo-Norman romance of *Horn* by 'Master Thomas', the narrator announces that there is not only the 'Tale of Horn' but also the 'Tale of Hadermod' Horn's son. This tale, however, he will not tell himself but will leave to his son Gilimot:

> Icest lais a mun fiz, Gilimot, ki·l dirrat,
> Ki la rime apré mei bien controverat –
> Controvures ert bon: e de mei [ce retendra].
> (ll. 5225–33) (Pope 1955–64: I, 173–74)
>
> This (story) I will leave to my son Gilimot to tell,/ who will well compose the verses (*la rime*) after me –/ he will be a good maker: and he will [get this] from me.

This is an intriguing passage, but too little is known of 'Master Thomas' and his art to have a clear idea of how he passed his heritage on to his son (and, of course, whether he did this orally or also in writing). The Irish poets (*filid*) and bards were organized in an

---

[45] On the role of memory and techniques of memorization in the Middle Ages, see Yates 1966; Carruthers 1990; Janet Coleman 1992; compare also the contributions in Roy and Zumthor 1985. On memorization in antiquity and the early Christian centuries, see Klauser 1950; on the role of memorization in medieval education, see Riché 1989. See further section 4.2 below.

elaborate system of ranks with corresponding skills and rights, and there is some information on this – such as the rules of avoiding flaws in making poetry in the *Auraicept na n-Éces* ('The Scholars' Primer', 10th c. ?). It is, however, difficult to be certain how these were taught, and works like 'The Scholars' Primer' point to written rather than oral instruction.[46] In his *ensenhamen* ('Instruction', PC 242a.1; composed *c.* 1160), the Catalan troubadour Guiraut de Cabreira (Guerau de Cabrera) criticizes his *joglar* Cabra for his lack of musical talent:

> Mal t'ensegnet
> cel que·t mostret
> los detz amenar ni l'arson
> (ll. 13–15) (Pirot 1972: 546)

He taught you badly,/ the person who showed you/ how to place the fingers and the bow (on the strings of the instrument)

By the same token, he enumerates a number of works, in particular *chansons de geste*, which the *joglar* masters only very imperfectly. Similar lists are found in other works; they tell us something about the repertoire (real or ideal) of a minstrel, but little or nothing about the way it is acquired. Musical skills are taught, as the verses from the *ensenhamen* make clear, and it is not unlikely that the singing of song and the chanting of epic poetry was also part of this instruction.[47]

For a better understanding of the teaching and transmission of oral poetry the evidence from oral traditions which are still observable is essential. Maurice Bowra, in his *Heroic Poetry*, quotes some Russian performers of *byliny* on how they learned their epic songs, and in *bylina* studies, the concept of regional 'schools of singers' has been developed by a number of scholars.[48] Bowra also mentions the oral tradition of Uzbek epic singers, a subject more closely analysed by Viktor Zhirmunsky, particularly in his monograph on Uzbek oral epic poetry, which he wrote together with the Uzbek folklorist Hādī Zarif. It was usual for a singer-to-be to stay with a master singer for a certain period. Generally, teaching and board were free in exchange for help in the household and on the farm. Learning an epic consisted in repeatedly listening to the performance of the teacher and in imitating what was heard by repeating the poems in smaller portions. These units were then composed into a larger whole. When the young singer was sufficiently trained, a public first performance was organized, where he received his teacher's blessing (called *fatiḥa*, an Arabic loan-word) and was 'released (from his articles)'.[49]

What Zhirmunsky and Zarif write about the training of Uzbek *bakhshi*s is also true of other traditions in the area. The Karakalpak epic singer with whom I have worked for

---

[46] See the tract 'Trefhocul' in Calder 1917: 148–69. On the *bard* and *fili*, see Murphy 1940 and Turville-Petre 1971; see also Williams 1971 and ch. 5 (J. Harris and K. Reichl), section 2.3 [pp. 162–63]; compare ch. 3 (M. Richter), pp. 114–16, and, on Old Irish, ch. 9 (J. F. Nagy).

[47] On the medieval *scholae mimorum*, where generally only instrumental skills were taught, see Salmen 1960: 180–84.

[48] See Bowra 1952: 428 ff.; Chicherov 1982; Novikov 2000: 176–266.

[49] See Zhirmunsky and Zarifov 1947: 36–37; for an English translation, see Reichl 2001: 221–22. For the 'singers of tales' of the Turkic peoples, among them the Uzbek *bakhshi*, see Reichl 1992: 57–91. For a similar account of how Persian narrators learn the oral performance of the *Shāh-nāma*, see Page 1979: 198-99; compare also chapter 25 (J. Rubanovich) in this volume.

a quarter of a century, Jumabay-jyrau Bazarov, had acquired three epics (as well as a number of shorter songs) from a master singer in very much the same way in the course of three years.⁵⁰ A similarly 'structured' transmission of oral heritage is also found in other cultures: Ruth Finnegan mentions the training of singers in Rwanda and the Maori 'schools of learning', and a number of scholars have studied the West African *griot* and other African oral artists and their training.⁵¹

When poetry is transmitted by word of mouth, its most noticeable feature is its fluidity. This fluidity can be of different kinds. In shorter poetry such as folk lyrics or ballads a certain stability in the wording of different versions can often be observed, which is doubtless the result of 'memory devices' such as metrical constraints (rhyme) and 'memorable' words and phraseological units.⁵² For longer poetry, such as epics, variation and divergence seems to be the rule in many traditions. The variability of oral epics has been well studied by Parry and Lord. According to their (as well as other Slavicists') research, the South Slavic singer of tales 'knows' an epic because he knows the story-line and its constituent motifs, masters formulaic diction to express the tale in verse and can manipulate the conventional themes (type-scenes) as building-blocks of the narrative. Every performance is different and the singer is said to 'compose in performance'. The fluidity and performance-dependent variability of the epic is nicely illustrated by an episode related by Matthias Murko, who in 1912 collected material on the South Slavic epics in Bosnia, Croatia and Dalmatia. A Muslim bey was dissatisfied with the singer's description of the hero and interrupted his performance by shouting: '*Nakiti momka, konja, nećeš mu za svoje pare kupovati*', 'Decorate the young man, the horse, you don't have to pay for it!'⁵³

## 4.2 Remembering vs. Memorizing

It is to be noted, however, that versions of an epic performed by the same singer are limited in their range of variation. An example from the Parry collection will exemplify this. In the second volume of *Serbocroatian Heroic Songs* three versions of the *Song of Bagdad* by Salih Ugljanin are published, of which two are complete (versions 1 and 3) and one is fragmentary (version 2). Of the two complete versions one comprises 1,620 and the other 1,368 lines; Lord lists 12 plot elements by which the two versions differ.⁵⁴ Such differences are, for instance, that in Version 1 it is told that Djerdjelez (Đerđelez) Alija and his army 'traversed land and countryside by easy stages from Bosnia to Stam-

---

⁵⁰ See Reichl 2000: 36 ff. The Karakalpaks live on the lower reaches of the Amu-Darya and the shores of the Aral Sea in north-western Uzbekistan.
⁵¹ Finnegan 1974: 55; on the training of *griots*, see Hale 1998: 172–92, on other African traditions, Okpewho 1992: 21–25. On the South Slavic singers' acquisition of their repertoire, see Lord 1960: 17–29. See also the discussion of learning in Merriam 1964: 145–63.
⁵² See Goody 1987: 167 ff.; Rubin 1998.
⁵³ Murko 1913: 22. On 'ornamentation' in the South Slavic epics, see the discussion of Avdo Medjedović in Lord 1991: 57–71.
⁵⁴ Versions 2 and 3 are not translated; version 2 was sung on July 24, 1934 and version 3 was dictated on July 23, 1934. See *SCHS*: I, 338–39. – On the versions of this song by Sulejman Fortić and Lord's later recordings, see Lord 1951; compare also Lord 1960: 117–18 and Lord 1981.

bol, and they arrived in the city of Stambol', while in Version 3 'Alija's army goes first to Salonika, where it embarks in ships for Stambol' (*SCHS*: I, 79 and 339). Looking at the lines in question, one can see that this is a very short passage and also a passage in which the 'framing-lines' (the first and last) are either verbally or at least semantically identical:

> Ej! Slaziše zemljom i svijetom,
> Lak' polako Bosni do Stambola,
> Ej! sidoše do grada Stambola.
> (ll. 897–99) (*SCHS*: II, 17)[55]

Ej! They went (down) on land and countryside,/ leisurely from Bosnia to Stambol,/ Ej! they went (down) to the city of Stambol.

> Sad odoše zemljom i svijetom,
> Pa šljegoše šeher Seljaniku,
> I u more nađoše đemije.
> Voziše se morom nesitijem,
> Dok izbiše kod grada Stambola.
> (ll. 647–51) (*SCHS*: II, 47)

Now they went (away) on land and countryside,/ then they reached the city of Saloniki,/ and at the sea they found ships./ They travelled on the insatiable sea,/ until they made it to the city of Stambol.

In Version 2 Alija and his companions cross the sea as in Version 3:

> Pa sljegoše zemljom i svijetom,
> Lak polako niz gradove ravne,
> A sidoše šeher Seljaniku,
> A Seljanika pitomu Primorju.
> Na obalu moru silaziše,
> E na more punahu đemije,
> Pa krenuše ka grada Stambola,
> Ka Stambolu gradu carevome.
> (ll. 692–99) (*SCHS*: II, 33)

Then they travelled on land and countryside,/ leisurely along low-lying towns,/ and they came (down) to the town of Saloniki,/ Saloniki on the pleasant coast./ They went (away) to the shore of the sea,/ eh, they put the ship on the sea,/ then set off to the city of Stambol,/ to Stambol the imperial city.

The variations are such that the verbal and semantic relationships between the passages are evident. These 'similarities in change' can be further underlined by looking at a passage at the beginning of the heroic song, where a journey in the opposite direction is described (in all three versions), with a ship crossing from Stambol to Saloniki:

| Version 1 | Version 2 | Version 3 |
|---|---|---|
| ll. 117–23 (II, 9) | ll. 100–106 (II, 27) | ll. 97–101 (II, 41) |
| | Tàtar vîknu, surūdîja pîsnu, | |
| | Pa krenuše sa grada Stambola, | |
| Dokljen skelji moru silazišе, | Ravno poljem na obalu moru. | Slježe Suka moru na obalu. |
| A na skelje moru dolaziše, | | |

---

[55] For *sidoše* read *sidoše*. For help with the texts I am grateful to Aida Vidan (Harvard University).

| | | |
|---|---|---|
| Pa na more vozi *ju* đemiju.<br>Uvoziše sebe i paripe,<br>Pa pušćaše pro mora đemiju,<br>Ka zvijezdu preko vedra neba,<br>Dok ispade šeher Seljaniku. | Kad na more nalazi đemiju,<br>Uvoziše sebe i menzile,<br>Pa pro mora pušćaše đemiju,<br><br>Dok ispade šeher Seljaniku. | Na obalu nalazi đemiju.<br>Uvoziše sebe i menzile,<br>Voziše se preko mora ravna<br><br>Dok ispade šeher Seljaniku. |
| **Version 1** (I, 69) | **Version 2** | **Version 3** |
| | The riders shouted, the drivers called out,<br>then he started on his journey from the city of Stambol, | |
| They travelled until they came to the shore of the sea,<br>and when they came to the shore of the sea,<br>they embarked in a ship on the sea.<br>They embarked themselves and their horses,<br>and then they cast the ship loose,<br>and (it sailed across the sea) even as a star across the clear heavens,<br>until he [i. e. Suka] went ashore at the city of Salonika. | and went straight down the field to the seashore.<br><br><br>When he found a ship at the sea,<br>they embarked themselves and their horses,<br>and then they cast the ship loose<br><br><br>until he went ashore at the city of Salonika. | Suka came to the shore of the sea,<br><br><br>at the shore he found a ship.<br><br>They embarked themselves and their horses,<br>they went across the flat sea,<br><br><br>until he went ashore at the city of Salonika. |

Without wanting to down-play the fluidity of the oral text, I would like to stress that a closer analysis often reveals a greater stability than is at first perceived. This is also true of Kirghiz oral epic. Wilhelm Radloff, in the introduction to his collection of Kirghiz epics of 1885, compared the art of the Kirghiz epic singer with that of the Homeric *aoidos*, stressing the facility with which a skilful narrator can 'improvise' with recourse to 'Vortragstheile' or 'Bildtheilchen', formulaic units ranging from a verse-line to typical scenes.[56] Radloff's comments, which foreshadow the results of Parry's and Lord's research, have often been interpreted as implying on the one hand a mechanical manipulation of pre-fabricated elements and on the other complete liberty on the part of the singer, resulting in entirely different versions of one and the same epic. The Kirghiz epic tradition is certainly characterized by fluidity, which is not surprising given the length of their epics: the cycle of epics on their main hero, Manas, comprises over 200,000 verse-lines in for instance the version of the Kirghiz bard Jüsüp Mamay (b. 1918) from the Kirghiz district of north-western China (Sinkiang) (Lang Ying 2001). Textual stability can, however, also be found, in particular in the elaboration of recurrent motifs and type-scenes (Reichl 1995). While the concept of the singer who has acquired a technique which provides him with the elements he needs to perform an epic is useful, it needs stressing that singers do not learn these elements in isolation from specific poems. When a singer knows a specific epic, he knows more than a collection of elements which he arranges according to the story-line; he knows a tale, a work of poetry, which has a specific shape and often also specific wording. This emerges from the study of Turkic

---

[56] Radloff 1885: xviff. (in the introduction to the German translation volume). For a partial English translation, see Radloff 1990.

traditions like the epics of the Karakalpak singer Jumabay Bazarov already mentioned (Reichl 2007: 81–97). In addition, within one and the same tradition some individual singers might be more conservative and others more innovative, which means that the degree of stability (or variability) might differ not only from tradition to tradition, but also from singer to singer.[57]

Sometimes the fluidity of oral poetry is restricted by the existence of written texts that have crossed the path of oral transmission. The performers of sung narrative poetry from West Sumatra (*sijobang*) have generally acquired their repertoire orally, as Nigel Phillips writes: 'Most of the *tukang sijobang* [epic singers] practising today say they learned by listening to their teacher recite a section of the story, and then singing it back to him, either at once or on a later occasion' (1981: 11). Nevertheless, some of the singers have also been in contact with written sources (11–14):

> At one extreme, Buyueng said that he had had no *guru* but had learned the story from a very large, old book written in Arabic script [...]. Jasa, now retired, apparently learned both by listening to his teacher and by reading passages from a book, which his teacher would then hear him sing. Sutan [...] is being taught by his uncle Sawi [...] by means of written versions of each episode, which Sutan is supposed to learn by heart. [...] although he is officially learning from written sources, it seems likely that Sutan learns much, perhaps most, by listening to other *tukang sijobang* [...]. A fourth *tukang sijobang*, Syaf, told me that when learning the first episodes he had made full notes from his teacher's recitation, and had kept them for a year or so, but for the remainder of the story had switched over to oral learning because he found it easier.

In the Arabic, but also Persian and Turkish (as well as generally Turkic) traditions written texts are used by the 'reader of tales', who might dispose of the fixed text quite freely, however (see chapters 24, 25, and 26 below). Apart from writing there might be other memory props that help to guarantee a certain stability of oral transmission. An interesting case is the performance of the epic of *Pābūjī* in Rajasthan: it is generally recited in front of a cloth (*paṛ*) depicting the various episodes of the epic tale. The performance is therefore aptly called 'reading the *paṛ*'.[58]

After this excursion into the world of primary orality, we return to the question of how longer narrative poetry could have been transmitted orally in the Middle Ages. Simplifying somewhat the situation found in various oral traditions, we can say that oral transmission can be both conservative, aiming at maximum closeness to the model learned, and innovative, audience-dependent, with a certain amount of flexibility. While it is comparatively easy to understand changes introduced in the course of oral transmission, the opposite, the stability of a text without the existence of a written text, is more in need of an explanation. Formulaic diction and formal constraints (metrical, musical, linguistic), typical scenes (themes) and 'runs' help to stabilize oral transmission. Furthermore, in traditions where exact imitation of aurally received poetry is the ideal and perhaps also part of the training, at least some stability in the course of the handing on of verbal art by word of mouth can be achieved. Although verbatim oral transmission of

---

[57] Alois Schmaus distinguishes two types of *bylina* singers, an 'intensive' conservative type and an 'extensive' innovative type (1958: 119–20).

[58] See Smith 1991; on the high degree of textual fixity, *ibid.*, pp. 25–27.

*1 Plotting the Map of Medieval Oral Literature* 29

texts like the *Vedas* has been both stressed and denied, cases of almost verbatim transmission in oral contexts have been reported. One is Somali oral poetry, about which John W. Johnson notes (2002: 194):

> The metrical templates of classical Somali poetry are so complex that they tend to eliminate all but the most predictable minor variation based on faulty memory and sometimes the 'corrective' manipulation of a reciter/memorizer. Add the range of acceptable topics for any given genre, and a musical structure which sometimes actually participates in the meter, and one is able to understand how the goal of verbatim memorization becomes the norm of this tradition.

There is no reason to doubt that medieval poetry was memorized in a comparable way without the help of written texts. Not all medieval poetry is formulaic to the extent that the South Slavic epics are and not all variant versions of poetic works (with a presumably oral background) show the kinds of variations that different recordings of a South Slavic heroic song show. In many cases, memorization is possibly a more likely alternative than 'remembering' and the resulting 'composition in performance'.[59]

For various medieval works a 'memorial' transmission has been proposed, with modifications and provisos, depending on the poetic tradition, work and period in question.[60] I have also argued for a memorial transmission of some types of Middle English popular romance (in particular in the tail-rhyme metre), motivated by my research on Turkic oral and popular narrative poetry (Reichl 2002). There is, however, one additional factor which is of importance in the present context. While textual stability can be found in purely oral transmission, it is doubtless greatest when oral and written transmission cross paths. This can be shown to be the case when in addition to the 'singer of tales' the 'reader of tales' is also active or when the singers have access to manuscripts or have come under the influence of printed editions. The written transmission of texts that were probably cultivated in an oral milieu is a fact – otherwise these works would not have been preserved. The dissemination of many of these texts, as far as it is accessible and reconstructible to us today, might have been restricted to manuscripts; others, however, might have had a parallel oral transmission, which intersected at various points with their circulation as written texts. This might explain why some of the variants that have been thought to be due to oral transmission are of a kind that cannot easily be reconciled with the types of variation encountered in oral poetry 'composed in performance'. The inapplicability of the Oral Theory to a medieval text does not automatically rule out oral transmission (Finnegan 1988: 139–74).

### 4.3 Oral Composition

So far only oral performance and oral transmission have been discusssed. In her survey of oral poetry, Ruth Finnegan underlines that 'oral poetry' means three things: 'The

---

[59] On Lord's concept of 'remembering' and his opposition to 'memorization' in oral tradition, see Lord 1995: 183 ff. ('Editor's Addendum'). Compare also Haferland 2004: 134–72.

[60] McGillivray 1990 provides a summary discussion of memorial transmission with regard to the Middle English romances; compare also Reichl 2002. On memorial transmission with reference to Middle High German heroic poetry, see Haferland 2004; compare Müller 2005. On 'mnemonic anchors', see ch. 6 (T. DuBois), esp. sections 3 and 4, in this volume.

three ways in which a poem can most readily be called oral are in terms of (1) its composition, (2) its mode of transmission, and (3) (related to (2)) its performance. Some oral poetry is oral in all these respects, some in only one or two.'[61] Oral composition is not to be confused with composition in performance, even if there is a relationship between the two and, as will be seen, a distinction is in some cases difficult. When a poem or tale is said to be orally composed, it is thought to be created basically in the same way as a written work, but of course without the help of writing. An oral poet invents or creates a work of verbal art either spontaneously or after a period of reflection.[62] Contest songs depend on the ability of the contestants to be quick at repartee and to master the lyric form employed for the song. Such songs are found in many oral traditions, among them in German folklore (*Schnaderhüpfel*), in Welsh, and in the song-repertoire of the Turkic-speaking peoples.[63] In the Middle Ages the Provençal genre of the *tenson* has been thought to have been 'improvised' or composed spontaneously. David Jones, in his monograph on the *tenson*, surveys the arguments for oral composition and comes to the conclusion that a number of these poems seem to have indeed been orally composed (improvised), but that their majority were not (1934:64). Praise poems (for instance those of the Zulu or Xhosa in Southern Africa) and contest poems are well-known examples of improvised oral poetry, that is, the creation of new poems in specific situations. Their newness, however, rests on traditional diction and is dependent on generic templates (metre, rhyme-words, phraseological units etc.). On closer analysis, some of these songs are highly formulaic; the ability to produce repartees on the spur of the moment depends very much on a knowledge of other songs and lines, which are then adapted to the new situation.[64]

A different case is the creation of longer narrative poems or epics. The traditional singer of tales does not as a rule consider himself the creator of narrative poetry: he thinks of himself rather as the bearer of tradition, a link in the chain of transmission. This is evidenced by his references to teachers or sometimes a whole genealogy of teachers or master-singers (see also section 4.1 above). It is noteworthy that these narrators only occasionally compose new epics or heroic songs. Murko remarks about the South Slavic singers that '(epic) songs about recent events are rarely sung.'[65] The Russian *bylina*-singer Marfa Kryukova was exceptional in having composed a narrative song about

---

[61] Finnegan 1977:17; similarly in Finnegan 1974. For an elaboration of the threefold distinction between (oral vs. written) composition, transmission and performance (private reading vs. public reading/ performance) with reference to medieval literature, see Bäuml 1984.

[62] For composition after a period of reflection as 'deliberative composition' and the distinction of various modalities, see Harris 1983:211ff.

[63] On the *Schnaderhüpfel*, see Beitl 1973; a specialized form of song-contest among Turkish popular poet-singers (*aşık*) demands that the contestants keep a needle between their lips while singing in order to avoid bilabial and labiodental consonants; it is called *dudak değmez* (the lips don't touch); see Gürsoy-Naskali 2000. On the medieval predecessors of the Welsh eisteddfod, see ch. 3 (M. Richter), pp. 115–16.

[64] On the formulaic element in the *Schnaderhüpfel* see Beitl 1973:643–47; on the relationship between formulaic diction, improvisation and memorization in Xhosa praise poetry, see Opland 1983:152–93.

[65] Murko 1913:32. Compare Chadwick and Chadwick 1932–40: II, 434–56, esp. the summary on pp. 437–39.

Lenin, and Central Asian epic singers have similarly been encouraged to create epics on recent history, although on the whole without much success.[66] Among Uzbek singers, the term *shāir* ('poet', from Arabic) denotes a singer who has composed poetry of his own. This type of poetry generally consists of shorter poems of topical or autobiographical character. In 1983, when I asked the Kirghiz singer Jüsüp Mamay (see p. 27 above) whether he would be able to compose an epic on a story I would tell him, he did not at first understand my question. After a while he realized what I meant and answered cheerfully: 'Oh, to turn prose into verse? Yes, I can do this!' The verse, of course, would have been the highly patterned verse of oral epic poetry. Bede's story of Caedmon comes to mind here: he was told new stories, on which he reflected – calling them back to mind and ruminating on them, as Bede says (*rememorando secum et* [...] *ruminando*) – and then turned prose into verse, the verse of oral tradition.[67] There is no reason to deny individual talent and individual creativity to singers of tales. It is equally incontestable that specific epics have originated with a specific singer at some point in time. What characterizes these works, however, is that they are grounded in an oral tradition, and this means that they are highly conventional in structure, form and content. It is this conventionality which makes it difficult and problematic to distinguish neatly between oral composition and composition in performance.

This is particularly true of poetic traditions where 'remembering' rather than 'memorizing' is the rule in oral transmission. One must, however, be wary of generalizations; every case has its own history. Jüsüp Mamay is not Caedmon, and the Bavarian *Schnaderhüpfel*-singer and his or her partner are not Cercamon and Guilhalmi as they debate in a *tenson* generally interpreted as a debate among jongleurs.[68] For medieval literature, oral composition is probably the least accessible aspect; we will have to be content in the main with recognizing traces of oral performance and oral transmission.

## 5 Oral Literature and Genre

In the *ensenhamen* by Guiraut de Cabreira from which I have quoted above (section 4.1) the troubadour finds fault with his *joglar* Cabra: he enumerates a vast repertoire of works which Cabra should master, but he apparently fails to perform to Guiraut's satisfaction. This is a witty poem and should not be taken literally; Cabra was in all probability not as incompetent as the poem makes him out to be, and it is unlikely that he was meant to perform all the works listed in the *ensenhamen*.[69] It is interesting to note

---

[66] On Marfa Kryukova, see Bowra 1952: 28, 116–17, 339–40, and *passim*; on Central Asian epics inspired by recent Soviet history, see Reichl 1992: 80–81.
[67] The Caedmon story has been discussed many times; for an interpretation of Caedmon as an oral singer, see Magoun 1955b and, from a comparative point of view, especially Zhirmunsky 1979. For text and translation of the story, see Colgrave and Mynors 1969: 414–21. See further the discussion by K. O'Brien O'Keeffe (ch. 4) below, pp. 123–27, and ch. 5 (pp. 146–47).
[68] For text and translation, see Rossi 2009: 130–35; compare *ibid.*, pp. 53–58. On debate poems, see also ch. 22 on the pastourelle (L. Spetia).
[69] The poem is comprehensively discussed in Pirot 1972 and edited and translated (into French) on pp. 546–54. On the genre of the *ensenhamen*, see Bossuat et al. 1964: 410–12, and Monson 1981.

that the ideal *joglar* was expected to perform both lyrics (or songs) and narrative poetry. Among the lyric genres explicitly mentioned are the *sirventes*, the *balada*, the *estribot*, the *rotrouenge*, the *tenson*, and also the *vers* of known troubadours such as Jaufre Rudel and Marcabru. This is a variegated group of lyrical genres: the courtly *canso* (*vers*), the satirical-critical *sirventes* (to which the *ensenhamen* belongs), the debate poem (*tenson*), the dance song (*balada*) and other forms of a probably popular character (*estribot* and *rotrouenge*).[70] Among the works of narrative poetry the *chansons de geste* figure prominently, with the 'great *geste* of Charlemagne' in the forefront (*gran jesta de Carlon*), but Arthurian romance (or *roman courtois*) is also represented, together with the *romans antiques* (*Roman de Thèbes*), the tales of Apollonius of Tyre and of Pyramus and Thisbe. Even if Guiraut's poem is satirical and no doubt exaggerated, his list reminds us that in actual practice genres co-occur and that a performer might be expected to have mastered more than one poetic genre or subgenre. Courtly romance and *chanson de geste*, dance song and *canso* do not exclude one another, at least not in the repertoire that Guiraut expects of his *joglar*.

All of the genres that Guiraut enumerates belong to the 'classic' literary genres of lyric and epic; non-fictional genres are absent. As the various terms for lyric poems indicate, genres were defined by differing criteria: by reference to form (*vers* 'verse'), content (*tenson* 'dispute'), function (*sirventes* 'serving a purpose') or performance (*balada* 'danse'). Although there is a good deal of evidence for medieval genre definitions – the codification of lyric genres in the fourteenth-century Provençal *Leys d'Amors* is a prominent example of this – a systematic classification of medieval genres is riddled with many problems, as Hugo Kuhn has shown with regard to Middle High German literature.[71] Nor is genre a difficult concept only for the Middle Ages. The genre theories developed from the eighteenth century onward for European literature are as problematic for the contemporary literary scene as they are for the Middle Ages. Various approaches to genre have been devised in order to do justice to historical genres and yet evade the pitfalls of normative poetics. Alastair Fowler (1982) has proposed that we distinguish between genres as historical kinds and modes such as 'tragic', 'comic', 'romance' etc., which constitute subgenres. Within the framework of anthropological linguistics and discourse analysis, various proposals for the classification and definition of 'communicative events' and 'discourse genres' have been made. There is much to be said for this approach, since from the point of view of performance, genres can be analysed as types of communicative events. This approach, however, presupposes the possibility of direct observation, a condition that imposes strict limitations on its applicability to medieval oral literature.[72]

---

[70] The *estribot* and the *rotrouenge* are ill defined and have been differently interpreted; on the former see Ricketts 1991, on the latter Bec 1977–78: I, 183–89. On Troubadour lyric genres, see also Paden 2000.

[71] See Kuhn 1956. For a discussion of medieval genres, see also Jauss 1972. For succinct information on the *Leys d'Amors*, see Bossuat et al. 1964: 928–30; on the genre of the *sirventes*, see *ibid.*: 1396–99.

[72] For a discussion see ch. 5 on performance and performers below, esp. pp. 142–46; see also ch. 6 on oral poetics (T. A. DuBois), esp. pp. 204–14.

## 5.1 Smaller Genres and 'niedere Dichtung'

Although Guiraut enumerates a number of works and several genres, there are also curious omissions. From the condemnation of minstrels who recite *verba turpia* in ecclesiastical texts we can deduce that they also told fabliaux, merry and very often risqué tales in verse. Genres that were probably current in oral tradition include proverbs, riddles, charms, and all kinds of wisdom and 'memorial poetry'. All of these are known to us only because they have been written down, and some were also composed in writing by literate authors. The Latin riddles by Aldhelm (d. 709) are outstanding representatives of this genre; his *enigma* were much read and admired and one of them is also found in Old English translation among the riddles of the *Exeter Book*.

Andreas Heusler, in his study of Older Germanic poetry, groups five genres together as 'lower genres' (*niedere Gattungen*): ritual poetry, charms, proverbial poetry, 'memorial poetry' (*Merkdichtung*), and short lyrics. These contrast with the 'higher genres' (*höhere Gattungen*), which consist of praise poetry and narrative lays and, according to Heusler, were the domain of the (oral) court poet. The 'lower genres', on the other hand, Heusler contended, were recited (and composed) at an early stage by anybody and everybody (1941: 26–113, esp. 108–13). This is partially validated by the findings of folklorists and ethnologists. Proverbs, riddles, and short lyrics might be the common property of society as a whole, but ritual poetry, charms and memorial verse (including genealogies) are as a rule the property of special groups such as shamans or public orators.[73] Some of these genres of predominantly oral circulation are discussed below, especially in connection with oral poetics and with ritual.[74]

In 1930 André Jolles published an influential study of short literary genres such as riddle, joke, proverb and legend. Jolles was not interested in the orality of these 'simple forms' (*einfache Formen*); he analysed these discourse genres as expressions in language of basic concerns and modes of thought, as verbal forms that carry the seeds of more complex genres.[75] Proverbs, riddles and similar smaller genres have been studied, apart from medievalists, mostly by folklorists and ethnologists, who have insisted that for the understanding of 'folklore genres' the respective ethnic classification system has to be taken into consideration. Generic labels borrowed from one tradition often fail when applied to others.[76]

## 5.2 The Case of Slavic Epic Poetry

It is mostly through the work of Milman Parry and Albert B. Lord that a wide circle of scholars in the field of epic poetry – Homerists, medievalists, folklorists – have been

---

[73] Under the heading of 'oral folklore', folklore handbooks like Dorson 1972 discuss folk narrative, narrative folk poetry, folk epic, proverbs, riddles and folk speech. For a theoretical discussion of the concept of folk poetry, see Toporov 1974; compare also Horálek 1974 on the history and typology of folk poetry. For a critical discussion of folklore genres, see Finnegan 1992: 135–57.
[74] See chapters 6 (T. A. DuBois) and 7 (P. Roilos); compare also the discussion of the 'heroic tale' in ch. 18 (S. N. Azbelev) and the detailed discussion of Heusler's position in ch. 8 on older Germanic poetry (J. Harris).
[75] See Jolles 1930; compare Ranke 1965 and von Sydow 1948.
[76] See Abrahams 1976; Ben-Amos 1976b; Voigt 1980; Honko 1989.

made familiar with the rich oral epic traditions of the South Slavs. Parry and Lord were, however, not the first to introduce the non-specialist to the Serbian, Croatian and Bosnian heroic songs. H. Munro Chadwick and Nora K. Chadwick devoted a long chapter to 'Yugoslav oral poetry' in the second volume of their monumental *Growth of Literature* (1932–40: II, 297–456). They in turn built on the research of an older generation of scholars, of the nineteenth and early twentieth centuries, Slavicists like Matthias Murko, Kosta Hörmann and Gerhard Gesemann. The renown of South Slavic oral epic poetry was, however, established at an even earlier date. Vuk Stefanović Karadžić, who wrote the first Serbian grammar book (Vienna, 1814) and who compiled a Serbian-German-Latin dictionary (Vienna, 1818), also edited and collected oral poetry. His edition of Serbian oral poems (*Srpske narodne pjesme*) became a landmark in South Slavic epic studies and has attained the status of a classic in South Slavic literature.[77] Vuk Karadžić was greatly encouraged in his efforts to bring Serbian into the circle of European written languages by Jacob Grimm, and his work on oral poetry sparked off a number of translations and interpretations in the Germany of the Romantic era. Goethe was one of the admirers both of Vuk Karadžić and of the poetry he published.

In an anthology of the epic poetry of the Slavic peoples, edited by the Russian folklorist P. G. Bogatyrev (1959), Serbian heroic songs and ballads hold an important place, as is to be expected. This is by no means the only Slavic tradition which can boast of oral epic poetry, however. In Bogatyrev's collection space is also given to the Bulgarians, a reminder of the fact that the South Slavic epic traditions comprise several branches – the epic songs of the Croats, the Serbs and Montenegrins, the Bosnians and Hercegovinians, the Bulgarians and Macedonians. The Albanians, who speak a non-Slavic Indo-European language, also have a strong oral epic tradition. In fact, some of the singers whom Lord and Parry recorded were bilingual and performed in Albanian also.[78] In Bogatyrev's anthology, the Eastern Slavs are represented by Russian *byliny* and historical songs and by Ukrainian *dumy* and historical songs.[79] Bogatyrev also included White Russian songs and folktales and numerous songs, many of them historical, from several West Slavic peoples (Polish, Czech, Moravian, Slovak, Upper Sorbian and Lower Sorbian).

One of the Sobian poems translated by Bogatyrev, a narrative song on the victory of the Sorbs over the Germans, illustrates some of the problems posed by the late documentation of poetry that was possibly composed in medieval times and transmitted orally to later centuries. The Sorbs are a small Slavic-speaking minority in the Lusatia area in the eastern part of Germany (with an estimated 20,000 to 30,000 speakers). Their language (consisting of two distinct dialects) was first written down in the first half of the six-

---

[77] His collection of lyric and epic songs was first published in four volumes in Leipzig and Vienna in 1823–33 and in a second edition in Vienna in 1841–62. The first volume contains lyrics (*ženske pjesme*), volumes 2 to 4 narrative poems (*junačke pjesme*); reprinted in Karadžić 1987.
[78] Among them Salih Ugljanin, mentioned above; see *SCHS*: I, 60.
[79] A representative choice of the various genres of Russian oral narrative poetry – *byliny*, historical songs (*istoricheskie pesni*), ballads and humoristic pieces (*skomoroshiny*) – is found in Putilov 1984; see his explanations on pp. 14ff., 212ff., 266ff., and 350ff. On the theory of folklore genres in Russian scholarship, see Putilov 1976: 128–76. The Ukrainian *duma* has many similarities to the Russian *bylina*; for a collection of texts with English translations, see Tarnawsky and Kilina 1979.

teenth century. The song in question was collected in the nineteenth century and edited by L. Haupt and J. E. Schmaler in 1841. In its twenty-five stanzas it narrates the victory of the Sorbs over the Germans, which prompted the 'king and prince' (*kral i fjeršta*) to give them valuable presents. The 'king and prince' is thought to have been the Polish duke and king Boleslav I (967–1025), whose reign was marked by his wars against Emperor Henry II.[80] In accordance with Axel Olrik's 'Law of Three' (*Gesetz der Dreizahl*) (1965: 133) the Sorbs defeat the Germans three times; after the first victory they receive new clothes and are drafted by the 'king and prince', after the second they are given clothes of sable and scarlet, and after the third sorrel horses and swords. The song is ballad-like in its repetitions, but also has faint echoes of medieval epic poetry, as when the Sorbs gather to do battle at the beginning of the song:

> Serbjo so do Njemcow hotowachu,
> Słowčka pak Njemski ńemóžachu,
>    Słowčka pak Njemski ńemóžachu.
>
> Swoje sej koniki sedowachu,
> Swoje sej wotrohi pšipinachu,
>    Swoje sej wotrohi pšipinachu.
>
> Swoje sej mečiki pšipasachu,
> Do runoh' pola so zjezdžowachu,
>    Do runoh' pola so zjezdžowachu.

> The Sorbs were marching against the Germans,/ they did not know a single German word,/ they did not know a single German word.// They saddled their horses,/ they put on their spurs,/ they put on their spurs.// They girded their swords,/ and rode out on the flat field,/ and rode out on the flat field.

The song is sung to a melody that cannot, however, be earlier than the fifteenth century. This melody is also used for another narrative song in the collection, a song about the tragic fall of a bridegroom from his horse on the way to his wedding; this song is mentioned by Francis Child in his discussion of parallels to the Scottish-English ballad of *Clerk Colvill* (1882–98: I, 386). Interestingly, the same expressions for the saddling of the horses, the putting-on of spurs, the girding of the sword and the riding together on the flat field occur. What seemed to be a medieval echo must therefore more properly be seen as a trait of Sorbian popular style.[81] This observation casts doubt on the antiquity of our song. While it is possible that the *kral i fjeršta* is a reference to Boleslav I, the connection of this song to medieval oral poetry is extremely tenuous. This example shows that while later survivals of medieval oral poetry must not be neglected, every case has to be assessed critically before a poem, song or narrative can be claimed as relevant in the context of this book.

None of the Russian *byliny* has been preserved in a medieval manuscript. The term *bylina*, literally meaning 'that which was', goes back to an Old Russian word but has been used as a technical term for oral epic poetry only since the nineteenth century. The

---

[80] Haupt and Schmaler 1841–43: I, 32; on the dating see I, 328; the melody is found on p. 31 (vol I). For a discussion of this song, see also Bogatyrev 1959: 360.
[81] The medieval ring is more prominent in the German translation in Haupt and Schmaler 1841, where the spurs are chinking and the swords are flashing.

plural is *byliny* in Russian; the Anglicized form 'bylinas' is also found. The earliest texts of *byliny* come from the seventeenth century, and the first collection was only made in the eighteenth century.[82] There is, however, one medieval Russian text which has been compared to other medieval epics, namely the celebrated *Song of Igor* or, as it is known in the original, *Slovo o polku Igoreve*, 'The tale [word] of Igor's campaign'.[83]

The text of this work was found in a manuscript possibly dating from around 1400 (according to other opinions, around 1500); it is thought to have been composed at the end of the twelfth century and was first published in 1800. The manuscript was destroyed in the Moscow fire of 1812; all that survives are some copies of the first edition and a transcript of the text made for Catherine the Great. The work is written in prose (comprising 218 sentences), but there are stretches of rhythmic speech throughout the text. In the *Song of Igor* the unsuccessful campaign of Prince Igor Svyatoslavich of Novgorod-Seversk against the Turkic Cumans (or Polovtsians) in 1185 is described. Eager to win glory in battle, Igor calls on his warriors to depart on a military expedition:

> 'Brethren and warriors! It is better to be killed in battle than to become a captive.
> Let us mount our swift steeds, brethren! Let us view the blue river Don.'[84]

Together with his brother Vsevolod and their warriors he marches into the steppe. They encounter the Cumans and engage in a fierce fight. The Russians are victorious on the first day, but their luck changes on the second and defeat looms on the horizon. In the end the Russians are completely defeated and Igor and his son Vladimir are held captive by the Cumans. Igor, however, manages to flee, and the *Song* ends with the singer's praise of Igor and his companions in arms:

> Igor rides along the Borichev to the Church of the Holy Virgin of Pirogoshch. The lands are jubilant. The cities rejoice.
> Once the glory of the princes of yore was sung, now glory will be sung for the young. Glory to Igor, son of Sviatoslav, to fierce aurochs Vsevolod, and to Vladimir, son of Igor.
> Hail to the princes and the armies who fight for Christendom against the infidel hosts.
> Glory to the princes and to the army. Amen

The language of the *Song of Igor* is rich in poetic images and has attracted poets to translate the Old Russian text into a modern language, among them Rainer Maria Rilke (into German) and Vladimir Nabokov (into English). From the images of the poem I will single out only the motif of the beasts of battle, which is well known from Older Germanic heroic and epic poetry:[85]

> Igor leads his warriors to the river Don.
> The birds in the forests of oak portend his misfortune. The wolves conjure the tempest in the ravines. The screeching eagles call the beasts to the feast of bones. Foxes bark at crimson shields.

---

[82] For a survey, see Chadwick and Chadwick 1932–40: II, 1–296; on early texts, see *ibid.*, pp. 6–7, 134.
[83] The following remarks are intended as an introduction to ch. 18 by S. N. Azbelev in this volume, which presupposes a knowledge of the *Song of Igor*.
[84] Quoted from the translation in Zenkovsky 1963: 137–60. I have ignored the rhythmic typographic arrangement of the text that is widely used for the text and translations; see Likhachev 1976: 121–46. In the original manuscript the text was written as prose.
[85] See Magoun 1955a; Honegger 1998.

The poem, in its vigorous evocation of heroic deeds, shares many stylistic traits with other heroic poetry; by the same token it has a certain personal-lyrical quality through the voice of the singer and narrator, who comments on the situation, laments the fate of the defeated and expresses his regret about the discord among the Russian princes in a time of need, exhorting them to take action. The *Song of Igor*, with its poetic language and its involved structure – the narrative flow is more than once interrupted, by Prince Svyatoslav's dream, the lament of Igor's wife, and the singer's comments – is anything but a simple battle narrative. On account of its style and the numerous historical allusions the poem bears a certain learned stamp. In genre it hovers between heroic song, historical poem and poetic admonition. In the text it refers to itself as *pesn'* 'song', but it is uncertain how this *poème en prose* was recited and whether it was ever sung.

The *Song of Igor* has given rise to a voluminous scholarly literature.[86] It has also provoked controversy. A number of scholars have doubted the genuineness of the poem and conjectured a forgery, not unlike Macpherson's *Ossian*. As the original manuscript was destroyed in the Moscow fire of the Napoleonic wars, doubts have never been completely allayed. It is fair to say, however, that the sceptics form a minority. There are a great number of good arguments for the authenticity of the text, arguments advanced by such eminent specialists as Albert B. Lord or Roman Jakobson (1952). Sergey Nikolaevich Azbelev, in this book, adduces further considerations for placing the *Song of Igor* in a context of medieval epic poetry, with an ultimate grounding in oral poetry (see ch. 18 below).

To what extent the *byliny*, collected at a late period and often in circumstances reflecting the last stages of oral tradition, are medieval and to be considered in the context of medieval oral literature is a moot point. In content many *byliny*, especially those of the Kiev Cycle, reach back to the Middle Ages. In the *byliny* about Il'ya Muromets, Dobrynya Nikitich and Alësha Popovich the heroic milieu evoked is that of Prince Vladimir (I) of Kiev (d. 1015) and his *druzhina*, his band of military companions and retainers. 'The poems of the Kiev Cycle relate to the tenth or eleventh centures, which, if we may trust the picture of this period as presented by the Ancient Chronicle [...] constituted the Heroic Age of Russia.'[87] The Chadwicks add, however, that '*byliny* continued to be composed in the traditional Kiev style long after heroic conditions had ceased everywhere', which makes it difficult to date particular poems. Ilias von Riuzen – who is none other than Ilya Muromets – appears in the Middle High German epic *Ortnit* of the thirteenth century, an indication of the existence of medieval narrative traditions about this *bylina*-hero.[88] The chronology of the *byliny* has been much discussed; while it is generally accepted that many *byliny* have medieval roots, the precise relationship between the poems collected in the nineteenth and twentieth centuries and their medieval ancestors remains a matter for speculation.[89]

---

[86] The various aspects of the 'Song of Igor' are extensively treated in the five-volume encyclopaedia edited by O. V. Tvorogov et al. 1995.

[87] Chadwick and Chadwick 1932–40: II, 69. For English translations, see Chadwick 1932 and Bailey and Ivanova 1998.

[88] Although there is no reason to doubt the identification of this figure in the Middle High German epic (as well as in the *Thidrekssaga*) with the hero of the *byliny*, critical voices deny that this implies a relationship to the extant *byliny* about Ilya Muromets; see Studer 1931: 24–63; Trautmann 1942.

[89] The classification of the *byliny* into groups according to (imputed) chronology was favoured by the

The situation is similar for South Slavic epic songs. While there is an early text from 1556, and some manuscript texts from the seventeenth and eighteenth centuries, serious collecting began only with Vuk Stjepanović Karadžić (Chadwick and Chadwick 1932–40: II, 300). Marko Kraljević, son of King Vukašin, is the hero of a widely diffused cycle of heroic songs. The historical Vukašin and Marko lived at a time when the Turkish attacks on the Serbian Empire were finally successful. During the decade after the defeat of the Serbs in 1371 'the Turks gradually took over the whole of Macedonia. Many Serbian princes there still retained a shadowy independence as vassals of the sultan, and the most famous of these was Marko Kraljević, son of Vukašin, and his successor at Prilep. It is somewhat ironical that Marko, a Turkish vassal, should have become the hero of so many Serbian legends and ballads' (Darby 1968: 99–100). Marko Kraljević is also the hero of the earliest heroic song extant, a poem included in Petar Hektorović's *Ribanje* ('Fishing') of 1556, *Marko Kraljević i brat mu Andrijaš* (Marko Kraljević and His Brother Andrijaš) (Rakić 2006: 132–36). One of the cycles of heroic songs is centred on the Battle of Kosovo of 1389, when the Turks under Sultan Murad I defeated the Christian army of Serbs, Albanians, Croats, Bulgarians and Hungarians under Prince Lazar, ruler of north Serbia.[90] It is possible that the roots of the Kosovo poems, as with those on Marko, go back to the fifteenth or even late fourteenth century. Such an early date can, however, only be assigned to a portion of the *junačke pjesme* that have been collected; and even with poems for which a medieval origin can be surmised the medieval form of these poems is beyond our reach. We have to be content that we are in the presence of a tradition with roots in medieval orality, but also with a post-medieval life. It is predominantly the latter that has been the object of scholarly study.

## 5.3 Epic and Romance

With reference to medieval European narrative, W. P. Ker (1908) linked the epic to the 'heroic age', the age of the Germanic migrations, and romance to the 'age of chivalry', the High Middle Ages. While epic is predominantly heroic, romance conveys 'some notion of mystery and fantasy' and is best represented in Arthurian romance. There is some justification for this distinction, but as the discussions of both genres in literary criticism show, there is no universally accepted definition of either genre. In Western literature, the definition of epic takes as its point of reference the Classical tradition, especially Homer and Virgil. Essential characteristics are claimed to be verse-form, epic breadth, a heroic outlook, and, as Hegel maintained in his *Aesthetics*, the poetic reflection of 'the world of a nation and a time'.[91] With the exception of verse-form, all these traits are open to differing interpretations and there is no unanimity among scholars in their use of the term 'epic' (or 'heroic epic') when applied to medieval works. The term 'romance' fares no better. As the *Princeton Encyclopedia of Poetry and Poetics* puts it: 'The meaning

---

'historical school' of Vsevolod Miller; for a detailed discussion of various evolutionary theories, see Putilov 1999: 69–106.

[90] On this cycle and its relation to the historical event, see Koljević 1980: 153ff; compare also Redep 1991.

[91] On the definition of epic, see Merchant 1971; Hainsworth 1991; R. Martin 2005.

of the term "romance" is complicated by the fact that both in medieval and modern times it has been used loosely' (Preminger et al. 1993:751). Nevertheless, most critics would agree that there is a difference between epic and romance even if this difference is difficult to pin down. Northrop Frye suggested that we distinguish between two types of romance, 'naive' and 'sentimental romance': 'By naive romance I mean the kind of story that is found in collections of folk tales and märchen, like Grimms' Fairy Tales. By sentimental romance I mean a more extended and literary development of the formulas of naive romance.' (1976:3). In the case of popular romances, narratives that have to be placed in an oral milieu, the borderline between 'naive romance' and 'sentimental romance' is blurred: they are more developed than folktales, but not in accordance with the canons of written literature. Romance, as opposed to epic, implies in Frye's and other critics' view a type of narrative in which the plot is characterized by adventures of a 'romantic' rather than 'heroic' nature, in which marvellous elements rather than realistic details predominate and in which there is a tendency to intercalate additional motifs and subplots in a comparatively loose and adaptable narrative structure (Radulescu 2009).

In literary criticism, a number of conventions in the use of these terms have become established. The distinction between epic and romance as it was made by Ker lies at the basis of the English use of these terms. We speak of the epic of *Beowulf* but of the romance of *Sir Gawain and the Green Knight*. The latter is an Arthurian romance, one of the few Middle English romances of a courtly orientation. In French we would speak of a *roman courtois*, in German of a *höfischer Roman* (a representative of *höfische Epik*). In the Persian, Arabic and Turkish medieval traditions discussed in this book, the nomenclature is further confused. Firdausī's *Book of Kings* (*Shāh-nāma*) is an epic by any standards; it is one of the great epics of world literature. Other Persian narratives, whether in verse or prose, might be called romances on account of their similarity to European romances (such as the Alexander romances) (see further ch. 25 by J. Rubanovich). In the Arabic tradition some of the narratives are in verse, some in prose, some in a mixture of verse and prose. Some are of a heroic nature, others belong more to the type of adventure stories. There are traditions where these works are transmitted orally and others where they are the domain of the public reader. In Western sources terms like 'epic', 'romance', 'popular novel' and others are found; the native genre term for most of these works is *sīra* (plural *siyar*), meaning 'life-story'. Depending on the narrative and narrative tradition one Western term or the other might be appropriate (see further ch. 24 by T. Herzog). In Turkish the situation is similar. There are narratives (or cycles of narratives) that correspond to what in English would be called epics or heroic epics, and there are others for which the genre-label 'romance' seems more appropriate. All of these narratives are, however, prosimetric, i. e. in prose with passages in verse; from the point of view of occidental genre distinctions the denomination 'epic' therefore seems questionable. Arguments for interpreting these works as epics rather than as romances can be advanced; but this means, of course, that some of the tenets of genre theory have to be re-thought (see further ch. 26 in this volume).

## 6 Orality, Folksong and Medieval Lyrics

Not all genres of the medieval lyric were sung poetry, but an overwhelming majority were meant to be sung and therefore orally performed (Stevens 1990). In troubadour and trouvère poetry as well as in Minnesang the poet, as a rule, was also the composer. This situation lasted into the late Middle Ages; Guillaume de Machaut (1300–1377) is generally considered the last important medieval poet-musician. Much medieval lyric poetry was not only orally performed but seems to have originated in an oral milieu. In many lyrics, in particular those that have reached us anonymously, we are able to hear the sound of folksong – in style, imagery, rhythm, as well as musical and poetic form. An image from nature, a sigh of unrequited love, an exclamation or an 'onomatopoeic' refrain like 'hey, troly, lo' or 'tandaradei' suggest that these lyrics have been inspired by folksongs, that they are echoes of folksongs. In some cases, the lyrics preserved might not only imitate folksongs but actually be folksongs. One way of characterizing the orality of these lyrics is, then, to link them to folksongs: either as echoes of folksongs or as remnants, sometimes no doubt fragmentary, of folksongs. This, of course, raises the question of what it means to call a poem a folksong.

Medieval lyrics for which a closeness to orality can be assumed have also been called 'popular'. The terms 'folksong' and 'popular lyric' overlap and are sometimes difficult to distinguish. Richard Greene, in his study of the medieval carol (1977), draws a distinction between 'popular by origin' and 'popular by destination' (cxviii). There is also the dichotomy between *poesia popolare* and *poesia d'arte* as advocated and discussed by Benedetto Croce (1946). By *poesia popolare* Croce understood, in Lo Nigro's words, 'poetry in a popular tone, expressing simple feelings in correspondingly simple modes, but also a traditional heritage, i. e. a poetic creation that has been transmitted orally and has therefore been subject to a continuous process of communal re-elaboration' (1964:5). It is unclear how these various terms can be related to orality; this is an issue which has to be addressed when looking at the medieval lyric.[92]

There is also a difference to be made between a lyric that is a folksong or an echo of a folksong on the one hand and a lyric poem on the other into which elements from folksong are incorporated or cited, often as contrasts.[93] An analogue from music is the *quodlibet*, which typically consists of the quotation of well-known melodies. A modern example is, for instance, Charles Ives' Second String Quartet, in which both folksongs and hymns are quoted.

---

[92] On the concept of 'poesia popolare', see also ch. 13 (R. Morabito), pp. 373 and 379. On the medieval lyric see the chapters in this volume by J.-D. Müller (ch. 10, sections 3.2 and 3.3), A. L. Klinck (ch. 20), K. Boklund-Lagopoulou (ch. 21), L. Spetia (ch. 22), and J. Monroe (ch. 23); see also the chapters by T. DuBois (ch. 6, esp. pp. 214–19) and P. Roilos (ch. 7, esp. pp. 229–33).

[93] As in the Middle English poem 'Blow, northerne wynd'; see Boklund-Lagopoulou below, p. 571, and Klinck, p. 545. On popular strains in the early Middle English love lyric, see also Reichl 1997.

## 6.1 Folksong

In his *English Folksong: Some Conclusions*, the eminent British musicologist Cecil Sharp, when commenting on the term 'folksong' and its derivation from German 'Volkslied', remarks:

> Unhappily it [the term 'folksong'] is used in two senses. Scientific writers restrict its meaning to the songs created by the unlettered classes. Others, however, use it to denote not only the peasant songs, but all popular songs as well, irrespective of origin, *i. e.* in the wider and looser sense in which it is sometimes used in Germany. (1907:2)

The scientific sense of 'folksong' which Sharp favours implies that this type of song was composed by 'the unlettered classes' or, as Sharp also says, by 'the common people'. By common people Sharp meant the non-educated strata of society, 'the unlettered, whose faculties have undergone no formal training whatsoever, and who have never been brought into close enough contact with educated persons to be influenced by them' (3–4). Sharp was writing at the beginning of the twentieth century, when the comparatively new science of folklore had as its goal the documentation and study of the manners and customs as well as the poetry, art and music found in areas and among parts of the population believed to be largely uncontaminated by the culture of modern city life (Karpeles 1973). No modern folklorist would restrict the scope of folklore in this way any more, just as modern dialectologists have moved on from the study of rural dialects to that of urban varieties. Nor are the creators and carriers of folksong as defined by Sharp easily identifiable as 'unlettered folk' in a modern industrial society. We understand what Sharp means, but would hesitate to use his terminology. Instead of the contrast 'urban' vs. 'folk', Robert Redfield (1956) has proposed the concept of the 'folk-urban continuum', insisting at the same time that 'folk' and 'peasant' are not synonymous. Precisely what is denoted by 'folk' depends very much on the society under investigation. In this respect, medieval societies differ from industrial societies, and Western societies differ from non-Western societies.

At this point it is perhaps helpful to make a few distinctions. One concerns the role of orality, in particular oral poetry, in a society. From an ethnological and sociological point of view we might put societies on a scale ranging from societies in which orality is the dominant form of the transmission of poetry (and knowledge) to societies in which orality plays at most a marginal role. Sir Maurice Bowra's book *Primitive Song* (1962) treats of poetry of the former type of society (or culture), while any study of folksong in the Western world after the invention of printing is concerned with societies of the latter kind, with various degrees of marginalization of orality. Coming back to the threefold understanding of 'oral poetry' as orally composed, orally transmitted, and orally performed (see above, p. 8), we can say that it is in the nature of folksong to be *orally performed*. Depending on time and place, *oral transmission* can also be assumed. There is, of course, no doubt about the existence of oral transmission in oral cultures. As for literate societies, matters differ. A German scholar who collected and studied folksongs at the end of the nineteenth century discovered to his surprise that his maid, aged twenty-four, knew by heart 123 folksongs from beginning to end as well as a number of fragments (Sahr 1912:18, n. 1). This does not mean that these folksongs had reached the young woman orally. It can be assumed that many of them existed in printed versions and that either she herself or some of her informants had learned the songs from printed sources. Still, the element of oral transmission cannot be ignored in her case and in similar cases, when people remember songs, know them by heart and are hence capable of passing them on orally.

Most difficult to answer is the question of *oral composition*. Sharp was of the opinion that folksongs actually originated from the 'common people'. This view is sometimes dubbed 'the production theory of folksong'. Although it maintains that folk poetry is composed by 'unlettered folk', this position does not subscribe to the opinion that *das Volk dichtet*, that the people create the poetry as an anonymous collective mass, as it has been expressed by some writers of the Romantic era and by scholars seeking the origin of traditional poetry in communal song and dance (Gummere 1901). There are always individuals at work, but their compositions use the traditional forms and they eventually become common property. The so-called 'reception theory of folksong', on the other hand, as formulated by John Meier, the founder of the German Folksong Archive, insists that only the wide popularity of folksong among the 'folk' and its general anonymity are defining traits of folksong (1906: i–cxliv). Folksongs are the creations of individuals, and these might come from both the educated and the uneducated classes. Once they become common currency, their authors are generally forgotten, and as orally performed – and as a rule also orally transmitted – poetry they take on a life of their own, with innumerable changes, variations and adaptations.

John Meier's reception theory does not equate folksong with popular song. Despite possible educated authorship, folksongs stay close to traditional ways of lyric expression. It is perhaps less misleading to characterize folksongs as traditional songs or as oral traditional songs. The constitutive elements of folksong are the same as those of folk music. Maud Karpeles, Sharp's collaborator and co-founder of the English Folk Dance Society, proposed the following definition of folk music at the 1954 conference of the International Folk Music Council as an emendation of the earlier provisional definition of the Council:

> 'Folk music is music that has been submitted to the process of oral transmission. It is the product of evolution and is dependent on the circumstances of continuity, variation and selection'.
> 
> This definition implies that folk music is the product of an unwritten tradition and that the elements that have shaped, or are shaping, the tradition are: (1) continuity, which links the present with the past; (2) variation, which springs from the creative impulse of the individual or the group; and (3) selection by the community which determines the form in which folk music survives.
> 
> The definition rightly leaves out of account the origin of folk music. The term can therefore be applied to music that has been evolved from rudimentary beginnings by a community uninfluenced by art music; and it can also be applied to music which has originated with an individual composer and has subsequently been absorbed into the unwritten, living tradition of a community. But the term does not cover a song, dance or tune that has been taken over ready-made and remains unchanged. It is the fashioning and re-fashioning of the music by the community that gives it its folk character.[94]

---

[94] Karpeles 1955: 6; see also Karpeles 1973: 3. For a comprehensive handbook on folksong, see Brednich et al. 1973–75.

By substituting 'folksong' for 'folk music' one arrives at a working definition of folksong or traditional song that can also be applied to the medieval situation. To be precise, no substitution of terms is necessary as folksong is by definition song and therefore part of folk music.

## 6.2 Folksong Collecting and Medieval Lyrics

Sharp, whose collection of English folksongs from the Appalachians of 1917 is a landmark of what today is called ethnomusicology (1932), followed in the footsteps of earlier collectors of folksongs and ballads and stood in a long line of scholars that reaches back to the eighteenth century at least. What began with Johann Gottfried Herder's collection of 'The Peoples' Voices in Songs' (*Stimmen der Völker in Liedern*), published in 1778–1779 (1975), was enthusiastically continued by the Romantics in the nineteenth century. In Germany, the poets Achim von Arnim and Clemens Brentano published three volumes of German folksongs under the title *Des Knaben Wunderhorn* between 1805 and 1808 (2003), and in 1844–1845 Ludwig Uhland published his collection of 'High- and Low-German folksongs', which were later followed by notes and an essay (1866). In his essay on the German *Volkslieder*, Uhland, who was not only a prolific poet but also a scholar and medievalist, noted that while medieval manuscripts mainly transmit lyrics that belong to the realm of courtly poetry, there was also a different type of song current at the time:

> Before and contemporary with such art compositions in castles and in court, there is plenty of evidence that songs were also sung by peasants, on the roads, by the people, and it is to be supposed that this ubiquitous song, as it treated of common topics, presented itself in a plainer style and in simpler forms: folksong in distinction to courtly song and art song. (1866:3)

In his essay Uhland discusses a great number of medieval lyrics as evidence for the echoes of folksong in the corpus of transmitted texts. In his discussion of medieval love lyrics, Uhland quotes a French poem of the thirteenth century:

> Bele Aliz matin leva,
> Sun cors vesti e para.
> Enz un verger s'en entra,
> Cink flurettes y truva.
> Un chapelet fet en a,
> De rose flurie.
> Pur Deu, trahez vos en la,
> Vos ke ne amez mie.[95]

Bele Aliz (Aelis) got up in the morning,/ got dressed and made herself beautiful./ She entered into a garden,/ there she found five little flowers./ She made a crown from them,/ of blooming roses./ By God, take yourselves away,/ you who have no love.

This is undoubtedly a traditional oral poem, possibly a dance song, at least in some of its variants. The different versions of this song as well as the contexts of their transmission provide a good example of the problems encountered in locating forms of folksong or

---

[95] Uhland 1866:421 (German translation), 518 (French text).

oral traditional song in medieval poetry. The poem quoted by Uhland comes from a thirteenth-century manuscript (London, BL MS Arundel 292), where it forms the motto for a sermon attributed to Archbishop Stephen Langton (d. 1228). In this sermon the poem is characterized as a dance song and, as is to be expected of a medieval sermon, is interpreted allegorically: 'Bele Aelis' is seen as none other than the Virgin Mary. The sermon is found in five manuscripts, and is followed in one of them by a sermon on another French poem, 'Sur la rive de la mer', similarly adapted to a religious purpose.[96] The allegorical interpretation of secular song has long been familiar from the religious interpretations of the *Song of Songs*, in both the Jewish and Christian traditions. It has helped to make secular love poetry acceptable in a religious milieu and also to preserve poetry which might otherwise have been lost.

In this case, however, 'Bele Aelis' poems have also been transmitted in a purely secular context. One source is the *Roman de la Rose* or *Roman de Guillaume de Dole*, attributed to Jean Renart (first half of the 13th c.).[97] This is a courtly verse romance, into which 48 songs are inserted, among them five poems in which 'Bele Aelis' figures. These lyric insertions generally occur in scenes describing the merry-making and pastimes of the courtly society gathered at Emperor Conrad's court. In one such scene the emperor's vièlle-player Juglés sings:

> Aaliz main se leva.
> *Bon jor ait qui mon cuer a!*
> Beau se vesti et para,
> Desoz l'aunoi.
> *Bon jor ait qui mon cuer a!*
> *N'est pas o moi.* (ll. 1579–84) (Lecoy 1963: 49)

Aaliz (Aelis) got up in the morning./ May the person who has my heart have a good day!/ She dressed herself beautifully and adorned herself,/ under the alder bushes. / May the person who has my heart have a good day!/ It is not with me (any more).

This (as well as the other 'Aelis' lyrics) is a *rondet de carole*, of which *Guillaume de Dole* contains seventeen. The *rondet* is an early form of the *rondeau*, a *forme fixe* in fourteenth- and fifteenth-century French poetry and music. The *rondet*s in *Guillaume de Dole* are the earliest lyrics of this kind in French literature. There is some debate among musicologists about the development and early form of this genre.[98] A defining trait of the *rondeau* is the use of refrains (printed in italics in the example above). The early *rondet* has as a rule a stanza of six lines, with the refrain in lines 5 and 6 and the first line of the refrain in line 2, making up the rhyme-scheme aAabAB (capitals symbolize refrains). Musically, the lines with rhyme *a* (or *A*) have one melody (α), while the lines with rhyme *b* (*B*) have another melody (β). The musical structure of this poem is then ααaβαβ. Unfortunately, the unique manuscript that contains the romance of *Guillaume*

---

[96] For a critical edition of these sermons and further comments, see Reichl 1973: 379–88. On the 'Aelis'-poems see also Stevens 1986: 177–78.

[97] Vatican, MS Reg. 1725; edited in Lecoy 1963. On *Guillaume de Dole*, see the essays in Durling 1997, among them, on *Guillaume de Dole* and medieval song, van der Werf 1997. On the performance of song in *Guillaume de Dole*, see Butterfield 2002: 64–71.

[98] On the older theory, see Gennrich 1921–27; this poem is edited in Gennrich 1921–27: I, 6–7 (no. 9). See also Wilkins 2001.

*de Dole* has no music. There are, however, sufficient other musical sources to allow a musical reconstruction of some of the poems. One of these musical sources for the 'Aelis' songs is a work from the *Chansonnier de Noailles*, an important source of the monophonic trouvère repertoire with about 500 songs, of which *c.* 360 are given with their melody (Paris, BnF MS fr. 12615, late 13th c.). This is a poem composed by Baude de la Quarière (or, de la Kakerie), a trouvère of the thirteenth century. It comprises five stanzas, each one beginning with a line of an 'Aelis song'. The poem (*incipit* 'Main se leva la bien faite Aelis') is basically a *cento* of refrains and has been called 'un pot-pourri de refrains' by Gaston Paris (1896:3). It is possible, as the poem's early editors surmised, that it was meant to be performed as a dramatic scene.[99]

## 6.3 Refrains

The presence of refrains in the *rondet* and *rondeau*, as well as in related lyrico-musical forms such as the *virelai*, the *villancico* or the carol, has been interpreted as pointing to an origin of these forms in a kind of round-dance or *carole*, with the singers alternatively dancing round in a circle and standing 'still' (presumably with rhythmical foot movements on the spot), corresponding with the singing of the refrain by all and the stanza by a soloist only. It is difficult to be certain exactly how these dances were performed and how the movements tally with text and music; in folklore a great profusion of round-dances with all kinds of variations can be found, a fact which is of little help in elucidating the choreography of the *carole*.[100] What is clear is that at least some of the refrain-songs inserted into the *Roman de Guillaume de Dole* are depicted as being sung and danced. In one of the scenes of courtly entertainment, we are told that 'les puceles et li vallet' (the young women and young men) were dancing the *carole* hand in hand and then, when one of the songs had just finished, the narrator continues:

> Ceste n'ot pas duré .III. tours,
> quant li fils au conte d'Aubours
> qui mout amoit chevalerie
> reconmencë a voiz serie:
> Main se levoit Aaliz [...] (ll. 528–32) (Lecoy 1963:17)

> This hadn't lasted for three turns,/ when the son of the Count d'Aubours,/ who loved chivalry very much,/ began again with an agreeable voice:/ 'Aaliz got up in the morning [...]'

French *tour* means 'circular movement': singing and dancing obviously went together.

While it is likely that refrain-songs have their origin in dance songs and while the tradition of singing and dancing might have continued all through the Middle Ages, refrain-songs like the *rondeau* as a *forme fixe* have certainly become dissociated from dancing and also from whatever folkloristic background from which they might at one time have arisen. The *rondeaux* composed by Guillaume de Machaut in the fourteenth century or by Charles d'Orléans in the fifteenth are a far cry from the *rondets* on 'Bele

---

[99] For the text, see Bec 1977–78: II, 155–58; see also Butterfield 2002:233–36; on p. 234 there is a facsimile of fol. 50v of the manuscript. See also Laforte 1981:209–21.
[100] See Sachs 1938:142–71; see also the article 'Round Dances' in Leach 1972:957–58.

Aelis' or 'Robin e bele Mariete' in the *Roman de Guillaume de Dole* and other sources of the thirteenth century.¹⁰¹ It is in the earlier lyrics that a layer of oral traditional song is still perceptible even if these *rondet*s and refrains meet us in literary works, where they might be quotations from folksong, echoes of traditional poetry or simply literary imitations in a popular tone.

With regard to refrains, some scholars propose a distinction between refrains as they appear in a poem and the mini-poems of one or more lines which seem to have been circulating on their own (from the twelfth to the beginning of the fourteenth century) since they generally appear in more than one poem. The lines 'Bon jor ait qui mon cuer a!/ N'est pas o moi' in the 'Aelis' poem cited above consitute such a refrain. They are on the one hand used as a refrain in the *rondet* inserted in *Guillaume de Dole*, but they are also found in other poems and are also 'refrains' in the sense of 'vagrant verses'. In addition to the *rondet*, Nico H. J. van den Boogaard, who has collected these refrains, also lists Baude de la Quarière's poem, where the lines make their appearance in the last stanza, and a motet ('Manoir me fait en folie') from the famous Montpellier codex.¹⁰² In this motet, which is also transmitted in another manuscript, these lines form the tenor of a bilingual two-part song. Some of the early motets of the thirteenth century make ample use of refrains, which has led to their being called 'refrain centos' (Everist 1994: 109–25). They certainly demonstrate the 'floating character' of these refrains. They also show the incorporation of poetry which evokes the world of folksong into the sophisticated art music of the thirteenth century.

## 6.4 Popular Voices from the Iberian Peninsula

It is from the art poetry of the Middle Ages that our knowledge of oral traditional songs mostly derives. As in the refrains of the *rondet*, the sound of popular song is heard in the refrains or refrain-like lines of other lyric forms as well. One of these is the *kharja* of Arabic and Hebrew poems from medieval Andalusia. The *kharja* is not a genre of its own, but is part of the *muwashshaḥ* and the *zajal*. These lyric forms originated in the Iberian Peninsula in the ninth century; the poem is called *muwashshaḥ* or *muwashshaḥa* when it is in Classical Arabic and *zajal* when it is composed in colloquial Arabic. The *muwashshaḥ* and *zajal* are poems with refrains and a very characteristic ending or *envoi*, called *kharja* (from Arabic *kharaja* 'to go out, to leave').¹⁰³ According to an Andalusian Arabic poet of the twelfth century (Ibn Sanā' al-Mulk), the '*kharja* is the spice of the

---

[101] For a collection of late-medieval *rondeaux* from Jehan de Lescurel via Machaut, Froissart, Deschamps, Christine de Pisan, and Chartier to Charles d'Orléans (with 14 music examples), see Wilkins 1969. On medieval dance-songs as poems and songs, see Stevens 1986: 159–98. On popular elements in Old French lyric poetry, see Spanke 1933.

[102] See van den Boogard 1969: 117 (no. 285). The 2-voice motet 'Manoir me fait en folie' in Montpellier, Bibliothèque de l'École de Médecine MS H 196, is edited in Rokseth 1935–39: III, 62–63 (no. 238); IV, 286. – On the refrains see Doss-Quinby 1984 and Butterfield 2002: 75–102.

[103] For a general introduction to this lyric genre, see Rosen 2000; the seminal modern study is Stern 1974: 1–122; in both Hebrew and Arabic, the form of the *muwashshaḥ* was also used for religious poems; see Stern 1974: 83–91. An anthology of Hispano-Arabic lyrics, including poems of the *muwashshaḥ* genre, with English translations and a detailed introduction is Monroe 1974.

*muwashshaḥ*, its salt and sugar, its musk and amber' (Stern 1974:34). This effect is achieved by various means, in particular by changing into a different register. Very often the *kharja* is put into the mouth of a woman and her words both complement and contrast with the sequence of thoughts in the preceding poem. The contrast is especially marked when the words are not in Arabic but in (Ibero-)Romance. With these short snippets in a Romance language we get a glimpse of what seems to have been a flourishing oral lyric tradition on the Iberian Peninsula.[104]

This tradition continued into the Renaissance and later periods and has been transmitted, not unlike medieval oral song, in the work of known poets and composers. Dámaso Alonso, together with José Manuel Blecua, has put together an anthology of Spanish lyrics in a book sub-titled 'lírica de tipo tradicional'.[105] Among the poems edited is the following anonymous lyric:[106]

> *Tres morillas m'enamoran*
> *en Jaén,*
> *Axa y Fátima y Marién.*
>
> *Tres morillas tan garridas*
> *Yvan a coger olivas,*
> *Y hallávanlas cogidas*
> *en Jaén,*
> *Axa y Fátima y Marién.*
>
> *Y hallávanlas cogidas,*
> *Y tornaban desmaídas*
> *Y las colores perdidas*
> *en Jaén,*
> *Axa y Fátima y Marién.*
>
> *Tres moricas tan loçanas,*
> *Tres moricas tan loçanas*
> *Yvan a coger manzanas*
> *en Jaén,*
> *Axa y Fátima y Marién.*

With three Moorish girls I am in love/ in Jaén:/ Aisha and Fátima and Marién. – Three such pretty Moorish girls / went to pick olives,/ and they found them picked already/ in Jaén:/ Aisha and Fátima and Marién. – And they found them picked already,/ and they returned weak/ and pale/ in Jaén:/ Aisha and Fátima and Marién. – Three such lively Moorish girls, / three such lively Moorish girls, / went to pick apples/ in Jaén:/ Aisha and Fátima and Marién.

---

[104] The *kharja* has been much discussed in connection with the origin of the Romance secular lyric; see Zwartjes 1997. The Romance *kharjas* are edited with the poems in which they occur in García Gómez 1975 (with translations into Spanish); on the *kharjas* in Hebrew poems, see García Gómez 1975:411–25. On the *muwashshaḥ* see further the chapter by J. T. Monroe below (ch. 23); see also pp. 529–31 in the chapter on woman's songs by A. L. Klinck (ch. 20).

[105] Alonso and Blecua 1964; see the detailed introductions by Dámaso Alonso (pp. vii–xxviii) and José Manuel Blecua (pp. xxix–lxxxiv); see also the introduction in Cummins 1977:1–36.

[106] Alonso and Blecua 1964:17 (no. 25); the poem is also edited in Cummins 1977:46. Alonso and Blecua have modernized the manuscript spelling; I am following the edition by Anglès 1947 (see below), which is closer to the manuscript.

This poem is a *villancico*, a lyric form very similar to the French *virelai* and the Middle English carol. It is introduced by a refrain (*estribillo*), of which lines 2 and 3 are repeated as refrains after every stanza (*vuelta*). The stanzas themselves consist of three mono-rhyme lines (*mudanza*), which are both repetitive and parallelistic. Hispanists see in the *villancico* – the term is a derivation of *villano* 'peasant' – a lyric form firmly rooted in folklore, with links to the *zajal* as well.[107] 'Tres morillas m'enamoran' is found in the *Cancionero de Palacio*, a manuscript from the end of the fifteenth or beginning of the sixteenth century (Madrid, Palacio Real, Biblioteca, MS 1335). It contains in its present form 463 musical pieces, of which over half are, like our song, anonymous. The music of this *villancico* is for three voices. Melodic structure and metric patterning complement one another. Metrically the poem consists of a three-line initial refrain (*estribillo*) and a two-line internal refrain (*vuelta*). Musically the third line of the mono-rhyme strophe (*mudanza*) is identical to the first line of the *estribillo*. Furthermore, the melody of lines 1 and 2 of each strophe is almost identical to that of the first line of the *estribillo*. The music stays the same for each stanza, but the rhyme of the *mudanza* is c in stanzas 1 and 2 and d in stanza 3. This results in the following structure: [108]

| Metric structure | Musical structure |
|---|---|
| $A_8$ | α |
| $B_3$ | β |
| $B_7$ | γ |
| $c_8$ | α' |
| $c_8$ | α' |
| $c_8$ | α |
| $B_3$ | β |
| $B_7$ | γ |

In all its simplicity – and perhaps because of its simplicity – this poem is somewhat puzzling. First these girls go to pick olives, but find the fruit harvested already, then they go to pick apples, and nothing more is heard of them. From their olive-picking they return weak and pale, but when they set out for their next tour they are *loçanas*, an epithet that can be glossed as 'vigorous, vivid, robust'. They are called *morillas* or *moricas*, diminutive forms of *mora* 'Moorish girl/woman', and they have Arabic names – Aisha (Axa) is the name of one of the Prophet's wives, Fatima the name of his daughter married to Caliph 'Alī, and Marién is an Arabic variant of (originally Hebrew) Maria. The poem's speaker is in love with them, but this is only stated once, in the first line. From a formal point of view the poem seems to have a flaw: while in the first two strophes the rhyme words vary, in stanza 3 the first and second line are identical (*tres moricas tan loçanas*). This looks like a case of textual corruption, and has certainly been treated like one by some editors (Beltrán 1998).

---

[107] See the detailed study by Le Gentil 1954; compare also Le Gentil 1952:244–62, and Baehr 1962:225–36. On the etymology of *villancico*, see Malkiel and Stern 1984.

[108] See the edition (with music) in Anglès 1947:29 (no. 24); the musical phrases α and α' only differ in their last note/ last two notes. On the *cancioneros* see Romeu Figueras 1949 and Reese 1954:581–86. Of this song a number of modern recordings are available. – Capital letters designate the refrain, subscript numbers the number of syllables per line.

An answer to some of these questions seems to be provided by the song which follows in the manuscript (Anglès 1947:30 [no. 25]). It is attributed to Diego Fernández, a Spanish composer from the end of the fifteenth and beginning of the sixteenth centuries. It has the same *estribillo* as our song and is also musically based on it, with some additional embellishments. Textually, the two-line *vuelta*, instead of having *Jaén* from the initial refrain in every strophe, has a different word or group of words. Instead of three, we have six stanzas, of which stanzas 3 to 6 have five instead of three lines in the *mudanza*. While these formal changes can be seen as no more than elaborations of the anonymous song, the content of the poems differs more noticeably. The second song is a variation on the theme of the pastourelle: the speaker sees a beautiful girl (prototypically, the encounter of a knight and a shepherdess), declares his love and either persuades the girl to enter into an amorous adventure or is rebuffed (see further ch. 22 on the pastourelle by L. Spetia). The latter is the speaker's lot here. The 'poet' sees three beautiful Moorish girls, who, on being questioned, tell him that they were *moras* but have become Christians. Rather than picking olives or apples, they go to the fountain for water. The speaker, accosted as *caballero* by the girls, swears by the *Alcorán* that he loves all three of them, but is told: *quien tres amigas ama/ No es amado de ninguna* (he who loves three girl-friends is loved by none). The knight will have to make his choice, but the outcome is not recounted.

Federico García Lorca has incorporated this poem as a *canción popular del siglo XV* (a popular song of the fifteenth century) into his lyrical *œuvre*, much inspired, not only in his *Romancero gitano* (Gipsy Ballad-Book) of 1928, by Spanish folk and popular poetry. Interestingly he gives an emended text: the *estribillo* and the *vuelta* are unchanged, and so are stanzas 1 and 2. The third stanza of García Lorca's text is parallel to stanza 1: the girls find the apples harvested just as they did with the olives:

> Tres moricas tan lozanas
> iban a coger manzanas
> y hallábanlas tomadas
> en Jaén:
> Axa y Fátima y Marién.

Three such lively Moorish girls/ went to pick apples/ and found them taken/ in Jaén:/ Aisha and Fátima and Marién.

This is no doubt a happy emendation as it also eliminates the repetition of the first line of this stanza. But García Lorca's text improves on the original even more. His text adds the first stanza of the second song, thus achieving a more satisfactory closure: the 'poet' declares his love and the identity of the three girls becomes somewhat more recognizable:

> Díjeles: ¿Quién sois, señoras,
> de mi vida robadoras?
> Cristianas que éramos moras
> en Jaen:
> Axa y Fátima y Marién. (García Lorca 1953:658–59)

I said to them: 'Who are you, ladies,/ robbers of my life?'/ 'Christians, who were Moorish girls/ in Jaén:/ Aisha and Fátima and Marién.'

Whether García Lorca took these changes to the anonymous song of the *Cancionero de Palacio* from folklore or 'emended' the text himself is unknown. Diego Fernández had already composed a variation on our song, almost certainly with borrowings from popular poetry. Popular and anonymous poems have no copyright. From a modern perspective, Lorca's text is more satisfactory than the fifteenth-century anonymous song: the fruit-picking motif is symmetrically balanced, the metrical 'flaw' of a repeated line in stanza 3 is removed and the narrative thread is rounded off by an additional last stanza. There is no knowing what the exact relationship of these two versions, Lorca's text and the manuscript text, to the tradition is. A less balanced or less coherent structure (assuming that balance and coherence can be clearly defined) are, however, not necessarily signs of textual corruption in a folk poem. Allusiveness, even fragmentariness, characterize a great number of lyrics in oral tradition and contribute to their charm. Every variant has to be accepted and interpreted on its own without the attempt to reconstruct an 'original'. This is not to deny that in the course of oral transmission occur textual changes which can be analysed as alterations based on misunderstandings and faulty memory, a process of *Zersingen*, as it is called in German (literally 'singing to bits'), where the misunderstood or forgotten form can sometimes be identified (Dessauer 1928). Despite these insights into textual changes, the oral poem is 'alive' only in performance, and it is the variant rather than a hypothetical 'original' that is the object of investigation. This is the lesson that folklorists and students of oral poetry have learned; it is a lesson that also applies to a great deal of medieval literature, not only literature with an oral background, as Paul Zumthor's concept of *mouvance* implies and as Bernard Cerquiglini has persuasively argued in his *Éloge de la variante* (1989).[109] The large number of musical recordings of the anonymous song in its traditional, unemended form testify to the attractiveness of this allusive poem even for a modern audience.

In its repetitiveness and with its unpretentious diction this poem is stylistically close to the medieval Galician-Portuguese *cantigas de amigo*, songs in which a woman expresses her longing for her absent friend.[110] Perhaps the most salient characteristic of these lyrics is an almost extreme form of parallelism, which results in a poetic texture of repetitions and variations on a very restricted lexicon.[111] Eugeno Asensio distinguishes three sub-types of 'synonymous parallelism' in Galician-Portuguese poetry, of which the first type is by far the most common. It consists in 'the repetition of a verse-line and its rhythmical movement, where only the end is varied by the replacement of the rhyming word with a synonym' (1970:78). A short poem by Martin Codax (13th c.) can illustrate this:

---

[109] See also above p. 22. On the style of medieval Spanish folksongs with or on *morenas*, girls of dark colour, see Wardropper 1980. Compare also ch. 22 on the pastourelle for possible Iberian echoes in Marcabru's pastourelle 'L'autrer jost una sebissa', p. 590.

[110] For an up-to-date encyclopaedia of medieval Galician and Portuguese literature, see Lanciani and Tavani 1993 (in Portuguese). See further ch. 20 by A. L. Klinck, pp. 541–42.

[111] Parallelism is a characteristic feature not only of the Hebrew Psalms but also of a great number of oral traditions. A substantial contribution to parallelism in folk poetry and medieval literature was written in 1898 by Aleksander Nikolalevich Veselovskiy (1940). For a detailed discussion of parallelism in the Galician-Portuguese but also the Spanish lyrics of the Middle Ages, see Asensio 1970.

Ai ondas que eu vin veere,
se me saberedes dizere
*porque tarda meu amigo sen min?*

Ai ondes que eu vin mirare,
se me saberedes contare
*porque tarde meu amigo sen min?*[112]

Oh waves that I came to see,/ can you tell me/ why my friend lingers away from me?// Oh waves that I came to look at,/ can you inform me/ why my friend lingers away from me?

The two stanzas are almost identical, with only slight variations being produced by replacing the rhymes of the first stanza with synonyms in the second. This minimalistic style has been interpreted as one of the main charms of this poetry. Parallelism and repetition are even more effective when the music is taken into consideration. While the later Spanish musical *cancioneros* transmit a wealth of melodies, Galician-Portuguese secular lyrics fare much worse. The music has been preserved for the poem quoted. This consists of three musical phrases, corresponding to the three lines of each stanza; the melody for the first and second line, however, is, with the exception of the first syllable, identical. The melody is predominantly melismatic (three or four notes per syllable), especially in the refrain. This results in a more involved melodic line than the verbal parsimony might suggest. In addition to the six lyrics by Martin Codax for which the music has been preserved, a further seven poems with music, this time *cantigas de amor* by Dom Denis (1261–1325), lyrics in the style of the troubadours, were discovered in 1990.[113] This is still a small corpus compared to the *c.* 250 troubadour melodies and the *c.* 1,400 trouvère melodies (van der Werf 1972: 14–15), but all the more precious for our knowledge of the music of the secular Galician-Portuguese lyric.

Martin Codax was a minstrel, in Portuguese terms a *jogral* or *segrel* (see ch. 5, pp. 183–84). Dom Denis, who also wrote *cantigas de amigo*, was one of the kings of Portugal. Clearly, echoes of folksong are to be found in poetry composed both by minstrels and by cultured authors, some of the latter of the highest possible social level. Another king of the Iberian Peninsula has left us a large legacy of medieval poetry, this time of a religious character: King Alfonso X of Castile, surnamed 'el Sábio' (1221–1284). The more than four-hundred *Cantigas de Santa Maria* compiled under the king's direction and in part composed by him largely consist of narrative miracle songs; every tenth *cantiga*, however, is a *cantiga de loor*, a song in praise of the Virgin. The songs are preserved in four manuscripts of the thirteenth and fourteenth centuries, beautifully illuminated and, what is more, in three manuscripts notated with their music.[114] The relevance of the *Cantigas de Santa Maria* in the present context lies with their form,

---

[112] Quoted from Ferreira 1986:135 (a full edition of the poems of Martin Codax, with commentary and facsimile, in Portuguese and English). Seven poems are found on the so-called 'Pergaminho Vindel' (discovered in 1914), but only six are notated, for one of them the staves have been left empty.

[113] The so-called 'Pergaminho Sharrer' was discovered by Harvey L. Sharrer; see Sharrer 1991. It has been edited (with commentary and facsimile, in Portuguese and English) by Manuel Pedro Ferreira (2005).

[114] On the *Cantigas de Santa Maria* and their music see the edition by Anglès 1943–64. 43 secular lyrics have also been attributed to the king; see Lanciani and Tavani 1993:36–41 (s. v. *Alfonso X*).

metrical and musical. They are refrain poems and, with only few exceptions, show the form of the *virelai*, i. e. the patterning that characterizes also the *villancico* discussed above and the earlier *zajal*. This, however, does not make them into popular lyrics or imitations of folksongs. The textual relationships to troubadour and trouvère lyrics have been noted and, as John Stevens has remarked, the *cantigas* 'are courtly [...] by patronage and immediate provenance' and seem 'to have been destined for a courtly audience.' As to the music, however, Stevens continues (with reference to the well-known *cantiga* 'Rosas das rosas'), 'the style and shape of the song remain entirely that of the dance-song tradition' (1990: 445–46, 447). No doubt, the sound of folksong might be heard more clearly in the music than in the text. On the one hand, the *Cantigas de Santa Maria* point to the world of popular religious poetry: the Italian *laude* (also in the *virelai*-form), the German *Geißlerlieder* (songs of the flagellants) and the Catalan and Latin pilgrims' songs in honour of the Black Madonna of Montserrat.[115] On the other hand, as *songs* they stress the importance of popular song and popular music for a fuller understanding of oral and traditional forms of medieval song.[116] This is an area that lies beyond the limits of this book; the brief comments in this section on orality, folksong and medieval lyrics can be no more than a reminder that word and music should ideally be considered together, at least in those (comparatively rare) cases where the lyrics have been preserved with musical notation.

## 7 Conclusion

The UNESCO list of representative and endangered works of the intangible cultural heritage of humanity comprises a number of works from oral tradition, such as Mongolian and Kirghiz heroic epics, the storyteller's art in Turkey, in Egypt and among the Palestinian Arabs, folksong traditions in Uzbekistan and Romania, and the puppet theatre in Indonesia and Sicily. Many of these works go back to medieval traditions, such as the performance of the *meddaḥ* (reader and narrator of tales) in Turkey, the *doina* (folksong) in Romania and the *opera dei puppi* in Sicily, where the medieval Italian versions of the *chansons de geste* via their transformation into prose tales (in the fourteenth-century *Reali di Francia*) have found a new (but now moribund) life in the Sicilian puppet theatre.[117] No apology is needed for the efforts spent by the UNESCO to safeguard these fast-disappearing remnants of tradtional verbal, musical, dramatic and other arts in various parts of the globe. One way of raising a general awareness of the importance of oral traditions in world culture is, of course, by teaching them. 'Teaching oral traditions' is the title of a book edited by John Miles Foley in the Modern Language Association's series 'Options for Teaching' (1998). In addition to theoretical and methodological contributions and to chapters on a number of living oral traditions, 'texts with roots

---

[115] On the *laude* see Stevens 1990: 433–42; edition (with music) by Liuzzi 1934. On the *Geißlerlieder*, see Hübner 1931; compare also Müller-Blattau 1975 on religious folksongs; on the Montserrat pilgrims' songs, see Suñol 1917.
[116] See, *inter alia*, Chailley 1956; Bukofzer 1960; Stevens 1961: 40–57.
[117] See the UNESCO's website at <http://www.unesco.org/culture/ich/>.

in oral traditions' are discussed. Among these we find poetry which figures also in this book: Old Germanic heroic epic, Middle English romance, the Old French *chanson de geste*, and the Old Icelandic saga (see chapters 8, 11, and 12 below). Unlike the works on the intangible heritage list, *Beowulf*, the *Chanson de Roland*, Arthurian romance or Icelandic saga are comparatively well protected; these works will remain on the syllabus of any course on medieval English or French or Norse literature (it is to be hoped), whatever their possible affiliations to orality.

What then does a study of oral roots contribute to an understanding of these and other medieval works? From their various perspectives, the chapters of this book will provide an answer – or at least a partial answer – to this question. Here, in this introductory chapter, I would like to highlight just a few aspects. For Milman Parry and Albert Lord it was clear that their study of South Slavic oral epic would contribute to a greater appreciation of the Homeric epics. Their systematic analysis of formulaic diction and their insight into the role of both formula and theme (type-scene) in performance and reception led them to a re-interpretation of the Homeric style. From the singer's point of view, formulaic diction helps him to perform without hesitation, it enables the narrator to compose in performance. From the audience's point of view, formula and theme give a structure of familiarity to what is heard, setting a network of associations and expectations in motion. If Homer's epic style is seen in the light of an oral tradition, the dynamics inherent in the performance situation can be grasped: the epic singer narrates a tale that is totally traditional and therefore fully familiar and yet his audience listens to something which they have not heard before in quite this way, to a new variant created in the course of performance. The writing-down of the epics and their later written transmission gives us only indirect access to the oral situation, but enough is left to be discernible and relevant for interpretation. Similar arguments can be made with regard to medieval works. Alain Renoir, in his interpretations of *Beowulf* and the *Hildebrandslied* (the Old High German *Lay of Hildebrand*) (1988), has shown how formulaic diction can be understood within a framework of verbal patterns, which enables the listener (and later the reader) to situate an expression or a motif in a wider traditional context and by this to appreciate its deeper resonance. In his *Immanent Art*, John Miles Foley proposes a methodology of recovering the underlying meaning of traditional poetry through the analysis of their verbal and thematic structuring, by following up the linguistic values and communicative functions of traditional language (1991 and 2002). A similar position is taken by Thomas DuBois, who, with reference to North-European oral lyric poetry, both modern and medieval, has suggested an interpretative hermeneutics that takes generic, associative and situational aspects into account (2006 and ch. 6 in this volume).

The search for an oral background to medieval poetry has, however, also been motivated by aims different from those of interpretation and appreciation. A main concern of literary studies in the nineteenth and twentieth centuries was the search for origins. 'Where does secular love poetry in the vernacular literatures of Europe come from?' is a typical question. 'From the poetry of the troubadours' is one answer. But, of course, the questioning continued, and a good number of theories of origin were consequently proposed for the troubadour lyric. Many paths on this quest for origins lead us to the Middle Ages: the beginnings of liturgical drama, of courtly literature, or of vernacular epic poetry can all be witnessed somewhere in the medieval period. In many cases an ultimate origin in the realm of orality has been sought and also found, although not always with convincing arguments. Since the latter part of the twentieth century questions of origin have been less hotly debated, if they have been debated at all. Peter Dronke has persuasively argued that no influence or external cause for the birth of the courtly lyric need be sought: idealization in love poetry is a universal phenomenon, found in such chronologically and geographically distant cultures as those of ancient Egypt and medieval Georgia (1968, esp. vol. 1). In a similar vein, Viktor Zhirmunsky had developed his historical-comparative approach to epic studies, insisting on the universality of the oral epic and the crucial role that social and cultural conditions play for its rise and development (1961). In these and similar works, the question of origin has been transformed into the typological and comparative study of poetry, both epic and lyric.

When the Oral Theory was first applied to medieval texts, scholars were mainly concerned with finding out whether a text was oral or not. If a text was oral that meant that it was orally composed and basically owes its written form to dictation: the dictation of a singer to a scribe or the dictation of a singer to himself once he has become literate. Not only has this picture been elaborated in subsequent scholarship, when it was realized that textualization is a more complicated process than simply writing down a dictated text, but the very question of whether or not a particular work is oral has receded into the background. In contemporary medieval scholarship it is generally considered more interesting and rewarding to study the way orality and literacy interact: the question is not *whether*, but rather *how* a text is oral. One of the reasons for this change of emphasis is the replacement of the orality-literacy dichotomy with the concept of an orality-literacy continuum, which certainly makes more sense for the medieval situation. Another reason is perhaps that the earlier analyses conducted within the Parry-Lord paradigm have in many cases led to opposing and irreconcilable views, while the focus on the vocality of much of medieval literature has found acceptance among a wide circle of scholars. Medievalists like Paul Zumthor and anthropological linguists like Dell Hymes have done much to shift the emphasis from the study of textual structures to the analysis of communicative situations and to raise awareness of the characteristics of performance, of which vocality and variation are important elements. This orientation also entails a new evaluation of ethnographic studies. Oral poetry as it still flourishes in many parts of the world, including Europe, is not only of interest for the search for origins or for providing parallels to poetic structures, but it also offers a unique opportunity to study what it means for poetry to be oral: when, why and how a performance occurs, how a performer learns and 'knows' his or her repertoire, what the performance sounds like, and how it is heard, appreciated and understood by the audience. This is not to say that insights from field-work are directly transferrable by simple equation to medieval literature. The variety and complexity of modern oral traditions on the one hand and of medieval oral literature on the other forbid such a procedure. Musicology is in a position similar to literary studies. Our understanding of the sound of medieval music is only partially helped by musical notations from the Middle Ages, which are often difficult to interpret, if they are interpretable at all. In addition, performance-related information is generally missing. For some time, musicians and musicologists have found inspiration in ethnic music like that of North Africa or the Levant. The 'museum pieces', as a critic has described the early recordings of medieval music by *Deutsche Grammaphon* in the 1950s, have meanwhile been replaced by recordings that sound like live music, where medieval fiddles are supported by Arabian drums. Music is only alive when it is heard. But this also applies to the poetry discussed in the chapters that follow: oral literature is literature that comes alive in sound.

* * *

The attempt to plot the map of medieval oral literature makes it clear that such a map can be drawn only on a very large grid and that it will contain many blank spaces. Furthermore, whatever we put on the map we do not see directly but through the window of written texts. Our map has a greater similarity to the maps plotted by early, premodern geographers than to those found in a modern atlas. R. M. Wilson has written a book on the lost literature of medieval England (1970). Medieval library catalogues, references in Latin chronicles or scribbles and scraps of poetry on the margins of manuscripts attest to the existence of works that are lost today. A similar book about the lost oral literature of the Middle Ages could be written, and would no doubt far exceed the size of this volume. But even the evidence we have about medieval oral literature suffices to double or treble the size of this book. It is hoped that the following chapters give a representative survey and provide in-depth discussions of a number of relevant aspects. There are, of course, areas which would have deserved a full chapter. Some of these I have discussed or at least circumscribed in this introductory chapter: late-medieval folksong and popular religious poetry; medieval Slavic oral epic poetry besides the *Song of Igor*; smaller genres such as riddles or proverbs; art forms contiguous to literature, especially music. This list could be extended. Some of the items on such a list, while not covered in a chapter of their own, do get attention in the individual chapters of this book (see also the index). The following chapters are organized in two blocks, six chapters on concepts and approaches, in which the impact of the Oral Theory on medieval studies (ch. 2), the interplay of orality and literacy (chs. 3 and 4), questions of performance and performers (ch. 5), oral poetics (ch. 6), and orality and ritual (ch. 7) are examined, and twenty chapters on traditions and genres. Some of the traditions include a variety of genres (the chapters on Older Germanic poetry [ch. 8] and on Medieval German Literature [ch. 10]), others are focused on one genre. The chapters on drama (ch. 27) and the ballad (ch. 16) are not restricted to one tradition, while the chapters on epic and lyric (with one exception, ch. 20) each look at one tradition in particular. Medieval oral-derived epic is studied with reference to Middle English romance (ch. 11), the Old French *chansons de geste* (ch. 12), the Italian *cantari* (ch. 13), Romanian epic songs (ch. 14), Hispanic epic and ballad (ch. 15), medieval Greek (ch. 17), and medieval Russian epic (ch. 18), Arabic epic narrative (ch. 24), Persian (ch. 25) and Turkish epic and romance (ch. 26); it is also treated in the chapters on Older Germanic (ch. 8) and Medieval German literature (ch. 10). In the chapters on medieval Hebrew traditions (ch. 19) and on Ireland (ch. 9) the emphasis is likewise on narrative. Pan-European in orientation among the chapters on the lyric is the chapter on woman's songs (ch. 20); the other lyric chapters focus on particular traditions (Middle English in ch. 21), subgenres (the pastourelle in ch. 22) or poems (a Hispano-Arabic *zajal* in ch. 23). As will be seen, all chapters show a high degree of unity in their common concern to explore the various dimensions of medieval oral literature, but they also reflect both the multiplicity of traditions, genres, and aspects and the variety of approaches and ways of coming to terms with the phenomenon of medieval oral literature. Every author has her or his own preferences, methodological direction, scholarly views and personal way of tackling and solving problems. While each chapter stands on its own, and can be read on its own, it is the *summa* of different chapters covering different (but often overlapping) regions on our 'map of medieval oral literature' that constitutes a map in the cartographer's sense: a source of knowledge about the shape and contours of an area and a guide to getting from one place to another. At the risk of overstraining the image of the map, I would like to conclude this introductory chapter by expressing the hope that our map, although it is no Ordnance Survey Map, will give a valid reflection of the terrain it has set out to map and will mark enough paths worth taking that the reader will not be left *vagus* (or *vaga*), 'unsteadily roaming about', at the end, *vagus*, that is, as Isidore of Seville defined it: '*Vagus* because without a way' (*Vagus, quia sine via, Etymologiae* X.280).

## References

Abrahams, Roger D. 1976. 'The Complex Relations of Simple Forms.' In Ben-Amos 1976a: 193–214.
Akinnaso, F. Niyi. 1982. 'On the Differences between Spoken and Written Language.' *Language and Speech* 25: 97–125.
Alonso, Dámaso, and José Manuel Blecua, eds. 1964. *Antología de la poesía española. Lírica de tipo tradicional*. 2nd ed. Madrid: Gredos.
Althoff, Gerd. 1997. 'Zur Bedeutung symbolischer Kommunikation für das Verständnis des Mittelalters.' *Frühmittelalterliche Studien* 31: 370–89.
–. 2003. *Die Macht der Rituale. Symbolik und Herrschaft im Mittelalter*. Darmstadt : WB.
Andersson, Theodore M. 1976. *Early Epic Scenery: Homer, Virgil, and the Medieval Legacy*. Ithaca, NY: Cornell UP.
Anglès, Higinio, ed. 1943–64. *La música de las Cantigas de Santa María, del rey Alfonso el Sabio*. 3 vols. Barcelona: Biblioteca Central.
–, ed. 1947. *La música en la corte de los Reyes Católicos. II. Polifonía profana: Cancionero Musical de Palacio (siglos XV–XVI)*. Vol. 1. Monumentos de la Música Española 5. Barcelona: Consejo Superior de Investigaciones Científicas, Instituto Español de Musicología.
Arlinghaus, Franz J., Marcus Ostermann, Oliver Plessow, Gudrun Tscherpel, eds. *Transforming the Medieval World: Uses of Pragmatic Literacy in the Middle Ages*. Turnhout: Brepols, 2006.
Arnim, Achim von, and Clemens Brentano. 2003. *Des Knaben Wunderhorn. Alte deutsche Lieder*. Ed. Heinz Rölleke. Frankfurt a. M.: Insel. [Or. 1806–8.]
Arnovick, Leslie K. 2006. *Written Reliquaries: The Resonance of Orality in Medieval English Texts*. Amsterdam: Benjamins.
Asensio, Eugenio. 1970. *Poética y realidad en el Cancionero peninsular de la Edad Media*. 2nd ed. Madrid: Gredos.
Assmann, Jan. 1992. *Das kulturelle Gedächtnis. Schrift, Erinnerung und politische Identität in frühen Hochkulturen*. Munich: Beck.
Baader, Renate. 1974. 'Ein Beispiel mündlicher Dichtung: Aucassin et Nicolette.' *Fabula* 15: 1–26.
Bächtold-Stäubli, Hanns, ed. 1927–42. *Handwörterbuch des deutschen Aberglaubens*. 10 vols. Berlin: de Gruyter. [Rpt. 1987.]
Baehr, Rudolf. 1962. *Spanische Verslehre auf historischer Grundlage*. Tübingen: Niemeyer.

Bailey, James, and Tatyana Ivanova, trans. 1998. *An Anthology of Russian Folk Epics.* Armonk, NY: Sharpe.
Bakker, Egbert J. 1999. 'How Oral is Oral Composition?' In *Signs of Orality: The Oral Tradition and its Influence in the Greek and Roman World.* Ed. E. Anne MacKay. Leiden: Brill. 29–47.
Bäuml, Franz H. 1980. 'Varieties and Consequences of Medieval Literacy and Illiteracy.' *Speculum* 55: 237–65.
–. 1984. 'Medieval Texts and the Two Theories of Oral-Formulaic Composition: A Proposal for a Third Theory.' *New Literary History* 14: 31–49.
–. 1993. 'Verschriftlichte Mündlichkeit und vermündlichte Schriftlichkeit: Begriffsprüfungen an den Fällen *Heliand* und *Liber Evangeliorum*.' In Schaefer 1993: 254–66.
–. 1998. 'Autorität und Performanz. Gesehene Leser, gehörte Bilder, geschriebener Text.' In Ehler and Schaefer 1998: 248–73.
Bec, Pierre. 1977–78. *La lyrique française au Moyen Âge (XII$^{ème}$- XIII$^{ème}$ siècles). Contribution à une typologie des genres poétiques médiévaux. Études et textes.* 2 vols. Paris: Picard.
Beitl, Klaus. 1973. 'Schnaderhüpfel.' In Brednich et al. 1973–75: I, 617–77.
Beltrán, Vicenç. 1998. 'Poesía tradicional: Ecdótica e historia literaria.' In *Lírica popular/ Lírica tradicional. Lecciones en homenaje a Don Emilio García Gómez.* Ed. Pedro M. Piñero Ramírez. Sevilla: Universidad Sevilla, Fundación Machado. 113–35.
Ben-Amos, Dan, ed. 1976a. *Folklore Genres.* Austin: U of Texas P.
–. 1976b. 'Analytical Categories and Ethnic Genres.' In Ben-Amos 1976: 215–42.
Benson, Larry D. 1966. 'The Literary Character of Anglo-Saxon Formulaic Poetry.' *PMLA* 81: 324–41.
–, gen. ed. 1987. *The Riverside Chaucer.* 3rd ed. Boston: Houghton Mifflin.
Bent, Ian, et al. 2001. 'Notation.' *New Grove²,* XVIII, 73–189.
Bloomfield, Morton W., and Charles W. Dunn. 1989. *The Role of the Poet in Early Societies.* Cambridge: Brewer.
Bogatyrev, P. G., ed. 1959. *Èpos slavyanskikh narodov. Khrestomatiya.* Moscow: Gos. uchebno-pedagogicheskoe izd. Ministerstva Prosveshcheniya RSFSR.
Bossuat, Robert, Louis Pichard, and Guy Raynaud de Lage, eds. 1964. *Dictionnaire des Lettres Françaises. Le Moyen Âge.* Édition entièrement revue et mise à jour sous la direction de Geneviève Hasenohr et Michel Zink. Paris: Fayard.
Bowra, C. M. 1952. *Heroic Poetry.* London: Macmillan.
–. 1962. *Primitive Song.* London: Weidenfeld and Nicolson.
–. 1972. *Homer.* London: Duckworth.
Brandin, Louis, ed. 1970. *Le Chanson d'Aspremont. Chanson de geste du XII$^e$ siècle.* CFMA 19, 25. 2 vols. 2nd ed. Paris: Champion.
Brednich, Rolf Wilhelm, Lutz Röhrich, and Wolfang Suppan, eds. 1973–75. *Handbuch des Volksliedes. I. Die Gattungen des Volksliedes. II. Historisches und Systematisches, interethnische Beziehungen, Musikethnologie.* 2 vols. Munich: Fink.
Briggs, Charles F. 'Literacy, Reading, and Writing in the Medieval West.' *Journal of Medieval History* 26 (2000): 397–420.
Brodeur, Arthur G. 1970. '*Beowulf*: One Poem or Three?' In *Medieval Literature and Folklore Studies: Essays in Honor of Francis Lee Utley.* Ed. J. Mandel and B. A. Rosenberg. New Brunswick, NJ: Rutgers UP. 3–26.
Brunner, Horst. 1997. *Geschichte der deutschen Literatur des Mittelalters im Überblick.* Stuttgart: Reclam.
Bukofzer, Manfred. 1960. 'Popular and Secular Music in England (to c. 1470).' In *Ars Nova and the Renaissance 1300–1540.* Ed. Anselm Hughes and Gerald Abraham. New Oxford History of Music 3. London: OUP. 107–33.

Burckhardt, Jacob. 1990. *The Civilization of the Renaissance in Italy*. Trans. S. G. C. Middlemore ; with a new introduction by Peter Burke and notes by Peter Murray. Harmondsworth: Penguin. [Or. 1860 in German.]
Butterfield, Ardis. 2002. *Poetry and Music in Medieval France: From Jean Renart to Guillaume de Machaut*. Cambridge: CUP.
Calder, George, ed. 1917. *Auraicept na n-Éces. The Scholars' Primer, Being the Texts of the Ogham Tract from the Book of Ballymote and the Yellow Book of Lecan, and the Text of the Trefhocul from the Book of Leinster*. Edinburgh: John Grant.
Calin, William. 1980–81a. 'L'Épopée dite vivante: réflexions sur le prétendu caractère oral des chansons de geste.' *Olifant* 8: 227–37.
–. 1980–81b. 'Littérature médiévale et hypothèse orale: une divergence de méthode et de philosophie.' *Olifant* 8: 256–85.
Carruthers, Mary. 1990. *The Book of Memory: A Study of Memory in Medieval Culture*. Cambridge: CUP.
Cerquiglini, Bernard. 1989. *Éloge de la variante. Histoire critique de la philologie*. Paris: Seuil.
Chadwick, N. Kershaw, trans. 1932. *Russian Heroic Poetry*. Cambridge; CUP.
Chadwick, H. Munro and N. Kershaw Chadwick. 1932–40. *The Growth of Literature*. 3 vols. Cambridge: CUP.
Chailley, Jacques. 1956. 'La chanson populaire française au Moyen Âge.' *Annales de l'Université de Paris* 26: 153–74.
Chicherov, V. I. 1982. *Shkoly skaziteley Zaonezh'ya*. Moscow: Nauka.
Child, Francis James, ed. 1882–98. *The English and Scottish Popular Ballads*. 5 vols. Boston.
Clanchy, M. T. 1993. *From Memory to Written Record: England 1066–1307*. 2nd ed. Oxford: Blackwell.
Coleman, Janet. 1992. *Ancient and Medieval Memories: Studies in the Reconstruction of the Past*. Cambridge: CUP.
Coleman, Joyce. 1996. *Public Reading and the Reading Public in Late Medieval England and France*. CSML 26. Cambridge: CUP.
Colgrave, Bertram, and R. A. B. Mynors, eds. and trans. 1969. *Bede's Ecclesiastical History of the English People*. Oxford: Clarendon.
Croce, Benedetto. 1946. *Poesia Popolare e Poesia d'Arte. Studi sulla Poesia Italiana dal Tre al Cinquecento*. 2nd rev. ed. Bari: Laterza.
Crocker, Richard. 1990. 'Medieval Chant.' In Crocker and Hiley 1990: 225–309.
–, and David Hiley, eds. 1990. *The Early Middle Ages to 1300*. The New Oxford History of Music 2. 2nd ed. Oxford: OUP.
Crosby, Ruth. 1936. 'Oral Delivery in the Middle Ages.' *Speculum* 11: 88–110.
Cummins, John G., ed. 1977. *The Spanish Traditional Lyric*. Oxford: Pergamon P.
Darby, H. C. 1968. 'Serbia.' In *A Short History of Yugoslavia from Early Times to 1966*. Ed. Stephen Clissold. Cambridge: CUP. 87–134.
Delbouille, Maurice. 1959. 'Les chansons de geste et le livre.' In *La Technique Littéraire des Chansons de Geste. Actes du Colloque de Liège (Septembre 1957)*. Bibliothèque de la Faculté de Philosophie et Lettres de l'Université de Liège. Fascicule 150. Paris: 'Les Belles Lettres'. 295–407.
Dessauer, Renata. 1928. *Das Zersingen. Ein Beitrag zur Psychologie des deutschen Volksliedes*. Germanische Studien 61. Berlin: Emil Ebering.
Doane, A. N. 1994. 'The Ethnography of Scribal Writing and Anglo-Saxon Poetry: Scribe as Performer.' *Oral Tradition* 9: 420–39.
Dorson, Richard M., ed. 1972. *Folklore and Folklife: An Introduction*. Chicago: U of Chicago P.
Doss-Quinby, Eglal. 1984. *Les refrains chez les trouvères du XII$^e$ siècle au début du XIV$^e$*. Frankfurt a. M.: Lang.

Dronke, Peter. 1968. *Medieval Latin and the Rise of European Love-Lyric.* 2 vols. 2nd ed. Oxford: Clarendon.
DuBois, Thomas A. 2006. *Lyric, Meaning, and Audience in the Oral Tradition of Northern Europe.* Poetics of Orality and Literacy 3. Notre Dame, IN: U of Notre Dame P.
Duggan, Joseph J. 1980–81a. 'La Théorie de la Composition oral des chansons de geste: les faits et les interprétations.' *Olifant* 8:238–55.
–. 1980–81b. 'Le Mode de composition des chansons de geste: analyse statistique, jugement esthétique, modèles de transmission.' *Olifant* 8:286–316.
Durling, Nancy Vine, ed. 1997. *Jean Renart and the Art of Romance: Essays on 'Guillaume de Dole'.* Gainesville: UP of Florida.
Ehler, Christine, and Ursula Schaefer, eds. 1998. *Verschriftung und Verschriftlichung. Aspekte des Medienwechsels in verschiedenen Kulturen und Epochen.* ScriptOralia 94. Tübingen: Narr.
Erll, Astrid, Ansgar Nünning, and Sarah B. Young, eds. 2008. *Cultural Memory Studies: An International and Interdisciplinary Handbook.* Berlin: de Gruyter.
Everist, Mark. 1994. *French Motets in the Thirteenth Century: Music, Poetry and Genre.* Cambridge: CUP.
Fähndrich, Hartmut. 1990. 'Der Begriff "adab" und sein literarischer Niederschlag.' In *Neues Handbuch der Literaturwissenschaft. V. Orientalisches Mittelalter.* Ed. Wolfhart Heinrich. Wiesbaden: AULA. 326–45.
Faulhaber, Charles. 1976–77. 'Neo-Traditionalism, Formulism, Individualism, and Recent Studies on the Spanish Epic.' *Romance Philology* 30:83–101.
Ferreira, Manuel Pedro, ed. 1986. *O Som de Martin Codax. Sobre a dimensão musical da lírica galego-portuguesa (séculos XII–XIV).* Lisboa: Unisys; Imprensa Nacional – Casa da Moeda.
–, ed. 2005. *Cantus Coronatus: 7 Cantigas d'El Rei Dom Dinis.* Kassel: Reichenberger.
Fine, Elizabeth C. 1984. *The Folklore Text: From Performance to Print.* Bloomington: Indiana UP.
Finnegan, Ruth. 1974. 'How Oral is Oral Literature?' *Bulletin of the School of Oriental and African Studies* 37:52–64.
–. 1977. *Oral Poetry: Its Nature, Significance and Social Context.* Cambridge: CUP.
–. 1988. *Literacy and Orality: Studies in the Technology of Communication.* Oxford: Blackwell.
–. 1992. *Oral Traditions and the Verbal Arts: A Guide to Research Practices.* London: Routledge.
Firth, Raymond, with Mervyn McLean. 1990. *Tikopia Songs: Poetic and Musical Art of a Polynesian People of the Solomon Islands.* Cambridge Studies in Oral and Literate Culture 20. Cambridge: CUP.
Foley, John Miles. 1990. *Traditional Oral Epic: The Odyssey, Beowulf, and the Serbo-Croatian Return Song.* Berkeley: U of California P. [Rpt. 1993.]
–. 1991. *Immanent Art: From Structure to Meaning in Traditional Oral Epic.* Bloomington: Indiana UP.
–, ed. 1998. *Teaching Oral Traditions.* New York: The Modern Language Association.
–. 2002. *How to Read an Oral Poem.* Urbana: U of Illinois P.
Fowler, Alastair. 1982. *Kinds of Literature: An Introduction to the Theory of Genres and Modes.* Oxford: Clarendon.
Fox, Adam. 2000. *Oral and Literate Culture in England 1500–1700.* Oxford: Clarendon.
Fromm, Hans. 1990. 'Kalevala and Nibelungenlied: The Problem of Oral and Written Composition.' In *Religion, Myth, and Folklore in the World's Epics: The Kalevala and its Predecessors.* Ed. Lauri Honko. Religion and Society 30. Berlin: Mouton de Gruyter. 93–114.
Frye, Northrop. 1976. *The Secular Scripture: A Study of the Structure of Romance.* Cambridge, MA: Harvard UP.
García Gómez, Emilio, ed. and trans. 1975. *Las jarchas romances de la serie árabe en su marco.* 2nd ed. Barcelona: Sex Barral.
García Lorca, Federico. 1953. *Obras completas.* Ed. Arturo del Hoyo. Madrid: Aguilar.

Gennrich, Friedrich, ed. 1921–27. *Rondeaux, Virelais und Balladen aus dem Ende des XII., dem XIII. und dem ersten Drittel des XIV. Jahrhunderts mit den überlieferten Melodien.* 2 vols. Gesellschaft für romanische Literatur 43, 47. Dresden and Göttingen: Gesellschaft für romanische Literatur.

Geuenich, Dieter, and Otto Gerhard Oexle, eds. 1994. *Memoria in der Gesellschaft des Mittelalters.* Veröffentlichungen des Max-Planck-Instituts für Geschichte 111. Göttingen: Vandenhoeck & Ruprecht.

Goetsch, Paul. 1985.'Fingierte Mündlichkeit in der Erzählkunst entwickelter Schriftkulturen.' *Poetica* 17:202–18.

Goetz, Hans-Werner. 1999. *Moderne Mediävistik. Stand und Perspektiven der Mittelalterforschung.* Darmstadt: WB.

Goody, Jack. 1987. *The Interface Between the Written and the Oral.* Cambridge: CUP.

–, and Ian P. Watt. 1963. 'The Consequences of Literacy.' *Comparative Studies in Society and History* 5:304–45.

Green, D. H. 1994. *Medieval Listening and Reading: The Primary Reception of German Literature 800–1300.* Cambridge: CUP.

–. 2002. *The Beginnings of Medieval Romance: Fact and Fiction, 1150–1220.* Cambridge: CUP.

Greene, Richard Leighton, ed. 1977. *The Early English Carols.* 2nd ed. Oxford: Clarendon.

Grundmann, Herbert. 1958.'Litteratus – illitteratus. Der Wandel einer Bildungsnorm vom Altertum zum Mittelalter.'*Archiv für Kulturgeschichte* 40:1–65.

Gummere, Francis. B. 1901. *The Beginnings of Poetry.* New York: Macmillan.

Gurevich, Aaron J. 1984.'Oral and Written Culture of the Middle Ages: Two "Peasant Visions" of the Twelfth – Early Thirteenth Centuries.' *New Literary History* 16 (1984): 51–66. [Also in Gurevich 1992:50–64.]

–. 1988. *Medieval Popular Culture: Problems of Belief and Perception* Trans. János M. Bak and Paul A. Hollingsworth. Cambridge Studies in Oral and Literate Culture 14. Cambridge: CUP.

–. 1992. *Historical Anthropology of the Middle Ages.* Trans. Jana Howlett. Cambridge: Polity P.

Gürsoy-Naskali, Emine. 2000.'*Dudak değmez*: A Form of Poetry Competition among the *Aşıks* of Anatolia.' In *The Oral Epic: Performance and Music.* Ed. Karl Reichl. Intercultural Music Studies 12. Berlin: Verlag für Wissenschaft und Bildung. 151–58.

Haferland, Harald. 2004. *Mündlichkeit, Gedächtnis und Medialität. Heldendichtung im deutschen Mittelalter.* Göttingen: Vandenhoeck & Ruprecht.

Hainsworth, J. P. 1991. *The Idea of Epic.* Berkeley: U of California P.

Halbwachs, Maurice. 1925. *Les cadres sociaux de la mémoire.* Paris: Librairie Alcan.

Hale, Thomas A. 1998. *Griots and Griottes: Masters of Words and Music.* Bloomington: Indiana UP.

Harris, Joseph. 1983.'Eddic Poetry as Oral Poetry: The Evidence of Parallel Passages in the Helgi Poems for Questions of Composition and Performance.' In *Edda: A Collection of Essays.* Ed. R. J. Glendinning and Haraldur Bessason. University of Manitoba Icelandic Studies 4. Winnipeg: U of Manitoba P: 210–42.

–. 1991.'Introduction.' In *The Ballad and Oral Literature.* Ed. J. Harris. Harvard English Studies 17. Cambridge, MA: Harvard UP. 1–17.

Haupt, Leopold, and Johann Ernst Schmaler, eds. 1841–43. *Volkslieder der Wenden in der Ober- und Nieder-Lausitz.* 2 vols. Grimma. [Rpt. Berlin: Akademie-Verlag, 1953.]

Havelock, Eric A. 1963. *Preface to Plato.* Oxford: Blackwell.

Heaney, Seamus. 1990. *New Selected Poems: 1966–1987.* London: Faber and Faber.

Herder, Johann Gottfried. 1975. *'Stimmen der Völker in Liedern'. Volkslieder. Zwei Teile 1978/79.* Ed. Heinz Rölleke. Stuttgart: Reclam. [Or. 1778–79.]

Heusler, Andreas. 1943. *Die altgermanische Dichtung.* 2nd ed. Potsdam: Athenaion.

Honegger, Thomas. 1998. 'Form and Function: The Beasts of Battle Revisited.' *English Studies* 79: 289–98.
Honko, Lauri. 1989. 'Folkloristic Theories of Genre.' *Studia Fennica* 33: 13–28.
–, ed. 2000. *Textualization of Oral Epics*. Trends in Linguistics 128. Berlin: Mouton de Gruyter.
Horálek, K. 1974. 'Folk Poetry: History and Typology.' In Sebeok 1974: 741–807.
Hübner, Arthur. 1931. *Die deutschen Geißlerlieder. Studien zum geistlichen Volksliede des Mittelalters*. Berlin: de Gruyter.
Huizinga, Johan. 1924. *The Waning of the Middle Ages: A Study of the Forms of Life, Thought, and Art in France and the Netherlands in the Fourteenth and Fifteenth Centuries*. Trans. F. Hopman. London: Arnold] [Or. 1919 in Dutch.]]
Hymes, Dell. 1981. *'In Vain I Tried to Tell You': Essays in Native American Ethnopoetics*. Philadelphia: U of Pennsylvania P.
Jakobson, Roman. 1952. 'The Puzzles of the Igor' Tale on the 150th Anniversary of its First Edition.' *Speculum* 27: 43–66.
Jänicke, Oskar, ed. 1866. *Biterolf und Dietleib. Laurin und Walberan*. Deutsches Heldenbuch, Part 1. Berlin.
Jauss, Hans Robert. 1972. 'Theorie der Gattungen und Literatur des Mittelalters.' In *Grundriss der romanischen Literaturen des Mittelalters. I. Généralités*. Ed. Hans Ulrich Gumbrecht. Heidelberg: Winter. 107–38.
Johnson, John William. 2002. 'A Contribution to the Theory of Oral Poetic Composition.' In *The Kalevala and the World's Traditional Epics*. Ed. Lauri Honko. Studia Fennica Folkloristica 12. Helsinki: Finnish Literature Society. 184–242.
Jolles, André. 1934. *Einfache Formen. Legende, Sage, Mythe, Rätsel, Spruch, Kasus, Memorabile, Märchen, Witz*. Tübingen: Niemeyer. [Rpt. Tübingen, 1974.]
Jones, David J. 1930. *La tenson provençale*. Paris: Droz.
Karadžić, Vuk Stefanović, ed. 1987. *Srpske narodne pjesme*. New ed. Vladan Nedić. 4 vols. Belgrade: Prosveta, Nolit. [Or. Vienna, 1841–62.]
Karpeles, Maud. 1955. 'Definition of Folk Music.' *Journal of the International Folk Music Council* 7: 6–7.
–. 1973. *An Introduction to English Folk Song*. London: OUP.
Ker, W. P. 1908. *Epic and Romance: Essays on Medieval Literature* 2nd rev. ed. London: Macmillan.
Kirk, G. S. 1965. *Homer and the Epic: A Shortened Version of 'The Songs of Homer.'* Cambridge: CUP.
Klaeber, Fr. 2008. *Klaeber's Beowulf and the Fight at Finnsburg*. 4th ed. rev. R. D. Fulk, Robert E. Bjork, and John D. Niles. Toronto: U of Toronto P.
Klauser, Theodor. 1950. 'Auswendiglernen.' In *Reallexikon für Antike und Christentum*. Ed. Theodor Klauser et al. Stuttgart: Hiersemann. I, cols. 1030–39.
Koch, Peter. 1997. 'Orality in Literate Cultures.' In *Writing Development: An Interdisciplinary View*. Ed. Clotilde Pontecorvo. Amsterdam: Benjamins. 149–71.
–, and Wulf Oesterreicher. 1985. 'Sprache der Nähe – Sprache der Distanz. Mündlichkeit und Schriftlichkeit im Spannungsfeld von Sprachtheorie und Sprachgeschichte.' *Romanistisches Jahrbuch* 36: 15–43.
Koljević, Svetozar. 1980. *The Epic in the Making*. Oxford: Clarendon.
Kuhn, Hugo. 1956. *Gattungsprobleme der mittelhochdeutschen Literatur*. Bayerische AW, Philosophisch-Historische Klasse, SB Jg 1954, Heft 4. Munich: Bayerische AW.
Laforte, Conrad. 1981. *Survivances médiévales dans la chanson folklorique. Poétique de la chanson en laisse*. Quebec: Les Presses de l'Université Laval.
Lanciani, Giulia, and Giuseppe Tavani, eds. 1993. *Dicionário da Literatura Medieval Galega e Portuguesa*. Lisbon: Caminho.
Lang Ying. 2001. 'The Bard Jusup Mamay.' *Oral Tradition* 16: 222–39.

Larrington, Carolyne. 1993. *A Store of Common Sense: Gnomic Theme and Style in Old Icelandic and Old English Wisdom Poetry*. Oxford: Clarendon.
Leach, Maria, ed. 1972. *Funk & Wagnalls Standard Dictionary of Folklore, Mythology and Legend*. San Francisco: Harper and Row.
Lecoy, Félix, ed. 1963. Jean Renart. *Le Roman de la Rose ou de Guillaume de Dole*. CFMA 91. Paris: Champion.
Le Gentil, Pierre. 1952. *La poésie lyrique espagnole et portugaise à la fin du Moyen Age. II. Les formes*. Rennes: Plihon.
–. 1954. *Le virelai et le villancico. Le problème des origines arabes*. Paris: 'Les Belles Lettres'.
Likhachev, D. S. 1976. *'Slovo o Polku Igoreve'. Istoriko-literaturny ocherk*. Moscow: 'Prosveshchenie'.
Liuzzi, Fernando. 1934. *La lauda e i primordi della melodia italiana* 2 vols. Rome: Libreria dello Stato.
Lo Nigro, Sebastiano. 1964. *Tradizione e invenzione nel racconto popolare*. Florence: Olschki.
Loomis, Laura Hibbard. 1942. 'The Auchinleck Manuscript and a Possible London Bookshop of 1330–1340.' *PMLA* 57: 595–627.
Lord, Albert B. 1951. 'Yugoslav Epic Folk Poetry.' *Journal of the International Folk Music Council* 3: 57–61. [Rpt. (with changes) in *The Study of Folklore*. Ed. Alan Dundes. Englewood Cliffs, NJ: Prentice-Hall, 1965. 265–68.]
–. 1960. *The Singer of Tales*. Cambridge, MA: Harvard UP. [Re-edition with a CD and a new introduction by Stephen Mitchell and Gregory Nagy, 2000.]
–. 1981. 'Memory, Fixity, and Genre in Oral Traditional Poetries.' In *Oral Traditional Literature: A Festschrift für Albert Bates Lord*. Ed. John Miles Foley. Columbus, OH: Slavica. 451–61.
–. 1991. *Epic Singers and Oral Tradition*. Ithaca, NY: Cornell UP.
–. 1995. *The Singer Resumes the Tale*. Ed. Mary Louis Lord. Ithaca, NY: Cornell UP.
Machan, Tim William. 1991. 'Editing, Orality, and Late Middle English Texts.' In *Vox intexta: Orality and Textuality in the Middle Ages*. Ed. A. N. Doane and Carol Braun Pasternack. Madison: U of Wisconsin P. 229–45.
McEvedy, Colin. 1961. *The Penguin Atlas of Medieval History*. Harmondsworth: Penguin.
McGillivray, Murray. 1990. *Memorization in the Transmission of the Middle English Romances*. New York: Garland.
McKitterick, Rosamond, ed. 1995. *The Uses of Literacy in Early Mediaeval Europe*. Cambridge: CUP.
Magoun, Francis P., Jr. 1955a. 'The Theme of the Beasts of Battle in Anglo-Saxon Poetry.' *Neuphilologische Mitteilungen* 56: 81–90.
–. 1955b. 'Bede's Story of Cædman: The Case History of an Anglo-Saxon Oral Singer.' *Speculum* 30: 49–63.
–. 1958. '*Béowulf A*': A Folk-Variant.' *Arv* 14: 95–140.
Makdisi, George. 1988. 'Schools, Islamic.' In *Dictionary of the Middle Ages*. Ed. Joseph R. Strayer et al. 13 vols. New York: Charles Scribner's Sons, 1982–89. XI, 64–69.
Malkiel, Yakov, and Charlotte Stern. 1984. 'The Etymology of Spanish *villancico* "Carol": Certain Literary Implications of this Etymology.' *Bulletin of Hispanic Studies* 61: 137–50.
Martin, Janet. 1995. *Medieval Russia, 980 – 1584*. Cambridge: CUP.
Martin, Richard P. 2005. 'Epic as Genre.' In *A Companion to Ancient Epic*. Ed. John Miles Foley. Oxford: Blackwell. 9–19.
Meier, John. 1906. *Kunstlieder im Volksmunde. Materialien und Untersuchungen*. Halle: Niemeyer.
Menéndez Pidal, Ramón. 1960. *La Chanson de Roland et la tradition épique des Francs*. 2nd ed. Rev. René Louis, trans. Irénée-Marcel Cluzel. Paris: Picard.
Merchant, Paul. 1971. *The Epic*. The Critical Idiom 17. London: Methuen.
Merriam, Alan P. 1964. *The Anthropology of Music*. Evanston, IL: Northwestern UP.

Moisl, Hermann. 1981. 'Anglo-Saxon Royal Genealogies and Germanic Oral Tradition.' *Journal of Medieval History* 7: 215–48.
Mölk, Ulrich. 1982. *Trobadorlyrik. Eine Einführung*. Munich: Artemis.
Monroe, James T., ed. and trans. 1974. *Hispano-Arabic Poetry: A Student Anthology*. Berkeley: U of California P.
Monson, Don Alfred. 1981. *Les 'ensenhamens' occitans. Essai de définition et de délimitation du genre*. Bibliothèque Française et Romane, C 75. Paris: Klincksieck.
Müller, Jan-Dirk. 2005. '"Improvisierende", "memorierende" und "fingierte" Mündlichkeit.' *Zs. für deutsche Philologie* 124 [Supplement]: 159–81.
Müller-Blattau, Joseph. 1975. 'Das ältere geistliche Volkslied von den Anfängen bis zum Ende des 16. Jahrhundert.' In Brednich et al. 1973–75: II, 421–37.
Murko, Matthias. 1913. *Bericht über eine Bereisung von Nordwestbosnien und der angrenzenden Gebiete von Kroatien und Dalmatien behufs Erforschung der Volksepik der bosnischen Mohammedaner*. Sitzungsberichte der Kaiserlichen AW in Wien, Philos.-Hist. Kl., 173, Abh. 3. Wien: Kaiserliche AW.
Murphy, Gerard. 1940. 'Bards and Filidh.' *Éigse* 2: 200–7.
Neusner, Jacob. 1987. *Oral Tradition in Judaism: The Case of the Mishnah*. New York: Garland.
*New Grove*[2]: *The New Grove Dictionary of Music and Musicians*. Ed. Stanley Sadie. 2nd ed. 29 vols. London: Macmillan, 2001.
Niles, John D. 1999. *Homo narrans: The Poetics and Anthropology of Oral Literature*. Philadelphia: U of Pennsylvania P.
Novikov, Yu. A. 2000. *Skazitel' i bylinnaya traditsiya*. St. Petersburg: Dmitriy Bulanin.
O'Brien O'Keeffe, Katherine. 1990. *Visible Song: Transitional Literacy in Old English Verse*. CSASE 4. Cambridge: CUP.
Oesterreicher, Wulf. 1993. '*Verschriftung* und *Verschriftlichung* im Kontext medialer und konzeptioneller Schriftlichkeit.' In *Schriftlichkeit im frühen Mittelalter*. Ed. Ursula Schaefer. ScriptOralia 53. Tübingen: Narr. 267–92.
–. 1997. 'Types of Orality in Text.' In *Written Voices, Spoken Signs: Tradition, Performance and the Epic Text*. Ed. Egbert Bakker and Ahuvia Kahane. Cambridge, MA: Harvard UP. 190–214.
Oexle, Otto Gerhard. 1994. 'Memoria in der Gesellschaft und in der Kultur des Mittelalters.' In *Modernes Mittelalter. Neue Bilder einer populären Epoche*. Ed. Joachim Heinzle. Frankfurt a. M.: Insel. 297–323.
Okpewho, Isidore. 1992. *African Oral Literature: Backgrounds, Character, and Continuity*. Bloomington: Indiana UP.
Olrik, Axel. 1965. 'Epic Laws of Folk Narrative.' In *The Study of Folklore*. Ed. Alan Dundes. Englewood Cliffs, NJ: Prentice-Hall. 129–41. [Or. published as 'Epische Gesetze der Volksdichtung.' *Zs. für deutsches Altertum* 51 (1909): 1–12.]
Olsen, Alexandra Hennessey. 1993. 'Formulaic Tradition and the Latin *Waltharius*.' In *Heroic Poetry in the Anglo-Saxon Period: Studies in Honor of Jess B. Bessinger, Jr.* Ed. Helen Damico and John Leyerle. Kalamazoo: Medieval Institute, Western Michigan U. 265–82.
Ong, Walter J. 1982. *Orality and Literacy: The Technologizing of the Word*. London: Methuen.
Opland, Jeff. 1983. *Xhosa Oral Poetry: Aspects of a Black South African Tradition*. Johannesburg: Ravan.
Pächt, Otto. 1962. *The Rise of Pictorial Narrative in Twelfth-Century England*. Oxford: Clarendon.
Paden, William D. 2000. 'The System of Genres in Troubadour Lyric.' In *Medieval Lyric: Genres in Historical Context*. Ed. William D. Paden. Urbana: U of Illinois P. 21–67.
Page, Mary E. 1979. 'Professional Storytelling in Iran: Transmission and Practice.' *Iranian Studies* 12: 195–215.
Paris, Gaston, 1896. 'Bele Aaliz.' In *Mélanges de Philologie Romane dédiés à Carl Wahlund à l'occasion du cinquantième anniversaire de sa naissance (7 janvier 1896)*. Mâcon.1–12.

Parkes, M. B. 1973. 'The Literacy of the Laity.' In *The Mediaeval World*. Ed. David Daiches and Anthony Thorlby. London: Aldus Books. 555–77.
Pasternack, Carol Braun. 1995. *The Textuality of Old English Poetry*. Cambridge: CUP.
PC: Alfred Pillet and Henry Carstens. 1933. *Bibliographie der Troubadours*. Schriften der Königsberger gelehrten Gesellschaft, Sonderreihe 3. Halle: Niemeyer.
Petrov, V. T. 1982. *Traditsii èpicheskogo povestvovaniya v yakutskoy proze*. Novosibirsk: Nauka, Sibirskoe otdelenie.
Phillips, Nigel. 1981. *'Sijobang': Sung Narrative Poetry of West Sumatra*. Cambridge: CUP.
Pirot, François. 1972. *Recherches sur les connaissances littéraires des troubadours occitans et catalans des XII$^e$ et XIII$^e$ siècles. Les "sirventes-ensenhamens" de Guerau de Cabrera, Guiraut de Calanson et Bertrand de Paris*. Memorias de la Real Academia de Buenas Letras de Barcelona 14. Barcelona: Real Academia de Buenas Letras.
Pope, Mildred K., ed. 1955–64. *The Romance of Horn by Thomas*. 2 vols. Anglo-Norman Text Society 9–10, 12–13. Oxford: Blackwell.
Preminger, A., T. V. F. Brogan et al., eds. 1993. *The New Princeton Encyclopedia of Poetry and Poetics*. Princeton: Princeton UP.
Pryce, Huw, ed. 1998. *Literacy in Medieval Celtic Societies*. Cambridge Studies in Medieval Literature 33. Cambridge: CUP.
Putilov, B. N. 1976. *Metodologiya sravnitel'no-istoricheskogo izucheniya fol'klora*. Leningrad: Nauka.
–, ed. 1984. *Russkaya narodnaya poèziya. Epicheskaya poèziya*. Leningrad: Khudozhestvennaya literatura.
–. 1999. *Èkskursy v teoriyu i istoriyu slavyanskogo èposa*. St. Petersburg: Peterburgskoe Vostokovedenie.
Radloff, Wilhelm, ed. and trans. 1885. *Proben der Volkslitteratur der nördlichen türkischen Stämme. V. Der Dialect der Kara-Kirgisen*. St. Petersburg.
–. 1990. 'Samples of Folk Literature from the North Turkic Tribes. Preface to Volume V: *The Dialect of the Kara-Kirgiz*.' Trans. G. B. Sherman and A. B. Davis. *Oral Tradition* 5: 73–90.
Radulescu, Raluca L. 2009. 'Genre and Classification.' In Radulescu and Rushton 2009: 31–48.
–, and Cory James Rushton, eds. 2009. *A Companion to Medieval Popular Romance*. Cambridge: Brewer.
Raible, Wolfgang. 1996. 'Orality and Literacy.' In *Schrift und Schriftlichkeit. Ein interdisziplinäres Handbuch internationaler Forschung*. Vol. 1. Ed. Hartmut Günther and Otto Ludwig. Handbücher zur Sprach- und Kommunikationswissenschaft 10. Berlin. 1–17.
Rakić, Bogdan. 2006. 'Subverted Epic Oral Tradition in South-Slavic Written Literatures, 16th – 19th Centuries.' *Serbian Studies* 20: 131–50.
Ranke, Kurt. 1965. 'Einfache Formen.' In *Literatur II*. Ed. Wolf-Hartmut Friedrich and Walther Killy. 2 vols. Das Fischer Lexikon. Frankfurt a. M.: Fischer. I, 184–200. [Rpt. in Kurt Ranke. *Die Welt der Einfachen Formen. Studien zur Motiv-, Wort- und Quellenkunde*. Berlin: de Gruyter, 1978. 32–46.]
Redep, Jelka. 1991. 'The Legend of Kosovo.' *Oral Tradition* 6: 252–65.
Redfield, Robert. 1956. *Peasant Society and Culture: An Anthropological Approach to Civilization*. Chicago: U of Chicago P.
Reese, Gustave. 1954. *Music in the Renaissance*. London: Dent.
Régnier, Claude, ed. 1969. *La Prise d'Orange. Chanson de geste de la fin du XII$^e$ siècle*. Bibliothèque Française et Romane, B.5. Paris: Klincksieck.
Reichl, Karl. 1973. *Religiöse Dichtung im englischen Hochmittelalter. Untersuchung und Edition der Handschrift B.14.39 des Trinity College in Cambridge*. Texte u. Unters. zur engl. Phil. 1. Munich: Fink.
–. 1991. 'The Middle English Popular Romance: Minstrel versus Hack Writer.' In *The Ballad and Oral Literature*. Ed. J. Harris. Harvard English Studies 17. Cambridge, MA: Harvard UP. 243–68.

–. 1992. *Turkic Oral Epic Poetry: Traditions, Forms, Poetic Structure*. New York: Garland.
–. 1995. 'Variation and Stability in the Transmission of *Manas*.' In *Bozkırdan Bağımsızlığa Manas*. Ed. Emine Gürsoy-Naskali. Ankara: Türk Dil Kurumu. 32–60. [English and Turkish.]
–. 1997. 'The "Charms of Simplicity": Popular Strains in Early Middle English Love Poetry.' In *Individuality and Achievement in Middle English Poetry*. Ed. O. S. Pickering. Cambridge: Brewer. 39–58.
–. 2000. *Singing the Past: Turkic and Medieval Heroic Poetry*. Ithaca, NY: Cornell UP.
–. 2001. 'Medieval Perspectives on Turkic Oral Epic Poetry.' In *Inclinate Aurem: Oral Perspectives on Early European Verbal Culture. A Symposium*. Ed. Jan Helldén, Minna Skafte Jensen, and Thomas Pettitt. Odense: Odense UP. 211–54.
–. 2002. *Spielmannsidiom, Dialektmischung und Kunstsprache in der mittelenglischen volkstümlichen Epik*. Nordrhein-Westfälische AW, Vorträge G 383. Paderborn: Schöningh.
–, ed. and trans. 2007. *Edige: A Karakalpak Oral Epic as Performed by Jumabay Bazarov*. FF Communications 293. Helsinki: Academia Scientiarum Fennica.
–. 2009. 'Orality and Performance.' In Radulescu and Rushton 2009: 132–49.
Renoir, Alain. 1988. *A Key to Old Poems: The Oral-Formulaic Approach to the Interpretation of West-Germanic Verse*. Foreword by Albert B. Lord. University Park: The Pennsylvania State UP.
Riché, Pierre. 1989. *Écoles et enseignement dans le Haut Moyen Âge: fin du $V^e$ siècle – milieu du $XI^e$ siècle*. 2nd ed. Paris: Picard.
Ricketts, Peter T. 1991. 'Estribot: Forme et fond.' In *Mélanges de langue et de littérature occitanes en hommage à Pierre Bec*. Par ses amis, ses collègues, ses élèves. Poitiers: Université de Poitiers. 475–83.
Rokseth, Yvonne, ed. 1935–39. *Polyphonies du $XIII^e$ siècle. Le Manuscrit H 196 de la Faculté de Médecine de Montpellier*. 4 vols. Paris: L'Oiseau Lyre.
Romeu Figueras, José. 1949. 'La poesía popular en los Cancionero Musicales españoles de los siglos XV y XVI.' *Anuario musical* 4: 57–91.
Rosen, Tova. 2000. 'The Muwashshah.' In *The Literature of Al-Andalus*. Ed. María Rosa Menocal, Raymond P. Scheindlin, and Michael Sells. Cambridge: CUP. 165–89.
Rossi, Luciano, ed. and trans. 2009. Cercamon. *Œuvre poétique*. CFMA 161. Paris: Champion.
Rothe, Hans. 2000. *Was ist 'altrussische Literatur'?* Nordrhein-Westfälische AW, Vorträge G 362. Wiesbaden: Westdeutscher Verlag.
Roy, Bruno, and Paul Zumthor, eds. 1985. *Jeux de mémoire. Aspects de la mnémotechnie médiévale*. Montréal: Presses de l'Université de Montréal; Paris: Vrin.
Rubin, David C. 1998. *Memory in Oral Tradition*. New York: OUP.
Rychner, Jean. 1955. *La Chanson de geste. Essai sur l'art épique des jongleurs*. Société de Publications Romanes et Françaises 53. Geneva: Droz.
Sachs, Curt. 1938. *World History of the Dance*. Trans. Bessie Schönberg. London: Allen and Unwin.
Sahr, Julius. 1912. *Das deutsche Volklied. I*. 3rd ed. Leipzig: Göschen.
Salmen, Walter. 1960. *Der fahrende Musiker im europäischen Mittelalter*. Die Musik im alten und neuen Europa 4. Kassel: Hinnenthal.
Schaefer, Ursula. 1992. *Vokalität. Altenglische Dichtung zwischen Mündlichkeit und Schriftlichkeit*. ScriptOralia 39. Tübingen: Narr.
–, ed. 1993. *Schriftlichkeit im frühen Mittelalter*. ScriptOralia 53. Tübingen: Narr.
Schmaus, Alois. 1958. 'La byline russe et son état actuel.' *La Table Ronde* 132: 115–27.
SCHS. 1953–. *Serbo-Croatian Heroic Songs (Srpskohrvatske junačke pjesme)*. Coll., ed., and trans. Milman Parry, Albert Lord, and David Bynum. Cambridge, MA: Harvard UP. [Vols. 1–2 co-published by the Serbian Academy of Sciences, Belgrade.] Vol. 1 *Novi Pazar: English Translations* (1954). Vol. 2 *Novi Pazar: Serbocroatian Texts* (1953).

Schupp, Volker. 1993.'Pict-Orales oder: Können Bilder Geschichten erzählen?' *Poetica* 25: 34–69.
Sebeok, Thomas A., ed. 1974. *Current Trends in Linguistics.* Vol. 12 *Linguistics and Adjacent Arts and Sciences.* Part 2. The Hague: Mouton.
Sharp, Cecil J. 1907. *English Folk-Song, Some Conclusions.* London: Novello.
Sharp, Cecil J., coll. 1932. *English Folk Songs from the Sourthern Applachians.* Ed. Maud Karpeles. London: OUP.
Sharrer, Harvey L. 1991. 'The Discovery of Seven *cantigas d'amor* by Dom Dinis with Musical Notation.' *Hispania* 74: 459–61.
Shippey, Thomas A. 1977. 'Maxims in Old English Narrative: Literary Art or Traditional Wisdom?' In *Oral Tradition, Literary Tradition: A Symposium.* Ed. Hans Bekker-Nielson, Peter Foote, Andreas Haarder, and Hans Frede Nielsen. Odense: U of Odense P. 28–46.
Shonk, Timothy A. 1985.'A Study of the Auchinleck Manuscript: Bookmen and Bookmaking in the Early Fourteenth Century.' *Speculum* 60: 71–91.
Smith, John D. 1991. *The Epic of Pābūjī: A Study, Transcription and Translation.* Cambridge: CUP.
Smithers, G. V., ed. 1952–57. *Kyng Alisaunder.* 2 vols. EETS ES 227, 237. London: OUP.
–, ed. 1987. *Havelok.* Oxford: Clarendon.
Spanke, Hans. 1933.'Volkstümliches in der altfranzösischen Lyrik.' *Zs. für romanische Philologie* 53: 258–86.
Spiegel, Gabrielle M. 1997. *The Past as Text: The Theory and Practice of Medieval Historiography.* Baltimore: The Johns Hopkins UP.
Steinen, von den, Wolfram. 1948. *Notker der Dichter und seine geistige Welt.* Editionsband. Bern: Francke.
Stern, Samuel Miklos. 1974. *Hispano-Arabic Strophic Poetry.* Ed. L. P. Harvey. Oxford: Clarendon.
Stevens, John. 1961. *Music and Poetry in the Early Tudor Court.* London: Methuen.
–. 1986. *Words and Music in the Middle Ages: Song, Narrative, Dance and Drama, 1050–1350.* Cambridge: CUP.
–. 1990.'Medieval Song.' In Crocker and Hiley 1990: 357–451.
Studer, Ella. 1931. *Russisches in der Thidrekssaga.* Sprache und Dichtung 46. Bern: Haupt.
Suñol, Dom Gregori M. 1917.'Els cants dels romeus (segle XIVe).' *Analecta Montserratensia* 1: 100–92.
Sydow, C. W. von. 1948. 'Kategorien der Prosa-Volksdichtung.' In his *Selected Papers on Folklore. Published on the Occasion of his 70th Birthday.* Ed. Laurits Bødker. Copenhagen: Rosenkilde and Bagger. 60–88, English summary 86–88.[Or. 1934.]
Tannen, Deborah, ed. 1982a. *Spoken and Written Language: Exploring Orality and Literacy.* Norwood, NJ: Ablex.
Tannen, Deborah. 1982b. 'The Oral/Literate Continuum in Discourse.' In Tannen 1982a: 1–16.
Tarnawsky, George, and Patricia Kilina, eds.and trans. 1979. *Ukrainian Dumy. Editio Minor.* Introduction by Natalie K. Moyle. Toronto: Canadian Institute of Ukrainian Studies; Cambridge, MA: Harvard Ukrainian Research Institute.
Tedlock, Dennis. 1983. *The Spoken Word and the Work of Interpretation.* Philadelphia: U of Pennsylvania P.
Toporov, V. N. 1974.'Folk Poetry: General Problems.' In Sebeok 1974: 683–739.
Trautmann, B. 1942.'Die Dietleibsage und die Bylinen-Dichtung.' *BGDSL* 66: 146–52.
Treitler, Leo. 1974.'Homer and Gregory: The Transmission of Epic Poetry and Plainchant.' *Musical Quarterly* 60: 333–72.
–. 1981.'Oral, Written, and Literate Process in the Transmission of Medieval Music.' *Speculum* 56: 471–91.
Tristram, Hildegard L. C., ed. 1996. *(Re)Oralisierung.* ScriptOralia 84. Tübingen: Narr.
Turville-Petre, Gabriel. 1971.'On the Poetry of the Scalds and the Filid.' *Ériu* 22: 1–22.

Tvorogov, O. V., et al., eds. 1995. *Èntsiklopediya 'Slova o polku Igoreve'.* 5 vols. St. Petersburg: RAN, Institut russkoy literatury (Pushkinskiy Dom).
Uhland, Ludwig. 1844–45. *Alte hoch- und niederdeutsche Volkslieder mit Abhandlung und Anmerkungen. I. Liedersammlung.* 2 vols. Stuttgart.
–. 1866. *Alte hoch- und niederdeutsche Volkslieder mit Abhandlung und Anmerkungen. II. Abhandlung.* Stuttgart.
van den Boogard, Nico H. J. 1969. *Rondeaux et refrains du XII$^e$ siècle au début du XIV$^e$.* Bibliothèque Française et Romane, D 3. Paris: Klincksieck.
van der Werf, Hendrik. 1972. *The Chansons of the Troubadours and Trouvères: A Study of the Melodies and their Relation to the Poems.* Utrecht: Oosthoek.
–. 1997. 'Jean Renart and Medieval Song.' In Durling 1997: 157–87.
Veselovskiy, A. N. 1940. 'Psikhologicheskiy parallelizm i ego formy v otrazheniyakh poèticheskogo stilya.' In his *Istoricheskaya poètika.* Ed. V. M. Zhirmunskiy. Leningrad: Khudozhestvennaya literatura. 125–99. [Or. 1898.]
Voigt, Vilmos. 1980. 'On the Communicative System of Folklore Genres.' In *Genre, Structure and Reproduction in Oral Literature.* Ed. Lauri Hono and Vilmos Voig. Bibliotheca Uralica 6. Budapest: Akadémiai Kiadó. 171–88.
Wardropper, Bruce W. 1980. 'Meaning in Medieval Spanish Folk Song.' In *The Interpretation of Medieval Lyric Poetry.* Ed. W. T. H Jackson. New York: Columbia UP. 176–93.
Wenzel, Horst. 1995. *Hören und Sehen, Schrift und Bild. Kultur und Gedächtnis im Mittelalter.* Munich: Beck.
Wilkins, Nigel, ed. 1969. *One Hundred Ballades, Rondeaux and Virelais from the Late Middle Ages.* Cambridge: CUP.
–. 2001. 'Rondeau (i).' In *New Grove$^2$*, XXI, 644–47.
Williams, J. E. Caerwyn. 1971. 'The Court Poet in Medieval Ireland.' *Proceedings of the British Academy* 57: 1–51.
Wilson, R. M. 1970. *The Lost Literature of Medieval England.* 2nd ed. London: Methuen.
Witthöft, Christiane. 2004. *Ritual und Text. Formen symbolischer Kommunikation in der Historiographie und Literatur des Spätmittelalters.* Darmstadt: WB.
Wolff, Philippe. 1971. *Western Languages AD 100 – 1500.* Trans. Frances Partridge. London: Weidenfeld and Nicolson.
Yates, Frances A. 1966. *The Art of Memory.* Harmondsworth: Penguin.
Zenkovsky, Serge A., ed. and trans. 1963. *Medieval Russia's Epics, Chronicles, and Tales.* New York: Dutton.
Zhirmunsky [Schirmunski], Viktor. 1961. *Vergleichende Epenforschung. I.* Deutsche AW zu Berlin, Veröffentlichungen des Instituts für Deutsche Volkkunde 24. Berlin: Akademie-Verlag.
–. 1979. 'Legenda o prizvanii pevtsa.' In his *Sravnitel'noe literaturovedenie. Vostok i zapad.* Leningrad: Nauka. 397–407. [Or. 1960.]
–, and Kh. T. Zarifov. 1947. *Uzbekskiy narodny geroicheskiy èpos.* Moscow: Gos. izd. khudozhestvennoy literatury.
Zumthor, Paul. 1972. *Essai de poétique médiévale.* Paris: Seuil. [*Toward a Medieval Poetics.* Trans. Philip Bennett. Minneapolis: U of Minnesota P, 1992.]
–. 1983. *Introduction à la poésie orale.* Paris: Seuil. [*Oral Poetry: An Introduction.* Trans. Kathryn Murphy-Judy ; foreword by Walter J. Ong. Minneapolis: U of Minnesota P, 1990.]
–. 1987. *La lettre et la voix. De la 'littérature' médiévale.* Paris: Seuil.
Zupitza, Julius, ed. 1887. *The Romance of Guy of Warwick.* Vol. 2. EETS ES 49. London.
Zwartjes, Otto. 1997. *Love Songs from Al-Andalus: History, Structure and Meaning of the 'Kharja'.* Leiden: Brill.

# Part I
## Concepts and Approaches

# 2 Oral Theory and Medieval Literature

## John Miles Foley and Peter Ramey

The survey we offer here is intended solely as an analytical review of the so-called Oral Theory in broad perspective, with selective historical background, a focus on the last two decades, and suggestions about possible avenues for future research and scholarship. As such, this chapter does not aspire to exhaustive inclusiveness, but rather aims to chronicle some of the most significant early and recent developments within the long history of the approach. We will further narrow the focus by concentrating chiefly on oral-derived Old English literature, generally recognized as the birthplace of the Theory in medieval literature, with some attention to Middle English works. We also include limited references to already influential and particularly promising parallel work on comparative oral traditions.

The overall organization of the survey falls into three major sections. Section 1, 'Origins and Early History', locates the background of the Oral Theory in the Homeric Question and in the philology and anthropology of the nineteenth and early twentieth centuries, and then looks very briefly at the well-documented contributions of Milman Parry and Albert Lord.[1] Thorough accounts of reactions to and continuations of their initiatives through about 1990 are readily available elsewhere and will therefore not be revisited here.[2] After that point, as we shall see, the Oral Theory begins to evolve away from a self-contained methodology and toward combination and integration with other approaches. Section 2 of the survey, 'Recent Contributions', examines some of the more influential related publications that have appeared during the last two decades, from approximately 1990 to the present, by identifying five major areas of inquiry: the traditional formula, comparative projects, Middle English literature, manuscript transmission, and performance/reception. The third and final section of the chapter examines several opportunities for future research and scholarship on oral tradition and medieval English literature.

---

[1] Part of the first section is based on Foley 1988:2–18, which includes a much fuller exposition of the roots of Oral Theory, with appropriate references. See further Foley 1981b and 1985:3–77.

[2] For summaries of pertinent research published before 1990, see especially Edwards 1986, 1988, and 1992 (on ancient Greek); Olsen 1986, 1988 (on Old English); Parks 1986 (on Middle English); and, on more than 150 different traditions, Foley 1985 (with updates in Tyler 1988 and Quick 1997).

# 1 Origins and Early History

## 1.1 The Homeric Question

The story of Oral Theory and medieval literature begins, as do so many other stories of how to understand verbal art, with Homer and the epics conventionally attributed to him.[3] Conceived of as the Homeric Question, this line of inquiry simply asked 'Who was Homer?' – not so daunting a query, we might suppose, from a modern point of view. But there was enormous uncertainty associated with looking back so far in time, and unavoidable complications inherent in any conclusions based on fragmentary evidence, which was then likely to be interpreted via anachronistic notions of authorship, epitomized literary work, literacy rates, text-making technology, and readership. These factors led to the formulation of many different answers to the Homeric Question, not a few of them representing radical departures from literary history and criticism as usually practiced.

As early as the first century CE, Flavius Josephus took the Greeks to task for their ancient illiteracy, and went on to link the *Iliad* and *Odyssey* to their mode of composition, which he understood as a piecemeal assemblage of smaller songs that, once stitched together, produced inconsistencies within the larger tableaus. A seventeenth-century (and Greekless) clergyman named François Hédelin, known also as the Abbé d'Aubignac, was later to use Josephus' assertions to deny Homer's very existence and to contend that literate redactors were responsible for the epics as we have them. The eighteenth-century classicist Richard Bentley likewise saw the Homeric poems as a 'loose collection of songs and rhapsodies', which, though written by Homer, were created to be performed by himself and others. Some fifty years later Robert Wood, an amateur classicist and traveler, took a major step by describing Homer as an oral bard: 'As to the difficulty of conceiving how Homer could acquire, retain, and communicate all he knew without the aid of letters, it is, I own, very striking. And yet, I think, it will not appear insurmountable, if, upon comparing the fidelity of oral tradition, and the powers of memory, with the Poet's knowledge, we find the first much greater, and the latter much less, than we are apt to imagine' (1767 [1976]: 259). In many ways Wood's remarks dramatically anticipated the efforts of many more modern scholars to discover a way to explain how these enormous poems – and textual remnants of other oral traditions from the ancient and medieval worlds – could possibly have emerged before the advent of textual technology as we know it.[4]

No scholar was more influential in regard to the Homeric Question than Friedrich Wolf, whose *Prolegomena ad Homerum* presented historical and archaeological evidence

---

[3] On Homer as a legendary anthropomorphization of ancient Greek oral epic tradition, with analogies to parallel figures in other traditions (including Widsith in Anglo-Saxon), see Foley 1999: 49–63.

[4] The notion that Homeric epic is too long to have been the product of an oral tradition is quickly dispelled by summoning analogs from central Asia and elsewhere that dwarf the *Iliad* and *Odyssey* in length. We also note the widely distributed practice of 'immanent epic', where performance of a part stands by idiomatic premise for the implied whole. On these two areas, see the summary remarks, with examples, in Foley 2004b: 173–81.

that writing could not have existed in Homer's time. Ascribing to the 'redactor theory' of how the epics were composed, he effectively set the stage for the nineteenth century's chief Homeric preoccupation: the Analyst-Unitarian controversy, the argument over whether the poems were the work of many poets or a single genius author. The Analysts cited discrepancies within the received texts to posit an amalgamation of pre-existing parts composed by many poets, and even went so far as to identify the boundaries of various poets' contributions. The Unitarian position, on the other hand, argued for a single (quite modern) craftsman behind the creation of both epics.[5] It was this pitched battle over the roots and provenience of the *Iliad* and *Odyssey* that Parry was to confront in his doctoral theses.[6]

## 1.2 Philology

Critical to Parry's eventual proposal of an oral traditional poetics were the insights of classical philologists Johann Ernst Ellendt, Heinrich Düntzer, and Kurt Witte, who pointed toward new ways of understanding the symbiosis of metre and phraseology in Homer, and also of his own mentor at the University of Paris, Antoine Meillet. In 1861 Ellendt, intent on expanding Immanuel Bekker's prior work on metrically shaped units of diction, actually linked patterned phrase-types to poets 'who did not write'.[7] Three years later Düntzer pointed out how metre influenced morphology and suggested that 'the epic mode of expression had assumed for itself a certain privilege, even to employ earlier forms, in order to ease the flow of the verse' (1864:88–89). In the process he specifically insisted that metre was the governing factor, and that contextual applicability of the famous epithets – their individual, literal meaning as detached from the units they helped to make up – was not a factor in the poet's selection. Just as clearly an influence on Parry was Witte's focus on the chronological development of the Homeric language, with his acknowledgment of both earlier and later forms side by side in the same *Kunstsprache* (1912a and b).

Meillet's impact on his protégé's thinking has been much underestimated. Writing on the Indo-European origins of the ancient Greek hexameter (which he denied), the great French philologist straightforwardly observed that 'the Homeric epic is made up entirely of formulas that are transmitted by the poets' and that the hexameter 'is verse wherein all is artificial and traditional: the vocabulary, full of archaic words; the grammar, in which the old forms are maintained alongside the new ones [...]; the phonology, a mixture of forms of various dates and from various dialects' (1923:61). These ideas clearly lie at the foundation of what Parry was to propose in his two French theses in 1928. Nor, as we shall see, was Meillet's contribution limited to insights from philology. He was also instrumental in introducing his student Parry to the work of his most significant anthropological influence.[8]

---

[5] See Wolf 1795 [1963] and Grafton, Most, and Zetzel 1985.
[6] See Parry 1928a and 1928b; both are translated in M. Parry 1971.
[7] Ellendt 1861:79. – Unless otherwise noted, translations from German, French, Greek, Old English, and South Slavic were done by J. M. Foley.
[8] Also worthy of mention as a frequently cited influence in Parry's work was the French theorist

## 1.3 Anthropology

A third area of substantial pre-Parry and Lord activity consisted of what we today call anthropology and ethnography, with an emphasis on insights derived not from textual analysis but directly from firsthand, on-site fieldwork.[9] In chronological terms, Wilhelm Radloff's study of Central Asian oral epic was the first of the most important influences on Parry, who cited *Der Dialect der Kara-Kirgisen* very frequently in his published scholarship.[10] Crucial features of Radloff's work included the recognition that oral epic singers demonstrably relied neither on rote memorization nor on invention *ex nihilo*, but rather varied their oral poems systematically and within limits from one performance to the next. He also describes narrative multiforms, later to be termed 'themes' or 'typical scenes' by Lord and a sequence of specialists in a variety of traditions, explaining that the performing bard 'has in readiness entire sets of "recitation-parts" [*Vortragstheile*] [...], which he joins together in fitting ways during the course of his narration' (1885: xvi). Speaking further of these 'idea-parts' [*Bildtheile*], Radloff provides a remarkably forward-looking account of the Kirghiz singers' compositional method (1885: xvii):

> The art of the singer consists only in arranging all of these ready-made idea-parts coherently, as the course of events requires, and in joining them together through newly composed verses. The singer is thus able to sing all of the previously mentioned idea-parts in very different ways. He knows how to sketch one and the same idea in a few short strokes, or describe it in detail, or enter into an extremely detailed description in epic breadth. The more adaptable to various situations the idea-parts are for a singer, the more diverse his song becomes and the longer he can sing without wearying his audience by the monotony of his images. The inventory of idea-parts and the skill in their manipulation are the measure of a singer's ability.

This report of the actual, observed practice of oral epic bards must have deeply impressed Parry as he explored multiform traditional structure in Homer and sought the reasons behind that phenomenon.

Among other significant contributors to the anthropological basis upon which the Oral Theory was built were Friedrich Krauss, Gerhard Gesemann, and Arnold van Gennep. The first two of these scholars located the compositional strategy of the South Slavic *guslari* in multiform patterns that served these singers as a specialized, adaptable register of language. Krauss called such commonplaces 'clichés' and Gesemann described several story-patterns or tale-types that he termed 'composition-schemata'.[11] It is significant that both investigators drew their insights from real-life experience with singers from the Former Yugoslavia. Correspondingly, van Gennep, though not himself an ethnographer, was able to digest the observations made by fieldworkers and offer this suc-

---

Marcel Jousse, whose 1925 monograph explored the 'mnemo-technical' nature of oral composition, with specific reference to the South Slavic oral epic tradition.

[9] We need not merely hypothesize about the most important of these influences on Parry, who explicitly identified Wilhelm Radloff, Gerhard Gesemann, and Matija Murko as the most dependable resources for information on and analysis of then-living oral epic (Parry 1933–35:440). We will also include a few words on the contributions of Friedrich Krauss and Arnold van Gennep, both of them mentioned explicitly in Parry's publications.

[10] See the wide-ranging studies of Karl Reichl (esp. 1992, 2000a), discussed below in sections 2.2 and 2.5, on central Asian oral traditions and medieval oral-derived texts, likewise based on *in situ* fieldwork.

[11] See Krauss 1908 and Gesemann 1926.

cinct (if somewhat overstated) summary of how South Slavic oral epic worked: 'the poems of the *guslars* consist of a juxtaposition of clichés, relatively few in number and with which it suffices merely to be conversant. The unfolding of each of these clichés proceeds automatically, following fixed rules [...]. A fine *guslar* is one who handles these clichés as we play with cards, who orders them differently according to the use he wishes to make of them' (1909:52). All three of these scholars tended strongly toward a structural and to some extent mechanistic view of the process of poetic composition, an attribute that was to transfer to the Parry-Lord Oral Theory as it emerged in its earliest form.

Of all of the anthropologists, armchair or not, far the most significant influence on Parry – both for his understanding of the oral tradition behind the *Iliad* and *Odyssey* and for the planning and execution of his and Lord's later fieldwork among the South Slavic *guslari* – was the Slovenian philologist-ethnographer Matija Murko.[12] In an essential sense, Murko's unique combination of fieldwork, his awareness of comparative implications, and his detailed observations on how South Slavic epic singers actually plied their trade served as the perfect catalyst for Parry's transition from viewing the Homeric poems as *traditional* to understanding them as also necessarily *oral* in origin. Among Murko's central contributions were insights gained from many summers of ethnographic research among practicing *guslari*; analogies explicitly drawn between South Slavic oral epic and Romance, Germanic, and other Slavic poetries; stories recounting performance events in the Former Yugoslavia that must have fired Parry's imagination; and a demonstrated acquaintance with the role of patterned phraseology and narrative structuring in real-life compositional practice. When one adds the crucial fact that Murko was himself present at Parry's defense of his two 1928 theses on Homer and epic tradition (at Meillet's invitation), it becomes apparent how important a force he represented in the development of the Oral Theory.

## 1.4 Milman Parry and Albert Lord

The trajectory of Parry and Lord and the evolution of the Oral Theory from 1928–1960, from Parry's doctoral theses through the publication of Lord's monumental *The Singer of Tales*, has been thoroughly documented elsewhere,[13] so we will add here nothing more than the broadest summary of what they accomplished. Suffice it to say that the first step consisted of Parry's analysis of the traditional epithet in Homer, together with his supplementary thesis on the relationship between formulas and the hexameter. With these two thorough and radical investigations of 1928 he managed not simply to answer the Homeric Question differently, but in effect to reshape the concept of Homeric epic entirely. In place of the ongoing duel between Analysts and Unitarians over one or many authors, Parry showed that a long tradition of poets lay behind the poems that have reached us. That the epics were traditional, passed down through gen-

---

[12] Once again, we do not have to theorize about this point; Parry himself acknowledged that 'it was the writings of Professor Murko more than those of any other which in the following years led me to the study of oral poetry in itself and to the heroic poems of the South Slavs' (1933–35:439). Parry's references were chiefly to Murko's 1929 French monograph, now available in English translation (Murko 1990); for reference to more of Murko's work, see Foley 1988:115, n. 25.

[13] See Foley 1988:19–56; also A. Parry 1971, Foley 1981a and 1985:3–77.

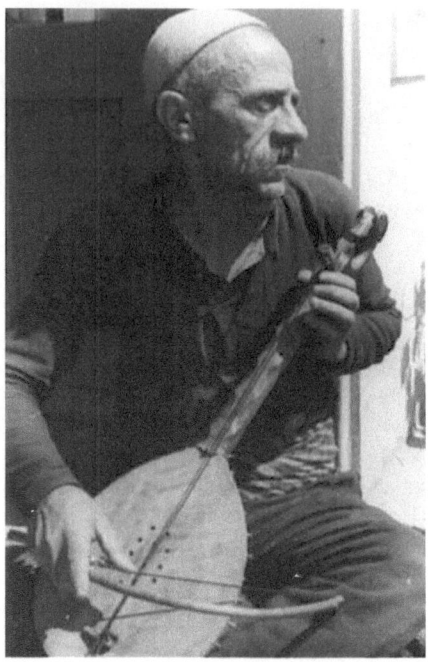

2 – Avdo Medjedović
No. 29 in Albert B. Lord's Photo Album. Its caption reads: 'Avdo Medjedovitch, peasant farmer, is the finest singer the expedition encountered. His poems reached as many as fifteen thousand lines. A veritable Yugoslav Homer!'

erations, was evident in their patterned diction (the primary exhibit being the noun-epithet formulas) and in the trademark symbiosis between metre and language. In place of the master redactor or the single inspired genius, Parry presented compelling evidence for a centuries-long succession of poets employing a common poetic language.

Reacting specifically to his mentor Meillet's criticism at the thesis defense, and to the unique insights derived from fieldwork by the anthropologists and ethnographers mentioned above, Parry swiftly moved in 1930–32 to the conclusion that such *traditional* verse-making must also necessarily have been *oral*. Only if the *aoidoi* composed in performance without the aid of writing, he reasoned, would they have needed to develop such an extensive system of ready-made phraseology. The first of the two articles in *Harvard Studies in Classical Philology* extends the concept of the *formula*, defined as 'a group of words which is regularly employed under the same metrical conditions to express a given essential idea' (1930: 272), in two interlocking ways – to cover all epic phraseology (and not simply the noun-epithet combinations) and to do so via the concept of the *formulaic system*.[14] In the second article, often underappreciated by later critics, Parry

---

[14] Parry defined the formulaic system as 'a group of phrases which have the same metrical value and which are enough alike in thought and words to leave no doubt that the poet who used them knew them not only as single formulas, but also as formulas of a certain type' (1930: 85).

made the case for a specialized poetic language or epic *koinê*, with contributions from multiple dialects and multiple chronological eras, as the dedicated language of an oral poetry. Citing the criterion of usefulness, which appears again and again in his writings, he envisioned an 'artificial' phraseology whose sole function was to enable the ready composition of ancient Greek epic in performance.[15]

Once having made what he came to understand as a necessary connection between traditional and oral, and inspired by Murko and others, Parry's next step was inevitable: together with his student Albert Lord, he would undertake the search for a living, flesh-and-blood Homer. He would journey to the living laboratory of then-Yugoslavia to study and record actual performances of oral epic by preliterate *guslari*, and compare what he discovered there to his theories derived from the Homeric texts. The proof for his claim of an oral Homer would be secured by analogy.

Starting in 1933 and continuing into 1935, the two American scholars canvassed six geographically defined regions in the able company of their native translator and interviewer, Nikola Vujnović, who was minimally literate and – very importantly – himself a *guslar*.[16] The result of their joint efforts was a collection of hundreds of oral epics in one of three formats: acoustic recordings of sung and instrumentally accompanied performances, acoustic recordings of recited and unaccompanied versions, or handwritten texts taken down (at a much slower pace) from dictation.[17] The three-person team also elicited substantial background information in the form of conversations managed by Vujnović, who as both an epic singer and a member of the fieldwork team maintained a foot in both worlds. This collected material was intended to serve as a living analog for the silent texts of Homer, so that they and others could investigate firsthand how the ecology of oral epic tradition actually functioned. They aimed to study Homer at one remove, as it were, by studying the practice, process, and products of the *guslari*.

With Parry's death in 1935 it was left to Lord to edit, translate, and publish the South Slavic epics in the series *Serbo-Croatian Heroic Songs* (*SCHS* 1953–), and to fulfill his mentor's plans for a comparative book-length study of oral epic poetry under the title *The Singer of Tales*.[18] The first of these projects, still ongoing today, has sought to present multiple versions of multiple songs by epic singers from within defined regions, and thus to illustrate how epic 'lives in the wild', so to speak, varying within limits from performance to performance, from one individual *guslar* to another, and from one singing community to another.[19] With the second project, far the most seminal work in Oral

---

[15] On the 'performance *koinê*' or compositional register of South Slavic epic, which reveals many of the same features as Homeric Greek, see Foley 1999: 65–88.

[16] For thorough accounts of the fieldwork expedition, see Lord's 'General Introduction', *SCHS* I: 3–20, and Mitchell and Nagy 2000. Lauri Honko (1998: 169–215) provides brief histories of 11 fieldwork projects that led to textualization of oral epics, including the Parry-Lord-Vujnović research.

[17] For a summary of materials collected during the 1933–35 trips, see Kay 1995; for a digest of collections during Lord's 1950–51 trip, see *SCHS* I: 41–45. For resources from the Milman Parry Collection available online, visit <http://chs119.harvard.edu/mpc/>.

[18] Lord 1960 was reissued in 2000 with a CD containing audio files of all the examples and a video clip with Avdo Medjedović.

[19] To date *SCHS* contains volumes representing the regions of Novi Pazar (vols. 1–2), Bijelo Polje (vols. 3–4 housing Avdo Medjedović's *The Wedding of Smailagić Meho*, about the length of the *Odyssey*; and vol. 6 presenting two additional epics by Medjedović), and Bihać (vol. 14). Both

Theory, Lord inaugurated a comparative approach that would rapidly spread to the study of literally scores of oral traditions over the next thirty years and beyond.[20] Soon Francis P. Magoun, Jr., writing in early response to the 1949 doctoral dissertation that became *The Singer of Tales* 11 years later, would bring the approach to Old English poetry in 1953,[21] and soon afterward a host of ancient, medieval, and modern literatures came under scrutiny. Lord went on to contribute a great many extremely influential publications to the ever-evolving Oral Theory, perhaps most notably *Epic Singers and Oral Tradition* and *The Singer Resumes the Tale*, shedding light on oral traditions as various as ancient and Byzantine Greek, Old English, South Slavic, Old French, Russian, Ukrainian, Bulgarian, Latvian, Finnish, Armenian, Turkish, Albanian, and various traditions from Africa, India, and Central Asia, as well as the oral traditions behind the New Testament. His work remains paradigmatic of the field as a remarkably diverse inventory of verbal art from oral tradition.[22]

## 1.5 A Third Stage of Development

If Lord's comparative extension to multiple traditions amounted to a second growth in the history of Oral Theory over the years between 1960 and the late 1980's, then the last few decades have seen a third, very promising subsequent growth. From about 1990 onward the Oral Theory began a new stage in its evolution, moving away from nearly exclusive attention to structure and to composition in performance on the model of the South Slavic *guslari* and toward a fuller awareness of the remarkable diversity that one actually finds in the world's oral traditions. New studies brought forward suggestive analogies that involved many different languages and traditions, which in turn revealed a host of different kinds of performers, different genres, and different media-contexts. It soon became apparent that we would need to enlarge and deepen our perspective in order to credit the numerous oral traditions – certainly the majority – that did not precisely follow the same rules postulated by the Oral Theory, founded as it was strictly on

---

manuscripts and audio records are becoming available through the online portal of the Parry Collection at <http://chs119.harvard.edu/mpc/>. See also my edition of *The Wedding of Mustajbey's Son Bećirbey* (Foley 2004a; also available as an eEdition at <http://oraltradition.org/zbm>) sung by the *guslar* Halil Bajgorić from the region of Stolac, where the Parry-Lord-Vujnović team began their fieldwork and collection. Note that their advocacy of regional investigation squares with the natural organization of the specialized language of South Slavic epic into idiolectal, dialectal, and pan-traditional forms (Foley 1990: 158–200, 359–87).

[20] For a sense of the Oral Theory's extraordinary comparative reach, see the bibliography of more than 2000 items in Foley 1985, with updates in Tyler 1988 and Quick 1997, which collectively include related research on more than 150 traditions; as well as Foley 1998, a survey of pedagogical applications to dozens of oral traditions.

[21] Magoun 1953. It should be noted here that Magoun was one of the readers of Lord's 1949 dissertation, and was thus exposed to comparative studies in oral tradition long before *The Singer of Tales* was published and generally available. Also of note is the fact that Old Germanic literatures in general, and Old English poetry in particular, already had a history of prior philological analyses of commonplaces, recurrent phrases, and the like (see Foley 1981b: 52–59).

[22] See Lord 1991 and 1995. For a bibliography of Lord's writings, see Foley 1992a.

the archetypal comparison between Homer and South Slavic oral epic.[23] Arguments over supposed binaries and singular models gave way to a more realistic grasp of complexity, especially in regard to interfaces and interactions between oral tradition and textual media.[24] Moreover, other approaches to oral tradition – especially Performance Theory and Ethnopoetics[25] – offered alternate (sometimes cognate) methods for understanding the dynamics, art, and meaning of non-literary verbal art. To an account of some major contributions to that third stage of development we now turn.

## 2 Recent Contributions

The past two decades have witnessed the expansion of Oral Theory into a number of new areas of studies in medieval literature, many of which its early proponents could hardly have anticipated. Some of these new areas include manuscript transmission and scribal practice, Middle English poems of unquestionably literate and literary provenance, Latin and prose vernacular works, as well as questions of audience and reception.

In the process, the approach itself has undergone alteration. Making such an expanded scope possible is a much-refined understanding of oral traditional poetics, which is increasingly viewed as compatible with writing. In fact, if anything like a consensus position can be found among scholars working in medieval English literature, it is that orality and literacy form a continuum, with considerable room for overlap and cross-fertilization, rather than contrasting, mutually exclusive categories. Concomitant with this shift, Oral Theory has grown less concerned with questions of composition *per se* and more interested in issues of meaning and aesthetics. As Mark Amodio puts it, 'in building upon and extending the project of oral-formulaic theory, contemporary oral theorists have begun to uncover and to understand more fully the aesthetics that underlie traditional oral poetries, aesthetics that had proved largely resistant to the literate

---

[23]   As brilliant and groundbreaking as the analogy between these ancient and modern traditions proved, it also artificially constrained the development of the Theory by tying it too parochially to the limited set of features shared by these two comparands. In other words, since Parry and Lord focused primarily on Bosnian Moslem epic from the South Slavic tradition (on the understandable ground that it more closely resembled Homeric epic than other forms from the same region; see further Foley 2002: 188–218 on the diverse ecology of oral genres found in the Former Yugoslavia), the resultant conception of oral tradition as a single, archetypal phenomenon was far too narrow. It did not take into account even the shorter Christian epic from the same and adjacent regions, not to mention any of the many other genres from that oral tradition that performed other functions for the society at large. As this extremely limited concept was applied outward away from then-Yugoslavia to other nations and ethnic groups across the globe and from the ancient world to the present day, problems of simple definition, as well as of dynamics, provenience, function, and the like, quickly arose and caused much serious (and unavoidable) disagreement among scholars. It was to air these differences and to provide a forum for appreciating the diversity of traditions that the journal *Oral Tradition* was founded in 1986.
[24]   Ruth Finnegan's *Oral Poetry* (1977) was particularly instrumental in helping scholars from various fields to understand the inherent diversity of oral traditions. See further Foley's *How to Read an Oral Poem* (2002: especially 38–52), which proposes a four-part heuristic for this diversity: oral performance, voiced texts, voices from the past, and written oral poetry.
[25]   See section 2.5 for a brief discussion of these two approaches.

interpretative strategies that had habitually, and with predictably unsatisfactory results, been brought to bear on them' (2005a: 6). In short, Oral Theory has broadened from a mode of compositional analysis to a more nuanced discourse capable of being applied to a variety of different kinds of texts and at the same time amenable to being fruitfully conjoined with a number of other approaches.

For the sake of this overview, these recent developments have been grouped into the five following subsections, although we stipulate from the start that there will be considerable overlap among them: expanded applications and definitions of the traditional formula; comparative approaches; oral poetics and Middle English literature; Oral Theory and manuscript transmission; and issues of performance and reception.

## 2.1 Expanding the Traditional Formula

The formula lies at the very origin of Oral Theory, and as the approach has evolved the concept of the formula has evolved along with it. These changes have come from many different quarters. One development has been formulaic analyses of previously uncharted areas, such as Anglo-Latin and Old English prose works. But perhaps the most significant shift has been in the overall change of emphasis. Less prevalent is the view of the formula as exclusively or even primarily a compositional unit; instead, it is now more often understood as an integer of traditional meaning. Scholarship has moved away from the rather sterile oral-versus-literate debates over the composition of Old English poems and turned toward assessing the expressive capacity of traditional verbal art forms and their continuing aesthetic role long after the advent of literacy in the British Isles.

The movement from composition to aesthetics is forcefully articulated, for example, in John Miles Foley's *Immanent Art*. Foley enlarges the concept of the formula (and its narrative counterpart, the theme or typical scene) by demonstrating how the traditional idiom is not so much descriptive as highly idiomatic or metonymic, operating with a much different dynamic of surface-to-deep structure than that frequently prized in literary works. In this understanding, formulas signify through metonymy as 'indexes of more-than-literal meanings, as special signs that point toward encoded traditional meanings', summoning rather than denoting the larger tradition. Foley terms this type of signification *traditional referentiality*, an operation that 'entails the invoking of a context that is enormously larger and more echoic than the text or work itself, that brings the lifeblood of generations of poems and performances to the individual performance or text' (1991:7). This highly reverberative idiom allows for the wider tradition to be referenced without being wholly re-created in each instance. Moreover, formulas and themes continue to be employed long after the establishment of literacy not 'out of a misplaced antiquarianism or by default, but because, even in an increasingly textual environment, the "how" developed over the ages still holds the key to worlds of meaning that are otherwise inaccessible' (1991:7). The traditional language continues to be used, Foley argues, because it remains a powerfully expressive tool that literary methods cannot readily replace or emulate.[26]

---

[26] See further Foley 2003, which demonstrates how Old English poetic formulas are able to cross over generic boundaries because of a shared verse structure.

As for the identity of the traditional units themselves, recent scholarship has shown that any definition of the formula must be tailored to its respective tradition. Old English verse, for example, because of its more flexible prosody, depends less on verbatim recurrent phraseology than on diction shaped by the more restrictive and encapsulating metres of Homeric or South Slavic oral epic. Old English poetry relies instead on alliterating morphemes and adaptable patterns, and as a consequence proves 'a far more flexible idiom that permits much more extensive variation around a relatively fixed core of one or more words or morphs' (Foley 1990: 355). This looser, stress-based organization of Old English versification leads to a formulaic language that is more elastic, including phrases often based around a single recurring word or lexical root. Foley goes so far as to suggest that 'the concept of "recurrence" itself may not be precise enough to describe the protean adaptability of Old English diction' (356). Instead, he describes the diction of *Beowulf* as 'a spectrum of phraseology that resists reduction to a single formulaic model' (390).

Yet the traditional language of Old English poetry proves no less resonant for its greater flexibility. In *Beowulf*, for example, Foley shows how the titles for Hrothgar – *helm Scyldinga* (protector of the Scyldings) – and *sunu Ecgþeowes* (son of Ecgtheow) – do much more than convey simple denotative significance. Rather, these epithets summon the larger values of Anglo-Saxon warrior society by indexing complex heroic personalities with great significative economy (1991: 30). And the formulaic phraseology works on a number of levels, corresponding to the elasticity of Old English prosody. Foley points out that a single lexeme such as the expletive *Hwæt!* ('Lo!') can function to summon the traditional idea of performance; or in other cases, such as Grendel's approach to Heorot, formulaic language is grouped into echoic clusters (31–33). The immanence of the surrounding tradition allows it to be invoked idiomatically through the traditional referentiality of formulaic language.[27]

Where Foley focuses on enlarging our understanding of the traditional formula to encompass aesthetics, Andy Orchard aims to enlarge its scope. Orchard's recent work challenges longstanding binaries of oral-literate, vernacular-Latin, poetry-prose, and pagan-Christian, arguing for a greater degree of continuity between these supposed poles in Anglo-Saxon England, particularly as demonstrated in and through the dissemination of traditional formulaic language.[28] He finds, for example, that the Old English homilies of Wulfstan 'rely on the formulaic repetition of rhythmical phrasing' in the case of common two-stress phrases frequently occurring in the prose works (1997: 109).[29] A similar perspective, he argues, can be applied to Anglo-Latin literature: 'since the same sort of formulaic patterning occurs in Aldhelm as in *Beowulf*, it seems reasonable to describe both as products of a traditional (and oral-derived) system of versification' (1994: 124).

Orchard finds further evidence for the Latin-vernacular overlap in the formulaic language of the Exeter Book, which in many cases combines Latin literary sources with

---

[27] For a brief introduction to the application of traditional referentiality to the shorter Old English elegy 'Deor', see Foley 1999: 263–70.
[28] A succinct overview of his approach is available in Orchard 2003.
[29] On homiletic prose, see Orchard 1993.

vernacular formulaic phrasing. He investigates this hybrid form to gauge the persistence and flexibility of the oral tradition (1997:114). His more recent work has analyzed the formulaic content of the Latin epistolary prose of Boniface and the subsequent generations of Anglo-Saxon missionaries to the continent.[30] He is currently at work on 'An Anglo-Saxon Formulary', a project that 'will exhaustively document formulaic phrasing in four key areas of Anglo-Saxon literature, namely (1) Old English poetry; (2) Anglo-Latin hexameter verse; (3) the Old English sermons of Wulfstan; (4) the Anglo-Latin letters of the Bonifatian correspondence' (2001:19).

For Anita Riedinger, the traditional formula can also serve as a means for expressive play. In her study of the Old English riddles, Riedinger argues that formulaic elements are used to deliberately lead the audience astray by establishing traditional (but misleading) associations that the actual solution contravenes. In such cases traditional connotation is harnessed for a specific sort of misdirection: the riddles 'exploit the tradition [...] in order to deceive' (2004:38). Erick Kelemen, on the other hand, has investigated the significance of a single Old English formula, *clyppan and cyssan* (to clasp and to kiss), as a 'formulaic expression of return from exile' (2001:1). As the oral-traditional phrase recurs throughout the corpus, including both prose and poetry, he discovers in it a complex 'idiomatic force' (7), encompassing multiple and competing connotations of Germanic heroism and Christianity, as well as a euphemism for the sexual act. For Kelemen the meanings embedded in the formula are not stratified layers but 'a system of active exchange and competition whose shared and contested elements are sometimes submerged, marginalized, or repressed but are nevertheless meaningful and current' (11).[31]

In addition, particular subtypes of the formula have been further delineated. In *Revising Oral Theory,* Paul Acker employs a linguistics-based approach to both Old English and Old Icelandic verse. Building on Paul Kiparsky's concept of the 'bound expression', Acker looks specifically at a subset of the formula – what he terms 'syndetic formulas' (formulas that recur as a fixed pair, such as *habban + healdan*) – to examine its role within the poetic corpus (1998:3). In 'A New Conception of Poetic Formulae Based on Prototype Theory and the Mental Template', John C. Ford suggests a more comprehensive definition of the formula for Middle English literature. Working with the Middle English *Amis and Amiloun,* he advocates an understanding of the formula based on a mental prototype rather than any specific lexical content. Employing John R. Taylor's concept of linguistic prototype, Ford argues that formulas are fashioned from a mental template, such as [preposition + *Seynt* + name]. From this point of view the defining properties of the formula are that it be a full lexical unit and a metrically useful item, and that it impart a non-particularized meaning that is open to general application (2002:225).

---

[30] See Orchard 2001. Alexandra Hennessey Olsen (2005) similarly finds that vernacular Anglo-Saxon oral poetics permeates the letters of the Boniface Collection via the operation of traditional themes and formulaic language.

[31] For Kelemen, 'the intertextual nature of formulaic language [...] is not a one-way dynamic of sources and influences but a culture field, a textual environment, which maps the complex exchanges and shared ideologies of the moment of production' (11).

## 2.2 Comparative Approaches

Foley's *Traditional Oral Epic* (1990) represents both a continuation and a beginning: it continues in the comparative vein that inaugurated Oral Theory in the South Slavic fieldwork of Parry and Lord, while at the same time it marks a significant break with prior research. As Foley notes, past comparative efforts were hampered by a lack of criteria for what could be appropriately compared, often with the result that differences are suppressed in order to emphasize shared characteristics. This volume seeks to redress this fundamental problem.

The overall aim of *Traditional Oral Epic* is to establish an oral traditional poetics that, while remaining distinct from literary criticism, avoids collapsing oral poetic traditions into a single, universalized category. Toward this end Foley sets up a 'reading program', a series of guidelines for approaching each tradition on its own terms while retaining the helpful pluralistic perspective of comparison. Its five criteria include: 1) text-dependence, or the comparability of the documents in question; 2) oral or oral-derived – whether the text can confidently be considered oral in origin, such as a recorded performance, or whether it is more prudently seen as oral-derived; 3) genre-dependence – that is, to what extent the comparands are generically suitable for comparison one to the next; 4) tradition-dependence, or attentiveness to the individual features of each tradition, so that each is understood in its own terms and significant differences between and among comparands are recognized; and 5) synchronic and diachronic contexts.

Applying this program to three epic traditions – *Beowulf*, the *Odyssey*, and the South Slavic Return Song – Foley finds that formulas and themes in the Homeric and South Slavic poetries correspond less directly to Old English poetry. From the vantage point of tradition-dependence, the operation of traditional features in symbiosis with the Germanic, stress-based prosody of *Beowulf* does not mirror the encapsulated, often verbatim texture of the formula as found in the quantitative and syllabic metres of the Homeric and South Slavic traditions. The stress-based and alliterative character of Old English metre makes for a less constrained, more flexible phraseology, so that the 'recurrent kernel of Beowulfian diction will seem to be the root morpheme, a still point surrounded by a looser aggregation of relatively less important words' (18) – a level of patterning typical of Anglo-Saxon oral-derived poetry in general. Greater flexibility is also found in the case of traditional themes or type-scenes. While these larger compositional units maintain a consistent narrative pattern, there is considerably less verbal correspondence than in the other two traditions (357). Overall, Foley's comparative approach reveals that Old English verse demonstrates a greater divergence between the deep structure of narrative units and their surface structure as recurrent phraseology.

Several other comparative studies have meshed Oral Theory with research involving different analogs. John D. Niles, for example, has examined Old English poetry in light of his personal fieldwork with Scottish balladry and storytelling.[32] Niles thus draws on living oral tradition to uncover how the oral poetics of traditional narrative performance

---

[32] Niles had already applied Oral Theory to questions of social meaning in *Beowulf: The Poem and Its Tradition* (1983). More recently, he further develops comparative studies in his *Homo Narrans: The Poetics and Anthropology of Oral Literature* (1999), as well as *Old English Heroic Poems and the Social Life of Texts* (2007); see also Niles 2003b.

is used to create social meaning.[33] He identifies traditional poetry most fundamentally as a form of 'mythopoesis'; oral narrative, he contends, is no less than 'the chief basis of culture itself' (1999:2). Scottish balladry usefully illustrates this role of oral narrative as 'social praxis' – a force that creates and maintains a communal identity and sets up social values, as well as provides a kind of forum for collective thought. Niles suggests that *Beowulf* 'served Anglo-Saxons as a mythlike tale that helped define their identity and preserve their equilibrium during a period of significant change' (31). By thoroughly examining both structure and context, he is able to demonstrate that traditional poetries do important cultural work, such as allowing the formation of a group identity, serving as a means of adapting that identity to change, and assisting in normative and sapiential functions.

Like Niles, Karl Reichl brings a concern with the context and function of oral poetry to his comparative research. Drawing on the living epic traditions of the Turkic peoples of Central Asia, among whom he has carried on extensive fieldwork, Reichl applies insights gathered from personal experience to illuminate the long-entexted heroic poetry of *Beowulf* and the Old French *Song of Roland*, as well as Middle English romance.[34] More recently, he has used Central Asian poetry to explore questions of performance in popular romance from the later Middle Ages, employing the diverse styles of performance in this living verbal art to map out possibilities for medieval performers we can know only from long-silent texts.[35] Ultimately, the comparison with living traditions allows Reichl to underscore 'the event-character of this type of poetry', a verbal art that was 'orally performed (sung/chanted/recited) to an audience at a particular occasion and for a particular purpose' (2003:76).

Building on the ever-accumulating evidence for the remarkable diversity of oral traditions and related forms, in 2002 Foley proposed a new heuristic for comparative investigation in *How to Read an Oral Poem*. In consonance with Ruth Finnegan's initial observations (1977) and in response to the variety reported over the previous 16 years in the journal *Oral Tradition* (1986–), he suggested a flexible and non-evolutionary system of four categories:[36]

|  | Composition | Performance | Reception |
|---|---|---|---|
| *Oral performance* | Oral | Oral | Aural |
| *Voiced texts* | Written | Oral | Aural |
| *Voices from the past* | O/W | O/W | A/W |
| *Written oral poems* | Written | Written | Written |

The first category is of course the most straightforward: live performance before an audience, as with genres worldwide from African American rap and hip hop to African oral epic. Voiced texts are composed in textual format but specifically for live performance, as

---

[33] Niles (1999:29–30) utilizes Foley's concept of 'word-power' (1992b; 1995:27–28) to explore the aesthetic and social force of traditional verbal art.

[34] The fullest treatment of these topics can be found in *Singing the Past: Turkic and Medieval Poetry* (2000a). See also his *Turkic Oral Epic Poetry: Traditions, Forms, Poetic Structure* (1992), which provides an in-depth study of Central Asian oral traditions, and his edition of an oral performance of the Karakalpak epic *Edige* (2007).

[35] See section 2.5 on performance and reception below.

[36] For a fuller explanation, see Foley 2002:38–52.

with the 'slam poetry' now gaining such currency in North American and European popular culture.[37] Medieval oral-derived poetries, as well as Homer's *Iliad* and *Odyssey*, belong to Voices from the past, which contains works that are in one way or another best taken as oral-derived. For if we are judicious and fair about weighing the facts at hand, we must acknowledge that poems surviving from these earlier eras occupy a middle, uncertain position: they reach us only in writing, but various kinds of internal and external evidence argue that they derive from oral traditions. Placing poems in such an intermediate category offers a realistic alternative to the simplistic (and far too constraining) binary of oral versus written, and leaves the way open to assess their oral traditional artistry. Finally, Written oral poetry names those works that employ a register of language developed in and for oral tradition, and consequently expect fluent reception on the same terms, even though they are composed and received without the involvement of orality or aurality of any kind. The traditional poems penned by the nineteenth-century Montenegrin bishop Petar Petrović Njegoš, as well as the Finnish *Kalevala* created by Elias Lönnrot from his collections and his own composition, can be understood through this model.

In the same volume Foley also includes a historical calendar of media-inventions, brief presentations of some central theoretical approaches to oral traditions, and a series of homemade proverbs meant to recall salient aspects of how oral poetries actually function. The species-calendar maps such inventions as numeracy, literacy, alphabetic writing, the printing press, and the Internet on a single twelve-month grid that represents the history of *homo sapiens*. Although we have no doubt used oral traditions to organize societies and transfer knowledge from near our beginnings (January), it turns out that the very earliest script traditions appear only on December 10th, about 94% of the way through our species-year (2002: 23). When one combines this diachronic perspective with the ubiquity of oral traditions worldwide today, the primacy of the unwritten technology is hard to escape. To investigate such a plethora of oral traditions, Foley next introduces the approaches known as Performance Theory, Ethnopoetics, and Immanent Art, with references to more extended accounts, advocating the value of multiple perspectives in coming to terms with such tremendous diversity. Finally, the interpretive 'proverbs' are intended as pseudo-traditional versions of important ideas that the textual world often obscures, such as 'Oral poetry works like language, only more so' (125–45) – a reminder that oral traditions are not warehouses of prefabricated items but highly coded forms of language that deserve faithful reception on their own terms.[38]

From a similar point of view, Margaret G. McGeachy's *Lonesome Words: The Vocal Poetics of the Old English Lament and the African-American Blues Song* looks at the affective dynamics of traditional lament forms as they would be vocalized within the community. What connects these two chronologically disjoined traditions, McGeachy

---

[37] Foley 2002: 156–65; see also Eleveld 2005.
[38] An insider's perspective on such encoding can be gained by considering oral poetry from the singers' rather than the text-based investigators' point of view. The South Slavic *guslari*, for example, perceive their discourse as composed of 'words' (*reči*) that run from a phrase to a scene to an entire tale in length. The same levels of 'thought-byte' appear in oral traditions as various as ancient Greek, Russian, Finnish, and Old English (where the singular 'word' often designates a whole speech). See further *ibid.*: 11–21.

discovers, is a traditional formulaic idiom that encodes a shared language of exile and loss. In both cases formulas serve a 'communicative role', connecting the performer to the wider community as they are vocalized in performance, since 'the formulas that evoke the theme of exile provide a template of emotional distress, deprivation, travel, and search in a very concise and efficient manner' and these 'formula-generated themes of loss and displacement assume a point of reference known to both poet and audience.'[39]

## 2.3 Middle English Literature

Over the two decades we are considering in section 2 of this chapter, Mark Amodio has taken great strides in applying Oral Theory to Middle English literature.[40] In his view traditional oral poetics as a 'highly metonymic idiom' and 'a powerful, supple, and highly associative expressive economy', does not disappear with Old English, but continues to flourish even within the literature of post-Conquest England (2004: 43; xvi). In *Writing the Oral Tradition: Oral Poetics and Literature Culture in Medieval England*, Amodio traces out the process whereby 'what was once a living tradition articulated only through the voices of singers engaged in public acts of (re)-composition comes to find expression through the pens of authors engaged in very different, private moments of composition.'[41]

Very importantly, Amodio carefully distinguishes between oral delivery and oral poetics, with the latter understood as 'largely nonperformative',[42] and this distinction allows for a new reading of the Middle English *Brut* of Layamon, a work that is by all accounts highly conscious of its textual status. He demonstrates that 'despite the stress laid on the *Brut*'s literate poetics by both poet and illuminator, its lexicon, thematics, syntax, metrics, narrative patterning, and verbal collocations all witness the centrality of oral poetics to Layamon's compositional process' (95). This fundamental character, Amodio contends, is not the result of an artificial and nostalgic archaism, but a logical continuation of the traditional poetic idiom. Post-Conquest authors employ oral poetics not because 'they wish to preserve an antiquated and archaic mode of composing verse', but because the 'oral poetics remains so freighted with traditional meaning(s) and because it continued to be compositionally useful (on both the lexical and narrative levels)' (130). As evidence for a living – rather than a literary and revived – tradition, he points out that in the case of the poem's diction Layamon 'was able not only to create new compounds that fit into an existing system but to coin new compound types that fit into established syntactic and lexical patterns' (104). It is far less likely, he argues, that the poet would have somehow accessed and imitated texts of Old English poems than

---

[39] 2006: 29, 63, 97–98. According to McGeachy, formulas such as 'I've got the blues' allow for the 'transformation of intensely personal utterance into a public expression of shared experience' (118). The emphasis is on this 'communicative' understanding of the formula rather than on actual oral performance: 'the formulaic nature of laments connects them to an oral tradition of performance, regardless of compositional techniques' (3).

[40] For an account of applications of the Theory in this area through the mid–1980's, see Parks 1986.

[41] Amodio 2004: xv. See also his 'Tradition, Performance, and Poetics in the Early Middle English Period' (2000), as well as 'Medieval English Oral Tradition' (2003), which explore the same subject.

that the traditional poetic language would have survived as a viable expressive medium beyond the Norman conquest.

Layamon's fluency in an inherited traditional poetics is examined in a number of ways. For instance, the idiomatic meaning associated with simplex *abelyen,* descending from the Old English *gebelgan,* would have been conventionally understood in Old English and later poetry as 'metonymically signaling the approach of an impending slaughter' (107). This example as well as others, Amodio contends, 'demonstrate[s] the continuing cohesion of this simplex's affective dynamics' (108). It is not only in the *Brut,* but to varying degrees in the *Ormulum* and even highly literary works such as *The Owl and the Nightingale,* that poets continue to utilize the traditional connotations, and even to humorously depart from the expectations that the tradition sets up. In the case of the simplex *abelyen,* Layamon employs this traditional marker of slaughter even where literal slaughter is avoided (109).

In concert with the interpretive program of Oral Theory, Amodio shows that the indexical force of oral tradition persists not just on the lexical but on the thematic level as well. In the case of the *Brut,* he identifies several traditional themes that are also found in Old English verse. Two such themes are the hero's battle with a monstrous creature, and the greeting and welcoming of a man by a woman via the offering of a cup. Amodio analyses these narrative patterns both for their traditional character and for the evidence they present of innovation, with these reverberative units at times fulfilling conventional expectations and at times upending them.[43]

Amodio has also been influential in his role as editor of two important collections of essays, *Oral Poetics in Middle English Poetry* and *New Directions in Oral Theory.*[44] Some of the most significant recent scholarship applying Oral Theory to Middle English literature has appeared in these volumes, and the following discussion is drawn primarily from these two works.

Of oral traditional approaches to works of Middle English, those treating the romance have proven especially rich. In 'Literacy, Orality, and the Poetics of Middle English Romance', Nancy Mason Bradbury argues for the implementation of a new oral poetics better equipped to deal with the romance, and one that might serve as a corrective to post-war New Critical readings that have devalued the recurrent narrative patterns typical of this genre. She calls for a specifically oral traditional perspective, noting 'the way in which their existence on the borders of literacy and orality affects the artistry of the English romances.'[45] Recurring narrative elements in the romance, she finds, are

---

[42] Amodio 2004: 98. This distinction is most fully expounded in Amodio 2005b.
[43] See especially 2004: 118–33. More recently, Jonathan Watson (2005) examines the complex integration of literary and oral poetics in the *Brut* by comparing how the two surviving manuscripts distinctly employ the traditional theme.
[44] See Amodio 1994 and 2005a. Another important collection for the expansion of Oral Theory into later medieval literatures that should be mentioned here is *Vox Intexta: Orality and Textuality in the Middle Ages* (Doane and Pasternack 1991). Several of the essays in this volume will be discussed in section 2.4 below.
[45] Bradbury 1994: 51. For a more extensive treatment of issues of orality in the Middle English romance, see Bradbury's *Writing Aloud: Storytelling in Late Medieval England* (1998a). Of related interest is her illustration of traditional referentiality in Scottish balladry (1998b). See also Bradbury 2002.

freighted with traditional meaning. The frequent exchanges or 'greetings' found throughout such works, for example, involve questions of identity and challenge, and conventionally lead to some form of struggle as 'each new exchange imports metonymically [...] the significance of previous exchanges' (55). Bradbury employs the terms 'resinging' and 'renarration' to describe the ways in which the same event is retold from the perspective of various characters within the same story as they 'isolate and emphasize the emotional core of a received story' (62). Finally, she also proposes a greater role for memory and recitation in the transmission of the romance.

Conceiving of orality and literacy as continuous rather than contrasting categories has also allowed for innovative approaches to Chaucer. In 'Oral Tradition and the *Canterbury Tales*', Ward Parks examines how the great fourteenth-century poet harnesses oral tradition in the depiction of his characters in a complex and even ambivalent way. Because of Chaucer's storytelling frame, 'the orality-literacy dynamic [...] insinuates itself into the basic conceit on which the *Canterbury Tales* is founded' (1994: 173). In the case of the metrical romance of *Sir Thopas*, his use of the oral tradition is 'sometimes sympathetic, sometimes critical' (158), Parks concludes, as the poet simultaneously employs and ridicules this native vernacular genre by the very act of textualizing it. Chaucer is able to satirize traditional oral poetics since in textual form this poetics appears inconsistent with the immediate narrative context. Furthermore, he employs traditional themes such as the arming of the hero and verbal dueling to 'set up expectations that the ensuing narrative emphatically does not satisfy' (162–63). A metonymic strategy, Parks explains, once textualized and 'stripped of its extratextual resonances, is liable to seem disconnected and full of holes.'[46] In this way oral poetics is submitted to a textual-based criticism as 'the textualization of an originally oral form of poetic narrative has ruptured that consensus that would supply a traditional coherency overriding temporary narrative breakdowns' (166).

Proverbs provide another venue where oral and literary poetics intersect. In 'The Role of Proverbs in Middle English Narrative', Lori Ann Garner explores how traditional proverbs draw on and confer authority by invoking the conventional meanings and associations encoded in them. She finds that the narratives can utilize traditional proverbs for a considerable variety of purposes. For example, in a work she considers closer to the oral end of the spectrum, *Havelok the Dane*, Garner discovers that while they are employed in various ways, the proverbs 'in all situations – even when applied inappropriately – retain their authority' (2005: 265). In contrast to this case, Chaucer's *Troilus and Criseyde* repeatedly questions and qualifies the traditional authority of proverbs. As Garner, Parks, and other scholars show, Middle English poets engage the oral tradition in a number of ways – some harness the tradition quite directly, while others explore, exploit, and critique it in a sophisticated and self-conscious manner.[47]

---

[46] Parks 1994: 163. This subject is also taken up in Parks 1991.
[47] There have been several other important essays that employ the perspective from oral poetics to better understand Chaucer. See especially Lerer 1994 and Arnovick 1994 on the *Canterbury Tales*.

## 2.4 Manuscript Transmission

Katherine O'Brien O'Keeffe's study of Anglo-Saxon manuscript variations, *Visible Song: Transitional Literacy in Old English Verse,* has proven to be a landmark publication for the expansion and evolution of Oral Theory. By arguing for the persistence of oral poetics *within* manuscript transmission – what she terms 'residual orality' – O'Brien O'Keeffe complicates the simplistic orality-literacy dichotomy and makes room for new investigations into their intersection and interaction. Residual orality occupies an intermediate position between the poles of orality and literacy as 'a state after the introduction of writing in a culture which nonetheless exhibits many features characteristic of "pure" orality' (1990: x). She contends that the manuscripts themselves can be mined for clues as to how the encoded texts were read and received. Thus, the degree to which the texts participated in an oral or written tradition – the extent to which the poetry was 'at home' on the page – is revealed by textual cues and concerns with spatialization, since 'literacy thus becomes a process of spatializing the once-exclusively temporal' (4). This transference means a greater reliance, for example, on textual conventions such as marking out or offsetting lines of verse. Thus it becomes possible to track the shift from orality to literacy by examining the conventions that the manuscripts employ to encode poetic texts over time.

She argues further that residual orality is also reflected in the phraseological variation within texts. Collocating lexical variations in the manuscripts containing 'Caedmon's Hymn', O'Brien O'Keeffe finds evidence of formulaic substitution by the copyists that mirrors the morphology typical of oral tradition. Comparing seven lexical variants in the *AE* (West Saxon) recension of Bede's *Ecclesiastical History,* she finds that scribes actually practice formulaic substitution, whereby variants are each 'semantically and grammatically appropriate' (39). The result is 'a dynamic of transmission where the message is not embellished but where the change within the formula is allowed' (39).[48] Such formulaic substitution, she contends, is evidence for a movement by degrees from orality to literacy that directly shaped the production of vernacular manuscripts; thus lexical variability 'is a consequence of its environment in a purely vernacular text [...] whose character as a living language kept it close to the oral status' (40). Because of proximity to oral tradition, 'reading and copying have actually been conflated with composing' (41).[49] O'Brien O'Keeffe's pioneering study awakened Oral Theory to the possibilities

---

[48] Alexandra Hennessey Olsen (1994) reaches a slightly different conclusion in her study of manuscript variation of the Middle English romance *Robert of Cisyle.* She argues for the impact of oral recitation upon manuscript transmission, making a distinction between scribal alterations, which she contends are based on aesthetic preference, against an oral improvisation deriving from recitation that retains the sense but not the wording.

[49] For a similar study on later English and Latin manuscripts, see Tim William Machan (1991). Like O'Brien O'Keeffe, Machan finds that scribes copying vernacular texts played a creative role in transmission, in contrast to the greater degree of stability characteristic of copying practices involving medieval Latin texts. On a striking parallel from a living oral tradition, see Nikola Vujnović, Parry and Lord's partner in fieldwork, who as a minimally literate *guslar* actually re-made acoustic recordings of oral epic songs as he transcribed them from the aluminum records into notebooks at the Parry Collection; see further 'Nikola Vujnović's Resinging' in Foley 2004a: 144–91.

of a dynamic interchange between writing and oral tradition, providing a concrete model for how oral tradition can permeate the world of writing.

Similarly, A. N. Doane's work also explores the interplay between oral tradition and scriptorium. Much like O'Brien O'Keeffe, he perceives the transmission of Old English texts as an open and creative process in which scribes fluent in the traditional oral poetry 'inevitably refashioned [the texts] according to their own competencies within the tradition' (2003: 62–63). As he puts it, 'whenever scribes who are part of the oral traditional culture write or copy traditional oral works, they do not merely mechanically hand them down; they rehear them, "mouth" them, "reperform" them in the act of writing in such a way that the text may change but remain authentic, just as a completely oral poet's text changes from performance to performance without losing authenticity' (1991: 80–81).

Highlighting this creative role of the scribe with the terms 'scribal performance' and the 'ethnography of scribal writing' (1994), Doane reads textual variants not as the corruption of an original exemplar, but as themselves instances and performances of the living tradition – an assertion that questions many of the assumptions of prior textual scholarship: 'Texts, especially traditional ones, were in any case from one writing to the next fluid, not fixed, open to the immense variational possibilities inherent in the tradition.'[50] He uses this perspective to determine the varying levels of traditional competency of the scribes of *Beowulf*. He argues that Scribe B, being perhaps older than Scribe A, is 'more orally inclined' and less concerned with the use of space or the stateliness of the manuscript appearance, and is generally less attentive to regularity of capitalization, fitt divisions, and word spacing (2003: 66–67). He explains that 'more writerly Latin-derived prose texts favour these purely iconic, visual features and the more "oral" poetic texts do not' (67). Finally, the frequent abbreviations of Scribe B suggest an expectation that the poem would fully emerge only via live vocalization. For Doane this is a reminder that 'it is best to see the poetic manuscript as an isolated "score"' intended to be realized in oral performance.'[51]

## 2.5 Performance and Reception

'Words are always situated', John Foley asserts at the beginning of *The Singer of Tales in Performance* (1995: xi), and this assertion is doubly true of traditional oral poetry. The socially situated nature of verbal art in the Middle Ages has become the subject of increasing attention in the last two decades. In many respects this is a natural outgrowth of the work of Parry, Lord, and others, who initially brought critical attention to the oral traditional aspects of medieval and ancient literature, particularly via the notion of oral composition. Indeed, an important implication of Oral Theory from its earliest form onward has been that meaning was created in the dynamic moment of performance,

---

[50] Doane 2003: 72. The concept of 'oral performance' is also applied by way of analogy in John Dagenais' study (1991) of medieval Spanish manuscripts of literary origin. Emphasizing the physicality of the text, Dagenais uses this analogy as a way to understand and value the manuscript variations of the *Libro de buen amor*. These variations, in his view, should not be understood as contaminations of an original exemplar, but as each a unique, material performance.

[51] Doane 2003: 72. More recently, Joyce Lionarons (2004) has applied considerations of scribal performance to the Old English sermons of Wulfstan.

and in recent years the perspectives from performance and reception have been extended to oral-derived and literary texts as well. In this connection, Oral Theory has been fruitfully combined with a number of other approaches – folklore, anthropology, sociology, history, and musicology, to name only a few – as issues of performance and reception have become central to the field of medieval studies.

In *The Singer of Tales in Performance,* Foley conjoins oral theory with two performance-centered approaches from folklore research – Performance Theory and Ethnopoetics – in order to explore how tradition is activated in the dynamic of performance. As he explains in the preface, 'from the Grimms on, prospective editors had resorted to a wide variety of (at best partially) successful techniques for reducing performed events to textual cenotaphs' (xiii). It is Foley's aim then, to recover some of the pre-textual, traditional meanings that would have been immanent in performance. To do so he connects the 'enabling referent of tradition' with the 'enabling event of performance' (xiv), the fusion of tradition and performance yielding what Foley calls 'word-power' (1992b) – the unique artistic and communicative channel created by this special situation.

Ethnopoetics, founded by Dennis Tedlock and Dell Hymes, provides a means of 'rebuilding the living organism of oral poetry' from its fossilized remains as text.[52] The aim of this approach is to 'represent oral poetry on its own terms and by doing so to foster the reader's more faithful *reperformance*' (2002: 96), working to restore to the verbal art form the native poetics that textualization has removed or obscured. Dovetailing with Ethnopoetics, Performance Theory examines the special communicative frame set up by what Richard Bauman terms performance 'keys', cues that signal the particular performance arena. One crucial key is the use of a specialized register of poetic discourse, for example the Old English *Kunstsprache* with its trademark vocabulary, metre, syntax, and phraseological and narrative structure.[53] Such cues indicate how the communication should be received.

Foley uses this performance-centered approach to understand how the Old English verse hagiography *Andreas* operates as an 'indexed translation' – created by a poet who undoubtedly depended on a Greek or Latin saint's life as the source, but then 're-wrote' that tale within the traditional Old English poetic register. 'Why', Foley asks at the outset, 'does the poet of the verse hagiography *Andreas* [...] continue to depend upon traditional forms as the foundation of his or her expressive repertoire?' (1995: 181) Concentrating on the sites where the poem departs most dramatically from its source, he goes on to demonstrate how this register is employed 'not for its expediency but for its unique significative capabilities: namely, it indexes the context in which [the poet] wants the communication to be received' (181). The poetic register, in other words, invokes the performance context.

From this point of view the manuscript-based *Andreas* embodies a mode of performance that is compatible with (and encoded in) writing, and perhaps more importantly is symbiotically linked with fluent reception for its meaning. As he observes, 'perhaps we can also understand how a syncretic poetics – a poetics that acknowledges the contributions of both text-based strategies such as typology and the rhetorically persistent dimension of word-power – helps us toward a continuity of reception and toward a better appreciation

---

[52] Foley 2002: 97. For an ethnopoetic rendering of the prologue of *Beowulf,* see 104–05. On the history of Ethnopoetics, with references, see Foley 1995: 17–27.

[53] On the history of Performance Theory, with references, see Foley 1995: 7–17.

of the remarkable performance by this singer of tales, both its undeniable creativity and its patently traditional resonance' (207). As *Immanent Art* and *The Singer of Tales in Performance* maintain, traditional verbal art is activated and actualized in performance even where represented textually, since the highly patterned and echoic register of oral traditional poetry is networked to an immanent context, not contained on the page.

Questions of performance become especially crucial for the study of Old English charms, since, as Lori Ann Garner points out, charms rely on 'performance context for their healing power' (2004: 38). Because the meaning and power of charms lie not in the information they convey on the page but on their capacity to activate a tradition, Garner sets out to partially reconstruct that larger context through comparative analysis of the Old English charm corpus. As she makes clear, understanding the underlying tradition is foundational in the case of the charms because 'the web of associations lying behind even highly literary works enables us to uncover traditionally encoded meanings across a broad spectrum of texts, and brings us at least somewhat closer to understanding these long-textualized medieval voices' (2003: 217).[54] For Garner, text and context are inextricably linked in the enactment of meaning.

A similar aim underlies *Written Reliquaries: The Resonance of Orality in Medieval English Texts,* where Leslie Arnovick attempts to unlock the textualized meanings of medieval English poetry by combining Oral Theory with the linguistically based approach of historical pragmatics. 'Reconstructing the discursive contexts that once animated' these texts, Arnovick contends, will allow us to 'hear' the speech-acts as they operate within and through the tradition (2006: 1). She applies this lens to the 'gibberish' of Old English charms, the invocations of the Pater Noster, and prayers to the saints, as well as Middle English proverbs, book curses, and a variety of speech-acts in Chaucer.

Interest in the realities of performance and its relation to medieval literature has informed a great deal of recent work. Although much of this scholarship lies beyond the scope of the present article, some of the larger trends may be briefly outlined here. One of these trends is represented in the work of Karl Reichl, who has drawn from comparative evidence from central Asia to formulate the performance modes of Old and Middle English poetry.[55] Likewise, the character and role of the *scop* within Anglo-Saxon society continues to be an active area of research.[56] Finally, the meaning and modes of recitation and its relation to writing within the cultures of the Middle Ages have provided the impetus for several prominent studies in the last decade.[57]

Of course, performance does not exist in isolation; it requires and assumes an audience fluent in the tradition in order to complete the communicative circuit of verbal art.

---

[54] Garner 2003: 217.
[55] See Reichl 2003, 2005. Of related interest are Reichl 2000b on performance and music in oral epic; and Harris and Reichl 1997 on prosimetric narrative. For performance of musical and lyrical song, see Leo Treitler, *With Voice and Pen: Coming to Know Medieval Song and How It Was Made* (2003).
[56] For example, performer and scholar Benjamin Bagby (2005) discusses his reconstruction of Old English and Old Norse; see further Bagby's re-creation of *Beowulf* as an oral performance (2006). Questions of the role of the *scop* for Anglo-Saxon society are addressed in Niles 2003a. For a lively account of the historiography of the *scop,* see Frank 2003. See also the earlier work by Jeff Opland (1980), which urges an analogy between Old English poets and Xhosa praise-poets.
[57] See especially O'Brien O'Keeffe 1998. For a recent collection of essays on this subject, see Vitz et al. 2005.

Performance and reception, in Foley's formulation, are 'two sides of the same coin' (2002: 138), a concept he underscores in *Immanent Art* where he melds Oral Theory with the receptionalist approaches of Wolfgang Iser and Hans Robert Jauss (1991: 38–60). This formulation serves as a forceful reminder that the audience – real or implied – is not merely an abstraction but a crucial constituent of meaning.[58]

Scholarship on medieval English literature over the past two decades has increasingly turned to questions of reception and to the conventions and expectations surrounding it, particularly as they are tied to modes of literacy and orality.[59] In regard to pre-Conquest England, Hugh Magennis surveys these questions succinctly in his essay 'Audience(s), Reception, Literacy', pointing out that 'even where composed in writing, Old English verse works in an oral-derived formulaic tradition' (2001: 92). Old English poems operate without any 'concept of an autonomous text' but depend heavily on context and often on aural reception (96). Magennis also explains how issues of literacy and orality underpin reception. He points out that literacy in Anglo-Saxon England existed in varying guises and served a number of purposes, from the Latin literacy of the clergy to the 'popular and "pragmatic" literacy' of those working in the secular world.[60] Finally, in 'Listening to Scenes of Reading: King Alfred's Talking Prefaces', O'Brien O'Keeffe similarly unites matters of literacy and reception, exploring the idea of 'corporate reading' within the context of King Alfred's court, as depicted by Asser in his *Life of Alfred*. From this scenario she argues that, while solitary reading was practiced, the three 'Prefaces' to Alfred's translations imagine a reception in social, aural 'scenes of reading' that would allow the participation of those with varying degrees of literacy.[61]

---

[58] Thomas DuBois makes reception the focal point of his comparative lyric study (2006), situating Old English poetry amid other traditional poetries of Northern Europe and devising an interpretative framework that addresses the complex interplay of audience, tradition, and performance in the generation of meaning. See also DuBois 1998 on Ethnopoetics and 2003 on opportunities for new directions.

[59] Questions of reception in the Middle Ages cannot be separated from larger issues of orality and literacy. The idea of modes of orality and literacy that are continuous and interdependent is first comprehensively advanced in the work of Ruth Finnegan (1977). Acknowledging their direct debt to Finnegan, Mark Chinca and Christopher Young state in the introduction to their recent collection, *Orality and Literacy in the Middle Ages*, that 'medieval literacy and orality must not be considered as two separate and largely unrelated cultures or modes of communication, but in their interpenetration, interplay and symbiosis' (2005: 1). This collection is dedicated to D. H. Green, whose studies of medieval German literature (especially 1994) argue for a third, intermediate mode apart from reading and listening. Additionally, see the work of Joyce Coleman (1996) on the prevalence of public reading, which she terms 'aurality' in contrast to the silent, solitary reception of literary works; and of Ursula Schaefer (1992, 1993; see Zumthor 1987, 1990), who advocates the similar idea of 'vocality' as intermediate between orality and literacy.

[60] 2001: 92, 90. Seth Lerer further explores the implications of literacy for Anglo-Saxon England in *Literacy and Power in Anglo-Saxon Literature* (1991). The degrees of developing literacy in the late Middle Ages in England are charted out in Paul Strohm's historical account of these modes (2006). Strohm builds on Brian Stock's concept of 'textual communities' (1983), contending that even illiterate individuals could participate in (usually religious) communities formed around a central text (466). For an investigation of the presence of non-ecclesiastical literacy in Anglo-Saxon England, see Lowe 1998.

[61] See O'Brien O'Keeffe 2005. [See also the chapter by Katherine O'Brien O'Keeffe in this volume (ch. 4).]

## 3 Opportunities for the Future

We began this chapter by observing that the Oral Theory traces its roots to a period before the paradigm-changing contributions of Milman Parry (especially 1928–35), who in providing a new answer to the Homeric Question drew from important philological and anthropological studies as far back as 1885 as well as undertook, along with Albert Lord, a collecting expedition in the Former Yugoslavia that was to yield the richest archive of oral epic in the world. With Lord's comparatively oriented *The Singer of Tales* in 1960 and the thousands of publications that have followed in its wake, an approach that was originally founded on the two-dimensional analogy between Homeric and South Slavic oral epic spread rapidly to more than 150 different traditions and many different disciplines. The last two decades have seen a third growth, during which Oral Theory has been extended and combined with other approaches to tackle the issues discussed in section 2 above.

With this history in mind, we now offer some suggestions for the future evolution of the Theory – some topics or themes that seem likely to receive fresh or continued attention over the next decade or so. These suggestions, couched in extremely general terms, concern three principal areas: comparative studies based on the ever more apparent diversity of oral traditions; issues of aesthetics and verbal art; and digital and web-based interventions.

### 3.1 Comparative Studies and Diversity

The archetypal comparison on which Oral Theory was founded has proven both a blessing and a curse. The close similarity between ancient Greek and South Slavic Moslem epic, as productive as it has been for those two genres (or subgenres), was also a false predictor; it suggested a single, unified model for all oral traditions that did not (indeed could not) exist.[62] Clearly, if all of written, em-booked literature cannot be accounted for by adducing, say, only the Renaissance sonnet, or the modern haiku, or the multi-volume Victorian novel, then how can we expect the inherently more numerous and diverse oral traditions of the world – which also support many more social functions than literature – to yield to a unique, self-contained model? In the coming years, as text-based and fieldwork-based investigations continue to reveal the diversity of oral traditions, we will need to take full account of the heterogeneity of models available to compare to medieval oral-derived works.[63] One size most certainly does not fit all.

Along similar lines, the valuable insights on oral-textual interactions that emerged over the last two decades have at last put the lie to the Great Divide binary of 'oral versus written'. Of course, the Oral Theory – like any pioneering approach – had to begin with such broad distinctions in order to create thinking space in which a new kind of verbal art could be imagined. And while reaction against the assumption of mutually exclusive categories was swift and expectable, from the perspective of the larger trajectory

---

[62] See note 23 above.
[63] See the flexible categories of Oral Performance, Voiced texts, Voices from the past, and Written oral poetry as described in Foley 2002: 38–52.

toward realistic complexity it was also absolutely necessary. Now, however, we need to examine the full implications of such heretofore unrecognized possibilities as orally composing scribes and texts written in oral traditional code as we seek to better understand the true provenience and expressive profiles of medieval English oral-derived works. Diversity of traditions and genres across cultures and eras, diversity and interaction among media-technologies – these are watchwords for more faithful, genuinely situated reception.

## 3.2 Aesthetics and Verbal Art

In the early stages of Oral Theory, with its emphasis on analyzing structures whose main function seemed to be to enable composition in performance, aesthetics was seldom a major issue. Even before Parry's mechanical definition of the formula as a metrical encapsulation of 'an essential idea', classical linguists had pointed toward metre as pre-empting phraseological choice and (by modern standards) creativity. Likewise, Magoun's introduction of the Theory into the study of Old English poetry advocated the lock-step utility of oral traditional formulas and themes, and even generated a mathematical litmus test for the 'orality' of poems from various medieval traditions. If a given work demonstrated a certain percentage density of formulaic phraseology, so went the claim, it could confidently be understood as oral.[64] Once again, reaction against this doctrinaire notion was quick and energetic, as critics called for less exclusive focus on the supposed exigencies of composition in performance and a returned attention to verbal artistry. If the poems in question were no more than exercises in formulaic composition, they asked, then how did these works qualify as art?

One answer to that very reasonable question emerged over the last few decades with the explanation from traditional referentiality.[65] This proposal, linked to the approach called Immanent Art, posited a non-literal, idiomatic relationship between expressive units (formulas, themes, story-patterns) and the ambient tradition that they index. Future research and scholarship along these lines might profitably aim at assembling lexicons not of textual words (defined as typographical or morphological bytes) but of oral traditional 'words' – the larger, resonant cognitive units that are the stock-in-trade, the poetic register, the *lingua franca* of poets who compose via oral traditional language. Consider the traditional pattern of 'exile', well documented as a structural pattern in numerous Old English poems for more than fifty years. The concatenation of typical imagery at lines 1255b–69a of the verse hagiography *Andreas*, for instance – with its recognizable blend of snow, winter, frost, bitter cold, hail showers, and the like – represents more than a lyric expostulation. It generically characterizes St. Andrew, imprisoned and beset by devils in the night, by idiomatically evoking the familiar stereotype cut off from society, community, kin, and even identity. Via this metonymic trope the poet in effect enlists the saint as a member of the *comitatus* of exiles in Anglo-Saxon tradition, along with the seafarer, the wanderer, Grendel, the 'last survivor' in *Beowulf*, and many

---

[64] For relatively recent and exacting mathematical analyses of formulaic structure and morphology in Homer, South Slavic oral epic, and Old French *chansons de geste*, see Sale 1993a and b, 1996.
[65] See section 2.1 above.

other figures in the elegies and elsewhere. Far more than a mere building block, the theme of exile – which by the way has no basis whatsoever in the Greek *Praxeis* from which the Old English poem was derived – offers a subtly but powerfully expressive tool. Its inherent traditional referentiality deepens and enriches our understanding of just what St. Andrew is enduring, and just how solitary and seemingly hopeless his situation is.[66]

### 3.3 Digital and Web-Based Interventions

The increasing importance of digital media and the Internet has affected all aspects of research and scholarship, and the evolution of Oral Theory is certainly no exception. In this brief section we offer a few examples of what has been accomplished in the last few years and point toward promising possibilities for the future.

Among projects that bear directly on oral tradition, Benjamin Bagby's DVD-based performance of *Beowulf* (2006) must occupy a special place. Accompanying himself on a replica of an early Germanic lyre, Bagby has been performing approximately the first third of the great epic at multiple venues throughout North America and Europe since 1990.[67] His commitment is to bring the story alive as an emergent experience shared by a latter-day *scop* with an audience, and toward this end he has developed a series of vocal and instrumental melodies to support his enactment of the Old English oral-derived text, as he explains on the DVD and in a 2005 article. Along with the video recording of the performance in the original Anglo-Saxon, glossed by modern English subtitles, the producers include a roundtable discussion with Bagby and several medievalists, and in the institutional version a 40-minute teacher's guide that includes specific commentary on *Beowulf* and oral tradition. Watching Bagby's re-creation of the poem as the living event it once was provides fresh perspective on the concerns and aims of Oral Theory – most crucially, to understand how oral tradition plays a unique role in the art of *Beowulf*. Hopefully, Bagby and others will continue to follow a trail so expertly blazed by creating oral performances of other Old English poems as well, perhaps (in the spirit of web democracy) as online, open-access entities.[68]

Actual electronic editions of oral and oral-derived poetry are now beginning to appear on the horizon, and they offer largely unexplored resources for representing as well as investigating the works for which they serve as vehicles. The radical potential of this approach stems from the counterintuitive but fundamental homology between the

---

[66] We trace the theme of 'exile' to Greenfield 1955; for more on this pattern, see Foley 1990:331 for a summary of scholarship to date, and Foley 1995:186–87 for more on the occurrence in *Andreas*.

[67] The DVD was recorded in January, 2006, at the Dunkers Kulturhaus in Helsingborg, Sweden, under the direction of Stellan Olsson.

[68] We mention in passing Richard Ringler's translation of *Beowulf* intended specifically for oral enactment (2007a), and his audio book that accomplishes that aim with a cast of performers (2007b); as well as Michael Drout's *Beowulf Aloud* (2007) and *Anglo-Saxon Aloud* (2008) in the original language. Also worthy of mention are two digital resources that, although focused on manuscript records, can be used to support the study of Old English verse from the perspective of Oral Theory: Kevin Kiernan's *Electronic Beowulf 2.0* (2004) and Daniel Paul O'Donnell's *Caedmon's Hymn: A Multi-media Study, Edition, and Archive* (2007).

media-technologies of oral tradition and digital/internet communication.[69] A case in point is *The Wedding of Mustajbey's Son Bećirbey as Performed by Halil Bajgorić*,[70] a South Slavic oral epic poem recorded acoustically by Parry and Lord in 1935. This eEdition harnesses the digital tool of hypertext to 'resynchronize the performance', that is, to integrate the original-language transcription, an English translation, an mp3 audio file, the commentary, and an idiomatic glossary (called an *apparatus fabulosus*, or 'story-based apparatus') on the same electronic page, using multimedia and hyperlinks. It thus removes the distance that conventional book-editions insert via their trademark insistence on spatialization and separation, and aims instead toward a facsimile reintegration of the experience as a whole. The entire eEdition is available free of charge and open-access at a public website (http://oraltradition.org/zbm). It is hoped that the basic set of strategies behind this eEdition can be utilized to more faithfully represent other oral and oral-derived poems as well, especially those from the Old English canon.

## References

Acker, Paul. 1998. *Revising Oral Theory: Formulaic Composition in Old English and Old Icelandic Verse*. New York: Garland.
Amodio, Mark C., ed. 1994. *Oral Poetics in Middle English Poetry*. New York: Garland.
–. 2000. 'Tradition, Performance, and Poetics in the Early Middle English Period.' *Oral Tradition* 15:191–214.
–. 2003. 'Medieval English Oral Tradition.' *Oral Tradition* 18:211–13.
–. 2004. *Writing the Oral Tradition: Oral Poetics and Literate Culture in Medieval England*. Poetics of Orality and Literacy 1. Notre Dame, IN: U of Notre Dame P.
–, ed. 2005a. *New Directions in Oral Theory*. Tempe: Arizona Center for Medieval and Renaissance Studies.
–. 2005b. 'Res(is)ting the Singer: Towards a Non-Performative Anglo-Saxon Poetics.' In Amodio 2005a: 179–208.
–, and Katherine O'Brien O'Keeffe, eds. 2003. *Unlocking the Wordhord: Anglo-Saxon Studies in Memory of Edward B. Irving, Jr.* Toronto: U of Toronto P.
Arnovick, Leslie K. 1994. 'Dorigen's Promise and Scholars' Premise: The Orality of the Speech Act in the *Franklin's Tale*.' In Amodio 1994: 125–49.
–. 2006. *Written Reliquaries: The Resonance of Orality in Medieval English Texts*. Amsterdam: Benjamins.
Bagby, Benjamin. 2005. '*Beowulf*, the *Edda*, and the Performance of Medieval Epic: Notes from the Workshop of a Reconstructed "Singer of Tales".' In Vitz et al. 2005: 181–93.
–. 2006. *Beowulf* (DVD), produced by Jon Aaron and Charlie Morrow. New York: Other Media.
Bradbury, Nancy Mason. 1994. 'Literacy, Orality, and the Poetics of Middle English Romance.' In Amodio 1994: 39–71.
–. 1998a. *Writing Aloud: Storytelling in Late Medieval England*. Urbana: U of Illinois P.
–. 1998b. 'Traditional Referentiality: The Aesthetic Power of Oral Traditional Structures.' In Foley 1998: 136–45.

---

[69] On this homology, see Foley 2008, 2009–, and 2011.
[70] Foley 2004a, which exists both as a conventional book in the Folklore Fellows Communications series (without the multimedia and hyperlinks mentioned here), and as an online, open-access hypertext facility (as described above).

—. 2002. 'Transforming Experience into Tradition: Two Theories of Proverb Use and Chaucer's Practice.' *Oral Tradition* 17: 261–89.
Chinca, Mark and Christopher Young, eds. 2005. *Orality and Literacy in the Middle Ages: Essays on a Conjunction and its Consequences in Honour of D. H. Green*. Turnhout: Brepols.
Coleman, Joyce. 1996. *Public Reading and the Reading Public in Late Medieval England and France*. Cambridge: CUP.
Dagenais, John. 1991. 'That Bothersome Residue: Toward a Theory of the Physical Text.' In Doane and Pasternack 1991: 246–63.
Doane, A. N. 1991. 'Oral Texts, Intertexts, and the Editor.' In *Influence and Intertextuality in Literary History*. Ed. Jay Clayton and Eric Rothstein. Madison: U of Wisconsin P. 75–113.
—. 1994. 'The Ethnography of Scribal Writing and Anglo-Saxon Poetry: Scribe as Performer.' *Oral Tradition* 9: 420–39.
—. 2003. '"Beowulf" and Scribal Performance.' In Amodio and O'Brien O'Keeffe 2003: 62–76.
—, and Carol Braun Pasternack, eds. 1991. *Vox Intexta: Orality and Textuality in the Middle Ages*. Madison: U of Wisconsin P.
Drout, Michael. 2007. *Beowulf Aloud*. Available at <http://michaeldrout.com>.
—. 2008. *Anglo-Saxon Aloud*. Available at <http://michaeldrout.com>.
DuBois, Thomas A. 1998. 'Ethnopoetics.' In Foley 1998: 123–35.
—. 2003. 'Oral Tradition.' *Oral Tradition* 18: 255–57.
—. 2006. *Lyric, Meaning, and Audience in the Oral Tradition of Northern Europe*. Poetics of Orality and Literacy 3. Notre Dame, IN: U of Notre Dame P.
Düntzer, Heinrich. 1864. 'Über den Einfluss des Metrums auf den homerischen Ausdruck.' *Jahrbücher für classische Philologie* 10: 673–94. [Rpt.in Latacz 1979: 88–108.]
Edwards, Mark A. 1986. 'Homer and Oral Tradition: The Formula, Part I.' *Oral Tradition* 1: 171–230.
—. 1988. 'Homer and Oral Tradition: The Formula, Part II.' *Oral Tradition* 3: 11–60.
—. 1992. 'Homer and Oral Tradition: The Type-Scene.' *Oral Tradition* 7: 284–330.
Eleveld, Mark. 2005. *The Spoken Word Revolution*. Bel Air, CA: Sourcebooks MediaFusion.
Ellendt, Johann Ernst. 1861. *Über den Einfluss des Metrums auf den Gebrauch von Wortformen und Wortverbindungen*. Königsberg. [Rpt. in Latacz 1979: 60–87.]
Finnegan, Ruth. 1977. *Oral Poetry: Its Nature, Significance, and Social Context*. Cambridge: CUP. [Rpt. Bloomington: Indiana UP, 1992.]
Foley, John Miles, ed. 1981a. *Oral Traditional Literature: A Festschrift for Albert Bates Lord*. Columbus, OH: Slavica.
—. 1981b. 'Introduction: The Oral Theory in Context.' In Foley 1981a: 27–122.
—. 1985. *Oral-Formulaic Theory and Research: An Annotated Bibliography*. New York: Garland. [With updates in Tyler 1988 and Quick 1997.]
—. 1988. *The Theory of Oral Composition: History and Methodology*. Bloomington: Indiana UP. [Rpt. 1992.]
—. 1990. *Traditional Oral Epic: The Odyssey, Beowulf, and the Serbo-Croatian Return Song*. Berkeley: U of California P. [Rpt. 1993.]
—. 1991. *Immanent Art: From Structure to Meaning in Traditional Oral Epic*. Bloomington: Indiana UP.
—. 1992a. 'Albert Bates Lord (1912–1991).' *JAF* 105: 57–65.
—. 1992b. 'Word-Power, Performance, and Tradition.' *JAF* 105: 275–301.
—. 1995. *The Singer of Tales in Performance*. Bloomington: Indiana UP.
—, ed. 1998. *Teaching Oral Traditions*. New York: Modern Language Association.
—. 1999. *Homer's Traditional Art*. University Park: Pennsylvania State UP.
—. 2002. *How to Read an Oral Poem*. Urbana: U of Illinois P. With eCompanion at <http://oraltradition.org/hrop>.

–. 2003. 'How Genres Leak in Traditional Verse.' In Amodio and O'Brien O'Keeffe 2003: 76–109.
–, ed. and trans. 2004a. *The Wedding of Mustajbey's Son Bećirbey as Performed by Halil Bajgorić*. FF Communications 283. Helsinki: Academia Scientiarum Fennica. Available as an eEdition at <http://oraltradition.org/zbm>.
–. 2004b. 'Epic as Genre.' In *The Cambridge Companion to Homer*. Ed. Robert Fowler. Cambridge: CUP. 171–87.
–. 2008. 'Navigating Pathways: Oral Tradition and the Internet.' *Academic Intersections* 2. <http://oraltradition.org/AI-article/1-Abstract.html>.
–. 2009–. *The Pathways Project*. An online facility at <http://www.pathwaysproject.org/pathways/show/HomePage>.
–. 2011. *Pathways of the Mind: Oral Tradition and the Internet*. Urbana: U of Illinois P.
Ford, John C. 2002. 'A New Conception of Poetic Formulae Based on Prototype Theory and the Mental Template.' *Neuphilologische Mitteilungen* 103: 205–26.
Frank, Roberta. 2003. 'The Search for the Anglo-Saxon Oral Poet.' In *Textual and Material Culture in Anglo-Saxon England: Thomas Northcote Toller and the Toller Memorial Lectures*. Ed. Donald Scragg. Cambridge: Brewer. 137–60.
Garner, Lori Ann. 2003. 'Medieval Voices.' *Oral Tradition* 18: 216–18.
–. 2004. 'Anglo-Saxon Charms in Performance.' *Oral Tradition* 19: 20–42.
–. 2005. 'The Role of Proverbs in Middle English Narrative.' In Amodio 2005a: 255–79.
Gesemann, Gerhard. 1926. *Studien zur südslavischen Volksepik*. Reichenberg: Stiepel.
Grafton, Anthony, Glenn W. Most, and James E. G. Zetzel, trans. 1985. F. A. Wolf. *Prolegomena to Homer*. 1795. Princeton: Princeton UP.
Green, D. H. 1994. *Medieval Listening and Reading: The Primary Reception of Germanic Literature 800–1300*. Cambridge: CUP.
Greenfield, Stanley B. 1955. 'The Formulaic Expression of the Theme of "Exile" in Anglo-Saxon Poetry.' *Speculum* 30: 200–6.
Harris, Joseph, and Karl Reichl, eds. 1997. *Prosimetrum: Crosscultural Perspectives on Narrative in Prose and Verse*. Cambridge: Brewer.
Honko, Lauri. 1998. *Textualising the Siri Epic*. FF Communications 264. Helsinki: Academia Scientiarum Fennica.
Jousse, Marcel. 1925. *Le Style oral rhythmique et mnémotechnique chez les Verbo-moteurs*. Paris: Gabriel Beauchesne. [Trans. as *The Oral Style* by Edgard Sienaert and Richard Whitaker. New York: Garland, 1990.]
Kay, Matthew W. 1995. *The Index of the Milman Parry Collection 1933–1935: Heroic Songs, Conversations, and Stories*. New York: Garland.
Kelemen, Erick. 2001. '*Clyppan* and *cyssan*: The Formulaic Expression of Return from Exile in Old English Literature.' *English Language Notes* 38: 1–19.
Kiernan, Kevin. 2004. *Electronic Beowulf 2.0*. London: British Library.
Krauss, Friedrich S. 1908. 'Vom wunderbaren Guslarengedächtnis.' In his *Slavische Volksforschungen*. Leipzig: Wilhelm Heims. 183–89.
Latacz, Joachim, ed. 1979. *Homer: Tradition und Neuerung*. Wege der Forschung 463. Darmstadt: WB.
Lerer, Seth. 1991. *Literacy and Power in Anglo-Saxon Literature*. Lincoln: U of Nebraska P.
–. 1994. '"Now holde youre mouth": The Romance of Orality in the *Thopas-Melibee* Section of the *Canterbury Tales*.' In Amodio 1994: 181–206.
Lionarons, Joyce Tally. 2004. 'Textual Appropriation and Scribal (Re)Performance in a Composite Homily: The Case for a New Edition of Wulfstan's *De Temporibus Anticristi*.' In *Old English Literature in Its Manuscript Context*. Ed. Joyce Tally Lionarons. Morgantown: West Virginia UP. 67–93.

Lord, Albert Bates. 1960. *The Singer of Tales*. Cambridge, MA: Harvard UP. [Re-edition with a CD and a new introduction by Stephen Mitchell and Gregory Nagy, 2000.]
—. 1991. *Epic Singers and Oral Tradition*. Ithaca, NY: Cornell UP.
—. 1995. *The Singer Resumes the Tale*. Ed. Mary Louise Lord. Ithaca, NY: Cornell UP.
Lowe, Kathryn A. 1998. 'Lay Literacy in Anglo-Saxon England and the Development of the Chirograph.' In *Anglo-Saxon Manuscripts and their Heritage*. Ed. Phillip Pulsiano and Elaine M. Treharne. Brookfield, VT: Ashgate. 161–204.
Machan, Tim William. 1991. 'Editing, Orality, and Late Middle English Texts.' In Doane and Pasternack 1991: 229–45.
Magennis, Hugh. 2001. 'Audience(s), Reception, Literacy.' In *A Companion to Anglo-Saxon Literature*. Ed. Phillip Pulsiano and Elaine Treharne. Oxford: Blackwell. 84–101.
Magoun, Francis P., Jr. 1953. 'The Oral-Formulaic Character of Anglo-Saxon Narrative Poetry.' *Speculum* 28: 446–67.
McGeachy, Margaret G. 2006. *Lonesome Words: The Vocal Poetics of the Old English Lament and the African-American Blues Song*. New York: Palgrave Macmillan.
Meillet, Antoine. 1923. *Les origines indo-européennes des mètres grecs*. Paris: Presses Universitaires de France.
Mitchell, Stephen A. and Gregory Nagy. 2000. 'Introduction to the Second Edition' of Lord 1960/2000: vii–xxix.
Murko, Matija. 1929. *La poésie populaire épique en Yougoslavie au début du XXe siècle*. Paris: Honoré Champion.
—. 1990. 'The Singers and their Epic Songs.' Trans. J. M. Foley. *Oral Tradition* 5: 107–30.
Niles, John D. 1983. *Beowulf: The Poem and Its Tradition*. Cambridge, MA: Harvard UP.
—. 1999. *Homo Narrans: The Poetics and Anthropology of Oral Literature*. Philadelphia: U of Pennsylvania P.
—. 2003a. 'The Myth of the Anglo-Saxon Oral Poet.' *Western Folklore* 62: 7–61.
—. 2003b. 'Prizes From the Borderlands.' *Oral Tradition* 18: 223–24.
—. 2007. *Old English Heroic Poems and the Social Life of Texts*. Turnhout: Brepols.
O'Brien O'Keeffe, Katherine. 1990. *Visible Song: Transitional Literacy in Old English Verse*. Cambridge: CUP.
—. 1998. 'The Performing Body on the Oral-Literate Continuum: Old English Poetry.' In Foley 1998: 46–58.
—. 2005. 'Listening to the Scenes of Reading: King Alfred's Talking Prefaces.' In Chinca and Young 2005: 17–36.
O'Donnell, Daniel Paul. 2007. *Cædmon's Hymn: A Multi-media Study, Edition, and Archive*. Cambridge: Brewer.
Olsen, Alexandra Hennessey. 1986. 'Oral-Formulaic Research in Old English Studies: I.' *Oral Tradition* 1: 548–606.
—. 1988. 'Oral-Formulaic Research in Old English Studies: II.' *Oral Tradition* 3: 138–90.
—. 1994. 'Oral Tradition in the Middle English Romance: The Case of *Robert of Cisyle*.' In Amodio 1994: 71–88.
—. 2005. 'Proteus in Latin: Vernacular Tradition and the Boniface Collection.' In Amodio 2005a: 107–24.
Opland, Jeff. 1980. *Anglo-Saxon Oral Poetry: A Study of the Traditions*. New Haven: Yale UP.
*Oral Tradition*, a journal devoted exclusively to the world's oral traditions and related forms. Also available at <http://journal.oraltradition.org/>.
Orchard, Andy. 1993. 'Crying Wolf: Oral Style and the *Sermones Lupi*.' *ASE* 21: 239–64.
—. 1994. *The Poetic Art of Aldhelm*. Cambridge: CUP.
—. 1997. 'Oral Tradition.' In *Reading Old English Texts*. Ed. Katherine O'Brien O'Keeffe. Cambridge: CUP. 101–23.
—. 2001. 'Old Sources, New Resources: Finding the Right Formula for Boniface.' *ASE* 30: 15–38.

–. 2003. 'Looking for an Echo: The Oral Tradition in Anglo-Saxon Literature.' *Oral Tradition* 18: 225–27.
Parks, Ward. 1986. 'The Oral-Formulaic Theory in Middle English Studies.' *Oral Tradition* 3: 636–94.
–. 1991. 'The Textualization of Orality in Literary Criticism.' In Doane and Pasternack 1991: 46–66.
–. 1994. 'Oral Tradition and the *Canterbury Tales*.' In Amodio 1994: 149–80.
Parry, Adam. 1971. 'Introduction' to M. Parry 1971: ix-lxii.
Parry, Milman. 1928a. *L'épithète traditionnelle dans Homère: Essai sur un problème de style homérique*. Paris: 'Les Belles Lettres'. [Trans. in M. Parry 1971: 1–190.]
–. 1928b. *Les formules et la métrique d'Homère*. Paris: 'Les Belles Lettres'. [Trans. in M. Parry 1971: 191–239.]
–. 1930. 'Studies in the Epic Technique of Oral Verse-Making. I. Homer and Homeric Style.' *Harvard Studies in Classical Philology* 41: 73–147. [Rpt. in M. Parry 1971: 266–324.]
–. 1932. 'Studies in the Epic Technique of Oral Verse-Making. II. The Homeric Language as the Language of an Oral Poetry.' *Harvard Studies in Classical Philology* 43: 1–50. [Rpt. in M. Parry 1971: 325–64.]
–. 1933–35. 'Ćor Huso: A Study of South Slavic Songs. Extracts.' In M. Parry 1971: 437–64.
–. 1971. *The Making of Homeric Verse*. Ed. Adam Parry. Oxford: Clarendon.
Quick, Catherine S. 1997. 'Annotated Bibliography 1986–1990.' *Oral Tradition* 12: 366–484.
Radloff, Wilhelm. 1885. *Proben der Volkslitteratur der nördlichen türkischen Stämme*, vol. 5: *Der Dialect der Kara-Kirgisen*. St. Petersburg.
Reichl, Karl. 1992. *Turkic Oral Epic Poetry: Traditions, Forms, Poetic Structure*. New York: Garland.
–. 2000a. *Singing the Past: Turkic and Medieval Poetry*. Ithaca, NY: Cornell UP.
–, ed. 2000b. *The Oral Epic: Performance and Music*. Intercultural Music Studies, 12. Berlin: Verlag für Wissenschaft und Bildung.
–. 2003. 'Comparative Notes on the Performance of Middle English Popular Romance.' *Western Folklore* 62: 63–81.
–. 2005. 'Turkic Bard and Medieval Entertainer: What a Living Epic Tradition Can Tell Us about Oral Performance of Narrative in the Middle Ages.' In Vitz et al. 2005: 167–80.
–, ed. and trans. 2007. *Edige: A Karakalpak Oral Epic as Performed by Jumabay Bazarov*. FF Communications 293. Helsinki: Academia Scientiarum Fennica.
Riedinger, Anita R. 2004. 'The Formulaic Style in the Old English Riddles.' *Studia Neophilologica* 76: 30–43.
Ringler, Richard, trans. 2007a. *Beowulf: A New Translation for Oral Delivery*. Indianapolis: Hackett.
–. 2007b. *Beowulf: The Complete Story: A Drama* (audio book). Madison: U of Wisconsin P.
Sale, William Merritt. 1993a. 'Homer and the *Roland*: The Shared Formular Technique, Part I.' *Oral Tradition* 8: 87–142.
–. 1993b. 'Homer and the *Roland*: The Shared Formular Technique, Part II.' *Oral Tradition* 8: 381–412.
–. 1996. 'In Defense of Milman Parry: Renewing the Oral Theory.' *Oral Tradition* 11: 374–417.
Schaefer, Ursula. 1992. *Vokalität: Altenglische Dichtung zwischen Mündlichkeit und Schriftlichkeit*. ScriptOralia 39. Tübingen: Narr.
–. 1993. 'Alterities: On Methodology in Medieval Literary Studies.' *Oral Tradition* 8: 187–214.
SCHS. 1953–. *Serbo-Croatian Heroic Songs (Srpskohrvatske junačke pjesme)*. Coll., ed., and trans. Milman Parry, Albert Lord, and David Bynum. Cambridge, MA: Harvard UP. [Vols. 1–2 copublished by the Serbian Academy of Sciences, Belgrade.]
Stock, Brian. 1983. *The Implications of Literacy: Written Language and Models of Interpretation in the Eleventh and Twelfth Centuries*. Princeton: Princeton UP.

Strohm, Paul. 2006. 'Writing and Reading.' In *A Social History of England 1200–1500*. Ed. Rosemary Horrox and W. Mark Ormrod. Cambridge: CUP. 454–72.

Treitler, Leo. 2003. *With Voice and Pen: Coming to Know Medieval Song and How It Was Made*. Oxford: OUP.

Tyler, Lee Edgar. 1988. 'Annotated Bibliography to 1985.' *Oral Tradition* 3: 191–228.

van Gennep, Arnold. 1909. *La Question d'Homère: Les poèmes homériques, l'archéologie, et la poésie populaire*. Paris: Mercure de France.

Vitz, Evelyn Birge, Nancy Freeman Regalado, and Marilyn Lawrence, eds. 2005. *Performing Medieval Narrative*. Cambridge: Brewer.

Watson, Jonathan. 2005. 'Writing Out "Oðinn's storm": The Literary Reception of an Oral-derived Template in the Two Versions of Lagamon's *Brut*.' In Amodio 2005a: 209–37.

Witte, Kurt. 1912a. 'Zur Flexion homerischer Formeln.' *Glotta* 3: 110–17. [Rpt. in Latacz 1979: 109–17.]

–. 1912b. 'Der Einfluss des Verses auf die Bildung von Komposita.' *Glotta* 3: 120–29.

Wolf, Friedrich August. 1795 [1963]. *Prolegomena ad Homerum sive (de) Operum Homericorum Prisca et Genuina Forma Variisque Mutationibus et Probabili Ratione Emendandi*. Halle. [Rpt. ed. Rudolf Peppmüller. Hildesheim: Olms, 1963.]

Wood, Robert. 1767 [1976]. *An Essay on the Original Genius of Homer*. [Rpt. Hildesheim: Olms, 1976.]

Zumthor, Paul. 1987. *La lettre et la voix: De la 'littérature' médiévale*. Paris: Seuil.

–. 1990. *Oral Poetry: An Introduction*. Trans. Kathryn Murphy-Judy. Minneapolis: U of Minnesota P.

# 3 The Written Word in Context: The Early Middle Ages

*Michael Richter*

Written material is of prime importance in any exploration of the past since the dawn of writing. Inevitably, however, written documentation only ever allows partial access to the past. This contribution[1] will explore the limitations of written culture in the Early Middle Ages as a necessary precondition for a substantial appreciation of the oral culture which has always formed the central element of social existence. Inevitably, this investigation will be carried out with the help of written sources, although by no means exclusively so. In recent decades the subject of literacy has enjoyed considerable vogue amongst medievalists, yet the concept itself is rarely analysed to any substantial degree.[2] In these works the written word is implicitly taken to have been of central importance in its society.[3] This attitude must, however, be questioned.[4] The following essay attempts to outline a cultural constellation as it has evolved from my work in this field over three decades: work which has gradually yet substantially transformed my perception of the medieval past.

The main aim of my contribution is to provide an outline of written culture in the early medieval West. Not without some reservations, I subscribe to Clanchy's statement that 'all writing depends on the prior formulation of language, and it makes no sense without speech; compared with language, writing is an ancillary and dependent technology.'[5] The context mentioned in my title refers to the ubiquitous predominance of oral culture. I will limit myself to the time-span of *c.* 400 to *c.* 1100; beyond this period, a considerable overall increase in the written record across Europe demands that different considerations be taken into account. Towards the end of this paper I will outline some aspects of oral culture.

Arguably the most important legacy of the Middle Ages was the fact that the European vernacular languages were turned into written form.[6] The history of written cul-

---

[1] In the formulation of the title I lean on the project 'Oral history in the Middle Ages: The spoken word in context', directed in February 2001 by Gerhard Jaritz and myself in the department of Medieval Studies at the Central European University, Budapest. For a first general discussion of the topic see Richter 1994. I owe the inspiration for that book to Leopold Genicot.
[2] See Mostert 1999: esp. 15–16. The discussion of the study of communication in the Middle Ages, whose beginning Mostert attributes to me, should be dated, if at all, to 1976 and not 1979; see Mostert 1999: 16, and bibliography no. 545.
[3] Michael Clanchy writes in his introduction to Mostert 1999: 'All Christianized medieval societies conferred extraordinary prestige on writing' (12). This is an unsubstantiated claim.
[4] Richter 2002 was a first attempt to grasp this nettle.
[5] Clanchy's introduction to Mostert 1999: 6.
[6] For a first sketch see Richter 1995.

ture in the Middle Ages is neither diffuse and diverse nor one of linear expansion. The origins of the writing of the European vernaculars, mostly with the help of the Latin alphabet, must be linked to the spread of the Christian religion, which was fundamentally built upon the written word. After the transcription of the European vernaculars had been mastered, its application varied considerably over time and space.[7] Nevertheless, the written record of medieval Europe with recourse to the Latin alphabet in the western and central parts of Europe, or its eastern cousin, the Cyrillic *azbuky*, in retrospect gives Europe a superficial appearance of cultural uniformity up to the present day.[8] This is one of the reasons why the term 'the Latin West' is widely used. Turning the numerous European vernacular languages into writing with the help of only two dozen symbols was an exceedingly demanding task; a number of devices were developed to do approximate justice to the specific sound system of each language. The issue of the effect of writing on a particular language lies beyond the range of the present investigation.

Any study of medieval oral as well as written culture will inevitably be based, like most other subjects, on written sources; in this case in particular, such sources need to be treated with caution, since many of their authors are far from ideologically impartial towards oral culture. However, it is also inevitable that the oral culture of the past may be recovered only indirectly, and thus at best only in some of its manifestations. The issue of the oral background to medieval literature will be handled in various contributions to the present volume.

Latin and the vernaculars occupied fundamentally different positions in medieval European societies. Outside Latin Europe (which I shall discuss later), Latin was, from the beginning, a foreign language.[9] Within Latin Europe, it became gradually more distant as the Romance vernaculars emancipated themselves from their Latin ancestor,[10] though the affinity of these children to their linguistic forefather remained close throughout the Middle Ages. On the other hand, a general acquaintance with Latin was linked virtually everywhere to the ability to read and, usually, also to write.

We must begin by looking at the Latin language in a more general framework. This language, with its multiple functions in the Middle Ages, was the legacy of antiquity. We will consider, albeit briefly, the latest stage in its development in order to assess its place in medieval society. This *lingua vulgaris* of the Roman world had been, in its written form, the principal instrument for the establishment and maintenance of the Roman Empire. Latin was the *lingua franca* throughout the empire and showed few regional variations in its written form. It must be assumed that the spoken manifestation of the Latin written record showed regional variations.[11] A considerable part of the western

---

[7] See e. g. Langosch et al. 1964 which, however, leaves out the Slavic as well as the Celtic literatures.

[8] An exceptional case is Glagolitic writing, developed in the 860s for writing the Western Slavic languages. It was ingenious but ultimately proved too cumbersome and was soon largely replaced by Cyrillic.

[9] 'Latin Europe' in the following is used synonymously with *Romania* in the sense of the area where Latin developed into the various Romance languages. On the term *Romania* and its various senses, see Tagliavini 1973: 125–27.

[10] From the wealth of literature I choose those works which have opened new ground for me: Banniard 1992; Wright 1982, which deals with France and Spain. We should include, in the western part of Europe, Italy and Raetia.

[11] This has best been studied with reference to Britain; see following note.

Roman world came to be wedded to the Roman language for good: Spain and Gaul in particular; the glaring exception is Britain.[12] In antiquity, Latin had been widely employed for a variety of aspects of civic life. Roman religion was not as tightly wedded to written culture as was later the case with the Christian religion; although there was a professional class of priests and priestesses, Roman religion was also practised at home – privately, as it were.

It is in the area of Christian religion that we encounter antiquity's most important legacy to the medieval West: the Latin Church. The Christian religion had taken roots in that part of the Roman Empire in which Greek was the *lingua franca*, and thus the works which eventually became the New Testament were originally written in Greek. Likewise, the decisive theological issues were discussed in the Greek world from 325 (Council of Nicaea) onwards; Latin, here, was the second cousin. As early as the second century, however, Latin, the official secular *lingua franca* of the empire, also came to be used for Sacred Scripture. Around the turn of the fifth century Jerome created a revised version of the available Latin translations (*vetus Latina*) and was responsible for the future standard version of the Latin Bible in the Roman Church. His work is now known, quite appropriately, as the Vulgate, since it was written in a language immediately accessible to the *vulgus* of the empire. Ulfila's translation of the Scriptures into Gothic in the fourth century took place on the borders of the Greek East and was in line with a widespread use there of non-Greek languages for the Christian cult.

The Christian religion, eminently a religion of 'the written word', and the official and exclusive religion of the empire since the late fourth century, benefited from the established written culture, building upon elements of Roman secular institutions. The Christian Church continued to use existing terminology for the religious sphere. The potentially problematic relationship between Christian and secular culture, including the language, was discussed from time to time but was never finally settled. Perhaps a solution was not possible, but as a result of these discussions Western Catholicism became distinctly Roman.

## 1 The Medieval 'Latin Church' and its Implications

It is imperative to view the Christian religion as it existed in any given society. The history of the 'conversion of Europe' was a lengthy and slow process. It may be said to have begun in the West with Ireland from *c.* 400 onwards and to have come to its formal conclusion with Iceland in the year 1000. Throughout this time, the Christian religion existed as part of these European societies. As well as shaping these, to an extent difficult to specify, it was in turn shaped by the societies within which it took root.[13] There was more cultural continuity in the Latin West than meets the eye in our sources.

In the Middle Ages the Latin language was used throughout our area of study as the language of the liturgy. Furthermore, the Latin Bible remained the norm; there were no translations of the Bible into the vernacular. Nevertheless, one must assume that in early

---

[12] In Britain Celtic prevailed, though heavily influenced by Latin; see Jackson 1953.
[13] For this see programmatically Southern 1970; also Hughes 1966.

medieval societies there was much use of the vernacular in the religious sphere which for a long time did not find its way into writing. This was especially the case with regard to preaching to lay audiences. The native clerics had grown up with their vernacular language: for them Latin was a professional second language which they may well have mastered to a high level, but they would not have lost their native language. The sermon literature surviving from the early medieval centuries is almost exclusively in Latin[14] and was thus immediately accessible outside Latin Europe only to *litterati*. By their very nature, sermons are an eminently oral form of communication; their written versions must be regarded as secondary or ancillary. The surviving material cannot therefore be regarded as representative of its genre, otherwise the spread of the Christian message would have to be considered minimal.

Before confronting the situation in the various areas of Western Europe, it is necessary to highlight the substantial changes in material aspects of written culture. The most widespread writing material in the Roman world had been papyrus, grown mainly in Egypt, but easily distributed throughout the empire as part of the functioning trading systems. The production of papyrus was inexpensive, and the transformation into writing material relatively easy; the one disadvantage of this material was its delicate physical state.

In the course of late antiquity a new raw material for writing emerged: animal skin, mainly that of sheep (parchment), but also calf (vellum) and other skins. One advantage was that the raw material 'grew' everywhere in the predominantly rural economy of the post-Roman West. Another advantage was that its material made for a good chance of survival in the damper climates north of the Mediterranean. The disadvantages, however, were twofold: the high price of the raw material and the laborious methods of preparing it for practical use in writing. The dominant form in which parchment was used, apart from its use for charters, was that of the codex (Roberts and Skeat 1983).

In many respects, the institution of the monastery was an ideal setting to overcome these barriers, providing an agrarian economy as well as the presence of various crafts within the community. Besides the necessity for religion to build on the written word, the material side helped in strengthening the institutions of Christianity as centres of written culture. Furthermore, for these very reasons, these institutions were taken into the service of secular government, and, as a result, the Christian dimension of early medieval society is once again, on the surface at least, fairly prominent. The close interaction of 'Church and State' has been a very significant feature of the medieval West, yet the material background to this has been hitherto largely neglected.

As far as our time-span is concerned, it may be stated that virtually all written documents are the products of clerics, which here still means members of the clergy. This is particularly important when considering the written documents in the various vernaculars, which are mostly of a secular quality, whereas written Latin was largely maintained for almost all ecclesiastical matter.

We now turn to the early medieval world, for which it is advisable to provide a historical outline. The phenomenon which used to be called 'the fall of Rome', a process

---

[14] There are extensive Old Irish passages in a Latin sermon fragment preserved in Cambrai, Bibliothèque Municipale MS 619, dated to 763x780, edited in Stokes and Strachan 1901–3: II, 244–47.

rather than an event, is now more appropriately labelled 'the transformation of the Roman world' into early medieval societies. This approach stresses continuities rather than ruptures. The main agents were ethnic groups organised as war-bands. In the early stage of that process, the transformation took place within the territory of the Roman Empire. Not surprisingly, the barbarian governments which replaced Roman rule continued to avail themselves of established institutions of administration, particularly Latin writing, which they modified according to their needs. For this usage they fell back on Roman personnel, who provided the necessary expertise. Writing was not used as widely as it had been by the Roman governments, and an exemplary case is that of the Roman senator Cassiodorus, for some time employed as secretary to the Ostrogothic king Theodoric (493–525). The collection of government correspondence formulated by Cassiodorus (*Variae*) opens with a letter from Theodoric to the Roman emperor Anastasius, which contains the programmatic phrase: *Regnum nostrum imitatio uestra est* (Our reign is the imitation of yours) (I.1; Fridh 1973: 9). Continuity rather than change therefore marked the field of the medium used.

The barbarian societies had existed without writing.[15] This is why the early stages of their structure and institutions are very difficult to grasp, since they come into view, if at all, only through the descriptions of outsiders, and are articulated in the language and concepts of these outsiders (Richter 1993). What has to be grasped is the fact that many of these barbarian societies had functioned successfully without writing; some political entities, however, did not survive the transformation of the Roman world.

We will present the various major linguistic regions separately, beginning with Gaul, followed by the Celtic languages and finally directing our attention to the Western Germanic languages. Spanish, the Northern Germanic and the Slavic languages appear in written form only towards the end of our time-frame. We will have to distinguish Latin as a scriptural medium from Latin as a spoken language; in the areas where Romance languages developed both forms of Latin coincided.

The following discussion will present two cases. On the one hand stands Latin Europe (the *Romania*), in which there is, at least superficially, a continuity of written culture from Roman to post-Roman times. On the other, there are parts of Europe in which there had been virtually no written culture and in which written culture arrived with Christianity and eventually impinged upon other social fields. Here our main emphasis will be on Celtic societies.

## 2 Latin Europe

When turning to the early medieval centuries in Western Europe, fluctuations in written culture become apparent in Latin Europe, which inherited the written legacy of the Roman Empire. Writing in the civic sphere decreased dramatically, for various reasons. The rising political forces, particularly in Merovingian Gaul, seem to have had less need for written documentation, and the institutional Roman infrastructure for education withered. The widespread use of writing is therefore increasingly linked to the Christian

---

[15] An exception, in a very limited way, are the runes of Scandinavia.

religion, to which it was indispensable. What needs to be kept in mind, however, is that the Latin of the church was still accessible to the general population until *c.* 800, and the institutions of the church eventually provided the infrastructure for written culture to serve their needs. It is very difficult to perceive continuity and change in the field of written culture in Gaul, but, looking at the volumes of the *Monumenta Germaniae Historica*, the leading collection of sources, it is hagiography which dominates the record.

In Latin Europe this constellation eventually brought about the social dichotomy of *litterati* and *illitterati* which was to characterise medieval European society for a considerable time to come. The surviving written sources from the early medieval centuries, and not only those written in Latin, are predominantly of clerical authorship, the consequences of which should be taken into account. This was a time in which *clericus* and *litteratus* were used synonymously. The written sources from Latin Europe are much richer than those from most other areas. In any case, their nature and presence must be seen as the result of the requirements of the Christian religion. Members of the clergy, the most likely group of *litterati*, were, numerically, a minority. Their written output must be considered a very partial representation of the society in which they worked. The overwhelming presence of written sources of a Christian quality from the Early Middle Ages has sometimes led to the conclusion that these societies were particularly Christian at this time. The circular nature of the argument is, however, obvious: the modern scholar is granted access to medieval societies through the minds of those who produced the written record.

We now come back to Michael Clanchy's statement that 'all writing depends on the prior formulation of language, and it makes no sense without speech; compared with language, writing is an ancillary and dependent technology' (1999: 6). Indispensable as written documents may be for us, in their own time they were above all ancillary products; what mattered ultimately was oral communication. This phenomenon has found its brilliant articulation in the works of Cicero, especially the *De Oratore*, in which he elaborates in great detail that public speaking entails much more than uttering words; rather, it was a demanding performance intended to impress, indeed seduce, the audience.[16]

Written material was put to such 'oratorial' use beyond antiquity by the almost universal custom of reading aloud. This had the important consequence that written material could reach people who were themselves unable to read, once the written material was presented in their native language (enabling active and passive participation). In this way, by means of performance, written material could take on an educational dimension in spreading language norms.

In Latin Europe, however, due to the fairly nuanced range of written material, we can at times go beyond the mere statement that written texts were read aloud; in fortunate instances, we can aim at recovering something of the quality of reading aloud. We

---

[16] See *De Oratore* I. v. 18: *Nam quid ego de actione ipsa plura dicam? quae motu corporis, quae gestu, quae vultu, quae vocis conformatione ac varietate moderanda est* [...] (And why should I go on to describe the speaker's delivery? That needs to be controlled by bodily carriage, gesture, play of features and changing intonation of voice [...]) (Sutton and Rackham 1948: 14/15). It is not accidental that in this context Cicero repeatedly refers to actors.

are grateful for small mercies. In the first place I want to refer to Isidore of Seville's discussion of the requirements of the lector in church, a normative text which has received detailed exegesis (Banniard 1975).

I want to look more closely at a specific instance which is particularly rich; it comes closest, in the Early Middle Ages, to what is nowadays called 'thick description'.[17] It is the story told by Gregory of Tours about a priest who, when reading mass, seems not to have done justice to his task, so that the audience mocked him for 'having spoken in such an uneducated manner' (*sic inculte loqui*) (Arndt and Krusch 1885: 159). Here we are confronted with variations in the register of one's language, not in the vocabulary but in the manner it was articulated. We are still in a world in which Latin was the language of the *vulgus* and passive participation in the Latin mass was unproblematic; indeed, it shows us a living language available in more than one manifestation in the spoken form.

On the other hand, the ideal of *sermo humilis* for the language of the clergy was applied to the written language. The term *sermo* may be taken as a representative case of the difficulty in clearly separating writing and speaking.[18]

The Romance vernaculars emerge in writing from the ninth century onwards. Until then, Latin was accessible to the Romance population.[19] It is all the more important that we witness a regression of written culture in the civic sphere, as in the exemplary case of private letter-writing.[20] However, the Latin language was not as static as the written products might suggest in the half-millennium following the demise of the western empire. As has been widely argued by Michel Banniard, one must assume that in the early medieval centuries Latin material was articulated with regional variations. When the Romance languages gradually found their way into written form, they simply made visible the previous existence of a variety of regional manifestations in the use of the Latin language.

## 3 Beyond Latin Europe

In looking at areas outside Latin Europe some general points need to be made. In the first place, the political entities were of a much smaller size than even the Roman provinces, let alone the empire. The situation in post-Roman Britain may be highly elusive, but there are indications nevertheless that small entities surfaced again. These were normally organised as war-bands under leaders, which stresses the closely integrated nature of the leading echelons of society, who had no need for writing. The *pax Romana* was gone, and no comparable *pax* would emerge again throughout the Middle Ages. There was much unrest and violence all over the early medieval West. The teachings of the Christian religion, with its central message of peace, were not heeded; on the contrary,

---

[17] The term was coined by the philosopher Gilbert Ryle and popularised by Clifford Geertz (1973: 5–10).
[18] See Richter 2005; see also the variety in terminology used by St Patrick (see the quotation from Bieler 1950: 61 below).
[19] The classic account is Banniard 1992, but he has also continued to work in this field; see e. g. Banniard 2005.
[20] See the exemplary study by Ralph Mathisen (1993).

the religion allowed itself to be drawn into the societies as they were. This was an ideal environment for a continued cultivation of worldly values, heroic deeds and their acclamation.

## 3.1 Ireland

Here we must begin with Ireland, for a number of reasons. It is generally assumed that Christianity came to Ireland around *c*. 400. In the year 431 Pope Celestine I deemed it necessary to send a Christian teacher, Palladius, from Gaul *ad Scottos in Christum credentes*.[21] Palladius was a native speaker of Latin. The only other person known by name to have taught Christianity to the Irish in the fifth century is Patrick. He came from Britain, and in one of his two surviving works, written in Latin, he writes explicitly that Latin was, for him, an acquired second language: *Nam sermo et loquela nostra translata est in linguam alienam, sicut facile potest probari ex saliva scripturae meae* (Because our speech and our language are translated into a foreign language, as can easily be seen by the flavour of my writing) (*Confessio*, ch. 9; Bieler 1950: 61). In his native Britain, bilingualism must have been widespread, comprising Latin and regional versions of British Celtic.

In Ireland the Latin language was retained for the Christian religion, as is evident from the written sources. The earliest written sources to survive were the penitentials, dating to the sixth century. In Ireland, therefore, for the first time in Western Europe, Latin assumed the place of a *lingua sacra* in the context of the Christian religion (Richter 2006). The first two centuries of Christianity in Ireland are virtually undocumented, but when the written record sets in, *c*. 600, Irish scholars were able to write clear and acceptable Latin. The first author to represent this achievement was Columbanus, whose diverse works date from the years between 590 and 615.

One can only assume – but one must, I think, assume – that from the beginning of Christianity Latin was taught in Ireland thoroughly and systematically. From around 600 the record of Latin grammars produced in Ireland sets in, all of which were based predominantly on the works of Donatus (Holtz 1981). It is a hazardous guess, but one that should nevertheless be aired, that systematic teaching of Latin in Ireland began as early as the fifth century, and I am inclined to go one step further and suggest that the circle around Palladius (who certainly had not gone on his own from Gaul to Ireland) had been active agents in this field.[22]

We must therefore assume that from the fifth century onwards the Latin and Irish languages co-existed in Ireland. The former was from the outset linked to writing; the latter was not yet written. On the other hand, we know from later sources that there were professionals of native culture and learning in Ireland from olden times who cultivated their skills orally. We will look at some of these in detail a little later. Here it is necessary to stress that the spoken language was cultivated and existed on a high level.

---

[21] Prosper of Aquitaine, *Chronicle*, s. *a*. 431 (Mommsen 1892: 473). The latest substantial synthesis by Thomas Charles-Edwards (2000) in my view overrates the success of Christianity in early medieval Ireland.

[22] In the surviving documentation from Ireland, Palladius is largely overshadowed by St Patrick, a phenomenon which has not been systematically investigated.

The professionals of the oral culture were highly respected and adequately remunerated for their skills; this oral learning carried enormous social prestige. It may be that one should posit that the new learning that arrived in Ireland with the Christian religion met a milieu open to learning *tout court*, and that for this reason Latin learning could take root.

The first steps for turning the Irish language into written form in the Latin alphabet can be traced ('seen' would be too strong a term) in dry-point glosses to Christian texts dated to the seventh century. However, it would appear that this new medium was applied to Irish language material quickly and extensively. The most astonishing achievement in this area is the vast body of Irish law, preserved in the Irish language and believed, on linguistic grounds, to have first been written around 700.

The corpus of written material from early medieval Ireland, in the two languages, is enormous and without parallel in Europe. It is insufficiently known for the simple reason that a command of Old Irish is not widespread, even though a large amount of the Old Irish material was translated into Western languages, particularly German, by the leading Celtic scholars around the turn of the twentieth century. It should be added that the corpus of Latin writing from Ireland declines from *c.* 800 onwards; from then on, Irish takes the lead.

Nevertheless, Ireland presents a fairly clear case of a society accommodating a foreign language used for a limited range of written documentation. A secondary effect was the application of the writing system to the native language for use in the vernacular. Early Irish society was never in a situation which could be characterized as having been built upon the written word.

## 3.2 Britain

Most of the island of Britain was a Roman province for more than three centuries, but when the last legions left shortly after 400, the population was still Celtic in speech. At this time one should use the term British Celtic, and this branch of the Celtic language family had, unsurprisingly, been strongly influenced by Latin (Jackson 1953). It would have existed in regional varieties, but only one of these has survived in written form: Cymric or, as the Saxons called it, Welsh. Owing to the Saxon invasions and later settlements in Britain, written material from the British has been preserved mainly from Wales. Here it is significant that in a general overview the written record is not nearly as plentiful as that from Ireland. This applies even to the text of the Bible. From before 1100 there is only one manuscript from Wales, the so-called *Lichfield Gospel*, compared with nearly a dozen from Ireland (where the *Book of Kells* is a manuscript of unrivalled quality). From Wales survive Latin inscriptions from the early medieval period (Nash-Williams 1950). We also have historiography in Latin from British authors in the early period such as Gildas and 'Nennius', and the sparse *Annales Cambriae* are likewise written in Latin. There is no documentation, apart from the onomastic material of the inscriptions, of writing British in the Latin alphabet.[23]

---

[23] An exceptional and difficult case are the Welsh-language elements in the Llandaff charters, allegedly going back as far as the sixth century, which cannot be discussed here. See Davies 1979.

The overall corpus of written material, in either language, is small in comparison to that of Ireland. The Welsh laws, for example, formulated in Latin and in Welsh, were not turned into writing until 1200. A possible explanation for this small corpus may be found in the legacy of the written Latin record, which may have stifled desires to write in the British language.[24] Alternatively, the Celtic legacy of professionals in the spoken word may have made the requirement to write less urgent. We know from the early period at least the names of two leading poets, Aneirin and Taliesin, even though the poetry attributed to them is preserved only in a thirteenth-century manuscript. The corpus of elegies known as *Y Gododdin* (see Illustration 3), allegedly commemorating battles around 600 between Britons and Saxons in Northern Britain south of Edinburgh has been preserved only in Welsh, although it was certainly not originally formulated in that variety of British.

The fact that written material survives only from Wales is due mainly to the political developments in Britain after the departure of the Roman legions. The invaders of Britain, whom the Celts to the present day call 'Saxons', managed to play a dominant role over the British population in the eastern parts of the island as regards settlement, religion as well as speech. The Saxons succeeded in Britain in two centuries, whereas the Romans had failed in almost double that time. That their country should eventually be called England, and the population English, is the questionable achievement of the Venerable Bede (Richter 1984).

The Saxons, who were organised in numerous political units which fought amongst themselves just as they fought the Britons, shunned the written Latin culture which they encountered. They were confronted with that culture only from the late sixth century onwards, with the Christian mission. This started among the Jutes (not the *Angli*, as Pope Gregory believed to the end of his days) with Augustine and his followers, who were sent from Rome. Despite Bede's lengthy account, this mission remained singularly unsuccessful. The limited success which the Roman missionaries nevertheless had in Kent was certainly helped by the fact that the Kentish king Aethelbert was married to a Frank called Berta, who was a Catholic and had a priest in her household. Clearly, written culture was already available when Augustine began his mission in Britain.

More successful was the missionary work of Irish Christians initiated in 635 by Oswald of Northumbria, to which Bede hardly did justice. However, he does report the use of the vernacular languages in preaching, reporting that King Oswald acted as an interpreter between the Irish missionaries and his Saxon subjects, translating the Irish into the Saxon language.[25] The Latin language does not figure at all in this account of Catholic Christianity.

## 4 The Carolingian Interlude

Around the year 790 the realm of Charlemagne had reached its full extent. It comprised nearly all of Gaul (except Brittany), a substantial part of Northern Italy and the regions

---

[24] For some thoughts on this, see Richter 2008.
[25] See Bede's account in his *Historia Ecclesiastica*, III.iii (Colgrave and Mynors 1969: 218–21).

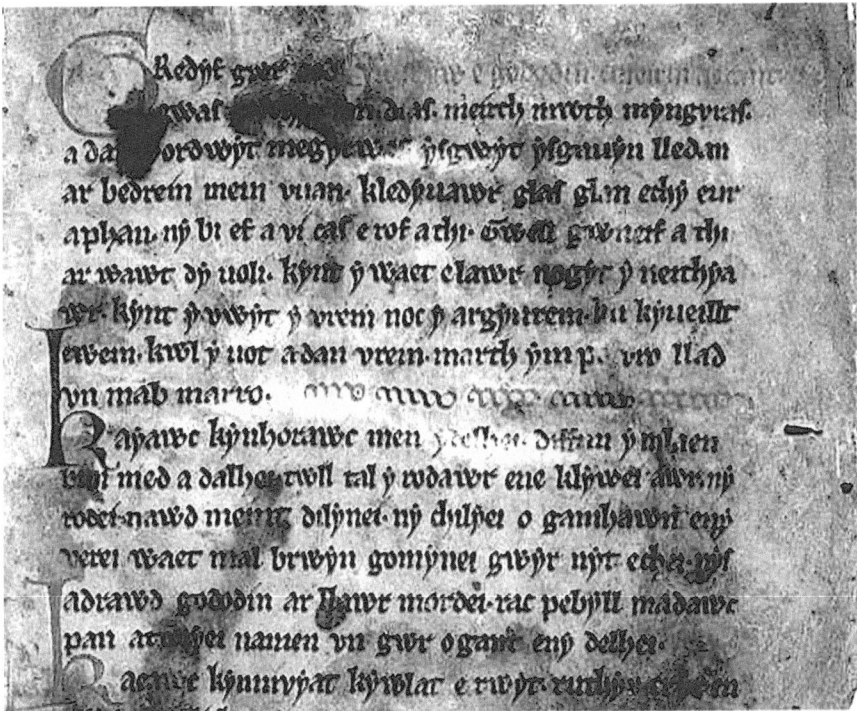

3 – Beginning of the *Gododdin* (Llyfr Aneirin, p. 1, *c.* 1265)

between the Rhine, the Elbe and the Alps. The population was in the majority Romanophone. Charles himself was a Frank and thus a native speaker of Frankish. Opinions differ as to his command of Latin, with my position being a minimalist one. This is not the place to discuss the 'Carolingian Renaissance', which I prefer to call 'Carolingian Humanism' since it manifests itself predominantly in literature. His rule is documented quite fully, and the overwhelming majority of these documents are in Latin. The alleged compilation of the various Germanic laws would have been in Latin, as were the *leges barbarorum* on the continent in general. The most impressive record, in any case, are the capitularies, specific formulations of the royal will on a wide range of topics. These are also all in Latin, and would have been made known regionally in all parts of the realm with the help of counts and bishops. There is enough evidence to show that Charles was anxious that the content of his legislation be understood by those whom it concerned. Latin written legislation was to be explained to the population orally, in such a manner that they would understand the royal will.[26]

---

[26] See Richter 1982. As far as Latin Europe is concerned, we may refer to the much-discussed chapter 17 of the Council of Tours of 813: *Et ut easdem omelias quisque aperte transferre studeat in rusticam Romanam linguam aut Thiotiscam, quo facilius cuncti possint intellegere quae dicuntur* (Werminghoff 1906: 288).

The instrument of the capitularies shows particularly clearly that Charlemagne intended to rule his territories with the help of the written word, showing himself an imitator of Roman practice in this respect. It is possible to think that a realm that size could not be ruled otherwise. Charlemagne is normally praised beyond reason by historians, not least because he found a biographer, Einhard, who glorified him, as courtiers tend to do, without any emotional distance. His words are generally taken as reliable factual information. I call the reign of Charlemagne an interlude because it did not create any lasting structures. The empire, in a bad state at the time of his death in 814, crumbled under the mismanagement of his son Louis the Pious and broke up for good after his death in 840; Louis did not even attempt to rule with the help of capitularies.

## 5 Glimpses of Oral Culture

*Quod loquimur transit, quod scribimus permanet* (The things we say pass, the things we write endure). This expression is taken from Pope Gregory I's *Moralia in Iob* (Adriaen 1979–85: 1675). I take it as a springboard for some ideas about oral culture in our period. In his attitude, probably widespread among *litterati*, Gregory appears very Roman and very Catholic. Gregory wrote a lot himself, and he may well have overestimated the social standing of writing in general and of his work in particular in his world.

Here it is advisable to make a general point: due to the nature of the medium, written culture may be glimpsed, however insufficiently, as it grows and spreads. By contrast, oral culture approached through the medium of written information may be grasped only occasionally. Since we approach it through the medium of the written word, we encounter it only sporadically, but at a stage in which it is firmly established. We will give some instances of this phenomenon below, taken from those societies introduced earlier in this paper.

*Quod loquimur transit* is a facile statement which lacks a sense of perception. Literally it may well be correct, but metaphorically it is far off the mark. I recall Clanchy's formulation of the ancillary nature of all writing; this includes Roman society. All the societies which bordered the Roman Empire in the West had existed without established recourse to writing. In the Roman world there were professional groups of scribes, even though oral performance was more highly regarded. In the barbarian societies there were professionals of the spoken word whose task it was to ensure that social knowledge was preserved and kept alive; these societies would not otherwise have been viable. Some features of the structural elements of oral culture will be highlighted.

### 5.1 Ireland

Not surprisingly, the most detailed and remarkable insight into the organisation of oral culture comes from Ireland, where, due to the lack of Roman occupation, there existed native institutions with a long ancestry.[27] I will confine myself to one quotation from the

---

[27] Unfortunately there is no comprehensive study devoted to the institutions of native learning in medieval Ireland.

law tract *Uraicecht na ríar*. The subtitle of the modern edition reads, 'The Poetic Grades in Early Irish Law'. This is somewhat misleading, in that it emerges from the text itself that the Irish term *fili* (pl. *filid*), denotes in that context the generic term for men of learning in a variety of skills; only in later times was *fili* the most respectful term for 'poet'.

> Cis lir gráda filed? Ní hansae: a secht: ollam, ánruth, clí, cano, dos, macfuirmid, fochloc. [...] caite dán 7 grád 7 lóg n-enech cach aí ó biuc co mór? Ní hansae: dán ollaman cétomus: secht cóecait drécht lais .i. cóeca cach gráid: is éola i cach coimgniu, 7 is éola i mbrithemnacht fénechais. Cethorcha sét a díre.
>
> How many grades of [men of learning] are there? Not difficult; seven: *ollam, ánruth, clí, cano, dos, macfuirmid, fochloc*. [...] What is the competence, grade and honour-price of each, from small to great? Not difficult: the competence of an *ollam* first: he has three hundred and fifty compositions, that is fifty for each grade; he is knowledgeable in all historical sciences, and he is knowledgeable in the jurisprudence of Irish law. His honour-prize is forty *sets*.[28]

According to a later gloss, the honour-price of the *ollam* would be the equivalent of 39 head of cattle.

Thus far the information from a law text dated to *c.* 700. We learn that there existed several grades amongst the men of learning, and to reach a higher grade it was necessary to accumulate more knowledge.

It is always impossible to know how such normative regulations were put into practice. In this respect there is, fortunately, an earlier reference to the existence of one type of oral scholar in Ireland which comes from a non-normative text. St. Patrick, in his 'Letter to the Soldiers of Coroticus' (*c.* mid-fifth century), mentions having met with legal experts during the course of his work in Ireland: *erogavi illis qui iudicabant per omnes regiones quos ego frequentius visitabam* (I gave to those who give judgment in all the regions which I most frequently visited) (*Confessio*, ch. 53; Bieler 1950: 86–87). He had thus encountered socially recognized legal experts apparently present throughout Irish society.

Members of the various sub-groups of the *oes dána* (men of learning) – amongst whom the legal experts, of course, figure prominently – were, ideally speaking, represented in the entourage of kings, showing their high social standing. There were many kings in Ireland, and consequently also many men of learning. The most frequently mentioned group are the *filid* who, with their poetry, acted as political arbiters. The rich corpus of their work found its way into writing in the High and Late Middle Ages.

## 5.2 Wales

It was stated earlier that the body of written documentation from Wales is not nearly as rich as that from Ireland. As regards established oral culture, I will here present information a little beyond the chronological framework of this article. An entry in a Welsh chronicle, originally composed in Latin but now available only in a Welsh translation, reports under the year 1176 a cultural contest initiated by a Welsh ruler:

---

[28] Breatnach 1987: 102–3 (translation slightly modified). For the wider context see Kelly 1988.

And then the Lord Rhys held a special feast at Cardigan, and he set two kinds of contest: one between the bard and the poets, and another between the crowders and the pipers and the various classes of string music. And he set two chairs for the victors in the contests. And those he enriched with great gifts. And then a young man from his own court won the victory for string music. And the men from Gwynedd won the victory for poetry. And all the other minstrels received from the lord Rhys as much as they asked, so that no one was refused.[29]

On the basis of this text it can be plausibly stated that the cultivation of poetry in Wales had had a long-standing tradition. Competition favoured quality, and its products were appreciated and highly valued. The infrastructure for this was a legacy of the past. A comparable situation existed with regard to instrumental music, a phenomenon that is much easier to grasp in view of the fact that music existed most of the time without writing, and that written music, down to the present time, is at best a skeleton brought to fruition by live performances.

The way the remuneration of the contestants is formulated shows the value that was attached to their skills; here it is significant that, according to the text, the artists could set the price of their activity.

## 5.3 The Carolingian World

Despite the relative richness of written documents under Charles, outside the religious sphere, and despite the much acclaimed Carolingian Renaissance and the production of literature in Latin[30] we are nevertheless afforded a glimpse of a prominent oral culture persisting under him as well. Einhard (in his *Vita Karoli Magni*, ch. 29) mentions Charlemagne's initiative to have a collection of the *carmina barbara et antiquissima* made, in which heroic ancestral deeds were celebrated (Pertz, Waitz and Holder-Egger 1911: 33). The wording of Einhart makes it more than likely that *barbarus* is a technical term referring to the vernacular language; that Charles ordered these songs to be collected testifies to his opinion about their quality. Lastly, Charles as well as Einhart was aware that this material was old, i. e. transmitted orally over several generations.

That a similar constellation existed in another context may be inferred from a sentence in Thegan's *Vita Ludowici* (ch. 19), allowing us a precious glimpse of normal festive life at the court of Charles's son Louis (the Pious): *Nunquam in risum exaltavit vocem suam, nec quando in summis festivitatibus ad laetitiam populi procedebant themilici, scurri et mimi cum coraulis et citharistis ad mensam coram eo, tunc ad mensuram ridebat populus coram eo, ille nunquam nec dentes candidos suos in risu ostendit* (He never raised his voice in laughter, nor, when for the peoples' entertainment during great feasts the entertainers, buffoons and mimes together with the flute-players and harpists went to his table and the peoples laughed accordingly in his presence, he never showed his white teeth in laughter) (Pertz 1829: 595). The material regularly performed here at court by professionals was doubtless secular in nature, and the audience reacted appropriately (*ad*

---

[29] *Brut y Tywysogyon* (The Chronicle of the Princes), Red Book of Hergest version; Jones 1955: 167. This is considered the earliest reference to the Welsh institution of eisteddfod, national competitions in word and music culture held annually in Wales since 1861; see Koch 2006: 664–65.

[30] The codification of the Hildebrandslied c. 800–830 is a stray example of extant heroic epic.

*mensuram ridebat populus*). According to the biographer, Louis had to tolerate this culture in his presence even though he detested it personally. As a matter of fact, this is the only reason for Thegan to bring this topic up. The text is not a normative one, but it does convey normal social behaviour in the presence of oral culture. The historian must add that the audience of the court of the emperor Louis included clerics as well as secular nobles. The aim of the performance was to bring joy to them all (*ad laetitiam populi*).[31]

## 5.4 The Continental Saxons

The closest we come to highly professional oral poets among the continental Saxons is a passage in the Latin preface to the continental Saxon poem *Heliand*, commissioned by the emperor Louis in the first half of the ninth century: *Praecepit namque cuidam viro de gente Saxonum, qui apud suos non ignobilis vates habebatur, ut vetus ac novum Testamentum in Germanicam linguam transferre studeret* (For he ordered a certain Saxon who was esteemed among his countrymen as a poet of no mean talents to endeavour to translate the Old and New Testaments into the German language).[32] Here it is hinted that the skill of this poet, labelled a *vates*, a Latin term of higher prestige than a mere *poeta*, gave that person a position of high social standing. The ruler availed himself of pre-existing talent that was to be applied to tell the story of salvation in the vernacular.

In Latin Europe, there are likewise references to the existence of professionals of the spoken word. In addition to the terminology of professionals as given in Thegan's *Vita Ludowici*, quoted above, one term commonly recurs: *ioculatores*.[33] This term apparently arose in the early medieval centuries and was to figure in all the Romance languages: the jongleurs. In the clerically inspired sources these are portrayed in a negative light, which is not surprising inasmuch as they articulated cultural values which were in many respects irreconcilable with Christian ethics. Nevertheless, they were widely attested, especially when appearing in the vicinity of churches, singing and dancing during Mass and obviously distracting those who attended the divine service.

In conclusion, it may be suggested that due to the basis of our information, namely the written medium, we can encounter oral culture only as part of a society which had a literate culture. While we can state empirically that oral culture had existed most of the time without writing, the arrival of writing drew much of its strength from continuing existing oral culture. The two were not mutually exclusive but instead mutually dependent (Richter 2000).

---

[31] I have explored this theme further in Richter 2001.
[32] The text is preserved only in an early print; Behaghel 1996: 1.
[33] Thegan's terms for the professional performers show him to have been a product of Carolingian Humanism. See Richter 1994: 106–11. [See also ch. 5, pp. 173–76.]

## References

Adriaen, Marcus, ed. 1979–85. *S. Gregorii Magnis Moralia in Iob*. 3 vols. CCSL 143, 143A, 143B. Turnhout: Brepols.

Arndt, W., and Br. Krusch, eds. 1885. *Gregorii Turonensis Opera. II. Miracula et Opera Minora*. MGH, Scriptores Rerum Merovingicarum I.2. Hannover.

Banniard, Michel. 1975. 'Le lecteur en Espagne wisigothique d'après Isidore de Séville: de ses fonctions à l'état de la langue.' *Revue des Études Augustiniennes* 21: 112–44.

–. 1992. *Viva Voce: Communication écrite et communication orale du IV<sup>e</sup> au IX<sup>e</sup> siècle en Occident latin*. Paris: Institut des Études Augustiniennes.

–. 2005. 'Niveaux de langue et communication latinophone (V<sup>e</sup> – VIII<sup>e</sup> siècle).' In *Comunicare e significare nell'Alto Medioevo, 15 – 20 aprile 2004*. Settimane di studio della Fondazione Centro Italiano di Studi sull'Alto Medioevo 52. Spoleto: Presso la Sede della Fondazione. 155–208.

Behaghel, Otto, ed. 1996. *Heliand und Genesis*. 10th ed. rev. by Burghart Taeger. Altdeutsche Textbibliothek 4. Tübingen: Niemeyer.

Bieler, Ludwig, ed. 1950. 'Libri Epistolarum Sancti Patricii: Introduction, Text, and Commentary.' *Classica et Mediaevalia* 11: 1–150.

Breatnach, Liam, ed. 1987. *Uraicecht na Ríar: The Poetic Grades in Early Irish Law*. Early Irish Law Series 2. Dublin: Dublin Institute for Advances Studies.

Charles-Edwards, T. M. 2000. *Early Christian Ireland*. Cambridge: CUP.

Colgrave, Bertram, and R. A. B. Mynors, eds. 1969. *Bede's Ecclesiastical History of the English People*. Oxford Medieval Texts. Oxford: Clarendon.

Davies, Wendy, ed. 1979. *The Llandaff Charters*. Aberystwyth: National Library of Wales.

Fridh, Å. J., ed. 1973. *Magni Aurelii Cassiodori Variorum Libri XII./ De Anima*, ed. J. W. Halporn. CCSL 96. Turnhout: Brepols.

Geertz, Clifford. 1973. *The Interpretation of Cultures: Selected Essays*. New York: Basic Books..

Holtz, Louis. 1981. *Donat et la tradition de l'enseignement grammatical. Étude sur l'Ars Donati et sa diffusion (IV<sup>e</sup> – IX<sup>e</sup> siècle), et édition critique*. Paris: CNRS.

Hughes, Kathleen. 1966. *The Church in Early Irish Society*. London: Methuen.

Jackson, Kenneth. 1953. *Language and History in Early Britain: A Chronological Survey of the Brittonic Languages, 1st to 12th c. A.D.* Edinburgh: Edinburgh UP.

Jones, Thomas, ed. 1955. *Brut y Tywysogyon or The Chronicle of the Princes: Red Book of Hergest Version*. Cardiff: U of Wales P.

Kelly, Fergus. 1988. *A Guide to Early Irish Law*. Early Irish Law Series 3. Dublin: Dublin Institute for Advanced Studies.

Koch, John T., ed. 2006. *Celtic Culture: A Historical Encyclopedia*. 5 vols. Santa Barbara, CA: ABC–Clio.

Langosch, Karl, et al. 1964. *Geschichte der Textüberlieferung der antiken und mittelalterlichen Literatur. II. Überlieferungsgeschichte der mittelalterlichen Literatur*. Zürich: Atlantis.

Mathisen, Ralph W. 1993. *Roman Aristocrats in Barbarian Gaul: Strategies for Survival in an Age of Transition*. Austin: U of Texas P.

Mommsen, Theodor, ed. 1892. *Chronica Minora Saec. IV. V. VI. VII*. Part I. MGH, Auctores Antiquissimi 9. Berlin.

Mostert, Marco. 1999. 'New Approaches to Medieval Communication?' In *New Approaches to Medieval Communication*. Ed. Marco Mostert with an introduction by Michael Clanchy. Utrecht Studies in Medieval Literacy 1. Turnhout: Brepols. 3–37.

Nash-Williams, V. E. 1950. *The Early Christian Monuments of Wales*. Cardiff: U of Wales P.

Pertz, Georg Heinrich, ed. 1929. *Scriptores Rerum Sangallensium. Annales, Chronica et Historiae Aevi Carolini*. MGH, Scriptores 2. Hannover: Hahn 1839.

–, Georg Waitz, and Oswald Holder-Egger, eds. 1911. *Einhardi Vita Karoli Magni*. 6th ed. MGH, Scriptores Rerum Germanicarum. Hannover: Hahn.
Richter, Michael. 1982. 'Die Sprachenpolitik Karls des Großen.' *Sprachwissenschaft* 7: 412–37.
–. 1984. 'Bede's *Angli*: Angles or English?' *Peritia* 3: 99–114.
–. 1993. 'Latein – ein Schlüssel zur Welt des Frühmittelalters?' *Mittellateinisches Jahrbuch* 28: 15–26.
–. 1994. *The Formation of the Medieval West: Studies in the Oral Culture of the Barbarians*. Dublin: Four Courts.
–. 1995. 'Writing the Vernacular and the Formation of the Medieval West.' In Michael Richter. *Studies in Medieval Language and Culture*. Dublin: Four Courts. 218–27.
–. 2000. 'Medieval Oral and Literate Culture: Siamese Twins?' In *Drugie srednie veka. K 75 letiyu A. Ya. Gurevicha* [The Other Middle Ages. Festschrift for Aron Gurevich on his 75th Birthday]. Moscow: Universitetskaya kniga. 288–96.
–. 2001. 'The Aesthetic Dimension of Oral Performances in the Early Middle Ages.' In *Verbal Art across Cultures: The Aesthetics and Proto-Aesthetic Forms of Communication*. Ed. Hubert Knoblauch and Helga Kotthoff. Tübingen: Narr. 273–80.
–. 2002. 'Vom beschränkten Nutzen des Schreibens im Frühmittelalter.' In *Vom Nutzen des Schreibens. Soziales Gedächtnis, Herrschaft und Besitz im Mittelalter*. Ed. Walter Pohl and Paul Herold. Forschungen zur Geschichte des Mittelalters 5; Österreichische AW, Phil.-Hist. Klasse 306. Vienna: Österreichische AW. 193–202.
–. 2005. 'Oral Communication.' In *Comunicare e significare nell'Alto Medioevo, 15 – 20 aprile 2004*. Settimane di studio della Fondazione Centro Italiano di Studi sull'Alto Medioevo 52. Spoleto: Presso la Sede della Fondazione. 448–67.
–. 2006. 'Concept and Evolution of the *tres linguae sacrae*.' In *Language of Religion – Language of the People: Medieval Judaism, Christianity and Islam*. Ed. Ernst Bremer et al. Mittelalterstudien des Instituts zur Interdisziplinären Erforschung des Mittelalters und seines Nachwirkens 11. Paderborn: Fink. 15–23.
–. 2008. 'Latin and the Rise of Old Irish and Old Welsh.' In *Latin écrit – roman oral? De la dichotomisation à la continuité*. Ed. Marieke van Acker, Rika van Deyck, and Marc van Uytfanghe. Corpus Christianorum, Lingua Patrum 5. Turnhout: Brepols. 115–23.
Roberts, Colin H., and T. C. Skeat. 1983. *The Birth of the Codex*. London: OUP.
Southern, R. W. 1970. *Western Society and the Church in the Middle Ages*. Harmondsworth: Penguin.
Stokes, Whitley, and John Strachan, eds. 1901–3. *Thesaurus Palaeohibernicus: A Collection of Old Irish Glosses, Scholia, Prose, and Verse*. 2 vols. Cambridge: CUP.
Sutton, E. W., and H. Rackham, eds. and trans. 1948. Cicero. *De Oratore. I. Books I, II*. London: Heinemann.
Tagliavini, Carlo. 1973. *Einführung in die romanische Philologie*. Trans. R. Meisterfeld and U. Petersen. Munich: Beck.
Werminghoff, Albert, ed. 1906. *Concilia Aevi Karolini*. I.1. MGH Concilia 2. Hannover: Hahn.
Wright, Roger. 1982. *Late Latin and Early Romance in Spain and Carolingian France*. Liverpool: Cairns.

# 4 Orality and Literacy: The Case of Anglo-Saxon England

*Katherine O'Brien O'Keeffe*

> Vnde ego te, lector, relegis qui haec sedulus, oro,
> Intentas adhibere sonis caelestibus aures.[1]

In the more than fifty years of debate over evidence of orality and literacy in the surviving records of Anglo-Saxon literature, interest has shifted from construing orality and literacy as discrete and impermeable social states to envisioning them as complex social conditions coexisting with one another and affecting each other to a greater or lesser degree.[2] Early approaches to medieval orality, which primarily focused on vernacular poetry (the test case of orality from the viewpoint of composition), have been enriched by the broader interests of later studies that examine conditions for the reception of vernacular poems, study the elements of oral poetics with literate culture, identify oral features in Anglo-Latin verse, and argue the evidence for orality in varieties of Anglo-Saxon prose, both Latin and vernacular.[3] To a greater or lesser extent, these latter approaches necessarily conceptualize and pursue orality and literacy less as two hypothetical states than as interconnected social conditions.[4] At some point in their lives all people are 'oral' peoples, and the evidence of early medieval European cultures shows the 'oral' and the 'literate' affecting and forming or deforming one another.[5] In the last two decades, a number of important studies have explored the varieties of orality and of literacy specific to medieval societies. Challenging the either/or of the strong hypothesis on the mutually exclusive states of orality and literacy, such studies have shown the extent to which vocality (*Vokalität*, with the sense of vocalizing when writing or reading aloud to an audience) and 'writtenness' (*Schriftlichkeit*, usefully nuancing 'literacy' in referring to the commitment of texts to writing) interact in complex ways.[6]

---

[1] 'Therefore I ask you, reader, as you carefully read and re-read this, to lend attentive ears to the sounds from heaven.' Riese 1906:50 (item 493a) (Schaller-Könsgen 5836). See p. 134 and n. 47 below.
[2] On the 'symbiosis between the spoken and the written word' see Green 1994:17. See now the important review of the interaction of orality and literacy in Grotans 2006: ch. 1.
[3] On oral poetics within literate culture see Amodio 2004. For oral features in Anglo-Latin verse see, for example, Lapidge 1979; Orchard 1994. For prose see, for example, Orchard 1992; Wieland 1997.
[4] On the so-called 'strong' and 'weak' theses of orality and literacy see Stock 1990: 5–11.
[5] For an incisive survey of approaches to orality and literacy (here made under the umbrella of 'medieval communication') see Mostert 1999: esp. 22–28, and his bibliography, 193–297.
[6] On *Vokalität* and *Schriftlichkeit* see Bäuml 1993:255; Bäuml 1997:123–24. For verse see Schaefer 1992.

To consider the interrelation of orality and literacy from such an interactive perspective requires a pragmatically social approach that investigates their appearance in a particular society at particular times, since the specific interrelation of the two hypothetical conditions is exquisitely driven by the social conditions in which these two ways of living in the world find themselves. In the following essay, I look at some ways in which elements of 'oral' and 'literate' ways of knowing may be seen to co-exist and affect each other at three particular moments in the written culture (that is to say that part of its culture for which records still exist) of Anglo-Saxon England – Bede's account of the testing of Caedmon's poetic gift; the literacies of King Alfred; and reading practice in the late Anglo-Saxon classroom. I will argue in what follows that Latin, the language of church and learning, was not immune to the power of the oral any more than the vernacular, the language of the cradle, was immune to the power and potential of writing. In these discrete moments, I should like to consider in what ways elements of each hypothetical state, orality and literacy, can be seen in interaction with the other; what social practices were represented in these moments; and what ideology was at work in representing the interaction of these conditions.

## 1 Bede and the Uses of Orality and Literacy

Interpreters of the now iconic scene of orality and literacy provided by Bede's account of Caedmon in the *Historia ecclesiastica* have generally read the story of Caedmon's divine gift in terms of a confrontation of two pure states, the oral, represented by Caedmon the unlettered cowherd, and the literate, represented by his learned interlocutors from the monastery of Whitby, in whose presence Caedmon's gift was tested (*doctioribus uiris praesentibus*) (Colgrave and Mynors 1969:414–20 [IV.24], at 416). Although this scene has been thought to reveal the very early operation of primary orality in the person of Caedmon (especially since the event must antedate 680, i. e. the death of Hild),[7] I should like to investigate the narrative as a measure of Bede's use of the interactions of these two modes of knowing.[8] To illustrate what I mean by such interaction requires considering how Bede's narrative represents the effect that Caedmon the illiterate has on the learned religious community that first tests and then incorporates him in their midst. Caedmon's innocence of reading is clearly of strategic importance to Bede's narrative, which carefully presents Caedmon as illiterate even after he had joined himself to Whitby by taking monastic vows. It is instructive to compare Felix's portrayal of Guthlac, Caedmon's later Mercian contemporary. Upon his conversion to the religious life, Guthlac, though he had spent his youth and young manhood in a warband, was set to

---

[7] Classically, Magoun 1955. See also Opland 1980; Fry 1981:288. For 'primary orality' see Ong 1982:11 and ch. 3.

[8] Irvine (1994) argues that Bede's account of Caedmon is 'not a story of a lost, reconstructable, oral past, but an especially valuable disclosure of the textuality of grammatical culture at work in Old English poems' (433–34). He reads Caedmon's *Hymn* as a 'gloss' (434) to contemporary Latin culture. Irvine is primarily interested in deconstructing the myth of origins to which Bede's account has lent itself. O'Donnell (2005:28) finds little to be learned 'about Cædmon's œuvre or methods of composition from Bede's account', instead reading Bede's narrative for its Christian ideology.

letters (*litteris edoctus*) upon joining the monastic community at Repton.[9] While Guthlac's continuous psalmody in his eremitic retreat at Crowland was doubtless a performance from memory, Felix portrays the saint at Repton as competently literate. We are told that Guthlac learns of the acts of the desert fathers that would inspire him to the anchoritic life by reading about them (cap. 24, *legebat*).[10]

While his subject's illiteracy suits Bede's narrative purposes, as I shall argue more fully below, we ought not interpret that condition as stigmatizing Caedmon in his new monastic community. Bede's description of the community of Whitby in the previous chapter (IV.23) suggests strongly that many, though not all, members of its community could read.[11] Neither is there any sense of inadequacy attached to Caedmon's labour of memory, by which he preserved the content of the religious history he heard from his learned teachers. Indeed, as we shall see, prodigious memory was not the sole preserve of the oral but was required for learning to read and for the contemporary practice of reading. However, Caedmon's continuing formal illiteracy suited Bede's narrative, not because it necessarily portrayed him as an oddity within the monastery, but because it enabled Bede to claim him as a pure vessel for receiving the matter of his poetry through the learned instruction of the brothers of Whitby. For the narrative of the capture of vernacular poetry for Christian purposes to do its work, it had to be clear that Caedmon's poetry was the effect of divine grace (*caelestem* [...] *gratiam*; *gratiam Dei*) (Colgrave and Mynors 1969:416, 418 [cap. 24]). God's continuing grace is highlighted by Caedmon's illiteracy, which represents for Bede a state of nature, if nature redeemed by a divine gift. By its counterpoint of illiteracy and grace, Bede's narrative of God's recuperation of vernacular poetry shows Caedmon not as an author in our sense (that is, an agent who 'makes' a text), but as a vessel (of God's gift and the brothers' teaching) and a vehicle (for the production of sanctified verse faithful to Christian teaching). In this way, the orthodoxy of his verse is ensured by the learning of the community (carefully extolled in IV.23) and Caedmon's own 'clean' processes of rumination and memorization (*rememorando* [...] *ruminando*).[12]

The dynamic and interactive elements of oral and literate processes are illustrated in Bede's description of the test of Caedmon's gift:

> [...] exponebantque illi quendam sacrae historiae siue doctrinae sermonem, praecipientes eum, si posset, hunc in modulationem carminis transferre. At ille suscepto negotio abiit, et mane rediens optimo carmine quod iubebatur conpositum reddidit.

---

[9] Colgrave 1956:84 (cap. 22). The *Vita* post-dates c. 720. Colgrave gives 674 as the probable date of Guthlac's birth (p. 2). Caedmon's gift is generally dated to somewhat before 680, the year of Hild's death. On the problem of dating Caedmon's gift, retirement to the monastery, and death see O'Donnell 2005:10, n. 6.

[10] One of Guthlac's miracles involves the recovery of a document written by another brother and snatched by a crow (cap. 37, 'membranas quasdam scribens'). See Wieland 1997:175, who examines 'entrenched oral thought patterns' in Felix's text.

[11] [...] *ut facillime uiderentur ibidem qui ecclesiasticum gradum, hoc est altaris officium, apte subirent plurimi posse repperiri* (that there might be no difficulty in finding many there who were fitted for holy orders, that is, for the service of the altar) (Colgrave and Mynors 1969:408–9).

[12] Colgrave and Mynors 1969:418 (cap. 24). For Bede's allegorical understanding of rumination see Wieland 1984.

They then read to him a passage of sacred history or doctrine, bidding him make a song out of it, if he could, in metrical form. He undertook the task and went away; on returning next morning he repeated the passage he had been given, which he had put into excellent verse. (Colgrave and Mynors 1969: 418–19)

I cite Colgrave and Mynors' translation here for its general accuracy, but also for an overtranslation that is material to this discussion. Colgrave and Mynors are right, I would argue, to translate *reddidit* as 'repeated'. The senses of this verb range from 'return' (i. e. to give back something unchanged) to 'represent' or 'render',[13] but Bede's language insists that Caedmon is changing nothing material in fashioning his 'acceptum' into English verse. That insistence drives the phrase *optimo carmine quod iubebatur conpositum*, for Bede's point is that Caedmon *repeated* what he had been assigned, returning it only 'arranged' or 'devised' in excellent verse. Since Bede's understanding of verse is that it does not change but merely adorns the 'sensus',[14] Bede himself could be faithful to the meaning of Caedmon's *Hymn* in his Latin translation of it, while explicitly acknowledging that he could not capture either the poem's style or its beauty.[15]

By contrast, in over-translating *exponebant* as 'read', Colgrave and Mynors force the scene of Caedmon's test into a simple confrontation of the oral and the literate. Bede's representation of the interaction of oral and literate ways of knowing in the *Historia ecclesiastica* in this chapter is considerably more subtle. For the book as such hovers precisely *outside* the chapter and scene in question. Had his examiners' test of the authenticity of Caedmon's gift been a reading of Scripture to the illiterate cowherd, what could Caedmon have made of the (Latin) language of their text? Bede's narrative at this point is not cleverly eliding an act of reading and translation in the account of Caedmon's test. Rather, Bede has the learned brothers of Whitby tell Caedmon a story from Holy Scripture in their shared language. *Exponebant* simply continues the earlier – and crucial – observation that whatever Caedmon learned of Scripture, he learned through interpreters (*quicquid ex diuinis litteris per interpretes disceret*) (Colgrave and Mynors 1969: 414). Caedmon's interlocutors' double function is implicit in the word *interpres* in both senses, that is, one who explains (in an exposition of Scripture) and translates (from one language to another).[16] But the source of knowledge to which both poet and teachers appeal, Holy Scripture (*diuinis litteris*), is the writing and the book that hover just outside this scene. On this understanding, their encounter, in pragmatic terms 'oral'

---

[13] Lewis and Short, s. v. *reddo*. Sense 1 is to 'return' or 'give back' or 'restore', but sense 4a suggests translation (whose synonyms are 'converto' and 'transferro'), and sense 4b suggests 'repeat, declare, report, narrate, recite, rehearse'. Senses 5–7 suggest giving back with changes: i. e. as 'represent' or 'render'.

[14] Lewis and Short, s. v. *compositus*, sense D1. See Colgrave and Mynors 1969: 416, where Bede himself preserves the 'sensus' in his Latin translation of Caedmon's *Hymn* at the expense of the Old English's *decoris ac dignitatis*. Carruthers (1990: 190) observes: 'There is, as it were, *an intention of the text* which can, and indeed must, be translated from one mind to another and adapted to suit occasions and circumstances. This adaptation was not believed to substantively alter the enduring *res* (or "sentence," as it was called in English), which is in a continual process of being understood, its plenitude of meaning being "perfected" and "corrected".' O'Donnell (2005: 19) believes that of primary significance to Bede was 'the beauty and power of his [Caedmon's] verse'.

[15] *Hic est sensus, non autem ordo ipse uerborum* (Colgrave and Mynors 1969: 416).

[16] Latham, Howlett, et al. 1975– : s. v. *interpres*, senses 2 and 4.

on both sides, illustrates the interconnection of readers and hearers in relation to a book (here Scripture) and exposes Bede's ideological use of both oral and literate ways of knowing.

4 – Caedmon's Hymn (Cambridge, MS Kk.4.1b, fol. 128v, top four lines)

Because the relation between Caedmon and his examiners in the narrative of the 'origins' of vernacular poetry is more complex than a simple confrontation of two categorical conditions, 'oral' and 'literate', it is important to capture the work *exponere* performs in the passage. *Exponebant* – with its senses of 'relate' and 'explain' as it echoes the phrase *per interpretes* at the introduction of the chapter – forefronts the status of Caedmon's monastic interlocutors as learned members of a community of textual interpretation.[17] At the same time, the force of that word in the scene of testing portrays an intimate economy of oral and literate modes of knowing, where the literati's knowledge of Christian history, imparted to Caedmon, is transformed into beautiful poetry without any loss of truth. That economy of knowledge – and its truth – depends upon their culture's acceptance of the trustworthiness of memory, both his learned interpreters' memory of sacred narrative as well as Caedmon's memory of the details of the accounts they had committed to his poetic gift.[18] It also depends crucially on the understanding that the *res* in a communication is not substantially changed by variation in individual expression. Across the divide of their differing relations to the written text is a shared reliance on memory – of each and of all – to preserve the sense of the sacred narrative imparted to Caedmon as well as the text that he fashioned from it. If Caedmon's literary production is represented as preserving, intact, the truth of his teachers' accounts, its

---

[17] Lewis and Short, s. v. *expono*, II B ('set forth, exhibit, relate, explain, expound'). On the simple requirement of a text (not a book), and audience, and at least one learned interpreter for a textual community to exist see Stock 1990: 37. See also Howe 1993: 69.

[18] The Old English translation of Bede's text makes the memorial nature of their charge to Caedmon clear: *Þa rehton heo him 7 sægdon sum halig spell 7 godcundre lare word* (Then they instructed him and uttered a holy narrative and words of divine teaching). See Miller 1890–98; I.2, p. 344, line 25. On *rehton* see Bosworth Toller, s. v. *reccan*, sense V 'to unfold the meaning of, to explain, interpret, expound'.

value added is a kind of sacred pleasure, which attracted to the truths of religion all who heard his verse. Just as the learned men of Whitby fill Caedmon's ears with the narratives of sacred history which he was able to learn by hearing (*quae audiendo discere poterat*), Caedmon, in his turn, reproduces his teachers as listeners (*doctores suos uicissim auditores sui faciebat*). In that activity, his teachers also become vessels which receive back by hearing the beautiful, vocalized truth they had explained to him.[19]

The reliability of Caedmon's textual production in Bede's account (where poetry simply adorns the *sensus*) depends on the trustworthiness (= orthodoxy) of the content of the explanation his *interpretes* convey. That trustworthiness is vouchsafed by the description of his interlocutors as *doct(i)ores* in the narrative of the *Historia ecclesiastica* IV.24 and by the preceding chapter (IV.23), which praises Hild's vigorous insistence on the study of Scripture and on the performance of good works by all in her monastery.[20] Her insistence on these twin activities is the reason, Bede suggests, why five men under her rule at Whitby became bishops. Of these five, Oftor, later bishop of Worcester, was sufficiently distinguished to study with Archbishop Theodore in Kent.[21] Although Hild's monastery, and Hild herself, were known for producing extremely learned and literate men, we have no way of assessing whether Hild was herself literate or simply the cause of literacy in others.[22] Bede is clear about Hild's strenuous encouragement of the reading of Scripture, and we know her protégé, Ælflæd, wrote a letter in Latin.[23] But whether the abbess herself could read and write is a matter of doubt on which Bede takes no opportunity to enlighten us. Bede does make clear, however, that the highly trained brothers of Hild's community test Caedmon's gift at Hild's command, and after the learned brothers of Whitby 'explained' (*exponebant*) a passage of Scripture and doctrine, Caedmon transferred (*transferre*) what he received into verse.[24]

The two events (the instruction and the composition) in Caedmon's test are inextricably linked in Bede's portrayal of the scene. Insofar as the instructors are lettered and the pupil is not, 'oral' and 'literate' practices contrast in the scene, but only to a limited degree. For all the superb Latin literacy of the *Historia ecclesiastica*, the book as a cultural object hovers just outside the scene we have been reading. Caedmon's learned interlocutors convey knowledge contained in books, but they do so in the vernacular and by voicing the sacred narrative that constitutes his test. Caedmon receives this information by listening. Nonetheless, in the test, Caedmon is thrust formally into the culture of the book: its contents are the measure of faithfulness on both sides.

---

[19] Colgrave and Mynors 1969: 418–19. Frantzen (1990: 142) deconstructs Bede's account of this scene to show the suppressed terms in a set of binaries, among them unlearned/learned.
[20] Colgrave and Mynors 1969: 416 (IV.24) and 408 (IV.23).
[21] Colgrave and Mynors 1969: 408 (IV.23). On Oftor see Sims-Williams 1990: 184–94; Bischoff and Lapidge 1994: 172 and 267; and Wallace-Hadrill 1988: 164.
[22] See Neuman de Vegvar 1996: 55–63. Lees and Overing (2001: 22) argue that Bede's structuring of the chapters of the *Historia Ecclesiastica* (IV. 23 and 24) occludes Hild's role in the story of Caedmon.
[23] See Fell 1981: 95–99. On Ælflæd see Colgrave 1968: 40. For Anglo-Saxon religious women who wrote in the seventh century see Stevenson 2005: II, 86.
[24] Frantzen (1990: 139) usefully points out that Caedmon's 'song became the center of an ever-widening interpretive community'.

As we have seen, Caedmon's continuing, positive status as unlettered in the narrative has a double ideological function: in the first instance it is meant to guarantee that his poetic ability does not come from men but from God; in the second instance it offers assurance that the content of his form is trustworthy as an effect of the orthodoxy of interpretation in the renowned abbey of Whitby. In the moment of instruction, the teachers recount and Caedmon listens; in the moment of performance, Caedmon sings and his teachers listen. These two events enact an oral economy apart from, but critically dependant, on the book. This is the point of the preceding chapter (IV.23), which functions importantly to set up the standards of the textual community that first tests then accepts Caedmon as an integral member of the monastery of Whitby in the *Historia ecclesiastica* IV.24.

By these observations I do not wish to argue that Caedmon and his learned interlocutors were 'equal' or that 'oral' and 'literate' practices were equally valued within a monastic economy. I do argue, however, that in Bede's narrative the oral poet Caedmon was prized in a particular way because of his illiteracy. Bede shows his incorporation into the community of Whitby for the value of what he produced, and that value was closely dependent on his innocence of writing: his gift was not the power to interpret (with which Bede associates reading) but the power to ornament what he heard. Interpretation, with its formal relation to written texts, was a practice reserved to the cowherd's learned teachers. Caedmon is shown to be of use to God (and to the community) as the medium through which an uncorrupt *sensus* was made attractive to others like him. That it also attracted and moved his monastic teachers speaks to the continuing position of honour that orality and its art forms played in the dynamic interaction between two ways of interacting with books.

## 2 The Literacies of King Alfred

The reading history of King Alfred, given the king's differing strategies of interacting with the culture of writing during his lifetime, provides a rich opportunity to examine some ways of interacting with books in the later ninth century. Our picture of Alfred and his use of books (as objects in themselves and as elements in the development of royal bureaucracy) is substantially complicated by the eagerness of his biographer, Asser, to portray the king as an ideal Christian ruler.[25] These complications are in part a consequence of Asser's understanding of literacy as the ability to read and write in Latin. But while that is portrayed as the goal of the king's education in literacy, Asser shows us a number of styles of interacting with books (in the vernacular as well as in Latin).

In the final chapter of the biography, Asser shows Alfred as the most penetrating of judges, committed to justice and truth, and in their service demanding that those functioning as judges in his kingdom learn to give better judgments (cap. 106). Alfred is shown to demand of incompetent and ignorant judges that they learn wisdom or lose their office: *Quapropter aut terrenarum potestatum ministeria, quae habetis, illico dimittatis, aut sapientiae studiis multo devotius docere ut studeatis, impero* (For that reason, I

---

[25] Stevenson 1959; Keynes and Lapidge 1983; Pratt 2007a.

command you either to relinquish immediately the offices of worldly power you possess, or else to apply yourselves much more attentively to the pursuit of wisdom).[26] Asser's explanation of the consequence of this order – that both ealdormen and reeves immediately turned to this task – makes a telling equivalence. While the king commands his judges learn wisdom, Asser's understanding of the command equates *sapientia* with learning to read. And so unlettered officials (*illiterati*) apply themselves to the unaccustomed labour of learning to read. While Asser is perfectly clear in equating acquiring wisdom with becoming lettered, he also indicates that in the case of anyone unable to learn how to read (because of age or inaptitude) the king ordered a son, or a kinsman, or a servant to read for him: *libros ante se die nocteque, quandocumque unquam ullam haberet licentiam, Saxonicos imperabat recitare* (ordered [him] to read out books in English to him by day and night, or whenever he had the opportunity).[27] And while this shift in acquiring knowledge – from reading for oneself to hearing a text read – is represented as satisfactory (the officials seem to have kept their offices), Asser closes the chapter with the frustration of non-readers. Those who couldn't read both congratulate the present youth on their enviable abilities in the liberal arts (*liberalibus artibus*) and regret their own lack, having neither learned in youth or been able to learn in old age. We have come a long way from Alfred's '*sapientiae* [...] *studium et operam*' (line 35) to mastery of the *artes liberales* which the untutored learn to esteem. As we will see, Asser's notion of full literacy meant reading in Latin. Nonetheless, in this final chapter of the biography, his portrayal of practical literacy for officials in Alfred's kingdom indicates that it was sufficient to acknowledge books as the source of wisdom, have books available, and have a lettered reader as interface with the world of writing.[28] By this means an unlettered judge might avail himself of wisdom by inserting himself aurally into reading.

Asser offers us two important scenes of Alfred's own reading which in different ways show the incorporation of someone otherwise unlettered into the world of writing. In effect, they show us differing 'literacies' in the same individual over time. In the first scene (cap. 23), where Osburh offers a book to whichever of her sons can learn its contents most quickly, we are shown the boy Alfred, incapable of reading, though led on by divine inspiration to learn, and thus acquire the book.[29] To win the competition, Alfred brings the book to a 'magister', who reads it aloud in order for the boy to learn its contents by memory. We have an approximate idea of when in the king's life this incident occurred. In the previous chapter (cap. 22) Asser reports that Alfred remained *illiteratus* until age twelve or later and blames it on the *incuria* (negligence) of both parents and tutors (Stevenson 1959:20 [cap. 22]). It is doubtful that by this statement Asser is claiming that education in reading was expected of royal children, but rather is shifting

---

[26] Stevenson 1959:93–94 (cap. 106, lines 36–39); Keynes and Lapidge 1983:110. Wormald (1999:429, 481–82) argues that although there were written laws, the law remained primarily an oral process.

[27] Stevenson 1959:94 (cap. 106, lines 52–54); Keynes and Lapidge 1983:110.

[28] On 'litteratus' referring to an individual who could read and write in Latin see Grundmann 1958. On 'pragmatic' as opposed to professional literacy see Parkes 1973:555–56.

[29] For readings of this scene see Lerer 1991: esp. 48, who explores Osburh's relation to reading. See also on this point Ong 1982:112–15. Lees and Overing (2001: esp. 47–48) contest the unexamined use of 'maternal' and 'paternal' in the structuring of royal literacy.

blame for the boy's inability to read from Alfred (portrayed as an eager learner) to those responsible for the youth.[30] We ought not to be misled by a simple translation of *illitteratus* by its Modern English reflex, 'illiterate'. As D. H. Green has argued, for a layman, exposure to literacy through the hearing of written works, did not constitute 'illiteracy' in any pure sense. Rather, Green would describe such an individual as 'quasi litteratus' on the basis of the individual's social interaction with written texts through hearing (1994:288). Around 861 (or so), that is, around age twelve, Alfred might fairly be described as unlettered, but his eager desire for the book his mother offers to her sons (so approvingly described by Asser) shows him already to be *within* a culture of reading, recognizing the power of written texts and desiring to be associated with them. It is this desire that Asser seems to extend to the unlettered ealdormen, reeves, and, thegns of the final chapter.

The attraction of being within reading is pointedly illustrated by Alfred's keeping of a prayer book, shortly thereafter. After winning Osburh's book of vernacular verse, Alfred learned some elements of the hours, the psalms, and a variety of prayers (cap. 24). Asser gives us no chronology beyond merely describing this activity as after the contest with the book (*post haec*). These liturgical texts, we are told, Alfred kept at hand in a book which never left his side. What was the practical function of this book, given two likelihoods at this point in his life – that the prayers were in Latin, and that Alfred couldn't read the book, since Asser reports that he was unable to read Latin until November 887 (cap. 87)?[31] It is most likely that what Latin prayers Alfred recited he had by rote memory. How then are we to regard the book he carried with him at this time? I suggest that at this stage of his life this book performed three functions in locating Alfred within reading: possessing it associated Alfred with the community of readers; carrying it made him a 'user' of books, and keeping it always by him (Asser says the book was *secum inseparabiliter*) was a sign of the atheling's pious disposition. From this perspective, the prayer book was a material substitute for what Asser claims Alfred wanted most of all, knowledge of the liberal arts, denied him by the lack of teachers (Asser's word is *lectores*) in England (cap. 24).

Almost a quarter century later, Alfred carries a book into another scene of reading, this time where the king was listening to his biographer, reading and commenting on an unnamed Latin text (cap. 87–89). As Asser was reading aloud to the king from 'a certain book' (*ex quodam* [...] *libro*) (Stevenson 1959:73 [cap. 88, l. 3]), the king suddenly produced his own book, which, Asser observes at this point, he carried with him always. Asser's descriptions of the contents of this book suggest that it was the same book of

---

[30] On skills suitable for an *ætheling*, see Abels 1998:95.
[31] Compare, for example, London, BL MS Harley 2965, a Latin prayer book known as the Book of Nunaminster and associated, perhaps, with Ealhswið, wife of King Alfred (Ker, *Catalogue*, no. 237; Gneuss, *Handlist*, no. 432). The so-called Book of Cerne (Cambridge, University Library MS Ll.1.10) is a Latin prayer book with a contemporary Old English 'Exhortation to Prayer' (fol. 2r) after which follow the Latin texts. Brown (1996) dates the making of the book to 820 X 840 in Mercia. Brown finds the Old English 'Exhortation' 'an essential adjunct to the compilation' (p. 130). Nonetheless, the following gospel excerpts, prayers, and breviate psalms are in Latin. Muir (1988: xxii) notes that liturgical manuscripts before 950 do not contain translations into Old English. For Alfred and prayer in the 890s see Kershaw 2001: esp. 210–13.

prayers mentioned in cap. 24. In that chapter, Asser describes the contents of Alfred's book as *cursum diurnum, id est celebrationes horarum, ac deinde psalmos quosdam et orationes multas* (the 'daily round', that is the services of the hours, and then certain psalms and many prayers); similarly, in cap. 88 the contents of the book Alfred produces are described as *diurnus cursus et psalmi quidam atque orationes quaedam, quas ille in iuventute sua legerat* (the day-time offices and some psalms and certain prayers which he had learned in his youth).[32] Alfred's following command that Asser copy into that book the Latin passage he had just explicated transforms the book and Alfred's relation to it. Because Asser found no room to add a passage in the book (had Alfred not noticed?), he prepares a fresh quire to add to the book so that it could accommodate further passages that the king might select from their conferences. At this point the book becomes quite a different kind of object from the prayer book that simply attested to the texts Alfred carried in his memory. In Asser's account of Alfred's relation to reading at this point, the new quire, swiftly filling up with passages in Latin copied at the king's command, inspires the king to imagine a new relation to Latin and to reading, to the book, and to other audiences. That is, the altered book alters Alfred's own relation to books and reading:

> Nam primo illo testimonio scripto, confestim legere et in Saxonica lingua interpretari, atque inde perplures instituere studuit [...]. Hic aut aliter [...] divinitus instinctus, praesumpsit incipere in venerabili Martini solemnitate. [Illosque] flosculos undecunque collectos a quibuslibet magistris discere et in corpore unius libelli, mixtim quamvis, sicut tunc suppetebat, redigere, usque adeo protelavit quousque propemodum ad magnitudinem unius pasl̇terii perveniret.[33]
>
> Now as soon as that first passage had been copied, he was eager to read it at once and to translate it into English, and thereupon to instruct many others [...]. [T]he king likewise [...] prompted from heaven, took it upon himself to begin on the rudiments of Holy Scripture on St Martin's Day [11 November] and to study these flowers collected here and there from various masters and to assemble them within the body of one little book (even though they were all mixed up) as the occasion demanded. (Keynes and Lapidge 1983:100)

This passage suggests some social dimensions of the interplay of orality and literacy at Alfred's court. The king as represented at the beginning of the scene is, in Green's sense, 'quasi litteratus', that is *within* reading (as one who benefits from books) without himself being able to read (at this point in Latin). With the preparation of a separate quire for collecting passages (and with the help of Asser as amanuensis), the king imagines his expanded book as a repository of knowledge that he might share with others through reading and translation. As Asser portrays it, on the feast of St. Martin, Alfred transforms himself into a *litteratus*, able to read Latin, and constantly in possession of his now psalter-sized enchiridion, from which he drew great comfort (*in quo non mediocre, sicut tunc aiebat, habebat solatium*).[34]

---

[32] Stevenson 1959:21 (cap. 24, ll. 1–3); Keynes and Lapidge 1983:75; and Stevenson 1959:73 (cap. 88, ll. 7–8); Keynes and Lapidge 1983:99. Keynes and Lapidge 1983 reasonably translate *legit* in cap. 23, l. 14 and *legerat* in cap. 88, l. 9 as 'learnt', given the difficulties posed by the construction 'et legit' in cap. 23, l. 14. See Keynes and Lapidge 1983:239, n. 48.

[33] Stevenson 1959:75 (cap. 89, ll. 15–19). I have adopted the Keynes' and Lapidge's suggested emendation of the text's nonsensical *quos* (at l. 15) to *illosque* (1983:269, n. 216).

[34] Stevenson 1959:75 (cap. 89, ll. 22–23). In this account, Asser foregrounds his own role in the

Asser's narrative in cap. 88 strongly suggests that his transformation of the book (by recording passages the king selected after hearing Asser read and explain them) from prayer book to enchiridion prompted Alfred's remarkable feat of learning to understand and read Latin on the same day. Once again, as Asser presents it, the impetus for Alfred's advance toward competence in reading was the presence of a book. In this case, the newly named 'Enchiridion' of cap. 89 had been transformed from a simple prayer book to a large miscellany. If the original prayer book was an object used primarily as a sign of the king's relation to books and reading, the newly developed enchiridion is deliberately designed (by Asser's strategies of preparing first one and then other quires) as a lure to get the king to perfect his abilities in understanding written Latin.

In these two scenes (cap. 23 and cap. 89) Asser scripts Alfred at two ends of the continuum of orality and literacy. In the first, the boy knows nothing of reading, in the last the king is shown miraculously to read and understand Latin. Despite Asser's narrative predilections, in neither case is Alfred ever purely 'oral' or 'literate'. Asser's portrait of Alfred, both boy and king, shows him always in relation to a book and thus always within reading. And his representation of the king in using books shows him for the most part partaking in a form of group reading. In cap. 77–78 (where Alfred gathers his learned helpers Wærferth, Plegmund, Athelstan, Werwulf, Grimbald, John, and Asser), Asser distinguishes between being able to read on one's own (*per se ipsum*), which the king cannot do at that point,[35] and reading/learning from books with the help of teachers who read aloud (*recitare*), which is the king's regular practice. I have elsewhere explored this mode of 'corporate reading' that Asser portrays for Alfred and that the works claiming Alfred as author presuppose. In these works interactive listening with a collective of learned interpreters appears to qualify the avid listener, who is not perfectly literate, as one of the readers.[36]

Asser's interest in portraying Alfred as an ideal king extends from scenes showing the increasing naturalization of the king within literate culture to the king's efforts to expand the reach of letters by requiring a functional bureaucratic literacy (that nonetheless concedes that listeners use books). A very different document from Asser's *vita* speaks to the interpenetration of speaking and writing, oral modes and literate modes, in a domain where oral practice is still dominant. I should like to conclude this section by looking at Alfred in quite another scene of reading, which combines oral and literate practice to affirm Alfred's right to bequeath his property.

The general Old English terms of art for the Anglo-Saxon will, *gewrit* and *cwide*, the one pointing to a document the other to an oral transaction, suggest the degree to which the conveyance of property among the elite combined, in complex ways, elements of

---

king's latter day education, and in so doing reveals his own attitude to what constitutes literacy. For Asser, one is only truly *litteratus* with an ability to read and comprehend Latin.

[35] By *legere* here, Asser means to read Latin.

[36] These works are: the Old English translation of Gregory's *Regula pastoralis* (Sweet 1899); the Old English translation of Boethius (Sedgefield 1899); the Old English Soliloquies (Carnicelli 1969); the Old English translation of the first 50 psalms (O'Neill 2001); and the Law codes (Liebermann 1903–16). I explore corporate reading in O'Brien O'Keeffe 2005: 19–24. Malcolm Godden (2007) doubts Alfred's authorship of any of the translations with which he is credited. David Pratt (2007b) supports Alfred's authorship.

speech and of writing.³⁷ These words, however, do not offer a neat map to a chronological development: H. D. Hazeltine observes that *gewrit* was used earlier in the period to signify 'will', and *cwide* later, and such usage warns us against making simplistic assertions about the role of the oral in bequeathal.³⁸ It is generally agreed, however, that in Anglo-Saxon England, the making of the will proper was an oral transaction before witnesses. The written document was not the 'will' (in our understanding of the act of bequeathal) but simply evidence of a prior oral act that was itself understood as fully performative.³⁹

In their study of some 62 Anglo-Saxon wills, Brenda Danet and Bryna Bogoch, argue that Anglo-Saxon wills 'are saturated with oral residue, illustrating in a host of ways the symbiotic relationship between the document and the oral ceremony which preceded it' (1994: 127). Investigating the wills for linguistic features that might exhibit performativity, they explore wills for what they consider evidence of a 'transition to literacy' and attempts to invest 'the written document with performative power'.⁴⁰ Rather than looking forward to the triumph of the document in itself becoming dispositive, I should like to look at the ways in which the written strategies of King Alfred's will persist in acknowledging the force of the oral.⁴¹

Because of the complex history of bequeathal and inheritance in both Æthelwulf's disposition of his property to his sons and the disposition of that property as each brother died in turn, Alfred's will begins with an elaborate historical account, preparatory to the record of the will. In this account, Alfred, in the first person, recounts the details of his agreement that his older brother, Æthelred, hold their mutual property until his death; their property arrangements at the assembly at *Swinbeorg*; and the lands he would succeed to upon the death of that last brother. All was agreed in the presence of witnesses. Alfred is careful to explain that upon Æthelred's death no one adduced any evidence – oral or written – that contradicted Alfred's claim to his inheritance. The Old English makes clear the complex interaction of oral and written in this transaction: *Þa ne cydde me nan mann nan yrfegewrit ne nane gewitnesse þæt hit ænig oðer wære butan swa wit on gewitnesse ær gecwædon* (Then no one made known to me any will or testimony showing that the position was other than as we had previously agreed before witnesses).⁴²

The words in the will *yrfegewrit* (for a written document) and *gewitnesse* (for oral testimony) direct us to the two different forms of proof of inheritance that Alfred and his court understand. In both cases they are records of the past, the one written, the

---

[37] *Dictionary of Old English*, s. v. *cwide* gives 'utterance, voice, speech; something said' as the primary sense (1.1) and 'will, bequest' as sense 9. Bosworth Toller, s. v. *gewrit* sense II, glosses 'of official, formal documents'. The word's primary sense is 'something written'.

[38] See Hazeltine 1930: xii–xv. See also Sheehan 1963: 20, who points out the word's connotation of orality at the same time as it referred to a written document. On the meaning of *cwide* as a legal procedure see *Dictionary of Old English*, s. v. *cwide*, sense 9. Alfred's will uses *yrfegewrit* specifying that this is a document about inheritance.

[39] Clanchy (1993: 254) argues that 'until the thirteenth century the will was essentially an oral act, even when it was recorded in writing'.

[40] Danet and Bogoch 1994: 107; see also Danet and Bogoch 1992: 99, 101 and 112.

[41] See Harmer 1914: 15–19 (item 11), with translation at pp. 49–53. For the most recent commentary on the will see Kelly, *Electronic Sawyer*, accessed 12 June 2008. For a closely accurate translation into English see Keynes and Lapidge 1983: 173–78, and Whitelock 1979: 534–37.

[42] Harmer 1914: 16, ll. 28–30; Keynes and Lapidge 1983: 174–75.

other recounted orally. To seal Alfred's contention that the property he is about to dispose of is legitimately his by right of inheritance, Alfred produces the will of his father, Æthelwulf. In this scene of reading that the first three paragraphs of Alfred's will construct, Alfred is at the center, represented as speaking to the assembled West-Saxon councillors. We 'hear' his voice arguing and disposing at the very time that he refers to the document, his father's will, whose witness he relies on to prove his property rights after the inheritance was disputed. The king recounts that he produced Æthelwulf's will at the assembly at *Langandene*, and caused it to be read aloud. Although it is unknown precisely when, between 872 and 888, Alfred made this will, it is likely, however, that at the time he was able to read English.[43] Having the will read was simply giving the task to a professional reader and, perhaps, additionally providing a show of objectivity by removing its performance from Alfred's voice.

Alfred's father's will functions in this account as a record by which the members of the *witan* can judge the validity of Alfred's oral claim of the right to dispose of the property. Their finding that Alfred had full right to the property, is, again, a record of an oral transaction in the presence of a written document: '*7 hy þa ealle to rihte gerehton 7 cwædon þæt hy nan rihtre riht geþencan ne mihtan ne on þam yrfegewrite gehyran*' (And then they all pronounced what was right, and said that they could not conceive any juster title, nor could they [hear] one in the will).[44] This record shows the weight of oral processes in the part that speaking and listening as well as hearing the (written) will play in the deliberations. The councillors' finding, made from the reading aloud of the will and transacted orally, was further sealed by verbal pledges and signs that they would support the king's disposition of the property.[45] After these three paragraphs of recorded procedure and testimony, Alfred's will proper begins in the first person: *Ic Ælfred Westseaxena cingc mid Godes gyfe 7 mid þisse gewitnesse, gecweðe hu ic ymbe min yrfe wille æfter minum dæge* (I, Alfred, king of the West-Saxons, by the grace of God and with this witness, declare what I desire concerning my inheritance after my lifetime).[46] The written document voices the king, registering his act in the past by reproducing his formal language in the first person, present tense. It encodes the performative of the will without replacing it. After the bequeathal of estates and of money made in the will proper, Alfred reveals that several copies were made, all with the same witness, of an earlier, now repudiated, will. In a statement that underlines the evidentiary impact of such documents, Alfred says he has retrieved and burned all the copies that he could find. This deliberate undoing of the force of the written records of an earlier will, lest their con-

---

[43] Keynes and Lapidge (1983: 173–74) argue that the will was likely the product of the 880's, that the first three paragraphs of the will (in Harmer's edition the narrative of Alfred's rights to the property he is about to dispose of) should be dated before 888, and that the will proper (the bequeathals) was a more recent statement of the king's wishes closer to his death.

[44] Harmer 1914: 17, ll. 5–7 (emphasis added); Keynes and Lapidge 1983: 175. I have inserted the more literal translation of *gehyran* into Keynes and Lapidge's translation to make the point. They note this meaning of *gehyran* at p. 316, n. 15.

[45] The councillors give 'hyra wedd [...] 7 hyra handsetene' (Harmer 1914; 17, ll. 9–10). Keynes and Lapidge (1983: 316, n. 16) observe that *handseten* usually refers to the witnessing of a document, but in this case might simply refer to a gesture confirming a pledge.

[46] Harmer 1914: 17, ll. 13–15; Keynes and Lapidge 1983: 175.

tinued existence interfere in the future with his present intentions, suggests that the written wills were recognized as evidence on a par with oral testimony.

Alfred, though qualifying in Asser's eyes at the end of his life as reading and translating Latin, clearly inhabited a world of texts where memorial strategies of acquiring and retaining knowledge were shared to a greater or lesser degree by lettered and unlettered alike. A written text might function as an archive or a magic object. Alfred's prayer book did both, as it positioned him within reading and attested to his participation in the world of written texts, even though the texts in question were retained in Alfred's memory and performed by him without necessary use of the book. The will functioned similarly: clearly Alfred knew the contents of his father's will. However, here too, he retained the text, though he had another read it for the benefit of the formal, oral disposition of his councillors. Though few of them were likely to be able to read, the circumstances of their disposition of Alfred's case by hearing Æthelwulf's written will inserted them too into writing.

## 3 Reading, Speaking, and Remembering in the Late Anglo-Saxon Classroom

This chapter has looked at the ways oral and literate modes of knowing interacted at two distinct moments in Anglo-Saxon England: Bede's early eighth-century presentation of the interaction of oral and literate individuals in the late seventh century, and some late-ninth-century representations of interactive styles of literacy that admitted substantially oral individuals into the domain of the book. In both circumstances is it clear that social reliance on prodigious feats of memory is the shared territory of both oral and literate people and the arena in which they approximated one another's functions. In concluding this consideration of the interaction of orality and literacy in Anglo-Saxon England, I wish to consider the epigram of the chapter, which, as it presupposes a written text, reminds us of the continuing oral contribution in the domain of reading. These lines are taken from the prefatory epigram found in a number of manuscripts of Prosper's *Epigrammata*, one of the basic texts of the early medieval classroom.[47] In their invitation to enjoy both the content and the pleasure of Prosper's epigrams, these verses address a reader (*lector*), who is enjoined to work over (*relegis* with the sense of re-read) the text of the *Epigrammata* with attentive ears (*intentas aures*). While this sentiment is hardly original in its combination of reading with hearing (it could be repeated from innumerable other comments by writers and copyists), it is apposite in the current context from its presence in English manuscripts of this school text, its function in the early English classroom, and its illustration of the interconnection – an indeed interdependence – of oral and literate practices.[48]

---

[47] Michael Lapidge (1996:459) identifies Prosper's *Epigrammata* as one of the fundamental texts of the Anglo-Saxon curriculum. He points out that much of the sporadic glossing of the English manuscripts of the *Epigrammata* seems to derive from a common source (469).

[48] For scribal observations on the role of the body in reading see O'Brien O'Keeffe 1998:46–58. The manuscripts in question are: London, BL MS Harley 110 (s. x$^{ex}$) (Gneuss, *Handlist*, no. 415); Cambridge, University Library MS Gg. 5. 35 (s. xi med.) (Gneuss, *Handlist*, no. 12); Cambridge, Trinity

In one of these English manuscripts, Trinity College MS O.2.31, these two excerpted lines are fully marked for construal, using both symbols (dots and strokes) and letters of the alphabet, marks over and above verbal glosses for parsing information that are shared with other manuscripts. Such markings were meant to assist readers in resolving the syntax of the Latin clauses, in the case of these lines by marking out the head word and verb of the clause, the pronominal subject and object, and then identifying the subject and verb of the embedded clause (*qui relegis* [...] *sedulus*). Letters of the alphabet (*a* and *b*) do double duty in identifying and connecting subject and verb of the indirect statement (letter *a*) and then the modifier and its object (*intentas* [...] *sonis caelestibus*, letter *b*). The system used here neither supplies word order nor mark identical cases, but rather sorts out syntactic relations by signs to aid reading.[49]

These syntax markers point us graphically to the visual element in the labour of the early medieval classroom. The aspiring *lector*, working to learn Latin texts whose word order and syntactical elements differed considerably from those of the vernacular, could use such graphic markers to piece together elements connected grammatically or syntactically, or to follow vernacular order through a kind of alphabetic breadcrumbs. Such markings could be copied (more or less accurately) by scribes, left piecemeal by previous readers, or inserted on a virgin page by an enterprising reader.

But the scene of *visual* reading that these markers suggest is only a partial one. The *aures* (and *ora*) of the aspiring *lectores* were fully used in the classroom, as the classroom experience of learning was bodily (that is, using eyes, hands, mouth, and ears) and formally incorporated pain as a technique to ensure accurate memorization of the daily assignment. The oral aspects of reading, inherited from classical training, were fully alive in the Anglo-Saxon classroom. Pierre Riché, in his studies of early medieval education on the continent and in England, has outlined the ways in which the teaching of children meant primarily memorial learning, where boys would sit around the master's chair for their lessons, which were voiced for memorization.[50] Given their scarcity and expense, books were the province of the master who would read aloud and comment on the text to be learnt.[51] Texts were taught twice, once at the level of syllable (for memorization and pronunciation) and then for content. As pupils progressed in learning to read, the master or his assistant would require them to read aloud singly or in groups both to assess progress and to ensure the learning of assigned material (Parkes 1997: 8–9). In the classroom, reading and writing were *aides memoires* to the memorization of individual lessons.[52] The lesson to be learnt, dictated by the master, would be copied onto wax tablets by the students for memorization and performance the following day. Because the tablets would have to be erased for the next day's lesson, learning a lesson

---

College MS O.2.31 (s. x/xi) (Gneuss, *Handlist*, no. 190); Cambridge, Corpus Christi College MS 448 (s. x¹ or x med.) (Gneuss, *Handlist*, no. 114).

[49] On syntax markers in Anglo-Saxon manuscripts see Robinson 1973: 445–75. See also Brunk 1973: ch. 1.

[50] In the absence of specific information on girls' education it has been assumed that their classroom experience was that of boys. On early medieval education see Riché 1989: esp. 218–23. See now Grotans 2006: esp. 104–6 and 111.

[51] When pupils copied, it was done on wax tablets.

[52] Carruthers 1990: 156; on the 'oral transmission from one memory to another', see *ibid.*, p. 161.

(*acceptum*) meant committing it perfectly to memory (Law 2000: 17–21). The consequence of an imperfect performance of a lesson was a beating. The grimly humorous treatment of beatings – beatings for imperfectly memorized assignments, corporate beatings for the errors of one pupil, or the daily dread of a pupil's expected beating – in a number of the Latin *Colloquies* of Ælfric Bata, speaks both to the premium placed on memorial learning and the understanding that the impression of the rod on the child's body ensured the continuing impression of the assigned text upon his mind.[53]

The fictional pupils of Ælfric of Eynsham's *Colloquy*, which sought to teach basic conversational Latin to the children of the monastery, accept whipping as the natural concomitant of daily lessons, and dutifully claim to prefer a beating to remaining ignorant (*flagellari pro doctrina quam nescire*) (Garmonsway 1978: 18, l. 7). The dialogue, first on different secular occupations, and later on the child's experience of the round of an ordinary day in the monastery, bespeaks the combination of oral and literate modes of learning joined in the bodily memory of their assigned lessons. We must assume that the *Colloquy* was designed to be performed *memoriter* by pupils whose task was to gain speaking ability in Latin beyond the rote performance of liturgical texts they voiced in the celebration of the Office. In this sense, the *Colloquy* worked to give English-speaking pupils an opportunity to develop oral skills in the Latin language they otherwise experienced textually. From the memorial recitation of the psalter (begun from their first days in the monastery), to the memorized syllables of their elementary texts, through the recited declensions and conjugations of Latin, to the tropes of interpretation they would come to internalize, the pupils of the monastic classroom illustrate the fundamentally oral learning on which the skill of reading rested. The interpenetration of these two modes of knowledge did not end in the classroom. One of the pupils in a colloquy by Ælfric Bata explains the point of their memorization: *ut quando senes eritis, tunc memoriter in cunctis libris latinis legere possitis et aliquid intellegere in illis* (so that when you're old you'll be able to read from memory in all Latin books and understand something in them).[54] For such a statement to make sense, we have to understand that reading *memoriter* meant that the skills of literacy simply supplemented the textual archive of an oral culture – memory.

As we have seen, Bede's portrayal of the interaction of orality and literacy in his treatment of the test of Caedmon's gift was substantially driven by the need to ensure the religious truth of Caedmon's verse. He did so by emphasizing Caedmon's innocence of letters and constructing him as a vessel into which the learned brothers of Whitby could pour the truths of Scriptural history. Although this would appear to demarcate a fairly sharp division between oral and literate apprehensions of the world, it was the function of memory for both teachers and pupil that united the activities of both. Memory ensured the accuracy of the brothers' (oral) teaching and the accuracy of Caedmon's poetic transformations. And in the economy of sharing Christian truth, each was shown as the vessel of the other. Asser gives us a very different purchase on the interaction of oral and literate ways of knowing, in that he permits us to see ways in which individuals unable to read (to a greater or lesser degree) could be included within reading and how

---

[53] Gwara 1996: e. g., 41, 69, 86–88; Gwara and Porter1997: 84–85; 92–93; 166–67.
[54] Gwara 1996: Colloquy 4, ll. 4–6; Gwara and Porter 1997: 87.

individuals might make use of books they could not formally read. It is Alfred himself, however, who shows us the cultural negotiations of the oral and the literate in both the performative of the will and the legal appeals to it which combined the testimony of memory with the reading of a document. Bringing these two together is the teaching practice of the early medieval English classroom. In its call upon the eyes, ears, and mouths of its pupils, it performed its understanding of the relation of oral and literate ways of knowing. To know a text by reading is, before all, to hold it in memory. To truly know a text, one must hear it.

## References

Abels, Richard. 1998. *Alfred the Great: War, Kingship and Culture in Anglo-Saxon England*. London: Longman.
Amodio, Mark C. 2004. *Writing the Oral Tradition: Oral Poetics and Literate Culture in Medieval England*. Notre Dame, IN: U of Notre Dame P.
Bäuml, Franz. 1993. 'Verschriftliche Mündlichkeit und vermündlichte Schriftlichkeit.' In *Schriftlichkeit im frühen Mittelalter*. Ed. Ursula Schaefer. Tübingen: Narr. 254–66.
–. 1997 'Scribe et Impera: Literacy in Medieval Germany.' *Francia* 24: 123–32.
Bischoff, Bernhard, and Michael Lapidge, eds. 1994. *Biblical Commentaries from the Canterbury School of Theodore and Hadrian*. CSASE 10. Cambridge: CUP.
Bosworth Toller: Bosworth, Joseph, and T. Northcote Toller. 1882–1972. *An Anglo-Saxon Dictionary*. Ed. and enlarged by T. Northcote Toller. Supplement by T. Northcote Toller, with revised and enlarged addenda by Alistair Campbell. 2 vols. Oxford: Clarendon.
Brown, Michelle. 1996. *The Book of Cerne: Prayer, Patronage and Power in Ninth-Century England*. London: The British Library.
Brunk, Gretchen. 1973. 'Syntactic Glosses in Latin Manuscripts of Anglo-Saxon Origin.' Ph.D. Thesis, Stanford University.
Carnicelli, Thomas A., ed. 1969. *King Alfred's Version of St. Augustine's 'Soliloquies'.* Cambridge, MA: Harvard UP.
Carruthers, Mary. 1990. *The Book of Memory: A Study of Memory in Medieval Culture* Cambridge: CUP.
Clanchy, Michael T. 1993. *From Memory to Written Record: England 1066–1307*. 2nd ed. Oxford: Blackwell.
Colgrave, Bertram, ed. and trans. 1956. *Felix's Life of Saint Guthlac*. Cambridge: CUP.
–, ed. 1968. *The Earliest Life of Gregory the Great*. Lawrence: U of Kansas P.
–, and R. A. B. Mynors, eds. and trans. 1969. *Bede's Ecclesiastical History of the English People*. Oxford: Clarendon.
Danet, Brenda, and Bryna Bogoch. 1994. 'Orality, Literacy, and Performativity in Anglo-Saxon Wills.' In *Language and the Law*. Ed. John Gibbons. London: Longman. 100–35.
–, and Bryna Bogoch. 1992. 'From Oral Ceremony to Written Document: The Transitional Language of Anglo-Saxon Wills.' *Language and Communication* 12: 95–122.
*Dictionary of Old English*: Healey, Antonette diPaolo et al. 1994–. *Dictionary of Old English*. Toronto: Pontifical Institute of Mediaeval Studies. (Microfiche edition; CD–ROM edition; Online version).
Fell, Christine, E. 1981. 'Hild, Abbess of Streonæshalch.' In *Hagiography and Medieval Literature: A Symposium*, ed. Hans Bekker-Nielsen, Peter Foote, Jørgen Højgaard Jørgensen, and Tore Nyberg. Odense: Odense UP. 76–99.
Frantzen, Allen J. 1990. *Desire for Origins: New Language, Old English, and Teaching the Tradition*. New Brunswick, NJ: Rutgers UP.

Fry, Donald K. 1981. 'The Memory of Cædmon.' In *Oral Traditional Literature: A Festschrift for Albert Bates Lord*. Ed. John Miles Foley. Columbus, OH: Slavica. 282–93.
Garmonsway, G. N., ed. 1978. *Ælfric's Colloquy*. Rev. ed. Exeter: U of Exeter P.
Gneuss, *Handlist*: Gneuss, Helmut. 2001. *Handlist of Anglo-Saxon Manuscripts. A List of Manuscripts and Manuscript Fragments Written or Owned in England up to 1100*. Medieval and Renaissance Texts and Studies 241. Tempe: Arizona Center for Medieval and Renaissance Studies.
Godden, Malcolm. 2007. 'Did King Alfred Write Anything?' *Medium Ævum* 76: 1–23.
Green, D. H. 1994. *Medieval Listening and Reading: The Primary Reception of German Literature 800–1300*. Cambridge: CUP.
Grotans, Anna A. 2006. *Reading in Medieval St. Gall*. Cambridge: CUP.
Grundmann, Herbert. 1958. 'Litteratus – Illitteratus.' *Archiv für Kulturgeschichte* 40: 1–65.
Gwara, Scott, ed. 1996. *Latin Colloquies from Pre-Conquest Britain*. Toronto Medieval Latin Texts 22. Toronto: Pontifical Institute of Mediaeval Studies.
–, and David W. Porter, trans. 1997. *Anglo-Saxon Conversations: The Colloquies of Ælfric Bata*. Woodbridge, Suffolk: Boydell and Brewer.
Harmer, Florence E., ed. and trans. 1914. *Select English Historical Documents of the Ninth and Tenth Centuries*. Cambridge: CUP.
Hazeltine, H. D. 1930. 'General Preface.' In Dorothy Whitelock, ed. and trans., *Anglo-Saxon Wills*. Cambridge Studies in English Legal History. Cambridge: CUP. vii–xl.
Howe, Nicholas. 1993. 'The Cultural Construction of Reading.' In *The Ethnography of Reading*. Ed. Jonathan Boyarin. Berkeley: U of California P.
Irvine, Martin. 1994. *The Making of Textual Culture: 'Grammatica' and Literary Theory 350–1100*. Cambridge: CUP.
Kelly, *Electronic Sawyer*: Kelly, S. E. *The Electronic Sawyer*. An online version of the revised edition of *Sawyer's Anglo-Saxon Charters*, section one [S 1–1602] and adapted for the WWW by S. M. Miller. <http://www.trin.cam.ac.uk/chartwww/eSawyer.99/S%201482–1539.html>
Ker *Catalogue*: Ker, N. R. 1990. *Catalogue of Manuscripts Containing Anglo-Saxon*. 2nd ed. with supplement. Oxford. Clarendon.
Kershaw, Paul. 2001. 'Illness, Power and Prayer in Asser's *Life of King Alfred*.' *Early Medieval Europe* 10: 201–24.
Keynes, Simon, and Michael Lapidge, eds. and trans. 1983. *Alfred the Great: Asser's Life of Alfred and Other Contemporary Sources*. Harmondsworth: Penguin.
Lapidge, Michael. 1979. 'Aldhelm's Latin Poetry and Old English Verse.' *Comparative Literature* 31: 209–31.
–. 1996. 'The Study of Latin Texts in Late Anglo-Saxon England: The Evidence of Latin Glosses.' In his *Anglo-Latin Literature, 600–899*. London: Hambledon P. 455–98, 516.
Latham, R. E., D. R. Howlett, et al. 1975–. *Dictionary of Medieval Latin from British Sources*. London: OUP.
Law, Vivien. 2000. 'Memory and the Structure of Grammars in Antiquity and the Middle Ages.' In *Manuscripts and Tradition of Grammatical Texts from Antiquity to the Renaissance*. Vol. I, ed. Mario De Nonno, Paolo De Paolis, and Louis Holtz. Cassino: Università degli studi di Cassino. 9–57.
Lees, Clare, and Gillian Overing. 2001. *Double Agents: Women and Clerical Culture in Anglo-Saxon England*. Philadelphia: U of Pennsylvania P.
Lerer, Seth. 1991. *Literacy and Power in Anglo-Saxon Literature*. Lincoln: U of Nebraska P.
Lewis and Short: Lewis, Charlton T., and Charles Short. 1879. *A Latin Dictionary*. Oxford.
Liebermann, Felix, ed. and trans. 1903–16. *Die Gesetze der Angelsachsen*. 3 vols. Halle: Niemeyer.
Magoun, Francis P. 1955. 'Bede's Story of Cædman: The Case History of an Anglo-Saxon Oral Singer.' *Speculum* 30: 49–63.

Miller, Thomas, ed. 1890–98. *The Old English Version of Bede's Ecclesiastical History of the English People*. EETS 95, 96, 110, 111. Oxford.
Mostert, Marco. 1999. 'New Approaches to Medieval Communication?' In *New Approaches to Medieval Communication*. Ed. Marco Mostert with an introduction by Michael Clanchy. Utrecht Studies in Medieval Literacy 1. Turnhout: Brepols. 3–37.
Muir, Bernard James, ed. 1988. *A Pre-Conquest English Prayer-Book (BL MSS Cotton Galba A. xiv and Nero A. ii (ff. 3–13))*. Henry Bradshaw Society 103. Woodbridge, Suffolk: Boydell and Brewer.
Neuman de Vegvar, Carol. 1996. 'Saints and Companions to Saints: Anglo-Saxon Royal Women Monastics in Context.' In *Holy Men and Holy Women: Old English Prose Saints' Lives and Their Context*. Ed. Paul E. Szarmach. Albany: State U of New York P. 51–93.
O'Brien O'Keeffe, Katherine. 1998. 'The Performing Body on the Oral-Literate Continuum: Old English Poetry.' In *Teaching Oral Traditions*. Ed. John Miles Foley. New York: Modern Language Association. 46–58.
–. 2005. 'Listening to the Scene of Reading.' In *Orality and Literacy in the Middle Ages: Essays on a Conjunction and its Consequences in Honour of D. H. Green*, edited by Mark Chinca and Christopher Young. Utrecht Studies in Medieval Literacy 12. Turnhout: Brepols. 17–36.
O'Donnell, Daniel Paul. 2005. *Cædmon's Hymn: A Multi-media Study, Edition and Archive*. Cambridge: Brewer, in association with SEENET and The Medieval Academy.
O'Neill, Patrick, ed. 2001. *King Alfred's Old English Prose Translation of the First Fifty Psalms*. Medieval Academy Books 104. Cambridge, MA: Medieval Academy of America.
Ong, Walter J. 1982. *Orality and Literacy: The Technologizing of the Word*. London: Methuen.
Opland, Jeff. 1980. *Anglo-Saxon Oral Poetry: A Study of the Traditions*. New Haven: Yale UP.
Orchard, Andy. 1992. 'Crying Wolf: Oral Style and the *Sermones Lupi*.' *ASE* 21: 239–64.
–. 1994. *The Poetic Art of Aldhelm*. Cambridge: CUP.
Parkes, M. B. 1973. 'The Literacy of the Laity.' In *The Mediaeval World*. Ed. David Daiches and Anthony Thorlby. London: Aldus Books. 555–77.
–. 1997. '*Rædan, areccan, smeagan*: How the Anglo-Saxons Read.' *ASE* 26: 1–22.
Pratt, David. 2007a. *The Political Thought of King Alfred the Great*. Cambridge: CUP.
–. 2007b. 'Problems of Authorship and Audience in the Writings of King Alfred the Great.' In *Lay Intellectuals in the Carolingian World*. Ed. Patrick Wormald and Janet L. Nelson. Cambridge: CUP. 162–91.
Riché, Pierre. 1989. *Écoles et enseignement dans le Haut Moyen Âge: fin du V$^e$ siècle – milieu du XI$^e$ siècle*. 2nd ed. Paris: Picard.
Riese, Alexander, ed. 1906. *Anthologia Latina*, I.2 Leipzig: Teubner.
Robinson, Fred. C. 1973. 'Syntactical Glosses of Latin Manuscripts of Anglo-Saxon Provenance.' *Speculum* 48: 445–75.
Schaefer, Ursula. 1992. *Vokalität: Altenglische Dichtung zwischen Mündlichkeit und Schriftlichkeit*. ScriptOralia 39. Tübingen: Narr.
Schaller-Könsgen: Schaller, Dieter, and Ewald Könsgen, with John Tagliabue. 1977. *Initia carminum Latinorum saeculo undecimo antiquiorum: Bibliographisches Repertorium für die lateinische Dichtung der Antike und des frühen Mittelalters*. Göttingen: Vandenhoeck & Rupprecht.
Sedgefield, W. J., ed. 1899. *King Alfred's Old English Version of Boethius, De Consolatione Philosophiae*. Oxford.
Sheehan, Michael M. 1963. *The Will in Medieval England: From the Conversion of the Anglo-Saxons to the End of the Thirteenth Century*. Toronto: Pontifical Institute of Mediaeval Studies.
Sims-Williams, Patrick. 1990. *Religion and Literature in Western England, 600–800*. CSASE 3. Cambridge: CUP.

Stevenson, Jane. 2005. 'Anglo-Latin Women Poets.' In *Latin Learning and English Lore*. Ed. Katherine O'Brien O'Keeffe and Andy Orchard. 2 vols. Toronto: U of Toronto P. II, 86–107.

Stevenson, William Henry, ed. 1959. *Asser's Life of King Alfred*. New impression with an article by Dorothy Whitelock. Oxford: Clarendon.

Stock, Brian. 1990. *Listening for the Text: On the Uses of the Past*. Baltimore: Johns Hopkins UP.

Sweet, Henry, ed. 1899. *King Alfred's West Saxon Version of Gregory's Pastoral Care*. EETS 45, 50. London.

Wallace-Hadrill, J. M. 1988. *Bede's Ecclesiastical History of the English People: A Historical Commentary*. Oxford Medieval Texts. Oxford: Clarendon.

Whitelock, Dorothy, ed. and trans. 1979. *English Historical Documents c. 500–1042*. English Historical Documents I. 2nd ed. London: Methuen.

Wieland, Gernot. 1984. 'Caedmon, the Clean Animal.' *American Benedictine Review* 35: 194–203.

–. 1997. '*Aures lectoris*: Orality and Literacy in Felix's *Vita Sancti Guthlaci*.' *Journal of Medieval Latin* 7: 168–77.

Wormald, Patrick. 1999. *The Making of English Law: King Alfred to the Twelfth Century. I. Legislation and its Limits*. Oxford: Blackwell.

# 5 Performance and Performers

## Joseph Harris and Karl Reichl

This chapter first attempts a general model of the performance of oral literature that may prove useful for medievalists specializing in various cultures and periods (by Reichl and Harris jointly). The ensuing survey of primary evidence (which in part tests the model) and of secondary literature is divided into an early medieval period (by Harris) and a high-to-late medieval period (by Reichl) and is largely structured according to concrete 'scenes of performance' or simply 'scenes'.[1] We have attempted to maintain a focus only on performance and performers, separating our subject here from the general conditions of orality and the textual structure of oral-derived literature, topics which tend to dominate in the chapters devoted to specific cultures, genres, or periods. The performance material surveyed represents a selection of examples we hope will prove suggestive, rather than a complete catalogue. In the early medieval section, the selection concentrates on the Germanic north and west of Europe, with lesser reference to Celtic traditions of performance. The Old Norse sagas, however, will be treated as a whole in the chapter on early Germanic oral literature (ch. 8, pp. 272–73). Philological notes on the earliest vocabulary connected with performance and a look at the special problem of music follow the general exposition here as separate sections (see sections 2.4 and 3.4 below). In the high-and-late medieval part of this chapter, there will be sections on the 'scenes of performance' as they can be reconstructed from our medieval sources, on the various types of performers and popular entertainers, on their repertoire and modes of performance, and on the relationship between performance and composition (section 3.3). The ethnically based, period, and genre chapters to follow in Part II will in many cases fill in further performance-related material.[2]

---

[1] We take the term from Lars Lönnroth (especially 1978). Such vignettes are usually reported for purposes distant from our own and embody a variety of points of view which are typically far from modern 'Wissenschaft'. We attempt, in all brevity, to extract performance information by comparison to Bauman's framework sketched here and of course to cite important studies cued by the 'scenes'.

[2] See in particular chapters 8–14 and 24–27 in this volume; see also ch. 2 on the impact of the Oral Theory on medieval literature (J. M. Foley and P. Ramey) and ch. 7 on oral literature, ritual, and the dialectics of performance (P. Roilos); see further ch. 1, section 4.3.

# 1 Performance and Medieval Performance: General Model

Performance has become a key-concept in recent studies in the 'human sciences' – the social sciences and humanities – a concept so multifaceted that it can hardly be grasped as the same idea across the many fields which it now is tasked with unlocking. Richard Schechner, the father of performance theory, says, perhaps not without irony, 'Performance is an inclusive term.'[3] Among the areas treated by Schechner are play, game, sport, ritual, and of course theatre, but the discourses of many more areas of life – law, economics, technology, for starters – make liberal use of the term.[4] 'Performance studies' is a new discipline presumably sprung up to study all kinds of 'performance', yet in fact restricted mainly to the theatrical, as far as we can see.[5] For students of medieval oral literature the conceptions of performance offered by American folklorists are probably the most directly pertinent since folklorists too are dealing with 'verbal art' or 'oral literature'.[6] From its beginnings in the late 1960s, but especially in the 1970s, the Performance School in folkloristics reflected impulses, on the humanistic side, from the works of Albert Lord and Milman Parry as well as from the socially oriented literary critic Kenneth Burke; more important, however, were from the outset influences from the social sciences. In its developed form the Performance School can be seen as the outcome of, especially, the anthropological thread in the genealogy of folkloristics;[7] but a significant input from sociology and sociolinguistics is easily recognized, along with a mutual feedback relationship with the contemporarily developing new fields of ethnography of speaking/communication and ethnopoetics.[8]

Probably the most prolific spokesman for the concentration of folkloristics on performance is Richard Bauman, and a thumbnail sketch of Bauman's conception will serve here as an introduction to the topic. Performance, then, is part of *communication* and implies the classic communication model: sender – channel – code – receiver.[9] Thus a performance requires a receiving *audience* but goes beyond the simple model in that the audience is prepared to *evaluate* the act of the sender, his performance; and for his part the sender becomes a performer when he *assumes responsibility for performance*, in other

---

[3] Schechner 1988: xiii; see also Schechner's introduction to performance studies (2006). As Henry Bial remarks in his introduction to a performance studies reader, '[...] performance is contingent, contested, hard to pin down' (Bial 2007: 1), – qualities that show up in spades in its study.

[4] For a clear overview, see Carlson 1996.

[5] See Carlson 1996 and the eclectic sampling in Bial 2007, especially Kirshenblatt-Gimblett 2007.

[6] Bauman 1977 with a full bibliography. See also the entries in Bauman 1992 (especially his chapter 'Performance', pp. 41–49) for more selective and recent bibliographies. Among older contributions, we mention especially the work of Dell Hymes, in particular Hymes 1975, as influential in the field. Particularly relevant to medievalists are works in the Performance-School vein by John Miles Foley; we mention especially Foley 1992, 1995, and 2002. On 'verbal art' and 'oral literature', see Harris 1991: 9–12; on 'oral literature' see also ch. 1, pp. 3–4.

[7] Zumwalt 1988; further, Bauman 1992 (especially his essay 'Folklore', pp. 29–40).

[8] Bauman 1977; 1992; Bauman and Braid 1998; Bauman and Briggs 1990. Some examples of ethnography of speaking are the supplementary essays by Roger D. Abrahams, Gary H. Gossen, and Joel F. Sherzer in Bauman 1977; further readings in this vein are listed in Sherzer 1992. A comprehensive presentation is Saville-Troike 1989.

[9] For a more elaborate version of this model and adaptation to poetry, see Roman Jakobson's famous 'Closing Statement' (Jakobson 1960).

words acknowledges evaluation. Thus performance in Bauman's sense is usually 'an aesthetically marked and heightened mode of communication, framed in a special way and put on display for an audience.'[10] The difference between a sender or addressor communicating some message to a receiver or addressee in everyday life and a performer addressing an audience consists in that communication is successful in the former case if the message is understood, in the latter case if in addition the presentation of the message exhibits the performer's skill. The performer's display of *communicative competence* may contribute to '*enhancement of experience*' in the audience: 'It is part of the essence of performance that it offers to the participants a special enhancement of experience, bringing with it a heightened intensity of communicative interaction which binds the audience to the performer in a way specific to performance as a mode of communication. Through his performance, the performer elicits the participative attention and energy of his audience, and to the extent that they value his performance, they will allow themselves to be caught up in it' (Bauman 1977: 43). Performance is part of an 'event' which can be described and located in time and place (its *setting*), in short a *context* which has various possible relations to performance itself.[11] Bauman, however, emphasizes the establishment of a 'frame' that fixes for the audience the verbal behaviour in question not as simple communication but as performance. Yet *framing* seems to exist in degrees, and the exact description of gradations along the cline would belong to the ethnography of performance in individual cultures, for the specifics of performance are *culture-bound* even though cross-cultural general features are sought. Signals establishing the frame constitute the '*keying*' of performance and may depend on elements of context or of the code, language features that signal performance, e. g. figurative language, parallelism, formulas, appeals to tradition or special paralinguistic features. Performances are patterned events in which the *participants* (performer and audience) have important structural functions. As Bauman points out, there is considerable cross-cultural variation concerning the eligibility and recruitment of performance-roles. 'One dimension along which this variation occurs has to do with conceptions of the nature of the competence required of a performer and the way such competence is acquired' (Bauman 1977: 30). Finally Bauman emphasizes the '*emergent*' nature of folklore performance, its flexibility and sensitivity to changing circumstances.

This model – though we have severely reduced Bauman's eloquent development and totally omitted his wide-ranging examples and have thus failed to represent the texture of his argument – can serve the medievalist as a minimal initial template for the performance mechanisms that will have produced our oral-derived texts. 'Text', however, leads immediately to the great discrepancy from the folklorist's template, namely that medievalists have texts but no directly experienceable contexts, while the Performance School gives relatively little attention to the output of performance except when struggling with the necessity of 'intersemiotic translation' from the oral medium to the writ-

---

[10] Bauman 1992: 41. Instead of 'interpretive frame', Foley proposes the term 'performance arena', 'understanding by that term the locus in which some specialized form of communication is uniquely licensed to take place' (Foley 1995: 8).

[11] 'We use the term "event" to designate a culturally defined, bounded segment of the flow of behavior and experience constituting a meaningful context for action' (Bauman 1977: 27).

ten.¹² Not all contemporary folklorists approve of this privileging of context over text, and in folkloristics the subject has been sharply debated.¹³ The medievalist is in any case necessarily bound first to the text, and only from that platform can he or she attempt to ascend to any oral milieu or specifically to informed speculation on the performances from which, logically, all our oral-derived texts originate. Medieval texts themselves vary greatly in their immanent power to reveal performance origins, but for us context, performance, and audience are always more or less reconstructions and the texts on which they are based, more or less contested sites.¹⁴

Medievalists will also be more interested in the 'input' of performances than is the Performance School, which values individual creativity (signalled by the term 'verbal *art*') over the older folkloristic's 'tradition'. The input of any performance can be considered the performer's sources; they would include the content as the performer received it, together with all the 'influences' that medievalists attempt to discover, such as other versions of the inherited content, relevant milieux and performance traditions, current styles, current political situations, the performer's life and individual interests, and so on.

If the content is narrative, we may, at a certain level of generalization, consider the input to be 'story' (*histoire*), the output to be realization as 'discourse' (*discours*).¹⁵ But such a model can be misleading since 'story' will already have been realized as 'discourse' in the input: any actual person knows a story as a particular version already manifested in language. And the story/discourse theorem misleads if it suggests that the circular process is ultimately static, whereas a closer consideration will show that performance produces discourse that ultimately changes story. The ballad's 'communal recreation', the process by which ballads evolve, is an example of the dynamic aspect of performance, for the 'communal' in this process is a name for nameless individual performers.¹⁶ But the ballad, which is after all not a quintessentially medieval genre, is unusual in offering many texts of 'same' and 'different' stories. For the most part students of medieval oral-derived literature are bound to one or a few extant texts (output of the performance mechanism), on which we are dependent for reconstructing the deep web of vanished texts (and their enabling performances) and conditions that constituted the decisive input behind our precious texts. Vésteinn Ólason has tersely defined 'tradition' as 'intertextuality', using a term elsewhere reserved for the interrelations of written literature (1985). While in the fields of folklore and anthropology performance studies focus understandably on observable cases, in medieval studies the evidence has to be scruti-

---

¹² See Fine 1984 and 1998.
¹³ The text/context debate among folklorists began in 1972; most of the discussion is summed up in Georges 1980 with references. But despite Georges's 'resolution', the subject remained contentious, as witness Zan 1988, and slumbers in its cave even now awaiting the profession's need.
¹⁴ Such reconstruction, as long as it attempts to remain strictly historical, is limited by textual evidence, which must, however, always be interpreted by the individual scholar. A more artistic type of reconstruction seems justified in the case of musical performance though here too rigorous historical musicology precedes intuition. We regard Benjamin Bagby as a preeminent contemporary exponent of 'historically informed reconstruction', with its highly disciplined role for intuition. See Bagby 2005 and the web site for *Sequentia*, <www. sequentia.org>; see also the performance website by New York University, 'Performing Medieval Narrative Today', at <www.nyu.edu/projects/mednar>.
¹⁵ See Chatman's introduction to narratology (1978: 19 ff.).
¹⁶ On communal recreation, see Gerould 1932: 189 ff. ; see also ch. 16 (T. Pettitt) in this volume.

nized carefully before it yields enough clues for the reconstruction of the dynamics of oral performance. As Timothy R. Tangherlini has stressed, in the afterword to a special issue of *Western Folklore* on 'models of performance in oral epic, ballad, and song', reconstruction is possible: philological analysis can successfully extract clues about performance from texts, by a methodology variously termed 'ethnoarchaeology', 'ethnopaleography' (Dennis Tedlock) and 'ethnophilology' (Joseph Harris). And furthermore, as with the elucidation of orality in the Middle Ages in general, comparative studies of living oral traditions and oral performances provide insights that help evaluate the medieval material: 'one of the keys to this process of reanimation of the textual remnants of once vibrant traditions is a clear understanding of contemporary performances.'[17]

The genealogy of the current vital interest in performance in the medieval period can be conveniently traced to Albert Lord's famous book, *The Singer of Tales*, of 1960, gathering force with developments in folkloristics through the 1970s and with wider anthropological and historical attention to orality and literacy. But the beginnings of these subjects do date from earlier times. Without attempting a history of the study of medieval performance, we will mention a few milestones. The works of the Swiss Andreas Heusler (1865–1940) can be considered the crest of the long, slow wave of older German-language scholarship on the largely preliterate early-medieval Germanic literatures; his *Die altgermanische Dichtung* of 1923 maps that field with some attention to what we would now call performance though Heusler's main interest lies ultimately in grand patterns of genre and mentality.[18] In England his contemporary, Hector Munro Chadwick (1870–1947), together with his wife Nora Kershaw Chadwick (1891–1972), developed a sophisticated sociological approach to the early and oral literature of the world that culminated in their great three volume *The Growth of Literature* (1932–40); here and in some of Mrs. Chadwick's copious later publications a precocious sense of the oral is already to be found. Among Romance scholars we mention Gaston Paris (1839–1903), Joseph Bédier (1864–1938), and Ramón Menéndez Pidal (1869–1968), whose views on the genesis of the *chanson de geste* and related works in the Romance languages have had a decisive influence on modern scholarship. The 'theory of *cantilènes*' as proposed by Gaston Paris in his *Histoire Poétique de Charlemagne* (1865), deriving the *chansons de geste* from earlier oral lays, was vehemently opposed by Joseph Bédier, who insisted on authorial composition and became the 'father' of 'individualism' in medieval epic studies. Outside the oral-formulaic school as represented by Milman Parry and Albert Lord, Ramón Menéndez Pidal is perhaps the most important student of the oral background to medieval literature, especially epic, whose neotraditionalism combines philological method with an openness to orality as still observable for instance in the modern ballad.[19] In the nineteenth and early twentieth centuries, scholars in other European languages and countries have also made decisive contributions to our knowledge

---

[17] Tangherlini 2003:146. This issue of *Western Folklore* (62, numbers 1 and 2, ed. by Joseph Falaky Nagy) contains contributions by John D. Niles, Karl Reichl, Barre Toelken, Joseph Harris and Richard P. Martin. On Terry Gunnell's ideas about the performance of the Edda (1995), singled out by Tangherlini, see below p. 157.
[18] The second revised and expanded edition was published in 1943.
[19] On neotraditionalism, see also ch. 1, section 3.1 (pp. 16–17); on the *chanson de geste* and orality, see also ch. 12 by D. Boutet.

of medieval oral literature, especially by collecting and editing huge corpora of texts such as the collection of popular ballads by Svend Grundtvig (*Danmarks gamle folkeviser*, 6 vols. 1853–1898) and Francis J. Child (*The English and Scottish Popular Ballads*, 5 vols. 1882–1898) or of folksongs by Clemens Brentano and Achim von Arnim (*Des Knaben Wunderhorn*, 3 vols. 1805–1808).[20]

Many other nineteenth- and early twentieth-century scholars showed a passing interest in 'performance' and especially in 'performers' – we could, for example, mention L. F. Anderson, who published a good monograph on the Anglo-Saxon poet in 1903 – but delving deeper than the great figures mentioned above will be, if at all, part of the task of the language-family chapters below. All that was required of these scholars to rank in the pre-history of performance approaches was a sense of literature and its purveyors as inhabiting a largely preliterate culture. But this is a hard-won insight that came little by little in the later twentieth century. We venture to name the Norwegian Sophus Bugge (1833–1907) as an example of a towering scholar of the early period who seems never to have acquired a sense of an oral tradition, at least to judge by some of the connections he proposes for essentially preliterate times.[21] And even the best synthesizer in the area of orality, Walter Ong, could have difficulty with the concept of 'literature' *avant la lettre* (1982).

For the post–1960 period no brief survey of performance scholarship could be adequate, but we cite John Miles Foley and many of his enterprises as providing copious material for such a survey.[22] (The effort to separate 'performance' from other aspects of oral literature is, however, not usual.) In many cases our chapters on language groups, periods, and genres will provide functional surveys. But we should add that in addition to literature rooted ultimately in the South Slavic model and in the performance school, some notice should be paid to a continuation of the sociological performance line effectively begun by the Chadwicks. *The Role of the Poet in Early Societies*, by Morton W. Bloomfield and Charles W. Dunn (1989), is a prime example of this strain, with special focus on early Germanic and Celtic poetries. In the field of Romance philology the studies by Ramón Menéndez Pidal, in particular his wide-ranging research on the medieval performer as it found expression in his *Poesía juglaresca y juglares* (1957), should be mentioned. Both works have proved valuable for the understanding of performance and performers in the early and later Middle Ages and will have to be referred to again in the following sections (see pp. 162 and 170 below).

## 2 Performance and Performers in the Early Middle Ages

The first 'scene' likely to spring to mind is the skald standing before his prince or the *scop* on the mead bench of a royal hall, but early medieval verbal performance itself seems not to be entirely bound to the warrior classes implied by that setting. The story

---

[20] See also ch. 1, section 6.2 (pp. 43–45).
[21] Harris 1983; Bugge and Moe 1897 as discussed in Harris (forthcoming).
[22] Foley 1985 and 1988; see the journal *Oral Tradition*, published since 1986, with annual bibliographies; the journal is now available online at <http://journal.oraltradition.org>.

of Caedmon begins English literature at the bottom of the social scale with a cow-herd and something like a *céilidh* (*convivium*, *gebeorscipe*) among his fellow *laboratores*.[23] Since Caedmon did menial work at the abbey and reported to the reeve, his singing company must also have been of low status though they knew well how to utilize the single harp that passed in turn to each of the colleagues. Bede's story famously tells how the performance-shy Caedmon would flee when the harp approached, how on one occasion he escaped to the barn where he was to look after the cattle and fell asleep, and how an angel in a dream turned Caedmon into a performer:

> 'Caedmon', he said, 'sing me a song.' 'I don't know how to sing', he replied. 'It is because I cannot sing that I left the feast and came here.' [...] 'But you shall sing to me.' 'What should I sing about?' he replied. 'Sing about the Creation of all things' [...][24]

Many scholarly speculations have been spun to reinterpret this incident of about 680 AD in modern terms. In our present context, something like Magoun's interpretation seems to fit: Caedmon had listened over the years to the kind of oral poetry practiced in Northumbria in the seventh century; perhaps he had secretly practiced or merely unconsciously assimilated its poetics; in any case, the dream galvanized his passive knowledge.[25] This scenario leaves unexplained the cultural miracle that it was given to this farm worker to put the secular traditional poetics to sanctified use; Caedmon's perhaps psychologically understandable 'breakthrough into performance' (to adapt the usage of Hymes 1975) is at once also a breakthrough in poetic practice (see also ch. 6, pp. 204 ff.). His monastic audience (including the noble abbess Hild) not only *evaluated* his performance highly but arranged his encores to be of spiritual value beyond their circle by writing at his dictation.

A somewhat less familiar breakthrough some three hundred years later is detailed in an incident of the thirteenth-century Icelandic *Saga of Erik the Red*. (Within a framework of performance typology these otherwise unrelated 'scenes' show some degree of similarity, and the comparability is itself perhaps evidence for the value of the kind of template suggested.) The scene is Greenland fifteen years before the Conversion, that is about 985; famine and disease have reigned through the winter, and the farmers at Herjólfsnes, including the wealthy Thorkell, respond by feasting a local woman known for her prophetic powers, Thorbjorg the 'Little Sybil' (*lítil-vǫlva*).[26] The *vǫlva* is courted with high honours because of the vanishing distinction (as we can read between the lines) between foretelling and foreshaping; and the saga gives an elaborate description of the spaewife (prophetess) and the rituals surrounding her. On the feast's second day, when all the other requirements of her magic had been met, the Little Sybil 'asked for the assistance of women who knew the spells needed for performing the witchcraft, known as Warlock-songs (*varðlok(k)ur*); but there were no such women available. So

---

[23] For a comprehensive treatment of Caedmon's story and the *Hymn*, see O'Donnell 2005.
[24] Crossley-Holland 1999: 161. Unattributed translations in section 2 of this chapter are mine [JH].
[25] Magoun 1955; but we distance the story from the oral theory, which was the central idea of Magoun's interpretation. For a discussion of this story, see also ch. 4 (K. O'Brien O'Keeffe), pp. 122–27.
[26] The saga is cited from Sveinsson and Þórðarson 1935: 193–237, at 206; the translation is from Magnusson and Pálsson 1965: 73–105, at 82–83.

inquiries were then made amongst all the people on the farm, to see if anyone knew the songs.'[27] The call is answered by a young girl, newly arrived with her family from Iceland; this Gudrid (Guðríðr) remembered the Warlock-songs from among the spells which her foster mother had taught her in childhood. But Gudrid at first refused Thorbjorg's request: '"This is the sort of knowledge and ceremony that I want nothing to do with," said Gudrid, "for I am a Christian."' The Sybil urges '"that you could be of help to others over this, and not be any the worse a woman for that,"' and Gudrid finally yields to pressure from her host Thorkell:

> The women formed a circle around the ritual platform on which Thorbjorg seated herself. Then Gudrid sang the songs so well and beautifully that those present were sure they had never heard lovelier singing. The prophetess thanked her for the song.
> 'Many spirits are now present,' she said, 'which were charmed to hear the singing, and which previously had tried to shun us and would grant us no obedience. And now many things stand revealed to me which before were hidden both from me and from others.'

Optimistic predictions for individuals and the community now followed, and in time the weather actually did improve. But before the prophetess wandered off to her next invitation, she forecast a great destiny for the girl – a theme the saga author has stretched as a red thread through the saga's variegated events.

Like Caedmon, Gudrid is a reluctant performer who is persuaded to find within herself the stuff of a performance she had not anticipated. The Little Sybil is not an angel but does have a direct connection to the supernatural, and both performances are mediated by a figure or figures that form a more active part of the audience. This 'director' is a part of the performance scene naturally noticed by more theatrically oriented theorists than by the folklorists; but it is clear that all members of an audience are not equal when it comes to influencing a performance.[28] Both our performers are of course positively evaluated by their audiences, and arguably both scenes imply two audiences: Gudrid's human and supernatural auditors are obvious, but Caedmon's 'now we should praise the Guardian of heaven [...]' would seem to have supernatural auditors beyond the instigating angel; his human audiences begin the next morning. Both performances not only give pleasure but ultimately effect good in the world.[29] Obviously the durability of this effect differs, and the sources, Bede and the saga, are hardly objective reports. The saga author, notably, manages to make this incident, which could have been seen as reprehensible pagan backsliding, into a good deed of his vaguely virtuous heroine, even though Gudrid's most concrete claim to Christian distinction lies in her progeny. Both performances constitute a landmark in the upward trajectory of the performer's life as both move from low to higher status. Bauman has written illuminatingly on poetic per-

---

[27] The second element of varðlokur is spelled –lokkur in one of the two principle manuscripts; but the detailed folkloristic understanding of this word and passage goes beyond the needs of the present context. See M. Olsen 1919:1–21, and Strömbäck 1935:124–39; also Siikala 1990:195–96, 200. According to my current understanding, the songs 'entice' (lokka) the favouring spirits (vǫrðr, verð-ir).

[28] Schechner 2007:8 is speaking mainly of theatre with his 'performance quadrilog – authors, performers, directors, and spectators'; compare Worthen 2007.

[29] The creation song in Beowulf (ll. 86–101) offers a parallel of sorts with a human audience and two supernatural ones, but Grendel's reaction is famously negative.

formance as creating 'honour' in thirteenth-century Iceland and, more generally, on the 'performance of honour' in that cultural moment.[30] But on the whole the scenes he analyses under this heading are already set in relatively high-status environments and do not show social advancement.

At the top of the social pyramid are a few scenes of royal poetic performance, beginning with the elegy of Gelimer, king of the Vandals (534): after months of hardship on his mountain retreat near Carthage, Gelimer wrote to his Eastern Roman (Byzantine) besieger asking cryptically for three items, including a lyre. The letter-bearer explained that 'being a skilful harpist he had composed an ode relating to his present misfortune, which he was eager to chant to the accompaniment of a lyre while he wept out his soul.'[31] Hrothgar, king of the Danes, would historically have been an older contemporary of Gelimer though of course he is portrayed not by a Procopius (thought to be an eyewitness of the campaign of his leader Belisarius in North Africa) but in the eighth-to-tenth-century English epic *Beowulf*. Hrothgar's singing to the harp after the slaying of Grendel is an event reported by Beowulf to his own king in Geatland: 'There was song and joy; the aged Scylding, / widely learned, told of far-off times; / at times the brave warrior touched the song-wood, / delight of the harp, at times made lays / both true and sad, at times strange stories / he recounted rightly. That great-hearted king, / gray-bearded old warrior wrapped in his years, / at times began to speak of his youth again, / his battle-strength; his heart surged within him / when, old in winters, he remembered so much.'[32] This is of course not historical information, and we may doubt especially that a king would have entertained as extensively as the *Beowulf*-poet here implies, but there is no reason to doubt that the image was plausible to its audience.

More usually early medieval kings formed the most important part of the audience for court performers. The most frequent settings of poetic performance derivable from sources in Old English and Old Norse – though our first two scenes show that it is not an exclusive one – are the interior of a hall and a ruler in the company of the men of his retinue. Though women are not totally absent, the earlier audiences would seem to have been warriors, their relationships governed by the customs of the *comitatus*.[33] The hall itself and the life of the comrades in the hall has been extensively discussed in recent literature,[34] and the aristocratic warrior milieu, especially of heroic poetry based on events of the Period of Migrations, is a common assumption in the older scholarship. These background factors seem to be reflected in the poetry; and when text and context

---

[30] Bauman 1986 is quite convincing and essentially traditional on 'honour' (usually *drengskapr*) as a reward for and often product of verbal art and its performance, also on the performative qualities of other concrete social acts, such as hospitality and even dying well; but we wonder if the argument does not threaten to become circular when Bauman seems to speak of directly performing honour as part of its semiotic system (e. g., p. 143).

[31] Procopius, *Vandalic War* IV.vi.27–34 (Dewing 1916:263). Klaus von See (1998:90–91) launches various arguments against this long-recognized landmark in the prehistory of Germanic verse. I can see no particular reason to doubt the historian here, but von See may be right to emphasize the thoroughgoing mediterraneanization of Gelimer and the Vandal ruling family; the argument would be more impressive, however, if similar elegies could be cited as sung by Roman rulers.

[32] Klaeber 2008: ll. 2105–2114; Liuzza 2000: 117.

[33] For bibliography and some 'customs', see Harris 1993.

[34] For bibliography on the hall as centre of poetic performance, see Niles 1999:79 and 218, n. 16.

mirror each other closely enough, some students of oral literature have spoken of a 'double scene'. This coinage of Lars Lönnroth's captures the homology that frequently recurs in performed literature between the scene of the action within the text and the scene of performance (including reception): 'A double scene is something that occurs in the course of an oral performance whenever the narrative appears to be enacted by the performer or his audience on the very spot where the entertainment takes place.'[35] Lönnroth discusses various examples, including, for the early medieval period, the arrival of an entertaining stranger; among other 'mead-hall motifs', we may instance the *Beowulf* poet's allusion to power under a metaphor that proves awkward for modern translators: 'Often did Scyld Scefing snatch away mead benches from [...] many tribes' (ll. 3–4) – literally unsettling, perhaps, to an audience perched on such benches. Hamlet's play-within-a-play presents a functional double scene, trebled for an audience of theatre-goers. Lönnroth hypothesizes plausibly that the 'original' performance scene leaves a stamp on the output of performance, the text, and that from those traces we can make deductions about the 'original' performance scene. The circularity is not complete, but it is damaging: these are insights, not laws. Nor is the double scene restricted to oral literature, but common also to scenes of reading (Chaucer, Dante) and difficult to separate from the general literary phenomenon of identification (especially of the reader/audience member with some agent in the text). Lönnroth himself, in his more sustained effort (1978), moves on from the 'furniture' of the double scene ('mead-benches') to the vaguer realm of ideological projections. With all due caveats for the hypothetical nature of ideas based on the double scene, however, one has to imagine that a king in the audience of *Beowulf*'s elegiac Hrothgar, quoted above, would have to be touched: the homology is close but flattering: such a one am I.

## 2.1 The Performance of Skaldic Poetry

The sparse earliest Latin and Greek references to Germanic oral poetry on the Continent actually give relatively little precise support for the court as the institutional setting of poetic performance. Scholars have concluded, however, that eulogy is the master genre that provides a deep generic link back to Indo-European times.[36] And two famous 'scenes' of migration-era eulogy – both set in the culturally Gothic court of Attila the Hun – should be mentioned as possible early forms of the later (after 850) poetic culture of the skalds. (1) Priscus, the Thracian secretary of an ambassador from Byzantium, wrote a history of the years 433–74 based on his own eyewitness experiences; it survives in Greek fragmentarily and as a source for Latin-language historians of the next century. His account of a mission to the multicultural empire of Attila in 448 includes a description of a banquet where two 'barbarians' declaimed poems before Attila, poems they had composed to celebrate his victories and brave deeds. The barbarians are regularly taken to be Goths, and the poetry to be an early form of the kind of eulogy that we know later in West and North Germanic forms. With regard to performance, the noteworthy features include the two poets, the personal 'authorship', and the apparent lack of music.

---

[35] Lönnroth 1979:95. See also Lönnroth 1978; Harris 2000c; and, more distantly, Nagy 2003.
[36] Opland 1980:29 and passim; West 2007:63–66.

The two latter features seem to carry over into the work of the skalds, but the partnered performance seems also to anticipate a minor feature of later eulogy (discussed below in connection with the dueling skalds Gunnlaug [Gunnlaugr] and Hrafn and with the Old English *Widsith*). Norse scholars have added a number of more distant parallels. (2) We owe also to Priscus (ultimately) an elaborate description of Attila's funeral (453) that includes the text or a paraphrase of a eulogy chanted by noble horsemen as they rode around his funeral bier. The riders are explicitly Huns, but Germanic connections are again usually assumed, especially when the passage is compared with Beowulf's funeral. The historical questions involved here are not simple, but as a 'scene of performance' we have to note the genre, the occasion, and the equestrian setting, all of which find some echo in later Germanic vernaculars.

From many Norse prose sources, mainly of the thirteenth century, the skald can be confidently described: in the ninth and tenth centuries these court poets were drawn from West Scandinavian lands generally, but starting in the eleventh century Icelanders gained a monopoly on the royal encomium.[37] The thirteenth century Icelandic *Skaldatal* (list of skalds) enumerates over one hundred court skalds (*konungs skald, hofuðskald* 'king's skald, chief skald' ) and the kings they performed for; but although the later Icelandic saga texts mention a great many 'scenes' of court performances, the vast majority are not rich in performance details. One typical example: In his saga Gunnlaug Serpent-tongue (so nicknamed for his biting satirical verse) travels around from court to court; when he comes to the London of King Æthelred (II, the Unready; the encounter would have happened about 1002), he goes before the king

> and greeted him politely and respectfully. The king asked what country he was from. Gunnlaug told him – 'and I have come to you, my lord, because I have composed a poem about you, and I should like you to hear it.'
> The king said that he would. Gunnlaug recited the poem expressively and confidently. The refrain goes like this [...]
> The king thanked him for the poem and, as a reward, gave him a cloak of scarlet [...]. He also made him one of his followers. Gunnlaug stayed with the king all winter and was well thought of.[38]

From such passages – our 'scenes' – one learns crucially that composition precedes performance in such longer poems, and of course to appear as a skald before a ruler is automatically to *take responsibility to an audience*. Typically the skald steps forward alone (compare 'confidently'), taking a stand before the patron, asks a hearing (*frame*), speaks his poem in a loud voice (*keying*), here 'expressively'. *Evaluation* is regularly expressed in terms of rewards from the patron, but the wider audience of court warriors (*drótt, hirð*) also reward the poet indirectly by social acceptance.

Occasionally these 'scenes' carry more information. When Gunnlaug later came to King Olaf (Óláfr) the Swede, another Icelandic poet from Gunnlaug's home district, Hrafn Qnundarson, was already in residence. Gunnlaug immediately requested a hearing for his poem, but King Olaf declined to hear it at that busy moment. Later Gunnlaug

---

[37] Among overviews of skaldic verse, see Whaley 2005 and Frank 1978.
[38] Nordal and Jónsson 1938:71; translation by Attwood 1997:315 (*Saga of Gunnlaug Serpent-tongue*, ch. 7).

tried again: '"Now, my lord, [...] I should like you to hear my poem."'[39] The king agrees, but Hrafn too wants to recite now. After the two young men quarrel over precedence – Gunnlaug living up to his nickname with a sharply worded claim of higher birth – the king decides, but with a hint of condescension, in favour of Serpent-tongue:

> Then Gunnlaug recited the *drapa* he had composed about King Olaf, and when he had finished, the king said, 'How well is the poem composed, Hrafn?'
> 'Quite well, my lord', he answered. 'It is an ostentatious poem, but is ungainly and rather stilted, just like Gunnlaug himself is in temperament.'
> 'Now you must recite your poem, Hrafn', the king said.
> He did so, and when he had finished, the king asked: 'How well is the poem put together, Gunnlaug?'
> 'Quite well, my lord', he replied. 'It is a handsome poem, just like Hrafn himself is, but there's not much to either of them. And', he continued, 'why did you compose only a *flokk* for the king, Hrafn? Did you not think he merited a *drapa*?'[40]

The conflict between the two Icelanders, which shapes the remainder of the saga and ends both their lives, thus grows directly out of literary criticism or, in terms of our template, out of performance *evaluation*.

The correlation of a poem with a poet's character is paralleled at least once in Old Norse writings[41] and, together with poetry-based nicknames like 'Serpent-tongue', suggests that this exchange actually reflects a form of critical thought. Soon after this scene Hrafn returns to Iceland, and from his parting declaration of hostilities we can reasonably deduce that it was not Gunnlaug's assertion of higher social status among Icelandic families nor even his hostile comparison of Hrafn himself to his poem that caused the breach between the former friends; after all, Hrafn's critique of Gunnlaug and his poem was parallel and only a little less harsh. Instead, the unforgivable factor was that final, extra critique of poetic form, Gunnlaug's embarrassing reference to Hrafn's use of the lesser poetic form *flokkr*, in contrast to the more prestigious *drápa*.[42] (One senses, when the saga author tacks this final sentence on with a shift to direct address to Hrafn, that Gunnlaug just could not restrain himself – he rarely did – from adding insult, the deadly supplement, to injury.[43]) How mischievous was the king's role in asking for *evaluation* from the competitors, in ceding his own place as chief voice of the audience to a segment of the audience certain, in the circumstances, to evaluate negatively? In any case, we can see the king here as both part of the audience and a kind of *director* in the sense that he mediates between performer and audience. One more performance issue

---

[39] Nordal and Jónsson 1938:79–80; Attwood 1997:319 (ch. 9).
[40] Nordal and Jónsson 1938:80; Attwood 1997:320.
[41] *Hreiðars þáttr heimska*; trans. Kellogg 1997:375–84, at 383–84 ('Hreidar's Tale').
[42] Nordal and Jónsson 1938:80, n. 1, quotes another scene in which the poet Þórarinn loftunga (praise-tongue) is threatened with death by Knut the Great for composing only a *flokkr* about him. Þórarinn saved himself by converting the more modest poem to a *drápa* by composing a refrain and adding material to some stanzas. The editors comment that this shows 'how much of an insult inheres in Gunnlaug's words to Hrafn before the king himself and what kind of serpent-tongue Gunnlaugr was.'
[43] Nordal and Jónsson 1938:80: '*eða hví ortir þú flokk um konunginn*', segir hann, '*eða þótti þér hann eigi drápunnar verðr?*' Hrafn's parting words: '*Lokit skal nú okkarri vináttu, fyrir því at þú vildir hræpa mik hér fyrir hofðingjum*' (81).

can be raised by the 'scene' at the court of Olaf the Swede, that of the intelligibility of skaldic verse. Skaldic verse, famously intricate and difficult for modern readers, was a Norwegian-Icelandic accomplishment, and by the date of the encounter of Gunnlaug and Hrafn, about 1004, it was exclusively Icelandic, at least at the court level. Did the Swedish king really understand more than the gist of these poems? It is noteworthy that he makes no judgment himself but consigns the evaluation alternately to the Icelandic poets. A few passages in Old Norse literature are explicit about this matter: Sneglu-Halli is a trickster who reports back to his Norwegian king about the poetic jokes he has perpetrated on the skaldically ignorant Danish and English kings.[44] More frequently the audience's limited understanding is touched on obliquely,[45] but according to a well-received theory of skaldic poetry (or more precisely of its major strand, the courtly), one of its functions may have been to separate the in-group of the (Norwegian) king's *drótt*, who will have had more familiarity with the skaldic skill, from outsiders, the poetically non-elect (Lindow 1975).

Another 'scene', that of Sturlu Þórðarson's shipboard performance (1263), contributes in a subtle way to this image of the limited intelligibility of skaldic verse.[46] But this short story (*þáttr*) is especially important as the most prominent moment in the very extensive quasi-historical literature in Old Norse where it is unclear whether a (prose) performance is purely oral or the oral realization of written sources, i. e., in some sense a 'reading': The Icelander Sturla (1214–1284) was in disfavour with the king but was allowed to join the company on the royal ship. He regales the ordinary sailors in the forecastle with his stories, until the queen persuades the king to relent and summons Sturla to the quarter deck to entertain her: 'and [bade him] bring his trollwife-saga with him.'[47] Hermann Pálsson, in particular, argued, against various oralists, that this meant that Sturla had a manuscript in his possession on the voyage.[48] Stephen Mitchell solves the dilemma by pointing out that the expression in question is attributed to the queen, a Dane of most cultured background, whose assumptions about entertainment would have been literate, reflecting the mixed 'Vokalität' of her upbringing.[49] Getting a foothold in the royal favour with his saga-telling, Sturla went on to recite his praise-poems on the king and the king's father. The anecdote thus also illustrates the relationship between poetic performance and status (or, with Bauman, honour).

---

[44] 'Sneglu-Halla þáttr' in Kristjánsson 1956: 281–95, at 192–93; trans. Clark 1997: 354–55 ('The Tale of Sarcastic Halli').
[45] See the discussion in Harris 1996a: 80–81 and 95, n. 32 (on 'Sturlu þáttr') and Frank 1985: 183; Williams 1971: 95.
[46] 'Sturlu þáttr' in *Sturlunga saga*, Guðni Jónsson 1954: III, xi, 367–83, at 379: After Sturla's praise-poem, the queen volunteers enthusiastically: 'I think that the poem was well-made.' The king responds ironically: 'Do you understand so well how to attend to it?' (*Dróttning mælti: 'Þat ætla ek, at kvæðit sé vel ort.' Konungr mælti: 'Kanntu mjök gerla at heyra?'*)
[47] Guðni Jónsson 1954: III, xi, 367–83, at 378: *En er menn váru mettir, sendi dróttning eftir Sturlu, bað hann koma til sín ok hafa með sér tröllkonusöguna.*
[48] Later Icelandic sources refer to such oral entertainment on a written basis as *sagnaskemmtun*, and Hermann Pálsson (1962) elevated this concept to a general model for much of Old Norse.
[49] Mitchell 1997: n. 6 cites some earlier discussions; the anecdote is also treated in Bauman 1986: 135–36 and widely. We adopt the concept of *Vokalität* from Schaefer 1992.

The rewards of skaldic performance – along with several other features of skaldic poetry as a lived reality – can be illustrated by the often-cited scene of Egill Skalla-Grímsson's daring performance in the hall of his arch-enemy, Erik Bloodaxe, expelled from his kingship in Norway and now reigning in York. Egill's comically treated reward for his extorted encomium was his own ugly head, hence the poem's name, 'Head-Ransom', *Hǫfuðlausn*. This extreme of honour or status through performance participates in a subtradition where the poet's very life is at stake; but as a whole the 'scene' confirms vividly a basic fact presupposed already in Gunnlaug's appearance before King Æthelred, namely the distinction between composition and performance in this genre. Egill's long and ornate poem was composed with difficulty in the course of a single night (another subtradition) entirely in the poet's mind; it is recited from memory. The poem and the 'scene' have been frequently parsed; but after allowance for the fanciful supernatural elements and the doubtful historicity of the events, the incident can stand with the force of a type, a rich, if imaginative, vignette on the composition and performance of courtly praise poetry in the North.

Early skaldic poetry offers several other models of composition and performance, more than can be discussed here. The majority of *short* skaldic poems, however, are presented by the later narrative prose (sagas) as having been simply spoken in a certain narrative context; the saga authors usually are interested only in content, but some 'scenes' of this kind make it clear that the verses are considered to be improvised and that a certain prestige attends that skill. For example, an anecdote about the poet Einarr Skúlason (12th c.) consists of three scenes of rapid composition and performance within the informal context of a Norwegian king at ease among his inner circle. Each time Einarr is challenged to recite a stanza on his immediate situation; in the third vignette the king demands a poem describing the passage of the ship belonging to a certain beautiful woman: 'Compose a verse now and have it finished before the ship sails out past the island of Hólm.' Einarr in turn challenges the king and his followers each to remember one line of the poem, then launches: 'The valliant dame with prows divides / the hollow waves [...]'. The king manages to remember the first and last lines, but the retainers retained nothing, whatever they may have understood. Einarr takes the agreed-on prize.[50]

The bantering tone of some skaldic performance may be balanced by the remains of a genre of ritual verse, the *erfikvæði* or funeral poem (Harris 2006). The most informative example of *erfikvæði* comes again from the repertoire of Egill Skalla-Grímsson and from the saga-biography about him, written about 1231. It is Egill's 25–stanza 'Lament for my Sons', *Sonatorrek*. And again the saga's account is too well known to be retold in detail, but we note that the poem is composed in Egill's mind and in solitude. When it is finished, Egill returns to his high-seat and recites *Sonatorrek* to his household as part of the death duties for his recently drowned favourite son. The saga author is convinced that the poem and its recitation constituted an important component in Egill's recovery from grief. *Sonatorrek*, as poem and performance, occupies a position at the opposite end of an ethical scale from the competitive snapshots of Einarr Skúlason, but one cannot speak definitively about the overall landscape of Old Norse oral poetry in skaldic metres.

---

[50] Harris 1996b in 2008: 337 and n. 66; translated 345–47.

Although the skaldic branch is well known to scholars of Nordic verse and to readers of Old Norse sagas and mythography, where skaldic poetry is chiefly preserved, there is no comprehensive modern study of its performance, and our 'scenes' have been almost random examples. In a very recent publication, however, a rich and insightful 'history' of Old Norse poetry and poetics, Margaret Clunies Ross does provide the beginnings of a systematic survey of the functional types of skaldic poetry; and her exposition of the recording and use of early poetry by the later prose writers makes clearer how intertwined the questions of original performance, re-performance, and reception can become (2005, esp. chapters 3–4).

## 2.2 The Performance of Eddic Verse

One 'scene of performance' introduces eddic verse as the inferior cousin of skaldic. King Harald the Hard-ruler (Haralds harðráði) invaded the north of England in 1066, to be famously defeated and killed at Stamford Bridge. This Harald is presented by many sources as a witty friend of oral literature, and the historical saga accounts depict him as reciting verse on the march upcountry. First he improvises (as it seems) a stanza in the old, common Germanic metre of eddic verse to the effect that they are marching toward battle without their mail-coats, which were left on shipboard. 'Then King Haraldr said: "That is a badly composed verse; now I'll do another one better," and he recited this [...]' (Finlay 2004: 227). The 'better' poem is a well-turned skaldic stanza stating that a certain woman (a battle-goddess or perhaps his mother?) had instructed Harald never to rely on artificial battle aides (such as mail-coats!). Whatever the real story underlying these two verses, the 'scene' presents both types of verse as improvised on a march; while its literary-critical aspect simply affirms the superiority of the more complex form, it seems reasonable to assume that this aesthetic reflected the age of the simpler eddic-type verse in contrast to the more contemporary skaldic. But while extracting facts of a real-life poetics is worthwhile, it would be wrong to overlook the artistry of the anecdote itself.

Norse sources present us with relatively little information on the composition and performance of the older – and to most readers more familiar – form. Eddic verse is anonymous and has no term for its 'poet' or 'performer', nothing corresponding to 'skald';[51] and the few 'scenes' of its performance tend to the laconic. Nevertheless, a great many commentaries have been offered by modern scholars though most do not rigorously separate performance and performers from the definition, history, content, and essence of eddic verse as we are here attempting.[52] Only five major passages in Old Norse literature constitute almost all the direct outside evidentiary material; here we will summarize four of these 'scenes' very briefly and expand somewhat on a final one. *Norna-Gests þáttr* shows a wandering entertainer/warrior of an ancient type performing saga-like material and also eddic verse before a king and his war-band; this Gestr also plays the harp, but it is not clear whether his music accompanies narrative. The frame story is

---

[51] 'Skald' is applied once to an originally eddic fragment, as discussed in Harris 1983: 229–31 in connection with 'skaldic revision' of 'eddic' verse.
[52] Primary and secondary references and commentary may be found in Harris 1983, 1985, 1996b, Gunnell 2005, 2008, and widely elsewhere.

traditional fiction (with mythic touches) rather than (traditional) history, but the locus of performance and evaluation agree largely with the settings of skaldic and some West Germanic narrative verse. The audience of warriors receives Gestr's stories of ancient heroes enthusiastically and sometimes with surprise (suggesting that not every story was always already familiar to every audience), and the king acts as 'director' managing the performances.[53] A more down-to-earth 'scene' is set at an Icelandic wedding held at a farmstead called Reykjahólar in 1119, that is, little more than a century after the official conversion of Iceland; the passage is realistic reportage in the context of a relatively historical saga written as little as fifty years after the events. Among the entertainments offered the wedding guests were two extensively described narrative performances by named poet-raconteurs. The passage presents several challenges but allows two fairly safe conclusions for eddic-style verse: first, eddic entertainment was not exclusive to royal contexts; and second, the prosimetrical base – narrative in unmarked language, prose, studded with verses just as we find in mythic-heroic sagas preserved from the late thirteenth century and later – goes far back in performance history (Harris 1997).

Two passages from Saxo Grammaticus, the Danish historian-cleric who wrote in Latin a history of the Danes about 1200, suggest that the performance of eddic-type verse could have functional intentions for audiences beyond simple entertainment. In 1131 a Saxon singer attempted, without breaching his own loyalty to the attackers, to warn the Danish king of a treacherous ambush by some of the king's relatives; the singer's method was indirect, the recital of a narrative poem known under a descriptive quasi-title, 'the very famous perfidy of Grimhild against her brothers'. In a somewhat similar scene, Saxo reports that preceding a battle in 1157 a minstrel (*cantor*) rode between the ranks 'rehearsing Sveno's murderous treachery in a famous song' and exciting 'the warriors of Waldemarus to battle by appealing to them loudly for revenge.' The outdoor, pre-battle setting in both cases is royal, but Danish, so very possibly influenced by German traditions; we do not know the form or content of the *perfidia Svenonis*, which might not be in any sense 'eddic', but the *perfidia Grimhildae erga fratres* seems to correspond to a known but lost poem in Old Norse (Harris 1976).

The last of this series of 'scenes' comes from Icelandic historical literature and tells how the skald Thormod (Þórmóðr) recited an eddic poem, the *Bjarkamál*, on the morning of the momentous battle of Stiklastaðir. The 'double-scene' effect is very strong here: *Bjarkamál* narrates the last stand of the ancient hero-king Hrolf the Ladder-pole (Hrólfr kraki), and the historical battle of 1030 was the doom of the Norwegian king Olaf the Stout, later St. Olaf. The poem opens with the waking topos as King Hrolf's men are awakened to their last battle, and Thormod's recitation does the same in the historical present. The strict historicity of Thormod's recitation is strongly disputed, and not without reason;[54] but if we can avoid entering into details of the controversies and varying interpretations, we can extract a few lessons from the 'scene.' A skald is the vector of an eddic re-performance here; as with the scenes from Saxo, the setting is outdoors and precedes a battle. Saxo's clear examples of the application of poetry to have an effect in a situation suggest that other eddic performances may have carried messages for their

---

[53] For bibliography and studies of *Norna-Gests þáttr* see Harris and Hill 1989 and Zernack 2004.
[54] von See 1976, 1981b; Harris 1985: 118–19; Klingenberg 1991.

original (real or imagined) audience; Thormod will have selected the *Bjarkamál* for its double scene, but its alternative title in tradition, *Húskarlahvǫt* 'Incitement of the Retainers', captures his principal motive.

Thormod, if we imagine him as reciting the whole of *Bjarkamál* as we know it from Saxo's Latin paraphrase, will have had to represent different voices (Hialto, Biarko, Ruta). In general eddic poetry has a strong dramatic edge. To what extent was its performance a dramatic event? Lönnroth (1971) and the tradition he follows imagine a single performer reciting more or less dramatically as narrative is interspersed with speech or certain poems are dramatic monologues; but another tradition insists on real drama, probably ritual drama for the *ljóðaháttr* poems, which are all speech and no narrative (except in the secondary prose of the manuscript). Terry Gunnell (1995, 2005, 2008) has argued the case for drama in the *ljóðaháttr* dialogue poems, especially *Vafþrúðnismál*, *Skírnismál*, *Lokasenna*, *Hárbarðsljóð*, and *Fáfnismál*, where the manuscript assigns speeches in marginal rubrics; this 'strongly suggests that the scribes viewed these pieces as similar in kind to the rudimentary dramas that were being recorded elsewhere, in England and northern France' (2005:96). This point is very likely right, but what the thirteenth-century Icelandic scribes may have thought, is less impressive to me than Gunnell's analysis and logic about the multi-voiced poems themselves; and the ancestry of the dialogue form may go deep into Indo-European culture (West 2007:68–69). Most eddic scholars probably remain skeptical toward dramatic realization as the mode of transmission through the Christian centuries,[55] but Gunnell has made a very persuasive case, in my opinion, that some of these very heterogenous poems remain marked by original or early dramatic performance, probably ritually reinforced.

## 2.3 West Germanic Oral Performance, with a Note on Celtic

In the earliest times Anglo-Saxon modes of performance must have resembled what we know of early skaldic poetry and its continental Germanic ancestor; as there, eulogy is the most solidly attested genre. Precious witnesses in Old English are two poems about poets, *Widsith* and *Deor*, which, along with *Beowulf*, offer several vignettes of oral performance and its contexts. We will glance briefly at a few of these familiar 'scenes'; but the secondary literature in Old English is markedly more plentiful than in Old Norse so that a different level of engagement is in order here. We have in particular one comprehensive study to rely on, Jeff Opland's 1980 classic *Anglo-Saxon Oral Poetry: A Study of the Traditions*, and Opland's work is also an adequate introduction to the basic evidence of oral poetry in other West Germanic language areas.[56] Beyond this book, there are a great many relevant studies of various kinds, too many for a comprehensive survey here, though such studies tend to treat oral (and oral-derived) poetry – and even the conditions of orality and literacy – more broadly than our close focus on performance allows.[57]

---

[55] For example, Clunies Ross 2005:29, n.
[56] Anderson 1903 is an honourable antecedant to Opland's work; among others, Wehrlich 1964 and 1967 should be still of interest to contemporary scholars.
[57] Surveys of the oral-formulaic studies on Old English can be found in Foley 1988 (index) and A. Olsen 1986, 1988; Foley 1985, together with his journal *Oral Tradition*, provides a full bibliogra-

*Widsith* (which we take to be quite old, perhaps from the eighth or ninth century) presents an optimistic picture of the wandering singer whose stock in trade is the praise of his patrons; the economy of praise is very direct: his panegyrics constitute the patrons' 'deathless fame'; their rewards of rings and gold support Widsith's cheerful life. He is a forerunner of the Nordic royal skald, and there are some oblique indications – the thulas or lists of rulers, heroes, and tribes and also the thumbnail narratives interspersed through Widsith's autobiography – that the same poet might also be a purveyor of narrative, genealogy, and even such a poem as *Widsith* itself (see ll. 54–56). Widsith praised not only Eormanric, the fierce king of the Goths, but also Eormanric's queen – something which would be a risky move in the later Norse milieu. But perhaps the most arresting performance detail to be derived from *Widsith* is that the lone skald-like eulogist may sometimes have partnered with a second singer, here named 'Scilling'. The dual singers, if that is the meaning of the text, may legitimately raise memories of the paired 'barbarian' eulogists at Attila's court and perhaps of competing skalds (like Gunnlaug and Hrafn). An English analogue for two singers is mentioned in the vita of the royal saint Æthelberht, who was murdered about 794, preserved in a manuscript of the early twelfth century; here two singers perform material about the ancestors of the king as entertainment on a journey and are rewarded with rings.[58] Less likely analogues for paired singers are those of Finnic folk tradition and of late medieval Icelandic folk verse.[59] The older Germanic dual singers may have been competitors; if so, *Deor* fits into the pattern (as discussed below). It has been sometimes argued that Scilling is only the name of Widsith's lyre (OE *hearpe*), and weapons, especially swords, do indeed sometimes bear names in early sources. As far as I know, however, Scilling would be the only named musical instrument; and, in any case, Malone points out that the wording at l. 104 ('before the victorious lord of us two') makes it unlikely that Scilling is a *thing* of any kind (Malone 1962: 50). All the non-anonymous performers seem to have speaking names, perhaps something like modern stagenames: *Widsith* 'far-travel(er)'; *Scilling* 'son of the resounding'; *Deor* 'bold one'; *Heorrenda* 'rattler'; *Healgamen* 'hall-entertainment'.[60]

All successful communications in *Beowulf* are oral,[61] and the many formal speeches, boasts, flytings, and so on might, in real life, have been 'performances' by modern standards. We will, however, stick to poetic performance (in the broad sense, which includes oral literature without specifying verse, prose, song, etc.). The most important scenes in

---

phy. But, again, we are endeavouring here to treat performance separately from the question of textuality (formulicity).

[58] Moisl 1981: 238–39; Opland 1980: 147–50 (excellent analysis).

[59] Einarsson 1963; Mustanoja 1959; for more references to dual singers see Harris 1985: 116.

[60] Malone 1962: 209–10 (*Widsiþ*; note the real person named *Oftfor* 'frequent travel(ler)' in Bede); Malone 1962: 50, 194 (*Scilling*); Malone 1966: 38 (*Deor*); Malone 1966: 39 (*Heorrenda*; compare de Vries 1977: 232). *Healgamen* (Klaeber 2008: l. 1066) is the new member of the club; Fulk discusses the *Beowulf* passage persuasively in the notes to Klaeber 2008 and in Fulk 2005: 195–97, giving many examples of 'epithets-turned-names' in Old English.

[61] The one instance of writing (ll. 1687–98b) communicates ironically with the poem's audience; but its actors look on uncomprehendingly. The notes to Klaeber 2008 give a full discussion and references. Especially challenging for my interpretation is Lerer 1991: 158–94; but see the comparable scene of non-reading in the eddic *Atlamál*, stanzas 9–12, and compare Harris 2000a: 91–92.

*Beowulf* are: (1) the (apparently) harp-accompanied, clear singing of a scop's creation hymn, a kind of dedication, as it seems, of the new hall Heorot (ll. 89b–98); (2) Hrothgar's scop Healgamen singing (or at least presenting in the context of song and harp) the heroic lay of Finnsburg, entertainment in Heorot in celebration of Beowulf's victory (ll. 1063–1160); (3) also in the hall, the aged king Hrothgar himself entertaining (ll. 2105–14) in a scene we compared above to Gelimer's elegy – the king's performances constitute part of Beowulf's report to his own king and a very complex passage.[62] (4) At Beowulf's funeral, twelve nobles ride around his barrow uttering (shouting? in unison or in series?) the eulogy of the king-hero that closes the epic (ll. 3169–82) – a passage rich in questions of several kinds.[63] (5) Finally, there is another horseback performance, the praise of Beowulf on the joyful return from Grendel's mere (ll. 853–917a).

Here we pause to point out some obvious and less obvious similarities to the scene from the *Life of Æthelberht* discussed above. Both entertainments, of course, take place while performers and audiences are riding on a journey, but both seem also to imagine multiple performers and attendant competition since 'many a man' (*manig*) expressed 'again and again' (*oft*) Beowulf's praise, his unique heroic status – though they did not mean thereby to criticize their own king (ll. 856b–64). Competition in song is inexplicit, but immediately we hear that the (younger?) men also raced their horses (*on geflit* 'in competition') where the ground suited. This passage on plural eulogists seems to lead up to the performance of 'the king's thane', a man freighted with old lore (ll. 867b–74a), who improvises a eulogy that apparently includes the positive exemplum of Sigmund and the negative one of Heremod – as if after the young amateur panegyrists, a master, who knew many old sagas, would show them how to vary words. Again, this famous passage can be parsed for performance information in various ways, but we suggest that the contrast of the *many* tersely mentioned eulogists, whose utterance is quickly summarized, with the *one* master poet, the content of whose poem is fully laid before us, suggests forms of competition as underlying motives.

The last of these primary witnesses, the poem *Deor*, does not actually contain any 'scenes of performance', but its autobiographical fiction does give a non-romantic idea of poetic competition. The poem is a collection of brief narrative vignettes from heroic legend spoken (as we learn in the last stanza) by the court poet Deor, whose story is that he has lost his position and his lord to the master poet Heorrenda; but the point of the small catalogue and the meaning of the poem as a whole depend on interpretation of the refrain that punctuates the irregular stanzas.[64] Both the poem's meaning and its historical context are contested, but its evidence for performance in an imagined early oral period remains.

The language of classical Old English poetry is largely descended from such an oral period and structured by the kind of performance culture we have been surveying, but in

---

[62] On all the Beowulf passages, see Klaeber 2008 for comments that represent the best contemporary opinion and very full references; but see especially Opland 1980: 199–201 on the difficulties of the scene of royal harping.

[63] Opland 1980: 51–53 (on Priscus and Attila's funeral), 205–07 (Beowulf's funeral); Frank 1982; Hill 2007.

[64] My interpretation (Harris 1989) seems not to have been widely embraced though the non-optimistic reading of Fulk and Cain (2003: 216–17) is a start.

literate Anglo-Saxon England this inherited poetic language absorbed influences from Latin and came to serve a variety of Mediterranean-influenced text-types, as well as late manifestations of early native genres forged in the older oral milieu (e. g., *The Battle of Maldon*, 991 or later). One speaks of 'oral-derived' poetry especially for works like *Beowulf*,[65] but in a very broad sense the whole structural basis of Old English poetic language is ultimately oral-derived; genres that originated in written circumstances and direct translations from Latin also utilize the common poetic dialect, at least until late in the Anglo-Saxon period. For verbal performance in Anglo-Saxon England, the interesting questions include not only the ultimate performative original of the language and literary forms (together, 'tradition') but also how products of this tradition were actualized. We recognize at least these modes: reading aloud and silently, oral improvisation and memorial recitation. It is obvious that the development of a literature is intertwined with the communication system as a whole, including technology (as the codex, the index, printing, the internet); and since oral performance is also communication, it too will reciprocally influence literary development. (Even in our time such mutual influence can surprise: a recent successful stage event has been an eight-hour reading of *The Great Gatsby*.) A full account of Old English literary history under the aspect of communication and performance remains a challenge.[66]

An interesting variation on these standard thoughts conceives of Anglo-Saxon manuscript transmission as itself a kind of performance. Katherine O'Brien O'Keeffe's well-received study of the textual variations of 'Caedmon's Hymn' shows how different the scribal approach to Latin verse in Anglo-Saxon England was from that of the scribe writing his own language (O'Brien O'Keeffe 1990: esp. 1–46). The scribe of vernacular verse, knowing his native poetic tradition, reads and writes in a state of 'transitional literacy' (48) somewhere 'between the fluid transmission of oral literature and the fixed text of a literate textual tradition' (Wilcox 2001:61). These insights are carried further and filled out in several strong articles by A. N. Doane.[67] The idea had been rather closely anticipated in Celtic studies by Edgar M. Slotkin, writing on Irish scribal habits,[68] but Doane's portrayal of the activity of the vernacular scribe as a kind of performance is especially thorough and stimulating. Here is the conclusion of his main statement of these ideas in the article of the series that deals most intensely with scribal performance:

> To sum up: performance as I have been defining it is to be understood as centering on the scribe as transmitter of traditional vernacular messages. Such a scribe differs in his behavior from a scribe preserving authoritative messages in Latin; the performing scribe transmits a traditional gist to an audience for present use, not for future generations. As such, the scribe is part of an emergent tradition, and he is responsible to that tradition, not to an unknown 'author' or to a dead piece of sheepskin, as he exercises his memory and competence to pro-

---

[65] This descriptor, now thoroughly naturalized in scholarship, is a coinage of John Miles Foley, apparently first appearing (JMF personal communication) in Foley 1990:5.
[66] The state of the art is Fulk and Cain 2003.
[67] Doane 1991, 1994a, 1994b, 2003.
[68] Part of Slotkin's conclusion: 'Given the attitude of scribes towards their work, we can think of each one of their productions as a kind of multiform of their original. In this sense the entire nature of a critical edition of a saga is a false concept. Surely, the "interpolation" of a late scribe may be traditional, meaningful, and necessary to the tale or that particular scribal performance of the the tale' (1977–79:450).

duce the tradition for a particular audience on a particular occasion. The tradition itself is the dynamic but unrealized amalgam of lore and story frameworks, of linguistic and cultural competencies that were stored in the heads of people linked within that tradition. The performing scribe produced the text in an act of writing that evoked the tradition by a combination of eye and ear, script and memory. (Doane 1994a: 435–36)

Before too enthusiastically welcoming the theory of the performing scribe, however, with its continual recreation of the text, oralists should consider that a radical interpretation of the theory stands at odds with the well-established survival of historical layers, even in the field of Old English verse. This controversy can be appreciated in two brilliant recent articles focused mainly on *Beowulf*, the first pushing the chirographic-recreation argument to its history-dissolving limit, the second re-establishing diachronic probability.[69]

Our interest in the interface of orality and literacy in the domain of performance should not imply a lack of performance in more ordinary senses even in late Anglo-Saxon England. A famous example is St. Dunstan, controversial harpist and singer, who performed partly in the vernacular (Opland 1980: 178–80). Early medieval oral performance is to be known only through its effects on text or through 'scenes' which served other purposes than ours; one is reminded of sciences which sometimes rely on perturbations of the context (dark matter, laryngeals) to predict unseen phenomena. Performance traces continue, of course, into Middle English. In the broad sense we have adopted from the Performance School, it is in fact hard to imagine any culture without 'performance'. Many of the themes we have touched on, especially the transition to Middle English, are dealt with comprehensively by Mark Amodio in *Writing the Oral Tradition* (2004), but we are not always in agreement with his point of view. Amodio's main point in the Old English sections of his book is the survival of an oral poetics into the written literature, through which alone we know everything we know about Old English poetry. True enough. But in speaking of performance, Amodio makes it clear that he still has the Parry-Lord paradigm exclusively in mind; he overlooks both oral performance as a *goal* of writing or writing down and also modes of composition that do not employ writing (i. e., are oral) but are not improvisatory. Hence Amodio's Anglo-Saxon verse must, for the most part, be 'nonperformative' (Amodio 2004: 28–29, 44, and passim; 2005).

One genre obviously based on oral performance (yet fueled by Christian learning) is preaching, whether we have in mind the 'sermon' or the 'homily' or do not distinguish between them. Old English scholarship is now beginning to grapple with the issues preaching raises for our understanding of its written remains. Andy Orchard, having just discussed formulaic patterning in Old English verse, comments on the 'growing realization' that such techniques were common also to performed prose, to wit the sermon (1997: 109). Orchard introduces comparative material from the repertoire of American, especially African-American, folk preachers (a topic made famous in oral studies especially by Rosenberg 1988) and comments: 'The value of such analogues lies in the emphasis they place on the role of performance in establishing the form and style of a text, and such examples illustrate an increasing tendency to look beyond the narrow

---

[69] Liuzza 1995: esp. 290–95 and Fulk 2003: esp. 16–25. I thank Leonard Neidorf for commentary on this point.

confines of the oral-formulaic theory as first applied to Old English verse, by focusing attention on other forms of discourse from Anglo-Saxon England, and attempting to address the issue of formulaic expression as a communal vehicle for interpretation' (1997:113–14). Orchard's earlier work in this vein (1992) concentrated on the archbishop and preacher Wulfstan; but most recently, with the work of Samantha Zacher (2009), the focus has shifted to the anonymous sermons of the Vercelli Book. In a related strand of scholarship the essential nature of such orally performed 'prose' is being reconsidered. Thomas Bredehoft, picking up an older discussion,[70] has argued that poetic prose of Wulfstan's older contemporary Ælfric is a form of 'late Old English verse', and now one can read in a new book by Tiffany Beechy a comprehensive aesthetic-linguistic theorization of the 'diversity of poetic phenomena across the Old English corpus' (2010:2). But the study of medieval sermon literature more generally – especially relevant to Old English is Carolingian (Amos 1989) – has gone further in considering preaching as 'event' (Thompson 2002). The external evidence (for example, in treatises on preaching, the *artes praedicandi*) intensifies starting in the twelfth century, but a student of Anglo-Saxon preaching as performance can find valuable suggestions outside the Anglo-Saxon field, especially in recent work of Beverly Kienzle, which is explicitly grounded in a contemporary understanding of performance.[71]

Some of the features of oral performance in West Germanic, especially Old English, have parallels in more or less contemporary (and contiguous) Irish and Welsh documents, and similar impediments exist to full understanding of performance. Fully qualified Celticists, however, might well emphasize the very significant differences that set Celtic apart; we offer here a few non-professional notes based on secondary literature.[72] A very accessible and authoritative account of Celtic poets and poetry, reaching back to extraordinary historical depths (the ethnographic writings of Posidonius, *c.* 135–51 BC) and forward to the end of the bardic order in Ireland in the seventeenth century, is to be found in Caerwyn Williams, 'The Court Poet in Medieval Ireland' (1971);[73] this article, which includes much material on performance itself, is a masterpiece, with a wealth of information and further references and also good comparative views to Welsh, Scots Gaelic, and Germanic. In Welsh, but particularly in Irish, the institution of poetry and the grades of poet are much more highly cultivated than in Germanic; Bloomfield and Dunn (1989) give an overall comparative view, as do the older works of the Chadwicks (1932–40; 1936). Both of the major Celtic traditions included formal training, with the Irish situation especially well attested: in the schools composition took place in prescribed contemplative situations,[74] and formal recitation was by a bard not identical with

---

[70] Bredehoft 2005, 2009; Momma 1997, with bibliography extending back at least to the 1920s.
[71] Kienzle 2002. For references to similar studies of Welsh sermons (as well as to performance in connection with medieval Welsh narrative) see Davies 2003.
[72] On general aspects of orality and literacy in Celtic sources see Ó Coileáin 1978, Nagy 1986, and Roberts 1988. We follow the traditional line on the age and continuity of Celtic, especially Irish, oral literature, but we recognize a well-received recent contrary strain in writings such as McCone 1989, 1990.
[73] See also Williams 1996; Williams and Ford 1992; Ford 1999; and J. T. Koch and Carey 1995.
[74] Bergin 1970:3–22; Knott 1960:56–57; Williams 1971:117–22. It is amusing, in the Old English context, to read in Knott (1960:56) about a controversy between late-sixteenth-century poets over the propriety of composing on horseback instead of the prescribed darkened room.

the poet (Knott 1960:57–58). The institutionalization and formal instruction appears to have been less strict in Wales (Williams 1978:14–15). The old genres of court poetry – eulogy, elegy, criticism or advice, and satire – are only partly homologous with Germanic, which also included narrative verse from an early point. These Celtic genres reflect an even closer poet-patron relationship than we are familiar with from Germanic. One extravagant conceit that brings this home is the Irish poet as spouse or (female) lover of his patron (Carney 1967), a lived metaphor that may have been Common Celtic or even older;[75] in death the 'wife' becomes a widow and overtones of suttee may even be heard in Germanic material (Simms 1989; Harris 1993). To conclude on an understatement: a new comparative study dedicated to Germanic and Celtic performance could be very rewarding.

## 2.4 The Problem of Music

One question that has never been satisfactorily solved for early Germanic is the role of music in oral performance; some external evidence from different times and places supports an important place for music in the preliterate poetics, but there is also weighty counterevidence.[76] The major words for 'poet' highlight, not a musical connection, but the satirical function: the best etymologies for OE *scop* and ON *skald* lead to the satirical context (compare Modern English *scoff* and *scold*), and this function, as in Celtic, is rightly viewed as the negative side of eulogy, the main function of the Indo-European poet.[77] The word-families of both *scop* and *skald* are attested in both North and West Germanic even though neither word can be claimed as *the* original Germanic designation for 'poet'; like Indo-European, Germanic seems to have had function-specific concepts in the area covered in modern times by the general or comprehensive terms 'poet' and 'makar'. One designation for 'poet' is the very old form OE *þyle*, ON *þulr* (Proto-Germanic *\*þuliz*);[78] this word and word-family clearly counts as Common Germanic, but the type of poet indicated seems unlikely to be responsible for the major genres of narrative and eulogy: ON *þylja* 'to mumble, rattle off (a list)', ON *þula* 'a list in verse', OE *þelcræft* 'oratoria'; most of the evidence for the agent nouns *þyle* and *þulr* favours 'councilor, spokesman'. Deeper etymological efforts have not produced any clarity (de Vries 1977:626).

In modern times English *singer* and German *Sänger*, carrying implications of musical accompaniment, have been applied to the early Germanic poet; but OE *songere, sangere*, OHG *sangari*, etc., and ON *sǫngvari* are found mainly in ecclesiastical contexts, often glossing *cantor* (Harris 2004). The word formation of this and words like Gothic *liuþareis* 'singer' is itself a borrowing from Italic. Secularization of the agent nouns

---

[75] See Mac Cana 1988 and West 2007:30.
[76] This question appears to be equally open in Celtic: see Ford 2005. Williams 1971 speaks as if music were generally involved (e. g., pp. 90, 91, 99); Williams 1996:216–17 has relevant remarks on the Lat. *cano* and related words.
[77] These lexical items, usually with their etymologies, are widely discussed; but we cite especially Klingenberg 1984a and 1984b; Heusler 1911, 1943; von See 1964; on the Indo-European depth, see West 2007:63–68.
[78] Klingenberg 1984a: 378; Poole 2005.

appears to begin in both English and German in the High Middle Ages, and the underlying meaning of the root seems to have to do with religion rather than music proper (Gothic *siggwan* 'sing, read out, present formally as by chanting'). Benveniste (1932) and others assign to the Proto-Indo-European root the meaning 'present in a religious manner'; this, together with the ON uses of *syngja*, *syngva* in the sphere of magical singing, suggests a reason for the early church's favouring this family. If this reasoning is correct, we also have to allow for early secularization of the verb 'to sing' in West Germanic.

The Greek and Latin references to Continental Germanic poetry leave no doubt that in the earliest traceable period, poetry was frequently sung or at least accompanied by the harp, and West Germanic material, when it begins to appear, continues the association; to give a single example from *Beowulf*: *Þær wæs hearpan sweg, / swutol sang scopes* 'there was the sound of the harp, the clear song of the scop' (ll. 89b–90a). We can refer again to Opland (1980) for an anglophone collection of witnesses; the 'harp' (OE *hearpe*), technically a lyre, has become even better known since Opland, however, due in part to the recent find of an almost perfectly preserved sixth-century lyre in southern Germany.[79] North Germanic sources and terminology preserve the archaic connection between music and verse in the magical sphere (see the 'scene' from *The Saga of Erik the Red* discussed above), though without instrumentation; but nonreligious narrative poetry is rarely and only debatably associated with the harp while skaldic eulogy seems never to be (Finnur Jónsson 1907–8). Heusler is the scholar who has most sharply defined this 'problem' ('schwierige Fragen', 1911:457) and most elegantly solved it: West Germanic has copious external evidence of sung narrative verse, but the preserved poetry in Old English, Old High German, and Old Saxon, with its enjambment and long anacruses, was 'by nature unsingable' ('innerlich unsangbar'). On the other hand North Germanic narrative verse had, in the main, a singable verse structure of end-stopped lines grouped in pairs but very little external evidence of musical accompaniment; and skaldic poetry was flatly unsingable.[80] Heusler's solution imagines the history of early Germanic verse as analogical losses with complementary retentions: the West Germanic references must be to the older, simpler end-stopped style as sung in the preliterate, mainly continental, period; after literacy took hold, harp and song were retired, and the West Germanic verse that survives is, with a few conspicuous exceptions, limited to the book-epic in unsingable run-on style. In the North, too, the harp and singing presentation were lost, along with almost all memory of it; but the older, singable style was retained in eddic poetry itself. Heusler's outline seems at least to offer a platform for further speculation, but Heusler, his gaze firmly backward toward the Common Germanic, does not attend to certain late Nordic musical traces associated with narrative (and skaldic) poetry.

Several modern scholars, though, have found the five melodies said to be traditionally connected with Old Norse poetry an interesting challenge. The tunes were published in a large ethnomusicological collection in Paris in 1780; and, despite some impressive skeptical scholarship, there is reason to trust the eighteenth-century witnesses to the extent of allowing some real connection between late medieval or early modern

---

[79] Theune-Großkopf 2006. For an up-to-date treatment of the music of oral epic, both in field studies and historically reconstructed, and an extensive bibliography see Reichl 2000a and b.
[80] The recent study by Gade (1994) reconfirms these results.

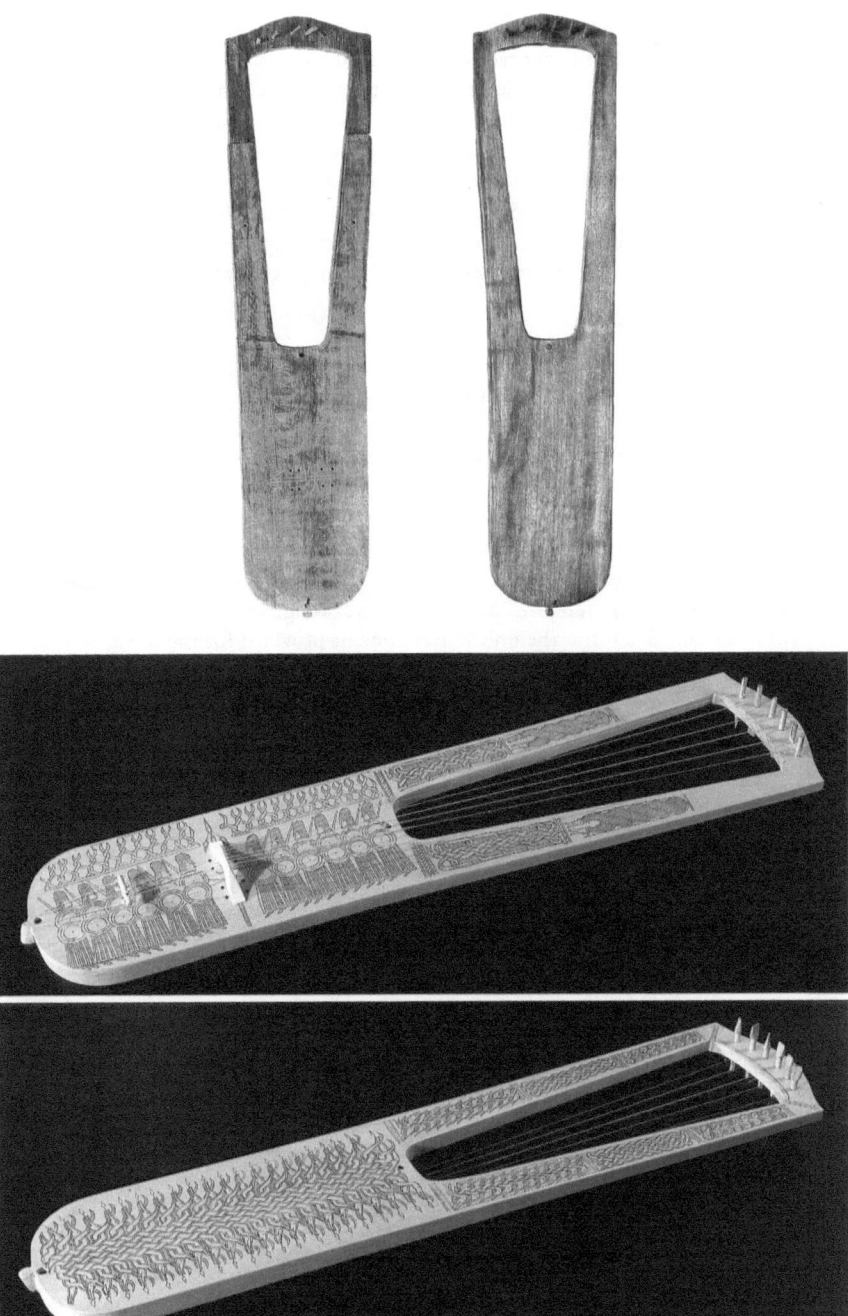

5 – Lyre, from Trossingen (6th c.), restored original (above) and reconstruction (below)

realization of Icelandic verse and these modern (or late early modern!) tunes.[81] A background of singing or half-singing receives some support from other writings of learned Icelanders of the late eighteenth and nineteenth centuries. The late medieval period (fourteenth century) saw the first attestations of a successor genre of both eddic poetry and skaldic in the *rímur*, rhymed stanzaic narrative verse traditionally sung in a kind of chant; the verb used for such performance is *kveða*, the same verb used for the performance of medieval poetry. Speculation about the concluding chapters of Norse performance history on the basis of these fragments is tempting, even though the resulting hypothetical would constitute but a minor part of the picture of early medieval performance in general.

## 3 Performance and Performers in the High and Late Middle Ages[82]

In the development of the Arthurian legend in the Middle Ages, Wace's *Roman de Brut*, completed in 1155 and dedicated to Aliénor of Aquitaine, wife of Henry II, is the first representation of Arthur and his court in a chivalric milieu. This milieu is strikingly evoked in the poet's description of the coronation feast. After a sumptuous meal the congregated knights go outside the town to amuse themselves with various games and contests, such as fencing, jumping, archery and wrestling, while the ladies watch from the town wall. But this is not the only entertainment provided for the feast:

> Molt ot a la cort jugleors,
> Chanteors, estrumanteors;
> Molt poïssiez oïr chançons,
> Rotruanges et noviaus sons,
> Vïeleüres, lais et notes,
> Lais de vïeles, lais de notes,
> Lais de harpes et de fretiaus,
> Lires, tympres et chalemiaus,
> Symphonies, psalterions,
> Monacordes, cymbes, chorons.
> Asez i ot tresgiteors,
> Joeresses et joeors;
> Li un dient contes et fables,
> Auquant demandent des et tables. (ll. 1997–2010)
>     (Arnold and Pelan 1962: 92)

There were many jongleurs at the court,/ singers and instrumentalists;/ you could have heard many songs,/ *rotrouenges* and new melodies,/ music for the *vièle*, *lais* and melodies,/ *lais* for the *vièle*, *lais* melodies,/ *lais* for harps and for flutes,/ lyres, drums and shawms,/ hurdy-gurdies, psalteries,/ monochords, cymbals and crowds./ There were a lot of *tresgiteors* there,/ musicians, male and female;/ some narrate stories and tales,/ others ask for dice and backgammon.

---

[81] Hofmann 1963; Jammers 1964; Hofmann and Jammers 1965; Harris 2003 (despite traumatic editing) and Harris 2000b together give a fair representation of the literature on 'eddic song'; a further cautiously favourable musicologist's position is K.-P. Koch 2002: 408–9.

[82] In section 3 'medieval' is to be understood as 'belonging to the High and Late Middle Ages'. – Unless otherwise indicated, all translations from primary and secondary sources are mine [KR].

This passage with its profusion of instruments is typical of similar descriptions in the literature of the High and Late Middle Ages. It is the earliest of its kind and also one which contains a number of technical terms that have given rise to some musicological and philological dispute. The instruments enumerated are the *vièle*, the medieval fiddle, the harp (*harpe*), the rebec (*lire*), a small bowed instrument, the hurdy-gurdy (*symphonie*), the psaltery (*psalterion*), the monochord (*monacord*), a one-stringed instrument, and the crowd or crwth (*choron*) as string instruments, the flute (*fretel*) and the shawm (*chalemel*) as wind instruments, and the small drum (*tympre*) and the cymbal (*cymbe*) as percussion instruments. The *rotrouenge* is a type of poem and song, generally with a refrain (Bec 1977–78: I, 183–89). The *lais* mentioned in this passage are almost certainly lyrical *lais*, a specific type of song, rather than the Breton *lais*, short narratives mainly associated with the literary activity of Marie de France.[83]

More interesting for the present discussion are the performers mentioned by Wace: the *jongleur*, the singer (*chanteor*), the instrumentalist (*estrumanteor*), the *tresgiteor*, and the female and male musician (*joeresse, joeor*). Their activity consists apparently in playing and singing music and in telling (*dire*) various kinds of narratives (*conte, fable*). It is not quite clear whether the game players mentioned in the last line are some of the entertainers or other members of the company assembled. While the purely musical terms for singers and instrumentalists are unequivocal, the figures of the *jongleur* and the *tresgiteor* are somewhat ambivalent. The word *tresgiteor* (*tresjetëor, tregetour*) is ultimately derived from Latin *traicere* (*transjicere*) 'to throw over', hence a *transjector* is a 'thrower (of balls etc.)' or a juggler. In the *Promptorium parvulorum*, a late-medieval English-Latin dictionary, the corresponding English word *tregettour* is glossed as 'mimus, pantomimus, joculator'. Both in medieval French and English the word often stresses the acrobatic and theatrical sides of the entertainer (*MED*, s. v. *tregetõur*).

It is passages like this which are our most important keys for an understanding of the late-medieval performer. These 'scenes' give us information about the various types of performers, their repertoire and modes of performance, and sometimes also about the impact of their performance on the audience. This information is, however, always in need of interpretation. The lines from Wace's *Brut* are a case in point. Leaving aside the fuzziness of some of the terms for musical instruments and of the genres performed, we can distinguish four activities of the entertainer: singing, playing a musical instrument, telling tales and providing further entertaining such as juggling and playing games. The various names used for the entertainers seem to overlap and might even be roughly synonymous: clearly the singer (*chanteor*) sings and the instrumentalist (*estrumanteor, joeresse, joeor*) plays an instrument, but in the same group are also the jongleur (*jugleor*) and the *tresgiteor*, and what they do is also sing and play. From the passage above it is not clear who is telling tales, but there seems to be an understanding that all are involved in the various forms of merry-making. From this passage then two preliminary conclusions can be drawn: on the one hand there seem to be different types of entertainers with possibly some kind of specialization, but on the other there is also a certain vagueness that characterizes terms like 'jongleur', which can denote a fairly broad spectrum of activ-

---

[83] On the interpretation of *lais* in this passage, see Foulet 1908: 161ff; see also Fallows 2001 and below p. 177.

ities comprising such diverse things as singing, playing music, juggling or telling tales. Many of the terms for the medieval entertainer are clearly under-differentiated (or over-generalized); sometimes the person denoted by such a term might have engaged in all the various activities listed above (playing, singing, reciting, juggling etc.), but sometimes more specialized skills are foregrounded in the 'scenes' found in our sources.

If we narrow down our view to performers of poetry, there are a number of questions that confront us. What kinds of poetry, what *genres*, did they perform? What was their *repertoire*? How did they perform, both with respect to the *mode* of performance (singing, chanting, speaking etc.) and the *manner* of performance (with or without musical accompaniment, face and body motions etc.)? What was the quality of their performance in terms of *evaluations* by the audience? What was the *role* of the performer in the processes of transmission and creation? What was the relationship to the poems he or she performed in terms of authorship, mental storage and verbal realization in the act of performance? Before addressing these questions, however, we have to take a look at the various terms for the medieval entertainer and the sources that help establish their meaning.

## 3.1 The Medieval Entertainer: Functions, Sources, Terms

Our sources for the medieval performer are manifold: some are pictorial, others literary, again others of a documentary nature. The literary sources are of the kind illustrated from Wace's *Brut*: descriptions of a minstrel's performance, typically at a feast. In addition we have the narrator's comments on his own performance, 'performative utterances' like 'Listen now, I'm going to tell you about so-and-so!' These and other 'traces of orality' in the texts are not always easy to interpret; they give, however, some indication about the mode of performance (see ch. 1, section 3). The documents relating to the medieval entertainer comprise various injunctions against vagrants and other non-sedentary folk, among them minstrels, many issued by the church at synods and in other contexts; they consist also of descriptions, definitions and discussions of minstrels in encyclopaedic and similar works, among them medieval glossaries and dictionaries. Information about minstrels is also found in chronicles as well as in household accounts, in which various musicians and their payment are listed. There are also numerous manuscript illuminations, carvings and sculptural representations. These various sources suggest that six major kinds of activities can be distinguished:
– playing a musical instrument,
– singing songs,
– doing acrobatics,
– telling jokes, humorous stories, anecdotes and *trivia* of various sorts,
– performing sketches, miming, putting on puppet-shows,
– reciting (longer) narrative poetry.

Needless to say, these activities overlap in many ways. An entertainer playing a musical instrument may also sing a poem or recite an epic; a juggler might also amuse his audience by telling them a spicy joke, and someone in whose repertoire there are fabliaux (humorous tales) might also perform narratives of a less frivolous nature. In the context of orality and literature, our interest focuses on those entertainers who perform poetry, be it in song or tale.

The entertainer as musician is profusely documented in art. Musicians are depicted in illuminations on the manuscript page, as figures in tapestries or glass windows, but also as sculptures on cathedral portals, on capitals or misericords, to name only the most common sources of visual representations.[84] The pictorial evidence also covers other aspects of the medieval entertainer. In a number of cases, the acrobatic aspect of the professional entertainer is depicted. Some of the earliest illuminations of this kind are found in one of the St. Martial manuscripts of the eleventh century (Paris, BnF MS lat. 1118). On fols. 107v and 112v, for instance, a flute player and a juggler of balls are represented; other illuminations show musicians (including King David, playing a crowd) and dancers. One of the dancers, a female figure, is ringing little bells while dancing (fol. 114r) [see Illustration 20]. In these illuminations we find a close symbiosis between music and dance, sound and movement, entertainment by music and by artistic performance. They underline the idea of the entertainer as musician, juggler, acrobat and dancer.

A rich mine of illustrations of musicians playing a wide gamut of instruments are two of the manuscripts of the *Cantigas de Santa Maria* by Alfonso X, the Wise (1221–1284). Well known is the illumination accompanying *cantiga* 120 in the Escorial MS j. b. 2 (E):

6 – Two musicians, from the *Cantigas de Santa Maria*

---

[84] For particularly well illustrated books on medieval musicians and minstrel-musicians see Munrow 1976; Bachfischer 1998.

Both musicians depicted are playing the lute; one of them is a Moor, the other presumably a Castilian. The latter not only strums his instrument but is clearly also singing. As Ramón Menéndez Pidal has put it, 'this illumination graphically shows the intimate collaboration of two performance traditions of the most diverse kind imaginable' (1957: 96, illustration on facing page). Here then we not only have an illustration of the singing of a song, of orally delivered lyrical poetry, but also of cultural contact and presumably influence. The duo reminds us that the mobility of musicians and minstrels was fairly high by medieval standards; they roamed over wide parts of Europe and are aptly referred to as *fahrendes Volk* (travelling people) in German.[85] For this reason a discussion of the medieval entertainer, while taking national developments into due consideration, must take a wider spectrum of traditions into account.

Evidence for the various functions of the minstrel comes also from chronicles, account books, encyclopaedic works, medieval vocabularies and dictionaries, as well as church documents, in particular the protocols and announcements of synods and councils. In account books musicians figure prominently. A good example is the payroll for the knighting feast of the future English king Edward II in 1306.[86] Among the names on the payroll we find Richard the harper, Nagary the crowder and Guillot the *vièle*-player, three musicians out of a group of twenty-six harpers, nine crowders and thirteen *vièle*-players. Only some belonged to the king, the others served various noble persons; even a *vièle*-player of the King of France and three fiddlers from Germany participated. The *menestrelli* of this feast, however, also comprised other persons, such as heralds, messengers and watchmen. Here *menestrellus* 'minstrel' has the general meaning of *ministerialis* 'a person in service, a functionary'. This is one of the senses of Old French *menestrel*; also the Middle English word *minstral* can have this sense, though only rarely. Apart from the musicians no other entertainers are mentioned by name on this payroll, with one exception, Matilda Makejoy, an acrobat:

> Several categories of instrumentalists are not represented on the Payroll, nor are there any identifiable conjurers, mimes, jugglers, funambulists, *gestours* and fools, although there is rich evidence in the records that such took part in royal household entertainment. There may be some among those whose names give no clue to their category, but Matilda Makejoy is the only one of whom we can be absolutely certain, because her name and category are recorded in the Wardrobe books. She was a *saltatrix* or female acrobat; not on wages and therefore not a royal domestic minstrel, yet she appears to have been attached, if that is the right word, to the royal household for at least 14 years. (Bullock-Davies 1978: 55)

Although minstrels are mentioned at various occasions by medieval historiographers, their descriptions are often disappointingly meagre. One of the most brilliant feasts in medieval German history was the *Mainzer Hoffest*, the celebrations of the imperial court of Frederick I in Mayence in 1184. The *Saxon World Chronicle* (mid–13th c.) characterizes this event as the 'greatest feast that ever took place on German soil'.[87] From the

---

[85] See Salmen 1960; see also Menéndez Pidal 1957: 81–99. The account of 'English wayfaring life in the Middle Ages' by Jusserand (1950: esp. 95–119) is still of interest.

[86] See Bullock-Davies 1978; Chambers 1903: II, 234–38 (Appendix C); some extracts from English account books are printed *ibid.*, 240–58 (Appendix E).

[87] *Sächsische Weltchronik*, MGH edition, p. 232. On this *Hoffest* see also Bumke 1986: I, 276–81.

*Chronicon Hanoniense* (Chronicle of Hainaut) by Gislebert of Mons (d. 1224) we learn that on the May 21, Henry and Frederick, the sons of Emperor Frederick I, were knighted and that 'in their honour many presents were given by them and by all the princes and many nobles to knights, prisoners and crusaders as well as to male and female minstrels, i. e. horses, precious clothes, gold and silver'.[88] There is no further qualification of these *ioculatores* and *ioculatrices*, nor is their performance described. Similarly we hear about the marriage celebration of Henry III of England in the *Chronica maiora* of Matthew Paris (d. 1259) that there was such a variety of minstrels (*histriones*) that London could barely contain them (Matthew Paris III, 336). Instead of providing an account of the entertainers' performance, however, he tantalizingly just asks the questions:

> How should I describe the over-flowing richness of the food and the different drinks at table? How the abundance of venison, the variety of fish, the delight given by the minstrels (*ioculatores*), the elegance of those serving? (III, 339)

Another source for the various functions of the medieval minstrel, in particular those which were found objectionable by ecclesiastical authorities, are statements put forth by churchmen and synods. Condemnations of the activities of popular entertainers – generally called *mimi* and *histriones* – began early in the growth of the Christian Church.[89] At the Synod of Elvira in Spain in *c.* 305, for instance, canon LXII allows chariot racers and pantomimes to become Christians only if they renounce their profession (Mansi II, col. 16). Among ecclesiastical admonishments and prohibitions from the later Middle Ages one of the most detailed sources of information on the medieval entertainer is provided by the *Summa de penitentia* (or *Summa confessorum*) of Thomas of Chobham (d. *c.* 1235). According to the *Summa* anyone with an occupation that is sinful has to give up this occupation if he or she wants to get absolution in confession. While for the participants in the Synod of Elvira all entertainers were intrinsically sinful, Thomas distinguishes between several types:

> Note that there are three types of entertainers (*histrio*). Some transform and contort their bodies through unseemly leaps or through foul gestures, baring their bodies in a shameful manner or putting on awe-inspiring armour or masks. All these will be damned unless they give their professions up.
>
> There are also other entertainers who have no occupation, but are busybodies who have no fixed place of abode, but haunt the courts of the great and spread scandal and disgrace about those who are absent. These will also be damned, since the Apostle (Paul) forbids to share the table with such people. They are called wandering buffoons (*scurra*), because they are good for nothing but eating and slandering.
>
> There is also a third type of entertainers, who have musical instruments to please people, and of these there are two kinds. Some take part in public drinking-bouts and licentious gatherings, where they sing licentious songs to induce people to lasciviousness. These shall be damned like the others. There are, however, others who are called minstrels (*ioculator*), who sing the deeds of noble men and the legends of saints and these give comfort to men in their afflictions or in their anxieties. They do not do many shameful things such as do the dancers,

---

[88] Gislebert of Mons, MGH edition, p. 143 (the feast is described on pp. 141–46).
[89] These prohibitions and injunctions are frequently discussed in the literature on the medieval entertainer; for a compact survey see Nicoll 1963: 136–50.

men and women, and others who put on a play with indecent representations and who, by magic or otherwise, create the illusion of some phantoms. If they do not do such things, but sing to the accompaniment of their instruments the deeds of noble men and other useful matter in order to bring comfort to men as has been said, then these can be well tolerated. This is shown by what Pope Alexander said when some minstrel asked him whether he could save his soul in his profession. The Pope asked him whether he knew of any other occupation from which he could live, and the minstrel answered, No. Therefore the Pope allowed him to get his living from his profession, as long as he abstained from the afore-mentioned indecent and shameful activities.[90]

Although Thomas adopts the official attitude of the church toward the popular entertainers, he does make an exception. His division into three types of *histriones* is illuminating, because it shows us that differences were recognized and made at the time. There are (1) the acrobats and jugglers as well as the masked performers, (2) the wandering buffoons, and (3) the entertainers who play musical instruments and sing. It is among the latter that he singles out the performers of heroic songs and saints' legends as acceptable, even praiseworthy. It is only those musicians and singers who incite their audience to sinful deeds that will be damned with the rest of the entertainers. By implication Thomas of Chobham also tells us that heroic narratives as well as religious narratives were sung rather than spoken. This is confirmed by musical evidence both for the *chansons de geste* and for saints' legends in the vernacular (see section 3.4 below).

Finally, it should be mentioned that glosses, glossaries and dictionaries also offer information on the various types of entertainer. The Middle English word *jogelour* is explained in the *Promptorium Parvulorum* of c. 1440 as 'mimus, histrio, pantomimus, balatro'. This is a late occurrence of *jogelour* in English; as early as the eleventh century, in Old English glosses to Aldhelm's prose *De virginitate* in a Brussels MS (Royal Library, MS 1650), we find the word *iugelere* as a gloss of *magus* and similar words meaning 'sorcerer, soothsayer, magician, snake-charmer' (Gretsch 1999: 406). These early and late glosses from Britain give us a spectrum of meanings, ranging from 'magician' (possibly 'illusionist') to 'pantomime' and 'buffoon' (*balatro*). Clearly, these meanings point to the theatrical activities of the entertainer. As to the glosses 'mimus' and 'histrio', they are not very helpful as they are merely the Latin equivalents of *jogelour*; their meaning 'entertainer' is just as vague as that of *jogelour*. What kind of entertainment the *mimus* or *histrio* provided cannot be deduced from a linguistic analysis of these terms.

This leaves us with the literary evidence. While chronicles are often disappointingly sparse in their descriptions of feasts with musicians and other kinds of entertainers, literary treatments of the same theme present in many cases a lavish picture. The enumeration of musicians and musical instruments as in the extract quoted above from Wace's *Brut* is a *topos*. In addition, there are a great number of descriptions that detail the various kinds of performers, their activities and, in the case of performers of poetry, their repertoire. No clear-cut terminology emerges from a consideration of these literary sources – words like *jogelour* or *minstral* retain their polysemy and hence ambiguity – but it is possible to piece together a somewhat fuller picture of the medieval performer, and his or her performance, than the documentary evidence affords.

---

[90] Broomfield 1968: 291–92 (Latin text). For a discussion of this passage, see Chambers 1903: I, 59 ff.; for the contemporary context, see also Rubel 1925.

Before we discuss the medieval entertainer as a performer of poetry, let us briefly review the main designations found in medieval sources. In Latin, the most common terms are *mimus*, *histrio* and *ioculator*, but other terms such as *scurra* (jester) are also found.[91] In French the two terms *jogelour/ joglëor* (later *jongleur*) and *menestrel* are the usual designations of entertainers.[92] The word *menestrel* becomes more common in the Late Middle Ages; derived from Latin *ministerialis* (a person in service), it generally denotes a person in steady employment.[93] Latin *ioculator* has continuations also in other Romance languages apart from French: Provençal and Catalan *joglar* (*juglar*), Spanish *juglar*, Portuguese *jogral* and Italian *giullare*.[94] In Portuguese there is also the term *segrel*, used (in the second half of 13th c.) for the *jogral* who in addition to being a performer and singer was also a composer of poetry (see pp. 183–84 below). In Italian the performer of *cantari* was called *cantastorie* (lit. 'singer of stories') or more generally *canterino* (singer).[95]

In Middle English we also find the word *jogelour*, in addition to other terms such as *minstral, disour, gestour, gleman*, and *rimour*. As the entries in the *Middle English Dictionary* and other lexicographical sources show, these terms overlap.[96] More specific seem to be the words *disour* (lit. 'speaker') and *gestour* (lit. 'teller of *gestes*'). Some of the evidence suggests that the word *disour* designated a performer of narrative, but this specialization is not consistently implied, and the *MED* offers in consequence the meanings: 'A storyteller or minstrel; also, an entertainer or jester'. A similar picture emerges in the case of *gestour*, where the *MED* glosses: 'One who recites metrical romances or tells stories, a minstrel; ?also, an entertainer, jester, mimic.' ME *gleman* goes back to OE *glēoman*, one of the terms for the Anglo-Saxon performer. Other terms in Old English and the other Older Germanic languages are discussed above (section 2.4). In Middle High German the entertainer is generally called a *spilman* (Modern German *Spielmann*). This term has been discussed widely, in particular in connection with the so-called *Spielmannsepen*, a group of epics thought to have been composed by minstrels on account of their style.[97]

---

[91] Although in many aspects superseded by later research, Reich 1903 contains a still useful collection of data and observations on the *mimus*, in particular with reference to his theatrical activities; compare also Allen 1909–11 (who contests Reich's idea that the medieval entertainer goes back to the *mimus* of antiquity) and Ogilvy 1963.

[92] The term 'Old French' is used to cover both Old French proper and what is more correctly called Middle French (c. 1310 to the end of the 16th c.); Anglo-Norman or Anglo-French is also subsumed under 'Old French' unless specified otherwise.

[93] The basic study of sources for the jongleur is Faral 1910. On the terms, see Tobler-Lommatzsch, s. v. *joglëor* and *menestrel* (with the meanings 'servant', 'worker, craftsman'; 'minstrel'; and figuratively, 'good-for-nothing'); compare also Morgan 1953–54 and Baldwin 1997. An informative discussion of the sources is found already in Sittard 1885; compare Wright 1990. On the jongleur, see also ch. 12 on the *chanson de geste* (D. Boutet).

[94] The entertainer on the Iberian Peninsula is comprehensively discussed in Menéndez Pidal 1957. On the Castilian *juglar*, see also Hilty 1995; on the Catalan *joglar*, see Tavani 1995.

[95] On the Italian *giullare*, see the study (and collection of texts) by Saffiotti 1990. On the *cantastorie* and *canterino*, see Levi 1914 and ch. 13 by R. Morabito in this volume.

[96] See *MED*, s. v. *jŏgelŏur, glē-man, minstral, rimŏur, disŏur, ğestŏur*; Carter 1961, s. v. *Iogelour, Gleman, Menestral, Gestour*. On the entertainer in medieval England, see also Burrow 1973; Grossmann 1906; Olson 1941; Southworth 1989; on the Middle English entertainers, see also ch. 11 by A. Putter in this volume.

[97] The concept of the *spilman* and his role in the composition of the so-called *Spielmannsepen* (*König Rother, Herzog Ernst* and others) as developed in the nineteenth century has been much criticised;

While the terminology for the medieval performer in the languages mentioned so far is generally familiar and fairly well researched, the corresponding terms in other medieval traditions also represented in this volume – Romanian, Greek, Russian, Hebrew, Arabic, Persian, and Turkish – are as a rule only known to the specialist. Romanian is documented only from the sixteenth century onward (excepting some Romanian words in Byzantine documents) and it is hence by the modern word for the performer, *lăutar* ('fiddler', etymologically derived from *lăută* 'lute'), that the medieval performer is designated in the literature (see further ch. 14 by M. Beissinger). When Pope Eusebius, in one of his decrees (310), forbade bishops to have entertainers at their table, he talked about 'the vain speeches of entertainers' (*acroamatum vaniloquia*) (Mansi II, col. 426). The term *acroama* has a Greek origin, where it means 'what is heard, recital, song'; in the Latin dictionary of Lewis and Short it is glossed as 'the entertainer at table, by music (a performer) or by reading (a reader), also a buffoon' (s. v. *ācrŏāma*). The general word for entertainer in the Byzantine world is, however, *mîmos* (μῖμος) and for the musician simply *mousikós* (μουσικός) (Tinnefeld 1974; Puchner 1983). Other terms, such as *tragoudistēs* (τραγουδιστής) 'singer', are of later date.[98]

Although there are early attestations of the word *shpil'man* in Russian (13th c.), obviously a loan-word from German *spilman*, the entertainer in medieval Russia was generally called *skomorokh*. The etymology of this word, first recorded in the eleventh century, is contested; one derivation connects it to words meaning 'impudent, immodest', but also 'cheerful, lively' in various Slavic languages.[99] The *skomorokh* was, like the jongleur, a musician, but could also perform all kinds of tricks and do acrobatics. The *skomorokhi* also recited *byliny* and played an important role in their transmission and public performance.[100] From medieval and post-medieval sources it can be gathered that they played the *gusli*, a plucked psaltery, or the *gudok*, a bowed fiddle.[101] *Byliny* were also recited by the *kaliki perekhozhie*, vagrant beggars and cripples, forming 'a confraternity of itinerant religious singers', a type of professional singer that has been described in detail in the Chadwicks' *Growth of Literature*. While the activity of the *skomorokhi* was forbidden in 1648 by Tsar Alexei Mikhailovich, the *kaliki perekhozhie* continued, not unlike the *Bänkelsänger*, *saltimbanco* and mountebanks and ballad-mongers further west, into the twentieth century. When the *byliny* were written down in the nineteenth century, the narrators (*skaziteli*) had ceased to be professionals. They were amateurs, almost exclusively peasants from the north of Russia.[102]

In the medieval Jewish world no professional entertainers in Hebrew seem to have existed, although story-*telling* (in Hebrew) was an important aspect of Jewish culture (see ch. 19 by Eli Yassif below). In the vernacular languages spoken by the Jewish popu-

---

see, e. g., Naumann 1924; Steinger 1930; Bahr 1954. For a survey, see Curschmann 1968, for a collection of studies, see Schröder 1977. *Spielmann* and *Spielmannsepen* are comprehensively discussed in Wareman 1951.

[98] On the singers of Modern Greek folk poetry (with regional types such as the Cretan *rimadóri* and Cypriot *pyitárides*), see Beaton 1980: 151–74.

[99] See Vasmer 1953–58, s. v. *shpil'man* and *skomorókh*.

[100] On the *skomorokhi*, see Zguta 1972 and 1978; Vlasova 2001; Findeizen 2008: I, 113–35.

[101] See Sadokov 1976; Findeizen 2008: I, 170–71 (*gudok*), 176–78 (*gusli*).

[102] See Chadwick and Chadwick 1932–40: II, 238–69 (*skaziteli*), 270–83 (*kaliki perekhozhie*); on the *byliny* compare also ch. 1, section 5.3; see also ch. 18 (S. N. Azbelev).

lation of Europe, on the other hand, oral and popular literature was cultivated, with plentiful evidence in particular in Yiddish. *Dukus Horant*, one of the Middle High German epics from the group of poems associated with the activity of minstrels – as performers and possibly composers – has been preserved in Hebrew script in a late fourteenth-century Cambridge manuscript from the genizah of the Ezra Synagogue in Cairo (edited and discussed in Ganz, Norman, and Schwarz 1964). While scholarly opinion is divided on the question whether this text belongs to Yiddish literature proper or is rather a Middle High German poem in Hebrew script (with some adaptations for a Jewish audience), other popular epics, mostly on biblical topics, from the end of the medieval period and the early modern period are undoubtedly works in Older Yiddish.[103] Max Weinreich discussed in his *Bilder fun der Yidisher Literaturgeshikhte* (Sketches from the History of Yiddish Literature) the medieval *zinger un ferleyener*, 'singer and public reader', and attributed an important role to the *spilman* for the performance and dissemination of Yiddish popular poetry (1928: 56–67). As in Middle High German research the 'romantic view of the *Spielmann*' has been criticized, so the role of the *spilman* in Yiddish culture has been similarly questioned:

> The diffusion of this literature inspired by feudal German epics has for a long time maintained the belief in the existences of professional wandering minstrels, the *spilmänner*, Jewish equivalents of the medieval troubadours. No precise source, however, seems to substantiate this theory. It is rather a romantic myth than a reality of Jewish society, especially as the perfect knowledge of the sources of the Jewish tradition makes one rather think that the authors were literates who composed the epics in Yiddish for the people of the ghettos.[104]

While the 'creative contribution' of the *spilman* to Yiddish oral literature is just as difficult to evaluate as that of his colleague in other medieval societies, his function as performer is uncontested, as is that of musician. From the sixteenth century onwards the musician and entertainer is called *klezmer* (from Hebrew *klei zemer* 'musical instruments'), a word still current today in 'klezmer music' (Salmen 1990).

Entertainers, in their various functions, were also found in other European countries in the Middle Ages, both locally and as visitors from other regions. The mobility of the medieval minstrels was surprisingly great and their travels correspondingly far-reaching, as Walter Salmen has pointed out with regard to the medieval entertainer-musician (1960: 145–205). In Hungary, for instance, three medieval terms for the entertainer are found, *regös*, *igric*, and *ioculator*. While the *regös* and the *igric* (the latter a Slavic loan-word meaning 'player') refer mostly to musicians, the Latin term, in a number of contexts, denotes the jongleur as a performer of narrative poetry (such as *chansons de geste*) (Falvy 1961). In Joinville's *Histoire de Saint Louis* we read of three Armenian *menestrier*, who, during the Sixth Crusade of 1248, surprised the Latin crusaders by their musical and above all acrobatic skills.[105] In medieval Armenia the minstrel was called *gusan*, a

---

[103] For a survey medieval epic and romance in Yiddish, see Baumgarten 2005:128–62; for the popularization of Romance chivalric epics in Yiddish by Elia Levita in the sixteenth century, see *ibid.*: 163–206.
[104] Baumgarten 1993:43. A similar opinion is expressed in Shmeruk 1986.
[105] Pauphilet 1952:317–18; already Thomas Percy, in his 'Essay on the Ancient Minstrels in England' (1765), drew attention to this passage (Percy 1886: I, 384–85).

loan-word from Parthian; this is still the term for the oral singer in modern Armenian (Boyce 1957: 12 ff.).

In the medieval Oriental literatures in Arabic, Persian and Turkish the situation is similar to that of other medieval traditions: whatever was composed, transmitted and performed orally is accessible to us only through written sources and hence dependent on interpretation. There is, however, one difference, and that is that some of these medieval traditions still have continuations or at least echoes in the modern world, and are hence available for direct observation. In all three language-areas orality and literacy are intimately intertwined and we can therefore find as one of the central figures the public reader, a 'reader', however, who is at times more of an actor and improviser than follower of a written text. With literacy memorization also plays a part in the structuring of performance. On the other hand, oral performance independent of writing and written transmission or composition can also be assumed, especially in the Turkic cultural word, where it has survived in some areas into the twenty-first century.[106]

I have used the masculine form of the various words for performers, but it should be borne in mind that many performers were women, not only among dancers and jugglers, but also among musicians, singers and (in some traditions) also 'singers of tales'.

## 3.2 Repertoire

Which genres of poetry and which works medieval minstrels performed can be deduced from various lists. These are of different kinds: the work lists that feature in the description of feast scenes, the repertoire lists of individual performers as they are given in their poetry, or the indications found in texts such as the *Summa de penitentia* quoted above.[107] A particularly detailed genre and work list is found in the Old Provençal verse romance *Flamenca* (*c.* 1240–1250). At Flamenca's and Archambaut's wedding feast, when the meal is over:

> Apres si levon li juglar;
> Cascus se volc faire auzir;
> Adonc aurizas retentir
> Cordas de manta tempradura. (ll. 592–95)
> (Lavaud and Nelli 1960: 674)

> Then the jongleurs got up;/ every one of them wanted to be heard;/ then you could have heard resound/ strings of various tuning.

In the course of over one hundred verse lines (ll. 592–709) the entertainment provided by the jongleurs is described; it consists of music played on various instruments, of *canzo*, *descort* and *lais* (l. 597), the *vers* of the troubadour Marcabru (l. 702), putting on a mar-

---

[106] On performers and performance in Arabic, see ch. 24 (T. Herzog), in Persian ch. 25 (J. Rubanovich), and in Turkish ch. 26 (K. Reichl).

[107] Various lists specifying the repertoire of the entertainer have been discussed in the literature; see, e. g., Wareman 1951: 66–72, 80–98; Hartung 1982: 9–20; compare also Chambers 1903: I, 70–86, and for a fairly extensive list of *témoignages relatifs aux jongleurs* (9th–13th c.), see Faral 1910: 272–327; for a list of literary documents referring to English minstrels, see Grossmann 1906: 58–66.

ionette play (l. 611), juggling and acrobatics (ll. 612–16), and most importantly of *diverses comtes* (l. 618), various narratives, which comprise a vast pool of narrative traditions: the legends of Troy and of Thebes, the stories of Pyramus and Thisbe and Apollonius of Tyre, the Alexander romance and the tale of Orpheus and Eurydice, narratives from the Bible (David and Goliath, Samson and Delilah, the Maccabees) and ancient history (Julius Caesar), Arthurian romances (Gauvain, Perceval, Erec and Enide, Yvain, Tristan) and *chansons de geste* (Charlemagne, Gui de Nanteuil). The *canzo*, *descort* and *lais* are sung and accompanied on musical instruments:

> L'uns viola-[l] lais del Cabrefoil,
> E l'autre cel de Tintagoil;
> L'us cantet cel dels Fins amanz,
> E l'autre cel que fes Ivans. (ll. 599–602)
> (Lavaud and Nelli 1960: 674)

One plays the 'Lai of the Honeysuckle' on the *vièle*,/ the other the 'Lai of Tintagel';/ one sings the 'Lai of the Courly Lovers',/ and the other the lai which Yvain composed.

As in the passage from Wace quoted above, *lais* are played and sung. It is possible that here narrative rather than lyric *lais* are denoted; at least names like 'Lai of the Honeysuckle' and 'Lai of the Courtly Lovers' point in this direction; they might refer to similarly named *lais* by Marie de France or rather to versions related to these *lais*.[108] Interestingly, for the narratives mentioned in the sequel the verbs *comter* (narrate) and *dizer* (say) are used. This might indicate the mode of performance: recite rather than sing or chant; but *dire* (*dizer*) can also mean 'to sing'.[109] On the other hand, it might be well not to put too much trust into this description. The list of stories contains a number of narratives that have reached us predominantly in literary versions, such as the *romans antiques* and the Arthurian romances, which are unlikely candidates for a minstrel's performance.

Similar doubts linger concerning other sources, where the hyperbolic or conventional nature of the representation makes it difficult to arrive at a clear picture. The *Cantare dei cantari* might be cited in this connection; this is not a description of a performance as in *Flamenca* or *Brut*, but the self-advertisement of a *giullare*. The Italian poem from the end of the fourteenth or beginning of the fifteenth century comprises 59 eight-line stanzas (in *ottava rima*) and enumerates a vast repertoire of stories offered by the minstrel to his listeners:

> I' veggio storie, favole e novelle,
> Nuove e antiche, tutte stare a schiera
> Dinanzi a me, co lor senbianze belle,
> Più che non sono e fior di primavera;
> E gli aultori, or di queste, or di quelle,
> M' inviton co s' dolce lor matera,

---

[108] See Marie's *Les Deus Amanz* and *Chevrefoil*, edited in Ewert 1944: 75–81 and 123–26 and translated in Burgess and Busby 1999: 82–85 and 109–10.

[109] The evidence of *dizer* is doubtful. In l. 702 we read *L'us diz lo vers de Marcabru* (Another 'says' the *vers* [= *canso*] of Marcabru). It is usual for troubadour *vers* to be sung, and as it turns out, the melodies of seven of Marcabru's poems have actually been preserved.

> Ch' i' non so quale in prima cominciare,
> O di qual più vi piaccia udir cantare.[110]

I see stories, tales and novellas,/ new and old, all stand in a crowd/ before me, with their beautiful appearance,/ more beautiful than are the flowers of spring;/ and the authors now of these, now of other stories,/ invite me with their tales ('matter') of such sweetness/ that I do not know which one I should first begin,/ or which it might please you more to hear (me) sing.

With so much to choose from, the *giullare* leaves the choice to his audience (st. 5) and begins his long list of alternatives with the biblical creation story. From there he proceeds to the legends of Classical Antiquity and tales from the history of Rome (st. 6–38). However, the *giullare* continues, if among the audience there might be someone in love, young or old, who would prefer to hear about Lancelot and Tristan, then they should make a sign and he will begin the tales of the Round Table (st. 39). There are many stories to be told gladly, but one displeases the narrator, the story of the destruction of the *Table Ronde* (st. 47). He therefore passes on quickly to tales about Charlemagne and his paladins, as well as other *chansons de geste* (st. 47–56), which he is happy to recite in French or in Italian (st. 48.8). The *giullare* concludes by assuring his audience that he can tell any tale from the various cycles and subject matters represented, in the vernacular or in Latin (st. 57.7), in rhyme (verse) or in the form of the *novelletta* (st. 59.7).[111] Clearly, such a huge list of narratives is hardly a realistic representation of the repertoire of a *giullare*; it is a hyperbolic boast of narrative skills.

The repertoire and the skills to be mastered by a jongleur are the subject of three Provençal *ensenhamen*s, poetic instructions, in which a troubadour addresses a jongleur and either criticizes his lack of knowledge and skill or positively advises him what to learn.[112] In 'Cabra juglar' (PC 242a.1) the Catalan troubadour Guiraut de Cabreira (Guerau de Cabrera) reproaches his jongleur Cabra that he plays and sings badly, that he cannot dance and juggle, and that his knowledge of tales to perform is minimal: 'of Roland you know as much as of something that has never existed' (*E de Rollan,/ sabs atretan/ coma d'aiso que anc non fon*, ll. 55–57).[113]

Criticism of a co-professional's competence and praise of one's own accomplishments is the tenor of an Old French text, 'Deux bordeors ribauz', classified as a fabliau and consisting of the attack of one *menestrel* on another and the latter's retort.[114] The

---

[110] Stanza 4; quotations are from the edition of Pio Rajna 1878 (where the poem is edited on pp. 425–37). On this work see also ch. 13 on the Italian *cantari* by R. Morabito (pp. 377–78).

[111] '*Intese avete oma' come cantare/ Vi posso* [... ]/ *Ogni ventura in rima o novelletta*' (You have heard now how I can *sing* to you [...] any adventure in rhyme [verse-form] or as *novelletta*). The use of the verb 'sing' speaks against understanding *novelletta* as meaning 'in prose'; what is probably meant is novellistic *cantari* (see ch. 13, p. 377 below).

[112] All three poems are edited, translated (into French) and extensively discussed in Pirot 1972. The third poem, by Bertran de Paris (PC 85.1), is less specific than the other two; see Pirot 1972: 596–614.

[113] Pirot 1972: 548. On this poem, see also ch. 1, p. 24.

[114] Second half of 13th c.; there is a third poem, also a retort, which gives, however, no information on a jongleur's repertoire. The poems are edited in Noomen 2003: 25–65, from which I quote. The word *ribaut* is glossed in Tobler-Lommatzsch, s. v. *ribaut*, as 'vagrant, tramp; riffraff following an army' but also without any pejorative meaning 'wandering minstrel'.

first 'talker' blames his interlocutor that he 'is not at all a minstrel' (*Tu n'es mie menestereus*, l. 38) and then launches into a praise of his own achievements:

> Mais ge sai ausi bien conter
> Et en roumanz et en latin,
> Aussi au soir com au matin,
> Devant contes et devant dus;
> Et si resai bien faire plus
> Quant ge sui a cort ou a feste,
> Car ge sai de chançon de geste [...] (ll. 58–64)

> But I can narrate well,/ in both French and Latin,/ in the evening as well as in the morning,/ in front of counts and dukes;/ and I can even do more/ when I am at court or at a feast,/ because I know *chansons de geste* [...]

The minstrel presents a long list of *chansons de geste*, but also *romans d'aventure*, noting that of one of them (*Partenoble de Blois*) he knows more than forty *laisses*.[115] The second minstrel rejects the criticism, saying that on the contrary 'I am a better *menestrel* than you' (ll. 4–5). He does not give quite such a long list of works, but is more explicit in some of his comments on his art. He is a *juglerres de viele* (l. 29), but can also play other instruments; he can sing, he knows games and is also an illusionist (*Bien sai un enchantement faire*, l. 40). And he has a good memory: he knows the 'whole story of the Loherans' (a cycle of *chansons de geste*)[116] *par sens et par memoire* and:

> De totes les chançons de geste
> Que tu savroies aconter
> Sai ge par cuer dire et conter. (ll. 144–46)

> From all the *chansons de geste*/ which you could enumerate/ I can recite and narrate by heart.

The exaggerations found in all these texts illustrating a minstrel's repertoire cast doubt on their use as evidence. What Pio Rajna has observed with regard to the *Cantare dei cantari* is, however, also valid for the other poems: 'But sometimes to tell lies does not mean to lie always'(*Ma, dir talvolta qualche bugia, non significa mentir sempre*; Rajna 1878: 225). No doubt these texts cannot be taken at their face value, but they also need not be discarded as worthless. They certainly imply that apart from songs jongleurs orally performed narrative poetry (by preference, but not exclusively, *chansons de geste*), and that in addition to their narrative skills they possessed the musical gifts of playing various instruments, prominently, it seems, the *vièle*. These texts in conjunction with other sources also give hints about the mode and manner of performance and the relationship of the minstrel to the poetry he performed in terms of authorship and, as it were, authority.

---

[115] In lines 88–89 the text interchanges *Blois* and *Galais*: 'Si sai de Perceval de Blois;/ De Partenoble le Galais/ Sai ge plus de quarante laisses.' It must be *Perceval le Galais* and *Partenoble de Blois*.

[116] 'Des Loherans tote l'estoire/ Sai ge par sens et par memoire', ll. 131–32. The cycle comprises five epics with a total of more than 60,000 lines: *Garin le Lorrain, Gerbert de Metz, Anseïs de Metz, Hervis de Metz*, and *Yon de Metz*.

## 3.3. Performer, Transmitter, Poet

In one of his love poems, the troubadour Bertran de Born (d. 1215) imagines a *domna soisseubuda*, a lady uniting the traits of various beauties, or as Ezra Pound translates, 'a borrowed lady'.[117] Bertran ends his poem with an envoi asking his *joglar* to sing his poem to Folquet de Marseille, a fellow-poet, designated by the *senhal* Aziman (magnet):

> Papiols, mon Aziman
> m'anaras dir en chantan
> qu'amors es desconoguda
> sai e d'aut bas chazeguda.

> Papiol, go to my 'Magnet'/ and tell him in singing/ that love is unappreciated/ here and is fallen from above to the ground.

Papiol is mentioned in nine of Bertran's poems; it is clear that he is the *joglar* whose task it was to get the poet's poems to their destination and to perform them in the appropriate places and circumstances.

Other troubadours had their *joglars* also. Arnaut de Mareuil (fl. 1195) names Pistoleta; Peire Cardenal (13th c.) is accompanied by a jongleur, Guiraut de Bornelh (second half of 12th c.) by two (Davenson [Marrou] 1961: 5–19). Bernart de Ventadorn (fl. *c.* 1150–1170) mentions a messenger (*messatgers*) in several poems, clearly a jongleur. He is told to sing the poem to the poet's lady, as in a poem addressed to Aliénor d'Aquitaine:

> Huguet, mos cortes messatgers,
> chantatz ma chanso volonters
> a la reina dels normans.[118]

> Huguet, my courtly messenger,/ sing my song gladly/ to the queen of the Normans.

However clear the distinction between troubadour and *joglar* might seem – the one the poet and creator, the other the performer and transmitter – it is by no means as clear-cut as these examples suggest. Troubadours were also the performers of their own poetry, and a number of troubadours were also *joglars*, as for instance Cercamon (12th c.), whose *vida* states in concise terms: 'Cercamon was a *joglar* from the Gascogne; he composed *vers* and *pastoretas* in the ancient manner. He roamed through the whole world, wherever he was able to go, and this is why he is called "Roam-the-World" (Cerca-mon)' (de Riquer 1975: I, 222). Other troubadours that were also called *joglars* include Marcabru, Alegret and Guiraut de Calanso. The nature of the evidence is not such that precise differentiations can be established. What is important to note in the present context, however, is the fact that performers termed *joglars* in medieval sources could also be composers of poetry.[119]

---

[117] 'Domna, pos de mi no·us cal' (PC 80.12), quoted from de Riquer 1975: II, 698–701, at 701; Pound's poem (originally published in his collection *Lustra*) is edited in Pound 1928: 85–87.

[118] 'Pel dous chan que·l rossignols fai' (PC 70.33), quoted from de Riquer 1975: I, 376–378, at 378.

[119] For a discussion of the differentation between *joglar* and *troubadour* in the case of early poets like Cercamon, see Jones 1931 and Harvey 1993; for a critical analysis of the distinction, see Noto 1998.

A companion piece to Guiraut de Cabreira's *ensenhamen* is a *sirventes* addressed by Guiraut de Calanso to his jongleur Fadet, 'Fadet joglar' (PC 243.7a), from the beginning of the thirteenth century. Once again various musical accomplishments and entertainment skills – juggling, acrobatics, putting on a puppet show – as well as a comprehensive mastery of narrative matter, mostly from ancient history and legend, are demanded. Only then is success assured: 'If you learn these new precepts, you will *trobar*, without lie' (*Comandamens/ nous, si·n aprens,/ i trobaras senes mentir*, ll. 214–16; Pirot 1972: 576). The gift of *trobar*, of composing poems, was promised already at the beginning of the poem (l. 13). This seems to imply that the *joglar* Fadet not only recites or sings poetry composed by others but also his own.

As the passage from *Flamenca* quoted at the beginning of section 3 suggests, Provençal *joglars* also performed narrative poetry. Although narrative genres like the *chanson de geste* and courtly romance are not as abundantly preserved from the south of France as from the north, a tradition connected to the performance of the *joglar contador* (the narrating jongleur) is nevertheless well substantiated. In *Daurel e Beton* a Provençal *chanson de geste* related to the Carolingian cycle, a leading role is played by Daurel, a *joglar*; it is not unlikely that the narrative originated in a minstrel milieu (Kimmel 1974). As Robert Lafont has argued, 'there can be no doubt about the existence of *jongleurs de geste* who have become poets' (1992: 262).

The same picture emerges for the followers of the troubadours in neighbouring countries – as in Catalonia and Italy (Cabré 1999) – and the trouvères of northern France. As Edmond Faral remarked in his study of the jongleur: 'Le trouveur, c'est simplement le jongleur considéré comme auteur'.[120] Among the poets of trouvère lyrics we find a figure like Colin Muset, a *menestrel* of the second third of the thirteenth century, from whom twenty lyrics have been preserved. In one of them (Raynaud-Spanke no. 476) he complains that his performance on the *vièle* has brought him no reward:

> Sire cuens, j'ai vielé
> Devant vous en vostre ostel,
> Si ne m'avez riens doné
> Ne mes gages aquité:
>     C'est vilanie! (Bédier 1938: 9)

Sir Count, I have played the *vièle*/ before you in your palace,/ but you have given me nothing/ nor paid my salary:/ this is disgraceful.

In another of his *chansons* (Raynaud-Spanke no. 967), he describes his vagrant life:

> L'en m'apele Colin Muset,
> S'ai maingié maint bon chaponnet,
> Mainte haste, maint gastelet,
> En vergier et en praelet,
> Et quant je puis hoste trover
> Qui vuet acroire et bien preter,
> Adonc me preng a sejorner
> Selon la blondete au vis cler. (Bédier 1938: 6–7)

---

[120] 'The troubadour/trouvère is simply the jongleur seen as author' (Faral 1910: 79). See Faral's chapter on the classification of jongleurs, pp. 66–86.

> I am called Colin Muset,/ and I have eaten many a good capon,/ many a roast, many a cake,/ in the orchard and on the meadow,/ and when I can find a host,/ who is ready to give credit and to lend money,/ then I make ready to stay/ near the fair woman with the radiant face.

This, of course, accords with the picture of the jongleur as someone ever in search of an audience and a patron in order to get rich recompense for his performance. However, entertainers like Cercamon or Colin Muset demonstrate also that the art of performing songs can include the art of composing poetry. A rigorous division between creative and merely reproductive jongleurs, at least as far as their lyrical repertoire is concerned, clearly does not do justice to the situation in the south and north of France in the period of the flowering of troubadour and trouvère poetry, i. e. the eleventh, twelfth and thirteenth centuries.

Similar observations can be made about the jongleur performing narrative poetry, in particular *chansons de geste*. Guiraut de Cabreira criticizes his *joglar* Cabra for being unable to sing a *chanson de geste* about Charlemagne's Saxon Wars:

> Del Saine cut
> c'ajas perdut
> et oblidat los motz e·l son:
> ren no·n diçetz
> ni no·n sabetz,
> pero no i ha meillor chanson. (ll. 49–54)

> Of the Saxon (the *Chanson des Saisnes*) I think/ you have lost/ and forgotten both the words and the melody:/ you don't say anything/ nor know anything of it,/ although there is no better *chanson*.

A *Chanson des Saisnes* has come down to us, in a version composed by Jean Bodel (d. 1210). Jean Bodel was a member of the 'Confrérie des Jongleurs et Bourgois d'Arras' and an extremely productive poet (if all the works ascribed to him are his).[121] In the introduction to his poem (in *c.* 8,000 alexandrines) we read:

> Cil bastart jougleour, qui vont par ces viliaus,
> A ces longues vïeles a depeciés forriaus,
> Chantent de Guitechin si com par asseniaus [...] (ll. 27–29)
>  (Brasseur 1989: I, 4)

> These bastard jongleurs who wander through the towns/ with their long *vièles* in their tattered cases,/ sing of Guitechin (= Widukind, the Saxon king) like madmen [...]

The jongleurs' lack of knowledge is criticized several times; the narrator promises to tell the story correctly and without the corruptions widely encountered. This kind of distancing from faulty jongleur performances is found in a number of *chansons de geste*. In Jean Bodel's case this does not imply a radical dissociation of the poet-narrator from the art of the oral poet, but rather a judgment of quality: Jean Bodel's version is going to be better than that of his competitors. He is, after all, a jongleur-poet and not a mere reciter of traditionally transmitted works (Jacob-Hugon 1995). It is important to realize

---

[121] His works comprise in addition to the epic nine *fabliaux*, five pastourelles, the *Jeu de Saint Nicolas*, and *Le Congés d'Arras*. Compare also D. Boutet's appraisal of Jean Bodel and his *Chanson des Saisnes* in ch. 12 of this volume, p. 361.

that the term 'jongleur' covers a wide spectrum of creative and reproductive skills. The same is true of the entertainer in other language areas; of the Italian *giullare* Michelangelo Picone remarks: 'On the one side we find the *giullare* degraded to the position of buffoon and on the other elevated to the position of poet' (1994: 29).

An important testimony for the distinction between various types of jongleurs is the petition by Guiraut Riquier addressed to King Alfonso X of Castile together with the king's answer (1274 and 1275).[122] Guiraut remarks that the estates of society are composed of various groups, all of which have their own names. Not so in the case of the jongleurs (*joglars/jograls*). There are some who are uneducated, conduct themselves disgracefully, are hardly able to play a musical instrument and, like beggars, lead a vagabond life. Then there are some who exhibit their art on market squares and in the taverns, some who show sleights of hand and make monkeys dance and put on puppet shows, and finally some who are able to compose poetry. All are called by the same name and Guiraut asks the king to mark these differences by different designations.

In his answer the king notes that in Latin different types of entertainers are distinguished: musicians who play an instrument are called *histriones*, poets *inventores*, and all the 'tumblers' *ioculatores*. In Spanish also distinctions are marked: the name *joglars* for those who play an instrument, *remendadors* for imitators, *segriers* for jongleurs-poets performing in courts, and *cazurros* for blind and deaf vagrants who discredit the jongleur class. In Provence, however, all are called *joglar*, and he therefore proposes a three-fold differentiation: the common entertainers, who make monkeys, goats and dogs jump, play the puppet theatre and sing among common people are the *bufos* (buffoons). The *joglar*, on the other hand, is a courtly performer, but only a performer and not a poet:

> E silh c'ap cortezia
> et ab azaut saber
> se sabon captener
> entre las ricas gens,
> per tocar esturmens,
> o per novas comtar
> d'autrui, o per cantar
> autrus vers e cansos,
> o per d'autres faitz bos
> ep plazens per auzir,
> podon ben possezir
> aquel nom de joglar (ll. 222–233)

And those who with courtly behaviour/ and sufficient knowledge/ can maintain themselves/ among rich people,/ by playing instruments/ or reciting narratives/ composed by others or by singing/ the *vers* and *cansos* of others/ may well have/ the name of *joglar*.

And finally, those who compose the words and the music of their poems are the *troubadours*. There is even a fourth degree, the *doctores de trobar*, the masters of poetry and song.

In Galician-Portuguese, the *jogral* (*joglar*) who was able to compose his own poetry was also called *segrel*, as indicated by the king's explanations (*segriers*). The distinction

---

[122] The text (from which I am quoting) is edited, translated (into Italian) and discussed in Bertolucci Pizzorusso 1966.

between *trovador* and *segrel* in Portuguese seems to have been mainly one of social position and, not unlike the situation found among Provençal troubadours, is not entirely clear (Resende de Oliveira 1993a, 1993b, 1993c). Once again, the reproductive performer merges into the creative performer, the reciter of the poetry of others into the reciter of his own poetry.

### 3.4 Performance Modes and Audience Interaction

The performance routine of a jongleur comprised also dramatic and miming skills. In the feast scene in *Flamenca* mentioned above some jongleurs are said to have put on a puppet show (*L'us fai lo juec dels bavastelz*, l. 611); puppets or marionettes are also listed as relevant for a minstrel's art in Guiraut de Calanson's *ensenhamen* (*bavastels*, l. 23).[123] Apart from putting on puppet shows, jongleurs seem to have been an important factor in the performance, no doubt sometimes mimed, and also in the composition (at least in France) of fabliaux.[124] A mimed performance of an English fabliau, the thirteenth-century story of 'Dame Sirith and the Weeping Bitch', with the minstrel changing his voice according to the character speaking, is to be inferred from the highly dialogised form of the poem as well as the indications of the different characters by their initials in the margins. The interpretation of this fabliau as a mimed performance is confirmed by a later 'Interlude of the Cleric and the Girl' (*Interludium de clerico and puella*), in which the same story is unambiguously set out as a series of speeches of the various characters, making it into 'the oldest secular play extant in English'.[125] Doubtless, the mimetic and dramatic performances of jongleurs have played a role in the development of medieval drama; this role, however, is not easy to assess in detail.[126]

The public performance of lyric poetry meant in the majority of cases that the lyrics were sung rather than recited. The melodies that have survived give us an idea of the sound of medieval song, despite the problems the interpretation of medieval notation poses. The musical aspect of medieval song has been extensively studied by musicologists, the textual by philologists and literary critics, and work has also been done on the relationship between words and music. The performance of medieval song, however, encompasses a far wider field than can be discussed in the context of this chapter.[127]

The focus of discussion, when it comes to the minstrel's performance of poetry, is on narrative, in particular extended narrative poetry such as the *chansons de geste*, the Middle High German *Spielmannsepen* or the Middle English romances. Albert Baugh, in one of his studies of the Middle English romances, assembles various quotations from

---

[123] Minstrels putting on puppet shows are repeatedly mentioned in medieval sources; see Chambers 1903: I, 71, II, 157–60.

[124] On jongleurs as authors of *fabliaux*, see Bédier 1925: 399–426; compare Faral 1910: 207–10. On the performance of *fabliaux*, see Levy 2005.

[125] Bennett and Smithers 1968: 196; for an edition and discussion, see *ibid.*: 77–95 and 196–200; see also Axton 1974: 19–23.

[126] Compare Faral 1910: 231–52; Rousse 1991; on medieval drama and orality, see further ch. 27 by T. Pettitt.

[127] See especially the discussion of minstrelsy in Page 1989 and of songs, instruments and performance practice in Page 1987.

primary texts about the performance of these romances. Some suggest that they were sung, some that they were recited, and some that they were read aloud. Baugh comes to the conclusion:

> In sum, I think the evidence is sufficient to show that romances were sometimes sung, sometimes recited, and sometimes read from a book. I suspect that it would not be too daring to see in the couplet in *Sir Generydes*
>
> > Forto sing, or forto rede,
> > Or forto speke of sum old dede
>
> a reflection of current minstrel practice.[128]

In the texts from which I have quoted in this chapter, we also find evidence for reading. The speaker of the *Cantare dei cantari* says that only one story meets with his disapproval, the story of the destruction of the Round Table. In this context he affirms: 'One tale only (of the Arthurian cycle) displeases me to read, to say (tell) or to sing' (*Un conto sol di costor me dispiace/ Di legere, o di dire, o di cantarlo*, st. 47–1–2). This suggests that our *giullare* might not only perform from memory but also read from written sources to an audience. Similarly, the second of the two *bordeors ribauz* boasts that he can also read and sing from liturgical texts (*Et lire et chanter de clergie*, l. 43).[129] From a number of passages in French romances thought to have been performed by jongleurs Madleine Tyssens has argued that perhaps the most common performance mode was that of reading.[130]

If jongleurs or minstrels recited from a written text it is improbable that they would have used any of the carefully produced and generally illuminated manuscripts of *chansons de geste* or of other narratives from the sphere of presumably oral literature. A cyclic manuscript of the French *chansons de geste* (cycle of Guillaume d'Orange) such as for instance BL, MS Royal 20 D XI, or a collection of Middle English romances such as the so-called Auchinleck MS are unlikely candidates for a minstrel's manuscript.[131] It is manuscripts of modest volume and appearance that have been thought to have been used by minstrels. In the nineteenth century Léon Gautier classified seven *chanson de geste* manuscripts as jongleur manuscripts (1878: I, 226, n. 1); Martín de Riquer added to these the Spanish manuscripts of the *Cantar de mio Cid* and the fragment of *Roncesvalles* (1959: 77). In English studies it has been proposed that on account of their size some manuscripts could have been 'holster books', manuscripts that could be kept in a

---

[128] Baugh 1967: 23. On the Middle English romances, see ch. 11 by A. Putter; specifically on questions of performance and music, see Reichl 2003, 2005, and 2009.
[129] Noomen translates 'Je sais lire et chanter à la messe comme un clerc' (2003: 45).
[130] Tyssens 1966. Although opposed to Jean Rychner's view of the jongleur (1955), she does admit that *chansons de geste* and similar narrative poetry were also (occasionally!) recited or sung without the help of a manuscript: 'On se gardera bien de conclure que jamais un jongleur n'a récité par cœur une chanson de geste' (695). On reading aloud, see also ch. 1 above, section 3.3.
[131] On British Library, MS Royal 20 D XI (beginning of the 14th c.), see the British Library website 'Catalogue of Illuminated Manuscripts' <http://prodigi.bl.uk/illcat/welcome.htm>; information on the manuscript and five illuminations can be found via 'Manuscript search' (Collection: Royal MS, MS number: 20 D XI). On the Auchinleck-Manuscript (Edinburgh, National Library of Scotland, Advocates MS 19.2.1; first half of 14th c.), see the website of the National Library of Scotland at <http://www.nls.uk/auchinleck/>.

saddle bag by a travelling minstrel (Guddat-Figge 1976:30–36). The idea of a minstrel manuscript has, however, also been opposed and called a 'myth' (Taylor 1991). Although it is difficult to prove that a specific manuscript was used for a minstrel performance, a belief in the performance of a minstrel with the help of a manuscript text implies that there were 'minstrel manuscripts'. Somewhat paradoxically, some scholars who favour the idea of a minstrel reading a text rather than reciting freely also deny the existence of minstrel manuscripts.[132]

When minstrels or jongleurs performed narrative poetry from memory they could either 'speak' or 'sing'. The verbs in the various medieval languages used for 'sing' and 'speak' are often ambiguous and overlap in their meanings. Some contexts make it clear that to 'sing a tale' can here only mean to 'tell a tale', while to 'speak a tale' in some other context must be interpreted as to 'sing a tale'. Formulaic diction – such as the use of word pairs like *singen und sagen* (sing and say) in medieval German – and exigencies of rhyme and metre have influenced the choice of verbs. While some narrative poems might have been recited by the medieval entertainer, there is ample evidence that genres such as for instance the *chansons de geste* were sung rather than spoken or recited, generally to the accompaniment of an instrument, usually the *vièle*. Johannes de Grocheio, in this theoretical treatise *De musica* (c. 1300), discusses various types of *cantus*, among them what he terms *cantus gestualis*:

> We call that kind of *cantus* a *chanson de geste* in which the deeds of heroes and the works of ancient fathers are recounted, such as the life and martyrdom of saints and the battles and adversities which the men of ancient times suffered for the sake of faith and truth, such as the life of St. Stephen, the first martyr, and the story of King Charlemagne. This kind of music should be laid on for the elderly, for working citizens and for those of middle station when they rest from their usual toil, so that, having heard the miseries and calamities of others, they may more easily bear their own and so that anyone may undertake his own labour with more alacrity. Therefore this kind of *cantus* has the power to preserve the whole city.[133]

Johannes de Grocheio estimates the singing of *chansons de geste* highly; like Thomas Chobham, he puts the jongleurs who sing *chansons de geste* in the same category with those who sing saints' legends (see pp. 171–72 above).

In addition to Grocheio's testimony, a number of melodies and melodic fragments that were indisputably meant for the singing of *chansons de geste* have been preserved. These melodies are of a comparatively simple, 'unflorid' kind; they are mostly syllabic (one syllable of text per note) and have an ambitus that does not exceed the fifth as a rule. Typically these melodies are 'stichic', i. e. the same tune, with possibly small varia-

---

[132] Some problems connected with memorization vs. remembering and with composition in performance I have discussed in ch. 1 above, sections 4.2 (remembering vs. memorizing) and 4.3 (oral composition).

[133] 'Cantum vero gestualem dicimus in quo gesta heroum et antiquorum patrum opera recitantur, sicuti vita et martyria sanctorum et proelia et adversitates quas antiqui viri pro fide et veritate passi sunt, sicuti vita beati Stephani protomartyris et historia regis Karoli. Cantus autem iste debet antiquis et civibus laborantibus et mediocribus ministrari, dum requiescunt ab opere consueto, ut auditis miseriis et calamitatibus aliorum suas facilius sustineant et quilibet opus suum alacrius aggrediatur. Et ideo iste cantus valet ad conservationem totius civitatis.' Text and translation from Page 1993:22 (text) and 23 (translation). On this treatise, see also Rohloff 1943.

tions, is repeated for every line.¹³⁴ This type of musical 'setting' is found in a great number of oral traditions where epics are sung, as for instance in the performance of the South Slavic guslars.¹³⁵ A similar type of melody is preserved in the manuscript of the thirteenth-century *chantefable* of *Aucassin et Nicolette* for the sung verse-parts of this prosimetric tale (Butterfield 1997: 71–73).

In addition to the *chansons de geste*, melodies for other medieval narrative tradtions have also been discussed. There is some musical evidence for the singing of Middle High German epic poetry.¹³⁶ In some cases we only know that medieval narrative poetry was musically performed, but have no music. In the register of St. Swithun's Priory, Winchester, we read that in 1338 a *ioculator* by the name of Herebertus sang (*cantabat*) the romance of *Guy of Warwick*.¹³⁷ Ezio Levi notes that numerous documents from medieval Florence and Perugia make it clear that the *cantari* were sung to the accompaniment of a musical instrument (1914: 20). Sometimes the evidence for musical performance is comparatively late and comes from ballads rather than longer narratives. The latter, of course, are, as principally sung poems, the domain of both the musicologist and the literary critic. Bertrand Bronson expressed the opinion that the ballad could only be studied when both text and music were equally taken into consideration.¹³⁸ The question of how far back the ballad melodies can be dated and how well they might preserve medieval traditions is difficult to answer. The Sefardi ballad tradition has strong roots in the Middle Ages, and there has been some debate about the conservative nature of Sefardi ballad tunes; it is possible that melodies recorded in modern times reflect medieval musical practice fairly faithfully.¹³⁹ Of course, the later a tradition has been recorded the more we know about the melodies of narrative song. Already in the first larger collection of Russian *byliny*, by Kirsha Danilov from the eighteenth century, tunes were given, and there are ample transcriptions and sound recordings from later times.¹⁴⁰ Although the melody type underlying the singing of the *chansons de geste* is widely disseminated in oral traditions, more 'florid' and melismatic melodies are also found, as for instance in the music of Greek ballads (Baud-Bovy 1958). Like the music of lyrical song, the music of medieval narrative poetry is an area lying outside the main concerns of this book and can only be touched upon in this section.

---

¹³⁴ On the music of the *chansons de geste*, see Gennrich 1923; Chailley 1948 and 1955; on the musical performance of medieval narrative in general, see Stevens 1986: 199–267 and 2000; compare also Gushee and Rastall 2001.
¹³⁵ See, *inter alia*, Erdely 2000; Pegg and Porter 2001; Reichl 2000b.
¹³⁶ See Bertau and Stephan 1956–57; Brunner 1970 und 1979; Lipphardt 1979. On the singability of Middle High German (popular) epic poetry, see also Heinzle 1978, 72–76; Curschmann 1986. On Old High German epic melodies, see section 2.4 above.
¹³⁷ See Grossman 1906: 54; compare also ch. 11 by A. Putter, pp. 348–49.
¹³⁸ 'Yet, I insist, if the student of the ballad is not prepared to give equal attention to the musical, as to the verbal, side of his subject, his knowledge of it will in the end be only half-knowledge. If he lacks the necessary acquaintance with musical rudiments, or is indisposed or unable to enlist the active and continual collaboration of others properly equipped, he had better turn to other fields.' Bronson 1969: 38. The tunes of the ballad tradition in English have been edited by Bronson 1959–72.
¹³⁹ See Katz 1962; Gerson-Kiwi 1964.
¹⁴⁰ On Kirsha Danilov's collections, see the re-edition by Gorelov 2000; for the music of Russian *byliny*, see Dobrovol'skiy and Korguzalov 1981. – For comments on the music of the Romanian oral epics/ ballads, see ch. 14 by M. Beissinger, section 7.

Despite the melodies that have been preserved, the descriptions of performances in literary and other texts and some pictorial representations, the 'communicative event' a medieval performance constituted is in its totality inaccessible to us and can only be partially reconstructed. In a communicative event all the participants are an important element, i. e. not only the performer but also his (or her) audience. Audience reactions and the interaction of performer and listeners have been studied in contemporary ethnographic works, but are difficult to assess for historically distant periods. Some medieval evidence does, however, allow us to speculate on this aspect of performance.

In the *Cantare dei cantari*, the *giullare* offers a rich repertoire to his listeners. Similarly, in one of the poems (*Spruch*) of the Middle High German poet *Der Marner (c. 1230 – c. 1280)*, we read:

> Sing ich dien liuten mîniu liet,
> sô wil der êrste daz
> wie Dieterîch von Berne schiet.
> der ander, wâ künc Ruother saz,
> der dritte wil der Riuzen sturm, sô wil der vierde Ekhartes nôt,
> der fünfte wen Kriemhilt verriet.[141]

> When I sing my songs to the people,/ then the first wants to hear/ how Dietrich parted from Berne./ The second wants to hear where King Rother lived and reigned,/ the third wants to hear the battle of the Riuzen, the fourth Ekhart's distress,/ the fifth who was betrayed by Kriemhilt.

The Marner's audience is choosy, some want to listen to narratives related to the cycle of Dietrich, others to a *Spielmannsepos* like *König Rother*, and some to epics from the Nibelung legend. As a good singer he will, of course, accommodate his audience's wishes, or so we may suppose. Although a great number of medieval manuscripts must have been lost and what has come down to us is therefore no certain guide, a certain popularity of some genres (or subgenres) is nevertheless suggested when texts are more plentifully transmitted. Texts such as, for instance, the corpus of tail-rhyme romances in England or the Franco-Italian *chansons de geste* in northern Italy certainly point to audience preferences.

Even less well documented are the listeners' reactions to the minstrel's performance, their 'enhancement of experience'. In Gottfried von Strassburg's *Tristan (c. 1210)* there is a scene in which Tristan performs two Breton lais. We are told that Tristan played the harp so skilfully (*harphete er sô schône*) and sang so sweetly (*sô suoze mit dem munde*)

> daz maneger dâ stuont under saz,
> der sîn selbes namen vergaz.
> da begunden herze und ôren
> tumben und tôren
> und ûz ir rehte wanken [...] (ll. 3589–3593) (Marold 1969: 55)

> that many a man sitting or standing there forgot his very name. Hearts and ears began to play the fool and desert their rightful paths [...] (Hatto 1960: 90)

---

[141] Haustein 1995: 222; see also *ibid*.: 222-26. On the Marner, see Wachinger 1987.

A good minstrel was sure to captivate his audience, even to move his listeners to tears.[142] Peter of Blois (1130/35 – 1211/12) mentions in his *Liber de Confessione Sacramentali* that people listening to minstrels narrating the misfortunes of Tristan and other heroes burst into tears out of compassion:

> [...] fabulosa quaedam referunt histriones, quorum auditu concutiuntur ad compassionem audientium corda, et usque ad lacrymas compunguntur. (Petrus Blesensis, PL 207, col. 1088)

> [...] The minstrels (*histriones*) narrate fabulous stories, which when heard awake compassion in the hearts of the listeners and move them to tears.

When a performance was received well ('positively evaluated'), it was, of course, also remunerated. Many descriptions of minstrels' performances at feasts and tournaments include a mention of the reward. A particulary sumptious list of gifts is enumerated in Heinrich von Veldeke's *Eneas*:

> daz tûre phellîne gewant,
> golt und aller slahte schat,
> silber unde goltvat,
> mûle und ravîde,
> phelle und samtîde
> ganz und ungescrôten,
> mangegen bouch rôten,
> dorchslagen goldîn,
> zobel unde harmîn [...] (ll. 13184–92)

(Kartschoke 1986:737)

> precious silk robes,/ gold and all kinds of valuable things,/ silver and golden vessels,/ mules and chargers,/ velvet and silk/ in uncut pieces,/ many red-golden embossed bracelets,/ sable and ermine [...]

We have seen above that the chronicler of the *Mainzer Hoffest* mentions equally lavish gifts (pp. 170–71). Presenting gifts to a minstrel was probably not only a noble gesture; we can assume that a jongleur who had been richly rewarded would be willing to sing the donor's praises and spread his fame (Dobozy 1992).

\* \* \*

In conclusion it has to be stressed again that the picture of the medieval entertainer – jongleur, minstrel, *spilman*, *skomorokh* and so on – is as variegated as the terms by which he – or she – is designated. From a sociological point of view, we can see that some entertainer types were highly regarded – such as the courtly *joglar* or the singer of *chansons de gestes* and saints' legends – while others, especially when their art consisted in juggling or buffoonery, were at the bottom of the social scale, excommunicated, or at least threatened with eternal damnation by the church, and as vagrants deprived of civil rights.[143] In the later Middle Ages the jongleurs were increasingly organized in guilds, such as the *Confrérie des jongleurs et bourgeois d'Arras* to which Jean Bodel belonged. By

---

[142] As Poggio Bracciolini (15th c.) relates, tears were shed when Roland's death was narrated; see ch. 13 (R. Morabito), p. 371.
[143] On the social position, see Klapper 1931 and Schreier-Hornung 1981.

the same token the *puys*, societies for the composition and cultivation of poetry, developed, especially in northern France and Flanders, but also in Britain; the (short-lived) London *puy* was founded at the end of the thirteenth century.[144] In the same manner the *Meistersinger* practiced the art of poetry in Germany, poetizing often in a pedantic and uninspired manner (Brunner 2001). With these good burghers we have entered a different world from that inhabited – and explored – by jongleur-poets like Cercamon, 'Roam-the-World'. In the later Middle Ages, the minstrel-musician became the professional musician, while the minstrel-singer-of-tales was more and more marginalized. He survived into the Renaissance, but now as the 'blind crowder', who sang 'the old song of Percy and Douglas' 'with no rougher voice than rude style', and whose performance Sir Philip Sidney, in his *Defence of Poetry* (1595), found moving despite its rudeness (Van Dorsten 1973:46). In the heartland of the Renaissance, the *cantastorie* or *canterino* experienced severe competition from the great poets, who took up his stories in the literary epics of fifteenth- and sixteenth-century Italy, Pulci's *Morgante* or Ariost's *Orlando Furioso*. Although we have moved into the domain of written literature, the conventions of oral performance linger. Ariosto casts himself into the role of narrator who addresses an audience of listeners. This is expressed repeatedly at the end of his cantos, as for instance in Canto XVIII:

> Ma chi del canto mio piglia diletto,
> Un'altra volta ad ascoltarlo aspetto.
> (Zingarelli 1973:190)

But whoever finds pleasure in my song,/ I expect him to come and listen to it another time.

'Come and listen to my song' is still the poet's invitation to his (reading) audience as it was the minstrel's address to his (listening) audience. Ariost's 'formula' shows us not only that oral forms are long-lived, but also that what appears to be oral need not be so. This is also true of the Middle Ages: however convinced we might be that we are in the presence of an orally performed text, the performance itself is beyond our grasp and the clues which our written documents offer are subject to interpretation and hence controversy. We have to learn, as Pio Rajna admonishes us (in connection with the *Cantare dei cantari*), 'to distinguish the real from the supposed' (*saper distinguere il reale dal suposto*; 1878:226). This is perhaps not as easy as it seemed to scholars embued by the positivistic optimism of the nineteenth century. Despite the indeterminacy of many of our sources, some advance has been made in our understanding of medieval performance, enough, it is hoped, to furnish a trustworthy foundation for future research.

# References

Allen, Philip Schuyler. 1909–11. 'The Medieval Mimus.' *Modern Philology* 7(1909/1910): 329–44; 8 (1910/1911): 1–44.
Amodio, Mark C. 2004. *Writing the Oral Tradition: Oral Poetics and Literate Culture in Medieval England*. Notre Dame, IN: U of Notre Dame P.

---

[144] See Chambers 1903: II, 258–62; Sutton 1992.

–. 2005. 'Res(is)ting the Singer: Towards a Non-Performative Anglo-Saxon Oral Poetics.' In *New Directions in Oral Theory*. Ed. Mark C. Amodio. Medieval and Renaissance Texts and Studies 287. Tempe: Arizona Center for Medieval and Renaissance Studies. 179–208.
Amos, Thomas L. 1989. 'Preaching and the Sermon in the Carolingian World.' In *De ore domini: Preacher and Word in the Middle Ages*. Ed. Thomas L. Amos, Eugene A. Green, and Beverly Mayne Kienzle. Studies in Medieval Culture 28. Kalamazoo: Medieval Institute, Western Michigan University. 41–60.
Anderson, L. F. 1903. *The Anglo-Saxon Scop*. Toronto: University Library.
Arnold, I. D. O., and M. M. Pelan, eds. 1962. *La partie arthurienne du Roman de Brut*. Bibl. Française et Romane, Série B: Textes et Documents 1. Paris: Klincksieck.
Attwood, Katrina C., trans. 1997. *The Saga of Gunnlaug Serpent-tongue*. In Hreinsson et al. 1997: I, 305–33.
Axton, Richard. 1974. *European Drama of the Early Middle Ages*. London: Hutchinson.
Bachfischer, Margit. 1998. *Musikanten, Gaukler und Vaganten. Spielmannskunst im Mittelalter*. Augsburg: Battenberg.
Bagby, Benjamin. 2005. '*Beowulf*, the *Edda*, and the Performance of Medieval Epic: Notes from the Workshop of a Reconstructed "Singer of Tales".' In Vitz, Regaldo, and Lawrence 2005: 181–92. [Also in German in *Basler Jahrbuch für historische Musikpraxis* 26 (2002): 31–46.]
Bahr, Joachim. 1954. 'Der "Spielmann" in der Literaturwissenschaft des 19. Jahrhunderts.' *Zs. für deutsche Philologie* 73: 174–96. [Also in Schröder 1977: 289–322.]
Baldwin, John W. 1997. 'The Image of the Jongleur in Northern France around 1200.' *Speculum* 72: 635–63.
Baud-Bovy, Samuel. 1958. *Étude sur la chanson cleftique*. Collection de l'Institut Français d'Athènes 53. Athens: Institut Français d'Athènes.
Baugh, Albert C. 1967. 'The Middle English Romance: Some Questions of Creation, Presentation, and Preservation.' *Speculum* 42: 1–31.
Bauman, Richard. 1977. *Verbal Art as Performance*. Prospect Heights, IL: Waveland P.
–. 1986. 'Performance and Honor in 13th-Century Iceland.' *JAF* 99: 131–50.
–, ed. 1992. *Folklore, Cultural Performances, and Popular Entertainments: A Communications-Centered Handbook*. New York: OUP.
–, and Donald Braid. 1998. "The Ethnography of Performance in the Study of Oral Tradition." In Foley 1998: 106–22.
–, and Charles L. Briggs. 1990. "Poetics and Performance as Critical Perspectives on Language and Social Life." *Annual Review of Anthropology* 19: 59–88.
Baumgarten, Jean. 1993. *Le Yiddish*. 2nd ed. Que sais-je? 2552. Paris: Presses Universitaires de France.
–. 2005. *Introduction to Old Yiddish Literature*. Ed. and trans. Jerold C. Frakes. Oxford: OUP.
Beaton, Roderick. 1980. *Folk Poetry of Modern Greece*. Cambridge: CUP.
Bec, Pierre. 1977–78. *La lyrique française au Moyen Âge ($XII^{ème}$- $XIII^{ème}$ siècles). Contribution à une typologie des genres poétiques médiévaux. Études et textes*. 2 vols. Paris: Picard.
Bédier, Joseph. 1925. *Les fabliaux. Études de littérature populaire et d'historie littéraire du moyen âge*. 4th ed. Bibliothèque de l'École des Hautes Études 98. Paris: Champion.
–, ed. 1938. *Les chansons de Colin Muset*. CFMA 7. Paris, Champion.
Beechy, Tiffany. 2010. *The Poetics of Old English*. Farnham: Ashgate.
Bennett, J. A. W., and G. V. Smithers, eds. 1968. *Early Middle English Verse and Prose*. With a glossary by Norman Davis. 2nd ed. Oxford: Clarendon.
Benveniste, Émile. 1932. 'Une racine indo-européenne.' *Bulletin de la societé de linguistique de Paris* 33: 133–35.
Bergin, Osborn. 1970. *Irish Bardic Poetry: Texts and Translations together with an Introductory Lecture*. Ed. David Greene and Fergus Kelly. Dublin: Dublin Institute for Advanced Studies. [Or. 1912.]

Bertau, Karl H., and Rudolf Stephan. 1956–57.'Zum sanglichen Vortrag mhd. strophischer Epen.' *Zs. für deutsches Altertum* 87:253–70.
Bertolucci Pizzorusso, Valeria. 1966.'La supplica di Guiraut Riquier e la risposta di Alfonso X di Castiglia.' *Studi mediolatini e volgari* 14:9–135.
Bial, Henry, ed. 2007. *The Performance Studies Reader*. 2nd ed. London: Routledge.
Bloomfield, Morton W., and Charles W. Dunn. 1989. *The Role of the Poet in Early Societies*. Cambridge: Brewer.
Boyce, Mary. 1957.'The Parthian *Gōsān* and Iranian Minstrel Tradition.' *JRAS* 1957.1/2: 10–45.
Brasseur, Annette, ed. 1989. Jehan Bodel. *La Chanson des Saisnes*. 2 vols. Textes littéraires français 369. Geneva: Droz.
Bredehoft, Thomas A. 2005. *Early English Metre*. Toronto: U of Toronto P.
–. 2009. *Authors, Audiences, and Old English Verse*. Toronto: U of Toronto P.
Bronson, Bertrand Harris, ed. 1959–72. *The Traditional Tunes of the Child Ballads*. 4 vols. Princeton: Princeton UP.
–. 1969. *The Ballad as Song*. Berkeley: U of California P.
Broomfield, F., ed. 1968. *Thomae de Chobham Summa Confessorum*. Analecta Mediaevalia Namurcensia 25. Louvain: Nauwelaerts.
Brunner, Horst. 1970.'Epenmelodien.' In *Formen mittelalterlicher Literatur: Siegried Beyschlag zu seinem 65. Geburtstag*. Ed. Otmar Werner and Bernd Naumann. Göppinger Arbeiten zur Germanistik 25. Göppingen: Kümmerle. 149–78.
–. 1979.'Strukturprobleme der Epenmelodien.' In Kühebacher 1979:300–28.
–. 2001.'Meistergesang.' *New Grove*[2], XVI, 294–300.
Bugge, Sophus, and Moltke Moe. 1897. *Torsvisen i sin norske form udgivet med en afhandling om dens oprindelse og forhold til de andre nordiske former*. Christiania.
Bullock-Davies, Constance. 1978. *Menestrellorum Multitudo: Minstrels at a Royal Feast*. Cardiff: U of Wales P.
Bumke, Joachim. 1986. *Höfische Kultur. Literatur und Gesellschaft im hohen Mittelalter*. 2 vols. Munich: Beck.
Burgess, Glyn S., and Keith Busby, trans. 1999. *The Lais of Marie de France*. 2nd ed. London: Penguin.
Burrow, J. A. 1973.'Bards, Minstrels, and Men of Letters.' *Literature and Western Civilization. The Mediaeval World*. Ed. David Daiches and Anthony Thorlby. London: Aldus Books. 347-70.
Butterfield, Ardis. 1997.'*Aucassin et Nicolette* and Mixed Forms in Medieval French.' In Harris and Reichl 1997:67–98.
Cabré, Miriam. 1999.'Italian and Catalan Troubadours.' In *The Troubadours: An Introduction*. Ed. Simon Gaunt and Sarah Kay. Cambridge: CUP. 127–40.
Carlson, Marvin A. 1996. *Performance: A Critical Introduction*. London: Routledge.
Carney, James. 1967. *The Irish Bardic Poet: A Study in the Relationship of Poet and Patron*. Dublin: Dolmen P.
Carter, Henry Holland. 1961. *A Dictionary of Middle English Musical Terms*. Ed. George B. Gerhard. Bloomington: Indiana UP.
Chadwick, H. Munro and N. Kershaw Chadwick. 1932–40. *The Growth of Literature*. 3 vols. Cambridge: CUP.
Chadwick, Nora Kershaw. 1936.'The Distribution of Oral Literature in the Old World.' *Journal of the Royal Anthropology Institute* 69:77–94.
Chailley, Jacques. 1948.'Études musicales sur la chanson de geste et ses origines.' *Revue de musicologie* 17:1–27.
–. 1955.'Autour de la chanson de geste.' *Acta Musicologica* 27:1–12.
Chambers, E. K. 1903. *The Mediaeval Stage*. 2 vols. London: OUP.
Chatman, Seymour. 1978. *Story and Discourse: Narrative Structure in Fiction and Film*. Ithaca, NY: Cornell UP.

Clark, George, trans. 'The Tale of Sarcastic Halli.' In Hreinsson et al. 1997: I, 342–57.
Clover, Carol J., and John Lindow, eds. 1985. *Old Norse-Icelandic Literature: A Critical Guide.* Islandica 45. Ithaca: Cornell UP. [Rpt. with a new bibliographical preface, Toronto: U of Toronto P, 2005.]
Clunies Ross, Margaret. 2005. *A History of Old Norse Poetry and Poetics.* Cambridge: Brewer.
Crossley-Holland, Kevin, trans. 1999. *The Anglo-Saxon World: An Anthology.* Oxford: OUP.
Curschmann, Michael. 1968. '*Spielmannsepik.' Wege und Ergebnisse der Forschung von 1907 – 1965. Mit Ergänzungen und Nachträgen bis 1967 (Überlieferung und Mündliche Kompositionsform).* Stuttgart: Metzler.
–. 1986. 'Sing ich dien liuten mîniu liet, ... Spruchdichter als Traditionsträger der spätmittelalterlichen Heldendichtung?' In *Kontroversen, alte und neue. Akten des VII. Internationalen Germanisten-Kongresses Göttingen 1985. 8. Ethische contra ästhetische Legitimation von Literatur. – Traditionalismus und Modernismus: Kontroversen um den Avantgardismus.* Tübingen: Niemeyer. 184–93.
Davenson, Henri [= Henri Irénée Marrou]. 1961. *Les troubadours.* Paris: Seuil.
Davies, Sioned. 2003. 'From Storytelling to Sermons: The Oral Narrative Tradition of Wales.' *Oral Tradition* 18: 189–91.
de Riquer, Martín. 1959. 'Épopée jongleresque à écouter et épopée romanesque à lire.' In *La technique littéraire des chansons de geste: Acte du Colloque de Liège (septembre 1957).* Paris: 'Les Belles Lettres'. 75–82
–, ed. and trans. 1975. *Los trovadores. Historia literaria y textos.* 3 vols. Barcelona: Planeta.
de Vries, Jan. 1977. *Altnordisches etymologisches Wörterbuch.* 3rd ed. Leiden: Brill.
Dewing, H. B., trans. 1916. Procopius. *History of the Wars.* Vol. 2 [Books 3–4]. Loeb Classical Library. London: Heinemann.
Doane, A. N. 1991. 'Oral Texts, Intertexts, and Intratexts: Editing Old English.' In *Influence and Intertextuality in Literary History.* Ed. Jay Clayton and Eric Rothstein. Madison: U of Wisconsin P. 75–113.
–. 1994a. 'The Ethnography of Scribal Writing and Anglo-Saxon Poetry: Scribe as Performer.' *Oral Tradition* 9: 420–39.
–. 1994b. 'Editing Old English Oral/Written Texts: Problems of Method (with an Illustrative Edition of Charm 4, *Wið Færstice*).' In *The Editing of Old English: Papers from the 1990 Manchester Conference.* Ed. D. G. Scragg et al. Cambridge: Brewer. 125–45.
–. 2003. '"Beowulf" and Scribal Performance.' In *Unlocking the Wordhord: Anglo-Saxon Studies in Memory of Edward B. Irving, Jr.* Ed. Mark C. Amodio and Katherine O'Brien O'Keeffe. Toronto: U of Toronto P. 62–75.
Dobozy, Maria. 1992. 'Beschenkungspolitik und die Erschaffung von Ruhm am Beispiel der fahrenden Sänger.' *Frühmittelalterliche Studien* 26: 353–67.
Dobrovol'skiy, B. M., and V. V. Korguzalov, eds. 1981. *Byliny. Russkiy muzykal'ny èpos.* Moscow: Sovetskiy kompozitor.
Einarsson, Stefán. 1963. 'Harp Song, Heroic Poetry (Chadwicks), Greek and Germanic Alternate Singing.' *Budkavlen* 42: 13–28.
Erdely, Stephen. 2000. 'Music of South Slavic Epics.' In Reichl 2000a: 69–82.
Ewert, A., ed. 1944. Marie de France. *Lais.* Oxford: Blackwell.
Fallows, David. 2001. 'Lai.' *New Grove*$^2$, XIV, 118–32.
Falvy, Zoltán. 1961. 'Spielleute im mittelalterlichen Ungarn.' *Studia Musicologica Academiae Scientiarum Hungaricae* 1: 29–64.
Faral, Edmond. 1910. *Les jongleurs en France au moyen âge.* Bibliothèque de l'École des Hautes Études 187. Paris: Champion. [Rpt. 1964]
Findeizen, Nikolai. 2008. *History of Music in Russia from Antiquity to 1800.* 2 vols. Trans. Samuel William Pring. Bloomington: Indiana UP. [Or. 1928, in Russian.]
Fine, Elizabeth. 1984. *The Folklore Text: From Performance to Print.* Bloomington: Indiana UP.

—. 1998.'Leading Proteus Captive: Editing and Translating Oral Tradition.' In Foley 1998:59–71.
Finlay, Alison, ed. and trans. 2004. *Fagrskinna: A Catalogue of the Kings of Norway.* Leiden: Brill.
Foley, John Miles. 1985. *Oral-Formulaic Theory and Research: An Introduction and Annotated Bibliography.* New York: Garland.
—. 1988. *The Theory of Oral Composition: History and Methodology.* Bloomington: Indiana UP.
—. 1990. *Traditional Oral Epic: The Odyssey, Beowulf, and the Serbo-Croatian Return Song.* Berkeley: U of California P.
—. 1992.'Word-Power, Performance, and Tradition.' *JAF* 105:275–301.
—. 1995. *The Singer of Tales in Performance.* Bloomington: Indiana UP.
—, ed. 1998. *Teaching Oral Traditions.* New York: The Modern Language Association.
—. 2002. *How to Read an Oral Poem.* Urbana: U of Illinois P.
Ford, Patrick K., trans. 1999. *The Celtic Poets: Songs and Tales from Early Ireland and Wales.* Belmont, MA: Ford and Bailie.
—. 2005. 'Performance and Literacy in Medieval Welsh Poetry.' *Modern Language Review* 100: xxx–xlviii.
Foulet, Lucien. 1908. 'Marie de France et la Légende de Tristan.' *Zs. für romanische Philologie* 32:161–83; 257–89.
Frank, Roberta. 1978. *Old Norse Court Poetry.* Islandica 42. Ithaca, NY: Cornell UP.
—. 1982 [for 1979]. 'Old Norse Memorial Eulogies and the Ending of *Beowulf*.' In *The Early Middle Ages*. [=Acta 6] Ed. W. Snyder. Binghamton: Center for Medieval and Early Renaissance Studies. 1–19.
—. 1985.'Skaldic Poetry.' In Clover and Lindow 1985:157–96. [Rpt. with a new bibliographical preface, Toronto: U of Toronto P, 2005.]
Fulk, R. D. 2003.'On Argumentation in Old English Philology, with Particular Reference to the Editing and Dating of *Beowulf*.' *ASE* 32:1–26.
—. 2005.'Six Cruces in the Finnsburg Fragment and Episode.' *Medium Ævum* 74:191–204.
—, and Christopher M. Cain. 2003. *A History of Old English Literature.* Oxford: Blackwell.
Gade, Kari Ellen. 1994.'On the Recitation of Old Norse Skaldic Poetry.' In *Studien zum Altgermanischen: Festschrift für Heinrich Beck.* Ed. Heiko Uecker. Berlin: de Gruyter. 126–51.
Ganz, P. F., F. Norman, and W. Schwarz, eds. 1964. *Dukus Horant*. Mit einem Exkurs von S. A. Birnbaum. Altdeutsche Textbibliothek, Ergänzungsreihe 2. Tübingen: Niemeyer.
Gautier, Léon. 1878. *Les épopées françaises: Études sur les origines et l'histoire de la littérature nationale.* Seconde édition, entièrement refondue. 3 vols. Paris.
Gennrich, Friedrich. 1923. *Der musikalische Vortrag der altfranzösischen Chansons de geste. Eine literarhistorisch-musikwissenschaftliche Studie.* Halle: Niemeyer.
Georges, Robert A. 1980. 'Toward a Resolution of the Text/Context Controversy.' *Western Folklore* 39:34–40.
Gerould, Gordon Hall. 1932. *The Ballad of Tradition.* Oxford: Clarendon.
Gerson-Kiwi, Edith. 1964.'On the Musical Sources of the Judaeo-Hispanic *Romance*.' *The Musical Quarterly* 52:31–43.
Gislebert of Mons: *Gisleberti Chronicon Hanoniense.* Ed. Wilhelm Arndt. MGH, Scriptores rerum germanicarum in usum scholarium, 29 (ed. Georg Heinrich Pertz). Hannover, 1869.
Gorelov, A. A., ed. 2000. *Drevnie rossiyskie stikhotvoreniya, sobrannye Kirsheyu Danilovym.* St. Petersburg: Tropa Troyanova.
Gretsch, Mechthild. 1999. *The Intellectual Foundations of the English Benedictine Reform.* CSASE 25. Cambridge: CUL.
Grossmann, Wilhelm. 1906. *Frühmittelenglische Zeugnisse über Minstrels (circa 1100 bis 1400).* Diss. Berlin.
Guddat-Figge, Gisela. 1976. *Catalogue of Manuscripts Containing Middle English Romances.* Texte u. Unters. zur engl. Phil. 4. Munich: Fink.

Gunnell, Terry. 1995. *The Origins of Drama in Scandinavia*. Cambridge: Brewer.
—. 2005. 'Eddic Poetry.' In *A Companion to Old Norse-Icelandic Literature and Culture*. Ed. Rory McTurk. Oxford: Blackwell. 82–100.
—. 2008. 'The Performance of the Poetic Edda.' In *The Viking World*. Ed. Stefan Brink in collaboration with Neil Price. London: Routledge. 299–303.
Gushee, Lawrence, and Richard Rastall. 2001. 'Minstrel.' *New Grove*², XVI, 732–36.
Harris, Joseph. 1976. '*Guðrúnarbrögð* and the Saxon Lay of Grimhild's Perfidy.' *Medieval Scandinavia* 9: 173–80. [Rpt. in Harris 2008: 127–36.]
—. 1983. 'Eddic Poetry as Oral Poetry: The Evidence of Parallel Passages in the Helgi Poems for Questions of Composition and Performance.' In *Edda: A Collection of Essays*. Ed. Robert J. Glendinning and Haraldur Bessason. [Winnepeg:] U Manitoba P. 210–42. [Rpt. in Harris 2008: 189–225.]
—. 1985. 'Eddic Poetry.' In Clover and Lindow 1985: 68–156.. 68–156. [Rpt. with a new bibliographical preface, Toronto: U of Toronto P, 2005.]
—. 1989 [for 1987]. '"Deor" and Its Refrain: Preliminaries to an Interpretation.' *Traditio* 43: 23–53.
—. 1991. 'Introduction.' In *The Ballad and Oral Literature*. Ed. J. Harris. Harvard English Studies 17. Cambridge, MA: Harvard UP. 1–17.
—. 1993. 'Love and Death in the *Männerbund*: An Essay with Special Reference to the *Bjarkamál* and *The Battle of Maldon*.' In *Heroic Poetry in the Anglo-Saxon Period: Studies in Honor of Jess B. Bessinger, Jr*. Ed. Helen Damico and John Leyerle. Studies in Medieval Culture 32. Kalamazoo: Medieval Institute, Western Michigan U. 77–114. [Rpt. in Harris 2008: 287–317.]
—. 1996a [for 1993]. 'Obscure Styles (Old English and Old Norse) and the Enigma of *Gísla saga*.' *Mediaevalia: A Journal of Medieval Studies* 19: 75–99.
—. 1996b. 'Romancing the Rune: Aspects of Literacy in Early Scandinavian Orality.' In *Atti, Accademia Peloritana dei Pericolanti*. Classe di lettere, filosofia e belle arti, LXX (anno accademico CCLXV (1994). Messina: Accademia peloritana dei pericolanti. 109–40. [Corrected rpt. in Harris 2008: 319–47.]
—. 1997. 'The Prosimetrum of Icelandic Sagas and Some Analogues.' In Harris and Reichl 1997: 131–63.
—. 2000a. 'Performance, Textualization, and Textuality of "Elegy" in Old Norse.' In *The Textualization of Oral Epic*. Ed. Lauri Honko. Trends in Linguistics: Studies and Monographs 128. Berlin: Mouton de Gruyter. 89–99.
—. 2000b. 'The Performance of Old Norse Eddic Poetry: A Retrospective.' In Reichl 2000a: 225–32.
—. 2000c. '"Double Scene" and "mise en abyme" in Beowulfian Narrative.' In *Gudar på jorden: Festskrift till Lars Lönnroth*. Ed. Stina Hansson and Mats Malm. Stockholm: Symposion. 322–38.
—. 2003. '"Ethnopalaeography" and Recovered Performance: The Problematic Witnesses to "Eddic Song".' *Western Folklore* 62: 97–117.
—. 2004. 'Sänger.' *RGA* XXVI, 79–86.
—. 2006. '*Erfikvæði* – Myth, Ritual, Elegy.' In *Old Norse Religion in Long-Term Perspectives: Origins, Changes and Interactions. An International Conference in Lund, Sweden, June 3–7, 2004*. Ed. Anders Andrén, Kristina Jennbert, and Catharina Raudvere. Vägar till Midgård 8. Lund: Nordic Academic P. 267–71.
—. 2008. *"Speak Useful Words or Say Nothing": Old Norse Studies by Joseph Harris*. Ed. Susan E. Deskis and Thomas D. Hill. Islandica 53. Ithaca, NY: Cornell UP.
—. Forthcoming. 'Eddic Poetry and the Ballad: Voice, Vocality, and Performance with Special Reference to DgF1.' In *Child's Children: Ballad Scholarship and its Legacies*. Ed. J. Harris and Barbara Hillers. Trier: WVT.

—, and Thomas D. Hill. 1989. 'Gestr's "Prime Sign": Source and Signification in *Norna-Gests þáttr*.' *Arkiv för nordisk filologi* 104: 103–22.

—, and Karl Reichl, eds. 1997. *Prosimetrum: Crosscultural Perspectives on Narrative in Prose and Verse*. Cambridge: Brewer.

Hartung, Wolfgang. 1982. *Die Spielleute. Eine Randgruppe in der Gesellschaft des Mittelalters*. Vierteljahresschrift für Sozial- und Wirtschaftsgeschichte, Beiheft 72. Wiesbaden: Steiner.

Harvey, Ruth E. 1993. '*Joglars* and the Professional Status of the Early Troubadours.' *Medium Ævum* 72: 221–41.

Hatto, A. T., trans. 1960. *Gottfried von Strassburg: Tristan. With the Surviving Fragments of the Tristran of Thomas*. Harmondsworth: Penguin.

Haustein, Jens. 1995. *Marner-Studien*. Tübingen: Niemeyer.

Heinzle, Joachim. 1978. *Mittelhochdeutsche Dietrichepik. Untersuchungen zur Tradierungsweise, Überlieferungskritik und Gattungsgeschichte später Heldendichtung*. MTU 62. Munich: Artemis.

Heusler, Andreas. 1911. 'Dichtung.' *Reallexikon der Germanischen Altertumskunde*. Ed. Johannes Hoops. 4 vols. Berlin: de Gruyter. I, 439–62.

—. 1943. *Die altgermanische Dichtung*. 2nd rev. ed. Potsdam: Athenaion.

Hill, Thomas D. 2007. 'Beowulf's Roman Rites: Roman Ritual and Germanic Tradition.' *JEGP* 106: 325–35.

Hilty, Gerold. 1995. 'La figura del juglar en la Castilla del siglo XIII.' *Versants* 28 [*Les Jongleurs en Spectacle*]: 153–73.

Hofmann, Dietrich. 1963. 'Die Frage des musikalischen Vortrags der altgermanischen Stabreimdichtung in philologischer Sicht.' *Zs. für deutsches Altertum* 92: 83–121.

—, and Ewald Jammers. 1965. 'Zur Frage des Vortrags der altgermanischen Stabreimdichtung.' *Zs. für deutsches Altertum* 94: 185–95.

Hreinsson, Viðar et al., eds. 1997. *The Complete Sagas of Icelanders, Including 49 Tales*. Introduction by Robert Kellogg. 5 vols. Reykjavík: Leifur Eiríksson.

Hymes, Dell. 1975. 'Breakthrough into Performance.' In *Folklore: Performance and Communication*. Ed. Dan Ben-Amos and Kenneth S. Goldstein. The Hague: Mouton. 11–74. [Rpt., revised and expanded in Hymes 1981: 49–141.]

—. 1981. '*In Vain I Tried to Tell You*': *Essays in Native American Ethnopoetics*. Philadelphia: U of Pennsylvania P.

Jacob-Hugon, Christine. 1995. 'Pour une lecture "jongleresque" de la *Chanson des Saisnes*'. *Versants* 28: 43–57.

Jakobson, Roman. 1960. 'Closing Statement: Linguistics and Poetics.' In *Style in Language*. Ed. Thomas A. Sebeok. Cambridge, MA: MIT P. 350–77.

Jammers, Ewald. 1964. 'Der Vortrag des altgermanischen Stabreimverses in musikwissenschaftlicher Sicht.' *Zs. für deutsches Altertum* 93: 1–13.

Jones, W. Powell. 1931. 'The Jongleur Troubadours of Provence.' *PMLA* 46: 307–11.

Jónsson, Guðni, ed. 1954. 'Sturlu þáttr.' In *Sturlunga saga*. 3 vols. n. p. [Reykjavík:] Íslendingasagnaútgáfan. III, 367–83.

Jónsson, Finnur. 1907–08. 'Das Harfenspiel des Nordens in der alten Zeit.' *Sammelbände der internationalen Musikgesellschaft* 11: 530–37.

Jusserand J. J. 1950. *English Wayfaring Life in the Middle Ages*. Trans. Lucy Toulmin Smith. 4th ed. London: Benn. [Or. 1884 French, 1889 English.]

Kartschoke, Dieter, ed. and trans. 1986. Heinrich von Veldeke. *Eneasroman. Mittelhochdeutsch/ Neuhochdeutsch*. Stuttgart: Reclam.

Katz, Israel J. 1962. 'Toward a Musical Study of the Judeo-Spanish *Romancero*.' *Western Folklore* 21: 83–91.

Kellogg, Robert, trans. 1997. 'Hreidar's Tale.' In Hreinsson et al. 1997: 375–84.

Kienzle, Beverly Mayne. 2002 'Medieval Sermons and their Performance: Theory and Record.' In Muessig 2002: 89–124.
Kimmel, A. S. 1974. 'Le jongleur héros épique.'*Actes du VI<sup>e</sup> Congrès international de la Société Rencesvals (Aix-enProvence, 29 août – 4 septembre 1973)*. Ed.Jean Subrenat. Aix-en-Provence: Université de Provence. 461–72.
Kirshenblatt-Gimblett, Barbara. 2007.'Performance Studies.' In Bial 2007: 43–55.
Klaeber, Fr. 2008. *Klaeber's Beowulf and the Fight at Finnsburg*. 4th ed. rev. R. D. Fulk, Robert E. Bjork, and John D. Niles. Toronto: U of Toronto P.
Klapper, Josef. 1931. 'Die soziale Stellung des Spielmanns im 13. und 14. Jahrhundert.' *Zs. für Volkskunde* 40: 111–13.
Klingenberg, Heinz. 1984a.'Dichter.' *RGA* V, 376–92.
–. 1984b.'Dichtung.' *RGA* V, 394–404.
–. 1991. 'Altnordisch *húskarl, Bjarkamál=Húskarlahvǫt* und stiklastad.' In *Festskrift til Ottar Grønvik på 75-årsdagen den 21. oktober 1991*. Ed. John Ole Askedal et al. Oslo: Universitetsforlaget. 183–211.
Knott, Eleanor. 1960. *Irish Classical Poetry*. 2nd ed. Dublin: Cultural Relations Committee of Ireland.
Koch, John T., and John Carey, eds. 1995. *The Celtic Heroic Age: Literary Sources for Ancient Celtic Europe and Early Ireland and Wales*. Malden, MA: Celtic Studies Publications.
Koch, K.-P. 2002.'Musik [§ 2].' *RGA* XX, 399–410.
Kristjánsson, Jónas, ed. 1956.'Sneglu-Halla þáttr.' In *Eyfirðinga sǫgur*. Íslenzk fornrit 9. Reykjavík: Hið íslenzka fornritafélag. 261–95.
Kühebacher, Egon, ed. 1979. *Deutsche Heldenepik in Tirol: König Laurin und Dietrich von Bern in der Dichtung des Mittelalters*. Bozen: Athesia.
Lafont, Robert. 1992. 'Épopée et *nòvas*: le texte du *joglar contador*.' *Revue des Langues Romanes* 96: 251–73.
Lanciani, Giulia, and Giuseppe Tavani, eds. 1993. *Dicionário da Literatura Medieval Galega e Portuguesa*. Lisbon: Caminho.
Lavaud, René, and René Nelli, eds. and trans. 1960. *Les Troubadours. Jaufre, Flamenca, Barlaam et Josaphat*. Bruges: Desclée de Brouwer.
Lerer, Seth. 1991. *Literacy and Power in Anglo-Saxon Literature*. Lincoln: U of Nebraska P.
Levi, Ezio. 1914. *I cantari leggendari del popolo italiano nei secoli XIV e XV*. Giornale Storico della Letteratura Italiana, supplemento 16. Turin: Loescher.
Levy, Brian J. 2005.'Performing Fabliaux.' In Vitz, Regalado and Lawrence 2005: 123–40.
Lewis and Short: Lewis, Charlton T., and Charles Short. 1879. *A Latin Dictionary*. Oxford.
Lindow, John. 1975.'Riddles, Kennings, and the Complexity of Skaldic Poetry.' *Scandinavian Studies* 47: 311–27.
Lipphardt, Walther. 1979. 'Epische Liedweisen des Mittelalters in schriftlicher Überlieferung.' In Kühebacher 1979: 275–99.
Liuzza, R. M. 1995.'On the Dating of *Beowulf*.' In *Beowulf: Basic Readings*. Ed. Peter S. Baker. New York: Garland. 281–302.
–, trans. 2000. *Beowulf: A New Verse Translation*. Peterbourgh, Ont.: Broadview.
Lönnroth, Lars. 1971.'Hjálmar's Death-Song and the Delivery of Eddic Poetry.' *Speculum* 46: 1–20.
–. 1978. *Den dubbla scenen: Muntlig dikning från Eddan till ABBA*. Stockholm: Prisma.
–. 1979.'The Double Scene of Arrow-Odd's Drinking Contest.' In *Medieval Narrative: A Symposium. Proceedings of the Third International Symposium organized by the Centre for the Study of Vernacular Literature in the Middle Ages, held at Odense University on 20–21 November 1978*. Ed. Hans Bekker-Nielsen et al. Odense: Odense UP. 94–119.
Lord, Albert Bates. 1960. *The Singer of Tales*. Cambridge, MA: Harvard UP. [Re-edition with a CD and a new introduction by Stephen Mitchell and Gregory Nagy, 2000.]

Mac Cana, Proinsias. 1988. 'The Poet as Spouse of His Patron.' *Ériu* 39: 79–85.
Magnusson, Magnus, and Hermann Pálsson, trans. 1965. *The Vinland Sagas: The Norse Discovery of America*. Harmondsworth: Penguin.
Magoun, Francis Peabody. 1955. 'Bede's Story of Cædmon: The Case History of an Anglo-Saxon Oral Singer.' *Speculum* 30: 49–63.
Malone, Kemp, ed. 1962. *Widsith*. 2nd rev. ed. Copenhagen: Rosenkilde and Bagger.
–, ed. 1966. *Deor*. 4th rev. ed. London: Methuen.
Mansi: *Sacrorum Conciliorum nova et amplissima collectio* [...], *quae Johannes Dominicus Mansi* [...] *evulgavit. Edition novissima. Tomus secundus. Ab anno CCCV. ad annum CCCXLVI.* Florence, 1759.
Marold, Karl, ed. 1969. *Gottfried von Straßburg: Tristan*. 3rd ed. rev. by Werner Schröder. Berlin: de Gruyter.
Matthew Paris: *Matthaei Parisiensis Chronica Majora*. Ed. H. R. Luard. 7 vols. Rolls Series (Rerum Britannicarum Medii Ævi Scriptores) 57. London, 1872–84. (III = 1876)
McCone, Kim. 1989. 'A Tale of Two Ditties: Poet and Satirist in *Cath Maige Tuired*.' In *Sages, Saints and Storytellers: Celtic Studies in Honour of Professor James Carney*. Ed. D. Ó Corráin, K. McCone, L. Breatnach. Maynooth Monographs 2. Maynooth: An Sagart. 122–43.
–. 1990. *Pagan Past and Christian Present in Early Irish Literature*. Maynooth Monographs 3. Maynooth: An Sagart.
*MED*: Hans Kurath, Sherman M. Kuhn, Robert E. Lewis et al., eds., *Middle English Dictionary*. Ann Arbor: U of Michigan P, 1954–2001.
Menéndez Pidal, Ramón. 1957. *Poesía juglaresca y orígenes de la literaturas romanicas. Problemas de historia literaria y cultural*. Sexta edicion corregida y aumentada. Madrid: Instituto de Estudios Politicos. [1st ed. 1924 under the title *Poesía juglaresca y juglares. Aspectos de la historia literaria y cultural de España*.]
Mitchell, Stephen A. 1997. 'Courts, Consorts, and the Transformation of Medieval Scandinavian Literature.' *NOWELE* 31/32: 229–41 (*Germanic Studies in Honor of Anatoly Liberman*).
Moisl, Hermann. 1981. 'Anglo-Saxon Royal Genealogies and Germanic Oral Tradition.' *Journal of Medieval History* 7: 215–48.
Momma, H. 1997. *The Composition of Old English Poetry*. CSAE 20. Cambridge: CUP.
Morgan, Raleigh, Jr. 1953–54. 'Old French *jogleor* and Kindred Terms: Studies in Medieval Romance Lexicology.' *Romance Philology* 7: 279–325.
Muessig, Carolyn, ed. 2002. *Preacher, Sermon and Audience in the Middle Ages*. Leiden: Brill.
Munrow, David. 1976. *Instruments of the Middle Ages and Renaissance*. London: OUP.
Mustanoja, Tauno. 1959. 'The Presentation of Ancient Germanic Poetry – Looking for Parallels.' *Neuphilologische Mitteilungen* 60: 1–11.
Nagy, Joseph Falaky. 1986. 'Orality in Medieval Irish Narrative.' *Oral Tradition* 1: 272–301.
–. 2003. 'Fighting Words.' *Oral Tradition* 18: 194–95.
Naumann, Hans. 1924. 'Versuch einer Einschränkung des romantischen Begriffs Spielmannsdichtung.' *Deutsche Vierteljahresschrift* 2: 777–94. [Also in Schröder 1977: 126–44.]
*New Grove*[2]: *The New Grove Dictionary of Music and Musicians*. Ed. Stanley Sadie. 2nd ed. 29 vols. London: Macmillan, 2001.
Nicoll, Allardyce. 1963. *Masks, Mimes and Miracles: Studies in the Popular Theatre*. New York: Cooper Square Publications.
Niles, John D. 1999. *Homo Narrans: The Poetics and Anthropology of Oral Literature*. Philadelphia: U of Pennsylvania P.
Noomen, Willem, ed. 2003. *Le jongleur par lui-même. Choix de dits et de fabliaux*. Louvain: Peeters.
Nordal, Sigurður, and Guðni Jónsson, eds. 1938. *Gunnlaugs saga ormstungu*. In *Borgfirðinga sǫgur*. Íslenzk fornrit 3. Reykjavík: Hið íslenzka fornritafélag. 49–107.
Noto, Giuseppe. 1998. *Il giullare e il trovatore nelle liriche e nelle 'biografie' provenzali*. Scrittura e Scrittori 13. Alessandria: Edizioni dell'Orso.

O'Brien O'Keeffe, Katherine. 1990. *Visible Song: Transitional Literacy in Old English Verse*. CSASE 4. Cambridge: CUP.
Ó Coileáin, Seán. 1978.'Oral or Literary: Some Strands of the Argument.' *Studia Hibernica* 17:7-35.
O'Donnell, Daniel Paul. 2005. *Cædmon's Hymn: A Multimedia Study, Archive and Edition*. Cambridge: Brewer with SEENET and The Medieval Academy.
Ogilvy, J. D. A. 1963.'*Mimi, Scurrae, Histriones*: Entertainers of the Early Middle Ages.' *Speculum* 38:603-19.
Ólason, Vésteinn. 1985.'Tradition and Text'. In *The Concept of Tradition in Ballad Research: A Symposium*. Ed. Rita Pedersen and Flemming G. Andersen. Odense: Odense UP. 87-100.
Olsen, Alexandra. 1986. 'Oral-Formulaic Research in Old English Studies: I.' *Oral Tradition* 1:548-606.
–. 1988.'Oral-Formulaic Research in Old English Studies: II.' *Oral Tradition* 3:138-90.
Olsen, Magnus. 1919.'Varðlokur. En bidrag til kundskap om gammelnorsk troldom.' *Maal og minne* (1919): 1-21.
Olson, C. C. 1941.'The Minstrels at the Court of Edward III.' *PMLA* 56:601-12.
Ong, Walter J. 1982. *Orality and Literacy: The Technologizing of the Word*. London: Routledge.
Opland, Jeff. 1980. *Anglo-Saxon Oral Poetry: A Study of the Traditions*. New Haven: Yale UP.
Orchard, Andy. 1992.'Crying Wolf: Oral Style and the *Sermones Lupi*.'*ASE* 21:239-64.
–. 1997.'Oral Tradition.' In *Reading Old English Texts*. Ed. Katherine O'Brien O'Keeffe. Cambridge: CUP. 101-23.
Page, Christopher. 1987. *Voices and Instruments of the Middle Ages. Instrumental Practice and Songs in France 1100-1300*. London: Dent.
–. 1989. *The Owl and the Nightingale: Musical Life and Ideas in France 1100-1300*. Berkeley: U of California P.
–. 1993. 'Johannes de Grocheio on Secular Music: A Corrected Text and a New Translation.' *Plainsong and Medieval Music* 2.1 (*Aspects of Medieval Song: Essays in Honour of John Stevens*): 17-41.
Pálsson, Hermann.1962. *Sagnaskemmtun Íslendinga*. Reykjavík: Mál og menning.
Pauphilet, Albert, ed. 1952. *Historiens et chroniqueurs du Moyen Âge. Robert de Clari, Villehardouin, Joinville, Froissart, Commynes*. Textes nouveaux commentés par Edmond Pognon. Paris: Gallimard.
PC: see Pillet and Carstens 1933.
Pegg, Carole, and James Porter. 2001.'Epics.' *New Grove²*, VIII, 265-269.
Percy, Thomas. 1886. *Reliques of Ancient English Poetry*. Ed. Henry B. Wheatley. 3 vols. London.
Petrus Blesensis. *Opera Omnia*. Ed. J.-P. Migne. PL 207. Paris, 1855.
Picone, Michelangelo. 1994. 'La carriera di un giullare medievale. Il caso di Ruggieri Apugliese.' *Versants* 25:27-51.
Pillet, Alfred, and Henry Carstens 1933. *Bibliographie der Troubadours*. Schriften der Königsberger gelehrten Gesellschaft, Sonderreihe 3. Halle: Niemeyer.
Pirot, François. 1972. *Recherches sur les connaissances littéraires des troubadours occitans et catalans des XII^e et XIII^e siècles. Les "sirventes-ensenhamens" de Guerau de Cacrera, Guiraut de Calanson et Bertrand de Paris*. Memorias de la Real Academia de Buenas Letras de Barcelona 14. Barcelona: Real Academia de Buenas Letras.
Poole, Russell. 2005.'Þulr.' *RGA* XXX, 544-46.
Pound, Ezra. 1928. *Selected Poems*. Ed. with an introduction by T. S. Eliot. London: Faber and Faber.
Puchner, W. 1983.'Byzantinischer Mimos, Pantomimos und Mummenschanz im Spiegel der griechischen Patristik und ekklesiastischer Synodalverordnungen.' *Maske und Kothurn* 29:311-17.

Rajna, Pio 1878. 'Il Cantare dei Cantari e il Serventese del Maestro di tutte l'Arti.' *Zs. für romanische Philologie* 2: 220–54; 419–37.
Raynaud-Spanke: *G. Raynauds Bibliographie des altfranzösischen Liedes*. Neu bearbeitet und ergänzt von Hans Spanke. Part 1. Leiden: Brill, 1980.
Reich, Hermann. 1903. *Der Mimus. Ein litterar-entwickelungsgeschichtlicher Versuch*. 2 vols. Berlin: Weidmannsche Buchhandlung.
Reichl, Karl, ed. 2000a. *The Oral Epic: Performance and Music*. Intercultural Music Studies 12. Berlin: Verlag für Wissenschaft und Bildung.
–. 2000b. 'Introduction: The Music and Performance of Oral Epics.' In Reichl 2000a: 1–40.
–. 2003. 'Comparative Notes on the Performance of Middle English Popular Romance.' *Western Folklore* 62: 63–81.
–. 2005. 'Turkic Bard and Medieval Entertainer: What a Living Epic Tradition Can Tell Us About Oral Performance of Narrative in the Middle Ages.' In Vitz, Regalado and Lawrence 2005: 167–78.
–. 2009. 'Orality and Performance.' In *A Companion to Medieval Popular Romance*. Ed. Raluca L. Radulescu and Cory James Rushton. Cambridge: Brewer. 132–49.
Resende de Oliveira, A. 1993a. 'Jogral.' In Lanciani and Tavani 1993: 339–40.
–, A. 1993b. 'Segrel.' In Lanciani and Tavani 1993: 609–11.
–, A. 1993c. 'Trovador.' In Lanciani and Tavani 1993: 639–41.
*RGA: Reallexikon der Germanischen Altertumskunde*. 2nd rev. ed. Ed. Heinrich Beck et al. 35 vols. Berlin: de Gruyter. 1973–2007.
Roberts, Brynley F. 1988. 'Oral Tradition and Welsh Literature: A Description and Survey.' *Oral Tradition* 3: 61–87.
Rohloff, Ernst, ed. and trans. 1943. *Der Musiktraktat des Johannes de Grocheo*. Media latinitas musica 2. Leipzig: Reinecke.
Rosenberg, Bruce A. 1988. *Can these Bones Live? The Art of the American Folk Preacher*. 2nd rev. ed. Urbana: U of Illinois P. [Or. 1970.]
Rousse, Michel. 1991. 'Le théâtre et les jongleurs.' *Revue des langues romanes* 96: 1–14.
Rubel, Helen F. 1925. 'Chabham's *Penitential* and its Influence in the Thirteenth Century.' *PMLA* 40: 225–39.
Rychner, Jean. 1955. *La Chanson de geste. Essai sur l'art épique des jongleurs*. Société de Publications Romanes et Françaises 53. Geneva: Droz. [Rpt. 1999.]
*Sächsische Weltchronik: Deutsche Chroniken und andere Geschichtsbücher des Mittelalters*. Ed. Gesellschaft für ältere deutsche Geschichtskunde. Vol. 2. MGH, Scriptores qui vernacula lingua usi sunt, 1.2. Hannover, 1877.
Sadokov, R. L. 1976. 'Vesëlye skomorokhi.' *Sovetskaya Ètnografiya* 1976.5: 126–45.
Saffioti, Tito. 1990. *I giullari in Italia. Lo spettacolo, il pubblico, i testi*. Milan: Xenia Edizioni.
Salmen, Walter. 1960. *Der fahrende Musiker im europäischen Mittelalter*. Die Musik im alten und neuen Europa 4. Kassel: Hinnenthal.
–. 1990. 'Das Bild vom Klezmer in Liedern und Erzählungen.' In *Dona Folcloristica. Festgabe für Lutz Röhrich zu seiner Emeritierung*. Ed. Leander Petzoldt and Stefaan Top. Franfurt a. M.: Lang. 201–12.
Saville-Troike, Muriel. 1989. *The Ethnography of Communication: An Introduction*. 2nd ed. Oxford: Blackwell.
Schaefer, Ursula. 1992. *Vokalität: Altenglische Dichtung zwischen Mündlichkeit und Schriftlichkeit*. ScriptOralia 39. Tübingen: Narr.
Schechner, Richard. 1988. *Performance Theory*. 2nd rev. ed. London: Routledge.
–. 2006. *Performance Studies: An Introduction*. 2nd ed. London: Routledge.
–. 2007. 'Performance Studies: The Broad Spectrum Approach.' In Bial 2007: 7–9.
Schreier-Hornung, Antonie. 1981. *Spielleute, Fahrende, Außenseiter: Künstler der mittelalterlichen Welt*. Göppinger Arbeiten zur Germanistik 328. Göppingen: Kümmerle.

Schröder, Walter Johannes, ed. 1977. *Spielmannsepik*. Wege der Forschung 385. Darmstadt: WB.
See, Klaus von. 1964.'Skop und Skald: Zur Auffassung des Dichters bei den Germanen.' *GRM* N. F. 14: 1–14. [Rpt. in von See 1981a: 347–60.]
—. 1976.'Hastings, Stiklastaðir und Langemarck: Zur Überlieferung vom Vortrag heroischer Lieder auf dem Schlachtfeld.' *GRM* N. F. 26: 1–13. [Rpt. in von See 1981a: 259–71.]
—. 1981a. *Edda, Saga, Skaldendichtung: Aufsätze zur skandinavischen Literatur des Mittelalters*. Heidelberg: Winter.
—. 1981b.'*Húskarla hvǫt*: Nochmals zum Alter der Bjarkamál.' In *Speculum Norroenum: Norse Studies in Memory of Gabriel Turville-Petre*. Ed. Ursula Dronke et al. Odense: Odense UP. 421–31. [Rpt. in von See 1981a: 272–82.]
—. 1998. 'Das Phantom einer altgermanischen Elegiendichtung. Kritische Bemerkungen zu Daniel Sävborg, "Sorg och elegi i Eddans hjältediktning".' *skandinavistik* 28: 87–100.
Sherzer, Joel F. 1992.'Ethnography of Speaking'. In Bauman 1992: 76–80.
Shmeruk, Chone. 1986.'Can the Cambridge Manuscript Support the *Spielmann* Theory in Yiddish Literature?' *Studies in Yiddish Literature and Folklore*. Research Projects of the Institute of Jewish STudies. Monograph Series 7. Jerusalem: The Hebrew University of Jerusalem. 1–36.
Siikala, Anna-Leena. 1990.'Singing of Incantations in Nordic Tradition.' In *Old Norse and Finnish Religions and Cultic Place-Name: Based on Papers Read at the Symposium on Encounters between Religions in Old Nordic Times and on Cultic Place-Names, held at Åbo, Finland, on the $19^{th}$–$21^{st}$ of August 1987*. Ed. Tore Ahlbäck. Scripta Instituti Donneriani Aboensis 13. Åbo: Donner Institute for Research in Religious and Cultural History. 191–205.
Simms, Katherine. 1989. 'The Poet as Chieftain's Widow: Bardic Elegies.' In *Sages, Saints and Storytellers*. Ed. Donnchadh Ó Corráin et al. Maynooth: An Sagart. 400–11.
Sittard, Josef. 1885. 'Jongleurs und Menestrels. Eine Studie.' *Vierteljahresschrift für Musikwissenschaft* 1: 175–200.
Slotkin, Edgar M. 1977–79.'Medieval Irish Scribes and Fixed Texts.' *Eigse* 17: 437–50.
Southworth, John. 1989. *The English Medieval Minstrel*. Woodbridge, Suffolk: Boydell and Brewer.
Steinger, Hans. 1930. 'Fahrende Dichter im deutschen Mittelalter.' *Deutsche Vierteljahrsschrift* 8: 61–81. [Also in Schröder 1977: 168–90.]
Stevens, John. 1986. *Words and Music in the Middle Ages: Song, Narrative, Dance and Drama, 1050–1350*. Cambridge: CUP.
—. 2000.'Reflections on the Music of Medieval Narrative Poetry.' In Reichl 2000a: 233–48.
Strömbäck, Dag. 1935. *Sejd: Textstudier i nordisk religionshistoria*. Nordiska texter och undersökningar 5. Stockholm: Geber.
Sutton, Anne F. 1992.'Merchants, Music and Social Harmony: The London Puy and its French and London Contexts, circa 1300.' *London Journal* 17: 1–17.
Sveinsson, Einar Ól., and Matthías Þorðarson, eds. 1935. *Eiríks saga rauða*. In *Eyrbyggja saga[,] Grœnlendinga sǫgur*. Íslenzk fornrit 4. Reykjavík: Hið íslenzka fornritafélag.193–237.
Tangherlini, Timothy R. 2003.'Afterword: Performing through the Past: Ethnophilology and Oral Tradition.' *Western Folklore* 62: 143–49.
Tavani, Giuseppe. 1995.'Els Joglars catalans.' *Versants* 28 [*Les Jongleurs en Spectacle*]: 131–52.
Taylor, Andrew. 1991.'The Myth of the Minstrel Manuscript.' *Speculum* 66: 43–73.
Theune-Großkopf, Barbara. 2006.'Die vollständig erhaltene Leier des 6. Jahrhunderts aus Grab 58 von Trossingen, Ldkr. Tuttlingen, Baden-Württemberg: Ein Vorbericht.' *Germania* 84: 93–142.
Thompson, Augustine, OP. 2002.'From Texts to Preaching: Retrieving the Medieval Sermon as an Event.' In Muessig 2002: 13–37.
Tinnefeld, F. 1974. 'Zum profanen Mimos in Byzanz nach dem Verdikt des Trullanums (691).' *Byzantina* 6: 321–43.

Tobler-Lommatzsch: Tobler, Adolf, Erhard Lommatzsch, and Hans Helmut Christmann, eds. 1925–2002. *Altfranzösisches Wörterbuch.* 11 vols. Berlin: Akademie-Verlag. [Electronic ed.by Peter Blumenthal, Stuttgart: Steiner, 2002.]
Tyssens, Madeleine. 1966. 'Le jongleur et l'écrit.' In *Mélanges offerts à René Crozet.* Ed. Pierre Gallais et Yves-Jean Riou. 2 vols. Poitiers: Société d'Études Médiévales. I, 685–95.
Van Dorsten, Jan, ed. 1973. Sidney. *A Defense of Poetry.* Corr. ed. Oxford: OUP.
Vasmer, Max. 1953–58. *Russisches etymologisches Wörterbuch.* 3 vols. Heidelberg: Winter.
Vitz, Evelyn Birge, Nancy Freeman Regalado, and Marilyn Lawrence, eds. 2005. *Performing Medieval Narrative.* Cambridge: Brewer.
Vlasova, Z. I. 2001. *Skomorokhi i fol'klor.* St. Petersburg: Izd. 'Aleteyya'.
Wachinger, Burghart. 1987. 'Der Marner.' In *Die deutsche Literatur des Mittelalters. Verfasserlexikon.* Ed. Wolfgang Stammler, Karl Langosch, Kurt Ruh et al. Vol. 6. Berlin: de Gruyter. Cols. 69–79.
Wareman, Piet. 1951. *Spielmannsdichtung. Versuch einer Begriffsbestimmung.* Ph.D. Thesis Amsterdam University.
Wehrlich, Egon. 1964. 'Der westgermanische Skop: Der Aufbau seiner Dichtung und sein Vortrag.' Ph.D. Thesis, Münster University.
–. 1967. 'Der westgermanische Skop: Der Ursprung des Sängerstandes in semasiologischer und etymologischer Sicht.' *Zs. für deutsche Philologie* 86: 352–75.
Weinreich, Max. 1928. *Bilder fun der Yidisher Literaturgeshikhte. Von di Anheybn bis Mendele Mokher-Sfarim.* Vilna: 'Tamar'.
West, M. L. 2007. *Indo-European Poetry and Myth.* Oxford: OUP.
Whaley, Diana. 2005. 'Skaldic Poetry.' In *A Companion to Old Norse-Icelandic Literature and Culture.* Ed. Rory McTurk. Oxford: Blackwell. 479–502.
Wilcox, Jonathan. 2001. 'Transmission of Literature and Learning: Anglo-Saxon Scribal Culture.' In *A Companion to Anglo-Saxon Literature.* Ed. Phillip Pulsiano and Elaine Treharne. Oxford: Blackwell. 50–70.
Williams, J. E. Caerwyn. 1971. 'The Court Poet in Medieval Ireland.' *Proceedings of the British Academy* 57: 1–51.
–. 1978. *The Poets of the Welsh Princes.* Writers of Wales. n. p. [Cardiff]: U of Wales P.
–. 1996. 'The Celtic Bard.' In *A Celtic Florilegium: Studies in Memory of Brendan O Hehir.* Ed. Kathryn A. Klar et al. Lawrence, MA: Celtic Studies Publications. 216–26.
–, and Patrick K. Ford. 1992. *The Irish Literary Tradition.* Cardiff: U of Wales P; Belmont, MA: Ford and Bailie.
Worthen, W. B. 2007. 'Disciplines of the Text: Sites of Performance.' In Bial 2007: 10–25.
Wright, L. M. 1990. 'More on the Meanings and Uses of *Jongleur* and *Menestrel*.' *Romance Studies* 17: 7–19.
Zacher, Samantha. 2009. *Preaching the Converted: The Style and Rhetoric of the Vercelli Book Homilies.* Toronto: U of Toronto P.
Zan, Yigal. 1988. 'The Text/Context Controversy: An Explanatory Perspective.' *Western Folklore* 41: 1–27.
Zernack, Julia. 2004. 'Gests Erzählungen: Germanische Mytholie und der ordo narrationis in der isländischen Geschichtsschreibung des Spätmittelalters.' In *Präsenz des Mythos: Konfigurationen einer Denkform in Mittelalter und Früher Neuzeit.* Ed.Udo Friedrich and Bruno Quast. Trends in Medieval Philology 2. Berlin: de Gruyter. 299–328.
Zguta, Russell. 1972. '*Skomorokhi*: The Russian Minstrel-Entertainers.' *Slavic Review* 31: 297–313.
–. 1978. *Russian Minstrels: A History of the 'Skomorokhi'.* Oxford: Clarendon.
Zingarelli, Nicola, ed. 1973. Ludovico Ariosto. *Orlando Furioso.* 7th ed. Milan: Hoepli.
Zumwalt, Rosemary Lévy. 1988. *American Folklore Scholarship: A Dialogue of Dissent.* Bloomington: Indiana UP.

# 6 Oral Poetics: The Linguistics and Stylistics of Orality

*Thomas A. DuBois*

> 'And now, Tarkheena, tell us your story. And don't hurry it – I'm feeling comfortable now.'
> Aravis immediately began, sitting quite still and using a rather different tone and style from her usual one. For in Calormen, story-telling (whether the stories are true or made up) is a thing you're taught, just as English boys and girls are taught essay-writing. The difference is that people want to hear the stories, whereas I never heard of anyone who wanted to read the essays.

Thus writes C. S. Lewis, one of the great religious essayists of the twentieth century, in the third volume of his *Chronicles of Narnia* series (1975: 32). For Lewis, the oral story-telling styles of traditional cultures represented a natural element of his exotic land of Calormen, a great human nation to the south of the animal kingdom of Narnia. Oral storytelling also helped distinguish this narrative world from the workaday realities of English childhood and education, where essay-writing had thoroughly and inexorably replaced the art of story-telling, except, of course, in the refuge of the children's bedtime story. Later in the narrative, as Aravis continues her narrative, one of her horse audience protests her embroidering of the events. Another audience member, Bree, declares, however: 'Hush, Ma'am, hush [...] she's telling it in the grand Calormene manner and no storyteller in a Tisroc's court could do it better. Pray go on, Tarkheena' (35). For Lewis, storytelling had its own aesthetic features, ones equally as valid as those of the written essay, and sometimes far more effective in capturing and maintaining the interest of an audience. This essay explores the skills and qualities inherent in oral performance, particularly as it existed in medieval Europe. By examining extant texts from the medieval period, and relating them to what scholars know about oral tradition and the workings of oral communication in general, we can suggest some of the main features of an oral poetics at work during the era. This system of aesthetic values and norms can be seen as distinct from that associated with modern written communication, as well as that typical of 'ordinary' oral speech.

Given that sound recording technology is little more than a century old, it is obvious that we have no direct examples of medieval oral tradition, ordinary or otherwise. All works which scholars have described as 'oral' or 'oral-derived' (Foley 1991) have come down to us, necessarily, through the processes of manuscript production and copying, or through sound recordings made much after the end of the medieval period. This mediation removes us from the direct experience of expressive culture as orally performed and/or composed during the medieval period, and compels us instead to reconstruct, as best we can, the relation between the written text and its putative oral antecedents. Are signs of the original oral work discernable in the written record? If so, how are these different from what we would have found if the work had been composed originally as a written document? Do seemingly oral features in an extant text represent a 'residue' from past oral performance, or do they reflect a written aesthetics that still values highly the modes and tendencies of prior oral art? This essay addresses these issues, examining the linguistics and stylistics of orality in general, particularly as we believe it to have existed within various traditions of oral poetry in medieval Europe.

## 1 Breakthrough into Performance

I began my essay with Lewis's account of Aravis in part because Lewis points to a crucial element of oral tradition which we can observe in modern verbatim or electronic recordings. It is an element which folklorists have termed 'breakthrough into performance'.[1] Ordinary speech proceeds at its own somewhat erratic pace, usually approximating to a degree the norms of a language's formal grammar, but often departing markedly from the rules that characterize language at its most idealized and formal. A speaker may hesitate, or break off altogether, lose and regain the floor, fill in pauses with words of little direct meaning, substitute vague nouns (like *thing, thingummy, doohickey* or *whatchamacallit*) for specific words, or, in multilingual situations, code-switch, or intersperse discourse in one language with terms or grammar from another. Modern sound recording has allowed ethnographers and linguists to document such actual speech in detail, revealing the degree to which spoken language differs from the standardized norms taught in schools or universities, even among people with a high degree of formal education. Amid this flow of speech, however, moments may occur when a speaker takes up the mantle of performance and launches into a different mode of verbal expression. Richard Bauman (1986: 3) describes the moment thus:

> I understand performance as a mode of communication, a way of speaking, the essence of which resides in the assumption of responsibility to an audience for a display of communicative skill, highlighting the way in which communication is carried out, above and beyond its referential content. From the point of view of the audience, the act of expression on the part of the performer is thus laid open to evaluation for the way it is done, for the relative skill and effectiveness of the performer's display [...]. Viewed in these terms, performance may be understood as the enactment of poetic function, the essence of spoken artistry.

The speaker, like the Tarkheena Aravis in Lewis's children's tale, becomes a performer, creating a new verbalization that engages the norms of a particular genre (e. g., a tale, a song, a riddle, a prayer, an incantation) and producing a performance that can be compared to others within the same tradition or personal repertoire. These distinctive speech acts display recognizable formal features and acquire a quality of temporal transcendence that promises to outlive the present moment and situation. They do so by appealing to and enacting the notion of tradition, a concept of shared norms that allows audience and performer alike to view the present performance as a piece in a long line of compar-

---

[1] See Ben-Amos and Goldstein 1975; Hymes 1981; Bauman 1986.

able performances stretching far into an esteemed past and living on in the present through the enactment at hand.

Given the tremendous expense and labour involved in producing medieval manuscripts – the involved processes of preparing page and ink, the toil of learning to read and write in a society with few forms of childhood education – it should not seem surprising that most or all of what comes down to us in such works can be regarded as heightened breakthroughs into performance. People simply did not use writing as a mode for idly jotting down inconsequential items, and even the marginalia on manuscript pages tended to play important, if sometimes transgressive, roles (Camille 1992). The genres displayed in such pages may vary however, with some (e. g., prose discourse regarding expenses or transactions at a particular court or church) probably coming closer to what may have been ordinary speech than others (e. g., epic songs, prayers, saints' *vitae*) whose highly artificed diction and lexicon mark them as obvious artistic creations. In any case, however, we should expect the texts that come to us from the medieval period to show signs of performative cognizance, incorporating features of word choice, metre, syntax, or imagery that seek to set off the communications as somehow special, and deriving directly from formal modes characteristic of the genres they encode. Naturally, certain elements of oral performance will not find expression in the relatively crude system for recording speech that we rely upon as written language (Tedlock 1972 and 1983). Depths and varieties of pause, vocal rhythms or tone, alternations in pace and volume: these important elements of oral expression seldom find demarcation even in modern print, not to mention in that of the medieval era. We must thus content ourselves with the rather narrow range of data regarding medieval modes of performance that have left their marks on the written page.

## 2 The Formal Markers of Breakthrough

To sense this artificiality, this performativity, of medieval written texts, let us examine a brief passage of medieval French poetry. The eleventh verse paragraph of the *Chanson de Roland* reads as follows:

> Bels fut li vespres e li soleilz fut cler.
> Les dis mulez fait Char[l]es establer.
> El grant verger fait li reis tendre un tref,
> Les dis messages ad fait enz hosteler;
> .xii. serjanz les unt ben cunreez.
> La noit demurent tresque vint al jur cler.
> Li empereres est par matin levet,
> Messe e matines ad li reis escultet.
> Desuz un pin en est li reis alez,
> Ses baruns mandet pur sun cunseill finer:
> Par cels de France voelt il del tut errer. AOI.
> (ll. 157–67) (Calin, 1968: 24)
>
> The evening was clear, the sunset bright:
> King Charles commands the ten mules to be stabled

> And has a tent pitched in the spacious orchard,
> In which the ten envoys are billeted;
> Twelve sergeants have attended to them well;
> They spent the night there till the break of day.
> The emperor has risen in the morning;
> The king has heard his matins and his mass,
> And then the king has gone beneath a pine
> And called his barons to conclude his council:
> He always wants the Frenchmen to advise him. AOI
> (Harrison 1970: 56)

Preserved in a single parchment copy dated to between 1125 and 1150 and known as Digby 23 of the Bodleian Library at Oxford University, the *Chanson de Roland* stands as a striking and transcendent textual rendering of medieval French epic performance, one which may have been sung with or without a musical accompaniment that has been lost to us entirely. It belongs to a wider genre of *chansons de geste*, syllabic song-poems with poetic assonance and later rhyme, often focusing on the exploits of the Carolingian era.[2] In the passage reproduced above, we see Charlemagne receiving the dishonest suit from his Moorish enemies to the south that will eventually lead to the tragic defeat of his doughty retainer Roland. It is likely that anyone of the text's era hearing this passage in its narrative context at the beginning of a Carolingian epic would easily recognize its ominous foreshadowing and sense the ironies of this gracious and good-willed evening of entertainment.

A modern reader perusing such a text for the first time, however, may be startled at its overtly artificed diction and imagery. Words and phrases recur within the text in a manner wholly different from what we associate with ordinary oral speech or from what we have come to expect in written literature. In the above example, we may note the conventionalized noun-adjective pairs: an evening that is 'beautiful' and a sun that is 'clear' (*Bels fut li vespres e li soleilz fut cler*), of visitors who remain until the break of day (*La noit demurent tresque vint al jur cler*), and of a king who starts his day off right by hearing his matins and mass (*Messe e matines ad li reis escultet*). It is easy to sense a certain stylization of action and description here that distinguishes such poetry from a straightforward narration of events. Indeed, medieval epics seem to team with such formulas, or commonplaces, which recur every time a hero, villain, or horse takes the stage, or whenever certain typical events occur. Nouns seldom go without an adjective, interactions seldom proceed without a formal dialogue. While clearly helping identify the discourse as belonging to a particular performative genre (the *chanson de geste*), and meeting the metrical requirements of the poetic/musical line, such features often seem the very building blocks by which medieval poetry is constructed.

Another medieval manuscript, a codex conserved in the Biblioteca Nacional de Madrid, and dating to the year 1307, contains the text of the Spanish epic *Cantar de Mio Cid*.[3] Replete in similar imagery and plot, the epic is also rich in poetic epithets, ones far distant from what must have been ordinary speech or behaviour during the era of the Cid Ruy Díaz (the late eleventh century) or the probable era of the poem's com-

---

[2] [On the *chanson de geste*, see further ch. 12 (D. Boutet) in this volume.]
[3] [On the *Cid*, see also ch. 15 (R. Wright) in this volume.]

position (the mid-twelfth century). Consider, for instance, the oration credited to a young girl when the unhappy Cid requests hospitality of her home in Burgos:

> Una niña de nuef años a ojo se parava:
> '¡Ya Campeador, en buen ora çinxiestes espada!
> El rey lo ha vedado, anoch dél e[n]tró su carta,
> con gran recabdo e fuertemientre sellada.
> Non vos osariemos abrir nin coger por nada;
> si non, perderiemos los averes e las casas,
> e demás los ojos de las caras.
> Çid, en el nuestro mal vos non ganades nada;
> mas el Criador vos vala con todas sus vertudes santas.'
> Esto la niña dixo e tornós' por su casa. (ll. 40–49)
> (Girón Alconchel and Pérez Escribano 1995: 73–4)
>
> A young girl of nine came before him.
> 'O Conqueror, in a happy hour you took up your sword!
> The King has sent word, his letter arrived last night,
> With a great guard and strongly sealed.
> We dare not open to you, nor give you aid for any price;
> Or else we would lose our possessions and our houses,
> As well as the eyes from our faces.
> Çid, in doing us harm you would gain nothing;
> May the Lord protect you with all of his holy faculties.'
> Thus spoke the young girl, and turned back to her house.

The passage, implausibly placed in the mouth of a little child, reflects the highflown and formulaic orations that recur throughout the text. The girl addresses the knight with a formula: *Ya Campeador, en buen ora çinxiestes espada* (O Warrior, in a happy hour you took up/strapped on your sword) a phrase which, along with the closely related *Ya Campeador, en buen ora fuestes naçido* (O Warrior, you were born in a happy hour) recurs virtually any time the hero is mentioned in the text. As such, the phrase does not function logically in an oration that is meant to turn the hero away without hospitality; rather, it seems to appear merely as an expected adjunct of the hero's name, conveying the respect and fame surrounding him. Likewise, the girl's claim that they will lose not only their possessions and houses, but also their eyes in revenge for ignoring the king's decree carries with it a quality of extreme cruelty that seems to run counter to any simple recounting of facts. The girl's blessing at the end of the oration further seems oddly out of place, particularly when coupled with her reminder that killing the family will bring the knight little glory. Crucial to the effect of the passage, of course, is the irony that the heroic and worthy Cid does not receive hospitality when so many despicable figures in epics – such as the conniving envoy from King Marsile/Marsilion in the *Chanson de Roland* – receive bountiful and generous welcomes from their hosts. Yet such is the stuff of epics, and part of the enjoyment of experiencing them comes in recognizing and appreciating the traditionality of the phrasing and formulas that fill the narrative.

A similar impression of traditionality may arise from the perusal of an anthology of English ballads, Middle English verse romances, a collection of traditional folktales, or any number of other genres that derive directly from oral tradition or that have become part of an oral tradition before being written down.[4] Clearly, on some fundamental level, oral traditions possess a distinct set of poetic features and tendencies, ones which may strike the literate reader as all the more noticeable when viewed from the perspective of modern literary aesthetics, where a great premium is usually attached to the notions of novelty, distinctiveness of diction and image, and avoidance of repetition. The traditional text may seem at first hopelessly redundant, predictable, or clichéd. In applying such 'modern' literate aesthetic criteria to works that come to us from an oral tradition, however, the reader may forget that literate criteria are not simply 'right'; they are instead a negotiated set of stylistic values that writers and audiences have come to share over the course of centuries. And further, the reader may miss the fact that – in a Western tradition in which literacy has long been equated with the elite and fine, and orality with the peasant and plain – these literate standards may themselves have been formulated so as to distinguish emphatically the pieces of writing produced by social superiors from the oral renditions of their inferiors.

An advance in conceptualizing these differences and the possible reasons for their existence occurred in the work of the Classicist Albert B. Lord, whose *The Singer of Tales* appeared in 1960. Following in the footsteps of his teacher Milman Parry, and drawing on the intriguing essay of the French scholar Marcel Jousse (1925), Lord collected and analyzed performances of South Slavic oral epic in an effort to understand the composition and stylistics of Homer's works. In Lord's view, Serbo-Croatian oral epic displays a remarkably labile form, varying in detail and wording each time a singer performs. Examining multiple variants of the same song from the same or different singers allowed Lord to notice recurrent wording, imagery, and stylistic features that underlie the performances. Noting these apparent building blocks of the epic, Lord posited: 'For the oral poet the moment of composition is the performance. [...] Singing, performing, composing are facets of the same act' (1960: 13). Lord identified the structural units of oral poetry as the 'formula' ('a group of words [...] regularly employed under the same metrical conditions to express a given essential idea'), the 'theme' ('groups of ideas regularly used in telling a tale'), and broader narrative arcs that Lord termed the 'song'.[5] In the epic examples cited above, we can recognize the Spanish *en buen ora çinxiestes espada* as a formula, the getting and giving of hospitality in both epics as a theme, and the story of dealing with underhanded enemies a narrative arc or 'song'.

Each of these structural levels provide a performance with an air of familiarity to a competent audience, who can appreciate both the use of traditional phrasing and structuring devices as well as the occasional departure from the norms for aesthetic effect. In essence, while focusing on the means by which epic songs were composed, Lord posited and described a set of standards by which an oral performance was aesthetically appraised, an 'oral style', as Jousse had termed it. Such features are not simply the signs of a creator's work, but also the means by which the work qualifies as art within its ambient culture.

---

[4] See Andersen 1985 (on English ballads); Bradbury 1998, Reichl 2002 (on Middle English verse romances); Virtanen and DuBois 2000 (on traditional folktales).

[5] See Lord 1960: 31 (formula), 68 (theme), and 100 (song). [On the oral-formulaic theory (or Oral Theory), see also ch. 2 (J. M. Foley and P. Ramey) in this volume.]

Walter J. Ong (1982) took Lord's ideas farther by positing that oral communication possesses certain features that distinguish it utterly from the written communication Westerners define as normative today. Where Lord saw formulas, themes, and narratives as formal elements of a song tradition, Ong regarded these, and other discursive features, as natural outgrowths of the state of primary orality. Written communication, Ong notes, has developed in only a tiny minority of the world's languages, and seldom achieves complete dominance, even in cultures with a high degree of popular literacy. In the Middle Ages, writing was only in its infancy as a technology, nor was it by any means widespread as a skill among individual members of society. The vast bulk of people hearing or even performing poems or songs had learned them only from oral tradition, sometimes with the mediation of a text in the distant or near past, but sometimes with no such mediation at all. Thus, it stands to reason, the practices and tendencies of orality should have dominated over those of writing.

In addition to the kinds of formulaic diction and stress on traditionality described by Lord, Ong identifies certain other features which he suggests may be typical of oral communication (36–50). Oral thought, Ong maintains, is 'additive rather than subordinative'; i. e., it tends to organize thoughts into parallel arrays linked by the conjunction *and* rather than into chains of phrases linked by various forms of subordination. Medieval texts seem highly prone to this tendency, which was facilitated in part by specialized graphemes for indicating the conjunction. The recurrent epithets and adjectives which occur in medieval poetic works can be seen, in Ong's view, as proof of the fact that oral thought is 'aggregative rather than analytic': i. e., possessed of a tendency to merge nouns with qualifying adjectives into singular, indivisible units that resist segmentation into separate components. Further, Ong posits, oral communication tends to be 'redundant' or 'copious' i.e 'ensuring adequate comprehension among an audience by explicitly repeating terms, and creating in the process texts', Ong notes, 'bloated with "amplification", annoyingly redundant by modern standards' (41). The texts are further grounded in concrete human experience or situations rather than abstractions, which are difficult to convey in a context of primary orality. In terms of emotional orientation, Ong states that orality tends to be 'empathetic and participatory' as well as 'agonistically toned': speakers approach topics with clear attitudes in mind and tend to favour narration of moments of conflict and aberration rather than those in which all unfolds as expected. Finally, oral communications tend to hold significance for the present, a tendency which Ong labels 'homeostatic'. In short, orality tends to show few of the tendencies toward distancing, abstraction, or detachment which eventually come to be associated with authoritative written discourse.

To illustrate the tendencies Ong describes, let us look at a piece of medieval prose. The medieval Welsh tale *Branwen Uerch Lyr* (Branwen, Daughter of Llyr) appears in both the White Book of Rhydderch (National Library of Wales) and the Red Book of Hergest (Bodleian Library), both dating from the fourteenth century, but undoubtedly containing material from an earlier era. It is one of the principle tales ('branches') of the Welsh *Mabinogi*, a collection of stories that hold the same kind of cultural and historical importance for Wales that the *Chanson de Roland* holds for France or *Cantar de Mio Cid* holds for Spain. At the outset of the tale, King Bendigeidfran of the Britons receives the suit of King Matholwch of Ireland for the hand of his sister Branwen. In the opening scene, King Bendigeidfran and his kinsmen are sitting on a rock by the sea as the Irish approach:

> Ac ual yd oedynt yn eisted yuelly, wynt a welynt teir llong ar dec, yn dyuot o deheu Iwerdon, ac yn kyrchu parth ac attunt, a cherdet rugyl ebrwyd ganthunt, y gwynt yn eu hol, ac yn nessau yn ebrwyd attunt.
> 'Mi a welaf longeu racco', heb y brenhin, 'ac yn dyuot yn hy parth a'r tir. Ac erchwch y wyr y llys wiscaw amdanunt, a mynet y edrych pa uedwl yw yr eidunt.'
> Y gwyr a wiscawd amdanunt ac a nessayssant attunt y wayret. Gwedy guelet y llongeu o agos, diheu oed ganthunt na welsynt eiryoet llongeu gyweirach eu hansawd noc wy. Arwydon tec, guedos, arwreid o bali oed arnunt.
> Ac ar hynny, nachaf un o'r llongeu yn raculaenu rac y rei ereill, ac y guelynt dyrchauael taryan yn uch no bwrd y llong, a swch y taryan y uynyd yn arwyd tangneued. Ac y nessawys y gwyr attunt, ual yd ymglywynt ymdidan. Bwrw badeu allan a wnaethont wynteu, a nessau parth a'r tir, a chyuarch guell y'r brenhin. E brenhin a'e clywei wynteu o'r lle yd oed ar garrec uchel uch eu penn.
> 'Duw a rodo da ywch', heb ef, 'a grayssaw wrthywch. Pieu yniuer y llongeu hynn, a phwy yssyd pennaf arnunt wy?'
> 'Arglwyd', heb wynt, 'mae ymma Matholwuch brenhin Iwerdon, ac ef bieu y llongeu.'
> 'Beth', heb y brenhin, 'a uynnhei ef? A uyn ef dyuot y'r tir?'
> 'Na uynn, Arglwyd', heb wynt, 'negessawl yw wrthyt ti, onyt y neges a geif.'
> 'By ryw neges yw yr eidaw ef?' heb y brenhin.
> 'Mynnu ymgyathrachu a thidy, Arglwyd', heb wynt. 'Y erchi Branwen uerch Lyr y doeth, ac os da genhyt ti, ef uyn ymrwymaw Ynys y Kedeirn ac Iwerdon y gyt, ual y bydynt gadarnach.'
> 'Ie', heb ynteu, 'doet y'r tir, a chynghor a gymwerwn ninheu am hynny.' Yr atteb hwnnw a aethy ataw ef.
> 'Minheu a af yn llawen', heb ef.
> Ef a doeth y'r tir, a llawen uuwyt wrthaw; a dygyuor mawr uu yn y llys y nos honno, y rwng e yniuer ef ac yniuer y llys.Yn y lle trannoeth, kymryt kynghor. (ll. 13–44) (Thomson 1976: 1–2)

As they were sitting thus, they could see thirteen ships coming from the south of Ireland, approaching them at a smooth and swift pace. The wind was behind them and they drew near rapidly.

'I see ships yonder', said the king, 'and they're coming boldly to land. Ask men of the court to arm and go find out their intentions.'

The men armed and went down to meet them. After seeing the ships up close, they were certain that they had never seen better equipped ships than those. Fair, shapely, splendid pennants of brocaded silk were aloft.

And then one of the ships pushed ahead of the others, and they could see a shield being raised above the ship's rail, the tip of the shield up, in a sign of peace. And the men drew near to them until they could hear each other's conversation. They put down boats and, as they approached the shore, greeted the king. The king could hear them from where he was on the rock above them.

'May God prosper you', he said, 'and welcome. Whose ships are these, and who is chief over them?'

'Lord', they replied. 'Matholwch, king of Ireland, is here; the ships are his.'

'What does he want?' asked the king. 'Does he wish to come to land?'

'He has business with you, Lord', they said, 'and he does not want to come to land unless he can accomplish his business.'

'What sort of business does he have?' asked the king.

*6 Oral Poetics: The Linguistics and Stylistics of Orality*

'He seeks an alliance with you, Lord', they said. 'He has come to ask the hand of Branwen daughter of Llŷr, and if it please you, he wishes to unite the Isle of the Mighty with Ireland that they might be stronger.'

'Well', said he, 'let him land, and we will take counsel about that.'

'I will go gladly', he said.

He landed and was welcomed. And there was a great assembly in the court that night between his retinue and that of the court. First thing in the morning they took counsel. (Ford 1977: 59–60)

Here we see, despite the significant differences in language, similar images and usage of epithets to that noted in the short passage from the *Chanson de Roland* above. Indeed, we could easily imagine little difference between the entertainment that the Irish men of the thirteen ships will receive at the court of Bendigeidfran and that enjoyed by the ten Moorish envoys at the court of Charlemagne. From the point of view of heroic narrative, of course, the moments are identical: serious suits are not addressed on the day that the envoy arrives, but rather after a night of entertainment and proper rest. The details signal to the knowing audience that a meeting of significance will unfold, and significantly, in both cases, the events which follow turn out to be of great sorrow to the kings in question. In this way, they share or presage a common story arc, just as they share similar traditional formulas and themes.

7 – *Branwen Uerch Lyr* in the White Book of Rhydderch (14th c.), fol. 10va
(*a cherdet* to *bwrd y llong* in the quotation above)

On a discursive level, however, as Ong's study predicts, we may also note striking repetitions of phrasing in the passage, so much so, in fact, that from the perspective of modern written communication the prose may seem stilted and redundant. For one thing, the text makes ample use of the conjunction *ac* (and), conforming in this way to Ong's characterization of oral communication as 'additive' rather than 'subordinative'. Referential redundancy is also evident at the very outset of the passage, where multiple verbs describing the advance of the boats recur in close succession, despite the fact that a modern reader might simply expect one mention to suffice: *teir llong ar dec, yn dyuot* (thirteen ships were coming), *ac yn kyrchu parth ac attunt* (and making toward them), *ac yn nessau yn ebrwyd attunt* (and approaching them swiftly). The issue of approaching and coming to shore recurs repeatedly in the subsequent paragraphs as well, as Bendigeidfran asks: '*A uyn ef dyuot y'r tir?*' (Does he wish to come to land?) and receives the response that Matholwch does not wish to come to land unless his suit will be successful. When finally Bendigeidfran states: '*doet y'r tir*' (let him come to land) followed by the rejoinder: *Ef a doeth y'r tir* (he came to land), one might easily have the impression that the whole issue of landing has received a surfeit of attention. The same kinds of repetitions occur in discourse connected with the ships and in the involved and formal way in which the suit is put forward, details which will become important later in the narrative, when Matholwch becomes convinced that he has been the victim of a grievous breach of protocol. We can also note the agonistic tone of the encounter, despite its great formality and friendly purpose, and the concrete situation at the heart of the encounter (i. e., that of courtship): all characteristics, Ong would contend, of the communicative workings of an oral culture.

Where Lord described such stylistic features as tools for the efficient and effective composition of songs in oral performance, and Ong saw these and other features as the natural consequence of orality as a mode of thought, scholars following in their wake have tended to view these same features as part of a conscious and aesthetically nuanced poetics inherent in the tradition itself. It is a poetics distinct from that which eventually grows up in written literature, but one of great subtlety and power nonetheless. John Miles Foley (1991), for instance, underscores the evocative power which traditional formulas and themes possess under the rubric 'traditional referentiality'. As an audience member compares a present instance of a formula or theme with others known from the tradition, a sense of the words' deeper significance arises, awakening thus in a knowing audience an apt understanding of a given narrative situation or character through the barest minimum of supplied detail. In Old English poetry, for instance, mention of ravens or predatory birds or beasts (eagles, wolves) at a scene of battle recurs frequently in the poetry that survives, and has been designated the 'Beasts of Battle' theme. Illustrative are the following lines from the Old English *Battle of Maldon*, as presented by Foley:

>     Þa wæs feohte neh,
> tir æt getohte. Wæs seo tid cumen
> þæt þær fæge men feallan sceoldon.
> Þær wærð hream ahafen, hremmas wundon,
> earn æses georn; wæs on eorðan cyrm.
>     Hi leton þa of folman feolhearde speru,
> gegrundene garas fleogan; (ll. 103b–9)

> Then the fight was near,
> glory at battle. The time was come
> that men fated to die had to fall there.
> An outcry was raised there. Ravens circled,
> the eagle eager for carrion. There was an uproar on earth.
> Then from their hands they let fly
> File-hard spears, cruelly ground lances. (Foley 1991: 226)

By analyzing the broader narrative situations in which such 'Beasts of Battle' imagery typically occurs, Foley is able to point to the meanings the device seems to have carried for its original performers and audiences. He writes:

> What the theme provides [...] is a map for interpreting this particular fight and all other such encounters; heroic achievement will take place under the always impinging threat of death and desecration, the lot of all who take up arms. By summoning this extratextual, extrasituational context, the poet and tradition make whatever specific combat is occupying the center stage more meaningful, precisely because the theme deepens the present action by institutionalized reference to parallel actions in the same context. (226)

Formulas and themes become metonyms, carriers of immanence, layers of meaning conveyed in a highly effective, but by no means perfunctory, poetic diction (Foley 1991, 1995).

Mark Amodio (2004) explores similar issues in his study of English oral poetics in both the Anglo-Saxon era and after the Norman Conquest. For Amodio, as for Foley, formulas, themes, and story arcs carry deep metonymic resonances which can be viewed as part of the poetic system itself. The lexical simplex *(x-) belgan (-mod)*, for instance, built on the verb 'to swell with anger', occurs in a variety of different Old English texts, ranging from renderings of biblical narratives to the epic *Beowulf* (59–61). In the nine instances of the simplex's occurrence in *Beowulf*, the words precede a scene of significant carnage. In lines 708–9, for instance, the hero Beowulf awaits Grendel *bolgen-mōd* (heart swollen with anger). As Amodio points out, Beowulf has no logical, discursive cause to be angry at this point in the narrative, and the descriptor appears to function on a different level: as a poetic signal of impending battle, a sense captured artfully in Seamus Heaney's translation of the words as 'spoiling for action' (1999: 24). Soon after (l. 723), Grendel will seize the hall's door *(ge-)bolgen* (swollen with anger), signaling the mutual enmity and rage which will mark the ferocious struggle between Beowulf and Grendel. Later still (ll. 2220 and 2304), the dragon will become *gebolgen* (swollen with rage) by the theft of a cup, and Beowulf *torne gebolgen* (swollen with anger) will prepare to meet him in battle (l. 2401), calling him out with words loosed from a breast *gebolgen* (l. 2550). In concise but powerful manner, then, use of the participle *(ge-)bolgen* allows the poet to signal a coming moment of enraged battle, in which equally committed combatants will struggle to the death.

Scholars describing these aspects of oral-derived texts often refer to the language of poems or other genres as a special form of diction or register. 'Diction' refers to specific words that are chosen as appropriate to a particular variety of communication. As Flemming Andersen (1985) has shown, for instance, ballad texts in English typically employ a distinct range of terms and epithets for typical characters and situations. Horses are called 'steeds'; young women are 'maidens fair'. Singers and audiences share these ballad terms and employ them regularly, even when they are otherwise absent from the dialect of English typically spoken in the locale. In many cases, they can come to carry all the associations and aesthetic merit described above as traditional referentiality. The linguistic term 'register' encompasses more than merely lexical items, allowing scholars to refer to a broad range of linguistic norms that can become attached to a specific situation over time. Phrasing, syntax, and even morphology can take on distinct forms deemed appropriate to particular situations, creating generic expectations that help audiences recognize and evaluate the new performances they hear. The resulting variety of language can take on a life of its own, thriving as a *Kunstsprache* or *Spielmannsidiom* among people whose own dialects may differ considerably from each other, as well as from some other prosaic standard. As Karl Reichl (2002) has shown, Middle English verse romances seem to have developed a kind of register of this sort, one which leveled dialect differences and created a form of English characteristic of the poems. Osborn Bergin notes the persistence of a similar phenomenon in Irish Bardic poetry over a period of centuries. Writes Bergin (1984: 13):

> Practically all bardic poetry is written in one standard literary dialect, which remained almost unchanged for five hundred years. All this time the local dialects were diverging more and more, and there was no capital to set a natural standard. Yet the trained profession poet wrote in such a style that it is impossible to tell from his language to what part of Ireland or Scotland he belonged, or to fix his date even approximately. It is hard to say what they ought to have done, but what they actually did is clear. They made an artificial standard. They normalized the language by admitting into their verse only such forms and usages as had the sanction of earlier poets of high repute, everything else being rigorously excluded.

Steeped in the mystique and power of tradition, such standardized language carried with it not the stigma of a literary cliché, but the authority of a prestigious idiom, one grounded in the achievements and glories of the past.[6]

## 3  Mnemonic Anchors and Poetic Form

Whereas the various characteristics described above can be seen as products of the urge to perform on the one hand, and the workings of the oral mind on the other, the oral-derived works of the medieval era also tend to display mnemonic frameworks that apparently helped performers remember and reproduce them over time (Jousse 1925). Such 'anchoring' can include the fixing of words and phrases through metre, rhyme, assonance, and alliteration, as well as the arrangement of phrases into meaningful sequences or patterned arrays. Narrative arcs can become associated with conceptual anchors as well: particular proverbs or place names, activities or entities that help demonstrate and underscore the existence and details of a narrative over time. Just as with forms of redundancy or formulaic diction, these varieties of discursive anchors can become aesthetically charged in themselves: constitutive of an artistry that combines the pragmatic work of memorization and recall with the aesthetic work of transcendence and appraisal.

---

[6]  [On Irish poetry and orality, see further ch. 9 (J. F. Nagy) in this volume.]

One of the most obvious and effective mnemonic anchors is that of metre. When combined with forms of alliteration, assonance or rhyme, metre can exert a powerful stabilizing effect on discourse, one that can help preserve pieces of poetic diction intact for generations, even centuries. Where ordinary speech may easily permit substitution or variation within utterances, metrically shaped communications exert strict control over the placement and quality of words and their relations to each other. Throughout medieval Europe, professional poets developed metrical systems that challenged the intellect as well as preserved poetry from performance to performance. Among Scandinavians, such was the case with the metres of the skalds, court poets who composed encomiums to the memory of chieftains or kings. Skaldic poems dating from the ninth century were still apparently in oral tradition by the twelfth and thirteenth centuries, when they began to be recorded in books. Consider, for instance, the Icelandic *Egils saga Skalla-grímssonar,* a thirteenth-century account of a ninth-century Icelandic poet named Egil. Preserved in a thirteenth-century manuscript known as *Möðruvallabók,* as well as in some other vellum works of the same or later periods, *Egils saga* includes a wide variety of poems that had apparently existed in oral tradition before being incorporated into the saga. One such poem is credited to Egil at the age of three:

> Kominn emk ern til arna
> Yngvars, þess's beð lyngva
> (hann vark fúss at finna)
> fránþvengjar gefr drengjum.
> Mon eigi þú þægir
> þrévetran mér betra
> ljósundinna landa
> linns óðar smið finna. (Jónsson 1931: 101)

> I have come in fine fettle to the hearth
> Of Yngvar, who gives men gold from the glowing
> Curled serpent's bed of heather [=treasure hoard];
> I was eager to meet him.
> Shedder of gold rings bright and twisted
> From the serpent's realm, you'll never
> Find a better craftsman of poems
> Three winters old than me. (Smiley and Kellogg 1997: 52)

The poem belongs to the metre known as *dróttkvætt,* an eight-lined verse form favoured by skalds of Egil's day (Gordon and Taylor 1957: 317–18). Each line contains three primary-stress syllables, with the final word of the line always consisting of a primary word stress followed by an unstressed syllable (e. g., *arna, lyngva*). In the odd lines, alliteration occurs between syllables that contain differing vowels (e.g, *fúss, finna; þú, þægir*), while in the even lines, syllabic rhyme occurs (e. g., *Yngvars, lyngva; þrévetran, betra*). Such rhyme always occurs between the first and third metrical foot, never between the first and second. These various rules make it difficult to substitute any other words for those originally incorporated into the verse, and thus act as a powerful stabilizing force over time. A relatively free poetic syntax and a penchant for elaborate metaphors (termed 'kennings') helped verse makers create poetry that obeyed these considerable strictures.

Rules of similar complexity govern Irish syllabic poetry. Knott illustrates one of the favoured metres with a stanza from the sixteenth-century poem entitled 'On the Cutting Down of an Ancient Tree':[7]

> Do bhíoth dhamh ag déanaimh eóil
>     an ghégsoin fa gar do mhaoin;
> fada siar ón tírsi thuaidh
>     aniar uain do-chínnsi an gcraoibh.
>
> The bough was wont to guide my way
>     It was a transient possession;
> Far back from this land in the north I could see
>     In the distance the branch behind me.

In the common metre known as *rannaigheacht mhór*, stanzas consist of four heptasyllabic lines, each line ending in a monosyllabic word (Knott 1934: 13–14). The final words of the second and fourth lines rhyme (i. e., *mhaoin* and *gcraoibh*), while those of the first and third *(eóil* and *thuaidh)* are consonate with them. There must be at least two internal rhymes within each couplet (e. g., in the first couplet *dhamh* and *gar*, *déanaimh* and *ghéagsoin;* in the second couplet *siar* and *aniar, tírsi* and *do-chínnsi)*, and the final word of the third line must rhyme with a word in the middle of the fourth line (i.e, *thuaidh* and *uain)*. Alliteration must occur between at least two words in each line (e. g., *dhamh* and *déanaimh)*, and the final word of the fourth line *(gcraoibh)* must alliterate with the stressed word that precedes it *(do-chínnsi)*. As the above examples show, rhyme was more broadly defined in Irish than in modern English, yet the combination of metre, alliteration and required rhymes expected in the various metres used by poets exercised a considerable stabilizing influence over the poetry, helping preserve it in oral form until it could be written down, as we shall discuss in the final part of this essay. Such artistry creates both an aesthetically pleasing whole as well as a product which could be remembered and reperformed effectively over time.

In examining oral narratives collected from Native American elders at the close of the nineteenth century, Dell Hymes (1981, 2003) has revealed the powerful use of pattern numbers as a means of organizing and aesthetically shaping extended narratives, regardless of whether they can be classified as poetry or prose. In highly valued narrative performances, when items occur in a series – be it a chain of events, a string of adjectives, or a set of characters – they will often be so arranged so as to match the dominant and secondary pattern numbers of the culture. In some Native cultures of North America, narrative sequences occur in groupings of two and four. In other cultures on the same continent, however, the typical groupings are of three and five. Thus, in one culture, characters will occur in pairs or foursomes, and will undertake tasks in a sequence of four attempts, while in other cultures – as in much of Europe (Olrik 1965) – characters will tend to occur in groupings of three, and undertake tasks in series of three or five attempts. These groupings recur within narratives at the level of lines or phrases, where they help organize the flow of discourse into verses, stanzas, scenes, and acts – terms which derive from the study of poetry and theater, but which receive new analytical significance. Such groupings are sometimes set off for the listening audience by overt

---

[7] Knott 1934: 9; see also Bergin 1984: 51–52, 232–33.

markers like counting, but more often they are signaled subtly through repeated parallel structuring or the recurrence of certain verbal particles or other linguistic features (2003: 304). These sorts of interlinear organization can occur in conjunction with more overt devices of poetic discourse (e. g., metre, rhyme), but they may also occur in discourse that at first resembles simple prose. Hymes labels this kind of verbal performance 'measured verse', suggesting that it bridges and helps undermine the rigid differentiation of poetry and prose that has come down to us through written literature. He labels the study of such features 'ethnopoetics', a term used with some variation by earlier scholars (e. g., Tedlock 1972, 1983). A passage from the earliest recorded piece of Finnish epic can illustrate such features. An oral ballad relating the martyrdom of Finland's patron saint Henrik, preserved in a manuscript from the eighteenth century but certainly representing earlier tradition, this text closes with an image of St. Henrik in joy, while his murderer Lalli suffers in eternal torment:

>     Pispa enkelein kansa laulelee
>         Ilon virttä veisailee.
>     Lalli hiidesä hihtelepi
>         Lylynensä luistelepi
>             Piinan savuhun sakiahan
>                 Sauvallansa satuttelee.
>     Pirut pahoin pistelevät
>         Helvetin heltehesä
>             Sielu parkaa vaivailevat.
>     (Kuusi, Bosley, and Branch 1977: 320)

>     The bishop is singing with the angels,
>         Chanting a verse of joy.
>     Lalli is skiing in Hiisi,
>         Sliding with his left ski,
>             Into the thick smoke of punishment
>                 Striking with his ski pole.
>     Demons are wickedly sticking him
>         In the heat of hell
>             Tormenting his sorry soul.

Although Finnish oral epic poetry in general displays formal parallelism, in which the contents of one line find close restatement in a matched second line, this passage displays a three-part structure built atop, and partly undermining, these obligatory line pairings (DuBois 1995). Each of the three parts of the passage focuses on a different actor engaged in a particular action, expressed through a succession of verbs ending in the frequentative suffix *-lla/ä*, translated above through the English present progressive. In the first part of the passage, we hear of the contented singing of the martyred St. Henrik, encompassed in the verbs *laulelee/veisailee* (singing/chanting). The couplet is clear and balanced, and follows the rules of formal parallelism closely. In the bridging middle part, Henrik's murderer Lalli is depicted in the frantic act of skiing, signaled by the active verbs *hihtelepi/luistelepi/satuttelee* (skiing/sliding/striking), distributed over four lines. Medieval skis were of differing lengths in Finnish culture, with the longer left ski *(lyly)* used for sliding and the shorter right ski *(kalhu)* for kicking. This fact serves as a semantic resource for building a parallel line to the one which announces Lalli's skiing, while the final verb in the section refers to the long staff or pole *(sauva)* used by skiers in place of matched ski poles. Lalli's act is located, rather picturesquely, in Hiisi, a term that refers originally to pre-Christian forest sacrificial sites, but which was eventually stigmatized as the equivalent of the Christian hell. It is depicted here with the darkness and cold of a forest grove, matching the ancient sense of the term. Finally, in the final three-line section, the poem depicts demons besetting Lalli, expressed through frequentative verbs of torture *pistelevät/vaivailevat* (sticking/tormenting) in a setting drawing more directly on the (imported) image of a flaming hell. Point of view is managed deftly in the passage, so that we can focus on each of the three situations in turn, while the parallelism of the verbs allows us to appreciate the contrasting outcomes of differing choices in life. Such interlinear groupings allow the poem to merge and shape its discourse into meaningful broader units, undercutting what might otherwise seem a jagged or perfunctory series of line pairs.

Hymes's ethnopoetic analyses have not as yet received as wide application among medievalists as have those of the Oral Formulaic school, but a number of scholars have begun to incorporate them into their frameworks, often in combination with the ideas of Lord and Ong.[8] Given the widespread nature of the phenomena Hymes describes, it is likely that groupings and techniques described under the rubric of ethnopoetics may obtain in other European traditions. In fact, certain of the tendencies which Hymes identifies as conscious aesthetic choices seem to come very close to the features which Ong attributed earlier to a seemingly innate oral psychology. The tendency for syntactic parallelism rather than subordination, for instance (Ong's 'additive' logic), as well as the recurrence of certain conjunctions or particles like *and,* may point to an aesthetic shaping, be it in poetry or in prose. Likewise, the lexical redundancy which Ong notes – the repetition of words more than once within a single sentence or passage – may, from the perspective of ethnopoetics, represent a conscious stylistic effect rather than merely an attempt to ensure oral comprehension. If, for instance, we reconsider the first section of the Welsh passage discussed above, we can note features that may have helped its creator, and audience, experience it aesthetically. Presenting it on the page as poetry helps reveal these features, as the following, accompanied with a closer English translation, illustrates:

> Ac ual yd oedynt yn eisted yuelly,
>     wynt a welynt teir llong ar dec,
> yn dyuot o deheu Iwerdon,
>     ac yn kyrchu parth ac attunt,
>     a cherdet rugyl ebrwyd ganthunt,
>         y gwynt yn eu hol,
>             ac yn nessau yn ebrwyd attunt.

> And as they were sitting thus,
>     they descried thirteen ships
> coming from the south of Ireland,
>     and making for them
>     sailing freely, swiftly along,
>         the wind at their backs
>             and they swiftly drew near.

---

[8] See, e. g., Zumthor 1972 and 1983; Foley 1995; Niles 1999; Amodio 2004.

Where this passage may have seemed at first clumsy and artless, ethnopoetic analysis reveals its careful shaping, and the uses made of parallelism and repetition in a discourse far different from what we may think of as prose today.

## 4 Mnemonic Anchoring through Content

The mnemonic anchoring achieved by metre, alliteration, rhyme, and parallelism may also occur through the medium of content. In the Welsh tale of Branwen discussed above, an angry Bendigeidfran pursues his former in-law-turned-enemy Matholwch across Ireland. The latter crosses the Shannon and destroys the bridge, banking on the magnetic stones at the bottom of the river to block the Britons' pursuit. The gigantic Bendigeidfran is not to be stopped, however, and lies down across the river as a bridge for his men. The troops place planks on top of him and march across to victory. The passage depicts Bendigeidfran's act as follows:

> 'Arglwyd', heb y wyrda, 'ti a wdost kynnedyf ur auon, ny eill neb uynet drwydi, nyt oes bont arnei hitheu. Mae dy gynghor am bont?' heb wy.
> 'Nit oes', heb ynteu, 'namyn a uo penn bit pont. Mi a uydaf pont', heb ef.
> Ac yna gyntaf y dywetpwyt y geir hwnnw, ac y diharebir etwa ohonaw. (ll. 291–95)
>     (Thomson 1976: 11)
>
> 'Lord', said his men, 'you know the peculiarity of the river, that none can go across it – nor is there a bridge over it. What do you advise for a bridge?'
> 'Nothing, except that he who is chief shall be a bridge', he replied. 'I will be a bridge.'
> Then was first uttered that saying, and it has become proverbial.
>     (Ford 1977: 67)

Bendigeidfran's statement, transformed into the proverb 'Like a bridge over troubled waters, I will lay me down', helps anchor the narrative, so that the saying – whenever it occurs – leads a listener to recall the narrative events, while the events of the narrative in turn help gloss and explicate the saying. John Miles Foley (1994) has pointed to a similar use of proverbs in South Slavic epic: they increase the traditional weight of the performance while helping extend the life of the proverb in oral tradition as well. The same sort of mnemonic anchoring can be observed in skaldic kennings, in which a single poetic epithet can encapsulate and recall an entire myth or heroic narrative. Thus, according to Snorri Sturluson, the kenning for gold *haddr Sifiar* (Sif's hair) derives from a complex tale in which the trickster Loki cuts off all of the goddess Sif's hair as a prank (Jónsson 1931: 122–25). Sif's husband, the god Thor, threatens Loki with death until he promises to engage dwarfs to create new hair for his wife. In the process, Loki assists in the creation of a variety of important implements of the gods, and ends up vindictively and humorously maimed by the dwarfs. Again, as with the Welsh proverb, the single kenning signals an entire narrative, while the narrative in turn confers meaning upon the otherwise cryptic metaphor, one useful in constructing verses that conform to the considerable requirements of skaldic poetry.

A further variety of content-based mnemonic anchors occurs in catalogues or listings, a characteristic particularly popular in medieval Welsh and Irish narratives. The same tale of Branwen discussed above is credited as containing one of the three most unfortunate slaps in the history of Britain, one of the three most fortunate interments of a corpse, and one of the three most unfortunate disinterments as well. The Irish tale of Mac Datho's Pig *(Scéla mucce Meic Dathó)* describes the landowner Mac Datho's home as one of the five chief hostels of Ireland of its time:

> Is <s>í sin in chōiced bruden ro·boī i nHērinn isind aimsir sin, ocus bruden Da-Derg i crích Cūalann ocus brudan Forgaill Manaich ocus bruden Me[i]c Da-Rēo i mBrēfni ocus bruden Da-Choca i n-īarthur Midi. (Thurneysen 1935: 1)
>
> This was one of the five chief hostels of Ireland at the time, and there was the hostel of Da-Derga among the men of Cualu, and the hostel of Forgall Monach, and the hostel of Da Reo in Brefne, and the hostel of Da Choga in Westmeath.
> (Cross and Slover 1936: 199)

Each mentioned hostel had its own tales and history, making the listing likewise a catalogue of potential tales, helping the storyteller keep track of a repertoire related to each. Such cataloguing works in a certain sense like metre and alliteration or rhyme, pulling into aesthetic 'equivalence' (Jakobson 1960) items of narrative that might not otherwise be regarded as related, and creating a new system of affinity between them that helps both explicate and recall the items included. This process, which Roman Jakobson (1960: 358) describes as the projection of the principle of equivalence from the 'axis of selection' into the 'axis of combination', lies at the heart of all poetics.

The tale of Mac Datho's pig provides illustration of a further mnemonic anchor favoured in medieval narratives: the association of tales with particular places and placenames. Thus, Ailbe, the exceptional hound of Mac Datho – the cause of a fierce conflict between rival kingdoms – becomes the source of the placename Mag n-Ailbi (the plain of Ailbe), while the place where its head falls after its death becomes known as Áth Cinn Chon (ford of the hound's head). The placenames again anchor the tale to the concrete environment, while the narrative helps explicate what might otherwise seem confusing names. The same use of onomastics recurs in many other medieval traditions, including the Icelandic sagas.

## 5 From Anchors to Attractors

Although features such as metre, rhyme, alliteration, classification and association certainly could exert considerable control over poetic utterances, the very conventionality of these features could lead in turn to a loss of specific detail. Folklorists examining the process of poetic transmission have noted the tendency of unique words or details in a song or tale to become replaced over time with more conventional ones. In time, as Tristram Coffin (1957) points out in his study of Anglo-American ballads, a unique historical account can become transformed into a thoroughly familiar and conventionalized rendering, containing little detail that would distinguish its narrated events from those of other songs or tales. Further, where pattern numbers can help a performer recall and recreate a series of events or details in performance, the aesthetic appeal of these numbers can easily force divergent series into adding or losing elements so as to conform to expectations. Unique or obscure characters or obscure places can similarly be replaced by more famous ones, a process known as 'narrative attraction', that can lead to particular deeds being credited to actors who may have lived centuries before or after the events in question, or in places far distant from where the legendary accounts stipulate. These effects can be regarded as the natural byproducts of the poetic and mnemonic systems operative in oral tradition, and certain medieval genres, such as the lyric song, display a high degree of conventionality which may be understood in relation to this process of transmission and change (DuBois 2006: 142–48). In those cases in which we are able to compare medieval epic or romance with drier historical accounts of the same events written closer in time to the events themselves, we frequently find alterations of detail or form which reflect these unspoken but powerful organizing tendencies. The poetics of medieval orality did not simply clothe events in an outward form suited to easy recall; rather, the events were often reshaped substantively into aesthetically effective and satisfying forms.

## 6 Acts of Composition

Assuming the responsibility of performance – breaking through – was a serious act in medieval culture, where the right to speak was regulated by strong considerations of class and decorum, and where verbal performances were carefully and rigorously evaluated. Performers who learned to enact valued genres artfully were praised for their skills and could at times build careers in a court or district. Novice performers, likewise, could be subjected to considerable training before taking the stage. Medieval literature often preserves legendary memories of particularly effective singers or poets, sometimes describing their careers in extended narratives, as the above discussion of *Egils saga* shows. Where such accounts occur, they tend to depict the act of composition as an involved skill, sometimes divinely granted, sometimes earned by dint of hard work. In any case, these acts of composition seem markedly different from the somewhat automatic creative work we might assume from an initial reading of Lord's great *Singer of Tales* or which we might at first assume from a lack of awareness of the aesthetic features of oral-derived works. Three examples illustrate this point and complete our essay.

In his eighth-century *Historia ecclesiastica gentis Anglorum* the Venerable Bede includes an account of the first man to adapt Anglo-Saxon heroic poetry to Christian themes.[9] A humble cowherd named Caedmon avoids taking up the harp out of embarrassment at his lack of musical skill. While sleeping in the cowshed, he sees a mysterious being (possibly an angel), who orders him to sing. When he awakes, he is able to perform a new religious hymn, a song of praise for God and his act of Creation as narrated in the Book of Genesis. Subsequently, Bede tells us, Caedmon became a member of the local monastic community and continued his newly found gift of poetic composition. His fellow monks read or related to him accounts from the Bible and these he reflected upon by himself until creating a poetic rendering. John Niles (2006) links this account to a

---

[9] Colgrave and Mynors 1969: 414–21. [See also ch. 4 (K. O'Brien I'Keeffe), pp. 122–27, and ch. 5 (J. Harris and K. Reichl), pp. 146–47 in this volume.]

more widely known Irish tale type 2412B 'The Man Who Had No Story' and suggests that Bede is here adapting a common folktale in order to make a point about religious poetry. Mark Amodio focuses similarly on the fictive qualities of the account, noting that 'If Caedmon did not exist, someone would have had to invent him' (2004: 25). He represents, in other words, a narrative point of origin for a new tradition of vernacular religious poetry that had become popular in England at the time of Bede (the eighth century) and after. Although, as these scholars point out, it is unwise to read the story of Caedmon as a straight historical account of an Anglo-Saxon poet's career, it is nonetheless useful to note that the depiction of poetic composition here is not one of creation through performance, but rather, of thoughtful meditation followed by a later performance.

The same two-part process is evident in the account of Egil Skallagrímsson's composition of the poem known as *Hǫfuðlausn,* or 'Head Ransom'. According to the account contained in the *saga,* Egil is magically drawn to the shores of Scotland, where his arch enemies King Erik Blood-axe and his queen Gunnhild have come to power.[10] Realizing that he has strayed into his enemies' hands, Egil goes directly to their court at York, where his friend Arinbjorn sues for his life. Arinbjorn promises that Egil will compose a long stanzaic poem (termed a *drápa*) of twenty stanzas in honour of Erik in order to restore good relations between them. Erik begrudgingly consents, and Egil is sequestered in a room by himself for the night in order to compose the poem. During the night, Egil is disturbed by a twittering bird – apparently the angry Gunnhild in magic disguise – until Arinbjorn chases the bird away and guards the poet's window for the rest of the night. In the morning, Egil has completed the poem, which he duly recites for the king, thus ransoming his head through poetic skill. A similar process of quiet composition followed by later performance occurs later in the saga as well, when Egil remains in seclusion in order to compose a lament for the death of two of his sons.[11]

In his *Memoirs of the Marquis of Clanricarde* of 1722, Thomas O'Sullevane presents a fascinating account of the training process of poets in eighteenth-century Ireland. The description has been discussed in detail by Osborn Bergin (1984: 5–7). According to this account, young men who wanted to make their way as court poets joined a kind of seminary for rhetoric, where they received daily instruction in poetic form and structures and were then given an evening assignment:

> The said Subject [...] having been given over Night, they work'd it apart each by himself upon his own Bed, the whole next Day in the Dark, till at a certain Hour in the Night, Lights being brought in, they committed it to writing. Being afterwards dress'd and come together in a large Room, where the Masters waited, each Scholar gave in his Performance, which being corrected or approv'd of (according as it requir'd) either the same or fresh subjects were given against the next Day. (6)

The poems thus created would be later performed by a different professional, a reciter *(reacaire)* with skills in oral delivery. Bergin suggests that this custom must have been very archaic in the eighteenth century and probably represents a continuation of medie-

---

[10] Jónsson 1888: 212–24, 350–6; Smiley and Kellogg 1997: 108–18.
[11] Jónsson 1888: 282–7; Smiley and Kellogg 1997: 149–58. [Compare also ch. 5 (J. Harris and K. Reichl), p. 154.]

val methods. In any case, it is difficult here to separate 'orality' from 'literacy', in that the mode of composition employed both in sequence. Nonetheless, it appears essential that the composition occur orally, and not through a process mediated by the new technology of writing. Perhaps this manner of creating a poem represents a medial stage between the oral composition described for Caedmon and Egil, and later, purely literate modes more familiar to poets ('writers') of today.

All three of these accounts share a rather wistful tone, as if to underscore the fact that the competences displayed by the poets in the texts were no longer commonplace within the literate milieu of the admiring scribes or authors of later centuries. New competences had replaced them, even while writers looked back with respect and sometimes envy on an era in which artistry consisted not in textual erudition but in the ability to create and convey works of beauty and significance through the transient strains of the human voice. Perhaps they, like Lewis's Bree, appreciated above all the performance of verbal art in the 'grand [...] manner' that orality affords.

## References

Amodio, Mark C. 2004. *Writing the Oral Tradition: Oral Poetics and Literate Culture in Medieval England.* Notre Dame, IN: U of Notre Dame P.
Andersen, Flemming G. 1985. *Commonplace and Creativity: The Role of Formulaic Diction in Anglo-Scottish Traditional Balladry.* Odense: Odense UP.
Bauman, Richard. 1986. *Story, Performance, and Event: Contextual Studies of Oral Narrative.* Cambridge: CUP.
Ben-Amos, Dan, and Kenneth Goldstein. 1975. *Folklore: Performance and Communication.* The Hague: Mouton.
Bergin, Osborn. 1984. *Irish Bardic Poetry.* Dublin: Dublin Institute for Advanced Studies.
Bradbury, Nancy. 1998. *Writing Aloud: Storytelling in Late Medieval England.* Urbana: U of Illinois P.
Calin, William, ed. 1968. *La Chanson de Roland.* New York: Appleton-Century-Crofts.
Camille, Michael. 1992. *Image on the Edge.* Cambridge, MA: Harvard UP.
Coffin, Tristram. 1957. '"Mary Hamilton" and the Anglo-American Ballad as an Art Form.' *JAF* 70: 208–14. [Rpt. in *Readings in American Folklore.* Ed. Jan Harold Brunvand. New York: Norton, 1979. 309–18.]
Colgrave, Bertram, and R. A. B. Mynors, eds. 1969. *Bede's Ecclesiastical History of the English People.* Oxford: Clarendon.
Cross, Tom Peete, and Clark Harris Slover, eds. 1936. *Ancient Irish Tales.* New York: Barnes and Nobles.
DuBois, Thomas A. 1995. *Finnish Folk Poetry and the Kalevala* New York: Garland.
–. 2006. *Lyric, Meaning, and Audience in the Oral Tradition of Northern Europe.* Notre Dame, IN: Notre Dame UP.
Foley, John Miles. 1991. *Immanent Art: From Structure to Meaning in Traditional Epic.* Bloomington: Indiana UP.
–. 1994. 'Proverbs and Proverbial Function in South Slavic and Comparative Epic.' *Proverbia* 11: 77–91.
–. 1995. *The Singer of Tales in Performance.* Bloomington: Indiana UP.
Ford, Patrick K., ed. and trans. 1977. *The Mabinogi and Other Medieval Welsh Tales.* Berkeley: U of California P.

Girón Alconchel, José Luis, and María Virginia Pérez Escribano, eds. 1995. *Cantar de Mio Cid.* Madrid: Editorial Castalia.
Gordon, E. V., and A. R. Taylor. 1957. *An Introduction to Old Norse.* 2nd ed. Oxford: Clarendon.
Harrison, Robert, trans. 1970. *Song of Roland.* New York: The New American Library.
Heaney, Seamus, trans. 1999. *Beowulf.* London: Faber and Faber.
Hymes, Dell. 1981. 'Breakthrough into Performance.' In his *"In Vain I Tried to Tell You": Essays in Native American Ethnopoetics.* Philadelphia: U of Pennsylvania P. 79–141.
–. 2003. *Now I Know Only So Far: Essays in Ethnopoetics.* Lincoln: U of Nebraska P.
Jakobson, Roman. 1960. 'Closing Statement: Linguistics and Poetics.' In *Style and Language.* Ed. Thomas A. Sebeok. Cambridge, MA: MIT Press. 350–77.
Jónsson, Finnur, ed. 1888. *Egils saga Skallagrímssonar.* Copenhagen: S. L. Møllers Bogtrykkeri.
–, ed. 1931. *Edda Snorra Sturlusonar.* Copenhagen: Gyldendalske Boghandel.
Jousse, Marcel. 1925. *Le style oral rythmique et mnémotechnique chez les verbo-moteurs.* Travaux du Laboratoire d'anthropologie rythmo-pédagogique de Paris 14. Paris: Beauchesne. [*The Oral Style.* Trans. Edgar Sienaert and Richard Whitaker. New York: Garland, 1990.]
Knott, Eleanor. 1934. *An Introduction to Irish Syllabic Poetry of the Period 1200–1600.* 2nd ed. Dublin: Dublin Institute for Advanced Studies.
Kuusi, Matti, Keith Bosley, and Michael Branch, eds. and trans. 1977. *Finnish Folk Poetry: Epic.* Helsinki: Finnish Literature Society.
Lewis, C. S. 1975. *The Horse and His Boy.* New York: Collier. [Or. published in 1954.]
Lord, Albert Bates. 1960. *The Singer of Tales.* Cambridge, MA: Harvard UP. [Re-edition with a CD and a new introduction by Stephen Mitchell and Gregory Nagy, 2000.]
Niles, John D. 1999. *Homo narrans: The Poetics and Anthropology of Oral Literature.* Philadelphia: U of Pennsylvania P.
–. 2006. 'Bede's Cædmon, "The Man Who Had No Story".' *Folklore* 117: 141–55.
Olrik, Axel. 1965. 'Epic Laws of Folk Narrative.' In *The Study of Folklore.* Ed. Alan Dundes. Englewood Cliffs, NJ: Prentice-Hall. 129–41. [Or. published as 'Epische Gesetze der Volksdichtung.' *Zs. für deutsches Altertum* 51 (1909): 1–12.]
Ong, Walter J. 1982. *Orality and Literacy: The Technologizing of the Word.* London: Methuen.
Reichl, Karl. 2002. *Spielmannsidiom, Dialektmischung und Kunstsprache in der mittelenglischen volkstümlichen Epik.* Nordrhein-Westfälische AW. Geisteswissenschaften. Vorträge G 383. Paderborn: Schöningh.
Smiley, Jane, and Robert Kellogg. 1997. *The Sagas of Icelanders: A Selection.* New York: Penguin Books.
Tedlock, Dennis. 1972. *Finding the Center: Narrative Poetry of the Zuni Indians.* Lincoln: U of Nebraska P.
–. 1983. *The Spoken Word and the Work of Interpretation.* Philadelphia: U of Pennsylvania P.
Thomson, Derick S., ed. 1976. *Branwen Uerch Lyr.* Dublin: Dublin Institute for Advanced Studies.
Thurneysen, Rudolf, ed. 1935. *Scéla Mucce Maic Dathó.* Mediaeval and Modern Irish Series 6. Dublin: Dublin Institute for Advanced Studies.
Virtanen, Leea, and Thomas A. DuBois. 2000. *Finnish Folklore.* Helsinki: Finnish Literature Society.

# 7 Oral Literature, Ritual, and the Dialectics of Performance

*Panagiotis Roilos*

## 1 Oral Traditional Literature: Comparative Perspectives

'Ritual' and 'oral literature' are concepts (and terms) that resist watertight definitions and categorizations; especially the second item in this dyad – in its English version as well as in its terminological equivalents in other European languages – constitutes a conspicuous nomenclatural oxymoron. 'Literature' (deriving from 'letter') points to *written* artistic discourse whereas 'oral' refers to vocal and auditory channels of communicative interaction. My reference from the outset to the truism of this inherent contradiction of the term that the English language uses to denote un-written verbal art aims at highlighting the notional, terminological, and methodological difficulties involved in any theoretical as well as historical discussion of what, drawing especially from my native language (Greek), I feel more comfortable to call 'orally produced and transmitted traditional verbal art' (*paradosiakê prophorikê logotechnia*).

The corpus of verbal art defined as 'oral literature' is distinguished from written literary forms on the basis of its 'orality'. Despite its apparent straightforwardness, this pivotal taxonomic criterion more often than not remains vague and elusive. The universalization of the applicability to different traditions of the notion of orality, as this was defined mainly through the systematic observation of composition-in-performance of traditional heroic songs in former Yugoslavia, has often been questioned on the basis of comparative evidence.[1] It is true that in preliterate societies entirely unaffected by literacy, a song or any other example of oral literature has to be orally composed, performed, and transmitted; however, the possibility of the coincidence of all these three phases in the communicative event of singing or performing seems to differ from tradition to tradition and, I would emphasize, from genre to genre within the same tradition.[2] For instance, these stages of the communication of oral traditional literary forms

---

[1] See, among others, Finnegan 1976 and 1977; for epic poetry, insightful remain Parry 1928, 1930, and Lord 1960; see also Lord 1995a. Informative critical overviews of research in oral tradition are provided in Foley 1985, 1988. [See also ch. 2 (J. M. Foley and P. Ramey) in this volume.]

[2] 'Genre' is another highly problematic concept that is often used unchallenged in discussions both of written and oral literature. Ben-Amos 1976 rightly put in question the validity of scholarly taxonomic criteria and emphasized, instead, the theoretical importance of indigenous perceptions and possible categorizations of oral literary forms. Yatromanolakis 2007, 2008, 2009a, 2009b offer some

are often subjected to (spatio)temporal differentiation due to the intervention of repeated rehearsals or of diverse mechanisms of memorization. The song culture of the Kaluli people in New Guinea provides a telling, and by no means exceptional, example of how differences in genre determine variations in terms of composition, performance, and transmission in traditional oral poetry. The only Kaluli genre that adheres to the descriptive model of oral poetry, which was based on Milman Parry's and Albert Lord's fundamental fieldwork on South Slavic heroic poetry, is *sa-yalab*, women's ritual lament; none of the remaining five kinds of indigenous songs seem to fit in the same model (Feld 1990a and 1990b: 254–55). Recent fieldwork on the traditional Chinese genres of *yüeh-fu* and *bimo* also puts in question the universalizing validity of the same analytical model.[3] Similar conclusions concerning the complexity of the circumstances and processes of composition, performance, and transmission of oral songs can be deduced from the study of Nepalese songs, especially those performed by women at the ritual of Tij.[4] Western European medieval literary texts that have been consistently perceived by scholars as results of oral composition also point to memorization as an important mechanism of transmission of such presumably orally composed texts.[5]

In Greek[6] oral literature, which – as we know it from examples sporadically surviving in manuscripts since the fifteenth century, published in a great number of nineteenth- and twentieth-century collections, or systematically recorded by specialists since the beginning of the last century – was produced, and it is still being (re)activated, in communities influenced to a lesser or greater degree by literacy, performers of short 'lyric' songs (wedding songs, laments, love songs) or other genres of traditional oral literature (such as spells, riddles, or proverbs) tend to reproduce versions of 'texts' they have previously heard from other agents of oral literary culture, and then memorized and rehearsed over time. However, idealization of alleged archetypal originals is not a rare characteristic of the indigenous 'metaliterary' discourses informants often employ to commend successful performances or, on the contrary, to justify their own or others' 'inability' to reproduce a time-honoured sample of their local literary tradition. In such cases, weak memory is as a rule used by members of a traditional community as an excuse of their failure to perform 'properly' a song or another kind of traditional oral 'text'. Tales as well as narrative songs are still transmitted and performed mainly through

---

of the most insightful interdisciplinary explorations of the concept of 'genre' in recent scholarship while also challenging all-too conveniently constructed, and thus easily established methodological preconceptions about 'genre' in premodern societies (see further Yatromanolakis' investigation of genre in Yatromanolakis and Roilos 2003: 43–59).

[3] Egan 2000; see Qubumo 2001, which also offers an interesting analysis of the flexibility of boundaries between sanctioned oral and written literary discourses in Nuosu culture in China.

[4] For the composition of such songs performed in the context of this ritual in Nepal, see Skinner, Holland, and Adhikari 1994: esp. 262–64.

[5] Fry 1981; Rosenberg 1981; Berlin 1995; Harris 1983: 211–12; Hoffman 1974; see also Reichl 1991, which also refers to examples of memorization in oral epic traditions of Inner Asia.

[6] In this chapter, 'Greek' refers to what classicists prefer to call 'modern Greek'; other periods in Greek tradition are denoted here through the use of relevant adjectives ('ancient' or 'medieval-Byzantine'). My employing of this unmarked form of 'Greek' to refer to the post-Byzantine period is anthropologically oriented and questions the essentializing and arbitrary use of this term – especially in modern Western European philological and historical discourses – only or primarily for classical antiquity.

the reactivation of habitually internalized thematic and formulaic elements, with the frequent exception of short lyrical songs and of 'einfache Formen'[7] of epigrammatic formulations of traditional knowledge like riddles, proverbs, and spells.

Ritual dirges from the region of Mani in Greece constitute an intriguing case in point, since almost always their composition coincides with their performance. Here is a representative example of this type of funerary songs collected in the early 1910s:

> I have been cursed by my fate,
> my fate and my fortune,
> and weather blows me here and there
> like a little bird on a branch.
> Every morning that I wake up
> I look downhill,
> in case I see the soldier,
> but nothing I see.
> Today, when I woke up
> and went down to the terrace,
> a crow passed by.
> Ah, crow, you who pass by
> with your all-black wings,
> go to Ioannina
> and the fortresses in Bizani
> and the mountains of Tzoumagia
> to find my brother,
> and give him this order:
> immediately he must come home,
> for he has left his widow with a child.
> Or bring me a sign of his,
> bring me his ring
> or his blond mustache,
> so that I might console myself,
> or otherwise I'll go crazy. (Kasses 1979: 297)

The central image in this lament is distinctively drawn from the stock of traditional motifs and symbolisms: in Greek oral literature, birds, especially 'sinister' ones such as owls or crows, are often encountered in ritual laments or mark a dramatic turn of events in other, mainly narrative, songs or in tales.[8] Fate is also evoked and often directly addressed in dirges or pathetic love songs;[9] and the metonymic substitution of a ring, cloth, or other significant token associated with a beloved person for his/her presence constitutes a recurrent *topos* both in oral literature and in specific ritual acts. Despite these affinities with traditional thematics and semantics – and by contrast to examples of the same genre from other Greek regions – the composer/performer of the specific ritual song focuses not so much on traditional imagery and relatively abstract, i. e. meta-

---

[7] For the concept of 'einfache Formen' ('simple forms'), see Jolles 1930.
[8] Interesting parallels can be found in a number of different traditions. A. B. Lord has commented on the importance of this motif in South Slavic songs (1995b: 27); Lord, who does not provide any broader contextual or intertextual discussion of this imagery, adds universalizing observations about the possible links of this motif to shamanism.
[9] For the role of fate in ritual laments, see M. Alexiou 2002a: 110–18.

phoric, formulations of her pain as rather on the particular circumstances of the death of the lamented person. The performer, who happens to be the sister of the deceased and a renowned lamenter in her own right, composes a short narrative about the death of her brother, who died heroically as a soldier in Epeiros during the Balkan Wars in 1913. In contrast to laments from other Greek regions, this dirge, like the majority of Maniat laments, is not a preset song but it is literally composed in performance so that it may address the performative and ritual exigencies of the specific occasion.

Other examples of this genre from the same area constitute even more marked articulations of individual pain and tragedy. Not rarely, the performance of such songs is employed by the lamenters as a discursive vehicle for openly conveying to the community a number of feelings, attitudes, and views normally suppressed, silenced, or disguised on unmarked occasions of everyday interaction. Dialogic exchanges composed in performance between different lamenters demarcate a marked spatiotemporal arena where ritual liminality encourages subversion on a number of discursive and social levels. In such cases, literal discourse tends to predominate over traditional formulaic metaphoric/allegorical *topoi* with a view to articulating an explicit *agôn* (contest) of arguments and statements of broader performative and social efficacy. Characteristic is the case of the dialogue performed on the occasion of the exhumation of the remains of a man (Lias Pereklakos) through the exchange of laments between his sister and his widow (Phragkogiannonyphe); the latter, who was married again after Lias' and their son's death and had another son from her second husband, was attacked in a lament by her former sister-in-law for allegedly being disloyal to Lias and rushing to marry another man just one year after Lias died. In her own lament, Phragkogiannonyphe called the participants in the ritual to listen to her *xagoria* (confession in public), and refuted the accusations of her former sister-in-law by exhibiting a disproportionate devotion to her first husband and son even at the expense of her present family, which she violently rejected. Next day, when Phragkogiannonyphe came back home, she died either out of excessive grief or, as rumors had it, struck by her new husband, who had been informed about his wife's daring performance of loyalty to her first husband (Kasses 1979: 370–73).

This ritually prompted dialectics of exceptional discursive individuality and collective witnessing finds its parallels in other examples of oral literature across different genres and traditions. Of great comparative interest is the case of Warao women's laments, which are often used as vehicles for conveying the lamenters' explicit anger against those whom they hold responsible for the death of their beloved deceased.[10] Even in such cases of composition-in-performance, use of formulas and repeated themes does not seem to constitute an omnipresent rule, as is often postulated. The majority of Maniat laments, for instance, depart conspicuously from such descriptive/prescriptive regularity, despite the fact that a large number of them belong to the longest Greek ritual songs.[11]

---

[10] Briggs 1992. For comparable cases of dynamic manipulation of the ritual performative context of lamentation in Greece, see the insightful studies of Caravelli-Chaves 1980 and 1986; Seremetakis 1991 offers penetrating readings of the same phenomenon in a similar rural Greek context; see also Herzfeld 1993. Bauman 1986 and 1992, and Turner 1971 are significant examples of context- and culture-specific analyses of medieval literary genres.

[11] In this respect, Nagler's approach to formula from the perspective of generative-transformative grammar points in the right direction, to the extent that it contributes to our understanding of the

## 2 Oral Literature in the Middle Ages: Beyond Polarizing Schemata and Scholarly Preconceptions

If the issue of 'orality', whenever not adequately defined, proves to be problematic in the study of the kind of literature that is amply documented from contemporary sources to be composed, performed, and transmitted orally, it ineluctably becomes even more complicated in the case of medieval literature and its possible connections to its synchronic oral tradition, which, in any case, might be only cautiously and hypothetically (re)constructed through the perplexing mediation of writing: no live performance or an absolutely accurate transcription of a text of medieval traditional, orally produced and transmitted verbal art can be accessible to us any more! The challenging gap separating the alterity of the Middle Ages from the modernity of our hermeneutic approaches can to a great extent be bridged through a systematic comparative and historical-anthropological study of the material that has survived from the past, on the one hand, and modern explorations of the compositional and performative conditions of oral literature across genres and cultures, on the other.[12]

Some supplementary fundamental questions should be kept in mind when we explore the interface of orality and literacy or, more specifically, of traditional oral and written literature both in modern times and in the past: to what extent is orality connected not only to particular morphological structures of expression but also to broader marked patterns of thought?[13] How is 'oral' related to 'traditional' and 'popular' in specific historical and sociocultural contexts?[14] Should the concept of 'oral literature' include all types of verbal discourse (e. g. tales, spells, proverbs, riddles) that deviate from the communicative norm of everyday speech in terms of form (aesthetics) and 'function' (performance)? If, as is indicated by scholarly practice in a number of fields, a positive answer to the last question seems to enjoy a significant consensus among researchers, approaches to the two other issues are more controversial and certainly more demanding, since they presuppose systematic investigations into specific synchronic textures of sociocultural interaction. This is not the place to provide specific solutions to these complex methodological matters other than pointing to the urgency of culture-specific methodologies dictated not by universalizing theoretical schemata but by available material,

---

dynamics of culture-specific deviations from a rigidly unifying model of oral-formulaic analysis (Nagler 1967).

[12] For the alterity of the Middle Ages and the methodological issues that this poses for modern researchers, see Jauss 1979; for the necessity of a historical anthropological approach to the Middle Ages with a focus on Byzantium, see Roilos 2005: 23–24.

[13] Ong 1982, Vansina 1985, and Goody 1987 (despite certain schematic generalizations put forward in them) are significant for a comparative understanding of the interaction of oral literature with broader patterns of thought.

[14] Burke 1978 and Gurevich 1988 remain important for the study of the concept and the complex manifestations of 'popular culture' in premodern Western Europe; Wardropper 1980 discusses what he calls medieval Spanish 'folksong' and the pervasiveness of popular culture in all social strata of Medieval Spain. For some observations concerning popular culture in Byzantium, see Roilos 2005: 100, 293–94. Yatromanolakis 2009a offers a brilliant analysis of the methodological problems involved in the use of the concept 'popular' in the study of ancient Greek literature and proposes a pathfinding approach to the so-called ancient Greek *carmina popularia*.

both textual and contextual. Easy polarizations such as, for instance, 'oral = popular = conservative = female vs. written = elitist = innovative = male', or 'oral = formulaic vs. written = non-formulaic' may be of some use in a number of cases but misleading in others.[15]

I want to clarify that 'orality' – as used in this chapter with respect to premodern literature that was produced in societies in which oral and written forms of communication and expression are known to have co-existed and that was transmitted to us from the distant past through writing – refers to the following categories: (1) a corpus of traditional oral literature (only hypothetically recoverable), which may have interacted with written literature, (2) either one or a combination of the three following major processes of the production and communication of literary art: composition, performance, transmission.[16]

The existence of traditional verbal art in European medieval societies (most notably song-making and story-telling) is beyond any reasonable doubt: scarcity of preserved 'original' texts *in many cases* cannot be taken as a conclusive indication of the absence of oral traditional literature from a given European medieval culture or, in case this type of literary art is explicitly attested in earlier eras of the same cultural or linguistic tradition, of its absolute and abrupt disappearance in later periods.[17] In this respect, the need to substantiate the possibility of the production and consumption of this kind of literature in medieval European cultures often constitutes a pseudo-problem rather than a real

---

[15] For instance, in an interesting reading of aspects of Marie de France's work, Frese (1991) questions the analogy 'women = orality'; see also the balanced approach to the interaction of orality and writing, and to the construction of memory in the early Middle Ages, with an emphasis on Notker of St. Gall's *Gesta Karoli* (late ninth century), in Innes 1998. Innes rightly questions analytical polarizations such as 'written-Church-Christian vs. oral-secular-unchristian' and teleological preconceptions often adopted in discussions of medieval orality. In a comparable vein, in his discussion of oral and literary modes of communication in Western European medieval literature, Green shows that the equations 'vernacular = listening' or 'Latin = reading' are also flawed (Green 1994: esp. 30–35, 270–315; see also Smith 1971; Olsen 1983; Stock 1983: esp. 12–87; 1990; Ziolkowski 1991). [On the interplay of orality and literacy in the early Middle Ages, see also chapters 3 (M. Richter) and 4 (K. O'Brien O'Keeffe) in this volume.]

[16] Bäuml 1984 offers an insightful revision of monolithic applications of what he calls 'secondary theory' of oral-formulaic composition to medieval texts, despite the fact that he fails to revisit the exaggerated and unjustifiably universalizing emphasis of the 'primary theory' on a number of aspects including, for instance, the coincidence of composition and performance; see also Bäuml 1980, where some careful observations about the different channels of transmission of Western European medieval literature are provided.

[17] In a seminal article on Byzantine popular poetry, Elizabeth and Michael Jeffreys appear overly skeptical and unnecessarily reluctant to accept the existence of oral poetry in Byzantium; however, some of the sources, to which they also refer, firmly establish the presence of forms of traditional oral poetry in Byzantine culture (Jeffreys, E. and M. Jeffreys 1986; see also my discussion below). It seems that this skepticism is based on the unjustified expectation that formulaic oral theory must be the principal guideline in our attempt to explore medieval traditional oral literature; hence this inflated focus on narrative poetry at the expense, for instance, of shorter ritual traditional oral songs like the *chelidonismata* (swallow songs) whose performance from late antiquity to Byzantium and to modern times is attested beyond doubt (on these songs, see discussion below). In a later contribution, a brief entry in *The Oxford Dictionary of Byzantium*, the Jeffreys rightly confirm the existence of different forms of oral poetry in Byzantium (E. Jeffreys and M. Jeffreys 1991). [See further ch. 17 by E. Jeffreys on medieval Greek epic poetry in this volume.]

issue. What, no doubt, remains as a rule problematic is our knowledge about concrete types (and texts) of traditional oral literature in particular medieval societies.[18] However, even when sources tend to be frustratingly vague or elusive, some sound inferences may be deduced from the available material.

Here I wish to focus on the case of Byzantium, not least because discussions of the European Middle Ages in general and of European medieval (written and oral) literature in particular tend to ignore it conspicuously and unjustifiably, often with ideologically charged and methodologically shaky and inaccurate conclusions.[19] The persistent adherence of medieval Greek literati to inherited modes of rhetorical sophistication and archaism is one of the most important reasons for the unfortunate fact that surviving evidence and material of Byzantine traditional oral literature is meager. In the twelfth century, Eustathios of Thessalonike, one of the most learned commentators of Homeric poetry ever, insightfully points to the conceptual and ideological tensions between written discourse and examples of simple, popular literature like children's swallow songs, and expresses the indirect complaint that his contemporaries were not interested in reporting such examples of popular culture in their writings.[20] A telling example of Byzantine intellectuals' usual highbrow attitude to popular discourse is provided by Anna Komnene, the 'purple-born' daughter of the Emperor Alexios Komnenos (c. 1057–1118) and writer of the *Alexias*, a historiographic and encomiastic account of her father's accomplishments. Writing also in the twelfth century (a few decades before Eustathios), in her discussion of a popular song about her father, Anna feels the need to convey the meaning of its 'low-style' wording in her own elevated archaizing style.[21]

However, I want to emphasize that, despite this sanctioned differentiation between 'high' and 'low' culture in the works of Byzantine intellectuals, in other fundamental aspects of medieval Greek culture, and especially in the institutionalized practice of religion, the gap between elevated and simpler linguistic registers in written and orally performed texts was not as deep as usually assumed, and certainly not as polarized as in Western European medieval societies, where the linguistic and cultural division between Latin and the vernaculars was by far more accentuated, if not, in certain cases, unbridgeable. The use of relatively simple linguistic registers in texts of liturgical literature such as passages from the Old and New Testament or hymnography as well as in preaching, was

---

[18] The perplexing, often contradictory, indications provided by preserved material in other Western European traditions make it clear that absolute certainty concerning the *composition* of specific texts usually treated in scholarship as oral or closely related to oral tradition such as *Beowulf* and other Old English or Germanic texts, or the Icelandic sagas, for instance, is as a rule impossible. See, *inter alia*, Amodio 2005b and the articles included in Amodio 2005a. [On Bede's account of Caedmon, see K. O'Brien O'Keeffe's discussion in ch. 4, pp. 122–27, and J. Harris' discussion in ch. 5, pp. 146–47; on the Old English *Beowulf* in the context of early Germanic poetry, see ch. 8 (J. Harris); on the *Nibelungenlied* in the context of Middle High German poetry, see ch. 10 (J.-D. Müller).]

[19] More often than not, discussions of 'European' Middle Ages tend to restrict themselves only to Western European cultures. Even sophisticated studies such as Stock 1983 or Green 1994 do not depart from established scholarly practices.

[20] *Commentarii ad Homeri Odysseam* 1914.54 (Eustathios 1825–25: II, 266).

[21] *Alexias* 2.4.9 (Reinsch and Kambyllis 2001).

conducive to the curtailing of both discursive and conceptual differences between different levels of socioaesthetic interactions in Byzantium.[22]

In addition to short popular acclamations or satirical songs addressed to emperors or other men of political and ecclesiastical power, which are attested since already the beginning of the seventh up to the twelfth century,[23] the existence of a number of other types of traditional songs throughout Byzantium can be accepted with a considerable degree of confidence, despite the fact that, as happens in the majority of other medieval European traditions, no specific text can be retrieved and reconstructed from the sources in its 'entirety' with absolute certainty: laments, love and wedding songs, lullabies, narrative songs are attested to have belonged to the repertoire of traditional Byzantine oral poetry.[24] Albeit scarce, indications of the performance of narrative songs of heroic character are detected in texts from the tenth to the fifteenth centuries.[25] Leaving aside the methodologically problematic issue of the relation of Greek traditional heroic songs collected in the nineteenth and twentieth centuries to the text(s) of *Digenes Akrites* (11th–12th c.?) and its possible oral tradition, the *Song of Armoures*, which is preserved in manuscripts of the fifteenth and sixteenth centuries, constitutes a rather solid example of traditional oral epic poetry from the late Byzantine period.[26]

As far as evidence allows us to see, specific types of oral traditional Byzantine poetry were associated with particular performative occasions, gender roles, or age groups. That traditional ritual threnodic songs throughout the Greek tradition were as a rule performed by women has been convincingly documented in Margaret Alexiou's seminal study of this genre (2002a). Other types of traditional oral songs are equally gender-marked; in an intriguing (but unjustifiably neglected) piece, Michael Psellos (11th c.) describes the feast of St. Agathe and the customs associated with it. A detail in his account indicates that, in addition to other ritual activities, dances and songs were also performed by women on that holiday. Psellos refers to two groups of songs sung on that occasion: some were of more general nature and applied to other performative contexts as well, while others were pertinent to the specific ritual event and composed most probably in performance. Interesting is also Psellos' reference to the instrumental role that

---

[22] Preaching in relatively simple register constituted one of the most effective discursive practices mediating between highbrow literacy and popular modes of thought (and expression) in the Greek Middle Ages. The relevant examples abound; here, I want to single out only the especially interesting but rather neglected sermons of Philagathos Kerameus, an eleventh-twelfth-century man of letters who lived in South Italy, in the margins, as it were, of the medieval Greek empire (Roilos 2005: 94, 100; 182; Kerameus' sermons are edited in Rossi-Taibi 1969). Margaret Alexiou insightfully discusses general but important aspects of the dialogue between popular culture and official church practices and discourses (M. Alexiou 2002b: 43–65).

[23] Maas 1912; Polites 1912; Koukoules 1948: 38–40; Spyridakes 1957; Beck 1971: 25–28.

[24] See Polites 1912; Kyriakides 1951; Beck 1971: 110–11, 162–63; Kyriakides 1978: 185–87. Much evidence has been collected in Koukoules 1948: 5–41; despite the various methodological problems of Koukoules' work, mainly deriving from its encyclopaedic nature, it still offers a considerable amount of accurate information concerning a number of aspects of Byzantine culture.

[25] See Theophanes Continuatus (Bekker 1838: 72); Nikephoros Gregoras, *Byzantina Historia* (Schopen 1829–55: I, 377); see Kougeas 1912–1913: 239; Spyridakes 1951; Kyriakides 1978: 291–92.

[26] On *Digenes Akrites*, see also Jeffreys 1998 [and ch. 17 in this volume]. On the *Song of Armoures*, see e. g. Beck 1971: 53–55; S. Alexiou 1985: 159–89.

old women played in the specific ritual: it was they, he emphasizes, who undertook to pass on the tradition to other participants and who would lead off singing and dancing.[27] His focus on older women's fundamental contribution to the perpetuation of certain ritual practices in this passage finds a parallel, I believe, in the rather realistic description of a rural funeral scene in Niketas Eugeneianos' novel *Drosilla and Charikles* (12th c.); there, it is again an old woman who leads off lamentation and initiates the young female protagonist, still a 'virgin', into the communal discursive territory of lamentation (Roilos 2005: 89).

Heroic narrative songs were performed by male, often itinerant, singers, while in certain cases seasonal ritual songs were performed by children. Important is the case of the *chelidonismata* (swallow songs) sung by children to celebrate the arrival of the swallows, symbols of nature's rebirth in the spring. Thematic as well as discursive similarities among ancient, medieval, and modern examples of this genre indicate that *chelidonismata* represent one of the oldest types of unequivocally and relatively comprehensively attested Greek popular songs from antiquity to the Middle Ages to modern times.[28]

## 3 Performability in Medieval and Early Modern Literature

Traces of oral traditional literature and the possible function of orality in medieval literary texts in a specific cultural tradition (as in any other period of premodern literature) may be detected mainly on the basis of comparative, anthropological methods (i. e. thanks to rare examples of premodern oral literature explicitly transmitted and confirmed as such in medieval literature or to oral 'texts' collected and studied *in situ* in modern times) or through close textual (and, whenever feasible, contextual) analyses of particular works from that period. The mediation of writing between an original text that scholars – in retrospect and often with a great deal of speculation and vagueness – deem 'oral' and its original composition and performance raises, as I indicated earlier in this chapter, a number of pivotal methodological issues. 'Orality' should be understood as a more flexible notion than 'oral traditional literature', since it may refer to all or any combination of the following processes of the creation and communication of verbal art: composition, performance, or transmission. More often than not orality in medieval literature, I argue, is to be understood in terms of the *performability* of a written text. Closely connected with the performative potential of a text is the vocality not rarely

---

[27] Sathas 1876: 530; Roilos 2005: 294. In a different context in his history (*Chronographia*), Psellos alludes to the close connection of specific events and the performance of songs commenting on them (*Chronographia* 5.38; see Sewter 1953: 103–4.).

[28] Tommasini 1901; Maas 1912:43–45; Krumbacher 1902; Polites 1912: 647–49; Baud-Bovy 1946–1949; Koukoules 1948: 7–9; Beck 1971: 27; Patala 1996; M. Alexiou 2002b: 87–94. As eloquent as Herzfeld 2005 may be, it remains highly speculative and unconvincing in its attribution of the continuation of this particular type of ritual song in modern times to the interference of hegemonizing educational agents in the formation of popular culture. There is no evidence to substantiate this far-fetched hypothesis, and Herzfeld's analysis does not account for the fact that performances of the same type of songs are attested not only in modern times and in antiquity but also in the Middle Ages: a twelfth-century version of this song is compellingly similar to the version recorded in Athenaios in the second/third century AD and to modern Greek *chelidonismata*.

inscribed in it. My use of 'vocality' here draws from the work of Paul Zumthor, who introduced this notion in his study of Western European medieval literature. Whereas in the case of traditional, orally composed and performed texts, composition, performance, and reception coincided (or, to be more anthropologically accurate, one should rather say that the last two of these three processes coincided), in the case of written works that were expected to be also orally transmitted (in part or in their entirety), writing, according to Zumthor, intervened between the composer and his listeners, thus separating the original voice of the former from the latter. This loss of the direct communication between the composer and his audience was often counterbalanced and to some degree replaced by the inscription of the author's voice into the text as a channel of (fictional) communicative immediacy, which could be activated any time the specific text was received by an audience. Vocality should thus be studied in close connection with the dialectics of performance involved in any specific case.[29]

To my mind, even the recurrent presence of an author's self-referential allusions to his authorial voice or of his extra-referential hints at a possible oral/aural performance and reception of his work by no means constitutes a decisive factor for determining the extent to which a specific text was composed with the expectation to be (also) orally acted out. A number of additional criteria should be explored in order for a scholar to determine whether such references may constitute valid indications of the performability of a text in terms of traditional, orally/aurally received literature, and not mere rhetorical *topoi*: language, metre, themes, contextual and intertextual allusions/evidence. Not rarely, written texts which presented a considerable number of formal and thematic features that deviated from the standards of their synchronic 'high' literature and were closer to oral literature and thus carried a symbolic capital that in a specific society was undervalued by the majority of literati (e. g. medieval Greek vernacular texts not intended for the exclusive consumption by the cultural or social elite) were also expected by both their authors and audience to be subjected to several modifications or adaptations during their transmission. This mobility, often attested in manuscript tradition, would invest such texts with additional textual flexibility and, as a result, bring them closer to the condition of orality.[30]

Late Byzantine/early modern (13th–16th c.) and Renaissance Greek literature (16th–17th c.) offers a number of examples of the intricate interaction between written discourse, on the one hand, and performability and vocality, on the other. In a number of works that survived from those centuries, authorial 'voice' is embedded in the written text in terms of a performable fictional reconstitution of the original composer's/performer's presence, which had been displaced through the interference of writing.[31]

---

[29] Zumthor elaborates on his idea of vocality in his 1987 book *La lettre et la voix*. Despite his occasionally over-romanticized understanding of 'voice' in (written and oral) literature, his discussion of vocality can be useful if applied with careful qualifications to specific cases of premodern poetry; see Schaefer 1991: 111; for comparable cases of the reinscription of discursive strategies associated with oral poetry in Old English *written* literature, see O'Brien O'Keeffe 1990.

[30] For the notion of mobility (*mouvance*) of medieval texts, see Zumthor 1991: 45–49.

[31] My brief discussion of the interaction of literacy and orality (which I define in terms of performability and vocality) in Renaissance Greek literature here draws from my earlier study of the topic in Roilos 2002 as well as from my more recent fieldwork in Crete (2002–2007). For comparable cases in late Byzantine vernacular literature, see Cupane 1994–95.

This vocality, when combined with a number of marked metrical, linguistic, and thematic features, points, I believe, to possible oral transmission and performance of such works. Especially Renaissance Cretan literature is characterized, as I have argued elsewhere, by an ostensible 'paradox', since some of the most refined written works produced during that period of Greek literature enjoyed exceptional popularity among people of diverse social and educational backgrounds for centuries. Parts of these texts used to be performed as oral songs/ballads or theatrical plays on certain ritual occasions in several parts of Greece until recently.[32] This idiosyncratic quality of Renaissance Cretan literature clearly indicates that polarizations such as 'popular versus learned', 'oral versus written', 'urban versus rural' often constitute misleading categorizations imposed *a posteriori* by scholars used to clear-cut taxonomic distinctions.

An important case in point is *Erotokritos*, the most popular and arguably the most elaborate work of Renaissance Cretan Literature. *Erotokritos*, an extensive romance (10,012 lines) with a considerable number of heroic elements, was written some time in the mid-seventeenth century by the Renaissance Cretan poet Vintsentzos Kornaros.[33] The story of this work follows the basic thematic pattern of fictional love narratives (novels/romances) as known to us in the European literary tradition since late Greek antiquity: a young man, Erotokritos, falls in love with a young lady, Aretousa, whom he marries after a long series of ordeals.

The earliest information about *Erotokritos*' popularity comes from Antonios Vortolis, the first editor of the poem. Writing in 1713, Vortolis notes that this 'old poem' was so popular that Cretan refugees took it with them to the Ionian Islands where they had fled after the conquest of their homeland by the Turks in 1669. Nineteenth-century travelers in Greece, such as Clarke and Leake, also point to its enormous popularity. Adamantios Koraes, one of the most important figures of the Greek Enlightenment, also attests to the poem's popularity mainly among illiterate Greeks by contemptuously calling its author 'Homer of vulgar poetry'. In his collection of Greek folksongs published in 1824, Fauriel included an excerpt from *Erotokritos*, which, to his mind, recalled traditional laments of departure from home and, therefore, should be taken as a popular song.[34] One hundred and thirty years after the publication of Fauriel's collection, James Notopoulos noted emphatically that 'this poem [*Erotokritos*] is so well known by Cretans, that its text, if lost, can be completely restored orally' (Notopoulos 1952: 228). As is evidenced from my own fieldwork in Crete in the period between 1995 and 2007 and from other earlier sources, *Erotokritos* has been very popular also throughout the previous century and well into this new one, despite the fact that broader sociocultural

---

[32] *The Shepherdess, The Sacrifice of Abraham, Erophile*, and *Erotokritos* are the most popular works of Renaissance Cretan literature. For further discussion and bibliography on this important aspect of Renaissance Cretan literature, see Roilos 2002. Especially interesting is the analysis of the case of *Erophile* in Puchner 1983 and 1991. M. Alexiou 1991 provides insights into the possible relations of *Apokopos* and *The Sacrifice of Abraham* with ritual laments. Interesting observations on orality in Cretan literature are found in Holton 1990.

[33] On the debates regarding the date of the composition of this poem, see the introduction in S. Alexiou 1994.

[34] Fauriel 1825: 213–17. In his collection of folksongs, Nikolaos Polites publishes a similar oral version of *Erotokritos* (Polites 1914: 256). For the reception of *Erotokritos*, see in detail Roilos 2002.

developments have considerably restricted the opportunities for its oral performance in recent years.³⁵

During my fieldwork in Crete I have had the opportunity to listen to a large number of performances of short passages from the poem that only rarely exceed twenty-five verses – the usual length of Greek folksongs, including ballads from mainland Greece.³⁶ Independently of their education, all the singers knew that the songs they performed came from an original written poem.³⁷ However, most of my informants assured me that they had not read these passages in the original written poem but rather heard them performed as songs on many traditional ritual occasions – at weddings, religious feasts, at the customary fortune telling on the 24th of June, the feast of John the Baptist – or at informal gatherings. I have repeatedly noticed that the performers of *Erotokritos* refer to the particular passages they sing or narrate by using titles that recall the corresponding predominant narrative theme around which these episodes are constructed: 'Erotokritos' leaving home', 'Erotokritos' return', 'The joust', 'The war', etc. This habit can be interpreted as a tendency of a large part of the audience of *Erotokritos* to receive this poem as a long tale consisting of shorter narrative units/ potential songs (ballads), which can be distinguished from one another on the basis of the thematic centre around which each unit has been constructed. Such episodes, and especially the scene of the joust, used to be performed not only as ballads but also as popular dramas in several parts of Greece at Carnival,³⁸ a practice that recalls the performance of similar public spectacles at Carnival time in Renaissance Crete.³⁹ By being performed on such occasions, *Erotokritos* assumed marked *ritual* dimensions; its transformation into a play performed on specific ritual occasions can be associated not only with the conspicuous theatrical structure of the poem but also with its stylistic and thematic affinities with traditional oral literature. These features enhanced the potential symbolic dimensions of *Erotokritos* and facilitated its function as a polysemic popular drama; in this way, Kornaros' poem was on certain occasions transformed from a liminoid written text to a liminal ritual *drômenon*.⁴⁰

As I have shown in detail elsewhere, the appropriation of this convoluted, extensive written work by a large part of agents of Greek traditional oral literature should be

---

35   According to S. Alexiou the last recorded performance of extensive passages from *Erotokritos* in Crete took place in 1971; this performance was based on a 'popular' edition of the poem (S. Alexiou 1994: ρα'). As recently as in the summer of 1991, while on fieldwork in the region of Gortynia in central Peloponnese, I noticed that many aged men and women were familiar with *Erotokritos* and some of them were also able to recite a few verses from the poem.

36   Ballads from other parts of the Greek-speaking world (e. g. Cyprus and regions in contemporary Turkey such as Asia Minor, Cappadocia, Pontos) tend to be longer.

37   Worth noting is the following comment of a Cypriot performer of an oral version of the *Erotokritos* on the written form of the original: 'a large piece of paper [...] a big piece of paper' (Papadopoulos 1977: 237, 708–9, 722–23).

38   For theatrical performances of *Erotokritos*, see S. Alexiou 1994: ρα'; in the early 1990s informants from Gortynia, Arcadia, would confirm to me that, as children in the 1920s to1930s, they used to dress up as Erotokritoi during Carnival.

39   On such performative contexts in Renaissance Crete, see Roilos 2002.

40   Turner distinguishes between 'individualized' or 'liminoid' works of art produced by learned privileged individuals in complex societies and 'liminal' and more 'ritualistic' works of art of a collective character (Turner 1982: 52–55).

viewed in connection with its dynamic performability, vocality, and traditional referentiality, and in terms of the ethnopoetic particularities both of its own composition and of broader traditional poetic intertexts.[41] The 'voice' of *Erotokritos*' writer was conveyed to his public through marked linguistic and metrical vehicles, which corresponded to the expectations of the widest possible audience. Written in the vernacular, in the dialect of Eastern Crete, in the fifteen-syllable *politikos* verse, which by the time Kornaros composed his work had been established as the most popular metrical system in oral and written Greek poetry, and exploiting thematic elements common in traditional fictional narratives, *Erotokritos* was invested with a dynamic traditional referentiality. The poet's 'voice', albeit separated from his recipients due to the mediation of the fixed written form of his poem, was inscribed in the text as a vicarious performing identity ('I') pointing to the 'present' of its expected future reactivation on different performative occasions, or foregrounding the envisaged communicative interaction between author/performer and his audience ('we').[42]

Despite the exceptionally long co-existence of *Erotokritos*' original written form along with its various oral versions for more than three centuries, the 'paradox' of its oral transmission and performance does not constitute an unparalleled case in premodern literature. Medieval and Renaissance Western European literature offers compelling analogous examples as, for instance, Dante's *Commedia* and especially Ariosto's *Orlando Furioso*, which was an immediate intertext of Kornaros' poem.[43] The fact that parts of Dante's *Commedia* were performed as popular songs by some of the poet's contemporary illiterate audience (*idiotae* or *illitterati*) gave rise to vehement criticisms on the part of highbrow intellectuals: Leonardo Bruni, for instance, urged his contemporaries to 'remove Dante from the ranks of the learned and leave him with the fullers and the millers', a view that recalls Koraes' condemnation of *Erotokritos*' popularity. An interesting, though much later, comparable case in point is also the reception of the *Kalevala*, Lönnrot's written (re)constructed corpus of Finnish epic poetry, by traditional singers of oral poetry in mid-late nineteenth-century Finland. Lönnrot's fixed texts were creatively assimilated into local singing traditions represented by individual traditional singers, who thus handled the *Kalevala* in manners comparable to the reception of *Erotokritos* throughout its long history of oral transmission and performance.[44]

---

[41] On ethnopoetics, see Hymes 1981 and 1996. On 'traditional referentiality', see the interesting discussion in Foley 1991a: 1–60; see also Foley 1991b and 1995; A. B. Lord would have called the same concept 'traditionally intuitive meaning' (Lord 1960: 66).

[42] Kornaros introduces self-referential comments already at the very beginning of his poem; other times he appeals to the communal 'we' shared by himself and his (future) audience. For these discursive strategies in *Erotokritos* and his affinities with traditional oral literature, see in detail Roilos 2002.

[43] Ahern 1981: 18. For the oral performance and transmission of *Orlando Furioso*, see Nelson 1976–77.

[44] For the impact of *Kalevala* on local Finnish oral traditions in nineteenth-century Finland, see DuBois 1995: 183–228; also DuBois 1996.

## 4 Ritual Poetics and Performance

In the case of premodern, especially medieval, literature that is believed to be related to aspects of 'orality' (as this category was defined earlier in this chapter), it may be safer to think of 'performance' in terms of performability rather than real acting-out of the original (written) text – at least when evidence does not allow us to retrace concrete steps of the oral/aural reception and transmission of a medieval/premodern text.

Performance, along with marked culture-specific textures and strategies of communication, is a crucial operational mode that oral literature shares with ritual. Like the latter, oral delivery of traditional, orally composed literature (as well as of written texts) involves a number of non-verbal channels of communication (e. g. gestures, body movements, facial expressions etc.), which are activated at the moment of performance.[45] This essential constituent of ritual is powerfully signified in the (ancient, medieval, and modern) Greek language through the word *teletê*, the principal Greek term corresponding to the English 'ritual'. Deriving from the verb *telô*, *teletê* points to the performative dynamics of ritual in the sense of acting out as well as of realization and 'accomplishment' of an underlying set of traditional ideas/beliefs – a concept akin to the principle of performance in transformational generative grammar. Relevant, though more marked, is the term *drômena*; deriving from *drân* and often employed in juxtaposition with *legomena* (sanctioned, usually sacred, discourses), *drômena* points to the performative potential of ritual both as spectacle (cf. *drâma*) and as enactment of collectively shared and communicated symbolic discourses.[46]

Rituals are notoriously protean processes/events that, like 'orality', elude, I stress, absolute categorizations and universalizing definitions. Being deeply aware of the culture-bound, and hence highly elusive, multivalence of the concept and actual manifestations of 'ritual' across different cultures or on diverse occasions in the same tradition, I would like, nevertheless, to highlight the following distinctive phenomenological components of this complex sociocultural category, which may further illustrate its fundamental relation to performance: formalization; sanctioned sequences of acted-out ideas or feelings that more often than not are symbolically encoded and communicated; traditionality; repetition or redundancy; activation of different, often synaesthetic, channels and media of semantic and performative interaction.

As has been proposed elsewhere, the performance of a ritual may be viewed in terms of a marked symbolic syntactic whole that is metonymically constructed out of interacting units of possible semantic polyvalence. Ritual should be understood in terms of a habitually acquired and (re)activated sense of ritual-making and ritual performance in a particular society.[47] Such an approach to this phenomenon in terms of culture-specific *habitus* brings to the fore the significance of the articulation of ritual textures as poten-

---

[45] For the importance of other, non-verbal, communicative channels as well as of marked objects in ritual, see Yatromanolakis and Roilos 2003; Finnegan 2005 also offers interesting comparative insights into this issue.

[46] Greek terms and concepts related to 'ritual' in connection with broader theoretical and methodological debates in anthropology are discussed in Yatromanolakis and Roilos 2003.

[47] For a systematic discussion of all these essential constituents of ritual acts, see Yatromanolakis and Roilos 2003: esp. 11–41.

tial receptacles for a number of (often symbolically articulated) contents – they even define the content of a ritual performance. Viewed from this perspective, 'ritual does not create semantic wholes out of nothing: it draws on common, everyday, or often traditionally defined, experiential elements, and by inscribing them into its demarcated performative frame invests them with particular communicative value' (Yatromanolakis and Roilos 2003: 32).

Albeit investing ritual with functional and semantic distinctiveness, marked spatio-temporal framing does not entail its absolute disconnection from broader socioaesthetic textures of communication; on the contrary, ritual performances tend to unfold as *mimeseis* of sanctioned 'scripts' of usually symbolically encoded acts and discourses, in which individual agents participate both as actors and audience/spectators embedded in – and thus metonymically embodying aspects of – wider nexuses of sociopolitical discourses and power relations. Rituals often proceed as performative arenas where such discourses and relations 'are constructed, deconstructed, reaffirmed, or subverted, and individual or group agents negotiate their positions in the established social, political, or ideological order, sometimes against, or in spite of, the counteractions of hegemonizing authorities – be these secular or sacred, directly (re)presented, or indirectly inscribed in the cosmological values of a given society' (Yatromanolakis and Roilos 2003: 40). These performances of complex nexuses of diverse discursive textures and dynamics may be studied in terms of what has been defined as 'ritual poetics'.[48] Situated at the intersection of a traditional sense of ritual-making and a habitual reactivation of this sense in other domains of sociocultural activities in a specific society, 'ritual poetics' involves the study of the homologies between the two constituents of this concept ('poetics' and 'ritual') as well as the exploration of the pervasiveness of the interaction of both in broader cultural discourses and practices.

Before I embark on an inevitably brief exploration of the multivalent dialectics of oral literature and ritual, I want to stress that the issue of the ontological/historical precedence of ritual over traditional oral literature or vice versa does not concern me at all here – or elsewhere. Debates about this pseudoproblem have been haunting the humanities but also, at least until not too many years ago and to a lesser degree, the social sciences – more often than not with rather shortsighted results.[49]

Ritual and oral traditional literature cannot be performed without the mediation of a number of channels, codes, modes, or, rather, textures of signification and expression

---

[48] The concept of 'ritual poetics' has been proposed and explored in Yatromanolakis and Roilos 2003; see further Yatromanolakis and Roilos (forthcoming).

[49] One of the most representative examples of this approach in the humanities, which even nowadays continues to be endorsed by some scholars, especially in those disciplines that study premodern cultures (most notably in classics), is the following view about a certain Ndembu ritual expressed by David Bynum, who, otherwise, has contributed insights into the study of oral literature; Bynum 1978: esp. 154–55: 'I say that the narrative pattern is prior to the Ndambu rites not only because the narrative is the entity of which the rites are only dismembered pieces, but also because one cannot even begin to trace such a ritual vignette of narrative motifs [...] over the spans of time and territory occupied by the story of the Two Trees'; see also Bynum 1981; Burke 1978: 181–82. Even such a sophisticated scholar of medieval literature as Paul Zumthor could not avoid absolute generalizations of this sort; see, for instance, the following statement: 'oral poetry was born from archaic rites – ontologically if not (who will know?) historically. The rite contained it' (Zumthor 1990: 211).

that in a specific society are recognized and received as marked communicative strategies or signs sanctioned through tradition. In this sense, both these cultural phenomena may be viewed in terms of reactivation of habitually established patterns of communication. Rituals tend to be articulated as sequences of long-established expressive mechanisms or building blocks not unlike traditional oral performances that resort to traditional, often formulaic, discursive patterns.[50] The adherence to such sanctioned means of communication does not preclude innovation; it rather 'circumscribes the always negotiable paradigmatic boundaries of continuously renewed syntagmatic constructions of signification' (Yatromanolakis and Roilos 2003: 31). The polyvalent, often symbolic, semantic potential of these expressive mechanisms and units is dynamically acted out in the context of the performative event, which sets into motion complex nexuses of interaction between different agents of tradition (performers and audience).

Rituals and products of oral traditional literature are most often performed in especially demarcated spatiotemporal territories that to a greater (rituals) or lesser degree (oral literature) interrupt the course of unmarked, everyday discursive and broader sociocultural interactions in a particular community. Although the performance of traditional oral literary texts in non-ritual contexts as a rule involves a much less accentuated situational markedness, occasionally it is also charged with ritualistic associations. It is reported, for instance, that some traditional storytellers in Italy used to begin their narrating by crossing themselves (Burke 1978:180); formulaic expressions framing the beginning and the ending of storytelling in Greek folktales functioned as comparable discursive and situational markers, despite their more secular character.

The dialectics between ritual and oral traditional literature is most dynamically activated when the latter contributes to the communicative efficacy of the former. In such cases, both the texts of oral literature that are acted-out as integral constituents of a ritual and the specific ritual performance are engaged in a creative interaction through which the one enriches or, at least, affects the communicative function of the other. That the thematic and performative potential of a song may be conducive or clearly related to a specific ritual does not, of course, require any detailed documentation. The so-called functional or ritual songs such as laments, wedding or seasonal songs, as well as examples of traditional folklore like spells are more often than not clearly associated with corresponding ritual occasions.

Old English charms constitute an interesting Medieval European case in point. In addition to articulating an evocative, often apotropaic, 'magical' discourse, some texts of this genre also include allusions to particular ritual acts and desired effects. Here is a representative example of a charm against 'wen':

> Wenne, wenne, wenchichenne,
> her ne scealt þu timbrien, ne nenne tun habben,
> ac þu scealt north eonene to þan nihgan berhge,
> þer þu hauest, ermig, enne broþer.
> He þe sceal legge leaf et heafde.

---

[50] As has become clear in my previous discussion, patterns of formulaic expression should not be necessarily understood in terms of oral-formulaic theory as developed in Parry's and Lord's pioneering works on South Slavic epics but on the basis of culture-specific analyses.

Under fot wolues,    under ueþer earnes,
under earnes clea,   a þu geweornie.
Clinge þu    alswa col on heorþe,
scring þu    alswa scerne awage,
and weorne   alswa weter on anbre [...]

Wen, wen, little wen, here you must not build, nor have any dwelling, but you must go north to the nearby hill where you have, miserable, one brother. He must lay a leaf at your head. Under the foot of a wolf, under the wing of the eagle, under the claw of the eagle, even may you diminish. Shrivel as a coal on the hearth, shrink as muck in the wall, and diminish as water in pail.[51]

The desired healing of the disease is described through a number of images, some of which point to the performance of marked ritual acts like the pouring of water. Furthermore, associations of this kind are established through the activation of homological notional structures: the gradual disappearance of the wen is connected to the slow but ultimate consumption of other substances – may this be natural (coal and muck) or mediated through human agency (water). No doubt, Old English or, for instance, medieval German charms[52] share such discursive and performative strategies with spells from many other premodern traditions; however, they are of particular significance for us as medievalists to the extent that they can shed light on the dialectics of orality, ritual, and performance in societies whose oral cultures we reconstruct only hypothetically.

Things are not always as straightforward as a convenient analytical equation of the type 'specific ritual = performance of especially assigned traditional oral literary "texts"' may imply. Ritual's typical power to assimilate the expressive potential of the media that it activates, traditional oral discourse included, as well as the latter's tendency to generic plasticity and performative flexibility render such categorial equivalences misleading; equally misleading and simplistic is also the notion of 'conflation', especially as applied in highly problematic approaches to ancient Greek drama.[53]

At times not only the same metaphorical imagery but precisely the same folksong can be performed on diametrically opposite ritual occasions. For instance, a wedding song from Thessaly, Greece, expressing the bride's anxiety as she departs from home can be performed in the same region as a lament at the funeral of a young woman (Roilos 1998). Homological ritual and discursive textures are responsible for this kind of performative mobility across an extended spectrum of ritual occasions. Comparable is the interchangeability of thematic and expressive *topoi* of wedding songs and dirges in Transylvania, Romania.[54] The singing of a song within the context of a particular ritual invests it with new symbolic or performative potential, even if the specific 'text' presents no obvious ritual associations. In this manner, the syntagmatic structure of a ritual event transforms the 'text' of oral traditional literature into a marked, often metaphoric vehicle of ritual meaning, of which it is otherwise disinvested. Characteristic is the example

---

[51] Text and translation in Garner 2004: 32–33; compare also e. g. the fundamental discussions of magical discourse in Malinowski 1922 and Tambiah 1985: 17–59.
[52] For a brief but insightful discussion of medieval German spells, see Klingenberg 1984: 399–401.
[53] I have in mind especially R. Rehm's *Marriage to Death* (1994). Rehm's book is heavily derivative and needs to be read with considerable caution.
[54] Kligman 1988; M. Alexiou 2002a: 105–7, 120–22, 155–57; Alexiou and Dronke 1971.

of the performance of certain traditional ballads at the ritual of fire-walking (*Anastenaria*) in Macedonia in Northern Greece. Usually sung as 'table' songs, when performed in this demarcated ceremonial context these ballads acquire additional symbolic connotations pointing to the risky liminality in which the performers find themselves. Indigenous interpretations do not necessarily articulate clear-cut or definite connections between the ritual and the songs they perform, thus alluding to emotional rather than noetic homologies between the state of the actors in the particular ritual and the story of the protagonists in the traditional ballads.[55] More often than not, ritual performative occasions call, therefore, for modifications of the form and the function of specific traditional oral texts, as happens, for instance, with the type of *bimo* epic narratives among the Nuosu people in China, the songs performed in middle India within the performative context of the female festival tradition of *bhojalî*, or the occasional interchangeability between ritual laments and wedding songs in Greece.[56]

In my discussion above of the Renaissance Cretan work of *Erotokritos*, I pointed to the importance of the ritualization of oral versions of this written poem and its symbolic potential. Especially the homonymous hero of the poem was appropriated by the performers of traditional Carnival *drômena* and assimilated into the marked socioaesthetic frame of their liminal acts. The history of the reception of Robin Hood, the protagonist of a number of oral narratives and ballads in early modern England, attests to similar ritual transformations of the legendary outlaw and his beloved, Maid Marion. For instance, it is recorded that at the celebration of May games in Reading in 1502 the two traditional characters were the royal May couple. The green colour of Robin's clothes and his associations with the greenwood were most probably responsible for the ritualization of his figure (Burke 1978: 180). Robin Hood's case exemplifies, I argue, the intricate metaphoric and metonymic mechanisms through which ritual and broader socioaesthetic textures are intertwined to produce a multilayered interdiscursivity.[57] Even the slightest expressive (verbal or other) detail, if employed in the context of a ritual performance, is charged with marked connotations that discern it from the communicative potential that it has on different occasions.[58] For instance, the image of the tree or similar symbolic elements drawn from the natural world, which in everyday discourse or in non-ritual contexts (e. g. traditional narratives such as tales and legends) convey less marked or even unmarked meanings, when used in wedding songs and especially in ritual dirges, activate a number of metonymic and metaphoric connections that dramatically move the praised or lamented person from her/his current ritual status to broader cosmological and symbolic systems of signification shared by the community and sanc-

---

[55] Danforth tries to find certain structural associations between these songs and the specific religious healing ritual (Danforth 1989: 103–22).

[56] For ritualization of epic poetry among the Nuosu, see Qubumo 2001. Flueckiger 1996 provides an interesting discussion of the interdependence of specific types of oral traditional Indian poetry and the rituals performed on the occasions of *bhojalî*. On ritual aspects of the performance of epic, see also Reichl 2003.

[57] For the concept of interdiscursivity, see Yatromanolakis and Roilos 2003, ch. 2; 2005: 15–18; Yatromanolakis 2007; 2008; 2009a; and Yatromanolakis and Roilos (forthcoming).

[58] Ploutarchos (first–second c. AD) offers some sensitive observations concerning the marked symbolic dimensions of objects associated with sacred spaces; see the discussion in Yatromanolakis and Roilos 2003: 28–29.

tioned through tradition. In addition to their discursive multilayeredness and semantic contribution to the wider verbal environment in which they are encountered (i. e. in the songs), this kind of metonymic and metaphoric associations enrich the performative potential of the ritual, since they are often acted out as dramatic constituents of the overarching ritual drama.[59]

The dynamic dialectics of ritual and oral traditional literature is also evinced in those cases in which details of the latter are better understood in the light of its ritual performative connections. I referred earlier to the close interrelation of the imagery in Old English (or, for that matter, in other premodern) charms and the performance of specific ritual acts. In this instance, the associations between the traditional oral text and its performative context seem to be more straightforward than, for example, in the case of songs whose performance is not necessarily accompanied by simultaneous ritual acts. In a German song about St. Martin, the saint is strangely associated with a goose-pen (*Gänsestall*). This rather bewildering detail can be deciphered if connected with the broader context of the feast in honour of the specific saint: we know that in premodern Germany on November 11th, his feast day, it was customary for the people who celebrated his memory to eat geese.[60] Beyond such implicit references to concrete constituents of ritual occasions and habitual reenactments of time-honoured customs, not rarely oral traditional literature activates marked ritual textures that contribute to the multivalence of its interdiscursivity and performativity. Broader ritual schemata or spatiotemporal markers are assimilated into the discourse of oral traditional literature – especially narrative stories or songs such as ballads or epics – thus investing them not necessarily with marked ritual functionality but rather with distinctive allusiveness to ritual, often symbolic, systems of communication and signification. Patterns and themes of liminality, either reproduced or subverted, play a principal role in the construction of stories and plots in traditional oral (prose or verse) narratives, especially heroic ones, including, for instance, *Beowulf* or *Digenes Akrites*.[61]

Particularly significant for our reconstruction of the dialectics in a specific culture, historical period, or genre between ritual and traditional oral literature are those examples of the latter in which extra-referential allusions to ritual practices are combined with distinctive self-referentiality commenting on the marked discourse employed in a text. As I have shown so far, ritual songs such as laments, spells, wedding songs, or songs performed on other special ritual occasions such as holiday feasts arguably constitute a most fertile field for such an investigation. Not rarely, the performance of these songs, as the cases of Maniat and Warao laments show, involves also negotiations of established power relations or of sanctioned modes of semantic (notably linguistic) and socioaes-

---

[59] I discuss the complex activation and performative dynamics of metaphoric and metonymic associations in ritual oral literature in Roilos 1998. For an insightful discussion of metaphor in ritual, see Fernandez 1986: 28–63.
[60] Burke 1978: 181. This custom is still preserved regionally in Germany, in particular in the Rhineland.
[61] Despite its well-known limitations, Propp's formalistic analysis of Russian wondertales remains instructive in several respects (Propp 1968). On ritual patterns of signification in vernacular medieval Greek literature, which occasionally seems to draw on oral narrative discourses, see Roilos 2007. For different but comparable ritual structures in Germanic epic tradition, see Tarzia 1989.

thetic interaction. Not rarely, the reconfiguration of these conventional patterns takes the form of dialogic exchanges between different performers, which is occasionally reflected in an extreme manipulation of the discursive liberty and self-reflexivity accorded to the singers on marked ritual occasions. This is the case, for instance, with traditional songs and *drômena* performed during Carnival, and with genres such as laments or couplets performed in the context of performative contests in Spain or in (ancient and contemporary) Greece.[62]

An intriguing example of marked self-referentiality and ritual discourse is also provided by Runo 3 in Lönnrot's *Kalevala*. Despite the notorious problems concerning the composition of this work, it is of comparative significance that the episode of the singing contest between the respected singer Väinämöinen and his much younger but overambitious rival Joukahainen is described in terms that foreground not so much a specific ritual occasion but, rather, the almost magical, that is ritual, potential of traditional singing in general; this is also illustrated in other examples of traditional oral Finnish literature. The contest between the two fictitious agents of traditional oral literature and lore is invested with aspects of the performative dynamics of shamanic incantatory discourse,[63] thus illustrating, I argue, in the most evocative way the complex nexuses of symbolic and broader socioaesthetic interaction that the methodological model of ritual poetics seeks to investigate.

## References

Ahern, John. 1981. 'Singing the Book: Orality in the Reception of Dante's Comedy.' *Annals of Scholarship* 2: 17–41.
Alexiou, Margaret. 1991. 'Literature and Popular Tradition.' In *Literature and Society in Renaissance Crete*. Ed. David Holton. Cambridge: CUP. 239–74.
–. 2002a. *The Ritual Lament in Greek Tradition*. 2nd ed. rev. by Dimitrios Yatromanolakis and Panagiotis Roilos. Lanham, MD: Rowman and Littlefield. [1st. ed. Cambridge, 1974.]
–. 2002b. *After Antiquity: Greek Language, Myth, and Metaphor*. Ithaca, NY: Cornell UP.
Alexiou, Stylianos, ed. 1985. Βασίλειος Διγενής Ἀκρίτης (κατὰ τὸ χειρόγραφο τοῦ Ἐσκοριὰλ) καὶ Τὸ Ἆσμα τοῦ Ἀρμούρη. Athens: Hermes.
–, ed. 1994. Βιτσέντσος Κορνάρος: Ἐρωτόκριτος. Athens: Hermes.
Alexiou, Margaret, and Peter Dronke. 1971. 'The Lament of Jephtha's Daughter: Themes, Traditions, Originality.' *Studi Medievali* 12: 819–63.

---

[62] In addition to the performances of Maniat laments discussed earlier in this chapter, I would like to refer to a characteristic example of ritual discursive self-referentiality in the same genre: in a dirge from this region, which belongs to the broader geographical area of Peloponnese (otherwise known as Morias), the lamenter extols the forcefulness of her own discourse that she proudly distinguishes from the unnerved language of the rest of Morias (Kasses 1979: 162). Fernandez 1986: 73–102 has been a groundbreaking study of the interaction of metaphoric and metonymic discursive modes in such songs in Spain. Herzfeld 1985 is an interesting exploration of the 'poetics of manhood' involved in comparable contexts in Crete; for an investigation into the complexities of similar performative occasions in ancient Greece, see Yatromanolakis 2009a: 271–75.

[63] I owe this interpretation of the specific episode to my graduate student Anita Nikannen (Department of Comparative Literature, Harvard University). For this episode, see Magoun's translation of the *Kalevala*, Magoun 1963: 14–21.

Amodio, Mark C., ed. 2005a. *New Directions in Oral Theory.* Tempe: Arizona Center for Medieval and Renaissance Studies.

–. 2005b. 'Res(is)ting the Singer: Towards a Non-Performative Anglo-Saxon Oral Poetics.' In Amodio 2005a: 179–208.

Bäuml, Franz. 1980.'Varieties and Consequences of Medieval Literacy and Illiteracy.' *Speculum* 55: 237–65.

–. 1984.'Medieval Texts and the Two Theories of Oral-Formulaic Composition: A Proposal for a Third Theory.' *New Literary History* 16: 31–49.

Baud-Bovy, Samuel. 1946–1949.'Sur le χελιδόνισμα.' Βυζαντινά-Μεταβυζαντινά [*Byzantina, Metabyzantina*] 1: 23–32.

Bauman, Richard. 1986.'Performance and Honor in 13th-century Iceland.' *JAF* 99: 131–50.

–. 1992. 'Contextualization, Tradition, and the Dialogue of Genres: Icelandic Legends of the *kraftaskáld*.' In *Rethinking Context: Language as an Interactive Phenomenon*. Ed. Alessandro Duranti and Charles Goodwin. Cambridge: CUP. 125–46.

Beck, Hans-Georg. 1971. *Geschichte der byzantinischen Volksliteratur*. Munich: Beck.

Bekker, Immanuel, ed. 1838. *Theophanes continuatus, Ioannes Cameniata, Symeon Magister, Georgius Monchus.* Bonn.

Ben-Amos, Dan. 1976.'Analytical Categories and Ethnic Genres.' In *Folklore Genres*. Ed. Dan Ben-Amos. Austin: U of Texas P. 215–42.

Berlin, Gail Ivy. 1995.'Memorization in Anglo-Saxon England: Some Case Studies.' In Nicolaisen 1995: 97–113.

Briggs, Charles L. 1992.'"Since I Am a Woman, I Will Chastise My Relatives": Gender, Reported Speech, and the (Re)Production of Social Relations in Warao Ritual Wailing.'*American Ethnologist* 19: 337–61.

Budelmann, Felix, ed. 2009. *The Cambridge Companion to Greek Lyric Poetry.* Cambridge: CUP.

Burke, Peter. 1978. *Popular Culture in Early Modern Europe.* London: Temple Smith.

Bynum, David. 1978. *The Daemon in the Wood: A Study of Oral Narrative Patterns.* Cambridge, MA: Harvard UP.

–. 1981.'Myth and Ritual: Two Faces of Tradition.' In Foley 1981: 142–63.

Caravelli-Chaves, Anna. 1980. 'Bridge between Worlds: The Greek Women's Lament as a Communicative Event.' *JAF* 93: 129–57.

–. 1986.'The Bitter Wounding: The Lament as a Social Protest in Rural Greece.' In *Gender and Power in Rural Greece*, Ed. Jill Dubisch. Princeton: Princeton UP. 169–95.

Cupane, Carolina. 1994–1995.'Δεῦτε, προσκαρτερήσατε μικρόν, ὢ νέοι πάντες: Note sulla ricezione primaria e sul pubblico della letteratura greca medievale.' *Diptycha* 6: 147–68.

Danforth, Loring. 1989. *Firewalking and Religious Healing: The Anastenaria of Greece and the American Firewalking Movement.* Princeton: Princeton UP.

Doane, A. N., and Carol Braun Pasternack, eds. 1991. *Vox Intexta: Orality and Textuality in the Middle Ages.* Madison: U of Wisconsin P.

DuBois, Thomas A. 1995. *Finnish Folk Poetry and the Kalevala.* New York: Garland.

–. 1996.'The *Kalevala* Received: From Printed Text to Oral Performance.' *Oral Tradition* 11: 270–300.

Egan, Charles H. 2000.'Were *Yüeh-fu* Ever Folk Songs? Reconsidering the Relevance of Oral Theory and Balladry Analogies.' *Chinese Literature: Essays, Articles, Reviews* 22: 31–66.

Eusthatios 1825–26. *Eustathii Commentarii ad Homeri Odysseam.* 2 vols. Leipzig.

Fauriel, C., ed. and trans. 1825.*Chants populaires de la Grèce moderne. II. Chants historiques, romanesques et domestiques.* Paris.

Feld, Steven. 1990a. *Sound and Sentiment: Birds, Weeping, Poetics, and Song in Kaluli Expression.* Philadelphia: U of Pennsylvania P.

–. 1990b.'Wept Thoughts: The Voicing of Kaluli Memoires.' *Oral Tradition* 5: 241–66.

Fernandez, James W. 1986. *Persuasions and Performances: The Play of Tropes in Culture.* Bloomington: Indiana UP.
Finnegan, Ruth. 1976. 'What Is Oral Literature Anyway? Comments in the Light of Some African and Other Comparative Material.' In *Oral Literature and the Formula.* Ed. Benjamin A. Stolz and Richard S. Shannon, Ann Arbor, MI: Center for the Coordination of Ancient and Modern Studies. 127–66.
–. 1977. *Oral Poetry: Its Nature, Significance, and Social Context.* Cambridge: CUP.
–. 2005. 'The How of Literature.' *Oral Tradition* 20: 164–87.
Flueckiger, Joyce B. 1996. *Gender and Genre in the Folklore of Middle India.* Ithaca, NY: Cornell UP.
Foley, John Miles, ed. 1981. *Oral Traditional Literature: A Festschrift for Albert Bates Lord.* Ed. John Miles Foley. Columbus, OH: Slavica.
–. 1985. *Oral-Formulaic Theory: An Introduction and Annotated Bibliography.* New York: Garland.
–. 1988. *The Theory of Oral Composition: History and Methodology.* Bloomington: Indiana UP.
–. 1991a. *The Immanent Art: From Structure to Meaning in Traditional Oral Epic.* Bloomington: Indiana UP.
–. 1991b. 'Orality, Textuality, and Interpretation.' In Doane and Pasternack 1991: 34–45.
–. 1995. 'The Implications of Oral Tradition.' In Nicolaisen 1995: 31–57.
Frese, Dolores Warwick. 1991. 'The Marriage of Woman and Werewolf: Poetics of Estrangement in Marie de France's "Bisclavret".' In Doane and Pasternack 1991: 183–202.
Fry, Donald K. 1981. 'The Memory of Cædmon.' In Foley1981: 282–93.
Garner, Lori Ann. 2004. 'Anglo-Saxon Charms in Performance.' *Oral Tradition* 19: 20–42.
Goody, Jack. 1987. *The Interface between the Written and the Oral.* Cambridge: CUP.
Green, D. H. 1994. *Medieval Reading and Listening: The Primary Reception of German Literature, 800–1300.* Cambridge: CUP.
Gurevich, Aaron. 1988. *Medieval Popular Culture: Problems of Belief and Perception.* Cambridge: CUP.
Harris, Joseph. 1983. 'Eddic Poetry as Oral Poetry: The Evidence of Parallel Passages in the Helgi Poems for Questions of Composition and Performance.' In *Edda: A Collection of Essays.* Ed. R. J. Glendinning and Haraldur Bessason. University of Manitoba Icelandic Studies 4. Winnipeg: U of Manitoba P. 210–42.
–, ed. 1991. *The Ballad and Oral Literature.* Cambridge, MA: Harvard UP.
Herzfeld, Michael. 1985. *The Poetics of Manhood: Contest and Identity in a Cretan Mountain Village.* Princeton: Princeton UP.
–. 1993. 'In Defiance of Destiny: The Management of Time and Gender at a Cretan Funeral.' *American Ethnologist* 20: 241–55.
–. 2005. 'Rites of Spring: Ritual, Resistance, and Taxonomic Regimentation in Greek Cultural History.' In Yatromanolakis and Roilos 2005: 371–82.
Hoffman, Werner. 1974. *Mittelhochdeutsche Heldendichtung.* Berlin: Erich Schmidt.
Holton, David. 1990. 'Orality in Cretan Narrative Poetry.' *Byzantine and Modern Greek Studies* 14: 186–98.
Hymes, Dell. 1981. *"In Vain I Tried to Tell You": Essays in Native American Ethnopoetics.* Philadelphia: U of Pennsylvania P.
–. 1996. *Ethnography, Linguistics, Narrative Inequality: Toward an Understanding of Voice.* London: Taylor and Francis.
Innes, Matthew 1998. 'Memory, Orality, and Literacy in an Early Medieval Society.' *Past and Present* 158: 3–36.
Jauss, Hans Robert. 1979. 'The Alterity and Modernity of Medieval Literature.' *New Literary History* 10: 181–230.

Jeffreys, Elizabeth, ed. 1998. *Digenis Akritis: The Grottaferrata and Escorial Versions*. Cambridge Medieval Classics 7. Cambridge: CUP.
–, and Michael Jeffreys. 1986. 'The Oral Background of Byzantine Popular Poetry.' *Oral Tradition* 1: 504–47.
–, and Michael Jeffreys. 1991. 'Poetry, Oral.' In *The Oxford Dictionary of Byzantium*. Ed. Alexander P. Kazhdan. 3 vols. Oxford: OUP. III, 1690.
Jolles, André. 1930. *Einfache Formen. Legende, Sage, Mythe, Rätsel, Spruch, Kasus, Memorabile, Märchen, Witz*. Tübingen: Niemeyer.
Kasses, Kyriakos D., ed. 1979. Μοιρολόγια τῆς Μέσα Μάνης. Ἀνέκδοτα κείμενα καὶ ἄγνωστα ἱστορικὰ μοιρολογιῶν καὶ οἰκογενειῶν. Athens: n. p.
Kligman, Gail. 1988. *The Wedding of the Dead: Ritual, Poetics, and Popular Culture in Transylvania*. Berkeley: U of California P.
Klingenberg, Heinz. 1984. 'Dichtung.' In *Reallexikon der germanischen Altertumskunde*. Ed. Heinrich Beck et al. Vol. 5. Berlin: de Gruyrer. 394–404.
Kougeas, Sokrates. 1912–13. 'Αἱ ἐν τοῖς σχολίοις τοῦ Ἀρέθα λαογραφικαὶ εἰδήσεις.' *Laographia* 4: 239–40.
Koukoules, Phaidon. 1948. Βυζαντινῶν Βίος καὶ Πολιτισμός, *A, II*. Collection de l'Institut Français d'Athènes 10. Athens: Institut Français d'Athènes.
Krumbacher, Karl. 1902. 'Review of Tommasini 1901.' *Byzantinische Zeitschrift* 11: 586–88.
Kyriakides, Stilpon P. 1951. 'Ταμήλιον δημῶδες βυζαντινὸν ᾆσμα.' *Annuaire de l'Institut de Philologie et d'Histoire Orientales et Slaves* 11: 179–83.
–. 1978. Τὸ Δημοτικὸ Τραγοῦδι. Ed. Alke Kyriakidou-Nestoros. Athens: Hermes.
Lord, Albert Bates. 1960. *The Singer of Tales*. Cambridge, MA: Harvard UP. [Re-edition with a CD and a new introduction by Stephen Mitchell and Gregory Nagy, 2000.]
–. 1995a. *The Singer Resumes the Tale*. Ed. Mary Louise Lord. Ithaca, NY: Cornell UP.
–. 1995b. 'Oral Composition and "Oral Residue" in the Middle Ages.' In Nicolaisen 1995: 7–29.
Maas, Paul. 1912. 'Metrische Akklamationen der Byzantiner.' *Byzantinische Zeitschrift* 21: 28–51.
Magoun, Francis Peabody, Jr., trans. 1963. *The Kalevala or Poems of the Kaleva District*. Compiled by Elias Lönnrot. Cambridge, MA: Harvard UP.
Malinowski, Bronislaw. 1922. *Argonauts of the Western Pacific: An Account of Native Enterprise and Adventure in the Archipelagoes of Melanesian New Guinea*. London: Routledge.
Nagler, Michael N. 1967. 'Towards a Generative View of the Oral Formula.' *Transactions of the American Philological Association* 98: 269–311.
Nelson, William. 1976–77. 'From "Listen, Lordings" to "Dear Reader".' *University of Toronto Quarterly* 46: 111–24.
Nicolaisen, W. F. H., ed. 1995. *Oral Tradition in the Middle Ages*. Medieval and Renaissance Texts and Studies 112. Binghamton: State U of New York at Binghamton.
Notopoulos, James A. 1952. 'Homer and Cretan Heroic Poetry: A Study in Comparative Oral Poetry.' *American Journal of Philology* 73: 225–50.
O'Brien O'Keeffe, Katherine. 1990. *Visible Song: Transitional Literacy in Old English Verse*. Cambridge: CUP.
Olsen, Alexandra H. 1983. 'Old English Poetry and Latin Prose: The Reverse Context.' *Classica et Mediaevalia* 34: 273–82.
Ong, Walter J. 1982. *Orality and Literacy: The Technologizing of the Word*. London: Methuen.
Papadopoulos, Thanasis. 1977. 'Ἐρωτοκρίτειοι ἀφηγήσεις ἐν τῷ Κυπριακῷ δημῶδει λόγῳ.' *Kypriakai Spoudai* 41: 211–42.
Parry, Milman. 1928. *L'épithète traditionnelle dans Homère. Essai sur un problème de style homérique*. Paris: 'Les Belles Lettres'.
–. 1930. 'Studies in the Epic Technique of Oral Verse-Making: Homer and the Homeric Style.' *Harvard Studies in Classical Philology* 41: 73–147.
Patala, Zoï. 1996. 'Les chants grecs du *Liber Politicus* du chanoine Benoît.' *Byzantion* 66: 512–35.

Polites, Nikolaos G. 1912. 'Δημώδη βυζαντινά ᾄσματα.' *Laographia* 3: 622–52.
—. 1914. Ἐκλογαὶ ἀπὸ τὰ τραγούδια τοῦ ἑλληνικοῦ λαοῦ. Athens: Estia.
Propp, V. 1968. *Morphology of the Folktale*. Trans. Laurence Scott, 2nd rev. ed. Austin: U of Texas P.
Puchner, Walter. 1983. 'Η Ἐρωφίλη στὴ δημώδη παράδοση τῆς Κρήτης.' *Ariadne* 1:173–235.
—. 1991. 'Tragedy.' In *Literature and Society in Renaissance Crete*. Ed. David Holton. Cambridge: CUP. 129–58.
Qubumo, Bamo. 2001. 'Traditional Nuosu Origin Narratives: A Case Study of Ritualized Epos in *Bimo* Incantation Scriptures.' *Oral Tradition* 16: 453–79.
Rehm, Rush. 1994. *Marriage to Death: The Conflation of Wedding and Funeral Rituals in Greek Tragedy*. Princeton: Princeton UP.
Reichl, Karl. 1991. 'The Middle English Popular Romance: Minstrel versus Hack Writer.' In Harris 1991: 243–68.
—. 2003. 'The Search for Origins: Ritual Aspects of the Performance of Epic.' *Journal of Historical Pragmatics* 4: 249–67.
Reinsch, Dieter R., and Athanasios Kambyllis, eds. 2001. *Annae Comnenae Alexias*. Corpus fontium historiae Byzantinae 40. Berlin: de Gruyter.
Roilos, Panagiotis. 1998. 'Ο νεκρὸς ὡς δέντρο στὰ ἑλληνικὰ μοιρολόγια. Ἡ μεταφορὰ στὴν παραδοσιακὴ προφορικὴ ποίηση τελετουργικοῦ χαρακτῆρα.' *Hellenika* 48: 61–85.
—. 2002. 'Orality and Performativity in the *Erotokritos*.' *Cretan Studies* 7: 213–30.
—. 2005. *Amphoteroglossia: A Poetics of the Twelfth-Century Medieval Greek Novel*. Cambridge, MA: Harvard UP.
—. 2007. 'Ekphrastic Semantics and Ritual Poetics: From the Ancient Greek Novel to the Late Medieval Greek Romance.' In *Literatur und Religion. Wege zu einer mythisch-rituellen Poetik bei den Griechen. II*. Ed. Anton Bierl, Rebecca Lämmle, Katharina Wesselmann. Berlin: de Gruyter. 335–54.
Rosenberg, Bruce A. 1981. 'Oral Literature in the Middle Ages.' In Foley 1981: 440–50.
Rossi-Taibi, Giuseppe. 1969. *Filagato da Cerami. Omelie per i Vangeli Domenicali e le Feste di Tutto l'Anno. I*. Palermo: Istituto siciliano di studi bizantini e neoellenici.
Sathas, Konstantinos. 1876. *Μεσαιωνικὴ Βιβλιοθήκη*. Vol. 5. Venice.
Schaefer, Ursula. 1991. 'Hearing from Books: The Rise of Fictionality in Old English Poetry.' In Doane and Pasternack 1991: 117–36.
Schopen, Ludwig, ed. 1829–55. *Nicephori Gregorae Byzantina Historia*. 3 vols. Bonn. [Vol. 3 ed. Immanuel Bekker.]
Seremetakis, Nadia. 1991. *The Last Word: Women, Death, and Divination in Inner Mani*. Chicago: U of Chicago P.
Sewter, Edgar R. A., trans. 1953. Michael Psellos. *The Chronographia*. London: Routledge and Kegan Paul.
Skinner, Debra, Dorothy Holland, and G. B. Adhikari. 1994. 'The Songs of Tij: A Genre of Critical Commentary for Women of Nepal.' *Asian Folklore Studies* 53: 259–305.
Smith, Colin. 1971. 'Latin Histories and Vernacular Epic in Twelfth-Century Spain: Similarities of Spirit and Style.' *Bulletin of Hispanic Studies* 48: 1–19.
Spyridakes, Georgios K. 1951. 'Ποιήματα δημωδῶν ᾀσμάτων εἰς Τραπεζοῦντα κατὰ τὸν 14ο αἰῶνα.' *Archeion Pontou* 16: 263–66.
—. 1957. 'Εἰδήσεις περὶ σκωπτικῶν ᾀσμάτων τοῦ λαοῦ ἐκ τῶν Βυζαντινῶν χρόνων.' *Hellenika* 15: 275–78.
Stock, Brian. 1983. *The Implications of Literacy: Written Language and Models on Interpretation in the Eleventh and Twelfth Centuries*. Princeton: Princeton UP.
—. 1990. *Listening for the Text: On the Uses of the Past*. Philadelphia: U of Pennsylvania P.
Tambiah, Stanley J. 1985. *Culture, Thought, and Social Action: An Anthropological Perspective*. Cambridge, MA: Harvard UP.

Tarzia, Wade. 1989. 'The Hoarding Ritual in Germanic Epic Tradition.' *Journal of Folklore Research* 26: 99–121.
Tommasini, Vincenzo. 1901. 'Sulle laudi greche conservate nel Liber Politicus del canonico Benedetto.' In *Scritti vari di filologia. Per il XXV anno di insegnamento a Ernesto Monaci*. Rome: Forzani. 377–88.
Turner, Victor. 1971. 'An Anthropological Approach to the Icelandic Saga.' In *The Translation of Culture*. Ed. Thomas O. Beidelman. London: Tavistock. 349–74.
–. 1982. *From Ritual to Theatre: The Human Seriousness of Play*. New York: PAJ Books.
Vansina, Jan. 1985. *Oral Tradition as History*. Madison: U of Wisconsin P.
Wardropper, Bruce W. 1980. 'Meaning in Medieval Spanish Folk Song' In *The Interpretation of Medieval Lyric Poetry*. Ed. W. T. H. Jackson. New York: Columbia UP. 176–93.
Yatromanolakis, Dimitrios. 2007. *Sappho in the Making: The Early Reception*. Cambridge, MA: Harvard UP.
–. 2008. 'Genre Categories and Interdiscursivity in Alkaios and Archaic Greece.' *Synkrise/Comparaison* 19: 169–87.
–. 2009a. 'Ancient Greek Popular Song.' In Budelmann 2009: 263–76.
–. 2009b. 'Alcaeus and Sappho.' In Budelmann 2009: 204–26.
–, and Panagiotis Roilos. 2003. *Towards a Ritual Poetics*. Athens: Foundation of the Hellenic World.
–, and Panagiotis Roilos, eds. 2005. *Greek Ritual Poetics*. Cambridge, MA: Harvard UP.
–, and Panagiotis Roilos. Forthcoming. *Interdiscursivity and Ritual: Explorations of Patterns of Signification in Greek Literature and Societies*. Munich.
Ziolkowski, Jan. 1991. 'Cultural Diglossia and the Nature of Medieval Latin Literature.' In Harris 1991: 193–213.
Zumthor, Paul. 1987. *La lettre et la voix. De la 'littérature' médiévale*. Paris: Seuil.
–. 1990. *Oral Poetry: An Introduction*. Trans. Kathryn Murphy-Judy. Minneapolis: U of Minnesota P.
–. 1991. *Toward a Medieval Poetics*. Trans. Philip Bennett. Minneapolis: U of Minnesota P.

# Part II
# Traditions and Genres

# 8 Older Germanic Poetry
## With a Note on the Icelandic Sagas

*Joseph Harris*

A relatively new initiative, the World Oral Literature Project from Cambridge University's Museum for Archeology and Anthropology, with the object of saving what it can of the vanishing oral literatures of the world, points out that '[g]lobalisation and rapid socio-economic change exert complex pressures on smaller communities' (http://www.oralliterature.org). Ironically it will take a 'global' effort to save *their* oral culture from *our* influence. We can imagine somewhat similar pressures – perhaps to be on the safe side I should add that academic parachute, '*mutatis mutandis*' – bearing on clan and tribal groups of northern Europe as they encountered socially and technologically advanced southern cultures, especially Roman; their oral literature was, however, saved into writing not by any organized initiative but only very sporadically and unsystematically. The 'smaller communities' in question here – the 'little traditions' encountering the 'great tradition' of Rome, to use some terminology from the anthropology of peasant cultures[1] – were historically related by language, poetics, custom and law, certainly also by intermarriage, and by at least some aspects of religion. Each community's assimilations of and to Latin culture in the Roman Iron Age (0–400 AD), and later to Byzantine and Roman Christianity, varied widely; and the study of these particular developments and of the historical fates of the various Germanic peoples are among the great subjects of European history.

A recent study by D. H. Green (1998) offers a comprehensive survey, admirably grounded in language, of the Germanic peoples' cultural relations with Rome in the early period, but Green deals with oral literature only incidentally. Insofar as early Germanic oral literature is our main concern in this chapter, the anthropological model from recent and contemporary times, though far removed from the Germanic historical base, can often be equally suggestive (Reichl 2000; Niles 1999). Of necessity the approach to the study of this largely lost, haphazardly preserved oral and oral-derived literature is also somewhat unsystematic, proceeding fragmentary record by fragmentary record. Underlying the fragmented prospective, however, are two factors that help to give shape to the enterprise: 1) the principles of dealing with oral literatures in general, tempered by the caveats just mentioned, and 2) the special aspects of the Germanic ethnic matrix at its nexus with orality and literacy. The former is the overall topic of this book as a whole;

---

[1] Wax 1969: 15; Wax draws these concepts from the anthropologist Robert Redfield.

the latter is the subject of this chapter and an old but still productive – in a sense, still essential – subject of study rooted in the recognition of certain ethnic commonalities.[2]

## 1 Oral Literature and Writing

Oral literature is both a product of and a part of 'culture', and the interrelated cultures of early Germanic Europe produced this product partly before and outside the influence of Rome. But it is saved, to the degree that it *is* saved, by writing, the archiving technology brought in with Latin civilization and especially with Roman Christianity. Almost as far back as we can see with any clarity, the basically oral cultures, the 'little tradition', of Germania were subject to influence by the Roman contact; and when scraps of Germanic oral literature are found written down through the Christian medium, it is difficult to tell exactly what the effects of the passage into letters – textualization – may have been (Honko 2000; 2003). The relatively anodyne discussion of textualization, however, is the recent, technologized successor of grittier cultural wars better left behind.

The purely oral culture ('primary orality') of a putatively isolated Germanic-speaking tribal community of the western Baltic in the pre-Roman Iron Age, that is before extensive contact with Rome, need not be doubted as a theoretical construct, and such a community will have had its oral literature. But historical times and more direct knowledge begin with information from Mediterranean writers. Especially rich, of course, is Tacitus's *Germania* (*c*. 98 AD), an ethnography that gives considerable attention to phenomena contemporary scholarship might denominate oral literature. At the same time an intra-Germanic tradition of writing was establishing itself within Germanic oral life, namely the runic writing that we thank for linguistic information and for at least hints about that oral life-world. The general view is that the futhark (or runic alphabet) was developed about the birth of Christ and that the earliest surviving examples are from the second century AD (Knirk 1993: 545–46). But the dates have been moved – tentatively and contentiously – back by finds in modern times, and Erik Moltke, for example, places the Meldorf fibula at about 50 AD and the development of the futhark 'as far back as 100–150 BC' or slightly more conservatively expressed: 'to say the year 0 +/− 100 (50) years'.[3]

The runic alphabet itself and its uses cannot be historically understood without Mediterranean sources and influences, and the same could be said also not only of some common types of inscriptions (e. g., maker claims), but also of some objects themselves (e. g., bracteates). My point is that Germanic literary culture, including its channels (oral, runes, manuscripts, etc.), has been impure, a hybrid from an early period. Newer studies of oral literature in medieval Europe are turning out to be studies of orality *and* literacy; for example, a contemporary collection of papers on the early medieval North is based

---

[2] A valuable recent work can serve as an introduction to the broader aspect of this chapter: Murdoch and Read 2004, with twelve mainly literary and cultural chapters by contemporary experts. Among predecessors of this book, an outstanding handbook of the field was (and still is) Schneider 1938, with nine somewhat more historically weighted chapters by great pre-War and transitional figures.

[3] Moltke 1985:64; similarly Moltke 1981:7; Antonsen 1998:150, citing Düwel and Gebühr 1981:161; and Düwel 1981.

on the idea of an orality-literacy continuum where surviving texts are to be placed without preconceptions; in other quarters the mixture of an all-pervasive background orality with influential elite literacy has been christened *Vokalität* and taken to characterize the early Middle Ages.[4] The ingredients and proportions vary by place and time, register and social class, genre and preservation; and in plotting any given text's position 'along the continuum' no automatic GPS can be trusted.

The old quibble about the oxymoron 'oral literature' should not detain us, even though Walter Ong's great synthesis introduces a subchapter with the title 'Did you say "oral literature"?' (1982: 10). Yes, the etymology of *literature* involves letters, and some folklorists still favour 'verbal art' for the unlettered equivalent. The problem of 'literature' (or equally of 'art') lies, however, not in how to conceive literature in the absence of writing (just one 'channel' among others) but in what, in essence, literature (or art) *is*. I will not attempt to answer the question 'What is literature?' But some traditional answers have contrasted literature with nonliterary discourse either because of a use of language that contrasts with ordinary language (as marked vs. unmarked; a subset of the grammar) or because of its fictive relation to the world ('the poet nothing affirmeth'), or both.[5] Roman Jakobson's famous discussion of the 'poetic function' would seem to be a theoretical vehicle well suited to the appreciation of 'literature' or 'verbal art' in a context of very limited background information like that on the oral literature of early Germanic *Vokalität*, where some of the haphazardly preserved snatches of discourse appear, as viewed retrospectively, to be striving toward verse, language on the way to literature.[6] But the hybridity of the cultural matrix cautions against rigid application of assumptions of purity.

The northern European pre-literary cultural traditions are grouped together primarily as a language group. Language is not DNA stock, and language and ethnicity do not always straightforwardly co-vary. But language is generally the non-negotiable central element of a culture, perhaps especially in the pre-modern world.[7] And when we find that a single basic poetics is shared across all the earliest Germanic peoples where verse is in evidence, it is reasonable to believe that the roots of this poetics follow the trail of the dialects back to the common proto-language. For the period of this common language – or grouping of closely related dialects – whose tight linguistic affinity began to fall apart about 200 AD, we can only imaginatively reconstruct an oral literature based on much later, but 'traditional', vestiges that happened to be recorded and preserved. But some of the earliest runic inscriptions do hint of the existence of a poetic language in the period of a Germanic proto-language still minimally differentiated into dialects. For example, a group of inscriptions on lance blades (the oldest being Øvre Stabu, 150–200 AD: **raunijaz** 'tester') has been persuasively interpreted as adumbrating a preform of the type of

---

[4] Ranković et al. 2010; Schaefer 1992; compare Amodio 2004.
[5] Ohmann 1971; 1974; Harris 1991: 10–12; 1979: 70–71.
[6] Jakobson 1960; now see also Beechy 2010. A recent discussion of 'Orality' precisely in the early Germanic context still echoes Ong on 'oral literature' (Dunphy 2004: 103); but despite views that differ from mine sufficiently to seem sometimes distinctly wrong, Dunphy's chapter should be read as one of the few recent efforts in precisely our area.
[7] See Watkins 1995: 7: 'Language is linked to culture in a complex fashion: it is at once the expression of culture and a part of it.'

verbal art we know much later from skaldic poetry,[8] and a few slightly later, but still Proto-Nordic, inscriptions are framed in alliterative language or use diction like that later marked as poetic.[9] By the time we get to the inscribed golden horn of Gallehus (c. 400), there is little doubt that the simple wording constitutes verse: *Ek Hlewa-gastiz Holtijaz horna tawido* 'I Hlewagastiz, son of Holta[gastiz], commissioned the horn.'[10]

If great literatures are supposed to begin with an epic,[11] this first preserved verse does not look auspicious; and if we adopt Erik Moltke's downbeat assessment – Hlewagastiz is an illiterate goldsmith, who copies the runes rather incompetently; the alliteration is accidental, the genre ordinary, and no verse is intended – it would be romantic to see even the seed of an *ars poetica* here. But there are good reasons for considering this line as a form of verse just antecedent to the forms we find in all early Germanic poetry. The second half-line scans nicely by Sievers' standards; the gratuitous presence of the patronymic provides alliterative adornment; and its clipping may show the language struggling toward the later attested syllabic patterning captured in Sievers' five types (1893). Even the mode of inscription suggests consciousness of verse: All words except *tawido* are incised with double lines, hatched to give the runes visual weight, but the line's last word (or foot), the least important and non-alliterating stress, is inscribed with single lines as if the 'author' wanted to mirror oral weight in script. Admittedly, *ek*, which is unstressed and even outside the metre, is incised with the same double lines; one could rationalize this as a visible symbol precisely that the pronoun is extrametrical and not here a proclitic. Wessén (1930) assumes plausibly, if prosaically, that lack of space is to blame for the single lines of *tawido*, and there is no denying the possibility. Simple as it is, however, this line of verse does undoubtedly deal at the beginning – or as close to the beginning of Germanic poetics as we can get with certainty – with *poesis* or 'making'.

In any case, we can with Winfred P. Lehmann and others,[12] take this early verse inscription as the humble first trace of the alliterative poetics, including metre, that

---

[8] Beck 2006; Harris 2010.

[9] Poetic language anticipatory of Gallehus may be found in the Kragehul spearshaft (Denmark c. 300), especially if Antonsen's reading is correct (1975:35–36): *ek erilaz Asu-gis$^a$las em. Uha haite* [...] (my capitalization and punctuation); Antonsen's translation: 'I am the *erilaz* of Ansugisalaz. I am called Uha [...]'; Krause's reading is less alliterative (1966:66). Another example is the Einang stone (Norway 350–400 AD; Antonsen 1975:39) with a metrical second half-line and the possibility of an originally alliterating name (*[ek Ra]da-gastiz runo faihido* '[I ...] painted the rune'; see Krause 1966:142–44); traditionally the name in Einang is completed with *[ek Go]da-*, but the alliterating element proposed here is common in names, and the whole name appears in Förstemann (1856:999: *Ratgast*).

[10] Text adapted from Antonsen 1975:41. The verb seems not to mean simply 'made' as in most translations (Wessén 1930:167–69; Lehmann 1956:28: 'contrived'); 'commissioned', i. e., 'brought about', is my guess based on the evidence I have seen. Antonsen and others who take the masc. nom. sg. *holtijaz* (an IE patronymic formation) as based on *holta-, a short form of *holta-gastiz, are surely right. Two equally possible etymologies of *hlewa-* are argued by different scholars (Antonsen 1975:41); I suppose I would favour PIE *k'lew-o- 'fame' (compare, e. g., Moltke 1985:88; Krause 1966:102).

[11] This canard of literary history looks different after one has read Watkins on the opening of a Trojan (Luvian) epic lay from the sixteenth century BC (1995:146–48)!

[12] Lehmann 1956:28–29; Russom 1998:1; von See 1967:1.

shapes Old Germanic poetry and lasts until remarkably late in outliers, as found in Iceland and in the Scottish/English alternative traditions, where, for one rare example, the young King James VI of Scotland wrote in his *Essayes of a Prentise, in the Divine Art of Poesie* (Edinburgh, 1584):

> Let all your verse be *Literall*, sa far as may be, quhatsumeuer kynde they be of, bot speciallie *Tumbling* verse for flyting. Be *Literall* I meane, that the maist pairt of your lyne, sall rynne vpon a letter, as this tumbling lyne rynnis vpon F:
> *Fetching fude for to feid it fast furth of the Farie.*

No need to comment on King James's taste. But his term for this accentual verse, 'tumbling', as opposed to 'flowing' syllabic verse, is not inappropriate; and his choice of genre, the flyting (a slanging match, competition of insults), is perfectly suited to the verse type. The late alliterative poets may have associated their own style with vigour and even violence: In his opening prayer the poet of the fifteenth-century *Alliterative Morte Arthure* asks God as Muse to let him 'werpe owte som worde at this tym'. Anyone seeking the historical roots of late tumbling verse or solid-built skaldic court-metre – indeed of any early Germanic verse and its late heirs – will be led back to Gallehus and, as the fountainhead, to the language features underlying it: the strong stress accent developed by Proto-Germanic in the last pre-Christian centuries and the linguistic features that devolve from the settlement of the variable Indo-European accent on the Germanic first syllable.[13]

## 2 'New' Comparative Poetics

Nineteenth-century scholars clearly recognized *affinity* as the key concept in comparing the poetics of Germanic languages; they further recognized dependence of the poetics on the languages themselves. But none of the older scholars mapped the territory of the intersection of language and poetics or clarified the chronological layering of the basic concepts involved more influentially than Andreas Heusler (1865–1940), especially in his *Die altgermanische Dichtung*.[14] Heusler, to whose brilliant work this chapter is a late tribute, sets out three basic concepts at the beginning of his study: *Urgermanisch* (Proto-Germanic); *Gemeingermanisch* (Common Germanic); and *Altgermanisch* (Old Germanic).

### 2.1 Ordering Affinity

'Proto-Germanic' refers to cultural features, most reliably linguistic features, which can be securely traced back to the period of linguistic community before about 200 AD and the departure of the East Germanic groups toward the Black Sea. Tacitus is the main

---

[13] For the dating of the accent shift see Voyles 1992:76–79; on initial accent in early Northwest Europe more generally, Salmons 1992. But my point is a standard one.

[14] The first edition was published in 1923; the edition of record is the corrected and augmented second edition, published posthumously in 1943 (the copyright is dated 1941, but the authoritative bibliography in Heusler's collected writings gives the later date). Important stages in Heusler's writings on the way to the version of 1923 were Heusler 1905, 1911–13, and 1920.

extra-linguistic witness to this cultural community, but his variegated picture shows that a 'cultural community' need not be imagined as uniform, whatever the logic of linguistic reconstruction. 'Common Germanic', strictly interpreted, should designate cultural features that were 'common to' all three branches, attested in North, East, and West Germanic, without reference to the history of the features (descent, diffusion, and, even in theory, polygenesis) or to any chronological criteria. (In other words, it does not matter to the Common Germanic quality of a feature whether it devolved from Proto-Germanic and therefore is material for reconstruction, whether it reflects intra- or extra-Germanic borrowing, or whether the feature originated separately under similar conditions.) Gothic, and East Germanic generally, have however left so little evidence of their poetics, that when the topic of discussion is literature, 'Common Germanic' has been more loosely applied, designating features shared by North and West Germanic (often called, within the restricted focus, North and South). Heusler's third category and the subject of his book, 'Old Germanic Literature', includes the Common Germanic – he instances, besides the alliterative metre itself, also genres such as magical charms and heroic poetry – but also all more or less native literature, even if it survived or developed in only one Germanic area, such as Iceland or England. This obviously much looser concept relies for full significance on our prior creation (mainly through linguistic comparison) of the Proto-Germanic and (mainly through cultural comparison) of the Common Germanic; with Old Germanic the operative criterion is negative, the *absence* of controlling influence from the Church or from Roman antiquity (1943: 6–8).

Such are the underpinnings, in Heusler's lucid interpretation, of this venerable approach. There are problems; for example, I have already suggested that it is impossible to get any real purchase on a period when absence of influence certainly existed, and for Heusler, who has plenty to say about outside influences (Irish, Roman, ecclesiastical), this definition is merely a starting point. The problems do not compromise what remains the most stimulating gateway into 'Old Germanic' literature and culture.

Heusler's great book, in its second edition of 1943, formed the crest of a long, slow wave of nineteenth- and early twentieth-century scholarship that took a comparative Germanic point of view. Since the Second World War, there have been excellent special studies[15] but little written for the general reader comparable to Heusler's *Die altgermanische Dichtung* – probably for obvious historical reasons. In the post-War period, reaction to the political appropriation of Germanic antiquity and growing internationalism have been among the forces reducing the prominence of the comparative Germanic approach. And yet in the thirty-seven volume (one more volume is in preparation) second edition of the encyclopedia of Germanic antiquity, the *Reallexikon der Germanischen Altertumskunde,* the post-War period has produced the apotheosis of detailed, professional scholarship in the area of older Germanic culture, history, archeology, and linguistics – a magnificent reference work (Beck et al. 1973–2008).

In English a very good guide book through Germanic poetics is – still – Winfried P. Lehmann's 1956 *The Development of Germanic Verse Form*, a book well written for the general reader by a prominent historical linguist with an appreciation and knowledge of

---

[15] One example is Beck 1965. More typically in the post-War period the reference field has become 'European' rather than 'Germanic'; two excellent examples, von See 1978, 1985.

poetry generally. One could carp (to use a favourite word of late English alliterative poetry) that its linguistics is not only mellowed out for this general reader but distinctly out of date. That may or may not matter; in any case, nothing comprehensive has replaced Lehmann.[16] A little more recent is Klaus von See's *Germanische Verskunst* (1967), a short, lively discussion stemming from the same kind of scholarly background as Lehmann's book and like his concerned to connect metrics and stylistics with history, literature, and humanistic issues – not, that is, only with linguistic issues. Von See largely rejects Heusler's most characteristic innovation in Germanic metrics, the isochronous interpretation of rhythm in terms of musically notated measures (*Takte* 'beats')[17] – a theory, by the way, based on the assumption of oral performance. But in its overall view, von See's 'art of Germanic verse' is a direct development from the great German-language tradition and especially from Heusler. Von See goes beyond Old Germanic, Viking-Age Scandinavian, and West Germanic verse (his three main chapters) to a brisk chapter on the decline of the tradition, the rise of end-rhyme, and modern survivals and revivals.

Too few English-language discussions in this area sit comfortably within the tradition of Lehmann and von See. An interesting recent article that does so is R. D. Fulk's 'Rhetoric, Form, and Linguistic Structure in Early Germanic Verse: Toward a Synthesis' (1996), an essay well worth pausing over. Fulk centrally stresses the dependence of poetics from language – a venerable theme. It is also Lehmann's central point – as von See recognizes (1967: 62–65) – and Russom too tries consistently to bolster Lehmann on this topic (1998: 204). Fulk, however, traces this dependence largely through *differences* among the Germanic traditions, a contrastive stylistics that mainly comes down to eddic vs. West Germanic. Lehmann, though of course he also discusses variety, more insistently asserts an underlying *unity* (e. g., 1956: 6); but perhaps this opposition is forced, just a 'half-full, half-empty' distinction. Fulk settles mainly on the difference in syntactic possibilities between stichic West Germanic (sponsoring long, complex sentences) and stanzaic North Germanic (which places severe restraints on complexity) and on the corollary of this difference in diction: emphasis on copia in West Germanic, less so in Old Norse, where the form favours spare narrative.[18] I am not sure, however, that 'steady pace' (Fulk 1996: 73) is a more apt description of eddic narrative than, for example, the 'leaping and lingering' of the ballad.[19] The *Hakenstil* of the epic, where enjambment rules and sentences frequently

---

[16] Crépin 2005 is a formidable handbook of poetics devoted to just *one* of the Germanic poetic corpora.

[17] Heusler 1925–29 (vol. 1, rpt. 1956); the theory is better known in its American variant by John C. Pope (1942). Von See's refutation takes in both forms (1967: 5–9).

[18] Fulk adds a possible 'more basic linguistic cause, as well. The loss of pretonic syllables in Norse, driving sentence particles such as articles, pronouns, and negative markers into enclitic position, discourages complex syntax' (1996: 75). This is truly interesting and truly linguistic (stanzaic form could be 'merely a cultural difference' (1996: 73) if 'merely' really applies here), but the explanation is too brief for my understanding. Compare Heusler 1920: 532–36 on syntactic enrichment.

[19] Lehmann strangely uses the term 'ballad' (1956: e. g., 26) where we would expect 'lay' (= *Lied* in the German tradition) for the short narrative poem; see Kittredge (Sargent and Kittredge 1904: xiv), who speaks of the Anglo-Saxons having 'ballads.' Today 'ballad' is reserved for the late medieval (and later) genre treated in ch. 16 by T. Pettitt (on the Late-Medieval ballad) in this volume; compare also ch. 15 by R. Wright (on Hispanic epic and ballad). On eddic poetry and the ballad, see Harris (forthcoming).

begin at mid-line, arguably provides 'a driving force forward' (Suzuki 2004:4, citing others), keeping an audience, as it were, on the hook as it waits for syntax at last to match verse structure. One can measure the richness of scholarly writing by the disagreements raised, and Fulk's well-grounded essay demonstrates the richness still left in this field.

Many works – 'rich' or not – have dealt with the metre, style, formulas, poetic diction and poetic syntax of specific texts (say, the *Heliand* or *Beowulf*) or groups of texts (the *Poetic Edda*),[20] and many of those make limited comparative forays within the Germanic literary world.[21] One difference from the wealth of pre-War writing in this vein is the cross-fertilization from oral studies and contemporary fieldwork.[22] Nineteenth-century scholars compiled repetitions and formulas,[23] but they usually treat such literature without special reference to the oral or mixed milieu in which it flourished until being recorded. Even the (often exciting) more recent essays on stylistic elements frequently lose sight of the oral conditioning of the poems; I mention only some examples that evince a pan-Germanic or a comparative perspective.[24] A clear desideratum, then, would be a new handbook, a version of Lehmann with input from von See, Fulk, and other recent scholars, but written with oral origins more consistently in mind.

## 2.2 Renewing Poetics

Besides more extensive attention to the conditions of orality and literacy, such an imagined handbook could incorporate a second 'new' element derived from Indo-European comparative poetics. In a recent, but already famous, book, *How to Kill a Dragon: Aspects of Indo-European Poetics* (1995), Calvert Watkins provides the theoretical structure and a massive exemplification of a 'new comparative philology' within the classic 'comparative method' (3–11; 1989), the newness inhering in philology's focus on poetics and perhaps in greater theoretical self-consciousness. In any case, a 'new' *Germanic* poetics in this spirit, as well as becoming self-aware as a subcomponent of Indo-European poetics, could constitute itself as a field for the same double action Watkins describes, from comparison of the descendents upward through the recognition of 'samenesses' toward reconstruction (compare Lehmann's emphasis on unity) and downward again through divergences toward derivation (difference, as in Fulk). This model, which is, in a sense, circular, though not 'vicious', would deal only with reconstruction to *Urgermanisch*, not with everything covered by Heusler's Common Germanic and Old Germanic, but as Watkins says of the comparative method in general, 'it is one of the most powerful theories of human language put forth so far and the theory that has stood the test of time the longest' (1995:4).

The categories of comparison on the Indo-European level – e. g., lexicon, formulas, themes/type scenes/topoi, syntax, rhetorical moves – yield to similar treatment on the

---

[20] For a stylistics bibliography of the *Poetic Edda* to c. 1984, see Harris 1985b: 131–32 and passim.
[21] A modern example: McTurk 1981 (on variation). A classic of Old English criticism dealing interpretively (and occasionally comparatively) with variation is Robinson 1985.
[22] 'Fieldwork' in ancient literatures begins at least with Parry and Lord, but for a recent example see Reichl (forthcoming).
[23] For example, Heinzel 1875; Meyer 1889; Paetzel 1913.
[24] Wolf 1965; Dronke 1978; Mittner 1955; Wilts 1968; Larrington 1993.

Germanic level; and according to Watkins' 'genetic intertextuality', even texts and text fragments may lend themselves to reconstruction. Watkins writes about Indo-European formulas that

> One of the characteristics of poetic language in many traditional societies is the extensive use of FORMULAS, whole phrases which are repeated with little or no variation, rather than recreated. Formulas play an important role in certain styles of improvised oral composition, where they have been much studied; but their usage is far more widespread, and reaches back into prehistory [...]. Formulas tend to make reference to culturally significant features or phenomena – 'something that matters' [...]. A proper linguistic theory must be able to account for the creativity of human language; but it must also account for the possible long-term preservation of surface formulaic strings in the same or different linguistic traditions over millennia. (1989: 792–93)

This emphasis on the 'ethnosemantics' of the formula, rather than on mere poetic utility, could be an important hint for a 'new' Germanic poetics. Admittedly, comparable intra-Germanic formula studies would be nothing strictly 'new'; for example, a model of ethnosemantic treatment of a cosmological formula is Lars Lönnroth's study of the cosmogonic formula 'iǫrð fannz æva né upphiminn' 'neither earth nor heaven existed' (1981). But a wider Indo-European frame of reference might help a small effort of mine: I identified a Norse and an Old English instance of a cursing formula, 'like a thistle', but the further parallels I cited and the background in Nordic texts seemed barely strong enough for the word 'tradition' I applied. If I could rewrite my 'Afterword' on the article (Harris 1975a [2002]), I would like to draw in Watkins's chapter '"Like a reed": The Indo-European background of a Luvian ritual' (1995: 335–42); the Luvian ritual is a curse with Indic parallels.

## 2.3 The Role of Metrics

Watkins labels the 'streams' of Indo-European poetics as 'formulaics', 'metrics', and 'stylistics' (1995: 12). Like Indo-Europeanists, Germanic scholars have mainly followed these as independent streams. Efforts at an integrated treatment (as in Lehmann or von See) will have to deal centrally with metrics, but metrics can be forbiddingly technical and difficult to link in detail with the rest of comparative poetics or with the larger field of comparative literature. As such, it will be the most difficult 'stream' or chapter in our imaginary update of Lehmann. Undoubtedly, linguistic training is crucial to the study of metrics, but I must agree with the complaints of one of the most recent contributors to the avalanche of scholarship on Old English metre (Bredehoft 2005: 4–5): It seems incongruous that at a time when the (few!) literary or cultural students of Old English verse are expected to know very little about the metrics of the poems they work through, 'critical studies of metre (or of the interaction between metre and syntax) have proliferated, with book length works by Hoover, Donoghue, Russom, Kendall, Cable, Fulk, Whitman, Hutcheson, Momma, and Blockley appearing since 1985' (4).[25] Besides his

---

[25] Hoover 1985; Donoghue 1987; Russom 1987; Kendall 1991; Cable 1991; Fulk 1992; Whitman 1993; Hutcheson 1995; Momma 1997; Blockley 2001.

own book, Bredehoft might have eked out his list with Obst, Creed, Suzuki, and Getty;[26] and this takes us only to 2005.

Despite the modest playing field implied by 'Old English metrics', these studies are engaged in serious intellectual work and not at all always with the *same* work. Fulk, in particular, uses metre to distinguish different chronological layers in a poetic corpus that at first seems relatively uniform (1992 and especially brilliantly in 2007). Bredehoft objects (2005: 7) that 'Fulk's *History [of Old English Meter]* is more properly a history of phonological issues in Old English verse' (than an actual history of its forms) – an objection that cannot obscure Fulk's enormous accomplishment. Bredehoft himself has some success in describing the verse component of a late Old English poetics developed from the classic form. Kendall, Donoghue, Momma, and Blockley are all especially interested in the complex integration of metrics with syntax;[27] but although many writers on Old English verse make some effort to address the oral and aural aspect and to accommodate the formulism of Old English verse, it is especially Kendall who actually builds in a Singer-of-Tales-like prehistory for his literate, probably monastic poet (1991: 2–4). In any case, this harvest of only two decades constitutes a tremendous block of difficult material for the hypothetical reviser of Lehmann; moreover, it does not encompass articles and contributions to reference works and focuses on only one of the poetic corpora constituting Germanic.

Old Saxon[28] and Old Norse, especially skaldic poetry,[29] have their own recent scholarly literature on metrics – though not a boom comparable to Old English. I mention only the most prominent or recent examples. But in the comparative context of our chapter, one group of writings on metrics deserves special reference here for their comparative thrust.[30] Geoffrey Russom's 1998 book applies his 'word-foot theory' (introduced in Russom 1987) to representative regular verses from the whole Germanic corpus (applied in Old Norse to *fornyrðislag*, not to the variant eddic metres or to skaldic). Though the book is technical and not comparable in humanistic appeal to that of Lehmann, the theory is not hard to follow on the basis of an acquaintance with Sievers' system such as a student of early Germanic poetry is likely to have. Russom examines the branches such as Old Saxon and Old Norse from within his system, however, not separately (like Lehmann and von See); but then the peculiarities of Continental West Germanic are separately discussed in chapters on Old Saxon and on the *Hildebrandslied*. Russom's final chapter summarizes, partly in the form of a history under Lehmann's title, 'the development of Germanic verse form'; and here Russom reaches back to cognate alliteration and initial word stress in the western Indo-European poetries and forward

---

[26] Obst 1987; Creed 1990; Suzuki 1996; Getty 2002.
[27] All centrally address Kuhn 1933, a study of verse syntax of primary importance for understanding style in Germanic poems.
[28] Hofmann 1991; Suzuki 2004 (with a copious bibliography on all aspects of the *Heliand* and Old Saxon *Genesis*). The preserved OS poetry is 'book epic', but Suzuki's literary introduction (1–7, with further references) shows the advantages of considering it against its more or less distant oral background.
[29] Gade 1995 (offering a bibliography for skaldic metrics). For Nordic, especially skaldic, poetics more generally see Clunies Ross 2005 (with full bibliography).
[30] A few further titles should be mentioned in this 'comparative' context: Fulk (forthcoming); Russom 2002; and Gade 2002, which is comparative within Scandinavian and fills a major gap there.

(in expectation of work to come) to the verse forms not yet covered by this history of the classic strain. F. H. Whitman (1993) makes a number of criticisms and proposals within Germanic verse, among them a rehabilitation of Heusler/Pope and musical notation at the expense of Sievers, and contributer some interesting thoughts about weak initial syllables (in types B and C and single-stress 'light' verses). But the most distinctive aspect (for the immediate purpose here) is Whitman's extensive comparison with other Indo-European metrics, especially western Indo-European (principally Italic, Old Latin, and Saturnian) accentual and alliterative metrics. Seiichi Suzuki has also written at length of this topic, with a derivation of Germanic metre from Indo-European.[31] Possibly a new 'development of Germanic verse form' would start, not with the old standard thoughts on the consequences of the accent shift learned from our language handbooks, but with further developments from this Indo-Europeanizing trend.

## 3 'Old' Comparative Literature

Whether or not poetics can be made 'new' (as discussed in the last *fitt*), it is not the only component of a comparative approach to early Germanic oral literature. We retreat from the linguistic brink to some account of studies of narrative content, genre and form, postponing for another day the topics that should follow: comparative function and literary history.

### 3.1 Heroic Legend and its Realizations

Who first noticed that certain stories, heroic or mythological, or their dramatis personae were widespread in the oral Germanic world? That OE *Weland* was ON *Völundr*, German *Wieland* (*Velent* in *Þiðreks saga*), that *Þeodric* was *Þjóðrekr*, *Dietrich*, and so on? The Preface to Snorri's *Prose Edda* (about 1220 if by Snorri) makes some equations with an English genealogy (e. g., 'Woden, whom we call Odin'). But a clearer recognition of narrative variation in connection with ethnic origin emerges from the Collector of the Codex Regius of the *Elder Edda*, the man responsible for assembling the main manuscript of the *Poetic Edda* about 1270 (or one of his predecessors). For example, the prose segment called *Frá dauða Sigurðar*:

> About the Death of Sigurd *In this poem* [the preceding *Brot af Sigurðarkviðu*] *the death of Sigurd is related and here it is said that they killed him outside. But some say this, that they killed him inside, sleeping in his bed. And Germans say that they killed him out in the forest. And the 'Old Poem of Gudrun' says that Sigurd and the sons of Giuki were riding to the Assembly when he was killed. But they all say that they treacherously betrayed him and attacked him when he was lying down and unarmed.* (Larrington 1996: 176)

Modern scholarship can be conveniently dated as beginning with Wilhelm Grimm's *Deutsche Heldensage* (1829) and the various prolegomena to it. Grimm's emphasis in this book was less on telling compelling stories (as in the *Household Tales* of 1812–15) than

---

[31] Suzuki 1988. Suzuki and others have produced quite a few articles relevant to the metrical relationship of Germanic to Indo-European; Suzuki 1988 must stand as representative.

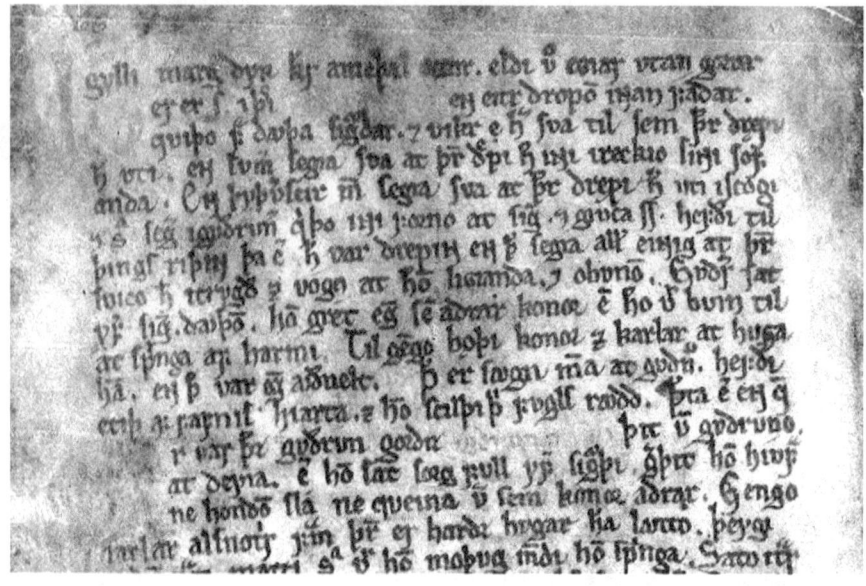

8 – *Frá dauða Sigurðar* in the *Poetic Edda* (Codex Regius, p. 66, beginning in line 2)

on collecting and listing 'witnesses' (*Zeugnisse*) to 'German' – by which he conventionally meant 'Germanic'[32] – heroic legend. The *Zeugnisse* range from major early sources (e. g., the old lay of Atli, *Atlakviða*, is No. 4) to brief seventeenth-century allusions, and later scholars (Müllenhoff, Jänicke) built separate collections of further *Zeugnisse* in the same spirit, which were included in the latest editions of Grimm.[33] An index made the *Zeugnisse* of 1829 usable for several purposes, but Grimm also concluded the book with an essay ('Ursprung und Fortbildung') that brought his thoughts on heroic legend together with brief story reconstructions – the prototype of all later treatments of the subject, whether popular or scholarly. Wilhelm Grimm's collection became the basis of a type of general presentation of Germanic heroic legend and, together with Jacob's *Teutonic Mythology* and the brothers' *Household Tales* and *German Legends*, has helped to shape the modern understanding of the major types of popular narrative tradition.

Hermann Schneider's *Germanische Heldensage* (three vols. 1933–34; vol. 1 in 2nd ed., 1962) and Heiko Uecker's *Germanische Heldensage* (about 140 pages; 1972) may stand as examples of the 'general presentations', but I intend no condescension by the term: these are vital scholarly works.[34] One might arrange the rest of the copious literature on heroic legend as grading off from broad coverage (for instance, Klaus von See's *Germanische Heldensage: Stoffe, Probleme, Methoden* of 1971) toward special studies

---

[32] There is now a definitive treatment of this often exasperating topic: Beck 2004.
[33] The exact additions and subtractions in the later editions are fairly confusing; see Grimm 1829 in the References to this chapter and Ehrismann's essay in the 1999 edition for some clarification.
[34] Two further standard surveys are Betz 1962 and Zink 1971.

(Caroline Brady, *The Legends of Ermanaric*, 1943).³⁵ Brady and Kemp Malone (e. g., 1959) are among the few examples of anglophone scholars who wrote specifically on Germanic heroic legend (or legends) from a position within this chiefly German-language tradition; among recent works, I am aware only of Haymes and Samples 1996, a book with an overview function like that of Uecker 1972 but covering a more limited segment of legend. Under the formula 'gods and heroes' one could cite popular surveys and storybooks. Von See's study of 1971, with its mixture of theory, criticism, and exposition, is the most challenging single title in the field of heroic legend and one of the best books I know on medieval narrative; its arguments will haunt much of the following brief discussion of larger topics within the field.

A distinction, obvious once noticed, must be made between the legend itself – that is, a story – and its realizations. The story of Sigurd's murder was known to the Collector in different 'multiforms', varieties of content; they must have been conveyed in different verbal or non-verbal representations. The distinction, a commonplace since structuralism's 'story vs. discourse' (compare the slightly longer discussion in ch. 5 above, p. 144), should be borne in mind when we read the provocative motto: 'Heldensage ist Heldendichtung' (heroic legend is heroic poetry). This exaggeration from the school of Heusler and Schneider did not really attempt to conflate story, 'heroic legend', with its realizations as specific instances of 'heroic poetry'. Rather the scholars meant that the mode of life of this kind of story was in its poetic realizations and especially that heroic legend was *transmitted* in poetic form. Clearly, however, a story, as a form of knowledge, is not identical with the vehicle by which it becomes known. Although knowledge is probably most widely transmitted in an oral world in question and answer, it is not impossible that the major, or even the exclusive, form of transmission of this (heroic) knowledge might be a very limited channel, but that seems very unlikely in this case. One important paper in the field reestablished the common-sense position against Heusler's turn-of-the-century aestheticism: Hans Kuhn's 'Heldensage vor und außerhalb der Dichtung' (1952; 'heroic legend prior to and independent of poems'). Kuhn's argumentation, however, is not theoretical (and certainly not structuralist), rising to general statement only in its concluding segment; though Kuhn's reasoning is so deeply immersed in the primary material (or for that reason!), this article should be high on the reading list of the present-day scholar in this area.³⁶

In practice most scholarship turns, not on disembodied story, but on the legend form of specific sources, often poems: does the difference between sources A and B reflect evolution or simple multiforms of the same story, or is poet C modifying the legend for identifiable purposes, and so on? Discussions that start with 'legend', i. e., story, usually default to poetry or confuse story with a prose rendering as *Sage* or saga; two recent essays on Germanic heroic legend add to their titles 'in/and Old English

---

³⁵ The bibliographies of Uecker 1972 are handy, but see also the fuller bibliography in Schneider 1933–34/1962 (covering 1928–60 by R. Wisniewski), continued to about 1985 in Beck 1988: 329–413 (by Beck and his students). The enormous evidence of these bibliographies makes any offhand attempt at order (like the gradation suggested here) seem hopeless, and yet Beck's bibliography is carefully arranged and potentially a great aid to study.
³⁶ Kuhn's essay acknowledges as predecessor Genzmer 1948 and was first published in Genzmer's festschrift. See further Uecker 1972: 13–15 on this topic.

literature/heroic poetry', sanctioning the default mechanism.[37] And yet something *can* be said about the stories themselves: for example, that they cater to an aristocratic audience, kings and their *comitatus*, that they run to tragedy, and so on. In his last chapter, von See (1971) successfully generalizes about the image of man in the heroic legend and finds the kernel of the tales in shocking scenes like Alboin's invitation to Rosimund to drink with her father, i. e., from the chalice made of his skull.

Discussions of essence (*Wesen*) often pose as questions of origin; and since its own origin with the Grimms, the scholarly conversation on the 'origin' of heroic legend has recognized three trends. Von See succinctly introduces them:

> What is the 'Germanic heroic legend' after all? Is it a stylized historical tradition, concentrated on human conflict? Or is it a historicized – and so also psychologized – myth which has sunk into non-sacred circumstances? Or is it a folktale (*Märchen*) that has been enriched and ennobled with tragic motifs?[38]

Von See's critical machine makes short work of the strong form of the fairytale theory, straightforward derivation, chiefly associated with Friedrich Panzer (1971:23–30; see Uecker 1972:7–9). *Beowulf*, probably Panzer's best-known case (1910), is still helpfully approached from narrative folklore (as in the excellent Stitt 1992); but folkloristics is not conceptually well suited to most of the field, and the differentiation from myth is itself a problem.

Both older and more productive is the coupling with myth. Uecker offers a quick typology of the greatly varying mythic approaches (1972:9–11). Most notable since the War are Otto Höfler's vision of deified heroes on a Greek pattern (his slogan converts the Heusler/Schneider thesis into 'Heldensage ist Heldenverehrung' 'hero worship')[39] and Franz Rolf Schröder's more flexible descent theory (especially in Schröder 1961). My article on Beow/Byggvir (1999) takes a Schröder-like approach and translates a useful passage, worth repeating here:

> It must be admitted that the Romantics – with their universal point of view, their deep understanding and spiritual sensitivity for extrasensory, religious, mythical realms – often saw things more clearly than did the later positivistic researchers and the purely aesthetic view of heroic legend which developed out of positivism. [Schröder might have in mind here Heusler's 'Geschichtliches und Mythisches in der germanischen Heldensage' and its patrimony.] But the Romantics went too far and wanted to derive *all* heroic legends from myths, and this insured an easy victory of the positivistic countercurrent. What they did not recognize (and in those days hardly could have recognized) is that every heroic legend ought to be investigated individually to see whether it has a mythic-cultic or an historical basis. Thus within the totality of the Germanic tradition two groups or layers are to be recognized that are different in structure and essence and at the same time present a sequence in time:
> 1. *the mythic-cultic layer*;
> 2. *the historical layer*.

---

[37] Frank 1991; Magennis 2010.
[38] Von See 1971:15: 'Was ist die "germanische Heldensage" also? Ist sie eine auf menschliche Konflikte konzentrierte, stilisierte Geschichtstraditon, oder ist sie ein in profane Verhältnisse gesunkener, historisierter und damit auch psychologisierter Mythos, oder ist sie ein mit tragischen Elementen angereichertes, veredeltes Märchen?'
[39] Höfler 1952, 1978 (the most developed of three versions of this study).
[40] Dumézil 1968–86. Von See thoroughly criticizes the ideas of Dumézil and his followers in von See 1988.

And to these can be added a

    3. *latest layer*, which has borrowed from *medieval narrative material* (fairytales, novellas, and the like). (1961:293)

Comparable to Schröder's point of view here is a contemporary monograph by Jan de Vries (1954), and one could speak of a resurgence of myth criticism after the period of positivism. Von See will have none of it, however (von See 1971:31–60; 1966). At one point he attempts to contrast myth with heroic legend by comparing a heroic lay to an *Aufreihlied*, a poem that lists the accomplishments of a god (32); the default mechanism is here in full force, diverting from story to vehicle and avoiding the question in what way the underlying stories resemble each other or not.

Not noticed by von See in this book of 1971 is another mode of myth theory for heroic legend, that of Dumézil, whose massive *Mythe et epopée* (beginning in 1968) was preceded by numerous publications of his own and his followers.[40] In general they tried to show how Indo-European myths, mythic schemas, religious functions, and socio-religious patterns had left their mark in 'historical' and heroic materials (some references and similar trains of thought in Old Norse in Harris 1999). Craig Davis (1996), in a valuable interpretative book on *Beowulf*, makes good use of the Dumézilian paradigm and also offers ideas on the end – rather than as usual, the origin – of heroic legend. Wilhelm Grimm, though, had already, in a passage of great beauty, intuited that heroic legend could be concerned with the demise of the heroic world it depicts and perhaps with its own demise.[41]

All scholars admit a major role for historical events in the rise of heroic legend; one could hardly come to another conclusion in view of historical figures such as Ermanaric, Theodoric (the Great), Attila, Odoaker, Theodoric (the Frank), Gundaharius (Gunther, etc.), Gibiche (Gjúki), and probably Brynhildr (if her prototype is the Frankish Brunichildis). And almost everyone agrees (mainly with Heusler) that historical events were personalized, psychologized, and made into family tragedies. But beyond this there are many shades of 'historical theory', for example the extent to which a real historical view or a political purpose should be read in. Von See (1971:61–95) and Uecker (1972:11–13) give good accounts and references. Probably we should with von See reverse Schröder's first two layers: the story from a historical context is privatized (doesn't rumour do that?) yielding the exorbitant or shocking kernel (Rosimund's toast); mythic motifs may enter, especially in the later Scandinavian versions, or, especially on the Continent, medieval folklore-related motifs (von See 1971:60). I would add sympathy for de Vries's idea of selection by homology with an 'archetype': 'From a historical event arises a heroic legend only then when an archetype has been recognized in its main figure.'[42]

---

[41]   'Wunderbare Werke ungenannter Dichter, erfüllt von reinster Poesie, schlicht und zwanglos, tiefsinnig und unausmeßbar, bewahren sie das Bild eines jugendlichen, in unverletzter Sitte kraftvoll blühenden Lebens. Sie verkünden zugleich den Untergang dieser Herrlichkeit und es scheint nicht, als ob spätere, wenn auch in anderer Hinsicht geistig begabte Zeiten, in welchen jener einfache Zustand und das Gefühl frischer Jugend verschwunden ist, fähig seyen, Werke dieser Art hervorzubringen.' (Grimm 1829:335 = 'Ursprung und Fortbildung', p. 1.)

[42]   de Vries 1954:162 (von See 1971:38): 'Aus einem geschichtlichen Ereignis entsteht erst dann eine Heldensage, wenn in seinem Träger ein Archetypus wiedererkannt worden ist.' De Vries uses 'archetype' here also in Éliade's sense, and the passage illustrates with cosmogonic motifs such as the slaying of a dragon.

Whatever else it is, an archetype is a repeated figure, and 'patterning', a recurring order, has played a significant role in the study of heroic legend, though more in folkloristic, structural, and cross-cultural traditions than in the Heuslerian strain we are chiefly examining. Olrik included heroic legend among the folklore forms that exhibited 'epic laws', structures of narrative more common in oral literature (1965 [1909]); Lord Raglan's well-known twenty-two point life pattern of 'the hero' included Siegfried, and this approach from 1936 had forerunners and successors in scholarship, where patterns were given psychological or ritual significance.[43] De Vries adopted neither wholly but shows considerable influence of the pattern approach to his question 'What is a hero?' (1963: 180–93; 1954: esp. 136–79). The consummation of this trend must be the recent and very substantial *The Epic Hero* by Dean A. Miller (2000), where various hero schemata come together with Dumézil and every imaginable reflex of structuralism and many influences from anthropology. Although the biography of 'the hero' shows only a few points of connection with the action of folktale, Propp's famous analysis has influenced students of *Beowulf*, offering an updated approach to the *Märchen* affinities of its narrative.[44] In fact, pattern has played such a large role in late nineteenth- and twentieth-century humanistic scholarship generally that it might be appropriate to ask why it is relatively less represented in the tradition of *Altgermanistik*.

## 3.2 Old Germanic Genres

Heusler had a firm sense of the text-types of his Old Germanic (oral) literatures, and they fell into 'higher' and 'lower' classes. The presentation of genres, with supporting material and discussion of problematic issues of individual texts and types, forms the core and bulk of *Die altgermanische Dichtung*. Heusler begins with the lower genres, supposed archaic and simple forms,

- from 'ritual poetry' (a wide variety of functional types somehow associated with ritual broadly defined, including hymn, prayer, legal verse, verse from wedding and funeral ritual, the magnificent Old Norse reconciliation oath, the *Tryggðamál*, and so on)
- on to 'magic charms' (again functional, often ritual, but a clear international type like the 'Second Merseburg Charm', with its echoes in the *Atharvaveda* and widely in Europe, and, for example, the Old English 'Nine Herbs Charm')
- and on to 'wisdom verse' (mostly the verse of 'sayings' and gnomes, but here also riddles),
- to 'memorial verse' (thulas, like the ancient lists of *Widsith*; the rune poems; sapiential poems of the *Edda*, which typically have lists at their core),

---

[43] Segal 1990 contains one forerunner complete, Otto Rank, *The Myth of the Birth of the Hero* (1909), Raglan's *The Hero* (1936), in excerpts, and Alan Dundes' long article 'The Hero Pattern and Life of Jesus' (1977), together with a good history of scholarship; one can look here, for example, for references and analysis on the famous pattern-study by Joseph Campbell, *The Hero with a Thousand Faces* (1949).
[44] Shippey 1969 and Barnes 1970.

- ending with the presumably most developed subgroup, the 'minor lyric' (a hodgepodge of short forms, including Old Norse improvised stanzas, *lausavísur,* and the flyting).

In this way Heusler leads his reader through the major representatives of virtually all the verse types in the poetic corpora of Old High German, Old English, and Old Norse and through all the most important early references (*Zeugnisse*) to this or that type of verse. There is no pretension (in this part) that we are reading a literary 'history', but implicitly we are encouraged to see the material as arranged in a cultural hierarchy from primitive word-magic to a degree of literary complexity that brings us to the threshold of the more aesthetically valuable literature. Heusler's is 'an order of words' not unworthy of Northrop Frye's phrase for the goal of the literary student.

Heusler's design in the book is thus elegant and powerful, leading 'up' to the higher genres, the sphere of the court poet and his aristocratic audience, and within this higher domain through the functionally transparent encomium finally to the heroic lay, his 'crowning genre' (124). The eulogy, widely paralleled on the Indo-European level, is attested from the Migration Period by Latin and Greek *Zeugnisse* (e. g., Priscus, Jordanes, Venantius Fortunatus), from the Merovingian period by *Beowulf*'s references to Hygelac's raid on the Rhineland, from the eighth century by Hrothgar's poet's improvisation on Beowulf's victory and by Widsith's self-promotion; beginning in the ninth century, we have, in Scandinavia, the riches of skaldic poetry. Tacitus's reference to the praise 'still' (*adhuc*) sung of Arminius (whose great victory over the Romans took place some ninety years before Tacitus wrote) causes Heusler problems: it must represent a 'forerunner' of the full-fledged praise poem (124). Heusler always seeks clear lines, and this genre should, like the heroic poem, be a creature of the militarization of the Migration Period, whatever its immediate origin. The fully extant West Germanic representatives, *Ludwigslied* (c. 881) and *Brunanburh* (c. 937) also require some special consideration (126–28); but in my opinion, the (oral)-literary ancestry of these poems is correctly placed within Heusler's overall plan.[45] The genre, which he names with the bipolar – or as recent scholars seem to think, schizoid – *Preislied/Zeitgedicht*, contains within it both tendencies: the tendency to list accomplishments of the patron and the tendency to narrate one or a few victories as 'news' or contemporary history. The model of the skaldic praise poems supports especially the encomiastic wing while these West Germanic battle poems support the other.

The twenty-five pages on 'The Common Germanic form of the heroic lay' (150–75) are arguably some of the most influential pages ever written in the historical humanities. Less than half the space is actually spent on historical matters: the earliest Latin and Greek allusions (*Zeugnisse*), chronicle summaries of lost heroic poems, the theory of Gothic origin within the limited period of the Migrations, possible outside stimulus (Armenian, Thracian, and the Roman *mimus*, for example), the theory of intra-Germanic narrative development out of praise poetry; a convincing picture of the life history (if not of the origin) of the heroic lay emerges with a South Germanic peak in the sixth

---

[45] Beck 1974; Harris 1985a: 249–51 (and other references, 274). For recent convincing modifications see Ebenbauer 1988 and Ghosh 2007.

century. The bulk of the chapter is Heusler's widely referenced phenomenology of the heroic lay, the description of form and structure, internal character, actors, types of fable, and especially verbal style. The following shorter chapter discusses all the types of lay attested only in Scandinavia and of course much later than the West Germanic remnants. It is a complex and strongly reasoned growth-chart of narrative: the lay (*kviða*) becomes a model for narrative mythological verse; there are younger heroic imitations of the old form and new forms treating the old Continental material or stories like it in dramatic or retrospective monologue. It is here that Heusler places most of the poems called elegies.

In the 1923 first edition, the penultimate chapter, 'Looking forward toward the epic' (*Ausblick auf das Epos*), is part of a coda of two symmetrical chapters: Old Germanic oral literature did not have epic in the sense of the long narrative poem about kings and heroes, only the short lay; real epic enters with writing and models like Virgil and his Christian imitators. *Beowulf* and even the *Heliand* are heirs of the heroic lay on one hand and of Virgil on the other. The original final chapter, 'Looking back over Germanic style' (*Rückblick. Germanischer Stil*), completed the coda, first, with caveats against such a thing as 'Germanic style' but finally with some success at capturing it, mainly under the concepts form, rhythm, and the dramatic. Heusler the philologist, habitually attendant upon the particular, seems uncomfortable with this basically art-critical concept; it seems as if his philological integrity undermines what must have been a desire for artistically strong closure.

Thus Heusler's treatment of the 'higher' genres, from the *Preislied/Zeitgedicht* through to 'book epic' shows literary entailment, cause and result, literary history in a largely oral zone, while the approach to the 'lower' genres presented static pattern except in the implicit evolution toward 'higher' (barbarian!) cultural forms. Together the picture presented is so elegant, complete, and convincing that I wonder that contemporary scholars in the area of oral literature or any branch of early Germanic do not feel obliged to begin with Heusler. They do not. But it is useful to distinguish between post-War German scholarship, where Heusler's views on the oral sources of the *Nibelungenlied* and 'epic' of the twelfth-to-thirteenth century seemed an obstacle to the newer understanding of those texts in their high-medieval context, and *our own* resolutely early medieval field.[46] In *Die altgermanische Dichtung* the 'prospect' (*Ausblick*) is one that looks ahead only as far as the ninth-century *Heliand* and the eighth- or ninth-century *Beowulf*. The serious effort to revise Heusler's model by Walter Haug is partly motivated by those high-medieval concerns (1975, 1980); Theodore Andersson's incisive response to Haug, however, not only gives a truer picture of Heusler on the early period but also explains for international or English-oriented readers the German reaction against him (1988).

There remain many points for productive disagreement. One is the place and history of elegy.[47] Another is the real existence of the lay as against (a looser sense of) epic, effectively the problem of idealization of literary categories, as debated by Haug (1975,

---

[46] For a pointed explanation of this resistance, see Andersson 1988; for a much broader treatment of the whole area covered by Heusler as background to the *Nibelunglied*, see Andersson 1987.

[47] My main thoughts on this subject: Harris 1983a, 1988, 1994, 2006, 2007.

1980) and Andersson (1988).[48] Still another is the possible existence of early oral epic on the South Slavic model (also a factor in the discussion of Haug and Andersson) as against memorial tradition.[49] I have already touched on the matter of 'story'. One particular very recent study of the origin and evolution of the heroic lay may be briefly discussed (Ghosh 2007). The author examines the historical background of his example, the fall of the Burgundians, with great care, caution, and skepticism (222–39); this carries over to the literary-historical portion of the article (239–52), although in the end his differences from Heusler seem to nuance rather than revolutionize (see the goals, 222). Some of Ghosh's points: oral heroic poetry will have evolved out of praise poetry, but forms will not have been frozen from the Migration period until the Carolingian period; the significance and function of the evolving heroic poetry will have changed when it was cultivated by distant folk groups (as the Franks took over the Burgundian narrative material); it will have taken longer (than Heusler seems to allow) for proper heroic legend to develop from eulogy, leading to a later peak for the lay. One might intervene that already for Heusler the genre we habitually call 'eulogy' (rather than 'eulogy-cum-contemporary history') contained historical impulses; Andersson (1988), in particular, demonstrates that Heusler did not rule out adventitious historical influences along the way of legendary development. The logic of Ghosh's modifications of the traditional picture is, however, persuasive; he makes room for legend as story (243) and by no means ignores Heusler's work.

*Die altgermanische Dichtung* is nearly ninety years old if we date from the first edition of 1923, and that dating seems proper when the two editions are compared: a great many details were changed in the second edition (1943: unnumbered first page of Foreword), but the only conceptual innovation is the addition of the chapters on the Icelandic sagas – important material but an excrescence on the elegance of the original form. It is a unique book in the annals of comparative literature – Hans Naumann's Foreword calls it 'innovative, totally one-of-a-kind, and inimitable'. I know of only one other closely comparable effort, Georg Baesecke's *Vorgeschichte des deutschen Schrifttums* (1940), which, though fiercely learned, is more compromised by its time, less literary, and intellectually not of Heusler's quality; one can learn from reading Baesecke but not imagine it as adaptable for contemporary use. Elsewhere we find only the Germanic prehistory of national literatures. A new version of Heusler's classic would have much to modify and amplify in the treatment of orality/literacy and performance and a vast updating responsibility for individual texts and groups of texts. A twenty-first-century comparatist would expect a more explicitly theoretical approach, especially to genre and the elements of composition below genre.[50] Assumptions about cultural evolution and the ethnic-historical background would become problematic, as they were not in Heusler's day.[51] Perhaps the 1920s was the last period when a comparative study of early Germanic poetry based on genetic relationship and cultural community could have been accomplished on the

---

[48] Stanley 1987; Frank 1991:96 and n. 13.
[49] Haymes 2000 and bibliography there; see also Mellor 2008 for a new beginning in eddic formula analysis and a fresh start on the relevance of oral theory. My views and early references on this subject are found in Harris 1983b, 1985b.
[50] My ideas in this area are to be found chiefly in Harris 1975b, 1979, 1990.
[51] For some notion of where studies in 'barbarian identity' stand today, see Ghosh 2007.

scale of *Die altgermanische Dichtung* – even if today we would settle for less self-assurance, clarity of argumentation, and verbal elegance. Even if a new version of Heusler's masterpiece is a less realistic idea than the same idea applied to Lehmann, it is perhaps not bad for a comparatist to retain it in mind as a distant model.

## 4 A Note on the Icelandic Sagas

Aesthetically speaking, Heusler spoiled the form of his 1923 book by the addition in the 1943 version of three chapters on the Icelandic sagas, inserted between his *Ausblick* and his *Rückblick* chapters. And despite the scholarly value of these pages (about 38 of them) on the saga, the topic is of debatable relevance. This Heusler may have recognized even as he made a good case: The sagas are literature (*Dichtung*) but prose and a uniquely Icelandic form of literature; they are arguably imbued with a heroic mentality, but this could be a new growth in the rulerless frontier settlement. In Heusler's day, however, it was common belief that the sagas were a late (thirteenth century) manifestation of Germanic continuity, a mentality that survived from the heroic age of the Migrations, and to some degree the literary heir of the heroic lay.[52] Sagas were certainly not 'Common Germanic'; but in the pre-War scholarly environment they fulfilled the criteria for 'Old Germanic', namely freedom from deep influence from the culture of the feudal court or from Roman antiquity.[53] Above all their 'root cause' (*Wurzelgrund*) lay in oral narrative art.[54]

Starting about 1960 new winds blew through scholarship on the saga literature, European winds that carried with them resistance to any alleged Germanic continuity and more affinity with the high-medieval period of actual saga writing. This cultural trend has only strengthened over the decades, but the question of orality and literacy in saga origin and continuity is still lively and of interest to readers of a handbook of medieval oral literature. Heusler (citing Liestøl 1930 as the chief authority) lays out the primary evidence for an oral narrative art, but he is well aware of the 'Icelandic School', writing in the 1930s about the sagas as the novel-like written composition of 'authors'. Heusler is usually identified with the codification of the positions into 'free prose' school and 'book prose' school, but near the end of his life he wanted to avoid these terms: 'They have something rigid about them and easily mislead into exaggeration, into distorted pictures of the opponent's point of view [...]. Is it so hard to think in terms of gradations, of shades of meaning?'[55] It was also in the 1960s that a new element was

---

[52] Andersson 1967:65-93 (ch. 3: The Heroic Legacy) gives a thorough history of research on this topic as well as his own new ideas. In the compressed context of the present article I speak simply of 'the saga' or 'sagas', but Heusler made careful distinctions among different classes within what we now refer to as 'the saga literature', sorting out the more or less native classes to which his criticism applied.

[53] The criteria of 1943 (202: 'das Vorrömische und Vorritterliche') deviate significantly from those of 1923 (1943:8: 'das von Kirche und antiker Bildung nicht greifbar bestimmte Germanentum').

[54] Heusler 1943:203: 'Wir sprachen eben von dem Wurzelgrund der isländischen Sagakunst [...]. Wir bekennen uns zu den Sätzen: Das Urphänomen der "Saga" ist eine mündliche Prosaepik.'

[55] 1943:216: 'Die Schlagworte "Freiprosa" und "Buchprosa" haben wir bis eben gemieden. Sie haben etwas Starres und verführen leicht zum Übertreiben, zu Zerrbildern der gegnerischen Ansicht [...]. Macht es soviel Mühe, sich in das Gradmäßige, das Abgeschattete hineinzudenken?'

introduced into the old free-prose/book-prose debate through Albert B. Lord's *The Singer of Tales* (1960). Although this strictly poetic theory did not directly apply to the prose sagas, the revitalized interest in the oral world in general did spread to saga scholarship. A great deal of interesting writing has ensued, the fortunes of the oral and written rising and falling in the kind of gradations Heusler desired. Luckily I do not have to trace these shadings or cite more than one recent work. Gísli Sigurðsson's book on the saga and oral tradition (2004) puts forth new ideas as well as summarizing the history of the subject (see the full bibliography). It can serve us as a contemporary handbook on this part of our subject, but a reading of Heusler on the sagas is still a rewarding pleasure.

## References

Amodio, Mark C. 2004. *Writing the Oral Tradition: Oral Poetics and Literate Culture in Medieval England*. Notre Dame, IN: U of Notre Dame P.

Andersson, Theodore M. 1967. *The Icelandic Family Saga: An Analytic Reading*. Harvard Studies in Comparative Literature 28. Cambridge, MA: Harvard UP.

−. 1987. *A Preface to the Nibelungenlied*. Stanford: Stanford UP.

−. 1988. 'Walter Haug's Heldensagenmodell.' In *Germania: Comparative Studies in the Old Germanic Languages and Literatures*. Ed. Daniel G. Calder and T. Craig Christy. Cambridge: Brewer. 127–41.

Antonsen, Elmer H. 1975. *A Concise Grammar of the Older Runic Inscriptions*. Tübingen: Niemeyer.

−. 1998. 'On Runological and Linguistic Evidence for Dating Runic Inscriptions.' In *Runeninschriften als Quellen interdisziplinärer Forschung. Abhandlungen des Vierten Internationalen Symposiums über Runen und Runeninschriften in Göttingen von 4.–9. August 1995*. Ed. Klaus Düwel and Sean Nowak. Ergänzungsbände zum Reallexikon der Germanischen Altertumskunde 15. Berlin: de Gruyter.

Baesecke, Georg. 1940. *Vor- und Frühgeschichte des deutschen Schrifttums, I. Vorgeschichte*. Halle: Niemeyer.

Barnes, Daniel R. 1970. 'Folktale Morphology and the Structure of *Beowulf.*' *Speculum* 45: 416–34.

Beck, Heinrich. 1965. *Das Ebersignum im Germanischen. Ein Beitrag zur germanischen Tier-Symbolik*. Quellen und Forschungen zur Sprache und Kulturgeschichte der germanischen Völker, N. S. 16 (140). Berlin: de Gruyter.

−. 1974. 'Zur literaturgeschichtlichen Stellung des althochdeutschen Ludwigsliedes und einiger verwandter Zeitgedichte.' *Zs. für deutsches Altertum* 85: 37–51.

−, ed. 1988. *Heldensage und Heldendichtung im Germanischen*. Ergänzungsbände zum Reallexikon der Germanischen Altertumskunde 2. Berlin: de Gruyter.

−, ed. 2004. *Zur Geschichte der Gleichung "germanisch-deutsch". Sprache und Namen, Geschichte und Institutionen*. Ergänzungsbände zum Reallexikon der Germanischen Altertumskunde 34. Berlin: de Gruyter.

−. 2006. 'Das *fuþark* und Probleme der Verschriftung/Verschriftlichung.' In *Das 'fuþark' und seine einzelsprachlichen Weiterentwicklungen. Akten der Tagung in Eichstätt vom 20. bis 24. Juli 2003*. Ed. Alfred Bammesberger and Gaby Waxenberger. Ergänzungsbände zum Reallexikon der Germanischen Altertumskunde 51. Berlin: de Gruyter. 61–79.

−, et al., eds. 1973–2008. *Reallexikon der Germanischen Altertumskunde*. 37 vols. Berlin: de Gruyter.

Beechy, Tiffany. 2010. *The Poetics of Old English*. Farnham, Surrey: Ashgate.

Betz, Werner. 1962. 'Die deutsche Heldensage.' In *Deutsche Philologie im Aufriß*. Ed. Wolfgang Stammler. 2nd rev. ed. Berlin: Erich Schmidt. III, 1871–1970. [1st printing 1957.]

Blockley, Mary. 2001. *Aspects of Old English Poetic Syntax: Where Clauses Begin*. Urbana: U of Illinois P.
Brady, Caroline. 1943. *The Legends of Ermanaric*. Berkeley: U of California P.
Bredehoft, Thomas A. 2005. *Early English Metre*. Toronto: U of Toronto P.
Cable, Thomas M. 1991. *The English Alliterative Tradition*. Philadelphia: U of Pennsylvania P.
Clunies Ross, Margaret. 2005. *A History of Old Norse Poetry and Poetics*. Cambridge: Brewer.
Creed, Robert P. 1990. *Reconstructing the Rhythm of 'Beowulf'*. Columbia: U of Missouri P.
Crépin, André. 2005. *Old English Poetics: A Technical Handbook*. Publications de l'association des médiévistes de l'enseignement supérieur, hors série 12. Paris: AMAES.
Davis, Craig. 1996. *'Beowulf' and the Demise of Germanic Legend in England*. New York: Garland.
de Vries, Jan. 1954. *Betrachtungen zum Märchen, besonders in seinem Verhältnis zu Heldensage und Mythos*. FF Communications 150. Helsinki: Academia Scientiarum Fennica.
–. 1963. *Heroic Song and Heroic Legend*. Trans. B. J. Timmer. London: OUP. [Dutch or. 1959.]
Donoghue, Daniel. 1987. *Style in Old English Poetry: The Test of the Auxiliary*. New Haven: Yale UP.
Dronke, Ursula. 1978. 'Le caractère de la poésie germanique héroïque.' In her *Barbara et Antiquissima Carmina* (with Peter Dronke). Publicaciones del Seminario de Literatura Medieval y Humanística. Barcelona: Facultad de Letras. 7–26.
Dumézil, Georges. 1968–86. *Mythe et épopée*. 3 vols. Paris: Gallimard. [Rpt. 1995.]
Dunphy, R. Graeme. 2004. 'Orality.' In Murdoch and Read 2004: 103–18.
Düwel, Klaus. 1981. 'The Meldorf Fibula and the Origin of Runic Writing.' *Michigan Germanic Studies* 7.1: 8–14 (with discussion, 15–18).
–, and Michael Gebühr. 1981. 'Die Fibel von Meldorf und die Anfänge der Runenschrift.' *Zs. für deutsches Altertum* 110: 159–75.
Ebenbauer, Alfred. 1988. 'Heldenlied und "Historisches Lied" im Frühmittelalter – und davor.' In Beck 1988: 15–34.
Föstemann, Ernst. 1856. *Altdeutsches Namenbuch*. Vol. 1. Nordhausen.
Frank, Roberta. 1991. 'Germanic Legend in Old English Literature.' In *The Cambridge Companion to Old English Literature*. Ed. Malcolm Godden and Michael Lapidge. Cambridge: CUP. 88–106.
Fulk, Robert D. 1992. *A History of Old English Meter*. Philadelphia: U of Pennsylvania P.
–. 1996. 'Rhetoric, Form, and Linguistic Structure in Early Germanic Verse: Toward a Synthesis.' *International Journal for Germanic Linguistics and Semiotic Analysis* 1.1: 63–88.
–. 2007. 'Old English Meter and Oral Tradition: Three Issues Bearing on Poetic Chronology.' *JEGP* 106: 304–24.
–. Forthcoming. 'Old Germanic Prosody.' In *The Princeton Encyclopedia of Poetry and Poetics*. 4th rev. ed. Ed. Stephen Cushman.
Gade, Kari Ellen. 1995. *The Structure of Old Norse 'Dróttkvætt' Poetry*. Islandica 49. Ithaca, NY: Cornell UP.
–. 2002. 'History of Old Nordic Metrics.' In *The Nordic Languages: An International Handbook of the History of the North Germanic Languages*. Ed. Oskar Bandle et al. 2 vols. Handbücher zur Sprach- und Kommunikationswissenschaft 22. Berlin: de Gruyter. I, 856–70.
Genzmer, Felix. 1948. 'Vorzeitsaga und Heldenlied.' In *Festschrift Paul Kluckhohn und Hermann Schneider gewidmet zu ihrem 60. Geburtstag herausgegeben von ihren Tübinger Schülern*. Tübingen: Mohr. 1–31. [Rpt. in Hauck 1961: 102–37.]
Getty, Michael. 2002. *The Metre of Beowulf: A Constraint-Based Approach*. Topics in English Linguistics 36. Berlin: Mouton de Gruyter.
Ghosh, Shami. 2007. 'On the Origins of Germanic Heroic Poetry: A Case Study of the Legend of the Burgundians.' *BGDSL* 129: 222–52.
Green, D. H. 1998. *Language and History in the Early Germanic World*. Cambridge: CUP.
Grimm, Wilhelm. 1829. *Die deutsche Heldensage*. Göttingen. [2nd ed. rev. Karl Müllenhoff. Berlin, 1867. 3rd ed. rev. Reinhold Steig. Gütersloh, 1889. 4th ed. rev. Siegfried Gutenbrunner.

Unter Hinzufügung der Nachträge von Karl Müllenhoff und Oskar Jänicke aus der *Zs. für deutsches Altertum*. Darmstadt: WB, 1957. New ed. Otfrid Ehrismann in Jacob Grimm and Wilhelm Grimm, *Werke*, Abt. II, Bd. 36, 1–2. 2 vols. Hildesheim: Olms–Weidmann, 1999.]

Harris, Joseph. 1975a. 'Cursing with the Thistle: "Skírnismál" 31, 6–8 and OE Metrical Charm 9, 16–17.' *Neuphilologische Mitteilungen* 76: 26–33. [Rpt. with an Afterword in *The Poetic Edda: Essays on Old Norse Mythology*. Ed. Paul Acker and Carolyne Larrington. New York: Routledge, 2002. 82–93.]

–. 1975b. 'Genre in the Saga Literature: a Squib.' *Scandinavian Studies* 47: 427–36.

–. 1979. 'The *senna*: From Description to Literary History.' *Michigan Germanic Studies* 5.1: 65–74.

–. 1983a. 'Elegy in Old English and Old Norse: A Problem in Literary History.' In *The Old English Elegies: New Essays in Criticism and Research*. Ed. Martin Green. Rutherford, NJ: Fairleigh Dickinson UP. 46–56. [Or. 1982.]

–. 1983b. 'Eddic Poetry as Oral Poetry: The Evidence of Parallel Passages in the Helgi Poems for Questions of Composition and Performance.' In *Edda: A Collection of Essays*. Ed. Robert J. Glendinning and Haraldur Bessason. Univerity of Manitoba Icelandic Studies 4. [Winnipeg:] U of Manitoba P. 210–42.

–. 1985a. 'Die altenglische Heldendichtung.' In von See 1985: 237–76.

–. 1985b. 'Eddic Poetry.' In *Old Norse-Icelandic Literature: A Critical Guide*. Ed. Carol J. Clover and John Lindow. Islandica 45. Ithaca, NY: Cornell UP. 68–156. [Rpt. Toronto: U of Toronto P. 2005.]

–. 1988. 'Hadubrand's Lament: On the Origin and Age of Elegy in Germanic.' In Beck 1988: 81–114.

–. 1990. 'Reflections on Genre and Intertextuality in Eddic Poetry (with special reference to *Grottasöngr*).' In *Poetry in the Scandinavian Middle Ages: Atti del 12° Congresso internazionale di studi sull'alto medioevo: The Seventh International Saga Conference, Spoleto 4–10 settembre 1988*. Ed. Teresa Pàroli. Spoleto: Centro italiano di studi sull'alto medioevo. 231–43.

–. 1991. 'Introduction.' In *The Ballad and Oral Literature*. Ed. J. Harris. Harvard English Studies 17. Cambridge, MA: Harvard UP. 1–17.

–. 1994. 'A Nativist Approach to *Beowulf*: The Case of Germanic Elegy.' In *Companion to Old English Poetry*. Ed. Henk Aertsen and Rolf H. Bremmer, Jr. Amsterdam: VU UP. 45–62.

–. 1999. 'The Dossier on Byggvir, God and Hero. *Cur deus homo*.' *Arv: Nordic Yearbook of Folklore* 55: 7–23.

–. 2006. '*Erfikvæði* – Myth, Ritual, Elegy.' In *Old Norse Religion in Long-Term Perspectives: Origins, Changes and Interactions. An International Conference in Lund, Sweden, June 3–7, 2004*. Ed. Anders Andrén et al. Vägar till Midgård 8. Lund: Nordic Academic P. 267–71.

–. 2007. 'Heroic Poetry and Elegy: *Beowulf*'s Lay of the Last Survivor.' *9. Pöchlarner Heldenliedgespräch: Heldenzeiten – Heldenräume*. Ed. Johannes Keller and Florian Kragl. Philologia Germanica 28. Vienna: Fassbaender. 27–41.

–. 2010. 'Old Norse Memorial Discourse, between Orality and Literacy.' In Ranković et al. 2010: 119–33.

–. Forthcoming. 'Eddic Poetry and the Ballad: Voice, Vocality, and Performance, with Special Reference to DgF1.' In *Child's Children: Ballad Study and its Legacies*. Ed. J. Harris and Barbara Hillers. Trier: WVT.

Hauck, Karl, ed. 1961. *Zur germanisch-deutschen Heldensage. Sechzehn Aufsätze zum neuen Forschungsstand*. Bad Homburg: Gentner.

Haug, Walter. 1975. 'Andreas Heuslers Heldensagenmodell: Prämissen, Kritik, und Gegenentwurf.' *Zs. für deutsches Altertum* 104: 273–92.

–. 1980. 'Normatives Modell oder hermeneutisches Experiment: Überlegungen zu einer grundsätzlichen Revision des Heuslerschen Nibelungen-Modells.' *Montfort: Vierteljahresschrift für Geschichte und Gegenwart Vorarlbergs* 32: 212–26.

Haymes, Edward R. 2000. 'Heldenlied und Eddalied.' In *Erzählen im mittelalterlichen Skandinavien*. Ed. Robert Nedoma et al. Vienna: Praesens. 9–20.

–, and Susann T. Samples. 1996. *Heroic Legends of the North: An Introduction to the Nibelung and Dietrich Cycles*. New York: Garland.

Heinzel, Richard. 1875. *Über den Stil der altgermanischen Poesie*. Strassburg.

Heusler, Andreas. 1905. *Lied und Epos in germanischer Sagendichtung*. Dortmund: Ruhfus.

–. 1911–13. 'Dichtung.' *Reallexikon der germanischen Altertumskunde*. Ed. Johannes Hoopes. 4 vols. Berlin: de Gruyter. I, 439–62.

–. 1920. 'Heliand, Liedstil und Epenstil.' *Zs. für deutsches Altertum* 57: 1–48. [Cited from rpt. in *Kleine Schriften*, 2 vols. Berlin: de Gruyter, 1969. I, 517–65.]

–. 1925–29. *Deutsche Versgeschichte mit Einschluß des altenglischen und altnordischen Stabreimverses*. 3 vols. Grundriss der germanischen Philologie 8/1. Berlin: de Gruyter. [2nd ed. 1956. Vol. 1.]

–. 1943. *Die altgermanische Dichtung*. 2nd rev. ed. Potsdam: Athenaion.

Höfler, Otto. 1952. *Der Runenstein von Rök und die germanische Individualweihe*. Germanisches Sakralkönigtum 1. Tübingen: Niemeyer; Cologne: Böhlau.

–. 1978. *Siegfried, Arminius und der Nibelungenhort*. SB der Österreichischen AW, phil.-hist. Kl. 332. Vienna: Österreichische AW.

Hofmann, Dietrich. 1991. *Die Versstrukturen der altsächsischen Stabreimgedichte Heliand und Genesis*. 2 vols. Heidelberg: Winter.

Honko, Lauri, ed. 2000. *Textualization of Oral Epics*. Trends in Linguistics: Studies and Monographs 128. Berlin: Mouton de Gruyter.

–. 2003. 'The Quest for the Long Epic: Three Cases.' In *Dynamics of Tradition: Perspectives on Oral Poetry and Folk Belief*. Ed. Lotte Tarkka. Helsinki: Finnish Literature Society. 191–212.

Hoover, David. 1985. *A New Theory of Old English Meter*. New York: Lang.

Hutcheson, B. R. 1995. *Old English Metre*. Cambridge: Brewer.

Jakobson, Roman. 1960. 'Closing Statement: Linguistics and Poetics.' In *Style in Language*. Ed. Thomas A. Sebeok. Cambridge, MA: MIT P. 350–77.

Kendall, Calvin B. 1991. *The Metrical Grammar of 'Beowulf.'* CSASE 5. Cambridge: CUP.

Knirk, James E. 1993. 'Runes and Runic Inscriptions.' In *Medieval Scandinavia: An Encyclopedia*. Ed. Phillip Pulsiano et al. New York: Garland. 445–52.

Krause, Wolfgang. 1966. *Die Runeninschriften im älteren Futhark*. (With contributions from Herbert Jankuhn.) 2 vols. Abhandlungen der AW in Göttingen, Philol.-hist. Klasse, 3rd series 65. Göttingen: Vandenhoeck & Ruprecht.

Kuhn, Hans. 1933. 'Zur Wortstellung und -betonung im Altgermanischen.' *BGDSL* 57: 1–109. [Rpt. in his *Kleine Schriften*. 4 vols. Ed. D. Hofmann et al. Berlin: de Gruyter, 1969–78. I, 18–103.]

–. 1952. 'Heldensage vor und außerhalb der Dichtung.' In *Edda, Skalden, Saga: Festschrift zum 70. Geburtstag von Felix Genzmer*. Heidelberg: Winter. 262–78. [Rpt. in Hauck 1961: 173–94.]

Larrington, Carolyne. 1993. *A Store of Common Sense: Gnomic Theme and Style in Old Icelandic and Old English Wisdom Poetry*. Oxford: Clarendon.

–, trans. 1996. *The Poetic Edda*. Oxford: OUP.

Lehmann, Winfred P. 1956. *The Development of Germanic Verse Form*. Austin: U of Texas P and Linguistic Society of America.

Liestøl, Knut. 1930. *The Origin of the Icelandic Family Sagas*. Trans. A. G. Jayne. Oslo: Instituttet for sammenlignende kulturforskning. [Norwegian or. 1929.]

Lönnroth, Lars. 1981. '"Iǫrð fannz æva né upphiminn": A Formula Analysis.' In *Speculum Norroenum: Norse Studies in Memory of Gabriel Turville-Petre*. Ed. Ursula Dronke et al. Odense: Odense UP. 310–27.

Lord, Albert B. 1960. *The Singer of Tales*. Cambridge, MA: Harvard UP. [Re-edition with a CD and a new introduction by Stephen Mitchell and Gregory Nagy, 2000.]

Magennis, Hugh. 2010. 'Germanic Legend and Old English Heroic Poetry.' In *A Companion to Medieval Poetry*. Ed. Corinne Saunders. Oxford: Wiley-Blackwell. 85–100.
Malone, Kemp. 1959. *Studies in Heroic Legend and in Current Speech*. Ed. Stefán Einarsson and Norman E. Eliason. Copenhagen: Rosenkilde and Bagger.
McTurk, Rory. 1981. 'Variation in *Beowulf* and the *Poetic Edda*: A Chronological Experiment.' In *The Dating of Beowulf*. Ed. Colin Chase. Toronto: U of Toronto P. 141–60.
Mellor, Scott A. 2008. *Analyzing Ten Poems from 'The Poetic Edda': Oral Formula and Mythic Patterns*. Lewiston, ME: Mellen.
Meyer, Richard M. 1889. *Die altgermanische Poesie nach ihren formelhaften Elementen beschrieben*. Berlin. [Rpt. Hildesheim: Olms, 1985.]
Miller, Dean A. 2000. *The Epic Hero*. Baltimore: The Johns Hopkins UP.
Mittner, Ladislao. 1955. *Wurd. Das Sakrale in der altgermanischen Epik*. Bibliotheca Germanica 6. Bern: Francke.
Moltke, Erik. 1981. 'The Origins of the Runes.' *Michigan Germanic Studies* 7.1: 3–7.
–. 1985. *Runes and their Origin: Denmark and Elsewhere*. Trans. Peter G. Foote. [Copenhagen]: National Museum of Denmark.
Momma, H. 1997. *The Composition of Old English Poetry*. CSASE 20. Cambridge: CUP.
Murdoch, Brian, and Malcom Read, eds. 2004. *Early Germanic Literature and Culture*. Rochester, NY: Camden House.
Niles, John D. 1999. *Homo narrans: The Poetics and Anthropology of Oral Literature*. Philadelphia: U of Pennsylvania P.
Obst, Wolfgang. 1987. *Der Rhythmus des 'Beowulf'. Eine Akzent- und Takttheorie*. Anglistische Forschungen 187. Heidelberg: Winter.
Ohmann, Richard. 1971. 'Speech Acts and the Definition of Literature.' *Philosophy and Rhetoric* 4: 1–19.
–. 1974. 'Speech, Literature and the Space Between.' *New Literary History* 5: 37–63.
Olrik, Axel. 1965. 'Epic Laws of Folk Narrative.' In *The Study of Folklore*. Ed. Alan Dundes. Englewood Cliffs, NJ: Prentice-Hall. 129–41. [Or. published as 'Epische Gesetze der Volksdichtung.' *Zs. für deutsches Altertum* 51 (1909): 1–12.]
Ong, Walter. 1982. *Orality and Literacy: The Technologizing of the Word*. London: Methuen.
Paetzel, Walther. 1913. *Die Variationen in der altgermanischen Alliterationspoesie*. Palaestra 48. Berlin: Mayer & Müller.
Panzer, Friedrich. 1910. *Studien zur germanischen Sagengeschichte. I. Beowulf*. Munich: Beck.
Pope, John C. 1942. *The Rhythm of 'Beowulf'*. New Haven: Yale UP. [2nd ed. 1966.]
Ranković, Slavica, et al., eds. 2010. *Along the Oral-Written Continuum: Types of Texts, Relations and their Implications*. Utrecht Studies in Medieval Literacy 20. Turnhout: Brepols.
Reichl, Karl. 2000. *Singing the Past: Turkic and Medieval Heroic Poetry*. Ithaca, NY: Cornell UP.
–. Forthcoming. '"Swutol sang scopes": Field Notes on the Performance of *Beowulf*.' In *Beowulf at Kalamazoo: Essays on Translation and Performance*. Ed. Jana K. Schulman and Paul E. Szarmach. Studies in Medieval Culture 50. Kalamazoo: Medieval Institute, Western Michigan U.
Robinson, Fred C. 1985. *Beowulf and the Appositive Style*. Knoxville: U of Tennessee P.
Russom, Geoffrey. 1987. *Old English Meter and Linguistic Theory*. Cambridge: CUP.
–. 1998. *Beowulf and Old Germanic Metre*. CSASE 23. Cambridge: CUP.
–. 2002. 'A Bard's-Eye View of the Germanic Syllable.' *JEGP* 101: 305–28.
Salmons, Joe. 1992. *Accentual Change and Language Contact: Comparative Survey and a Case Study of Early Northern Europe*. Stanford: Stanford UP.
Sargent, Helen Child, and George Lyman Kittredge, eds. 1904. *English and Scottish Popular Ballads*. Edited from the Collections of Francis James Child. Boston: Houghton, Mifflin and Co.
Schaefer, Ursula. 1992. *Vokalität: Altenglische Dichtung zwischen Mündlichkeit und Schriftlichkeit*. ScriptOralia 39. Tübingen: Narr.

Schneider, Hermann. 1933–34. *Germanische Heldensage*. 2 vols. in 3. Berlin: de Gruyter. [Vol. 1: *Deutsche Heldensage*, 2nd ed. with bibliographical appendix by R. Wisniewski. Berlin: de Gruyter, 1962.]
–, ed. 1938. *Germanische Altertumskunde*. Munich: Beck. [2nd printing, corrected, 1951.]
Schröder, Franz Rolf. 1961.'Mythos und Heldensage.' In Hauck 1961:285–315. [Rev. from or. in *GRM* 36 (1955): 1–21.]
See, Klaus von. 1966. 'Germanische Heldensage: Ein Forschungsbericht.' *Göttingische Gelehrte Anzeigen* 218:52–98. [Rpt. in his *Edda, Saga, Skaldendichtung: Aufsätze zur skandinavischen Literatur des Mittelalters*. Heidelberg: Winter, 1981. 107–53.]
–. 1967. *Germanische Verskunst*. Stuttgart: Metzler.
–. 1971. *Germanische Heldensage: Stoffe, Probleme, Methoden. Eine Einführung*. Frankfurt a. M.: Athenäum.
–, ed. 1978. *Europäische Heldendichtung*. Wege der Forschung 500. Darmstadt: WB.
–, ed. 1985. *Europäisches Frühmittelalter*. Neues Handbuch der Literaturwissenschaft 6. Wiesbaden: AULA.
–. 1988. *Mythos und Theologie im skandinavischen Hochmittelalter*. Skandinavistische Arbeiten 8. Heidelberg: Winter.
Segal, Robert A., ed. 1990. *In Quest of the Hero*. Princeton: Princeton UP.
Shippey, Thomas A. 1969.'The Fairy-Tale Structure of *Beowulf*.' *Notes and Queries*, N. S. 16:2–11.
Sievers, Eduard. 1893. *Altgermanische Metrik*. Halle: Niemeyer.
Sigurðsson, Gísli. 2004. *The Medieval Icelandic Saga and Oral Tradition: A Discourse on Method*. Trans. Nicholas Jones. Publications of the Milman Parry Collection of Oral Literature 2. Cambridge, MA: The Milman Parry Collection of Oral Literature, Harvard University.
Stanley, Eric Gerald. 1987. 'The Germanic "Heroic Lay" of Finnesburg.' In his *A Collection of Papers with Emphasis on Old English Literature*. Publications of the Dictionary of Old English 3. Toronto: Pontifical Institute of Mediaeval Studies. 281–97.
Stitt, J. Michael. 1992. *Beowulf and the Bear's Son: Epic, Saga, and Fairytale in Northern Germanic Tradition*. New York: Garland.
Suzuki, Seiichi. 1988.'The Indo-European Basis of Germanic Alliterative Verse.' *Lingua* 75:1–24.
–. 1996. *The Metrical Organization of Beowulf: Prototype and Isomorphism*. Berlin: Mouton de Gruyter.
–. 2004. *The Metre of Old Saxon Poetry: The Remaking of Alliterative Tradition*. Cambridge: Brewer.
Uecker, Heiko. 1972. *Germanische Heldensage*. Stuttgart: Metzler.
Voyles, Joseph B. 1992. *Early Germanic Grammar: Pre-, Proto-, and Post-Germanic Languages*. New York: Harcourt-Brace.
Watkins, Calvert. 1989.'New Parameters in Historical Linguistics, Philology, and Culture History.' *Language* 65:783–99. [Rpt. in *Selected Writings*. 2 vols. Innsbrucker Beiträge zur Sprachwissenschaft. Innsbruck: Institut für Sprachwissenschaft der Universität Innsbruck. I, 315–31.]
–. 1995. *How to Kill a Dragon: Aspects of Indo-European Poetics*. Oxford: OUP.
Wax, Rosalie. 1969. *Magic, Fate, and History: The Changing Ethos of the Vikings*. Lawrence, KS: Coronado.
Wessén, Elias. 1930. 'Runinskriften på Gallehus-hornet. Några anmärkningar.' *Fornvännen* 25:165–74.
Whitman, F. H. 1993. *A Comparative Study of Old English Metre*. Toronto: U of Toronto P.
Wilts, Ommo. 1968.'Formprobleme germanischer Spruchdichtung.' Ph.D. Thesis, University of Kiel.
Wolf, Alois. 1965. *Gestaltungskerne und Gestaltungsweisen in der altgermanischen Heldendichtung*. Munich: Fink.
Zink, Georges. 1971.'Heldensage.' In *Kurzer Grundriß der germanischen Philologie bis 1500*. Ed. Ludwig Erich Schmitt. 2 vols. Berlin: de Gruyter. 2:1–47.

# 9  Oral Tradition and Performance in Medieval Ireland

*Joseph Falaky Nagy*

In a survey of references to oral tradition in the literature of the European Middle Ages, Karl Reichl, citing the work of the poet Gottfried of Strassburg, singles out the figure of the young Tristan in the court of King Mark, playing the harp (only one of the many instruments he can play), and singing a Breton lay, switching back and forth among the various languages he knows, as a 'paradigm of performativity' (2005: 167–68). This observation has special resonance for a Celticist, beyond the salient fact that it highlights the 'Breton lay', a genre of medieval narrative poetry the subject matter of which was attributed to a Celtic-language tradition. In his observation Reichl associates the 'live', dynamic background to medieval literature with a figure whose story, more than that of any other member of the extensive cast of characters featured in the medieval narrative repertoire known as the 'Matter of Britain', brings together the various peoples of northwest Europe that in modern times we have come to call the 'Celts'. According to that story in a nutshell, the heroic knight Tristan (a figure of medieval British tradition alternatively, depending on the source, associated with the Picts, the Welsh, or the Cornish) enters the service of the king of Cornwall, woos on his behalf and then is compelled by a love potion into a relationship with an Irish princess, and in the end marries a Bretonne, with tragic consequences. Reichl's nomination of the musical storyteller Tristan as paradigmatic medieval performer also alights upon a connection between narrative transmission and the professional players of plucked instruments such as the harp that may prove one of our most valuable clues in reconstructing the history of oral tradition in medieval Ireland.

By way of background, we should note that the Irish (and their offshoots, the Scottish and the Manx) and the Welsh (along with their British Celtic cousins, the Cornish and the Bretons) represent only a portion of what was once a much grander spectrum of Celtic languages and cultures extending in the ancient world from Asia Minor all the way to the Iberian Peninsula. The societies and customs of these various peoples, referred to as 'Celts' or 'Gauls' in classical sources, were the subject of considerable ethnographic comment in the writings of many Greek and Roman authors.[1] Caesar in the first century BC said of the druids, the designated tradition-bearers of the Celtic tribes he was conquering, that they refused to preserve or convey their knowledge in writing, even though they used the Greek alphabet for more practical matters (*Conquest of Gaul*,

---

[1] All but the last of the passages from classical authors cited in this paragraph are conveniently brought together in Tierney 1960.

6.14). Other classical writers add further details to our picture of pre-medieval Celtic oral tradition, mentioning the cultural importance among the Celts of the 'bard' who sings the praises of patrons at banquets and recounts deeds of heroes of old, and of specialists in the performance of divination (Strabo, 4.4.1). Even those Celts who were not professional talkers or singers enjoyed the reputation of being fond of and adept at boasting and riddling (Diodorus Siculus, 5.31). The stereotype of the rhetorically skilled Celt is perhaps of a piece with Caesar's observation that the chief god among the peoples of *Gallia* is 'Mercury', whom he describes as the inventor of all the arts and the divine patron to whom one prays for good bargains (6.17) – the arts presumably including the verbal, and bargaining being to a great extent a matter of persuasive speech (an attribute of both the Roman Mercury and his Greek counterpart Hermes). As for what the Celts valued in their gods and heroes, the second-century AD Greek writer Lucian describes a depiction he claims to have seen of the 'Celtic Heracles', an old man with chains leading from his tongue to the ears of his followers, signifying that his power lay in his speech.[2]

In commercial and cultural contact with the literate cultures of the Mediterranean world well before the vast majority of them were conquered by the Romans toward the end of the first millennium BC, the Celts, those having developed written forms of their languages, left a body of inscriptions, a few of which preserve magical formulas and hints of rituals, redolent of oral culture (Meid 1994: 38–47). The establishment of Celtic literary traditions, however, had to wait for the coming of Christianity to Britain (the southern part of which the Romans conquered in the first century AD, and which subsequently was affected by Christianity along with the rest of the empire), and to Ireland (to which the new religion was introduced in the fifth century, probably from both Britain and the Continent). With the gradual development of classes of ecclesiastical elites focused on reading sacred scriptures, and the receding of the western Empire, the innovative idea of inventing a written form of the vernacular based on the Latin alphabet emerged on both sides of the Irish Sea during the second half of the first millennium AD. Knowledge of the Latin of the Western church and a familiarity with the surviving literature of the Roman Empire continued to be cultivated in Ireland and Britain, providing a *lingua franca* that supported bridges of intellectual exchange among Irish, British, and continental clerics. At the same time, literary forms of insular Celtic languages gradually became vehicles for the production of not only commentary on Latin texts and works of a homiletic or hagiographic nature, but also poetry, law tracts, and prose narratives.[3] Surviving specimens of these last three literary categories bear unmistakable signs of literary composition or at least re-composition (including the traces of influence from available biblical, patristic, and classical sources). Moreover, the motivations and methods of the Christian literati of early Ireland and Wales were far more complex than those of the imaginary crypto-druids whom overenthusiastic scholars and the popular imagination have envisioned as the driving forces behind early medieval Celtic literature. Clearly, however, the conventions of poetic discourse that characterize Irish and Welsh poetic

---

[2] Lucian's *Heracles* is edited with an English translation in Harmon 1913: 62–71; see 62–64.
[3] While Irish and Welsh are not the only Celtic languages to have survived into the post-medieval period, they are the only ones in which substantial and diverse corpora of literature produced in the Middle Ages have survived. See, however, Brett 1989 and Padel 2005.

genres, the formulas and idiom of the substantial corpus of legal literature from early medieval Ireland (as well as the corpus of somewhat later date that developed in Wales), and the narrative patterns and motifs of medieval Irish and Welsh narrative texts derived to a considerable extent from the pre-existing oral traditions of the Celtic peoples of Ireland and Britain.[4] These traditions, moreover, clearly did not die out with the establishment of a literary elite producing texts, but thrived in a synergistic relationship with the new literate culture, well into the Middle Ages and arguably even into the early modern period. Some if not most of those elite, as we shall see at the end of this survey, engaged in oral performance, depending on it for the transmission of their lore and art, not to mention their livelihood.

Roughly in the same period that Béroul, Thomas, Eilhart, and Gottfried were telling and developing the tale of Tristan as it has come down to us, a gigantic Irish text was taking shape, the *Acallam na Senórach* (Dialogue of the Ancients),[5] a mélange of prose and verse centred on the heroic figure of Finn mac Cumaill and his band of fellow warrior-hunters known collectively as the *Fían* (often referred to in the plural, *Fianna*). This Irish term (from which the adjective in English used to designate this cycle of heroic tales and songs, *Fenian*, derived much later) designates a classic example of the Indo-European *Männerbund*, composed of young men living adventurously beyond the pale of society in preparation for their re-entry as adults, under the supervision of older males (Finn and the other senior members of the *Fían*), who, while intimately familiar with society and its values, have chosen to live beyond the boundaries of social convention. Real counterparts to Finn's larger-than-life *Fían* may well have existed in Ireland before the coming of Christianity in the fifth century, and even into the early Christian era. By the time of the *Acallam*, however, the institution of the *Fían* survived only in the realm of story, while new cultural factors were starting to reshape the image of the Fenian heroes, such as the contemporary reality of mercenaries supported by and fighting for the competing kings of medieval Ireland, and notions of chivalry seeping in from Britain and the continent (especially via the Anglo-Normans, who in 1169 invaded and established a long-term presence in Ireland [Ó Néill 1997]).

The author(s) of the *Acallam* assembled a cornucopia of stories about Finn and the *Fían*, at least to some extent culled from the oral tradition of the time. In Irish vernacular literature of earlier centuries, going back to its sixth-century origins, there are relatively few references to Finn, the *Fían*, or Fenian story, so the *Acallam* offers a windfall of information about an extensive narrative tradition whose roots very likely extended back into the pre-Christian era. The premise of the text is that, in the style of legendary sleeping heroes who awake to renewed celebrity in an era later than their own, a few members of the *Fían* survive the end of their pre-Christian heroic age, living well past the death of Finn and their other companions, under the auspices of a mysterious hos-

---

[4] Some groundbreaking and reliable discussions of the issue of the oral element in medieval Celtic literatures include Mac Cana 1975; Ó Coileáin 1977–78; Roberts 1988; Davies 2005. The studies in Tranter and Tristram 1989 and Pryce 1998 give a sense of the range of texts and scholarly perspectives on them that figure in these discussions.

[5] The author's translations are based on the text in the Stokes 1900 edition of the earliest surviving recension of the *Acallam*, now available online (see references, Stokes 1900). A translation of the complete text is available in Dooley and Roe 1999.

9 – *Acallam na Senórach*, Bodl. Library, MS Laud Misc. 610, fol. 124rb

tess. When they emerge from their otherworldly suspension, Caílte (Finn's right-hand man), Oisín (Finn's son, a poet as well as a warrior-hunter, like the other members of the *Fían*), and their companions find themselves in the time of St Patrick and the conversion of Ireland (5th c. AD). The saint's ecclesiastical retinue encounters the old-timers, who at first frighten the Christian missionaries on account of their gigantic size. Despite this bad start to the relationship, the saint and the ancient warriors almost immediately warm up to each other. Patrick continues his tour of Ireland in the company of his new friends, but only after the saint exorcises as well as baptizes them, and receives assurance from divinely sent messengers that it is permissible to listen to the stories these pagan 'ancients' can tell and the poems they can sing or recite (in response to questions from Patrick and other people they meet along the way), provided these performances are *written down and preserved for posterity*.[6] Whether or not this conceit of an old storyteller as the source of the material framed in the *Acallam* accords at all with the reality of whence the material of the text derives, it is a bold premise for a work composed in a literary milieu that prided itself on its bookishness and had been sustained since its beginnings by learned clerics who often insisted that they were only faithfully following and building upon what they had already found in writing.[7]

As eager as Patrick, the high-king of Ireland, kings of the provinces, and others in the *Acallam* who win the chance to talk with the Fenian heroes are to be entertained by their stories and poems as well as to record them, no one is as intent on mentally collecting as much of this lore as possible as Cass Corach, a character who, in the redundant style of the *Acallam*, describes his mission thus: 'I am compelled by the desire to acquire the knowledge, wisdom, storylore, and great deeds of valour of the Fian from Caílte mac Rónáin.'[8] Not at all a clerical scribe but an otherworldly being who proudly introduces himself to Caílte as a master musician and player of the *timpán* (a small harp), Cass Corach attaches himself to the old hero and, serving as back-up to Patrick and his scribe Broccán, proceeds to elicit and collect Caílte's lore – not, however, by writing it down. Furthermore, the hero and his musician-'sidekick' engage in a series of adventures that sometimes take them into the *síde* (the fairy dwellings that house the erstwhile gods of Ireland), whence Cass Corach originally emerged to make contact with Caílte in order to expand his Fenian repertoire.

The *síd* musician gives some powerful performances in the course of the *Acallam*. When he first meets Patrick, the saint requests a demonstration of his art (whether this involves only playing his instrument or singing as well is never clear):

'Sing for us', said Patrick, 'something [representative] of your craft and art' [...] And he took up his *timpán*, tuned it, and played it, so that he put a *cairche cíuil*[9] on it, and they had never

---

[6] Stokes 1900, ll. 290–303. The word used in this passage to describe the effect the written-down stories and poems will have upon future generations (presumably when they hear them read aloud), *gairdiugudh* (translatable as 'entertainment'), literally means 'shortening', specifically as in shortening the time (Poppe 1999: 37). Thus the audiences of Fenian lore will experience something like the temporal transcendence that animates the Fenian narrator-hero of the *Acallam*, enabling Caílte to share what he knows with Patrick and to bring his era to life.

[7] The alternation between attribution to the spoken word and attribution to pre-existing text, a dynamic that underlies the Irish literary tradition, is the subject of Nagy 1997.

[8] Stokes 1900, ll. 3353–55. Among other meanings, *cas(s)* can mean 'skilled', and *corach* 'musical', according to the Royal Irish Academy *Dictionary of the Irish Language* (see references, *DIL*).

[9] 'Strain of music' perhaps. *Ceól* is the Irish word for 'music', also 'song, musical performance'. It is perhaps significant that the obscure word *cairche* also appears in the *Acallam* in the phrase *cairche teined*, referring to the fire an otherworldly marauder launches from his mouth, like a fiery utterance, after he has lulled his human victims to sleep by playing his *timpán* – a performance dramatically different in outcome from the one given in this passage by Cass Corach to Patrick, but similar in its soporific effect. In the medieval heroic saga known as the *Táin Bó Fraích* (Cattle Raid of Fráech), entertaining harpers unintentionally 'slay' some members of the audience with the exquisiteness of their performance (Meid 1974, ll. 98–99).

heard anything as beautiful with the exception of the chanting (?) of godly scripture and praise of the King of Heaven and Earth. Then, under the influence of the plaintive music of the *síd*, the clerics fell into a sleep-like trance. He finished his performance. 'Pay me for the performance, holy cleric', said Cass Corach. 'What payment do you seek?' 'Heaven for me myself, for that is the best payment of all, and grace to my art forever, and to my colleagues who will come after me henceforth.' 'Granted', said Patrick, 'and henceforth it will be one of the three art forms from which anyone can derive a living in Ireland. For all time, even if the inhospitality facing him is formidable, it will disappear once a colleague of yours performs music or tells stories. He will always share the bed of a king, thanks to your art, and musicians will prosper, unless they grow neglectful.'

'Fine [the demonstration of your] art you have given us', said Broccán. 'Fine indeed', said Patrick, 'and if there were not a touch of *síd* magic in it, there would be nothing more like the music [played for] the King of Heaven.' 'If there is music in heaven', said Broccán, 'why shouldn't there be music on earth? It would be unfair to ban musical performance.' 'I said nothing of the kind', said Patrick, 'only that one should not put too much trust in it.' (Stokes 1900, ll. 3461–86)

Remarkably, in this initial encounter with Patrick, there is no need for the otherworldly *airfitech* 'musician, entertainer' to be exorcised, a requirement for Caílte and his Fenian companions before the Christian clerics could engage in dialogue with them. Cass Corach's *elada* 'art' gives him and his colleagues a free pass into the new world being ushered in by the saint. Even more remarkably, the musician's salvation and the good fortune of his successors are not even made contingent on their being baptized, but only on their maintaining their professional competence (not becoming neglectful). And so the *Acallam* in the person of the authorizing Patrick not only gives its imprimatur to the writing-down of oral tradition but guarantees a livelihood for those who perpetuate it as a dynamic performance tradition – that is, for the practitioners of Cass Corach's art, which is here said explicitly to combine storytelling with music-making,[10] and which as a repertoire favours stories and songs having to do with Finn and his *Fian*. The caution issued by Patrick, not to 'put too much trust' in music or musical performance, is mild to the point of being perfunctory, unlikely to inhibit anyone from following in the footsteps of the otherworldly performer.

In his remarkable statement guaranteeing a receptive audience to the successors of the *airfitech*, it would appear that Patrick (that is, the author of the *Acallam*) is privileging the professional musician over the amateur storyteller Caílte, who after all is just a warrior retelling what he knows and has experienced. What, however, is Cass Corach expected to do with the stories he hears from Caílte? Is the *airfitech* so eager to learn the old hero's tales, a 'multi-tasker', capable of switching between two or more different modes of entertaining and performing?[11] Perhaps the heritage that Cass Corach

---

[10] The combination envisioned here may be an alternation between the two activities, depending on the context and the audience's wishes, or the harper's storytelling may provide background to and context for the song he sings (as when, in the *Acallam*, Caílte tells a story and caps it off by reciting, or singing, pertinent verse), or the accompanied song itself could be construed as narrative in nature.

[11] A thirteenth-century Irish poet chides his noble patron for giving *timpán* players a horse as their reward for telling him stories about Finn's *Fian* – better payment than what the poet received for composing verse praising the patron (Mac Cana 1980, 12–13). In a narrative text produced three centuries or so earlier, the legendary Leinster king Labraid Loingsech receives pivotal assistance in

bequeaths to his performer-heirs is an expanded repertoire of accompanied songs that chronicle Fenian adventures. In fact, we find preserved in Irish manuscripts from as early as the twelfth century many poems that relay stories involving Finn and his *Fian*.[12] These poems (*laoithe*) have been characterized by some scholars as 'balladic' in that they narrate in the elliptical, dialogue-heavy style that has been taken to be characteristic of the ballad as it has been identified and studied in various European traditions from the late Middle Ages down to recent times. *Laoithe* are also 'balladic' in the sense that the process of their composition and transmission probably involved both literary and oral input.

To return to the *Acallam*, we find that the dangers of 'putting too much trust' in the engrossing performance of a *timpán* player become shockingly apparent in a later episode. Ironically, the victims are not Patrick's fellow humans, to whom he issues the warning in the passage quoted above, but they are, like Cass Corach, supernatural beings. In this episode, Caílte and the musician devise an ingenious plan to attract the three wolves who are marauding the property of one of their hosts. Cass Corach knows that they are really *síd* women who magically transform themselves into animal shapes in order to wreak all the more damage. There is only one 'crowd' (*drong*) to which they will pay any heed, he explains: those who play the harp (*cruit*) or *timpán*. Thus, Caílte assigns Cass Corach the task of attracting the wolves with his musical performance, while the lying-in-wait Caílte will do the job of slaying them. First, the performer by himself tries out his power to attract the deadly females, and the experiment works. When they come for a second evening's entertainment, Cass Corach, at Caílte's prompting, asks them to remove their wolfskins, for as humans, he slyly says, they will enjoy the performance all the more. It is only after they do so, thereby presumably rendering themselves more vulnerable, that Caílte slays them, skewering all three of them with his spear (Stokes 1900, ll. 7674–717).

Even though elsewhere the *Acallam* presents musical performance as emanating from the otherworld with the result that it can make a saint uneasy, its effect here is to *humanize* the listeners, or, its effects are said to be maximized if the audience is human. In other words, the type of performance that Cass Corach gives, and that perhaps employs the Fenian lore he is gathering, constitutes what anthropologists and folklorists would call a *cultural performance*. There is something fundamental to the definition of the human as understood in *Acallam* that the audience of an *airfitech* hears, and that is conveyed in the act of performing the music and telling the stories that make up the *airfitech*'s repertoire. The demise of the women who take off their animal skins vividly highlights the vulnerability woven into the definition of civilized humanity experienced through performance.

This transformation brought about by music affects the performer Cass Corach as well. When he is first introduced into the text of the *Acallam*, his reputation is that of

---

his rise to power from his poet and harper, who work together to further their patron's interests, almost like a team: see Ó Cathasaigh 2002a:12–13. On the high status of the harper in medieval Irish society compared to other skilled craftsmen, and on the even higher status of members of the poetic order, see Kelly 1988: 64, 43–49. References in contemporary sources to the 'performing arts' of pre-modern Ireland, including music and poetry, are surveyed in Fletcher 2000: 9–60.

[12] On the interplay of written and oral in the history of the development of the Fenian *laoi* (possibly related to French *lai* 'lay'), see the contributions to Carey 2003, and MacInnes 1987.

an otherworldly virtuoso destined for a career in the *síd*. The last time we see him, Cass Corach has just been appointed to the position of 'best' or first (*ollam*) among performers *in this world*, by the high-king of Ireland. Along with this privileged position comes marriage to a human princess, arranged for Cass Corach by Caílte himself. He assures the girl, in fact, that the musician will be the only member of the pre-Christian otherworld who will *not* be banished by Patrick into the hills and underground (ll. 7889–95, 7410–546). Thus not only does Cass Corach's *elada* survive the radical passage from paganism to Christianity, from 'oral' culture to 'written' culture, but it absorbs the makings for a dramatic increase in repertoire (with Cass Corach's unlimited access to Caílte and his store of knowledge), and witnesses the transformation of its paradigmatic exponent from a supernatural being straying from the *síd* to a full-fledged human, with security of employment.

This easy transition could be explained as a sign of the relatively easy-going attitude of the author(s) of the *Acallam* and of twelfth-thirteenth-century Irish literati in general toward their pre-Christian past, which lay centuries behind them and no longer posed a threat to the no-longer-new religion. And yet in some Latin saints' lives from the seventh century, among the earliest productions of the Irish literary tradition, we find a comparable embrace of the figure of the musical performer, and the same sense that civilized social existence, whether Christian or pagan, is unthinkable without the element of professional music-making and oral composition. For instance, in the following episode from one of the lives of St. Brigit (who along with Patrick and Columba forms the triumvirate of great saints celebrated in the hagiography of the early Irish church), the saint not only tolerates music-making but miraculously endows non-musicians with skill as wondrous as that of a Cass Corach. The welcoming attitude toward musical performance exhibited here by Brigit, supposedly a contemporary of Patrick's, strikingly resembles that on display in the *Acallam*, a vernacular text of considerably later date that, while indebted to hagiography for some of its narrative motifs, represents a very different kind of literary production, with very different agenda:

> Saint Brigit was asked to go to a certain king in Mag Cliach to secure the release of a man whom the king had in chains. And Brigit went and entered the king's house but did not find the king in his house. However, his friends were there, that is, the man who had fostered the king, he and his wife and sons. And Brigit saw harps in the house and said to the people, 'Play your harps for us.' The king's friends replied, 'There are no harpists in this house just now. They've gone out.' Then another man who was with Brigit's companions said jokingly to the (king's) friends, 'Play the harps for yourselves and may saint Brigit bless your hands that you may carry out what she bids you and obey her word.' And the king's friends said, 'Let us do it. May Brigit bless us!' Thereupon the unskilled harpists picked up the harps and played. Then the king came back home and hearing the sound of the music said, 'Who is making this music?' Someone answered him, 'Your foster-father and foster-mother and their children were at Brigit's bidding.' And the king went into the house and asked to be blessed by Brigit. And Brigit said, 'Do you in return release the prisoner to me.' Whereupon the king freely gave her the prisoner. Indeed the king's friends were harpists till their death and their descendants were held in high esteem by kings for many ages. (Connolly 1989: 36–37)

Brigit, anticipating her saintly colleague in the *Acallam*, has no intention of doing without musicians, even going so far as to manufacture some for her delectation while she waits for the king. She thus accords a legitimate place in Christian society for such entertainment (including, one presumes, singing and storytelling), but, like the Patrick of the *Acallam* who shifts Cass Corach's affiliation from the otherworld to this world, Brigit also engages in some reorganization, putting newcomers in the place of those who had been the designated players of the king. Furthermore, the talent and training with which she miraculously endows them are inheritable traits. Thus the saint's playing mischief with the *status quo* both violates and upholds assumptions of continuity (such as the Celtic expectation that harping, like other crafts, passes from father to son) and rehabilitates the idea (explicitly expressed in the *Acallam*) that the best musical expertise derives from the otherworld. The harpers featured in the Brigit *Vita* indeed owe their artistry to something unearthly, but it is the power of a saint.

In constructing this 'myth' that disrupts the conventions of performers and performance in order to validate the carry-over of the multifaceted art of harpers into the Christian era, the hagiographic tradition resorts to a powerful traditional narrative 'trick' also to be found in a medieval account of how the hero Finn of Fenian tradition acquired his poetic talent and mantic knowledge (through which, according to the *Acallam*, he could even know of the existence of the Christian God and the coming of Christianity). According to the *Boyhood Deeds of Finn* (a text contemporary with or slightly earlier than the *Acallam*), the hero becomes a prophet and poet *accidentally*, when he touches a magical salmon containing knowledge meant for a master poet, and which the young Finn, his pupil, is assigned the task of cooking (Nagy 1985: 155–63). The randomness of the choice of Finn as poet, like the serendipity of the king's foster relatives and their descendants becoming harpers by virtue of Brigit's miraculous *fiat*, signals a renewal of the poetic and musical tradition. Finn as a paradigm of the 'new' poet leads the institution out toward the margins of society and into the wilderness, where he and other *fénnidi* (the members of a *fían*) dwell in freedom from the restrictions of regular social existence. Brigit, the *impresaria* who makes professionals out of amateurs, leads this new empowered generation of performers not out into the realm of nature but deep into the mainstream of the coming-into-being Christian era.

This sea-change represents new life and possibilities for poets and musicians, but it also creates victims: those who not only are but *must be* left out of the new order in order for the latter to develop successfully. In the case of the episode from the *Vita*, it is the king's original harpers, who come home with their lord to find themselves rendered superfluous; in the *Boyhood Deeds*, it is the master poet, who was not destined to consume the salmon after all. In the *Acallam*, it is the people of the *síd*, who are condemned to obscurity in the wake of Cass Corach's rise to fame and fortune in the human realm.

Explicit indications as well as lurking hints that a person or thing vital to the setting of performance is paradoxically and pointedly missing from it, can be detected in various descriptions of poetic and musical conventions, as well as in legends about performers attested in Celtic traditions ancient, medieval, and modern (Nagy 2003). Given the close connection between saints and performers we are finding so far in the texts under discussion, it may not surprise us that this syndrome finds its counterpart in a recurring Irish hagiographic scenario wherein the saint either loses someone who is his counterpart or 'sidekick', rescues someone who is missing or in captivity, or himself eludes capture and imprisonment. In the Brigitine episode just discussed, for example, the mission that brings the saint to the king's court and leads to the miraculous replacement of the harpers involves *liberating a prisoner*. (Of course, the king, impressed by Brigit's bagatelle with performers and performance, agrees to Brigit's request that he release the captive.) Could the bringing together here of these seemingly disparate story elements – the saint's quest to free a prisoner, and her/his intervention in matters performative – be meaningful? Pity for a captive drives the third of the most revered saints of early Christian Ireland, Columba (Latin 'Dove') or (his Irish name) Columcille (Dove of the Church), in a legend first attested in our surviving sources roughly around the same time as the story of the encounter between Patrick and the ancient members of Finn's *Fían*. Columcille, after he undertakes a self-imposed exile from Ireland and goes to live in Scotland, allows a monumental exception and returns to his native soil, in order to attend a convention of the men of Ireland, summoned by their king. Not wishing to break his vow of exile, Columcille brings earth from Scotland with him, lest he step on Irish ground, and he keeps his face veiled, lest he see his homeland. Officially, what compels the 'absent' saint to come home is the urgent request of his fellow Irishmen that he settle some very thorny controversies. Yet there is also a personal reason for Columcille's return: his desire to free a royal protégé of his, who is being kept in chains by the king of Ireland. Despite the latter's unwillingness, the captive is freed and delivered to Columcille by divine intervention (Nagy 1997: 174–82).

Before Columcille can return to his exile in Scotland, there is still an outstanding issue of the utmost cultural importance to the Irish on which he has to take a stand. The people of the island and their king, as much as they depend on poets to praise the righteous ruler and satirize the unjust, as well as to preserve traditional knowledge and values, have decided to banish all poets, practitioners of an art that upholds society but who themselves have grown tiresome in their arrogance and self-promulgation. Columcille, who himself enjoys the reputation of a poet (more so, for that matter, than any other traditional Irish saint), recognizes the grave danger society will face if it obliterates the poetic institution altogether, and intercedes on the poets' behalf. He arranges an agreement whereby poets modify their professional behaviour and expectations of support in return for the Irish allowing them to stay in Ireland.

In gratitude, the chief of poets (the *ollam* 'greatest' among poets, as Cass Corach was the *ollam* of musicians) composes a poem commemorating Columcille and begins to perform it for him. The saint, however, protests: such praise is suitable only after its recipient has died. So Dallán (Blind One) the poet is not to perform the poem in public until after he is informed (via the miracle, as specified by Columcille, of his temporarily regaining sight) that the saint has died. The poem in question is the *Amrae Choluim Chille* (Praise Poem for Columcille), one of the earliest extended verse compositions to have survived in the 'new' literary language of Old Irish, a work that reflects both the Christian learning of the early Irish church as well as formulas and compositional devices that derive from a venerable encomiastic tradition. The *Amrae*, in other words, emblematizes the complex weave of written and oral influences at work in medieval Irish literature. Does the legend of its deferred performance refer to the watershed event in the history of Irish tradition, whereby it became possible to 'fix' a vernacular text and gain repeated access to it in a written form, even apart from the context of performance? Subject (Columcille) and poet are separated, as are audience and performer, per order of the saint, but the poem, as a result of its being 'canonized' in the emerging literary tradition, becomes an even more powerful instrument for the protection of the saints' devotees. To recite the *Amrae* daily without flaw, claims the literary tradition, is to receive the full benefit of the saint's protection (Nagy 1997: 154–57).

While the deferred encomiastic performance of a single, superlative poet successfully enters into the literary tradition not only as a paradigmatic story but a talismanic text that goes along with that story, the legend of Columcille's return also features a 'choral' musical performance by a whole group of poets that, like Dallán's *Amrae*, is fashioned to express the profession's gratitude to the saint. This presentation, however, because of its dangerous seductive impact on even a man as holy as Columcille, persists as a detail in the narrative, but its contents are suppressed from the literary record. According to an eleventh-century preface to the *Amrae* that tells the legend of the saint's return to Ireland:

> Then the poets came to the assembly, bringing with them a poem of praise for Columcille. This type of musical composition was known as *aidbse*. It was an outstanding kind of music [...]. And they all performed that music for Columcille simultaneously. As a result, the cleric experienced a fit of pride, so that the air above his head was swarming with demons. This was revealed to [the saint's clerical companion] Baithéne, who proceeded to chide Columcille. The cleric then lowered his head and did penance [for the sin of having fallen under the sway of the music]. And when he raised his head, a great cloud of mist exploded from it. The demons fled, scattered by that mist. (Nagy 1997: 170, slightly revised)

According to another preface to the *Amrae* from roughly the same period, the effect of this mysterious *aidbse* on the saint could only be countered by the application of an indisputably literary weapon, the writings of the church father Basil the Great, which, when read aloud to Columcille by Baithéne, broke the grip of the poets' song.

> [...] After this incident he would not let allow entertainers (*cliara*) to come near him while he was alive, and he did not permit Dallán to compose his poem of praise for him while he, Columcille, was alive. (*ibid.*)

The saint may have kept his distance from the spell cast by these siren-like performers, even if he was the subject of their compositions, but he is after all their great protector, and consequently their musical compositions expressing their thanks to Columcille, and the tradition of performing these compositions, live on, albeit extra-literarily. Whether or not it is specifically the *Amrae* or the obscure *aidbse* to which the following episode from the seventh-century Adomnán's (Latin) Life of Columcille refers, we see that the power of the saint *in absentia* can be invoked by way of special Columban songs, even when those singing them are not professional performers:

> Not to be overlooked is the incident in which certain converted laymen, miscreants stained with blood, were saved from the hands of their enemies who had encircled the house in which they were singing songs in praise of the blessed man in the Irish tongue and commemorating his name, escaping unharmed from amidst the flames, the blades, and the lances. Miraculously, a few of them, who did not wish to sing those songs, as if they thought little of them, perished in that onslaught of their rivals. (Nagy 1997: 149)

These marauders who, despite being 'stained with blood' and engaging in anything but devout or learned activity, know enough to put their trust in the saint and express it in songs passed down to them. Escaping miraculously from a deadly confinement, Columcille's ruffian devotees seem to be the literary forerunners of Caílte and the other Fenians featured in the *Acallam* – themselves erstwhile 'miscreants', who win a lease on life by performing their way into a holy man's good graces.[13]

Apart from Patrick's cordial encounter with an exponent of otherworldly musical art and his encouragement of Caílte's recollections of Fenian lore (including poetry) in the *Acallam*, there is little in the extant literary dossier on this saint demonstrating any affinity with or patronage of entertainers such as those featured in the legends about Brigit and Columcille discussed above.[14] There is, however, a strong and old Patrician connection with poets and their closely allied colleagues, the jurists, in their capacity as guardians of native traditions (like Caesar's druids), who assist the saint in redacting this body of knowledge and technique for literary storage and use in the new Christian society of Ireland (Nagy 1997: 199–208). But it is as if Patrick, pre-*Acallam*, were too 'intellectual' to be concerned with issues having to do with what should constitute performative art and entertainment for the post-pagan Irish. And yet, in the seventh-century Muirchú's Life of Patrick (a Latin work), we find the following account of how Patrick confronted a trap as deadly as that in which Columcille's devotees found themselves, and escaped from it by means perhaps not so dissimilar from those employed by those 'bloodstained' singers:

> [...] The [stubbornly pagan] king [of Ireland] came, impelled by fear, and bent his knees before the holy man, and pretended to do him reverence though he did not mean it; and after they had parted and the king had gone a short distance away, he called holy Patrick with false words, wishing to kill him by any means. Patrick, however, knew the wicked thoughts of the wicked king. He blessed his companions, eight men with a boy, in the name of Jesus Christ, and started on his way to the king, and the king counted them as they went along, and suddenly they disappeared from the king's eyes; instead, the pagans merely saw eight deer with a fawn going, as it were, into the wilds. And king Loíguire, sad, frightened, and in great shame, went back to Tara at dawn [...] (Bieler 1979: 91)

Scholars examining the early Irish *lorica* or 'breastplate' (a kind of poetic charm) titled 'The Deer's Cry'(*Fáeth Fiada*), attributed to Patrick and associated by literary tradition with this incident in the saint's life, have noted (most recently Borsje 2008: 126) that the shapeshifting power the saint employs in this rescue of his companions and himself bears a striking resemblance to that on display in a seemingly very different narrative context, far in its concerns from saints and Christianity – namely, an episode from a text that is the closest medieval Irish literary tradition came to producing an epic, the *Táin Bó Cúailnge* (Cattle Raid of Cúailnge):[15]

---

[13] On the affinity between the recurring hagiographic figure of the brigand and the *fénnid* (such as Finn and his companions), see Sharpe 1979.

[14] An unpleasant encounter Patrick has with entertainers is the subject of Nagy 1999. Compare a story told about Columcille and some avaricious poets (Nagy 1997: 165–66). Musicians similarly harass Saint Cóemgen of Glendalough in an episode from his Irish lives (Plummer 1922: I, 129, 150, 163).

[15] On both the traditional and innovative aspects of this work, another example of the confluence of oral and written traditions on display in medieval Irish literature, see Ó Cathasaigh 2002b.

Then the harpers of Caín Bile came to them from Ess Ruaid, to entertain them [that is the host invading the province of Ulster] with music. But they thought that the harpers had come from the Ulstermen to spy on them. So they hunted them until they went before them into the pillar-stones at Lía Mór in the north, transformed into deer, for (in reality) they were druids possessed of great occult knowledge. (O'Rahilly 1976: 151)

The powerful pre-Christian symbolism of deer stands out as a common denominator in these episodes from contrasting genres of early Irish literature (secular epic, saint's life). Assuming the form of this swift animal, the Christian holy man and the pagan druids alike demonstrate both their own (verbal) power and the powerlessness of their enemies, who cannot keep up with the deer. For our purposes, however, it is also worth observing that the druids in the *Táin* passage are *harpers* as well, musicians who can also be druids and change themselves into wild animals, seemingly as easily as the musician Cass Corach of the *Acallam* could charm the supernatural females out of their wolfskins, thus rendering them easy prey. And if, as seems likely, the Patrick-as-deer vignette plays on its audience's knowledge of the traditional motifs on display in the *Táin* episode and is making a point about the affinity among saints, druids, musicians, and deer, then it gives us an illuminating background to the *Acallam* and to the harmonious relationship that obtains therein among the saint recording everything for literary posterity, the music-maker who shape-shifts from 'otherworldly' to 'human', and the storytelling warrior-hunter Caílte, whose chief companion and fellow survivor from the days of Fenian glory is named 'Fawn' (Finn's son Oisín, whose otherworldly mother could assume the appearance of a doe [Nagy 1985:95]). It is an abiding interest in maintaining and enriching musical performance, which alternates with or includes storytelling, that brings together these characters, just as it creates a continuum between pre-Christian and Christian, and oral and written traditions.[16]

# References

Bieler, Ludwig, ed. and trans. 1979. *The Patrician Texts in the Book of Armagh*. Scriptores Latini Hiberniae 10. Dublin: Dublin Institute for Advanced Studies.
Borsje, Jacqueline. 2008. 'Druids, Deer and "Words of Power": Coming to Terms with Evil in Medieval Ireland.' In *Approaches to Religion and Mythology in Celtic Studies*. Ed. Katja Ritari and Alexandra Bergholm. Newcastle: Cambridge Scholars Publishing. 122–49.
Brett, Caroline. 1989. 'Breton Latin Literature as Evidence for Literature in the Vernacular, A. D. 800 – 1300.' *Cambridge Medieval Celtic Studies* 18: 1–25.
Carey, John, ed. 2003. *Duanaire Finn: Reassessments*. Irish Texts Society Subsidiary Series 13. London: Irish Texts Society.
Connolly, Seán. 1989. 'Vita Prima Sanctae Brigitae: Background and Historical Value.' *Journal of the Royal Society of Antiquaries of Ireland* 119: 5–49.
Davies, Sioned. 2005. '"He was the best teller of tales in the world": Performing Medieval Welsh Narrative.' In Vitz et al. 2005: 15–26.
DIL: *Dictionary of the Irish Language: Based Mainly on Old and Middle Irish Materials*. Compact ed. Dublin: Royal Irish Academy, 1983. – *Electronic Dictionary of the Irish Language*. Ed.

---

[16] The point that it was music and the setting of performance (mostly unaccounted for in the Celtic medieval written record) that made texts 'come alive' is forcefully made in Ford 2005, specifically in regard to medieval Welsh poetry.

Gregory Toner, Maxim Fomin, Thomas Torma, Grigory Bondarenko. Available at <http://www.dil.ie/index.asp>.
Dooley, Ann, and Harry Roe, trans. 1999. *Tales of the Elders of Ireland: A New Translation of Acallam na Senórach*. Oxford: OUP.
Fletcher, Alan J. 2000. *Drama, Performance and Polity in Pre-Cromwellian Ireland*. Toronto: U of Toronto P.
Ford, Patrick K. 2005. 'Performance and Literacy in Medieval Welsh Poetry.' *Modern Language Review* 100.4: xxx–xlviii.
Harmon. A. M., ed. and trans. 1913. Lucian. *I.*, Phalaris. Hippias or The Bath. Dionysus. Heracles. Amber or The Swans. The Fly. Nigrinus. Demonax. The Hall. My Native Land. Octogenarians. A True Story. Slander. The Consonants at Law. The Carousal (Symposium) or The Lapiths. Loeb Classical Library. London: Heinemann.
Kelly, Fergus. 1988. *A Guide to Early Irish Law*. Early Irish Law Series 3. Dublin: Dublin Institute for Advanced Studies.
Mac Cana, Proinsias. 1975. 'On the "Prehistory" of *Immram Brain*.' *Ériu* 26: 33–52.
–. 1980. *The Learned Tales of Medieval Ireland*. Dublin: Dublin Institute for Advanced Studies.
MacInnes, John. 1987. 'Twentieth-Century Recordings of Scottish Gaelic Ballads.' In *The Heroic Process: Form, Function and Fantasy in Folk Epic*. Ed. Bo Almqvist, Séamas Ó Catháin, and Pádraig Ó Héalaí. Dublin: Glendale P. 101–30.
Meid, Wolfgang, ed. 1974. *Táin Bó Fraích*. Rev. ed. Mediaeval and Modern Irish Series 22. Dublin: Dublin Institute for Advanced Studies.
–. 1994. *Gaulish Inscriptions*. Archaeolingua, Series Minor 1. Budapest: Archaeolingua Alapítvány.
Nagy, Joseph Falaky. 1985. *The Wisdom of the Outlaw: The Boyhood Deeds of Finn in Gaelic Narrative Tradition*. Los Angeles: U of California P.
–. 1997. *Conversing with Angels and Ancients: Literary Myths of Medieval Ireland*. Ithaca, NY: Cornell UP; Dublin: Four Courts P.
–. 1999. 'The Irish Herald.' In *Ildánach Ildírech: A Festschrift for Proinsias Mac Cana*. Ed. John Carey, John T. Koch, and Pierre-Yves Lambert. Celtic Studies Publications 4. Andover and Aberystwyth: Celtic Studies Publications. 121–30.
–. 2003. 'The Poetics of Absence in Celtic Tradition.' Sir Thomas Parry-Williams Memorial Lecture. Aberystwyth: U of Wales Centre for Advanced Welsh and Celtic Studies.
Ó Cathasaigh, Tomás. 2002a. 'The Oldest Story of the Laigin: Observations on *Orgain Denna Ríg*.' *Éigse* 33: 1–18.
–. 2002b. '*Táin Bó Cúailnge*.' In *The Epic Voice*. Ed. Alan D. Hodder and Robert E. Meagher. Westport, CT: Praeger. 133–47.
Ó Coileáin, Seán. 1977–78. 'Oral or Literary? Some Strands of the Argument.' *Studia Hibernica* 17–18: 7–35.
Ó Néill, Pádraig. 1997. 'The Impact of the Norman Invasion on Irish Literature.' *Anglo-Norman Studies* 20: 171–85.
O'Rahilly, Cecile, ed. and trans. 1976. *Táin Bó Cúailnge. Recension I*. Dublin: Dublin Institute for Advanced Studies.
Padel, O. J. 2005. 'Oral and Literary Culture in Medieval Cornwall.' In *Medieval Celtic Literature and Society*. Ed. Helen Fulton. Dublin: Four Courts P. 95–116.
Plummer, Charles, ed. and tr. 1922. *Bethada Náem nÉrenn. Lives of the Irish Saints*. 2 vols. Oxford: Clarendon.
Poppe, Erich. 1999. 'Reconstructing Medieval Irish Literary Theory: The Lesson of *Airec Menmann Uraird maic Coise*.' *Cambrian Medieval Celtic Studies* 37: 33–54.
Pryce, Huw, ed. 1998. *Literacy in Medieval Celtic Societies*. Cambridge: CUP.
Reichl, Karl. 2005. 'Turkic Bard and Medieval Entertainer: What a Living Epic Tradition Can Tell Us about Oral Performance of Narrative in the Middle Ages.' In Vitz et al. 2005: 167–78.

Roberts, Brynley F. 1988. 'Oral Tradition and Welsh Literature: A Description and Survey.' *Oral Tradition* 3:61–87.
Sharpe, Richard. 1979. 'Hiberno-Latin *laicus*, Irish *láech*, and the Devil's Men.' *Ériu* 30:75–92.
Stokes, Whitley, ed. 1900. *Acallamh na Senórach*. Irische Texte 4.1. Leipzig: Hirzel. Also available at <http://www.ucc.ie/celt/published/G303000/index.html>.
Tierney, J. J. 1960. 'The Celtic Ethnography of Posidonius.' *Proceedings of the Royal Irish Academy* 60, Sect. C. 189–275.
Tranter, Stephen N., and Hildegard L. C. Tristram, eds. 1989. *Early Irish Literature: Media and Communication / Mündlichkeit und Schriftlichkeit in der frühen irischen Literatur*. ScriptOralia 10. Tübingen: Narr.
Vitz, Evelyn Birge, Nancy Freeman Regalado, and Marilyn Lawrence, eds. 2005. *Performing Medieval Narrative*. Cambridge: Brewer.

# 10 Medieval German Literature: Literacy, Orality and Semi-Orality

*Jan-Dirk Müller*

## 1 The Semi-Oral Culture of the German Middle Ages

### 1.1 Orality vs. Literacy, Latin vs. the Vernacular

The German Middle Ages were based on the one hand upon the literate Mediterranean culture of the Roman Empire, and on the other upon the culture – which was largely still oral – of the 'barbarian' peoples from Northern and Central Asia, who threatened and ultimately overran the borders of the empire during the Migration Period. The relationship between the written and spoken word was correspondingly complex, and may be differentiated temporally, spatially, functionally and in terms of social estate.

*Temporal*: with the decline of late antique educational establishments, the active and passive use of writing receded dramatically within the realm of the former Roman Empire between the fifth and the eighth centuries AD; beyond these borders, which intersect what was to become the German-language region, the use of writing was almost marginal. Yet a counter-movement set in from the eighth century with the establishment of the Frankish Empire under the Carolingians; this gave rise to the gradual expansion of writing and the suppression of oral culture in a number of phases lasting until the end of the Middle Ages. Over the course of the Middle Ages, the relationship between orality and literacy, or rather, between an oral and a literate culture, therefore underwent significant changes pertaining to institutional conditions, social distribution and the proportion of illiterate to educated language. Nevertheless, large sectors of society at the end of the Middle Ages still managed without writing, and particularly in the spheres of song, story-telling and teaching, there were traditions of oral 'literature'[1] which were only gradually recorded in written form.

*Spatial*: as had been the case within the Roman Empire, literacy dwindled from the Mediterranean centre towards the periphery. With the process of Christianisation, areas

---

[1] Despite etymological qualms, the following article refers also to oral 'literature,' by which are meant 'texts' (for textuality, see Ehlich 1989, 1994) which are rooted in oral traditions, which have come down to us thanks to secondary scripting or textualisation and which may be regarded from a modern point of view as belonging to the system of 'literature' thanks to their form and function. Ong's polemic against the phrase as etymologically incorrect and prompting unwelcome connotations (1982 : 11–15) is valid, yet he is unable to suggest an alternative term.

beyond the empire also came under the influence of literate culture. Yet whereas Northern and Eastern Europe long remained peripheral, the highly developed monastic culture of Ireland and England spread through Central Europe in the Early Middle Ages. During the Early Middle Ages there existed a cultural incline primarily from the west to the east and from the south to the north in Germany; the German Empire, on the other hand, radiated towards the East and North. In the beginning, literacy was 'insular', i. e. based around a small number of religious centres (monasteries, episcopal sees) and was embedded in an environment largely devoid of writing. From these ecclesiastical centres, literacy made inroads into political and economic centres, capturing the courts and the cities along with its functional elite and upper class (both connected with the landed gentry), and progressing increasingly thereafter into urban trade and craft as well. Only at the end of the Early Modern Period, however, did this literacy expand comprehensively to include rural areas as well.

*Functional*: in the Early and still in the High Middle Ages, the use of writing was largely the province of a communications elite, the *clerici*, who had received a clerical education which usually led to an ecclesiastical post. In the Early Middle Ages, the use of writing was therefore predominantly associated with Latin, the language of scholarship and religion. From the twelfth century, however, the literacy of the *laici* in the vernacular became increasingly significant, as much in literature as in everyday writing or in governing, legal and administrative practice. Nevertheless, only around the end of the Middle Ages the prominence of the *clerici* over laymen diminished in this area too.

*Social Estate*: on the whole, the use of writing was more widespread in the feudal and urban upper classes than in the middle and lower classes. Within the upper classes, greater value was placed upon a thorough upbringing which, certainly amongst the nobility – and in the Early Middle Ages even in royal dynasties[2] – consisted primarily of physical training for young men, and did not necessarily include either an active or a passive use of writing; women, on the other hand, were more frequently literate.[3] As a rule, the male lay nobility had no direct stake in literate culture. In Germany this situation slowly began to change from the late twelfth century; in the ruling dynasties, education in the written language was increasingly deemed a requirement for the duty of governance. Even in the Late Middle Ages, however, large factions of the aristocracy were still illiterate. This did not exclude them from literate culture at all. In the service of other institutions and social groups, the *clerici* moved beyond their true sphere of activity, the church and monastery. The representatives of the estates, once more ranked according to their position in the estate system, were therefore able to participate at least indirectly in literate culture. The *clerici* were also drawn to some degree from the nobility, and the ecclesiastical hierarchy was integrated within the system of ruling estates. Thus the higher clerical offices were also attractive for noblemen. In order to qualify for these posts, younger sons, and in particular those who were partly or fully ruled out of inheriting, frequently received at least a rudimentary clerical training. If later there was any change to the succession, these men were then *litterati* amongst the *laici*. Finally,

---

[2] See Haubrichs 1995:45f.; Bumke 1986:603–5.
[3] See Grundmann 1936; Haubrichs 1995:43–51. [On literacy and orality in the Early Middle Ages see also chapters 3 (M. Richter) and 4 (K. O'Brien O'Keeffe) in this volume.]

competence in the written language was the most important vehicle for ascent through the social ranks, sometimes from the very bottom to the very top, in the ecclesiastical hierarchy as much as in the posts occupied by *clerici* in the court or in the principalities.

Complex and multifaceted combinations of orality and literacy emerge from the overlap between these four parameters, calling for a differentiated consideration of individual cases. The functional distinction between *clerici* and *laici*, literacy and orality, Latin and the vernacular was intersected by the stratified estate system of the Middle Ages. The boundary of the sphere in which writing was used did not at first correspond to this stratification, but instead divided the *clerici* from the rest of society, the *laici*. In medieval Germany this boundary slowly shifted, both temporally and spatially, in favour of the written word.

We can refer to primary orality (Ong 1982: 16 ff., 31 ff.) only at best within certain marginal zones and peripheral groups in Europe during the Middle Ages. Medieval society in Germany was semi-oral or partially oral, which is to say that the use of writing was established within certain groups and certain spheres of life, not at all within others, and that there were many hybrid forms of written and spoken communication. Orality and literacy are interwoven. Christian Kiening has therefore proposed that the rigid opposition of these terms be replaced by the polarity *Körper* and *Schrift* (body and writing), both of which are always involved in acts of communication in such a semi-oral society. Particularly in the vernacular, texts in the written language are 'embodied', that is, orally delivered and converted back into a 'voice'; the body is a surface on which meaning is inscribed, and is to be 'read', too. The two concepts 'designate aspects of a partially oral culture in which the word, even in its written form, remains coupled with a collaborative activity, a social practice, a habitualised performance.'[4] To a certain extent this is true not only of the vernacular but also of Latin literate culture. The means of communication – 'hearing and seeing, writing and image'[5] – are closely connected and interchange with one another, particularly in lay society.

Until the twelfth century, *illiteratus* for the most part signifies 'unable to read or write' and not 'uneducated',[6] inasmuch as it does not exclude active participation in oral culture (historical and genealogical interests, the reception of epic, songs and so forth) and certainly not passive participation in ecclesiastical culture. Illiterate laymen could acquire the knowledge of written works when they were read aloud and translated (Bumke 1986: 607–10). It was only in the course of the Middle Ages that the meaning of *litteratus* changed from 'elementary knowledge of reading and writing' to 'education in the arts and sciences'.[7]

---

[4] Kiening 2003: 13 ('kennzeichnen Aspekte semi-oraler Kulturen, in denen das Wort, auch wenn es schriftlich ist, an ein gemeinschaftliches Tun, eine soziale Praxis, einen habitualisierten Vollzug gekoppelt bleibt.')
[5] 'Hören und Sehen, Schrift und Bild', the title of Wenzel 1995.
[6] See Grundmann 1958; Bumke 1986: 602.
[7] See Grundmann 1958; Bumke 1986: 607.

## 1.2 'Literature' under Oral Conditions: Verse – Rhyme – Strophe – Formula

Like other oral cultures, the culture of lay society in the Early and High Middle Ages cultivated its own manner of preserving traditions, of rendering speech more permanent (*Verdauerung*),[8] and as a result generated specific forms of a 'literature' which was rooted in orality. Admittedly, not all relevant traditions had to be recorded without the help of writing, since the central bodies of knowledge – legal norms, ethics, binding religious beliefs and suchlike – were enshrined in written form by the *clerici*, custodians of the written Latin culture. Of course, in this process it was the *clerici* whose criteria regarding relevance were of primary importance; they decided what was and was not important or central. Non-literary strategies of preserving traditions, by contrast, had to be implemented for all traditions 'beneath' or 'beyond' their selectional interests (thus, for instance, for local legal traditions, rules of everyday conduct, practical knowledge or know-how, customs, non-liturgical religious acts, non-canonical philosophies of belief and the like). Such strategies were elaborately applied, however, mainly in traditions relating to memory, history, norms and ways of life, and after that also to the amenities of the lay upper class.

In contrast to those cultures in which everything deemed worthy of transmission was systematically fostered – by a caste of priests, for instance – there were no specific institutions available in the European Middle Ages for safeguarding oral traditions. They therefore had to avail themselves of informal linguistic means such as a certain kind of (long-line) verse, strophes, alliteration, end-rhyme and formulaic patterns.[9] By these means, noteworthy matters could be collected in texts and these texts better remembered. The adaptation of memorised texts might have been the subject of specific training and a specific profession without this being necessarily still perceptible; Anglo-Saxon sources speak of the scop, Nordic sources of the skald.[10] Texts which were originally oral are only attested insofar as they are recorded in writing or even edited in written form, i. e. when they have been *verschriftet* (scripted) or *verschriftlicht* (textualised). Since oral literature of the Middle Ages is therefore accessible to us only through the medium of writing, the characterisation of its genuine form is fraught with a great deal of uncertainty given that we cannot reliably state to what degree oral traditions have been altered in this new medium. Furthermore, each of the mechanisms for preserving oral tradition may also be used beyond this pragmatic function, in texts genuinely composed in the written language. In this case it is a purely stylistic device. In the hybrid oral-literate culture of the Middle Ages, therefore, the affiliation of texts to one side or the other cannot be demonstrated with certainty; at best, we can make a conjecture as to their disposition.

Oral tradition is dependent upon memory. To avoid over-burdening this faculty, oral tradition must be economical in both the selection and the stylisation of material to be memorised. In preserving a statement, importance is placed only upon its (semantic) core rather than its word-for-word reproduction.

---

[8] See Ehlich 1994. Such more 'durable' oral speech should also be labelled 'text' here, and the concept of text is not restricted to the written form.
[9] The characteristics described above designate oral texts at large; see the remarks of Ong 1982: 33–36.
[10] [On the Anglo-Saxon scop and the Nordic skald, see ch. 5 on performance and performers in this volume (section 2 by J. Harris).]

Verse can be remembered more easily than prose. A recurrent verse structure safeguards the content which is to be remembered and offers a degree of protection against alterations, additions and reductions. To this end, early German literature usually employed the 'alliterative long-line', composed of an *a*-verse and a *b*-verse (*Anvers* and *Abvers*), each with two or more stressed syllables, and a caesura in between. Aside from the stressed syllables ('lifts'), it is *Füllungsfreiheit* (the free use of unstressed syllables) which dominates, i. e. only the number of lifts is determined, whereas the number of unstressed syllables ('anacruses' or 'dips') between the lifts may vary. The verse may begin with or without an unstressed syllable ('anacrusis') or, as the case may be, even with several unstressed syllables. Dips may be employed many times or not at all; the former generates feet of three syllables or more; in the latter, two lifts collide in an 'augmented lift' (*beschwerte Hebung*). Older German verse therefore allows for many variations, until that time at which anacrusis as well as the distribution of lifts and dips was fully and bindingly regulated (as in the Opitzian verse reform of 1624). In the early German verse the standard ancient differentiation between iambic and trochaic, anapaestic and dactylic metre was dropped. The long-line verse is just as suitable for improvisation as for memorisation: in fashioning a verse, only a certain number of lifts need be realised on significant syllables, and in subsequent renditions it is adequate to remember a limited number of significant words.

In the Early Middle Ages texts which have their roots in orality are largely 'stichic,' i. e. composed of a series of (long-line) verses in the same form. Strophic verse appears only after the end of the twelfth century, possibly under the influence of lyric. In comparison with an arbitrarily extensive sequence of equal long-line verses, strophe further limits the variations possible, since variously constructed verses recur in a fixed sequence. In this sense, strophe ensures a higher degree of stability but makes greater demands in terms of composition, in that whilst metrical variation is preserved, an additional rule is specified for the adaptation of spoken material. Strophe is therefore suited less for oral improvisation than for memorising and retaining a relatively firmly constituted text.

Strophic structure is to be found above all in shorter texts (songs, sayings). In epic, complex strophic forms appear only at a relatively late date. It is possible that a written record was already added as a mnemonic device at this stage; in any case the text was further received by means of oral delivery. Most epic strophes seem to have developed out of stichic precursors. In Otfrid of Weissenburg's Old High German *Evangelienbuch* ('Book of Gospels', also called 'Krist') the 'strophe' is composed of two equally constructed long-line verses, the first of which is accentuated in each case by a larger initial letter; the long lines are in turn composed of two short-lines in rhyming pairs, each of which has two accented syllables. We therefore become aware of the strophic character only in its written form. With regard to the *Nibelungen*-strophe it was likewise supposed that each strophe was at first composed of four equally constructed long-verses rhymed in pairs with two sets of three accented syllables. Only later the fourth verse was lengthened by one foot (Heusler 1921:37f., 53). Melodies for recitation also survive for most epic strophes.[11]

---

[11] [On the music, see further ch. 5, sections 2.4 (J. Harris) and 3.4 (K. Reichl).]

The effective retention of oral speech was fostered not only by verse structure but by rhyme, which unites two verses or verse-sections. Rhyme appears too in stereotypical prose phrases, in the form of end-rhyme (*klein, aber fein*, 'small but excellent') as well as initial-rhyme (*mit Mann und Maus*, 'all together', lit. 'with man and mouse'); the second form is also known as alliteration. On this basis a fixed structure of initial rhyme developed in the Germanic region: the *Stabreim*, a kind of alliterative verse. Alliterative verse connects two or three of the (usually) four syllables which bear the primary stress of the long-line verse (in this case, connecting two in the first verse-section and one in the second) by means of the same initial consonantal sound (or, in the case of a vocalic beginning, by a glottal stop, not indicated in graphic form).[12] Only the syllables of nouns and primary verbs – and not proforms, auxiliary verbs, adverbs, conjunctions etc. – are able to bear this primary stress. Accordingly, in Germanic long-line verse there is usually a total of three syllables at most which alliterate (*staben*), and *Stabreim* is therefore not to be confused with the bursts of alliteration found in the imitations and parodies of Richard Wagner's style. By means of such economy only two or three meaningful words per verse need be memorised accurately, whilst the remainder may be supplemented in a suitable fashion. Therefore, apart from the syllable nucleus, as elsewhere in long-line verse, a high degree of variation prevails.

In the German-speaking area the technique of alliterative verse was already in decline by the time of the first written attestations of formerly oral poetry in the eighth and ninth centuries. Thus although the *Hildebrandslied* was originally composed in alliterative long-line verse, in its written form this alliteration had already been partially destroyed or damaged. Nevertheless, traces of alliterative verse technique may still be detected in much later texts with other forms of rhyme.[13]

From the ninth century, final-syllable rhyme or final-rhyme (the *Ludwigslied*, Otfrid of Weissenburg's *Krist*) took over from initial-rhyme, at first in the form of assonance. Assonance connects one or two syllables which have the same or similar vowel colour (*faterlos / buoz*) but a different consonantal setting (*Krist / iz*), final-syllable rhyme connects the last syllables of a verse (e. g. *scinhaft / craft*), and final-rhyme connects the two final stressed syllables in a verse, which may then be followed by a weakly stressed syllable (the 'masculine' single-syllable cadence: *al / scal* vs. the 'feminine' two-syllable cadence: *gimuato / guato*). From the twelfth century the trend towards 'pure' rhyme prevails. In this form the vowel (or vowels) and the concluding consonantal syllable must accord entirely.

A further device for rendering oral texts more permanent is their formulaic nature. Formulas are not only linguistic units fully identical in their verbal form, articulating, always in the same fashion, similar actions (*die degene einander liefen an*), stereotypical characterisations (*der rîche künec her*), typical value judgements (*daz was übele getan*) and so forth; rather, they are also semantic/syntactical and textual 'construction kits' which may be stocked with a variety of linguistic material, yet which are nevertheless always recognized thanks to their recurrent structure. Such construction kits may be short syn-

---

[12] See Heusler 1925: I, 276–84; März 2003.
[13] See Splett 1964 on the *Nibelungenlied*, although there the number of *Stäbe* (alliterative accents) varies greatly, so that the intersection with alliteration is fluid.

tagmata (e. g. article + attribute + subject/object + predicative), complete syntactic units (subject + predicate + object), or even more complex sentence patterns with greater leeway for semantic variation, and finally textual schemata for the portrayal of situations and actions.

Formulas make it possible for episodes with different players, a different sequence of events, different contexts etc. both to be differentiated according to their distinctive features yet also to be grasped in a manner familiar and recognisable to all. Thus formulas in a broader sense also signify schemata in which the world is experienced and reproduced in a manner which is ever the same. They are patterns in which a narrative habitually takes place (e. g. the progress of a battle as a series of duels) or which clearly structure and motivate complex sequences of events (e. g. political conflicts as a dangerous bridal quest). A formula makes actions of all kinds manageable and memorable by reducing their semantic and syntactic complexity; it guarantees that even the new appears in trusted and familiar form. Formulas facilitate the invention of a text, the clothing of something new in old and familiar patterns ('improvised orality'), as well as memorisation, the integration of the unfamiliar into the stock of that which is already known ('memorised orality').[14]

In conjunction with the rhythmic patterns prescribed by the structure of the verse, formulas allow a considerable quantity of semantic information to be processed over long passages without expending too much imagination.[15] Repetition is a common feature of the devices of oral preservation of tradition: repetition of a rhythmic structure, of a sound, of the linguistic material and its syntactic organisation, of certain stereotypical contents – including the prototypes for a wide range of situations and deeds. Also the problem of the greater complexity of meaning is solved by varying repetition, i. e. by the parataxis of similar (though not identical) units, rather than by hypotaxis, as is generally the case in the written language. By varying the repeated material, change, reassessment and reversal may be expressed.

Cultures without writing are cultures of memory. Cultures of memory are homeostatic, in that they tend to minimise changes and to perceive and digest the new within the horizons of the old.[16] Naturally developed memory ('communicative memory'), which is based on narratives told by the older generation, usually (apart from a few outstanding occurrences) extends back no further than two generations (Assmann 1992). In an oral culture there is no interest in an abstract chronological framework which spans individual phases of life. The viewpoint from which the past is viewed moves constantly forward. Oral literature, by contrast, safeguards matters which lie beyond this natural sphere of memory, but which are nevertheless always pertinent to the present. In consequence, oral literature flattens historical differences, portrays the contemporary as age-old and the age-old as contemporary (thus in Germany, for instance, the genealogical prehistory in the *Buch von Bern*, 'Book of Bern') or places events which historically are not contemporaneous in the same time-period (thus in the *Nibelungenlied*, for instance,

---

[14] See Curschmann 1979; Haferland 2002; 2003; 2004:331–39.
[15] See Parry 1971; Lord 1960.
[16] See Goody and Watt 1963:307–10; Ong 1982:46–49.

we see the courtly stylisation of a history from the time of the Migration Period). This conception of history continues to have an effect on written material.

## 2 Periods

### 2.1 The Early Middle Ages

With the decline of ancient literate culture and its institutions over the course of the Migration Period, writing in Western, Central and Northern Europe became the province primarily of the church and its office-holders. That is not to say that the use of writing was restricted to matters within the church itself, but rather that the use of writing in all political and social spheres probably lay largely in the hand of the *clerici*, and that the acquisition of both an active and a passive use of writing took place predominantly within ecclesiastical educational establishments. Literacy was thus bound up with the Latin language. The oral culture of the common people and the nobility, whether it be the handing-down of laws, history or sayings, whether songs of praise, heroism, mockery or love, is recorded no more than haphazardly, and is therefore largely lost.

The earliest written texts in the vernacular in Germany are for the most part subsidiary to a dominant oral practice, i. e. they underpin or record oral communication, or reprocess elements of the Latin literary tradition for the oral sphere. Occasionally traces of the vernacular in Latin texts (e. g. legal terms in the codification of tribal laws) point to a largely dominant oral practice, and unwritten executed legal acts may be documented retroactively in written form (the Hammelburg Boundary description, which refers back to a walk round the boundaries; the Oaths of Strasbourg, which the sons of Louis the Pious swore in front of their armies).

In the first place, ancillary devices for oral communication were transmitted in written form – elementary word-lists (*Abrogans, Paris Glosses*) which gloss Latin lemmata in the vernacular and so render them available for oral use (ed. S. Müller 2007). Secondly, translations of ritual texts in Latin (such as the Lord's Prayer, baptismal vows, the Creed, formulas for confession) were recorded, so that they might be used orally in missionary and clerical work with an illiterate lay society. Thirdly we have records of spoken or sung ritual texts (prayers, the *Petruslied, Galluslied*, etc.) and even magical formulas (magic spells and incantations of blessing). Fourthly there are documented portions of vernacular text which support the oral explanation of a written (Latin) text, e. g. from the lessons delivered in monastic schools; the texts are glossed lemma by lemma (partly by marginal or interlinear glosses in drypoint, so-called *Griffelglossen* [Glaser 1996]) or word-group by word-group (listed over the text, in the margin or embedded in the Latin text). In each case, vernacular literacy is simply an instrument for oral communication.

In the latter case, however, the crossover with translation (which may also be received as a written text) is fluid. Translations break away from the word-order and syntax of their source. Basic texts of the Christian faith (Tatian's *Gospel Harmony*, the *St. Matthew's Gospel* of Monsee/Vienna) or of spiritual guidance (the Old High German translation of Isidore's 'De fide catholica [...] contra Iudaeos') were translated. Thus the beginnings of a written vernacular culture emerged, a culture which adapted the authoritative knowledge preserved in the language of scholars for the *laici*. Even vernacular *Buchdichtung* (book poetry) like Otfrid's *Evangelienbuch* (*Krist*) derives its poetic medium from oral tradition, but leans upon scholarly exegetical traditions in its reworking of the biblical material.

Whenever vernacular poetry which was originally oral finds its way into writing, this poetry remains marginal, as – in a very literal sense – with the *Hildebrandslied*, which filled in the remaining space on the outer sides of the flyleaves at either end of a Latin codex, and was only fragmentarily recorded, since space was insufficient to write out the complete text (see Illustration 10, p. 316). This is the sole attestation of a Germanic heroic poem of the kind that must have been orally disseminated in large numbers throughout the Middle Ages, as is shown by indirect sources and by the textualisation, centuries later, of heroic epic material from the Migration Period. The song, which was probably itself already copied out from an older record, is of Upper German, perhaps ultimately Langobardic, origin (8th c.?). The form of the language and certain characteristics of oral narrative style – its formulaic character, the alliterative long-line metre – had either been corrupted already by the time the scribe encountered them, thanks to a long process of reception without the support of writing, or were deemed unworthy of observation by him since they had no role to play in the medium of writing.

There must have been further texts of this kind, but they are not transmitted in written form. Related, however, are literary stylisations of contemporary events such as the *Ludwigslied*, which celebrates the victory of the West Frankish King Louis III over the Normans, or the Latin-German poem *De Heinrico*, which takes as its subject the meeting of two rulers. Both already feature the new technique of assonance.

Charlemagne, according to his biographer Einhard (*Vita Karoli*, chapter 29), is said to have initiated a collection of ancient vernacular songs (*barbara et antiquissima carmina*) – therefore obviously orally disseminated texts – whose subjects were the martial deeds of prehistoric kings (*veterum regum actus et bella*). That is not to say that this must necessarily have been a collection of exclusively heroic songs, for it might also have included related poems – songs of praise, of historical events etc. (Haubrichs 1989). The collection would have archived the (originally) oral tradition in the manner that it was recited, most notably by bards at the residence of rulers; nothing of it survives, however.

Poetic forms originating in orality also influenced religious poems in the written vernacular, whether these, like the Old Saxon *Heliand* (mid–9th c.), recount the life of Jesus in alliterative verse for an aristocratic society of soldiers, or, like the Old Saxon *Genesis*, treat of the history of creation, like the *Muspilli*, adapt Christian eschatology for the comprehension of the laity, or, like Otfrid of Weissenburg's *Krist*, render biblical history and exegesis into the East Frankish vernacular. A poem like *Christ and the Samaritan Woman*, set out in dialogic form, reveals traces of oral mediation.

As is particularly evident in the *Evangelienbuch*, which is doubtless to be seen as the late fruit of Carolingian educational policy, such works owed their existence to specific personal and institutional circumstances which fostered vernacular poetry in the context of a Latin education. The early vernacular written form was therefore admitted in an 'insular' fashion into a culture of scholarly literacy and lay orality.

The short phase of scripting and textualising the oral vernacular broke down, with a few exceptions, towards the end of the ninth century. Most of these exceptions are closely associated with ecclesiastical institutions – thus the translations of Notker of St. Gall ('the German'), who edited the Psalter and the key texts of an academic education (Aristotle, Boethius, Martianus Capella; other texts, including poetry, are lost) for the pupils of his monastic school, or Williram von Ebersberg, who laboured over an ambitious rendition of the Psalter. These translations no longer formed a mere support for oral communication or an aid in the comprehension of Latin texts; instead, as may be seen from the attempt at a regulated orthography transcribing the oral use of language as accurately as possible, they were concerned with a sophisticated use of written language in the vernacular, even when they still related to Latin sources and above all to educated literary practice within the monastery.[17] Poetry beyond the ecclesiastical educational institutions, on the other hand, remained manifestly limited to the oral sphere, so that hardly any vernacular texts survive from the tenth and eleventh centuries.

## 2.2 The High Middle Ages

The written record of vernacular literature started afresh at the beginning of the twelfth century, yet was now increasingly focused on the lay nobility. At the beginning it was clearly related to their oral traditions, which were still alive. The court became the centre of this literary communication sustained by the written language – in the first instance the court of the king, followed by those of the great imperial princes.[18] From the very start, the court was the zone of contact between clerical literacy and lay orality (Jaeger 1965). It was in this contact zone that the textualisation of the vernacular began (Bumke 1986:631). The early vernacular use of writing is measured against the clerical literate culture, but draws from the oral tradition and is in part influenced by its forms, although it is a matter of debate as to what extent and how this was the case in the different genres. This writing aimed at vocal realisation, and as a rule was thus listened to rather than read (Kiening 2003:12f.). Nevertheless, it would be incorrect to speak of a 're-oralisation', since its conceptual basis lay in the written form.[19] It is in keeping with the common form of reception that, up until the thirteenth century, the texts were overwhelmingly composed in verse. In this context verse no longer, as in oral poetry, functioned as an aide-mémoire – instead, writing fulfilled this function. Resources which helped with memorising were therefore phased out; the verse-form became an acoustic ornament in the recitation, and as such was developed in a variably complex fashion according to genre (lyric vs. epic).

Written vernacular literature orientated itself polemically against the oral tradition. The Early Middle High German *Annolied* (early 12th c.) points to its connection with oral epic not just in formal terms, through its strophes, which vary in length and are composed in (now short-line) verse based on assonance – but also in its specific criticism, in the opening strophe, of orally delivered profane poems (*singen von alten dingen*,

---

[17] See Haubrichs 1989:160–69; on the usage in schools: 170–229.
[18] See Bumke 1986:624ff.; Wenzel 2005:10f.
[19] See Egidi 2002:353 (on *Sangspruchdichtung*).

ll.1 f.). A narrative of a spiritual subject-matter is to take their place: the life of the bishop St. Anno (ed. Bulst 1961). The somewhat later *Kaiserchronik* (mid–12th c.), a history of the Roman emperors and popes from Augustus and St. Peter up to the mid-twelfth century (ed. Schröder 1892), likewise conducts a polemic in the prologue and in the section about King Theoderic the Great against an oral tradition which distorts the historical truth and does not withstand that chronological examination which was standard in the written tradition. Here the criticism is directed against the tendency in oral poetry to amalgamate different historical figures and events into one. In the oral heroic epic adaptation, figures such as Ermanrich, Dietrich von Bern and Etzel jostle in temporal proximity and a single contextual framework. In order to correct this, the *Kaiserchronik* fabricates intermediate links which separate figures who are not contemporaries (therefore bringing in a second Dietrich von Bern, grandfather of the first, who might very possibly have been a contemporary of Etzel's). This carries the principle of chronological coherence, characteristic of the written language, over into the oral tradition, yet does not fundamentally challenge it. The continued dependence of the vernacular upon oral tradition is evident insofar as the stories it tells are not abandoned, but instead an attempt is made to salvage them by means of (untenable) auxiliary fabrications.

That the oral tradition was still regarded as an – admittedly not learned, but nevertheless serious – body of knowledge from the past is evident also in that this tradition left traces behind in Latin historiography: thus the Dietrich saga in the *Annals of Quedlinburg* (around 1000; the relevant entry is probably a later interpolation), in the *Würzburg Chronicle* (11th c.) and in the work of Frutolf von Michelsberg (around 1100), who, like the later *Kaiserchronik*, is concerned with bringing the information of the vernacular *cantilenae* into conformity with the chronology found in the scholarly historiography.

In this respect the written tradition remained the yardstick by which oral traditions were measured. Accordingly, in the textualisation of these traditions in full-scale epic, books are frequently invoked as reliable sources,[20] or it is claimed that an orally disseminated history like the Nibelungen legend may be traced back to a written record, conceivably even one in Latin (J.-D. Müller 1996). In both cases it is alleged that religious institutions safeguard the written transmission of a vernacular text intended for the lay world; thanks to the written source, this text is then deemed authentic even when it is disseminated, as reported, in oral form. Information of that kind would nowadays be regarded as the fictitious citing of a source (*Quellenfiktion*), yet it attests to the superior prestige of the clerically administered written culture, which was also supposed to legitimate the vernacular traditions. In a breathtaking *Quellenfiktion* in *Parzival*, Wolfram von Eschenbach, who emphatically rejects the help of writing (*der buoche stiure*, 115.29 f.), parodied the alleged relationship between the vernacular epic tradition and the written word by feigning to follow questionable, but obviously learned authorities for his epic.[21]

The Middle High German term for early vernacular epic is usually still *liet* (lit. 'song'). This reminds us, and not just in heroic epic material (*Nibelungenlied*, *Rolandslied*, *chanson de geste*), of its provenance in orality. Yet the term is used also for texts in

---

[20] See Coxon 1998 on *Wolfdietrich* D.
[21] *Parzival* 115.29 f.; 453.11–455.16 (Lachmann 1926); see Strohschneider 2006.

the written tradition, such as the *Alexanderlied* of Pfaffe Konrad (ed. Ruttman 1974) or *Herzog Ernst* (ed. Bartsch 1896). Even the formula *singen unde sagen* (to sing and to say), used particularly in textualised heroic epics, refers back to their original realisation in oral form.

Whereas in Middle High German heroic epic, oral dissemination is presupposed even when a book is invoked corroboratively as a source, the courtly romance, which was imported from France in the last third of the twelfth century, emphasises its written status, setting itself apart from the muddled and unverified stories provided in the oral recitations of entertainers (jongleurs). Chrétien de Troyes contrasts the crude fictions of these entertainers with the *bel conjointure* of the highly structured work produced in written form (*Erec et Enide*, ll.14f.). The first German adaptor of his romances, Hartmann von Aue (*Erec, Iwein*), connected the new genre with the educational changes of the High Middle Ages, the literacy of the lay knights. He articulated the knight's pride in education, he who *geleret was, daz er an den buochen las* (*Der arme Heinrich*, ll. 1f.; see 1–17; *Iwein*, ll. 21–30) and was therefore able to adapt written models. Gottfried von Strassburg 'reads' the histories about Tristan and recounts them from his *lesen* (ll. 132–34; 147–49).[22] The vernacular courtly romance is therefore of genuinely written form. Yet Wolfram von Eschenbach's polemic against *der buoche stiure* (*Parzival*, ll. 115, 29f.) still sets itself expressly against the written literary traditions of the *clerici*; Wolfram styles himself as a *poeta-vates* inspired by the Holy Spirit.[23] The role of Wolfram shaped the image of the 'wise layman' in the thirteenth century, who successfully grappled with the learned cleric (*phaffe*) Klingsor; this role reflected the self-awareness of the new lay culture, which, even though it had not been purely oral for some time, still rejected the literary traditions of the clergymen.[24]

There is a conflict between the primarily written production and the primarily oral reception of vernacular texts. Even the courtly romance was delivered predominantly in oral form and was received by listening. In fact it was on these grounds that the courtly romance conceptualised face-to-face scenarios of oral communication, conversations between the narrator and his public or with other narrative authorities, such as the personifications of courtly values (Frau Minne, Frau Aventiure). Thus the narrator 'Hartmann' simulates a conversation with his listeners about the properties of Enite's saddle (*Erec*, ll. 7493–7525), or feigns a dialogue with another narrator, Frau Minne (Lady Courtly Love), about the correct manner in which to narrate Iwein's separation from Laudine (*Iwein*, ll. 2971–3028). Here seemingly oral communication already serves as a fictionalisation of the narration, in which the ostensibly present (oral) narrator, or rather, one of his masks (Frau Minne), delivers the narration as a performance by the grace of the (absent) author.

---

[22] On Hartmann's works, see the editions by Scholz 2007 (*Erec*), Benecke et al. 1968 (*Iwein*), and Paul 1984 (*Der arme Heinrich*).

[23] On the controversy over Wolfram's education, see Ohly 1961–62 vs. Grundmann 1967. When Wolfram purports to understand nothing of the art of books (see *Parzival*, 114, 12–30; *Willehalm*, 2.17–22), this must primarily be a pose, as research into his immense body of learned knowledge has shown. For the text of *Willehalm*, see Kartschoke and Schröder 2003.

[24] See Ragotzky 1971; Kellner and Strohschneider 2005.

Writing allows for larger-scale epic dimensions and permits more complex structural forms which are nevertheless influenced by oral traditions. Thus the principle of repetition customary in oral epic is incorporated, but is integrated into a complex structure of progression (the symbolic structure of the Arthur romances: the double cursus).[25] Furthermore, the courtly romance is composed in verse, but in short-line rhyming couplets. Verse was now a chiefly ornamental form rather than a mnemonic aid, and was just as suitable for private reading as for oral recitation.

With the emergence of a vernacular literacy, the roles of narrator and author separated, whereas under oral conditions they had been indistinguishable. This creation of an authorial profile is apparent in that the names of composers of courtly romances are consistently known, whereas those in the orally rooted heroic epic remained largely anonymous (Höfler 1961). In heroic epic exceptions are rare, thus the *Goldemar* fragment, whose poet is named Albrecht von Kemnaten, or the name of Heinrich der Vogler, who is named as the compiler or perhaps only the commentator of the *Buch von Bern*, or the mysterious Heinrich von Ofterdingen, to whom a version of *Laurin* is attributed. Such attributions are invariably secondary and reflect the incorporation of formerly oral traditions into written culture. No matter how large his actual stake in the recited text, the deliverer of oral poetry acts only as the latest figure to continue a long collective tradition. This continued to have an impact on vernacular literacy, as even an author identified by name still understood himself not as the 'inventor' of his text, but as the 'reteller' and adapter of already existing stories.[26] On the other hand, the earliest vernacular epics recorded in written form (*Annolied, Kaiserchronik*) are still anonymous.

Other vernacular genres, like courtly *Minnesang* or *Sangspruchdichtung*, were also designed for recitation. Their elaborate strophic forms and plays on sound were directed towards a listening audience. Yet as a rule they already presupposed a written conception (Cramer 1998). Certainly in the first instance they appear to be predominantly orally disseminated, which exposed them to the erosion typical of oral tradition. Only some generations after their genesis – and characteristically without the notation necessary for musical delivery – were they recorded in written form. The *Minnesang* was collected in songbooks; now songs and *Sangsprüche* became written literary genres.

The impulse towards textualisation which was marked by courtly epic had its basis in a much more widespread process of textualisation in all areas of everyday life, and accelerated in the thirteenth century. Germany still has no study equivalent to Clanchy's work on the textualisation of legal acts in the twelfth to fourteenth centuries in England (1993), but conditions in Germany were probably similar. The *Sachsenspiegel* (first third of the 13th c.), a codification of legal norms for peasants and knights ('common law' and 'feudal law') in the old Duchy of Saxony, which stands at the start of similar records in Germany, documents a legal practice which was still oral and establishes legal acts which were to be enacted orally, yet it does so in written form (Schmidt-Wiegand 1980).

In historiography and technical literature in general, from the end of the thirteenth century verse is replaced by prose; fictional narrative literature followed.[27] Yet there

---

[25] See Kuhn 1969; Haug 1989d; 1992:91–107.
[26] See Worstbrock 1999; J.-D. Müller 2005b.
[27] See Schnell 1984; J.-D. Müller 1985.

might have been a high proportion of oral transmission which is attested at best indirectly, and even prose texts are not specifically destined only to be read (for oneself), but also to be heard (when read out aloud). Up until the end of the Middle Ages we must therefore deal with both forms of reception in all literary genres. As a result, a broad zone of transition between literacy and orality emerges. Medial orality does not necessarily imply conceptual orality, and the same applies to literacy (Koch and Oesterreicher 1985).

The oral delivery of a text which is fixed in writing nevertheless meets with terms of communication different from those in primary orality, since the audience of a written text has the option of distancing themselves from the narrative, in accordance with a 'contract of fictionality' (with the narrator). No clear-cut distinction can be made between genuine (only subsequently scripted) orality and genuine literacy (only disguised as orality) – as indeed the majority of research in recent decades has insinuated of the *Nibelungenlied* – because the pertinent characteristics cannot be unequivocally apportioned in a text which has come down to us only in written form.[28]

## 2.3 The Late Middle Ages

The gradual move away from a purely orally enactive dissemination of knowledge deemed worthy of transmission continued in the late Middle Ages. This move was reflected in a technical vernacular prose which encompassed all fields of knowledge (Friedrich 1997). Education became dissociated from participation in action and from oral communication,[29] and moved towards a cognitive mechanism mediated through writing. The 'explosion' of literacy (Kuhn 1980: 136f.) took over even areas in which writing was virtually dysfunctional, although this type of writing had no future. Examples are the combat manuals of the late Middle Ages (J.-D. Müller 1994). Their scripting of oral instructions and directions about posture and bearing are all but unintelligible in their written form, and require prose commentary and visual depiction. Here and in comparable genres the tendency towards textualisation therefore never fully prevailed (J.-D. Müller 1994: 357f.).

From the thirteenth century first the monarchs expanded their chancelleries, and then from the fourteenth century the imperial princes followed suit (Bumke 1986: 624–33), whereupon Latin was gradually pushed back by the vernacular from the thirteenth century onward (633–37). Administrative and legal acts were increasingly executed and documented in writing. The rise of cities, the expansion of commercial relationships and the boom and differentiation of trade and craft promoted the proliferation of writing more than ever. The municipal school system, i. e. a system which was no longer carried out primarily by ecclesiastical institutions, was expanded. In addition to the civic Latin schools, unauthorised, privately organised schools (*Winkelschulen, Klippschulen*) appeared, in which an elementary knowledge of reading, writing and arithmetic was transmitted. Up until the end of the Middle Ages, therefore, the balance

---

[28] See Curschmann 1967 and 1979; Egidi 2002: 27.
[29] On this form of upbringing in the court, see Wenzel 1995: 128–192.

between the domains of Latin and the vernacular shifted ever further in favour of the latter, the more the acquisition of the cultural skills of reading and writing moved away from ecclesiastical institutions of education. With the increasing literacy of the upper class and a section of the middle class, above all in urban populations, processes of oral transmission lost their relevance.

Not only the practices of the clerical communities but also the piety of the lay society in the late Middle Ages increasingly required the medium of writing for worship, meditation and religious edification, as is attested by the numerous Books of Hours, texts of legends and visions, Tractates of the Passion, small books of solace and the like which have survived. In addition to public reading (e. g. collations in religious convents), private reading emerged. Despite this, in many areas of religious life writing remained merely subservient to the dominant form of oral communication, as with the retrospective documentation of public sermons or the compilation of sermons and their themes in large sermon-collections for the purpose of future (oral) use. Performances of liturgical dramas, which presented the central events of the Christian history of salvation to a mass audience in dramatic form, depended upon written texts in their staging. Songs and stories, which might in principle be disseminated without the help of writing, were collected or recorded so as to be reused.

In this respect large areas of culture in the late Middle Ages were broadly based upon oral transmission; participation in this culture did not necessarily require the use of writing. Larger pieces of writing were still costly to compose and expensive to possess. The introduction of paper in the place of the more expensive parchment (which took place in Germany from the end of the fourteenth century) made written products cheaper, as did the introduction of new procedures for the reproduction of manuscripts in commercially operating scriptoria (Saurma-Jeltsch 2001). We see the beginnings of a rudimentary market for the production of writing. Yet, as before, the price of written texts had a prohibitive effect (Brandis 1984). Thus a large proportion of literary communication continued to take place orally. Only the invention of the letterpress with adjustable letters and the optimisation of the new technology led gradually to a reduction in costs after the 1480s significant enough that a larger proportion of the population could obtain access to communication in written form. Even so, large areas still remained the province of orality. In particular, the lower classes in both town and country were excluded from literate culture. Despite the expansion of the school system, the level of literacy on the eve of the Reformation was slight, particularly in the countryside. Efforts in this regard during the Reformation[30] were successful at first chiefly only in large municipalities like Strasbourg. Only at the end of the eighteenth century were public elementary schools established all over the country.

The pamphlet campaign of the years 1520/1530, to which the early Reformation owes its success, although it relied upon (printed) writing, primarily adapted oral forms of communication (especially talks) for its propaganda. In order to have a large-scale effect, the written text had to be suitable for oral performance.[31] Information and pro-

---

[30] Thus already Luther's letter 'An die Rathherren aller Städte deutsches Lands' of 1524 (edited in Luther 1899).
[31] See the collection edited by Lenk 1968.

clamations also frequently continued to be disseminated in the form of songs or maxims in rhyming couplets.[32] When these were fixed in writing or even printed, and thus directed at a reader, writing could also serve as a support for oral delivery. Up until the large campaigns for literacy in the late eighteenth and early nineteenth centuries, sensations, important military events, political propaganda and sectarian polemics were mediated through pamphlets, which reached a large audience first through oral communication via newspaper-hawkers, colporteurs and the like.

Literary communication still took place to a large extent orally. Early prints recommend themselves as works for both reading and being listened to. Thanks to their organisation into small sections, printed works destined predominantly to be read sought to accommodate the perceptive faculties of a public still largely unpractised in the use of writing. Farces and other short narratives were fixed in written form in large collections, so that they might be retold orally: on a journey, at soirees or in similar social situations. Collections like *Rastbüchlein*, *Wegkürtzer*, *Katzipori* and the like are intended not just to be read aloud from; rather, they provide a narrative repertoire at one's own disposal, to be learned by rote or even for individual rearrangement. In these cases writing is simply the storage mechanism which preserves material for oral communication.

In addition to these we have songbooks, collections of proverbs (Sebastian Franck, Christoph Egenolf) and fairy-tales; these anthologies come to a definite end in the early nineteenth century (*Des Knaben Wunderhorn*). The collection of the Brothers Grimm (Grimms' *Fairy Tales*) is already a latecomer with an academic, conservational agenda. The Grimms already had to assert the oral provenance of their material, as opposed to its actual written literary transmission, by devising an old Hessian story-teller as their source. In this respect, the history of oral literary traditions does not come to an end with the Middle Ages. Up to the end of the eighteenth century, orality had a substantially higher stake in literary communication than it does today: in narratives told in social settings, in reading aloud, in recitations. Even the representation of literary subjects in 'living' tableaux belongs to this context, as it provides an occasion for oral exchange. In certain spheres oral dissemination is primary still today (urban legends).

## 3 Genres

From the Early Middle Ages, oral poetry had been the domain of entertainers, narrators, singers and speakers, who as a group are not often clearly demarcated from other artists in the sources (acrobats, fire-eaters, mime artists, musicians and so forth), and who were defamed as irresponsible riffraff from the perspective of the *clerici*, who were skilled in writing. Yet they seem to have been firmly established in the lay culture of the Middle Ages. Their social status seems to have been extremely varied, from prestigious court singers to groups of itinerant minstrels (whose status is difficult to grasp) and finally to the outcast. With the textualisation of their repertoire, a tendency towards professionalisation was introduced.[33]

---

[32] See J.-D. Müller 2004a; Liliencron 1865.
[33] [On the medieval performer, see also ch. 5 in this volume (J. Harris and K. Reichl).]

Given the partial orality of the Middle Ages, there are transitional zones between orality and literacy in almost all literary genres. Writing can serve to record oral communication subsequently, or can be a helpful device for oral communication. Writing is then merely subsidiary to orality. In such cases the usual rules of the written language are abandoned in favour of a mimetic adherence to the spoken language. In addition, texts conceived in written form were consistently received in oral form – especially the epics and romances of the High Middle Ages; but even prose texts could be destined for oral delivery (thus the sermon), or others, like the prose romance, optionally so. In epic verse, situations of oral communication were still frequently simulated in written form; this may be a relic of an oral practice, but in the written text it is also a signal of its fictionality, since such a practice now seems just to be staged. Finally, oral poetry may be archived in collections, fixed in written form. Unlike modern transcriptions of oral speech, its oral character is often abandoned in favour of the rules for textualising the written language.

If, in this respect, vernacular literature in the Middle Ages is to be located as a whole in the transitional zone between orality and literacy, then certain genres – in their production as much as their reception – are nevertheless more strongly rooted in and characterised by orality. These will be discussed again in the following analysis.

### 3.1 Heroic Epic

Epic is the medium of preliterate tradition. Its primary manifestation in the German Middle Ages is in heroic epic, although its stylistic traits may be found in other types of historical tradition. Whereas in other cultures, religious, mythical and cultic traditions are also the subject-matter of oral poetry, we do not find this type of poetry in the German Middle Ages, for such themes are the concern of the literate clerical culture. The epic tradition is restricted to knowledge of the past. As a result, the recollection of important rulers and dramatic events cannot be divided neatly from that of the fortunes of exceptional heroes. Heroic epic too was fundamentally understood as knowledge about a distant past.

The appropriation of the past tended towards the 'reduction and assimilation' of noteworthy events; which is to say that these were compressed and adapted to the prevailing conditions of comprehension.[34] This does not mean a freely available poetic technique but the adaptation of habitualised patterns of apperception which allow societies primarily devoid of writing or with only a limited use of writing to learn of and interpret the past according to known patterns which have proven themselves since time immemorial and which will long continue to do so. 'Reduction and assimilation' are manifested in the form of a personalisation of anonymous and collective processes, their apparent dehistoricisation and the compression of complex contextual frameworks.[35] Traces of analogous revision are also to be found far beyond the oral tradition of history, indeed even in the erudite Latin historiography of the Middle Ages, insofar as this draws on oral traditions (Haug 1989e).

---

[34] See Heinzle 1994: 25; 1999; see also Haug 1989b; 1989c; 1995b.
[35] See Haug 1995b: 61f.; 1995c: 90; Heinzle 1999: 204f.

In a traditional society, institutions are poorly developed. Political action therefore largely takes place in the form of personal interaction. Longer and more complex chains of action are reduced to the interaction of individual people, so that they may be passed on in a form more easily remembered: e. g. the conflict between two *gentes* is reduced to the hatred between their leaders, the demise of a people to the personal vengeance and treachery of its individual members, the change of a dynasty to murderous intrigues in the royal house, and so forth. This engenders typical forms of narration, as, for instance, when adversaries clash in a hall (hence the popularity of the paradigmatic situation 'Struggle in the Hall').

Single events are worthy of recollection only if they are of exemplary significance. The once-only/specific is therefore stylised to become timeless/typical. Whilst the practical historical context sinks back into oblivion, the single event is retained ('dehistoricised') as an isolated component of knowledge relevant to the present. The same applies to events which were remembered due to their excessiveness; from the outset they outshine the historical context in which they had occurred. Their importance for the *mémoire collective* lies beyond history and chronology. History and historical thinking, on the other hand, require the use of writing so as to permit the precise chronological attribution of events and chains of events.

Since memory, as the medium of oral transmission, has to function economically, there is a tendency to shift things which are widely separated into close proximity. The 'heroes' and the other performers of memorable deeds are therefore located in one and the same context in terms of time and storyline, which may be expressed in retrospect as an 'age of heroes'. Temporal distances, transitions and intermediate links, by contrast, are meaningless.

Because of this tendency towards stylisation, the epic tradition of history-writing is deemed unreliable and confused, particularly as it varies widely as a result of its being retold in a continually new form. It is therefore consistently criticised in scholarly historiography, or at least in the historiography based on written sources. When heroic epic was textualised – largely first in the High Middle Ages – the written text was preceded by a century-long oral tradition of heroic songs and stories about heroes. On the continent, apart from a few fragments, this tradition has been lost. Yet indirect evidence, as well as parallel traditions in Northern Europe and England, supports the notion that there must have been such a tradition here as well. Closely related are songs of praise, songs about contemporary events such as battles, spectacular misadventures and the like, the subjects of which were likewise recorded in written form from the High Middle Ages.

In the first half of the twentieth century Heusler had still assumed that the precursors to the heroic epic of the High Middle Ages were always fashioned texts, and therefore poetry, and in his attempt to reconstruct the prior history of the *Nibelungenlied* he had hypothetically proposed a succession of such orally transmitted poems (*Heldenlieder* or heroic lays), which he supposed to have been joined together in the twelfth century to form a short epic, the *Ältere Not*. The *Ältere Not* was itself then used as the basis for the *Nibelungenlied*.[36] In contrast to this, it has been recognised that in addition to poems

---

[36] Heusler 1921: 17–49. For an edition of the *Nibelungenlied*, see de Boor 1959.

there must have been a wide, and evidently very diverse, tradition of different versions of sagas, even in informal recitations (Curschmann 1984; 1989). Thus, around the middle of the thirteenth century, the *Thidrekssaga* – which collected in prose the material about Dietrich von Bern, along with the Nibelungen legend – refers to poetic sources and other tales from sailors and merchants which were in circulation in Northern Europe.[37] Without the storage mechanism of writing, fashioned and unfashioned narratives of heroic sagas and other major events drifted ever further from their historical basis over the course of the centuries, and gradually reshaped the material quite radically, so that it is no longer possible to decide which version of the legend is authentic, or to ascribe a particular feature of the saga to a particular source.

The precise shape of the oral tradition is a matter for debate, given that apart from the Old High German *Hildebrandslied* we have no other heroic lay in German from the Early and High Middle Ages. We must therefore attempt to read characteristic features from the *Hildebrandslied*. The lay offers an extract from a comprehensive tradition of which prior knowledge is assumed, and which is therefore present only in allusive form; the tradition is not narrated in full,[38] but rather, attached to certain great names, recalls a single event worthy of recollection, stylised into an easily memorable situation. Its period and region remain uncertain (and are therefore variously interpreted). The emphasis lies on a collective conflict which is framed as a personal one (here upon the strife between father and son meeting between opposing armies). The broad scope of the allusion and the absence of any explanatory context for its comprehension are typical of oral poetry, since in oral communication one can ask questions if common prior knowledge proves insufficient. A *Jüngeres Hildebrandslied* and the song of *King Ermanaric's Death*, both of which first survive from the Late Middle Ages, testify that similar material must have been disseminated in short narratives throughout the Middle Ages. These two texts differ in their construction and their contents, however, from the basic types of the Early Middle Ages.

Early heroic song might have stood in a literary context similar to that of its successors in the Late Middle Ages: with songs of historical events, songs of praise and of censure, tidings of battles, sensational crimes, marvellous events and the like. The little evidence of this type from the Old High German period, which should not be restricted to heroic material, likewise represents a broad spectrum of themes. The *Ludwigslied* and *De Heinrico* also share the characteristic of genuinely oral poetry not to explain all details which are required for its comprehension, but rather, merely to allude to a prior knowledge (which is situational, specific to a certain group or which refers to a common present). When this prior knowledge is lost, as with the macaronic German-Latin *De Heinrico*, then the text remains opaque. The *Georgslied* transfers the heroic mode of representation to the legendary material of the holy knight (a processional song?). It might equally stand for a common pre-literary type of eulogistic or narrative songs about saints, the representatives of which have otherwise perished (Haubrichs 1995: 330 f.).

The adaptation of material is subject to historical modification, but as a whole appears relatively stable. The 'formulaic' style of narration led to the supposition that

---

[37] Bertelsen 1905–8: I, 2 (*Thidrekssaga*); Erichsen 1924: 61.
[38] On this as a peculiarity of heroic epic, see Adler 1975.

the heroic epics of the High Middle Ages had preserved the form of older oral epic. This supposition was supported by the research into 'oral-formulaic poetry', which still recognised similar stereotypes in oral epic of the twentieth century.[39] Its theses were primarily adapted to the *Nibelungenlied*, the oldest large-scale epic of Middle High German, which became a model for other strophic heroic epics. In the *Nibelungenlied* it was believed that one could detect the practices of oral improvisation supposed to have been preserved in the recording of the epic.[40] This thesis, however, was soon weakened.[41] Reference was made to the large-scale construction of the *Nibelungenlied*, unusual for an oral poem, or the relatively close interweaving and precise development of episodes and scenes, or the relatively high degree of consistency in the text, as well as the high degree of variation in the stock of formulas.[42] Its dependence upon an oral narrative style is not contested, but this is interpreted as a sign of a particular stylistic conception, a contrived oral idiom – in the formulation of Michael Curschmann, as the artificial language *Nibelungisch* (1979; 1987:955–58). The strophic form, which corresponds metrically to a lyric strophe, the so-called Kürenberger *Ton*, which supplants the stichic construction of older epic poetry formed from alliterative or assonant long-line verses, and which was modified in other Middle High German heroic epics, might also be taken as evidence for such an artificial language.

The hypothesis of simulated orality was long the consensus view until Harald Haferland cast doubt upon the possibility of such stylistic imitation in the Middle Ages, and insisted once more upon the genuine orality of the epic. He was not taking into account an 'improvising' orality, however, but rather a 'memorising' orality, i. e. a painstakingly calculated conception of the epic as a fixed text, yet one without the support of writing, rehearsed via rote learning and subsequently disseminated in oral form; this relatively stable text was supposed to have been set out in writing at a later date, possibly by means of dictation (2002; 2003; 2004). Haferland's hypotheses about a secondary textualisation remain speculative, of course, but his considerations nevertheless demand a re-evaluation of the place between orality and literacy occupied by the *Nibelungenlied*. The versions of the epic transmitted from the thirteenth century in manuscript form are unquestionable instances of a *Buchepos*. They were probably already conceived in written form, even if they also used orally formulated material. This corresponds to the fact that from the very beginning the text of the epic was always transmitted in conjunction with the *Nibelungenklage*, a work of undisputedly written form and composed in rhyming couplets; this combination predominated in the Later Middle Ages. The significant divergences in the versions of the best manuscripts are scarcely to be understood as the result of oral improvisation, but only as deliberate interferences in a text of written form. Likewise, other semantically neutral ('iterative') variations in the text are not necessarily the products of oral transmission, but are instead typical of the vernacular

---

[39] See Parry 1971; Lord 1960. For a collection of seminal articles in German or German translation, see Voorwinden 1979. [On Parry's and Lord's Oral Theory, see further ch. 2 in this volume (J. M. Foley and P. Ramey).]
[40] See Haymes 1975; 1986; Bäuml 1978; 1980; 1984; 1986.
[41] See the overview of scholarship in J.-D. Müller 2005a: 28–39.
[42] See Wolf 1987; 1988a; 1988b; 1991; 1995; Curschmann 1967; 1977; 1979; J.-D. Müller 2005a: 51–55.

tradition as a whole in the Middle Ages – also including the written literary tradition – a tradition which did not strive towards a word-for-word approach.

Independently, however, the textualised *Nibelungenlied* also remained in continued interchange with oral transmission.[43] Thus the so-called *Darmstädter Aventiurenverzeichnis* testifies that a variant, evidently solely oral tradition about Siegfried's battle with the dragon (in which he rescues Kriemhild, as in the *Hürnen Seifried*) was absorbed into the contextual framework of the epic. In late medieval manuscripts we find additional episodes or motifs which can be explained only by the influence of oral traditions; the *Heldenbuchprosa*, too, an overview of heroic poetry which was attached to late medieval collections of heroic epics, indicates that variant plots of the legend must have existed which are unattested in written form.

Its strophic form and formulaic nature indicate without doubt that the *Nibelungenlied* is orientated towards recitation in oral form. That being so, it is impossible to estimate its stake in an originally oral tradition. Not just particular characteristics, and perhaps also particular phrases, but even overarching structural patterns might derive from a phase of orality. These would all then be fused into the *Buchepos*. Traces of incessant reworking may be recognised in the epic, which continued after its written conception and recording. Again, however, later changes reworking the written text conform quite naturally to the established form. So there is absolutely no need to think in terms of a conscious quotation of style when a narrative form established in orality was absorbed, amended and further developed in writing.

By contrast, the *Nibelungenklage*, which was appended to almost all *Nibelungenlied* manuscripts, documents the total passage of the heroic tradition into literacy. The work is based in a related, probably oral tradition of material; it may indeed have originated before the final redaction of the epic, but is in any case typologically later. Like the courtly romance, the *Nibelungenklage* is written in rhyming couplets (which permits its reception as much by individual reading as by recitation); it presupposes a knowledge of the legend, and at most briefly recapitulates its plot in certain manuscripts, talking about it in plaintive, laudatory, reflective terms. It narrates, moreover, how the lore about the demise of the Nibelungen found its way from informal narration into writing, and how this lies at the root of the Nibelungen poems (the *Nibelungenlied?*): the oral tradition is conceived from the perspective of literacy (J.-D. Müller 1996).

In the remaining heroic epics too, shaped and unshaped oral traditions must have preceded their written documentation (from the thirteenth century). Recollections of a typical oral style are developed very differently in the individual texts, and most of all in structure, plot and strophic form. The protagonist is usually Dietrich von Bern, a legendary form of Theoderic the Great, king of the Ostrogoths. In some epics (the so-called 'historical' Dietrich epic poetry: the *Buch von Bern*, the *Rabenschlacht*, and also *Alpharts Tod*) he is the legendary *princeps* and King of Dietrichsbern (Verona), who loses his kingdom to King Ermanaric, flees to the king of the Huns and seeks in vain to regain his sovereignty in a series of battles. It is this constellation, the struggle – as much heroic and exemplary as it is ultimately unsuccessful – of *armer Dietrich*, who always wins, and yet who continually suffers new losses, which clearly engages the imagination and which

---

[43] See Curschmann 1989; Heinzle 1998: 204 f.

10 – Beginning of the Old High German *Hildebrandslied*, Kassel MS, fol. 1r (8th/ 9th c.)

constantly provokes new stories. In the *Buch von Bern* (*Dietrichs Flucht*) and the *Rabenschlacht*, this constellation of victory and defeat, which is always the same, is treated four times consecutively in four battles. These battles are only roughly ordered into a consistent context. Nevertheless, the *Buch von Bern* was evidently understood as a reliable historical source, which is why it was employed together with written traditions of scholarly provenance in a historiographical compilation like the *Weltchronik* of Heinrich von München, and was brought into alignment with them. Another type shows Dietrich von Bern in disputes with giants, dwarfs and monsters (*Sigenot, Eckenlied, Laurin, Virginal,* and also *Goldemar* and *Der Wunderer*). The majority of these texts survive in numerous versions, which, although by no means directly reducible to oral tradition, attest to the persistent influence of oral traditions on already textualised poems. With the histories of the dwarf-king Laurin in particular we may observe the dependence upon and crossover with local legends which have been preserved in South Tyrol up to the present day.

Related to the Dietrich legend are the cycles of Ortnit and Wolfdietrich, which were probably originally independent, and which are genealogically linked with one another (ed. Kofler 2001). *Kudrun* goes back to an older, different tradition of legends, which, on the basis of a now only broadly comprehensible legend from the area of the North Sea and the Baltic, was probably composed as a large-scale epic in the thirteenth century, as a counter to the *Nibelungenlied*, but which was first recorded in written form only at the start of the sixteenth century. To these may be added epics which were secondarily derived from older heroic epic (*Wormser Rosengarten, Biterolf and Dietleib*). Furthermore, oral heroic legends left traces in other written texts (*König Rother*).

Traces of the heroic legends may also be found in other genres.[44] Heroic epic material clearly belongs to the repertoire of professional reciters, as is shown by the programmatic strophe of the *Sangspruch* poet Marner (XV, 14; ed. Strauch 1876). As a tradition of lay history, heroic epic appears to have had a wide audience, and pictorial representations on aristocratic estates testify to its vibrancy. From the perspective of religious and moral didaxis, it was held to be of low quality (Hugo von Trimberg, *Der Renner* [1833–34]). As a tradition of the uneducated from time immemorial, heroic epic still received the attention of educated humanistic history-writing which sought to interpret it as allegorically encoded historical truth (J.-D. Müller 1982: 197–203). When this tradition was attached to the *rustici*, it referred not to the social status of the peasants but to the education level of the public (who spoke the vernacular).

The form of heroic epic indicates a varying proximity to orality. The earliest attestation of textualised heroic epic is a strophe of the *Eckenlied* in the *Codex Buranus* (from 1230). In contrast rhyming couplets – by far the most prevalent form of written narrative literature in the vernacular – indicate the transition of heroic epic material into writing. This we find in the *Buch von Bern*, in the *Nibelungenklage* (which belongs to the learned tradition of the *planctus*),[45] in *Laurin* (with the exception of one version), in *Biterolf and Dietleib*, which was complied from heroic epic motifs, and in a late version of *Der Wunderer*. The medieval audience, however, attached no significance to the for-

---

[44] See the documentation in Grimm 1957.
[45] See Knapp 2005 and the edition and translation by Bartsch and Lienert 2000.

mal difference between epic poetry in rhyming couplets and that in strophic form, and therefore to the difference between a genre belonging to a primarily written and one belonging to a primarily spoken tradition; this we see in the combination of *Nibelungen-Lied* and *Nibelungen-Klage* or the *Buch von Bern* and the *Rabenschlacht*.

The great majority of heroic epic is strophic (rather than stichic), yet composed in long-line verses.[46] Whereas rhyming couplets were recited in spoken form, it can be supposed that strophes were performed in sung form. For the epic strophes several regular types can be distinguished, with a signifcant number of variants. Most strophic forms are derived from the Nibelungen strophe: four long-line verses with a caesura in the middle, and the last verse lengthened by an additional foot (*Takt*) in the second half-line. The *Hildebrandston* (in *Ortnit*, most versions of *Wolfdietrich* and the *Wormser Rosengarten*, and – alongside the Nibelungen strophe – also in *Alpharts Tod*) simplifies this strophe by constructing the last verse in the same manner as the three preceding verses, so that – metrically (although not in a melody from the sixteenth century which survives along with it) – it gives the impression of long-line verses rhymed in pairs. A variant is the *Heunenweise*, in which not just the long-line verses as a whole, but also the first parts (*Anverse*) of the long lines rhyme with one another, forming the impression of cross-rhymed short-line verses (*Dresdner Laurin*, *Dresdner Rosengarten*, *Dresdner Wunderer*, *Dresdner Wolfdietrich*, one print of *Wolfdietrich* and two of *Der Wunderer*). The epic of *Kudrun* consists of strophes in which the last verse of the Nibelungen strophe is lengthened once again by a foot. The strophe in the *Rabenschlacht* combines the last two verses of the *Nibelungen*-strophe with the last of the *Kudrun*-strophe. It has an internal rhyme between *Anvers* and *Abvers* (which reproduces the impression of rhyming couplets).

A special stanza is called *Bernerton* (*Eckenlied, Sigenot, Virginal, Goldemar*), a thirteen-verse strophic form which incorporates the (lyric) canzone form (two similarly constructed three-verse *Stollen* and a differently constructed seven-verse *Abgesang*). The distribution of one- and two-syllable cadences and the number of accents in the last verse varies. Given its correspondence with lyric forms of the last third of the twelfth century, its genesis is assumed to have been late.

The strophic form of Wolfram von Eschenbach's romance *Titurel* is derived secondarily from heroic epic, yet from the very beginning was conceived in written form. With a further formal complication, this stanza was adapted in Albrecht's *Jüngerer Titurel* as well as in Püterich von Reichertshausen's *Ehrenbrief* (a catalogue of chivalric epics from the High Middle Ages) and Ulrich Fuetrer's *Buch der Abenteuer*, a cycle of romances from the end of the fifteenth century. In each of these cases the strophic form quotes oral poetry, yet this is oral poetry as an artefact set out in written form.

The strophic form points to oral delivery even in the heroic epics of the Late Middle Ages; the fact that the manuscripts eschew illustration also argues for this. With a few exceptions pictures are lacking as a reading aid in private reading up until the fifteenth century.[47] As in genuinely oral poetry, textual variation in textualised heroic epic is high. This therefore inhibits conventional textual criticism and the attempt to recover

---

[46] On the strophic forms, see Heinzle 1999.
[47] On the late illustration of heroic epic, see Ott 1987.

a common archetype. As a rule, multiple versions are transmitted, and cannot be derived from one single text (*Eckenlied*, *Laurin*, *Sigenot* and *Virginal* are particularly numerous).

It is only with the *Heldenbücher* of the fifteenth century that the transition into *Buchepik* is conclusively accomplished. In these, different types of heroic epic were collected. The aforementioned *Heldenbuchprosa* is adjoined to some of these; it contains an overview of the 'Heroic Age,' a form of herogony and 'twilight of the heroes' (Heinzle 1999: 49). The *Heldenbücher*, at first in manuscript, later in printed form, were aimed at a reading public; in these, therefore, reading is supported by numerous illustrations.

In addition to heroic poetry in its narrower sense, we must take into account the oral transmission of historically significant events in the earlier Middle Ages. This is likewise manifested only to the extent that it entered the written chronicles. Entertaining or educational small-scale epic (myths, farces, exempla, paradigms) is rooted in orality, too. It is recorded in written form only relatively late, from the thirteenth century. Even in a textualised form, it is orientated towards the enactment typical of oral narration (communication amongst those present, appeal to the listeners, insinuation of an everyday context; calls for collective drinking, for the compensation of those reciting, and the like). Yet this could also be a mere gesture of staging. In early *Märendichtung* the plot largely advances by means of dialogues (Werner 1966), which allows for an effective oral presentation of the narrative through speech and response. In the sixteenth-century collections of small-scale epic, the context of oral communication is often invoked only in the title of the collection, or is recalled in the preamble (*Rollwagenbüchlein*, *Nachtbüchlein* and the like).

## 3.2 Sangspruchdichtung

From the Early Middle Ages we have evidence that not only songs of praise, shorter and longer texts with historical or heroic epic material, but also proverbial songs concerning questions of common interest were performed orally at courts. Their possible thematic spectrum can only be conjectured from the *Spruchdichtung* set out in written form in the thirteenth century and beyond: questions about everyday life and advice about the appropriate lifestyle, ethics, knowledge of all kinds, explanation of binding collective norms and religious beliefs, the existential problems of the *Spruch* poet, commentaries on current events, speeches of invective, polemics etc.[48]

After a pre-literary phase which is documented only indirectly, we have *Spruchdichtung* in written form from the twelfth century. From this point on, *Spruchdichtung* stood between orality and literacy, since on the one hand it was delivered orally and incorporated oral traditions (proverbs etc.), but on the other it was predominantly conceived and set out in written form, and stood in interchange with scholarly literary traditions. The oldest texts transmitted in written form are restricted to elementary questions from an aristocratic ethical standpoint, and have a high degree of generality (Ortmann 1989). That these were recorded early on ought to be connected with the fact that they were not bound to a narrow situation, but could continually be 'adapted' afresh to

---

[48] See Bumke 1986: 616f.; Tervooren 2001; Brunner and Tervooren 2000.

different conditions; this stood a greater chance of being recorded than those which pertained only to the instant; these latter, however, must also have existed.

The *Spruch* strophes are relatively easily composed, more easily than the strophes of the courtly love-lyric, which were textualised at roughly the same time, yet the transmitted melodies attest likewise that they were sung (in contrast to the *Reimrede*, which was composed in rhyming couplets, and which was widely disseminated in the Late Middle Ages: it was probably already destined for reading). This is expressed by the term *Sangspruch* in German studies. In principle, a *Sangspruch* consists of a single strophe. Sometimes, however, similarly constructed strophes were associated into strophic groups (although not into a unity as in *Minnesang*) by means of thematic and formal recurrences.[49] That, however, is not the rule. There are multi-strophic *Töne* with a wholly heterogeneous subject matter in single unlinked strophes.

The *Ton*, i. e. the unity of strophic form and melody, is deemed the actual accomplishment, and therefore the intellectual property, of the *Spruch* poet; the accusation *du doenediep* (you stealer of *Töne*) is therefore a serious charge against a competitor.[50] For this reason, the use of another master's *Ton* is exceptional.[51] Whilst most *Sangspruch* poets of the thirteenth and fourteenth centuries used several *Töne*, in the thirteenth century an author like Reinmar von Zweter still based most of his *Sangsprüche* on just a single strophic form.

With Walther von der Vogelweide, the canzone form, which was developed for the *Minnelied*, was also established for the *Spruch* strophe. In scholarship Walther's *Sprüche* are labelled according to the thematic focus of single *Spruch* strophes (*Reichston*, first and second *Philippston* etc.). These labels are modern, yet we have contemporary names for the *Töne* from the thirteenth century onwards. They associate the name of the inventor with a certain content or with certain formal properties (Marner's Long *Ton*, Boppe's or Muskatsblüt's Courtly *Ton*, Regenbogen's Long or Grey *Ton*, Reinmar's *Frau-Ehren Ton*, etc.). The names, in part highly fanciful, were adopted from the urban *Meistersänger*, who collected the *Töne* of the 'old masters' (in part with uncertain or false attribution) and used them as the basis for their multi-strophic songs.[52]

*Sangspruch* poetry engaged in political disputes (strophes of praise and censure) and was therefore an instrument in the battle of opinions which had to be staged orally in a predominantly illiterate society. A further favoured theme is the (courtly) *Minne* (e. g. Frauenlob). Here the transition into courtly *Minnesang* becomes blurred (Egidi 2002). Moreover, *Sangspruch* poetry is the medium of lay didaxis and ethics (conduct in courtly love, as a host, towards dependents, the uncertainty of life as a traveller, etc.) as well as a

---

[49] The controversy over multi-strophic *Sangspruch* forms, above all in Walther von der Vogelweide, which was argued in particular by Maurer and Ruh (Maurer 1972; Ruh 1972; Moser 1972b), has by now been decided in favour of the single strophe. Certainly, however, frequently close intertextual relations between strophic groups are demonstrated; see the overview of scholarship in Tervooren 2001.

[50] Der Marner XI 39 against Reinmar von Zweter; see Wachinger 1973: 121–31on its contested interpretation.

[51] Although see Kornrumpf and Wachinger 1979; Wachinger 1987:76f.

[52] See Brunner 1975; Schanze 1983–84.

hub for the communication of academic knowledge – religious, historical, natural historical – to a lay community unversed in Latin (e. g. Heinrich von Mügeln).

Many *Sangspruch* poets were highly educated; they sought to outdo each other, especially from the second half of the thirteenth century, by means of their *recherché parlance* ('flowered' style, i. e. enriched with *flores rhetorici*) and their sophisticated, often dark thoughts. This can considerably hamper comprehension of their texts, which were destined for oral use. Whereas, to a significant extent, courtly *Lieddichtung* remains the poetry of the amateur (although here too we see an increase in professional poets from the thirteenth century), *Sangspruch* is a field of professionalisation. This professionalisation expresses itself in severe polemic between authors and in fierce competition for the grace of patrons. In *Sangspruch* a pronounced authorial consciousness is articulated, and this stands in tension with the usually subordinate position of the author.

The song-like communication of all kinds of knowledge, as well as songs of political propaganda, are still found in late medieval courts (Michel Beheim). Up until the early modern period, 'speakers' keep their hold there, functioning as publicists by composing and publicly reciting rhyming couplets or songs.[53] A considerable proportion of reformation publicity was composed in verse and sought to capitalise upon the impact of *Sangspruch* for new doctrines. Pamphlets in verse are the precursors of the newspaper-hawkers and colporteurs who still disseminated the tidings of substantial or just spectacular events even in the nineteenth century.

### 3.3 Minnesang / Lied

*Minnesang*, unlike modern love poetry which is written, is courtly love poetry performed in sung form. Dance songs and love poetry (*winileodos*) antedate the written tradition and are only indirectly attested.[54] Such songs – underneath the art poetry (*Kunstpoesie*) of the court – had probably existed in all strata of society up until the Late Middle Ages. They are virtually never transmitted to us, and efforts to collect them began only in the sixteenth century.

In Germany the oldest textual evidence for *Minnesang* dates back to the middle of the twelfth century, in the so-called *Donauländischer Minnesang*, which shares several traits with orally rooted epic (long-line verse, strophic form). In the last third of the twelfth century, this indigenous love poetry came under the influence of (Provençal) troubadour and (Northern French) Trouvère poetry, the *grand chant courtois*. This also crucially changed the amorous conceptions of the German *Minnesang*. Its heyday lies between the end of the twelfth and the thirteenth centuries.

To begin with, *Minnesang* was above all the art of aristocratic amateurs who were probably predominantly illiterate; soon, however, professional poets appear to have joined their ranks (Reinmar, Walther von der Vogelweide), and these presumably had a formal education at their disposal (Bumke 1986: 688 f.). The most important type is the *Werbekanzone*, in which a first-person speaker woos an unnamed lady in front of an attendant court circle and bewails his unfulfilled love in his song. In addition to this we

---

[53] See Liliencron 1865; J.-D. Müller 2004a.
[54] See Bumke 1986: 616. [See also ch. 20 on woman's songs in this volume (A. Klinck).]

find *Rollenlieder* (role poetry of a lady, or of a messenger), *Wechsel* (alternating monologic strophes of a man and a woman who speak not with, but about, each other) and dawn songs, which reflect upon the situation of lovers parting after a night spent together. The songs are recited; they are directed at an audience which is imagined as present, and the narrative persona of the speaker or singer is also imagined to be present. The song may explicitly refer to the recital's performance itself (*ich minne/ ich singe*) and set it in tension with the actual appearance of the singer in front of the audience (J.-D. Müller 1999). The *Minnesang* is staged as an oral interaction (Tervooren 1996).

Any interpretation therefore has to elucidate the poem solely on the grounds of its written form, even if the genre was designed for recitation. The original performance situation can no longer be reconstructed, but only posited in an abstract fashion. In recent years this has favoured investigations which place the 'pragmatic' function of courtly song poetry at the centre, and see its function in the context of its performance. Yet in the process, a definite 'performance situation' was frequently assumed for which any evidence in the sources is lacking (Willaert 1999). Notions of concert-like performances at a courtly celebration in front of an assembled court society are romanticising back-projections from the nineteenth century. We do indeed have information – predominantly from literary texts – about the singing of love songs (Horant in *Kudrun*, alone outside or in the ladies' chambers in front of the women) – but it is by no means certain that this refers to *Minnesang*.

Love songs evidently belong to the entertainment programme of a courtly chivalric society, yet the exact appearance of this entertainment remains unclear. When Tristan recited love songs at the court of Isolde Weisshand, these might also be balladic tales of unhappy love. Information that a particular *Minnelied* was sung everywhere as a 'hit' for a season (as Ulrich von Liechtenstein testifies),[55] do not tell us where, at whose hands and on which occasion – in front of a courtly circle? – this took place. 'Uolrich' also relates how he sent his lady some songs in written form, or how songs were presented by one of his messengers for her to hear.[56] The author's performance of a *Minnelied* before a courtly audience, possibly in the presence of the lady, is therefore only at best one option for its realisation. The songs could have been reproduced by other singers (which sometimes results in their name being attached as the name of the author [Bein

---

[55] See *Frauendienst* (ed. Spechtler 1987), strophes 1370, 1621, 1633, 1738, 1779; one song accompanies the knights at the joust (1352); one song is danced to (1359); one *reie* 'is well received' (1381); similarly at 1383, 1395, 1644; see Kartschoke 1980.

[56] In *Frauendienst*, at most the season is usually stated; sometimes we hear that a song was sung *ze dienste* (out of devotion to) the lady (1620, 1649, 1688, 1695), and one time the singer sings only 'for himself' (1726). The forms of communication are varied: strophe 66 reports that he had sung a song about his lady – where? – which his niece is to present for the lady's hearing; the niece reads it aloud to her – after its written recording? – (*las*, 74.2). The next song that he sang is to be sent to the lady together with a letter (strophes 108–13), and is therefore to be read. The next is sent, via two intermediaries, as a letter with a *büechelin* (strophe 165). Sometimes it is not said how the lady comes to hear the song which Uolrich sings 'about her,' but at any rate scarcely by means of a recitation in front of her (strophes 1343 f., 1347 f.). Many songs come to the lady's ear – since it is not only Uolrich who sings them, but because they are sung everywhere? – (strophes 1362 f.). The Leich is *guot ze singen*, but was also read by the lady (1374.1 f.).

1998]) or even repeated in wider circles. We must restrict ourselves to the minimal statement that *Minnesang* was clearly intended for oral realisation, but that we can no longer reconstruct the exact nature of its performance.

More recently interest has begun to shift once more from the assumed communicative framework to the (written) literary structure of the songs themselves (Braun 2010). This, however, does not form an inherent contrast. The poetic devices suitable for a sung performance should be borne in mind even when we then analyse the written form. Certainly the songs are not to be assigned unequivocally to one form of reception or the other (Egidi 2002: 24–29, 349–54). The texts transmitted in the song-manuscripts are essentially stylised as 'communication amongst those present.' This means that the speech is embedded in a 'deictic space' (Karl Bühler) to which the song may refer, and that it presupposes a counterpart to which it directly or indirectly addresses itself. As a rule, this counterpart is not the beloved lady, but the courtly company (or one of its representatives, such as the messenger). As in oral communication, those present are generally assumed to possess a common knowledge of the situation, and the speaker can allude to this without impairing the intelligibility of his speech. This is expressed grammatically in the frequent use of deictic forms and pro-forms (Tervooren 1996) and in the lack of explanations of the conditions in which the song is situated. In oral delivery, non-verbal indications, such as gestures, can also be added. The circumstances of the performance itself can be fictionalised and turned into a matter of expert artistry. Thus the Minnesinger Neidhart plays with such putative prior knowledge when in his *Minnesang*, which is transplanted into a rustic world, he summons incessant figures and events without ever fully explaining their history, whilst simultaneously acting as if everybody knows to what he is referring.

The poetic tools of *Minnesang* predominantly aim at acoustic effects: responses in the form of rhyme and other aural modes, the tension between rhythmic flow and semantic structure. The sensuous quality (*suoze*) with which a song is credited alludes above all to its beautiful singing. Gottfried von Strassburg thus compares the singers of Minnesang with nightingales; their songs imitate the singing of birds in the vernal wild (*Tristan*, ll. 4749–99). The only textual form to survive today therefore impedes our view of the intended aesthetic impression, in which the semantics can be subordinate to the sound. In this respect, the virtuoso aural feats and the plays upon rhyme in late *Minnesang* only radicalise a tendency which had been established in *Minnesang* from the very start (Braun 2007).

Written recordings of *Minnelieder* first survive in large compilations from the late thirteenth and the fourteenth centuries. The fact that *Minnesang* was conceived for recital does not imply that it was composed without the aid of writing. The form and extent to which this was the case, however, is disputed. Some ornamental poetic devices (visual rhyme, acrostics etc.) are revealed only when read, and are therefore aimed from the first at the reader (Cramer 1998). Nevertheless, the *Minnelied* was initially in oral circulation and could be disseminated orally by being sung back in imitation. From the beginning, however, there must have been ephemeral documentation on single sheets or wax tablets recording the song for reuse. These appear to have been collected in smaller compilations which comprised, for instance, the repertoire of a singer or the verses of a particularly favoured poet. The later books of songs presuppose such older collections.⁵⁷ The musical component of the performance seems to have been communicated almost entirely orally; at any rate, musical notation has been preserved for only a few songs.

The tendency towards textualisation is reflected in the efforts (attested above all in France) to place a song in the context of a *vida* (the biography of its author) or to indicate in a *razo* the situational context from which it arose. The situationally bound nature of oral communication was thereby abandoned; the 'life-setting' of the poem was subsequently communicated to the recipient in written narrative form. Ulrich von Liechtenstein's *Frauendienst* is the sole example of a *vida* and *razo* in Germany. The *Frauendienst* combines both types: that focusing strongly on biographical narrative, primarily in the first section, and, towards the end of the work, that more rationalising kind providing the occasion for the song. A separate transmission of Ulrich's songs, however, attests that they were originally destined for oral recital in various situations. The *Frauendienst* reveals how purported biographical cause and the more general concerns of reception may diverge.⁵⁸

The large song-collections are entirely the products of literate culture. While in the earlier written recordings of the songs writing was subordinate to the recitation (which was reproducible at will), the collections are not any more meant as helps for recitation. In the *Weingartner Liederhandschrift* or the *Große Heidelberger (Manesse) Liederhandschrift*, only a few miniatures point to the original form of reception in the form of sung performance (possibly with instrumental accompaniment). The collections probably go back to the circles of aristocratic connoisseurs and amateurs in the German South-West, whose interest as collectors was by this time no longer directed towards the performance but towards archiving literary holdings. In the so-called *Manesse* manuscript, verses by Johannes Hadlaub are preserved, telling of the gathering of *Minnelieder* through the agency of the two Zurich Manesse patricians.⁵⁹ These verses depict, probably with some accuracy, the literary interest in what was originally an oral genre. In the Late Middle Ages there are more collections of previously oral texts. In his *Hausbuch*, for instance, Michael de Leone, the protonotary to the Bishop of Würzburg, had similarly recorded songs of Reinmar and Walther, together with other popular texts in the vernacular (Kornrumpf 1987).

In these collections, thanks to the desire to record as fully as possible all the verses of a *Ton* which were in circulation, song-units appear which had never been recited in that form. Writing therefore distorted the oral poetry. Occasionally, stages in the process of collection are still discernible, as when a previously unknown strophe is inserted into an already recorded sequence of verses at the margins or at the lower end of a page, or when at a later point in the manuscript one or more additional strophes are appended to the same *Ton* (here the scribe usually confines himself to adding those verses which he had not yet recorded). These strophes apparently never did belong to one and the same

---

⁵⁷ On the complicated processes of transmission, see Holznagel 1995.
⁵⁸ So, for example, two songs in which Uolrich claims to articulate *zorn* at his Lady were labelled as *tanzwîse* (nos. 21, 22), and the second became an audience favourite (1370).
⁵⁹ Hadloup in Schiendorfer 1990, no. 2. By now the verses are no longer related self-evidently to the C manuscript in which they are transmitted; perhaps they talk about a different sponsor of a *Minnesang* collection.

song-unit. The different manuscripts also may contain diverse strophes and combinations of strophes. Older philological scholarship tended, wherever possible, to unite all the verses transmitted in the manuscripts into a single song. In doing so, a philology orientated towards literacy was transferred to oral poetry. Supplements and verse-divergences may point to rival orally recited versions. We can no longer reconstruct the concrete shape of these rival versions. The manuscript tradition offers a certain support to feasible hypotheses, as there are frequent variations in the number and order of verses and in wording. In fact, the texts transmitted divergently in the manuscripts might, but need not, trace back to rival delivered versions. In all, however, written archiving can provide no information about the formerly orally recited form of a song. Again, the variance and changeability of texts which are rooted in orality can only be presumed in broad terms, not described in its actual manifestations.

*Minnesang* is the poetry of the nobility. Beneath the topmost social stratum there must have existed a similar practice of song; this remained oral, however, and is transmitted fragmentarily at best from the Late Middle Ages. Individual upper-class authors like Oswald von Wolkenstein are influenced by this practice. After some sporadic precursors, these songs were first collected in the sixteenth century; it was the nineteenth century which was first interested in them systematically under the category of folksong and folk poetry.

### 3.4 Religious and Secular Drama

The religious and secular dramas of the Late Middle Ages are also located on the threshold between orality and literacy.[60] Vernacular religious drama is closely related to religious cult (J.-D. Müller 2004b). Liturgy certainly belongs to literate clerical culture and was fixed and transmitted in written form. The same holds for paraliturgical celebrations (*Feiern*), which were affiliated with the liturgy of high feasts and which are recorded in the Latin language from the Early Middle Ages (Lipphardt 1975–90). Religious drama incorporated elements of liturgy and of celebrations and integrated them into a continuous theatrical plot. This took place by means of verbal (Latin) citation, by paraphrase and by adopting certain structural elements.

The theatrical portrayal of central events in the life of Jesus (Christmas, the Passion, Easter), of world history interpreted as salvation history (plays about the Creation, the Old Testament, Corpus Christi, the Last Judgment) or of the acts of the saints were designed to render biblical and extrabiblical events accessible to the illiterate masses, with the aim of emotional participation and the communication of their theological significance. Common scenes of medieval daily life are embedded in the biblical or hagiographical context. Salvation history is made 'present'.

The structure of communication in the religious dramas is asymmetrical, for, as a rule, the playwright and/or director probably belonged to the literate *clerici* – as a priest, teacher or some such – whereas most of the actors and the audience in particular were of the laity, for whom as a whole the knowledge and use of writing cannot be assumed.

---

[60] See Linke 1978 and 1987; Meier et al. 2004. [See also ch. 27 in this volume (T. Pettitt).]

Above all, when a religious drama was attached to an ecclesiastical solemnity, it remained closely related to the written literary tradition by means of the gospel text, liturgical chants and because it followed the dramaturgical sequence of the celebration. This relationship is explicitly emphasised in the plays, in that the literate language of Latin was generally adopted for quotations from the Bible or for liturgical antiphons and hymns. We may well assume that the actors too had a minimal comprehension of the meaning of these texts and could in this respect participate in the literate clerical culture, whereas for the public the aim perhaps lay simply in the authority of the cultic language rather than any understanding of the words. On the other hand, there are (predominantly comic) scenes taken from everyday life which have absolutely no basis in written literature, whose textual basis is sometimes only crudely outlined in written form and which are evidently orientated towards improvisation in speech and play-acting. Religious drama is thus located at the intersection of orality and literacy.

That which survives in textual form from the religious dramas is of correspondingly varied status. There are the theatrical texts which served as the template for entire performances, and those which documented a prior performance, as well as those which merely gave indications and support for the manner in which a text was to be spoken and acted. The relationship between written text and the words spoken/enacted in a performance in the medieval vernacular is therefore fundamentally different from that of drama in the modern era. The performance relies upon writing, but this writing is only a supplement to the theatrical practice. Religious dramas are therefore composed in verses which need to be rendered in spoken form, and the written text therefore displays just as small a degree of stability as do other texts which are rooted in orality. Related theatrical texts which were performed multiple times or in many places show traces of ever new and different arrangement.

Writing serves only to a very limited extent as a medium of preservation. In those cases in which manuscripts preserve a play for re-performance, we find traces of the alterations to the text: deletions and insertions, permutations of parts of the text, adaptations to the availability of performers and the possibilities for performance etc. Such variations, however, are not to be seen as variations upon one text and one text only (as is the case today with the adaptation of a dramatic text for performance), for this one text does not exist as a base point; the text is the sum of its realisations in changing performances. Since documentation increased towards the end of the Middle Ages, the influence of a genuinely oral practice on writing may be strikingly observed in the variance between the texts of the dramas. Editions are therefore confronted with a scarcely resolvable problem. When they document all variants, they can show the mutability of plays actually performed, yet they no longer reveal a coherent text.[61] When they orientate themselves around a key text, they privilege one arbitrary realisation above all alternatives. Parallel editions become confusing because of the restructuring of entire scenes or even of smaller text complexes (Janota 1996–2004). The problem of adequate editions of written texts which were current under oral practices is therefore exacerbated even further in comparison with editions of lyric poetry.

---

[61] See the edition of *Weltgerichtsspiele* in Linke 2002.

Writing fulfils a variety of functions in the transmission of dramatic texts. Writing can be destined – and only here do we leave the sphere of orality altogether – for the subsequent, recapitulatory reading of a text which formed the basis of a performance; these manuscripts fulfil the same function as tractate-like meditational texts. Writing can provide a template for future performances which need to be adapted according to particular circumstances. It can serve as a support for the memory in individual roles (*Einzelrollentexte*), either for the rehearsal of the actors themselves or for the director who needs to rehearse the role with an actor. For the director, the written form may assemble the sections of text to be performed (*Dirigierrolle*), in which case only the first verse is listed for the individual speakers, rather than their entire text, which must be completed from memory. Even in records of whole plays, 'well-known' sections of texts (e. g. liturgical chants, Biblical verses) are often cited by their first word only, and must be completed during the performance. With the exception of the first case, the text fixed in writing is not authoritative; writing merely refers to that which is to be orally realised.

Clearer yet is the case of so-called secular drama, which is transmitted in written form from around the fourteenth century (Simon 2003). In contrast to sacred drama, secular drama as a rule lacks any reference to literate culture (liturgy, Holy Scripture, paraliturgical celebrations). Secular drama seems to have a closer relationship to (seasonal, regional) customs, to courtly or civic celebrations or to single prominent events. We may suppose that long before their written documentation, plays of this kind were performed, sections of text, such as they existed, were improvised or were only roughly fixed, and writing played no role at all or only a subordinate role. In the oldest indirect evidence it is impossible to draw a clear distinction between dramas and other customs or merriments of the feast days, particularly those associated with carnival: processions, receptions, combat sports, competitions, masqued festivals, dances, festive hunts and the like. The oldest surviving texts of dramas display traces of a connection with and embeddedness in such events,[62] and even the theatrical practice of the second half of the fifteenth century which is documented in written form has not detached itself from these, and competes with other feast-day entertainments. As with the religious dramas, there were mobile theatrical venues, so that the drama could be part of a procession (English and Low German pageant).

Interest in documenting such dramas remained meagre. Thus, of the innumerable Lübeck Shrovetide plays of the fifteenth century, only the titles, not the texts, are preserved with two exceptions, both considerably later and located in a different literary context (Simon 2003:279–86). The case is similar for an overwhelming proportion of the dramas which are attested during the carnival period in particular (i. e. between the beginning of the year and the start of the Lenten period) in numerous cities of the Empire. The Nuremberg *Fastnachtspiel* is an exception, and is well preserved thanks to its subsequent documentation. In Nuremberg these plays were chiefly *Einkehrspiele*, i. e. dramas performed by a theatrical troupe in private houses; they claimed a considerable place within the Shrovetide amusements. Here the interest in written documentation appears to have emanated from the organisers. In addition, we also have reports from Nuremberg of public dances (without text), masquerades and processions (like the

---

[62] See Simon 2003:38 f.; for later periods, *passim*.

*Schembartlauf* of the patrician sons) (Roller 1965). The *Einkehrspiele* are sometimes dependent upon their structure (*Moriskentanz*, 'morris dance'). Their texts were collected in other areas (Augsburg, South Tyrol) and were partially adapted to the theatrical traditions in those places.

In terms of content, the demarcation between secular and religious dramas is problematic, since in the former it is by no means only 'secular' material which is performed. It seems more sensible to distinguish between plays which stand in close relation to religious solemnities and those which were performed at other times, in particular during carnival or within the framework of seasonal customs. In both cases it was the cities above all which were responsible. In all, the degree of literary preservation of secular dramas lags behind that of the religious ones.

## 4 Conclusion

The Middle Ages remained semi-oral in Germany, although, when seen as a whole, we may observe the inroads of literacy at the cost of orality. Yet even up to the present day there are areas in which oral communication and oral transmission continue to prevail. We may also observe a contemporary process of re-oralisation. Nevertheless, with the invention of the letterpress, orality was pushed back to the fringes of literary history – or else was archived in writing.

## References

Adler, Alfred. 1975. *Epische Spekulanten. Versuch einer synchronen Geschichte des altfranzösischen Epos.* Munich: Fink.
Assmann, Jan. 1992. *Das kulturelle Gedächtnis. Schrift, Erinnerung und Identität in frühen Hochkulturen.* Munich: Beck.
Bäuml, Franz H. 1978. 'Medieval Literacy and Illiteracy: An Essay Toward the Construction of a Model.' In *Germanic Studies in Honor of Otto Springer.* Ed. Stephen J. Kaplowitt. Pittsburgh: K&S Enterprises. 41–54.
–. 1980. 'Varieties and Consequences of Medieval Literacy and Illiteracy.' *Speculum* 55: 237–65.
–. 1984. 'Medieval Texts and the Two Theories of Oral-Formulaic Composition: A Proposal for a Third Theory.' *New Literary History* 16. 31–49.
–. 1986. 'The Oral Tradition and Middle High German Literature.' *Oral Tradition* 1. 398–445.
Bartsch, Karl, ed. 1869. *Herzog Ernst.* Vienna: Braumüller. [Rpt. Hildesheim: Olms, 1969.]
–, ed., Elisabeth Lienert, trans. 2000. *Die Nibelungenklage.* Schöninghs mediävistische Editionen 5. Paderborn: Schöningh.
Bein, Thomas. 1998. *'Mit fremden Pegasusen pflügen.' Untersuchungen zu Authentizitätsproblemen in mittelhochdeutscher Lyrik und Lyrikphilologie.* Berlin: Erich Schmidt.
Benecke, Georg Friedrich, Karl Lachmann and Ludwig Wolff, eds., Thomas Cramer, trans. 1968. Hartmann von Aue. *Iwein.* Text of the 7th ed. Berlin: de Gruyter.
Bertelsen, Henrik, ed. 1905–8. *Þiðreks saga af Bern.* 2 vols. Samfund til Udgivelse af Gammel Nordisk Litteratur 34. Copenhagen: Møller.
Brandis, Tilo. 1984. 'Handschriften- und Buchproduktion im 15. und frühen 16. Jahrhundert.' In *Literatur und Laienbildung im Spätmittelalter und in der Reformationszeit. Symposium Wol-*

*fenbüttel 1981*. Ed. Ludger Grenzmann and Karl Stackmann. Germanistische Symposien, Berichtsbände 5. Stuttgart: Metzler. 176–93.
Braun, Manuel. 2010. 'Spiel – Kunst – Autonomie. Minnesang jenseits des Pragma-Paradigmas.' University of Munich Habilitationsschrift. Munich.
Brunner, Horst. 1975. *Die alten Meister. Studien zu Überlieferung und Rezeption der mittelhochdeutschen Sangspruchdichter im Spätmittelalter und in der frühen Neuzeit*. MTU 51. Munich: Beck.
–, and Helmuth Tervooren. 2000. *Neue Forschungen zur mittelhochdeutschen Sangspruchdichtung*. Zs. für deutsche Philologie, Sonderheft. Berlin: Erich Schmidt.
Bulst, Walther, ed. 1961. *Das Anno-Lied. Hg. von Martin Opitz. Diplomatischer Abdruck*. Heidelberg: Winter.
Bumke, Joachim. 1986. *Höfische Kultur. Literatur und Hofgesellschaft im hohen Mittelalter*. 2 vols. Munich: dtv.
Clanchy, Michael T. 1993. *From Memory to Written Record: England 1066–1307*. 2nd ed. Oxford: Blackwell.
Coxon, Sebastian. 1998. 'Zur Form und Funktion einiger Autorendarstellungen in mittelhochdeutscher Heldenepik: "Wolfdietrich" und "Dietrichs Flucht".' In *Autor und Autorschaft im Mittelalter. Kolloquium Meißen 1995*. Ed. Elizabeth Anderson, Jens Haustein, Anne Simon and Peter Strohschneider. Tübingen: Niemeyer. 148–62.
Cramer, Thomas. 1998. *Waz hilfet âne sinne kunst? Lyrik im 13. Jahrhundert: Studien zu ihrer Ästhetik*. Philologische Studien und Quellen 148. Berlin: Erich Schmidt.
Curschmann, Michael. 1967. 'Oral Poetry in Mediaeval English, French, and German Literature: Some Notes on Recent Research.' *Speculum* 42: 36–52.
–. 1977. 'The Concept of the Oral Formula as Impediment of Our Understanding of Medieval Oral Poetry.' *Mediaevalia et Humanistica* 8: 63–76.
–. 1979. 'Nibelungenlied und Nibelungenklage: Über Mündlichkeit und Schriftlichkeit im Prozeß der Episierung.' In *Deutsche Literatur im Mittelalter. Kontakte und Perspektiven. Hugo Kuhn zum Gedenken*. Ed. Christoph Cormeau. Stuttgart: Metzler. 85–119.
–. 1984. 'The Prologue of Thidreks Saga: Thirteenth Century Reflections on Oral Traditional Literature.' *Scandinavian Studies* 56: 140–51.
–. 1987. '"Nibelungenlied" und "Klage".' In *Die deutsche Literatur des Mittelalters. Verfasserlexikon*. Ed. Kurt Ruh et al. 2nd ed. Vol. 6. Berlin: de Gruyter. 926–69.
–. 1989. 'Zur Wechselwirkung von Literatur und Sage: Das "Buch von Kriemhild" und Dietrich von Bern.' *BGDSL* 111: 380–410.
de Boor, Helmut, ed. 1959. *Das Nibelungenlied. Nach der Ausgabe von Karl Bartsch*. 15th ed. Wiesbaden: Brockhaus.
Egidi, Margreth. 2002. *Höfische Liebe. Entwürfe der Sangspruchdichtung. Literarische Verfahrensweisen von Reinmar von Zweter bis Frauenlob*. GRM, Beiheft 17. Heidelberg: Winter.
Ehlich, Konrad. 1989. 'Zur Genese von Textformen. Prolegomena zu einer pragmatischen Texttypologie.' In *Textproduktion. Ein interdisziplinärer Forschungsüberblick*. Ed. Gerd Antos and Hans P. Krings. Tübingen: Niemeyer. 84–99.
–. 1994. 'Funktion und Struktur schriftlicher Kommunikation.' In *Schrift und Schriftlichkeit – Writing and Its Use. Ein interdisziplinäres Handbuch internationaler Forschung – An Interdisciplinary Handbook of International Research. I*. Ed. Hartmut Günther and Otto Ludwig. Berlin: de Gruyter. 18–41.
Erichsen, Fine, trans. 1924. *Die Geschichte Thidreks von Bern*. Thule 22. Jena: Diederichs. [Rpt. with an afterword by Helmut Voigt, Darmstadt: WB, 1967.]
Friedrich, Udo. 1997. 'Fachprosa.' In *Reallexikon der deutschen Literaturwissenschaft. Neubearbeitung des Reallexikons der deutschen Literaturgeschichte. I*. Ed. Klaus Weimar et al. Berlin: de Gruyter. 559–62.

Glaser, Elvira. 1996. *Frühe Griffelglossierung aus Freising. Ein Beitrag zu den Anfängen althochdeutscher Schriftlichkeit.* Göttingen: Vandenhoeck & Ruprecht.
Goody, Jack, and Ian Watt. 1963. 'The Consequences of Literacy.' *Comparative Studies in Society and History* 5: 304–45.
Grimm, Wilhelm. 1957. *Die Deutsche Heldensage.* Ed. Karl Müllenhoff and Reinhold Steig. 4th ed. Darmstadt: WB. [Or. 1829.]
Grundmann, Herbert. 1936. 'Die Frauen und die Literatur im Mittelalter. Ein Beitrag zur Frage nach der Entstehung des Schrifttums in der Volkssprache.' *Archiv für Kulturgeschichte* 26: 129–61.
—. 1958. 'Litteratus – illiteratus. Der Wandel einer Bildungsnorm vom Altertum zum Mittelalter.' *Archiv für Kulturgeschichte* 40: 1–65.
—. 1967. 'Dichtete Wolfram von Eschenbach am Schreibtisch?' *Archiv für Kulturgeschichte* 49: 132–37.
Haferland, Harald. 2002. 'Der auswendige Vortrag. Überlegungen zur Mündlichkeit des Nibelungenliedes.' In *Situationen des Erzählens. Aspekte narrativer Praxis im Mittelalter.* Ed. Ludger Lieb and Stephan Müller. Quellen u. Forschungen, N. F. 20. Berlin: de Gruyter. 245–82.
—. 2003. 'Das Gedächtnis des Sängers. Zur Entstehung der Fassung C des Nibelungenliedes.' In *Kunst und Erinnerung. Memoriale Konzepte der Erzählliteratur des Mittelalters.* Ed. Ulrich Ernst and Klaus Ridder. Köln: Böhlau. 87–135.
—. 2004. *Mündlichkeit, Gedächtnis und Medialität. Heldendichtung im deutschen Mittelalter.* Göttingen: Vandenhoeck & Ruprecht.
Haubrichs, Wolfgang. 1989. 'Veterum regum actus et bella. Zur sog. Heldenliedersammlung Karls des Großen.' In *Aspekte der Germanistik. Festschrift für Hans-Friedrich Rosenfeld.* Ed. Walter Tauber. Göppingen: Kümmerle. 17–46.
—. 1995. *Von den Anfängen zum hohen Mittelalter. Teil 1: Die Anfänge: Versuche volkssprachiger Schriftlichkeit im frühen Mittelalter (ca. 700–1050/60).* 2nd rev. ed. Geschichte der deutschen Literatur von den Anfängen bis zum Beginn der Neuzeit I,1. Tübingen: Niemeyer.
Haug, Walter. 1989a. *Strukturen als Schlüssel zur Welt: Kleine Schriften zur Erzählliteratur des Mittelalters.* Tübingen: Niemeyer.
—. 1989b. 'Andreas Heuslers Heldensagenmodell. Prämissen, Kritik und Gegenentwurf.' In Haug 1989a: 277–92. [Or. 1975.]
—. 1989c. 'Normatives Modell oder hermeneutisches Experiment: Überlegungen zu einer grundsätzlichen Revision des heuslerschen "Nibelungen"-Modells.' In Haug 1989a: 308–25. [Or. 1980.]
—. 1989d. 'Die Symbolstruktur des höfischen Epos und ihre Auflösung bei Wolfram von Eschenbach.' In Haug 1989a: 483–512 [Or. 1971.]
—. 1989e. 'Der aventiure meine.' In Haug 1989a: 447–63. [Or. 1975.]
—. 1992. 'Chrétiens "Erec"-Prolog und das arthurische Strukturmodell'; 'Programmatische Fiktionalität: Hartmanns von Aue "Iwein"-Prolog.' In his *Literaturtheorie im deutschen Mittelalter. Von den Anfängen bis zum Ende des 13. Jahrhunderts.* Darmstadt: WB. 91–107; 119–33.
—. 1995a. *Brechungen auf dem Weg zur Individualität. Kleine Schriften zur Literatur des Mittelalters.* Tübingen: Niemeyer.
—. 1995b. 'Mündlichkeit, Schriftlichkeit und Fiktionalität.' In Haug 1995a: 59–71. [Or. 1994.]
—. 1995c. 'Die Grausamkeit der Heldensage.' In Haug 1995a: 72–90. [Or. 1994.]
Haymes, Edward R. 1977. *Das mündliche Epos: Eine Einführung in die 'Oral Poetry' Forschung.* Stuttgart: Metzler.
—. 1986. *The Nibelungenlied: History and Interpretation.* Urbana: U of Chicago P.
Heinzle, Joachim. 1994. *Das Nibelungenlied: Eine Einführung.* Rev. ed. Frankfurt a. M.: Fischer.
—. 1998. 'Zur Funktionsanalyse heroischer Überlieferung: das Beispiel Nibelungensage.' In *New Methods in the Research of Epic. Neue Methoden der Epenforschung.* Ed. Hildegard L. C. Tristram. ScriptOralia 107. Tübingen: Narr. 201–22.

—. 1999. *Einführung in die mittelhochdeutsche Dietrichsepik*. Berlin: de Gruyter.
Heusler, Andreas. 1921. *Nibelungensage und Nibelungenlied: Die Stoffgeschichte des deutschen Heldenepos*. Dortmund: Ruhfus. [Rpt. Darmstadt: WB, 1982.]
—. 1925. *Deutsche Versgeschichte*. 3 vols. Berlin: de Gruyter.
Höfler, Otto. 1961. 'Die Anonymität des Nibelungenliedes.' In *Zur germanisch-deutschen Heldensage. Sechzehn Aufsätze zum neuen Forschungsstand*. Ed. Karl Hauck. Wege der Forschung 14. Darmstadt: WB. 330–92.
Holznagel, Franz-Josef. 1995. *Wege in die Schriftlichkeit. Untersuchungen und Materialien zur Überlieferung der mittelhochdeutschen Lyrik*. Bibliotheca Germanica 32. Tübingen: Francke.
Hugo von Trimberg. 1833–34. *Der Renner. Ein Gedicht aus dem XIII. Jahrhunderte*. Bamberg: Dresch.
Jaeger, C. Stephen 1985. *The Origins of Courtliness: Civilizing Trends and the Formation of Courtly Ideals, 939–1210*. Philadelphia: U of Pennsylvania P.
Janota, Johannes, ed. 1996–2004. *Die Hessische Passionsspielgruppe*. 3 vols. Tübingen: Niemeyer.
Kartschoke, Dieter. 1980. 'Ulrich von Liechtenstein und die Laienkultur des deutschen Südostens im Übergang zur Schriftlichkeit.' In *Die mittelalterliche Literatur in Kärnten. Vorträge eines Symposions in St. Georgen/Längsee vom 8. bis 13. 9. 1980*. Ed. Peter Krämer. Wiener Arbeiten zur germanistischen Altertumskunde und Philologie 16. Vienna: Halosar. 103–43.
—, and Werner Schröder, eds. 2003. Wolfram von Eschenbach. *Willehalm*. 3rd ed. Berlin: de Gruyter.
Kellner, Beate, and Peter Strohschneider. 2005. 'Wartburgkriege. Eine Projektbeschreibung.' In *Deutsche Texte des Mittelalters zwischen Handschriftennähe und Rekonstruktion. Berliner Fachtagung 1.–3– April 2004*. Ed. Martin J. Schubert. Beiheft zu Editio 23. Tübingen: Niemeyer. 173–202.
Kiening, Christian. 2003. *Zwischen Körper und Schrift: Texte vor dem Zeitalter der Literatur*. Frankfurt a. M.: Fischer.
Knapp, Fritz Peter. 2005. '"Tragoedia" und "Planctus". Der Eintritt des "Nibelungenliedes" in die Welt der "litterati".' In *Nibelungenlied und Nibelungenklage. Neue Wege der Forschung*. Ed. Christoph Fasbender. Darmstadt: WB. 30–47. [Or. 1985.]
Koch, Peter, and Wulf Oesterreicher. 1985. 'Sprache der Nähe – Sprache der Distanz. Mündlichkeit und Schriftlichkeit im Spannungsfeld von Sprachtheorie und Sprachgeschichte.' *Romanistisches Jahrbuch* 36: 15–43.
Kofler, Walter, ed. 2001. *Ortnit und Wolfdietrich D. Kritischer Text nach Ms. carm. 2 der Stadt- und Universitätsbibliothek Frankfurt am Main*. Stuttgart: Hirzel.
Kornrumpf, Gisela. 1987. 'Michael de Leone.' In *Die deutsche Literatur des Mittelalters. Verfasserlexikon*. Ed. Kurt Ruh et al. 2nd ed. Vol. 6. Berlin: de Gruyter. 491–503.
—, and Burghart Wachinger. 1979. 'Alment. Formentlehnung und Tönegebrauch in der mittelhochdeutschen Spruchdichtung.' In *Deutsche Literatur im Mittelalter. Kontakte und Perspektiven. Hugo Kuhn zum Gedenken*. Ed. Christoph Cormeau. Stuttgart: Metzler. 356–411.
Kuhn, Hugo. 1969. 'Erec.' In his *Dichtung und Welt in Mittelalter*. Stuttgart: Metzler. 133–50. [Or. 1948.]
—. 1980. 'Versuch über das 15. Jahrhundert in der deutschen Literatur.' In his *Liebe und Gesellschaft*. Ed. Wolfgang Walliczek. Vol. 3 of his *Kleine Schriften*. Stuttgart: Metzler. 135–55.
Lachmann, Karl, ed. 1926. Wolfram von Eschenbach. *Parzival*. 6th ed. Berlin: Reimer.
Lenk, Werner, ed. 1968. *Die Reformation im zeitgenössischen Dialog. 12 Texte aus den Jahren 1520 bis 1525*. Berlin: Akademie-Verlag
Liliencron, Rochus von, ed. 1865. *Die historischen Volkslieder der Deutschen vom 13. bis 16. Jahrhundert*. Leipzig. [Rpt. Hildesheim: Olms, 1966.]

Linke, Hansjürgen. 1978. 'Das volkssprachige Drama und Theater im deutschen und niederländischen Sprachbereich.' In *Europäisches Spätmittelalter. Neues Handbuch der Literaturwissenschaft. VIII*. Ed. Klaus von See. Wiesbaden: Athenaion. 733–63.
–. 1987. 'Vom Sakrament bis zum Exkrement. Ein Überblick über Drama und Theater des deutschen Mittelalters.' In *Theaterwesen und dramatische Literatur. Beiträge zur Geschichte des Theaters*. Ed. Günter Holtus. Tübingen: Francke. 127–64.
–, ed. 2002. *Die deutschen Weltgerichtsspiele des späten Mittelalters. Synoptische Gesamtausgabe.* Tübingen: Francke
Lipphardt, Walther, ed. 1975–90. *Lateinische Osterfeiern und Osterspiele*. 9 vols. Berlin: de Gruyter.
Lord, Albert Bates. 1960. *The Singer of Tales*. Cambridge, MA: Harvard UP. 2nd ed. with DVD, 2000. [German trans. under the title *Der Sänger erzählt. Wie ein Epos entsteht*. Munich: Hanser, 1965.]
Luther, Martin. 1899. 'An die Rathherren aller Städte deutsches Lands, daß sie christliche Schulen aufrichten und halten sollen.' [1524]. In *D. Martin Luthers Werke. Kritische Gesamtausgabe*. Vol. 15. Weimar. 27–53.
Marold, Karl, ed. 1977. Gottfried von Straßburg. *Tristan*. Reprint of the 3rd ed. by Werner Schröder. Berlin: de Gruyter.
März, Christoph. 2003. 'Stabreim, Stabreimvers.' In *Reallexikon der deutschen Literaturwissenschaft. Neubearbeitung des Reallexikons der deutschen Literaturgeschichte. III*. Ed. Jan-Dirk Müller et al. Berlin: de Gruyter. 489–91.
Maurer, Friedrich. 1972. 'Walthers "Sprüche".' In Moser 1972a: 146–71.
Meier, Christel, Heinz Meyer and Claudia Spanily, eds. 2004. *Das Theater des Mittelalters und der frühen Neuzeit als Ort und Medium sozialer und symbolischer Kommunikation*. Symbolische Kommunikation und gesellschaftliche Wertesysteme 4. Münster: Rhema.
Moser, Hugo. 1972a. *Mittelhochdeutsche Spruchdichtung*. Ed. Hugo Moser. Wege der Forschung 154. Darmstadt: WB.
–. 1972b. '"Lied" und "Spruch" in der hochmittelalterlichen deutschen Dichtung.' In Moser 1972a: 180–204. [Or. 1961.]
Müller, Jan-Dirk. 1982. *Gedechtnus: Literatur und Hofgesellschaft um Maximilian I*. Forschungen zur Geschichte der älteren deutschen Literatur 2. Munich: Fink.
–. 1985. 'Volksbuch/Prosaroman im 15./16. Jahrhundert: Perspektiven der Forschung.' *Internationales Archiv für Sozialgeschichte der deutschen Literatur*. Sonderheft 1: Forschungsreferate. 1–128.
–. 1994. 'Hans Lecküchners Messerfechtlehre und die Tradition schriftlicher Anweisung für eine praktische Disziplin.' In *Wissen für den Hof: Der spätmittelalterliche Verschriftungsprozeß am Beispiel Heidelberg im 15. Jahrhundert*. Ed. Jan-Dirk Müller. Münstersche Mittelalter-Schriften 67. Munich: Fink. 355–84.
–. 1996. 'Der Spielmann erzählt. Oder: Wie denkt man sich das Entstehen eines Epos?' In *Erzählungen in Erzählungen. Phänomene der Narration in Mittelalter und Früher Neuzeit*. Ed. Harald Haferland and Michael Mecklenburg. Forschungen zur Geschichte der älteren deutschen Literatur 19. Munich: Fink. 85–98.
–. 1999. 'Performativer Selbstwiderspruch. Zu einer Redefigur bei Reinmar.' *Beiträge zur Geschichte der deutschen Sprache und Literatur* 121: 379–405.
–. 2001. 'Nibelungenlied und kulturelles Gedächtnis.' In *Arbeiten zur Skandinavistik 14. Arbeitstagung der deutschsprachigen Skandinavistik München 1999*. Ed. Annegret Heitmann. Frankfurt a. M.: Lang. 29–43.
–. 2004a. 'Publizistik unter Maximilian I. Zwischen Buchdruck und mündlicher Verkündigung.' In *Sprachen des Politischen. Medien und Medialität in der Geschichte*. Ed. Ute Frevert and Wolfgang Braungart. Göttingen: Vandenhoeck & Ruprecht. 95–122.

–. 2004b. 'Realpräsenz und Repräsentation. Theatrale Frömmigkeit und Geistliches Spiel.' In *Ritual und Inszenierung. Geistliches und weltliches Drama des Mittelalters und der Frühen Neuzeit.* Ed. Hans-Joachim Ziegeler. Tübingen: Niemeyer. 113–33.
–. 2005a. *Das Nibelungenlied.* 2nd rev. ed. Klassiker Lektüren 5. Berlin: Erich Schmidt.
–. 2005b. '"Improvisierende", "memorierende" und "fingierte" Mündlichkeit.' In *Retextualisierung in der mittelalterlichen Literatur.* Zs. für deutsche Philologie, Sonderheft 124. Ed. Ursula Peters. Berlin: Erich Schmidt. 159–81.
Müller, Stephan, ed. 2007. *Althochdeutsche Literatur. Eine kommentierte Anthologie. Althochdeutsch / Neuhochdeutsch. Altniederdeutsch / Neuhochdeutsch.* Stuttgart: Reclam.
Ohly, Friedrich. 1961–62. 'Wolframs Gebet an den Heiligen Geist im Eingang des Willehalm.' *Zs. für deutsches Altertum* 91: 1–37.
Ong, Walter J. 1982. *Orality and Literacy: The Technologizing of the Word.* London: Methuen.
Ortmann, Christa. 1989. 'Der Spruchdichter am Hof. Zur Funktion der Walther-Rolle in Sangsprüchen mit milte-Thematik.' In *Walther von der Vogelweide. Hamburger Kolloquium 1988 zum 65. Geburtstag von Karl-Heinz Borck.* Ed. Jan-Dirk Müller and Franz Josef Worstbrock. Stuttgart: Hirzel. 17–35.
Ott, Norbert H. 1987. 'Die Heldenbuch-Holzschnitte und die Ikonographie des heldenepischen Stoffkreises.' In *Heldenbuch. Nach dem ältesten Druck in Abbildung.* Ed. Joachim Heinzle. Vol. 2. *Kommentarband.* Litterae 75/II. Göppingen: Kümmerle. 245–96.
Parry, Milman. 1971. *The Making of Homeric Verse.* Ed. Adam Parry. Oxford: Clarendon.
Paul, Hermann, ed. 1984. Hartmann von Aue. *Der Arme Heinrich.* 15th ed. by Gesa Bonath. Altdeutsche Textbibliothek 3. Tübingen: Niemeyer.
Ragotzky, Hedda. 1971. *Studien zur Wolframrezeption: Die Entstehung und Verwandlung der Wolframrolle in der deutschen Literatur des 13. Jahrhunderts.* Studien zur Poetik und Geschichte der Literatur 20. Stuttgart: Kohlhammer.
Roller, Hans-Ulrich. 1965. *Der Nürnberger Schembartlauf. Studien zum Fest und Maskenwesen des späten Mittelalters.* Volksleben 11. Tübingen: Tübinger Vereinigung für Volkskunde.
Ruh, Kurt. 1972. 'Mittelhochdeutsche Spruchdichtung als gattungsgeschichtliches Problem.' In Moser 1972a: 205–26.
Ruttman, Irene, ed. 1974. *Das Alexanderlied des Pfaffen Lamprecht (Straßburger Alexander). Text. Nacherzählung. Worterklärung.* Darmstadt: WB.
Saurma-Jeltsch, Liselotte. 2001. *Spätformen mittelalterlicher Buchherstellung. Bilderhandschriften aus der Werkstatt Diebold Laubers in Hagenau.* Wiesbaden: Reichert.
Schanze, Frieder. 1983–84. *Meisterliche Liedkunst zwischen Heinrich von Mügeln und Hans Sachs.* 2 vols. MTU 82, 83. Munich: Artemis.
Schiendorfer, Max, ed. 1990. *Die Schweizerischen Minnesänger.* Newly edited from the edition by Karl Bartsch. Tübingen: Niemeyer.
Schmidt-Wiegand, Ruth. 1980. 'Eike von Repgow.' In *Die deutsche Literatur des Mittelalters. Verfasserlexikon.* Ed. Kurt Ruh et al. 2nd ed. Vol. 2. Berlin: de Gruyter: 400–9.
Schnell, Rüdiger. 1984. 'Prosaauflösung und Geschichtsschreibung im deutschen Spätmittelalter. Zum Entstehen des Frühneuhochdeutschen Prosaromans.' In *Literatur und Laienbildung im Spätmittelalter und in der Reformationszeit. Symposium Wolfenbüttel 1981.* Germanistische Symposien 5. Ed. Ludger Grenzmann and Karl Stackmann. Stuttgart: Metzler. 214–48.
Scholz, Manfred Günter, ed. 2007. Hartmann von Aue. *Erec.* Frankfurt a. M.: Deutscher Klassiker Verlag.
Schröder, Edward, ed. 1892. *Die Kaiserchronik eines Regensburger Geistlichen.* MGH, Deutsche Chroniken und andere Geschichtsbücher des Mittelalters I,1. Hannover.
Simon, Eckehard. 2003. *Die Anfänge des weltlichen deutschen Schauspiels. 1370–1530; Untersuchungen und Dokumentation.* MTU 124. Tübingen: Niemeyer.
Splett, Jochen. 1964. 'Der Stabreim im Nibelungenlied. Vorkommen und Stilistik.' *BGDSL* 86: 247–78.

Spechtler, Franz Viktor, ed. 1987. Ulrich von Liechtenstein. *Frauendienst*. Göppingen: Kümmerle.
Strauch, Philipp, ed. 1876. *Der Marner*. Straßburg. [Rpt. Quellen und Forschungen 14, Berlin: de Gruyter, 1965.]
Strohschneider, Peter. 2006. 'Sternenschrift. Textkonzepte höfischen Erzählens.' In *Text und Text in lateinischer und volkssprachiger Überlieferung des Mittelalters. Freiburger Kolloquium 2004*. Ed. Eckart Conrad Lutz. Wolfram-Studien 19. Berlin: Erich Schmidt. 33–58.
Tervooren, Helmut. 1996. 'Die "Aufführung" als Interpretament mittelhochdeutscher Lyrik.' In *'Aufführung' und 'Schrift' in Mittelalter und Früher Neuzeit*. Germanistische Symposien 17. Ed. Jan-Dirk Müller. Stuttgart: Metzler. 48–66.
–. 2001. *Sangspruchdichtung*. 2nd rev. ed. Sammlung Metzler 293. Stuttgart: Metzler.
Voorwinden, Norbert, ed. 1979. *Oral Poetry. Das Problem der Mündlichkeit in mittelalterlicher epischer Dichtung*. Wege der Forschung 555. Darmstadt: WB.
Wachinger, Burghart. 1973. *Sängerkrieg: Untersuchungen zur Spruchdichtung des 13. Jahrhunderts*. MTU 42. Munich: Beck.
–. 1987. 'Der Marner.' In *Die deutsche Literatur des Mittelalters. Verfasserlexikon*. Ed. Kurt Ruh et al. 2nd ed. Vol. 6. Berlin: de Gruyter. 70–79.
Wenzel, Horst. 1995. *Hören und Sehen – Schrift und Bild. Kultur und Gedächtnis im Mittelalter*. Munich: Beck.
–. 2005. *Höfische Repräsentation. Symbolische Kommunikation und Literatur im Mittelalter*. Darmstadt: WB.
Werner, Otmar. 1966. 'Entwicklungstendenzen in der mittelhochdeutschen Verserzählung zur dramatischen Form. Studien zum Stricker: Das heiße Eisen.' *Zs. für deutsche Philologie* 85: 369–406.
Willaert, Frank. 1999. 'Minnesänger, Festgänger?' *Zs. für deutsche Philologie* 118: 321–35.
Wolf, Alois. 1987. 'Nibelungenlied, Chanson de geste, höfischer Roman: Zur Problematik der Verschriftlichung der deutschen Nibelungensagen.' In *Nibelungenlied und Klage: Sage und Geschichte, Struktur und Gattung*. Passauer Nibelungengespräche 1985. Ed. Fritz Peter Knapp. Heidelberg: Winter. 171–201.
–. 1988a. 'Altisländische theoretische Äußerungen zur Verschriftlichung und die Verschriftlichung der Nibelungensagen im Norden.' In *Zwischen Festtag und Alltag: Zehn Beiträge zum Thema 'Mündlichkeit und Schriftlichkeit.'* Ed. Wolfgang Raible. ScriptOralia 6. Tübingen: Narr. 167–89.
–. 1988b. 'Die Verschriftlichung von europäischen Heldensagen als mittelalterliches Kulturproblem.' In *Heldensage und Heldendichtung im Germanischen*. Ed. Heinrich Beck. Ergänzungsbände zum Reallexikon der Germanischen Altertumskunde 2. Berlin: de Gruyter. 305–28.
–. 1991. 'Medieval Heroic Traditions and Their Transitions from Orality to Literacy.' In *Vox intexta: Orality and Textuality in the Middle Ages*. Ed. A. N. Doane and Carol Braun Pasternack. Madison: U of Wisconsin P. 57–88.
–. 1995. *Heldensage und Epos: Zur Konstituierung einer mittelalterlichen volkssprachlichen Gattung im Spannungsfeld von Mündlichkeit und Schriftlichkeit*. ScriptOralia 68. Tübingen: Narr.
Worstbrock, Franz Josef. 1999. 'Wiedererzählen und Übersetzen.' In *Mittelalter und frühe Neuzeit. Übergänge, Umbrüche und Neuansätze*. Ed. Walter Haug. Fortuna vitrea 16. Tübingen: Niemeyer. 128–42.

## 11  Middle English Romances and the Oral Tradition

### Ad Putter

Are the Middle English metrical romances 'oral', and in what way? Advances and trends in modern scholarship have not made the question any easier to answer and, in the current climate of uncertainty and scepticism about this orality, the issue cannot be approached without much circumspection and argumentation.

No such caution seemed necessary in the early days of modern scholarship. In 1765, when Bishop Thomas Percy published his *Reliques of Ancient Poetry*, he had no hesitation in describing the romances he had discovered in the folio named after him[1] as the work of 'ancient minstrels' (1886: I, 381). According to Percy, these romances had been composed without the aid of writing, and would have been recited from memory by minstrels, accompanied by harp or fiddle. Much later, in 1936, Ruth Crosby could still write that the popularity of the minstrel 'cannot be overestimated', and that the 'surest evidence of the intention of oral delivery' was 'the use of direct address not to the reader but to those listeners who are present at the recitation' (93, 102). Today, things no longer seem so clear. In his study of the Percy Folio romances, Joseph Donatelli doubts that any of the Percy romances were transmitted orally: 'there is very little evidence', he writes, 'of oral or musical context in the Percy Folio manuscript'; the compiler's 'sphere of activity must have been the library rather than the nursery, tavern, or street. From there [he] was not well placed to hear the dying voice of a minstrel tradition' (1993: 130). As for the evidence of direct addresses to listeners, many critics now construe these as textual ploys. Rosalind Field, for example, argues that the 'romantic image of the minstrel is internalized into the romance genre to provide the audience with a sense of the past and of community. It is a powerful device, blocking the view of a more prosaic actuality – that of the lone reader, the clerics using their library, the family book.'[2] Though not everyone agrees with Field and Donatelli (as not everyone in the past agreed with Percy), it is true to say that earlier generations of readers had more faith in minstrels than do modern critics.

---

[1] The Percy Folio, now BL MS Add. 27879, is a manuscript from the middle of the seventeenth century, which Percy personally rescued from a heap of scrap papers with which Sir Humphrey Pitt's chambermaid was hoping to light the fire. Many of the Percy Folio romances (e. g. *Sir Lambewell*, *Eger and Grime*, *Sir Triamore*, *Sir Eglamour*, *Sir Degree* [alias *Sir Degaré*]) descend from Middle English romances that survive in manuscripts and/or early printed editions: see Rogers 1991.

[2] Field 1999:168. Field's view is widely held. E. g. Taylor (1992) suggests that expressions of oral delivery were intended 'to offer the solitary reader the pleasures and consolations of an imaginary community' (62).

What has caused this change in the climate of opinion? If we look back at the scholarship on the question of orality in the Middle English romances, we can detect several important revisionist ideas – some salutary and some themselves in urgent need of revision. I would like to begin with the seminal work of A. C. Baugh. In a series of articles published in the 1950s and 60s (1950; 1959; 1967), Baugh insisted on the important distinction between orality of composition and orality of transmission, pointing out that the Middle English romances cannot in the main be called oral in the first sense. Where evidence about their genesis is available, this evidence usually points to composition with the aid of writing. For instance, many romances can be shown to be close translations from French. A case in point is the tail-rhyme version of *Ipomadon*, which is so close to the Anglo-Norman source that it has been used to correct or clarify obscure lines in the latter (Purdie 2001: lxi-lxx). One of our earliest Middle English romances, *Havelok* (*c.* 1280), was evidently also produced 'quill on vellum', for the poem ends with a request to pray 'For him þat haueth þe rym maked, / And þer-fore fele nihtes waked' (ll. 2999–3000), that is, for a writer who has been burning the midnight oil to bring his poem to completion (Smithers 1987: 82). The orality of Middle English romances, as Baugh rightly argues, should therefore be seen as an aspect of their mode of reception and dissemination. And there was more than one such mode. Quite apart from oral minstrel recitation, romances were frequently read aloud from a written text (by professional entertainers or household members);[3] and they were also read in private by the small minority of English men (and the even smaller minority of English women) who could read and had access to books. Private reading, however, must always have been the exception rather than the rule in a period when levels of literacy were low.[4] On the rare occasions when books and writing feature in popular romance, they tend to be surrounded by an aura of mystery.[5] In this light, it is unlikely that 'lone readers' could ever have constituted a standard 'prosaic actuality' behind the direct addresses to listeners in popular romance.

Richard Firth Green's landmark study *Poets and Princepleasers* (1980) further undermined the role of the minstrel as the purveyor of romance. The picture he sketches is one in which the minstrel was slowly but steadily ousted by the court poet, so that 'by the end of the fourteenth century the minstrel had virtually lost whatever claim he once had to a share in the literary life of the court' (105). The minstrels that still appear in the records are not storytellers but specialised musicians, and poetry has become the reserve of the professional man of letters. This development is reflected in a semantic

---

[3] The normality of public reading has been well documented by Coleman 1996. See also Sánchez Martí 2004.

[4] It has been estimated that in 1500 an average of five percent of adult males and one percent of adult females could sign their names in England. Since the ability to write and the ability to read were not co-extensive in the Middle Ages, the percentage of readers is likely to have been higher by 50%. See Fox 2000: 18.

[5] See Bradbury 1998: 102–5. Bradbury cites *The Seege of Troye*, ll. 515–18: 'Þer-on was in lettrure / Lettres of seoluer, ful fair scripture, / Þat uche clerk myȝte hit rede, / Þat to bok was set or to scole ȝeede.' Note also *Beues of Hamtoun* ll. 1323–26 (Terri meets Beues, who is carrying a letter): 'Me þenkeþ, þou are a masager / Þat in þis londe walkes her; / Icham a clerk and to scole ȝede: / Sire, let me þe letter rede' (Kölbing 1885–93: 65).

narrowing of the word 'minstrel', which in refined language begins to refer exclusively to music-making. *Sir Gawain and the Green Knight* (*c.* 1380) illustrates the point well. Twice in the romance the poet uses the word 'minstrelsy'. On the first occasion he is describing Arthur's New Year's banquet – 'Wyth all maner of mete and mynstralcie boþe' (l. 484) – and on the second Bertilac's equally sumptuous Christmas dinner at Castle Hautdesert, 'With merþe and myntralsye, with metez at hor wylle' (l. 1952). 'Minstrelsy' here refers to the instrumental music accompanying the feast, and the entertainment following the feast similarly consists of elegant music and song, not romances recited by minstrels:

> At þe soper and after, mony aþel songez,
> As coundutes of Krystmasse and carolez newe
> With al þe manerly mete þat mon may of telle [...] (ll. 1654–56)
>   (Tolkien and Gordon 1967:46)

> During and after supper, many splendid songs such as Christmas part-songs and new carols, with all the seasonal food that anyone can mention [...]

Green's findings have been confirmed by John Southworth's study of English minstrels (1989), which also points to increasing specialisation of the profession and the consequent decline of the all-round entertainer.

If we want to follow the storyteller's demise in the royal records, the terms to look out for are not *minstrel* (which came to designate musicians), but *harpour* (the harp being used not only as a solo instrument but also to accompany the monophonic singing of narrative verse), *gestour* (the teller of *gesta*, the 'deeds' of great men), and *rimour* (composer/teller of rhymed tales). In the household accounts of Edward I, these reciters of tales still appear in good number; Edward II continued to employ some of the reciters he inherited from his father, but they appear to be a dying breed and their decline intensifies during the reign of Edward III; thereafter they all but disappear from accounts of the royal household.[6] The harper's decline, as Southworth points out (1989: 98), reflects the triumph of the physical book: written texts increasingly make the minstrel redundant as a transmitter of stories.

Green's research has been enthusiastically cited by scholars arguing against minstrel transmission of romances, but it needs to be emphasized that Green focused on the royal and princely courts. Outside that exclusive milieu, minstrels continued to ply their trade as all-round entertainers long after the end of the Middle Ages. As Adam Fox has shown, in the early seventeenth century 'it was still common to find medieval-style entertainers travelling the country, "rymers (who perhaps were fidlers too) that upon any subject given, would versifie extempore half an hower together." They performed for the crowds at fairs and festivals, while "every gentleman almost kept a harper in his house; and some of them could versifie."'[7] The continuing vitality of minstrelsy will only come as a surprise to those who suppose that the conditions of the royal court also prevailed in the provincial manor hall or in such popular settings as inns or fairs. In fact,

---

[6] Some 'last survivors' mentioned in household accounts are the 'blind harper' William Dodmore, and William Percival, *gestour* (Richard II), Alexander Mason, *geyster* (Richard III). See, in addition to Southworth 1989, Chesnutt 1987.

[7] Fox 2000: 27. The quotations are from John Aubrey.

the writers of popular romances could only guess what went on at the royal court – which is why they have no difficulty imagining that kings would still be listening to minstrel romances, as in the following description of a royal entertainment in *Sir Cleges* (*c.* 1400):

> The kyng was sett in hys parlere,
> Myrth and revel forto here;
> Syre Cleges theder wente.
> An harper had a geyst i-seyd,
> That made þe kyng full wele a-payd,
> As to hys entente. (ll. 481–86)[8]

The king was seated in his parlour, to hear merriment and revel. There Cleges went. A harper had told a story that pleased the king greatly and was to his liking.

If only the poet could have read Richard Firth Green, or had known more about the royal court, he might have realised that kings were not in the habit of listening to minstrel recitals any more. Yet the poet did not intend this description of a minstrel in action as a nostalgic evocation of olden times. Notice, for instance, that the king is listening to the story in his 'parlour', having retreated there from the hall, as was the latest fashion amongst the rich.[9] The scene is evidently a projection of the kind of entertainment which was still being served up for the lower nobility, and about which the poet of *Sir Cleges* knew much more than he did about the pastimes of kings.

That we are not dealing with a fiction 'internalized into the romance genre' is indicated by the following passage from Langland's *Piers Plowman*, *c.* 1388:

> Clerkes and knyhtes welcometh kynges munstrals
> And for loue of here lord liþeth hem at festes;
> Much more me thynketh riche men ouhte
> Haue beggares byfore hem þe whiche ben goddes munstrals,
> [...]
> Forthy y rede ȝow ryche, reueles when ȝe maketh,
> For to solace ȝoure soules suche munstrals to haue:
> The pore for a foul sage sittynge at thy table,
> With a lered man to lere the what oure lord suffrede
> For to saue thy soule from Satan thyn enemye
> And fithele the withoute flaterynge of god Friday þe geste,
> And a blynd man for a bordor or a bedredene womman
> To crye a largesse tofore oure lord, ȝoure good loos to schewe.
> Thise thre manere munstrals maketh a man to lauhe
> And in his deth-deynge they don hym greet confort
> That by his lyue lened hem and louede hem to here.
> (*Piers Plowman*, C VII, 97–112) (Pearsall 1994: 133)

Clerks and knights welcome the king's minstrels, and for the love of their lord listen to them at feasts. Much more, I think, rich men ought to have beggars before them who are God's

---

[8] Treichel 1896: 386 (Oxford, Bodleian Libary MS Ashmole 61).
[9] In the good old days, lords entertained in the hall, as William Langland writes: 'Elenge [= wretched] is the halle, ech day in the wike, / Ther the lord and the lady liketh noght to sitte. / Now hath ech riche a rule – to eten by hymselve / In a pryvee parlour [...]' (*Piers Ploughman* B X, 96–99; Schmidt 1995: 146).

minstrels [...]. Therefore I advise you rich people, when you are feasting, to have such minstrels to comfort your souls: the poor, instead of a professional fool, sitting at your table, together with a learned man to teach you what our lord suffered, in order to save your soul from Satan your enemy, and to fiddle you without flattery the story of Good Friday, and a blind man or a bed-ridden woman instead of a jester, so that they may ask for a bonus before our lord and spread your good name. These three kinds of minstrels make a man laugh and in his last hour they give him great comfort, for during his life he supported them and loved to hear them.

In a note to this passage, Derek Pearsall tells us that by king's minstrels we are to understand 'high-class professional musicians, not to be confused with popular entertainers'. This is fine as a summary of current knowledge about royal minstrels, but it does not quite correspond with what Langland is saying. There are, Langland says, two kinds of minstrels: there are those that entertain rich folk, the king's minstrels, and then there are God's minstrels, i. e. beggars. The latter are the kind that rich people should welcome: they will sing you the story of good Friday, and will give you a good report before God when they call on the heavenly Lord's 'largesse'. In other words, God's minstrels do what the king's minstrels do, but in a spiritually beneficial way. So instead of regaling you with secular stories, they will 'fiddle' you the *gest* of Good Friday. If Langland's contrast is to work, it is no good imagining the king's minstrels as 'high-class musicians'; on the contrary, Langland thinks of them, too, as verbal entertainers, as retailers of witticisms (*fool sage*), jesters (*bordor*), and tellers of story (*geste*). Possibly, the king's minstrels adapted themselves to local circumstances as they toured the country, or possibly Langland imagined that king's minstrels were not very different from other lords' minstrels who, if they were worth their salt, had a range of skills. As Langland tells us in his description of Haukyn, those skills included music-making, the telling of 'fayre gestes', juggling, fiddling and farting at feasts:

> Munstracye can y nat moche bote make men merye;
> [...]
> Y can not tabre ne trompy ne telle fayre gestes,
> Farten ne fythelen at festes, ne harpe,
> Iape ne iogele ne genteliche pipe,
> Ne noþer sayle ne sautrien ne syngen with þe geterne. (C XV, 197–208)
>   (Pearsall 1994: 255–56)

I don't know much minstrelsy except to make people laugh; [...] I can't play on the tabor or the trumpet or tell noble stories, I can't fart or fiddle at feasts or play the harp, I can't crack jokes or juggle or play the flute nicely, I can't dance or play the psaltery or sing to the gittern.

There is no evidence from contemporary writers such as Langland or the poet of *Sir Cleges* that telling stories (*gestes*) had ceased to be part of the repertoire of late-fourteenth-century minstrels. If the minstrel had become more or less exclusively a musician at the royal court, some contemporaries seem to have been quite unaware of that development, presumably because it was not happening in the world they knew.

A second argument that needs further examination is one that bases itself on the fact that romances are often referred to as being *read*, so often indeed that the phrase 'romance-reading' became a standard alliterative collocation. David Burnley noted that 'romance-reading' is mentioned as a form of household entertainment in a number of

Auchinleck romances[10] such as *Beues of Hamtoun* (l. 3895) and *Reinbrun*: 'Meche ȝhe 
kouþe of menstralcie, / Of fiþele, of sautri, / Of romance reding' (ll. 142–44). From this, 
he concluded that they should be regarded as texts intended for public reading rather 
than minstrel recitation (1996: 88). However, this is a one-sided view. Although the 
Auchinleck manuscript is indeed a family reading book, the romances could assume oral 
as well as written forms. Significantly, a number of Auchinleck romances portray exactly 
the kind of situation that Burnley disregards. For example, when the king in *Horn 
Childe* hears news that his enemy is approaching, he has to interrupt a 'lay' ('story' or 
'song') mid-flow:

> He bad þe harpour leuen his lay:
> 'For ous bihoueþ anoþer play,                      behooves
>    Buske armour & stede.' (*Horn Childe*, ll. 157–59)   get ready
>         (Mills 1988: 86)

The narrators of the Auchinleck romances speak for all the world as if they, too, were 
minstrel performers, requesting their audience to be quiet, asking for a drink to wet the 
whistle (e. g. *Guy*, ll. 2449, 3997, 4298, 5515, *Beues*, l. 4436), and sometimes referring to 
their performance as song:

> Lordinges, herkneþ to my tale!
> Is merier þan þe niȝtingale,
>    Þat y schel *synge*. (*Beues of Hamtoun*, ll. 1–3)
>       (Kölbing 1885–94: I, 1 [italics mine])

The argument that these postures are fictional runs up against the problem that they are 
corroborated by external evidence. Especially interesting in this regard is the testimony 
provided by the poet of *Speculum Vitae* (fl. 1400), who names some of the romances 
favoured by 'mynstreles' and 'gestours'. Auchinleck titles are well represented:

> I warne ȝow ferst at þe begynnyng,
> I wil make no veyn spekyng
> Of dedes of armes ne of amours,
> Os don mynstreles and oþer gestours
> Þat make spekyng in many a place
> Off Octouian and Isanbrace
> And of many other gestes,
> And namely whan þei come to festes,
> Ne of Beues of Hamptoun
> Þat was a knyght of gret renoun,
> Ne of sir Gy of Warewyk [...] (*Speculum Vitae*, ll. 35–46)[11]

These and comparable passages (such as the ones from *Piers Plowman*) offer *prima facie* 
evidence that 'mynstreles' did recite Middle English romances. Of course, this is not to

---

[10] This manuscript, copied *c.* 1330, is the most important medieval anthology of Middle English 
romances (and other pieces). A number of romances discussed in this chapter (*Sir Tristrem, Guy of 
Warwick*) are also found in this manuscript. The MS has been reproduced in facsimile: Pearsall and 
Cunningham 1979. A digital edition by David Burnley and Alison Wiggins is available at <http://
auchinleck.nls.uk/>

[11] Quoted by Baugh 1967: 10.

deny that these same romances were also read (in private and more commonly in company); it is simply to say that minstrel recitation continued to exist as an alternative mode of reception.

Moreover, recitation from memory is not merely an alternative to 'romance reading'; it is an activity that may even be designated by that phrase as it was used and understood in Middle English. A brief discussion of the semantic history of 'romance reading' provides a revealing insight into the different ways in which Middle English romances were received. The modern sense of 'private reading' is only rarely indicated for Middle English uses of 'romance reading.' Geoffrey Chaucer – as the Eagle's comment in the *House of Fame* implies – was remarkable for sitting 'domb as any stoon' (l. 656) while reading (he did not even mumble to himself).[12] In the prologue to the *Book of the Duchess* Chaucer tells us how 'this other night / Upon my bed I sat upright / And bad oon reche me a bok / A romaunce,[13] and he hit me tok [= gave]/ To rede' (ll. 45–49). More commonly, 'reading romance' is used in contexts where it can hardly be translated literally into modern English. When, for example, Criseyde tells Pandarus in Chaucer's *Troilus and Criseyde* 'This romaunce is of Thebes that we rede' (II, 100), 'reading' is a communal activity. Perhaps the best translation is 'this story that we are hearing read to us'. This is an instance of the kind of communal household reading (from a book, as witness *Troilus* II, 111) that Burnley postulated for the Auchinleck romances. However, in Middle English the verb 'read' could simply mean 'tell', 'recite' and need not imply the presence of a book at all. The verb derives from Old English *rædan* (advise, interpret) and originally concerned oral communication, as it still does in modern German where *reden* (speak) is quite distinct from *lesen* (read) – though, interestingly, German *lesen* and French *lire* could in the medieval period also mean, not only 'read', 'read aloud', but also 'tell, recite' *in the absence of any book*.[14] 'Tell, recite' is certainly recorded in the

---

[12] All quotations from Chaucer are taken from Benson 1987.
[13] The story (Middle English *romaunce*) that Chaucer reads is that of Ceyx and Alcione from Ovid's *Metamorphoses*.
[14] Middle Dutch has a number of idioms in which *reden* explicitly occurs without a written text; see Verwijs and Verdam 1927–52: s. v. *lesen*, sense 4: *lesen sonder brief* means 'to read without an epistle', i. e. 'to relate'; *sonder boeke lesen*, means 'to recite from memory'. *Lesen* in Middle High German has the same sense. As D. H. Green (1994: 316–23) has shown, the basic sense is to 'read a piece of writing', by oneself or to others, but in a few cases the context rules out this sense. One of the earliest examples is Gottfried von Strassburg's *Tristan*: when Isolde warns Mark about the gossip that he will cause if he banishes Tristan from his court, she says '*so wirt des maeres viel gelesen*' ('the tale will be often told', l. 14125). Evelyn Vitz (1999: 114) has suggested that Old French *lire* may have the same ambiguity. Although the dictionary examples are not conclusive, Vitz's suggestion is supported by an interesting passage from the *Moniage Guillaume* (1st version). Guillaume d'Orange has become an old man, and after the death of his wife he decides to join a monastery; the abbot interrogates him about his qualifications for the monastic vocation: 'Mais or me dites, savés chanter ne lire?' / 'Oïl, sire abes, sans regarder en livre./ Vous estes maistres, vos savés bien escrire / En parchemin et en tables de chire.' / L'abes l'entent, si commencha a rire, / Et tout li moine qui erent en capitre (ll. 130–35; Cloetta 1906–11: I, 6). ('But tell me now, can you sing or read?' 'Yes indeed, sir abbot, without looking in a book. You are educated, you know well how to write on parchment and on wax tablets.' The abbot heard him and began to laugh, as did all the monks who were in the chapter.) In Guillaume's usage, 'reading' is conceivable without book. Like any other layman, he knows his basic prayers by heart. The sense of *lire* here (for saying prayers) might be compared with that of German *lesen* in the poem *Die Erlösung*, where Christ, in the Garden of Gethsemane, 'reads'

*Middle English Dictionary* (s. v. *reden*, sense 5), but many attestations listed there are spurious. To take just the first (*c*. 1250), 'In boke is ðe turtres lif writen o rime / ic it wile gu reden' (*Bestiary*, ll. 574–55), here *reden* means 'to read aloud', as the presence of *bok* suggests. Yet in a number of cases, *reden* really does seem to mean 'narrate'. For example, in *King Alisaunder* (Lincoln's Inn MS, ll. 4608–9), the narrator declares 'Ac þeo doel þat Alisaunder made / No may I nouʒt fully rede';[15] 'rede' should probably be glossed as 'declare, tell'. This gloss sheds light on a very interesting passage from Robert Mannyng's *Chronicle*,[16] which makes mention of the many oral legends about Havelok (l. 533) and the silence of the written record:

> Bot I haf grete ferly þat I fynd no man
> þat has writen in story how Hauelok þis lond wan:
> [...]
> Bot þat þise lowed men vpon Inglish tellis,
> right story can me not ken þe certeynte what spellis.
> Men sais in Lyncoln castelle ligges ʒit a stone
> þat Hauelok kast wele forbi euerilkone,
> & ʒit þe chapelle standes þer he weddid his wife,
> Goldeburgh, þe kynges douhter, þat saw is ʒit rife,
> & of Gryme, a fisshere, *men redes ʒit in ryme*
> þat he bigged Grymesby, Gryme þat ilk tyme.
> Of all stories of honoure þat I haue þorgh souht,
> I fynd þat no compiloure of him tellis ouht.
> Sen I fynd non redy þat tellis of Hauelok kynde,
> turne we to þat story þat we writen fynde. (II, 519–20, 527–38)
> (Sullens 1996: 499–500 [italics mine])

But I am truly amazed that I can find no-one who has written down in any history how Havelok won this land. [...] But as for what ordinary folk say in English, true history cannot tell me whether it is true. People say that in Lincoln castle lies a stone which Havelok threw much further than anyone else. And the chapel where he married his wife, Goldeburgh the king's daughter, is still standing – that story is widespread. And about Grim, a fisherman, people still tell rhymed stories, that Grim built Grimsby at that same time. Having consulted all the chronicles of repute, I find that no compiler says anything about him. Because I do not find anyone who says anything about Havelok's kin, let us now turn to the history that we find in writing.

The opposition here is between respectable written history (*story*) and the legends circulating orally: these include the story of Grim the fisherman that people *redes in ryme*, i. e. recite as a rhymed tale. Mannyng apparently knew the romance of Havelok (or something like it) from oral recitation but, unwilling to rely on hearsay, he returns at the end of the passage to the evidence of written chronicle.

The point of this philological excursus is that the collocation *reden romance* cannot be relied upon as evidence that Middle English romances were always 'read' in the mod-

---

his prayers: *Sin gebet der herre las* (48730), and with English *reden* in Walter Kennedy's *Passioun of Crist*, where Christ, again in the Garden of Gethsemane, *red þe grace* (IV, 321; Meier 2008: 29). The verbs *las* and *red* here should be glossed as 'recited'.

[15] 'But I cannot fully tell the lament that Alexander made.' Smithers 1952–57: I, 258.
[16] For a fuller discussion, see Bradbury 1998: 68–70.

ern sense: the phrase may refer to the reading of a written text (in private or in company), but sometimes it simply means 'to tell a story'.[17] A revealing example of the latter sense may be found in an episode from John Barbour's *Bruce* (c. 1375). In the course of a mass retreat, the King and his soldiers have to cross Loch Lomond in makeshift fashion. After a long search, a boat is found, which is so small that only three men fit in it. While his men are gradually being ferried across, Robert Bruce entertains his companions with the story of Fierabras:

> The king the quhilis meryly
> Red to thaim that war him by
> Romanys off worthi Ferambrace
> That worthily our-cummyn was
> Throu the rycht douchty Olyver [...] (III, 435-39)

> Meanwhile the king 'read' cheerfully to those who were with him the story of worthy Fierabras, who was honourably beaten by the most doughty Oliver. (Duncan 1997: 132 [translation], 133 [text])

It is hardly plausible that the King in this situation has a book to read from: the sense dictated by context is 'he narrated to those around him the story of noble Ferumbras'.

When we lack any context to determine the sense of 'read', we need to stay openminded. *Sir Tristrem*, preserved in the Auchinleck manuscript, illustrates the problem of interpretation. The first occurrence of the verb is in the prologue. Here the narrator tells us that he knows the story because he has heard it from the legendary poet and prophet Thomas Erceldoun:

> I was at Ertheldoun
> With Thomas spak Y thare;
> Ther herde Y *rede in roune*[18]
> Who Tristrem gat and bare
> [...]
> Thomas telles in toun
> This aventoures as thai ware. (*Sir Tristrem*, ll. 1-4, 10-11; italics mine)

Are we to imagine Thomas reading from a book, reciting from memory, or indeed singing? It is hard to say. Consider next the following passage, which introduces us to Ysonde:

> The king had a douhter dere;
> That maiden Ysonde hight
> That gle was lef to here
> And romaunce to rede aright.
> Sir Tramtris hir gan lere
> Tho with all his might
> What alle pointes were,
> To se the sothe in sight,
>   To say.
> (*Sir Tristrem*, ll. 1255-63)

---

[17] The point was made by Hoops 1929: 37: '*Romaunce reden* bedeutet gelegentlich nicht "eine Romanze lesen", sondern "erzählen".'

[18] I. e. 'recounted in a poem'; *roun* means 'conversation, discussion, song'. – I have used the edition by Lupack 1994: 191(ll. 1255-63), 192 (ll. 1283-85), 171 (ll. 551-59).

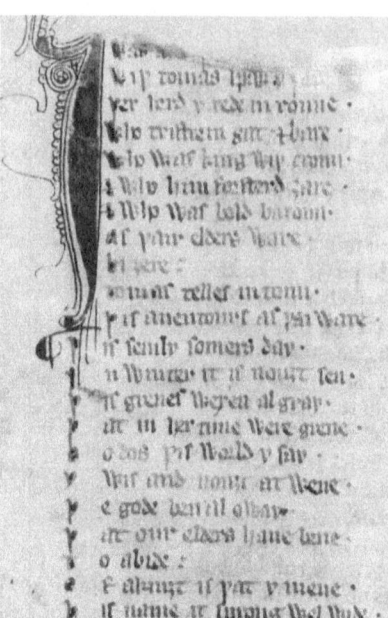

11 – Beginning of *Sir Tristrem*, Edinburgh, Nat. Lib. of Scotland MS Advocates 19.2.1, fol. 281ra

The king had a beloved daughter, whose name was Ysonde, and who loved to hear music and to tell stories properly. Sir Tramtris [alias Tristrem] then began to teach her, as best he could, what all the techniques were for seeing the truth in sight and for saying it.

Ysonde loves to hear minstrelsy, and likes to *rede romaunce aright*: does this mean she likes *reading* stories to others or does she like *telling* them? And when Tristrem instructs her in the finer points of romance reading (which involve *seeing* the truth 'in sight') are we to imagine him initiating Ysonde into the art of public reading or of memorial story-telling? A later passage sheds some further light on the problem:

> Ysonde he dede understand
> What alle playes were
> In lay. (ll. 1283–85)

He made Ysonde understand what all the stories were with their musical accompaniment.

Is Tristrem, who is exiled in Ireland, drawing these stories from books? I very much doubt it. Stories in this poem seem to be told, and disseminated, by word of mouth. Thomas Erceldoun has told the story to the narrator and he tells it to us, Tristrem tells stories to Ysonde, and he himself is evidently to be imagined as an old-fashioned harper whose repertoire is stored in memory. So it is that Tristrem outdoes a harper in what we must surely imagine as an impromptu performance:

> An harpour made a lay
> That Tristrem aresound he.
> The harpour yede oway,

> 'Who better can, let se.'
> 'Bot Y the mendi may,
> Wrong than wite Y the.'
> The harpour gan to say,
> 'The maistri give Y the
>     Ful sket.' (ll. 551–59)

A harper composed a lay, and Tristrem deprecated it. The harper went away: 'if anyone can do better, let's see it.' 'If I cannot I can improve on you I was wrong to blame you.' The harper said: 'I concede victory to you straightaway.'

The oral context that is inscribed in the romance is also relevant to *Sir Tristrem* itself, for we have sound evidence that it, too, was transmitted orally. Robert Manning tells us the romance of Tristrem was his personal favourite, but unfortunately, he continues, there are few people who can tell the story as Thomas of Erceldoun intended it to be told. As a result, the recitations heard nowadays are garbled versions of the 'fine saying' of yore:

> But I here it no man so say,
> þat of some copple, som is away.
> So þare fayre sayng here beforn
> is þare trauayle nere forlorn [...]
>     (I, 101–4) (Sullens 1996: 93)

But I can't hear anyone tell it without part of a couplet being missed out, and so all the effort that was put into the beautiful storytelling in the past is almost completely wasted.

Finally, let us consider the famous description of the festivities in celebration of Havelok's coronation as King of Denmark; the passage contains the first attestation of the phrase 'romance-reading':

> Hwan he was king, þer mouthe men se
> Þe moste ioie þat mouhte be –
> [...]
> Wrastling with laddes, putting of ston,
> Harping and piping ful god won,
> Leyk of mine, of hazard ok,
> Romanz-reding on þe bok.
> Þer mouthe men here þe gestes singe,
> Þe glevmen on þe tabour dinge [...]
>     (*Havelok*, ll. 2321–30) (Smithers 1987: 64)

When he was king, one could see there the greatest joy that ever could be [...]. Young men wrestling, stone throwing, harp and flute music a-plenty, backgammon and dice, romance reading from the book; there you could have heard the stories being sung, and the musicians banging the tabor.

According to A. C. Spearing, this passage 'can only be part of a bookish poem's intermittent fiction of minstrelsy' (2005: 50–51) – a fiction punctured by the line 'romanz-reding on the bok' – which shows that in real life romances were being read from manuscript. We need to ask, however, why the poet thought it necessary to say *on the bok* at all. If *romance reading* necessarily entailed a written book, there would have been no need to specify its presence. The obvious explanation is that *romance reading* for this poet meant 'telling stories' – either from a book or without it, as perhaps in the singing of *gestes* in the next line (both, it may be noted, clearly distinguished from the purely instrumental glee of harp, pipe, and tabor).[19] The phrase *on the bok* is therefore not redundant but disambiguates the activity.

There are, to sum up my argument thus far, a couple of misconceptions that have bedevilled discussions of the orality or otherwise of Middle English romances. One misconception is that minstrels (*qua* storytellers) were becoming extinct in the later Middle Ages. It is true that, in aristocratic (and later civic) contexts, the term 'minstrel' began to designate professional musicians rather than storytellers – but, in other spheres of life, storytellers (variously referred to as minstrels, harpers, rhymers) continued to thrive. It is also true that the word 'romance' (story) frequently occurs in collocation with the verb 'read', but 'reading romance' in Middle English could mean several things, and the three forms of romance dissemination that need to be borne in mind – private reading, reading aloud, and oral recitation from memory – are all neatly encompassed in the semantic range of the phrase.

Having cleared up these misconceptions, I would like to say a little more about the positive evidence we have for oral transmission, focusing on two romances, *Eger and Grime* and *Guy of Warwick*. *Eger and Grime* is a late medieval Scottish romance, today extant only in late texts: there are three early prints by Sanders (1669 and 1687, the Huntington version) and Laing (a reprint of a 1711 edition) and there is the Percy Folio.[20] The text of the prints is very similar and for purposes of comparison the text of the Huntington version (edited by Caldwell in parallel with the idiosyncratic Percy version) may be regarded as representative of the printed editions. Though the surviving texts are late, the story goes back to the medieval period. It is mentioned, for example, in the accounts of the Lord High Treasurer in Scotland, which record that on 19th April 1497 James IV gave nine shillings to 'twa fithelaris that sang Graysteil to the King' (Caldwell 1933: 6).

*Eger and Grime* is a substantial couplet romance (2,860 in the Huntington edition, 1,474 lines in the Percy Folio), and the 'idea of singing a poem of this length arouses strong resistance in the modern mind', but, as John Stevens continues, 'this resistance has to be overcome; it is quite anachronistic' (1986: 220). The evidence of the medieval German epic and the Old French *chanson de geste*, both discussed by John Stevens, and the comparative evidence of Slavic epics (which survive in oral tradition to this day) show quite clearly that lengthy narratives were sung to unobtrusive melodies.[21] In the case of *Eger and Grime*, the music for a sung version miraculously survives: the early-seventeenth-century Straloch lutebook (now lost, but transcribed in 1847) gives the tune of 'Greysteel', and the music itself confirms that it was meant to accompany words: 'The character of the repetition of notes is not an instrumental one. It is the kind of repetition that represents sung syllables' (Purser 1996: 146).

---

[19] As a form of entertainment, the *singing* of stories is again well attested in all manner of sources. Note, for example, the following lines from *Femina* (a French teaching manual, *c.* 1400), ed. Rothwell 2005: 'En sale chaunterez les gestez / Pur oblier les grevez molestez.' The Middle English translation reads: 'In halle ȝe shulle synge þyse gestez / To foryete þyse grevous hurtes' (30.10–11).

[20] See the edition of the romance by Caldwell 1933: 6. The first Sanders print (BL C.57.aa.44) was not known to Caldwell.

[21] See the essays in Reichl 2000 and Vitz, Regalado, and Lawrence 2005, and Reichl 2003.

Inevitably, since 'spoken language does not fossilize' (Havelock 1982: 162), our evidence that the popular romances once flourished in oral tradition is indirect. What remains today, apart from traces of oral performance in the written record, are printed and handwritten copies. In the case of *Eger and Grime*, however, comparison of the printed versions with the Percy Folio makes it abundantly clear that the Percy Folio text had passed through at least one stage of memorial transmission before the scribe committed the text to paper. The type of error that we find in the Percy Folio version is evidence of this. To simplify a complex matter, scribal transmission and memorial transmission manifest themselves in different kinds of mistakes.[22] In the case of scribal reproduction, errors tend to be due to misreading of the written exemplar (eye-skip, mistaken anticipation of copy-text, and so on). In oral transmission, error (or, more charitably, variation) is due to memory loops and miscues.[23] For example, verbal material belonging to separate episodes in a remembered text may get confused or transposed because the episodes are similar in narrative function and/or contain identical verbal material that triggers further duplication. The Percy Folio text of *Eger and Grime* is full of such 'slips' of memory.[24] Let us consider one example. In the printed editions, Eger tells Graham of his defeat at the hands of Graysteel and of the kindness of a lady (Lillias) who nursed him back to health:

> Such drink then as she gave me there,
> Saw I never in my fare,
> That so much could me so restore,
> For I was vanquisht all before [...]
> (Huntington, ll. 311–14)

When, many lines later, Graham does battle with Graysteel, he, too, benefits from the drink provided for him by Lillias:

> He set it to his head and drank,
> And said, the Lady serveth thank,
> For there was neither aile nor wine,
> That came to me in so good time.
> (Huntington, ll. 1635–39)

The Percy Folio text contains a curious conflation of these two different incidents. When in the Percy Folio Eger tells Sir Graham of Lillias's kindness, his words are:

> shee gaue me drinke for to restore,
> for neere hand was I bled before;
> there was neuer alle nor wine
> came to mee in soe good a time [...]
> (Percy, ll. 245–48)

---

[22] The following paragraph is based on the discussion of memorial transmission in my 'Historical Introduction' to Putter and Gilbert 2000: 1–15.
[23] See Rubin 1995 and, with specific application to the popular romances, McGillivray 1990.
[24] For full discussion of these examples see Curnow 2002: 132–78. Quotations from Caldwell 1933: 199 (Huntington, ll. 311–14), 283, 285 (Huntington, ll. 1635–39); 198 (Percy, ll. 245–48) (italics mine).

Two originally separate episodes have become mixed up in the Percy text because of a similarity of content (the hero drinks ...). Such 'long-range transfer' of verbal material between episodes that are far apart in a written copy points to transmission from memory, since in remembered form all parts of a romance are simultaneously present and so potentially vulnerable to cross-contamination. In scribal transmission, on the other hand, cross-contamination normally affects only passages that are adjacent in the scribe's exemplar.

In the case of *Guy of Warwick* we also have strong evidence of oral transmission. The written source of the Middle English romance (extant in many different versions) is an Anglo-Norman romance (*Gui de Warewic*), but the story did not lead only a lettered life. In 1338 a minstrel (*joculator*) named Herbert recited two stories in the hall of Winchester Cathedral priory, the first a song (*canticum*) of Colbrand, the legendary giant defeated by Guy, the second a tale (*gestum*) of the unjustly-accused Queen Emma (Bradbury 1998: 1–2). The popularity of Guy of Warwick was undiminished in the sixteenth century, when George Puttenham in the *Art of English Poesie* (1560) spoke of 'blind harpers or such like tavern minstrels that give a fit of mirth for a groat, and their matters being for the most part stories of old time, as the tale of Sir Thopas, the reportes of *Bevis of Southampton, Guy of Warwicke* [...] and such other old Romances or historicall rimes' (Burrow 1983: 78). The word 'reportes' here needs to be understood in relation to the verb 'report', meaning 'to repeat (something heard), to relate as having been spoken by another' (*OED* s. v. *report*, sense 2b), as illustrated by Chaucer's Pardoner: 'For lewed peple loven tales olde; / Swiche thynges kan they wel *reporte* and holde' (*Pardoner's Tale*, 437–38). *Bevis*, *Guy* and *Thopas* were evidently 'tales olde' of this kind, so memorable that they passed down 'by report' to the sixteenth century.

Interestingly enough, the Percy Folio tail-rhyme version of *Guy*, entitled *Guy and Colebrand*, is based on the very same episode as the one recounted by Herbert the minstrel, namely Guy's fight with Colbrand, an episode which circulated independently from the rest of the story.[25] And again a comparison of the Percy version with other versions of *Guy of Warwick* shows that the Percy Folio text had been reconstituted from memory at some stage in its textual history. Like the Percy text of *Eger and Grime*, *Guy and Colebrand* abounds in cases of memorial cross-contamination.[26] For example, verbal material which in the manuscript tradition belongs to Guy's fight against the giant Amoraunt –

> And for the hete of the daye
> He [= Amoraunt] was grevyd for thyrste so sore,
> That he muste drynke, or dye ryght thore. (C 8278–80)[27]

has in the Percy Folio become associated with a different giant, Colbrand:

> then the Gyant thirsted sore;
> some of his blood he had lost thore;
> & this he sayd on hye [...] (268–70)[28]

---

[25] The fragmentary inventory of books in the *Paston Letters* (Davis 1971: 516–18) makes mention of 'a boke lent Mideltion, *and* therein is Bele Da<...> Mercy, Þe Parlement off Byrdys, Balade <...> off Guy *and* Colbronde, Off the Goos [...]'.
[26] For full discussion see Curnow 2002: 197–215.
[27] C = Cambridge, Caius College, MS 107. I cite the edition by Zupitza 1883–91: 467.
[28] References are to Hales and Furnivall 1868: II, 509–49, at 536.

It could perhaps be argued that such 'long-range transfers' are due to authorial re-composition, but there seems nothing artful or deliberate about the long-range repetitions that characterise the Percy text. Compare, for example, the following two incidents from *Guy and Colebrand*:[29]

1) The King's messenger goes to Felice to ask for Guy's armour:

> The Kings messenger *to warwicke* went,
> *The Countesse soone he ffound.*
> before her he kneeled him on his knee,
> prayed her of the armor belonged to *Sir Guy* (ll. 134–37)

2) Guy sends his page to Felice to summon her to his death bed:

> the little lad made him bowne
> till he came *to warwicke* towne.
> *the Countesse soone he ffound;*
> before her he kneeled on his knee;
> saith, 'well greeteth you my Lord, *Sir Guy*!' (ll. 561–66)

Only the second of these passages is paralleled in the other versions (cf. A 289.1–6, C 10889–92, F 10603–6). The obvious explanation for the wholesale repetition in the Percy version is that it is due to the short-circuiting of memory, prompted by the similarity of the situation and/or the recurrence of 'to warwick'. The rhyme *knee : Sir Guy* seems also to have stuck in the poet's mind.

Donatteli's claim that 'there is very little evidence of oral or musical context in the Percy Folio manuscript' is, for all these reasons, untenable.[30] Throughout the medieval and early modern period, romances were transmitted orally and indeed musically. Although we encounter them today frozen in writing, many of them, as *Eger and Grime* and *Guy and Colebrand* illustrate, would not have made it into written form if they had not previously been carried in the living memories of storytellers. The widespread scepticism about the oral transmission of medieval popular romances (despite the many medieval voices telling us the contrary), and, conversely, the readiness to believe that the signs of orality and minstrelsy in popular romance were planted there by clever authors seeking to efface the traces of their bookishness, are symptoms of our own modernity, reflexes of the habits and conditions of literate people with literate minds.

# References

Baugh, Albert C. 1950. 'The Authorship of the Middle English Romances.' *MHRA: Annual Bulletin* 22: 13–28.

–. 1959. 'Improvisation in the Middle English Romance.' *Proceedings of the American Philosophical Society* 103: 418–54.

–. 1967. 'The Middle English Romance: Some Questions of Creation, Presentation, and Preservation.' *Speculum* 42: 1–31.

Benson, Larry D., gen. ed. 1987. *Riverside Chaucer*. Boston: Houghton Mifflin.

---

[29] Hales and Furnivall 1868: II, 531 and 546–47 (italics mine).
[30] Donatelli 1993: 130 (citing Bertrand Bronson).

Bradbury, Nancy Mason. 1998. *Writing Aloud: Storytelling in Late Medieval England*. Urbana: U of Illinois P.
Burnley, David. 1996. 'Of *Arthour and Merlin*.' In *The Arthur of the English*. Ed. W. R. J. Barron. Cardiff: U of Wales P. 83–90.
Burrow, John. 1983. '*Sir Thopas* in the Sixteenth Century.' In *Middle English Studies Presented to Norman Davis*. Ed. Douglas Gray and E. G. Stanley. Oxford: Clarendon. 69–91.
Caldwell, James Ralston, ed. 1933. *Eger and Grime: A Parallel-Text Edition of the Percy and the Huntington-Laing Versions of The Romance, with an Introductory Study*. Harvard Studies in Comparative Literature 9. Cambridge, MA: Harvard UP.
Chesnutt, Michael. 1987. 'Minstrel Reciters and the Enigma of Middle English Romance.' *Culture and History* 2: 48–67.
Cloetta, Wilhelm, ed. 1906. *Les deux rédactions en vers du Moniage Guillaume, chanson de geste du XII<sup>e</sup> siècle*. 2 vols. SATF. Paris: Firmin-Didot.
Coleman, Joyce. 1996. *Public Reading and the Reading Public in Late Medieval England and France*. Cambridge: CUP.
Crosby, Ruth. 1936. 'Oral Delivery in The Middle Ages.' *Speculum* 11: 87–110.
Curnow, Demelza Jane. 2002. 'Five Case Studies on the Transmission of Popular Middle English Verse Romances.' Ph.D. Thesis, University of Bristol.
Davis, Norman, ed. 1971. *Paston Letters and Papers of the Fifteenth Century, Part I*. Oxford: OUP.
Donatelli, Joseph. 1993. 'The Percy Folio Manuscript: A Seventeenth-Century Context for Medieval Poetry.' *English Manuscript Studies 1100–1700*. Vol. 4. Ed. Peter Beal and Jeremy Griffiths. London: British Library. 114–33.
Duncan, A. A. M., ed. and trans. 1997. John Barbour. *The Bruce*. Canongate Classics 78. Edinburgh: Canongate.
Field, Rosalind. 1999. 'Romance in England, 1066–1400.' In *The Cambridge History of Medieval English Literature*. Ed. David Wallace. Cambridge: CUP. 152–81.
Fox, Adam. 2000. *Oral and Literate Culture in England 1500–1700*. Oxford: Clarendon.
Green, D. H. 1994. *Medieval Listening and Reading: The Primary Reception of German Literature, 800–1300*. Cambridge: CUP.
Green, Richard Firth. 1980. *Poets and Princepleasers: Literature and the English Court in the Late Middle Ages*. Toronto: U of Toronto P.
Hales, John W., and Frederick J. Furnivall, eds. 1868. *Bishop Percy's Folio Manuscript: Ballads and Romances*. 3 vols. London.
Havelock, Eric A. 1982. *The Literate Revolution in Greece and Its Cultural Consequences*. Princeton: Princeton UP.
Hoops, Reinald. 1929. *Der Begriff 'Romance' in der mittelenglischen und frühneuenglischen Literatur*. Heidelberg: Winter.
Kölbing, Eugen, ed. 1885–94. *Sir Beues of Hamtoun*. 3 vols. EETS ES 46, 48, 65. London.
Lupack, Alan, ed. 1994. *'Lancelot of the Laik' and 'Sir Tristrem'*. Kalamazoo: Medieval Institute, Western Michigan University.
McGillivray, Murray. 1990. *Memorization in the Transmission of the Middle English Romances*. New York: Garland.
Meier, Nicole, ed. 2008. *The Poems of Walter Kennedy*. The Scottish Text Society, Fifth Series 6. Cambridge: Boydell and Brewer.
Mills, Maldwyn, ed. 1988. *Horn Childe and Maiden Rimnild*. Middle English Texts 20. Heidelberg: Winter.
Pearsall, Derek, ed. 1994. Langland. *Piers Plowman: The C-Text*. 2nd ed. Exeter: Exeter UP.
–, and I. C. Cunningham, eds. 1979. *The Auchinleck Manuscript: National Library of Scotland Advocates' Ms. 19.2.1*. London: Scolar P.

Percy, Thomas. 1886. *Reliques of Ancient English Poetry, Consisting of Old Heroic Ballads, Songs, and other Pieces of our Earlier Poets.* Ed. Henry B. Wheatley. 3 vols. London. [Rpt. New York: Dover, 1966.]
Purdie, Rhiannon, ed. 2001. *Ipomadon* EETS 316. Oxford: OUP.
Purser, John. 1996. 'Greysteil.' In *Stewart Style, 1513–1542: Essays on the Court of James V.* Ed. Janet Hadley Williams. East Linton: Tuckwell P. 142–52.
Putter, Ad, and Jane Gilbert, eds. 2000. *The Spirit of Medieval English Popular Romance.* London: Pearson.
Reichl, Karl, ed. 2000. *The Oral Epic: Performance and Music.* Intercultural Music Studies 12. Berlin: Verlag für Wissenschaft und Bildung.
–. 2003. 'Comparative Notes on the Performance of Middle English Popular Romance.' *Western Folklore* 62: 63–81.
Rogers, Gillian. 1991. 'The Percy Folio Manuscript Revisited.' In *Romance in Medieval England.* Ed. Maldwyn Mills, Jennifer Fellows, and Carol Meale. Cambridge: Brewer. 39–64.
Rothwell, William, ed. 2005. *Femina.* Anglo-Norman On-Line Hub. Available at <http://www.anglo-norman.net/texts/femina.pdf>.
Rubin, David C. 1995. *Memory in Oral Tradition: The Cognitive Psychology of Epic, Ballads, and Counting-Out Rhymes.* New York: OUP.
Sánchez Martí, Jordi. 2004. 'Reading Romance in Late Medieval England: The Case of the Middle English *Ipomedon*.' *Philological Quarterly* 83: 13–19.
Schmidt, A. V. C., ed. 1995. Langland. *The Vision of Piers Plowman. A Critical Edition of the B-Text Based on Trinity College Cambridge MS B.15.17.* 2nd ed. London: Dent.
Smithers, G. V., ed. 1952–57. *Kyng Alisaunder.* 2 vols. EETS 227, 237. London: OUP.
–, ed. 1987. *Havelok.* Oxford: Clarendon.
Southworth, John. 1989. *The English Medieval Minstrel.* Woodbridge, Suffolk: Boydell and Brewer.
Spearing, A. C. 2005. *Textual Subjectivity: The Encoding of Subjectivity in Medieval Narrative and Lyrics.* Oxford: OUP.
Stevens, John. 1986. *Words and Music in the Middle Ages: Song, Narrative, Dance and Drama, 1050–1350.* Cambridge: CUP.
Sullens, Idelle, ed. 1996. Robert Mannyng of Brunne. *The Chronicle.* Medieval and Renaissance Texts and Studies 153. Binghamton: State University of NY at Binghamton.
Taylor, Andrew. 1992. 'Fragmentation, Corruption, and Minstrel Narration.' *Yearbook of English Studies* 22: 39–62.
Tolkien, J. R. R., and E. V. Gordon, eds. 1967. *Sir Gawain and the Green Knight.* Rev. ed. by Norman Davis. Oxford: Clarendon.
Treichel, A. 1896. 'Sir Cleges. Eine mittelenglische Romanze.' *Englische Studien* 22: 345–89.
Verwijs, E., and J. Verdam, eds. 1927–1952. *Middelnederlandsch Woordenboek.* 10 vols. Den Haag: Nijhoff.
Vitz, Evelyn Birge. *Orality and Performance in Early French Romance.* Cambridge: Brewer.
–, Nancy Freeman Regalado, and Marilyn Lawrence. eds. 2005. *Performing Medieval Narative.* Woodbridge, Suffolk: Boydell and Brewer.
Zupitza, Julius, ed. 1883–91. *Guy of Warwick.* 3 vols. EETS ES 42, 49, 59. London.

# 12 The *Chanson de geste* and Orality

## *Dominique Boutet*

While it has been possible to approximate the *chanson de geste* to South Slavic or African oral epics, the fact that the *chanson de geste* belongs to a culture in which writing plays a considerable role makes this *rapprochement* questionable and clouds that which we can perceive only at a distance. The question of the relationship between *chanson de geste* and orality must be broken down into in a number of questions, all of which are problematic:
- a question of textual evolution: what is the role of orality in the composition of the *chansons de geste* and their transformations over the course of time?
- a question of technique and aesthetics: to what degree is the art that characterizes these works due to the needs or the mode of oral performance?
- a question concerning the history of the genre: was there a period of pure orality before the appearance of the first written documents?

Before discussing these questions, it will be appropriate to distinguish the different stages at which orality is likely to intervene and to recall the conditions of the diffusion of the *chansons de geste*.

Paul Zumthor has proposed that we distinguish five states in the life-cycle of literary works: production, transmission, reception, conservation and repetition (1983:32–33). The simultaneous manner of the transmission and reception of a work of verbal art defines the situation of oral performance; in the case of written literature, however, publication and reading are not simultaneous. Furthermore, for one and the same poem, the modalities of orality and of writing/reading can occur simultaneously, a fact which invalidates any monolithic theory.

## 1 The Conditions of Oral Communication

Everyone is in agreement that the *chansons de geste*, at least until the end of the thirteenth century, were meant to be sung by a jongleur to an audience. In his treatise on music, Johannes de Grocheio, at the end of the thirteenth century, evokes the genre of the *chanson de geste* in the following terms:

> We call that kind of *cantus* a *chanson de geste* in which the deeds of heroes and the works of ancient fathers are recounted, such as the life and martyrdom of saints and the battles and adversities which the men of ancient times suffered for the sake of faith and truth [...]. This kind of music should be laid on for the elderly, for working citizens and for those of middle

station when they rest from their usual toil, so that, having heard the miseries and calamities of others, they may more easily bear their own and so that anyone may undertake his own labour with more alacrity. Therefore this kind of *cantus* has the power to preserve the whole city. (Page 1993: 23)

He also specifies that in this *cantus* the same melody must be repeated for each verse; the chanted recital is therefore the normal performance mode of these works. Nevertheless, paradoxically, no manuscript of a *chanson de geste* gives any indication about the melody, as distinct, for example, from the *chansonniers* which transmit lyric poetry. Only the *Jeu de Robin et de Marion* by Adam de la Halle quotes a verse from the parodic *chanson de geste* of *Audigier* together with its musical notation.[1] On the other hand, a great number of prologues to *chansons de geste* allude to recitation by a jongleur with such frequency that this motif becomes conventional in the last quarter of the twelfth century. Some comments by the jongleur, in the middle of the work, appeal to the audience to be generous or to return on the following day to hear the continuation (as in *Huon de Bordeaux*, *Le Couronnement de Louis* or *Baudouin de Sebourc*). As will be seen, the stylistic traits characteristic of the *chanson de geste* are specially adapted to the needs of a jongleur's performance.

The jongleurs can be defined as professional entertainers: bear-leaders, acrobats, jugglers, musicians and reciters of poetry.[2] Some could be all of these at once, but others were probably specialized in the spreading of saints' lives and *chansons de geste*, since the Church condemned the jongleur profession, with the exception of the latter specialization. The audience was varied: at fairs, in public squares and in holy places all social strata were in contact with one another, and the itinerant character of the jongleurs was a notable factor in the propagation of literary works across a whole language area. But the audience could also be more restricted, when a jongleur sang the *geste* in a castle for a feudal lord and his whole household. Thus, in order to enhance the high quality of the poem, some prologues evoke the presence of a king, duke or count.

The recitation of the *chanson de geste* poses a first problem with regard to its segmentation into 'sittings' and consequently the dimension of the recited text. Taking South Slavic singers as his model, Jean Rychner estimates that a session could extend to 2,000 verse lines at the most, and from this perspective he examines nine *chansons de geste* of the twelfth century, which form the basis of his study (1955: 46–67). The results are unequal: four of them, which comprise each fewer than 2,000 lines, could have been recited at one sitting (*Pèlerinage de Charlemagne*, the oldest part of the *Chanson de Guillaume*, *Charroi de Nîmes*, and *Prise d'Orange*); the *Chanson de Roland* (4,000 lines) shows no trace of a division into sessions; the *Couronnement de Louis*, which is incidentally structured as a succession of independent episodes, has divisions around lines 310 and 1350–1375; the three episodes of the second redaction of the *Moniage Guillaume* (Guillaume in the convent, Synagon, Ysoré) could correspond to three sessions: in the first hundred lines or so of each references to the situation and announcements of the forthcoming story are made; according to Jean Rychner, these are typical of the begin-

---

[1] [On the musical performance of medieval epic poetry, see further sections 2.4 and 3.4 in ch. 5 on performance and performers in this volume (J. Harris and K. Reichl).]

[2] On the jongleurs, see Faral 1910. [See also ch. 5, section 3.3., in this volume (K. Reichl).]

nings of a performance session, where the jongleur positions himself and attracts an audience by presenting his wares; in *Raoul de Cambrai*, on the other hand, the situation is more fluid and dependent upon the episodes. In numerous *chansons de geste*, still of the thirteenth century, the narrative thread is taken up anew in various places, with a summary of what has happened before and a preview of what is to follow, sometimes accompanied by appeals to the audience. But these interventions of the jongleur need not necessarily be interpreted as the beginnings of a new session. In *Jehan de Lanson* (c. 1240), for instance, they can be found in the middle of a laisse: here we have instead a literary device by which the narrative threads are brought together explicitly before a moment that is meant to be dramatic (Boutet 1988: 194–95 and 205–6).

The lack of a tight structure, even of coherence, in many *chansons de geste* is in Jean Rychner's eyes a sign and a consequence of this distribution of the performance into various sessions. The *Couronnement de Louis* can be recited in independent episodes, which have as their common element the activity of Guillaume in the service of the king of France and of Christendom. The overall composition diminishes in importance when one knows that the audience would change from one session to another. In a way, an exception like the *Chanson de Roland* proves the rule; besides, Jean Rychner states that it comprises a fairly reduced number of explicit markers of orality. It will nevertheless be noted that the long prose romances of the thirteenth century, which by definition lie outside the performance of a jongleur, show no tighter a structure. While, in the case of the *chansons de geste*, it is impossible to exclude the influence of the conditions of their diffusion, it is equally impossible to derive a convincing argument from these conditions.

## 2 The Style of the *Chansons de geste* and Orality

The strongest arguments for the oral nature of the *chansons de geste* are based on their style and the way the laisse functions. The laisse is in the first place a musical unit; the research of the musicologist Jacques Chailley has shown that one has to distinguish between an intonation melody, particular to the first line of each laisse, a concluding melody and a developing melody, which is repeated in each of the other lines and can alternate with the intonation melody.[3] Furthermore, assonance, and later, rhyme, guarantee the unity of the sound of the laisse. Ideally (and this is generally the case in the *Chanson de Roland*) the laisse is also a narrative unit. Of variable length – three or four lines, but also several hundred lines are found – it can just as well relate a whole episode as delineate a remarkable element, the feat of a hero, a crossing of swords, or a *planctus*. This flexibility makes the laisse into an instrument that is well adapted to oral diffusion: the jongleur can modify its length according to his inspiration, can lengthen or shorten it, or he can pour into this mould a stereotyped motif like that of the attack with a lance. Another technique, widely spread in oral literatures, is added to this flexibility: repetition (*reprise*) or linking (*enchaînement*). Numerous laisses repeat in their first line(s) the substance of the last line(s) of the preceding laisse, with variation of the order of words,

---

[3] See Chailley 1948; Chailley's terms are *timbre d'intonation, timbre de développement, timbre de conclusion*.

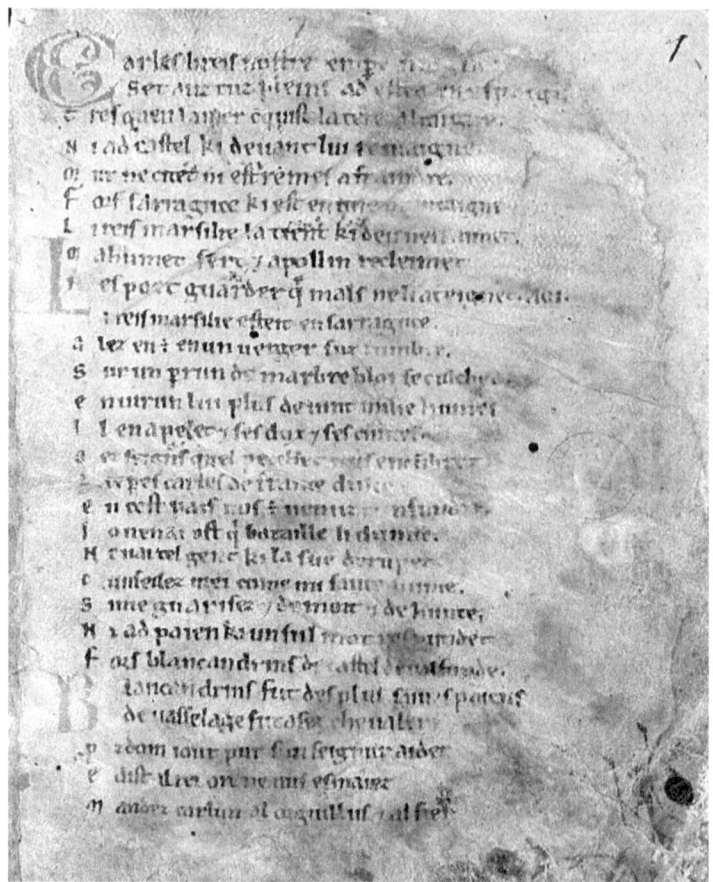

12 – Beginning of the *Chanson de Roland*, Oxford, Bodl. Lib. MS Digby 23, fol. 1r

the words themselves or even the formulation in its entirety. This technique can also have a mnemonic function: by keeping to the linking device, the jongleur at the same time knows the assonance of the following laisse. In addition, the intonation verses are built on the model of only few types and are therefore highly memorable, as the coupling of the name of the hero with a verb of action or an epithet ('Carles li reis, nostre emprere magnes' [Charles the king, our great emperor], 'Li reis Marsilie out sun counseill finét' [King Marsile had his council finished]), epic inversion ('Halt sunt li pui et li val tenebrus' [High are the hills and the valleys shadowy], 'Vait s'ent Guillaumes sans nul arestement' [Guillaume leaves without any delay]), apostrophe ('Singneur, ce dist duc Naimes' [Lords, this said Duke Naimes], 'Sire Guillelmes, dist li rois Looÿs' [Sir Guillaume, said King Louis]), constructions with *or* (now) followed by a verb and the subject of the action ('Or fu Guillelmes as fenestres au vent' [Now Guillaume was at the window], 'Or fu Guillelmes dolant et correços' [Now Guillaume was sad and angry]). Similarly, the concluding verse often shows a sententious turn, summarizing the action developed in the laisse or expressing the reaction, opinion or response of an interlocutor ('Dist Oliver : "Gente est nostre bataille"' [Oliver said: 'Noble is our battle'], 'Baisset sun chef, si cumence a penser' [He inclined his head and began to think]). A statistical study shows that these different types are clearly more frequent in this position (beginning or end) than in the body of the laisse. 'Verbal intonation and conclusion melodies'[4] then overlay the music of the verses to underline the shape of the laisse. It is evident that not all *chansons de geste* show the same firmness, but the study of *Jehan de Lanson* reveals that in the middle of the thirteenth century this principle of composition was still very much alive. It is uncertain, however, whether this principle is due solely to the convenience of oral diffusion; as will be seen, these techniques also help to underline the aesthetics of this genre.

On the example of the South Slavic epic, Jean Rychner considers the stereotyped style of the *chanson de geste*, i. e. its rhetorical motifs and formulas, the essential prop for the memory and improvisation of the jongleur. But here, too, the difference between theory and practice has to be taken into consideration.

It is apposite to distinguish with Jean-Pierre Martin (1992) between narrative motifs and rhetorical motifs, the former stereotypes of narration and the latter stereotypes of expression. Both can be closely related to orality.

The narrative motifs of epic poetry in fact complement those of Stith Thompson's index of folklore motifs (1955–58); Philip Kennedy has compiled a motif-index of medieval French epics on this model (1966). Thus the motif of the single combat between two champions, which is found in most of the *chansons de geste* (be it a combat that will decide a collective fate or a judicial duel destined to make manifest the truth in connection with an often mendacious accusation), is listed by Stith Thompson under the numbers H217.1 ('Decision of victory by single combat between army leaders') and H218 ('Trial by combat'). Jean-Pierre Martin remarks correctly that this motif 'corresponds perfectly to Propp's functions H ("The hero struggles with the villain") and J ("Victory over the villain").'[5] These are motifs characterized by the repeated occurrence in a given corpus, in the present case, that of oral folktales, put down in writing fairly late (essentially from the nineteenth century onwards), but also represented in the narrative literature of the Middle Ages. After a close analysis of the *chanson de geste* of *Beuve de Hantone* (twelfth century), carried out with the instruments provided by folkloristics, Jean-Pierre Martin, however, comes to the conclusion that 'the hinge-like position of the *chanson de geste* between the strict tradition of folklore and the literary aesthetics typical of the epic invalidates a classification system that was conceived for folklore alone' (1992:44). The system actually takes no account of the contextualization of the motifs, which is particularly complex in a work comprising several thousands of lines, nor of the specific traits of the *chanson de geste*, which provide a generic contextualization and endow a motif with a generally recurring orientation, which can, however, undergo different variations. In fact, the conclusion must be reached that the majority of the motifs

---

[4] Jean Rychner (1955:69–74) adapts to the words the terminology that Jacques Chailley had applied to the music of the laisse (*timbres verbaux d'intonation et de conclusion*).
[5] Martin 1992:80; compare Propp 1968.

encountered in the *chansons de geste* are typical of the genre and interfere only rarely with those of folklore. In addition, they bear the stamp of the feudal system. This is not incompatible with the formulaic style characteristic of the oral art of the jongleurs, but the possible, if not frequent interrelationships with the politico-feudal reality tend to give the different occurrences of a motif a specific orientation, which may be ideological, polemic or simply topical at the time of composition, an orientation which presupposes a deeply thoughtful use of the motif and which moves the motif to the side of writing rather than that of improvisation as suggested by stereotyped oral structures. This kind of use of recurring narrative motifs, however, is an indubitable fact; some hundred motifs suffice to cover the ca. 50,000 lines of the corpus studied by Jean-Pierre Martin.

Rhetorical motifs are units which, on the microstructural level, decompose a narrative element into a variable number of clichés, which in turn are expressed by stereotyped formulas. They are found in all oral epics, from Homer to the South Slavic songs, and Jean Rychner saw them as arising from the needs not so much of performance as from the jongleur's presence of mind, on which improvisation partly depends. The use of formulaic expressions frees the performer's memory to allow him to think ahead of the following sequences rather than to lose himself in the recall of detail in expression: 'The profession of the jongleur, the public song, absolutely forbid the patient searching for a singular and original expression [...]. In reality then, the jongleur treats his topic in an almost totally traditional way, thanks to stereotyped motifs on the level of narration as well as expression' (1955: 127). Such motifs are, for example, 'the knight in arms', 'the attack with the lance', 'the prayer in the greatest danger', 'the epic panorama' or 'the general battle'. Thus, the rhetorical motif of the attack with the lance comprises ideally, in its complete form, seven elements: giving one's horse the spurs, brandishing the lance, striking, smashing the opponent's shield, breaking his coat of mail, stabbing the lance through his body *versus* missing him, and throwing him from his horse. Jean Rychner, however, remarks that this motif is hardly ever complete and that the last four elements have variants which amount to narrative options (the coat of mail breaks or does not break, the shield is or is not completely pierced through etc.). A great number of motifs are incidentally found in different degrees of realization, ranging from the canonical form (in which all or almost all clichés are expressed) to the ornate form (i. e. developed along the lines of amplification: short history of the weapons, richness of the material etc.), but also often in a short or schematic form, in which the clichés that constitute the motif are replaced by a simple general statement. Sometimes a disjunct form also occurs: an extraneous element is interpolated in the two clichés of a motif. All this gives a jongleur a great deal of freedom; in this way he can distinguish himself from his colleagues by modulating the detail of a story according to his preferences, by foregrounding certain elements and pushing certain others into the background, yet staying entirely within the framework of traditional art.

For all that, a careful study shows that matters are more complex. Jean-Pierre Martin notes that regarding a motif like that of the 'planctus' (or lamentation) in the *Chanson de Roland*, Jean Rychner and Paul Zumthor are in agreement neither about the number of occurrences nor about their delimitation: twenty-three according to Paul Zumthor *versus* eight according to Jean Rychner, and the beginning of the motif is more or less clearly marked according to the respective case.

Formulas, too, have variable realizations, and critics have come to talk of a 'stock of formulas'. Thus, for the cliché of 'giving one's horse the spurs' we can find variants like *Le destrier broche* (he gives the charger the spurs), *Son destrier broche* (he gives his charger the spurs), *Le cheval point* (he spurs the horse): variants with minimal lexical changes and an identical rhythmic-syntactic structure; but there are also variants like *Broche le bien* (he spurs him well), *Bien fu brochiés* (he was well spurred): variants with a totally different prosodic and syntactic pattern. Variation therefore plays as important a role as repetition, but from the perspective of traditional art and oral performance (without the possibility of going back in the text), variation probably goes more or less unnoticed, as in the audience's mind a variant is received as the simple realization of a cliché and as such does not change; only the cliché is of importance.

Whatever the role of formulas, one cannot reduce the formulaic style to a repertoire of formulas from which the jongleur would choose at the moment of performance. Numerous studies have shown that a formula in its wider sense is defined as a template that is at the same time semantic, rhythmic (in the case of the decasyllabic verse normally divided into 4 + 6) and syntactic and provides a schema for lexical variations. Michael Nagler has proposed a generative view of the formula, which posits a deep-structure template on the part of the oral poet, 'what he terms a "preverbal Gestalt", an ideational nexus of traditional meaning which can take a variety of verbal forms.'[6] The semantic aspect of the formula can be understood in a very wide sense, comprising connotation and not only denotation. Thus in *Jehan de Lanson*, the formula *dans la salle voutie* (in the vaulted hall) alternates, according to the rhyme of the laisse, with *dans le palais listé* (in the great hall decorated with stripes): the basic idea is clearly that of a rich and splendid place. The possibilities of variation are such that one might ask oneself whether the recourse to a formulaic style is due to the needs of the jongleur's profession and whether it should be seen as the inscription of these needs in the text.

## 3 The Discussion of the Theory of Improvisation

Maurice Delbouille was the first to lead a counteroffensive by defending the position that the *chansons de geste* are in the first place written works, products of literary creation and not of the jongleurs' improvisation. The debate moved in this way from the domain of transmission/reception (the performance situation) to that of production, while Jean Rychner had constantly maintained (except for the *Chanson de Roland*) the impossibility of distinguishing between the two, as in his view the performance was the site of the creation or re-creation of a song.

According to Maurice Delbouille, the importance of variants confuses the notion of traditional form, for motifs as well as for formulas: 'Every jongleur had his formulas, one will say. This may be so; and every poet has his ways and, after him, every scribe his mannerisms or his preferences. But from this point onwards, one can no longer talk of a vast treasury of *traditional* formulas, from which everybody could serve himself accord-

---

[6] See Nagler 1967; see the discussion of his definition in Foley 1988: 100–2 (from where the quotation is taken; p. 101). Compare also the comments in Zumthor 1968: 117.

ing to the demands of improvisation, at the moment of the song' (1959: 370). In opposition to oral composition, more or less collective and ephemeral (every jongleur produces his version, which can be different each time), as seen by the representatives of traditionalism, Maurice Delbouille, as a true disciple of Joseph Bédier, maintains the presence of a poet from the very beginning, a poet who has brought his work to maturity and has transferred it onto parchment before handing it on to the jongleur. This would not in principle exclude the notion that the stereotyped style and the taste for repetitions are linked to the needs of the performance by a jongleur (Molière, in his masterfully composed comedies, takes account of the needs of representation!), but Maurice Delbouille prefers to see in this style 'one of the great principles of medieval art, the stylization of forms, which are intentionally simplified and repeated in their essential traits, but animated by having recourse to variations based on a virtuosity that is felt to be the essence of all art' (370–71). Certain scholars (Hans-Erich Keller, Cesare Segre) have even gone so far as to derive the style of the *chansons de geste* from that of saints' legends like the Provençal *Boèce* or the *Vie de saint Alexis*, a position that has been opposed by Jean Rychner, who thought that this argument could be reversed, as the *chansons de geste* were certainly in existence before the end of the eleventh century and therefore before the saints' legends.

What complicates the problem (concerning questions of origin and composition) is that 'conservation' and 'repetition', to take up Paul Zumthor's terms again, can be transmitted orally or in writing, but it is through manuscripts that the *chansons de geste* have come down to us, and not by means of oral traditions. The differences between the manuscripts can speak for divergent traditions, based, for example, on different recitations written down from the mouth of the performers. In such a case, the manuscript is simply the testimony of an oral event. The same is true if the text found in a manuscript was dictated by a jongleur or based on the memory of a member of the audience. Certain manuscripts could have been produced under such circumstances. A case in point, according to Claude Régnier, is manuscript D of the *Prise d'Orange* (Paris, BnF MS fr. 1448), where the order of laisses is disturbed throughout an entire passage and becomes incoherent, and where groups of verse lines found in the other manuscripts appear in the middle of passages which have been taken from other sources (1966: 83–86). In general, however, the fact that the recension of manuscripts succeeds in establishing a *stemma codicum* speaks in favour of an essentially written manuscript transmission for the majority of the *chansons de geste*.

It should be added that the theory of improvisation (even of a previously written work) cannot be generalized; one has to distinguish clearly between the *chansons de geste* and their Serbian or African equivalents. Many prologues make this clear: in order to attract the audience, the jongleur stresses that he is not one of these bad performers who distort the poem for lack of knowing it perfectly through memorization. It is therefore a question of recitation and not of improvisation, and the jongleur who appears in one of the manuscripts of *Gaydon* declares: 'Mais je la sçay dès le commencement/ Jusqu' à la fin, car j'en ai le rommant' (But I know it from the beginning/ Till the end, because I have its *roman*), that is, in this context, the text written down in a manuscript. In an analogous fashion, the epilogue of *Fierabras* wishes a long life to the person (scribe? author?) who has 'written' this *roman* (narrative in the vernacular), of which the *chanson de geste* is the recital. A great number of *chansons de geste*, incidentally, pretend to be the works of clerics, who have versified some text (of a chronicle?) found in an abbey. The semi-improvised traditional oral performance and the recitation of a written text therefore coexisted, but in twelfth- and thirteenth-century France the former was considered a by-product and only the latter worthy of a first-rate audience. Rather than presenting itself as the product of an oral tradition, which would confer worth and authenticity upon it, the *chanson de geste* pretends (often ficticiously, but the argument alone plays a role) to take its subject matter from a historical work and its form from an artist conscious of his art. Furthermore, some *chansons de geste* are not anonymous: around 1200 Jean Bodel (who is also the author of the *Jeu de saint Nicolas* and of several fabliaux) in his *Chanson des Saxons* denigrates *cil bastart jougleour* (these bastard jongleurs) who mix up the history of the Saxon Guiteclin, 'car il ne sevent mie les riches vers nouviaus/ Ne la chançon rimee que fist Jehans Bodiaus' (because they don't know at all the new magnificent verses/ Nor the *chanson* in rhymes that Jean Bodel composed). This claim to novelty, however exceptional it might be, is nevertheless significant: the conception of epic creation that Jean Bodel had is completely on the side of writing. In the fourteenth century, the *chanson de geste* of *Hughes Capet*, among others, demonstrates that the authority of the written word is indispensable in the middle of an oral performance: in narrative anticipation, the jongleur announces to the audience that the events will happen 'ainsi comme vous orrez au lyvre retraitier' (as you will hear the book report them), and he announces in the prologue that he will *read* the life of an admirable warrior ('Et pour ce vous lyrai la vie d'un guerier' [And therefore I will read you the life of a warrior]).

The research undertaken by Jean-Pierre Martin on the *chansons de geste* of the end of the twelfth or the beginning of the thirteenth century has confirmed this point of view, which privileges the written word in the elaboration of the *chansons de geste*, despite the traits of orality that they contain: 'The formulaic style characteristic of oral poetry is exploited in an autonomous fashion by each work, conforming to the conditions of individuality which belong to written literature' (1992: 197). W. M. Hackett had stated already, with reference to *Girart de Roussillon* (dated to the middle of the twelfth century), that the person she called the poet 'employs a formulaic style, as well as other forms of repetition, not by necessity but by choice, as the style suitable to the genre he has chosen; and the manner in which he uses it excludes, it seems to me, all idea of improvisation' (1973: 352). The study of *Jehan de Lanson*, which belongs to the following generation, shows that the frequent complexity of the linking of the laisses, the deliberate structure of a great number of the latter, the distanced, almost parodic, use of certain motifs (as for example that of disguise) unquestionably place this *chanson de geste* in the vicinity of writing (Boutet 1988). There is a subtle relationship between the traditional form, adapted to the conditions of orality, as has been seen, and the searching for special effects which exceed the framework of stereotyped expressions and play with variation and repetition for specific purposes, something which is incompatible with the very philosophy of a traditional oral art. This *chanson de geste* thus invalidates the premature judgement given by Hans-Robert Jauss, for whom the *chansons de geste* of the second generation manifest a pure reproduction of stereotypical models: 'When a text is content to reproduce the typical elements of a genre, to introduce another subject matter in already tried models, to simply take up again the traditional *topoi* and metaphors, a stereotyped literature arises, where one can see the decline of genres that have been successful, like the *chanson de geste* in the twelfth and the fabliau in the thirteenth centuries. The limit thus reached is that of simple utility value or the character of an article for daily use' (1970: 86). This is precisely that of which the prologues of the *chansons de geste* of that period, accomplished works of poets (who could be clerics as well as jongleurs), accused the bad jongleurs, who disfigured the works that they recited.

## 4 An Aesthetics of the Voice

It can be taken for granted then that, while the style of the *chansons de geste* is well adapted to the conditions of recitation, it transcends oral performance and has a properly literary aim, at least in the majority of the *chansons de geste* that have come down to us and have been written down on parchment. Jean Rychner was the first to have been able to see in the *chansons de geste* a combination of narrative and lyric, by bringing to light the technique of the parallel laisses, of the similar laisses and of certain forms of linking which disturb the perception of temporal sequence. At the beginning of the nineteenth century, Claude Fauriel saw in the long repetitions a sign of decay, due to unintelligent scribes who had various manuscripts before them and who recopied the different versions of the same laisse in succession. Gaston Paris has followed this view in his *Histoire poétique de Charlemagne*, and Léon Gautier, in the first edition of his *Epopées françaises*, interpreted the parallel laisses of *Jehan de Lanson* as the result of innovations effected by successive adaptors.[7] The frequency of repetitions in general had impressed Gaston Paris, who interpreted this as the naive outcome of the inner feelings of the poet in view of the grandeur of his subject, again and again repeating the same idea in order to express it more completely (1865: 24). Naive art or textual corruption of the scribes: all these theories referred to writing and not to orality. Jean Rychner, when analysing the two parallel series of three laisses in the *Chanson de Guillaume* – relating respectively the death of Girard and that of Guichard, built with the same narrative elements and with analogous formulas, but diverging in their final element, since Girard dies a good Christian, while Guichard, a converted pagan, renounces God in favour of Muhammad – sees in them an undoubted sign of orality: 'The author of *Guillaume* has cast the death of Guichard in the mould that had served him for the death of Girart, with the parallelism underlining the divergence at the end. We are in the presence of a full oral style, of which the resumption of a theme, leading to variations on this theme, is in fact one of the fundamental traits. The resumption or recommencement facilitates re-memorization or recitation. It does not demand a great effort to memorize and it gives the performer the leisure to think ahead, to devote his attention to what is going to follow' (1955: 85). Nevertheless, he does not hesitate to see in the similar laisses, in which the actor and the action do not change (with the exception

---

[7] Gautier 1865–68 (first ed.): I, 290–93; in the second edition (1878–97: I, 357–66) he no longer proposes this interpretation as one of the possible explanations of this phenomenon. Fauriel's analysis is quoted in the second edition (1878–97: I, 362). See Heinemann 1993: 17–18 and n. 12.

of small variations of the same act, as in the laisses that depict Roland's death), 'a stop in the narration which permits the display of lyricism' (93). Clearly, Jean Rychner recognizes an aesthetic quality to this phenomenon, beyond its technical usefulness.

It was Paul Zumthor's merit to have brought out the synthesis of technique and aesthetics, by insisting, beyond orality, on the *vocality*, the corporeality of the voice, i. e. on its effects, which are both dynamic and aesthetic in the course of a jongleur's performance: 'In the heat of simultaneously present bodies in performance, the poetic voice has no other function or power than that of exalting that community in its agreement or its resistance' (1985: 12). From this point of view, vocal expression, formulaic style, content and function are insolubly linked, and it is evidently from this perspective that the general thinking about the *chanson de geste* must be conducted in the future. As I have noted in my book *La chanson de geste* (1993), the *chansons de geste* are caught in a 'tension between the exteriorization of collective memory via the ritual of sound and the system of authentication that refers to a written authority, to a memory preserved on the parchment of abbeys, a tension between what one might call a living memory and a dead memory, which endlessly demands to come back to life' (102). Even if the epic style is not necessarily, or exclusively, born from the jongleur's performance, it is evident that in the effects for which it aims it is inseparable from the reciting voice, and that writing is no more than the medium of the text's creation and preservation. To mention just one case: the similar laisses, when they are read in a manuscript, impede the view and the narrative progression, whereas when they are recited, as will be seen, they unfold all their power.

Edward A. Heinemann has paid close attention to the patterns of rhythms, of dynamic effects and of echoes in the texture of the *chansons de geste*, without taking sides in the debate on their oral or written origin, since, according to him, 'the subtle rhythms of a text demand neither a written composition for their creation nor a reading for their appreciation. The illiterate singer and his audience pass through the same scale of sensibilities as the writer and his readers' (1993: 42). The perspective is not that of literary history (we will come back to this) but that of the genre's aesthetics.

When observing the frequent coincidence between phrase and verse in a paratactic structure – at least in the oldest *chansons de geste* and in particular in the *Chanson de Roland* – Paul Zumthor suggested that there was a 'vital exchange' between syntax and rhythm, 'which engenders a new form, both rhythm and discourse: the verse' (1965: II, 770). E. A. Heinemann starts from this idea in order to expose the recurrent but complex metrical templates and to underline the notion of 'impulse' for the rhyme and the caesura: an impulse that can be zero (a logical halt), linking (when the following verse depends on the preceding one, as, e. g., expansion or correction) or anticipatory (when the essential syntactic or semantic element is found in the following verse). He then applies this notion logically to macrostructures, i. e. the laisses (in comparison with which the verses are microstructures). From this perspective, the *chanson de geste* takes the form of an organism, animated by an internal dynamics, a dynamics that is evidently sensitive particularly during the performance of a jongleur, – while in the act of reading the manuscript the eyes could move directly to the following verse without being affected by the rhythm caused by the impulse.

The linking of the laisses, which slows down the course of narration in order to dwell on a specific element (whose narrative importance can be highly variable, ranging from a major crisis to a simple transitional factor), combines with the impulse of the other characteristic trait of the epic style, repetition. E. A. Heinemann connects repetition to the group of echo phenomena that the *chanson de geste* cultivates. The echo actually appears on several levels: repetition of passages within the same text ('verbal echo', which can be consecutive or disjunctive according to the degree of distance of the occurrences), templates common to successive verses ('metrical echo'), and finally echoes characteristic of 'traditional language', i. e. motifs and formulas ('external echo'). In this way the whole poetics of the *chanson de geste* is taken into account, from a perspective that is necessarily that of an oral aesthetics: the cases of recurrence due to the combination of syntactic rules and the 'metrical rule' 'open the way to facilitating composition and improvisation but also to poetic utilization' (1993: 223–24). The disjunctive echo, i. e. the non-immediate repetition (from one laisse to another or to verses several hundred lines apart) of a passage of a certain length (more than one line), is in the eyes of this scholar an essential element in the narrative and lyrical organization of the *chanson de geste*. According to him, the consecutive echo is a purely lyrical procedure, especially in the course of the recurrence of metrical templates (and in particular of the impulse for the caesura). E. A. Heinemann realizes, however, that the aesthetic interpretation of these echoes is sometimes difficult: some produce a lyrical and poetic effect (and can therefore be interpreted as an indication of a consciously poetic composition), but others can have the appearance of facilitating turns or weaknesses (of the jongleur's improvisation – or owing to the negligence of the scribes?), or can even 'stem from the subconscious functioning of language' (303).

It seems to me that the rhythmic effects, linked on the one hand to the metrical templates, on the other to the play of the impulse (on the level of both the succession of verses and the succession of laisses), are indications of a poetics of *energy*, which corresponds exactly to the precarious nature of vocality that is typical of the jongleur's performance. It is here that the aesthetic originality of the *chanson de geste* lies as well as its generic qualification by the epic register, of which the distinctive trait is the *souffle épique*, the epic breath.

The similar laisses are the most remarkable manifestations of this aesthetics of repetition, of energy and ritual. The canonical example, by reason of its effects, is the death of Roland in the Oxford manuscript. Two series of similar laisses follow one another. In the first (laisses 171–73), the hero tries in vain to break his sword, symbolic object of the warrior function, on a rock; in the second (laisses 174–76), he prepares himself for death and beats his breast to commit his soul to God. For the first series, one can hesitate between qualifying the passage as a passage of similar or of parallel laisses: are the blows struck on the rock successive or are they the same blows repeated three times? In other words, has the repetition a narrative value or an exclusively lyrical value? The text nevertheless seems to invite the second alternative: already in laisse 174 it is said that Roland strikes ten blows on the rock, a detail that is not repeated in the two following laisses, and the regrets spoken over the sword are of the same nature in laisses 172 and 173 (Roland remembers the conquests that his sword has allowed him to make for the greater glory of Charlemagne), where the second laisse only amplifies the motif of the conquests by providing details. The final laisse of the series introduces a major and ideologically essential variation by replacing the motif of the conquests by that of the relics contained in the pommel, which sanctify the sword and effect a change of perspective from the feudal world centred on the activity of a knight to the religious one, fundamental for the ideology of the Crusades. These three similar laisses are therefore not limited to telling an action: their composition and their juxtaposition, by means of the effects of rhythm (slowing down through repetition) and of variation, result in a real ritual, which is from the narrative perspective that of the hero, and from the ideological perspective that of the values that must knit together the community gathered around the jongleur, values that form the foundation of medieval society.

The second series of laisses is centred entirely on the hero. Their global similarity is accompanied, in each laisse, by a slight progression, with each laisse taking up the narrative at the same point (Roland, stretched out under a pine-tree, feels death coming): at the end of laisse 174, Roland, having beaten his breast, offers his glove to God for the remission of his sins; at the end of laisse 175, angels descend from heaven towards him; at the end of laisse 176, his soul is carried to Paradise by the angels. One could compare the aesthetic effect produced by this conjunction of a repetitive stamping and a slow progression with an intensely dramatic passage in Richard Wagner's *Tristan*, Isolde's death, where the same melodic cell is repeated for a long time, but with a continual slight chromatic rise which culminates in a kind of explosion in the moment of death. This underlines the lyrical value of the construction of the laisses of the *Chanson de Roland* and, in the aesthetics postulated here for the similar laisses, the important role played by the recitation of the words, by the force of the voice and by its emotive power over an assembled audience.

It might be appropriate to emphasize that the *chanson de geste*, with its aesthetics of repetition, corresponds perfectly to the perception of time, typical of twelfth-century man: time was viewed as essentially repetitive, be it the return of the same hours (one thinks of time regulated by the monastic hours and the rituals that accompany them), the return of the seasons in the profane world and even more the return of the same liturgical feasts from year to year, but with the Augustinian hope, at that time still very much alive, that every year humanity distances itself slightly further from the 'terrestrial city' in order to move towards the 'celestial city'.

The formulaic style, the echoes of every kind, the impulses, the song itself that orchestrates all this and realizes all its energy, perfectly express this relationship of human society to human time as it was lived and conceptualized in a Christian worldview. The acknowledgement of the essential role played by orality, not only in the history of the *chanson de geste* and its techniques, but more profoundly in its aesthetics, has motivated a group of scholars, united for a number of years in the 'Réseau euro-africain de recherches sur l'épopée' (Euro-African Network of Research on the Epic), to study systematically the correspondences in technique, theme, anthropology and aesthetics between Western medieval epics and the epics of West Africa.[8] This kind of comparative approach is in no way incompatible with the recognition of the essentially literary character of the works transmitted in our manuscripts, which can actually be discerned even better in this way.

---

[8] The proceedings of the founding seminar, which was held in Dakar in November 2000, are published in Suard, Boutet, and Kesteloot 2002.

## 5 Orality and the History of the Genre

From this aesthetic and comparative perspective, the old debate about the origin of the style of the *chanson de geste* and about an originally purely oral poetic activity acquires a new dimension. Until the 1960s this question was ultimately based on the idea that writing produces more sophisticated literary works than orality and on a conception of literature that privileged the individual as well as the act of reading on one's own, while in the opinion of these scholars, the performance of the jongleur was secondary to the written text. We can now see that orality can be the carrier of an aesthetics, and in order to be persuaded of this at once, it is sufficient to have heard a griot sing an African epic.

The critical point is that the *chansons de geste* have come down to us in manuscripts, with variants which, as we have seen, can be attributed to the activity of scribes as well as to different recitations by jongleurs, and that none of these manuscripts takes the trouble to transcribe the musical accompaniment to which Johannes de Grocheio alludes and which prompts him to discuss the *c h a n s o n de geste* in his treatise on music. Does this mean that the music was secondary in the eyes of the scribes and their patrons, who were only interested in the written text and who consequently thought of the *chansons de geste* as literary works (in the proper sense of Latin *littera*)? We know that the chansonniers, manuscripts which transcribe the troubadour poems and the lyrics of the trouvères, give the melody for each poem. Does this mean that the melody, or rather the *melopœia*, of the *chansons de geste* was left to the discretion of the jongleur, as he was not dealing with complex music, and that the mode of singing was without interest, since it had no substantial relationship to the text? If the *chanson de geste* was simply chanted in the manner of Gregorian chant, with only some specifications concerning the melodic patterns of the intoning and concluding phrases, it is normal that the manuscripts should not be concerned with the music. It is at any rate noteworthy that at the end of the thirteenth century the *chanson de geste* is called *cantus gestualis* in Latin by Johannes de Grocheio, an expression that seems to connect the *chanson de geste* with the gesticulations of the jongleur and not with the epic subject matter, the feats or *gesta* of a hero or a people.

Even if the oldest *chanson de geste* to have been preserved, the *Chanson de Roland* in the Oxford manuscript, is likely to be the planned and written work of a poet (as, incidentally, Jean Rychner also thinks),[9] it seems certain nevertheless that the degree of elaboration of its style presupposes a fairly long maturation period. Some documents attest to an oral poetic activity before the end of the eleventh century. The oldest testimony is that of Einhard (beginning of the ninth century), which relates that Charlemagne ordered that the old pagan poems (*barbara et antiquissima carmina*) which narrated the history of the ancient kings be written down; these poems, whose subject matter is therefore earlier than the Carolingian era, do not seem to have left any trace. In the same period, or probably somewhat later, a group of manuscripts of Einhard's *Vita Karoli Magni*, in which the battle of Roncevaux in 778 is evoked, mention among the warriors

---

[9] Joseph J. Duggan (1973), on the other hand, is of the opinion that this text is typical of a purely oral composition, since he has been able to find 32% of the hemistichs repeated; a style, however, can imitate orality without being its direct result.

killed in battle *Hruodlandus, Britannici limitis praefectus* (Roland, Lord of the Breton Marches).[10] Between the end of the tenth and the first third of the eleventh century, a very fragmentary Latin prose text, the so-called *Fragment de La Haye*, which imitates an original composed in hexameters, mentions a battle in which Charlemagne and a certain number of heroes from the Guillaume-Cycle of *chansons de geste* take part. Paul Aebischer has noted that this text, although inspired by memories of Latin poetry (Virgil and Ovid in particular), uses the technique of repetitions and the linking of laisses, of which traces remain despite the prosaic form, a fact that makes one think that a *chanson de geste* which possessed these stylistic characteristics already lies at the core of this fragment (1957: 34 ff.). Furthermore, in the years 1065 to 1075, the *Nota Emilianense* alludes to the disaster of 778 and names several of the Twelve Peers who figure in the *Chanson de Roland*, such as Guillaume with the telling nickname 'Alcorbitanas', a form that is divergent from the Latin point of view (the normal Latin form is *curbinasus*) but which can be perfectly explained with reference to the French surname *al corb nés* (with the crooked nose).[11] Finally, we know from the testimony of chroniclers (Guy of Amiens in his *Carmen de Hastingae proelio* and William of Malmesbury in his *Gesta regum Anglorum*) that jongleurs took part in the Battle of Hastings and, to fire the courage of the combatants, sang the feats of Roland and Oliver.[12] An oral tradition has thus been growing gradually since at least the Carolingian era, but there is no way of knowing at which moment the forms and techniques with which we are familiar began to make an appearance.

In the twelfth and thirteenth centuries manuscripts compete with orality, at first for preservation and reproduction (some manuscripts which are of humble appearance, small format and which have come down to us in a fairly poor condition have been thought to be 'jongleur manuscripts', props for the performer's memory, but this hypothesis has remained controversial), and then also for reception. This is especially true of the so-called cyclic manuscripts, which collect the *chansons de geste* that celebrate the feats of the same hero or the members of his clan (*Cycle de Guillaume*) or which, often from a chronological perspective, put together epics about the glory of Charlemagne (*Cycle du roi*) or, conversely, about rebellious vassals (*Cycle de Doon de Mayence*). Clearly, these manuscripts attempt to create a continuum between the various *chansons de geste*, radically different from the jongleur's recitation in a single sitting. Manuscript H 247 of the library of the Faculté de Médecine of Montpellier introduces transitions between the *chansons de geste*, in this way blurring the border, for instance, between *Gaufrey* and *La Chevalerie Ogier*. The cyclic manuscripts of the *grand cycle* of Garin de Monglane (of which the *Cycle de Guillaume* is a part) had to solve the delicate organizational problem posed by the existence of chronologically parallel *chansons de geste*; they have adopted the technique of 'incidences': this word is placed in the margin and indicates that a *chanson* or one of its episodes has been inserted into the text of another *chanson*. This is the case in Manuscript B1 (London, BL MS Royal 20 D XI), where the *Enfances Guillaume* are

---

[10] See Thorpe 1969: 64–65 (translation), 181–83 (commentary).
[11] On the *Nota Emilianense*, see Alonso 1953.
[12] The relevant passages are found in the original and in English translation in Morton and Muntz 1972: 26/27 (Guy of Amiens) and Mynors, Thomson, and Winterbottom 1998–1999: 1, 454/455 (William of Malmesbury).

placed as 'incidence' in the *chanson de geste* of *Les Narbonnais*, in which the beginnings of Guillaume's and his brothers' career are narrated. The text can thus be read like consecutive chapters of a huge narrative. According to Madeleine Tyssens (1967), the circumstances of collecting the *chansons de geste* into cycles explain the divergences between the redaction of one and the same *chanson* just as well, if not better, than the hypothesis of transformations due to the performance of jongleurs. It is certain at any rate that by the fourteenth century the individual reading of a manuscript had widely replaced orality. These manuscripts are library copies, which have sometimes been magnificently illuminated, and the majority of new compositions were meant for reading. Orality nevertheless continued to be present as a characteristic stylistic technique defining the genre of the *chanson de geste*, and the voice of the jongleur and the rhythms of orality continued to be inscribed artificially in the text, as witnessed by late *chansons* like *Tristan de Nanteuil* or the *Chanson de Bertrand du Guesclin*, which together comprise more than 20,000 lines. A final victory of the voice over the letter!

# References

Aebischer, Paul. 1957. 'Le Fragment de La Haye.' *Zs. für romanische Philologie* 73: 20–37.

Alonso, Dámaso. 1953. 'La primitiva épica francesa a la luz de una "Nota Emilianense".' *Revista de Filología Española* 37: 1–94.

Boutet, Dominique. 1988. *Jehan de Lanson. Technique et esthétique de la chanson de geste au XIIIe siècle*. Paris: Presses de l'Ecole normale supérieure.

–. 1993. *La chanson de geste. Forme et signification d'une écriture épique du Moyen Âge*. Paris: Presses Universitaires de France. [2nd ed. 2003.]

Chailley, Jacques. 1948. 'Études musicales sur la chanson de geste et ses origines.' *Revue de musicologie* 27: 1–27.

Duggan, Joseph J. 1973. *The Song of Roland: Formulaic Style and Poetic Craft*. Berkeley : U of California P.

Faral, Edmond. 1910. *Les jongleurs en France au moyen age*. Bibliothèque de l'École des Hautes Études 187. Paris: Champion. [Rpt. 1964]

Foley, John Miles. 1988. *The Theory of Oral Composition: History and Methodology*. Bloomington: Indiana UP.

Gautier, Léon. 1865–68. *Les épopées françaises. Étude sur les origines et l'histoire de la littérature nationale*. 3 vols. Paris . [2nd ed. in 4 vols. Paris, 1878–92.]

Hackett, W. Mary. 1973. 'Le style formulaire dans "Girart de Roussillon".' In *Mélanges de langue et de littérature médiévales offerts à Pierre Le Gentil*. Ed. Jean Dufournet and Daniel Poirion. Paris : S. E. D. E. S. & C. D. U. Réunis. 345–52.

Heinemann, Edward A. 1993. *L'art métrique de la chanson de geste. Essai sur la musicalité du récit*. Geneva : Droz.

Jauss, Hans-Robert. 1970. 'Littérature médiévale et théorie des genres.' *Poétique* 1: 79–101.

Kennedy, Philip Houston. 1966. 'Motif-Index of Medieval French Epics Derived from Anonymous Sources in the Early Twelfth Century.' Ph.D. Thesis, University of North Carolina. [See *Dissertation Abstracts*, A. 27, 1967, May-June, p. 2842–A.]

Martin, Jean-Pierre. 1992. *Les motifs dans la chanson de geste. Définition et Utilisation (Discours de l'épopée médiévale, I)*. Thèse de Doctorat de Troisième Cycle soutenue devant l'Université de Paris III. Université de Lille III: Centre d'études médiévales et dialectales.

Morton, Catherine, and Hope Muntz, eds. 1972. *The Carmen De Hastingae Proelio by Guy Bishop of Amiens*. Oxford: Clarendon.

Mynors, R. A. B., R. M. Thomson, and M. Winterbottom, eds. and trans. 1998–1999. William of Malmesbury. *Gesta Regum Anglorum*. *The History of the English Kings*. 2 vols. Oxford: Clarendon.

Nagler, Michael N. 1967. 'Towards a Generative View of the Oral Formula.' *Transactions of the American Philological Association* 98: 269–311.

Page, Christopher. 1993. 'Johannes de Grocheio on Secular Music: A Corrected Text and a New Translation.' *Plainsong and Medieval Music* 2.1 (*Aspects of Medieval Song: Essays in Honour of John Stevens*): 17–41.

Paris, Gaston. 1865. *Histoire poétique de Charlemagne*. Paris.

Propp, V. 1968. *Morphology of the Folktale*. 2nd ed. Trans. Laurence Scott, rev. and ed. Louis A. Wagner. Austin: U of Texas P.

Régnier, Claude. 1966. *Les rédactions en vers de la Prise d'Orange*. Paris : Klincksieck.

Rychner, Jean. 1955. *La chanson de geste. Essai sur l'art épique des jongleurs*. Société de Publications Romanes et Françaises 53. Geneva: Droz. [Rpt. 1999.]

Suard, François, Dominique Boutet, and Lilyan Kesteloot, eds. 2002. *Epopées d'Afrique de l'Ouest, épopées médiévales d'Europe*. Littérales 29. Nanterre: Centre des sciences de la littérature.

Thompson, Stith. 1955–58. *Motif-Index of Folk-Literature*. 6 vols. Rev. ed. Bloomington: U of Indiana P.

Thorpe, Lewis, trans. 1969. Einhard and Notker the Stammerer. *Two Lives of Charlemagne*. Harmondsworth: Penguin.

Tyssens, Madeleine. 1967. *La Geste de Guillaume d'Orange dans les manuscrits cycliques*. Bibliothèque de la Faculté de Philosophie et Lettres de l'Université de Liège 178. Paris: 'Belles Lettres'.

Zumthor, Paul. 1965. 'Le vers comme unité d'expression dans la poésie romane archaïque.' In *X$^e$ Congrès International de Linguistique et Philologie Romanes, organisé sous les auspices de la Société de Linguistique Romane par Le Centre de Philologie et de Littératures Romanes de la Faculté des Lettres de l'Université de Strasbourg du 23 au 28 avril 1962. Actes*. Ed. Georges Straka. 3 vols. Paris: Klincksieck. II, 763–74.

–. 1983 *Introduction à la poésie orale*. Paris: Seuil.

–. 1985. 'Les traditions poétiques.' In *Jeux de mémoire. Aspects de mnémotechnie médiévale. Recueil d'études*. Ed. Bruno Roy and Paul Zumthor. Paris: Vrin. 11–21.

# 13 The Italian *Cantari* between Orality and Writing

## *Raffaele Morabito*

In the research on Italian literature of the fourteenth and fifteenth centuries, the importance of the *cantari* has long been known: an intensification of research between the second half of the twentieth century and the beginning of the new millennium provides ample proof of this, as does the quality of attention this genre has received. It is not that the *cantari* went unnoticed before (even today, nineteenth- and early twentieth-century collections of materials and texts deserve to be mentioned), yet in more recent times these texts have been regarded less as 'popular' creations or analysed merely as part of 'higher' phenomena – studied as the antecedents of works which have been universally recognized (the most obvious instance here being Pio Rajna's study on the sources of the *Orlando Furioso*);[1] instead, an effort has been made to examine the *cantari* for their own sake, and not as the mere by-product of a literary culture which manifests itself significantly only in the works of the 'great names' (hence the studies regarding the formal structures of the *cantari* as an autonomous phenomenon and not simply in relation to more authoritative genres which have received greater recognition).

For the non-Italian reader, however, it may be helpful to elaborate on the *cantari*'s characteristics in their quality as a typical genre of Italian poetry in the fourteenth and fifteenth centuries (and indeed continuing into the following centuries). In one of the *facezie* (written between 1438 and 1452), Poggio Bracciolini speaks of a 'homo simplex' who went to listen to 'unum e grege cantorum (qui gesta heroum ad plebem decantant)' (one of those minstrels who tell the people of heroic enterprises); the singer having promised to tell, on the next day, the story of the death of Hector: 'noster [...] pretio redemit, ne tam cito Hectorem virum bello utilem interficeret' (our friend [...] offered him some money with the plea not to kill a hero as great as Hector so early). On the following days he kept paying to prolong the hero's life ('pro vitae dilatione'), until, left with no money, 'tandem mortem eius multo fletu ac dolore narrari audivit' (he was forced to listen to that tale of death, gripped by great sadness).[2] This story is related to another (which precedes it in Bracciolini's collection) remembered by Ezio Levi, who, at the beginning of his work on Italy's *cantari leggendari*, recalls the anecdote about a citizen of Milan who was moved to tears by a story of the death of Orlando he heard from a

---

[1]  See Rajna 1975, originally published in 1900.
[2]  See Poggio Bracciolini's *facezia* LXXXIII; Cicutto 1983:202 (for the Latin text) and 203 (for the Italian).

*canterino* (a singer or minstrel performing *cantari*) on the streets.[3] Both anecdotes offer proof of a gullible and popular audience's identification with the characters and stories which figure in the plays and public recitals they witnessed; the anecdotes are not surprising at all and are expressions of a phenomenon not untypical of gullible spectators: analogous episodes, for example, are mentioned again by Ettore Li Gotti in relation to the *opera dei pupi* (puppet plays) in the nineteenth century (1959: 37-38). It remains interesting, however, that this 'fabella stultitiae' is told with detached superiority by a humanist like Poggio, who thinks himself far removed from the world of the *cantari*. For him, obviously, these no longer represent suggestive and fascinating stories, as the 'Arturi regis ambages pulcerrimae' (the most beautiful tales of King Arthur) did for Dante (*De vulgari eloquentia*, I, X); anyone who allows himself to identify overly with the events of those stories is accused of 'insulsam mœstitiam' (silly sadness).[4] Detachment of this kind can be traced as early as the end of the fourteenth century in Franco Sacchetti's novella CXIV (this one, too, is mentioned by Levi), in which Dante himself chides a blacksmith who recites his *Commedia* poorly: 'cantava il Dante come si canta uno cantare e tramestava i versi suoi, smozzicando e appiccando' (he sang Dante the same way a *cantare* is sung, and he turned his verses upside down, maiming them and adding sections) (Lanza 1984: 231); as a result the blacksmith puts Dante's book away 'e se volle cantare, cantò di Tristano e Lancelotto, e lasciò stare il Dante' (and when he felt like singing he sang of Tristan and Lancelot, and let Dante be) (232). Like Poggio, therefore, Sacchetti feels that there is a great difference in quality between the literary genres which are part of high literature, and those less refined and more coarsely written; the *cantari* belong to the latter.

13 – *Cantastorie* (with vièle), from a popular print (16th c.) in the Biblioteca Nazionale Marciana of Venice

---

[3] See Levi 1914a: 3-4. Poggio Bracciolini's *facezia* LXXXII is found in Ciccuto 1983: 200, 202 (Latin), 201, 203 (Italian).
[4] For Dante's text, see Botterill 1996: 22 (Latin), 23 (English).

The term *cantare*, as is well known, is used for a form of narrative poem very common in Italy, and specifically in Tuscany (although also in other parts of Italy, from the Veneto to Umbria and Naples; Ragni 1973: 484), between the fourteenth and fifteenth centuries, and which was publicly recited on city squares by professional singers (the *canterini*) who had often themselves written or re-elaborated the poems. The recital was accompanied by music (the most common instrument being the viol or vièle), and covered a broad range of topics: Levi has proposed a classification of these topics, distinguishing chivalric *cantari* (of Breton or Carolingian setting) from legendary, religious and classic *cantari*, with two more categories added by F. A. Ugolini (1933): those treating of contemporary history and those of an obscene, novella-like character. But of course such classifications remain approximations and are not very strict: Levi himself defines his own as 'empirical and summary' (1914a: 21). Emilio Pasquini has recently sketched out another classification of sub-genres (1995), whereas a collection published with the title *Cantari Novellistici* comprises a few texts which had been classified differently in other collections, as, for example, *Bel Gherardino* or *Ponzela Gaia* or *Liombruno*, which for Levi were part of the legendary *cantari* (1914b). Additionally, a definition based on an obscene and novella-like content does not quite encompass a story like *Ginevra degli Almieri*, which unravels in novella-like fashion but which can hardly be defined as obscene; or that about Griselda, taken directly from the last novella of Boccaccio's *Decameron*, which has no place at all for what might be defined as obscene, and in which, quite to the contrary, its highly symbolic qualities can be observed.[5]

It stands as a fact that although some of the basic characteristics of the genre may be recognized, it has not yet been satisfactorily circumscribed, and neither should it be seen as a rigid category. One element normally considered defining is 'popularity': the reference to the humble dimension 'of the people' and to the cultural limitation implied by this is also expressed in the brief and keen-sighted comprehensive study by Eugenio Ragni (1973). Maria Predelli (1979) has pointed out the different meanings the term may assume (a degradation of art literature; work of bourgeois origin, educated but not overly so; or an orally circulating piece of work addressed to an unlettered audience). A distinctive trait of the genre is assumed to be the texts' oral and public transmission: this has been studied by scholars such as Levi and Branca, of whom the latter identifies it as a primary and defining trait (1936). Others have deemed it necessary to draw a distinction between shorter *cantari* (a few dozen stanzas) and longer ones, for which the hypothesis of oral transmission seems rather less plausible.[6] It is, of course, always problematic to draw clear lines of demarcation, and between an oral and a written transmission – just as between literary texts and popular texts – there are gradations and shades of details which may be endless and difficult to determine; nevertheless, there can be no doubt that, for a genre such as the *cantari*, oral circulation plays a major role. This peculiarity is closely connected to a phenomenon noted in 1960 by Domenico De Robertis, who, during the course of a convention on the problems of textual criticism, pointed out the constitutional difference between the *cantari* and major literary genres. Insofar as these are texts stemming from a re-elaborative tradition – i. e. the objective of those

---

[5] See, in particular, Branca 1956.
[6] See Ageno 1959–60; Franceschetti 1973; Pasquini 1995.

compiling the manuscripts in which the texts are transmitted is less to reproduce a text than to re-elaborate it according to their own needs – a philological practice aiming at the restitution of the work's original form remains necessarily inadequate. Instead, each witness has its own autonomous value, by virtue of representing a specific moment in a continuous process of re-elaboration. This has an impact both on the dating of the works and on the editorial practice: each manuscript must be taken as the attestation of a specific outcome in a tradition which is contemporary to the manuscript itself; the manuscript cannot represent an earlier stage of that tradition: 'the date of a redaction is practically that of the codex which contains it' (1961:103). For the modern editor this means that: 'there are practically no good or bad variant readings: there is only the reading of this or that redaction' (108). De Robertis' paper has re-affirmed the status of the *cantari* as not being part of high literature, stressing how the modalities of the texts' tradition in writing denote their oral existence and transmission. Additionally, this paper constitutes an important moment in research into the genre insofar as it finds points of reference for modern editorial practice, which must not try to produce the 'best text' of a given work, but should aim instead at offering a 'representation of the tradition's history which is explained to the reader in the best manner possible' (98). In another paper, some twenty years later, De Robertis himself reaffirmed 'that the text, in the course of its history, is made up of a succession of indifferent variations' and that 'we find ourselves in front of the reflections of a series of performances' (1984:21). It is in the light of such understanding that we have to read the justification inserted by De Robertis into the preface to the most important collection of *cantari* published in recent years (2002), an explicit justification as to why the work does not include such texts as *Geta e Birria*, a poem in two canti by Ghigo Brunelleschi and Domenico da Prato, which goes back to the classical model of Plautus's *Amphitruo*, through the mediation of Vital de Blois; or the version in *ottava rima* of the *Novella del Grasso legnaiolo*, a story in which one of the protagonists – and in fact the artifex of the jest on which the story is focused – is one of the greatest Renaissance artists, Filippo Brunelleschi (who is joined by Donatello and other extraordinary intellectuals of humanist Florence – a Florence shown as the new city of a classicist culture); just as in *Geta e Birria*, although in a more controversial and unsettling fashion, this story questions the same notion of an individual's personal identity, the perception of which constituted one of the major achievements for the new Renaissance concept of the world: challenging this, or calling it into question, implies that an awareness of such identity had already been attained.

The transmission of the *cantari* was oral, by public performance and with the *ottava rima* as its favourite metre.[7] This is in fact characteristic to such an extent that the critics' dispute about the origin of the *ottava rima* has become closely connected to the discussion about the history of the *cantari* genre. Nineteenth-century theories[8] claiming that the invention of this metre occurred in the popular sphere have been credibly called into question by Carlo Dionisotti (1989), who instead attributed the invention to Boccaccio; this theory was also used as a starting-point by Aurelio Roncaglia (1965), who considers the *ottava rima* to have been derived from transalpine metrical forms imported

---

[7] The *ottava rima* is a verse form consisting of eight lines, rhyming abababcc.
[8] For a review of theories concerning the origin of the *ottava rima*, see Menichetti 1984:383.

from France through the Anjou court. Guglielmo Gorni (1993) builds upon the same theory, reasserting Boccaccio's crucial role in the creation of the *ottava rima*: he is supposed to have deduced it from lyrical models (and in particular from Cino da Pistoia). Aldo Menichetti (1984), too, situates himself on the same line as Dionisotti and Gorni, in favour of the Boccaccian paternity; Armando Balduino, on the other hand, voiced a certain reserve regarding Boccaccio's authorship and came forward with a hypothesis proposing the derivation of the *ottava rima* from examples to be found in religious poetry from Umbria (1981 and 1982). It is clear that the question remains intricate, and the discussion, rather than being based upon certainties, is rooted in hypothesis and possibility. And while it is true that one cannot make an argument without some basis in the material we have and its ascertained date, it is also true that we have no form of documentation at our disposal which certifies the date of origin of this metrical form and that we are advancing on purely circumstantial ground. The opinion expressed by Giosue Carducci in his speech in honour of Giovanni Boccaccio (1875) seems, all in all, well-balanced even today, so much so that it was proposed again, in the main, by Balduino[9] and by Franceschetti:

> That there were poems in *ottava rima* before Boccaccio's time remains to be proven; it has been proven, however, that he was at least the first to diginify the *ottava rima* by introducing it into literary poetry. He was aware that the *terzina* had been born and made with Dante's poem, and for the subjective vision that is part epic, part didactic and part dramatic; he was aware that for his own poetry, for the poetry of the coming generations, popular and bourgeois, a new metre was needed, one that was less solemn and possibly less sad than Dante's, more varied than the one used for the feudal epics from France, a metre in which the creator-poet's imagination could move with ease, the imagination of a poet who no longer sang or contemplated, but instead narrated. And whether he decided to shorten the Sicilians' *nona rima*, or took the already shortened *ottava rima* from the poetry of Naples, the fact is that by picking up a metre from the people to ensure that it was filled with vitality and ready to stand up to the centuries, he displayed the sagacity of a real artist. (Franceschetti 1973: 321–22)

In fact, during the fourteenth century the *ottava rima* was not yet the obvious metre of choice for narrative poetry. Dionisotti gives examples of stories in verse for which different metres were used, and yet more could be added to those. An example from the period between the fourteenth and fifteenth centuries is the ballad of *Solazzo* by Simone Prodenzani, who was also the author of *O chiaro robino*, a *cantare* in *ottava rima*; this is a novella of Boccaccian tone which tells of the mishaps of a group of clerics looking for erotic adventures.[10] Seen from this point of view, the *cantari* seem to be a poetic genre which – whoever was the first to adopt the *ottava rima* – cleared the field and prepared the ground for the likes of Boccaccio, who, since his œuvre was much more deliberately composed and more refined than that of the *canterini*, essentially contributed to the way in which the *ottava rima* affirmed itself as the narrative metre par excellence for Italy's poetic tradition. We could say that whereas Boccaccio worked on an aristocratic level, the *canterini* worked on the most humble levels: their works were much coarser and

---

[9] See Balduino 1970: 5–21 ('Introduzione').
[10] See Prodenzani 2003: 29–198 and 1–28.

cannot be compared to those of a master as cultivated as he; nevertheless, they remained widely diffused works, which, in various social strata, introduced and strengthened the conscious perception of the *ottava rima* as the proper metre of narrative poetry. In texts like *Filostrato* or *Ninfale fiesolano*, Boccaccio bestowed on the *ottava rima* an unquestionable patent of nobility through the stylistic mastery he had acquired; and in the *Teseida*, a long narrative poem in twelve cantos, he invites comparison with that sublime paradigm, the *Aeneid*, so as to assert the value and power of expression of his own metrical tool. Thus he laid the foundations for a tradition which would see its greatest fruits in poems like those of Boiardo, Ariosto, Tasso; and, later on, through Marino all the way to the Romantic novellas in verse, which are perhaps the genre most characteristic of Romantic literature in Italy (Van Tieghem 1969); although the *ottava rima* was widely spread it did not lead to works of great importance. It continued, however, to prosper on a lower level in anonymous texts of popular origin: so that in the nineteenth century a story like that about Pia Tolomei told by Dante Alighieri (see *Purgatory*, V, 130–36) could be found in an anonymous edition of popular origin (reprinted some 30 years ago in a small amateur's edition) or in another, more culturally ambitious version (though, in the end, one humble in its outcome) by a professional writer like Bartolomeo Sestini from Siena.[11]

To give a defining criterion for the genre of the *cantari*, Eugenio Ragni (1973) suggests that 'the fairy-tale atmosphere', 'the fantastic might be among the most important elements of identification, even though, if applied, it would automatically exclude many compositions that share the main exterior traits of a *cantare*', in particular the historical ones dealing with recent history ('mainly with current events of local or at best regional impact'; 481), and those of religious content that can be attributed to educated authors, such as are the texts in a collection edited by Varanini (1965). Referring to religious *cantari*, Ragni takes up the remarks expressed by Varanini in the appendix of the aforementioned collection, which, significantly, he chose to call *Cantari religiosi senesi del Trecento* (Religious *cantari* of fourteenth-century Siena), thus unreservedly stressing their status as part of that genre. Varanini does not forget the very specific character of the poems he has edited: they are not generally addressed to a common street audience but 'to specific religious communities, lay confraternities, to the pious persons close to these and, generally, as far as Siena is concerned, to that part of the lay citizenship towards which, directly or indirectly, the religious actions of Caterina of Siena and her disciples was directed' (1965: 454). He does point out, though, that 'they are indeed true *cantari*, even though they have usually been described, in general terms, as short religious poems, without stressing that they belong to the *cantari*-tradition. Moreover, there seems to be a common tendency to regard as *cantari* only those of chivalric and legendary character' (452), even though 'the processes of composition are undoubtedly identical, even as far as concerns the use of the source and the structure derived from it' (453). Narratives of a more bourgeois nature, taken directly from the novellistic tradition (as in the case of the *Cantare di Masetto di Lamporecchio*, of Boccaccian origin), would have to be excluded, as well as those closely related to the genre of the novella (from *Lusignacca*

---

[11] His novella *La Pia* in *ottava rima* was published in 1821; see Sestini 1833. For an edition of the anonymous *Pia de Tolomei*, see Amerighi 1975.

to *Ginevra degli Almieri*). In fact, the range of topics addressed by the genre is very wide. An example of this is given by the *Cantare dei cantari*, in which the anonymous author spreads out his repertory in front of the audience:[12] a repertory which includes narratives from the Bible, from both the Old and New Testaments, from *Genesis* to the life of Christ and further to the early Christian era; the stories of the Trojan cycle, from the founding of Troy to the war and the flight of Aeneas and his arrival in Italy; further, the Theban cycle, the narratives of Theseus – in relation to which he recalls the twelve books of the *Teseida* 'composed by messer Giovano Boccaccio' (XXVI, 4) – and of Ulysses, Medea, Dido, Deianeira; the founding of Rome, the history of republican Rome and after that the deeds of (Julius) Caesar; followed by the Breton cycle, Merlin, the Round Table, King Arthur, Tristan and Iseult, Lancelot and Guinevere, Parcival and the Grail; the cycle of Charlemagne and his Paladins; that of Alexander the Great; and beyond that 'Fortune nuove, francesche e latine, / e novellette dirò sanza fine' (French and Latin new tales and little novellas I will tell without end; LVII, 7–8) (Rajna 1878: 436). These last verses include the novellistic *cantari* in the genre; additionally, in one of the most renowned anthologies of the genre – that compiled by Balduino, which contains *cantari* of the fourteenth century – the editor does not hesitate to include the *Storia del calonaco di Siena*, which recounts, actually in novellistic style, the love adventures of a canon, and the *Cantare della guerra degli otto santi*, recounting an episode of Florence's contemporary history.[13] As pointed out above, classifications of this kind can only have empirical value: thus the *Ponzela Gaia* or *Liombruno*, edited by Levi in the group of *cantari leggendari*, can be presented later as *cantari novellistici*.[14] In order to delimit the genre of the *cantare*, it is therefore more useful to refer not to the topic of the narratives but to the transmission modalities of the texts as well as to certain internal characteristics, above all of a stylistic nature.

I have already spoken of the importance that scholars have accorded the modalities of the texts' transmission. An 'insider's point of view' on the work of the *canterino* is being offered in *Liombruno* (II, 2), where a reference is made to the singer's need to recover the contents of his own narrative from his memory:

> De mio coragio convene ch'io me mova,
> ché liegere né scrivere non so io;
> datime, Signore mio, a·ffare prova
> in ogni cosa che a vui sia in dixio;
> spetïalmente a questa cosa nova,
> possa bene rimare, Signore Idio,
> sí ch'el mio cantar a ciascaduna volta
> diletti e piaccia a ciascaduno che lo ascolta.
>     (Benucci, Manetti and Zabagli 2002: 321–22)

---

[12] Dated by its modern editor, Pio Rajna (1878), as originating between the last two decades of the fourteenth and the first two of the fifteenth century.

[13] See Balduino 1970: 147–60 (*Storia del calonaco di Siena*), 237–51 (*Cantare della guerra degli otto santi*).

[14] See Levi 1914b: 29–58 (*Ponzella Gaia*), 59–87 (*Liombruno*); Benucci, Manetti and Zabagli 2002: 407–60 (*Ponzella Gaia*), 301–39 (*Liombruno*).

I have to muster up my courage,/ since I cannot read or write;/ Lord, please grant that I do well/ in all that you ask of me;/ especially that on this new occasion/ I may rhyme well, my God,/ so that each time my singing/ will please and entertain anyone who listens to it.

Manetti describes this as 'quite extraordinary and interesting information regarding the modes of production and transmission', and from it there emerges the image of an illiterate *cantore* who is forced to rely on his memory without the possibility of falling back on a written aid; if this is the case, Manetti wonders, 'has the written document of the second *cantare* of *Liombruno* been recorded by a witness to the impromptu performance of an illiterate *canterino*-rewriter?' (Benucci, Manetti and Zabagli 2002: 321 n.). In truth, I find the hypothesis of a text transcribed by a spectator who witnessed the minstrel's performance rather less probable, but this explicit statement inserted into the recital shows that at least the hypothesis of an illiterate *canterino* relying solely on his memory would have been plausible. Regarding the mnemonic capabilities of the author of the *Cantare dei cantari* a certain amount of reserve has been voiced concerning the trustworthiness of his affirmations, which are clearly hyperbolic in nature: referring to the history of Rome alone, for example, he boasts to know 1106 *cantari*. But, as has been said, it remains just that: a boast, made with the intention of being self-promotional, highlighting the author's own ability (Ugolini 1933: 22–27). Regardless of the author's truthfulness when admitting his own illiteracy, however, it is more interesting to note the emphasis placed on oral performance as the means of transmitting the text – or rather, the story, since the concept of the text which has to be preserved in its distinctive form, a concept typical of written literature, seems foreign to the *cantari*.

If in recent times, as I have already pointed out, scholars have insisted upon the pre-eminent role of orality in the transmission of the *cantari*, in an earlier phase, between the last decades of the nineteenth and the first half of the twentieth century, it was the subject-matter of the narratives which drew most attention: the stories and plots had been thoroughly studied, with a particular interest in the reciprocal relations between the various texts, pointing out, first and foremost, all the elements that had passed into high literature from a pre-existent, and less illustrious, tradition. Thus Pio Rajna, in *Le fonti dell'Orlando Furioso*, his most renowned piece of work, goes through Ariosto's narrative poem looking for the specific precedent for each episode. He traces them back to the classics of antiquity, from Ovid to Virgil, Statius to Apollonius Rhodius, but also the poems of 'our earlier chivalric literature', mainly the Carolingian cycle and that of the Round Table; and he remarks that if Ariosto takes only the raw material or subject-matter from the latter ('only the original ideas and the thought', as he puts it), then from the former he takes 'the form as well'. 'It is obvious that this does not reduce the work's greatness in the least', Rajna claims; 'in regard to all of his models, Ariosto has one governing thought: to preserve their beauty, to augment them, to correct their defects, to give everything an elegant appearance.' Rajna's studies seem to affirm 'that the essence of the poem really lies in the mastery of the art' and that, in fact, 'art abounds everywhere in *Orlando Furioso*.' Although, he adds, 'the inventiveness is often poor.' And although he at first affirms that 'it is obvious that this does not reduce the work's greatness in the least', immediately after that, considering the author and not the piece of work, he asks himself: 'Does the fact that Ariosto took a great deal from elsewhere, in imitation or adaptation, diminish his merits?' And he answers more or less in the affirmative: 'I know that I go against the opinion of many by not answering with a resolute "no"'; adding: 'What would the greats do without material to work on? [...] The truth is that the forces of a single man are never enough to create an immortal work. An entire age, an entire people, and at times even a multitude of ages and a multitude of people labour in silence until the times are right and there comes a mind that is able to profit from this long and slow preparation' (1975:608–10).

Rajna's book constitutes the best-known example of the kind of source-based criticism that Benedetto Croce disliked so much, even though their critical conclusions regarding *Orlando Furioso* were in the end less different than it might seem. Croce defined Ariosto as the poet of harmony, whereas for Rajna he was the poet of art.[15] The difference lies in the reflection on the act of crafting present in a poet's work; Rajna stresses the importance of the material's re-elaboration, while Croce depreciates this aspect of the creative process, insofar as, from his perspective (which focused on grasping the features of lyrical intuition within the works of poetry), it was not essential. It is not, however, the valuation of Ariosto's œuvre which is of interest here. Among the sources of *Orlando Furioso* discovered by Rajna, alongside the texts mentioned above, are others attributable to the tradition of the *cantari*, or at least closely connected to it (from *La Bella Camilla*, the *Cantari di Carduino* and *La Ponzella Gaia* to *Ancroia* and *Historia di Bradiamonte*). There are, in truth, few citations, but they are significant in the perspective from which those texts were regarded: that is, as constituting a single uninterrupted line in which the poems *d'autore* (by a greater, known author such as Pulci, Boiardo, Ariosto etc.) occupy the higher ranks, while the more popular texts occupy the lower ones, without ever breaking the continuity. A few decades later, Natalino Sapegno, too, draws a distinction between popular poetry (which includes the *cantari*) and art poetry, not only – as Croce said – in the 'basic quality of impressiveness and emotions evoked', but also in the 'distinctiveness of greater or lesser stylistic awareness' (1981:567).

In the second half of the twentieth century not only has the study of narrative material refined its techniques, thanks to the better calibrated instruments of textual criticism, which have permitted deeper and more reliable research; but more sensitive attention has also been paid to the specific modes of textual circulation. Their oral diffusion has now been recognized as one of the defining elements of the *cantari* as a genre. Abundant testimonies of the communicative practices of the *canterini* have remained – as I have mentioned already –, which are found not only outside the genre, but also in the texts themselves, in particular in the frequent references to the moment of performance. In truth, the assumption that the oral performance of the poetic text constitutes the characteristic and specific moment of its transmission has been engraved into Western poetry. I have already pointed out elsewhere that in the Italian literary tradition – and not only Italian, we may say, but in the occidental literary tradition in general – 'writing truly seems to be set up, at least hypothetically, as *ancilla elocutionis*' (Morabito 1984:173): it is only in the nineteenth century that poetic writing separates itself from the oral execution of the text. Still, despite the presence – if only virtual – of the voice, the specific weight of the written word has continually gathered importance, and the

---

[15] See Croce 1968; Rajna 1975: '[...] the fact has to be agreed that, although in *Orlando Furioso* art abounds everywhere [...], there often is a lack of invention, especially when it comes to plot'(608).

autonomy of writing in the communicative process has continued to grow over time. For the likes of Petrarch, who retreated to his *cameretta* (tiny room) to study (*Canzoniere*, CCXXXIV), or for the reader who should hunker down over the pages of that *opera d'inchiostro* (literally 'work of ink') which is the *Orlando Furioso* (I.III, 6), the moment for the enjoyment of poetry was one of solitude, in which its sound reverberated in the mind rather than physically inside the walls of the room. In the case of the *cantari*, on the contrary, the oral dimension is to be understood as the real condition of communication: real and exclusive. If, beyond that, the texts were to experience a written existence, then this was partly due to the *canterino*'s practical necessities concerning memorization; in part it constituted an attempt to move onto a higher level which continued to differentiate itself more and more from 'popular' poetry; to move on to the poetry by lettered poets for a lettered audience, which was attempting to establish itself in the fifteenth and sixteenth centuries as 'classic', to stake out room for itself and to earn a status of literary nobility equal to that of the classics: texts written in Latin, a dead language that could be heard, if at all, echoing through the gatherings of scholars, texts that lead a fundamentally written life, with mere episodes of orality.

As Balduino pointed out, it is surely appropriate to keep in mind that the *canterino*'s appearance may well differ from case to case: on one occasion he might be a minstrel who merely picked up the texts of others, perhaps adapting them to the demands of the moment as best he could; on another he might recite texts he composed himself *ex novo* (of course still drawing on a pre-existing tradition of stories on the same subject); or again he might produce a text of his own in the role of author and then commit it to others for recital in public (1970: 11). And his talent as a poet was just as diverse as his cultural level and ability; the range spans between the crudest of street-singers to more refined authors like that of the anonymous *Cantare di Florio e Biancifiore* (one of the oldest and best products of the *cantari*-genre), and on to figures whose features remain more clearly depicted, from the best known and most prolific, Antonio Pucci from Florence (ca. 1310–1388), to Neri Pagliaresi, Niccolò Cicerchia and brother Felice Tancredi da Massa. These last are typical members of a prominent cultural sphere in fourteenth-century Italy, that is, the circle of followers devoted to the moral teachings of Caterina of Siena, whose lessons in the religious sphere they not only pursued, but also practised. Still, beyond these not-insignificant internal differences, the phenomenon of the *cantari* presents itself with a certain unity: the texts, apart from their mode of performance and transmission, have also formal characteristics in common, in both content and style.

In the first place, the metre of the *ottava rima* is used in all *cantari*. I have already mentioned the discussion regarding its origin; its importance in cultured Italian literature, on the other hand, is too well known to be pointed out. It is a form of *ottava rima* which differs in quality from that used by Ariosto, and is of such fluidity as to remind Foscolo of the endless succession of waves on the ocean.[16] It is a form which is syntactically more fragmented and with cadences that usually indicate strong pauses after every second verse, with a tendency towards coordination and parataxis with frequent irregularities, and with recurring hypermetric or hypometric verses: cases of hypermetricity or

---

[16] See chapter X of *Notizia intorno a Didimo Chierico*; Foscolo 1951.

hypometricity, however, can often be regarded as purely graphic facts and as such are easily corrected when actually recited.[17] Being meant for oral performance implies an underlying narrative structure calibrated to the audience's capacity for listening: the *cantari* can normally be found to extend to some forty or fifty stanzas, which is as many as could be sung in an average recital (the *cantari* of greater length are of a later date, and even the *cantari* in which the story is composed of multiple textual units seldom exceed this number of lines in each of the single units: for example, the fourteen parts of which Pagliaresi's *Leggenda di Santo Giosafà* consists are all made up of fifty stanzas each, except for the last one, which amounts to fifty-three).

The specific traits of the *canterino* style have been studied and inventoried multiple times.[18] Among the first traits to be noted is an initial introductory gesture which normally consists of one or two stanzas of invocation of God or the Madonna, or of angels and saints as well. Symmetrical to this introductory move is a conclusion that refers to the will of God and the circumstances of the performance, addressing the audience in formulas directly connected to the oral means of the diffusion of the texts. An example is the concluding verse of *Madonna Eléna*: 'Questo cantare è detto al vostro onore' (this *cantare* has been spoken in your honour). This verse is found in identical form at the end of the first of the two *cantari* which constitute *Bel Gherardino*; and likewise, the conclusion of *Ultime imprese e morte di Tristano*: 'Signori, i'ho cantato al vostro onore' (Ladies and gentlemen, I sang in your honour).[19] Likewise the apostrophes directed at the audience by the *canterino* refer to the same situation (an example might be the *ottava* of *Liombruno*, as quoted above), which is equally to be found in popular works and in texts of a more artistic and original character, as, for example, *La Leggenda di Santo Giosafà*. Another trait typical of the genre is the swiftness of transition from one narrative situation to the next. An example comes from *Florindo e Chiarastella*, LXVII, 7–8: 'Ormai vi vo' lassar costor da canto / e de Florindo ragionare alquanto' (And now I'll leave those to one side / and tell you something of Florindo).[20] Further traits are the frequent use of hyperbole to stress the exceptionality of the situations; the use of synonymous word-pairs, the ornamental use of adjectives and the use of stereotypical formulas; and, apart from the word-pairs, whole series of words, listings of common objects, adjectives or proper names. Very well known is the series 'Avino Avolio Ottone e Berlingeri', introduced as brothers, and sons of the Duke Namo di Baviera in *Vanto dei paladini* (VIII, 8);[21] they are also found in the tenth *cantare* of *Guerra dell'Aquila* (X, xxvii, 6–7): 'Aviano, Avolio, Ottono e Verlenzeri / tacase omai' (Aviano, Avolio, Ottone and Verlenzeri/ be silent now) (De Matteis 1996: 177). This became a fixed expression and was handed down to the 'refined poets', to Boiardo (I.II.LVII, 3; II.VII.XVIII, 8; II. XXXI.XXXVIII, 7; III.IV.XIV,7) and Ariosto (XVI.XVII, 8;XVII.XVI, 5; XVIII.VIII,

---

[17] See Limentani 1961 on the development of this metre and on the characteristics of the *canterini*'s *ottava rima*.
[18] For a full list of traits see the summaries by Balduino 1970 and Ragni 1973 as well as the works of Limentani 1992 and Cabani 1988.
[19] The texts can be found in Benucci, Manetti and Zabagli 2002: 341–68 (*Madonna Eléna*), and Balduino 1970: 71–99 (*Il Bel Gherardino*) and 101–27 (*Ultime imprese e morte di Tristano*).
[20] The text can be found in Benucci, Manetti and Zabagli 2002: 615–48.
[21] Edited in Barini 1905: 33–41.

8), to be explicitly parodied by Ariosto himself in *Cinque canti* (III.LXVI, 2–4): 'fu da Carlo eletto / Ottone, Avolio e il frate Berlingiero: / ch'Avino infermo era già un mese in letto' (there were chosen by Carlo / Ottone, Avolio and the brother Berlingiero: / since Avino, being sick, had already been in bed for a month).

A peculiar instrument of the *cantari*'s popular style, in addition, is a particular use of repetition, which, far from being avoided for fear of slowing down the discourse, can instead assume a wholly constructive value. Thus, for example, in the first of the *Cantari di Griselda* from the fourteenth-century manuscript Parmense 2509

> in stanzas VI–XVI there is a high density of instances of the verb *volere* (14 instances, with a total of 19 in the whole of the *cantare*), of *contento* (6 out of 8 in total, apart from one instance of *contentasse* in IV, 6), of *piacere* (6 out of 9): it is the moment in which the bride is being chosen, and the lexical solutions stress that a precise will is at work, the authority of whoever can pursue such a will and allow for one's own subjective preferences, the general satisfaction, apart from Gualtieri's, with the chosen bride. The lexical choices with their insistence give decisive directions to the reader, pointing toward the narrative's critical motive [...]. Those phenomena are certainly not exceptional in the literature of the *canterini*. (Morabito 1988: 9)

In the *Cantare di Florio e Biancifiore* repetition is used in the same way to single out

> a few lexical elements with a characterizing function (*cristiana* – and, in contrast, *saracina* –, *bella*, *reina*) that recur in stanzas VI–XII, and then appear less frequently in the course of the narration. These are concentrations that might well be spontaneous [...] they could also be seen as a symptom of a possible lexical poverty of the *canterino* [...]. What remains important to point out, however, is the manner in which these accumulations help to single out fundamental narrative sections. (9–10)

This specific use of repetition is a manifestation of the *canterini*'s 'popular' style, in which the formal aspects of discourse can take on a different value from that in high literature; this is due to a difference in the configuration of the narrative and to the specific communicative situation, an audience 'di piazza', rather than an academic one.

It is in the light of such observations on the style of the *canterini* that quotations from 'high texts', such as the Bible, Dante's *Commedia* or from Petrarch's *Canzoniere* are to be understood; instead of evoking precise narrative situations, these quotations are used as of ready-made formulas, since they have been tested in elevated and sacred contexts. The use of stereotyped formulas is, in fact, another trait typical of the *cantari*. Thus, a lovely young woman is often a *rosa di spina* 'a rose on the briar'. Examples are *Madonna Eléna*, IV, 8: 'che fu più bella che roza di spina' (who was more beautiful than a rose on the briar); *Ultime imprese e morte di Tristano*, LXII, 6: 'Tristano istà co' la rosa di spina' (Tristan is with the rose on the briar); *Cantari di Griselda*, III.XV, 8: 'era suo moglie, la rosa de spina' (it was his wife, the rose on the briar). Formulas sometimes assume the function of an actual expletive. Examples are from *Storia del calonaco di Siena*, XXXIV, 1: 'Ma io non saccio bene, *a dire il vero*' (but I don't know for sure, to tell the truth); from *Ginevra degli Almieri*, LIV, 4: 'e un grosso pippion, *per quel ch'io sento*' (and a great fool, from what I hear).[22]

---

[22] For editions of these texts, see Balduino 1970: 147–60 (*Storia del calonaco di Siena*) and 101–27 (*Ultime imprese*); Morabito 1988 (*Cantari di Griselda*); Benucci, Manetti and Zabagli 2002: 341–68 (*Madonna Eléna*) and 559–88 (*Ginevra degli Almieri*).

Such conventionalized and widely spread modules are matched by a way of constructing the narrative which aims not so much at tracing a logical series of events, but rather at presenting a succession of situations that might arouse the listeners' interest; situations in which the audience is being captured in such a way that, involved in the narration, they are kept from paying attention to the logical connections between the various scenes of the story. More than the narrative logic, however, it is the single scenes that count, and the more conventionalized and thus more recognizable they are, the more easily the audience can identify with them. Thus at the beginning of *Bel Gherardino* the protagonist finds himself facing a snake and a bear that attack him on the road leading him to the White Fairy's castle: they are obviously beasts guarding the fairy and her home, but nowhere in the text is this explicitly expressed: there probably was no need to do so, since the audience, well acquainted with the genre, could easily make that connection themselves. It remains to be said, however, that beyond the reciprocal functional relations, the narrators were intent on making use of certain materials that figured among the most typical of a specific tradition, putting them together in order to create a typical narration – which should contain as many characteristic elements of the genre as possible. Accordingly, even if the events told in the *Ultime imprese di Tristano* could acquire meaning in the greater contexts of the Breton cycle and the exploits of Tristan and Lancelot, in the *cantare* itself, however, the single narrative events do not connect reciprocally through links of functional implications.

As I have remarked above, the plot too can be traced back to conventional patterns. This is a kind of poetry in which adapting to the canon is more important than any display of individual originality. The *canterino*'s performance is aimed at activating a sense of community based on an immediate sharing of values: positive heroes and negative characters, right and wrong have to be clearly identified and defined, set against each other. This moral order of the narrative universe is further strengthened for the audience as the facts are not usually presented as the *canterino*'s inventions, but as though they had been taken from a book in which that specific story could be found: a truth-telling, authoritative book which the *canterino* himself quotes to support his own storytelling, a book which not only supplies the plot but also authenticates the subject-matter of the narration (a trick which can also be found in Renaissance narrative poems of chivalry, composed in *ottava rima*, from Pulci and Boiardo to Ariosto).

It is not surprising in such a context that the characters show a complete lack of real psychological depth: it seems unnecessary to explain their behaviour on this level, or to describe what drives them internally; they do not possess their own personal space and instead express themselves through direct action. A case like that of *Leggenda di Vergogna*, in which the protagonist's reflections are expressed to some extent, is the exception rather than the rule. And whereas in the fourteenth century, with the establishment of the novella a genre had emerged in which the problematic character of facts and of the human world is of crucial importance (Neuschäfer 1969), in the *cantari* the moral order of the world is secure and without hesitation: on one side stand the hero and his companions, on the other, the antagonists. In this respect, the *cantari*'s world is closer to the *exemplum* than to the novella.

Certainly, the degree of refinement and complexity in the construction of the story varies from text to text.[23] In the *Leggenda di Santo Giosafà* by Neri Pagliaresi, for example, certain metrical figures alone are enough to affirm the composition's higher level of 'literariness'. And that is the significance of the presence of enjambments between verses, as in II.L, 7–8: 'Or vi dirò come Barlaàm a lui / venne' (I will tell you now how Barlaàm came / to him), or between stanzas, as in III.XLI, 7–III.XLII, 1: 'ma perché Giosafà è casto e netto / vergine e puro senza alcun difetto, / veder potrà la pietra e ciò che è in ella' (but since Giosafà is chaste and limpid / a virgin still and pure without a fault, / he'll see the stone and what is within). It is no coincidence that these examples are taken from a piece of work whose author is not anonymous, but known, a work *d'autore*, for which – as mentioned above – the modern editor Varanini has himself pointed out an area of circulation that differs from that of the more 'typical' *cantari*. In general, however, it can be said that the features I have noted as the *cantari*'s most characteristic describe a genre of which the single texts, speaking strictly in terms of literature, are certainly minor. This, to a certain extent, is what happened to the *commedia dell'arte*: so long as it was regarded as a literary manifestation, rather than as a major phenomenon of Italian and European theatre history, it was not properly valued. The *cantari* will doubtless be taken into account not only from this perspective, however, but also as a fact of communication and public performance involving the less cultured and the unlettered strata of society, an involvement which high contemporary literature could not achieve to such an extent. This is thus an audience which, according to Dionisotti, was selected and restricted socially to a greater extent during a more archaic period in the thirteenth and fourteenth centuries (1989: 242–43). Then, during the fourteenth century, and even more so in the fifteenth, it broadened and became more of a 'mass phenomenon'. As mentioned above, the connections the *cantari* have to fifteenth-century art narrative poetry, as well as to chivalric poetry in general, have always been evident and have, as such, been emphasized many times.[24] Still, it is during the fourteenth century that the growing chasm between *cantare* and art poetry became apparent. This phenomenon is in fact part of the process of dissociation between popular culture, tied to orality, and high culture, connected to writing. I am not saying that high culture is in itself written, but that at this time the creation of a new notion of textuality had begun, first in Italy, and then in the whole of the West. While for the *canterino* the important things to transmit are the plot and the values, the 'spirit' of the story, for the educated poet (the 'philologist') it is essential to pay attention to the 'letter', to the verbal form of the story; this new attention to form goes back to the belief that only by carefully and scrupulously transmitting that verbal surface can those values be transmitted, values which are closely connected to the individuality of the author who created them, and to the specific form in which they were created. These two paths branch out and diverge ever more clearly, and communication between the higher and the lower path becomes harder and harder; the poetry of academics, courts and educated people becomes more and more estranged from that which circulated amongst a popular audience – the *cantari*'s audience. From this point of view, the anecdote recounted earlier, told by Sacchetti in the *Trecentonovelle*

---

[23] For a structural study of the *cantari*'s plots, see A. Mariani 1989.
[24] See, for instance, Branca 1936; G. Mariani 1953; Bronzini 1966.

in relation to Dante, can assume a certain importance as early as towards the end of the fourteenth century: even to a man who is as much 'discolo e grosso' (a brute without education) as Sacchetti,[25] the sacred texts of high literature deserved respect – which was not the case for more vulgar pieces of work as, for instance, the *cantari*.

## References

Ageno, Franca. 1959–60. 'La *Ponzela Gaia* e il *Cantare di Liombruno*.' *Romance Philology* 13: 59–65.
Amerighi, Guglielmo, ed. 1975. *Pia de Tolomei. Composizione in ottava rima secondo la tradizione cantata*. Florence: Libreria Editrice Fiorentina.
Balduino, Armando, ed. 1970. *Cantari del Trecento*. Scrittori Italiani. Milano: Marzorati.
–. 1981. 'Le misteriose origini dell'ottava rima.' In Picone and Bendinelli Predelli 1984: 25–47.
–. 1982. '*Pater semper incertus*. Ancora sulle origini dell'ottava rima.' *Metrica* 3: 107–58.
Barini, Giorgio, ed. 1905. *Cantari cavallereschi dei secoli XV e XVI*. Collezione di opere inedite o rare 82. Bologna: Romagnoli Dall'Acqua.
Benucci, Elisabetta, Roberta Manetti, and Franco Zabagli, eds. 2002. *Cantari novellistici dal Tre al Cinquecento*. Introduzione di Domenico De Robertis. 2 vols. I novellieri italiani 17. Rome: Salerno Editore.
Botterill, Steven, ed. and trans. 1996. Dante. *De vulgari eloquentia*. Cambridge Medieval Classics 5. Cambridge: CUP.
Branca, Vittore. 1936. *Il cantare trecentesco e il Boccaccio del Filostrato e del Teseida*. Florence: Sansoni.
–. 1956. *Boccaccio medievale*. Florence: Sansoni.
Bronzini, Giovanni B. 1966. *Tradizione di stile aedico dai cantari al 'Furioso'*. Biblioteca di 'Lares' 23. Florence: Olschki.
Cabani, Maria Cristina. 1988. *Le forme del cantare epico-cavalleresco*. L'Unicorno 2. Lucca: Maria Pacini Fazzi.
Carboni, Fabio, ed. 2003. Simone de' Prodenzani. *Rime*. Dal codice al libro 25. Manziana (Rome): Vecchiarelli.
Carducci, Giosue. 1936. 'Ai parentali di Giovanni Boccaccio.' In *Edizione Nazionale delle Opere di Giosue Carducci. XI. Petrarca e Boccaccio*. Bologna: Zanichelli. 311–34. [Or. 1875.]
Ciccuto, Marcello, ed. and trans. 1983. Poggio Bracciolini. *Facezie*. Con un saggio di Eugenio Garin. Milan: Rizzoli.
Croce, Benedetto. 1968. 'Ariosto.' In his *Ariosto, Shakespeare e Corneille*. Bari: Laterza. 1–68. [Or. 1920.]
De Matteis, Carlo, ed. 1996. *La guerra dell'Aquila. Cantare anonimo del XV secolo*. L'Aquila: Edizioni Textus.
De Robertis, Domenico. 1978. 'Problemi di metodo nell'edizione dei cantari.' In his *Editi e rari. Studi sulla tradizione letteraria tra Tre e Cinquecento*. Milan: Feltrinelli. 91–109. [Or. 1961.]
–. 1984. 'Nascita, tradizione e venture del cantare in ottava rima.' In Picone and Bendinelli Predelli 1984: 9–24.
–. 2002. 'Introduzione.' In Benucci, Manetti and Zabagli 2002: ix–xxxviii.
Dionisotti, Carlo. 1989. 'Appunti su cantari e romanzi.' *Italia Medioevale e Umanistica* 32: 227–61.
Foscolo, Ugo. 1951. *Prose varie d'arte*. Ed. Mario Fubini. Florence: Le Monnier.
Franceschetti, Antonio. 1973. 'Rassegna di studi sui cantari.' *Lettere Italiane* 51: 556–74.
Gorni, Guglielmo. 1993. 'Un'ipotesi sull'origine dell'ottava rima.' In his *Metrica e analisi letteraria*. Bologna: Il Mulino. 153–70. [Or. 1978.]

---

[25] Sacchetti himself in the *Proemio* of *Trecentonovelle*; Lanza 1984: 1.

Lanza, Antonio, ed. 1984. Franco Sacchetti. *Il Trecentonovelle*. I classici italiani. Florence: Sansoni.
Levi, Ezio. 1914a. *I cantari leggendari del popolo italiano nei secoli XIV e XV*. Giornale Storico della Letteratura Italiana, supplemento 16. Turin: Loescher.
–, ed. 1914b. *Fiore di leggende. Cantari antichi. I. Cantari leggendari*. Scrittori d'Italia 64. Bari: Laterza.
Li Gotti, Ettore. 1959. *Il teatro dei pupi*. Florence: Sansoni.
Limentani, Alberto. 1961.'Struttura e storia dell'ottava rima.' *Lettere italiane* 13: 20–77.
–. 1992.'Il racconto epico: funzioni della lassa e dell'ottava.' In his *L'Entrée d'Espagne' e i signori d'Italia*. Ed. Marco Infurna and Francesco Zambon. Medioevo e Umanesimo 80. Padova: Antenore. 243–72. [First publ. in Picone and Bendinelli Predelli 1984: 49–74.]
Mariani, Annajulia. 1989. *Le fate, i cavalier, l'arme e gli amori. Per una morfologia del 'cantare'.* Studi e Testi 7. Salerno: Edisud.
Mariani, Gaetano. 1953. *Il Morgante e i cantari trecenteschi*. Florence: Le Monnier.
Menichetti, Aldo. 1984.'Problemi della metrica.' In *Letteratura Italiana Einaudi. III. Le forme del testo. I. Teoria e poesia*. Turin: Einaudi. 349–90.
Morabito, Raffaele. 1984.'La poesia italiana dall'oralità alla scrittura.' In his *Parola e scrittura. Oralità e forma letteraria. Studi critici*. L'analisi letteraria 24. Rome: Bulzoni. 171–89.
–, ed. 1988. *Cantari di Griselda*. L'Aquila, Rome: Japadre.
Neuschäfer, Hans-Jörg. 1969. *Boccaccio und der Beginn der Novelle. Strukturen der Kurzerzählung auf der Schwelle zwischen Mittelalter und Neuzeit*. Theorie und Geschichte der Literatur und der schönen Künste 8. Munich: Fink.
Pasquini, Emilio. 1995.'Letteratura popolare e popolareggiante.' In *Storia della letteratura italiana. II. Il Trecento*. Ed. Enrico Malato. Rome: Salerno. 921–90.
Picone, Michelangelo, and Maria Bendinelli Predelli, eds. 1984. *I cantari. Struttura e tradizione. Atti del convegno internazionale di Montréal: 19–20 marzo 1981*. Biblioteca dell' 'Archivum Romanicum' 186. Florence: Olschki.
Predelli, Maria. 1979.'Sulla letteratura popolare nella Toscana del Trecento.' *Quaderni Medievali* 7: 57–74.
Ragni, Eugenio. 1973.'Cantari.' In *Dizionario critico della letteratura italiana. I*. Ed. Vittore Branca. Turin: Utet. 480–88.
Rajna, Pio. 1878.'Il Cantare dei Cantari e il Serventese del Maestro di tutte l'Arti.' *Zs. für romanische Philologie* 2: 220–54, 419–37.
–. 1975. *Le fonti dell'Orlando Furioso. Ristampa della seconda edizione del 1900 accresciuta d'inediti*. Ed. Francesco Mazzoni. Florence: Sansoni.
Roncaglia, Aurelio. 1965.'Per la storia dell'ottava rima.' *Cultura Neolatina* 25: 5–14.
Sapegno, Natalino. 1981: *Il Trecento*. 4th rev. ed. Storia letteraria d'Italia 5. Milan: Vallardi. [Or. 1933.]
Sestini, Bartolomeo. 1822. *La Pia. Leggenda romantica*. Rome: Ajani.
Ugolini, Franceso A. 1933. *I cantari di argomento classico*. Florence: Olschki.
Van Tieghem, Paul. 1969. *Le romantisme dans la littérature européenne*. Paris: Albin Michel. [Or. 1948.]
Varanini, Giorgio, ed. 1965. *Cantari religiosi senesi del Trecento. Neri Pagliaresi – Fra Felice Tancredi da Massa – Niccolò Cicerchia*. Scrittori d'Italia 230. Bari: Laterza.

# 14 Court Poetry, Village Verse: Romanian Oral Epic in the Medieval World

*Margaret H. Beissinger*

Little is known about Romanian oral epic before the nineteenth century. There are few early historical documents that substantiate the early performance of the genre, and those that do date from long after the medieval Romanian Principalities were established. Likewise, there are no extant texts of Romanian epic from the Middle Ages, the oldest transcribed collections deriving from less than two centuries ago. Yet there are bits of historical evidence, comparative analogues, contemporary transcribed texts, and recorded fieldwork that hint at a rich epic tradition that has endured arguably for over 500 years. When and where was early Romanian epic performed? Who sang these tales, and for whom? What stories were told? How were they performed? My goal in the pages ahead is to piece together a portrait of Romanian epic primarily in the Middle Ages, employing available historical, comparative, textual, and ethnographic findings. I examine what historical documents say about medieval Romanian epic and how they have been interpreted, how comparative epic traditions of the European world inform the Romanian genre, and how the performance of Romanian epic in the nineteenth and twentieth centuries sheds light on how it may have existed in the Middle Ages.

Reaching back into the distant, imagined past, we can speculate not only that an oral narrative poetry might have existed in pre-feudal Romania, but that an epic genre performed by Romani (Gypsy) poet-musicians for the nobility and elite of the medieval courts may well have arisen by the late fourteenth century. By the sixteenth century, Romanian epic was documented (though still not recorded) by travelers and chroniclers, but it was not until almost 300 years later that it was first collected and transcribed. At that time, epic consisted largely of heroic narratives sung in verse that were performed primarily by traditional Romani musicians in village settings.

Romanian oral epic songs, believed to be in existence since at least the Middle Ages, are called *cântece bătrânești* (ancient songs). The first significant publications of the genre were issued in Iași in 1852 and 1853 by Vasile Alecsandri (1821–1890), one of the most influential cultural and political figures of nineteenth-century Romania. Alecsandri appropriated the western term 'ballad' (*baladă*) in these and later publications in order to put Romanian epic on the folklore map of Europe.[1] Although some Romanian

---

[1] He seems to have succeeded: by 1855 a French translation of the collection had come out, and two years later, a German one. In 1866, Alecsandri combined and expanded the two earlier volumes and published *Folk Poems of the Romanians (Poesii populare ale românilor)*.

scholars use the term 'ballad' to refer to all narrative song, I adopt 'oral epic', synonymous with 'ancient song', to mean mythological, heroic, feudal-court, and pseudo-historical sub-categories; ballads, by contrast, which I do not treat here, are a more recent sub-genre and reflect domestic themes as well as dramatic and lyric elements.[2] Romanian epic is no longer sung, but up until very recently, it was performed by Romani bards called *lăutari* (sg. *lăutar*), who sang and played mostly stringed instruments in small ensembles, serving originally as court musicians for the elite. *Lăutari* – who now perform mainly lyric song and dance music – are traditional professional musicians who transmit their occupation from generation to generation through the male kin line.[3] *Lăutar* derives from the medieval instrument *lăută* (lute), a strummed instrument which early *lăutari* played.[4]

The epic song known to twentieth-century collectors and listeners is performed by small ensembles (*tarafuri*, sg. *taraf*) of male Romani musicians on traditional instruments, among them the violin, double bass, guitar, cymbalom or hammer dulcimer, and accordion.[5] The song begins with an instrumental introduction struck up by the whole ensemble and is followed by vocal sections sung by the epic singer, who usually plays a violin or guitar, resting with his instrument in hand when he sings. He sings vocal sections of varying lengths, much like the *laisses* of Old French epic, stopping intermittently in order to play instrumental interludes with the other musicians.[6] At the end of the song, an instrumental finale is played by all. The songs are roughly 200–400 verses long. Corresponding to 8-beat melodic lines, the standard textual verse is a 7- or 8-syllable, generally trochaic, line. The poetry reflects a considerable degree of formulaic composition as singers rely on repeated syntactic and lexical patterns that are employed according to the narrative context.[7] The epics that circulated among Romanians were largely heroic and belonged to the Balkan Christian tradition.[8]

---

[2] There is no indication that ballads played a role in medieval Romania. I follow the terminology used by Mihai Pop, who distinguishes between oral epic – which includes a class of heroic songs (including those about 'heroic deeds [...] and [...] brigands and rebellions') and historical songs (including those about historical and contemporary events) – and ballad, with 'novella-like themes' (Pop 1998: 110–11). In my translations, I employ the term 'ballad' only when Romanian scholars use *baladă*, and 'ancient song' when they use *cântec bătrânesc;* when they utilize *epic* or *epos*, I translate them directly as cognates into English. [On European balladry, see ch. 16 by T. Pettitt in this volume; on Hispanic epic and ballad, see ch. 14 by R. Wright.]

[3] For a fuller treatment of Romani epic singers and Romanian epic, see Beissinger 1991 (ch. 1–3); on identity (occupational and ethnic) among Romani musicians, see Beissinger 2001a.

[4] *Lăută* is originally an Arabic word, which is found in a number of European languages besides Romanian (English *lute*, German *Laute* etc.).

[5] *Taraf* is borrowed from Arabic via Turkish.

[6] On relationships between the text and music in Romanian and Old French epic, see Beissinger 2000.

[7] For a discussion of formulaic composition in Romanian epic, see Beissinger 1991 (ch. 4–5); on text and music, see ch. 6.

[8] The Balkan Christian epic tradition is distinctive to the Serbs, Croats, Bulgarians, and Romanians and is contrasted with the Bosnian Muslim tradition. Romanian and South Slavic oral epic reflect similarities in the larger historical and cultural continuum that they share. Both are attested from at least the late fourteenth century, and like the South Slavic, the Romanian epic mirrors the Ottoman presence in the Balkans. The core of the heroic narrative deals with confrontations between native

The earliest Romanian epic, it is generally believed, rendered tales with mythological and supernatural content. Epic from the fourteenth-century founding of the Romanian Principalities to centuries of Ottoman suzerainty was chiefly heroic and pseudo-historical, as local protagonists prevailed over Turkish foes.[9] Narrative songs relating to the feudal court and conflicts of love, loyalty, and power were also typical, especially starting in the sixteenth century. And by the eighteenth century, heroic narratives about local brigands (*haiduci*, sg. *haiduc*) were circulating. Reflected in the collections made since the mid-nineteenth century, epics of all of these categories continued to be performed in the modern period, in addition to ballads.[10]

## 1 Story in Song: The Imagined Past

Romanians are the descendants of an indigenous population that inhabited the ancient territory of Dacia (much of present-day Transylvania), which the Romans occupied in the second-third centuries AD, during which time Christianity was introduced. Latin mixed with the Dacian language, eventually emerging as Romanian.[11] What is now Romania was later invaded by Slavs (in the sixth-seventh centuries), Hungarians (starting in the eleventh century), and Turks (from the fourteenth century on). Sometime after the tenth century, a Romanian ruling class developed, exerting its dominance and power over the local state and church. The independent medieval Romanian Principalities were established in the fourteenth century: Valachia around 1310, and Moldova circa 1352.[12]

Whether there was a Romanian narrative song tradition in existence before the fourteenth century is largely speculative. This would have been preceding the establishment of the medieval Romanian Principalities, before the Ottoman threat commenced in southeastern Europe, and prior to the settling of the Roma (Gypsies), some of whom became *lăutari*, the first recognized performers of epic. Comparative perspectives support the view that the singing of narrative verse by the common people did exist in some form in early Balkan history. Svetozar Koljević reflects on pre-Christian times when the 'Slav singers in the Balkans seem to have been ordinary people sharing in a popular entertainment.'[13] Albert Lord likewise argued that stories in verse were already in place

---

populations and Turks; tales of rescue, return, and weddings are also common. The Christian songs are generally several hundred lines long and are stichic.

[9] 'Pseudo-historical' refers to songs that contain references to historically identifiable names, places, and events yet whose stories are not historical per se (Lord 1972: 299).

[10] My own fieldwork collecting epic, mainly from *lăutari*, took place in south-central Romania between 1979 and 1987.

[11] Transylvania is in central and northwestern Romania. Little is known about Dacian.

[12] Valachia includes the historic regions of Muntenia (southeast-central Romania, the capital of which is Bucharest) and Oltenia (southwest-central Romania, in which Craiova is located), while Moldova, of which Iași is the capital, is in the northeast of the country. Most scholars agree that the Middle Ages started in Romania in the fourteenth century due to the imminent establishment of the Romanian Principalities; Georgescu considers the early eighteenth century as bringing to a close the medieval period.

[13] Koljević 1980: 304. Among the south Slavs, this would mean prior to the mid–ninth century. Koljević also points out that 'in the early Christian times [epic singers] were already known as professionals in Hungary and among some other nations' (304).

by the time the Ottomans started their ascent into the Balkans in the 1300s (1972: 299). Suggesting that Romanian epic 'has its roots in the most long-ago historical conditions of [the Romanian] people', Alexandru Amzulescu asserts that these ancestors 'created their own narrative songs many centuries [ago]'.[14] Mihai Pop and Pavel Ruxăndoiu maintained that Romanian epic as an ancient genre was originally peasant in character but 'later generated the classic *lăutar* form of the epic song which has survived until the present time' (1978: 294).

The most ancient epics are those that include mythic and supernatural content but are devoid of historical components. They constitute the kernel of many oral narrative traditions.[15] Lord argued that '"mythological" narratives formed the main repertory of the singers, Slavic, Greek, Romanian, or Albanian' in the pre-Ottoman Balkans, stating that 'the Christian tradition did retain some of the mythic songs rather well.'[16] Indeed, an ancient body of narratives with mythological, supernatural, and ahistorical themes is shared by Romanians and South Slavs. Early Romanian epic relates narratives about cosmic and natural forces, telling of heroes who vanquish dragons, serpents and other supernatural creatures. Among the most frequently performed early epics collected since the mid-nineteenth century are 'The Sun and the Moon', 'The Serpent', and 'Iovan Iorgovan', which find parallels in nineteenth-century collections of what is considered the oldest Serbian epic.[17] As Amzulescu points out,

> from the oldest times among the Romanians [there were narrative songs] with fantastic-mythological content, rising out of [...] ancient myths and beliefs, developing parallel and being fed from the same heroic-poetic substance as the folktale [and ritual poetry]. (1964: I, 38)

Many of these narrative songs are composed in a variant short metre consisting of 5- or 6-syllable verses, a hallmark of early Romanian epic.[18]

---

[14] Amzulescu 1964: I, 38, 37. He bases this view on 'comparative epic research of neighbouring countries, the few pieces of evidence that are known about the existence of Romanian epic in the preceding centuries, the distribution of the repertory gathered in the past 100 years, and what is known about the spread of [the epic] at the present' (1964: I, 36).

[15] Lord wrote of the 'generic narrative of the "monster-slayer"', an ancient pattern found in the epics of *Gilgamesh* and Heracles, as well as in Homer, Hesiod, and others (1995: 106–7). See the twentieth-century debate between Petru Caraman and Dimitrie Caracostea on the role of history in Romanian epic (Caracostea 1969; Caraman 1932–33).

[16] Lord 1972: 299, 300. He noted the 'richest of the mythic material in Christian tradition collected around [heroes involved in] [...] the slaying of dragons or dragon figures [...] and of relations with female supernaturals [...] [as well as] the justly famous stories of human sacrifice required for building a bridge or other edifices [...]. This kind of song one can rightly place at the core of Balkan oral ballad and epic tradition before the coming of the Turks' (1972: 299–300).

[17] 'The Sun and the Moon' ('Soarele şi luna') tells of incest on a celestial scale as the Sun attempts to marry his sister the Moon; 'The Serpent' ('Şarpele') relates how a young champion overcomes a dragon; and 'Iovan Iorgovan' renders the hero Iovan's rescue of a maiden captured by a monster (Amzulescu 1964, vol. 1). In the multi-volume anthology *Serbian Folk Songs* (*Srpske narodne pjesme*) compiled by Vuk Stefanović Karadžić, the categories 'mythological songs' and 'the oldest songs' include heroic epics involving the slaying of dragons and are comparable to the oldest, mythological Romanian songs, even with a parallel Jovan Jorgovan, such as in 'Jovan and the leader of the giants' ('Jovan i divski starješina') and other analogues such as 'The Dragon Bridegroom' ('Zmija mladoženja'), both from volume 2.

[18] In Amzulescu's comprehensive 'Thematic Index' of 352 types of Romanian narrative song (in his

## 2 Early Epic: The Heroic Age

The quintessential 'heroic age', as H. M. Chadwick famously articulated, is 'characterized by an aristocratic and military ethos, itself reinforced by the existence of court minstrels who praise the dominant warrior princes' (Finnegan 1977: 247). Historical circumstances throughout Europe in the Middle Ages set the stage for heroic poetry to develop. Romania's heroic age was shaped by the creation in the fourteenth century of the medieval states and rise of the feudal courts, the Ottoman advance, and the enslavement of newly arrived Roma, who provided a major source of labour for the elite, including, as *lăutari*, the performance of music and song in the courts. Against the backdrop of an emerging feudal society, Roma, having migrated northward several centuries earlier from upper India, were arriving and settling in southeastern Europe in the fourteenth century. Many formed communities in Valachia and Moldova, and within a relatively short time, had begun to be systematically enslaved by the Romanian nobility and clergy. The first written evidence of Romani subjugation is a deed dated 1385 recording a gift of forty Gypsy slave family groups from a Valachian prince to a monastery.[19]

The feudal period in Romania was dominated by the ruling elite, the military leaders, and the Church.[20] It furnished the milieu in which oral narrative songs glorified the feats of heroes and noblemen present at court banquets and reflected the culture of the upper classes. In medieval France and the Balkans, as elsewhere, a feudal class and its courts, defense against sustained foreign threats (be they Saracens or Ottomans), and specialized bards (from jongleurs to Serbian *guslari* and Romanian *lăutari*) created the context for the singing of heroic epic. Embellishing on the notion put forth by the Chadwicks that heroic poetry is 'primarily composed as celebratory accounts of the deeds of contemporary warrior princes and heroes' (Finnegan 1977: 248), C. M. Bowra noted that heroic poets 'assume that their task is to give pleasure through their art' (1952: 29). The Romanian feudal courts provided the principal settings for the jubilant feasts that the nobility regularly held especially after military victories. There the festivities included lavish praises for the exploits of the soldiers and other heroes. As Botnaru remarks, the princes 'would organize great "banquets" where ceremonies would take place in which those who had distinguished themselves in battle would be admitted into the ranks of the knights and boyars' (2005: 169). Indeed, Amzulescu comments that at these occasions, *lăutari* 'were pressured excessively to flatter the princes and glorify their exploits at any price while entertaining them at the banquets' (1964: I, 37).

---

*Balada populare romînești*, 1964), about 10% (or 36) song types are classed as 'Fantastic', and about half of those are in the shorter (5/6-syllable) metre. The other half are in the long (7/8-syllable) verse, as are virtually all other Romanian epic songs.

[19] Achim 1998: 21. A number of other late fourteenth- and fifteenth-century documents also make reference to Romani slaves in monasteries and estates.

[20] The time frame for medieval Romania is roughly early fourteenth to early eighteenth century. On the degree to which Romania was feudal, Georgescu argued that 'In the mid-fourteenth century when the two principalities were newly founded, [...] the relationship between the prince (*domn*) and noble (*boyar*) resembled vassalage in some respects, and the relationship between boyar and peasant and the structure of land ownership often took feudal forms' (1991: 19).

Church Slavonic, having been adopted in the tenth century, was the written language of the Romanian clergy and nobility, as well as of legal documents and chronicles. But medieval society at large was dominated by a predominantly oral culture. As such, one could argue that it was epic songs that provided the 'literature', admittedly oral, of the times. Alexandru Lambrior (1846–1883) was the first to claim, in 1875, that the cradle of Romanian epic was to be found in the early medieval courts (1976: 172–74). He posited that the genre was originally sung at gatherings of the elite and represented the highest form of verbal art for the nobility of the Romanian Middle Ages. It was, however, the well-known historian Nicolae Iorga who – in 1925 – developed and elaborated most fully the theory of aristocratic Romanian epic origins, maintaining that the genre developed in the courts of the early medieval princes and boyars and that it comprised narratives of their heroic exploits. Iorga argued that the court epic was sung in the vernacular, maintaining that 'it was in Romanian – and not in the language of the State or the Church – that the *lăutari* sang, telling tales of heroism that had just barely taken place [...]' (1925: 27). Iorga projected that a *lăutar* would have sung at the banquet of a prince, 'when, between glasses [of wine], his Highness would have requested to be told about the deeds of those who had sat in the same throne and had battled on the same fields' (26). I. C. Chiţimia elaborated on this, asserting that the epic in Romania (and Serbia, for that matter) was the supreme literary (albeit oral) form of the boyars of the Middle Ages. He wrote, 'it is clear that the ballad in the past was the genre that comprised the highest literary manifestation of the boyar court, alongside the medium of the popular masses' (1968: 235). Appearing posthumously (in 1969), P. P. Panaitescu likewise argued that an early medieval court epic tradition existed in the Romanian Principalities, as well as elsewhere in eastern Europe, where 'an oral literature of the court developed in the language of the land in formal contact with the popular language' (2000: 324).

South Slavic and Romanian epic were in close contact between the fourteenth and sixteenth centuries. Especially in Valachia, shared borders (and in some cases languages), culture, history, and religion nurtured close Romanian-Serbian ties. They mutually experienced patriarchal village life and the Ottoman Empire, not to mention sharing the Eastern Orthodox faith. Epic songs – including story patterns, heroes, and motifs – overlapped in the larger Balkan cultural continuum that was emerging at this time. Koljević characterizes the pre-sixteenth-century South Slavic 'world of medieval feudal song' as 'performed by foreign and native *jongleurs*, by various types of medieval entertainers, singers, actors, and drummers' (1980: 304). Serbian epic singers (*guslari*, sg. *guslar*) traveled and performed in the Romanian courts by at least the mid-fifteenth century, surely influencing to some extent both *lăutari* and their repertories.[21] Other foreign singers – such as the French jongleurs – may well have also sung in Romania and may have even had some influence on Romanian epic performance.[22]

---

[21] *Guslari* were oral poets who played the bowed, one-stringed *gusle* and sang epic in the south Slavic medieval courts as well as in villages in Serbia, Bosnia, Montenegro, and Croatia (see Koljević 1980).

[22] Little is written about this, although Iorga infamously argued that the roots of Romanian epic were to be found in medieval western Europe – especially in France – and that epic as a genre traveled eastward, as early as the thirteenth and fourteenth centuries, to the south Slavic lands, and then on

The Turkish presence in Romania and the Balkans was critical to the development of the epic. It united the Romanians with their Orthodox Christian neighbours to the south, who had already some years earlier succumbed to Ottoman control (Bulgaria in 1396 and Serbia by 1459). Despite fierce struggles and celebrated attempts to fend off foreign rule, however, Valachia become a permanent vassal to the Sultan *c.* 1476 and Moldova by 1512. Both Romanians and South Slavs found effective ways – through epic – to articulate their fears as well as their defiance of the Ottoman political and military threat, and it is clear that the narrative base that arose out of this historical condition became the bedrock of both of their epic traditions.[23] Heroic songs provided for all of them a means to express their resistance and formed the core of their sung narrative epic traditions; as Lord remarked, the 'whole genre' of Balkan epic 'depends on the Turks' (1972: 299). Reflecting a 'heroic age', an aristocratic, feudal world that was dominated by military concerns and threatened especially by the Ottoman Empire, both Romanian and South Slavic epic are filled with anti-Turkish themes, many of which could well have originated in the fourteenth and fifteenth centuries. Indeed, an entire corpus of Romanian epic includes tales of individual heroes fighting single or small groups of Turks in hyperbolic terms. Although we can make no assumptions about how early specific songs were sung, many appear to have roots in the medieval period as the Turks advanced northward into the Balkans.[24] As Ottoman control expanded, Turks supplemented the monsters and dragons as the adversaries of the earlier epic.

Several foreign documents refer to Romanian singing and singers – possibly of epic – in the late fourteenth century. The Byzantine chronicler Michael Doukas, who wrote a history of the Ottoman Empire, described how Sultan Bayazid I (1360–1403) was routinely entertained by young 'Greeks, Serbs, Romanians, Albanians, Hungarians, Transylvanian Saxons, Bulgarians, and Latins, each singing in their own language.'[25] Moreover, a manuscript at Marienburg from September, 1399 cites 'ein walachischer Spielmann' (Pop 1997: 36). By the fifteenth century, ceremonious banquets, such as at the court of the Moldovan Prince Stephen the Great (Ştefan cel Mare, ruled 1457–1504), were well-established occurrences and furnished typical venues at which heroic songs of praise were performed. In a manuscript from 1481, an anonymous chronicler briefly mentioned a triumphant feast after a battle at Râmnicu Sărat (Botnaru 2005: 169). The

---

into Romania. He maintained that the shorter epic songs of the Balkans were spin-offs from longer, more grandiose epics, in particular the Old French tradition (1925: 14–15). This view never took hold among Romanians and has been repeatedly discredited (see Amzulescu 1964: I, 37; Vrabie 1966: 19).

[23] Panaitescu even went so far as to suggest that Romanian and South Slavic oral poetries of the court represented 'for the fourteenth and fifteenth centuries a Romanian-Balkan literary collaboration, based in political terms on the common struggle of the Romanians, Serbs, and Bulgarians against the Turkish invasion' (2000: 237).

[24] As Rosetti et al. remarked, 'the heroic resistance struggle against the greed of the [Ottoman] invaders comprised the principal historical content and definitive thematic source in the development of the Romanian epic starting in the fourteenth century' (1970: 102).

[25] Ducas 1958: 86. The history covered 1341 to 1462 (Bayazid I ruled 1389–1402). The singing took place in northwestern Turkey. Pop read this as 'the custom in which young captive cavaliers who were Slavic, Magyar, and German, as well as Valachian, would sing heroic songs in their native languages at the banquets of the Sultan Bayazid' (1997: 36).

Moldovan chronicler Grigore Ureche gave an account – 150 years after it happened – of a similar event that took place in 1497 after a local victory over the Poles, writing that the prince 'put on a great banquet for all the boyars and all their heroes, and furnished them with expensive gifts' (quoted in Botnaru 2005: 169). But epic culture also transcended the banquets. When Prince Stephen led his armies against the Turks, he was accompanied by *lăutari*, who sang his praises in addition to other heroic poetry on the battlefront. In short, by the fifteenth century, Romanian court life included many occasions for the performance of music and song. Epic played a major role in this milieu; it was, as Chițimia pointed out, 'indispensable to the meals and festivities of the boyars' (1957: 614).

## 3 Epic in Medieval Manuscripts: Travel Accounts and Chronicles

During the sixteenth and seventeenth centuries, the anti-Ottoman struggle was fiercely fought in the Romanian Principalities. In cultural and social terms, this period witnessed the beginnings of Romanian literature in the vernacular and the rise of an urban class. These circumstances had a significant impact on epic. Although there are no extant song texts from this period, the heyday of Romanian epic is considered to have taken place between the sixteenth and eighteenth centuries. Performances took place in the courts of the nobility, where at festive meals and weddings, epic – along with lyric and love songs as well as dance genres – was heard. Epic often provided spontaneous praise and recognition of the deeds of the princes and warriors present and related local events that had happened. Many of those songs were short-lived and slipped into oblivion as time and exalted heroes passed; they no doubt included local, contemporaneous details that were lost for posterity.[26]

The earliest extant Romanian language manuscripts date from sixteenth-century Transylvania. At the same time, vernacular Romanian was gradually replacing Old Slavonic as the official language of the Moldovan and Valachian nobility. It was during the seventeenth century that Romanian supplanted Slavonic, this being, as Petre Brâncuși notes, 'the most significant cultural moment in the history of the Romanian Middle Ages' (1969: 49). In 1673, the earliest poetry in Romanian was published, and by 1688, the 'Bucharest Bible' was translated into the vernacular.[27] The establishment of Romanian as the primary language of written and spoken usage during the second half of the sixteenth century paralleled the rise of the urban boyar class. Ottoman control also intensified at this time, and as that happened, Turkish culture (including music) came into vogue. Moreover, urban areas were becoming larger centres for commerce and merchant trade. Boyars increasingly moved to the cities, establishing additional urban estates and monasteries and bringing with them their respective slaves, including *lăutari*, who performed at the courts. In fact, it is at this time that the first references to Romani slave

---

[26] According to Pop and Ruxăndoiu, 'many of the heroic songs must have originally resembled historic songs, with their tendency to relate events as close as they could to the authentic facts that generated them' (1978: 328).

[27] The poet was the Moldovan Bishop Dosofteiu, while the 'Bucharest Bible' was translated with the assistance of the Prince of Valachia, Șerban Cantacuzino (1624–1693; ruled 1678–1688).

*lăutari* were made. In 1558, *lăutar* slaves of the Prince of Valachia were mentioned in a document; while in 1565, a group of Romani slaves, including a *lăutar*, were purchased. A charter from 1570 provides the first mention of Romani *lăutari* in Moldova; specific names are found on a list of purchases, bequests, and inheritances by the Prince.

Travel accounts by foreign visitors furnish the initial concrete evidence of epic in the medieval Romanian Principalities. Maciej Stryjkowski, a Polish chronicler who visited Moldova, Valachia, and Dobrogea (among other places in the Balkans) in 1574–1575, wrote about epic:

> This glorious, ancient custom is still maintained today in Greece, Asia, Thrace, the Romanian Lands [Valachia; and Moldova], Transylvania, Hungary, and in other lands as I myself saw and heard with my own ears at virtually every gathering. [...] [I]n the public squares, the deeds of famous men are sung in verse, accompanied by the violin, which we call Serbian, (or) lutes, kobzas, and harps, to the great joy of the common people, who listen to the deeds of renown of the princes and celebrated knights. (Quoted in Amzulescu 2000: 6)

Referencing Stephen the Great, who had died 70 years before Stryjkowski witnessed his praises in song, he went on to note that

> At all their gatherings, Moldovans and Muntenians on their Serbian fiddles announce in their language: 'Stephen, Stephen the Prince [...] has beaten the Turks, he's beaten the Tatars, he's beaten the Hungarians, Russians, and Poles.' (Quoted in Botnaru 2005: 12)

Stryjkowski also transcribed a song (in octosyllabic metre) that he heard repeatedly, including the rhyming couplet:

> Ştefan, Ştefan, Domn cel Mare
> Seamăn pe lume nu are.

Stephen, Stephen, the great Prince/ Has no equal in the world.
(Quoted in Brâncuşi 1969: 56)

Stryjkowski's observations are revealing: he saw and heard wonderful performances considered traditional that were ('still') carried on. In just a few words, he fit Romanian epic into a broad comparative sphere of Balkan and Central European traditional narrative song. The singing of epic also seems to have been ubiquitous, including in public spaces, and while the passage unmistakably cites epic outside of the courts, it also mirrors the court and its most celebrated military hero, Stephen the Great. Stryjkowski remarked that the songs were accompanied by stringed instruments and were sung in the vernacular, neglecting only to address who exactly performed them.

Epic also provided a means of celebrating military campaigns as they happened. Paraphrasing an account by the Hungarian chronicler Szamosközy, Iorga wrote that in 1599, as Michael the Brave (1558–1601)[28] entered Alba Iulia after a victorious battle (in which Valachia, Moldova, and Transylvania were momentarily united),

> the *lăutari* went by his side, [...] and the songs they sang on such a day contained nothing but the tales of his triumphant deeds and the memories of the exploits of other Romanian princes so that they would never be forgotten. Along with the bugles, drums, and flutes, a different

---

[28] Mihai Viteazul; ruled 1593–1601.

sound was heard at the front of the procession: voices in Romanian glorifying the deeds of war. Accompanied by kobzas, the Prince's Gypsies were singing ballads.
(Iorga 1925: 27)

Here 'Gypsy' *lăutari* praised illustrious warriors in narrative song in Romanian as they played the kobza.

Seventeenth-century *lăutari* were frequently engaged at festivities for the elite, fairs and markets located at the boyar and monastery estates, and local inns. Extant documents from this time reveal that *lăutari* performed a wide variety of song (lyric, ritual and narrative) and dance genres and comprised a significant presence in Romanian society. The second significant surviving commentary on epic singing in Romanian by a foreign traveler is from 1632. It is the account of Paul Strassburgh, a German envoy of the Swedish King (Gustavus Adolphus II), who encountered the genre en route to Constantinople. He paid a visit to the court of the Valachian Prince, where soldiers who had fought with Michael the Brave were present. Strassburgh 'was accompanied at his departure by the Prince [...] [who brought] a guard of horsemen and pedestrians, with buglers and drummers.' Following them, he relates,

> important officials and the boyars of the land came forward on both sides, riding Asiatic horses and wearing brilliant attire. Next to the prince were *lautari* and a chorus of musicians who passionately sang an ancient song [epic] in Romanian. (Quoted in Botnaru 2005: 12)

This too is a telling passage. While Stryjkowski opens our eyes to the lower classes enjoying epic, Strassburgh reinforces our understanding of the genre as sung in aristocratic, martial settings, meant to impress foreign dignitaries.

As writing and literacy increased among the elite in the seventeenth century, written records of court performances by *lăutari* also multiplied. In one of the first written accounts of a court wedding in Moldova from 1652, we learn that the groom was piqued by the songs performed by various (ethnic Romanian and Turkish) musicians at the banquet. Only after an ensemble of Romani *lăutari* was brought in 'was he able to shake off his sullen mood' (Posluşnicu 1928: 582). Records of the early chroniclers also provide portraits of court events. In addition to Grigore Ureche, mentioned earlier, the Moldovan Miron Costin offered an account of two days of feasting and celebrating in June 1655 after a crushing defeat by the Romanians. He observed music-making on the first day, including performances on the bagpipe and zurla,[29] as well as the subsequent praise poetry, presumably epic:

> On the second day after the troops dismounted, Racoţii [the host] put on a great banquet and [the musicians] glorified both princes [the Moldovan Gheorghe Ştefan and the Muntenian Constantin Şerban]. [Racoţii] was at the head of the table; on his right, Prince Ştefan, and on his left, Prince Constantin. ( Quoted in Amzulescu 1964: I, 46)

At the wedding of the daughter of another Moldovan Prince in 1681, *lăutari* also delighted the guests with the entertainment they provided – apparently a great variety of both song and dance (although epic is not explicitly mentioned). Constantin Bobulescu noted that according to chroniclers of the day, 'royal court weddings lasted weeks

---

[29] The traditional Balkan zurla (*surlă* in Romanian) is a Middle Eastern wind instrument typically played by Romani musicians.

on end, even fifty days' and that much of their commentary on weddings focused on the entertainment provided and the many genres they heard: 'all of this merry-making and dancing was unmistakably due to the *lăutari*' (1922: 114).

Further references to late seventeenth-century epic are found in two somewhat anomalous examples. The first is from the biography that the well-known Prince of Moldova, Dimitrie Cantemir (1673–1723), wrote of his father in 1714–1716.[30] It refers to a Polish victory at the Battle of Iași in 1686. Paraphrasing, Bobulescu tells us that after the elder Cantemir fled Iași,

> the great king of Poland [Jan III Sobieski (1629–1696), ruled 1674–1696] [...] spent time there putting on banquets for his soldiers, and he parodied the custom of the heroic songs that were told at the Princes' meals when he began to sing mockingly of [Cantemir], who had just abandoned his own throne:
>
>> Constantine, fuge bine.
>> Nici ai casă, nici ai masă,
>> Nice dragă jupăneasă.
>>
>> Hey, Constantin, run away quickly,
>> You have neither a home nor a table [meal],
>> Nor your dear little mistress.
>> (Quoted in Bobulescu 1922: 70–71)

That a satirical imitation such as this was generated (even by a foreign victor) points to the institutionalized nature of this 'praise poetry' and provides a trenchant counterexample to the apparently more typical pure admiration in verse for the rulers that others left for posterity. In the second instance, the Valachian chronicler Constantin Cantacuzino wrote in 1694 that the songs performed 'by *lăutari* and other singers' relating the exploits of princes, heroes, and others did not provide reliable historical sources since they either excessively extolled the deeds or overly denounced the misdeeds of their protagonists. Either way, he shrewdly pointed out, such examples of 'history' were not historical. Notwithstanding, the Moldovan historian Ioan Neculce apparently borrowed details for his chronicles from the 'ancient songs he had the privilege to hear so many times at the princely meals or on the road to battle with soldiers' (Iorga 1925: 29).

Many of the stories of Romanian – as well as Balkan – heroic epic are rooted in the fundamental struggle between native autonomy and Ottoman control. In southeast Europe, as Lord pointed out, 'most of the historical and pseudo-historical oral narrative traditional songs are post-Turkish invasions' (1972: 299). Numerous Romanian heroic songs collected in the nineteenth century and later tell tales that fit into the medieval period dominated by the Ottoman Empire. Despite the illustrious Romanian leaders who resisted Ottoman control during the Middle Ages, however, few identifiable heroes figure in the songs.[31] Virtually all of the songs elaborate on a basic pattern in which native heroes are challenged by and defeat hostile Turks who seek to slay, kidnap, or rob

---

[30] He ruled 1693 and 1710–1711. His father, Prince Constantin Cantemir, lived *c.* 1614–1693 and ruled 1685–1693.

[31] Even Michael the Brave, who is regarded as one of the noblest Romanian leaders of the past and who triumphantly – but briefly – joined Valachia, Moldova, and Transylvania in 1599, does not appear in Romanian epic (see Fochi 1985).

the locals. In 'Tănislav', 'Badiul the Innkeeper', and 'Sick Doicin', local heroes masterfully defeat malicious Turks who attempt to overcome them. In 'Chira Chiralina' and 'Şandru's Ilincuţa', maidens are abducted in boats by roving Turks. In the former, Chira is rescued by her brothers, and in the latter, Ilincuţa escapes, usually preferring to drown than be taken prisoner. Songs about Novac and Gruia (an amusing father and son pair who are always up to heroic deeds) were also among the most popular.[32]

Not all of the heroic songs are specifically anti-Turkish, although they contain motifs and narrative patterns widespread in the Balkans. Such is the case with the imprisoned protagonist in 'Corbea', who manages to escape when he alone can mount his magnificent horse. Moreover, 'The Old Man' is a return song: a soldier arrives home on the day of his own wife's wedding to another, reclaims her, and restores order to his household, while 'The Best Man's Song' is a classic narrative wedding song, complete with the tests of the bridegroom and bride capture.[33] Both of these were routinely sung by *lăutari* at traditional weddings in Romania until very recently and indeed are found in multiform throughout the Balkans.[34]

Feudal-court epic songs, which depict social conflicts and tensions within the ruling elite, emerged during the later medieval period.[35] They illustrate rivalries and jealousies among the nobility, as well as romantic and kin-related dramas, and often present historical figures, although the narrative details in them are largely fictional.[36] Reflecting what must have been a persistent concern, treachery is common in these sordid tales. In 'Aga Bălăceanu', young Costin kills his godfather, Aga Bălăceanu, in order to win the favour of Constantin Brâncoveanu, the Valachian prince, but is in turn killed by Brâncoveanu, who fears that if Costin could betray his own godfather, he could also betray his prince. Also concerned with fictive kin, 'Vartici' is a melodrama of illicit passion initiated by a boyar's wife, Ileana, who loves her godson Vartici. He rejects her but is either hanged by her husband or kills himself, after which Ileana commits suicide. In 'Radu Calomfirescu', the hero joins a party of boyars who are conspiring against him with news that his home and women-folk have been pillaged by the Turks. Radu succeeds in rescuing them but is killed when he reveals the boyars' treachery. And in 'Dobrişan', the prince covets the bejeweled sheep and precious staffs of the shepherd Dobrişan and orders his decapitation, but just before the ax descends, he and Dobrişan are revealed as brothers and are reconciled. South Slavic epic of the same vintage also contains comparable narrative

---

[32] 'Badiul cârciumarul', 'Doicin bolnavul', 'Ilincuţa Şandrului', and Novac and Gruia songs (see Amzulescu 1964). Amzulescu includes 51 anti-Turkish epics in his Thematic Index–somewhat over 14% of all the titles. Comparing Vuk's Serbian epic collections that came out in the early 1800s, similar songs – most of them heroic – provide parallels, e. g., 'Bolani Dojčin' is 'Sick Doicin'; and Novak and Grujica songs abound in the South Slavic tradition (see Karadžić 1987, vols. 2 and 3).

[33] The two narrative wedding songs are 'Moşneagul' or 'Uncheşeii' and 'Cântecul naşului' (see Amzulescu 1964).

[34] A well-known Serbian Christian return song is 'The Captivity of Stojan Janković' ('Ropstvo Jankovića Stojana'; see Karadžić 1987, vol. 3); on Balkan return songs, see Beissinger 2001b.

[35] They developed in the courts of the princes and nobles 'toward the end of the feudal period', as Emilia Comişel notes, 'when the anti-Ottoman struggles settled into a slower tempo, after the glorious epochs of Stephen the Great and Michael the Brave' (1986: 106).

[36] In a listing of 25 names in Romanian feudal-court epic, most of them derive from the sixteenth and seventeenth centuries; but the stories surrounding them are ahistorical (Fochi 1985: 94–101).

songs in which feudal topics, especially family and court dramas as well as tragedies that reflect the medieval world, take centre stage. Like the Romanian genre, they tell of filial loyalty, betrayal, generational tensions, and other family conflicts.[37] A telling world of intrigue and at times graphic melodrama is depicted in these contemporaneous Balkan narrative forms.

Despite their popularity, many of the feudal-court songs did not survive into the mid-nineteenth and twentieth centuries (Pop and Ruxăndoiu 1978: 318). And as for those that did, Amzulescu warns against 'considering them exact "remnants" of the feudal ballad' (1964: I, 51). Nonetheless, descriptions within the songs that mirror a distinctly medieval milieu may well be hints of relative age. For example, nobles are portrayed as fighting each other with swords on horses, a feature that was distinctive to boyars of that period, contrasting with the way in which peasants fought: on the ground, with bows.[38] Furthermore, Romanian epic collected since the mid-nineteenth century (heroic, feudal-court, and mythological songs alike) includes cases of archaic speech, among the most conspicuous being Turkish, reflecting usage during the Ottoman period. The most common Turkish terms in the poetry refer to titles representing political or military status and institutions (political, territorial, and religious). Words related to taxation, money, and clothing, as well as interjections or greetings are also frequent.[39] They are emblems of the larger Ottoman influence that characterized so much of medieval Romanian epic.

Epic songs of the Middle Ages, though composed in the aristocratic milieu, were also, as Amzulescu argues, 'taken over and disseminated among the common people by *lăutari*' (1964: I, 51). *Lăutari* increasingly performed not only among the elite but also among the ordinary folk, where oral poetry formed a significant part of traditional culture, including seasonal and life-cycle ritual repertory. In fact, until the seventeenth century and even later, the differences between the song and dance repertories perpetuated by *lăutari* for boyars and peasants were minimal (Ciobanu 1969: 12–13). In other words, *lăutari* performed epic at court as well as at village weddings and other such events. As Dimitrie Caracostea neatly put it, Romanians had a narrative-song listening 'public in both the upper as well as lower classes.'[40]

---

[37] See 'The Building of Ravanica' ('Zidanje Ravanice'), 'The Wedding of Prince Lazar' ('Ženidba kneza Lazara') in Karadžić 1987, vol. 2.
[38] E. g., in 'Radu Calomfirescu' and 'Vartici' (see Panaitescu 2000: 325–26).
[39] Examples of Ottoman lexicon in Romanian epic (some of which is now obsolete) include *caimacan* (caimacam), *ceauș* (former civil servant), *deliu* (soldier from Turkish light cavalry), *pașa* (pasha), *spahiu* (spahi), *divan* (council), *firman* (administrative order by Sultan), *sangeac* (sanjak), *mecet* (small mosque), *haraci* (annual tribute), *irmilic* (silver Turkish money), *mahmudea* (gold Turkish money), *caftan* (kaftan), *ipingea* (man's cloak), *șalvari* (shalwar), *aferim* (bravo), *selamalic*, *temenea* (salaam [greeting]).
[40] Quoted in Botnaru 2005: 7. Caracostea also pointed out that this distinguished the epic culture of Romanians from the other epic cultures south of the Danube.

## 4 Epic Songs Move to the Villages and Towns

The Phanariot period, imposed in 1711, generally marks the end of the Middle Ages in Romania. It consolidated Turkish control in the Romanian Principalities through Ottoman-appointed Greek rulers and lasted for over a century. Ottoman cultural influence was strong at that time and made an imprint on *lăutar* music and song. Musical entertainment for the elite and the celebrations of seasonal and life-cycle events – much of it performed by *lăutari* – were essential to the eighteenth-century boyar households.[41] Describing a royal wedding, Cantemir wrote in 1714 that the musicians who 'are brought in [...] are always Gypsies, and [the wedding guests] feast in the house while music is made by singing and playing instruments.'[42]

Yet while *lăutari* were very much in favour at the courts of the nobility, they were progressively settling and performing in Romanian villages and towns. They typically lived on the outskirts of cities and towns, often called the *mahala*, in specifically *lăutar* neighbourhoods such as 'Scaune' in Bucharest; such ghettoes existed in Iași and other cities as well.[43] *Lăutari* found a professional niche at weddings, village dances, and family celebrations; they also performed for local inhabitants at inns, taverns, and fairs set up at boyar estates and monasteries. In many cases *lăutari* became the primary performers of traditional music in public, the most significant event being the wedding. Reflecting their emergent professionalism, guilds of Romani *lăutari* were established in the eighteenth century: by 1775 in Valachia and in 1795 in Moldova.

Pseudo-historical narrative songs characterized more and more the epic repertory in the eighteenth century. 'Constantin Brâncoveanu' is the sensational tale of the death by decapitation in Constantinople of the Valachian prince by the same name for his refusal to convert to Islam. A similar event took place in 1714, but the song fictionalizes the details, relating that Brâncoveanu's corpse was put in a basket and thrown into the sea, which miraculously burned for three days.[44] Meanwhile, the French Count d'Hauterive noted that the Moldovans he met in 1787 continued to exalt Stephen the Great in their oral poetry, writing that 'the tales of his deeds even today [...] are the joy of get-togethers and celebrations' (quoted in Bobulescu 1922: 64). But epic as a court genre was in decline. It was, as Iorga wrote, 'the hour of the demise of the ballad "of the princely banquet"' (1925: 30). Epic no longer served the purpose of glorifying the elite; it yielded to newer genres and styles in tune with Phanariot culture, especially Turkish music. The growing culture of literacy within the eighteenth-century elite also affected the decline of epic in the courts. Romanian literature was beginning to supersede the virtually all-oral literary culture that had existed for centuries. Written literature was replacing oral

---

[41] *Lăutari* at that time were 'highly valued by the dominant class. Now no one could even imagine celebrations without them. Just about every important boyar had to have a musical ensemble for his own court' (Cosma 1996: 18).
[42] Cantemir 1973: 240. Weddings then – as always – were the most festive (and exhausting) events at which *lăutari* played. Poslușnicu noted that in the eighteenth century, they would begin to play for wedding festivities already at least three and up to seven days before the actual nuptials (1928: 583).
[43] Pl. *mahalale*, a Turkish word (of Arabic origin).
[44] Brâncoveanu (1654–1714) ruled 1688–1714 and was beheaded by the Turks, an event that was widely publicized in Europe at the time for its barbarity (Chițimia 1957:17–18).

epic; early written poetry became the 'new epic'.[45] Furthermore, while formerly epic had been seen as a means to 'document' historical events, as Romanian chroniclers and historians in the latter seventeenth and eighteenth centuries progressively preserved for posterity the events that happened around them in writing, one of the purposes of epic was becoming obsolete. As Vlad Georgescu noted, a 'newer historiography' was taking place; and with the publication, in particular, of Cantemir's enlightened, fact-based histories in 1716 and 1723, 'the Romanians moved into solid history writing'.[46]

Epic had been performed in tandem in both court and village for some time – at least since the latter sixteenth century. When *lăutari* began to relocate en masse to the countryside, they increasingly appropriated the genres they heard around them (including narrative song) as well as transplanted what they had sung in the courts, thus actively performing epic for several more centuries. With these migrations, the contrasts between urban and rural music performed by *lăutari* became progressively more distinct. By the first half of the nineteenth century, urban *lăutari* were abandoning epic and picking up urban romances and international dance forms such as the waltz, polka, mazurka, and quadrille. Meanwhile, rural *lăutar* repertory was characterized primarily by native Romanian forms: traditional dance as well as lyric, ritual, and narrative song.

It is clear that heroic, feudal-court, and mythological songs were firmly embedded in the rural *lăutar* repertory by the time they were collected in the mid-nineteenth century and must have made up the majority of the epic sung in the Middle Ages. But another significant body of epic poetry was beginning to develop as the medieval period was coming to a close in the eighteenth century: outlaw (*haiduc*, pl. *haiduci*) songs, heroic songs that recounted the deeds of independent local brigands. As an outgrowth of the earlier anti-Turkish epic, they reflected a society relinquishing the feudal heroic age dominated by Ottoman rule. Moreover, while the antagonists in earlier heroic epic were Turks, in *haiduc* songs they were native boyars or representatives of the power elite. Sometimes verifiable names of local *haiduci* surfaced in these tales; the events related, however, were by and large generic. The songs were widespread not only in Romania, but throughout southeastern Europe, where comparable South Slavic *hajduk*, as well as Greek and Albanian klephtic songs similarly evolved. *Haiduc* songs typically depict a dashing outlaw who always has a trusty horse and is himself a little bit of a rogue, though mostly a champion of the underclass in his community. They have at times an elegiac tone, as *haiduci* are caught, incarcerated, and even sometimes perish at the hands of the ruling elite. As Iorga noted, they were full of 'fleeting love affairs, heroic fights, suffering in prison, the joy of escaping' (1925: 47). *Haiduc* songs were stories for the village underprivileged par excellence. They were sung far and wide by *lăutari* in the eighteenth and nineteenth centuries: 'at *haiduc* feasts in the forest or while seated around a table at an inn with [the innkeeper's beautiful wife or daughter]' (Iorga 1925:

---

[45] Ion Budai-Deleanu (1763–1820) from Transylvania; members of the Valachian Văcărescu family (e. g., Ienăchiță 1740–1797, Alecu 1769–1799, and Iancu 1786–1863); and the Moldovans Costache Conachi (1778–1849) and Gheorghe Asachi (1788–1869) were the best-known poets at that time.

[46] Georgescu 1991: 70; see Cantemir, *Historia incrementorum atque decrementorum aulae othomanicae* and *Descriptio Moldaviae* (1716); *Hronicul vechimii romano-moldo-vlahilor* (Chronicle of the antiquity of the Roman-Moldovan-Valachians) (1723).

47). Many of these songs were simply titled after the *haiduci* whom they celebrated. 'Toma Alimoş' relates how a *haiduc* drinks with his faithful horse and is confronted by a perfidious boyar who succeeds in killing him, but not before Toma deals him a final blow. In another, 'Iancu Jianu', the *haiduc* is captured, along with his horse, and imprisoned; he then sings a vindictive song behind bars denouncing the wealthy class.

Joining a substantial body of *haiduc* songs in the Romanian tradition are songs that concern horse theft.[47] Both contain traditional heroic patterns and motifs. One popular song tells of a clever horse thief who first steals a prize horse, is then captured, and finally escapes with it, leaping over a bulwark ('Codrean'). Both *haiduc* and horse-thief songs, emerging in the eighteenth century, drew heavily from an existing bedrock of heroic patterns and motifs, including the role of the hero's horse, capture and rescue, and the hero's acts of valiance.

## 5 Oral Epic: Transcribed Texts and Ethnographic Findings

The nineteenth-century Romantic nationalism that swept through Eastern Europe was instrumental in generating interest in the discovery and public promotion of native oral traditions. The calls to nation-building through folklore resonated deeply. Balkan scholars and enthusiasts turned their attention en masse to oral poetry. Vuk Stefanović Karadžić issued his debut collection of Serbian oral poems in 1814.[48] The Transylvanian poet Ion Budai-Deleanu was among the first to show interest in the gathering of Romanian epic in the early 1800s.[49] Enthusiasm for Romanian oral traditions, especially epic, was kindled by the mid-nineteenth century as a sense of a national cultural identity began to be forged. By the time epic was discovered in the 1840s, it was associated with the 'folk' – ordinary people – and was performed only in non-elite settings, mainly in villages. Meanwhile, Greek Phanariot rule had ended in 1821 in the Romanian Principalities, which came under Russian protectorate, and the Union of the Principalities of Valachia and Moldova took place in 1859. The Emancipation of Roma occurred officially in 1864, an event that was significant in terms of its impact on *lăutari*.[50] Many musicians left the estates and institutional venues at which they had served as they joined guilds and performed in cities, towns, and villages. In 1878, the Congress of Berlin signaled Romania's independence from Ottoman domination, while in 1881, the Kingdom of Romania was established.

Alecsandri started gathering oral poetry in 1840 in his native Moldova, and by 1849 and 1850 had brought out individual epic texts in issues of the publication *Bucovina*. The first published epic collections came out in 1852 and 1853 in Iaşi in two book-

---

[47] In Amzulescu's Thematic Index, he lists 83 *haiduc* song types and 70 song types for songs about theft.
[48] *Mala prostonarodnja slaveno-serbska pjesnarica* (A Simple Little Slaveno-Serbian Songbook), Vienna.
[49] Budai-Deleanu wrote about epic that he heard at markets and fairs: 'songs that are still sung today by *lăutari*' (Pop 1997: 37). I was unable to locate a source for this since there was no reference provided.
[50] Emancipation was begun in 1855 and 1856 in Moldova and Valachia respectively.

lets titled *Folk poetry: Ballads collected and edited by Vasile Alecsandri*.[51] In the preface to the edition from 1852, Alecsandri mapped out three large categories of songs, the first being what he called 'Ancient songs or ballads', defined as 'short poems about historical events and great exploits'; the other two categories were lyric (1866: xi–xii). He continued to collect oral poetry and brought forth a second, definitive anthology in Bucharest in 1866: *Folk poems of the Romanians collected and arranged by Vasile Alecsandri*.[52] Included here were variants of epic texts that Alecsandri had published in the earlier volumes.[53] Within a few years Romanian epic – and folklore in general – had become a powerful symbol of the nation and an integral part of scholarly culture. Alecsandri inspired numerous other Romanian folklorists to collect and record narrative songs, most notably in Valachia, considered the richest zone of Romanian epic.[54]

In the nineteenth century, epic was sung in public (at inns, pubs, or fairs) and at traditional weddings, baptisms, and other family celebrations throughout Valachia and Moldova. By the mid-twentieth century, it was performed almost exclusively at weddings in southern Romania (Valachia). Although the audiences had changed from the medieval times to the present, epic was still sung most often at banquets, feasts, and mealtimes, and still by *lăutari*. In the traditional village wedding, epic was performed during the Sunday evening banquet, the culmination of the several-day-long traditional nuptial celebration. Epic songs would be requested by the wedding guests, the new 'boyars' and 'princes'. Many an epic song collected during the past 150 years is framed precisely by evocations to the 'boyars' who are in the audience, internal evidence that corroborates the courtly banquet setting of early epic. A 1955 epic performance is brought to a close with the following formulaic passage, sung by the skilled *lăutar* Mihai Constantin:

> Ascultaz', boieri, de-aminî
> Fost-ai cîntecu deplin,
> Să mai bem f-un pa'r de vin,
> Macar fie de rachiu,
> Sîn' nepo' lu' Costandinî,
> Vă fac altu, mai bătrînî [...]
> Vă fac altu, mai bătrîn!

> Listen, boyars, [I tell you] amen!
> It was a good [full] song,
> Let's drink another glass of wine,
> Or at least some brandy,
> I am Costandin's nephew,
> I'll sing you another, an even older one [...]
> I'll sing you another, an even older one![55]

---

[51] *Poezii poporale. Balade adunate și îndreptate de Vasile Alecsandri*. It was a volume of oral poetry, including epic, collected in Moldova.
[52] *Poesii populare ale Românilor adunate și întocmite de Vasile Alecsandri*.
[53] Under 'Ballads: ancient songs' there are 55 titles; in this edition, 'ballad' has become the primary term used, whereas over a decade earlier, Alecsandri had used 'ancient song'.
[54] Among the most important collectors and years in which they published epic include G. Dem. Teodorescu (1885), Grigore G. Tocilescu (1900), Nicolae Păsculescu (1910), Constantin Brăiloiu (1932), and Alexandru I. Amzulescu (1974).
[55] Amzulescu 1974: 16. Constantin (1912–1970) was a superb *lăutar* from Desa, Dolj (Oltenia).

Constantin conveys a multiplicity of messages in this passage. He addresses his peasant audience as 'boyars'; lays claim to the fine quality of the song he has just sung; urges his listeners to keep drinking, thus requesting more songs for which he will be recompensed; reminds them of his *lăutar* pedigree as the male heir of another fine *lăutar*; and promises another, better song. He calls it an 'older' song, evoking the generic term 'ancient or old song'.

Romanian epic told of heroes and deeds that, by the time it first began to be collected, represented stories from a by-gone era when principalities had flourished but later submitted to Ottoman dominance. Included in all of the published collections of epic, from Alecsandri's through the twentieth century, epic texts are mythological, heroic, pseudo-historic, and feudal-court songs. Regardless of what we may label as a general period in which any given song or song type 'belongs', all categories were still being performed when epic was first collected by scholars. In other words, the genre did not proceed in a neat step-by-step progression whereby one theme was replaced by a later one, and so on, but rather, layer upon layer of songs appear to have developed, progressively enhancing the larger collective repertory.

Twentieth-century Romania saw two world wars, the union of Transylvania with the historic Romania (1918), the communist period (1944–1989), the revolution (1989), and the post-communist transition. Yet epic remained a vibrant genre; collectors found and published epic performed by accomplished *lăutari* well into the communist period. Moreover, twentieth-century technology made audio recordings possible. Thus, in addition to textual transcriptions, numerous epic performances have been registered electronically.[56] I too found inspiring singers in villages in southern Romania performing fine examples of epic in the late 1970s and 1980s. As a 'class' of professional traditional musicians performing not only epic but a broad spectrum of genres at social celebrations, *lăutari* effectively kept epic alive throughout most of the twentieth century.[57] Indeed, *lăutari* – or Romani musicians, as they now are perhaps more appropriately called – still perform at traditional events, especially weddings, and boast large and diverse repertories: traditional and popular lyric, ritual, and dance forms. And although epic is no longer part of their active repertory, it passed away as a genre only very recently.[58] The communist system had also contributed to epic's survival: as long as communist control was in place, all public music and song was regulated and censored, thus epic remained in traditional wedding performances. But once the central state dominance over cultural expression was punctured, epic was doomed to make way for other more contemporary, flashier genres. After the revolution in 1989, thus, as Romania's cultural, social, and political borders opened up, epic all but disappeared.[59]

---

[56] The Institute of Ethnography and Folklore 'C. Brăiloiu' in Bucharest has the largest archive in Romania.
[57] See Beissinger 2011.
[58] Contemporary musicians who perform at weddings and other family celebrations are often called *manelişti*, performers of the most popular Balkan-pop song genre sung today, the *manea*. See Beissinger 2007.
[59] On the music and instruments of Romanian epic see the additional commentary at the end of this chapter.

## 6 Conclusion

In the preceding pages, I have attempted to shed light on medieval Romanian epic by synthesizing historical, comparative, textual, and ethnographic evidence pertinent to the genre. While a more fully documented history would have been useful, what has been left to posterity answers at least some of our basic questions of performance: who sang, when, where, and what? Moreover, comparable European medieval oral epic traditions, especially the South Slavic and Old French, constructively inform our knowledge of the early Romanian genre and its role in society. Finally, recordings and ethnographic accounts of oral epic since the mid-nineteenth century furnish us with many useful models that shed light on how epic was formerly performed. A more difficult question to answer concerns how – or even whether – epic collected since the mid-nineteenth century derives from earlier, possibly medieval, performances. There is no doubt that the narrative patterns found in Romanian epic are ancient; but how old the epic texts (and melodies) are is another matter. Certainly the overriding spirit of the Middle Ages – resistance to Ottoman control – was kept alive for centuries. I myself collected heroic anti-Turkish songs more than 100 years after Ottoman suzerainty had ended in Romania and longer still since the Turks had marauded through the countryside. But songs discovered in the nineteenth and twentieth centuries cannot have survived wholesale over centuries of performance. What we have today is not what was sung verbatim in the Middle Ages but rather concrete examples of what might have been sung.[60]

Bowra claimed that heroic poetry is set 'apart in a curious kind of past'.[61] Surely by the time Romanian epic was put down on paper (and later on tape), most of the songs were already part of a past, an imagined past, yet a past that struck a chord with the then-present. Driven in part by a curiosity as to how the past informed the present, Alecsandri himself, as well as the great folklorist B. P. Hașdeu, tried unsuccessfully to locate epic songs from the illustrious reign of Stephen the Great, including missing songs about him.[62] And while archaic and obsolete Turkish lexicon, not to mention references and imagery, index a long-ago time in many of the songs, they are surely simply remnants of the world they depicted. There is no mistaking that the epic songs that have endured maintain vestiges of a vibrant medieval and post-medieval world, especially of heroism though also social conflict and drama. But taken as a whole, they are most of all timeless tales of human exploits, dilemmas, and experiences that resonate precisely because they transcend both history and the past.

We may lament the demise of Romanian epic, though comparable cultures tell us that this is inevitable, but it is also remarkable that the genre existed as long as it did. Launched by *lăutari* at the courts in the 1400s, if not earlier, Romanian epic lasted for

---

[60] On epic songs collected over the past 150 years, as Chițimia commented, 'they were only variants of the old ballads, found in a new stage of development' (1968: 236).
[61] Bowra 1952: 25. And addressing confusions she finds in the theorizing of the Chadwicks regarding the 'heroic age', Ruth Finnegan has noted that 'it is often unclear [...] whether this term refers to the period in which the poems were composed, or to the society actually depicted in the poems' (1977: 247–48).
[62] Iorga 1925: 27. One is reminded of how Vuk also looked in particular for songs (e. g., about the Battle of Kosovo) that would ignite the fires of nationalism in Serbia in the nineteenth century.

over 500 eventful years, functioning well into the twentieth century as a dynamic genre in traditional, mainly village, life. Although the epic voices of *lăutari* continued to be heard until very recently, the upheavals that followed the revolution in 1989 – the dramatic overturning of culture and powerful transformations ignited by the sudden globalism – signaled the end of performances at their last stronghold, the traditional wedding. Romanian epic lives on, however, in thousands of written transcriptions and taped performances that preserve the genre in endlessly varied forms.

## 7 Additional Commentary on the Music and Instruments of Romanian Epic

The music of epic has received far less scholarly attention than the texts; it was not until the twentieth century that its serious study began. Epic songs are, as Gheorghe Ciobanu noted, 'very old, most of them dating from the medieval period, some even from the early Middle Ages' (1969: 32); he bases this on the use by *lăutari* of certain chromatic modes associated with medieval Middle Eastern music. The verses of the poetry are sung to 8-beat melodic formulas whose contours include small intervals that are varied and combined in various ways as the song proceeds; the tunes are predominantly pentatonic. Framed by distinctive initial and final melodic formulas, musical strophes of irregular lengths comprise the larger *laisse*-like vocal sections (also of varying lengths) that are punctuated by instrumental interludes. This is how epic was sung in the nineteenth and twentieth centuries. We can assume that early epic performances resembled this form as well.

For as long as epic has been collected in Romania, the vocalists have played stringed instruments and have been accompanied by a small group of other instrumentalists in an ensemble called a *taraf*. Traditional stringed instruments associated with the singing of Romanian epic include the strummed kobza (*cobză*) and lute (*lăută* or *alăută*), both attested since the sixteenth century. In Cantacuzino's seventeenth-century translation of the Bible (mentioned earlier), *lăutari* are referenced as 'they sing with their *alăute*' (Cosma 1996: 9–10). Guitars were also played starting in the late seventeenth century (Bobulescu 1922: 33). In a manuscript from the seventeenth century (written by the Prince of Valachia), we read that at banquets for the nobility, where epic was likely heard, 'it is typical to have at your table [*lăutari* playing] various guitars, drums, *gusle* (a type of Serbian violin), and lyres' (quoted in Costăchel et al. 1957: 532). The *gusle* played a not insignificant role in early Romanian epic performances, underscoring the contacts between Romanian and Serbian performers.

Violins were first attested in 1633 in Moldova; they gained great favour throughout Romania and continue to dominate *lăutar* music-making. Seventeenth-century Moldovan *lăutari* are documented as playing in ensembles consisting of the violin (sometimes called *scripcă*), kobza, trumpet, and zurla (Bobulescu 1922: 12). It was during the eighteenth century that the violin – long considered the quintessential *lăutar* instrument – became widespread throughout Romania (the violin is so closely associated with the word *lăutar* that Romanians often translate it as 'fiddler'). An eighteenth-century observer remarked, 'At the table, between one toast and another, the Gypsies draw their bows across the strings of their violins, so that the song requested by the Prince will be heard

[...]' (quoted in Poslușnicu 1928: 583). Pictorial representations from the late eighteenth century on reveal that *lăutari* performed in ensembles that virtually always included violins. In an illustration from 1787, four musicians sit at a table; they play the violin, long-necked strummed instrument, hammer-dulcimer-like instrument (labeled *organ*), and pipe held vertically; a man next to them is directing them (Bobulescu 1922: 121). In another, three *lăutari* stand as they play the violin, kobza, and panpipes (*nai*) (Bobulescu 1922: 159). And a drawing from 1837 renders a pair of *lăutari* – presumably a father on the violin and his son on the kobza – as a small group of listeners surrounds them (Bobulescu 1940: 77).

By the mid-nineteenth century, *lăutar* instruments included the 'simple violin with four strings', the kobza, sometimes replaced by guitar, and 'the *keman* with two rows of strings' (Bobulescu 1922: 33). In an illustration of a *taraf* from this time, three *lăutari* play the violin, while the fourth is on the kobza and fifth on the panpipes (Cosma 1996: 120; see Illustration 14). By the twentieth century, the ensembles in which epic was sung – found mainly by then in southern Romania – frequently included the violin, bass viol, cymbalom or hammer dulcimer, guitars (ordinarily replacing kobzas in Oltenia), and accordion. In my fieldwork in the late 1970s through the 1980s, ensembles for epic included combinations of these instruments; the vocalist was the violinist (Muntenia) or guitarist (Oltenia). The epic *taraf*, then, comprised of the vocalist on a stringed instrument and his fellow (mostly stringed) instrumentalists, has endured for at least several hundred years.

14 – *Taraf* of Dumitrache Ochialbi (Painting by Carol Popp de Szathmáry, 1812–1888)

# References

Achim, Viorel. 1998. *Țiganii în istoria României*. Bucharest: Editura enciclopedică.
Alecsandri, Vasile. 1852–53. *Balade adunate și îndreptate de Vasile Alecsandri*. 2 parts. Iași.
—. 1866. *Poesii populare ale Românilor, adunate și întocmite de Vasile Alecsandri*. Bucharest.
Amzulescu, Alexandru I. 1964. *Balade populare romînești*. 3 vols. Bucharest: Editura pentru literatură.
—. 1974. *Cîntece bătrînești*. Bucharest: Editura Minerva.
—. 2000. *Valori de patrimoniu ale cântecului bătrânesc din Oltenia*. Bucharest: Editura 'Grai și suflet – Cultura Națională.'
Beissinger, Margaret H. 1991. *The Art of the Lăutar: The Epic Tradition of Romania*. New York: Garland.
—. 2000. 'Creativity in Performance: Words and Music in Balkan and Old French Epic.' In *The Oral Epic: Performance and Music*. Ed. Karl Reichl. Intercultural Music Studies 12. Berlin: Verlag für Wissenschaft und Bildung. 95–113.
—. 2001a. 'Occupation and Ethnicity: Constructing Identity Among Romani (Gypsy) Musicians in Romania.' *Slavic Review* 60: 24–49.
—. 2001b. 'Gender and Power in the Balkan Return Song.' *Slavic and East European Journal* 45: 403–30.
—. 2007. '"Muzică Orientală": Identity and Popular Culture in Post-Communist Romania.' In *Balkan Popular Culture and the Ottoman Ecumene: Music, Image, and Regional Political Discourses*. Ed. Donna A. Buchanan. Lanham, MD: Scarecrow P. 95–141.
—. 2011. 'Why Does Epic Survive? A Comparison of Balkan Oral Traditions.' In *Balkan Epic: Song, History, Modernity*. Ed. Philip Bohlman. Lanham, MD: Scarecrow P. 55–82.
Bobulescu, Constantin. 1922. *Lăutarii noștri: din trecutul lor*. Bucharest: Tip. 'Națională' Jean Ionescu.
—. 1940. *Lăutari și hori în pictura bisericilor noastre*. Bucharest: Sindicatul Artiștilor Instrumentiști.
Botnaru, Sorin Th. 2005. *Toma Alimoș: Un cântec aristocratic din secolul al XVI-lea*. Bucharest: Concept Valah.
Bowra, C. M. 1952. *Heroic Poetry*. London: Macmillan.
Brâncuși, Petre. 1969. *Istoria muzicii românești: Compendiu*. Bucharest: Editura muzicală a Uniunii Compozitorilor din Republica Socialistă România.
Cantemir, Dimitrie. 1973. *Descrierea Moldovei. Descriptio antiqui et hodierni status Moldaviae*. Ed. and trans. Gh. Guțu. Bucharest: Editura Academiei Republicii Socialiste România. [Or. 1716.]
Caracostea, Dimitrie. 1969. 'Balada zisă istorică: Metoda identificărilor istorice in folclor: Balada Crivățului.' In *Poezia tradițională română*. Vol. 2. Bucharest: Editura pentru literatură. 74–128. [Or. 1943.]
Caraman, Petre. 1932–33. 'Contribuții la cronologizarea și geneza baladei populare române.' *Anuarul arhivei de folclor* 1: 53–106; 2: 21–28.
Chițimia, Ion Const. 1957. 'Poezia populară narativă. Balada.' *Studii și cercetări de istorie literară și folclor* 6: 595–651.
—. 1968. 'A. Lambrior, folclorist.' In *Folcloriști și folcloristică românească*. Bucharest: Editura Academiei Republicii Socialiste România. 217–72.
Ciobanu, Gheorghe. 1969. *Lăutari din Clejani: Repertoriu și stil de interpretare*. Bucharest: Editura muzicală a Uniunii Compozitorilor din Republica Socialistă România.
Comișel, Emilia. 1986. 'Contribuții la cunoașterea folclorului muzical din evul mediu (sec. IX–XVI).' In her *Studii de etnomuzicologie*. Bucharest: Editura muzicală. 98–108.
Cosma, Viorel. 1996. *Lăutarii de ieri și de azi*. 2nd ed. Bucharest: Editura du Style.

Costăchel, V., P. P. Panaitescu, and A. Cazacu. 1957. *Viața feudală în Țara Romînească și Moldova (sec. XIV–XVII)*. Bucharest: Editura științifică.
Ducas, Mihai. 1958. *Istoria turco-bizantină (1341–1462)*. Bucharest: Editura Academiei Republicii Socialiste România.
Finnegan, Ruth. 1977. *Oral Poetry: Its Nature, Significance, and Social Context*. Cambridge: CUP. [Rpt. Bloomington: Indiana UP, 1992.]
Fochi, Adrian. 1985. *Cîntecul epic tradițional al românilor*. Bucharest: Editura științifică și enciclopedică.
Georgescu, Vlad. 1991. *The Romanians: A History*. Trans. Alexandra Bley-Vroman. Columbus: Ohio State UP.
Iorga, Nicolae. 1925. *Istoria literaturii Românești*. Vol. 1. Bucharest: Editura librăriei Pavel Suru.
Karadžić, Vuk Stefanović, ed. 1987. *Srpske narodne pjesme.* New ed. Vladan Nedić. 4 vols. Belgrade: Prosveta, Nolit. [Or. Vienna, 1841–62.]
Koljević, Svetozar. 1980. *The Epic in the Making*. Oxford: Clarendon.
Lambrior, Alexandru. 1976. 'Obiceiuri și credințe la români.' In *Studii de lingvistică și folcloristică*. Iași: Editura Junimea Iași. 172–190. [Or. 1875.]
Lord, Albert B. 1972. 'The Effect of the Turkish Conquest on Balkan Epic Tradition.' In *Aspects of the Balkans: Continuity and Change*. Ed. H. Birnbaum and S. Vryonis, Jr. The Hague: Mouton. 298–318.
–. 1995. '*Beowulf* and Oral Epic Tradition.' In his *The Singer Resumes the Tale*. Ed. Mary Louise Lord. Ithaca, NY: Cornell UP. 96–116.
Panaitescu, P. P. 2000. *Introducere la istoria culturii românești. Problemele istoriografiei române*. Bucharest: Editura Minerva.
Pop, Mihai. 1997. 'Însemnări despre folclorul românesc.' *Revista de etnografie și folclor* 42: 31–58.
–. 1998. 'Caracterul istoric al epicii populare.' In: *Folclor românesc. II*. Bucharest: Editura grai și suflet – Cultura națională. 109–20.
Pop, Mihai, and Pavel Ruxăndoiu. 1978. *Folclor literar românesc*. 2nd ed. Bucharest: Editura didactică și pedagogică.
Posluşnicu, Mihail Gr. 1928. *Istoria musicei la români. De la renaştere până'n epocă de consolidare a culturii artistice*. Bucharest: Cartea românească.
Rosetti, Al., Mihai Pop, I. Pervain, and Al. Piru. 1970. *Istoria literaturii române. I*. 2nd ed. Bucharest: Editura Academiei Republicii Socialiste România.
Vrabie, Gheorghe. 1966. *Balada populară română*. Bucharest: Editura Academiei Republicii Socialiste România.

# 15 Hispanic Epic and Ballad

*Roger Wright*

There are two main kinds of evidence for the medieval Hispanic oral tradition; the surviving ballads, and written texts from the past. Studying both together can lead to an appreciation of the nature of the old genre.

## 1 Ballads

From as far as we are able to see backwards in time, there has been a flourishing tradition of oral ballads in the Hispanic languages. Even now, in many parts of the Iberian Peninsula, the New World, and the Sephardic communities of the Middle East, investigators are finding new versions of old themes. The genuinely oral Hispanic ballad genre resists periodization, since it seems to have remained essentially the same in many aspects for at least eight hundred years and probably from earlier than that. Inevitably, it also changes over time as it adapts to a changing world, but even so the nature of the oral ballad genre as attested in the present is probably a good guide to its nature in the Middle Ages, perhaps even a more accurate one than are the surviving texts that were recorded from the fifteenth century onwards.

The Spanish ballads (*romances*) are defined according to their form. If a verse is structured with predominantly eight-syllabled lines, and vocalic assonance at the end of every even line, then it comes into the category, regardless of its length or subject matter.

Much detailed scholarship has been devoted to Hispanic ballad texts, both those preserved in writing before the twentieth century and those recorded on tape since then.[1] Each ballad theme has been allotted a name, which need not appear in the words of every attested version, allied to a particular assonance pattern: e. g. *Delgadina (á.a)*; as a result, newly recorded performances can usually be slotted into existing categories.[2] This is a genuinely oral tradition. That is, the ballads have usually been learnt from other singers, not from texts. Performers still usually perform from memory, although they are

---

[1]   In this chapter scholarship is reviewed in separate sections; for the Hispanic ballads, see section 3 below. [On European balladry, see also ch. 16 by T. Pettitt in this volume.]

[2]   For Sephardic versions of this romance, see the website 'Folk Literature of the Sephardic Jews', based on the collections of Samuel G. Armistead, Joseph H. Silverman and Israel J. Katz, at <http://www.sephardifolklit.org/flsj/>. The ballad is listed under 'Delgadina á-a' in the archive at <http://www.sephardifolklit.org/flsj/explore/searchBallads.html>.

not necessarily illiterate. Some of the themes first attested textually in the nineteenth century must be older than that; significantly, the Sephardic tradition, performed by descendants of those expelled from the Peninsula after 1492, has survived best in communities that did not have the Roman alphabet. Since the geographical range is so wide, we know now more than the performers do about the variability inherent in the genre. New versions of well-known tales are often found which are slightly but definitely different from previously-known ones, for there is no set text and each ballad, in a phrase which has itself become formulaic, *vive en variantes*. There is fairly clear evidence of the genre's flourishing existence in the twelfth century, three hundred years before we find written texts of any ballad. It may have existed even earlier.

Written texts of oral ballads have existed from the mid-fifteenth century onwards, and these may in practice have influenced the subsequent development of the genre. Huge *Cancioneros* were produced in the late fifteenth and early sixteenth centuries. Most of their texts are not ballads, since the ballads were seen as unacceptably rustic; but a few are, and the purpose of the collections seems to have been to provide texts that could be sung. *Canciones* are by definition songs with words. Then in the mid-sixteenth century, perhaps catalysed by the increasing availability of printing, the old *romances* became fashionable. It was partly their very oldness which appealed to the compilers of the collections of *romances* known as *Romanceros* (on the analogy of *Cancioneros*). These big volumes can hardly have been practical aids to performance; that role was taken by the loose-leaf printed sheets known as *pliegos sueltos*. Not many of these survive now, naturally, but there were originally large numbers of them; and their purpose was to encourage and enable performances. In this way some versions of the varying tradition could come to be much better known than others. The main sources for some *Romanceros* were probably those printed *pliegos sueltos*, but Martín Nucio, who produced the first such volumes at Antwerp in 1548 and 1550, tells us that he took texts from actual performances. Several others were produced later in the sixteenth century; scholars have felt justified in regarding them as genuine evidence of the oral tradition, even though it is likely that the collectors, or the printers, tidied up their texts in several ways, including Castilianizing the dialect.

Many of the earliest attested written ballads are based on striking historical events. The collectors seem to have preferred such narrative material, often ignoring the decontextualized tales of lovers and princesses which appealed to the Romantics three centuries later and must have been in existence then too. Modern editions of *romances* usually divide up the ballads accordingly into two main types, the historical and the fictional (or 'novelesque'), but the distinction in reality is not as sharp as it is in theory, because over time a ballad originally inspired by actual events tended to lose that connection as the reality faded out of the collective memory of both performers and listeners. In place of many of the original details 'historical' ballads tended to gain features more generically characteristic of the genre. This process, known as *novelización*, has led to a rough assumption that the more historically accurate a ballad is, the closer its composition to the events. This is a valid generalization, but several cases are counter-evidence, both in modern times and in the Middle Ages: for ballad-composers have often been inspired by a need to create political propaganda, particularly at times of civil war. This was the motivation of composers of *corridos* (as *romances* are known in Mexico) in the Mexican

15 – *El libro de los cincuenta romances* (The Book of Fifty *romances*), 1550–1551

Civil War of 1910–1918, for example, as it had been for participants in the Trastamaran civil wars of 1350–1369.

These latter ballads, composed for propaganda purposes, are the earliest ballads whose date of composition we can be sure of. But the composers, the red-top gutter press of the age, cannot have been avant-garde litterateurs inventing a new genre; they were adapting a type of popular verse already traditional and much performed. The civil wars continued from the accession of King Pedro of Castile in 1350 until he was killed personally in 1369 by his illegitimate half-brother, Enrique de Trastámara, who thus became the next king; since he lost, Pedro has been known ever since as Pedro el Cruel. Most of the surviving ballads were composed by his enemies, presenting Pedro as evil and murderous, but there are also echoes and hints of ballads composed by Pedro's supporters. The fact that the genre could be exploited for such a direct practical purpose suggests that many of the ostensibly 'historical' ballads (that is, originating in the historical events they describe, rather than implying any historical accuracy) could perhaps have been first composed by participants in those events, even when they are of the tenth or eleventh century.

Composition of ballads by participants in contemporary events was common after the accession of Enrique I, at least in the southern part of the Peninsula. One of the

King Pedro ballads, *Cercada tiene a Baeza*, set on the frontier between Christian-ruled Andalucía and Muslim Granada, expresses hostility towards Pedro for being an ally of the Muslims. This ballad, and others like it, set a trend. Between then and the capture of the city of Granada in 1492 many ballads seem to have been composed about, and by participants in, the stirring confrontations between the two sides of that frontier. These are now known as *romances fronterizos*. Granada was the only part of Muslim Spain to continue in Muslim control after the death of King Fernando III of Castile in 1252; they maintained their independence for the next 240 years through luck, skill, diplomacy, determination and economic efficiency. The Christian Castilians could not understand why fifteenth-century Muslim Granada was so much more prosperous than they were. We can sense from several ballads that theirs was a hostility tinged with admiration; so much so, that it used to be suggested that they could be translations from Arabic originals.

This admiration is evident in the ballad *Abenámar*. In 1431 King Juan II of Castile led an army southwards into the kingdom of Granada, guided by a dissident Granadan exile known in the ballad as Abenámar. On 27th June they arrived on the hills to the north of the city, and could see it beneath them shining in the sun; this panorama included the Alhambra and other buildings since destroyed. In the ballad, Abenámar explains what they can see below. The king falls in love with the city, and proposes marriage; the answer comes back on the wind, as the city replies that she is already married to her Moorish master (*el moro que a mí me tiene*). Battle is then joined outside the walls, and the Castilians go home with loads of booty (which seems to have been the point all along, rather than conquest). The conversations and the battle all happen in 52 octosyllables, in the version which survives from 120 years later; such a length might seem laconic enough, but the other Golden Age versions which have survived stop after 30 lines, with the city's negative reply; singers and audiences of this later age preferred a romanticized vision to the practicalities of the second half of the original, which rang more of a bell at the time of composition. The descendant found in modern Morocco (now available in a commercial recording) confines itself to the first ten lines of the original, where Abenámar is explaining the beauties of the city; the historical context has been lost, Abenámar is a romanticized figure, and the result is the musical performance of an emotional experience rather than a narrative; in all, a striking extended case of *novelización*.

This concentration on emotions has been a constant of the genre. All events, whether historical in inspiration or not, tend to be important mainly for the effect they have on the protagonists of the ballad. Deaths are not often described for their own sake, and often occur off-stage; the contact point for the ballad's listeners lies in the pain felt by the living after the event. Thus the death of the Count of Niebla at Gibraltar in 1436 is described, but mainly because it was the cause of great scenes of mourning at the Castilian court. This despair connected with the original singer's and audience's own worries, yet this tendency also applies to events from the distant past, where none of the listeners could have had any direct knowledge of the circumstances. Thus the dead knight Beltrán, killed during the Battle of Roncesvalles, has his death described baldly at the start of the ballad: *En los campos de Alventosa / mataron a don Beltrán* (on the battlefields of Alventosa they killed Don Beltrán); the other 78 lines concern his father's desperation as he searched for the body. Even Roland's death is mentioned specifically for the effect that the news has on Doña Alda, his bride.

These latter two ballads come into the category of 'Carolingian' ballads. These are descended from stories which came into the Iberian Peninsula from France, mostly near the start of the fifteenth century. The 'frontier' ballads represented and inspired the emotions of those who lived near the southern frontier, and they may not have been well known in the North of Castile; conversely, the Carolingian ballads, and the general atmosphere of late chivalry which pervades Castilian culture during much of the fifteenth century, were in comparison inappropriate for the South, where battles were real. Maybe, for a while, the geographical distribution of the two types was even complementary. The Carolingian ballads are so called because many of the tales were set at the time of the Emperor Charlemagne, but it is generally accepted that they can hardly be called 'historical' in any serious sense. Some of the Spanish ballads came over time to lose all direct connection with their transpyrenean original; at times their literary relationship can be restored by modern scholarship, but at times it cannot, and this can leave an enigmatic air hanging over a story which in origin could have been more banal. A good example is the ballad of *Rosa Florida*: she lives in a magic castle in Castile, being courted by many Italian suitors, but is in love with the French Count Montesinos, whom she has never met; she tells her page to take Montesinos a letter inviting him to come to see her, whereupon she will give him not only her body (second in beauty within Castile only to that of her sister, otherwise unmentioned) but seven castles. Since the emotion of the protagonist is, as usual, the point of the ballad, it stops there without informing us of Montesinos's reply. This episode seems inexplicable out of context, and that is now part of its charm; it is slightly disappointing to discover that it derives from the French tale *Aiol*, in which the reference to her sister makes straightforward sense.

This category of Carolingian ballads, in which fact has over the years turned into fiction, thus merges into that of those assumed to be fictitious in their origin: the novelesque ballads. Some of these are ancient folktales, presenting themes well known to performers and folklore specialists all over Europe, or even the world. Thus fables, in which animals are given simplified human characteristics, are not common in the Spanish ballad tradition, but those that appear may relate in some sense to wider traditions than just the Hispanic. For example, in the ballad of *Fonte Frida* we meet a widowed turtle-dove angrily rejecting a deceitfully propositioning nightingale. This is not really a tale of one bird rejecting another, of course, but a representation of raw human emotions in non-human form, which is a useful technique when the emotions are ones which human beings naturally tend to dissimulate and hide; and comparisons with similar birds in other folk traditions help us appreciate what an appropriate reaction is. For such reasons specialists feel justified in alluding to Stith Thompson's *Index* of folk-motifs (which was unknown to the original performers and audiences). There are two ways in which geographically wide comparisons might be illuminating. We may, firstly, feel that the recurrence of a motif, such as the adulterous wife attempting to mislead her husband in certain specific ways, is a symptom of universal constants of human psychology, unconscious, subconscious or conscious; or we may instead see the manifestations of such motifs in disparate parts of Europe as manifesting direct historical links with an older pan-Indo-European folk tradition. Almost by definition, both approaches are interesting but also unprovable. It seems to me less likely that adducing pan-European ballad examples helps us understand a frontier ballad rooted in a specifically Hispanic context, however, as it has recently proved fashionable to imply (with reference to *Moraima*) (Smith 1964: 191–92).

Throughout all these sub-genres, the effect on the audience seems to be the performer's primary concern. The ballads are not meant to be read but recited; and not just sung for the singer's own entertainment, but to catch the attention and feelings of listeners. The process is mutual; the listeners hope to be moved, to feel the emotions of love, or anger, or horror, or conflicts of duty, etc. They also hope to be amused, and indeed some ballads strike us as being humorous at least in part, but the atmosphere is not frivolous. Even the ballad of *Gallarda*, who hangs the severed heads of her hopeful but unfortunate lovers from the rafters of her house, eventually being killed with her own dagger by an intended victim, is a tale of revenge, relief and poetic justice rather than merely a good joke. The living genre is not well represented by written texts, without the music or the context of performance, and in the event some of the best studies of the modern ballad tradition have been undertaken by anthropologists (such as Judith Seeger), who are able to analyse the ballad as a group activity relying on the creation and development of an atmosphere, largely in the hands of the performer (rather than directly on any aspect of the original text). Different performers can thus give radically different performances of essentially the same text. It seems, for example, judging from the remarkably varied modern attitudes to it, that the frontier ballad of *Álora* could either be presented in such a way as to arouse sympathy for the Christian besiegers, whose leader is treacherously shot dead by a Muslim arrow during a period of truce, or in such a way as to arouse admiration for the skill of the Muslim marksman; which suggests that the intention of the original creator of the ballad (for every ballad, however anonymous, must have had a first time and an original inventor) could easily slip away over time and yield to the intentions of a performer. This anthropological approach makes the ballad genre seem to be a variety of drama. We might indeed have here the lost genre of medieval Spanish drama; even though it was essentially a one-man (or one-woman) show, the performers, like theatrical producers, saw and see their main aim as catching an audience's attention and creating an atmosphere in a dramatic arena.

This perspective on the genre leads us to the most controversial question which surrounds the old Hispanic ballads. What was their relation to epics?

## 2 Epics

There is only one genuine extant medieval Castilian epic, the *Poema de Mio Cid*, attested in one manuscript only, datable to the late thirteenth or early fourteenth century.[3] This is a copy of an earlier manuscript dated explicitly to the year 1245 of the Spanish era; that is, 1207 AD. Whether 1207 is the date of its original composition as a

---

[3] For scholarship on the Hispanic epic, see section 4 below. [On epic in the Romance languages, see also the chapters by D. Boutet on the *chansons de geste* (ch. 12), by R. Morabito on the Italian *cantari* (ch. 13), and by M. Beissinger on Romanian epic poetry (ch. 14).]

written text, or the date of the initial preservation in written form of an earlier oral composition, or the date of a late rewriting of a version already available in written form but oral in origin, is still controversial. Other Hispanic compositions of the age have been called epics, but only in an approximate sense; there is a fragment of an otherwise unknown text usually now referred to as the *Cantar de Roncesvalles*, but being a single page there is no way of knowing if the whole was originally long enough to be classified as an epic rather than a long ballad. The *Poema de Fernán González* is not itself an epic, but may have been based on one which is now lost. The fourteenth-century *Mocedades de Rodrigo* is not itself an epic either, but there may have been a related one on the topic (the Cid's youth). Several episodes in the enormous Histories produced at the court of King Alfonso X of Castile (1252–1284) derived from poetic compositions, but it is still a moot point whether those compositions, usually called in the Histories non-committally *cantares*, 'songs', were long enough for us to call them 'epics'. The possible relationship of epics with the ballads is mainly postulated on the basis of these reconstructable epics glimpsed in the Alfonsine Histories, since many ballads recount what may have also been episodes in those now lost epics. There are, for example, a number of surviving ballads on the highly dramatic siege of Zamora of 1072, which recount the tale more or less in sequence; it is widely thought that this ballad 'cycle' is evidence of the previous existence of a (now lost) single epic on that siege, which was prosified for the benefit of the Histories and fragmented later into separate ballad-shaped episodes. This theory became associated with the great genius of Spanish medieval studies, Ramón Menéndez Pidal, who saw many of the surviving ballads, attested textually from a much later date, as being 'fragments' of earlier epics. That is, the fashion for epics (in this view) disappeared during the fourteenth century, as the Heroic Age of the Reconquest slipped into the past and out of general experience and memory, but many of the individual episodes were so striking and memorable that they survived as brief tales, often performed out of any wider context. (Not all cycles could be explained this way, including most obviously the earliest, the ballads on the Trastamaran Wars.)

This theory is plausible in many instances. But it has also become clear that the ballad genre almost certainly existed at the same time as the postulated lost epics, in the thirteenth century and probably earlier, such that the verse compositions apparently attested in the Histories could well have been separate short compositions all along. For the *Poema de Mio Cid*, the only undoubtedly existing medieval Castilian epic, did not fragment that way; there are two surprisingly prosaic ballads descending from the text attested in the mid-sixteenth-century collections, but it is generally thought that these came from a prose account composed in that century rather than directly from the older epic poem. The fourteenth-century *Mocedades de Rodrigo* is undoubtedly closely related to several ballads, but it is likely that ancestors of the surviving versions of those ballads predated the *Mocedades* and in part inspired it.

This view of the ballads does not imply that I am sceptical of the existence of oral epics in Castile altogether. Some scholars have been so. But the suggested co-existence of ballads and epics in the thirteenth century and perhaps earlier does not necessarily imply that they were totally separate genres. Indeed, the genres were very similar. The *Poema de Mio Cid* (of 3730 lines) is structured according to lines roughly twice as long as the ballad's octosyllables, but commonly with a caesura; this means that the assonance found at the end of every line in the *Poema* is heard at the same intervals as the assonance found at the end of every alternate line in the ballads. As usually printed, the *Poema* has 152 *tiradas* (laisses), sequences within which most or all lines end in the same vowel assonance pattern; these section divisions are not in the manuscript, but it is a reasonable assumption that a performer would have been likely to pause when the assonance pattern changed. But neither the length of line nor the uniformity of assonance within each laisse are mathematically accurate. This fact has led several of the many editors that the *Poema* has attracted to 'emend' the unique manuscript in order to create lines having more equal numbers of syllables and less variable assonance (and thereby coincidentally to make the individual *tiradas* seem even more like ballads), but this instinct is probably anachronistic in that it corresponds to French or Italian instincts of a later age rather than to the native verse patterns of the Peninsula, which depended more on stress patterns than on syllable count. As with most aspects of the *Poema*, this matter remains controversial.

It is important for present purposes to separate fact from fiction within the *Poema*, to see if the fictional aspects can be explained by the nature of the oral tradition. On the whole, the *Poema* is fiction, but based on fact. It concerns the last part of the life of Rodrigo (Ruy) Díaz, the Castilian hero who came to be known by the Muslims of Valencia as 'El Cid'; that is, *Sidi*, the Arabic for 'boss'. It used to be thought, from the fifteenth to the late nineteenth century, that he was fictional; then the exhaustive research of Menéndez Pidal (1869–1968) proved beyond doubt that he had been real, and established most of what we know about his life and the legends that accumulated around him. In particular, Menéndez Pidal edited the anonymous twelfth-century partial Latin biography of Rodrigo written in the East of the Peninsula, usually known now as the *Historia Roderici*. This *Historia* is sober in approach, but it becomes clear that Rodrigo's life was full and fascinating.

He was born in Vivar, just outside Burgos, the capital of Old Castile, between 1040 and 1043. In the legends, and probably in life, he was an *infanzón*, a member of the minor nobility roughly equivalent to a country squire. There are several fictionalized stories about his youth in later compositions such as the *Mocedades* of the fourteenth century, or the seventeenth-century plays by Guillén de Castro and Corneille, and several ballads, which have no echo in the epic. But it does seem to be true that by his late twenties Rodrigo was commander-in-chief of the Castilian army. We know this because of the historical accounts of the Siege of Zamora of 1072. This was the final episode in the conflicts that followed the death of King Fernando I of León-Castile in 1065. Fernando divided up his kingdom among his children, which led to civil war between Sancho II of Castile and Alfonso of León. Sancho defeated Alfonso, and by 1072 their sister Urraca, in Zamora (a walled town on the Duero), was the only obstacle to a Castilian takeover of the whole kingdom. So the Castilian army besieged Zamora, and it seemed inevitable that they would win. But the story (possibly true in essence) is that a Zamoran, Vellido Dolfos, left the town and came to the Castilian camp, claiming treacherously to be a deserter who could show them how to enter the town through the gate he had just used to leave it; having gained the confidence of the king, Vellido Dolfos then assassinated him and rode back to Zamora in triumph, closely pursued (according to the historical accounts, the ballads, and the reconstructed epic) by Rodrigo Díaz, our hero. Rodrigo failed to catch him, a failure which suggests that the episode might well be roughly true. The war abruptly stopped, because Sancho had no heir and the kingdom was inherited by his brother Alfonso, despite being recently defeated. Rodrigo Díaz may have had in reality the role as regent attributed to him in the historical and ballad traditions, although this may not have included the blood-chilling oath that Rodrigo (in the ballads) made the new king Alfonso perform before the coronation, swearing that he had not arranged the treacherous assassination of his brother (the 'Oath of Santa Gadea', St Agatha's Church in the centre of Burgos). The many attested ballads on the dramatic events of 1072 form a cycle, and lie at the heart of the modern arguments over the relationship between histories, ballads, and reconstructable epic, but the siege has no direct echo in the *Poema*.

From 1072 to 1080 Rodrigo Díaz was in the service of the new king, Alfonso VI. Alfonso VI became one of the most influential rulers of medieval Castile, but everybody knew that he succeeded to the throne in dubious circumstances. Modern scholars have assumed that this coloured the relationship between Alfonso and the general who had defeated him before his accession; but even if so, they were working together during these years, as exemplified strikingly by the wedding document, which still survives, of Rodrigo's marriage to Ximena, a cousin of the Royal family, in 1074. Latent hostility may, though, be part of the explanation for the king's exiling Rodrigo in 1081. The proximal cause derived from the hostility between Castilians and Leonese. During this period the Northern Christian kings had the ability to send armies south demanding protection money (*parias*) from several of the separate independent Muslim kingdoms of the Peninsula (the *taifas*). In 1080, Rodrigo went with some Castilian soldiers to the *taifa* kingdom of Sevilla on such a mission, while the Leonese General García Ordóñez went to the *taifa* kingdom of Granada. They seem not to have realized that Sevilla and Granada were currently at war, and both Northern groups became involved in the Battle of Cabra; Sevilla won the battle, and Rodrigo captured his fellow-commander García Ordóñez. The story goes – it might be true – that Rodrigo humiliated his Leonese colleague by pulling out pieces of his beard. But he missed the next trick, because the Leonese were able to get their version of events back to the king first, saying that Rodrigo had been embezzling some of the parias for himself, rather than giving them to the king. As a result, the king exiled Rodrigo from his kingdom. This version of events relies on guesswork and inference from sources that may not be reliable, but is the best we can do now.

So Rodrigo went into exile, and this is the point at which the *Poema de Mio Cid*, in its surviving form, begins. But there is uncertainty even about its starting-point, since the first folio of the manuscript is missing and the text starts *in medias res*. An appreciation of the *Poema* depends on the listeners knowing about the preceding events; García Ordóñez's beard plays a crucial role, for example.

In real life, we know that on being exiled Rodrigo and his loyal soldiers offered their services as mercenaries to the Count of Barcelona. The offer was not accepted; it is the *Poema* to which we are indebted for an explanation of why not, telling us that Rodrigo had got into a fight with a nephew of the Count. This shows us neatly how awkward it is to evaluate many of the details of the tale, since the epic may be right; but it could invent causalities of its own. Our hero's motivating force, for example, is continually said and shown in the epic to be his desire to return from exile into the king's favour, which seems not to have been the case in reality. The epic has no doubt about Rodrigo's innocence of the charges of embezzlement laid against him, a certainty which underlies the early scene in which Rodrigo borrows some money on his way out of Castile and leaves a chest as surety with the money-lenders, which they suppose to contain the embezzled treasure but in reality contains nothing of value; and he never pays them back. But this episode is not to be seen as a case of Rodrigo cheating, precisely because the money-lenders should never have believed those stories in the first place. For the purposes of the epic, our hero is simply right and those who doubt him are simply wrong. Thus the Count of Barcelona who rejected his offer of employment is captured by Rodrigo some time afterwards, and presented in the epic as a figure of fun who deserves the humiliation which he receives.

Rodrigo spent five successful years (1081–1086) in the service of the Muslim ruler of Zaragoza. Rodrigo gained a reputation as a soldier who never lost a battle, which may even be true. In particular, he successfully relieved a fierce siege imposed on the fortress of Almenar by the Count of Barcelona and his allies in 1082, an episode which inspired the first extant literary work about him: the Latin hymn of 128 and a half lines in rhythmic sapphics, known now as the *Carmen Campi Doctoris*. It was once suggested that this *Carmen* was an oral composition, but that view has fortunately been discarded. The *Historia Roderici* mentions Rodrigo's five-year career as a mercenary for Zaragoza with considerable admiration, but the *Poema* neither mentions nor even hints at it. The surviving version of the *Poema* was elaborated at a time when the Northern Christian kingdoms were recruiting soldiers for a planned mass attack on the Muslims of the South, so these five years, if the poet even knew about them, would not have seemed suitable material. This is not a crusading poem, however. In the event the Muslims in the *Poema* are not the villains; the Leonese (including García Ordóñez) are villains, and there is a good Muslim, Abengalbón, who rescues the Cid's daughters.

Rodrigo played no part in the two most dramatic military events of his lifetime, the capture of Toledo by Alfonso VI in 1085, and the subsequent arrival of the fundamentalist Almorávides from Morocco, who defeated Alfonso at Sagrajas (Badajoz) in 1086. The first is not hinted at in the *Poema*, and the second only mentioned because Rodrigo had to confront them. After the loss at Sagrajas, Alfonso recalled Rodrigo from exile; but they could not work together, and he was exiled again in 1088. The return and the second exile are omitted in the *Poema*, probably again because the 1207 poet did not know about them. From then on Rodrigo and his soldiers were fighting on their own account, and, remarkably, captured the wealthy Muslim city of Valencia on 15 June 1094. They defended it against the Almorávides. Rodrigo gained his nickname of El Cid, perhaps as a direct result. Rodrigo reigned there as king, eventually dying, apparently of natural causes, in 1099. His wife Ximena inherited the kingdom, but the Muslims returned; she was allowed to go home, with the bodies of her husband and his horse. They were both buried at San Pedro de Cardeña (Burgos), and became the centre of a tomb cult and a tourist trade.

The epic recounts the victory at Valencia in surprisingly perfunctory fashion; for it is not primarily interested in politics. The first third of the epic has a base in reality, but after the conquest of Valencia the focus of interest shifts to the Cid's daughters and the plot becomes fictional. Two Leonese noble brothers, the Infantes de Carrión, ask the king to arrange marriages for them with the Cid's daughters, Elvira and Sol. Rodrigo is taken aback when he hears about this, since his desire to return to the king's favour cannot allow him to reject the king's proposal of an ostensibly advantageous marriage for his daughters. A sense of foreboding thus comes into the epic, which turns out to be justified. Two years later, when the Cid and his soldiers have repelled the Almorávides, the Infantes ask the Cid for permission to take their wives home to their lands in León. The Cid agrees, but he knows (as do the audience) that the Infantes are up to no good, so he sends trusted colleagues after them. Sure enough, the Infantes beat up their wives and leave them to die in the wild forest, and the Cid's daughters are only rescued by the Cid's own providence and his friend Abengalbón, the good Muslim.

The final part of the epic revolves around the Cid's attempt to get legal redress for his daughters. The attack automatically dissolved the marriages; the point at issue now concerns the Cid's family honour and social status. Rather than riding after the Infantes and cutting off their heads (as many epic heroes would), he appeals to the king to take the Infantes to court. When the king decides to grant this request, this decision signals the end of the Cid's exile (the theme of the first part of the epic) and the start of his triumphant exaltation over all his enemies (the theme of the last). The king summons a meeting of his Cortes for Toledo. After lengthy argument, theatrically presented, between the Cid's supporters and his Leonese opponents, including García Ordóñez, the Cid is vindicated, the Infantes are disgraced, and the epic ends with envoys from the royal houses of Aragón and Navarra seeking the daughters in marriage for their own princes. The Cid has completed his journey from penniless exile to wealthy ruler, on a social level with royalty.

The marriages and their violent dissolution are fiction; the calling of a meeting of the Cortes in Toledo is both fictional and anachronistic. Toledo may have been chosen by the poet to show that the king is literally meeting the Cid halfway, being equidistant from Valencia and Burgos; but the choice of Toledo could have an extra-literary point. The first such meeting in Toledo that we know of was held in January 1207, which is also the date found at the end of the epic's only manuscript; it has been suggested that this written version may be a copy of the script for, or a record of, an oral performance at that meeting. But although the epic is well known to modern Hispanists, it was not well known in Toledo later in that century; the greatest historian of the age, the Archbishop of Toledo (from 1208) Ximénez de Rada, mentions Rodrigo but does not call him Cid, and seems not to know of the *Poema* (though he does know the oral tradition deriving from the Siege of Zamora, including Rodrigo's part in that). One of the Histories of Alfonso X presents a slightly adapted prose account of the *Poema*; otherwise the Cid's life survives in popular memory in several other strands of historical or legendary reminiscence, rather than as the hero of the plot of the *Poema*.

Excellent studies have been written setting the *Poema* in its thirteenth-century context, seen from social, economic, political and historical viewpoints. Less attention, surprisingly, seems to have been paid recently to setting it in its contemporary literary context, or to explaining why the fictional elements in the tale were developed as they were. But if the oral tradition of the ballads was already in existence during the twelfth century, in a shape similar to that of the surviving later written evidence, features of that tradition may explain why and how the fictional elements of the *Poema* came to be as they are.

The ballads overwhelmingly revolve around the personal lives of young women, for example. This is true not only of the completely fictional ones but also of the originally 'historical' ones. If they have such an aspect, some episodes can survive in the popular memory long after the historical events themselves have been lost in the mist, regardless of whether they have a basis in fact. For example, the Muslim invasion of 711 is presented in several ballads as being the revenge taken by Julián, the Governor of Ceuta (on the African coast), for the rape of his daughter La Cava by King Rodrigo, the last of the Visigothic kings; this king's defeat is thus seen as a deserved punishment for his own sins, rather than as a wider geopolitical event. Other ballads about King Rodrigo's defeat, however, do not mention La Cava at all, which is an argument against the view that these ballads are all fragments of a single epic-sized whole. Similarly, the gruesome tale of the Siete Infantes de Lara, which probably had a historical event at its root whose exact nature is irretrievable now, depends for its satisfactory dénouement on a Muslim princess who takes the sexual initiative with a Christian prisoner. Over time, some of the events of the Siege of Zamora came in the general memory to depend on a supposed previous love affair between Rodrigo Díaz and Queen Urraca, whose conflict at Zamora is thus presented in some ballads as the result of a lovers' tiff. In much the same way, most of the fictional elements introduced into the *Poema de Mio Cid* depend on the marriages of the Cid's daughters to the Infantes and their consequences, and the culminating climax comes with the royal betrothal of those same daughters. Historical events usually fade from collective memory and gradually lose the ballad audience's involvement unless there is love or sex interest, so this is often inserted; similarly, films about the Battle of Britain, or Vietnam, etc., often include invented love interest for the main participants even when the broad outline of events is otherwise true. It would be inappropriate to criticize such accretions for being historically inaccurate; they are constants of both these quasi-dramatic genres, ballad and film, introduced to attract the audience, and such a criticism, even if true, would generally be thought to be pointless.

Other fictional elements of the epic are more recognizable to connoisseurs of the Spanish ballad than to students of epics in general. It tends to surprise modern readers, for example, to find the Cid portrayed as a gentle and thoughtful family man, whose strongest emotions are felt when he is parted from his wife and daughters and goes into exile without them; the pain is described in a striking image (one of the few in the epic), *asis parten unos dotros como la uña dela carne* (they part from each other like the fingernail from the flesh) (l. 375). This distress is both personal and dynastic, since the future of his family is a concern both of the fictional Cid and the poet. But this aspect of the hero's personality follows the expectations of the genre of Hispanic oral literature. That is, many ballads in the tradition feature a princess whose love life worries her father; two of the best known are *Gerineldos*, in which the princess seduces the king's eponymous bodyguard, and *Conde Claros*, who is wrongly accused of seducing the princess who has in fact seduced him. It is still true that the general public are exceptionally interested in the love lives of royal princesses, partly because all love lives are of direct interest to all humans with similar experiences, but also because the marriages of royal children directly affect the future of their subjects.

Graphic violence similarly catches an audience's attention, and the combination of sex and violence in the scene of the Infantes stripping, beating and abandoning their wives (the *Afrenta de Corpes* episode, *tiradas* 128–30) could certainly be used by the performer to do that. Women who have been attacked by men are often the protagonists of ballads, although the ballads tend to portray the revenge of a victim rather than the initial rape. The final resolution in the *Poema* exemplifies such revenge: the legal justice there is also the 'poetic justice' which we all long for, and is common in folklore but so disappointingly absent from our experience.

There are other similarities between the fictional aspects of the epic and the contemporary oral tradition. For example, it is the king in the epic whose eventual change of heart towards the exiled hero leads to the desired conclusion; kings in ballads often have similar functions (it is the unnamed king who releases the unfortunate *Prisoner*, and another similarly releases Virgil at the end of the striking ballad in which Virgil was unjustly imprisoned for rape),[4] so anyone who is elaborating an essentially fictional narrative with a happy ending can easily be led by the clichés of the oral tradition to give the king a leading part in that. There is no reason to suppose that such a reliance on kings was based on real experience of the behaviour of actual wise kings. There are also many ballads on the theme of exiled and reinstated heroes. Many tell of a long-lost husband's return from foreign wars; the ballad of *Arnaldos* concerns a long-lost prince inadvertently rediscovered by the sailors sent to look for him; the ballad of *Espinelo* tells of a royal twin cast into the sea after his birth, who (in most versions) eventually returns to his rightful inheritance; and the *Poema de Mio Cid* is based on the theme of an exile who returns triumphantly to royal favour at the end. This last triumph was required by the literary expectations, for it is not historically accurate; at the end of the *Poema* Rodrigo is back in favour with the Castilian king, as the structure of the oral poem demands, but in real life he remained in exile from 1088 until his death.

Thus, for several reasons, it seems clear that the oral epic, as attested in its written counterpart, the *Poema de Mio Cid*, and the old oral ballads of the same time, as attested in later records and recordings, were related parts of the same genre. This is not to claim that the epic was a long ballad, or a sequence of many ballads, for it has a coherent structure of its own as a single entity. But the same people performed them (*juglares*), both were called *cantares*, both had musical accompaniment; they have similar verse structures, plots, themes and atmosphere; they tend to present the tensest and most arresting moments in dramatic dialogue, so that the performers can ham it up and grasp the listeners' attention all the better; and whether the later ballads on originally historical themes are fragments of earlier epics, or coexisted with them at the same time, or the reconstructed epics are modern fantasies and the only performances in medieval reality were of the shorter *romances* – all these views are plausible in themselves – it is reasonable to see them all as manifestations of the one genre; which we can for convenience call the genre of Medieval Spanish Oral Literature.

---

[4] The *Romance del Prisionero* is printed and commented upon in Smith 1964: 207–8; on the *Romance de Virgilios*, see Sleeman 2004.

## 3 Scholarly Discussion of Ballads

Extensive critical bibliographies have been produced by Samuel Armistead and his colleagues, including Antonio Sánchez Romeralo and Suzanne H. Petersen (see Armistead 1971; Armistead et al. 1979 and 1980). The Seminario Menéndez Pidal also produced several volumes on individual ballads attested in multiple versions, under the general title of *Romancero tradicional* (Catalán et al. 1969–85); *Gerineldo*, for example, recovered now in about a thousand versions, was the subject of volumes 6–8 (1975–76). Volumes have been dedicated to particular geographical areas: most notably the Canary Isles (e. g. Catalán et al. 1969; Trapero 2003); several areas of the New World have yielded ballad treasures, e. g. to Cruz-Sáenz (1986), who subsequently worked in Aragón (1995). Portuguese ballads have been studied by Manuel da Costa Fontes (e. g. Fontes 2000); the collection made forty years ago by the late Joanne Purcell in the Azores is now being published (thanks to Samuel Armistead and his colleagues; vol. 1, 2002). Armistead's own *Folk Literature of the Sephardic Jews* series started in 1971, usually in collaboration with Joseph H. Silverman, and with Israel J. Katz for expert descriptions of the music (see also note 2 above). Israeli scholars have recorded and disseminated their still living (and still fascinating) tradition, including Susana Weich-Shahak (see Alexander et al. 1994). The modern performances can give us an insight into the old tradition as far as the words are concerned; the study of the modern music is more tantalizing, since we cannot be sure how much of the music recorded in recent decades descends directly from earlier ages. Two intriguing studies of the Judeo-Spanish tradition by British scholars deserve mention: Pomeroy (2005) and Sleeman (2004, one of four Hispanic contributions to this volume); Estrea Aelion, the star of Sleeman's study, was a Judeo-Spanish singer who immigrated from Greece into London, and died in 1988 at the age of 104. For anthropological studies see Seeger 1987 and 1990.

Studies of the modern oral tradition probably give us a better idea of the nature of the medieval one than textual collections from the past, but the great *Romanceros* of the Golden Age are also available; most were published by Antonio Rodríguez Moñino, including Martín Nucio's *Cancionero de Romances* of 1550 (Rodríguez Moñino 1967); Nucio's first collection was edited by Ramón Menéndez Pidal (1945). There are many student collections available, such as Di Stefano (1993); Smith (1964 [1996]) is widely used by English-speaking students; 71 ballads, mostly taken from the old *Romanceros*, with performable translations, appear in Wright (1987 and reprints). Monographic studies of Medieval Hispanic ballads usually consider just one ballad or group of ballads; the relationship between history and oral literature is studied by Mirrer-Singer (1986); for a fascinating comparison of ballad, literary and historiographical treatments of the same minor event on the fifteenth-century Andalucía-Granada frontier, see López Estrada (1998). Specifically literary studies include Deyermond (1996) and Vasvári (1999).

## 4 Scholarly Discussion of the Epic

The historical Rodrigo Díaz has been presented by Menéndez Pidal (1929 and reprints), which includes the Latin text of the *Historia Roderici*; Horrent (1973); and Fletcher (1989). Barton and Fletcher (2000) include an English translation of the *Historia Roderici*.

Bibliographies have been dedicated to the *Poema* by Magnotta (1976), Deyermond (1977b), Webber (1986), and more recently Pattison (2000: 125–34). Also in this latter volume, Martin (2000) insists on the need for investigators to consult and quote the manuscript, which has been produced in an attractive facsimile edition (*Poema de Mio Cid* 1988), since every one of the many editors has 'emended' (that is, misrepresented) the text to fit anachronistic ideas of what it 'must' have been like originally; see also Bayo (2001, 2002). Smith's edition (1972) has been translated into Spanish, as has Ian Michael's (1975); Montaner Frutos's edition (1993) has copious literary and historical notes.

Studies of the epic's composition and presentation include Smith (1983), who did not believe that it was oral literature at all; the opposing view has been presented by e. g. Walsh (1990) and Montgomery (1998). Most scholars probably now accept that there was an oral tradition of songs about Rodrigo, even if the attested text is not that of an actual performance. For the exploitation of Cid material in Alfonsine Histories, see Dyer (1995). For the place of the *Poema* in the literary context of the early thirteenth century, see Jeremy Lawrance (2002). For the relationship between the fictional parts of the epic and the contemporary ballad tradition, see Wright (1995: chapters 19–21); for the relationship between the *Poema* and the postulated wider Hispanic epic tradition, see Deyermond (1988). Duggan (1989) allies historical and literary viewpoints. Powell and West (1996) contains studies on both ballads and epic; Smith (1977) and Russell (1978: 13–204) collect many articles on the *Poema*.

Thus there is an enormous bibliography available on the epic, which has not led to a consensus on whether the *Poema*, the only extant text in the medieval tradition, represents an oral genre or not. The ballad evidence, in contrast, is growing all the time, even as the oral tradition itself seems to be fading away. Between them, the two strands of scholarship are capable of providing us with a plausible and clear notion of the oral tradition in the Hispanic Middle Ages.

## References

Alexander, Tamar, Isaac Benabu, Yaacov Ghelman, Orad (Rodrigue) Schwarzwald, and Susana Weich-Shahak. 1994.'Towards a Typology of the Judeo-Spanish Folksong: *Gerineldo* and the *Romance* Model.' In *Jewish Oral Traditions: An Interdisciplinary Approach*. Ed. Israel Adler, Frank Alvarez-Pereyre, Edwin Serousse, and Lea Shalem. Yuval: Studies of the Jewish Music Research Centre 6. Jerusalem: Magnes P. 68–163.

Armistead, Samuel G., ed. 1971. *The Judeo-Spanish Chapbooks of Yacob Abraham Yoná*. Folk Literature of the Sephardic Jews 1. Berkeley: U of California P.

–, Antonio Sánchez Romeralo, and Diego Catalán, eds. 1979. *El Romancero hoy: historia, comparatismo, bibliografía crítica. 2.º Coloquio Internacional/ The Hispanic Ballad Today: History,*

*Comparativism, Critical Bibliography. 2nd International Symposium.* Madrid: Cátedra Seminario Menéndez Pidal. [Bibliography on pp. 197–310.]
–, Antonio Sánchez Romeralo, and Suzanne H. Petersen. 1980. *Bibliografía del Romancero Oral.* Madrid: Seminario Menéndez Pidal.
Barton, Simon, and Richard Fletcher. 2000. *The World of El Cid: Chronicles of the Spanish Reconquest.* Manchester: Manchester UP.
Bayo, Juan Carlos. 2001.'Poetic Discourse Patterning in the *Cantar de Mio Cid*.' *Modern Language Review* 96: 82–91.
–. 2002.'La datación del *Cantar de Mio Cid* y el problema de su tradición manuscrita.' In *Mio Cid Studies: 'Some Problems of Diplomatic' Fifty Years On.* Ed. Alan Deyermond, David G. Pattison, and Eric Southworth. London: Department of Hispanic Studies, Queen Mary and Westfield College. 15–31.
Catalán, Diego, et al., eds. 1969–85. *Romancero Tradicional.* 12 vols. Madrid: Seminario Menéndez Pidal.
–, María Jesús López de Vergara et al, eds. 1969. *La flor de la Marañuela. Romancero general de las Islas Canarias.* Madrid: Seminario Menéndez Pidal.
Cruz-Sáenz, Michèle S. de, ed. 1986. *Romancero tradicional de Costa Rica.* Prefacio de Samuel G. Armistead, transcripciones musicales de Christina D. Braidotti. Newark, DE: Juan de la Cuesta.
–, ed. 1995. *Spanish Traditional Ballads from Aragon.* Collected and edited with the help of Teresa Catarella; with musical transcriptions by Christina D. Braidotti and a foreword by Samuel G. Armistead. London: Associated UPs.
Deyermond, Alan D., ed. 1977a. *'Mio Cid' Studies.* London: Tamesis.
–. 1977b.'Tendencies in Mio Cid scholarship, 1943–1973.' In Deyermond 1977a: 13–47.
–. 1988. *El 'Cantar de Mio Cid' y la épica medieval española.* Barcelona: Sirmio.
–. 1996. *Point of View in the Ballad: 'The Prisoner', 'The Lady and the Shepherd' and Others.* London: Department of Hispanic Studies, Queen Mary and Westfield College.
Di Stefano, Giuseppe, ed. 1993. *Romancero.* Madrid: Taurus.
Duggan, Joseph J. 1989. *The 'Cantar de mio Cid': Poetic Creation in its Economic and Social Contexts.* Cambridge Studies in Medieval Literature 6. Cambridge: CUP.
Dyer, Nancy Joe. 1995. *El mio Cid del taller alfonsí: Versión en prosa en la 'Primera Crónica General' y en la 'Crónica de veinte reyes'.* Newark, DE: Juan de la Cuesta.
Fletcher, Richard. 1989. *The Quest for El Cid.* London: Hutchinson.
Fontes, Manuel da Costa. 2000. *Folklore and Literature: Studies in the Portuguese, Brazilian, Sephardic, and Hispanic Oral Traditions.* Albany: State U of New York P.
Horrent, Jules. 1973. *Historia y poesía en torno al 'Cantar del Cid'.* Trans. Juan Victorio Martínez. Letras e Ideas Maior 2. Esplugues de Llobregat [Barcelona]: Ariel.
Lawrance, Jeremy. 2002.'Chivalry in the *Cantar de Mio Cid*.' In Deyermond 1977a: 37–60.
López Estrada, Francisco, ed. 1998. *Poética de la frontera andaluza (Antequera, 1424).* Salamanca: Ediciones Universidad de Salamanca.
Magnotta, Miguel. 1976. *Historia y bibliografía de la crítica sobre el Poema de Mío Cid (1750–1971).* North Carolina Studies in the Romance Languages and Literatures 145. Chapel Hill: University of North Carolina, Department of Romance Languages.
Martin, Georges. 2000.'Gestas de arena.' In Pattison 2000: 23–33.
Menéndez Pidal, Ramón. 1929. *La España del Cid.* 2 vols. Madrid: Plutarco.
–, ed. 1945. *Cancionero de romances impreso en Amberes sin año.* Madrid: Consejo Superior de Investigaciones Científicas.
Michael, Ian, ed. 1975. *Poema de Mio Cid.* With English Prose Translation by Rita Hamilton and Janet Perry. Manchester: Manchester UP. [Spanish translation, Madrid: Castalia, 1976.]

Mirrer-Singer, Louise. 1986. *The Language of Evaluation: A Sociolinguistic Approach to the Story of Pedro el Cruel in Ballad and Chronicle*. Purdue University Monographs in Romance Languages 20. Amsterdam: Benjamins.
Montaner Frutos, Alberto, ed. 1993. *Cantar de Mio Cid*. Madrid: Crítica.
Montgomery, Thomas. 1998. *Medieval Spanish Epic: Mythic Roots and Ritual Language*. University Park: Pennsylvania State UP.
Pattison, David G., ed. 2000. *Textos épicos castellanos: problemas de edición y crítica*. London: Department of Hispanic Studies, Queen Mary and Westfield College.
*Poema de Mio Cid*. 1988. 2 vols. Burgos: Ayuntamiento. [Vol. 1 facsimile, vol. 2 transcription and commentaries.]
Pomeroy, Hilary S., ed. 2005. *An Edition and Study of the Secular Ballads in the Sephardic Ballad Notebook of Halia Isaac Cohen*. Newark, DE: Juan de la Cuesta.
Powell, Brian, and Geoffrey West, eds. 1996. *Al que en buen hora naçio: Essays on the Spanish Epic and Ballad in Honour of Colin Smith*. Liverpool: Liverpool UP.
Purcell, Joanne B., ed. 2002. *Romanceiro tradicional das Ilhas dos Açores. I. Corvo e Flores*. Estudo preliminar de Joanne B. Purcell, organização de Samuel G. Armistead e outros. Angra do Heroísmo, Açores: Governo Regional dos Açores, Secretaria Regional da Educação e Cultura.
Rodríguez Moñino, Antonio, ed. 1967. *Cancionero de Romances (Anvers, 1550)*. Madrid: Castalia. [Martín Nucio's Antwerp edition of 1550.]
Russell, Peter E. 1978. *Temas de 'La Celestina' y otros estudios*. Barcelona: Ariel.
Seeger, Judith. 1989. 'The Living Ballad in Brazil: Two Performances.' In *Hispanic Balladry Today*. Ed. Ruth H. Webber. New York: Garland. 175–217. [Also: *Oral Tradition* 2 (1987): 573–615.]
–. 1990. *Count Claros: Study of a Ballad Tradition*. New York: Garland.
Sleeman, Margaret. 2004. 'Estrea Aelion, Salonica Sephardic Tradition and the Ballad of Imprisoned Virgil.' In *The Singer and the Scribe: European Ballad Traditions and European Ballad Cultures*. Ed. Philip E. Bennett and Richard Firth Green. Amsterdam: Rodopi. 153–68.
Smith, Colin, ed. 1964. *Spanish Ballads*. Oxford: Pergamon. [Rev. ed., Bristol: Classical P, 1996.]
–, ed. 1972. *Poema de Mio Cid*. Oxford: Clarendon. [Spanish translation, Madrid: Cátedra, 1985.]
–. 1977. *Estudios cidianos*. Madrid: CUPSA.
–. 1983. *The Making of the Poema de Mio Cid*. Cambridge: CUP.
Trapero, Maximiano, ed. 2003. *Romancero general de Lanzarote*. Taro de Tahíche (Teguise), Lanzarote: Fundación César Manrique.
Vasvári, Louise O. 1999. *The Heterotextual Body of the 'Mora Morilla'*. London: Department of Hispanic Studies, Queen Mary and Westfield College.
Walsh, John K. 1990. 'Performance in the *Poema de Mio Cid*.' *Romance Philology* 44: 1–25.
Webber, Ruth House. 1986. 'Hispanic Oral Literature: Accomplishments and Perspectives.' *Oral Tradition* 1: 344–80.
Wright, Roger, ed. and trans. 1987. *Spanish Ballads with English Verse Translations*. Warminster: Aris and Phillips.
–. 1995. *Early Ibero-Romance: Twenty-One Studies on Language and Texts from the Iberian Peninsula between the Roman Empire and the Thirteenth Century*. Newark, DE: Juan de la Cuesta.

# 16 The Late-Medieval Ballad

## Thomas Pettitt

Like most ballad questions, the relationship between the late-medieval ballad and oral tradition must be approached via post-medieval evidence. There are simply not enough ballads surviving from the medieval period to work on, even in a European perspective, although this is predictably a matter of definition.[1]

For the editor of what became the definitive Anglophone collection, Francis James Child, 'ballad' meant simply a narrative song, but his *English and Scottish Popular Ballads* concerned the particular category specified in the title: as he assured the Danish folklorist Svend Grundtvig in a letter of 1875, 'I shall omit everything that is not strictly a Popular Ballad.'[2] Given the indebtedness of Child's project to Grundtvig's example, 'popular ballad' was evidently intended as an equivalent to the Danish *folkevise*, but 'popular' proved an unfortunate choice. At the time it will still have signalled that these songs qualified as 'popular antiquities' – traditional cultural practices formerly vital and significant for society as a whole, but of late confined to its more backward (provincial, rustic, uneducated) segments.[3] The field was however already in the process of being rechristened 'folklore', leaving 'popular' free to drift in the direction of commercial, vulgar forms of entertainment available via the mass-media. And among the earliest and most powerful of the media in what we now call 'popular culture' were the hastily-composed, mass-produced and cheaply-sold printed broadsides (Würzbach 1990). They mostly contained songs, many of them narrative, and while dismissed by Child as 'veritable dunghills' they were regularly called 'ballads' by the people who wrote, printed, bought and

---

[1] While the evidence adduced in what follows will be predominantly from Anglo-Scottish traditions, the aim is to achieve insights valid for a wider range of European language areas, into which occasional forays will duly be undertaken. For pan-European surveys of ballads and/or ballad research see Entwistle 1939; Danckert 1970; Armistead 2000; Seemann 1973. For the Scandinavian ballads a vital resource is Jonsson et al. 1978, a complete catalogue of all 838 Scandinavian songs qualified (in the compilers' view) as ballads, each provided with a summary in English; for Denmark see also Præstgaard Andersen 1981. A substantial anthology of European ballads with parallel English translations has been published by the Council of Europe (Seemann et al. 1967). Sigurd Kværndrup's massive investigation of East-Nordic balladry in a European perspective, including in-depth discussion of the oral aspect of tradition, has a comprehensive Summary in English (Kværndrup 2006: 651–72). [On Hispanic ballads, see ch. 15 by Roger Wright in this volume; on Romanian ballads/ oral epics, see ch. 14 by Margaret Beissinger in this volume.]
[2] Bold 1979: 20. – Child 1882–98 (ballads are cited by number; commentary by volume and page).
[3] On other aspects of the scholarly climate in which Child worked (and which he subsequently influenced) see Harris 1991: 1–10; Bell 1988; Riewerts 1995; Andersen 1995.

sang them (Bold 1979:13), and indeed over a third of the ballads in his collection also appeared on broadsides .[4]

Beyond a contribution to *Johnson's Universal Cyclopedia* of 1874 with generalizations of the order of 'Its historical and natural place is anterior to the poetry of art' (1875:58), Child never got round to elaborating fully on what distinguished the 'popular' ballad as a category of narrative song, and the consistency and wisdom of his selections have been repeatedly questioned.[5] But the collection was the result of a decades long struggle to pin down a particular kind of narrative song (Rieuwerts 1994), and that it was neither acknowledged as a distinct genre nor called 'ballad' in the late-medieval or early-modern periods does not necessarily mean that the distinction is invalid. Earlier song traditions did not always feel the need for explicit taxonomies: 'The truth of the matter is that very few medieval songs are called anything and that those terms that do occur from time to time are not used consistently' (Bohnet 1978:18).

Terminology and criteria for categorization are accordingly at the discretion of scholarship, and different scholarly traditions have taken different options. French research has largely ignored the 'ballad' as conceived of by Anglo-Scandinavian conventions (Bennett 2004), preferring to categorize narrative song in terms of context (*chansons de toile*) and content (*chansons de mal mariée*; *chansons d'aventure*), but will have encompassed any individual songs within these genres that also qualify as ballads. Conversely the French categories are virtually ignored in English and Scandinavian ballad studies, but not necessarily the individual songs, since a few English and Danish ballads may qualify as the one or the other.[6]

Other international perspectives are more encouraging: 'The conviction of some sort of generic unity in the English and Scottish ballads is enhanced by comparison with other European bodies of song which not only have similar stylistic features but also treat similar narratives.'[7] The fact that one of the larger Danish manuscript songbooks, from *c.* 1570 (the Karen Brahe Folio), contains *only* songs that modern scholarship acknowledges as *folkeviser* suggests an early if unformulated generic awareness, and at the opposite chronological extreme modern Scottish travellers are aware of their 'big ballads' or 'muckle sangs' as a distinct group: 'They feel different [...]. I can feel the difference when I'm singing' (Andersen 1991:26–27, quoting Stanley Robertson).

## 1 The Ballad as Narrative: Towards a Contextual Formalism

From the late sixteenth century to the late nineteenth, most European countries had both broadside ballads and what out of deference to convention will here be called 'oral ballads', although since both were sung (and so strictly-speaking 'oral') and heard (and so strictly-speaking 'aural'), the real distinction lies in the media by which a song reached a given singer, by which it was preserved between performances, and from which it was

---

[4] See Atkinson 2002:19; Andersen 1982.
[5] See Reppert 1974; Harker 1981.
[6] See Colbert 1978; Shields 1989.
[7] Shields 1991:40; see also Neumann 1980:25–28.

generated in performance. For broadside ballads the medium in all three cases constituted a printed text (transmission is textual-oral). For oral ballads the medium in the first process was the aural reception of an oral performance, in the second and third the singer's mind (transmission is aural-mental-oral): 'For the nonliterate singer the process necessitated his storing the material in this mind so that he could reproduce the stories readily in performance' (Buchan 1973:2). 'Oral tradition' will be deployed here to encompass the collective sum of these aural-mental-oral processes over time, without presumption concerning the precise way they deal with the verbal material of the 'oral ballads' thus transmitted. To the extent the broadsides inherited their format from widely distributed handwritten sheets (Wehse 1975:325) or their function from the performances of minstrels, this pattern of dual ballad traditions may be a continuation of late-medieval conditions, and so potentially shed light on them.

The distinction is in the first instance purely contextual, acknowledging that a very large number of songs migrated from one medium to the other (Wehse 1975) and in so doing technically shifted category. *The* ballad question, encompassing or impinging on most other ballad questions, is to what degree these purely contextual categories have generic implications. Do ballads transmitted under oral auspices differ in any systematic way from those distributed as broadsides? Is the oral ballad a sub-genre with characteristics recognizably distinct from those of other narrative songs, particularly broadsides, and directly related to its particular mode of transmission?

Since they share many topics and themes with broadside ballads any distinctive features of oral ballads are most likely to be in terms of form, and there is a strong current in ballad research, from the early nineteenth-century Scottish collector Motherwell onwards (Brown 1996), which sees an organic relationship between oral tradition and the characteristic form of the songs belonging to it, which is determined by what David Buchan elegantly calls 'the aesthetic conditions of non-literacy' (1978:100). More prosaically: 'The folk of the oral tradition were nonliterate and it is their method of composition and transmission that has given the distinguishing traits to what we normally think of as "the" ballads' (1973:2). Alan Bold states the thesis uncompromisingly and with a Darwinian turn: 'all the stylistic features we associate with balladry can be explained by the fact that to survive they had to be unforgettable' (1979:14).

In these statements, as in most literary histories, 'ballad' is used in the specific sense of the narrative songs with the characteristics best fitted to survive in oral tradition, and the present study will follow suit from here on (specifying 'oral' where there is need to distinguish them from broadside ballads). This is not tantamount to *defining* the ballad genre as oral, but rather the result of applying a contextual formalism which explores whether and how contextual factors – like oral tradition – influence or determine the way similar or even the same narrative material is handled, so that songs in one context have or acquire formal features differing from those in other contexts.[8]

The matter will be explored here in relation to the ballad traditions of Scandinavia, German-speaking areas of Europe, and (particularly) the English-speaking cultures of the British Isles and North America, whose characteristic metrical vehicle is some variant of

---

[8] 'Contextual formalism' is my coinage: a plain man's version of the 'context-oriented genre theory' impressively applied to broadside and traditional ballads by Natascha Würzbach (1983).

the 'ballad' stanza: usually 4 but up to 8 lines, each corresponding to a musical phrase, typically verbal material with four stresses or three stresses and a pause (Bronson 1969: 38–39). In this they differ from the short stychic traditional narratives of other areas (Finland; Greece; Iberia)[9] and the metrical and musical unit of performance will influence not merely the way the narrative material is distributed through the song,[10] and the latter's emotional and aesthetic impact in performance (Bronson 1969:131), but the way it responds to the opportunities and challenges of oral transmission: 'A melody repeating every stanza produces a unit that can be moved, omitted, and put into an organization.'[11]

While broadside ballads and oral ballads share the same stanza forms (and indeed the same melodies), the oral ballad differs substantially in the way it handles narrative, both the strategies of narration and the tactics of verbalization. But the difference is one of degree rather than kind (Atkinson 2002:24). Like most folklore genres (Harris 1995), the ballad is not a definable category with conventional norms which can be consciously followed or self-consciously breached (Wehse 1979:193–205). The situation calls for an adjective rather than a noun, in that some narrative songs are more 'balladic' than others, approaching more closely an ideal ballad paradigm (Moreira 1997:105).

The paradigm is familiar enough from ballad studies, and is common to several traditions of stanzaic narrative song in Europe.[12] The mode is impersonal, with no narrative voice imposing itself between the narrative and the listener, and (not least thanks to this lack of commentary) efficient, with little or no prefatory setting the scene for the critical moment with which the narrative opens, and along the way little description of persons, objects or places. Ballads are 'dramatic' by virtue of focusing on critical scenes comprising fateful confrontations, largely in the form of a dialogue characteristically lacking specification of the speaker. But drama and efficiency are far from compatible qualities in a narrative context, and their combination contributes significantly to a narrative mode with a characteristic 'leaping and lingering' progress. While we leap into the first scene with little preamble, and from one scene to another with little transition, the scenes themselves are lingered over in a singularly inefficient manner. This in turn is due to the presence of so much dialogue, and to the extensive use of various repetition patterns, some of which involve much verbal redundancy.[13]

Together with the narrative structuring many of them enhance, these repetition patterns are among the most definitive characteristics of the verbal style of ballads, ranging from simple, static reiterations, through balances between question-answer, order-fulfilment, etc., the rendering of similar events in near-identical formulations, and the resolution of narrative segments into stages rendered by 'incremental repetition'. But when W. Edson Richmond asserted, in a standard introduction, that '[...] repetition is

---

[9] France seems in many respects to be a transitional area (Simonsen 2003)
[10] See Entwistle 1939:18; 25; Rubin 1995:266.
[11] Rubin 1995:277; see also Wallace and Rubin 1988; Friedman 1983:235. See also Holzapfel 1980:85–86 for a brief discussion of the differing narrative techniques of Finnish-stychic and Danish-stanzaic modes and Holzapfel 1978a: 114–15 for a brief comparison of the way the same story is handled in the two forms.
[12] See Hodgart 1962:27–32; Jonsson 1956; Richmond 1990; Gerould 1957:84–130.
[13] For a more systematic survey see Andersen 1985:68–79.

not only the hallmark of folk poetry, it is the very sum and substance of its being', he was thinking not so much of these 'internal' repetitions, as the 'external' repetitions which occur when a given ballad deploys phrases, from half a line or so to a stanza, which are also to be found, in more or less recognizable variants, in other ballads (1972: 88). The latter represent not so much the intertextuality familiar from literary narrative, although one ballad sometimes does borrow material directly from another, as a corpus of commonplaces or formulas common to a given tradition as a whole. Internal and external repetition can of course be linked in that the former occurs whenever the same formula is used twice in a given ballad.

But there is a decisive second proviso to the generic status of the ballad as represented by the narrative features just reviewed. It is not so much that some *ballads* are more balladic than others, as that some *versions* of a given ballad are more balladic than others. It is not enough with both a noun and an adjective, we also need a verb to cover the process by which a given narrative song is *balladized* under the auspices of oral tradition.

German scholarship can be seen somewhat laboriously moving towards this insight in the mid-twentieth century, but generating a useful terminology in the process. The first step was the realization that the changes occurring within oral tradition could amount to singing into shape, *zurechtsingen*, as well as singing to pieces, *zersingen*.[14] The second step was to introduce a generic perspective, the appreciation that the reshaping of the songs by oral tradition also encompassed the development of balladic features such as the focusing of the narrative, impersonality, the generation of repetitions and the introduction of formulas.[15]

These insights were readily applicable to English balladry (Schmidt-Hidding 1933), and from a similar point of departure in J. R. Moore's belief that precisely these balladizing processes were symptoms of balladry's degeneration due to 'the increasingly low average of intelligence among those who transmit the ballads' (1916: 389), Anglo-American scholarship followed a similar trajectory (McMillan 1964), culminating in Tristram P. Coffin's influential thesis that a narrative song passed through a 'ballad stage' on its way to a lyric, 'emotional core' (1961).

## 2 Oral Tradition: The Theories

In oral tradition therefore, the performance of a ballad can be associated with the reformulation of its verbal material, and that reformulation can vary not merely in terms of its deliberation and its extent, but also in terms of its relationship to the ballad paradigm.

Reformulation can be premeditated or take place in the course of the performance itself, in which case it might range from conscious improvisation to unconscious alteration. It can vary in extent from minor verbal adjustment to massive reconstruction which can virtually qualify as re-composition. It can be neutral with regard to ballad

---

[14] Catarella 1994: 471; see Röhrich 1973a: 16.
[15] See Röhrich 1973b: 32–34; Danckert 1970: 11–13; Hruby 1949: 4–5.

qualities, or contribute to the balladizing of the song by enhancing them: Pondering why some Nordic songs achieve ballad characteristics more than others, and how their balladic character increases over time, Vésteinn Ólason suggests the useful concept of a 'ballad competence', exercised by the singers as much as or even more than the composer of the original song.[16] Such clarifications may be helpful in understanding oral tradition and in identifying more precisely the issues in the debates to which this topic has given rise.

With regard to the manner and the date of ballad origins, for example, in relation both to the individual ballad and to the emergence of the genre (or rather the ballad paradigm), a good deal of confusion is resolved when it is appreciated that a ballad can be created by the balladizing of an existing narrative song, as well as by the composition of a new song displaying the full panoply of balladic features. Indeed one of the residual mysteries of ballad 'origins' is whether the latter extreme ever occurred; and if it did it will probably remain invisible (inaudible): most creative ballad activity, not least that registered in the surviving texts and recordings, probably involved generating further balladic features in songs which already had them in one degree or another.

Ballad composition is therefore closely linked to ballad transmission, which in the last few decades of the twentieth century became the major focus of debate in ballad studies. While there has been some interest in the way the content of a given ballad has changed in relation to its shifting socio-cultural context,[17] controversy has mainly concerned the actual mechanisms of oral tradition.

The 'oral-formulaic theory', which has been the major occasion of controversy, also operates with a substantial overlap between composition and transmission, but in a distinct permutation of the aspects involved.[18] It is designed to deal with a mature balladry in which narrative songs have already achieved their optimum ballad mode, and performance accordingly involves reformulating a song within that mode: It has little to contribute on how a narrative song becomes a ballad. The theory postulates a radical recasting of the verbal material, amounting to re-composition, consciously undertaken, and above all not premeditated, but improvised in performance. As David Buchan puts it, the ballad singer 'learned both ballad-stories and a method of ballad composition, and in performance re-created the ballad-story by this method of composition to produce a ballad text. Each performance, then, resulted in a freshly composed ballad-text' (1973: 2; see Buchan 1977). There was a tendency to reserve the term 'oral' for this process of improvised in-performance reconstruction (Buchan 1977: 56), and to deny or ignore the possibility of a 'memorial' reproduction of relatively stable verbal material which was other or more than rote or verbatim memorization.

Transmission is also intimately related to the diametrical opposite of ballad origins – their final fate in oral tradition, and the demise of oral tradition itself. There is a link to both the origin and transmission debates just touched on, in that if a characteristic of a healthy oral tradition is its ability to remould narrative songs into ballads, then the loss of that particular ballad competence will be a symptom of distress. Correspondingly,

---

[16] See Ólason 1991: 122; see also Amodio 2004: 31.
[17] See Atkinson 1989 and 1992; Gammon and Stallybrass 1984–85.
[18] [See also ch. 2 by J. M. Foley and P. Ramey in this volume.]

adherents of the oral-formulaic theory tended to project the 'oral' phase of re-creative, improvisational performance into a past golden age of balladry, the more recent periods when most ballads were recorded a merely 'verbal' phase in which recreative processes were undermined by increasing literacy and access to printed songs (broadsides).

There is also the question of what happens to the individual narrative song within a viable oral tradition after it has been moulded into close conformity with the ballad paradigm: will it thereafter change only within the ballad mode, or will those same processes take it to some state 'beyond the ballad'? This may explain the character of some celebrated narrative songs sometimes offered as 'typical' ballads, such as *The Maid Freed from the Gallows* (Child 95), *Edward* (Child 13), and *Lord Randal* (Child 12), and their continental analogues. Focusing not merely on a single episode but its climactic scene, and comprising exclusively dialogue, to the extent these songs once had more narrative elements they have subsequently been reduced to their dramatic core, distinct from but probably overlapping with the 'emotional core' which Tristram P. Coffin sees as the fate of American ballads taken beyond the balladic, when 'unessential details drop off until lyric emerges' (1961:249).

The alternative for Coffin is a 'meaningless jumble', and oral tradition is certainly familiar with fragments which are nonsense or make no sense on their own. But both the criteria and the judgement should be the exclusive right of performer and audience within the tradition. In a pioneering and provocative study Mary-Ann Constantine and Gerald Porter have sought to understand these criteria, on the basis of the premise that 'Without direct evidence from a singer that a song is inadequate, there is every reason to assume otherwise' (2003:16).

It is an attractive thesis. In a tradition which knows the whole ballad, the performance of a selection of stanzas, or even a single stanza, can be enough to evoke the whole. It is recurrently reported by those in direct contact with singers that ballads are accompanied by a *midrash* of prose elaborations and explanations which make the performance as a whole less fragmentary or incoherent than the song actually recorded (Abrahams 1970:148). But whatever its authenticity and integrity from this perspective there is also a moment when such a reduced song has so little narrative that it is no longer a ballad as understood here.

## 3 The Evidence

The processes of oral tradition are clearly central to the understanding not merely of transmission but also of the origin and end of ballads, and those processes can ultimately be understood only on the basis of the ballads themselves. Assumptions, however reasonable, and arguments, however plausible, are inadequate in themselves, and ballad singers are no more reliable on this aspect of their craft than the South Slavic *guslars* who insisted that they performed their epics word for word as they had heard them, even as Parry and Lord were recording the evidence that this was not the case. The celebrated Arkansas singer Almeda Riddle distinguished a category of 'classic songs' (including all the Child ballads in her repertoire) which were not to be changed, while other songs might be, but Roger D. Abrahams is right to add 'in theory' (1970:153). A New Hampshire singer, confronted with a version of a ballad she had performed on a previous occasion differing markedly from what she had just sung, 'listened incredulously. No, she had never heard it before' (Anders 1974: 115–16).

Of the various procedures available for exploiting the evidence provided by the ballads, the least satisfactory is the analysis of the individual performance to detect features claimed as symptoms of one or other form of transmission. This procedure loomed large in the earliest applications of the oral-formulaic approach to ballads, reflecting the dubious logic that since the improvised South Slavic epics studied by Lord and Parry were formulaic, the presence of formulas in other traditions must demonstrate that they too were recreated anew at each performance. Systematic analyses duly demonstrated that ballads were to a substantial degree formulaic,[19] but failed to take sufficiently into account the technical differences between ballads and epics,[20] and the evidence could equally be taken to indicate that the formulas contributed to the *stability* of a ballad's formulation (Thigpen 1973).

A revealing instance is Patricia Conroy's work on the significant ballad traditions of the Faroe islands, which takes it as axiomatic that 'it is the relative quantities of formulas and formulaic expressions that distinguish an orally re-created text from a memorized literary one' (1980: 35). As it happens the material subjected to analysis, the seventeen ballads in the repertoire of a Faroese ballad-singer, Hans Johannessen, collected in the first half of the nineteenth century, does not unambiguously meet the criteria applied to demonstrate oral recreation, but other insights are achieved along the way, including the existence of separate corpora of formulas for couplet and quatrain ballads.[21]

The formulaic intensity of the singer's couplet ballads was 'considerably below' the level to be expected for improvisation in performance, but for statistical reasons Conroy undertook two analyses: one in which a line qualified as a formula if it occurred more than once in the singer's repertoire, one in which it so qualified if it occurred more than once *within the same ballad*. The latter of course also qualify as internal repetitions, and a discernible discrepancy between the two usefully revealed that 'repetitive wording is a feature of a given couplet ballad rather than a compositional device facilitating improvisational performance' (1980: 40).

The quatrain ballads were more formulaic, but the implications ultimately ambiguous, as were the results of an analysis of how this singer used the 'theme' of the sea journey. Conroy seeks to explain this ambiguity in terms of the dual contexts of Faroese ballad singing. When the ballads were sung during evening work periods, the audience, who had heard the ballads often, would react to any deviation from the known text; when they were performed at social gatherings to accompany the dance, the singer could make *ad hoc* decisions on whether to include material or not, depending on how the performance was going – it was also customary, if memory flagged, to repeat a stanza,

---

[19] See Jones 1961; Anders 1974.
[20] See Friedman 1961; Roth 1977.
[21] The contemporary practice of ballad-dancing on the Faroe Islands is to a substantial degree a revival tradition, the result of what Michael Chesnutt calls a 'refolklorization' for political reasons in the late nineteenth century (Chesnutt 1993); the performances discussed by Conroy date from before these developments, however.

perhaps with a minor adjustment to the wording. This is not particularly recreative, and as Conroy indeed points out, 'the high level of group participation in singing the [dance-] ballad undoubtedly inhibits improvisation': while the lead singer decided which stanza would come next, the dancers would join in as soon as they recognized it (48).

An indisputable contribution of the oral-formulaic theory has been the respect it accorded to the formula as something other and more than a shop-worn commonplace or cliché. As with repetitions, formulas are evidently of various kinds, in terms both of the way they are generated (McCarthy 1990: 145–55), and of their function. Some formulas are purely decorative, or seem designed to fill up a line (particularly one which ends with a rhyme), and are perhaps best accorded a humdrum term such as 'commonplaces', but in several linguistic traditions a special class of formulas has been identified which both express significant ballad actions, and – individually and collectively – do important narrative work.[22]

On the denotative level the individual 'narrative formulas'[23] relate important events, but also have a connotative function, in that performer and audience will have heard a given formula in many other ballads, and will have built up a notion of the narrative and thematic context in which it is deployed. The formula therefore conveys information about situation, character, intention and likely sequel which would otherwise need to be formulated explicitly (further contributing to narrative efficiency). Narrative formulas effectively constitute a now lost ballad language which modern scholarship needs to reconstruct as a significant interpretative resource.

And when several different narrative formulas are deployed in a given ballad they can provide it with an underlying narrative rhythm, since they come in sub-categories geared to the major structural developments in a ballad narrative: introduction, situation, transition, conclusion (Andersen 1985); or opening situation, confrontation, alarm/action, reaction (Holzapfel 1980: 89; 1982: 151).

While the occasional study of the supra-narrative functions of such narrative formulas may assume them to be part of an improvisatory system (McAlpine 1996), for Otto Holzapfel, who pioneered this line of research in relation to German and Danish traditions, they are rather part of a 'stereotyping which suited the conditions for oral transmission, that is to say above all singing from memory' 1991: 32 [my translation]). Indeed both he (1987b: 120) and Flemming Andersen (the latter in a significant extension of this approach to Anglo-Scottish balladry; 1985: 91) estimate that narrative formulas *stabilize* a text in oral tradition.

A comprehensive restructuring and refocusing of the oral-formulaic approach, designed expressly to encompass a wide range of the ballad's special narrative characteristics, was powerfully argued and substantially illustrated in David Buchan's watershed study of Northern Scottish balladry, *The Ballad and the Folk* (1972). Obliged to explain

---

[22] See Holzapfel 1980 (English Summary 102–7) and 1982 for Danish and German, Andersen 1985 for English and Scots, and Del Giudice 1994 for Italian.

[23] The term 'epic formulas' by which they are often referred to in English misleadingly implies a relationship with the epic as genre: in the original Danish and German publications 'epic' (*episke / epische*) means simply 'narrative' as opposed to lyric and dramatic; an analogous process produced the equally misleading 'epic laws' of Danish folklorist Axel Olrik.

his view 'simply and crudely' for a later anthology, Buchan obliged with a succinct statement which also brings out the adaptation of the theory to suit the particular qualities of ballads:

> [...] the oral maker controls his material by patternings. For easy mental storage he reduces a heard ballad-story to its bare narrative essence, and then, in the act of composition expands the nuclear story into a full-blown ballad-text through structural and formulaic patternings. These structural patternings enable him both to advance the story's episodes dramatically and to control proportionately the individual episodes in their relationship to each other and to the story as a whole (1973: 2–3).

Formulaic patternings are also deployed, but '[...] it is arguable that [...] the structuring bulked larger in importance'.

Buchan's book provides a thorough and illuminating survey of the types of structuring involved, in terms of stanzas, narrative units, direct and indirect speech, and the distribution of characters between scenes, and as framing, annular, balancing and triadic structures, but the diagnostic claims of such structuring as evidence of 'oral composition' are no stronger than the analogous claim made for the formula. And like the formula, repetition patterns have also been seen as 'a strong aid to memory' (Rubin 1995: 275), or as Albert B. Friedman put it in his second 'Re-rebuttal' of the oral-formulaic theory as applied to ballads: 'most elements of ballad style can be interpreted as devices that came into habitual use to facilitate memorial transmission' (1983: 230).

Buchan's approach was closely followed almost two decades later by William McCarthy's detailed study of the ballads of Agnes Lyle of Kilbarchan, as recorded in the early nineteenth century by William Motherwell. The well-documented and intelligently analysed annular, binary and trinary patterns of organization in the individual ballad are here too taken as revealing the manner of its transmission (1990: 13), but McCarthy supplements this with the claim that it is also the 'consistent and distinctive' characteristics of Agnes Lyle's repertoire which reveal 'an orally recreative "singer of tales"' (20). But while the consistency demonstrated in the repertoire is its (balladic) *style*, the distinctiveness of the repertoire (more important for understanding the ballad competence of the individual singer) is largely demonstrated in terms of *content*. There is little attempt to explore if and how Agnes Lyle's handing of annular, binary and trinary patterns differs from that of other singers performing the same ballad.

But ultimately this is less significant than McCarthy's substantial reformulation of what is at stake. A well-balanced review of the controversy sparked by the irruption of the oral-formulaic theory into ballad studies, and recourse to the original enunciations of Lord and Parry, culminate in the view that 'Improvisation is not the essence of the oral-formulaic theory' (1990: 8). Texts in ballad tradition are normally 'stable', although McCarthy insists this is not the same as 'fixed', since reformulation, and even improvisation, can occur; in a viable tradition ballads 'will always be open to improvisation and innovation. The inspiration of the moment, a better idea, or the influence of another version can at any performance induce changes, minor or major' (159). But reformulation is particularly characteristic not so much of actual performances as of those proto-performances in which a singer is practicing or singing for himself, and McCarthy sees systematic oral recreation mostly as the process by which a singer develops an individual version of a song (which is thereafter 'stable'), rather than a means of generating each performance.

Reformulation is indeed the key, and both understanding oral tradition and appreciating the skills of the ballad singer can be achieved only by comparative analyses of multiple performances of a given song which identify the changes and ponder their implications. But the nature and value of what such comparisons can tell us depend on the exact relationship between the performances compared, and indeed whether that relationship is ascertainable. The many procedures feasible can be resolved into two general categories: macro-tradition studies in which the versions studied are at some distance from each other in terms of time and/or place, and micro-tradition studies involving versions recorded very close to each other not merely in these terms but with regard to performer, at their closest multiple performances of a particular ballad by an individual singer. Ideally the two approaches should be combined, as each has its strengths and weaknesses.

Macro-tradition studies have the advantage of demonstrating the larger, strategic reformulations achieved in oral tradition, but by the same token the external relationship between the versions concerned is less certain. G. M. Laws' valuable examination of verbal change in American song tradition (1964:71–82) is regularly punctuated by regrets that while differences between versions of a song can be discerned, the direction of change can generally not be determined (although the extent of reformulation can confirm the general verbal conservatism of this tradition).

A valuable example of both the value and the limitations of the approach is provided by W. Edson Richmond's juxtaposition (1972:93–94) of two versions of *The Death of Queen Jane* (Child 170). As recalled from oral tradition in 1776 and communicated to Sir Thomas Percy (Child 170A), this is structured around the queen's two appeals that her child be delivered by Caesarean section, and the responses to them, each exchange expressed in similar wording, and prefaced and linked by the calling on of the person to whom the appeal could be addressed. As recorded from Scottish tradition in the late nineteenth century (Child 170E), it is organized around three – identically formulated – requests for the fetching of increasingly authoritative figures, each of whom is asked not for a decision but to summon the next, culminating with the one who has the requisite authority. This is a striking example of the traditional skills of ballad-craft applied to achieve alternative permutations of patterns in a song which already has many balladic features. To the extent the later version has more patterning, with more extensive verbal repetition, and has excised the introductory scene-setting and cut down on the narrative aftermath (the christening of the child and the funeral of the queen), this is also an example of reformulation which takes the song several steps closer to the ballad paradigm, but we cannot say how many performances it took, by how many singers, to achieve the changes observed, or even if the two performances are in the same line of transmission.

Such longitudinal studies, when based on texts of uncertain relationship, are best deployed in ascertaining very long term and general changes, say over several centuries, in which the progress of balladization is usually very clear, for example *Sir Lionel* (Child 18) in England and Scotland (Pettitt 1982a), *Robin Hood and Little John* (Child 125) in

England and America (Kirkland 1940), *Frau von Weißenburg* in Germany;[24] *Fier Margrietken* in Holland.[25] They are at their most reliable when it can be claimed with some confidence that the basis for comparisons is the original form, for example a more literary artsong, subsequently encountered in oral tradition, an approach pioneered by John Meier's classic *Kunstlieder im Volksmunde*.[26] But the general applicability of the results remains in doubt, the simple availability of the original defining these as special cases: Oral tradition might not have had the same impact on artsongs as on its more usual fare.

The otherwise inconvenient proximity of broadsides to ballads is in this respect an advantage, and comparative analysis of an original broadside and its oral derivatives recorded decades or centuries later should – with a similar reliability – reveal processes with a more frequent incidence and so broader validity. A celebrated instance is the version of *Robin Hood and the Tanner* (Child 126) recorded by Cecil Sharp in Somerset in 1905 from the singing of Henry Larcombe, and offered in evidence of 'the amazing accuracy of the memories of folk singers' during his influential discussion in *English Folksong, Some Conclusions*, being 'word for word the same as the corresponding stanzas of a much longer black-letter broadside preserved in the Bodleian Library' (1936: 17). This is both inaccurate and inadequate. Two thirds of the lines common to both versions have substantial differences, the result of both coherent reformulation and garbling, and Larcombe's version (Bronson 126.2, from Cecil Sharp's papers)[27] has two complete lines that do not appear in the Bodleian broadside (Child 126a). It is actually a good example of the balladizing competence which involves retaining only what is essential to the dramatic narrative, the selection of stanzas strategic and ruthless. It retains only one episode (the most dramatic: Robin's fight with the Tanner) out of the three in the original, its selection of seven (not eleven) stanzas of the original's twenty-two made up of from one to three stanzas from each of the narrative sub-units constituting that episode. In the process the proportion of stanzas including direct speech has increased from 50% to 70%.

But as with all studies comparing broadsides with oral versions there is a residual uncertainty as to whether the former, although invariably earlier, is indeed the original from which the latter is directly derived. The later version could in theory stem from an even earlier oral tradition to which the broadside itself was indebted (Atkinson 1992: 362–67). The latter scenario is presumably less likely on those very rare occasions when a broadside with balladic oral derivatives is attributed to a known author, as is the case with two ballads in Child's collection which as issued on mid-seventeenth century broadsides were signed with the initials L. P., almost certainly balladeer Laurence Price.

---

[24] See Hruby 1949: 19. – For an edition of this ballad, see Meier 1935–36: I, 210–18 (no. 30).
[25] See Putter 2004; Putter's exploration of the Dutch hagiographical ballad *Fier Margrietken*, first encountered as a narrative song printed in 1544, then as a folksong recorded from oral tradition in west Flanders in 1900, is less clear in its implications, as the juxtaposition seems rather designed to demonstrate the oral character of the original than exploit the known oral status of the later text to demonstrate the effect or oral tradition on narrative song.
[26] See Meier 1906; see also Rossel 1971 (English Summary 261–62); Barry 1912; 1961.
[27] Bronson 1959–72 (ballads are cited by number; commentary by volume and page).

In one case at least some of the changes, thematic and formal, can be attributed to the workings of oral tradition.[28]

A more reliable option is to take as the point of departure journalistic broadsides reporting recent events, typically crimes and trials. While they are very likely influenced by an existing paradigm for the kind of narrative involved, their journalistic function ensures that we are indeed dealing with the *Urform* of a given song. Several comparative analyses of such songs indicate, amidst much variation and confusion, a general trend in the direction of the balladic.[29] Material inessential for the narrative is omitted, and the narrative that remains is not merely more impersonal and efficient as a result, but more focused on the personal tragedy of the persons involved than on the judicial process that led to trial and punishment. Any additions will be of motifs familiar from other songs in ballad tradition. The narrative tends more to leap and linger, the relative proportion of dialogue increasing; repetition patterns develop, and formulas are substituted for original formulations.

The remaining uncertainty of such investigations is that while we are confident of having the original song and a later derivative from oral tradition, we cannot rule out the intervention of non-traditional processes in the meantime, not least the publication of a recomposed broadside, as assumed by G. M. Laws in pursuing the development of an English murder ballad in America (1957:119). The risk can at least be reduced by taking into consideration any intermediate broadsides which can be located.

The overlapping between ballads and broadsides is an endemic problem of the field,[30] and a related complication is the textual instability of the broadsides themselves, even when not subjected to deliberate and wholesale revision. In a comparative analysis of 21 different printings of a nineteenth-century highwayman ballad Roger de V. Renwick discerned 'characteristics similar to transmission in "oral tradition"' (2002:81), the changes ranging from altered punctuation to the addition or omission of whole lines or even complete stanzas. As with analogous studies of oral tradition the insights are limited by uncertainty about the relationships between the various versions, but in a particular case where one printing is known from external evidence to derive from another, a compositor can be seen adding changes of the kind which can also be encountered in oral transmission, such as regularizing the metre, and adding an 'and' at the beginning of lines (82). Some other changes also suggest that the compositors are treating the ballad as a sequence of sounds rather than symbols, adopting what Renwick reasonably calls an 'oral attitude' towards it, suggesting perhaps that although they are clearly copying the text from a sheet in front of them, as they read its text they are effectively singing the ballad in their minds, and printing what they hear.

In this field without absolute categories it should occasion no more surprise that printing can involve change than that oral tradition can involve verbal stability, and Renwick actually fails to note a classic instance of internal verbal contamination in which a couplet appearing only once in the original (assuming it is the original) appears twice in one of the other printings, creating a repetition pattern characteristic of the

---

[28] See Atkinson 1989; Pettitt 1997a: 115–17.
[29] See Andersen and Pettitt 1985; Pettitt 1994 and 1997b.
[30] See Donatelli 1995; Atkinson 2002: 18–25.

balladic mode. But there are so many other oddities in this particular version that Renwick himself concludes it may actually be a transcript of an oral version.

A more striking example, invoked by David Atkinson in his sustained discussion of broadsides versus oral transmission (2002:22), is Dianne Dugaw's juxtaposition of four versions of the female warrior ballad, *Maid in Sorrow*, two broadsides and two versions from oral tradition. Comparison leads to the conclusion that

> the commercially printed texts [...] exhibit the same range and kind of variation as the non-commercial oral ones. All four versions exhibit continuity, variation, and selection. Stylistically indistinguishable, all four versions clearly represent a single song tradition. (Dugaw 1984: 102)

The overall extent of the variation may indeed be commensurate in the two pairs, but the nature of the variation differs, and is related to differences in style. It is a matter of degree rather than kind, but the oral and broadside versions nonetheless, in the way they are and the way they change, approximate to different generic paradigms and reflect different processes. Given its purpose the comparative analysis should be alert to ballad-specific factors such as repetition patterns, and indeed the two broadsides and their variation evince more 'balladic' features than Dugaw reports: but the oral versions do so to a degree which is noticeably greater. A small but telling illustration is provided by the way the four texts refer to the captain who hires the disguised heroine as she sets off to find her beloved:

| Boadside versions | | Oral versions | |
|---|---|---|---|
| London | Glasgow | Nova Scotia, 1952 | Ireland, 1937 |
| She bargain'd with a captain | the captain | *the captain* | a sea captain |
| The captain did sigh and say | [The] captain | *he* | the captain |
| O hold your tongue, dear captain | dear captain | *dear captain* | sea captain |
| She said farewell, dear captain | dear captain | *dear captain* | sea captain |
| | | *dear captain* | sea captain |
| O, hold your tongue, dear captain | dear captain | *dear captain* | sea captain |

One of the references, the heroine's farewell, has bifurcated into two in oral tradition, symptomatic of the more frequent and more systematic verbal repetition characterizing the latter's style. The extent of the variation also differs: in the broadsides it amounts to only 'the captain' versus 'a captain' in one instance; the oral versions have variant formulations in *every* instance. And this is due to a *kind* of variation which is more prominent in the oral versions than the broadsides, in which reformulation follows (and reinforces) existing repetition patterns: if one 'dear captain' is changed to 'sea captain', then all are (and a mere 'captain' is reformulated to follow suit). Both traditions are verbally unstable, but the oral versions are reformulated with a greater degree of ballad competence than the broadsides.

Ideally, macro-tradition studies should take as their point of departure the original version of a narrative song composed under the auspices of oral tradition, and in a companion piece to her formulaic analyses of Faroese balladry Patricia Conroy (1979) examines an instance which comes close to fulfilling this ideal, exploring the changes undergone by a particular ballad in a local tradition between recordings in 1821 and 1848, the first version recorded from a singer reputed by local lore to be its composer. This original has some traditional features, but they are substantially increased in the derivative versions which have been subjected to both the automatic effects and purposeful interventions of oral transmission. The changes involve the song acquiring more formulas and more repetitions, some resulting from internal contamination, some from the bifurcation of a stanza into two, some from adding a given formula more than once, others from downright additions: 'Most often [...] stanzas were added by the ballad man in order to recount similar episodes in a more parallel manner' (37). Features which were not in conformity with traditional style (like a scene-shift within a single stanza) were adjusted to become so.

The most reliable insights into the nature of oral tradition are achieved by microtradition comparative analyses of multiple performances of a given ballad by a single singer, or by two or more singers in a close network of relationships (Niles 1999:154). In the first flush of oral-formulaic enthusiasm following the publication of *The Singer of Tales* in 1960, W. Edson Richmond was confident he had found evidence of improvisational composition-in-performance in two versions of a ballad, *The Unfaithful Husband* collected in Norway in the second half of the nineteenth century. They tell the same story, with the same motifs in the same order, but with massive verbal discrepancy. Moreover both versions are full of verbal formulas and commonplaces, but not the same ones (1963:79; 75–76).

This has no greater evidential force than other comparisons between versions of unknown relationship, but the information Edson Richmond supplies actually demonstrates that the norm in at least one of the micro-traditions concerned was the reproduction of stable verbal material. One of the versions he discusses was recorded, sometime before 1863, not merely from a particular singer, but also from her brother, both on that occasion and again in 1867: the brother's versions differed from the sister's and from each other in only 'minor variations' (79).[31]

More or less the same can be said of an analogous and near-contemporary instance from Scotland, in which the ballad *Earl Crawford*, having been collected from a singer sometime between 1867 and 1873 (Child 229Aa), was collected from her daughter in 1890 (Child 229Ab). The words have remained relatively stable over the twenty or so years and between the performers, although interestingly the more substantial reformulations are connected with verbal repetition patterns (and have made the daughter's version somewhat more balladic than the mother's), while the formulas are clearly a stabilizing factor (Andersen 1985:86–91).

Denmark's heritage of Renaissance ballad manuscripts is matched by the rich harvest of songs recorded from oral tradition in the nineteenth century by collectors such as Evald Tang Kristensen with surprisingly modern notions about recording the song accurately as performed and noting details of the singer. In a substantial and significant recent study of Danish ballad tradition, Sigurd Kværndrup invokes several multiple performances from one of the singers recorded at this time, Sidsel Jensdatter, in support of his contention that while by then unusual, improvisation could still occur.[32]

---

[31] Multiple performances by the same singer, largely from American tradition, studied by Wolfhart Anders, similarly show a degree of variation in otherwise stable verbal material (Anders 1974:109–26).

[32] See Kværndrup 2006:227–28. Kværndrup devotes most attention to a humorous song, recorded from this singer three times by Evald Tang Kristen in 1869, whose length varied from 12 to 35

Sidsel Jensdatter was recorded on three separate occasions singing the historical ballad *Queen Dagmar in Denmark* (*DgF* 133):[33] twice in 1866 by a local schoolteacher (133B. b.β and 133B. b.γ), and once in 1868 (133B. b.α) by Evald Tang Kristensen. Kværndrup does not elaborate on the differences, and they are relatively straightforward. The two versions of 1866 are virtually identical except for a stanza missing in one of them, and small-scale variations on the level of 'silver and gold' versus 'gold and silver'. They are less than half the length of the 1868 version (9–10 stanzas to its 25), but mainly by virtue of stopping half way through, so that they are effectively wry stories of a princess (Dagmar) who for dynastic reasons was married off to an ugly king, and end when she sees him waiting on the shore and exclaims in disgust. The 1868 version lacks their two-stanza exchange in which the princess wonders who the ugly man is and is told the disconcerting truth, but inserts a four-stanza account of her departure and journey, and continues the narrative to what happens after her wedding. There are two discrepancies in the line sequence between the 1866 and 1868 versions, but not enough to unduly complicate the impression of relatively simple variation achieved by including or omitting a given sequence of stanzas. This might conceivably have happened in performance, but the *DgF* editors were less struck by this aspect than by Sidsel Jensdatter's introduction (in all three versions) of a sequence of four stanzas deriving from another ballad on Queen Dagmar, prompting the remark that 'occasional free reformulations of the received material' are an idiosyncrasy of this singer (*DgF* X: 283). Sidsel Jensdatter effectively provides the opportunity for multiple performance studies which the repertoire of Agnes Lyle did not offer, with results somewhat living up to William McCarthy's expectations.

More revealing is *DgF* 47 *Elveskud* [Elf-shot], recorded twice by Evald Tang Kristensen, at an interval of a few days, in 1869.[34] According to Kværndrup the versions use different formulas to tell the story in different ways, but the differences (as in the preceding instance) are as much a matter of narrative sequences. The two versions begin together with Sir Peder out hunting, and stay in step for his encounter with an elf woman, the mortal wound he receives for refusing to dance with her, his arrival home with boots full of blood, and his demand for a priest and a bed. (The second performance, *DgF* 47R, adds a three-stanza exchange in which his mother sees though his explanation that he has had an accident.) They end together with the multiple deaths and funerals of the protagonists (the first version, which omits the death of the mother, inconsistently following two deaths with three funerals).

The two performances part company decisively in their selection of quite different sequences for what happens between Sir Peder's arrival home and the multiple deaths,

---

stanzas. But rather than juxtaposing the variant texts Kværndrup invokes musical evidence suggesting that at least the difference between the long version and the two shorter ones was due to Sidsel Jensdatter operating with parallel versions, suitable, respectively, for recreational singing and dance accompaniment – which is not the same as improvising a new version each time.

[33] For the edition of *DgF* (*Danmarks gamle Folkeviser*), see Grundtvig et al. 1853–1976.
[34] Kværndrup mentions a third version, *DgF* 47X, attributed to Sidsel Jensdatter in *DgF*'s index of singers, but not in the headnote to the text; it was recorded by the schoolteacher involved in recording *Dronning Dagmar* but in a different town. Either way it is clearly a different version of the ballad, with even a different name for the protagonist.

both in the traditional balladic mode. The first performance attempts the more familiar sequel with the arrival of Sir Peder's betrothed hard on the heels of his death, and his mother's attempts, in a series of questions and answers, to conceal what has happened. The second performance substitutes a small family drama in which the dying Sir Peder, concerned at what will happen to his betrothed, asks his youngest brother to marry her.

Whether this reflects re-composition, or a repertoire with alternative versions of the same ballad, as suspected by Tang Kristensen and the *DgF* editors, is less important than Evald Tang Kristensen's revealing account of the circumstances of the recordings, which undermines Kværndrup's conclusion that this and the other song are evidence that although Sidsel Jensdatter mainly memorizes her ballads (about half of which can be traced back to broadsides), if she was nonetheless at times able 'to reproduce new versions of oral texts there and then in front of a learned collector' then under more natural conditions and with a supportive audience 'actual oral-formulaic "improvisation" might happen'.[35] On the first occasion, Tang Kristensen reports:

> she couldn't remember it properly, and there were several gaps. We left it for a few days, so she could think it over in the mean time, which she did, and I got the whole song, but it was partly changed [...][36]

The changes were evidently a result of deliberation between performances, not improvisation in performance.

Such micro-tradition analyses are usually more informative, and more reliable, the more recent the performances concerned, but by the same token the tradition they represent may be the more interfered with by the literacy of the singers and the availability of printed songs. Thomas A. McKean's study of an illuminating instance of sequential versions in a family tradition is alert to these factors. Elizabeth Stewart, from 'one of Scotland's outstanding singing families' sings traditional ballads learnt from her aunt, Lucy Stewart (1901–1982), who was extensively recorded in the first wave of the rediscovery of balladry among the Scottish travellers. McKean concludes from a consideration of their attitudes and practice that despite considerable literacy their way with ballads was still 'oral in nature'. Thus in singing her aunt's songs – in a very different singing style – Elizabeth Stewart introduces small-scale changes in almost every other line ('The beggar's bed ...' becomes '*Oh* the beggar's bed ...'; 'Een was fair ...' becomes 'Een *o them* wis fair ...', etc.). But this is all: otherwise 'Lucy's and Elizabeth's versions of songs reveal a high degree of exactitude, with only minor variations' (2003b: 193).

This is ostensibly at odds with McKean's insistence that oral tradition involves change, and can thoroughly reshape a song (199), but the contradiction can be resolved by a factor, scarcely unique to this family and entirely compatible with traditional attitudes and practices: the conservative influence of the respect felt by a singer for the song as received from a predecessor who looms large in their sense of identity as both individual and singer.

McKean's study is a useful reminder that in the English-speaking world the Scottish travellers and the English gypsies offer special opportunities for research, having almost

---

[35] Kværndrup 2006:231, my translation; see also English Summary, 662. Kværndrup also invokes Agnes Lyle, as studied by William McCarthy (see above) in support of this conclusion.
[36] Supplied by Kværndrup 2006:227, n. 183 from *DgF* IV 841, n.

up to the present performed ballads under auspices strikingly close to authentic oral tradition, the singers frequently illiterate, the ballads a living aspect of their cultural traditions and sense of identity: 'the travelling people have become the real custodians of English and Scots traditional song' (MacColl and Seeger 1977: 15).

In the case of the Scottish singers the many recordings of live performances offer ample evidence that singers adapt songs, but little for significant improvisation in performance (Henderson 1973: 28; 32). Changes between multiple performances by the same singer may even reflect precisely the intense interest of the folklorists who collected the songs and the celebrity on the folk scene which sometimes ensued. In a disturbing ethnomusicological study of multiple performances of *My Son David* (Child 13, *Edward*) by the most celebrated of the Scottish travellers, Jeannie Robertson, James Porter (although with other ends in view) documents how her characteristic slow, self-projecting style developed in response to her growing fame, as 'she began to see herself as a "folk singer", a "performer", and was partially conforming to her idea of what a "folk singer" should be like' (1976: 14). Her performance doubled in duration in the period covered by the study, and she developed a standard nine-stanza version of the song which had previously varied between eight and eleven stanzas.

Recording from the English gypsies seems to have been less intense and may have been less disruptive: 'theirs was a tradition that was being carried on quite separately from folk clubs or festivals' (Stradling 2007: 9). They have something of a notoriety for the instability of their songs, but rather than disciplined improvisation it takes the form of switching from one song to another, like a train changing tracks, at points constituted by narrative motifs common to several ballads (MacColl and Seeger 1977: 13). Other observations suggest that this is not so much instability in a given song as an endemic disregard for the distinctions between songs (Yates 2006: 23–24). But equally it could reflect the style of some individual singers or groups who have attracted particular attention (Constantine 2003: 87 ff.): The several singers in the much respected Brazil family of Gloucestershire have a repertoire of narrative songs which are both coherent and unjumbled.[37]

The many recordings of the family, undertaken over two decades or more, provide opportunities for the comparative analysis of multiple performances, be they by the same singer or two siblings, in the latter case any differences reflecting individual reformulations of a song both probably learnt from their father.[38] In one instance, *Three Brothers in Fair Warwickshire*, it is possible to combine these multiple performance analyses with a longitudinal study of how the oral tradition of which these performances are the culmination has dealt with this song, by comparing them with the original, a news broadside reporting a highway robbery in 1818 (Pettitt 2008).

And in a manner we more associate with fieldwork in far away places, the evidence also includes revealing comments from singers and audience in connection with performance. In a fascinating incident in January 1966, when Peter Shepheard was recording a performance of the narrative folksong *The Old Riverside*, the singer faltered in

---

[37] See Rod Stradling's remarks in the booklet accompanying the 3–CD set *The Brazil Family: Down by the Riverside* (MTCD 345–7; Stroud: Musical Traditions Records, 2007), p. 8.

[38] *The Brazil Family* (n. 37) has some instances.

rendering the last stanzas, and one of the listeners prefaced an ultimately unsuccessful attempt of her own with an apologia whose implications merit further thought: 'I knows a lot of the words, but I can't rhyme 'em together, you see.'[39]

In exceptional circumstances multiple-performance studies can be undertaken in relation to much earlier phases of ballad tradition, and it is evident that ballad studies have not heard the last from or about the celebrated Anna Gordon Brown of Falkland, the Professor's daughter and clergyman's wife much courted by Scottish ballad collectors in the last two decades of the eighteenth century. Between 1783 and 1800 she provided them with 35 different ballads, all of which were accepted into the Child canon, and indeed may have contributed to shaping what Child felt a ballad should be (Pettitt 1984: 17–18). Many of them were recorded more than once, providing the opportunity for multiple performance analyses which have duly been seized in studies seeking to determine the mechanisms of oral tradition, although their outcome can be complicated by the circumstances of recording.

The situation is particularly frustrating in relation to the thirteen ballads which appear in both of the song manuscripts she compiled in 1783, the duplication itself not surprising given that the second was designed to supply the music for some of the ballads whose words only had been supplied the first time around. The implications of comparative analysis are ambiguous. Surveying the group as a whole Bronson concludes that 'for Mrs. Brown there was nothing sacred about the mere words of her ballads' but this is evidently not to be taken as meaning more than that the changes are due, in Bronson's own summary, to corrections of memory, rationalizing, metrical conditions, regularizing dialectal features and aesthetic adjustment (1969: 69; 67). On the basis of a similar survey of this group plus a closer look at one ballad (Child 98: *Brown Adam*) Holger Olof Nygard concludes more emphatically: 'Mrs. Brown's ballads are essentially repetitions of a text, not recreations of a story maintained in fluid solution subject to a free variation in successive singings' (1978: 79). But analysing another individual instance (Child 6: *Willie's Lady*) David Buchan finds that while the wording of the individual stanzas is relatively stable they have been rearranged into a new structure of repetition patterns very much in accordance with his notions of re-creation in performance (1972: 142–43). The issue might be decided by commensurate comparative analyses of all the other ballads in the group, but the motivation to do so is undermined by the uncertain status of the second set of performances. An explanatory letter written by Mrs. Brown subsequently suggests very strongly that as she 'performed' the songs the second time around the manuscript with the transcripts of the earlier performance was available to her, decisively compromising the 'oral' nature of the recording (cited in Buchan 1972: 69–70).

The results of the other comparative analyses of multiple performances enabled by the Brown repertoire are ambiguous in a more straightforward way. In a second phase of collection in 1800 Mrs. Brown recorded another set of ballads, two of them, *Child Waters* (Child 63) and *The Lass of Roch Royal* (Child 76), already featuring in the 1783 collection. The same year William Jamieson recorded a small cluster of ballads she had not provided elsewhere, but in retrospect, feeling that the version of *Bonny Baby Livingston* (Child 222) she had supplied was, in her own words 'imperfect', and finding that 'I

---

[39] *The Brazil Family* (n. 37), track 4.

had the whole story in my memory', she wrote it out 'entire' and sent it to him (Andersen and Pettitt 1979:9).

Comparative analysis of *Child Waters* and *Bonny Baby Livingston* reveals, amidst some limited reformulation which might have been improvised (see also Anders 1974:116–22), a dominant verbal reproduction which may have triggered Buchan's startling concession that 'the re-creative method produces story-texts remarkable for stability rather than innovation' (Buchan 1972:166). As McCarthy was to do later, Buchan seeks to resolve this 'paradoxical' combination of 're-creative technique' and 'narrative conservatism' (167) with the notion that a ballad can settle down with a stable set of structural and formulaic patterns.

But the concession may have been premature, for *The Lass of Roch Royal* behaves in a manner altogether more in conformity with the verbal *instability* and re-structuring we should expect from the re-creative processes of Buchan's improvisation theory, and in this instance it is the opponents of recreation in performance who are faced with the challenge of explaining it away. It is possible for example that between 1783 and 1800 Mrs. Brown may have been influenced by the version printed in Herd's *Scottish Songs*, or in 1800 she may have been engaging rather in *literary* emendation.[40] Or she may simply have known two distinct versions of this ballad[41] – the evidence for which is concrete but convoluted.

Astonishingly, multiple performances of a ballad from the same singer are available from Sweden over a century earlier. Recorded in the 1670's in the context of an official campaign to document the history and cultural independence of a nation emerging into regional great power status, a farmer's widow, Ingierd Gunnarsdotter, supplied 47 ballads (of the more than three hundred she was said to know), of which five were recorded twice, one three times, and one four times. Bengt Jonsson reports that the differences between the multiple versions of her songs 'are, as a rule, slight', and offers by way of illustration the alternative formulations of the second and fourth lines of a stanza in a ballad narrating the myth of how a giant stole Thor's hammer (1991:144–45):

| (first performance:) | (second performance:) |
|---|---|
| Thor's hammer have I taken | Thor's hammer have I taken |
| I do not hide it in my speech* | I do not hide it from him with a word |
| Fifteen fathoms and forty | Fifteen fathoms and forty |
| it lies there buried. | it lies under the earth. |
| [*i. e. I do not deny it] | |

This would seem to conform to the general trend of the evidence that – however achieved – verbal reproduction accompanied by occasional reformulation is the norm for how oral tradition handles ballads.

---

[40] See Duffin 2004:146–49; Pettitt 1984:24–30.
[41] See Andersen and Pettitt 1979:21–23; Nygard 1978:83.

## 4 The Oral Ballad in the Later Middle Ages

The simple fact that ballads change over time effectively rules out using post-medieval versions to document medieval balladry, but the supplementary fact that ballads can also develop out of existing narrative songs, which compounds this difficulty, also means that medieval narrative songs evincing substantial ballad features are very likely products of balladizing in oral tradition.

But such songs are not easy to find. The early-modern evidence is everywhere limited or problematic, and the late-medieval texts extremely sporadic.[42] And although Scandinavian scholarship speaks of the 'medieval ballad' as a genre (Jonsson 1991), the amazing Danish heritage of forty manuscript songbooks with versions of half of the 539 *folkeviser* in the ballad canon belongs to the sixteenth and seventeenth centuries. The older view that the songs go back to medieval antecedents (Steenstrup 1914) is challenged by the possibility that some may be almost contemporary with the manuscripts, or even derive from antecedent broadsides.[43]

Equally some undoubtedly medieval songs which present themselves with apparently good credentials can prove disappointing. A cautionary instance is a reference in Boccaccio's *Decameron* to a song recounting a recent and dramatic domestic tragedy, the story, later made familiar by Keats, of the young woman whose secret lover is murdered by her brothers – very much the stuff of balladry. When he reveals his fate to her in a dream she conceals his head in a pot of basil, dying of grief when it is taken from her: 'But after due process of time, many people came to know of the affair, and one of them composed the song [*canzone*] which can still be heard to this day' (McWilliam 1995: 330). Effectively a fourteenth-century account of the composition of a medieval narrative song and its subsequent oral transmission, the incident is appealed to by Peter Dronke in pursuing, deep into the Middle Ages, a tradition of ballads on the appearance of a dead lover to his grieving sweetheart.[44] For although Boccaccio's story is fictional the song itself is real enough: Boccaccio himself quotes half a stanza from it, and it survives in a fourteenth-century manuscript and sixteenth-century songbooks. But on inspection the song does not narrate the story of Isabella, with which it has indeed no connection: it belongs to a quite different tradition of (lyric) folksongs in which a girl laments the loss of her maidenhead, lightly allegorized in the loss or breakage of some appropriate object ('sprig of thyme' is a familiar English analogue) (Belden 1918). Boccaccio has developed his Isabella narrative as a spoof explanation for the song (Marcus 1989), but his intertextual jest at least suggests that fourteenth-century readers would find plausible the composition of a stanzaic song (a proto-ballad) commemorating a notorious domestic tragedy.

A German *Volkslied* which attracted a lot of attention because of its possible links to a Germanic heroic lay from the Dark Ages proves, in its earliest recorded text from 1472 to be a rather lengthy stanzaic song with few ballad features.[45] The *Jüngeres Hil-*

---

[42] See Buchan 1978; Richmond 1978.
[43] See Sønderholm 1978; Piø 1977 and 1985.
[44] See Dronke 1984: 200–1 (in his chapter 'Learned Lyric and Popular Ballad in the Early Middle Ages', 167–208).
[45] See von der Hagen and Büsching 1825: II.2, 219–21, and for other versions Meier 1935–36: I, 35–42 (no. 1).

*debrandslied* narrates somewhat laboriously in 29 eight-line stanzas how after years in exile the old warrior Hildebrand returns and unbeknowingly faces his son in combat, until the latter's fighting style reveals his identity: a somewhat sentimental family reunion duly ensues. The focus on a limited sequence of connected scenes involving dramatic confrontations with a good deal of dialogue, and the abrupt opening and transitions, take the first steps on the ballad road, but there are no classic narrative formulas, and no verbal repetitions of note. We are told who speaks, and the song ends with a narrator's *explicit* ('[...] we will stop this and sing no more of it: may God be with us').

That it was intended to be performed is confirmed by another manuscript with songs specified as being sung to 'the tune of Hildebrand' (Classen 1996: 368–69), but with over a score of printings in the sixteenth century there must be few songs whose early oral transmission was more compromised by the broadside trade. The broadsides actually show rather more balladic tendencies than the earliest version in omitting a peripheral episode and introducing some formulas and verbal repetitions (Rosenfeld 1973: 74), but it is not certain whether these record the impact of subsequent oral tradition or a late-medieval oral tradition which the manuscript version adapts (or the oral habits of broadside compositors), and the song has not been recovered from later tradition (Meid 1988: 31). As we have it this song demonstrates the existence of the ballad in late-medieval Germany only to the extent the latter is defined as 'strophic narrative songs with rounded melodies' (Ward 1978: 46): in the terms applied here it is at best a proto-ballad, which might have moved towards the ballad paradigm under the right auspices. German scholarship tends to agonize over whether what we have should not rather be classified as a 'minstrel song' (Hruby 1949: 9): it is almost as if it was composed in readiness for the forthcoming invention of the broadside.

In England the situation is similarly complicated by the availability of narrative songs that have not yet been shaped by oral tradition into ballads, or which belong rather to the forms (spoken 'rhymes'; minstrel songs; quasi narrative lyrics) from whose coalescence the stanzaic narrative song was shortly to emerge.[46] The balladic status of the celebrated border ballads and Robin Hood ballads are particularly compromised in this respect, but the insights achieved by the methods outlined above may ultimately contribute to resolving this uncertainty.

England's two surviving medieval ballads based on biblical narrative or hagiographical material are better qualified in this respect, and probably represent a sub-tradition that was stronger in the pre-Reformation period (and can be supplemented by a number of post-medieval religious ballads). The fifteenth-century *St Stephen and Herod* (Child 23) from the celebrated Sloane Manuscript, has had its credentials under several of the criteria deployed above thoroughly approved in two similar but independent analyses[47] – it is demonstrably more balladic than the semi-narrative caroles in the same manuscript – and is offered as an example of a medieval ballad in current popular surveys.[48]

Inevitably more of a challenge is the thirteenth-century *Judas*, which, if it is a ballad, is the only surviving instance from anywhere in Europe from before the fifteenth cen-

---

[46] See Boklund-Lagopoulou 2002; Fowler 1968; Green 1997.
[47] See Pettitt 1982b; Boklund-Lagopolou 2002: 78–81.
[48] See Hirsch 2005: 125–26. [On Middle English popular song, see also ch. 21 by K. Boklund-Lagopoulou in this volume.]

tury.⁴⁹ Narrating a legend of Judas's betrayal of Christ, it is very much at home in the Dominican or Franciscan devotional compilation of English, French and Latin poems where it is preserved (there are no later versions).⁵⁰ Having been entrusted with thirty pieces of silver to buy food, Judas loses them, and when offered a bribe to betray Jesus, specifies this as the price. Unusually in the Judas legends, the money is stolen by his sister (or with her connivance), who lulls him to sleep in her lap (not the last ballad lady to use this device), encompassing the song, despite its holy setting, within traditional balladry's endemic fascination with family conflicts in general and problematic brother-sister relationships in particular (Lüthi 1973: 96).

It comprises fifteen long couplets or ballad quatrains with (most of the time) the traditional metre and rhyme-scheme. In the right margin beside three of the lines is a '.ii.', probably signalling that (as the rhyme scheme clearly indicates) they are part of extended stanzas for which the musical phrase accompanying the second line should be repeated for the third (Axton 1990: 191) – useful in suggesting that this is indeed a song, and metrical features indicate it conforms to a stanzaic and musical form encountered in more recent tradition (Mitsui 1995). [See Illustration 16.]

In a sustained assessment from several perspectives Karin Boklund-Lagopoulou argues that the song displays many stylistic qualities, which are 'closely related to the techniques of oral composition', and that the narrative mode in particular has a dramatic intensity deriving from features – economy, action and direct speech with little or no transitions, extensive repetition (including incremental repetition) – which are 'characteristics of the ballad'; not so much generic conventions as '[...] aspects of the process of oral composition and performance' (2002: 59). She hesitates (61) to claim that this proves *Judas* is a ballad, but from the perspective applied here that is precisely what 'ballad' means.

For Scandinavia, the entire existence of a medieval balladry hinges on the only surviving text of more than one stanza antedating the broadsides and the Renaissance song collections, a seven-stanza fragment in Danish from a Norwegian manuscript of c. 1500 (*DgF* 67A, *The Knight in a Deerskin*).⁵¹ A lascivious knight who has dreamt of a maiden orders his squires to go and woo her for him. They do so and are rebuffed. When they report back he resolves to don his 'deerskin' and win her that way. A casual addition on a blank sheet following a vernacular sermon collection, the ballad text breaks off at the bottom of the page, depriving us of the sequel, in which (as can be gathered from later versions) the maiden is lured by this charming 'deer' to a lonely spot where the knight reveals himself and resolves to have his wicked way with her, only to be foiled by a clever ruse on her part.

The fragment has no narrative formulas in the strict sense, but does deploy the commonplace 'Now it's of [person N.]', very widespread in Danish balladry. Stanza-form and refrain, narrative structure, the leaping between scenes dominated by repetitive dialogue, and various types of verbal patterning all conform to the ballad norm, and the material is very compatible with the ballad universe. Several later versions survive in

---

⁴⁹ Discussed here on the basis of Axton 1990: 191–92.
⁵⁰ See Axton 1990: 190; for an edition and study of the manuscript as a whole see Reichl 1973.
⁵¹ See Jonsson 1991: 146–47; Colbert 1989: 53–56.

early modern song manuscripts, their twenty to twenty-five stanzas all including a stanza sequence covering the same events in near-identical phrases or clearly related formulations, including the dream-refrain. The ballad has not however been found in later oral tradition.

If the conclusions reached in the earlier discussion are valid, then this is just enough to demonstrate that Scandinavia too, by the late-medieval period, had narrative songs which were either composed as ballads, or more likely reshaped by the ballad competence of oral tradition.

16 – The Ballad of Judas, Cambridge, Trinity College MS B 14. 39, fol. 34r

# References

Abrahams, Roger D., ed. 1970. *A Singer and Her Songs: Almeda Riddle's Book of Ballads.* Baton Rouge: Louisiana State UP.
Amodio, Mark C. 2004. *Writing the Oral Tradition: Oral Poetics and Literate Culture in Medieval England.* Notre Dame: U of Notre Dame P.
Anders, Wolfhart H. 1974. *Balladensänger und mündliche Komposition.* Munich: Fink.
Andersen, Fleming G. 1982. 'From Tradition to Print: Ballads on Broadsides.' In Andersen, Holzapfel and Pettitt 1982: 39–58.
–. 1985. *Commonplace and Creativity: The Role of Formulaic Diction in Anglo-Scottish Traditional Balladry.* Odense: Odense UP.
–. 1991. 'Technique, Text and Context: Formulaic Narrative Mode and the Question of Genre.' In Harris 1991: 18–41.
–. 1995. '"All there is ... as it is." On the Development of Textual Criticism in Ballad Studies.' *Jahrbuch für Volksliedforschung* 39: 28–40.
–, and Thomas Pettitt. 1979. 'Mrs. Brown of Falkland: A Singer of Tales?' *JAF* 92: 1–24.
–, Otto Holzapfel, and Thomas Pettitt. 1982. *The Ballad as Narrative: Studies in the Ballad Traditions of England, Scotland, Germany and Denmark.* Odense: Odense UP.
–, and Thomas Pettitt. 1985. '"The Murder of Maria Marten": The Birth of a Ballad?' In *Narrative Folksong: New Directions. Essays in Appreciation of W. Edson Richmond.* Ed. Carol L. Edwards and Kathleen E. B. Manley. Boulder, CO: Westview P. 132–78.
Armistead, Samuel G. 2000. 'Ballad.' In *Medieval Folklore: An Encyclopedia of Myths, Legends, Tales, Beliefs, and Customs.* Ed. Carl Lindahl and John McNamara. 2 vols. Santa Barbara: ABC–CLIO. I, 61–71.
Atkinson, David. 1989. 'Marriage and Redistribution in "James Harris (The Dæmon Lover)".' *Folk Music Journal* 5: 592–607.
–. 1992. 'History, Symbol, and Meaning in "The Cruel Mother".' *Folk Music Journal* 6: 359–80.
–. 2002. *The English Traditonal Ballad: Theory, Method and Practice.* Aldershot: Ashgate.
Axton, Richard. 1990. 'Interpretations of Judas in Middle English Literature.' In *Religion in the Poetry and Drama of the Late Middle Ages.* Ed. Pietro Boitani and Anna Torti. Cambridge: Brewer. 179–97.
Barry, Phillips. 1912. 'William Carter, the Bensontown Homer.' *JAF* 25: 156–68.
–. 1961. 'The Part of the Folk Singer in the Making of Folk Balladry.' In Leach and Coffin 1961: 59–76.
Bekker-Nielsen, Hans, Peter Foote, Andreas Haarder, and Hans Frede Nielsen, eds. 1977. *Oral Tradition, Literary Tradition: A Symposium.* Odense: Odense UP.
Belden, H. M. 1918. 'Boccaccio, Hans Sachs, and the Bramble Briar.' *PMLA* 33: 327–95.
Bell, Michael J. 1988. '"No Borders to the Ballad Maker's Art": Francis James Child and the Politics of the People.' *Western Folklore* 47: 285–307.
Bennett, Philip E. 2004. 'The Suppression of a Ballad Culture: The Enigma of Medieval France.' In Bennett and Green 2004: 105–21.
–, and Richard Firth Green, eds. 2004. *The Singer and the Scribe: European Ballad Traditions and Ballad Cultures.* Amsterdam: Rodopi.
Bohnet, Artur. 1978. 'Ballads, *Ballata, Ballade* – and "À l' entrade del tens clar".' In Conroy 1978: 17–25.
Boklund-Lagopoulou, Karin. 2002. *'I have a yong suster': Popular Song and the Middle English Lyric.* Dublin: Four Courts P.
Bold, Alan. 1979. *The Ballad.* London: Methuen.
Brednich, Rolf, Lutz Röhrich, and Wolfgan Suppan, eds. 1973. *Handbuch des Volksliedes. I. Die Gattungen des Volksliedes.* Munich: Fink.

Bronson, Bertrand Harris, ed. 1959–72. *The Traditional Tunes of the Child Ballads*. 4 vols. Princeton: Princeton UP.
–. 1969. *The Ballad as Song*. Berkeley: U of California P.
Brown, Mary Ellen. 1996. 'The Mechanism of the Ancient Ballad: William Motherwell's Explanation.' *Oral Tradition* 11: 175–89.
Buchan, David. 1972. *The Ballad and the Folk*. London: Routledge and Kegan Paul.
–, ed. 1973. *A Scottish Ballad Book*. London: Routledge and Kegan Paul.
–. 1977. 'Oral Tradition and Literary Tradition: The Scottish Ballads.' In Bekker-Nielsen et al. 1977: 56–68.
–. 1978. 'British Balladry: Medieval Chronology and Relations.' In Holzapfel 1978c: 98–106.
Catarella, Teresa. 1994. 'The Study of the Orally Transmitted Ballad: Past Paradigms and a New Poetics'. *Oral Tradition* 9: 468–78.
Cheesman, Tom, and Sigrid Rieuwerts, eds. 1997. *Ballads into Books: The Legacies of Francis James Child*. Bern: Lang.
Chesnutt, Michael. 1993. 'Aspects of the Faroese Traditional Ballad in the Nineteenth Century.' In *The Stockholm Ballad Conference 1991*. Ed. Bengt R. Jonsson. Stockholm: Svenkst Visarkiv. 247–59.
Child, Francis James. 1875. 'Ballad Poetry.' In *Johnson's Universal Cyclopedia*. 1875; rpt. *The Anglo-American Ballad: A Folklore Casebook*. Ed. Diane Dugaw. New York: Garland. 58–67.
–, ed. 1882–98. *The English and Scottish Popular Ballads*. 5 vols. Boston. [Rpt. New York: Dover, 1965.]
Classen, Albrecht. 1996. 'The *Jüngeres Hildebrandslied* in its Early Modern Printed Versions: A Contribution to Fifteenth- and Sixteenth-Century Reception History.' *JEGP* 95: 359–81.
Coffin, Tristram P. 1961. 'Mary Hamilton and the Anglo-American Ballad as an Art Form.' In Leach and Coffin 1961: 245–56.
Colbert, David W. 1978. 'The Danish Bower Ballad: A Seminal Type.' In Conroy 1978: 7–16.
–. 1989. *The Birth of the Ballad*. Stockholm: Svenskt Visarkiv.
Conroy, Patricia, ed. 1978. *Ballads and Ballad Research*. Seattle: U of Washington P.
–. 1979. 'Creativity in Oral Transmission: A Example from Faroese Ballad Tradition.' *Arv: Nordic Yearbook of Folklore* 35: 25–48.
–. 1980. 'Oral Composition in Faroese Ballads.' *Jahrbuch für Volksliedforschung* 25: 34–50.
Constantine, Mary-Ann. 2003. '"God was in France all Friday": Incoherence from the Inside.' In Constantine and Porter 2003: 77–100.
–, and Gerald Porter. 2003. *Fragments and Meaning in Traditional Song: From the Blues to the Baltic*. Oxford: OUP.
Danckert, Werner. 1970. *Das Europäische Volkslied*. 2nd ed. Bonn: Bouvier.
Del Giudice, Luisa. 1994. 'Oral Theory and the Northern Italian Ballad Tradition: An Ethnographic Approach to the Ballad Formula.' *Journal of Folklore Research* 31: 97–126.
*DgF*: see Grundtvig et al. 1853–1976.
Donatelli, Joseph M. P. 1995. '"To hear with Eyes": Orality, Print Culture, and the Textuality of Ballads.' In Porter 1995: 347–57.
Dronke, Peter. 1984. *The Medieval Poet and his World*. Rome: Edizioni di storia e letteratura.
Duffin, Charles. 2004. 'Echoes of Authority: Audience and Formula in the Scots Ballad Text.' In Bennett and Green 2004: 135–51.
Dugaw, Dianne M. 1984. 'Anglo-American Folksong Reconsidered: The Interface of Oral and Written Forms.' *Western Folklore* 43: 83–103.
Entwistle, William J. 1939. *European Balladry*. Oxford: Clarendon.
Fowler, David C. 1968. *A Literary History of the Popular Ballad*. Durham, NC: Duke UP.
Friedman, Albert B. 1961. 'The Formulaic Improvisation Theory of Ballad Tradition: A Counterstatement.' *JAF* 74: 113–15.

—. 1983. 'The Oral-Formulaic Theory of Balladry – A Re-rebuttal.' In *The Ballad Image: Essays Presented to Bertrand Harris Bronson*. Ed. James Porter. Los Angeles: Center for the Study of Comparative Folklore and Mythology. 215–40.
Gammon, Vic, and Peter Stallybrass. 1984–85. 'Structure and Ideology in the Ballad: An Analysis of "Long Lankin".' *Criticism* 26: 1–20.
Gerould, Gordon Hall. 1957. *The Ballad of Tradition*. New York: OUP. [Or. Oxford, 1932.]
Green, Richard Firth. 1997. 'The Ballad and the Middle Ages.' In *The Long Fifteenth Century: Essays for Douglas Gray*. Ed. Helen Cooper and Sally Mapstone. Oxford: Clarendon. 163–84.
Grundtvig, Svend, et al., eds. 1853–1976. *Danmarks gamle Folkeviser*. 12 vols. Copenhagen: Universitets-Jubilæets Danske Samfund.
Harker, Dave. 1981. 'Francis James Child and the "Ballad Consensus".' *Folk Music Journal* 4: 146–64.
Harris, Joseph, ed. 1991. *The Ballad and Oral Literature*. Cambridge, MA: Harvard UP.
Harris, Trudier. 1995. 'Genre.' *JAF* 108: 509–27.
Henderson, Hamish. 1973. 'The Oral Tradition.' *Scottish International Review* 6: 27–32.
Hirsch, John C., ed. 2005. *Medieval Lyric: Middle English Lyrics, Ballads and Carols*. Oxford: Blackwell.
Hodgart, M. J. C. 1962. *The Ballads*. New York: Norton.
Holzapfel, Otto. 1978a. 'Svandinavian Folk Ballad Symbols, Epic Formulas and Verbal Traditions.' In Conroy 1978: 113–21.
—. 1978b. 'Skandinavische Volksballadenformeln: Merkmal traditioneller Improvisation oder literarischer/verbaler Tradierung?' *Sumlen* 50: 102–21.
—, ed. 1978c. *The European Medieval Ballad*. Odense: Odense UP.
—. 1980. *Det balladeske. Fortællemåden i den ældre episke folkevise*. Odense: Odense UP.
—. 1982. 'Narrative Technique in the German and Danish Ballads – a Stylistic Sample.' In Andersen, Holzapfel and Pettitt 1982: 101–52.
—. 1991. *Spuren der Tradition*. Studien zur Volksliedforschung 6. Bern: Lang.
Hruby, Antonin. 1949. 'Zur Entstehungsgeschichte der ältesten deutschen Balladen.' *Orbis Litterarum* 7: 1–30.
Jones, James H. 1961. 'Commonplace and Memorization in the Oral Tradition of the English and Scottish Popular Ballads.' *JAF* 74: 97–112.
Jonsson, Bengt R. 1956. 'Balladdiktning.' In *Kulturhistorisk Leksikon for nordisk middelalder*. Ed. Johannes Brøndsted et al. Copenhagen: Roskilde and Bagger. I, col. 316–21.
—. 1991. 'Oral Literature, Written Literature: The Ballad and Old Norse Genres.' In Harris 1991: 139–70.
—, Svale Solheim, and Eva Danielson, eds 1978. *The Types of the Scandinavian Medieval Ballad: A Descriptive Catalogue*. Stockholm: Svenkst Visarkiv.
Kirkland, Edward Capers. 1940. 'The Effect of Oral Tradition on "Robin Hood and Little John".' *Southern Folklore Quarterly* 4: 15–21.
Kværndrup, Sigurd. 2006. *Den østnordiske ballade – oral teori og tekstanalyse – Studier i 'Danmarks gamle Folkeviser'*. Copenhagen: Museum Tusculanums Forlag and University of Copenhagen.
Laws, G. M. 1957. *American Balladry from British Broadsides*. Philadelphia: American Folklore Society.
—. 1964. *Native American Balladry*. 2nd ed. Philadelphia: American Folklore Society.
Leach, M., and T. P. Coffin, eds. 1961. *The Critics and the Ballad*. Carbondale: Southern Illinois UP.
Lüthi, Max. 1973. 'Familienballade.' In Brednich et al. 1973: 89–100.
MacColl, Ewan, and Peggy Seeger, eds. 1977. *Travellers' Songs from England and Scotland*. London: Routledge and Kegan Paul.
Marcus, Millicent. 1989. 'Cross-Fertilizations: Folklore and Literature in *Decameron* 4,5.' *Italica* 66: 383–98.

McAlpine, Kaye. 1996. '"I'd gie them a": The Formula in "Geordie"and Other Ballads.' *Folklore* 107:71–76.
McCarthy, William Bernard. 1990. *The Ballad Matrix: Personality, Milieu, and the Oral Tradition*. Bloomington: Indiana UP.
McKean, Thomas A., ed. 2003a. *The Flowering Thorn: International Ballad Studies*. Logan: Utah State UP.
–. 2003b. 'The Stewarts of Fetterangus and Literate Oral Tradition.' In McKean 2003a: 181–201.
McMillan, Douglas J. 1964.'A Survey of Theories Concerning the Oral Transmission of the Traditional Ballad.' *Southern Folklore Quarterly* 28:299–308.
McWilliam, G. H., trans. 1995. Giovanni Boccaccio. *The Decameron*. 2nd ed. Harmondsworth: Penguin.
Meid, Volker. 1988. 'Glückliche Heimkehr. Zur Ballade vom alten Hildebrand.' In *Gedichte und Interpretationen: Deutsche Balladen*. Ed. Gunter E. Grimm. Stuttgart: Reclam. 29–37.
Meier, John. 1906. *Kunstlieder im Volksmunde. Materialien und Untersuchungen*. Halle: Niemeyer.
–, ed. 1935–36. *Balladen*. Das deutsche Volkslied 1–2. 2 vols. Leipzig: Reclam.
Mitsui, Tori. 1995.'How was "Judas" Sung?' In Porter 1995:241–50.
Moore, John Robert. 1916.'The Influence of Transmission on the English Ballads.' *Modern Language Review* 11:385–408.
Moreira, James. 1997.'Genre and Balladry.' In Cheesman and Rieuwerts 1997:95–109.
Neumann, Friedrich Wilhelm. 1980.'Zur Theorie und Ästhetik der Ballade.' In *Balladenforschung*. Ed. Walter Müller-Seidel. Hanstein: Athenäum. 24–36.
Niles, John D. 1999. *Homo Narrans: The Poetics and Anthropology of Oral Literature*. Philadelphia: Pennsylvania UP.
Nygard, Holger Olof. 1978.'Mrs. Brown's Recollected Ballads.' In Conroy 1978:68–87.
Ólason, Vésteinn. 1991.'Literary Backgrounds of the Scandinavian Ballad.' In Harris 1991:116–38.
Pettitt, Thomas. 1982a. '"Bold Sir Rylas" and the Struggle for Ballad Form.' *Lore and Language* 3.6A: 45–60.
–. 1982b. '"St Stephen and Herod" and the Songs of the Sloane Manuscript.' In Andersen, Holzapfel and Pettitt 1982:19–38.
–. 1984.'Mrs. Brown's "Lass of Roch Royal" and the Golden Age of Scottish Balladry.' *Jahrbuch für Volksliedforschung* 29:13–31.
–. 1994. '"Worn by the Friction of Time": Oral Tradition and the Generation of the Balladic Narrative Mode.' In *Contexts of Pre-Novel Narrative: The European Tradition*. Ed. Roy Eriksen. Berlin: de Gruyter. 341–72.
–. 1997a. 'The Ballad of Tradition: In Pursuit of a Vernacular Aesthetic.' In Cheesman and Rieuwerts 1997:111–23.
–. 1997b. 'Ballad Singers and Ballad Style: The Case of the Murdered Sweethearts.' In *The Entertainer in Medieval and Traditional Culture: A Symposium* Ed. Flemming G. Andersen, Thomas Pettitt, and Reinhold Schröder. Odense: Odense UP. 101–31.
–. 2008.'From Journalism to Gypsy Folk Song: The Road to Orality of an English Ballad.' *Oral Tradition* 23:87–117.
Piø, Iørn. 1977.'On Reading Orally Performed Ballads: The Medieval Ballads of Denmark.' In Bekker-Nielsen et al. 1977:69–82.
–. 1985. *Nye veje til Folkevisen* [New Approaches to the Ballad]. Copenhagen: Gyldendal.
Porter, James. 1976.'Jeannie Robertson's *My Son David*: A Conceptual Performance Model.' *JAF* 89:7–26.
–, ed. 1995. *Ballads and Boundaries: Narrative Song in an Intercultural Context*. Los Angeles: Department of Ethnomusicology and Systematic Musicology.
Præstgaard Andersen, Lise. 1981.'The Development of the Genres – the Danish Ballad.' *Sumlen* 53:25–35.

Putter, Ad. 2004. '*Fier Margrietken*: A Medieval Ballad and its History.' In Bennett and Green 2004: 69–88.
Reichl, Karl. 1973. *Religiöse Dichtung im Englischen Hochmittelalter: Untersuchung und Edition der Handschrift B.14.39 des Trinity College in Cambridge*. Texte u. Unters. zur engl. Phil. 1. Munich: Fink.
Renwick, Roger de V. 2002. 'The Oral Quality of a Printed Tradition.' *Acta Ethnographica Hungarica* 47: 81–89.
Reppert, James. 1974. 'F. J. Child and the Ballad.' In *The Learned and the Lewed*. Ed. Larry D. Benson. Cambridge, MA: Harvard UP. 197–212.
Richmond, W. Edson. 1963. '"Den Utrue Egtemann": A Norwegian Ballad and Formulaic Composition.' *Norveg* 10: 59–88.
–. 1972. 'Narrative Folk Poetry.' In *Folklore and Folklife: An Introduction*. Ed. Richard M. Dorson. Chicago: U of Chicago P. 85–98.
–. 1978. 'A New Look at the Wheel: An Essay in Defining the Ballad.' In Holzapfel 1978c: 86–97.
–. 1989. *Ballad Scholarship: An Annotated Bibliography*. New York: Garland.
–. 1990. 'Esse est percipi: A Poetic Genre Created by Perceptions.' In *Inte bara Visor*. Ed. Eva Danielsen et al. Stockholm: Svenskt Visarkiv. 313–38.
Rieuwerts, Sigrid. 1994. '"The Genuine Ballads of the People": F. J. Child and the Ballad Cause.' *Journal of Folklore Research* 31: 1–27.
–. 1995. 'From Percy to Child: The "Popular Ballad" as "a Distinct and very Important Species of Poetry".' In Porter 1995: 13–20.
Röhrich, Lutz. 1973a. 'Vorwort.' In Brednich et al. 1973: 7–18.
–. 1973b. 'Die Textgattungen des populären Liedes.' In Brednich et al. 1973: 19–35.
Rosenfeld, Hellmut. 1973. 'Heldenballade.' In Brednich et al. 1973: 57–87.
Rossel, Sven Hakon. 1971. *Den litterære vise i folketraditionen* [Artsongs in Folk Tradition]. Copenhagen: Akademisk Forlag.
Roth, Klaus. 1977. 'Zur mündlichen Komposition von Volksballaden.' *Jahrbuch für Volksliedforschung* 22: 49–65.
Rubin, David. C. 1995. *Memory in Oral Traditions: The Cognitive Psychology of Epic, Ballads, and Counting-out Rhymes*. New York: OUP.
Schmidt-Hidding, Wolfgang. 1933. 'Die Entwicklung der englisch-schottischen Volksballaden.' *Anglia*. 57: 1–77; 113–207.
Seemann, Erich. 1973. 'Die europäische Volksballade.' In Brednich et al. 1973: 37–56.
–, Dag Strömbäck, and Bengt R. Jonsson, eds. 1967. *European Folk Ballads*. European Folklore Series 2. Copenhagen: Rosenkilde and Bagger.
Sharp, Cecil J. 1936. *English Folksong: Some Conclusions*. 2nd ed. London: Novello, Simpkin Marshall.
Shields, Hugh. 1989. 'Chanson de toile et ballade populaire: problématique d'une comparaison.' In *Ballades et Chansons Folkloriques*. Ed. Conrad Laforte. Quebec: CÉLAT, Université Laval. 319–31.
–. 1991. 'Popular Modes of Narration and the Popular Ballad.' In Harris 1991: 40–59.
Simonsen, Michèle. 2003. 'The Corpus of French Ballads.' In McKean 2003a: 285–94.
Sønderholm, Erik. 1978. 'The Importance of the Oldest Danish Ballad Manuscripts for the Dating of the Ballad Genre.' In Conroy 1978: 231–37.
Steenstrup, Johannes C. H. R. 1914. *The Medieval Popular Ballad*. Trans. Edward Godfrey Cox. Boston: Ginn. [Rpt. Seattle: U of Washington P, 1968.]
Thigpen, Kenneth. 1973. 'A Reconsideration of the Commonplace Phrase and Commonplace Theme in the Child Ballads.' *Southern Folklore Quarterly* 37: 385–408.
von der Hagen, Friedrich Heinrich, and Johann Gustav Büsching, eds. 1818–25. *Deutsche Gedichte des Mittelalters*. 2 vols. Berlin.

Wallace, Wanda T., and David C. Rubin. 1988. '"The Wreck of the Old 97": A Real Event Remembered in Song.' In *Remembering Reconsidered: Ecological and Traditional Approaches to the Study of Memory*. Ed. Ulric Neisser and Eugene Winograd. Cambridge: CUP. 283–310.

Ward, Donald. 1978. 'The Origin of the Ballad: Urban Setting or Rural Setting?' In Conroy 1978: 46–57.

Wehse, Rainer. 1975. 'Broadside Ballad and Folksong: Oral Tradition versus Literary Tradition.' *Folklore Forum* 8: 324–34.

–. 1979. *Schwanklied und Flugblatt in Großbritannien*. Frankfurt a. M.: Lang.

Würzbach, Natascha. 1983. 'An Approach to a Context-Oriented Genre Theory in Application to the History of the Ballad: Traditional Ballad – Street Ballad – Literary Ballad.' *Poetics* 12: 35–70.

–. 1990. *The Rise of the English Street Ballad, 1550 – 1650*. Trans. Gayna Walls. Cambridge: CUP.

Yates, Mike. 2006. *Traveller's Joy: Songs of English and Scottish Travellers*. London: English Folk Dance and Song Society.

# 17 Medieval Greek Epic Poetry

*Elizabeth Jeffreys*

## 1 Preamble

Greek has a very long linguistic and literary tradition, with a complex history. In the ancient world Greek speakers were proverbially scattered round the Mediterranean like frogs round a pond (Plato, *Phaedo*, 109.b), but the heartland of Greek speech was to be found in the Balkan peninsula.[1] From here in the fourth and third centuries BCE, in the wake of the conquests of Alexander the Great, the use of Greek spread widely throughout the East beyond the fringes of the Mediterranean. Great cities established by Alexander, most notably Alexandria, became centres of a Greek literary culture. From the second and first centuries BCE, following the rise of Rome, Greek became the language of culture for the Romans (for whom skill *utrius linguae*, that is, in both Latin and Greek, was the mark of a civilised person), although throughout late antiquity a linguistic divide continued, with Latin the dominant language for day-to-day purposes in the Western Mediterranean and Greek in the East. Latin however remained the language of government throughout the Roman Empire. Subsequently, from the late sixth century CE, Greek became the main language of administration, education, literature and the church for the Byzantine world, the continuation of the Roman Empire in the East, based in Constantinople. The Byzantine Empire endured for nearly a millennium, with fluctuating boundaries and an interlude of Frankish domination in the thirteenth century following the diversion of the Fourth Crusade in 1204. Reduced to little more than the city of Constantinople itself, it finally fell to the Ottoman Turks in 1453. Throughout the period of the Tourkokratia, that is, the period when the Balkans and Anatolia were under the control of the Ottoman Empire prior to the independence movement of 1821 and the creation of the modern Greek state, Greek retained its cultural and linguistic significance in these areas – largely because of the major role taken by the Orthodox Church, in politics and education as well as in religious matters.[2]

Given then that there is a linguistic continuity in Greek in the east Mediterranean and given also that the South Slavic oral tradition analysed by Parry and Lord in the 1930s came from part of this region, *prima facie* it might not be unreasonable to look

---

[1] In areas now more or less co-terminous with the modern Greek state. For a convenient survey of the development of spoken Greek, see Horrocks 2010.
[2] The Ottoman *millet* system, defining subject peoples by religious affiliation, devolved much authority to their religious leaders, in this case, the Greek Patriarch; see, e. g., Clogg 1992: 10–15.

for a continuity of oral epic poetry. The factors that had led to the creation of the Homeric epics, that is, bards who composed orally on traditional subjects, might have lingered in the Greek-speaking world over the millennia with an unbroken tradition of orally narrated tales. Certainly this thought is present in Lord's writings, and the medieval Greek epic-romance *Digenis Akritis* is one of the texts examined in *Singer of Tales* (1960: 207–20).

However, unsurprisingly, this approach is too simplistic and produces meagre results. Examination of literature in medieval Greek for poetry with connections to an oral poetic tradition must proceed without reference to the ancient world.

## 2 Medieval Greek

Some background points are needed. Like all languages Greek has evolved, but whereas Latin, the dominant language of the Roman empire in the West, broke up into the modern Romance languages with the dissolution of the empire in the first centuries CE, the Greek of that time remained a unity. While there developed some distinct regional dialects, most notably now Cypriot and Pontic Greek, the differences have never become such as to lead to mutual incomprehensibility.[3] For this there were arguably two reasons. Greek had become the language of administration of the Byzantine empire, which was extensive, and on the whole stable; in a virtuous circle, regional vernaculars were not needed, as they were in the West, to confirm separate identities and ensure accurate communication, and so were under no pressure to stress their differences. Furthermore, Greek remained the language of an education which enshrined a culture whose linguistic rules, standards and literary canon had been established during the so-called Second Sophistic of the second and third centuries CE, a literary movement which urged a return to the norms of fifth-century BCE Attic Greek.[4] Christianity added another privileged stratum, based on the Septuagint and the Gospels. A consequence of this quasi-canonisation of different strata of the language was the development of what might be called a *diglossia*, the expectation that distinct registers of the language would be used for different purposes. In the case of Byzantine, or medieval, Greek, the register required for formal purposes – state administration, ecclesiastical texts, literature (however defined) – aimed at a close approximation to the Attic Greek of the Second Sophistic, and had to be formally learned by all Byzantines. Ecclesiastical texts used the Biblical register. The register for spoken Greek, which differed from the others in vocabulary, syntax and morphology (which had simplified steadily since the early years CE in the direction of today's Modern Greek),[5] was censored out of writing – with very occasional exceptions. Linguistic censorship of this sort does not provide conditions conducive to the recording of the special spoken discourse of oral epic or ballads. It is important to remember this when searching for evidence for epic or oral poetry in the medieval literature of Byzantium.

---

[3] Horrocks 2010: 84–88, 281; Mackridge 1985: 4–6.

[4] The First Sophistic was the period of the sophists and rhetors of the fourth century BCE, to whose literary and linguistic standards the Second Sophistic harked back; see Anderson 1993, Whitmarsh 2005.

[5] Gignac 1976–81: II, 414–21; Browning 1983: 29–38; Horrocks 2010: 273–324.

This leads to a further background point. Modern terminology for the registers of post-classical Greek can give rise to confusion. A convention has grown up, in English-based scholarship at least, that restricts 'Byzantine' to the Greek used for texts written in the higher linguistic registers (which, seen from today's perspective, represent a literary and linguistic dead-end) whilst the register used for texts written in something that approximates to the vernacular (and which may be seen as an antecedent for literature in Modern Greek) is termed 'medieval'; the implication is that these are two different forms of the language. However, this terminological distinction is misleading (M. Jeffreys 2007). Gradations between registers were flexible and dependent on context and training. Greek was constantly evolving in every register, whether formal or informal.[6] While committing a text to writing imposed one of the formal linguistic registers, nevertheless informal and vernacular forms were in use for spoken communication at all levels of society, elite and non-elite alike, whether measured by social status or level of education; orally circulating songs, ballads or stories in the vernacular would have been universally accessible.[7] However, literacy in the vernacular developed in Greek more slowly and less comprehensively than it did in the Romance languages (McKitterick 1994), and the taboos produced by linguistic censorship were broken only rarely between the sixth and the twelfth centuries, and not frequently after that.[8] When the taboos are broken one needs to ask why.

There are two moments when the Byzantine linguistic watch-dogs relaxed their vigilance and writing in the vernacular appeared in literary contexts: the first was in Komnenian Constantinople in the middle years of the twelfth century and the other came in the late thirteenth and early fourteenth centuries under the Palaiologan emperors.[9] The texts discussed in this chapter are the products of each phase, *Digenis Akritis* from the twelfth century and the remainder from the fourteenth.

## 3 Twelfth-Century Background

The middle years of the twelfth century were one of the most fertile periods in Byzantine literary history. For reasons that are not well understood, from the 1120s onwards there were present in Constantinople more lively well-trained writers and scholars than

---

[6] As demonstrated in every chapter of Horrocks 2010.
[7] The evidence for this is scattered, dependent on haphazard recording and transmission; examples would be the vernacular phrases occasionally cited in the *Peira*, the records of an eleventh-century judge (M. Jeffreys 2007: 63–64).
[8] The standard handbook on the texts involved in the breaking of these taboos is Beck 1971; M. Jeffreys 1996 offers some suggestions for the scenarios involved.
[9] Komnenian emperors: Alexios I (1081–1118), John II Komnenos (1118–1143), Manuel I Komnenos (1143–1180), Alexios II Komnenos (1180–1183), Andronikos I Komnenos (1183–1185). Palaiologan emperors: Michael VIII Palaiologos (1259–1282), Andronikos II Palaiologos (1282–1328), Michael IX Palaiologos (1294–1320), Andronikos III Palaiologos (1328–1341), John V Palaiologos (1341–1391), John VI Kantakouzenos (1341–1354), Andronikos IV Palaiologos (1376–1379), John VII Palaiologos (1390), Manuel II Palaiologos (1391–1425), John VIII Palaiologos (1425–1448), Constantine XI (XII) Palaiologos (1448–1453). For an over-view of these periods, see Mango 2002: 169–213, 248–83.

in the previous generation. There were also patrons who were willing to commission texts of all sorts. Sometimes these were encomiastic celebrations of national or domestic events or short dedicatory epigrams to accompany items of liturgical furnishing but they also included longer, more ambitious material, in prose as well as verse, though verse predominated. The patrons ranged over the social scale from the emperors through their courtiers and their families to abbots of monasteries.[10] The experiments produced under this patronage ranged from a verse chronicle to four novels which were pastiches in verse of the novels of late antiquity, to a handful of verse satires on contemporary Constantinopolitan life which switched from formal to vernacular levels for literary effect.[11] The satires are known as the *Ptochoprodromika* (Poems of Penniless Prodromos [the Fore-Runner]).[12] Of the writers perhaps the most versatile was Theodore Prodromos (*c.* 1100–*c.* 1157). In addition to producing commentaries on ecclesiastical texts, some hagiography, letters and much encomiastic verse (and quite probably also the *Ptochoprodromika*),[13] he dedicated his novel, much indebted to Heliodorus' *Aithiopika*, to a Caesar, almost certainly Nikephoros Bryennios, who died in 1138.[14] For their plots all four of the Komnenian 'novels'[15] draw heavily on the novelists from late antiquity,[16] but much of their content can be viewed as a loosely linked sequence of *ekphraseis* (descriptions) or other rhetorical exercises set against tales of hazardous elopement in a vaguely sketched ancient world. These are products of a competitive educational environment where bright young men are demonstrating their skills to prospective employers, often in a *theatron* or literary salon where texts were performed and discussed. The novels are but one of the literary genres inherited from antiquity to be the subject of *mimesis* (imitation) at this time;[17] they will have a place in the discussion of *Digenis Akritis*. The *Prochoprodromika* and the other texts that slip into the vernacular are a little different, though the intention was undoubtedly also to attract notice from prospective employers.[18]

---

[10] Magdalino 1993a: 335–356, with a list of patrons at 510–12.
[11] For the standard account of these texts, see Hunger 1978: I, 419–22, II, 119–42, and Beck 1971: 101–9.
[12] The best edition is Eideneier 1991.
[13] For a full list of his works, see Hörandner 1974: 37–72. The authorship of the *Ptochoprodromika* is a vexed issue, further confused by the existence of a contemporary anonymous poet conventionally known as Manganeios Prodromos (*ODB* s. v.).
[14] E. Jeffreys 2000; Agapitos 2000. Nikephoros Bryennios, son-in-law of Alexios I, brother-in-law of John I and husband of Anna Komnene, was a man of letters (author of a history and member of a literary salon) as well as a man of war: E. Jeffreys 2003.
[15] *A&K*: Manasses' *Aristander and Kallithea*; *D&Ch*: Eugenianos' *Drosilla and Charikles*; *H&H*: Makrembolites' *Hysmene and Hysmenias*; *R&D*: Prodromos, *Rhodanthe and Dosikles*. A convenient edition of all these, with an Italian translation, is Conca 1994; note also a forthcoming English translation (E. Jeffreys 2012).
[16] For an excellent analysis of the use made of Achilles Tatius by Makrembolites in his *H&H*, see Nilsson 2001; for a thoughtful analysis of all novels, see Roilos 2005.
[17] On Byzantine educational goals, see Markopoulos 2008. On *mimesis*, the classic statement is Hunger 1969–70. Other genres for which pastiches were produced in the first half of the twelfth century include tragedy (*Katomyomachia*, *Christos Paschon*) and essays in the style of Lucian (*Charidemos*, *Timarion*): Hunger 1978: II, 142–56.
[18] The chief texts are the poem of advice known as *Spaneas*, the poem from prison of Michael Glykas, the *Eisiterioi* for Agnes of France and some passages in Manganeios Prodromos' petitions to the

There the shifts in register might be attributed to the poets' response to the developing tastes of their imperial patrons, influenced perhaps by the realisation, following the influx of crusading Westerners, that the vernacular could be used to good effect.[19] The results however were limited in extent and brief in duration.

## 4 *Digenis Akritis*

At this point the discussion turns to *Digenis Akritis* (*DA*), the only text that can be classed as a medieval Greek – or Byzantine – epic, though that classification is frequently challenged. Primarily it is epic because the central figure, Digenis, is male, performing valiant deeds against wild beasts and other foes, both human and supernatural, in a historical setting that is reminiscent of one of Byzantium's more heroic periods in the ninth and tenth centuries. But there is a certain amount of romance, in two love-stories, first between Digenis' parents and then between Digenis and his bride. The hero is literally 'di-genis', that is, 'double-born' or 'of Double Descent'. He is also a man of the frontier: his life was spent patrolling the territory lying between the shifting Byzantine-Arab borders (*akra*). Digenis' father was an Arab emir, who is the major character of the first part of the story, part of which is told from an Arab point of view. The emir, on a raid into Byzantine Cappadocia, seized a Greek girl, daughter of the provincial governor. Out of love for her, when defeated by her brother in single combat, he decided to be baptised, to marry her and to come over to the Byzantine side. When their son Digenis was born, he grew up very quickly, passed a *rite de passage* in hunting, and then followed family tradition by stealing a bride from another Byzantine castle. After a sumptuous wedding, he settled down to a solitary life (with his wife) as a kind of policeman of a large tract in the east of the Byzantine Empire, near the river Euphrates and the Arab border. But the criminals he defeated seem to be largely Christian Greek irregular troops or shape-changing *drakontes* rather than the Arab forces who were the most prominent of Byzantium's external foes. He finally built a palace by the Euphrates and died young and childless, with his wife immediately expiring beside him from grief.

This episodic tale survives in six manuscripts dating from the early fourteenth to the mid-seventeenth centuries, discovered and published between 1871 and 1926. All manuscript versions tell recognizably the same story but with variants in wording and choice of episodes. All are written in the fifteen-syllable line, first found in written form in the tenth century and later becoming the standard metre for Greek folk-song.[20] From 1871, when a version of the text was found (in the Soumela monastery near Trebizond), it was immediately recognised as an extended version of the tales about Digenis or Akritis long known from ballads sung and collected in Anatolia and throughout Greek-speaking lands.[21] The text was commandeered to serve as the National Epic of the Greek

---

emperor; all are written in the fifteen-syllable line. In all these imperial patronage plays a role. Dedicatees of the *Ptochoprodromika* include the emperors John II and Manuel I.

[19] The points made in E. Jeffreys 1980 are still valid.
[20] The fifteen-syllable line became the national metre of Modern Greece; on its history see M. Jeffreys 1974 and Lauxtermann 1999.
[21] This version is referred to as T. All manuscripts (= versions) of *DA* are conventionally known by

state, the modern equivalent of Homer or the European *Beowulf* or *Cid*. These nationalistic overtones have long haunted *DA*, exacerbated by the Greek Language Question, the long struggle between the vernacular (*demotike*) and learned (*katharevousa*) versions of Greek for the status of national language. The two primary versions of *DA* could be seen as forerunners of these two registers. In the language debates of the late nineteenth and early twentieth centuries it was important to know which was the authentic language of the nation's epic.[22]

17 – Digenis and a Princess, Byzantine glazed plate (12th c.), Archaeological Museum of Ancient Corinth

Work over the last thirty years has clarified much about the transmission of the six versions.[23] It is now clear that the four sixteenth- and seventeenth-century manuscripts are derived from an early sixteenth-century compendium (lost long ago; it has been christened Z by Erich Trapp). Whilst of interest in their own right, these later versions can be

---

initials of their find spots or first editors. On the ballads, see Beck 1971: 87–93, Beaton 1980: 78–82.

[22] Browning 1983: 100–15; Mackridge 1985: 6–10.

[23] For bibliography and a survey of earlier work, see Beck 1971: 63–97. Subsequent bibliography can be found in the standard editions: Trapp 1971, Alexiou 1985, E. Jeffreys 1998.

left to one side when the origins of the poem are considered.[24] For this, focus has to be on the two earliest, the Grottaferrata version (= G) and the Escorial version (= E).[25] Further back than these two in the reconstruction of the earliest form of the text it is impossible to go. While extensive passages show a virtually identical sequence of episodes (see Table on p. 478 for the structure of *DA*) and much wording in common[26] this commonality of material frequently breaks down, and is then obscured further by variations of register when choices have to be made at the lexical level. The question then arises as to whether G, in a more learned but also clumsy register of Greek, or E, in a much more fluid vernacular, better represents the text which must lie behind them both. The academic debate was not aided by the fact that E was for long only available in a poor edition – a situation remedied with Stylianos Alexiou's interventionist edition in 1985 which revealed the text's quality. Recent editorial work has suggested that both G and E need to be accepted as equally valid representatives of a text that has been through a complex transmission process; they are probably also equally deficient representations of earlier forms.[27] It has also become quite clear that both in their present forms are the product of a copying process, as Alexiou's work on E has demonstrated.[28] G is plainly a version created in writing, but the irregularities of E in its old edition were such that plausible suggestions were made that it could be an oral dictated text (notably Morgan 1960).

It is possible to comment on the nature of the text that lies behind G and E, which for convenience can be called *Digenis*. It was episodic and abrupt,[29] made up of discrete events loosely strung together to make a biography of the hero, as can be seen from the sections listed in the Table;[30] its language combined both vernacular and high-level features;[31] and names and incidents involving its characters arguably reflect scattered incidents in the wars of the ninth and tenth centuries against Arab invaders and heretic Christians.[32] However both G and E, and so *Digenis* also, echo some of the romantic interests, and phrases, found in the novels of the 1130s–1150s and derived from models

---

[24] The interdependence of manuscripts T (Trebizond), A (Athens), P (now in Thessaloniki), O (Oxford) was shown by Kyriakidis 1946, whose conclusions were put into practice in Trapp's edition (1971). On the nature of Z, see Trapp 1971: 26–33 and M. Jeffreys 1975.

[25] G is a South Italian manuscript of c. 1300; editions: Trapp 1971, E. Jeffreys 1998 (with English translation). E is late fifteenth century; editions: Alexiou 1985; E. Jeffreys 1998 (with English translation).

[26] Beaton 1993a; E. Jeffreys 1998: 26–30.

[27] Editorial theory for the treatment of texts like *DA* was the subject of the conference Neograeca Medii Aevi IVa (Hamburg, 1999), published as Eideneier, Moennig and Toufexis 2001: debate was vigorous and the conclusions mixed.

[28] E. g. the word division at E792 demonstrates that the text was copied from a manuscript with a lacuna; see further Alexiou 1985: ιζ'-κβ'.

[29] Alexiou 1985: λβ'-λς'; Ricks 1989.

[30] On the development of biographical love-stories which end with the death of one or both of the protagonists, which include *DA*, *Ach* and *A&S* (for abbreviations see notes 49–51 below), see Moennig 2004: 46–49, 65–69.

[31] Beaton 1993b, using a computer generated concordance of G and E, lists core material attributable to the 'Lay of the Emir' which demonstrates the shifts in register. For the concordance, see Beaton, Kelly, and Lendari 1995.

[32] See Oikonomidès 1979 for a good discussion of the issues, and also Alexiou 1985: νδ'-ξη'.

from the Second Sophistic, especially Achilles Tatius.[33] Moreover the lion-wrestling scene from G4.112–29 is parodied in the *Ptochoprodromika* (I.160–177), dedicated to John I Komnenos (d. 1143) and almost certainly by Theodore Prodromos, author of one of the novels.[34] There is thus a good case that *Digenis should be attached to the novel-writing movement of Komnenian Constantinople. One could argue that it represents the results of a, not very successful, experiment, an attempt to set a 'novel' in Byzantium's own recent past rather than a blurred late antiquity, taking some intriguingly vernacular ballads and structuring them as a biography ending in death rather than as a romance with a happy end in the protagonists' marriage, as in the novels.[35]

From this it follows that, although *DA* is set in Byzantium's eastern frontier on the Euphrates, the connection with the Constantinopolitan literary elite makes the capital the most likely, indeed the only probable, place for the poem's composition.[36] Arguably the raw material for the 'epic', by this scenario consisting of ballads dealing with the hero's exploits on the frontier and his father's battles in the Byzantine-Arab wars of ninth and tenth centuries,[37] circulated orally in his 'home territory' and was then brought to Constantinople. It has been suggested that refugees were responsible for this, in the wake of Turkish invasions in the decades around the battle of Manzikert in 1071.[38] Movement between Constantinople and the frontier areas was constant and from the late eleventh century onwards the appearance of the Western Crusading armies added to the traffic. Byzantine armies, whose leaders included Nikephoros Bryennios, the probable dedicatee of Prodromos' *R&D*, were in Cilicia, and Digenis territory, in the 1130s.

All that has been said thus far deals with the written aspects of the *Digenis* text as we now have it, referring back to ballads on Digenis's exploits hypothetically circulating in an oral form from the ninth and tenth centuries onwards. Certainly ballads with Digenis as the central figure were sung in Greek-speaking areas until very recent times (though contamination from electronic as well as written versions is now very likely) (Beaton 1986). It is simpler to deal with the later ballads first since the evidence for their existence is undeniable. Examples were collected from the late eighteenth and early nineteenth century onwards with an influential collection edited and translated by Fauriel in

---

[33] E. g. G4.276–80, see Achilles Tatius 1.4.4–5 (effects of love); G7.14–41, E1657–8, see Achilles Tatius 1.15.1–8 (a garden); G6.782, see Achilles Tatius 1.1.11, *H&H* 2.4.3 (a girl's tunic).

[34] The scene is also found in E764-77 but without the phrases for cap, kilt and club that here link G and the *Ptochoprodromika*. Ptochoprodromos 4.539-52 refers to John's son Manuel as a second Akritis. Eideneier cautions that the dedicatory titles of the *Ptochoprodromika* are not necessarily reliable.

[35] Not all students of this subject would agree with this formulation; Beaton, for example, puts the composition of the earliest form of *Digenis* in the late eleventh century (Beaton 1996a: 50). The present author, whilst linking *Digenis with the fashion for writing novels, has previously suggested a date in the 1150s, when Manuel I was on campaign on the Euphrates borders (E. Jeffreys 1998: lvi-lvii). Debate continues.

[36] Evocations of a Syrian monk musing on the deeds of Digenis deal with the physical but not the literary context of the poem (e. g. Mavrogordato 1956: lxxix).

[37] Names cited in the emir's genealogy have been identified with the Paulician heretics Chrysocheir (d. 878/9), Karbeas (d. 863) and 'Umar, emir of Melitene (d. 863), who fought with the Muslims against Basil I (Lemerle 1973: 85–103).

[38] Magdalino 1993b; Beaton 1996b.

1824–1825; other collections followed.[39] An early written witness to ballad material is found in a seventeenth-century manuscript, with musical notation attached, now kept in the Iviron monastery on Mount Athos (Bouvier 1960); this group of songs is of especial interest because one seems to link the Digenis-story of the nineteenth-century ballads to the medieval narrative. Do the Iviron texts show a continuous tradition of transmission from the middle Byzantine period through to the early years of the Tourkokratia and beyond? There is no satisfactory answer: the seventeenth-century texts are brief and the resemblances to either later or earlier texts are of episode rather than details of wording. There are some marked resemblances between the wording, metrical usages and line structure of some of the nineteenth-century ballads and the text in E, and this has given rise to debate as to whether the ballads are really independent survivals or merely a worn-down reflection of the Byzantine text (Beck 1971: 48–63). There are enough tantalising similarities to indicate a relationship of some sort.[40] But it must be remembered that copies of the Z text were available in the Balkans in the eighteenth century and could well have contaminated whatever singing tradition was in existence. Two at least of these manuscripts were seen by the learned monk Kaisarios Dapontes (1714–1784), who lamented that *Digenis* had never been printed.[41] The wider question whether the oral ballads of the Tourkokratia still preserve something of the ballads from the ninth and tenth centuries (the likely origin of *Digenis) is even more problematic. Evidence for the very existence of these earlier ballads is slight: besides hazy memories of the past surviving in G and E, there are scanty references in historians, most notably the comment in Psellos' *Chronographia* (c. 1080) on the tales (not necessarily songs) told of the Doukas clan. It is noteworthy that this is a family which figures prominently in Digenis' genealogy.[42] Yet Digenis himself shows no interest in historical epic; though the hero has been well instructed in the art of music (G4. 396–40, E826–34), he sings love-songs, not tales of heroic valour.

A search in formal aspects of G and E for signs of contact with an oral past gives limited results. The presence of repeated phrases and lines is usually taken as one of the most indicative tests as they may be oral formulas. There are a few repeated phrases in G and rather more in E. Lines already mentioned as virtually identical in both manuscripts[43] are evidence for the existence of the earlier *Digenis, not formulaic density. Other repeated phrases and lines, whether appearing only in one version or – less commonly – in both, suggest that both versions (and so *Digenis) are drawing on a shared pool of phraseology, arguably oral in origin (Beaton 1993b). But the statistics which these phrases generate are very low,[44] with most consisting of name and epithet, of the type 'Akritis the bold' (*Akriten ton gennaion*, Ἀκρίτην τὸν γενναῖον). When G and E are examined separately, G emerges as having been thoroughly worked over in a literate and

---

[39] Fauriel 1824–25; Passow 1860.
[40] Prombonas 1985; Sifakis 1989; Fenik 1991.
[41] Dapontes' paraphrases of the texts he had seen (one in an illustrated manuscript) allow these to be connected to the O version of Digenis, which has a (probably authorial) date of 1670; his comments are cited from (the still) unpublished *Biblos Basileion* (Book of Kings) by Lambros 1880: xcix–ci.
[42] E. Jeffreys 1998: xxxix, and genealogy at xxxvi.
[43] Beaton 1993a for the 14 lines completely identical in both and lists of others that are nearly so.
[44] E. Jeffreys 1998: lv; Lord 1960: 213.

literary manner by a redactor who added gnomic sayings and allusions from hagiography.[45] E, however, which – as noted above – shows rhythms and phrases that have parallels with later folk song, including songs independent of the *Digenis* material, also has rather more repetitions (Alexiou 1985: πς-πθ). These are the features that have driven the arguments that E both reflects the genuine, uncorrupted language of the people and must be closest to the original form of the *Digenis* poem.

Very striking is the *Son of Armouris*, a poem of some 200 lines, essentially a long ballad, which is preserved in two manuscripts of which one is dated scribally to 1461 and is thus more or less contemporary to E.[46] Many phrases and many of the plot situations in the *Son of Armouris* echo the Arab-Byzantine environment envisaged in the *Digenis* poem and, more particularly, details found in E. This suggests that the *Digenis* material continued to circulate, though whether orally (as the style implies) or only in written form is debatable: both manuscripts of the *Song of Armouris* have palaeographical errors produced in copying and so neither was transcribed from performance (Alexiou 1985: 160).

Byzantium's only epic poses many riddles. Its generation and transmission must at some point have involved orally disseminated material: stories, almost certainly in verse, about the legendary past and a lone hero of Arab-Byzantine parentage would have circulated in the frontier areas on the banks of the Euphrates. Our evidence for their existence comes from Psellos' comments on tales told of the Doukas family. At some point these ballad stories were brought to Constantinople. Using the evidence of G and E it can be argued that they were limited in scope: they reflected the Arab-Byzantine society of the frontier and told of the hero's clashes with groups of bandits, how he hunted wild beasts, abducted a bride, built a palace and met an early death. It was probably in the 1130s and 1140s, when it became fashionable in Constantinopolitan literary circles to write narratives in the manner of the novelists of late antiquity, that an attempt was made to string this material about the hero Digenis into a biographical sequence and trim it with appropriate romantic elements. It may well have been this material's vernacular background that attracted those who were then experimenting with varied genres and language levels. This novel, or romance, on Digenis was never rounded out and it remained a sketch, a loosely linked sequence of episodes: it is this, *\*Digenis*, which lies behind G and E. It would have been in the fifteen-syllable line, linguistically and metrically awkward, with imitations of Achilles Tatius and Heliodoros at some key points. It thus exemplified the difficulties that even the boldest spirit faced when attempting to break through the cultural barriers imposed by Byzantium's linguistic taboos. Before the middle of the twelfth century one of its episodes was lampooned in the *Ptochoprodromika*.

## 5 The Fourteenth Century and Oral Poetry

However, even if linguistic censorship has removed almost all the possible written evidence for Byzantine epic, there are sufficient pointers of other sorts from texts of the

---

[45] Odorico 1989; Trapp 1976.
[46] The best edition is that in Alexiou 1985; English translation in Ricks 1990.

fourteenth century, to construct arguments that oral traditions existed and exerted influence at that date. The works concerned are all in the fifteen-syllable verse, and also in a register of Greek which, despite variations, is closer to the vernacular in morphology and syntax than was normally permitted. Their language also includes a puzzling mix of forms which normally belong to different dialects or different temporal strata of Greek.[47] There are some indications that these features made up an artificial poetic language for the fifteen-syllable verse, but also that the Greek of the period was itself full of linguistic variants. The texts appeared at some point in the early fourteenth century (and possibly the late thirteenth), in Palaeologan Constantinople and the Greek-speaking lands in which Frankish rulers had established states following the division of Byzantine territory after the sack of Constantinople in 1204. The most significant of these Franco-Greek areas was that of the Morea, in the Peloponnese.[48] The texts are, with one possible exception, anonymous and their dates of production continue to be debated. They include chronicles;[49] romances, some with French, Italian or Turkish originals, others apparently original compositions;[50] animal-fables and satire, including a retelling with fourteenth-century overtones of the legendary career of the sixth-century general Belisarios;[51] and narratives of contemporary warfare.[52]

Despite their disparate subject-matter, these texts share sufficient common characteristics to justify their being treated as a group, notably their metre and their language. Furthermore, when a text survives in more than one manuscript then the variants are such that it is impossible to collate the readings into one primary version by conventional editorial principles. Finally, these texts share a noticeably large number of repeated lines, repeated both within a given poem and also across several, even the whole corpus. Because none of these features were fostered by the regular Byzantine education, these texts have had low esteem, derided as the inefficient products of semi-literate would-be poets.[53] However it was precisely this combination of features that led Constantine Trypanis (1963) to claim for this group an oral poetic composition of the type described in *The Singer of Tales*, thus vindicating their 'uncouth' style and other oddities. This initial

---

[47] Browning 1983: 5–12, 69–87; Horrocks 2010: 342–67.
[48] The history and culture of this area is usefully surveyed in Lock 1995.
[49] *CoM*: Chronicle of the Morea (Schmitt 1904); *ChTocco*: Chronicle of Tocco (Schirò 1975). On the texts listed in this and the following three notes, see Beck 1971; Knös 1961 is also worth consulting, particular on post–1453 material.
[50] *A&S (Alexander and Semiramis)*: Moennig 2004 (version of Persian-Ottoman *Ferec ba'd eş-şide*); *Ach (Tale of Achilles)*: Cupane 1995; *ByzIl (Byzantine Iliad)*: Nørgaard and Smith 1975; *K&Ch (Kallimachos and Chrysorrhoe)*: Cupane 1995; *I&M (Imberios and Margarona)*: Kriaras 1955 (version of French *Pierre de Provence et la belle Maguelonne*); *L&R (Livistros and Rhodamne)*: Agapitos 2006a (recension α), Lendari 2007 (ms.V); *Ph&P (Phlorios and Platzia-flora)*: Cupane 1995 (version of Tuscan *Cantare di Florio e Platzia flore*); *V&Ch (Velthandros and Chrysantza)*: Cupane 1995; *Peri E&D (On Good and Bad Fortune)*: Cupane 1995; *WoT (War of Troy)*: Papathomopoulos and Jeffreys 1996 (version of Benoît de Ste Maure's *Roman de Troie*).
[51] *Poul (Poulologos)*: Tsavari 1987; *Quadrupeds*: Nicholas and Baloglou 2003; *Belis (Belisarios)*: Bakker and van Gemert 1988.
[52] Such as the *Battle of Varna* of 1444 (Legrand 1875). For post-1453 examples, such as Achelis' *Siege of Malta* (1572) or Diakrousis and Bounialis on the Veneto-Turkish Cretan Wars, see Knös 1961: 227–32 and, e. g., Kaklamanis 2005.
[53] Often classified in manuscript catalogues as written 'graeco-barbare'.

claim was taken up by others in close studies of several texts, most notably the romance *I&M* and the chronicle *CoM*.[54] These studies accepted from the start that these works were composed and circulated in writing, though their poets were under fairly direct influence from oral poets. Trypanis himself, on the other hand, went on to make sweeping claims for the role of oral composition throughout Greek literature of the time (1981:498–505).

The most convincing evidence that this group of fourteenth-century texts has been produced against a background in oral poetry takes the form of a high 'formula' count in certain of them, using the terminology and definitions of Milman Parry and Albert Lord (1960: 3–12). The text that has been used most rigorously to demonstrate a formulaic texture is the *CoM*:[55] analyses by Michael Jeffreys produced a formulaic density of 31.7%. This figure (meaningless in itself) is to be contrasted with a formulaic density of 12% in an almost exactly contemporary text, the Byzantine *Alexander Poem*, in the same metre and similar language, thus suggesting different circumstances of composition.[56] Analyses of several more texts in this group demonstrated that they show a formula count which ranges from around 35% to a barely perceptible level, around 12%.[57] The *WoT*, with a high formula count (29.3%),[58] is also a translation of the twelfth-century *Roman de Troie* of Benoît de Ste Maure; the relationship is sufficiently close that the French original can often be used in the selection of readings from the Greek manuscript variants. This is a classic combination of a text undoubtedly produced by literate means with elements of an orally based style, with parallels, for example, in the Middle High German texts examined by Bäuml (1980 and 1984). His conclusion that the stylistic features represent an attempt to give texts validation by reference to an earlier authoritative traditional style is relevant to the Greek situation. Moreover, the *WoT* is not unique: *Ph&P* is similarly close to its Italian original and similarly has a significant proportion of repeated phrases.

Other indices are regularly used as signs of the influence of oral composition, for example, themes. Recent work by Teresa Shawcross on *CoM* shows that this text has a thematic system for the presentation of speech acts arguably deriving from a degenerate oral poetry.[59] The analysis made by Ulrich Moennig of narrative techniques in *A&S* also reveals a patterning of meetings and speeches (2004: 115–30).

Attempts to find references to singers in contemporary Byzantine writers have produced disappointingly scanty – though nonetheless suggestive – results, such as the references in the historical work of Gregoras to travellers singing of the 'deeds of men' (E.

---

[54] E. Jeffreys and M. Jeffreys 1971; M. Jeffreys 1973.
[55] As will be discussed below this was composed in the fourteenth century and survives in several languages; see Shawcross 2005 and 2009, for a careful recontextualising of the Greek and the French versions.
[56] M. Jeffreys 1973: 11 (formulaic density of *CoM*), 12 (formulas in *Alexander*),
[57] M. Jeffreys 1993:54, note 12; other figures for formulaic density: *I&M* 35.7%, *Ach* (Oxford version) 35%, *Belisarios* 34.2%, *Ach* (Naples version) 29.2%, *Ph&P* 22.4%, *V&Ch* 19.4%, *K&Ch* 12.1%; preliminary investigations into *L&R* suggest that this has a high formula count. Moennig 2004: 146–55 discusses the formulaic texture of *A&S*.
[58] E. Jeffreys and M. Jeffreys 1979; 119; Papathomopoulos and E. Jeffreys 1996: lxxxi–lxxxvi.
[59] Shawcross 2005. *DA* is more productive of themes: Fenik 1991.

Jeffreys and M. Jeffreys 1986: 507–9). Within the texts themselves and most notably in *L&R*, as with *DA* earlier, characters are not infrequently shown singing, but songs of love rather than brave deeds. However, many of the texts include a conventional summons to an audience to gather round to hear the tale that is to be told.[60]

This is an ambivalent situation, of a sort regularly encountered in the literatures of medieval Europe, where a high incidence of repetitions is balanced against a relative paucity of other markers of orality. The explanation for the Greek texts must be, as elsewhere, that they were composed in writing by poets who were familiar with a tradition of orally composed and performed poetry and wished to emulate this in a written form. Other relevant issues concern the audience to whom these texts were directed and whether the texts were to be heard or read.

Detailed suggestions made in the 1970s that the repeated phrases and lines could be interpreted as a marker of indebtedness to traditions of oral composition were read as claims for direct oral composition. One immediate reaction, without addressing the issue of internal repetitions, was that the common lines shared between several texts were due to a school of poets who plagiarised each other's work (e. g. Spadaro 1975, 1976 and 1978). Subsequently Arnold van Gemert suggested, with good examples from the problematic ending to *Ach*, that copyists might have been responsible for some of the variants (van Gemert and Bakker 1981). Hans Eideneier, who has different arguments for an oral stratum in medieval Greek literary texts, pointed out examples of errors in manuscripts apparently attributable to an internal dictation, introducing another aspect of orality (1982–83 and 1999). Roderick Beaton attempted a compromise position which allowed for elements of a traditional oral style in combination with a school of poets (1996a: 164–88). Others remained in general unsympathetic to the texts under analysis (to discover the formula-level of the *CoM* did not make it any the better as poetry)[61] and were unwilling to accept that an oral background gave any insights into their nature: a major stumbling block would appear to be the differences between the medieval texts and the folksong and ballads in Modern Greek, thus postulating (improbably) the existence of two distinct traditions. Others again did not confront the issue of oral backgrounds overtly but responded by implication. Thus Panagiotis Agapitos has pointed out the bookish features of the manuscripts in which many of these texts survive: the integral role of rubrics and illustrations, the learned scribes, the internal references to reading and literate composition.[62] His insights are driven by detailed work on the structures and narrative devices of *L&R*, *K&Ch* and *V&Ch* which show an authorial mind-set developed in a literate literary culture (1991).

Since the early stages of this debate a number of issues have been clarified, to a greater or lesser extent. These include: the texts' language, their manuscripts, the scribes, their indebtedness to twelfth-century antecedents, the court environment to which they allude. On-going editorial work has resulted in clearer insight into dating. Editorial tech-

---

[60] Cupane 1994–95. For an intricate discussion of the interweaving of recitation and writing in the Palaeologan romances see Agapitos 2006b.
[61] Mackridge 1990, reporting a colloquium debating the nature of orality, set up in response to current debates stimulated by modish interest in Walter Ong's *Orality and Literacy* (1982).
[62] Agapitos and Smith 1994; Agapitos 2006b.

niques have been problematised.⁶³ It cannot be sufficiently stressed that it has long been clear that all these texts were produced by written means, and that not one can be an oral dictated text: they are the products of a literate culture which has retained some of the trappings of orality.

*Language.* The mixed nature of the vernacular of these texts had caused much debate in the early years of the twentieth century when tensions over the Language Question in Greece were high.⁶⁴ Suggestions that this phenomenon might have a parallel in the mixed Homeric language, preserved by metrical pressures, were mentioned in the initial proposals for an oral background to the fourteenth-century texts (M. Jeffreys 1973: 193). These proposals assumed too much regularity in the spoken language of the time which contained many variations. In particular, an appreciation of the language of vernacular prose, admittedly largely post-Byzantine rather than Palaeologan, indicates the morphology and syntax found in vernacular verse is not as unusual as once thought.⁶⁵

*Manuscripts and scribes.* It is now much better understood that careful consideration must be given to each manuscript in which a text of this type survives, that each has played an individual role in the transmission of the text and that to attempt to produce a unified edition is often unrealistic. Each manuscript has its own validity as a version of the text. It is significant too, as Chatizyakoumis has pointed out (1977), that most of the manuscripts are late (i. e., sixteenth century) and a noticeable proportion were copied in the West for western scholars. Furthermore, many others make up collected volumes, put together when vernacular Greek culture was under pressure of dissolution in the early years of the Tourkokratia.⁶⁶ A number of the scribes can be shown to have copied material in a range of registers (ecclesiastical and high-register secular as well as vernacular).⁶⁷ The rubricated titles, and also the illustrations (or rather, spaces for illustrations), that accompany many of the texts (*WoT, L&R, Peri E&D,* etc) have been shown to be authorial and not scribal (Agapitos and Smith 1994), thus firmly locating these texts in a literate environment.

*Indebtedness to twelfth-century novels.* One of the motifs that recurs in the romances in this group of texts is that of the castle, its associated garden and the heroine it protects: it appears in *L&R, K&C, B&C, Ach, Peri E&D*. The origins and function of this motif have been debated at length but inconclusively.⁶⁸ However, a consensus is now emerging that, for example, the elaborately allegorical castles of *L&R*, with their figures of the Virtues and the Months (*L&R* recension α 1023–1252, *L&R* ms. V 801–1012),

---

⁶³ See the discussions in Eideneier, Moennig and Toufexis 2001. Each text imposes its own issues and editorial solutions: these include reliance on stemmatic relationships (*Poul*: Tsavari 1987; *WoT*: Papathomopulos and Jeffreys 1996), presentation of versions synoptically (*Belis*: Bakker and van Gemert 1988), edition of single manuscripts (*Ach*: Smith 1990, 1999), or eclecticism (*L&R*: Agapitos 2006a).

⁶⁴ The chief protagonists in this aspect of the debate were Jean Psycharis (1824–1929) and Georgios Chatzidakis (1848–1941); Browning 1983: 9–10, 107–8.

⁶⁵ See the studies on early vernacular prose by Eleni Kakoulidou-Panou and her team of researchers in E. Jeffreys and M. Jeffreys 2005: 461–539.

⁶⁶ Such as Vindob. theol. gr. 244. See the papers in Holton 2005, deriving from a conference which focused on the nature of collected manuscripts of Byzantine and early vernacular Greek texts.

⁶⁷ E. g. Reinsch 2005; Hinterberger 2005.

⁶⁸ Recent useful discussions include Cupane 1978, Littlewood 1979, Agapitos 1991.

were devised with full knowledge of the equally elaborate *ekphraseis* of the twelfth-century *H&H*.

*Court environment.* Studies on *K&C*, *V&C*, *A&S* and to a lesser extent *L&R* have shown the extent to which references to procedures derived from practices of the Palaeologan imperial court, such as *proskynesis* (ritual prostration), titles of officials, the issuing of decrees, are embedded in the settings of the romances.[69] However, the presence of such details does not necessarily imply composition at court.

*Insights into dating.* The cumulative effect of recent work is to push the dating of several of the texts in this group towards the middle of the fourteenth century. The *CoM* survives in multiple versions, in Greek, French, Aragonese, and Italian; each has its own rationale and for each it is possible to suggest a date. From a combination of internal evidence and manuscript watermarks, it can be concluded that the basic version was initially constructed *c.* 1320, while the oldest surviving Greek version (in verse) dates from the 1380s and the French prose version from *c.* 1340; Teresa Shawcross (2009) argues both that the Greek and the French versions conform to the contemporary conventions of the language in which they are composed, and that Greek was the language of the original text.[70] This text can only have been produced in the Morea, the Peloponnese. There are now several new points that can be made about dating the romances, to supplement the long-standing suggestion placing *K&Ch c.* 1310–1340 with Andronikos Palaiologos, cousin of the emperor Andronikos II (1281–1328), as author (Knös 1962). The work of Panagiotis Agapitos on *L&R* has produced a convincing series of arguments on the transmission history of this romance which take its composition back before 1330, though his attribution to Laskarid Nicaea and the thirteenth century is less well-founded.[71] Spadaro (1966) made a good case for linking the introduction of the Italian text on which *Ph&P* is based to the entourage of Niccolo Accaiuoli, who came to the Morea in 1348. Maria Politi has shown that the watermark of the Leipzig manuscript for *Peri E&D* can be dated to the mid-fourteenth century (Politi-Sakellariadi 1987: 286). The Ottoman model for *A&S* circulated widely with the first attested copy dated to 1382 (Moennig 2004: 24). It is however still not clear at what point in his long career as a teacher and ecclesiastical administrator did Theodore Meliteniotes (*c.* 1320–1393), putative author of *To Chastity*,[72] produce this amalgam of romance motifs with echoes of *DA* and *L&R*. However, whilst this work confirms the clustering of the romances towards the middle and in the first half of the fourteenth century, little more can be added about their relative dating, which remains problematic.[73]

It might be noted that references in this discussion have been made to romances and one chronicle while the relevant texts were initially stated to include animal-fables and satire. Lack of discussion here of these latter types is not an indication of intrinsic

---

[69] Notably Hunger 1965 and 1968; most recently Gaul 2007.
[70] Jacoby 1968 remains a convenient summary for the dating issues.
[71] Agapitos 2006a: 197–98 for composition before 1330, 51–53 for composition in Nicaea *c.* 1240–160. The grounds for this are the indebtedness of *L&R* to the Komnenian novels, copies of which are found in thirteenth-century manuscripts, and an innovation in coronation ritual (which became the norm subsequently).
[72] On *To Chastity* (*Eis te Sofrosynen*) see most recently Schönauer 1996, with older literature.
[73] Despite the arguments presented in Agapitos 1993.

stylistic difference but rather a reflection of the balance of recent scholarly investigations – as well as the pressures of space in this chapter. However, now that the issue of orality versus literacy, or literariness, has ceased to be a fashionable matter for discussion, for the most part there seems to have developed a tacit acceptance that the stylistic features and peculiarities of this group of late Byzantine verse texts are best explained against a background of orally composed and orally disseminated poetry.[74]

Although much still remains obscure, with a better understanding of the nature of this poetry and a more nuanced appreciation of interaction between Byzantine writers, some suggestions might be made that take into account both the traditional style and the signs of authorial interaction, though the texts have still to lose their anonymity. Much of the earlier discussion about schools of poets and their exchange of material was conducted in a vacuum, with little attempt to pin down dates or places. Here it seems relevant to draw analogies with the social and literary environment of Komnenian Constantinople which produced the twelfth-century novels and *DA*. At that time, it can be argued, a group of teachers and taught vied in literary virtuosity, combining learned and vernacular elements across the breadth of the Greek linguistic and literary heritage, pushing at the boundaries of cultural conventions and parading their wares before each other and their patrons. Palaeologan Constantinople after 1261 saw a similar grouping of teachers, with figures such as Maximos Planoudes (c. 1255–c. 1305), the best known, Theodore Hyrtakenos (early 1300s), Manuel Bryennios (c. 1300) and others.[75] This was a continuation of the revival of education that had begun in Nicaea after 1204 at the instigation of the emperor Theodore Laskaris, in an attempt to reaffirm Byzantine cultural values after the disaster of 1204. The taught are perhaps less visible, except as recalcitrant youths who were inclined to prefer the excitements of the streets to the classroom, as Planoudes complains in his letters; the more conscientious worked through the system to become the prelates and administrators of the next generation. It would seem a not unreasonable scenario that some lively individual, who was stimulated – once again – by knowledge of Western vernacular texts and romances and familiar with the Greek vernacular traditions (folktales with witches, magic horses and cruel *drakontes* told in a traditional style), combined these with the Greek learned literary tradition (this time adding the twelfth-century novels to those from late antiquity): the result would have been a text like *K&C*, which then challenged others. Is it significant that Planoudes, the most distinguished of the teachers, translated Ovid's *Heroides* and his *Ars Amatoria*, one of the key texts for the Western writers of romance,[76] and that Hyrtakenos, one of his fellow teachers, wrote an *ekphrasis* of the garden attached to a monastery dedicated to St Anne that can only be compared to the garden *ekphraseis* of the romances, especially that of *Ach*?[77] As in Komnenian Constantinople, all this takes place at an elite level, socially and educationally. The audience for these texts would have been, once again, partly fellow-students, partly members of the court or aristocratic house-

---

[74] As was evident in many of the contributions to the conference *Neograeca Medii Aevi VI: Glossa, paradose kai poietike*, held in Ioannina, Greece, in September 2005.
[75] Constantinides 1982: 90–110; Mergiali 1990: 49–50.
[76] *Heroides*: Papathomopoulos 1976; *Ars Amatoria*: Easterling and Kenney 1965. I owe this point to Tina Lendari.
[77] Dolezal and Mavroudi 2002.

holds, who would have appreciated the mixture of traditions. Yet it need not be restricted to these since the language register was very accessible. In 1326 Anna of Savoy, accompanied by a train of Italian courtiers, arrived in Constantinople to marry the young emperor Andronikos III. One is tempted to think that this might have been a pivotal moment in the energising of competing poets. Once again a *theatron*, with an attendance composed of the erudite and the fashionable, women as well as men, would have provided the environment for a reading, a performance, a display. This line of argument suggests that these texts are indeed the work of a small group of writers exchanging ideas, though not in a minutely plagiarising way. Rather they would be drawing on a pool of commonly recognised phrases, and – in good Byzantine manner – using the style appropriate to their chosen genre; one might even call this *mimesis*.

But it is wrong to focus on Constantinople to the exclusion of other areas. Indeed some previous discussions of these texts assumed that they were produced away from the capital in areas where Frankish customs predominated and where Greek linguistic censorship was meaningless to multi-cultural communities (Beck 1971:7–8). A significant region on which to focus is the Morea, the Peloponnese, where the Frankish state of Achaia and its successive suzerains co-existed with the Byzantine Despotate in Mistra, which had wrested back much territory from the post–1204 invaders and which maintained an active Greek cultural presence (Zakythinos 1975). It was from this environment that the *CoM* appeared, probably in the 1340s, as a document in both Greek and French which was to appeal to the symbiotic society of Greeks and Franks. The resonances carried by *WoT* in its original French form and also in the translated Greek version suggest that it too has to be located in the Peloponnese, at some date that can only be guessed at.[78] However, its phraseology is thoroughly part of the mix found in *L&R* and other poems of the romance group; indeed some phrases apparently adopted by the translator of the *WoT* in an attempt to render the *Roman de Troie* precisely into Greek (E. Jeffreys and M. Jeffreys 1979) are also found in *L&R*; the implications of this have yet to be resolved. The Morea was no isolated backwater: in the Greek sphere traffic back and forth from Constantinople was frequent while the Frankish communities were closely tied to the Angevin kingdom in South Italy.

Ultimately, at this stage of our knowledge, there are no clear answers to the inter-relationship of the Palaeologan vernacular verse texts. Despite the advances that have been made, not least in rehabilitating much of this material as worthwhile literary constructs, there is much scope for further research. The time is probably right for a new book-length study that covers all these texts, replacing Beck's encyclopaedic *Handbuch* (1971), expanding the scope of Beaton's *Medieval Greek Romance* (1996), and considering both the continuing influence of a vernacular poetry rooted in a tradition of orally composed material as well as the more literary influences. One question worth pursuing, for example, is the knowledge of *DA* shown by the Palaeologan poets: *DA* is strongly present in the *Ach* and *A&S* at the level of plot structure, in *I&M* at the level of individual scenes and also offers phrases common to *L&R* and Melitiniotis' *On Chastity*. Does this suggest that *DA* was viewed as part of the traditional oral material which provided the phraseology for the style emulated by the Palaeologan poets, or was it seen as part of

---

[78] E. Jeffreys 1993: I, 310–24; Shawcross 2003.

the group of literary novels that were to be emulated? Does it indicate that there was little else available?

## 6 Epic

Thus the case concerning verse romances and chronicles in the vernacular in the fourteenth century can be said to be parallel to that of the twelfth century and *DA*. In both cases there is circumstantial evidence for the existence of orally disseminated poetry (internal evidence from the nature of the texts and scanty external references to poets) but the surviving texts have either been thoroughly revised according to the contemporary literary conventions or composed with a homage to the oral styles. The Byzantine linguistic censorship prevented the preservation in their raw form of texts expressed in the spoken form of the language, leaving a tantalisingly circular situation in which glimpses of what might once have existed serve also as evidence for that existence.

There are a few other texts which might come under a broad definition of epic. These include *Belis*, already referred to. But though this deals with a sixth-century figure and there are signs that the story (or legend) developed in the twelfth century the text as it now exists (in several versions, thoroughly interwoven into the net of Palaeologan romance vocabulary) is a literary construct of the late fourteenth century.[79] The *CoM* is a more complex case and has been referred to at several points in this chapter. It functioned as the foundation epic of the post–1204 Frankish kingdoms of the Morea; multiple versions exist of which the primary are those in Greek verse and French prose. The Greek has a high formula count but while it offers little scope for thematic analysis it does show many other stylistic features ultimately derived from techniques of oral composition – an instance of validation via a now lost oral poetry (Shawcross 2005 and 2009). The *ChTocco* (written 1429 and surviving in what may be an authorial copy) shows some of the markers of the traditional style, notably a number of repeated phrases, and would repay deeper investigation.[80]

The enduring validity of this style for quasi-epics recording heroic conflicts can be observed in the series of texts from the sixteenth and seventeenth centuries recording the Veneto-Turkish wars and the wars in the Balkan principalities, using the fifteen-syllable verse and with a network of common lines – though of a different order from the Palaeologan texts (Vlassopoulou 2000).

## 7 Conclusion

Thus, the issue of epic and oral poetry composed in medieval Greek in the Byzantine world, where Greek was the language of communication for most of the territories covered by the long-lasting empire of East Rome, produces a series of conundrums. Deeply instilled literary conventions dictated the types of texts that were esteemed and pre-

---

[79] As set out in Bakker and van Gemert 1988.
[80] Schirò 1975; Ilieva 1995.

served. A small number of examples, however, produced in certain circumstances where the conventions were flouted, have been preserved in writing, bearing witness to material and styles that were normally censored out of existence. These are *DA* in the twelfth century, when a literary effervescence encouraged rule-breaking and experimentation in general, and a mixed group, with romances predominating, from the fourteenth, when there was again a period of literary effervescence. These breaches in censorship have usually been attributed to pressures resulting from upheavals in the Byzantine world, either after the unruly passage of the Crusades in the late eleventh and early twelfth centuries or after the traumas of 1204. That must be part of the answer. Other parts of the answer lie in a deliberate intention to shatter conventions. In both the twelfth- and the fourteenth-century situations there was a superfluity of bright young intellectuals looking for employment and seeking to display their employability (Ševčenko 1974). It need be no surprise that both periods saw the expected norms of style and genre pushed to their limits. A further element may be found in the fact that Constantinople under both the Komnenian and the Palaeologan emperors saw influxes of travellers, mercenary soldiers and indeed residents from western Europe, from areas where the vernacular was becoming an accepted tool for literary expression.

It cannot be stressed too highly that in both periods the types of texts surveyed in this chapter were exceptions. The preferred genres of Byzantine literature, as preserved and as produced (to judge by comments from the Byzantines themselves), were theology, hagiography, historiography, epistolography, and epideictic oratory. Writing in verse normally entailed composition in the highest registers of Greek, according to the rules of ancient prosody. Based on a syllable length that had long since become meaningless, these conflicted with the stress rhythms of Byzantine Greek, and the exercise focused on demonstrating the writer's expertise in this most stylistically demanding of techniques. Recent modern discussion of the small number of exceptions produced in verse in vernacular, or near-vernacular, Greek has been obscured by an unwillingness to recognise this, by an unwillingness to see these texts in the entire context of the society and literary culture that produced them, and by an obsession with viewing them only as forerunners of the literature of the modern Greek state.[81]

**Postscript.** Since this chapter reached its final form an argument has been developed that places the composition of the *WoT* in the Peloponnese in the years between 1267 and 1281; it would thus be the earliest of the group of texts whose characteristics it shares (E. Jeffreys 2011).

---

[81] This discussion has left out of account the contemporary literature of Veneto-Greek Crete and writers such as Stephanos Sachlikis (*c*.1331–after 1391) and Leonardo Dellaporta (*c*. 1346–*c*. 1420); Dellaporta alludes to *L&R* (Agapitos 2006a: 123–36).

TABLE. *Digenis Akritis*: outline of contents in the Grottaferrata and Escorial versions (from E. Jeffreys 1998).

| Episode | G | E |
|---|---|---|
| *Lay of the emir* | | |
| The emir raids, carries off the girl; her brothers pursue and defeat the emir | 1.1–197 | [lacuna in E] 1–55 |
| They cannot find their sister, emir produces her, converts, marries; birth of DA | 1.198–337; 2.1–49 | 56–224 |
| Emir's mother writes, he quarrels with the brothers, leaves his bride, returns to Syria, converts his mother and returns | 2.50–300; 3.1–343 | 225–609 |
| *Romance of DA* | | |
| Education of DA | – | 610–20 |
| Digenis visits Philopappos and asks to join the guerrillas | – | 621–701 |
| Emir's exploits; education and first hunt of DA | 4.1–47; 4.48–253 | 702–91 |
| Digenis serenades the girl and carries her off | 4.254–855 | [lacuna in E's exemplar] 792–1065 |
| The wedding of DA and the gifts | 4.856–952 | 1066–88 |
| DA on the borders with the girl | 4.953–70 | 1089–94; 1095–96 DA's parents die |
| Visit from the emperor | 4.971–1093 | – |
| *DA's exploits* (1st pers. narrative) | | |
| DA's encounter with Aploravdis' daughter | 5.1–289 | – |
| Meadow in May, the encounter with the serpent, lion and guerrillas | 6.1–175 | 1097–196 |
| Defeat of the three guerillas | 6.176–310 | 1197–315 |
| Guerrillas summon Maximou and Melimitzis | 6.311–475 | 1316–420 |
| DA defeats guerrillas and Maximou | 6.476–713 | 1421–351> |
| DA defeats Maximou again and commits adultery | 6.714–805 [lacuna at 785/6] (6.795–8 kills Maximou) | 1352–605 |
| (*end of exploits* and 1st p. narrative) | | |
| *Palace and garden* | | |
| Garden and palace by Euphrates; DA keeps peace on borders | 7.1–229 (7.106–55 death and burial of father; 7.189–98 death of mother) | 1606–59, 1660–94 tomb on bridge |
| *Death* | | |
| DA falls ill, recalls his past life with the girl, advises her; they both die | 8.1–141; 8.142–98 | 1695–793; 1794–867 |
| Funeral and mourning | 8.199–313 (8.238–44 tomb at Trusis) | – |

## References

For abbreviated titles of primary works (apart from *DA = Digenis Akritis*), see notes 15, 49, 50 and 51.

Agapitos, Panagiotis A. 1991. *Narrative Structure in the Byzantine Vernacular Romances: A Textual and Literary Study of Kallimachos, Belthandros and Libistros.* Miscellanea Byzantina Monacensia 34. Munich: Institut für Byzantinistik und neugriechische Philologie der Universität.
–. 1993. 'Η χρονολογική ακολουθία των μυθιστορημάτων Καλλίμαχος, Βέλθανδρος και Λίβιστρος.' In Panayotakis 1993: II, 97–134.
–. 2000. 'Poets and Painters: Theodore Prodromos' Dedicatory Verses of his Novel to an Anonymous Caesar.' *Jahrbuch der Österreichischen Byzantinistik* 50: 173–85.
–, ed. 2006a. *Αφήγησις Λιβίστρου και Ροδάμνης. Κριτική έκδοση της διασκευής α.* Βυζαντινή και Νεοελληνική Βιβλιοθήκη 9. Athens: Morfotiko Idrima Ethnikis Trapezis.
–. 2006b. 'Writing, Reading and Reciting (in) Byzantine Erotic Fiction.' In *Lire et écrire à Byzance.* Ed. Brigitte Mondrain. Paris: Association des Amis du Centre d'Histoire et Civilisation de Byzance. 125–76.
–, and Ole L. Smith. 1994. 'Scribes and Manuscripts of Byzantine Vernacular Romances: Palaeographical Facts and Editorial Implications.' *Hellenika* 44: 61–80.
Alexiou, Stylianos, ed. 1985. *Βασίλειος Διγενής Ακρίτας (κατά το χειρόγραφο του Εσκοριάλ) και Το άσμα του Αρμούρη.* Φιλοσοφική Βιβλιοθήκη 5. Athens: Ermis.
Anderson, Graham, 1993. *The Second Sophistic: A Cultural Phenomenon in the Roman Empire.* London: Routledge.
Bakker, Wim, and Arnold van Gemert, eds. 1988. *Ιστορία του Βελισαρίου.* Βυζαντινή και Νεοελληνική Βιβλιοθήκη 6. Athens: Morfotiko Idrima Ethnikis Trapezis.
Bäuml, F. H. 1980. 'Varieties and Consequences of Medieval Literacy and Illiteracy.' *Speculum* 55: 237–65.
–. 1984. 'Medieval Texts and the Two Theories of Oral-Formulaic Composition: A Proposal for a Third Theory.' *New Literary History* 16: 31–49.
Beaton, Roderick. 1980. *Folk Poetry of Modern Greece.* Cambridge: CUP.
–. 1986. 'The Oral Traditions of Modern Greece: A Survey.' *Oral Tradition* 1: 110–33.
–. 1993a. '*Digenes Akrites* on the Computer: A Comparative Study of the E and G Versions.' In Panayotakis 1993: II, 42–68.
–. 1993b. 'An Epic in the Making.' In Beaton and Ricks 1993: 55–72.
–. 1996a. *The Medieval Greek Romance.* 2nd ed. London: Routledge.
–. 1996b. 'Cappadocians at Court: Digenes and Timarion.' In *Alexios I Komnenos. I. Papers.* Ed. Margaret Mullett and Dion Smythe. Belfast: Belfast Byzantine Enterprises. 329–38.
–, and David Ricks, eds. 1993. *Digenes Akrites. New Approaches to Byzantine Heroic Poetry.* Centre for Hellenic Studies, King's College London. Publications 2. Aldershot: Ashgate.
–, James Kelly, and Tina Lendari. 1995. *Concordance to Digenes Akrites, Version E.* Irakleio: Panepistemiakes Ekdoseis Kritis.
Beck, Hans-Georg. 1971. *Geschichte der byzantinischen Volksliteratur.* Munich: Beck.
Bouvier, Bertrand. 1960. *Δημοτικά τραγούδια από χειρόγραφο της Μονής των Ιβήρων.* Μουσικό λαογραφικό αρχείο 24. Athens: Ekdoseis tou Gallikou Instiotou Athenon.
Browning, Robert. 1983. *Medieval and Modern Greek.* 2nd ed. Cambridge: CUP.
Chatziyakoumis, Manolis, ed. 1977. *Μεσαιωνικά ελληνικά κείμενα.* Athens: n. p.
Clogg, Richard. 1992. *A Concise History of Greece.* 2nd ed. Cambridge: CUP.
Conca, Fabrizio. 1994. *Il Romano bizantino del XII secolo. Teodoro Prodromo – Niceta Eugeniano – Eustazio Macrembolita – Costantino Manasse.* Turin: Unione tipografico-editrice torinese.
Constantinides, C. N. 1982. *Higher Education in Byzantium in the Thirteenth and Early Fourteenth Centuries (1204–ca. 1310).* Texts and Studies in the History of Cyprus 11. Nicosia: Cyprus Research Centre.

Cupane, Carolina. 1978. 'Il motivo del castello nella narrativa tarda bizantina. Evoluzione di una allegoria.' *Jahrbuch der byzantinischen Byzantinistik* 27: 229–67.
—. 1994–95. 'Δεῦτε, προσκαρτερήσατε μικρόν, ὦ νέοι πάντες. Note sulla ricezione primaria e sul pubblico della letterature greca medievale.' *Diptycha* 6: 147–68.
—, ed. 1995. *Romanzi cavallereschi bizantini. Callimaco e Crisorroe -Beltandro e Crisanza – Storia di Achille – Florio e Plaziaflore – Storia di Apollonio di Tiro – Favola consolatoria sulla Cattiva e la Buona Sorte.* Turin: Unione tipografico-editrice torinese.
Dolezal, Mary-Lyon, and Maria Mavroudi. 2002. 'Theodore Hyrtakenos' *Description of the Garden of St. Anna* and the Ekphrasis of Gardens.' In *Byzantine Garden Culture*. Ed. Antony Littlewood, Henry Maguire, and Joachim Wolshke-Bulmahn. Washington, DC: Dumbarton Oaks Research Library and Collection.
Easterling, P. E., and E. J. Kenney, eds. 1965. *Ovidiana Graeca: Fragments of a Byzantine Version of Ovid's Amatory Works*. Cambridge Philological Society, Supplement 1. Cambridge: Cambridge Philological Society.
Eideneier, Hans. 1982–83. 'Leser- oder Hörerkreis? Zur byzantinische Dichtung in der Volkssprache.' *Hellenika* 34: 119–50.
—, ed. and trans. 1991. *Ptochoprodomos. Einführung, kritische Ausgabe, deutsche Übersetzung, Glossar*. Neograeca Medii Aevi V. Cologne: Romiosini.
—. 1999. *Von Rhapsodie zu Rap. Aspekte der griechischen Sprachgeschichte von Homer bis heute.* Tübingen: Narr.
—, Ulrich Moennig, and Notis Toufexis, eds. 2001. Θεωρία καὶ πρᾶξη τῶν ἐκδόσεων τῆς ὑστεροβυζαντινῆς ἀναγεννησιακῆς καὶ μεταβυζαντινῆς δημώδους γραμματείας. Πρᾶκτικα τοῦ διεθνοῦς συνεδρίου Neograeca Medii Aevi IVa, Ἀμμπούργο 28.–31.1.1999. Irakleio: Panepistemiakes Ekdoseis Kritis.
Fauriel, C. C., ed. and trans. 1824–25. *Chants populaires de la Grèce moderne*. 2 vols. Paris.
Fenik, Bernard. 1991. *Digenis: Epic and Popular Style in the Escorial Version*. Irakleio: Crete UP.
Gaul, Niels. 2007. 'The Partridge's Purple Stockings: Observations on the Historical, Literary and Manuscript Contect of Pseudo-Kodinos' Handbook on Court Ceremonial.' In *Theatron: Rhetorische Kultur in Spätantike und Mittelalter*. Ed Michael Grünbart. Berlin: de Gruyter. 69–103.
Gignac, Francis T. 1976–81. *A Grammar of the Greek Papyri of the Roman and Byzantine Periods*. 2 vols. Testi e documenti per lo studio dell'antichità 55. Milan: Istituto editoriale cisalpino-La goliardica.
Hinterberger, Martin. 2005. 'Ὁ Ἀνδρέας Λιβαδηνός, συγγραφέας/ γραφέας λογίων κειμένων, ἀναγνώστης/ γραφέας δημωδῶν κειμένων: ὁ ἑλληνικός κώδικας 525 τοῦ Μονάχου.' In Holton 2005: 25–42.
Holton, David, ed. 2005. *Copyists, Collectors and Editors: Manuscripts and Editions of Late Byzantine and Early Modern Greek Literature. Papers from a Conference held at the Danish Institute in Athens, 23–26 May 2002, in Honour of Hans Eideneier and Arnold van Gemert*. Irakleio: Panepistemiakes Ekdoseis Kritis
Hörandner, Wolfram, ed. 1974. *Theodoros Prodromos. Historische Gedichte*. Wiener Byzantinische Studien 11. Vienna: Österreichische AW.
Horrocks, Geoffrey. 2010. *Greek: A History of the Language and its Speakers*. 2nd ed. Maldon, MA: Wiley-Blackwell.
Hunger, Herbert. 1965. 'Die Schönheitskonkurrenz in "Belthandros und Chrysantza" und die Brautschau am byzantinischen Kaiserhof.' *Byzantion* 35: 150–58.
—. 1968. 'Un roman byzantin et son atmosphere: Callimaque et Chrysorrhoé.' *Travaux et Mémoires* 3: 405–22.
—. 1969–70. 'On the Imitation (mimesis) of Antiquity in Byzantine Literature.' *Dumbarton Oaks Papers* 23/24: 17–38.
—. 1978. *Die hochsprachliche profane Literatur der Byzantiner*. 2 vols. Munich: Beck.

Ilieva, Aneta. 1995. 'Images of Towns in Frankish Morea: The Evidence of the "Chronicles" of the Morea and of the Tocco.' *Byzantine and Modern Greek Studies* 19: 94–119.
Jacoby, David. 1968. 'Quelques considerations sur les versions de la *Chronique de Morée.' Journal des Savants*: 1–55.
Jeffreys, Elizabeth. 1980. 'The Comnenian Background to the "romans d'antiquité".' *Byzantion* 50: 455–86.
–. 1993. 'Place as a Factor in the Edition of Early Demotic Texts.' In Panayotakis 1993: II, 310–24.
–, ed. 1998. *Digenis Akritis. The Grottaferrata and Escorial Versions.* Cambridge Medieval Classics 7. Cambridge: CUP.
–. 2000. 'A Date for *Rhodanthe and Dosikles?*' In *Der Roman im Byzanz der Komnenenzeit*. Ed. Panagiotis A. Agapitos and Diether F. Reinsch. Meletemata 8. Frankfurt a. M.: Beerenverlag. 127–36.
–. 2003. 'Nikephoros Bryennios Reconsidered.' In *The Empire in Crisis (?): Byzantium in the 11th Century (1025–1081)*. International Symposium 11. Athens: National Hellenic Research Foundation, Institute for Byzantine Research. 201–14.
–. 2011. 'Byzantine Romances: Eastern or Western?' In *Renaissance Encounters: Greek East and Latin West*. Ed. Marina Brownlee and Dimitris Gondicas. Princeton: Princeton UP.
–. 2012. *Four Byzantine Novels: Prodromos, Makrembolitis, Eugenianos and Manasses*. Liverpool: Liverpool UP.
–, and Michael Jeffreys. 1971. '*Imberios and Margarona*: The Manuscripts, Sources and Edition of a Byzantine Verse Romance.' *Byzantion* 41: 122–60.
–, and Michael Jeffreys. 1979. 'The Traditional Style of Early Demotic Greek Verse.' *Byzantine and Modern Greek Studies* 5: 115–39.
–, and Michael Jeffreys. 1986. 'The Oral Background of Byzantine Popular Poetry.' *Oral Tradition* 1: 504–47.
–, and Michael Jeffreys, eds. 2005. *Approaches to Texts in Early Modern Greek. Papers from the Conference Neograeca Medii Aevi V. Exeter College, University of Oxford, September 2000*. Oxford: Sub-faculty of Modern Greek.
Jeffreys, Michael. 1973. 'Formulas in the *Chronicle of the Morea.' Dumbarton Oaks Papers* 27: 163–95.
–. 1974. 'The Nature and Origins of the Political Verse.' *Dumbarton Oaks Papers* 28: 142–95.
–. 1975. 'Digenis Akritas Manuscript Z.' *Dodone* 4: 163–201.
–. 1993. 'Early Modern Greek Verse: Parallels and Frameworks.' *Modern Greek Studies (Australia and New Zealand)* 1: 49–78.
–. 1996. 'The Silent Millennium: Thoughts on the Evidence for Spoken Greek between the Last Papyri and Cretan Drama.' In *ΦΙΛΕΛΛΗΝ. Studies in Honour of Robert Browning*. Ed. Costas N. Constantinides, Nikolaos M. Panayotakis, Elizabeth Jeffreys, and Athanasios D. Angelou. Venice: Istituto Ellenico di Studi Bizantini e Postbizantini de Venezia. 133–49.
–. 2007. 'Modern Greek in the 11th century – or What Else Should We Call It?.' *ΚΑΜΠΟΣ: Cambridge Papers in Modern Greek* 15: 61–89.
Kaklamanis, Stephanos. 2005. 'Ο Άνθιμος Διακρούσης αναγνώστης της *Μάλτας πολιορκίας* του Αντωνίου Αχέλη.' In E. Jeffreys and M. Jeffreys 2005: 251–58.
Knös, Börje. 1961. *Histoire de la literature néo-grecque. La periode jusqu'en 1821*. Stockholm: Almqvist & Wiksell.
–. 1962. 'Qui est l'auteur du roman de Callimaque et de Chrysorrhoé?' *Hellenika* 17: 274–95.
Kriaras, Emmanouel. 1955. *Βυζαντίνα ἱπποτικά μυθιστορήματα*. Βασική Βιβλιοθήκη 'Αετοῦ' 2. Athens: Aetos.
Kyriakides, Stilpon P. 1946. 'Ἀκριτικαὶ μελέται.' In *Miscellanea Giovanni Mercati*. 6 vols. Studi e Testi 121–26. Rome: Biblioteca Apostolica. III, 399–430.

Lambros, Spyridon, ed. 1880. *Collection de romans grecs en langue vulgaire et en vers publié pour la première fois d'après les manuscripts de Leyde et d'Oxford.* Paris: Maisonneuve.

Lauxtermann, Marc D. 1999. *The Spring of Rhythm: An Essay on the Political Verse and Other Byzantine Metres.* Byzantina Vindobonensia 22. Vienna: Österreichische AW.

Legrand, Emile, ed.. 1875. *Les oracles de Léon le sage; La bataille de Varna; La prise de Constantinople: poèmes en grec vulgaire publiés pour la première fois d'après les manuscrits de la Bibliothèque nationale.* Collection de monuments pour servir à l'étude de la langue grecque, N. S. 5. Paris.

Lemerle, Paul. 1973. 'L'histoire des Pauliciens d'Asie Mineure d'après les sources grecques.' *Travaux et Mémoires* 5: 1–145.

Lendari, Tina, ed. 2007. Αφήγησις Λιβίστρου και Ροδάμνης *(Livistros and Rodamne). The Vatican Version.* Βυζαντινή και Νεοελληνική Βιβλιοθήκη 10. Athens: Morfotiko Idrima Ethnikis Trapezis.

Littlewood, Antony. 1979. 'Romantic Paradises: The Role of the Garden in the Byzantine Romance.' *Byzantine and Modern Greek Studies* 17: 83–103.

Lock, Peter. 1995. *The Franks in the Aegean, 1204–1500.* London: Longmans.

Lord, Albert Bates. 1960. *The Singer of Tales.* Cambridge, MA: Harvard UP. [Re-edition with a CD and a new introduction by Stephen Mitchell and Gregory Nagy, 2000.]

Mackridge, Peter. 1985. *The Modern Greek Language: A Descriptive Analysis of Standard Modern Greek.* Oxford: OUP.

–. 1990. 'Orality in Modern Greek Poetry: Introduction.' *Byzantine and Modern Greek Studies* 14: 123–38.

Magdalino, Paul. 1993a. *The Empire of Manuel I Komnenos, 1143–1180.* Cambridge: CUP.

–. 1993b. '*Digenes Akrites* and Byzantine Literature: The Twelfth-Century Background to the Grottaferrata Version.' In Beaton and Ricks 1993: 1–14.

Mango, Cyril, ed. 2002. *The Oxford History of Byzantium.* Oxford: OUP.

Markopoulos, Athanasios. 2008. 'Byzantine Education.' In *The Oxford Handbook of Byzantine Studies.* Ed. Elizabeth Jeffreys, John Haldon and Robin Cormack. Oxford: OUP. 785–95.

Mavrogordato, John, ed. and trans. 1956. *Digenes Akrites.* Oxford: Clarendon.

McKitterick, Rosamond. 1994. *Books, Scribes and Learning in the Frankish Kingdoms, 6th–9th Centuries.* Collected Studies Series 452. Aldershot: Ashgate

Mergiali, Sophia. 1990. *L'enseignement et les lettrés pendant l'époque des Paléologues (1261–1453).* Athens: Etaireia ton filon tou laou.

Moennig, Ulrich, ed. 2004. *Die Erzählung von Alexander und Semiramis.* Supplementa Byzantina. Texte und Untersuchungen 7. Berlin: de Gruyter.

Morgan, Gareth. 1960. 'Cretan Poetry: Sources and Inspiration.' *Kretika Chronika* 14: 7–68, 203–70, 394–404.

Nicholas, Nick, and George Baloglou, trans. 2003. *An Entertaining Tale of Quadrupeds: Translation and Commentary.* New York: Columbia UP.

Nilsson, Ingela. 2001. *Erotic Pathos, Rhetorical Pleasure: Narrative Technique and Mimesis in Eumathios Makrembolites' 'Hysmine & Hysminias'.* Acta Universitatis Upsaliensis, Studia Byzantina Upsaliensia 7. Uppsala: University of Uppsala.

Nørgaard, Lars and Ole L. Smith, eds. 1975. *A Byzantine Iliad: The Text of Par. Suppl. Gr. 926 Edited with Critical Apparatus, Introduction and Indexes.* Opuscula Graecolatina 5. Copenhagen: Museum Tusculanum.

ODB. *The Oxford Dictionary of Byzantium.* Ed. Alexander P. Kazhdan, Alice-Mary Talbot, Anthony Cutler, Timothy E. Gregory, and Nancy P. Ševčenko. 3 vols. Oxford: OUP.

Odorico, Paolo. 1989. 'La sapienza del Digenis: matierali per lo studio dei *loci similes* nella recenzione di Grottaferrata.' *Byzantion* 59: 137–63.

Oikonomidès, Nikos. 1979. 'L'épopée de Digénis et la frontière orientale de Byzance aux Xe et XIe siècles.' *Travaux et Mémoires* 7: 375–97.

Ong, Walter J. 1982. *Orality and Literacy: The Technologizing of the Word*. London: Methuen.
Panayotakis, Nikolaos M., ed. 1993. *Origini della letteratura neogreca: atti del secondo Congresso Internazionale 'Neograeca Medii Aevi', Venezia, 7–10 novembre 1991*. 2 vols. Bibliothèque de l'Institut hellénique d'études byzantines et post-byzantines de Venise 14–15. Venice: Istituto ellenico di studi bizantini e postbizantini di Venezia.
Papathomopoulos, Manolis, ed. 1976. *Μαξίμου Πλανούδη μετάφρασις τῶν Οβιδίου Επιστολῶν*. Ioannina: Panepistemion Ioanninon, Filosofiki scholi.
–, and E. M. Jeffreys, eds. 1996. *Ο πόλεμος της Τρωάδος (The War of Troy)*. Βυζαντινή και Νεοελληνική Βιβλιοθήκη 7. Athens: Morfotiko Idrima Ethnikis Trapezis.
Passow, Arnold, ed. 1860. *Popularia carmina graeciae recentioris*. Leipzig.
Politi-Sakllariadi, Maria. 1987. 'Προβλήματα της έκδοσης του "Λόγου Παρηγορητικού περί Δυστυχίας και Ευτυχίας".' In *Neograeca Medii Aevi. Text und Ausgabe. Akten zum Symposim Köln 1986*. Ed. Hans Eideneier. Cologne: Romiosini. 285–94.
Prombonas, Ioannes K., 1985. *Ακρίτικα Α'*. Athens: n. p.
Reinsch, Dieter R. 2005. 'Ο Νικολάος Αγιομνήτης ως γραφέας και λογίων και δημωδών κειμένων.' In Holton 2005: 43–66.
Ricks, David. 1989. 'Is the Escorial *Akrites* a unitary poem?' *Byzantion* 59: 184–207.
–, ed. and trans. 1990. *Byzantine Heroic Poetry*. Bristol: Bristol Classical P.
Roilos, Panagiotis. 2005. *Amphoteroglossia: A Poetics of the Twelfth-Century Medieval Greek Novel*. Cambridge, MA: Harvard UP.
Schirò, Giuseppe, ed. and trans. 1975. *Cronaca dei Tocco di Cefalonia di Anonimo; prolegomeni, testo critico e traduzione*. Corpus fontium historiae byzantinae 10. Series Italica. Rome: Accademia nazionale dei Lincei.
Schmitt, John, ed. 1904. *The Chronicle of Morea: A History in Political Verse, Relating the Establishment of Feudalism in Greece by the Franks in the Thirteenth Century*. London: Methuen.
Schönauer, Sonja. 1996. *Untersuchungen zum Steinkatalog des Sophrosyne-Gedichtes des Meliteniotes mit kritischer Edition der Verse 1107–1247*. Meletemata 6. Wiesbaden: Beerenverlag.
Ševčenko, Igor. 1974. 'Society and Intellectual Life in the Fourteenth Century.' In *XIV[e] Congrès International des Etudes Byzantines, Bucarest, 6–12 Septembre, 1971. Rapports I*. Bucharest: Editions de l'Academie de la Republique Socialiste de Roumanie. 69–92.
Shawcross, Teresa. 2003. 'Re-inventing the Homeland in the Historiography of Frankish Greece: The Fourth Crusade and the Legend of the Trojan War.' *Byzantine and Modern Greek Studies* 27: 120–52.
–. 2005. 'Oral Residue and Narrative Structure in the *Chronicle of Morea*.' *Byzantion* 75: 310–333.
–. 2009. *The Chronicle of Morea: Historiography in Crusader Greece*. Oxford: OUP.
Sifakis, Gregory M. 'Ζητήματα ποιητικής του Διγενή Ε και των ακριτικών τραγουδιών.' *Ariadne* 5: 125–40.
Smith, Ole L., ed. 1990. *The Oxford Version of the Achilleid*. Opuscula Graecolatina 32. Copenhagen: Museum Tusculanum Press.
–. ed. 1999. *The Byzantine Achilleid: The Naples Version*. Edited and prepared for publication by Panagiotis A. Agapitos and Karin Hult. Wiener byzantinische Studien 21. Vienna: Österreichische AW.
Spadaro, Guiseppe. 1966. *Contributo sulle fonti del romanzo grec-medievale 'Florio e Platziaflore'*. Κείμενα και Μελέται Νεοελληνικής Φιλολογίας 26. Athens: n. p.
–. 1975. 'Problemi relativi ai romanzi greci dell'eta dei Paleologi, I. Rapporti tra *Ιμπέριος και Μαργαρόνα* e *Φλόριος και Πλατζιαφλόρε*.' *Hellenika* 28: 302–7.
–. 1976. 'Problemi relativi ai romanzi greci dell'eta dei Paleologi, II. Rapporti tra la *Διήγησις τοῦ Αχιλλέως*, la *Διήγησις τοῦ Βελισαρίου* e l' *Ιμπέριος και Μαργαρόνα*.' *Hellenika* 29: 287–310.
–. 1978. 'Problemi relativi ai romanzi greci dell'eta dei Paleologi, III. *Achilleide, Georgillàs, Callimaco, Beltandro, Libistro, Florio, Imperio*, e *Διήγησις γεναμένη ἐν Τροία*.' *Hellenika* 30: 223–79.

Trapp, Erich, ed. 1971. *Digenes Akrites. Synoptische Ausgabe der ältesten Versionen.* Wiener byzantinische Studien 8. Vienna: Böhlau.
—. 1976. 'Hagiographische Elemente im Digenis-Epos.' *Analecta Bollandiana* 94: 175–87.
Trypanis, Constantine A. 1963. 'Byzantine Oral Poetry.' *Byzantinische Zeitschrift* 56: 1–3.
—, ed. and trans. 1981. *Greek Poetry from Homer to Seferis.* London: Faber and Faber.
Tsavari, Isavella, ed. 1987. *Ο Πολουλόγος.* Βυζαντινή και Νεοελληνική Βιβλιοθήκη 5. Athens: Morfotiko Idrima Ethnikis Trapezis.
van Gemert, Arnold, and Wim Bakker. 1981. 'Η *Achilleida* και η *Ιστορία του Βελισαρίου*.' *Hellenika* 33: 82–97.
Vlassopoulou, Maria. 2000. 'Literary Writing and the Recording of History: A Study of Marinos Tzane Bounialis' "The Cretan War" (17th Century).' Ph.D. Thesis, Cambridge University.
Whitmarsh, Tim. 2005. *The Second Sophistic.* Greece and Rome: New Surveys in the Classics 35. Oxford: OUP.
Zakythinos, Dionysios A. 1975. *Le despotat grec de Morée.* Édition revue et augmentée par Chryssa Maltézou. 2 vols. London: Variorum.

# 18 The *Song of Igor* and its Medieval Context in Russian Oral Poetry

## S. N. Azbelev

Are all basic genres of Russian oral poetry sufficiently known to scholarship? Such a question is justified when we talk not about the contemporary or recent state of folklore, but about a more or less distant past. The traditional ideas about the generic composition of Russian oral poetry is almost exclusively based on material which was written down in the nineteenth and in the first half of the twentieth century. If the scholarly collection of works of oral poetry had begun only half a century ago, after the great collections of the nineteenth century, then, for instance, the characterization of the *bylina* as one of the basic genres would only be hypothetical.[1] For its substantiation one would have to compare the rare and fairly worthless transcriptions from the second half of the twentieth century with the 'Collection of Kirsha Danilov' and with the scanty records of the seventeenth century, which have sometimes undergone considerable literary adaptation.[2] The study of other classical genres would present a similar picture.

It is clear that the disappearance of several types of oral poetry and their substitution by others also happened earlier. There is no foundation for the assertion that in the records of the nineteenth century all genres that were widely distributed, for instance, in the twelfth or fourteenth centuries, are appropriately reflected. The great historical upheavals as well as the economic and social changes that took place in the sixteenth, seventeenth and eighteenth centuries, the radical break-down of the traditions of the Old Russian civilization which began in the time of Peter the Great, all this was certainly reflected in the further history of folklore genres, in the same way in which, for instance, the social cataclysms of the twentieth century are reflected in the fortune of the *byliny*. One can assume *a priori* that those forms of oral poetry which completed the period of their productive development at an earlier time and which existed as a heritage that was only barely continued by new creations were destined to disappear from a living repertoire.

---

[1] [For a general background to this chapter, see ch. 1, section 5.2, pp. 33–38 above. In English, for the plural of the word *bylina* both the Russian form (*byliny*) and the Anglicized form *bylinas* is found. The former is used in this book.]

[2] [The *byliny* collected by Kirsha Danilov in the second half of the eighteenth century were first published in 1804 under the title 'Old Russian Poems' (*Drevnie russkie stikhotvoreniya*). The standard edition is Evgen'eva and Putilov 1977.]

The sixteenth, seventeenth and parts of the eighteenth centuries are correctly known as the time of the highest development of the Russian historical song.[3] There are only very few historical songs that date from an earlier time, and even then their dating is sometimes questioned. It would be difficult to explain the almost complete absence of older historical songs by the fact alone that this material was badly preserved. It is more natural to suppose that at an earlier time historical poetry was the domain of a different genre. When the historical song arose, this other genre, pushed to the periphery of the oral repertoire, was only preserved by virtue of its inertia, but disappeared later, as it did not adapt to changed circumstances.

If one accepts this conclusion, this would help to explain, in particular, why in the living repertoires of the nineteenth and twentieth centuries the most incisive historical events of the struggle to shake off the Tatar yoke are only comparatively weakly reflected in folk poetry. The hypothesis that before the sixteenth century the historical awareness of the people had not yet reached a sufficiently high level might provide another explanation, but this hypothesis is itself in need of factual support. Neither the data of the Russian literature of this time nor the comparative material of the folklore of other peoples that are in a similar phase and in similar conditions of their historical development support such a hypothesis. The search for the traces of a developed oral historical poetry from the tenth to the fifteenth century is therefore in itself fully justified. The outcome of this search can provide new material for our ideas about the evolution of the reflection of historical reality in folklore.

Among oral historical narratives that were written down in the nineteenth century one encounters occasionally somewhat mysterious works which are so striking that editors and scholars did not at first recognize them as the texts of legends, but classified them provisionally sometimes as historical tales, sometimes also as *byliny*, or simply commented on their strange and unusual structure, which, although works of oral poetry, resembles nevertheless some forms that are commonly attributed to the literary works of medieval Rus'. According to their contents, however, not all of these works can be traced back to a medieval tradition. Thus, for instance, E. V. Barsov published a narrative in rhythmic form about the encounter of Peter I with the Swedes. 'This narrative', stated E. V. Barsov, 'is in its artistic aspect so outstanding that we do not know anything comparable in Russian narrative literature. In places we can place it on the same level with the *Song of Igor*' (1872: V, pt. 1, 306).

As another example, belonging to an even earlier period, the so-called Altay version of the *bylina* about Sukhan can be cited.[4] V. Ya. Propp stated in print his belief that this is 'a work of a different poetic system than that of the *bylina*'. According to Propp the given text 'is an oral narrative' (1957a). This very term 'oral narrative' (*ustnaya povest'*) is not fully adequate: it would be more suitable to call such narratives 'heroic tales' (*geroicheskie skazniya*).

In his time, C. W. von Sydow, on the basis of international material, gave a general characterization of the special variety of folklore called *Heldensagen* (heroic legends). By

---

[3] [The Russian term is *istoricheskiy pesn'*. For a short definition and discussion of this genre, see Costello and Foote 1967: 149–52.]

[4] Published from the manuscript of the collector in Malyshev 1956: 153–54.

their contents these are emotionally heightened, ostensibly trustworthy narratives about the feats of actually existing heroes. The narrative can, however, greatly differ from reality, by using motifs and artistic means which are borrowed from the works of other genres. In this way the events which actually took place and served as the starting-point of the tale are ornamented and complemented by the fruits of popular imagination. The heroic tales do not give the full biography of a person, but concentrate only on those moments which can effect an emotional uplifting of the listeners. Such narratives are characterized by what von Sydow called *gebundene Form* (bound form), meaning by this a rhythmic or metrical organization of speech. He noticed, however, that such a form can alternate with that of traditional tales in prose; the narrative can even be completely in prose. C. W. von Sydow noted that the heroic tales are variable and not very long-lived: 'Heroic or family legends which are in a state of disintegration on account of the disappearance of their tradition bearers – a process that comes about, for instance, at large-scale cultural revolutions – break up into their components; these can live on as *Erinnerungssagen* (memorial legends) or as fabulous stories' (1948:79).

The Altay text mentioned above was written down from a performer who maintained that he transmitted a narrative about the battle on the Kulikovo Pole in 1380 in answer to the collector's question what he knew about the mighty battle of Mamay.[5] S. K. Shambinago suggested that the Altay version goes back to a literary source, to an Old Russian tale about the *Mighty Battle of Mamay* (1909: 510–15). Indeed the correspondence in the plot is here beyond doubt. There are also stylistic parallels, a fact that was later noticed by B. M. Sokolov (1912), who was in agreement with S. K. Shambinago's results. As, however, S. Rozhnetskiy soon showed (1914), the parallels do not testify to borrowings from the tale. One must therefore agree with V. Ya. Propp, who wrote that 'these correspondences prove the opposite: they passed from the epic into literature, not the other way round, since the popular contents of the tale called also for a popular style' (1959: 587). To this one can add that in general the use of oral works about the battle of Kulikovo Pole in the *Tale of the Mighty Battle of Mamay* is a proven fact and that therefore the Altay text itself must naturally be considered a remnant of one of the tales that existed in oral tradition in the course of several centuries.

This is also supported by a number of other records from the nineteenth century; of these I will shortly deal with only one, the extensive heroic tale about the deeds of the Russian ambassador Zakhariy Tyutchev, which was written down by A. Kharitonov and published by A. N. Afanas'ev.[6] With reference to this work it is possible to show by textological analysis that it was one of the sources of the *Tale of the Mighty Battle of Mamay*. The latter undoubtedly made extensive use of some of the early versions of this very narrative, a narrative which was re-shaped more than once by the composers of different redactions of the *Tale*. This proves that the *Tale* made use of oral narratives and not the other way round.[7]

---

[5] [One of the major victories over the Golden Horde under Khan Mamay was won on 8th September 1380 by the Russian Grand Duke Dmitriy on the Kulikovo Pole (Snipe Field) on the Don.]

[6] Barag and Novikov 1985: II, 377–83 (text); 458–59 (notes). [The ambassador's name varies in different versions; in Afans'ev's tale his name is Zakhariy Tyutrin.]

[7] This is argued in Azbelev 1982: 90–119.

As to the *Tale of the Mighty Battle of Mamay* itself – according to O. F. Miller's expression 'a free semi-historical, semi-epic tale' (1887:364) – it is today known in about ten redactions, extant in hundreds of manuscripts. Almost all redactions draw directly to some degree on oral sources. These were evidently tales of the participants in the battle of 1380, historical legends on the basis of such tales as well as heroic narratives. One of the first students of the *Tale* justly wrote that despite the fact that on the whole it 'exhibits a serious edifying character in the Christian spirit', in its descriptions it again and again clearly manifests 'a spirit of warlike manliness, eager for honour and fame. This energetic spirit of warlike daring and courage leaves its impression also in the language, which is to the point, quickly moving, rapid, sparkling with picturesque comparisons, which are directly taken from the folk epic' (Nazarov 1858:56–57).

The early redactions of this tale are by their style related to the heroic narratives about the battle on the field of Kulikovo, more or less in the same way as the written re-tellings of *byliny*, known in texts of the seventeenth and eighteenth centuries and published formerly in the series 'Monuments of Russian Folklore', are related to the oral *byliny* (Astakhova, Mitrofanova, and Skripil' 1960). All in all, however, the *Tale of the Mighty Battle of Mamay* is indebted to a literary tradition. The quotations from oral heroic narratives can in most cases be comparatively clearly distinguished on stylistic grounds, and not one of the copies of the *Tale* is a transcript or even an adaptation of an oral text in its entirety.

18 – Battle on the Kulikovo Pole, from a manuscript of *The Mighty Battle of Mamay* (17th c.)

The situation is different with another well-known document, which is extant only in six manuscripts and bears different titles in these: 'The Tale about the Battle on the Don', 'The Tidings of the Grand Duke Dmitriy Ivanovich [...]' and others. In the scholarly literature it is generally called *Zadonshchina* ([The exploits] beyond the River Don), although Academician I. I. Sreznevskiy had already remarked long ago that in the original text the word 'Zadonshchina' was not used as the name of a literary work, but rather as the designation of the battle on the Kulikovo Pole, which took place *beyond the Don* (*za Donom*). The oral origin of this work was first pointed out 150 years ago by the same I. I. Sreznevskiy. At that time only two manuscripts of the *Zadonshchina* and a correspondingly small number of copies of the *Tale of the Mighty Battle of Mamay* were known. The later finds of new texts gave new support to the ideas of Sreznevskiy, one of the greatest Russian philologists. 'When collating the two manuscripts of the *Zadonshchina*', Sreznevskiy wrote, 'I can see so many differences, variations in expressions, substitutions of places and substitutions of names and persons that cannot come from copying; they are at least as frequent and as arbitrary as one would expect of someone who does not copy from a book or a notebook, but writes from memory. In addition I can see such a great number, such an accidental collection, of grammatical errors which are not found in the copies of other documents, no matter how illiterate the scribe. And from that it seems to me that the *Zadonshchina* was not written down from a finished variant, but from memory, and if not in these collections, where it is found, then in others, from which it found its way into these manuscripts. If it were written down in a book from memory, then it belonged to memory, travelled from person to person like a legend, was recited at different occasions or was sung, just like the *bylina*, the *duma*,[8] poems or riddles, and was one of them [...]. If this is correct, we have in the *Zadonshchina* a specimen of a special kind of popular poem with historical content' (1858: 340).

After Sreznevskiy had expressed his opinion about the oral-poetic nature not only of the *Zadonshchina* but also of the *Song of Igor*, he asked whether 'on account of the general peculiarity of a great number of such poems' there were characteristic traits which were not only found in these works and whether there were analogous antecedents in oral poetry already for the *Song of Igor*. He wrote:

> These traits are no less distinct than others, if not more so, and the poems differ in narrative presentation and in style from the *Song of Igor*. But one notices these characteristic features also where they would not be expected. Once one notices them, one instinctively remembers the *Song of Igor*, because nothing else brings these traits so clearly to mind. From this, however, it does not follow that they could belong only to the *Song of Igor*. Their very distinctiveness in the *Song* demonstrates, it seems to me, that it was not in the *Song* that they made their first appearance, but rather that these traits reached their full development in it on account of the fact that there had been a prior preference for them. These traits can also be noticed in works equally old, but extant only in fragmentary form; they can also be detected in works of popular oral literature that are transmitted up to the present. What is noticeable is that they cannot be put on the same level as imitations of the *Song of Igor*: this demonstrates in an even more positive way that the characteristics that recall the *Song* were still in a process of development and were not due to its influence. In the *Zadonshchina* some traits seem to be taken literally from the *Song of Igor*; but we find such a literal similarity also between works of

---

[8] [The *duma* is an Ukrainian oral narrative poem or ballad.]

different genres (saints' legends, religious poems, historical narratives, folktales, *byliny, dumy*, songs) – and this need not trouble us in the least. Together with these traits we find in the *Zadonshchina* much that, even if it is additional, differs from the *Song of Igor* by content and expression. From where is this taken? In the tales and narratives about the *Mighty Battle of Mamay* there are also such passages that differ from everything around them in exactly the same manner, concerning both representation and style or only representation; and among them there are some that occur neither in the *Song of Igor* nor in the *Zadonshchina*. These passages are clear insertions and demonstrate, on the one hand, that they enjoyed popularity, and on the other that there was a source from which they could be borrowed. What kind of source? For this as for everything else of a similar nature, the source is one and the same: the spirit and conception of poems like *The Song of Igor*. (1858: 341–43)

Twenty years later, Academician V. Jagić wrote in his well-known work on Slavic folk poetry about the *Song of Igor* and the *Zadonshchina* as about 'unique remains of the Old Ukrainian and South-Russian epic poetry'. He expressed the same opinion as Sreznevskiy: '[...] it is possible that many poetic forms and phrases travelled by way of borrowing from one song to the other, as the common property of everybody, as material which is more or less known in every *bylina* or *duma*' (1876: 102–6).

It would not be difficult to name a whole range of philologists and historians of the nineteenth and twentieth centuries who expressed similar thoughts about the oral-poetic nature of the *Zadonshchina* and the *Song*. Academician A. N. Pypin, speaking in his 'History of Russian Literature' about the *Zadonshchina*, quoted I. I. Sreznevskiy's opinions, to which I have referred, in great detail and gave further support to them by the assumption that for the existence of works of oral poetry like the *Zadonshchina* that have not been preserved 'speaks above all the *Song of Igor*, among other direct references to old songs; for it speaks also the epic *bylina*, which, however, is not truly old, but is yet a trace from old times' (1902: I, 204). The hypothesis about the oral-poetic origin of these literary works was also argued for in the research of I. P. Khrushchov, P. N. Polevoy, P. A. Bessenov, S. M. Solov'ev and other scholars.[9] About the oral origin of the *Song of Igor* later wrote also Academician A. A. Shakhmatov (1915: 386).

In the latest scholarly literature I. I. Sreznevskiy's idea was supported by further arguments by V. F. Rzhiga, who came to the conclusion that 'the predominantly song-like character of the *Zadonshchina* is fairly obvious' and noted in particular that in the manuscripts 'there are mistakes in the text' which 'clearly indicate its spoken rather than its written origin.' V. F. Rzhiga assumed that 'Sofoniy[10] imitated the *Song of Igor* not via written sources but via hearing and remembering' (Tikhomirov, Rzhiga, and Dmitriev 1959: 398, 399, 400). V. P. Adrianova-Peretts, in her review of this book, offered a number of independent observations of her own, similar to those of V. F. Rzhiga, and wrote that they 'support I. I. Sreznovskiy's ideas, elaborated by V. F. Rzhiga, about the oral source of the copies of the *Zadonshchina*' and that the latter's opinion about 'the role of a beginning in song' is 'extraordinarily fruitful' (1960: 157, 158).

The suggestion that the copies of the *Zadonshchina* go back to oral originals was made by I. I. Sreznevskiy on the basis of two manuscripts known at the time. The older Kirillo-Belozerskiy copy, dating from the second half of the fifteenth century, is found in

---

[9] For details on these works, see Azbelev 1968: 79–81.
[10] [The assumed author of the *Zadonshchina*]

a manuscript that comes from the hand of the scribe Efrosin.[11] In this copy there are small distorting alterations and interpolations which could not be present in a direct transcript of an oral text from performance or from memory. Consequently the copy itself was written down earlier than the appearance of this oldest manuscript. As to the later manuscripts of the *Zadonshchina*, it has also been argued that they go back to oral originals, based on an analysis of their textual peculiarities; in this connection V. P. Adranova-Peretts wrote about the 'oral source of the copies of the *Zadonshchina*'.[12]

One has to mention in particular the study of the famous folklorist (and at the same time specialist of Old Russian literature) A. I. Nikiforov. This work (a typescript comprising about 2,000 pages) was defended by him as his doctoral thesis in the spring of 1941. A year later A. I. Nikiforov died during the Leningrad siege. He managed to publish only the first chapter of his study (1940); some extracts were printed with introductory explanations posthumously (1978 and 1981). By developing the central idea of I. I. Sreznevskiy, A. I. Nikiforov conducted his research to show that in medieval Rus' there existed a tradition of high oral-poetic art, whose traces have reached us mainly in the form of a number of written monuments (which, however, are of oral origin): *The Song of Igor*, *The Tale of the Destruction of the Russian Land* and several variants of the *Zadonshchina*.[13] The questions that arose in this connection were considered by the author from different points of view. The central position in his study was taken by the *Song of Igor* (which, according to A. I. Nikiforov's conclusions, was transmitted in oral tradition until the end of the fourteenth century). The scholar devoted 240 pages to the *Zadonshchina*, of which more than half was allocated to the textological analysis of all six copies.

It has already been remarked that A. I. Nikiforov's work is practically unknown to later specialists of Old Russian literature. Thus the author of the most detailed book about the research on the *Song of Igor*, published half a century ago, gave only a short notice of this work and wrote: 'In the secondary literature, A. I. Nikiforov's fundamental work on the study of the *Song* is completely ignored; no one mentions it, although his research and popularization can offer a number of remarkable observations and much interesting material' (Golovenchenko 1955: 377). After forty years Nikiforov's research was taken notice of in the *Encyclopedia of the Song of Igor*.[14] This, however, did not entail that the works of Russian medievalists showed any consideration of the results of his study, which is kept in the manuscript department of the Institute of Russian Literature (Pushkinskiy Dom) of the Russian Academy of Sciences.[15]

---

[11] The attribution of the manuscript to Efrosin was established by N. V. Ruzskiy (1891: 19, 27–28). A. D. Sedel'nikov characterized Efrosin as a 'remarkable scribe of his kind', considering the number of his literary interests (Sedel'nikov 1929: 626). Among recent studies of Efrosin's activity, see Shibaev 2005.

[12] For a full annotated edition of the *Zadonshchina*, see Likhachev and Dmitriev 1966: 535–56.

[13] [The *The Tale of the Destruction of the Russian Land* (*Slovo o pogibeli Russkoy zemli*) is a short fragmentary text from the period of 'the Mongol-Tatar yoke'; it begins with an extensive praise of the Russian lands under Vladimir of Kiev. For an English translation, see Zenkovsky 1963: 173–74.]

[14] [See Rudi 1995.]

[15] Section V, collection 120, files 1–4 (A. I. Nikiforov, 'Slovo o polku Igoreve' – *bylina* XII veka). The members of the degree committee who conferred the degree of doctor of philology to Nikiforov on

When studying the metre and rhythm of the *Zadonshchina*, A. V. Pozdneev came to the conclusion that the text shows traits of the *kondakarny*-system[16] and has the tendency to introduce verse lines with the same number of stresses (1965: 18–19). This conclusion can also be applied to those portions of the *Tale of the Mighty Battle of Mamay* which I. I. Sreznevskiy assumed to have the same origin as the *Zadonshchina*. At present, the opinion that the manuscript version of the *Zadonshchina* goes back to the transcription of an oral text is principally shared by the majority of scholars writing about this literary document.[17] The textual correspondences between several passages of the *Tale of the Mighty Battle of Mamay* and the *Zadonshchina* are fairly numerous. L. A. Dmitriev suggested that such passages in the *Tale* 'are not copies from a written text of the *Zadonshchina*'; the author of the *Tale* knew apparently this text 'by heart' and occasionally inserted from it 'either whole extracts, without changes or adaptations, or individual phrases and words from different passages, which he combined to form poetic images of their own' (Dmitriev and Likhachev 1992: 444).

Stylistically the additions from the *Zadonshchina* differ fairly sharply from those parts of the *Tale* which apparently do not go back to transcriptions of oral heroic narratives. Let us look at one of these additions in context:

Учрежено войско их: князь Федор Семенович, князь Семен Михайлович, князь Александр Кемский, князь Глеб Каргомьский и Андомския князи; приидоша же Ярославские князи со всеми силами: князь Андрей Ярославский, князь Лев Суропский и инии многи. – *Уже бо, братья, не стук стучит и не гром гремит, стучит сильная рать великого князя Дмитрея Ивановича в славном граде Москве, а гремят русские сынове злачеными доспехи.* – Князь же великий Дмитрей Иванович поим с собою брата своего князя Владимира Андреевича и все князи русские православныя и еде к живоначальной Троице, ко отцу своему духовному преподобному старцу Сергию, благословение получити от тоя обители святыя.[18]

Their army is formed up: Prince Fëdor Semënovich, Prince Semën Mikhailovich, Prince Aleksandr Kemskiy, Prince Gleb Kargom'skiy and the Princes of Andom; also the Princes of Yaroslavl' have come with all their forces: Prince Andrey Yaroslavskiy, Prince Lev Suropskiy and many others. – *Already, brothers, neither a thump thumps nor a thunder thunders, it is the strong host of the Grand Duke Dmitriy Ivanovich in the famous city of Moscow that thumps, and it is the Russian sons with their golden armour that thunder.* – The Grand Duke Dmitriy Ivanovich takes with him his brother Prince Vladimir Andreevich and all Orthodox Russian princes and goes to the lifegiving (monastery of Holy) Trinity, to his ghostly father, the saintly *starets* (monk) Sergiy, to get the blessing from this holy monastery.

There are, however, also many examples which, while neither by content nor by form extracts, are similar to the *Zadonshchina*, but do not stand out from the context of the

---

account of his dissertation denied, with good reasons, the author's attribution of the works studied in his dissertation to the genre of the *bylina*.

[16] [The *kondakarny* notation was used for Church Slavonic chants; the word is derived from Byzantine Greek *kontakion*, the name of a religious hymn; a *kontakarion* or *kondakarion* is a collection of such hymns; the melodic style of these hymns is melismatic (several notes to one syllable).]

[17] See, e. g., Solov'ev 1958; Zimin 2006: 89–94. D. S. Likhachev wrote, with reference to the oldest manuscript of the *Zadonshchina*, that 'the whole copy is written down from memory by Efrosin, a lover of popular works' (1964: 475).

[18] Quoted from the manuscript: Gosudarstvennyy Istoricheskiy Muzey (Moscow), Otdel rukopisey, Sobranie Uvarova, No. 802, p. 175.

*Tale.* It is in precisely these cases that the context itself turns out to be a large addition from an oral narrative. It can be shown that various phrases and word combinations agree with those in the *Zadonshchina* in similar passages and that furthermore parallels to the *Song of Igor* can also be found. I will give one example:

> Тогда же возвеяша силни ветри по Бервице широте, воздвигошеся велицы князи, а по них рускии сынове успешно грядут, аки медвяны чаши пити и стебле винны ясти. Но не медвяны чаши пити, не стебле винны ясти грядут: хотят укупити чести и славнаго имяни во веки земли Руской, великому князю Димитрею Ивановичю похвалу и многим государем. Дивно и грозно бо в то время слышати, а громко в варганы бьют, тихо с поволокою ратные трубы трубят, многогласно и часто коне ржут. Звенит слава по всей Руской земли. Велико вече бьют в великом Новеграде, стоят мужи новъгородцы у Святыя Софеи Премудрости Божия, а ркучи межу собою таковое слово: Уже нам, братие, на помощь не поспети к великому князю Димитрию; уже бо яко орли слеталися со всеи Руской земли, съехалися дивные удалцы, храбрых своих пытати. Не стук стучит, не гром гремит, по зоре стучат и гремят руские удалцы.[19]

Then strong winds arose on the plain of Bervitsa; the great princes set out, and the Russian youths approach them, as if to drink honey-flavoured cups and to eat grapes.[20] But they do not approach to drink honey-flavoured cups nor to eat grapes: they want to gain honour and a famous name on the eternal Russian land as well as praise for the Grand Duke Dmitriy Ivanovich and many lords. It is wonderful and terrible to hear how they beat noisily the *vargans*,[21] how they play melodiously with feeling the war trumpets, how the horses neigh repeatedly with many voices. Fame resounds over the whole Russian land. The great host fights in great Novgorod, the men of Novgorod stand next to Holy Sofia the Godly Wisdom and speak among themselves these words: 'We have, brothers, no time to lose to help the Grand Duke Dmitriy.' Like eagles they have already flown together from all the Russian lands; glorious heroes have ridden out to put their valour to the test. Neither a thump thumps nor a thunder thunders, it is the Russian heroes who thump and thunder in the dawn.

This extract is identical to the *Zadonshchina* with respect to the ideas expressed and the art exhibited. It coincides with the *Zadonshchina*, however, only in some of its parts. Several parallels to the *Song of Igor* are also found.[22] Nevertheless, it is the same text, of the same nature as also the other poetic passages of the *Tale of the Mighty Battle of Mamay* that have no textual parallels neither to the *Song* nor to the *Zadonshchina*. The natural explanation lies in the fact that the *Song* and the *Zadonshchina* (or rather their oral originals) go back to the same heroic narratives of oral origin that came into being on the basis of a common poetic tradition.

When one makes comparisons one must of course take account of a certain lack of perfection in medieval texts. We do not know to what degree the oral originals are correctly transmitted in the manuscripts that contain copies of the narrative about the *Zadonshchina* and in the numerous excerpts from the *Tale of the Mighty Battle of Mamay*, but also in other Old Russian texts of an analogous kind, which are devoted to different topics and which cannot be fully discussed but only referred to in the present

---

[19] Quoted from Snegirev 1838: III, bk.1, 26–27.
[20] [Literally 'wine-stalks'; *steble* 'stalks' might stand for Old Russian *stafili* 'grapes'.]
[21] [In Modern Russian *vargan* means 'jew's harp', in Old Russian 'trumpet'; here some kind of drum seems to be meant. 332–50.

chapter. The manuscript tradition itself must have deformed the original text in various degrees. There are passages that have plainly been corrupted in the course of copying and there are also clear interpolations by the scribes themselves. By the same token it is evident that the scribes, when copying the written originals, corrected these on the basis of the oral variants of the narratives about the *Zadonshchina* or other tales of a similar nature that were known to them. The existence of copies in the manuscript tradition acted in this way as some kind of correction of the oral tradition. In the transcriptions of the nineteenth century that have become part of the classic collections, a completely exact transmission of oral originals is also hardly ever found. If we accept this fact also, for instance, in connection with the collection of A. N. Afanas'ev,[23] then there is, of course, no reason to think insufficient exactness an obstacle for folkloristic research when it comes to written documents of the fifteenth, sixteenth or seventeenth centuries. Insofar as in the written form of that time the rhythmic structure of the text is fairly clear, one can consequently assume that the defects of these written texts are on the whole comparatively insignificant.

I will try to characterize briefly the general traits that connect the scholarly transcriptions of Russian heroic tales, made in the nineteenth century, and the corresponding medieval texts (taking in this connection not only account of the *Song of Igor* and the tales about the battle of Kulikovo, but also of narratives on other topics). The number of relevant texts, if one has full transcripts and sizable fragments in mind, runs to about seventy. From the group of medieval texts only those are, of course, among this number which reflect directly or indirectly the use of an oral tradition and are not simply the results of later redactions in manuscript transmission.

The heroic tale gives a direct account of specific historical facts, being thus close to the historical legend and the historical song. The narration is characterized by a definite historicism in distinction to the conventional historicism of the *bylina*. The heroes of the tales are persons of real existence, who are correctly named and act not in a conventional epic world, but in the historical situation of their time.

In the *byliny* about the utter defeat of the invading enemies, the hero Il'ya Muromets figures as the main character; his folkloristic shape developed by reference to a historical prototype who lived apparently before the raids of the Polovtsian armies and before the Mongol-Tatar invasions of Rus' (Azbelev 2007: 35–60). Matters are different in the *Song of Igor* and in the tales about the battle of Kulikovo: here the deeds of Prince Igor' Svyatoslavich of Novgorod-Severskiy and his brother Vsevolod are described, of Grand Duke Dmitriy Ivanovich of Moscow and his cousin Vladimir Andreevich as well as of their correctly named contemporaries, whose names and deeds have also been documented in historical sources, independent of folkloristic tradition. The subjects of similar works also agree in their general outline with the information provided by these sources.

The heroic tale, however, in distinction to the historical legend, has an orientation that is not primarily directed towards information about facts, but rather towards the

---

[22] [A. N. Afanas'ev (1826–1871) collected Russian folktales; his collection in eight volumes first appeared in 1855–1863; for later editions see Propp 1957b and Barag and Novikov 1985.]

praise of the deeds of its characters. This is visible both in the choice of the initial material and in the structure of the narrative.

In the period when heroic tales flourished a fairly elaborate poetic system was typical of them. A. I. Nikiforov showed conclusively by a great number of examples that these poetic modes have very many parallels in other genres of East Slavic folklore. As a homogeneous system, however, none of these modes is found in any of them. The very parallels indicate, it appears, that many genres of oral poetry not only exerted an influence but were also themselves subjected to the influence of the more highly developed poetics of the heroic tales.

The best specimens of such tales are works of great poetic refinement. This genre demanded a high professional culture. The heroic tales had to be composed and performed by masters, whose position, if one can say so, was on the highest level of qualification attainable for the bearers of an oral poetic tradition.

There existed apparently in Old Rus' a phenomenon that was in some respects similar to the poetry of the skalds. According to the conclusions reached by D. M. Sharypkin, who analysed the *Song of Igor* especially in this regard, 'the work of Boyan[24] is from a developmental-typological point of view akin to the poetry of the skalds', as 'can be judged by the text of the *Song*'; in the very praise songs of Boyan 'the skaldic modes and forms created a firm stylistic structure' (1976: 16, 22). As is well-known, the poetry of the skalds furnished an example of the phenomenon that in the Middle Ages the oral tradition of a people could reach an even higher level of elaboration than their contemporary written literature.[25] The reflections of oral heroic tales in the Old Russian written literature provide material for a typological comparison with some peculiarities of skaldic poetry. There are grounds for thinking that the heroic tales had a number of varieties, which can be brought to light by a more detailed study of the texts that are preserved in medieval Russian writing. It would be wrong to assume that there was at no time in Rus' anything like skaldic poetry (although there are no supporting Russian texts). But it seems that there existed a type of oral poetic culture which is comparable to the skaldic tradition in a number of its characteristics. There existed a poetry that represented the same phase in the development of the creative process as was expressed in the literary compositions of the skalds.

It is natural that poetry of such a kind must gradually become extinct with the change of the historical conditions that created it. The disappearance of heroic tales from the living oral repertoire was, however, apparently caused not only by historical transformations and the gradual vanishing of the social environment whose requirements this genre served in the first place. Insofar as the plot of a heroic tale had to follow the outlines of its factual basis, the compositional possibilities were comparatively small. Inevitably, the entertaining character of the narrative had to recede into the background. The epic hyperbolic style, so organic and captivating in the *byliny*, is hardly characteristic of the heroic tale and is found mostly in the very latest variants, which have already come under the influence of the poetics of the *byliny*. The poetics peculiar

---

[23] [Boyan is mentioned in the *Song of Igor* and in the *Zadonshchina* as a singer of heroic poetry.]
[24] See Steblin-Kamenskiy 1958. [See also in ch. 5 on performance and performers section 2.1 (J. Harris), pp. 150–55 above.]

to the tale, on account of its refinement, could hardly be fully appreciated by any audience and could not be adequately performed by any performer. The complicated nature of the poetic system of the heroic tale was accompanied by the limitations of its inherent potentialities, which might have assured its preservation in the oral repertoire after the loss of its historical topicality. Clearly, in this way the relatively short-lived existence of works of this genre can to a large degree be explained. The heroic tales ceded gradually the place to historical songs, with their less complicated figurative style, their simpler composition and, on account of their form as songs, their greater ease to be retained in memory.

The rise of a national consciousness, aroused in all strata of Russian society by the victory on the Kulikovo Pole, evidently called forth the last wave of heroic narratives, of which numerous traces have reached us in the form of written texts and reminiscences in the literature of the fifteenth to the seventeenth centuries. The latest echoes of these tales are evidenced by some rare copies which collectors were still able to make in the nineteenth century.

But even the best late copies, independent of all their qualities, are already witnesses of the decline of the genre. An example of this is a text written down by A. Kharitonov, which nevertheless is excellent in some respects. Although V. Ya. Propp, not without reason, noticed, when commenting on this copy, that it has much in common with the *Zadonshchina* (1957b: III, 415), one can see the manifest break with its poetic system, the clear tendency to come close to the *byliny* by the simultaneous simplification of the poetic structure and the noticeable decay of the rhythm. With regard to rhythm the Altay text of the *Mighty Battle of Mamay* looks much more regular, but by its content it is already a contamination with the *bylina*, which allowed a number of scholars to regard this text as a special version of the *bylina*.

The tendency of heroic tales to become contaminated by *byliny* led to the emergence of new *bylina* plots (Azbelev 1971). One can see the genetic connection of the heroic tales not only to the epic poetry of the *byliny*, but also to historical legends and historical songs. The South Slavic song on the Kulikovo battle, known from two copies of the nineteenth century (by Vuk Karadžić and Manoilo Korduna š), is certainly not only by content connected to the heroic tale written down by Kharitonov and to corresponding folkloristic fragments of the *Tale of the Mighty Battle of Mamay*. This song contains also fairly clear parallels to the *Zadonshchina* (Azbelev 1982: 102–12).

It is essential to realize that there is no impermeable borderline to be found between the conventional historicism of the *byliny* and the concrete historicism of such genres as the heroic tale, the historical song and the historical legend. It is important to take into consideration that the heroic tale, the historical legend and the historical song could in a number of cases serve as mediating links between the *bylina* and the historical fact.

# References

Adrianova-Peretts, V. P. 1960. [Review of Tikhomirov, Rzhiga, and Dmitriev 1959.] *Izvestiya AN SSSR. Otdelenie literatury i yazyka* 1960.2: 156–60.
Astakhova, A. M., V. V. Mitrofanova, and M. O. Skripil', eds. 1960. *Byliny v zapisyakh i pereskazakh XVII–XVIII vekov*. Pamyatniki russkogo fol'klora. Moscow, Leningrad: Nauka.
Azbelev, S. N. 1968. 'Kulikovskaya bitva v slavyanskom fol'klore.' *Russkiy fol'klor. 11. Istoricheskie svyazi v slavyanskom fol'klore. Materialy i issledovaniya*. Moscow, Leningrad: Nauka. 78–101.
–. 1971. 'Byliny ob otrazhenii tatarskogo nashestviya ("Ermak i Kalin", "Kamskoe poboishche", "Il'ya i Kalin").' *Russkiy fol'klor. 12. Iz istorii narodnoy poèzii*. Leningrad: Nauka. 162–80.
–. 1982. *Istorizm bylin i spetsifika fol'klora*. Leningrad: Nauka.
–. 2007. *Ustnaya istoriya v pamyatnikakh Novgoroda i Novgorodskoy zemli*. St. Petersburg: Dmitriy Bulanin.
Barag, L. G., and N. V. Novikov, eds. 1985. *Narodnye russkie skazki A. N. Afanas'eva*. 3 vols. Moscow: Nauka.
Barsov, E. V., ed. 1872. 'Pëtr Velikiy v nardonykh predaniyakh Severnogo kraya.' *Beseda* 1872.5: 295–309.
Costello, D. P., and I. P. Foote, eds. 1967. *Russian Folk Literature: Skazki, Liricheskie pesni, Byliny, Istoricheskie pesni, Dukhovnye stikhi*. Oxford: Clarendon.
Dmitriev, L. A., and O. A. Likhachev, eds. 1992. *Skazaniya i povesti o Kulikovskoy bitve*. Literaturnye pamyatniki. Leningrad: Nauka.
Evgen'eva, A. P., and B. N. Putilov, eds. 1977. *Sbornik Kirshi Danilova. Drevnie rossiyskie stikhotvoreniya, sobrannye Kirsheyu Danilovym*. 2nd ed. Literaturnye pamyatniki. Moscow: Nauka.
Golovenchenko, F. M. 1955. *'Slovo o polku Igoreve'. Istoriko-literaturny i bibliograficheskiy ocherk*. Moscow: Izdanie Moskovskogo gosudarstvennogo pedagogicheskogo instituta.
Jagić, Vatroslav. 1876. 'Gradja za slovinsku narodnu poeziju.' *Rad Jugoslavenske Akademije Znanosti i Umjetnosti* 37: 33–137.
Likhachev, D. S. 1964. 'O nazvanii "Zadonshchina".' In *Issledovaniya po otechestvennomu istochnikovedeniyu. Sbornik statey, posvyashchennykh 75–letiyu professora S. N. Valka*. Trudy Leningradskogo otdeleniya Instituta istorii Adademii nauk SSSR 7. Moscow, Leningrad: Nauka. 474–75.
–, and L. A. Dmitriev, eds. 1966. *Slovo o polku Igoreve i pamyatniki Kulikovskogo tsikla. K voprosu o vremeni napisaniya 'Slova'*. Moscow, Leningrad: Nauka.
Malyshev, V. I. 1956. *Povest' o Sukhane. Iz istorii russkoy povesti XVII veka*. Moscow, Leningrad: Nauka.
Miller, O. F. 1887. *Istoriya russkoy literatury*. St. Petersburg. [Lithographic edition.]
Nazarov, I. 1858. 'Skazaniya o Mamaevom poboishche.' *Zhurnal Ministerstva narodnogo prosveshcheniya*. St. Petersburg. 99, no. 7, section 2: 31–107.
Nikiforov, A. I. 1940. 'Problema ritimiki "Slova o polku Igoreve".' *Uchënye zapiski Leningradskogo gosudarstvennogo pedagogicheskogo instituta imeni M. N. Pokrovskogo* 4: 214–50.
–. 1978. 'Fol'klor i "Slovo o pogibeli Rusyya zemli".' Ed. S. N. Azbelev. In *Iz istorii russkoy fol'kloristiki*. Leningrad: Nauka. 189–98.
–. 1981. 'O fol'klornom repertuare XII–XVIII vv. Na materiale "Slova o polku Igoreve", "Zadonshchiny", "Povesti o razorenii Ryazani", Pskovskoy letopisi, Azovskikh povestey i drugikh pamyatnikov.' Ed. S. N. Azbelev. In *Iz istorii russkoy sovetskoy fol'kloristiki*. Leningrad: Nauka. 143–204.
Pozdneev, A. V. 1965. 'Stikhoslozhenie drevney russkoy poèzii.' *Scando-Slavica* 11: 5–24.
Propp, V. Ya. 1957a. [Review of Malyshev 1956.] *Russkiy fol'klor. Materialy i issledovaniya*. 2. Moscow, Leningrad: Nauka. 348–50.
–, ed. 1957b. *Narodnye russkie skazki A. N. Afanas'eva*. 3 vols. Moscow: Gosudarstvennoe izd. khudezhstvennoy literatury.

–. 1959. *Russkiy geroicheskiy èpos.* 2nd ed. Moscow: Gosudarstvennoe izd. khudozhestvennoy literatury.
Pypin, A. N. 1902. *Istoriya russkoy literatury.* 2nd ed. 4 vols. St. Petersburg: n. p.
Rozhnetskiy, S. 1914.'Otvet g. B. Sokolovu.' *Izvestiya Otdeleniya russkogo yazyka i slovesnosti Imperatorskoy AN* 19, pt. 1: 345–49.
Rudi, T. R. 1995. 'Nikiforov Aleksandr Isaakovich.' In *Èntsiklopediya 'Slova o polku Igoreve'.* Ed. O. V. Tvorogov et al. 5 vols. St. Petersburg: RAN, Institut russkoy literatury (Pushkinskiy Dom). III, 315–18.
Ruzskiy, N. V. 1891. 'Svedeniya o rukopisyakh, soderzhashchikh v sebe "Khozhdenie" v Svyatuyu zemlyu russkogo igumena Daniila v nachale XII veka.' *Chteniya v Obshchestve istorii i drevnostey rossiyskikh pri Moskovskom universitete* 3, pt. 2: 1–172.
Sedel'nikov, A. D. 1929. 'Literaturnaya istoriya povesti o Drakule.' *Izvestiya po russkomu yazyku i slovesnosti* 2, pt. 2: 652–59.
Shambinago, S. K. 1909. 'Istoricheskie perezhivaniya v starinakh o Sukhane.' In *Sbornik statey, posvyshchennykh V. O. Klyuchevskomu.* Moscow: n. p. 503–15.
Shakhmatov, A. A. 1915. 'Fëdor Evgen'evich Korsh.' *Izvestiya Otdeleniya russkogo yazyka i slovesnosti Imperatorskoy AN* 9, no. 5: 389–91.
Sharypkin, D. M. 1976. 'Boyan v "Slove o polku Igoreve" i poèziya skal'dov.' *Trudy Otdela drevnerusskoy literatury Instituta russkoy literatury AN SSSR* 31: 14–22.
Shibaev, M. A. 2005. 'Zagadki biografii inoka Efrosina – knizhnika Kirillo-Belozerskogo monastyrya vtoroy poloviny XV v.' In *Istoriya i kul'tura: Aktual'nye problemy.* St. Petersburg: Nauka. 85–93.
Snegirev, I., ed. 1838. 'Povedanie i skazanie o poboishche velikogo knyazya Dmitriya Ivanovicha Donskogo.' In *Russkiy istroicheskiy sbornik.* Moscow. Vol. 3, bk. 1: i–xvi, 1–80.
Sokolov, B. M. 1912. 'Nepra-reka v russkom èpose.' *Izvestiya Otdeleniya russkogo yazyka i slovesnosti Imperatorskoy AN* 17, no. 3: 198–214.
Solov'ev, A. V. 1958. 'Avtor "Zadonshchiny" i ego politicheskie idei.' *Trudy Otdela drevnerusskoy literatury Instituta russkoy literatury AN SSSR* 14: 183–97.
Sreznevskiy, I. I. 1858. 'Zadonshchina velikogo knyazya gospodina Dmitriya Ivanovicha i brata ego Volodimera Ondreevicha.' *Izvestiya Otdeleniya russkogo yazyka i slovesnosti Imperatorskoy AN* 6, no. 5: 337–62.
Steblin-Kamenskiy, M. I. 1958. 'Proiskhozhdenie poèzii skal'dov.' *Skandinavskiy sbornik* 3: 175–204.
Sydow, C. W. von. 1948. 'Kategorien der Prosa-Volksdichtung.' In his *Selected Papers on Folklore. Published on the Occasion of the 70th Birthday.* Ed. Laurits Bødker. Copenhagen: Rosenkilde and Bagger. 60–88, English summary 86–88. [Or. 1934.]
Tikhomirov, M. N., V. F. Rzhiga, and L. A. Dmitriev, eds. 1959. *Povesti o Kulikovskoy bitve.* Moscow: Nauka.
Zaliznyak, A. A. 2004. *'Slovo o polku Igoreve': Vzglyad lingvista.* Moscow: Yazyki slavyanskoy kul'tury.
Zenkovsky, Serge A., ed. and tr. 1963. *Medieval Russia's Epics, Chronicles and Tales.* New York: Dutton.
Zimin, A. A. 2006. *Slovo o polku Igoreve.* St. Petersburg: Dmitriy Bulanin.

# 19 Oral Traditions in a Literate Society: The Hebrew Literature of the Middle Ages

*Eli Yassif*

Since the time of the Koran and early Islam, the Jews have been known as the 'People of the Book'. This phrase has a double meaning: not only did the Jews give the world the Bible, the 'Book of Books', but books have always been central to the life of the nation.[1] That being the case, it might be thought that oral traditions have never played a major role in Jewish culture. As we shall see, however, research into the Jewish world of the Middle Ages reveals that, like many other cultural notions, this perception is based on mistaken assumptions. The fact is that the status of written sources was inferior to that of oral traditions, at least in the early part of the Middle Ages.

Among the most influential figures in early medieval Judaism were the heads of the large *yeshivot* (religious academies) in Iraq, who were considered religious and social authorities of nearly royal standing. Among them was R. Aaron Sargado, head of the Pumbeditha Yeshiva from 943–960. In a Geonic (formal head of the academy) responsum regarding his *yeshiva*'s reading of a Talmudic text, R. Sargado maintained that 'our whole *yeshiva*, of which it is known that its version [of the Talmud] comes from the mouths of the great ones [...] most of them [the members of the *yeshiva*] do not know anything of a book.' As his school's version of the Talmudic text was based on an unbroken oral tradition that reached back to the Talmudic masters themselves (about 400 years previously), he argued, it should be accepted as the more authoritative version (Ephrat and Elman 2000: 114).

Thus, in the mid-tenth century, in an effort to demonstrate the superiority of his institution over others, the head of the Pumbeditha Yeshiva, one of the most prominent figures in the Jewish religious world at the time, boasted that his scholars relied on no books whatsoever, but only on ancient oral traditions that could be traced back directly to the period of the Talmudic masters themselves. He therefore made a claim for the greater authority of his textual version on the basis of the differences between the oral and written texts, and the unquestioned superiority of the former. The words of R. Sargado illustrate a basic premise regarding the oral tradition: it was believed to be passed down by word of mouth from generation to generation in precise, literal, and authorita-

---

[1] For the sources of the phrase and its implications see Jeffrey 1996: xi–xii. The centrality of the book in Jewish culture since antiquity and the concept of canonization are discussed by Halbertal 1997.
[2] Oxford, Bodleian Library MS Or. 135, fol. 362b–363a; see Yassif 1988–89: 890–91.

tive form. The written text, on the other hand, did not bear the same ancient cachet, and therefore lacked the authority and authenticity of the oral text.

It would be mistaken to believe that this view of oral vs. written traditions was current only among the scholars of the time or was restricted to a certain geographical region. Our second example comes not only from a different literary genre, but also from a completely different cultural space. In the second decade of the thirteenth century, a simple Jew by the name of Menachem ben Peretz ha-Hevroni returned to his home in France after several years in the Holy Land. He brought with him stories he had heard in the Land of Israel, legends about a vicious beast with a single horn (a combination of the European unicorn and the Middle Eastern hyena), a magical tree that played sweet melodies when the wind blew through it, a land of midgets, and the figure of Abraham the Patriarch appearing to a widow in the Cave of the Patriarchs in Hebron. But most of his stories were about holy gravesites. He described them, identified the people buried there, and told of the miracles that happened to the pilgrims who visited them. In addition to being one of the first Jewish folklorists known to us by name and conducting what is tantamount to ethnographic fieldwork, Menachem ben Peretz provides us with intriguing information in the introduction to his stories, avowing:

> I received this from the people in the Land of Israel and I, Menachem ha-Hevroni, have written it down from beginning to end. If any of the distinguished men whose names appear above should read this, let them not suspect that I have written it to find favour with them or to demand money from them. For as God is my witness, I heard it from the people in the Land of Israel. And if the reader should ask how these people know of the graves of the holy men who have been buried there for three thousand years, I the writer will answer, *they come from the mouths of the people of the Land of Israel and not from the written word*. Those who live today in the Land of Israel have never left it to this day [...]. The sons of their sons are still living in the Land of Israel and each of them heard it from his father since the time of the destruction of the Temple and so they know of it and so I, Menachem ha-Hevroni, heard it.[2]

What is so surprising about Menachem's statement is the supreme authority which he attributes to the oral tradition. As these stories and others like them were never written down, yet seem to have enjoyed a large measure of credibility among the Jewish community in the Land of Israel at the time, one might be expected to wonder about the source of their authenticity. Menachem's reasoned response is based on the perception that oral tradition is more reliable than the written text. And it seems obvious from what he says that this is not merely his own opinion, but reflects the attitude both of those from whom he heard the stories and the audience to which his words are addressed.[3]

This is the extent of the similarity between the two examples. Whereas R. Sargado was referring to a precise, authoritative legal text, Menachem the traveler was not alluding to the accurate preservation and transmission of the exact words of a specific text, but to folk traditions about holy gravesites which, as he was well aware, could take a

---

[3] On these concepts compare Reiner 2005a.

variety of different forms even though they told the same story. This, in fact, is the essential distinction between scholarly and folk oral traditions.

R. Sargado's contention is less surprising in light of the findings on the Mishnah and the Talmud that have appeared in research since the mid-twentieth century. The Mishnah, the most important text in the Jewish world after the Bible, was given final form around 200 CE and the two versions of the Talmud in the fourth and fifth centuries CE. Yet they continued to exist as oral traditions and were set down in writing only in the ninth and tenth centuries.[4]

Both in the Talmud itself and in Geonic literature there is considerable evidence of the manner in which these central sources were transmitted orally for over five hundred years. There was a position in the *yeshiva* that was held by *Tanaim* who were not scholars, but rather served as 'remembers', or, as Lieberman dubs them, 'living books'. It was their function to memorize the laws handed down by the rabbis in the course of their studies in the *yeshiva*. Committing them to memory word by word and organized by subject, they then passed them along to the next generation. Whenever the rabbis were in need of the precise wording of a law for purposes of teaching or debate, they would summon the 'living books', who would recite the words from memory as they had been passed down orally for hundreds of years. Presumably, at least some of these people made notes for their own use, but these written reminders had no scholarly or legal value. We also know that the 'remembers' were tested periodically by the *yeshiva* head, when the accuracy and reliability of the texts they had committed to memory were examined.

Today we also know the answer to the question of why the *yeshivot*, all of whose members were literate, did not choose to record the ancient traditions in writing in order to give them permanence and authority. It was a strategic decision taken by the *yeshivot* in Babylon to ensure their religious and political predominance (Ephrat and Elman 2000). Anyone anywhere in the Jewish world who was in need of an accurate version of the Mishnah or Talmud – and everyone was – had no alternative but to turn to the Babylonian *yeshivot*. Had these books been available in writing, each community would have had its own authoritative copy. In other words, the familiar contention that control over literacy was a means for certain social classes to ensure their dominion over society operated in the opposite direction in the Jewish world until the tenth century. It was control over the oral traditions that enabled the *yeshivot* to maintain their authority.

Most of the texts transmitted orally, and the mechanisms devised to preserve them, belong to the genre of Halakhic law. Although the Mishnah – and particularly the two versions of the Talmud – also contains numerous non-legal Aggadic texts, these were always considered of lesser importance. Nevertheless, their precise wording was also committed to memory for purposes of instruction. In contrast, the local legends that Menachem ben Peretz heard on his travels in the Land of Israel in the thirteenth century took many forms, changing from one storyteller to the next, as he himself noted. All Galileans may have identified a particular place as the same holy site or grave, but each informant would have related a different legend about it, or a different version of the

---

[4] This theory was developed over many years. Some of the most significant studies are: Lieberman 1950, Gerhardsson 1961, Neusner 1979, Drory 1988: 55–80, and the most comprehensive account of the sources and their study by Sussman 2005.

same legend. These discrepancies had no significance for Menachem. On the contrary, he regarded the various traditions as confirmation of the reliability of the basic information to which they bore witness. Thus the two examples that we have offered demonstrate the two major models of oral traditions in the Jewish world in the Middle Ages, the scholarly and the folk traditions, each with its own genre, social role, and function.

Jewish society was distinct from the two dominant societies of the Middle Ages, the Muslim and the Christian, in that all members (or at least all males) were literate. This was the result of the religious injunction to teach every boy to read and write from about the age of five so that he could read the Torah.[5] Consequently, any discussion of Jewish oral tradition of the period must take into account the fact that every member of the community could have opened a book in Hebrew and read from it (although they may not always have understood what they were reading). In this sense, medieval Jewish society is a clear example of what Brian Stock calls 'weak orality', that is, a society in which rich written literature exists side by side with diverse oral traditions (1990: 5–6). Unlike the situation in other medieval societies, however, the written texts were accessible to at least half the members of the Jewish community (the men), and not merely to a small class of scholars, as was the case for Christians and Muslims.

This fact is clearly reflected in the familiar religious/social ritual of the annual Passover Seder. Here the extended family members and guests gather around the ritually laid table to read the same text, the Haggadah, which tells the story of the exodus from Egypt and its religious and historical significance according to Jewish tradition. This is a perfect example of the combination of oral and written traditions in a literate society. The core of the text was passed down to medieval communities from ancient Jewish sources, most likely orally, as described above. This core was then expanded and modified by the different communities, a fact attested to by the large variety of versions of the Haggadah that have survived from the Middle Ages.[6] The Seder ritual can help demonstrate how oral and written traditions come together in the Jewish world. Today, each participant, including the children, holds their own copy of the Haggadah which they follow as the leader of the Seder reads aloud from it, periodically joining in the recitation or singing. This was probably not the case in the Middle Ages, however. At that time, a Haggadah was quite expensive, and therefore relatively rare. Thus on most Seder tables there would have been a single copy of the book. Poorer families might not even have been able to afford that luxury, and would have recited the text entirely from memory, or perhaps with the help of notes they had jotted down for themselves from a Haggadah in the community. This practice is also familiar from the medieval European university

---

[5] See for example the astonishing testimony of one of Abelard's students, writing in 1140: 'When Christians send their sons to school, they do not send them for the love of God, but for lucrative reasons [...]. But the Jews, moved by piety and by the love for the law of the Lord, send to school all their children, so that everyone of them may understand the law of God [...]. A Jew, even poor, would he have ten sons, will send all of them to school, not in order to obtain any [material] advantages, as Christians do, but for the study of the law of God, and [he will send] not only his sons but also his daughters' (Graboïs 1975: 633). See also Marcus 1996 and the vast literature presented on the subject there.

[6] Major publications of the earlier sources and their studies are Goldschmidt 1960, Kasher 1967, both in Hebrew, and in English, the condensed and updated entry, with good additional bibliography and text-sources, by Goldschmidt et al. 2007.

## 19 Oral Traditions in a Literate Society: The Hebrew Literature of the Middle Ages

19 – Seder Table, Second Nuremberg Haggadah (15th c.)

and Muslim madrassa, where due to the scarcity of written manuscripts, each classroom contained a single copy of the textbook from which one student would read while the others listened. There is an essential difference between these two customs, however, as Jews gathered around the Seder table in the Middle Ages not to study, but for social reasons: to strengthen family and community ties and to shape the collective memory of the nation's past and its hopes for the future.

The Seder ritual combined reading from a book – and as we have mentioned, all the male members of the family were literate – with hearing and remembering the oral traditions heard on previous Seder nights and the ritual traditions of the family or community. The written text provided the formal framework for conducting the ceremony, while the fact that only one or two participants actually had a book in front of them made it an oral tradition and enabled oral traditions from other sources to be incorporated as well into the formal framework, producing the open diverse nature of the event. This is evidenced not only by the different versions of the Haggadah, but also by its concluding portion, which is seemingly informal. This section contains the poems and folksongs that appear at the end of the text and are different from one Haggadah to the next and from one community to the next. The lyrics were undoubtedly sung rather than read, using the words and melodies passed down to the participants from previous generations and influenced by the local culture to which they belonged, including the non-Jewish culture.[7] The blend of written and oral traditions in a literate society may explain the diverse, dynamic nature of the Passover Haggadah, which exists side by side with the unchanging literary framework in which the different materials are 'encaged'. It may also account for the huge popularity of the ritual throughout the ages. Fondness for it cannot be attributed solely to religious observance, but doubtlessly derives also and perhaps primarily, from the social and creative aspects that result from combining the two types of tradition.

Like the poems and folk materials that have come down to us through the various versions of the Haggadah, other oral traditions from the Middle Ages have survived only in written sources. In other words, they exist today after extensive alteration at the hands of the scholarly elite. This situation obviously limits our ability to understand them as they were in the 'original'. The historian Aaron Gurevich claims that a scholar engaging with medieval folk culture should not be discouraged by the fact that all the sources are essentially in the form of scholarly literature. What is important, in his opinion, is the dialogue between them, as well as the recognition that this symbiosis with educated society was the only means by which the folk culture of the period could have survived (1992:64). In an attempt to comprehend the spiritual world of a sixteenth century Friulian miller by the name of Menocchio, Carlo Ginzburg demonstrates how the combination of local folk traditions and the books that he chanced upon shaped the miller's unusual, subversive views (1992:27–32, 58–62). The testimony from surviving court records of his Inquisition trial (again, his activities are recorded in the writings of scholars, his most bitter enemies) also reveal how important it was to the miller to present his ideas and attitudes to church officials and other erudite individuals in order to receive their opinion. Thus, the dialogue between the local folk culture and educated society was one of the major forces that forged Menocchio's views and intellectual activity.

As we have seen, in the Jewish world, in which the book was held as sacred at least from the height of the Middle Ages, the dialogue between local oral culture and scholarly society was particularly intense. What were originally oral traditions have been preserved in every type of written source from the period: commentaries on the Bible and Talmud, the profuse Halakhic literature, historical writing, chronicles of journeys, mystical literature, and *maqamat* (rhymed prose). Each of these instances of the oral tradition within scholarly literature generated both a dialogue and tension between the two primary forms of contemporary communication which appear side by side and one within the other. This dialogue and tension are central to any such understanding of Jewish culture of the time.

Let us consider two typical examples which illustrate not only the nature of the dialogue, but also the methodological significance of the oral/written relationship in the medieval Jewish world. The first is a text whose source in oral traditions is not in ques-

---

[7] On these see the separate entries on Jewish music, and studies of the specific folksongs like Ḥad Gadya, Eḥad mi Yodea, Dayyenu, Adir bi-Melucha and many more, in the *Encyclopedia Judaica*, under these specific names or in the central entry (Goldschmidt et al. 2007).

tion. Benjamin of Tudela (from the second half of the twelfth century) is one of the most well-known and important of Jewish travelers, largely due to the journal in which he described in detail what he saw on his long journey.[8] In one famous episode during his stay in Jerusalem, which was then ruled by the Crusaders, he relates that a local man told him of an event that had taken place there several decades earlier. When the workers repairing a church removed stones to use as building materials, they uncovered a deep cave. Climbing down in the hope of finding hidden treasure, they discovered beautiful palaces, but when they tried to enter, a fierce wind from below blew them back out. A friend carried them home, unconscious, and the next day they were found dead in their beds. The storyteller explained that the cave was the burial place of the kings of the House of David, and the workers were punished for their sacrilege in entering the site. As recorded by Benjamin of Tudela, the story has all the hallmarks of an oral tradition. It is offered with contextual accuracy, told to the traveler by an 'eye witness' who was present at the event and who most likely pointed out the precise place where it occurred. The style is also indicative of the colloquial language of speech, containing idiomatic expressions, folk sayings, and formulaic repetition of key phrases. Benjamin appears to have considered the story to be of particular significance, and therefore recorded it almost word for word as it was told to him.

Scholars have noted that the story is an analogy for the conflict between Jews and Christians over control of the religious sites in the Holy Land. It implies that it is the Jews who hold true knowledge of the sacred biblical sites and dominion over them, not the Christians who conquered them by force.[9] To a large extent, the book as a whole expresses the same idea by means of detailed descriptions of the Jewish communities in the Middle East which stress their ancient heritage and wide dispersion. By including this story in the chronicles of his journey, Benjamin was calling on local folk traditions to reinforce the journal's message. The story makes use of devices typical of folktales: the mysterious cave, a taboo that is broken, a supernatural force emerging from the depths, and an unearthly punishment. It is incorporated into the realistic description of a journey, replete with geographical and economic details and insights, thus constituting a different communicative form whose genre contrasts with the majority of the book, yet which has its own purpose and intent.

If this example represents texts whose oral origins are undeniable, the second represents those whose roots in the oral tradition are assumed rather than explicit, since their source is not immediately obvious. Most of the textual evidence of oral traditions that has come down to us in the works of medieval scholars and writers belongs to this category.

An important genre of Jewish literature is the Hebrew collections of tales which began to appear on the scene around the ninth century (Yassif 2004). Probably originating in Eastern Jewish communities (Iraq, Persia), the tales drew their narrative materials from two major sources. As was only to be expected, the first was Talmudic and Midrashic literature, rich in stories. As this literature achieved its hallowed status in the Mid-

---

[8] For text and translation, see Adler 1909; essential information and bibliography is found in Roth 2007; see also the important study by Prawer 2005.
[9] See Reiner 2005b, which includes the Benjamin text.

dle Ages and was considered to be the foundation of Jewish life and culture, it is not surprising that its narratives appeared again and again in collections of Hebrew tales from the period. This transfer might be said to be emblematic of the realm of elite scholarly literature: like their contemporaries in Europe, the writers and editors of the collections of tales borrowed from classical sources (Yassif 2004: 9–30). However, it might also be seen as a more complex process in which the Aggadic narratives from the Talmud and Midrash themselves became an oral tradition in the Middle Ages. In other words, they were taken from Talmudic literature and told, that is, transmitted orally, to broader sectors of the population. It was from these oral traditions, rather than from the books themselves, that they were then written down and compiled as collections of tales.[10]

One of the best ways to distinguish between the two processes is to examine the differences between the stories in the rabbinical sources and those in the collections from the Middle Ages. If the discrepancies are merely a matter of a word here and there or an insignificant detail, it may be assumed that they are solely philological and stem from differences in the particular manuscript to which the writer of the tale had access. On the other hand, if there are essential differences which include reference to a reality or attitude characteristic of the Middle Ages, it is logical to infer that they were the product of the second process, that is, that they were written on the basis of an oral tradition deriving from the Talmudic texts.

The tales in the eleventh-century collection entitled *An Elegant Composition Concerning Relief after Adversity* clearly illustrate the latter process. Written by R. Nissim ben Jacob ibn Shahin, one of the leading Halakhic authorities in Kairuan in North Africa, it offers a perfect example of the dialogue between scholarly and popular culture (Brinner 1977). Here a distinguished scholar, whose thorough knowledge of Talmudic literature cannot be questioned, wrote a collection of tales in the local dialect (the variety of Arabic spoken by North African Jews). Although many of the narratives are taken from Talmudic literature, they are presented in entirely different versions, with which R. Nissim was obviously familiar. Presumably, they evolved in the following way. At the *yeshiva* that he headed, R. Nissim would take advantage of various occasions to orally impart stories from the Talmudic sources in order to convey a moral or didactic lesson to his students and the community at large. However, he customarily modified the tales, adapting them to the times, his audience, or his purposes. Only later were his stories written down, either by himself or by his students. Thus the *Elegant Composition* shows evidence of the two methodologies described above: the dialogue between scholarly and oral literature and the oral tradition underlying the written tales, even if their initial source was Talmudic written material.

Whereas the written sources of medieval oral traditions, like those of early rabbinical literature, are readily discernible, the other source of the narratives – folk traditions, whether Jewish or otherwise – are harder to identify and to investigate. The claim that a given text derives from a folk tradition can be based primarily on two features: the fact that a certain narrative cannot be found in any earlier source in Jewish literature; and the existence of parallels in the folk narratives of the cultures among which the Jews lived, either in the Muslim East or in Christian Europe. We know that few Jews at the

---

[10] See Yassif 1999a: 250–64 ('Rabbinic Agaddah as Folk Narrative in the Middle Ages').

time read books in foreign languages, and those who did were interested in philosophy or science (such as Maimonides), not narrative traditions. It may therefore be assumed that traditions which are absent from early Jewish literature and have parallels in folk non-Jewish literature entered the medieval Jewish world through oral channels.

The following example of an early collection of tales, probably from the ninth century, is presented here in detail in order to illustrate, in concrete rather than solely theoretical form, many of the issues addressed thus far. Known as *Midrash of the Ten Commandments*, it is arranged in the order of the Biblical commandments, offering a few comments on the importance of each, followed by a series of tales aimed at demonstrating the moral precept as manifested in the real world. The fifth chapter is thus devoted to the fifth commandment, 'Honour thy father and thy mother'. The second story in the chapter is the tale of 'The Child and the Book of Genesis'. After much prayer and supplication, a pious, rich, and childless man was given a son in his old age. Every day, he would carry his son to school on his shoulders. When he inquired of the teacher with which book of the Torah he would start teaching his son, the teacher replied, 'with Leviticus'. 'Start my son with the Book of Genesis', said the father, 'which declares the praises and greatness of the Holy One, Blessed be He' (Bin Gorion 1990: 163). One day, when the boy refused to be carried to school and went alone carrying the Book of Genesis in his hand, he was kidnapped by a knight from a faraway kingdom. After many days, the king of that land fell ill, and asked to be read to. The Book of Genesis was chosen at random from his library, and as no one could read it, one of his ministers recalled the Jewish child-slave in his house. The boy was brought, and read and translated for the king, who was fascinated with the wonders and greatness of God. He recovered, and sent the boy back home with great honour and riches (Bin Gorion 1990: 163–64).

The story of 'The Child and the Book of Genesis' has come down to us in dozens of versions, the earliest of which, including that in *Midrash of the Ten Commandments*, have been dated to around the ninth century.[11] The supposition that the majority of the stories in this collection originated in independent folktales that were brought together by an editor who sought a normative framework for the tales in oral traditions, gains credence from the fact that the connection between the fifth commandment and the story is tenuous at best. The child's refusal to be carried on his father's shoulders was not related to the issue of honouring his father (as enjoined by the fifth commandment), but to his desire not to be mocked by the other children. Hence, it seems likely that the story did not evolve within the literary context of this commandment, but in some other, independent, context.

At first glance, the power and popularity of the tale lies in its simplicity. The father and son observe the religious commandments (prayer and supplication, teaching Torah to one's children, honouring one's father and mother), and are rewarded in this world and the next. Thus by means of the psychological mechanism of reward and punishment, of putting fear in the hearts of sinners or promising great benefit to the pious, the story conveys its message without sermonizing. It employs a much more persuasive method, the narrative. It is the same technique used in the medieval *exemplum*, which was very popular in the two dominant religious cultures of the time, Christianity and

---

[11] Compare Bin Gorion 1990: 163–65; Levin 2004.

Islam (Berlioz and Polo De Beaulieu 1992), as well as in the minority religion, Judaism, as illustrated here.

The same explanation of the meaning and function of this tale in Jewish society can be applied to dozens of other stories from the Middle Ages. What makes 'The Child and the Book of Genesis' stand out from all the rest, however, is the middle episode of the fabula, in which the father asks the teacher with which book he will start and instructs him to begin not with the Book of Leviticus, but with the Book of Genesis so that the boy may learn of the greatness of God. The father's request is an indication that he was familiar with the educational curriculum for young children and that he objected to it, demanding an alternative approach for his son.

Indeed, a close reading reveals this exchange to be the narrative focal point of the story. In whatever version the tale is told, this episode is the turning point of the plot, since it is immediately followed by a change of direction: the child is kidnapped and the story shifts to a different geographical region and society. The father's behaviour raises two questions. First, how could a Jew of this period dare challenge the explicit precept: 'R. Assi said: Why do young children commence with [the Book of] The Law of the Priests [Leviticus] and not with [the Book of] Genesis? – surely it is because young children are pure, and the sacrifices are pure; so let the pure come and engage in the study of the pure.'[12] This was obviously the accepted norm in his community. Secondly, how would the story have been different had the teacher begun with the Book of Leviticus, and if this were the book that the child was carrying when he was kidnapped?

It is impossible to understand the events in the story without being aware of the dispute in the Geonic period between different communities, and possibly within communities themselves, over didactic issues. We know that despite the explicit rabbinic instructions, several communities determined that the teaching of young children should begin with the Book of Genesis, whereas others continued to adhere to rabbinic instructions.[13] The explanation for making the change is expressly stated in the story: a child should first be acquainted with the Creator and His deeds, the Creation and the beginning of all. Although the Book of Leviticus deals with pure animal sacrifices in the Temple, they derive from God's greatness and should therefore be taught subsequently.

The story also alludes to another, possibly more fundamental and problematic issue. Imagine that the kidnapped child had been holding the Book of Leviticus, rather than the Book of Genesis, and had read and translated it for the king. What would the king and his court have known of Judaism? That its rituals are filled with bloodshed in the House of God? That the God of Israel is bloodthirsty? Instead, they heard the universal

---

[12] *Midrash Vayikra Raba*, 8, 3 (Margulies 1972: I, 156).

[13] Yassif 2004: 18–19; Levin 2004: 346, n. 1. An outstanding piece of evidence, from early eleventh-century Kairuan (Tunisia), is given in Rabbi Nissim ben Ya'akov of Kairuan's collection of tales, *An Elegant Compositon Concerning Relief After Adversity*. After telling this story (in Arabic, like all the tales narrated there), he concludes by saying that when he was a little boy and read from the book of Leviticus in front of his father, 'the head' of the great *yeshiva* of Kairuan, he stopped and asked his father why it is that children start with Leviticus and not with the first book of the Torah. His father explained that after the destruction of the Temple, as there are no more sacrifices, the reading of the sacred words of Leviticus becomes the atonement for one's sins in their absence. This evidence presents the opposing attitudes which were heard in the Jewish communities. See Brinner 1977: 88–89.

message of the Book of Genesis, the creation of a world that belongs to all human beings. Thus, the choice of the Book of Genesis was not only a didactic issue, but one of *weltanschauung* as well. It was the choice between particularism and introversion in the Book of Leviticus in contrast to the Book of Genesis, which manifests an openness to the nations of the world and an attempt to bring them closer and to present the universality of Judaism. These were more than merely theoretical issues in the Middle Ages; they were existential concerns shared by Jewish communities both in Muslim countries and in Christian Europe.

In this interpretation, the story 'The Child and the Book of Genesis' offers an answer to a fundamental existential question of medieval Jewish society. The members of this society had a choice between two books of the Torah, both of which strengthened their bonds to the Jewish past and to the sacred literature in which their identity was grounded. The question of which to choose could not be answered simplistically with 'study both', as the choice itself was symbolic. It represented the choice between two essentially different approaches and worldviews. By setting the Book of Genesis against the Book of Leviticus, the story defines the character and meaning of each, otherwise what difference would it make with which of the two books the child began his studies?

The issue of the source of the story is extremely pertinent here. The tale has no precedent in earlier Jewish literature; it appears for the first time in that context in the Middle Ages. On the other hand, contemporary folktales contain many of the same motifs: a childless couple blessed with a child late in life; God answering the prayer for a child; a child being kidnapped and treated brutally; the wisdom of a child being recognized far from home, and so on.[14] In other words, the two hallmarks of oral traditions noted above characterize this tale, as do many of the stories in *Midrash of the Ten Commandments*. It seems clear that the author/editor became acquainted with them through the oral traditions of the Jewish society in which he lived, or the tales he heard in non-Jewish (Arabic or Persian) society. He later wrote them down after revising them in a manner that is difficult for us to recreate today. The many Hebrew collections of tales produced in the Middle Ages are therefore a rich and important source for understanding the oral Jewish literature of the period.

Our analysis of 'The Child and the Book of Genesis' brings us back to a key feature of medieval oral traditions, the dialogue between folk and scholarly literature. Both as an exemplum and a folktale, the story was created by and for a broad cross section of Jewish society. It reflects the deep commitment of members of the community to Jewish education and the teaching of its religious legacy, as well as the equally deep anxiety regarding non-Jewish society and its sucking in of Jews, whether willingly or by force. It is also an expression of the unshakable faith that better days awaited the Jews –present hardship, separation, wandering, violence, and so on notwithstanding – and that these days would come only if Jewish society preserved its identity and ethos. These were

---

[14] For the Middle Ages, see Tubach 1969, s. v. 'Child', 'Children'; see also in Thompson 1955–59 the motifs B543.3 and R311.3: Stolen Child; S300–S359: Abandoned children; H1292 and J129: Wisdom learned from child; compare also the rich source material in Boswell 1988 and Finucane 1997.

[15] See Dan 2007 and 1990, especially vol. 1, pp. 107–65.

supreme values shared by all members of the community in one form or another, regardless of education, and they are distinctly present in the story in the 'naive' context of reward and punishment. Nevertheless, as indicated, the story also adopts a firm stance in a scholarly debate. It deals with didactic and philosophical issues of immanent historical significance. It may be assumed that the Jewish public at large was not concerned with the question of how to educate the next generation and how this decision would impact on relations with the non-Jewish world, or indeed on Jewish existence in the Diaspora as a whole. In the Middle Ages, this was a philosophical and historical issue that belonged to the realm of scholars, thinkers, and educators. Yet the two dimensions exist side by side in the story and are inseparably intertwined. A Jewish scholar who heard the tale, say in a debate over the program of studies in the community school, would also have been exposed to its simpler exemplary meaning. Similarly, if the story were told to broader sectors of the community, in the synagogue for example, they would have learned of the dispute over whether to begin the children's studies with the Book of Genesis or the Book of Leviticus, even if they did not understand its full implications. In addition, it is of considerable significance that this folktale centers on a book. It includes the desire for a book, dependence upon it, and its determining the fate of a society. The fact that the nature of Jewish existence is defined here by 'the book' is a fine illustration of the symbiosis between the oral and written traditions in medieval Jewish culture.

Our discussion thus far makes it clear that the distinction between oral and written traditions in Jewish society was not based on social class or status. That is, oral traditions were not restricted to the lower classes and the uneducated, and written traditions were not the exclusive domain of scholars. Instead, the distinction was primarily a matter of content. R. Nissim of Kairuan, the author (or teller) of *An Elegant Composition Concerning Relief after Adversity*, was a preeminent scholar and religious leader who belonged to a dynasty of Jewish scholars. Yet he was intensely involved in oral literature, most likely telling his stories both to the students in his *yeshiva* and to the community at large in the synagogue, in homilies delivered to the public, etc. R. Nissim was unique not because he told these tales, as many others did so as well, but because of their content. Most are oral versions of stories from the Talmud and classic Midrash. That is to say, he made deliberate use of his religious knowledge and status to transfer classic stories to the oral tradition and to tell them to the community in its colloquial language, Jewish-Arabic, changing their narrative form and adapting their content to contemporary life.

Another example indicative of the fact that the oral/written dichotomy was not associated with social divides comes from Rabbi Judah he-Ḥasid (the pious). A leading Jewish scholar of the Middle Ages, he was the founder of Ashkenazi Hasidism and the primary author of the influential book *Sefer Ḥasidim*, as well as the author of numerous works of commentary, philosophy, mysticism, and ethics.[15] The more than four hundred exempla and folktales in *Sefer Ḥasidim*, along with the numerous demonological stories in his other books, provide ample evidence of Judah he-Ḥasid's keen interest in the narrative world (Yassif 2005). From his students we know that he habitually told them stories, all of which he included in his books. One account in particular is so clearly

---

[16] *Sefer ha-Gan*, attributed to R. Isaac ben R. Eleazar of Worms, Venice 1606, pp. 9b–10a.

pertinent to our discussion that I offer it here in its entirety. The speaker is the anonymous author of *Sefer ha-Gan*, a fourteenth century commentary:

> When I studied in Speyer before Rabbi Yedidiah of blessed memory, I found in his school the handwriting of Rabbi Zaltman [son of R. Judah the Pious]. This is [what it said]: My father and teacher, the Pious, told me that in his time there was an incident involving a wealthy man in Speyer who used scissors to shave his beard. My father and teacher would approach him and protest against [this practice]. The wealthy man did not heed his words, saying, 'a refined person (*istenis*) am I, and I cannot suffer the beard.' My father and teacher told him: 'You should know that you will know a bitter end, for after your death, demons resembling cows [will] trample your beard. This is the lot of those who cut their beards. And you will know the truth of the verse, "You shall not round the corners of your heads, neither shalt thou mar" (Leviticus 19:27), which is an acrostic [the Hebrew word for] "cows" (*parot*)' And when that man of means passed away, all the great men of Speyer sat near [the corpse], and my father and teacher was there. He wrote a name and threw it on that wealthy man, and he [the dead man] stood up. And all those who had been sitting there ran out [in fear of the dead]. Then the dead man began to pluck at his head and pull his hair. My father and teacher said to him: 'What [is happening] to you?' He said to him: 'Woe is me that I did not heed you.' My father and teacher said to him: 'Please explain what is happening to your soul?' He said to him: 'When my soul left [my body], a demon, looking like a great cow, came with a vessel full of pitch, sulphur, and salt, and imprisoned it in it, so that [the soul] could not get out. The harsh justice ensued and took the vessel with the spirit [within] from the demon and brought it before the Creator of Souls. A divine voice sounded, and said to me: "Have you studied and repeated?" I said to him: "I have studied and repeated." At once he ordered that a *Humash* (Pentateuch) be brought and said to me: "Read it." As soon as I opened the book I found written, "neither shalt thou mar the corners of thy beard" and I did not know what to answer. Then I heard a voice declaring: "Put this one's soul on the bottommost level." As they were bearing [my] soul to the bottommost level, a divine voice sounded: "Wait. My son Juda is more righteous than he and has now asked mercy. His soul will not descend to She'ol."' Until this point (in his words).[16]

The manuscript was found in the *yeshiva* where R. Judah's son had studied several years earlier, and the handwriting is identified as his by the writer. Like our first example, the story told to Benjamin of Tudela in Jerusalem, this tale has come down to us in a version as close as possible to that told by R. Judah to his son (perhaps in the presence of others as well). It is a folk legend in every sense of the word, with the central motif of a divine injunction and the punishment that follows its infringement. Bringing the dead back to life by means of a magical name, the description of hell and the demons populating it, and the punishment that fits the crime were all common themes in medieval folklore.[17] In other words, we see a scholar and religious leader making use of the hallmarks of folklore – the oral tale and its narrative model and motifs – in order to tell a story with both an overt objective and a covert agenda.

On the surface, it is a typical exemplum focusing on a particular commandment or taboo, the Biblical injunction against cutting one's beard and the punishment incurred

---

[17]  See Patch 1950, and with special reference to the discussion of oral/literacy see Gurevich 1992: 50–64 ('Oral and Written Culture of the Middle Ages: Two "Peasant Visions" of the Late Twelfth to the Early Thirteenth Centuries'). The folkloric origins are described in: Gatto 1979, Gardiner 1993, and in Jewish culture, in Yassif 2001: 99–111, 460–68.
[18]  See Dan 1961, 1990, and 2007; Yassif 2005.

for infringing it. After hearing this story from an authority such as R. Judah he-Ḥasid, any Jew who believed in the next world and the punishment it inflicted – as did the overwhelming majority of the community in Ashkenaz at the time – would clearly have thought twice before deciding to ignore the injunction and shave his beard. But it is equally clear that the story also had a tacit purpose: to bolster R. Judah's leadership status in the community by reinforcing it among the stronger and wealthier sectors of the population. In essence, the conflict between R. Judah and the wealthy 'refined' man did not centre on the performance of some commandment or another. It was a struggle for power and standing, a question of whether the social or religious leaders would determine the behavioural code of the community, and of which group was subordinate to which.

This is another example of the complex function of the oral tradition, and here, at least, the oral nature of the story is not in doubt. It served both the intents and interests of the broadest sectors of Jewish society and the narrower concerns of its leaders and scholars, for whom the disputational aspects and the issue of authority were crucial. As we can see, these matters were not addressed solely in philosophical or Halakhic literature, but in oral narratives as well. That is, the leaders borrowed the popular forms of expression in order to draw attention to issues of importance to them. Thus the oral traditions served as loci of conjunction and communication between the differing, albeit not contradictory, interests of Jewish society at large on the one hand, and its leaders and scholars on the other.

It is not by chance that the concluding episode in R. Judah's tale brings to mind Dante's *Inferno*. Characterizations of the fearsome demons who torture the dead in hell, the different levels of hell, and recognizing the dead man as someone who was formerly a distinguished figure in the storyteller's own town and one who was involved in political intrigues are all central motifs in Dante's poem. The significance of these parallels is that each man, R. Judah he-Ḥasid in Germany and Dante Alighieri in Italy, took the motifs from the oral folklore current in his own time and place. Indeed, R. Judah's writings contain numerous materials familiar from European folk culture of the period, both Jewish and Christian, including descriptions of demons (vampires, witches, strigae), narrative motifs, and folk legends.[18] From this perspective, R. Judah might even be seen as a sort of amateur ethnographer who recorded the local folktales and folk-beliefs that piqued his curiosity. His aim, of course, was not folkloristic, but rather religious and social. However, he used these tales and myths to reinforce the religious truths he expounded and to instill them in the Jewish community at large. And so, while this was never his intention, the fact remains that the hundreds of narrative texts preserved in his writings provide invaluable evidence of the diverse oral traditions popular in the Jewish community in central Europe in the twelfth century.

R. Judah was not the only figure to borrow from local folklore. The anonymous author of *Midrash of the Ten Commandments* did not invent the dozens of stories in his collection either. The large majority of them were tales being told in Jewish communities in the East in the eighth and ninth centuries. And like R. Judah, he too did not display an interest in them for what we would define today as folkloristic, but instead

---

[19] See Reiner 2005a; Limor 2005.

sought out those stories that could best illustrate the fundamental values expressed in the Ten Commandments. Nonetheless, his decision to create a collection of stories rather than to write moral lessons on the commandments is an indication both of his fascination with them and of his belief, shared by numerous Eastern and European preachers and moralists, that the tales were a more effective means of influencing the community as a whole. And whatever his primary intention, by the very act of collecting or collating the tales, the anonymous author also established himself as an early ethnographer, documenting the oral traditions of his community in the awareness that human memory, on which the survival of this tradition depends, is unreliable. Hence, their cultural legacy could best be preserved for future generations by means of a written text.

Thus far we have seen two types of ethnographers. The first were Jewish travelers such as Benjamin of Tudela and Menachem ben Peretz ha-Hevroni. Other well-known travelers included R. Pethachiah of Regensburg, Jacob ben Nathaniel, and Samuel bar Samson, to name but a few. These individuals had two major interests. The first was to report on the size and conditions of Jewish communities throughout the world, thereby fostering a sense of nationhood and social unity. The second was to describe the holy places in the Land of Israel, which provided a historical link with the magnificent past of the nation and helped sustain the hope that its former glory would one day be restored. In order to achieve these goals, the travelers listened to the stories related in the various Jewish communities that they visited and retold them to their own community on their return. They were written down either by the travelers themselves, or, in most cases, by other writers who considered it important to preserve these materials for the generations to come.[19] We have seen examples of this sort of documentation in Benjamin's story of the burial place of the House of David and Menachem ben Peretz's tales of the wonders of the Holy Land.

The second type of 'ethnographer' was the educators and religious teachers. The author of *Midrash of the Ten Commandments*, R. Nissim of Kairuan, the writer of *An Elegant Composition Concerning Relief after Adversity*, and R. Judah he-Ḥasid all collected stories from the local oral traditions in both their own communities and in the dominant Christian or Muslim societies among which they lived in order to use them to disseminate moral precepts. Recognizing that these tales had more influence on the conduct of the community at large than did any moral lessons, they took advantage of any narrative, whether Jewish or otherwise, that would serve to demonstrate proper behaviour or, alternatively, conduct that deviated from religious or social norms. Consequently, like the wealth and diversity of exempla in the Christian world, the collections of tales documented by these educators are a rich source of knowledge of the oral traditions of their period and their role in the cultural reality of the time.

Medieval Jewish society also saw a third type of collector and recorder of oral traditions: the chroniclers and historians. It is a well-known fact that historians in the Middle Ages made considerable use of oral legends which recounted historical events of significance to the local community or to society as a whole.[20] The authenticity of these legends was derived from a complex system which relied on factors such as the credibility

---

[20] On the vast research on this topic, see Yassif 1999a: 519–20, and Yassif 1999b.

of the people who told them, their grounding in an explicit historical time and familiar geographical location, their similarity to other legends recounting the same event, and most importantly, their meaning and function in the society in which they were related. Historical legends from medieval Jewish society have survived in a wide variety of sources that are not necessarily historical in nature, such as midrashim, commentaries on the Bible and Talmud, books of Halakha and ethics, liturgical poetry, and so on. Nonetheless, the most salient sources from this period remain the historical writings and chronicles based on legends taken largely from oral traditions. Such works include the tenth-century *Yosippon*, the eleventh-century *The Chronicle of Yerachme'el* or its expanded version as a fourteenth-century *Book of Memories*, the thirteenth-century *Sefer ha-Kabbala* (Book of Tradition), and the *Shalshelet ha-Kabbala* (Chain of Tradition) from the sixteenth century.

*The Chronicle of Ahimaaz* is a family history from southern Italy written in 1054 by Ahimaaz ben Paltiel. It presents the annals of the author's family from their arrival in Italy in the Roman era to the time of its writing, conveyed in the form of tales concerning its most prominent members. The chronicle was unknown until it was discovered in the archives of the Toledo cathedral in the mid-nineteenth century (Yassif 2004: 97–135). Since then it has made a substantial contribution to numerous areas in the study of the period. In the context of our present discussion of medieval Jewish oral traditions, its major importance lies in the fact that it seems never to have gone beyond the confines of the family, and that a single copy, most likely in the author's own handwriting, has survived, after making its way to Spain in some unknown manner. As *The Chronicle of Ahimaaz* was totally obscure, it could not have influenced parallel traditions, that is, similar tales that appear in other contemporary sources. Therefore, they could only have had their source in independent oral traditions which can be analyzed and compared with the stories in the chronicle. In the words of Ahimaaz himself, as recorded in the introduction and conclusion to his book:

> In the name of Him that dwelleth in the heavens of splendor, I will begin to tell the story, diligently to investigate, arrange and present a collection of the traditions of my forefathers, to unfold them in proper order, to explain them with notes, to trace without confusion the genealogy whose parts must be collected like stubble[...]. That I may inculcate lessons of truth [...] in the seat of the elders, in the company of the learned [...].
>
> He has granted me with what I have so ardently asked of Him. I have pondered and examined and have found what my heart desired, the lineage of my family. With God's help I have arranged and written it in poetic form [...]. In a book I have collected and compiled and narrated it for the generation to come. (Salzman 1924: 60, 101)

In other words, Ahimaaz ben Paltiel's overriding aim was to record, 'in a book', his family lineage for future generations. To do so, he 'collected and compiled', words clearly associated with oral traditions, and made explicit reference to 'elders' and 'the learned', that is, the members of the community who remembered the events, or the traditions that contained accounts of them. Further evidence that *The Chronicle of Ahimaaz* relied largely on oral sources is the great esteem in which the author holds the 'book'. Had he had in his possession any written documents recording the family history, he would undoubtedly have indicated as much, as this would have enhanced the credibility of his composition. The fact that no mention is made anywhere in the chronicle of even a single document from which he drew his information allows us to conclude that most, if not all, of it was derived from oral traditions.

The chronicle contains dozens of tales of miracles, exorcisms, raisings of the dead, the use of magical names, and struggles both within the Jewish community and between it and non-Jewish society in southern Italy. Byzantium and its history are present in the background. Momentous events, such as the reconquest of North Africa from the Vandals and Ostrogoths, the establishment of a Byzantine dynasty in Egypt, and so on, are all attributed to the writer's forefathers, members of the Ahimaaz line, going back two hundred years.

The stories in *The Chronicle of Ahimaaz* suggest the existence of sustained oral traditions that served to reinforce the status of wealthy and distinguished families. These traditions belong entirely to the genre of folk-legend: stories passed by word of mouth that are anchored in an explicit historical time and a familiar geographical location, and which are regarded as reliable histories by the community despite their supernatural motifs. The chronological order of the legends (which we are told is the work of the writer) presents the historical memory of both the family itself and its community. *The Chronicle of Ahimaaz* thus constitutes important evidence of an entire body of oral traditions, rather than a single narrative, which was preserved by the family and which shaped its collective memory over the course of two hundred years. Admittedly, the amateur ethnographer Ahimaaz ben Paltiel did not conduct objective fieldwork. He had a specific agenda which he states clearly: to demonstrate the importance of his family. As a result, he undoubtedly manipulated the material he collected and made considerable modifications to suit his purpose. Nevertheless, the material itself, the manner in which it is presented (its arrangement, rhyming pattern, and style), and his interpretation of it make an enormous contribution to our understanding of the historical oral traditions of the period.

A further example of the oral sources used by early Jewish historiographers is *Shevet Yehudah*. Written around 1520 by Solomon ibn Verga, it documents the blood libels against the Jews in Spain which led to their expulsion in 1492 (Shochat 2007). Here is how the writer describes his sources:

> *I heard* this from the mouth of a great sage of Ashkenaz who came as an emissary [...]. *I also heard from the mouth* of a kabbalist sage who had come from France, that in one city [...] a decree was proclaimed [...]. From such a pious and wise man as R. Abraham ibn Arama *I heard* that a miracle was performed by my master, R. Judah ibn Verga of Seville. I will write of it here [...]. *I heard* from elders, emigrants from Spain, that one ship came here because of the plague. (Baer 1947: 91, 92, 122)

Solomon ibn Verga composed his account some thirty years after the expulsion. At the time, the expulsion of 1492 and those that preceded and foreshadowed it were subjects of consuming interest to Jewish society. Historical narrative traditions of these events were widespread, and were told in numerous communities, yet few were worthy of being enshrined in ibn Verga's book. Still, the sources he records indicate that the majority of tales that he did include, like those in other historiographical works, were created, developed, and disseminated in Jewish communities as oral narrative traditions before ever being set down in writing (see also Loeb 1892).

These two historiographers, Ahimaaz ben Paltiel in eleventh-century Italy and Solomon ibn Verga some three hundred and fifty years later in Spain, as well as all the Hebrew writers between them, provide distinct evidence of the significant role played by oral traditions in perpetuating the collective memory and promoting a social agenda (the status of the Ahimaaz family or remembrance of the Jews expelled from Spain). Both Ahimaaz and ibn Verga were well aware that the history of their community was preserved in its oral traditions, and therefore drew on them as they were recounted by any source they regarded as reliable: community elders, rabbis, religious authorities, social leaders, or family members. They received their materials in the form of historical legends relating to particular events bound to a certain time and place, and saw it as their primary task to incorporate them into a comprehensive historical record. We must not forget that this record only came into being when the individual traditions were brought together and written down. As oral traditions they remained the province of different tellers in different places, so that no cohesive historical account existed. These two works are thus of paramount importance for the examination of oral traditions and the changes they undergo when transferred into writing.[21]

The fragmentary nature of oral traditions in medieval Jewish culture, as opposed to the comprehensive and cohesive character of its written works, may also explain why there are no epic Jewish oral narratives from this period. Nothing has been found to compare to the great French or German epic poems from the Middle Ages (*The Song of Roland, Nibelungenlied*) or the South Slavic epics. The closest we can come would be the Passover Haggadah, which might be considered a combined oral and written work used for the communal ritual of telling the story of the Exodus. Other epic works in the Jewish literature of this time are all written compositions for which there is no evidence to indicate that they were ever oral traditions. We can therefore state with considerable certainty that the oral culture produced in the Middle Ages in literate Jewish society was principally local and fragmentary. It created folktales and legends, myths and rumours that related to life and society in a particular region and a specific historical and geographical reality. Such were the traditions recorded by Jewish travelers like Menachem ben Peretz or Benjamin of Tudela, and such were the many Galilean traditions regarding Jesus/Yeshu'a – whether Jewish, Christian, or Muslim – which similarly reflected the geographical and social reality of the local population.[22]

These examples attest to the importance of uncovering and reconstructing oral traditions in a society that is not only literate, but that expressly reveres the written word and discounts oral accounts. Investigations of this sort reveal a cultural product whose qualities, purposes, and meanings are distinct from those which the religious and social hierarchy strives to present. It is here that the tension between scholarly literature and the traces of oral traditions within it manifest themselves most conspicuously. This is the task which future research should set itself, to find in the written work that which scholarly authorities would prefer to remain enshrouded. The perception of the Jews as the 'People of the Book' has cast a shadow over a major aspect of medieval Jewish society –

---

[21] This was suggested already in the pioneering work of Jan Vansina (1965: 19–30, 'Tradition as a Chain of Testimonies').
[22] See the seminal study by Reiner 1996.

its oral traditions. Preconceptions regarding the educated elite versus the unlearned populace and the book as the focus of culture versus inferior oral literature have led generations of cultural development and the study of Jewish literature since the nineteenth century to ignore this key feature of the Jewish world.

## References

Adler, Marcus Nathan, ed. and trans. 1909. *The Itinerary of Benjamin of Tudela: Critical Text, Translation and Commentary.* New York: Feldheim.
Baer, Yitzhak, and Azriel Shochat, eds. 1947. Shlomoh Ben Yehuda Verga. *Sefer Shevet Yehuda.* Jerusalem: Mosad Bialik.
Berlioz, Jacques, and Marie Anne Polo De Beaulieu, eds. 1992. *Les exempla médiévaux. Introduction à la recherche.* Carcassonne: Garae/ Hesiode.
Bin Gorion, M. J. and E., coll. 1990. *Mimekor Yisrael: Classical Jewish Folktales.* Ed. Dan Ben-Amos, trans. I. M. Lask. Bloomington: Indiana UP.
Boswell, John. 1988. *The Kindness of Strangers: The Abandonment of Children in Western Europe from Late Antiquity to the Renaissance.* New York: Pantheon.
Brinner, William M., trans. 1977. Nissim ben Jacob ibn Shahin. *An Elegant Composition concerning Relief after Adversity.* New Haven: Yale UP.
Dan, Joseph. 1961. 'Sipurim demonologiim mi-kitvei R' Yehuda he-Hasid' [Demonological Tales from the Writings of R. Judah the Pious]. *Tarbiz* 30: 273–89.
–. 1990. *Hasidut 'Ashkenaz be-toldot ha-mahashavah ha-yehudit* [*Ashkenazi Hasidism in the History of Jewish Thought*]. Tel-Aviv: The Open University of Israel.
–. 2007. 'Judah ben Samuel he-Hasid.' In *Encyclopedia Judaica*, XI, 490–91.
Drory, Rina. 1988. *Reshit ha-maga'im shel ha-sifrut ha-yehudit 'im ha-sifrut ha-'aravit be-me'asir-it* [*The Emergence of Jewish-Arabic Literary Contacts at the Beginning of the Tenth Century*]. Tel-Aviv: The Porter Institute.
*Encyclopedia Judaica.* Ed. Fred Skolnik et al. 2nd ed. 22 vols. Detroit: Macmillan, 2007.
Ephrat, Daphna, and Yaakov Elman. 2000. 'Orality and the Institutionalization of Traditions: The Growth of the Geonic Yeshiva and the Islamic Madrasa.' In *Transmitting Jewish Traditions: Orality, Textuality, and Cultural Diffusion* . Ed. Yaakov Elman and Israel Gershoni. New Haven: Yale UP. 107–38.
Finucane, Ronald C. 1997. *The Rescue of the Innocents: Endangered Children in Medieval Miracles.* New York: Macmillan.
Gardiner, Eileen. 1993. *Medieval Visions of Heaven and Hell – A Sourcebook.* New York: Garland.
Gatto, Giuseppe. 1979. 'Le voyage au paradis: La christianisation des traditions folkloriques au Moyen Age.' *Annales ESC* 34: 929–42.
Gerhardsson, Birger. 1961. *Memory and Manuscript. Oral Tradition and Written Transmission in Rabbinic Judaism and Early Christianity.* Uppsala: Gleerup; Copenhagen: Munksgaard.
Ginzburg, Carlo. 1992. *The Cheese and the Worms: The Cosmos of a Sixteenth Century Miller.* Baltimore: The Johns Hopkins UP.
Goldschmidt, E. Daniel 1960. *The Passover Haggadah: Its Sources and History.* Jerusalem: The Bialik Institute.
–, et al. 2007. 'Haggadah, Passover.' *Encyclopedia Judaica*, VIII, 207–17.
Graboïs, Aryeh. 1975. 'The *Hebraica Veritas* and Jewish-Christian Intellectual Relations in the Twelfth Century.' *Speculum* 50: 613–34.
Gurevich, Aaron J. 1992. *Historical Anthropology of the Middle Ages.* Trans. Jana Howlett. Cambridge: Polity P.

Halbertal, Moshe. 1997. *People of the Book: Canon, Meaning, and Authority*. Cambridge, MA: Harvard UP.
Jeffrey, David Lyle. 1996. *People of the Book: Christian Identity and Literary Culture*. Grand Rapids, MI: Eerdmans.
Kasher, Menachem M., ed. 1967. *Hagadah Shelemah. Seder Hagadah shel Pesach 'im ḥilufei nusḥa'ot, he'arot ve-ziunim ve-yalqut perushim* [*Hagadah Shelemah: The Complete Passover Hagadah. Text with Variant Reading*]. 3rd ed. Jerusalem: Torah Shelema Institute.
Levin, Dina. 2004.'Ma'aseh be-sefer Bereshit' [The Tale of the Book of Genesis] In *Enziqlopediyah shel ha-sipur ha-yehudi. Sipur 'oqev sipur* [*Encyclopedia of the Jewish Story. Sippur Okev Sippur*]. Ed. Yoav Elstein, Avidov Lipsker and Rella Kushelevsky. Ramat Gan: Bar-Ilan UP. 333–49.
Lieberman, Saul. 1950.'The Publication of the *Mishna*.' In Saul Lieberman. *Hellenism in Jewish Palestine: Studies in the Literary Transmission, Beliefs and Manners of Palestine in the I Century B. C. E. – IV Century C. E*. Texts and Studies of the Jewish Theological Seminary of America 18. New York: The Jewish Theological Seminary of America. 83–99.
Limor, Ora. 2005.'Bemo 'eynav: 'oleh ha-regel mesaper' ['With his Own Eyes': The Pilgrim Narrates]. In Limor and Reiner 2005:325–51.
–, and Elchanan Reiner, eds. 2005. *'Aliyah le-regel. Yehudim, noẓrim, muslemim* [*Pilgrimage: Jews, Christians, Moslems*]. Ra'anana: The Open University of Israel.
Loeb, Isidore. 1892.'Le folk-lore juif dans la chronique du Schébet Iehuda d'Ibn Verga.' *Revue des Études Juives* 24:1–29.
Marcus, Ivan G. 1996. *Rituals of Childhood: Jewish Acculturation in Medieval Europe*. New Haven: Yale UP.
Margulies, Mordecai, ed. 1972. *Midrash Vayiqra' rabah. Yoẓe' le'or 'al-pi kitvei-yad ve-sridei ha-gnizah 'im ḥilufei nusḥa'ot, he'arot ve-be'urim* [*Midrash Wayyikra Rabbah. A Critical Edition Based on Manuscripts and Genizah Fragments with Variants and Notes*]. 5 parts in 2 vols. 2nd printing. Jerusalem: Vahrmann Books.
Neusner, Jacob. 1979.'Oral Torah and Oral Tradition: Defining the Problematic.' In Jacob Neusner. *Method and Meaning in Ancient Judaism*. Brown University, Brown Judaic Studies 10. Missoula, MT: Scholars Press. 59–75.
Patch, H. R. 1950. *The Other World According to Descriptions in Medieval Literature*. Cambridge, MA: Harvard UP.
Prawer, Joshua. 2005. 'Te'urei-masa' 'ivriim be-'ereẓ-Yisra'el ba-tequfah ha-ẓalbanit.' [Hebrew Travel-Descriptions of Eretz Yisrael in the Crusade Period]. In Limor and Reiner 2005:372–440.
Reiner, Elchanan. 1996.'Ben Yehoshu'a le-Yeshu'a: mi-sipur miqra'i le-mitos meqomi' [Between Joshua and Yeshu'a: From Biblical Story to Local Myth]. *Zion* 61:281–317.
–. 2005a.'"Mi-pi bnei ma'arava"': 'al darkhei rishumah shel masoret ha-meqomot ha-qedoshim be-'ereẓ-Yisra'el be-yemei ha-benayim' ['From the Mouth of the Sons of Eretz Yisrael': On Inscription of Jewish Holy Land Traditions in the Middle Ages]. In Limor and Reiner 2005:441–58.
–. 2005b.'Ha-sheqer ha-galuy ve-ha-'emet ha-nisteret: noẓrim, yehudim ve-meqomot qedoshim be-'ereẓ Yisra'el ba-me'ah ha-y"b' [The Exposed Lie and the Hidden Truth: Christians, Jews and Holy Places in Eretz Yisrael of the 12th Century]. In Limor and Reiner 2005:268–98.
Roth, Cecil. 2007.'Benjamin (Ben Jonah) of Tudela.' *Encyclopedia Judaica*, III, 362–64.
Salzman, Marcus, trans. 1924. *The Chronicle of Ahimaaz*. Columbia University Oriental Studies 18. New York: Columbia UP.
Shochat, Azriel. 2007.'Ibn Verga, Solomon.' *Encyclopedia Judaica*, IX, 695–96.
Stock, Brian. 1990. *Listening for the Text: On the Uses of the Past*. Philadelphia: U of Pennsylvania P.

Sussman, Yaakov. 2005. '"Torah she-baʻal peh" pshutah ke-mashmaʻah' [Oral Torah: Its Accurate Meaning]. In *Mechqerei Talmud. Gimel. Qovets mehqerim be-talmud ve be-thumim govlim, muqdash le-zechro shel prof. Efraim E. Urbach* [*Talmudic Studies 3.Talmudic Studies Dedicated to the Memory of Professor Ephraim E. Urbach*]. Jerusalem: The Magnes Press. 209–384.

Thompson, Stith. 1955–1959. *Motif Index of Folk-Literature*. 6 vols. Copenhagen and Bloomington: Indiana UP.

Tubach, Frederic C. 1969. *Index Exemplorum: A Handbook of Medieval Religious Tales*. FF Communications 204. Helsinki: Akademia Scientiarum Fennica.

Vansina, Jan. 1965. *Oral Tradition: A Study in Historical Methodology*. Harmondsworth: Penguin.

Yassif, Eli. 1988–89. '"Pna'i" ve "Ruah rehavah": Halachah ve maʻaseh be-hithavut ha-sipur ha-ʻivri be-shilhei yemei-ha-benayim' ['Leisure' and 'Generosity': Theory and Practice in the Creation of the Hebrew Narrative in the Middle Ages]. *Qiryat Sefer* 62: 887–905.

–. 1999a. *The Hebrew Folktale: History, Genre, Meaning*. Bloomington, IN: Indiana UP.

–. 1999b. 'Agadah ve-historiyah: historionim qor'im be-ʻagadot ʻivriyot mi-yemei ha-benayim' [Legend and History: Historians Read Medieval Hebrew Stories]. *Zion* 64: 187–220.

–, ed. 2001. *Sefer ha-Zikhronut. Hu Divrei ha-yamim le-Yerahmeʼel* [*The Book of Memory – that is The Chronicles of Jerahmeʼel*]. Tel-Aviv: Tel-Aviv UP.

–. 2004. *Ke-margalit be-mishbezet. Qovets ha-sipurim ha-ʻivri be-yemei ha-benayim* [[*Like a Pearl in its Setting.*] *The Hebrew Collection of Tales in the Middle Ages*]. Tel-Aviv: Hakibbutz Hameuchad.

–. 2005. 'The Medieval Saint as Protagonist and Storyteller: The Case of Judah he-Hasid.' In *Creation and Re-Creation in Jewish Thought: Festschrift in Honor of Joseph Dan*. Ed. Rachel Elior and Peter Schäfer. Tübingen: Mohr Siebeck. 179–92.

# 20 Woman's Song in Medieval Western Europe

*Anne L. Klinck*

## 1 What is Woman's Song?

In Shakespeare's *Twelfth Night*, the sentimental Duke Orsino asks for a song that is 'old and plain', and goes on to describe it thus:

> The spinsters and the knitters in the sun,
> And the free maids that weave their thread with bones,
> Do use to chant it. It is silly sooth,  [simple truth]
> And dallies with the innocence of love,
> Like the old age.  (II.iv.41–47)[1]

The Duke seems to be asking for a 'woman's song'. What he actually has in mind turns out to be an affected lament by a *man* expiring of love. He has, however, evoked a whole world of women's oral traditions. One might expect a woman's song to be composed by a woman; in fact, the term, a translation of *chanson de femme* and *Frauenlied*, refers to a particular kind of song or poem – in a traditional style and usually about love – in a woman's voice. In the plural, 'woman's songs' is preferable to 'women's songs', since the latter is more likely to be misunderstood. The concept has long been familiar to continental medievalists; it is less common in English scholarship.[2] Linguists would call it a 'fuzzy concept', because it is by no means well defined at the edges.[3] Typically, woman's song is characterised by stanzaic structure, often with repeated lines or phrases creating parallelism or refrain; simplicity of vocabulary and syntax; lack of narrative and descriptive detail; emotional, often exclamatory language; focus on certain natural objects – water, trees, birds, animals; and a strong physical element in the speaker's account of

---

[1] Quoted from Warren and Wells 1994.
[2] As far as I know, the first English-language volume devoted to woman's song was *Vox Feminae*, an essay collection edited by John Plummer in 1981. This volume contains the editor's introduction on early medieval woman's song in various languages, followed by essays on Medieval Latin, Galician-Portuguese, German, Irish, Middle English, and French. The more recent collection edited by Klinck and Rasmussen (2002) contains essays on Old English, Iberian, Occitan, Old French, German, and Middle English texts, as well as on musical performance, and on parallels between ancient and medieval woman's song. Most of the scholarship on Continental woman's songs continues to be written in languages other than English.
[3] Semanticists find 'fuzzy concepts' a necessary component of discourse. See O'Grady and Archibald 2004: 232.

herself and her feelings. Often the opening is addressed to the speaker's mother, lover, or confidante(s).

## 2 An Oral or Popular Mode?

German and French writers influenced by Romantic attitudes became interested in medieval poems of this kind, and detected in them reflections of 'the oldest folk poetry'.[4] From Goethe and Jakob Grimm in the earlier years of the nineteenth century to Alfred Jeanroy and Gaston Paris at the end of it, they looked to preliterate compositions spontaneously created by groups of singing, dancing women and girls.[5] Woman's song was for them an essentially popular kind of verse, the creation of the folk. Although this Romantic view of the origins of woman's song is too simple,[6] and many, perhaps most, of the surviving specimens are the work of sophisticated, highly literate *men*, this type of poetry is to a large extent the product of a long-standing oral tradition.

Poems of this kind are typically also songs, sometimes intended to be accompanied by music, and sometimes by dance. Sadly, in most cases the music has been lost, and although we still call these pieces woman's *songs*, we tend to think of them in terms of the written text rather than the live performance.[7] Though necessarily preserved in writing, the mode is essentially an oral one.[8] Oral transmission is suggested by the existence of variants, or of differences in the order and number of stanzas, making it hard to decide what constitutes a distinct and separate poem.[9] Composers and singers would often have been the same persons. Probably then, as now, the singer cultivated a stage persona.[10] In general, poet-composers enjoyed a higher status than mere performers. Professional, public, entertainment was not an occupation for respectable women and tended to be linked with the performance of other services. In a couple of Spanish romances, high-born women who sing take pains to point out that 'I am not a *joglaresa*'

---

[4] See Mölk 1988:63–88, at 67, referring to the reaction of Goethe, Grimm, and others to Serbian folk songs. Mölk's essay is reprinted as the introduction to his *Romanische Frauenlieder* (Mölk 1989:13–47). On woman's song from the Balkans, see further below.

[5] For the history of the term *Frauenlied*, see Mölk 1988:64–67; also Mölk 1990. Earlier influential studies of woman's song include Jeanroy 1925; Paris 1891–92; Frings 1949; Spitzer 1952; Malone 1962; Dronke 1996:86–108 (ch. 3); Davidson 1975.

[6] Ruth Finnegan notes that 'the key strands in the [Romantic] approach to national and "folk" literature are, first, the view of the artless spontaneity of such literature, and, second, the yearning for another, more organic and natural world from the analyst's own' (Finnegan 1977:34).

[7] For the music of the troubadours and trouvères, see van der Werf 1995; Aubrey 1996 and 2001; Rosenberg et al. 1998; Switten et al. 2001 (CD-ROM). On women's performance of medieval lyric more generally, see Boynton 2002 and Cohen 2002.

[8] The text in isolation leaves us missing much of the effect. Compare Finnegan 1977 on the need to consider 'the nature of the audience, the context of performance, the personality of the poet-performer, and the details of the performance itself' (p. 29; see also p. 133 on the importance of performance).

[9] Variations in stanza number and arrangement are problematic in German lyrics; variants are an issue in the Spanish songbooks. See, respectively, notes 84 and 103, below.

[10] See pp. 438–39, below, in connection with the German poet Reinmar, and compare Bonnermeier 2002 on modern *chanteuses*.

20 – Woman Dancer, from Paris, BnF MS lat. 1118, fol. 114r (first half of 11th c.)

(female public performer).[11] Though young women sing and dance for their own pleasure, there is a long tradition of female performance at male entertainments.[12] An illumination in a Latin liturgical manuscript of the first half of the eleventh century from the south of France shows a *joglaresa* (or French *jougleuresse*), singing and dancing while holding up two bells (see Illustration 20).[13] Similar depictions in the Cancioneiro da Ajuda, a collection of medieval Portuguese lyrics, are linked by Frede Jensen to Moorish singers and dancers as well as to the 'girls from Cadiz' Roman writers speak of.[14] One

---

[11] *Libro de Apolonio*, l. 490 (Alvar 1976), and *Libro de Alexandre*, l. 1723 (Willis 1934). See Cohen 2002:68.

[12] On sanctions against respectable women performing in public see Boynton 2002:58, Cohen 2002:68. On the low status of the travelling *Spielleute* (minstrels), and specifically the female minstrel (*spilwif*), see Kasten 1990:16. Coldwell links *jougleuresses* with servants and courtesans, and notes that 'The tradition of singing and dancing slave girls and harem members extends back into Near Eastern Islamic history' (Coldwell 1986:43).

[13] Paris, BnF MS lat. 1118, fol. 114r. The picture is intriguing, as William Paden observes, commenting on it in the Introduction to his *Medieval Lyric: Genres in Historical Context* (Paden 2000:1). [On medieval performers, see also ch. 5 by J. Harris and K. Reichl in this volume.]

[14] Jensen 1978:30–31. The celebrated or notorious 'girls from Cadiz' (*puellae gaditanae*), in southern Spain, are mentioned in Pliny, Juvenal, Martial, and Statius; for citations, see Klinck 2002b: 213, n. 44.

thinks also of Salome dancing for Herod,[15] and of *hetairai* (courtesans or prostitutes) providing entertainment at male gatherings in ancient Greece.[16]

Most of the songs in a woman's voice would have been transmitted orally, instead of, or as well as, in writing. However, some of them are definitely literary, and even those that seem otherwise may be skilful imitations of traditional oral songs. The relationship between these traditional songs and similar works composed in writing is problematic, to say the least. Recent scholarship has preferred to think of woman's song as a mode adopted by all kinds of people, literate and illiterate, male and female, high and low.[17] If woman's song is popular, it is so in the sense of belonging to the whole population, rather than a particular segment of it, like courtly literature, or literature composed in Latin. Leaving aside the difficult question of whether or not we are dealing with oral provenance in specific cases, we can at least admit that the mode of woman's song is probably ancient and may be universal.[18]

## 3 Defining the Parameters of Woman's Song

Definitions have tended to focus on erotic content. Thus, in his seminal study of the origins of French lyric, Alfred Jeanroy speaks of 'a woman's monologue', claims that 'All these pieces relate to love', and notes, 'Happy love is fairly rare in them.'[19] More recently, Pierre Bec describes *chansons de femme* as 'a rather varied corpus of poetic genres generally characterised by a lyric monologue, with mournful connotations, placed in the mouth of a woman.'[20] Bec speaks in terms of a 'popularising register' rather than popular origins, making a distinction between *popularisant* and *aristocratisant*,[21] and similarly between the *féminité textuelle* found in *chansons de femme* and the *féminité génétique* that means female authorship.[22] Ulrich Mölk defines the *Frauenlied* as 'a love-song in a popular register in which the woman's perspective is realised as monologue, dialogue, or reported speech'.[23]

---

[15] Matthew 14.3–11. Matthew identifies her only as 'the daughter of Herodias' and thus Herod's stepdaughter. She 'pleased Herod', and so 'he promised with an oath to give her whatsoever she would ask.' Herodias prompted her daughter to ask for the head of John the Baptist because he had rebuked Herod for breaking Jewish law by marrying the wife of his brother.

[16] See, for example, Philocleon's remarks about the flute-girl in Aristophanes' *Wasps* 1346 (Hendersen 2002).

[17] See Rasmussen 2006. For some reservations about calling woman's song 'popular', see Klinck 1999.

[18] As argued by Frings 1949.

[19] '[...] un monologue de femme [...]. Toutes ces pièces sont relatives à l'amour [...]. L'amour heureux y est assez rare' (Jeanroy 1925: 158).

[20] '[...] un corpus assez varié de genres poétiques globalement caractérisés par un monologue lyrique, à connotations douloureuses, placé dans la bouche d'une femme' (Bec 1977–78: I, 57).

[21] Bec 1969: 1325–28. Paul Zumthor deliberately avoids class implications in his distinction between the *registre de la requête d'amour, spécifique du grand chant courtois*, and the *registre de la bonne vie*, associated with game, dance, *repas champêtre*, and love (Zumthor 1972: 251–52). Christopher Page distinguishes between the 'high' and the 'lower' styles (Page 1987: 16).

[22] Bec 1979: 235–36. In his *Chants d'amour des femmes-troubadours: Trobairitz et chansons de femme*, Bec brings together songs in the two registers, but groups them separately, and regards them as distinct (Bec 1995).

[23] '[...] ein Liebeslied des volkstümlichen Registers [...], in dem die Perspektive der Frau als Monolog, Dialog oder Erzählerbericht realisiert ist' (Mölk 1988: 88).

Some years ago I attempted a definition myself (1994: 14), in terms of four criteria, to which I will add a fifth here:
1. the femininity lies in voice rather than authorship;
2. the utterance is perceived as in some way contrastive to male-voice song;
3. the language and style are simple, or affect simplicity;
4. the subject is the loves, loyalties, and longings of the speaker;
5. in the context of medieval Europe, this poetry is secular, not religious.

The first criterion has already been mentioned, and the second will be explored as we continue. The third raises some tricky issues. I have deliberately refrained from defining woman's song as popular, but criterion 3 involves a diction which might well be regarded in that way, by virtue of being, or pretending to be, natural and untaught. It should go without saying that simplicity of vocabulary and syntax does not imply simple-mindedness.[24] The use of simple language should be seen as a choice, and not as a reflection of essential femininity. Nevertheless, this choice does draw on a widespread cultural construct that characterises women's speech by limited vocabulary and paratactic syntax, with little subordination.[25] Criterion 4 captures, I hope, a poetry of the affections. Usually, woman's songs treat erotic subjects, but one might include poems of friendship, laments, lullabies, and so on. Women also sing on other topics: their work, for example, or people they *don't* like.[26] These are not 'woman's songs' in the present sense. Criterion 5 excludes the poetry of affective piety, some of which, especially the lyrics devoted to the Virgin Mary, has strong affinities with secular love poetry, but generically belongs elsewhere.

Often, woman's song is regarded as uncourtly, or even anti-courtly. And it may be, especially in France – though its ethos is as often urban-bourgeois as rustic. In Germany, however, woman's song can be very much a part of the courtly culture, as Ingrid Kasten remarks in the introduction to her collection of *Frauenlieder*.[27] Although many woman's songs are anonymous, many, especially in certain ethnic contexts, are the work of known

---

[24] To take a prose example far removed from woman's song but sharing with it an appearance of 'simple' orality, much of Plato's Socratic dialogue is characterised by a pleasantly limpid conversational style, yet no one would regard it as simple-minded.

[25] Jennifer Coates comments on some unscientific assumptions about language, including those relating to male and female usage and to the belief that the subordinating syntax of formal written prose is superior. She does herself believe that women's writing tends to the structures of orality. See Coates 1986: 15–34 (ch. 2, on 'Folklinguistics').

[26] A couple of examples from the ancient world come to my mind: a line from a washing song and a bit of satire. The first is attributed to Anacreon but may be appropriated by him from songs he had heard; the p sounds could have accompanied stamping or pounding: *ek potamou 'panerchomai, panta pherousa lampra* ('I'm coming from the river bringing everything bright', *Poetae Melici Graeci* no. 385 [D. Page 1962]). The other, a refrain the philosopher Thales heard a woman singing while grinding her grain, lampoons the current dictator on the island of Lesbos: 'Grind, mill, grind; / for Pittacus is grinding, / the ruler of great Mytilene' (*Poetae Melici Graeci* no. 869 ). For various kinds of songs, some performed by women, described by St. John Chrysostom in late antiquity, see below. Most of the songs of the women troubadours are on the subject of love, but one, the *sirventes* (polemic or satire) by Gormonda de Monpeslier treats a politico-religious topic; Bec 1995 omits it from his collection for that reason.

[27] Kasten 1990: 21; in addition to German poems, this collection includes a few medieval Latin, Occitan, and French examples. On the integration of German *Frauenlieder* into courtly conventions, see also Kasten 2000: 11.

male authors. Again, the poetry of the trobairitz, the aristocratic women troubadours of Southern France, adopts the posture of the outspoken, desiring, earthy *femna*, combined with that of the lofty *domna*, who features, silently, as the object of adoration in the poetry of their male counterparts.[28] These complications need to be borne in mind when one applies Bec's scheme of the two contrasting registers.[29] Further, woman's songs may show the influence of learned sources; and they may be written in the learned language, Latin. For all these reasons, it is desirable to expand the term somewhat, without losing sight of an appeal that is popular in the broad sense. Thus, we can accommodate within the category of woman's song 'compositions that may be aristocratic in origin, complex in intent, and authored by either men or women' (Klinck 2002a: 5).

Theodor Frings, whose work on the subject is still valuable, though now dated, detected in medieval woman's song the outgrowth of a substratum that had always lain beneath the courtly lyrics of the Middle Ages, a kind of poetry common to all peoples and all periods. Claiming universality for the mode is rather sweeping. Still, there is evidence for continuing traditions of songs on the subject of love performed by girls or women, from ancient into modern times. Female choruses in Greece often delivered admonitions on the perils of love.[30] A separate women's tradition persisted in the oral culture of the Balkans until quite recently, as the materials gathered by Milman Parry and Albert Lord in the area of the former Yugoslavia show. Some of the songs collected were specifically labelled 'women's songs' by the locals, in this case on the basis of performance rather than voice. Whereas 'men's songs' were about fighting, 'women's songs' were about love. Women and girls gathered in their homes and sang them at their embroidery.[31]

## 4 Medieval Terms for Woman's Songs

Thus far, I have been outlining the characteristics of a widespread mode. Medieval poets must have been aware of it, but there seems to have been no medieval term for it, at least in western Europe, partly because vernacular poetry was not, like Latin, the subject of theoretical analysis, and partly because the poets and their public focused on the narrower genres they cultivated. The closest medieval equivalent to 'woman's song' – though not co-terminous with it – is a phrase that begins to appear in Portugal not long after 1300: *cantiga de amigo*, a woman's-voice 'song about a lover' (literally, 'about a friend'), as opposed to the man's voice *cantiga de amor*, 'song about love', the former

---

[28] See Klinck 2002a: 8–9. Traditionally, the works of the aristocratic *trobairitz* have been excluded from the corpus of woman's songs. See Plummer 1981: v. For an overview of the *trobairitz*, see Bruckner 1995, and, succinctly, Paden 1995. On the *trobairitz* as situating themselves both inside and outside the conventions of troubadour poetry, see Findley 2006: 298–99.

[29] See Grimbert 2001: 7–11, and 2003: 117–24.

[30] See, for example, the (Louvre) Partheneion by the archaic poet Alcman (*Poetae Melici Graeci* no. 1, ll. 15–19 and 39–101;); also the choruses in Euripides' *Hippolytus* 525–54 (addressed to the love-sick, tragic Phaedra) and *Medea* 629–53, both passages on disastrous love, which the chorus pray will not befall them. On sex and vengeance in Greek tragedy, see Loraux 1998: 55 and 57–58.

[31] See Lord 1960; also Foley 1995: 106, 112, and Vidan 2003: 82–83, 87, 93 (from Part I); most of the examples printed in Part II are about star-crossed lovers. For woman's song in contemporary Mediterranean and Middle Eastern countries, see Cohen 2002: 77–78.

composed in a more popular, the latter in a more courtly register, often by the same poets.³² That an important kind of woman's-voice poetry could be defined by the expression 'song about a friend' is corroborated by the independent occurrence of a Germanic term meaning exactly the same thing in a Carolingian capitulary of 789 CE. Section 3 prohibits nuns from writing *winileodas*,³³ a Latinised form of a compound containing the elements 'friend' (*wini*) and 'songs' (*leodas*). In Germanic as well as Romance languages, 'friend' often has an erotic connotation.

## 5 Old English

We have no contemporary account of what the Carolingian *winileodas* were like, but we do have two Old English love laments uttered by women: *The Wife's Lament* and *Wulf and Eadwacer*. These two poems draw on the conventions of Germanic alliterative verse, which was, at least in the written record, overwhelmingly male-oriented. At the same time, they offer a perspective that is distinctively female.³⁴ We have no idea who their authors were; monastics is the most likely guess – quite possibly men, but they could have been women.³⁵ There is a sexual intimacy about these two poems unlike anything else in the preserved Old English corpus. This tone is established by some significant details in the text: by the use of the dual 'we two'; the longing for one particular individual rather than a social group; the reminiscence of embraces as the Wife thinks of lovers keeping their bed together (*Wife*, ll. 33b–34) and the *Wulf* narrator of her man's animalistic mating, about which she has mixed feelings (*Wulf*, ll. 11–12).³⁶

Woman's song is especially the poetry of love and lament, the two themes often coinciding, as they do in the *Wife's Lament* and *Wulf and Eadwacer* – and in other poems from early northern Europe.³⁷ While *Wife* and *Wulf* need to be related to the

---

³² In the *Arte de Trovar*, a fragmentary 'Ars Poetica' found at the beginning of one of the main manuscript collections ('Cancioneiro da Biblioteca Nacional'; Lisbon, Biblioteca Nacional MS 10991; copied in the late fifteenth or early sixteenth century), *cantiga de amigo* designates a song in which a woman's voice begins the poem, *cantiga de amor* a song in which a man's does. See Greenfield 2000: 175–76; Corral 2002: 81–82.
³³ *Capitulare generale anni 789*, section 3; in Pertz 1835: 68.
³⁴ On these poems as woman's songs, see Belanoff 1990 and 2002.
³⁵ There has been some attempt to recuperate them as women's writing. See Desmond 1990, who argues that *Wulf* and *Wife* should be treated as woman-authored. The two poems are also included as women's writing in Thiébaux 1994, an anthology entitled *The Writings of Medieval Women*. On the desirability of treating anonymous poetry in a woman's voice as woman-authored, see also Bruckner in the Introduction to her edition of *The Women Troubadours* (Bruckner et al. 1995: xlv); also Bruckner 2002: 128–35. Similarly, on the case for the existence of the women trouvères, see Grimbert 2001: 1–6. On the general question of whether anonymous medieval poetry in a woman's voice should be regarded as woman-authored, see Klinck 2003.
³⁶ The Wife contrasts the 'friends' who lie together (*Frynd synd on eorþan, / leofe lifgende leger weardiað*, 'There are lovers on earth, dear ones living, keeping their bed') with herself pacing her solitary cave at dawn (*Wife*, ll. 33b ff.). The *Wulf* narrator remembers how *mec se beaducafa bogum bilegde* ('the man keen in battle laid his arms about me', *Wulf*, l. 11). *Bog* is a word used for the forequarters of an animal; see Klinck 1987.
³⁷ Most of the examples of woman's song that follow will be found with accompanying translation in my *Anthology of Ancient and Medieval Woman's Song* (Klinck 2004). In the present chapter my

international phenomenon of woman's song, they do have other connections, notably with the group of Old English poems of lament and melancholy reflection that we call the elegies. Like their male counterparts, the figures of these bereft, isolated women are projected against a background of hostile nature – very different from the genial spring setting that frames so much of later medieval lyric. The Wife, in her cave under an oak tree, lives in a forbidding briar-enclosed, mountain-overshadowed scene; the *Wulf* narrator on an inaccessible island surrounded by fen, weeping, in rainy weather. They are, like their male counterparts who miss the communal joys of the hall, exiles. Both, like the male Wanderer and Seafarer (the title characters of two other Old English poems), are separated by water from what they hold dear. The Wife, especially, uses the language of heroic poetry, speaking of her estranged 'lord', and calling herself a *wineleas wrǣcca* ('friendless exile', l. 10).[38] The *Wulf* narrator's language is much less formulaic, and perhaps derives from a different poetic tradition; the verse form, with its refrain-like repetition of lines 2–3 in 7–8,[39] and its varying line-lengths, stands outside conventional Old English metrics.[40] Both poems convey a specifically feminine sorrow, and thus align themselves with the poetry of women's mourning. Both end with an exclamation of despair, the *Wulf* narrator reflecting that it is easy to break what was never really united, the banished Wife proclaiming woe for one who must with longing wait for a dear one. The two poems can just as well be designated laments as *wineleodas*.

## 6 Early Celtic and Norse

The early Welsh poems in the cycle of Llywarch Hen ('the Old')[41] are similar to the Old English elegies in their contemplation of ruins and their laments for the joyful hall-community of former days. One of the lamenting figures is Heledd, sister of Cynddylan, Prince of Powys; she bewails the destruction (by the Anglo-Saxons) of Cynddylan's hall at Pengwern (modern Shrewsbury). Bereft of brothers, sisters, and home, 'wandering' Heledd (*Heled hwyedic*, stanza 78), who had betrayed her family in some way (stanzas 46, 57, 86), mourns for herself, weak and ill (stanza 62); once she had fine horses, but now she has not even a mantle (stanza 72).[42] Love song and death song coincide in the

---

quotations use the texts in that volume where possible; here I have occasionally modified the translations in that volume to make them more literal.

[38] The Old English elegies are edited in Klinck 1992; see also Muir 2000. The whole corpus of Old English poetry is collected in the six-volume *Anglo-Saxon Poetic Records* (1931–53); the Exeter Book, containing the elegies interspersed with other material, is edited in volume 3 (Krapp and Dobbie 1936).

[39] *Willað hy hine aþecgan gif he on þreat cymeð. / Ungelic is us* (They will take him if he comes into their troop. / Unalike are our lots).

[40] Interestingly, in the Balkan tradition recorded by Parry, Lord and others, women's songs are lyrical ballads about love in a symmetrical octosyllabic metre (4–4), and men's songs are epic, in an asymmetrical decasyllabic (4–6). See Foley 1995: 106, 112.

[41] Edited with commentary in Welsh by Williams 1970; with English translation and commentary by Rowland 1990. I cite from the latter. See *Canu Heledd* (The Song of Heledd); text 429–47; translation 483–96.

[42] On similarity between *The Wife's Lament* and *Canu Heledd*, see Jacobs 1989 and Bray 1995, who both prefer to place these woman's songs within the context of heroic poetry rather than *Frauen-*

early Irish Lament of Créde for Cáel, one of the poems incorporated in the prose *Acallam na Senórach* (*Tales of the Elders of Ireland*). Créde laments for her warrior husband, who has died in battle, drowned when he chased an opponent into the sea; the waves, the birds, and the animals mourn aloud with Créde.[43] In the Norse *Poetic Edda*, Guthrun laments at the death of her husband Sigurd, murdered by her brothers. The *First Lay of Guthrun* in the *Edda* narrates the scene of mourning, in which one woman after another recites the story of her own woes, before Guthrun speaks.[44] Like Heledd, she laments the consequences to herself, specifically the loss of her own status: now she is as insignificant as a little leaf on a tree (stanza 19). These poems from northern Europe are all set, perhaps retrospectively, in a heroic society of constantly warring tribal groups. Their ethos is to a large extent pre-Christian.[45] Their literary ties lie with epic more than with lyric as we see it in its later manifestations.

## 7 Hispano-Arabic

Another corpus of early European woman's song, very different from these northern poems, is to be found in Hispano-Arabic Spain, after the Moorish conquest. Here, Muslim women, from slaves to aristocrats, composed poetry.[46] The best known of these Muslim women poets is Wallāda, a princess of the Umayyad dynasty. She participated in the circles of male poets, and was the lover of one of them, Ibn Zaydūn. Her poems, in Arabic, are like those of the women troubadours of Southern France, frank, outspoken, and imbued with a strong sense of her own worth. Wallāda, who was criticised by some of her contemporaries for her unorthodox behaviour, wore the following provocative lines embroidered on her sleeves:

> I am, by God, made for glory,
> and I go my own way with pride.
> I give my lover power over my cheek,
> and I offer my kisses to him who desires them.[47]

---

*lieder*. In some of the Heledd sequences the speaking voice is not particularly characterised and might well be attributed to one of Cynddylan's warriors. It has often been suggested that, like the Welsh Llywarch Hen and Heledd poems and some of the poems in the Norse *Edda*, *The Wife's Lament* has a background in legend. This may be the case, but if so, no particular legendary tale has been convincingly proposed. On the various suggestions made in this direction, see Klinck 1992: 53–54.

[43] [On the *Acallam na Senórach*, see ch. 9 by J. F. Nagy in this volume.]
[44] The *Edda* is edited in German by Neckel 1968–83. For an English translation, see Larrington 1996. [On the *Poetic Edda* see further ch. 8 by J. Harris in this volume.]
[45] Dating these poems is notoriously difficult. The Old English ones are undoubtedly from before 1000 CE; the Celtic and Norse poems are preserved in later manuscripts. All three contain far earlier material; just when the texts crystallised in more or less their present form is a question about which scholars continue to disagree.
[46] On the poetry of women in Muslim Spain as more sincere, less conventional, and less sensual than that of their male contemporaries, see del Moral 1993.
[47] I am indebted to Teresa Garulo for assistance with Wallāda's poetry. The Andalusian women poets of the eighth to fourteenth centuries are collected, in Spanish translation, in Garulo 1986. For an

In early Andalusia (southern Spain), Muslims, Christians, and Jews coexisted.[48] They shared a culture largely Arab in its literary traditions, and all were familiar with the local Mozarabic dialect of Romance heavily influenced by Arabic. One characteristic verse form was the *muwashshaḥa*, a composition in classical Arabic, or sometimes Hebrew, usually a panegyric or a homoerotic love poem. The male-voice *muwashshaḥa* closed with a *kharja*, literally 'exit', a contrasting coda in colloquial language, which could be Arabic or Mozarabic, and was often in the voice of a young woman.[49] The frequent lack of fit between the *muwashshaḥa* and *kharja*, and the occurrence of the same *kharja* attached to more than one *muwashshaḥa*, suggest that the *kharja* had had a previous independent existence. For example, the *kharja* 'Adamey filiolo alieno' (I loved someone else's little son)[50] closes three *muwashshaḥa*s and may express either hetero- or homosexual love.[51] Typically, the woman's-voice *kharja*s are outspokenly erotic. Scholars disagree as to whether these bits of poetry represent an independent, oral, women's tradition. More recent scholarship has tended to emphasise their Arab or Hebrew context.[52] At any rate, the nubile vulnerable maidens depicted in them are a far cry from Wallāda and her like.

In a *kharja* from the Hebrew poet Yehuda Halevi also found in two Arabic *muwashshaḥa*s, a young girl protests at aggressive sexual overtures: 'Don't touch me, oh my lover; it still hurts me. / My bodice is fragile. Enough! I say no to this' (*Non me tanqesh, ya habibi; fa-encara dannosho. / Al-gilala raksa a toto. ¡bashta! me refusho*). Another maiden exclaims, 'Mercy, my lover! Don't leave me alone. / Kiss my little mouth well – you won't want to go so quickly' (*¡Amanu, ya habibi! Al-wahsh me no ferash. / Bon beija mia bokella awshak tu no irash*).[53] It has been argued, convincingly I believe,

---

English translation of Arabic poetry, by both men and women, from Andalusia, see Monroe 1974; Middleton and Garza-Falcón 1993. [On Andalusī–Arabic poetry and in particular the *zajal*, see also ch. 23 by James Monroe in this volume.]

[48] On the multiculturalism of medieval Iberia, see the essays in Hamilton et al. 2004.

[49] Galmés de Fuentes notes that the woman's voice is typical of the Romance *kharjas* but almost entirely absent from the Arabic ones (Galmés de Fuentes 1998: 50–51). The *kharjas* are edited mainly in Spanish. The versions cited here are based on Solá-Solé 1973; see also Solá-Solé 1990. They were earlier edited by García Gómez (1965; 3rd ed. 1990). Heger 1960 (German) includes fifty-three *muwashshaḥa*s with their *kharjas*. Since these poems are recorded in Arabic characters, with no vowels, by scribes who did not understand Romance, the texts are highly uncertain, and transliterations as well as translations differ.

[50] Also translated as 'I loved a foreign boy'.

[51] Solá-Solé 1973: 131–36, no. 14c. See Valencia and Boyarin 2004. The authors of this paper do not comment on the gender-change.

[52] Margit Frenk links the Mozarabic *kharjas* in a woman's voice to 'a more or less uniform common base of woman's song, probably linked to chant and dance, and spread throughout western Europe, perhaps diverging at certain centres of dispersal impossible to determine' ('una base común más o menos uniforme de canciones de mujer probablemente legadas al canto y al baile y difundidas por la Europa occidental, quizas a partir de ciertos focos de irradiación imposibles de determinar', Frenk 1979:78). Samuel Armistead traces identical motifs and metrical patterns in the *kharjas* and the later Spanish *villancicos* (Armistead 2003). Conversely, Richard Hitchcock emphasises the learned, Arab, context rather than a possible oral, Romance, provenance (Hitchcock 1991). And Federico Corriente, responding to Armistead, emphasises the need to take account of massive Islamic influence on a (partially) Romance poetry with pre-Islamic roots (Corriente 2004).

[53] Solá-Solé 1973: 204–9 (no. 29c) and 309–11 (no. 53), respectively; *kharja* 29 reads *mordesh* ('bite')

that an utterance of this type is more likely to be the work of a male author for a male public than a specimen of traditional song composed and performed among women (Spitzer 1952:21–22).

## 8 Woman's Song in a 'Latent State': Evidence from the Church

Both the Old English woman's songs and the *kharja*s have been seen as evidence for a vernacular European tradition in the early Middle Ages, with roots going back to ancient times. Most of the songs in this oral tradition would never have been recorded, but would have existed in what Ramón Menéndez Pidal called an *estado latente* (latent state).[54] The ecclesiastical councils repeatedly mention the public staging of 'pagan' songs, especially erotic ones performed by women. Thus, the Council of Auxerre (561–605 CE) forbids the performance of 'girls' songs' (*puellarum cantica*) in church; the Council of Chalons (647–53 CE) condemns the singing of 'obscene and shameful songs' (*obscina et turpea cantica*) with choruses of women at religious festivals; and the Council of Rome (853 CE) complains that there are many people, especially women, who desecrate feast days by dancing and singing 'dirty words' (*verba turpia*) and having 'choruses' in the manner of the pagans.[55] These are just one genre, cheerful ring songs, apparently, accompanied by dancing, and thus different from solo lament like the Old English elegies, or love complaint like the *kharja*s. As Peter Dronke emphasises in the first chapter of his *Medieval Lyric*, all kinds of songs must have existed. Dronke quotes, in translation, a passage from St. John Chrysostom's exposition on Psalm 41, in which he expatiates on the wondrous power of music, and the delight the human spirit takes in singing. Chrysostom ('Golden Mouth') eloquently describes the singing of men and women at their daily tasks; he mentions among his examples lullabies and songs accompanying spinning and weaving.[56]

## 9 Occitan

Medieval lyric suddenly bursts into full flower at the end of the eleventh century in the south of France with William, Ninth Duke of Aquitaine and Seventh Count of Poitou, and the troubadours who came after him. In their poetry we find the first expression of what they called *fin amors* (refined love) and what modern scholars have called 'courtly love', a term less current these days,[57] although it continues to be useful to define the

---

instead of *tanqesh* ('touch') in the a and b versions (see Jones 1988:173–74), making it even more titillating; 29a's *muwashshaḥa* has the girl lying naked with her lover.
[54] See Menéndez Pidal 1951:266–67. Somewhat similarly, Claude Charles Fauriel saw in the women's songs and dances of early medieval France a continuation of Graeco-Roman festivities; see Fauriel 1846: I, 166–67. The publication of the Mozarabic *kharja*s by S. M. Stern in 1948 prompted some enthusiastic responses connecting them with medieval (and later) woman's song more generally. See, for example, Ganz 1953.
[55] See, respectively, de Clerq 1964:266 and 307; Hartmann 1984:328.
[56] Dronke 1996:13–31, at 15; see Migne 1862:155–58.
[57] The term 'courtly love' (*amour courtois*) was first used by Gaston Paris; see Paris 1883:518–19. On the use of the term, see Burnley 1998:148–75 (ch. 9, 'Courtly Love').

aristocratising literary convention whereby a devotee serves his lady – often another man's wife – and aspires to be worthy of her. Secrecy is mandatory, *lauzengier* (tattle-tales) are feared, and the *gilos* ('jealous' husband) is given short shrift. The troubadour genre *par excellence* is the *canso*, a monologue love complaint in the courtly style.

Woman's song is often regarded as contrastive to the poetry of *fin amors*, but the songs of the women troubadours provide a locus where the two conventions overlap in interesting ways. Thus, the Comtessa de Dia and Na Castelloza, to take two of the best known *trobairitz*, are high-born ladies well aware of their own worth; but instead of being the silent objects of male devotion, they proclaim their right to woo, with an outspokenness that resembles the frankly desiring language of popular woman's song. The Comtessa, composing at the end of the twelfth century, declares, 'How I wish I could hold my knight / one night naked in my arms' (*Ben volria mon cavallier / tener un ser en mos bratz nut*) and 'For I take more delight in him / than Floris did in Blanchefleur' (*car plus m'en sui abellida / no fetz Floris de Blanchaflor*), appropriating the active male role by equating herself with the male partner Floris in a medieval romance. Similarly, Castelloza, perhaps a generation later, assumes the posture of the devoted (male) suitor wooing an unresponsive beloved: 'If you render me evil for good / I still love you well, nor will cease to do' (*e si·m fasetz mal per be, / be·us am e no m'en recre*).[58]

Perhaps because of the prestige attached to courtly conventions, which dominate the literary record, very few *chansons de femme* of the popular or popularising type are preserved in Occitan, the language of Southern France. There are one or two: 'Quant lo gilos er fora' (When that jealous man's away) and 'Coindeta sui' (I'm pretty), both anonymous and both *baladas*, or dance songs.[59] The first is also a *chanson de mal-mariée*, 'song of an ill-married wife'. The others include 'A l'entrade del tens clar' (At the beginning of the fair season), a lively *balada*, featuring a little mime involving the 'April Queen', preserved in Occitan modified by Northern French; and a love complaint which combines aristocratising and popularising elements, 'Quan vei los praz verdesir' ('When I see the fields grow green').[60] In the last poem, the speaker thinks of the time when her lover was imprisoned in her chamber, a sexual double-entendre that we shall find in other woman's songs.

A couple of genres frame woman's song in dialogue or reported speech: the dawn song of parting lovers,[61] in which the word *alba* (dawn) is repeated in a refrain, and the pastourelle (Occitan *pastorela*), in which a smooth-talking male sophisticate attempts to

---

[58] Quotations from, respectively, Comtessa de Dia, 'Estat ai en greu cossirier' (I have been in sore distress), Pillet and Carstens 1933 (abbreviated as PC): no. 46.4, stanza 2; Na Castelloza, 'Mout avetz faich lonc estatge' (Long is the time you've been away), PC 109.3, stanza 2. For the poems of these two authors, along with the other *trobairitz*, see Bruckner et al. 1995. The *trobairitz* poems are edited very thoroughly, in German, by Rieger 1991, but she excludes the *genres popularisants* (see pp. 77–81).

[59] 'Coindeta sui', PC 461.69, but not 'Quant lo gilos', PC 461.201, is included in Bruckner et al. 1995: 130–33. The latter poem is edited with German translation by Mölk 1989.

[60] 'A l'entrade', PC 461.12, is edited in Hill and Bergin 1973; 'Quan vei', PC 461.206, in Mölk 1989 and Rieger 1991.

[61] Sigal 1996 discusses dawn songs in medieval Occitan, French, German, and English. For an extremely comprehensive survey of dawn songs in traditions the world over, see the collection of 50 essays in Hatto 1965.

seduce a simple peasant girl, with varying success. The former genre is often courtly in language and setting; the latter exploits a class conflict. Both focus especially on the situation of the woman. Instead of the usual castle chamber, a spring meadow with blossom and song birds forms the setting for the anonymous *alba* 'En un vergier sotz fuella d'albespi' (In an orchard, under the leaves of a hawthorn tree); the speaker drinks in the sweet vapour of her lover's breath, wants to do everything in spite of the *gilos*, and exclaims in the poem's refrain 'Oh God! Oh God! the dawn! How soon it comes!' (*Oy Dieus! Oy Dieus! de l'alba tan tost ve!*).[62] The twelfth-century poet Marabru's 'L'autrer jost' una sebissa' (The other day, by a hedgerow), the earliest unmistakable example of a pastourelle in a European vernacular, plays deftly with class and manners as the shepherdess sees through the knight's wiles and sends him off with a flea in his ear: 'gape, you fool, / open-mouthed at noon!' (*bada fols bada, / en la muz' a meliaina!*, stanza 8).[63] Elements of the pastourelle are also to be found in Marcabru's 'A la fontana del vergier' (At the spring in the orchard), in which the male speaker encounters a girl passionately crying out against the Crusade that has deprived her of her lover – except that here the maiden is 'daughter of a castle's lord' (stanza 2), not a peasant.[64]

## 10 Northern French

The lyric genres of Occitania infiltrated other countries and other languages, blending with indigenous traditions. Among poems constructed wholly or partly in a woman's voice, the *aube* (*alba*) and pastourelle are represented in Northern France, and the popularising *chanson de femme* is widespread, functioning as a counter to the *canso*, or *grand chant courtois*, its Northern French equivalent.[65] Often the *chansons de femme* are dance songs, and typically the metre is simple, with much repetition of lines, in contrast to the more complex metres and absence of refrain in the *grands chants*. Most of these countercourtly poems are anonymous, and have been assumed to be the work of male authors, although, as mentioned earlier, there is now a tendency to recuperate anonymous female-voice poetry as women's writing.[66] It is worth noting, however, that poems definitively attributed to women authors (Wallāda, the named women troubadours and trouvères) do not depict their female speakers merely as saucy wantons or pathetic victims, in the way that poems known to be male-authored often do.[67]

---

[62]  'En un vergier', PC 141.113, is included in Bruckner et al. 1995: 134–35.

[63]  For a few examples of eleventh- and early twelfth-century poems – Latin, Iberian, and Northern French – that have some affinities with the pastourelle, see the Antecedents section of Paden's comprehensive collection (Paden 1987: 8–33; original text with facing translation). [For a discussion of the pastourelle, with focus on Marcabru's 'L'ultrer jost'una sebissa', see ch. 22 by Lucilla Spetia in this volume.]

[64]  'A la fontana', PC 293.1, and 'L'autrer', PC 293.30, are edited, with translation, in Rosenberg et al. 1998, and Gaunt et al. 2000 [see also text and translation of 'L'autrer' from Gaunt et al. in this volume, pp. 594–96].

[65]  A succinct account of the Northern French *chanson de femme* is provided by Rosenberg 1995.

[66]  For the previously conventional and still widely accepted opinion, see Bec 1979: 236; Rosenberg 1995. For the more recent tendency, see Grimbert 2001: 1–6, and n. 35, above. Doss-Quinby et al. 2001 include 'all the songs [entirely in the female voice] listed as anonymous' (Grimbert 2001: 6).

[67]  On this topic see Klinck 2003, and Klinck 2004: 13.

Various genres of *chanson de femme* can be identified, often overlapping: the *chanson d'ami*, a term corresponding to *winileod* and *cantiga de amigo*, a maiden's song of love-longing; the *chanson de délaissée*, or song of the girl who has been deserted; the often more courtly *chanson de croisade* (Crusade song);[68] the *chanson d'aventure*, which might well also be a pastourelle, featuring a young man riding out and encountering a young woman. Two varieties especially characteristic of Northern France are the *chanson de toile*, attested only there, and the *chanson de mal-mariée*.

The archaising, ballad-like *chanson de toile* (sewing song) is said to have been sung by women at their needlework. In its simple exposition and dramatic dialogue it resembles the Old French epic or *chanson de geste*, to which it forms a feminine counterpoint, much as the lyrical ballads that used to be sung until recently by women in former Yugoslavia contrast with the men's epic songs (see p. 526, above). Orsino's words quoted at the beginning of this chapter evoke a humbler version of the *chanson de toile*. And, as we saw, St. John Chrysostom knew of such songs in the Byzantium of late antiquity. The Old French genre is quite sharply defined. The song focuses on a girl and her feelings for a lover; usually the setting is a castle room, and frequently the opening line begins with *Bele* and the heroine's name. Thus, Bele Erembors and Bele Yolande both sit in a chamber embroidering rich cloth and thinking about their lovers. Erembors pines for Raynaut in the poem's refrain, 'Oh Raynaut, my love' (*E Raynauz, amis*). The more feisty Yolande stands up to her scolding mother, who finally backs off in the face of her married daughter's determination to keep seeing Count Mahi, and, in the last line, changes her tune from 'I'm scolding you, fair Yolande' (*Chastoi vos en, bele Yolanz*) to 'Suit yourself, fair Yolande' (*Covegne t'en, bele Yolanz*). Both girls – Erembors, who accosts Raynaut from her window and convinces him of her fidelity, and Yolande, who scorns her mother as well as her husband and his relatives – take the initiative in getting their man.[69]

The *chansons de mal-mariée* are lively little songs that would have lent themselves to accompaniment by dancing. In a thirteenth-century rondeau or round by Adam de la Halle of Arras, Picardy, a young wife mocks her tiresome husband: *Fi, maris, de vostre amour, / car j'ai ami!* and goes on to tell him that her *ami* is handsome, cuts a fine figure, and serves her both night and day. The contrast with the handsome, dashing lover implies that the husband is old and repellent – and very likely impotent too. In other poems, the rough reality of an abusive marriage lies behind the poem – but does not dampen the narrator's spirits. For example, in the anonymous *ballette* (dance song) 'Por coi me bait mes maris, / laisette?' (Why does my husband beat / poor wretched me?) the crude husband gets his just deserts as the wife pays him back for his brutality: 'I know what I'll do / to take my revenge. / I'll lie with my lover / naked' *(Or sai bien que je ferai*

---

[68] In addition to 'A la fontana', mentioned above, see, for example, Rinaldo d'Aquino's 'Già mai non mi conforto', on which I comment briefly below. The French *chansons de croisade* are edited in Bédier and Aubry 1909.

[69] Compare Burns 2002. The 'Bele Erembors' song (Linker 1979: no. 265.1485) begins, *Quant vient en mai, que l'on dit as lons jors* (When it befalls in May, called the time of long days); the other (Linker 1979: no. 265.222) *Bele Yolanz en chambre koie* (Fair Yolande, quiet in her chamber). The poems are edited by Zink 1977.

/ et coment m'an vangereai: / avec mon amin geirai / nüete). The saucy tone is conveyed in part by diminutives like *laisette* and *nüete*.⁷⁰

Equally sprightly, but more dignified, Maroie de Diergnau (near Lille) refuses to be cast down by winter: 'Mout m'abelist quant je voi revenir / yver' (It pleases me a lot when I see / winter return), but, being a *bele pucele* (good-looking girl), she will sing of love to raise her spirits, 'for my noble heart, full of desire for love / won't let my great joy fail' (*car mes fins cuers plains d'amorous desir / ne mi fait pas ma grant joie faillir*). Only one stanza is preserved, which seems to be part of a *grand chant*, like the *canso*s of the *trobairitz*.⁷¹

## 11 Medieval Latin

While some of the genres of woman's song are limited to a particular culture and language, many are broadly disseminated. These cross-cultural forms may have originated in Occitania, where vernacular lyric had its first great flowering, or may have come from Latin into the embryonic Romance languages.⁷² There is the possibility of a learned as well as a popular background. Ovid was widely read in the Middle Ages,⁷³ and his *Heroides* (Heroines), love-epistles addressed by various legendary abandoned women to their lovers, may have served as a model for some poems. It has been suggested, for example, that they may have influenced the *canso*s of the *trobairitz*.⁷⁴ Some of the earliest specimens of lyric genres are actually found in Latin poems. The tenth-century dawn song 'Phoebi claro nondum orto iubare' (When the bright radiance of Phoebus has not yet risen) – a military reveille with Christian overtones, not a lovers' parting – contains the characteristic word *alba* in its Occitan refrain.⁷⁵ The eleventh-century 'Plangit nonna, fletibus' (A nun is lamenting with tears), is the lament of a reluctant nun forced into the grim asceticism of a convent when she would like to wear pretty clothes and make love – but at least she can kill herself. This poem treats with savage bitterness a theme that reappears, less disturbingly, in the vernaculars.⁷⁶ 'Nam languens / amore tuo' (For longing / with love of you), from the late tenth- or early eleventh-century *Cambridge*

---

⁷⁰ 'Fi maris' (Linker 1979: no. 2.45) is edited in a collection of rondeaux and refrains by van den Boogaard 1969, and in the collected works of Adam de la Halle by Badel 1995 (with music); 'Por coi' (Linker 1979: 265.1346) in Doss-Quinby et al. 2001: 153–54. Zumthor 1972 picks out the use of diminutives in feminine adjectives as one of the characteristics of the *registre de la bonne vie*. See n. 21, above.

⁷¹ *Mout m'abelist* (Linker 1979: 178.1) is edited with accompanying music in Doss-Quinby et al. 2001: 116–18.

⁷² Elvira Gangutia has argued for a line of influence running from the Middle East, through Greece and north Africa, into Spain and thence Occitania. This is one possibility, but it is unlikely to be the only or even the major source. See Gangutia 1972, 1991, and 1994.

⁷³ On Ovid's influence see Martindale 1988.

⁷⁴ See de Riquer 1975: II, 80; Blakeslee 1989: 74. Commenting on woman's songs in medieval Latin, Anne Schotter finds in the *Heroides* a more positive Ovidian influence as compared with a dismissive attitude to women in Ovid's *Ars Amatoria*, *Remedia Amoris*, and *Amores* (Schotter 1981: 23). On Ovidian influence more generally, see Klinck 2002b: 26.

⁷⁵ For English translation and Latin text, see Wilhelm 1990: 8–9 and 299–301.

⁷⁶ Text and translation in Dronke 1968: 357–60.

*Songs* – actually a collection from Germany –, is a 'boat song' voiced by a girl waiting by the sea for her lover's ship, and foreshadows a genre common in Hispanic lyrics.[77]

The use of Latin or macaronic verse (the latter composed in a mixture of two languages, one of them usually Latin) can allow poets to speak of unsavoury matters with greater freedom. 'Plangit nonna' is graphic in its descriptions of the filthy conditions in which the speaker has to live – her smelly underwear, her lice-infested hair. The presence of the learned language can also convey certain implications about education, class, and status. Thus, the pastourelle genre, the essence of which is an encounter between a knight or clerk and a peasant girl, sometimes draws on Latin to underline the man's sophistication versus the girl's simplicity. In Marcabru's 'L'autrer, jost una sebissa', the courtly suitor and the down-to-earth shepherdess speak in different registers of the same language, Occitan. Latin heightens this social contrast, and adds gender implications. Although some medieval nuns became proficient in Latin, it remained to a very large extent a male preserve. Two songs from the thirteenth-century *Carmina Burana* collection, a miscellany of sacred and secular lyrics in German and Latin, exploit the implications of knowing or not knowing the learned language.[78] One, 'Huc usque, me miseram' (Until now, poor wretched me), is a *chanson de délaissée* with overtones of pastourelle. The other, 'Ich was ein chint so wolgetan' (I was such a lovely girl) is rather similar: a pregnant girl bewails her fate and the heartlessness of the man who has seduced her. Poems like these two – the former entirely in Latin, the latter mixing Latin and German – ironise the plight of young women in a language they cannot understand. Poems of this type are, I think, more likely to have been composed by and circulated among male clerics than to have been created by and for women.[79]

The speaker in 'Huc usque' suffers public humiliation when people see her big belly, nudge each other, and point. The girl in 'Ich was ein chint' tells of her seduction under a linden tree by a crude fellow. He pulled up her shift and broke into her little fortress with his erect spear (ll. 57–60). The poem closes with a brisk 'End of the game!' (*ludus compleatur!*) and a reiteration of the refrain: 'Hoy and oë! / Cursed be the linden trees / planted by the way!' (*Hoy et oe! / maledicantur tilie / iuxta viam posite!*).[80] Both flippant and bitter, the tone of these poems is ambivalent, the jauntily rhyming Latin making light of a suffering that is, nevertheless, inescapable.[81]

---

[77] Poem no. 14A. Text and translation of the *Cambridge Songs* in Ziolkowski 1994 (this text, pp. 68–69).

[78] The *Carmina Burana* (*CB*) are edited with German translation by Vollmann 1987; with French translation by Gérard 1990. The love songs of the *CB* are edited by Hilka and Schumann 1941, and translated into English by Blodgett and Swanson 1987.

[79] Schotter, while making a distinction between those (Latin) poems in which the woman's voice is treated satirically and those in which it is presented in a sensitive way, believes that both kinds must have been composed by men. See Schotter 1981: 19 and 26. Jane Stevenson, in her study of *Women Latin Poets* from ancient times on, argues for female authorship of the more sensitive poems (Stevenson 2005: 103–7).

[80] See *CB* 126 ('Huc usque') and *CB* 185 ('Ich was ein chint').

[81] While Schotter points to the cynicism of 'Huc usque', Dronke emphasises its tragedy (Dronke 1996: 302). With 'Ich was ein chint' compare the use of macaronic verse in the late twelfth-century *tenso* (debate poem) between Raimbaut de Vaqueiras and a Genoese woman. In a similar vein to Marcabru's *pastorela*, Raimbaut woos in Occitan, the elite language, while she responds very bluntly in her native dialect. The poem's irony is commented on by Gaunt 1988 and Deyermond 1996.

A fragmentary poem from the *Cambridge Songs*, 'Veni dilectissime' (Come sweetheart), presents a frank invitation to a sexual encounter by a speaker who says she is longing for sex (*venerem desidero*) (no. 49). The lover is invited to come with his key and enter, in language reminiscent of the Song of Songs in the Old Testament (Song 5.4–8);[82] the lines alternate with the exclamation 'ah and oh!' (*et a et o!*). Like some of the other erotic poetry in this collection, 'Veni, dilectissime' has been erased by a medieval censor. Here, the Latin language provides a certain distancing for material that might be considered rather *risqué*.

## 12 German

The two great collections of medieval Latin lyric, the *Cambridge Songs* and the *Carmina Burana*, both come from Germany. In the German vernacular, *Frauenstrophen* (woman's stanzas) are found in the earliest *Minnesang* (love poetry), which seems not yet to have been touched by the conventions of courtly love.[83] A Latin love-letter from the twelfth century, very likely written by a nun, ends with the following lines in German – one is reminded of the Carolingian strictures against *winileodas* mentioned above:

> Du bist mîn, ich bin dîn.
> des solt du gewis sîn.
> du bist beslozzen
> in mînem herzen,
> verlorn is daz sluzzelîn:
> dû muost ouch immêr darinne sîn.

You are mine, I am yours:/ of that you should be sure./ You're locked up/ in my heart,/ and the key is lost./ So you must always stay there.

Here, the woman's heart is a sweet prison that confines the absent lover. The image resembles that in 'Quan vei los praz verdesir'; the key-and-lock motif is shared with 'Veni dilectissime' – but without the blatant eroticism of the Latin poem. Another *Frauenstrophe*, appended to a Latin poem in the *Carmina Burana* but probably earlier than the (thirteenth-century) manuscript, adds a local specificity to the commonplace that one's beloved is 'all the world to me':

> Wære diu werlt alle mîn
> von deme mere unze an den Rîn,
> des wolt ich mich darben,
> daz chunich von Engellant
> læge an mînen armen.

Were all the world mine,/ from the sea to the Rhine,/ I'd relinquish it all/ to have the King of England/ lying in my arms!

---

[82] On references to the Song of Songs in medieval literature, see Astell 1990.
[83] A useful brief account of *Minnesang* for the English reader is provided by Rasmussen 2006. A substantial selection of texts, along with modern German translation and commentary, is contained in Kasten and Kuhn 1995. [See also ch. 10 by Jan-Dirk Müller in this volume, esp. section 3.3.]

With sharpness and economy, these two mini-poems focus on a single motif, possession in the one, desire in the other. Both are anonymous; both quite possibly composed by women, but we cannot be sure.[84] Interestingly, the latter poem has been altered by crossing out the manuscript *chunich* (king) and writing *diu chuenegin* (the queen) above, so that the speaker who longs to embrace a noble and inaccessible person becomes a man and by a single touch the whole ethos of the poem is changed.

Another famous woman's song, concentrated in two short stanzas, is 'Ich zôch mir einem valken' (I trained me a falcon), probably dating from the mid-twelfth century. In this, effectively anonymous, poem by Der von Kürenberg, 'the man from Kürenberg' (possibly Kürnberg castle, near Linz in Austria) the bird seems to represent the woman's lost lover. After she had trained him for over a year, he flew away to 'other lands'. Since then she has seen him in splendid flight, trailing silk ribbons from his feet. It is not clear whether the other lands represent the territory of another woman, or something more transcendental, like the next world.[85]

None of this early German woman's song is definitively attributed to women, and much of it was composed by named male poets. Among these, Reinmar der Alte (the Old) and Walther von der Vogelweide, both composing in the late twelfth and early thirteenth centuries, are noted for their representations of a woman's voice. Reinmar has six monologues in a woman's voice, Walther two. Both compose poems with a male and a female speaker, Reinmar favouring the *Wechsel* (exchange) in which the two speakers address the same topic but not each other, and Walther the dialogue.

In 'War kan iuwer schoener lîp' (Where has your beauty gone?), Reinmar evokes the turbulent feelings of a woman separated from her lover by 'spiteful ones' (*nîde*, stanza 2), but nevertheless eagerly anticipating a reunion.[86] 'War kan' incorporates courtly conventions like the *Frauendienst* (service to a woman) expected of a knight, and the resentment felt towards malicious outsiders (the *nîde* here corresponding to the Occitan *lauzangier*, 'tattletales'). At the same time, the poem presents the frankly sensual, desiring persona characteristic of so much woman's song. In 'Sage daz ich dirs iemer lône', a dialogue between lady and messenger, the woman's words reflect subtle and shifting feelings. She respects the man who is wooing her and desires his company – but not as a lover. This poem actually quotes from another one by Reinmar, in which the poet devotedly serves a lofty lady; the present song offers an intimate glimpse of her feelings, and, if

---

[84] Both poems are edited in the classic *Minnesangs Frühling* collection (*MF*) (Moser and Tervooren 1977–88), *MF* 3.1 and 3.7, respectively. In the following discussion, poems are identified by the number of the first stanza in this edition; the arrangement in different manuscripts varies.

[85] *MF* 8.33 and 9.5. Moser and Tervooren print the two stanzas together as one poem. Kasten comments that the speaker in this poem has been variously interpreted – and not always as a woman, the symbolism implied by the falcon being the only evidence for his maleness and her femininity. Thus, the subject has been taken to be a man who has lost his sweetheart, a father whose daughter has been taken away, a falconer whose bird has escaped. See Kasten 2000: 15. On different interpretations of this poem, see also Balbuena Torezano 2003. For the interpretation of the poem in the light of a newly found manuscript version, see Kern 2001.

[86] Reinmar's œuvre is edited in *Minnesangs Frühling*. See also Jackson 1981, for a study of Reinmar's woman's song; and Kasten 1987 and 2002, for a contrast between Reinmar and the Occitan Comtessa de Dia.

not autobiographical, refers to a very specific relationship between the Reinmar persona and his lady, a relationship also alluded to in three of his other *Frauenlieder*.[87]

Walther's *Frauenstrophen* and *Frauenlieder* are poetically very rich, belying a superficial appearance of simplicity.[88] To take the most famous example, *Under der linden* is a four-stanza monologue influenced by the pastourelle genre, but the speaker in this case rejoices in the encounter:[89]

> Ich kam gegangen
> zuo der ouwe,
> dô was mîn friedel komen ê.
> dâ wart ich empfangen,
> hêre frowe,
> daz ich bin sælic iemer mê.
> kuster mich? wol tûsent stunt,
> tandaradei,
> seht, wie rôt mir ist der munt. (stanza 2)

I came on my way/ to the meadow,/ where my lover had come before./ There I was taken – / Holy Mary! – / and I'm happy for it evermore./ He kissed me a thousand times – / tandaraday – / see how red is my mouth.

This is a much happier story of sex under a lime tree than 'Ich was ein chint'. But on closer inspection the *Lindenlied* is an enigmatic poem. Is the speaker an innocent village maiden or an assured woman of rank? Is she being modest or arch? The parenthetical 'honoured lady' (*hêre frowe*) could be an exclamation of rapture or a reference to her own social status.[90] Both exuberant and diffident, she confides her adventure only to the nightingale who witnessed their love-making, and whose song echoes in the refrain.

Contemporary with Walther, Wolfram von Eschenbach is better known for his long romances. He did compose love lyrics too, including *Tagelieder*, or dawn songs.[91] 'Sîne klâwen / durch die wolken sint geslagen' (Its claws / tear through the clouds) begins with the striking image of dawn as a cruel bird of prey. The poem, like the classic Occitan *alba*, focuses on a dialogue between a woman in the arms of her lover and the castle watchman warning her that her friend must go. She protests, 'You keep snatching him from me, / from white arms, but never from the heart' (*du hâst in dicke mir benomen / von blanken armen, und ûz herzen niht*, stanza 4). Wolfram suggests both the feelings of the woman and her physical being: 'Against his breast she pressed her little breasts' (*ir brüstlîn an brust si dwanc*, stanza 5). Her persona thus also implies the presence and the perspective of her lover.[92] In the hands of poets like Reinmar, Walther, and Wolfram,

---

[87] The present poem is *MF* 177.10; the others 178.1, 186.19, and 195.25. See Kasten 1987 and 2002; Kasten and Kuhn 1995: 867–70; Haferland 2006. The last writer sees Reinmar's lyric 'I' as very much a performance persona (375, n. 27).

[88] On Walther's experimentation with genres, see Ashcroft 2000.

[89] Walther's poetry is edited in German by Cormeau 1996 (a revision of editions by Lachmann et al.), and by Schweikle 1998, with modern German translations. On Walther's woman's song, see Rasmussen 2002.

[90] For doubts that this poem is a *Mädchenlied*, see Bennewitz 1989.

[91] On medieval German *Tagelieder*, see Hatto 1965: 428–72.

[92] Edited in Moser and Tervooren 1977–88 (the 38th edition of *Minnesangs Frühling*, not in earlier editions); also in Kraus 1978.

highly conventional genres become the vehicle for complex perspectives and finely delineated shades of feeling.

## 13 Italian

The poetic genres of Occitania also move into Italy, where love lyric in the troubadour style appears in the thirteenth century, first of all at the court of Frederick II of Sicily. Much of this poetry is very derivative, including some of the pieces in a woman's voice.[93] Like other male-authored woman's songs, they tend to construct desiring women overpowered by their emotions. 'Dolze meo drudo, eh! vatène?' (My sweet love, are you leaving?), by King Frederick, features a woman protesting her lover's departure, while he promises that his heart will remain with her. Dramatic and exclamatory, 'Già mai non mi conforto' (Never shall I find comfort), by Rinaldo d'Aquino, possibly the brother of Thomas Aquinas, voices a woman protesting that the Cross which should save is destroying her by taking away her lover. The anonymous 'Compiangomi, laimento e di cor doglio' (I lament, bewail, and grieve from my heart) presents a regretful woman who has alienated her lover by her cruelty and now wishes to make amends. More strikingly, the sonnet 'Tapina in me, c'amava uno sparvero!' (Alas for me, I loved a hawk!) symbolises the roving lover by a tamed hunting bird that flies off from the lady he has served to another. The poem is reminiscent of Der von Kürenberg's 'Falkenlied', but in the present case the symbolism is clear, and the presence of a woman rival explicit (Kasten 2000: 16).

More unusual than 'Già mai non conforto', 'Ormai quando flore' (Now when things are in bloom), also by Rinaldo d'Aquino, begins with a typical spring setting describing flowers and singing birds, and only in line 28, with the feminine inflection in *so amata* (I am loved) do we realise that the speaker is a woman. Her heart is refined with love (l. 21); a boy suffers torment for her (l. 34). Although these are conventional *topoi*, the speaker's reciprocal passion and her conflicting feelings make the poem more distinctive and more complex. She anticipates gratification in a shady place in the fresh wood (ll. 25–27). Swept away like a leaf by the wind (ll. 38–39), she fears for her reputation (l. 41). Finally, she protests that she will not give way (ll. 43–45) – a rejection that is almost an invitation.

A handful of Italian woman's songs are attributed to women, most plausibly three sonnets by La Compiuta Donzella ('The Accomplished Young Lady') of Florence, whose poetry offers a different take on young women and romance. 'A la stagion che'l mondo foglia e fiora' (In the season when the world puts out leaves and flowers), uses the spring setting when 'joy grows in all noble lovers' (*acresce gioia a tutti fin' amanti*, l. 2) to protest against the speaker's father's intention of marrying her off against her will. In the poem that follows in the manuscript, she expresses her desire to enter a con-

---

[93] For a selection of the poetry of the Sicilian School with English translation, see Jensen 1986. For a similar selection from northern Italy, see Jensen 1994. Mölk 1989 includes twenty Italian examples of woman's songs (with German translation). The ones that follow here, except for the last two, are edited by Panvini 1962–64.

vent. 'A la stagion' at the same time echoes the *mal-mariée* song of the dissatisfied wife and counterpoises the lament of the unwilling nun.[94]

Another poem from northern Italy, the earthy and outspoken, 'Mamma, lo temp' è venuto' (Mother, the time has come) is a spirited dialogue between a young girl eager to marry her lover, and her parent, who wants to put the brakes on.[95] The mother, presumably exaggerating, tells her daughter that she would be risking death if she had dealings with a man (ll. 43–44, 47–48). The daughter envisages having her lover closer to her than her shift and embracing him so it will delight her heart (ll. 55–59). As in the popularising French *chansons de femme*, much of the poem is taken up by the refrain: *Mamma, lo temp' è venuto / ch' eo me voria maritare / d' un fante che m' è sí plazuto / no' l te podria contare* (Mother, the time has come / when I'd like to be married / to a boy who's so pleasing to me / that I couldn't describe it to you.)

## 14 Galician-Portuguese and Castilian

While Italian woman's song is represented by only a fairly small number of poems, the Iberian peninsula provides us with an abundance, mainly in Galician-Portuguese and Castilian (standard Spanish), but including a few in Catalan (the language of the northeast, as well as the Mediterranean coast and islands). The widespread genres noted earlier are found here too: the pastourelle, the song of the woman left behind (but the Hispanic *despedida*, 'farewell', is not a poem of unhappy rejection), the laments of the reluctant nun and the ill-married woman, and the *alba* – usually as the *alborada*, 'dawn meeting', rather than the dawn parting. Most typical is the song of the young girl, sometimes addressed to her lover, sometimes confiding in her mother or girl friends. The *romaria*, 'pilgrimage song', in which the setting for a lovers' meeting is the shrine of a saint, is only found in Spain and Portugal.

In the Galician-Portuguese *cantigas de amigo,* the central figure is usually a country maiden who engages in rustic activities like washing her clothes in a stream or dancing under the trees.[96] These *cantigas*, like the later Castilian *villancicos* (peasant songs), cultivate an engaging simplicity, reflecting or imitating a tradition that is oral and popular (Jensen 1992: xxiv). Typical is a parallelistic structure with *leixa pren* (leaving and taking up), that is, the incorporation of an earlier line into a later stanza. Simple in syntax, conventional in vocabulary, these poems can nevertheless reflect considerable artistry, in their melodiousness, their subtly varied incremental repetition, and their evocation of powerful feelings.[97]

---

[94] The poem is edited by Contini 1960. Cherchi 1989 argues that La Compiuta Donzella was a real person but that her poetry is not necessarily autobiographical. He regards two other supposed thirteenth-century Italian women poets, Gaia da Camino and Nina Siciliana, as fictitious.
[95] Edited by Contini 1960; also Orlando 1981.
[96] Edited by Nunes 1926–28; Jensen 1992 (with English translations); Brea 1996. Selected translations in Fowler 1996.
[97] Finnegan (1977: 90, 129–30) regards repetition – of sound, syntax, or meaning – as the most marked feature of oral poetry.

The natural setting common in medieval lyric assumes especial importance in these poems. Particular symbols recur. Swelling or stormy water suggests dangerously powerful feelings, as well as real fear and danger. In Mendinho's 'Sedia-m'eu na ermida de San Simion' (I was at the sanctuary of St. Simon), both a *marinha* (sea-song) and a *romaria*, the narrator describes how she stood at the island sanctuary waiting for her lover, as the huge waves rolled around her, and she felt that she would die. In Johan Zorro's 'Pela ribeira do rio salido' (By the bank of the swelling river), a girl admits to her mother that she has been busy (*trebelhei*) with her lover, and wishes she had not. In 'Ondas do mar de Vigo' (Waves of the Bay of Vigo) by Martin Codax, one of the few songs for which music is preserved in this corpus, the speaker again and again asks the waves of the stormy sea if they have seen her beloved, praying that he will come soon.[98] In poems by Pero Meogo, such as the dialogue 'Digades, filha, mia filha velida' (Tell me, daughter, my lovely daughter), stags, with their wildness and virility, symbolise the intrusion of the girl's lover into her sheltered world. The young girl in 'Digades, filha' tells her mother she has been delayed at the stream by the mountain stags who came and muddied the water. More light-heartedly, Airas Nunez's 'Bailemos nós ja todas tres, ai amigas' (Let us dance now, friends, all three) evokes the youth, beauty, and high spirits of a group of young girls dancing under the flowering hazel trees.

Nuno Fernandes Torneol's *alba* 'Levad'amigo, que dormides as manhanas frias' (Rise, my friend, sleeping in the chill morning) begins with the expected morning awakening while birds sing of love, but in the course of the poem we find that the speaker's 'friend' has broken the branches where the birds perched, and dried up the streams where they drank. The birds and their haunts suggest the happy, innocent love he has destroyed. When the girl tells her lover to rise, she is actually ordering him to leave; her refrain *leda m'and'eu* (joyful go I) becomes ironic.[99] 'Cabelos, los meus cabelos' (Flowing hair, my flowing hair), a mini-dialogue by Johan Zorro, also has dark implications. The king has asked for a girl's luxuriant hair. What shall she do? Cynically, her mother tells her to give the king his wish. Evidently, it is not just her hair that the king desires.

The femininity in these poems is constructed largely by externals, albeit deftly and delicately, a feature that tends to suggest the perspective of the male author, as does the narrator's autopanegyric.[100] 'Lovely as I am, I'll die in the deep sea' (*morrerei fremosa no alto mar*, l. 22), says the speaker in 'Sedia-m'eu'; 'I'll go, in loveliness' (*louçana irei*), she reiterates in the refrain of Martin Ginzo's 'Treides, ai mia madr', en romaria' (Come, my mother, on pilgrimage). Similarly, the maidens in 'Bailemos nós ja' reiterate in their refrain, with variations, that they are pretty (*velida, louçana, ben parecer*).

The absence of Castilian lyric from the earlier written record is in all likelihood attributable to a sense that Galician-Portuguese was the language for lyric, Castilian for

---

[98] As well as being included in two large manuscript collections, the seven surviving poems of Martin Codax are preserved on a single manuscript leaf, the Pergaminho Vindel, where they appear with musical notation.
[99] On 'Levad' amigo' and its varying interpretations, see Jensen 1978:75; also Wright 1998.
[100] See Beltrán 1987:54; Corral 2002:83. Masera 1993 considers the question of whether the auto-referentiality of the female voice in early Hispanic lyric can be a test of male versus female authorship, but comes to no conclusions.

epic.[101] Preserved mainly in manuscripts and early printed books from the late fifteenth to early seventeenth century, Castilian lyrics contain material of earlier provenance, but in their present form many of these poems are the work of highly literate authors.[102] Usually, the *villancicos* in a woman's voice consist of an *estribillo* (refrain) and an elaboration in a *glosa* (literally, 'gloss'). Like the *cantigas de amigo*, they construct the voice of a young girl frankly expressing her feelings. The typical genres include the *romaria* and the *alborada*, also found in the Galician-Portuguese *cantigas*, and the *morena* (song of a Moorish girl).[103]

A single-stanza *morena* seems to have a proverbial source, but is also reminiscent of 'I am black but comely' in the Song of Songs 1.5: *Aunque soi morena, / no soi de olbidar, / que la tierra negra / pan blanco suele dar* (Although I'm dark / you shouldn't forget / that the black earth / gives white bread). Another poem contains the proverbial *estribillo Niña y viña, / peral y havar, / malo es de guardar* (A girl and a vine, / a pear tree and a bean-plant – / it's hard work to guard them). 'Niña y viña' is the song of a girl who went to cut roses in the clear morning and gave a 'bad vine-tender' (*viñadero malo*, ll. 9 and 19) the token he asked for. Like the flowing hair demanded by the king in Johan Zorro's poem, the cut roses and the sash given to the gardener suggest the girl herself and her virginity. In the *estribillo* to a short lament by an unwilling nun, the speaker complains, *Agora que soy niña / quiero alegría, / que no se sirve Dios / de mi mongía* (Now, while I'm young, / I want to have fun. / It's no use to God / my being a nun). The theme is like that in 'Plangit nonna', but the seamy details are absent. The *romaria* 'So ell enzina, enzina' (Under the oak-tree, oak-tree) voices a girl's conflicting feelings about making love while going on pilgrimage. Like the speaker in the Old English *Wulf and Eadwacer*, she takes delight (*goçaba*, stanzas 8 and 9) in her lover's embraces, but also feels sad and distressed (*pésome, cuytada*, stanzas 7 and 8). Hauntingly musical in its varied repetitions, the *alborada* 'Al alva venid, buen amigo / al alva venid' again and again begs a lover to come at dawn. The two-line *estribillo* is interlaced with a two-line *glosa*.

Very few medieval lyrics from Spain and Portugal are attributed to women authors. However, women performers are mentioned, especially the Galician *soldadeiras* (paid women), who are the subject of satirical poems by male authors. Maria Balteira, for

---

[101] See Jensen 1992: cxiv–cxv. However, some scholars caution against assuming that poems in a traditional style from the fifteenth to seventeenth centuries are relics of a lost medieval corpus. See Beltrán 1998.
[102] In the *Prólogo* to her *Corpus de la antigua lírica popular*, Margit Frenk comments on the difficulty of picking out the popular from the learned (Frenk 1987: vi–vii). She notes that some of the pieces in these Renaissance *cancioneros* are archaic, others composed in that style, others old but touched up, and others newly minted (Frenk 1987: vii). See also her *Nuevo corpus* (Frenk 2003: 15, n. 10). Frenk emphasises the prominence of woman's song in the popular lyric, and to a large extent aligns the male/female with the popular/aristocratic divide (Frenk 1992), an alignment which often holds but is a little sweeping.
[103] The poems quoted here are edited by Alín 1991 and Frenk 2003. I follow Frenk's texts, which reconstruct repeated lines: Frenk nos. 140 ('Aunque soi morena'), 314C ('Niña y viña'), 207 ('Agora, que soy niña'), 313 ('So ell enzina, enzina'), 452 ('Al alva venid, buen amigo'). All except the first are also to be found in Alonso and Blecua 1964; 'Niña,' 'So ell encina,' and 'Al alva' also in Pérez Priego 1989. For an anthology of male- and female-voice lyric from this period, with English translations, see Cummins 1977. As a glance at the selections in Frenk will show, it can be hard to distinguish between separate poems and variants of the same poem. 314C, for example, is very similar to 314A and B.

example, is mocked for never 'locking her trunk'.[104] There are no surviving poems by named women authors in Galician-Portuguese, but a couple of later pieces in the other languages of the Iberian peninsula are preserved. These poems, like those of the Provençal *trobairitz*, are aristocratic in their reference and courtly in their style, but have affinities with woman's song of the popular or popularising kind. From the Queen of Mallorca, in the mid-fourteenth century, we have a Catalan *despedida*, 'E-z ieu am tal que es bo e bell' (I love a man who's noble and handsome), lamenting her husband James III's absence in France.[105] Very similar in its motivations, Mayor Arias' Castilian *despedida* 'Ay mar braba, esquiba' (Oh rough, cold sea), prompted by her husband's departure with an embassy to Tamburlaine in Samarkand in 1403, is also a *marinha* or *barcarola* (boat song) apostrophising the sea in a way reminiscent of the poems of Martin Codax.[106]

## 15 Middle English

We now turn to the last group of poems to be discussed here, those from late medieval England.[107] Although there is some continuity between Old and Middle English poetry – especially in the treatment of religious themes like the transience of the world and its pleasures, for the most part Middle English lyric seems to be a new phenomenon. As in the Continental countries, we find the pastourelle, the *chanson d'aventure*, and the *chanson de délaissée*. A favourite theme of Middle English woman's song is the girl seduced by a clerk or priest, often called John or Jankyn. Like their counterparts in other languages, these 'jolly Jankyn' poems, all anonymous, move between pathos, cynicism, and cheerful insouciance. The fact that the seducer is so often a cleric makes it probable that clerical circles were largely responsible for this verse. Nevertheless, as we saw in Latin and Latin-German poems, the inherent tragedy of the abandoned and pregnant girl can come across with painful reality.

Most of these Middle-English woman's songs are carols, that is, songs originally composed for dancing, with 'burdens', refrains that begin the song and are repeated after each stanza. My titles here are taken from the first line of the burden, rather than of the first main stanza. In 'Now springes the spray', dating from the late thirteenth or early fourteenth century, a cheerful fellow riding out comes across a country maiden in an arbour singing of how her lover has proved untrue.[108] Her words are bitter: *The clot him clinge! / Wai es him i love-longinge / sal libben ay* (Let the earth to him cling! / Woe for one who in love-longing / must live always). He thinks only of the pleasantly vernal setting and the delightful melody of her song, which echoes through the poem in the burden: *Now springes the spray, / al for love iche am so seek / that slepen I ne may.* The

---

[104] Cohen 2002:73. For the *cantigas d'escarnho* (mocking songs) making fun of *soldadeiras*, see Lapa 1995.
[105] James III had two wives, so the queen may be either his first wife Constance or his second wife Violant. The poem is edited in Castellet and Molas 1969:65–67, and translated into English verse in Wilhelm 1990:259.
[106] Printed in López Estrada 1999. On this poem, see Whetnall 1984:149–50; Cohen 2002:73–74.
[107] [On the Middle English lyric, see also ch. 21 by Karin Boklund-Lagopoulou in this volume.]
[108] *Index of Middle English Verse (IMEV)* no. 360. Edited in Brown 1932. This and all other Middle English poems discussed here are included in Greene's edition of carols (Greene 1977).

girl's bitter outburst is surprisingly like the ending of *The Wife's Lament*. But the burden's motif of spring as the time of burgeoning shoots and branches, awakening hearts to love, is light years away. In fact, the poem may be based on an Old French original, 'L'autrier defors Picarni'.[109]

'Rybbe ne rele ne spynne yc ne may', i. e., 'I cannot scrape, wind, nor spin [the flax]' and 'Alas, alas, the wyle' both narrate the seduction of a servant girl amid the festivities of a public holiday (doubtless a common occurrence), her subsequent pregnancy, and her mistress's wrath.[110] Both are characterised by explicit detail and earthy dialogue. The fifteenth-century 'A dere God, what I am fayn, / for I am madyn now gane' is a lyric that has been interpreted in radically different ways. I am inclined to read this poem of a pregnant *délaissée* as the disillusioned words of an unhappy young woman (understanding *fayn* as 'vain', 'worthless', rather than 'glad', and *gane* as 'gone', 'no more', rather than 'again'), not the satisfaction of one who has miraculously recovered her maidenhood.[111]

Two contrasting poems on the seduction-by-a-clerk theme are the cheerful 'Hey noyney! / I wyll love our Ser John and I love eny' and the pathetic 'Kyrie so kyrie'.[112] In the former, the speaker seems to be doing rather well: Sir John the parish priest brings her presents and charms her altogether. In the latter, she falls for the wiles of Jankyn the holywater clerk. The poem alternates English with words from the mass, including the refrain *Kyrieleyson* (Lord have mercy), and ends *Benedicamus Domino, Cryst fro shame me shylde. / Deo gracias therto – alas, I go with chylde*. The mechanical Latin words learned by rote contrast with the woman's very real personal feelings and her sharp fear for her future.

In the love complaint 'Wolde God that hyt were so', gender has been changed by altering key words throughout.[113] The speaker laments that the man that she loved best of all does not reciprocate her affection and treats her coldly. When she would like him to stay he leaves without even saying farewell. *In places ofte when I hym mete, / I dar noght speke but forth I go; / with herte and eyes I hym grete, / so trewe of love I know no mo* (stanza 3). Touching as the poem is, it can quite easily metamorphose into the plaint of the typical male lover pining for a cruel lady. Conversely, the male-voice love poem of which the opening stanza begins 'Ichot a burde in boure bryht' contains a burden whose melodiously repetitive words, evoking a figure standing by the seashore and awaiting the lover's return, could well have originally been voiced by a woman:

> Blow, northerne wind,
> send thou me my sweting,
> blow, northerne wind,
> blow, blow, blow![114]

---

[109] See Bartsch 1870: 111 (II, no.7); edited (and translated) together with the Middle English poem in Reichl 1987: 37–40.
[110] *IMEV* nos. 225 and 1849, respectively. These and the following two Middle English poems are edited in Robbins 1955.
[111] *IMEV* no. 3594. Cartlidge 1998 takes the optimistic view of this poem.
[112] *IMEV* nos. 2494 and 377, respectively.
[113] *IMEV* no. 3418. See Robbins 1955: 16–17 (notes on Poem 22).
[114] *IMEV* no. 1395. See Boklund-Lagopoulou 2002, who argues that the male speaker of this poem 'could well in the burden [which she finds less courtly than the rest of the poem] be more appropriately replaced by a female voice' (30). Compare Davis, who, in his edition of *Medieval English*

## 16 Mode and Gender: Markers of Author and Voice

As we have seen, woman's song is represented by some typical genres, the narrower ones culture-specific.[115] At the most obvious level, a female speaker is often indicated by gender-markers in the opening lines of a poem; these markers may be grammatical, designating the speaker as feminine or her lover as masculine, or they may reflect social conventions. An apostrophe to a mother or to female friends signals a woman's song, especially in Hispanic tradition. The need to mark femininity may arise from the performance context. If the performer is a man, it will be necessary to indicate in the words of the song that he is playing a feminine role. Very likely, too, the social dominance of the male point of view prompts the need to mark femininity, whereas the male voice can remain unmarked.[116] Sometimes the femininity of the speaker is associated with a very specific symbol or situation: the male lover as stag or falcon; the watching by the sea for the lover or his boat. Often, too, the female speaker is stationary or confined, the male lover mobile, both literally and figuratively.

Significant but less salient features have been picked out by critics examining the language of male- and female- authored poetry. For example, Joan Ferrante, Sarah Kay, and Sophie Marnette have all analysed the language of the troubadours and *trobairitz*, and come to separate but somewhat similar conclusions, finding that the women authors use a more direct language and less elaborate metres.[117] The most detailed and rigorous analysis is Marnette's, who finds that women poets as compared with men more often present the female speaker as subject, use twice as many commands and usually in the negative, more frequently speak of the lovers in the first person, and tend to present a love triangle rather than a bilateral relationship.

The woman's voice in poetry is always a construct, but male and female authors do seem to construct it differently. Since the number of attested female authors is very small, inferences must be tentative. That said, male authors tend to focus on appearance and dress and to present women emotionally dependent on men, while female authors – usually speaking in their own personas – are more interested in thoughts than appearance, and, even when they protest the vehemence of their passion, display a strong sense of their own dignity and worth. While anonymous poems should not be simply assumed to be either male- or female-authored, if we consider these tendencies, most of the anonymous texts resemble woman's songs known to be composed by men more closely than those composed by identifiable women.

Finally, the features identifying the woman's voice are not fixed in stone. There are short poems that with the adjustment of very small touches can be transposed into the

---

*Lyrics*, observes that the burden may well be that of a popular song and that its character is quite different from the rest of the poem (1963: 317).

[115] Compare Simon Gaunt at the beginning of his *Gender and Genre in Medieval French Literature*: 'I shall argue that [...] the distinct ideologies of medieval genres are predicated in part at least upon distinct constructions of gender' (1995: 1).

[116] But Thomas Cramer 2000 argues that in the *Minnesangs Frühling* edition of medieval German lyrics, there are far more stanzas where the speaker's gender is uncertain than was previously thought; he adds a category of *androgyne Strophen* alongside *Männerstrophen* and *Frauenstrophen*.

[117] See Ferrante 1989 and Kay 1989; Marnette 1997.

male voice. The narrator of the *kharja* 'I loved someone else's little son' changes gender in different contexts. The 'heroic' woman's songs from early England and Wales use a formulaic language that resembles male-voice lament. Evidence of manuscript alteration is rare, but telling. It occurs in the German 'Waere diu werlt' and the Middle English 'Wolde God that hyt were so'. Thus, slight changes can make profound differences. It is a good possibility that such adaptations were common in performance – as they are now. This kind of slippage may explain how Orsino in *Twelfth Night*, when he spoke of an old song chanted by 'the spinsters and the knitters in the sun, and the free maids that weave their threads with bones' could misapply words that so hauntingly evoke the deep tradition and simple rural life at the root of woman's song.

## References

Akehurst, F. R. P., and Judith M. Davis, eds. 1995. *A Handbook of the Troubadours*. Berkeley: U of California P.
Alín, José María, ed. 1991. *Cancionero tradicional*. Madrid: Castalia.
Alonso, Dámaso, and José Manuel Blecua, eds. 1964. *Antología de la poesía española. Lírica de tipo tradicional*. 2nd corr. ed. Madrid: Gredos.
Alvar López, Manuel, ed. 1976. *Libro de Apolonio*. 3 vols. Madrid: March.
Armistead, Samuel G. 2003. '*Kharjas* and *Villancicos*.' *Journal of Arabic Literature* 34: 3–19.
Ashcroft, Jeffrey. 2000. 'Frauenstimmen in der Minnelyrik.' In Cramer et al. 2000: 95–102.
Astell, Ann W. 1990. *The Song of Songs in the Middle Ages*. Ithaca, NY: Cornell UP.
Aubrey, Elizabeth. 1996. *The Music of the Troubadours*. Bloomington: Indiana UP.
–. 2001. 'Introduction to the Music.' In Doss-Quinby et al. 2001: 44–51.
Badel, Pierre-Yves, ed. and trans. 1995. *Adam de la Halle. Oeuvres complètes*. Paris: Librairie Générale Française.
Balbuena Torezano, María del Carmen. 2003. *Frauenlied-Frauenstrophe: El discurso feminino en la lírica de Der von Kürenberg*. Huelva: Universidad de Huelva.
Bartsch, Karl, ed. 1870. *Romances et pastourelles françaises des XII$^e$ et XIII$^e$ siècles. Altfranzösische Romanzen und Pastourellen*. Leipzig.
Bec, Pierre. 1969. 'Quelques réflexions sur la poésie lyrique médiévale. Problèmes et essai de caractérisation.' *Mélanges offerts à Rita Lejeune*. 2 vols. Gembloux: Duculot. II, 1309–29.
–. 1977–78. *La lyrique française au Moyen Âge (XII$^{ème}$- XIII$^{ème}$ siècles). Contribution à une typologie des genres poétiques médiévaux. Études et textes*. 2 vols. Paris: Picard.
–. 1979. 'Trobairitz et chansons de femme: Contribution à la connaissance du lyrisme féminin au Moyen Âge.' *Cahiers de Civilisation Médiévale* 22: 235–62.
–. 1995. *Chants d'amour des femmes-troubadours*. Paris: Stock.
Bédier, Joseph, and Pierre Aubry, eds. 1909. *Les chansons de croisade*. Paris: Champion. [Rpt. Geneva: Slatkine, 1974.]
Belanoff, Patricia A. 1990. 'Women's Songs, Women's Language: *Wulf and Eadwacer* and *The Wife's Lament*.' In *New Readings on Women in Old English Literature*. Ed. Helen Damico and Alexandra Hennessey Olsen. Bloomington: Indiana UP. 193–203.
–. 2002. '*Ides ... geomrode giddum*: The Old English Female Lament.' In Klinck and Rasmussen 2002: 29–46.
Beltrán, Vicente. 1987. *Canción de Mujer, Cantiga de Amigo*. Barcelona: Promociones y Publicaciones Universitarias.
–. 1998. 'Poesía tradicional: ecdótica e historia literaria.' In Piñero Ramírez 1998: 113–35.
Bennewitz, Ingrid. 1989. '"vrouwe/maget." Überlegungen zur Interpretation der sogenannten Mädchenlieder im Kontext von Walthers Minnesang-Konzeption.' In *Walther von der Vogelweide:*

*Beiträge zu Leben und Werk. Günther Schweikle zum 60. Geburtstag.* Ed. Hans-Dieter Mück. Stuttgart: Stöffler & Schütz. 237-52.

Blakeslee, Merritt. 1989. 'La chanson de femme, les *Héroïdes*, et la *canso* occitane à voix de femme. Considérations sur l'originalité des *trobairitz*.' In *Hommage à Jean-Charles Payen*. Caen: Université de Caen. 67-75.

Blodgett, E. D., and R. A. Swanson, trans. 1987. *The Love Songs of the Carmina Burana*. New York: Garland.

Boklund-Lagopoulou, Karin. 2002. *'I have a yong suster'*: *Popular Song and the Middle English Lyric*. Dublin: Four Courts.

Bonnermeier, Andreas. 2002. *Frauenstimmen im französischen Chanson und in der italienischen Canzone. Ein Genre und seine Interpretinnen.* Hamburg: Kovač.

Boynton, Susan. 2002. 'Women's Performance of the Lyric Before 1500.' In Klinck and Rasmussen 2002: 47-65.

Bray, Dorothy Ann. 1995. 'A Woman's Loss and Lamentation: Heledd's Song and *The Wife's Lament*.' *Neophilologus* 79: 147-54.

Brea, Mercedes, ed. 1996. *Lírica profana galego-portuguesa. Corpus completo das cantigas medievais, con estudio biográfico, análise retórica e bibliografía específica*. 2 vols. Santiago de Compostela: Centro Ramón Piñeiro.

Brown, Carleton, ed. 1932. *English Lyrics of the XIIIth Century*. Oxford: Clarendon.

Bruckner, Matilda Tomaryn. 1995. 'The Trobairitz.' In Akehurst and Davis 1995: 201-33.

–. 2002. 'Fictions of the Female Voice: The Women Troubadours.' In Klinck and Rasmussen 2002: 127-52. [Rpt., with modifications, from *Speculum* 67 (1992): 865-91.]

–, Laurie Shepard and Sarah White, eds. 1995. *Songs of the Women Troubadours*. New York: Garland.

Burnley, David. 1998. *Courtliness and Literature in Medieval England*. London: Longman.

Burns, E. Jane. 2002. 'Sewing Like a Girl: Working Women in the *chansons de toile*.' In Klinck and Rasmussen 2002: 99-126.

Cartlidge, Neil. 1998. '"Alas, I Go with Chylde": Representations of Extra-Marital Pregnancy in Middle English Lyric.' *English Studies* 79: 395-414.

Castellet, J. M., and Joachim Molas, eds. 1969. *Ocho siglos de poesía catalana*. Madrid: Alianza.

Cherchi, Paolo. 1989. 'The Troubled Existence of Three Women Poets.' In Paden 1989: 197-209.

Coates, Jennifer. 1986. *Women, Men, and Language: A Sociolinguistic Account of Sex Differences in Language*. London: Longman.

Cohen, Judith. 2002. '*Ca no soe joglaresa*: Women and Music in Medieval Spain's Three Cultures.' In Klinck and Rasmussen 2002: 66-80.

Coldwell, Maria V. 1986. '*Jougleresses* and *Trobairitz*: Secular Musicians in Medieval France.' In *Women Making Music: The Western Tradition, 1150-1950*. Ed. Jane Bowers and Judith Tick. Urbana: U of Illinois P. 39-61.

Contini, Gianfranco, ed. 1960. *Poeti del Duecento*. 2 vols. La letteratura italiana, storia e testi 2. Milan: Ricciardi.

Cormeau, Christoph, ed. 1996. *Walther von der Vogelweide: Leich, Lieder, Sangspruche*. 14th ed. With contributions by Thomas Bein and Horst Brunner. Berlin: de Gruyter.

Corral, Esther. 2002. 'Feminine Voices in the Galician-Portuguese *Cantigas de Amigo*.' Trans. Judith R. Cohen with Anne L. Klinck. In Klinck and Rasmussen 2002: 81-98.

Corriente, Federico. 2004. 'Again on (Partially) Romance Andalusi *Kharajāt*.' *Journal of Arabic Literature* 35: 139-51.

Cramer, Thomas. 2000. 'Was ist und woran erkennt man eine Frauenstrophe?' In Cramer et al. 2000: 19-32.

–, John Greenfield, Ingrid Kasten, and Erwin Koller, eds. 2000. *Frauenlieder: Cantigas de Amigo*. Stuttgart: Hirzel.

Cummins John G., ed. 1977. *The Spanish Traditional Lyric*. Oxford: Pergamon.

Davidson, Clifford. 1975. 'Erotic "Women's Songs" in Anglo-Saxon England.' *Neophilologus* 59:451-62.
Davis, R. T., ed. 1963. *Medieval English Lyrics: A Critical Anthology*. London: Faber.
de Clercq, Charles, ed. 1964. *Concilia Galliae, A.511–A.695*. CCSL 148a. Turnhout: Brepols.
del Moral, Celia. 1993. 'Poesía de mujer, poesía de hombre: la diferencia del género en la lírica andalusí.' In *Árabes, judías y cristianas: Mujeres en la Europa medieval*. Ed. Celia del Moral. Granada: Universidad de Granada. 173–93.
de Riquer, Martín. 1975. *Los trovadores: Historia literaria y textos*. 3 vols. Barcelona: Planeta.
Desmond, Marilyn. 1990. 'The Voice of Exile: Feminist Literary History and the Anonymous Anglo-Saxon Elegy.' *Critical Enquiry* 16:572–90.
Deyermond, Alan. 1996. 'Lust in Babel: Bilingual Man-Woman Dialogues in the Medieval Lyric.' In *Nunca fue Pena Mayor: Estudios de Literatura Española en Homenaje a Brian Dutton*. Ed. Ana Menéndez Collera and Victoriano Roncero López. Cuenca: Universidad de Castilla-La Mancha. 199–221.
Doss-Quinby, Eglal, Joan Tasker Grimbert, Wendy Pfeffer, and Elizabeth Aubrey, eds. and trans. 2001. *Songs of the Women 'Trouvères.'* New Haven: Yale UP.
Dronke, Peter. 1968. *Medieval Latin and the Rise of European Love-Lyric*. 2nd. ed. Oxford: Clarendon.
–. 1996. *The Medieval Lyric*. 3rd ed. Cambridge: Brewer.
Fauriel, Claude Charles. 1846. *Histoire de la poésie provençale*. 3 vols. Paris.
Ferrante, Joan M. 1989. 'Notes Towards the Study of a Female Rhetoric in the *Trobairitz*.' In Paden 1989:63–72.
Findley, Brooke Heidenreich. 2006. 'Reading Sincerity at the Intersection of Troubadour/Trobairitz Poetry: Two Poetic Debates.' *Romance Quarterly* 53:287–303.
Finnegan, Ruth. 1977. *Oral Poetry*. Cambridge: CUP.
Foley, John Miles. 1995. *The Singer of Tales in Performance*. Bloomington: Indiana UP.
Fowler, Barbara Hughes, trans. 1996. *Songs of a Friend: Love Lyrics of Medieval Portugal*. Chapel Hill: U of North Carolina P.
Frenk, Margit. 1979. 'La lírica pretrovadoresca.' In *Grundriss der romanischen Literaturen des Mittelalters*. Ed. Hans Robert Jauss, Erich Köhler et al. II.1, fasc. 2. Heidelberg: Winter. 25–79.
–, ed. 1987. *Corpus de la antigua lírica popular (siglos XV a XVII)*. Madrid: Castalia.
–. 1992. 'Lírica aristocrática y lírica popular en la Edad Media española.' In *Heterodoxia y ortodoxia medieval*. Ed. Concepción Abellán et al. Mexico City: Universidad Nacional Autónoma de México. 1–19.
–, ed. 2003. *Nuevo corpus de la antigua lírica popular hispánica (siglos XV a XVII)*. Mexico City: Facultad de Filosofía y Letras, Universidad Nacional Autónoma de México.
Frings, Theodor. 1949. *Minnesänger und Troubadours*. Vorträge und Schriften, Deutsche AW zu Berlin 34. Berlin: Akademie-Verlag.
Galmés de Fuentes, Alvaro. 1998. 'Las jarchas mozárabes y la tradición lírica románica.' In Piñero Ramírez 1998:27–53.
Gangutia Elícegui, Elvira. 1972. 'Poesía griega "de amigo" y poesía arabigo-española.' *Emerita* 40:329–96.
–. 1991. 'La temática de los "cantos de amigo" griegos.' *Poesía estrófica*. Ed. F. Corriente and A. Sáenz-Badillos. Madrid: Universidad Complutense. 121–35.
–. 1994. *Cantos de mujeres en Grecia*. Madrid: Ediciones Clásicas.
Ganz, Peter. 1953. 'The "Cancionerillo Mozarabe" and the Origin of the Middle High German "Frauenlied".' *Modern Language Review* 48:301–9.
García Gómez, Emilio, ed. and trans. 1990. *Las jarchas romances de la serie árabe en su marco*. 3rd ed. Madrid: Alianza.
Garulo, Teresa, trans. 1986. *Dīwān de las poetisas de al-Andalus*. Madrid: Hiperión.

Gaunt, Simon. 1988. 'Sexual Difference and the Metaphor of Language in a Troubadour Poem.' *Modern Language Review* 83: 297–313.
–. 1995. *Gender and Genre in Medieval French Literature*. Cambridge: CUP.
–, Ruth Harvey, and Linda Paterson, eds. 2000. *Marcabru: A Critical Edition*. Cambridge: Brewer.
Gérard, Marcel, ed and trans. 1990. *Les chansons d'amour des Carmina Burana*. Luxemburg: Saint-Paul.
Greene, Richard Leighton, ed. 1977. *The Early English Carols*. 2nd ed. Oxford: Clarendon.
Greenfield, John. 2000. 'Kleine Typologie der galego-portugiesischen *Cantigas de Amigo*.' In Cramer et al. 2000: 173–90.
Grimbert, Joan Tasker. 2001. 'The Case for the Women Trouvères.' In Doss-Quinby et al. 2001: 1–26.
–. 2003. 'Songs by Women and Women's Songs: How Useful is the Concept of Register.' In *The Court Reconvenes: Courtly Literature across the Disciplines*. Selected Papers from the Ninth Triennial Congress of the International Courtly Literature Society, University of British Columbia, 25–31 July 1998. Ed. Barbara K. Altmann and Carleton W. Carroll. Cambridge: Brewer. 117–24.
Haferland, Harald. 2006. 'Subjektivität, Fiktion und Realität in Reinmars Frauenlieder.' *Zs. für deutsches Altertum* 125: 368–89.
Hamilton, Michelle M., Sarah J. Portnoy, and David A. Wacks, eds. 2004. *Wine, Women and Song: Hebrew and Arabic Literature of Medieval Iberia*. Newark, DE: Cuesta.
Hartmann, Wilfried, ed. 1984. *Die Konzilien der karolingischen Teilreiche 843–859*. MGH, Leges, Concilia 3. Hannover: Hahn.
Hatto, Arthur T., ed. 1965. *Eos: An Inquiry into the Themes of Lovers' Meetings and Partings at Dawn in Poetry*. The Hague: Mouton.
Heger, Klaus. 1960. *Die bisher veröffentlichten Ḫarǧas und ihre Deutungen*. Beihefte zur Zs. für romanische Philologie 101. Tübingen: Niemeyer.
Henderson, Jeffrey, ed. and trans. 2002. *Aristophanes*. 4 vols. Loeb. Cambridge, MA: Harvard UP.
Hilka, Alfons, and Otto Schumann, eds. 1941. *Carmina Burana 1.2. Die Liebeslieder*. Heidelberg: Winter.
Hill, R. T., and T. G. Bergin, eds. 1973. *Anthology of Provençal Troubadours*. New Haven: Yale UP.
Hitchcock, Richard. 1991. 'The Girls from Cádiz and the *Kharjas*.' *Journal of Hispanic Philology* 15: 103–16.
*IMEV*: Carleton Brown and Rossell Hope Robbins. *The Index of Middle English Verse*. New York: Columbia UP, 1943. / Rossell Hope Robbins and John L. Cutler. *Supplement to the Index of Middle English Verse*. Lexington, KY: U of Kentucky P, 1965. / Julia Boffey and A. S. G. Edwards. *A New Index of Middle English Verse*. London: The British Library, 2005.
Jackson, William E. 1981. *Reinmar's Women: A Study of the Woman's Song ('Frauenlied' and 'Frauenstrophe') of Reinmar der Alte*. German Language and Literature 9. Amsterdam: Benjamins.
Jacobs, Nicholas. 1989. 'Celtic Saga and the Contexts of Old English Elegiac Poetry.' *Études Celtiques* 26: 95–142.
Jeanroy, Alfred. 1925. *Les origines de la poésie lyrique en France au Moyen Âge. Études de littérature française et comparée suivies de textes inédits*. 3rd ed. Paris: Champion.
Jensen, Frede. 1978. *The Earliest Portuguese Lyrics*. Études romanes de l'Université d'Odense 11. Odense: Odense UP.
–, ed. and trans. 1986. *The Poetry of the Sicilian School*. New York: Garland.
–, ed. and trans. 1992. *Medieval Galician-Portuguese Poetry: An Anthology*. New York: Garland.
–, ed. and trans. 1994. *Tuscan Poetry of the Duecento: An Anthology*. New York: Garland.
Jones, Alan. 1988. *Romance 'Kharjas' in Andalusian Arabic 'Muwaššaḥ' Poetry: A Paleographical Analysis*. London: Ithaca P.

Kasten, Ingrid. 1987. 'Weibliches Rollenverständnis in den Frauenliedern Reinmars und der Comtessa de Dia.' *GRM* N. F. 37: 131–46.
–, ed. and trans. 1990. *Frauenlieder des Mittelalters*. Stuttgart: Reclam.
–. 2000. 'Zur Poetologie der "weiblichen" Stimme: Anmerkungen zum "Frauenlied".' In Cramer et al. 2000: 3–18.
–. 2002. 'The Conception of Female Roles in the Woman's Song of Reinmar and the Comtessa de Dia.' Trans. Ann Marie Rasmussen. In Klinck and Rasmussen 2002: 152–67. [Based on Kasten 1987.]
–, ed., and Margherita Kuhn, trans. 1995. *Deutsche Lyrik des frühen und hohen Mittelalters*. Bibliothek des Mittelalters 3. Frankfurt a. M.: Deutscher Klassiker Verlag.
Kay, Sarah. 1989. 'Derivation, Derived Rhyme and the Trobairitz.' In Paden 1989: 157–82.
Kern, Peter. 2001. 'Die Kürenberg-Texte in der Manessischen Handschrift und im Budapester Fragment.' In *Entstehung und Typen mittelalterlicher Lyrikhandschriften. Akten des Grazer Symposiums 13.–17. Oktober 1999*. Frankfurt a. M.: Lang. 143–63.
Kibler, William W., and Grover A. Zinn, eds. 1995. *Medieval France: An Encyclopedia*. New York: Garland.
Klinck, Anne L. 1987. 'Animal Imagery in *Wulf and Eadwacer* and the Possibilities of Interpretation.' *Papers on Language and Literature* 23: 3–13.
–. 1992. *The Old English Elegies: A Critical Edition and Genre Study*. Montreal: McGill-Queen's UP. [Rpt. with updated bibliography 2001.]
–. 1994. 'Lyric Voice and the Feminine in Some Ancient and Mediaeval *Frauenlieder*.' *Florilegium* 13: 13–36.
–. 1999. 'The Oldest Folk Poetry? Medieval Woman's Song as "Popular" Lyric.' In *From Araby to Engelond: Medieval Studies in Honour of Mahmoud Manzalaoui on His 75th Birthday*. Ed. E. A. Christa Canitz and Gernot R. Wieland. Ottawa: Ottawa UP. 229–52.
–. 2002a. 'Introduction.' In Klinck and Rasmussen 2002: 1–14.
–. 2002b. 'Sappho and her Daughters: Some Parallels Between Ancient and Medieval Women's Song.' In Klinck and Rasmussen 2002: 15–28.
–. 2003. 'Poetic Markers of Gender in Medieval "Woman's Song": Was Anonymous a Woman?' *Neophilologus* 87: 339–59.
–, ed. 2004. *An Anthology of Ancient and Medieval Woman's Song*. New York: Palgrave Macmillan.
–, and Ann Marie Rasmussen, eds. 2002. *Medieval Woman's Song: Cross-Cultural Approaches*. The Middle Ages Series. Philadelphia: U of Pennsylvania P.
Krapp, George P., and Elliott Van Kirk Dobbie, eds. 1936. *The Exeter Book*. The Anglo-Saxon Poetic Records. Vol. 3. New York: Columbia UP.
Kraus, Carl von, ed. 1978. *Deutsche Liederdichter des 13. Jahrhunderts*. 2nd ed. 2 vols. Rev. by Gisela Kornrumpf and Hugo Kuhn. Tübingen: Niemeyer.
Lapa, Manuel Rodrigues, ed. 1995. *Cantigas d'escarnho e de mal dizer*. 4th ed. Lisbon: da Costa.
Larrington, Carolyne, trans. 1996. *The Poetic Edda*. Oxford: OUP.
Linker, Robert White. 1979. *A Bibliography of Old French Lyrics*. Romance Monographs 31. University, MS: Romance Monographs, Inc.
López Estrada, Francisco, ed. 1999. Ruy González de Clavijo. *Embajada a Tamorlán*. Madrid: Castalia.
Loraux, Nicole. 1998. *Mothers in Mourning: With the Essay of Amnesty and Its Opposite*. Trans. Corrine Pache. Ithaca, NY: Cornell UP.
Lord, Albert Bates. 1960. *The Singer of Tales*. Cambridge, MA: Harvard UP. [Re-edition with a CD and a new introduction by Stephen Mitchell and Gregory Nagy, 2000.]
Malone, Kemp. 1962. 'Two English *Frauenlieder*.' *Comparative Literature* 14: 106–17.
Marnette, Sophie. 1997. 'L'expression féminine dans la poésie lyrique occitane.' *Romance Philology* 11: 170–93.

Martindale, Charles, ed. 1988. *Ovid Renewed: Ovidian Influences on Literature and Art from the Middle Ages to the Twentieth Century.* Cambridge: CUP.
Masera, Mariana. 1993. "'Yo, mi madre, yo, que la flor de la villa me so." La voz feminina en la antigua lírica popular hispánica.' In *Voces de la Edad Media.* Ed. Concepción Company et al. Mexico City: Universidad Autónoma de México. 105–13.
Menéndez Pidal, Ramón. 1951. 'Cantos románicos continuadores de una lírica latina vulgar.' *Boletin de la Real Academia Española* 31: 187–270.
*MF*: see Moser and Tervooren 1977–88.
Middleton, Christopher, and Leticia Garza-Falcón, trans. 1993. *Andalusian Poems.* Boston: Godine.
Migne, Jacques-Paul, ed. 1862. '*Expositio in Psalmum XLI.*' In *S. Joannis Chrysostomi Opera omnia.* Vol. 5. PG 55. Paris. 155–58.
Mölk, Ulrich. 1988. 'Die frühen romanischen Frauenlieder. Überlegungen und Anregungen.' In *Idee, Gestalt, Geschichte. Festschrift Klaus von See.* Ed. Wolfgang Weber. Odense: Odense UP. 63–88.
–, ed. 1989. *Romanische Frauenlieder.* Klassische Texte des Romanischen Mittelalters 28. Munich: Fink.
–. 1990. 'Chansons de femme, trobairitz et la théorie romantique de la genèse de la poésie lyrique romane.' *Lingua e stile* 25: 135–46.
Monroe, James T., ed. 1974. *Hispano-Arabic Poetry: A Student Anthology.* Berkeley: U of California P.
Moser, Hugo, and Helmut Tervooren, eds. 1977–88. *Des Minnesangs Frühling.* 3 vols. 36th ed. (vols. 2 and 3), 38th ed. (vol. 1). Stuttgart: Hirzel.
Muir, Bernard J., ed. 2000. *The Exeter Anthology of Old English Poetry.* Rev. and enl. 2nd ed. Exeter: U of Exeter P.
Neckel, Gustav, ed. 1968–83. *Die Lieder des Codex Regius nebst verwandten Denkmälern. I. Text. II. Kurzes Wörterbuch.* 2 vols. Rev. Hans Kuhn. 5th ed. (vol. 1), 3rd ed. (vol. 2). Heidelberg: Winter.
Nunes, José Joaquim, ed. 1926–28. *Cantigas d'amigo das trovadores galego-portugueses.* 3 vols. Coimbra: Imprensa da Universidade.
O'Grady, William, and John Archibald. 2004. *Contemporary Linguistic Analysis.* 5th ed. Toronto: Pearson Longman.
Orlando, Sandro, ed. 1981. *Rime dei Memoriali Bolognesi 1279–1300.* Turin: Einaudi.
Paden, William, ed. and trans. 1987. *The Medieval Pastourelle.* 2 vols. New York: Garland.
–, ed. 1989. *The Voice of the Trobairitz: Perspectives on the Woman Troubadours.* Philadelphia: U of Pennsylvania P.
–. 1995. 'Trobairitz.' In Kibler and Zinn 1995: 927–28.
–, ed. 2000. *Medieval Lyric: Genres in Historical Context.* Urbana: U of Illinois P.
Page, Christopher. 1987. *Voices and Instruments of the Middle Ages: Instrumental Practice and Songs in France 1100–1300.* London: Dent.
Page, D. L., ed. 1962. *Poetae Melici Graeci.* Oxford: Clarendon.
Panvini, Bruno, ed. 1962–64. *Le Rime della Scuola Siciliana.* 2 vols. Florence: Olschki.
Paris, Gaston. 1883. 'Études sur les romans de la Table Ronde: *Lancelot du Lac*.' *Romania* 12: 459–534.
–. 1891–92. 'Les origines de la poésie lyrique en France.' *Journal des Savants*: (1891) 674–88, 729–42; (1892) 155–67, 407–30. [Review of A. Jeanroy, *Les origines de la poésie lyrique en France au Moyen Âge*, 1st. ed., Paris, 1889.]
PC: Alfred Pillet and Henry Carstens. 1933. *Bibliographie der Troubadours.* Schriften der Königsberger gelehrten Gesellschaft, Sonderreihe 3. Halle: Niemeyer.
Pérez Priego, Miguel Angel, ed. 1989. *Poesía feminina en los cancioneros.* Madrid: Castalia.

Pertz, Georg Heinrich, ed. 1835. 'Karoli Magni capitularia.' In *Capitularia regum Francorum*. MGH, Leges 1. Hannover. 32–194.
Piñero Ramírez, Pedro M., ed. 1998. *Lírica popular / lírica tradicional: Lecciones en homenaje a Don Emilio García Gómez*. Seville: Universidad de Sevilla.
Plummer, John F., ed. 1981. *Vox Feminae: Studies in Women's Song*. Kalamazoo: Medieval Institute, Western Michigan U.
Rasmussen, Ann Marie. 2002. 'Reason and the Female Voice in Walther von der Vogelweide's Poetry.' In Klinck and Rasmussen 2002: 168–186.
–. 2006. 'Woman's Song.' In *Women and Gender in Medieval Europe: An Encyclopedia*. Ed. Margaret Schaus. New York: Routledge. 845–46.
Reichl, Karl. 1987. 'Popular Poetry and Courtly Lyric: The Middle English Pastourelle.' *REAL: The Yearbook of Research in English and American Literature* 5: 33–61.
Rieger, Angelica, ed. 1991. *Trobairitz: Der Beitrag der Frau in der altokzitanischen höfischen Lyrik: Edition des Gesamtkorpus*. Tübingen: Niemeyer.
Robbins, Rossell Hope, ed. 1955. *Secular Lyrics of the XIVth and XVth Centuries*. 2nd ed. Oxford: Clarendon.
Rosenberg, Samuel N. 1995. 'Women's Songs.' In Kibler and Zinn 1995: 987.
–, Margaret Louise Switten, and Gérard Le Vot, eds. 1998. *Songs of the Troubadours and Trouvères: An Anthology of Poems and Melodies*. New York: Garland.
Rowland, Jenny. 1990. *Early Welsh Saga Poetry: A Study and Edition of the Englynion*. Cambridge: Brewer.
Schotter, Anne Howland. 1981. 'Woman's Song in Medieval Latin.' In Plummer 1981: 19–33.
Schweikle, Günther, ed. and trans.. 1998. *Walther von der Vogelweide: Werke*. 2 vols. Stuttgart: Reclam.
Sigal, Gale. 1996. *Erotic Dawn Songs of the Middle Ages*. Gainesville: U of Florida P.
Solá-Solé, Josep M., ed and trans. 1973. *Corpus de poesía mozárabe*. Barcelona: Hispam.
–, ed. and trans. 1990. *Las jarchas romances y sus moaxajas*. Madrid: Taurus.
Spitzer, 1952. 'The Mozarabic Lyric and Theodor Frings' Theories.' *Comparative Literature* 4: 1–22.
Stern, S. M. 1948. 'Les vers finaux en espagnol dans les muwaššaḥas hispano-hébraïques.' *Al-Andalus* 13. 299–346.
Stevenson, Jane. 2005. *Women Latin Poets: Language, Gender, and Authority, from Antiquity to the Eighteenth Century*. Oxford: OUP.
Switten, Margaret, et al. 2001. *Teaching Medieval Lyric with Modern Technology*. CD–ROM. South Hadley, MA: Mount Holyoke College.
Thiébaux, Marcelle, trans. 1994. *The Writings of Medieval Women: An Anthology*. New York: Garland.
Valencia, Adriana, and Shamma Boyarin. 2004. '"Ke adame filiolo alieno": Three *Muwaššaḥāt* with the same *Kharja*.' In Hamilton et al. 2004: 75–86.
van den Boogaard, Nico H. J., ed. 1969. *Rondeaux et refrains du XII$^e$ siècle au début du XIV$^e$*. Paris: Klincksieck.
van der Werf, Hendrik. 1995. 'Music.' In Akehurst and Davis 1995: 121–64.
Vidan, Aida. 2003. *Embroidered with Gold, Strung with Pearls: The Traditional Ballads of Bosnian Women*. Cambridge, MA: Harvard UP.
Vollmann, Benedikt Konrad, ed. and trans. 1987. *Carmina Burana*. Bibliothek des Mittelalters 13. Frankfurt a. M.: Deutscher Klassiker Verlag.
Warren, Roger, and Stanley Wells, eds. 1994. William Shakespeare. *Twelfth Night*. Oxford: Clarendon.
Whetnall, Jane. 1984. 'Lírica Feminina in the Early Manuscript Cancioneros.' In *What's Past is Prologue: A Collection of Essays in Honour of L. J. Woodward*. Ed. Salvador Bacarisse et al. Edinburgh: Scottish Academic P. 138–50.

Wilhelm, James J., ed. and trans. 1990. *Lyrics of the Middle Ages: An Anthology.* New York: Garland.
Williams, Ifor, ed. 1970. *Canu Llywarch Hen.* 3rd ed. Cardiff: U of Wales P.
Willis, Raymond S., Jr., ed. 1934. *El Libro de Alexandre.* Princeton: Princeton UP.
Wright, Janice. 1998. 'The Enemy Within: A Galician-Portuguese Dawn Song.' *La Corónica* 26: 5–8 and 77–90.
Zink, Michel, ed. 1977. *Les chansons de toile.* Paris: Champion.
Ziolkowski, Jan M., ed. and trans. 1994. *The Cambridge Songs (Carmina Cantabrigiensia).* New York: Garland.
Zumthor, Paul. 1972. *Essai de poétique médiéval.* Paris: Seuil.

# 21 Popular Song and the Middle English Lyric

## Karin Boklund-Lagopoulou

### 1 Orality and Literacy in England after the Norman Conquest

Virtually all scholars agree that the vernacular lyric poetry of medieval Europe has its roots in an oral tradition of popular song. What the songs of this tradition may have been like, however, is not easy to determine. By definition, whatever medieval poetry has survived has come to us in the form of written texts, and the intentions of their scribes was not generally to record for posterity the lyrics of a popular song.

We may take it as given that orally transmitted songs were in circulation in England during the Middle Ages.[1] Songs and stories are still circulating orally in our own society, where literacy is well-nigh universal and printed books are easily available; in medieval Europe, where literacy was much less widespread and the materials for writing much less accessible, oral transmission must have been much more common.

England in the Middle Ages was by no means a preliterate culture; medieval Europe had been a literate society for centuries.[2] But it was not a universally, or even a predominantly literate society. The dominant 'high' culture, the culture of the Church and the nobility, was certainly largely a culture of the written word, although even here a case can be made for more orality than we usually recognize. But access to this written culture was limited. Access to the courtly culture of the nobility, though not literally limited to those of noble birth, was nonetheless regulated by the kind of informal social training acquired by participation in a noble household. Access to ecclesiastical culture depended on formal schooling in Latin. Oral culture, by contrast, was non-exclusive. It was a popular culture, not in the sense that it was practiced exclusively by the 'folk', but in the sense that it was available to all. Participation was open to rich and poor, noble and commoner, literate or illiterate.[3]

Of course, the *influence* of written culture was not limited to the upper classes. Especially the culture of the Church was a genuine hegemonic culture, omnipresent and

---

[1] Middle English literature refers to the period after the Norman Conquest of 1066; in practice, Middle English lyrics begin to appear in manuscripts in the early thirteenth century.
[2] The following discussion is based on material from Boklund-Lagopoulou 2002.
[3] Peter Burke, employing Robert Redfield's distinction between the 'great' or learned tradition and the 'little' or popular tradition, argues that 'there were two cultures in early modern Europe, but they did not correspond symmetrically to the two main social groups, the elite and the common people. The elite participated in the little tradition, but the common people did not participate in the great tradition' (Burke 1978:28).

overwhelmingly familiar to medieval men and women in all social ranks. Courtly culture, too, filtered down through the gentry to the urban middle class. But equally, high culture was not exclusively a written culture. Up to the end of the fourteenth century much courtly literature, both lyrics and narrative verse, was meant to be performed orally. Even within the Church, many hymns and prayers, and most of the liturgy, though they of course existed in written form, would have circulated among the clergy as much orally as in writing.

Thus, orality in the Middle Ages is not necessarily limited to popular literature. A degree of orality characterizes many texts of both courtly and clerical origin.[4] There is a good deal of interaction between written and oral culture; literate members of the gentry, merchants and lower clergy seem to have been instrumental in preserving popular texts in writing. Many texts seem to have moved back and forth between oral and written forms of transmission.

It should not be necessary, in the context of the present volume, to defend the artistic quality of oral poetry. Our modern concept of verbal art is very closely related to the kinds of aesthetic effects that can be produced in a written text. Especially when dealing with lyric poetry, we tend to assume that these effects are the very essence of art as such. The result of such an assumption, as has been pointed out by several scholars, is that only a written tradition is seen as capable of producing art, and the forms of artistry peculiar to an oral tradition are either not recognized at all, or undervalued. The oral tradition is perceived as secondary to and dependent on the written; oral compositions tend to be seen as poor imitations of the art of the written culture.[5]

In the face of the mass of evidence gathered by ethnologists from contemporary oral cultures, such a view is simply untenable. As Ruth Finnegan in particular has argued (1977 and 1988), an oral culture is just as much a culture, with its acquired skills and its trained specialists, as is a written tradition. But two circumstances of medieval English society in particular also argue against it. The first is its *de facto* limitation on social mobility. Access to high culture required wealth, social standing, and power. Intelligence and ability were of course important, then as now, if one wanted to improve one's position in society, but the scope of even the greatest ability was much more limited than it is in modern society. Thus, men and women with artistic talent would not all gravitate to the centres of high culture, but many would remain and exercise their abilities within the context of the popular, oral culture which was available to them. This is amply documented for early modern Europe by Peter Burke (1978:91–108), and there is every reason to believe that it was the case in earlier centuries as well.

The second of the circumstances that favoured the survival of an oral poetic tradition in Middle English is the linguistic situation resulting from the Norman Conquest in 1066. With Norman French replacing Anglo-Saxon as the language of government and as the preferred literary language of the nobility, and given the predominance of Latin in learned and ecclesiastical culture, English virtually disappears from the written

---

[4] Walter Ong (1982:26) argues that '[o]ral habits of thought and expression, including massive use of formulaic elements, still marked prose style of almost every sort' as late as the Tudor era.
[5] See Lord 1960; Tristram 1992; Finnegan 1988; Ong 1982.

records up to the end of the twelfth century. During this time, literary production in English must have been almost exclusively oral.

After the twelfth century, Anglo-Norman probably was not truly a spoken mother tongue in England outside the ranks of the very high nobility. But throughout the thirteenth century it appears to have remained the preferred *literary* language, the most appropriate medium for fashionable vernacular poetry, both lyric and romance.[6] It was not limited to the nobility. Elizabeth Salter (1983: 21) considers that Anglo-Norman literature 'catered for many different levels of society', and a large proportion of the population must have been at least partly bilingual (or tri-lingual, if one includes some knowledge of Latin). However, although there seems to have been a flourishing oral tradition in both English and Anglo-Norman, the tradition of *written* poetry was more highly developed in French.[7] For poets who wanted to work in Middle English, on the other hand, the most immediate models were oral.[8]

We no longer believe that the acquisition of literacy automatically disqualifies an individual as bearer of an oral tradition. We might add that literacy, in thirteenth-century England, meant literacy primarily in Latin, secondarily and to a lesser extent in French. It would not necessarily interfere with an individual's ability to operate within an oral tradition in English, though access to Latin literate culture especially would tend to make one feel that the vernacular oral culture was less valuable.

## 2  Types of Orality in Middle English Lyrics

Franz Bäuml (1984) has pointed out that there are two different ways in which a poem can be considered 'oral'. First, it can be composed using specifically oral techniques of composition. Secondly, it can be transmitted and performed orally, as part of a society's oral tradition. Although Bäuml is writing of the heroic epic, these different types of orality clearly apply to lyric poetry as well. That medieval lyrics were transmitted and performed orally is well documented. It is more difficult to find historical evidence of oral composition. European folksongs in more recent times do not use formulae and are rarely composed in performance, and as far as we can tell this was probably true of medieval oral lyrics as well. There is, however, ample evidence that oral lyrics whether modern or medieval rely heavily on conventional themes, imagery, diction, and style, which are analogous in function to the formulaic systems of heroic verse; they may also be subject to limited recreation in performance, and certainly often involve direct audience

---

[6] See Richter 1995; Crane 1999. [See also chapters 3 (M. Richter) and 4 (K. O'Brien O'Keeffe) in this volume.]

[7] See also Jeffrey and Levy (1990: 3): 'for the writer of a certain class and training, his vernacular models were written in that language.'

[8] Indeed, until recently, many scholars (e. g. Robbins 1952: lii; Woolf 1968: 2; Oliver 1970: 131) argued that properly 'courtly' lyric poetry essentially was not written in Middle English until the end of the fourteenth century. With the recent work of Carter Revard (2000) on the Harley scribe and Karl Reichl's identification of the manuscript leaf of *Mirie it is while summer ilast* as a fragment of an early–13th-century English *chansonnier* (Reichl 2005a: 24–33), this view will have to be revised.

participation in refrains and dances. We are thus justified in speaking of techniques of oral composition for the lyric, modern or medieval.

It is helpful to think of the various kinds of Middle English lyrics as situated on a continuum. Hildegard Tristram (1992) envisions this continuum as two converging lines, the first referring to manner of composition and the second to medium of transmission: from poetry oral both in conception and transmission, to poetry orally composed but transmitted partly in writing, to poems composed in writing but for oral performance, to written lyrics meant for private reading. Where on this continuum any particular text is to be situated depends largely on the social milieu in which the poem circulated and the functional use to which it was put, but for these we usually have only circumstantial evidence.

## 3  Forms of Transmission: Records of Popular Song

What fragments we have of the oral poetry of medieval England have necessarily reached us in writing. Since the primary custodian of the written word in medieval Europe was the Church, it comes as no surprise that the earliest Middle English verse has been recorded in manuscripts of clerical provenance. In such a context, how can we recognize material from an oral tradition?

In some cases, the manuscripts themselves tell us. On one famous occasion, the twelfth-century chronicler Thomas of Ely records a song that was improvised by King Canute, as he was being rowed by Ely Abbey:[9]

> Merie sungen ðe muneches binnen Ely
> ða Cnut cning reu ðer by;
> Roweþ, cnites, noer the land,
> And here wve þes muneches saeng.

Merrily sang the monks in Ely/ As King Knut rowed by there;/ Row, ye knights, nearer the land/ And let us hear these monks' song

It is, of course, not certain that the chronicler is recording an actual event here; it may just as well be simply a local legend. But that the song was part of an oral poetic tradition (and that there was more to it than these four lines) is clear from the chronicler's comment 'et caetera, quae sequuntur, quae usque hodie in choris publice cantantur et in proverbis memorantur' (and other verses which follow, which are still sung today at public dances and remembered in proverbs).

Other clerics also mention popular singing and dancing, usually with disapproval. In the opening lines of an early-thirteenth-century sermon we read:[10]

> Atte wrastlinge my lemman I ches
> And ate ston-kasting I him for-les.

---

[9] Cambridge, Trinity College MS O.2.1; Brook 1968:4. The text is as printed by Greene 1977: xlix. *Index of Middle English Verse (IMEV)* no. 2164.
[10] Cambridge, Trinity College MS B.1.45, quoted in Greene 1977: xlix-l. *IMEV* no. 445.

Mi leue frend, wilde wimmen & golme i mi contreie, wan he gon o þe ring, among manie oþere songis, þat litil ben wort þat tei singin, so sein þei þus: 'Atte wrastli[n]ge mi lemman' etc.

At the wrestling my lover I chose/ And at the stone-casting I lost him

My dear friends, wanton women and men (?) in my country, when they go in the ring, among many other songs that little be worth that they sing, they say thus: 'At the wrestling my lover', etc.

The preacher has taken as the text of his sermon two lines of a song, which he specifies is sung and danced by the women in his home region. His sermon is a moralizing allegorical interpretation of these lines. Interestingly, the preacher's quotation contains a 'mistake'. The same song appears in another manuscript, in a slightly different form:[11]

Atte ston castinges my lemman i ches,
and atte wrastlinges sone i hym les;
allas, þat he so sone fel;
wy nadde he stonde better, vile gorel?

At the stone-castings my lover I chose/ And at the wrestlings soon I lost him/ Alas, that he fell so soon;/ Why didn't he stand better, the vile pig?

The second couplet specifies that the speaker abandoned her lover because he 'fell so soon'; logically, he must have fallen in the wrestling match, not at the shot-putting.[12] This is the kind of variation that we would expect in a song circulating orally, though if the preacher's audience recognized it, it must have rather upset his allegory.[13]

Both the secular clergy and the monastic orders were instrumental in recording popular lyrics. Siegfried Wenzel cites dozens of fragments of lyrics preserved in sermons.[14] A particularly important role was played by the preaching friars; Rosemary Woolf points out that Middle English vernacular lyrics 'first appear in quantity, and in the body of the text not in the margins, in manuscripts that were preaching note-books of the friars' (1968: 373). The friars, who arrived in England in the 1220s, made it their special mission to preach to the populace, and for this purpose they systematically both used popular material for their sermons (Owst 1961) and themselves composed vernacular lyrics as preaching aids (Jeffrey 1984: 307). Richard Greene (1977: cl-clvii) credits them with the composition of the vast majority of the religious carols, written to be sung to the melodies of secular dance songs in oral circulation.

A special case of fragments of popular songs quoted in a clerical manuscript are the songs in the *Red Book of Ossory*. This is a collection of Latin hymns apparently composed mainly by Richard de Ledrede, bishop of Ossory (1317–1360), in an attempt to dissuade his clergy from the singing of secular songs.[15] To indicate the intended tune for the composition, a few lines of a vernacular song are prefaced to each Latin text; some are

---

[11] Cambridge, University Library MS Ii.3.8, as printed by Robbins 1952: xxxix.
[12] There is probably a sexual pun on his inability to 'stand' as well; see Dronke 1990: 10–11.
[13] For the allegory, see Greene 1977: cxlvii.
[14] Wenzel 1974; 1986: 209–56. For a recent discussion of the lyric in the sermon, see Fletcher 2005.
[15] The widespread practice of *contrafactum*, composing religious lyrics to a secular tune, goes back at least as far as Thomas of Bayeux, Archbishop of York (d. 1100), of whom William of Malmesbury reports that 'if anyone sang a profane song in his hearing he at once converted it into a hymn of

religious, but many are apparently secular love songs. For these fragments, then, we know that they were songs, and we can reasonably assume that they were in popular circulation, at least in Bishop Ledrede's diocese in the mid-fourteenth century.

What were these popular songs like? The few lines of each that we have are scarcely enough material for analysis. But one of the song fragments from the *Red Book of Ossory* appears in two other fourteenth-century sources. It is quoted briefly in a sermon found in Worcester Cathedral Library MS F. 126, where it is called a *karole*, a dance song,[16] and it is also included among the so-called Rawlinson lyrics. These are twelve short poems or fragments of English and French verse, written on a single strip of parchment dated to the second quarter of the fourteenth century, which was incorporated into the binding of Oxford, Bodleian Library MS Rawlinson D. 913.

Most scholars today would agree with Greene that the Rawlinson lyrics are 'either genuine folksong or something closely modeled upon genuine folksong' (1977: lii). John Scattergood considers them representative of 'an extensive tradition, probably popular, probably largely oral' (2005: 51). The piece of parchment on which they are written seems to have been a little scroll, something that could be rolled up and carried easily in a bag or pocket. The texts recorded on it are very short, often abbreviated so that more material could be squeezed into the limited space. It seems to be a set of personal notes, perhaps to be copied into more permanent form when occasion arose.

The first item on the parchment scroll is a love song with a spring setting:[17]

>    Of euerykune tre,
>    of euerykune tre,
>    þe hawe-þorn blowet suotes
>    Of euerykune tre.
>    my lemmon sse ssal boe
>    my lemmon sse ssal boe
>    þe fairest of euery kinne
>    my lemmon sse ssal boe.

Of every kind of tree,/ of every kind of tree,/ the hawthorn blossoms sweetest/ Of every kind of tree./ My lover she shall be/ my lover she shall be/ the fairest of every kind [kin?]/ My lover she shall be.

After three brief fragments (only a line or two of each poem has been written down) and two French songs, there follows 'Ich am of Irlaunde':

>    Ich am of Irlaunde
>    Ant of the holy londe
>    Of Irlaunde.
>
>    Gode sire, pray ich thee
>    For of sainte charity

---

praise' (quoted in Brook 1968: 16); it sounds as though Bishop Thomas may have been composing his hymns orally. See also Dronke 1965.

[16] The lyric probably 'circulated orally in various forms, and therefore [...] was a popular song. [...] by calling the Middle-English lyric a *karole* this preacher [...] thought of a secular song and probably of a dance song' (Wenzel 1974: 72–74).

[17] Text quoted as emended by Dronke 1961. *IMEV* nos. 2622 ('Of everykune tre') and 1008 ('Ich am of Irlaunde').

> Come ant daunce wit me
> In Irlaunde.

The next item is 'Maiden in the mor lay', the dance song that is also found in the *Red Book of Ossory*. The Latin text of Bishop Ledrede has been used to reconstruct the stanza form of the English poem:[18]

> Maiden in the mor lay,    [moor]
>    In the more lay
> Sevennight fulle –
> Sevennight fulle –
> Maiden in the mor lay,
>    In the mor lay,
> Sevennights fulle –
> Sevennights fulle –
>    Fulle ant a day.
> Well was hir mete.    [meat, food]
>    What was hir mete?
> The primerole ant the –    [primrose]
> The primerole ant the –
> Well was hir mete.
>    What was hir mete?
> The primerole and the –
> The primerole and the –
>    And the violet.
> Well was hir dring.    [drink]
>    What was hir dring?
> The chelde water of the –    [cold]
> The chelde water of the –
> Well was hir dring.
>    What was hir dring?
> The childe water of the –
> The childe water of the –
>    Of the welle spring.    [well-spring]
> Well was hir bour.    [bower, chamber]
>    What was his bour?
> The rede rose ant the –
> The rede rose and the –
> Well was hir bour.
>    What was hir bour?
> The rede rose ant the –
> The rede rose ant the –
>    Ant the lilie flour.    [flower]

The last English pieces include two short love songs, 'Alnist by þe rose' and 'Al gold Ionet is þin her', and another dance song (partly illegible):

> Ye sir þat is idronken    [drunk]
>    dronken dronken ydronken

---

[18] As printed by Burrow 1977, but expanded according to the suggestions by Duncan 2005b: 32–35. *IMEV* nos. 3891 ('Maiden in the mor lay') and *24 ('Ye sir þat is idronken').

>           [...] atta dronken
>                as tabart atte wyne.        [Tabard]
>           hay [...] malikin                [Malkin]
>                suster walter peter         [sister]
>           þe dronke al depe                [they drank all deeply]
>                ant ichulle eke             [and I shall also]
>           Stondet alle stille              [all stand still]
>                stille stille stille
>           Stondet alle stille
>                stille as any ston
>           trippe a lutel wit þi fot        [trip a little with your foot]
>                ant let þe body go.

If we look at these poems together with Wenzel's fragments of popular songs, can we identify any characteristics of a Middle English tradition of popular oral poetry?

The first characteristic that strikes us is that all these fragments appear to be songs, and several of them are specifically identified as dance songs. 'Atte wrastlinge my lemman I ches' was sung by 'wilde wimmon & golme ... wan he gon o þe ring', and no less than three of the Rawlinson lyrics, 'Maiden in the mor lay', 'Ich am of Irlaunde', and 'Ye sir þat is idronken', are dance songs or dance games (the last one especially seems to imply dance movements mimicking a drunkard).[19] This points to one powerful context for the transmission of oral material: music and dance.[20]

Another feature that we can identify immediately is the directness and simplicity of the language. There are no Latinisms, no learned vocabulary. There is no lack of a subjective voice, especially in the love songs, but even these have a certain impersonality: we learn nothing specific about either the singer or the object of his/her song.

However, the simple language does not necessarily make these poems easy to understand. Burrow (1977: xxiv) has commented on the 'intractable problems of interpretation' of many of these texts. This is not only due to their fragmentary nature. While we are fairly well informed about the imagery and the conventions of courtly or religious poetry, there are no sources that explain to us the beliefs and practices behind the lyrics of the oral tradition. These seem to have been so widely familiar in their own time that they were not felt to require any explanation.

A formal feature characteristic of later European folksong which is prominent in several of these pieces is the use of repetition. Repetition characterizes many kinds of poetry. In songs, for instance, it is closely related to the nature of the melody, so that the existence of a refrain, or of a solo singer alternating with a chorus, tends to encourage the repetition of whole lines or groups of lines. This is clearly one of the reasons for the repetitions in 'Maiden in the mor lay'. But there is also another mechanism at work in this poem. The repetitions are not exact, but involve slight alterations: a line in the form of a statement is followed by an almost identical line in the form of a question, or

---

[19] For dance games and the songs that accompanied them, see Dronke 1996: 186–206, and Axton 1974: 47–60.

[20] The presence of music is not in itself proof that a poem is of oral provenance; some medieval music is highly sophisticated, and the nature of a medieval musical score is not always easy to judge for a non-specialist. Nonetheless, there is a strong relationship between dance music and popular song; see Stevens 1982 and 1986: esp. 159–98.

a line is left incomplete, to be completed only in a last repetition in the final closing of the stanza. The effect is one of postponed closure, of expectations raised to be fulfilled only after tantalizing delay, of questions reluctantly answered and an invitation to share in a secret universe to which access is apparently offered but then teasingly withdrawn. This effect cannot all be due to our incomplete knowledge of the belief world behind the poem; part of it at least is built into the structure of the song. This is what folksong scholars call incremental repetition, repetition creating a peculiar tension in the text with the very gradual revelation of small but important pieces of information, through a slight but significant alteration, with each repetition, of the form and function of the repeated phrase.[21]

It is perhaps also possible to tentatively identify some recurrent motifs. Several scholars have remarked on the use of nature imagery in these lyrics. The songs associate the love between man and woman with spring, nature and fertility.[22] In 'Of euerykune tre' the human world of the lovers and the natural world are seen as parallel, and the poem seems to want to align the human world with the fertility and promise of nature: as the hawthorn blossoms, so will their love flourish. A similar pattern is shown by the stanza below, allegorized in an early fifteenth-century parish priest's notebook, which Wenzel argues from the manner of its insertion into the manuscript context is a secular love song. Here we again find elements of nature (the spring, the thorn tree) in close association with a young woman in love ('fulle of loue y-bounde'), and the association is marked as positive ('bote of bale'):[23]

> At a sprynge-wel vnder a þorn
> Þer was bote of bale, a lytel here a-forn;
> Þer by-seyde stant a mayde,
> Fulle of loue y-bounde.
> Ho-so wol seche trwe loue
> In hyr hyt schal be founde.

At a spring-well underneath a thorn-tree/ There was relief from sorrow, a little while ago;/ Beside it there stands a maid,/ Full of love bound./ Whoso would seek true love,/ In her it shall be found.

The association with nature is not always a happy one. The *Red Book of Ossory* contains a fragment of what appears to be a lover's lament that sounds astonishingly modern; Greene points out that willow branches are traditional in English song as the badge of a forsaken lover:[24]

> Gayneth me no garlond of greene,
> Bot hit ben of wythowes ywroght.      [of willow-branches wrought]

---

[21] The term 'incremental repetition' seems to be the invention of Francis B. Gummere (1907: 117–34 and *passim*). A definition of the term and a discussion of its functions in folksong can be found in Greene 1977: cxviii–cxxix; see also Burke 1978: 136–46.

[22] Renwick (1980: 54–69) has a very interesting discussion of the persistent use of nature imagery in modern folksongs of sexual liaisons (a group he calls 'symbolic' songs).

[23] From Oxford, Magdalen College MS 60, one of the notebooks of John Dygoun, a parish priest and canon lawyer who became a recluse at Sheen Priory in 1435, as printed by Wenzel 1986: 230. *IMEV* no. 420.

[24] As printed by Greene 1974: xvi. *IMEV* no. 891.

The love lament, which we usually think of as the typical genre of courtly lyric, seems to be well established in the oral tradition. An 'amorosa cantilena' bewails the unfaithfulness of a lover:[25]

> Ich aue a loue vntrewe  [I have a love untrue]
> Þat is myn herte wo.
> Þat make me of rueful hewe
> Late to bedde go.
> Sore me may rewe  [sorely I may rue]
> Þat euer Hi louede hire so.  [that I ever loved her so]

The expression 'to go y-bounde' for love or with love seems to be part of the traditional diction of love songs. Wenzel quotes one suggestive couplet from a collection of sermons of the thirteenth century:[26]

> Ne sal it wite no man, wite no man,  [no man shall know it]
> Hu Ich go ibunde for mi lemmon.

Another sermon refers to 'illud canticum Anglicum':[27]

> Wo is me, wo is me,
> For loue Y go ibunden.

Songs of girls who have been seduced and abandoned lent themselves well to didactic interpretation:[28]

> Weylawey þat iche ne span  [that I didn't spin]
> Whan Y to þe ringe ran.

These lines are also quoted in another manuscript, with a slight variation ('to þe wude' instead of 'to þe ringe', phrases functionally equivalent in this semantic context and thus open to improvisation in performance) and followed by a second couplet:

> Waylaway wy dude Ich so  [why did I so]
> Vor nou ic am in alle wo.  [for now I am]

One item is identified by the preacher who quotes it as a lullaby, though the words strike us today as rather odd for lulling a child to sleep:[29]

> Wake wel, Annot  [guard]
> þi mayden boure;
> & get þe fra Walterot  [stay away from]
> for he es lichure.  [is a lecher]

---

[25] From Cambridge, University Library MS Ii.3.8, as printed by Wenzel 1986:22. *IMEV* no. 1301.
[26] From Oxford, New College MS 88, a collection of sermons and sermon notes of the second half of the thirteenth century, as printed by Wenzel 1986:225.
[27] From Cambridge, University Library MS Ff.1.17, as printed by Wenzel 1986:222.
[28] From London, BL MS Harley 505. *IMEV* no. 3900.5.
[29] 'Karissimi, bene scitis quod iste mulieres [...] þat lulle þe child with þair fote & singes an hauld song, sic dicens [...]', from a Latin sermon in London, BL MS Cotton Faustina A.v, quoted by Robbins 1952: xxxix. *IMEV* no. 3859.5.

Finally, there seems to have been a whole group of dance songs explicitly for women. They are documented in irate ecclesiastical references from long before the thirteenth century. There is a whole section devoted to women dancing in a late thirteenth-century collection of sermon materials, from which Wenzel prints the following two songs:[30]

>            Of my husband giu I noht            [I care nothing]
>            Another hauet my luue ybohit,       [has got my love]
>            For tuo gloues wyht ynoht.          [two gloves, very white]
>            If Hic him luue, Y naue no woht.    [I have no idea]

and

>            Lete þe cukewald syte at hom        [cuckold]
>            And chese þe anoþer lefmon.         [choose for yourself]
>            Late þe churl site at hom and pile, [scratch himself]
>            And þu salt don wat þu wile –       [you shall do]
>            God hit wot hit nys no skile!       [God knows it isn't difficult]

The point of these songs, then, seems to be that the women claim the right to choose their own lovers – or to have no man at all:

>            We schun makyn a ioly castel
>            On a bank bysyden a brymme,
>            Schal no man comyn theryn
>            But yuf he kun swymme,
>            Or buth he haue a both of loue
>            For to seylen ynne.[31]

We shall make a jolly castle/ On a bank beside a shore./ No man shall come therein/ Unless he can swim,/ Or unless he has a boat of love/ For to sail in.

In addition to songs about love in all its various aspects, the preachers' notebooks occasionally preserve other material of popular provenance. One of the earliest manuscripts of this kind, Cambridge, Trinity College MS 323, contains a couplet that may be a riddle:[32]

>            Ic chule bere to wasscen doun i þe toun     [I shall carry]
>            Þat was blac ant þat was broun.

In the same section of the manuscript we find the following verses:

>            'Say me, viit in þe brom,
>            Teche me, wou I sule don
>            Þat min hosebonde
>            Me louien wolde.'
>            'Hold þine tunke stille
>            Ant hawe al þine wille.'

'Tell me, wight in the broom [bush],/ Teach me how I should do/ So that my husband/ Will love me.'/ 'Hold your tongue still/ And have all your will.'

---

[30] From Dublin, Trinity College MS 347, as printed by Wenzel 1986: 216–17.
[31] From Cambridge, Jesus College MS 13, as printed by Wenzel 1986: 228–229. *IMEV* no. 3870.22.
[32] The texts are from the edition of the manuscript by Karl Reichl 1973. The poem known as *Judas*, perhaps the earliest English ballad, is in the same section of the manuscript. *IMEV* no. 1389.5.

The same verses, with slight variations, also occur in another manuscript, where they are included (in English) in an *exemplum* written in Latin:[33]

> 'Sey, wist y þe brom,
> Þwat ys me for to don?
> Ich haue þe werreste bonde        [worst]
> Þat ys in oni londe.'
>
> *responsio sortilege anglice*
> 'Þyf þy bonde ys ylle           [if your husband is bad]
> Held þy tonge stille.'

The differences between the two versions, slight as they are, are not entirely without consequences for the interpretation of the poem. In the second text, the problem is how to manage a bad marriage, and the solution proposed is the traditional one of wifely silence and obedience. In the first version, the goal is a loving relationship ('Þat min hosebonde Me louien wolde'), and the wight in the broom suggests a rather subversive strategy: by adopting a conventionally subordinate role, the woman will in fact have things her own way. Apparently the poem can to some extent be adapted to different situations and contexts, characteristic of material from an oral tradition.

A more unusual context for the deliberate recording of oral poetry in a monastic manuscript is exemplified by the famous 'Cuckoo Song':[34]

> Svmer is icumen in.
> Llude sing cuccu!                    [sing loudly, cuckoo]
> Groweþ sed and bloweþ med            [seed is sprouting] [meadow is blossoming]
> and springþ þe wde nu.               [the forest is leafing now]
> Sing cuccu!
>
> Awe bleteþ after lonb                [the ewe bleats after the lamb]
> llouþ after calue cu,                [the cow bellows after the calf]
> Bulloc sterteþ, bucke uerteþ.        [the bullock leaps, the buck farts]
> Murie sing cuccu!                    [merrily]
> Cuccu, cuccu,
> Wel singes þu cuccu.                 [well do you sing]
> ne swik þu nauer nu!                 [may you never fail now]
>
> Pes:   Sing cuccu nu, Sing cuccu!
>        Sing cuccu, Sing cuccu nu!

MS Harley 978, according to Brown (1932:168–89), is a commonplace book from Reading Abbey. It begins with a section of musical pieces, including this poem (the only one in English), which has instructions in Latin for singing as a round. This is a not unlikely setting for a popular song which struck a music-interested monk as having an unusual melody or manner of performance.[35]

---

[33] From London, BL MS Addit. 11579. The context is given in Brown 1932:180–81. *IMEV* no. 3078.

[34] From London, BL MS Harley 978, as printed by Brown 1932:13; a recent discussion can be found in Boffey 2005:6. *IMEV* no. 3223.

[35] That it was the music which was of interest is also indicated by the *contrafactum*, the alternative religious text provided for it in Latin. The manuscript is dated, on the basis of both internal textual

21  *Popular Song and the Middle English Lyric*

21 – 'Svmer is icumen in', BL MS Harley 978, fol. 11v

So far, we have been discussing material which the manuscript context identifies (or allows us to identify) as of oral provenance. There are also cases where oral lyrics have been preserved simply by accident. The Rawlinson lyrics are perhaps the best example of this; the parchment scroll on which they were recorded would have had very slim chances of surviving to the present day if it had not been used to stiffen the binding of

---

evidence and handwriting, to around 1240. As Richard Crocker has pointed out, 'After much discussion there now seems to be agreement that it [the polyphonic song] can be dated 1240–60; indeed, there is no stylistic reason requiring a date later than, say, 1220' (Crocker 1990: 712).

an entirely unrelated manuscript. Another poem was recorded because it was cited as evidence in a lawsuit in 1331; it had been sung as a lament for the death of Robert de Neville some fifty years earlier:[36]

> Wel, qua sal thir hornes blau        [who shall their horns blow]
> Haly Rod thi day?                    [on the day of the Holy Cross]
> Nou is he dede and lies law          [low]
> Was wont to blaw thaim ay.           [to blow them always]

This manner of accidental preservation is still common, especially for poetry from the oral tradition, throughout the fifteenth century.

## 4 Orality in Written Lyrics

There are, however, also poems with no indication that they are popular songs that nevertheless show signs of being composed in an oral poetic tradition. One type of poetry which shows clear marks of orality, and which we frequently find in clerical manuscripts, is the kind of rather grim moral and didactic verses exemplified by 'Erþe toc of erþe' (copied into London, BL MS Harley 2253, around the year 1340):[37]

> Erþe toc of erþe erþe wyþ woh;
> Erþe oþer erþe to þe erþe droh;
> Erþe leyde erþe in erþene þroh.
> Þo heuede erþe of erþe erþe ynoh.

> Earth took of earth earth with woe;/ Earth other earth to the earth drew;/ Earth laid earth in an earthen grave./ Then had earth of earth earth enough.

It is impossible to say if these verses were first composed orally or in writing, though we can with some certainty say that they circulated widely in both forms. The Harley version is the earliest recorded one, but the poem occurs in various expanded forms in several later manuscripts.[38] Verses of a mnemonic, moral and generally didactic character are among the earliest and most persistent of Middle English texts. They range from the very popular to the very learned, and were clearly favourite material for both poets and preachers. 'Erþe toc of erþe' shows many characteristics of oral poetry, notably in its use of repetition with an elegant and ironic shift in meaning which has a cumulative, incremental effect. It feels like a popular proverb. But it could just as well be the work of a learned poet whose written, monastic culture had long ago appropriated and incorporated this aspect of the vernacular poetic tradition.[39]

---

[36] Recorded in London, BL MS Lansdowne 207; printed by Wilson 1970: 186–87.
[37] For the provenance of London, BL MS Harley 2253, and its scribe, see the volume edited by Susanna Fein (2000). The text is as printed by Brook 1968: 29. *IMEV* no. 3939.
[38] Brown 1932: 224; Gray 1972: 196–98.
[39] See the comment by Vincent Gillespie 2005: 68–69: 'It is in the nature of pre-literate and partially literate societies that their moral values and ethical principles will be encoded in and transmitted by memorial verse.' The moral and penitential lyrics of the Middle English period were 'part of a wide spectrum of didactic writing in which portable piety and aphoristic wisdom played a central role'.

There is no reason to believe that only illiterate singers composed oral poetry. The techniques of oral composition could very well have been known to members of the clergy, and to anyone wanting to compose in English rather than Latin, the style and diction of the oral tradition might well have felt more natural. This is perhaps the explanation for the quatrain that Carleton Brown entitled 'Sunset on Calvary':[40]

> Nou goth sonne vnder wod, –
> me reweth, marie, þi faire Rode.
> Nou goth sonne vnder tre, –
> me reweth, marie, þi sone and þe.

Now the sun goes down under the forest –/ I pity, Mary, your fair face./ Now the sun goes down under the tree –/ I pity, Mary, thy son and you.

This little poem appears in the text of St Edmund of Abingdon's *Speculum Ecclesie*, a devotional treatise probably written in 1239–1240. It occurs in a meditation on the Crucifixion. Immediately preceding the English poem there is a passage in irregularly rhyming, rhythmical French, relating Mary's weeping to Naomi's lament and to the bride of Canticles who says that she is not fair but burnt by the sun. At this point, the English lines are inserted with the comment 'E pur ceo dit un Engleis en teu manere de pité.'[41] The context for the poem is thus clearly learned and devotional. There is no indication that it is a song, and it was probably included because it was felt to be suitable for private reading and meditation, not oral performance. It is theologically rather sophisticated: as the purpose of this kind of devotional exercise is for the meditating reader to identify emotionally with the personages of sacred history, the poem telescopes time and space, so that the sunset on Calvary becomes the 'now' of an English countryside.[42] But the verse itself is closer to folksong than it is to written lyric. It has no direct Latin or French model. It shows none of the didacticism or moralizing found in thirteenth-century written religious lyric, but is composed in simple, direct language, at the same time objective and personal, intense but not sentimental. It makes delicate use of the method of incremental repetition, in which both the repeated and the new elements acquire added significance from each other. It was probably composed by a cleric, but I think he was working with the techniques of an oral literary tradition.[43]

Interaction between oral and written modes can also occur in transmission. The Middle English hymns composed by the friars are a particularly fruitful area for this kind of interaction. When we have more than one manuscript copy of a poem, the various texts often show variations that cannot be due simply to scribal mistakes but seem to indicate that the poem has been circulating orally. In the introduction to his volume of

---

[40] Brown 1932:1. *IMEV* no. 2320.
[41] Brown (1932:165–66) suggests that the poem was written by St Edmund himself, a view recently revived by Alan Fletcher (2005:200–2). Wilshere (1982:xvi) judges it to have been interpolated, probably by the translator, into the French translation made shortly after his death.
[42] See Woolf 1968:19–30; Gray 1972:18–30; Whitehead 2005:101; Fletcher 2005:200–2.
[43] Rosemary Woolf comments on this poem that 'in style it is quite unlike any other religious poetry of this period, unless one were to [...] guess that "I syng of a myden þat is makeles" is also an early poem. There are stylistic affinities between the two, in that both combine the incremental repetition of the ballads, with verbal subtlety and an oblique, emotive, use of symbolism' (Woolf 1968:242).

*English Lyrics of the Thirteenth Century,* Carleton Brown noted several such 'overlappings' between thirteenth-century manuscripts of religious verse. He remarks that comparison of the texts 'shows many variations of phrase, though in almost all cases the retention of the rhyme-words', and frequently a shift in the position of one or more stanzas, exactly the kinds of changes one would expect if the poems were taken down from memory or oral recitation. He concludes that 'these English lyrics must have circulated orally ... even though we are here dealing with clerks and friars rather than with "lewed folk".[44]

A macaronic hymn to the Virgin in English and French from London, BL MS Harley 2253, would seem an unlikely place to look for traces of oral poetry. But consider the first stanza of 'Mayden moder milde':[45]

> Mayden moder milde,
> *oiez cel oreysoun;*
> from shome þou me shilde,
> *e de ly mal feloun.*
> for loue of þine childe
> *me menez de tresoun;*
> Ich wes wod ant wilde,
> *ore su en prisoun.*

Maiden mother mild,/ *hear this prayer;/* shield me from [doing] sin,/ *and from the evil one./* For love of your child/ *protect me from treason;/* I was mad and wild,/ *now I am in prison.*

Brook observes that the concluding prayer at the end of the *Ayenbite of Inwit* repeats the English (but not the French) lines of this stanza, in a different order and with the addition of two intermediate lines that he calls 'common tags'. In the manuscript the lines are written as prose; I reproduce them below as verse:[46]

> Mayde and moder mylde
> uor loue of þine childe         [for]
> þet is god an man
> me þet am zuo wilde             [that am so]
> uram zenne þou me ssylde        [from sin]
> ase ich þe bydde can.           [as I pray you]

It is not really possible to derive the one form of this poem from the other by means of a series of written copies, however corrupt. But it is fairly easy to imagine how the different versions might have come about if the lines were being reproduced from memory in different contexts.

A different kind of interaction between oral and written is the incorporation of a piece of popular song as the refrain of a courtly lyric.[47] One of the most complex and

---

[44] Brown 1932: xxvi–xxvii. Julia Boffey (2005: 17) also comments that many of the Middle English lyrics must have circulated orally as well as in writing.
[45] Brook 1968: no. 28. *IMEV* no. 2039.
[46] I quote from Brook 1968: 86–87, who reprints the lines from London, BL MS Arundel 57. *IMEV* no. 2034.
[47] Both Gray (2005: 146) and Reichl (2005b: 168–69) have commented on the burdens from popular songs being used in courtly lyrics or sophisticated religious carols.

sophisticated of the Harley lyrics, 'Ichot a burde in boure bryht',[48] has a burden very different from the elegant courtly diction of the rest of the poem; characteristically, while the poem is written from a male perspective, in the burden we cannot tell if the speaker is supposed to be male or female:

> Blow, northerne wynd,
> sent þou me my suetyng!     [sweetheart]
> Blow, norþerne wynd,
> blou! blou! blou!

Karl Reichl mentions the popular-sounding burden of an early *chanson d'aventure* in carol form, in which a 'litel mai' curses an unfaithful lover:[49]

> Nou sprinkes the sprai,
> al for loue icche am so seeke
> that slepen I ne mai.

Now the branch is blossoming,/ all for love I am so sick/ that I cannot sleep.

Even the famous Harley lyric known as 'Alisoun' has a burden that, with its strong rhythm, feels very much like a popular dance song:[50]

> An hendy hap ichabbe yhent,
> ichot from heuene it is me sent;
> from alle wymmen mi loue is lent,
> ant lyht on Alysoun.

A happy chance I have received,/ I believe it is sent to me from heaven;/ from all women my love is taken/ And settled on Alison.

It is characteristic that the poems to which these lines belong are songs. Music remains one of the strongest links between the oral and written lyrical traditions well into the sixteenth century, and burdens, like melodies, can move easily between different songs. The following quatrain is the burden of a courtly madrigal included in an early sixteenth-century manuscript of music played at the court of Henry VIII:[51]

> Westron winde, when will thou blow?
>     The smalle raine downe can raine.
> Christ, if my love were in my armes,
>     And I in my bed againe.

The first two lines of the quatrain are echoed in a nineteenth-century ballad (*The Unquiet Grave*) and in a Scottish popular song ; John Stevens identifies it as a well-known popular song used as the basis for a fashionable piece of music.[52]

By the mid-fifteenth century, book ownership was becoming more common, and we have several manuscripts from the fifteenth century that are carol collections or song-

---

[48] Brook 1968: no. 14. *IMEV* no. 1395.
[49] Reichl 2005b: 167. – From London, Lincoln's Inn MS Hale 135, as printed by Brown 1932: 119. *IMEV* no. 360.
[50] Brook 1968: no. 4. *IMEV* no. 515.
[51] London, BL MS Royal Appendix 58.
[52] See Stevens 1961: 130. See Child 1882–98, nos. 78 and 204.

books. Most of the items in these manuscripts are religious poems, and most (though not all) are in carol form. The carol is a traditional popular dance song, usually with several verses and a burden; many of the lyrics allegorized in sermons that we discussed above are identified as carols. The majority of carols that have been preserved are what Richard Greene (1977: cxxix) has called 'popular by destination' rather than by provenance, written compositions intended to replace popular songs. They were part of the educational programme of the Franciscans, who often consciously imitated popular song. They tend to be rather didactic and moralizing, though at times the effort to compose lyrics in imitation of the oral tradition can produce quite attractive pieces.

Not only the Franciscans but other religious establishments as well seem to have made a systematic effort to preserve and transmit carols in writing, as is evident by the considerable number of texts that are found in more than one manuscript. But several carols also show evidence of having simultaneously circulated orally (Greene 1977: cxviii–cxxxviii). Usually, with the carols, oral transmission results in poorer texts; when the poems include Latin or French lines, for example, these tend to become jumbled. Occasionally, however, oral transmission seems to have had other kinds of effects. There is, for example, a carol from the second half of the fifteenth century about the Five Joys of Mary (here apparently the Annunciation, Nativity, Epiphany, Resurrection and Assumption):[53]

    Of a rose, a louely rose,
        Of a rose I syng a song.
[...]

    The [first] branch was of gret honour;
    That blyssed Mary shuld ber the flour,    [bear the flower]
    Ther cam an angel ovght hevyn tour    [out of heaven's tower]
        To breke the develes bond.

    The second branch was gret of might,
    That sprong vpon Cristmas night;
    The sterre shone and lemeghd bright,    [shone bright]
        That man schuld se it both day and nyght.

    The third branch gan spryng and spred;
    iii kynges than to branch gan led
    Tho to Owr Lady in hure childbed;
        Into Bethlem that branch sprong right. [...]

A later version of this carol shows up in the commonplace book of Richard Hill, a merchant of London in the early sixteenth century.[54] Here the connection with the events represented by the Five Joys is confused, and instead the poem adds a sixth 'branch' that refers to all the five joys together. But there is also a third version, recorded apparently some years *earlier* than the first, in which the connection with the Five Joys is completely lost:[55]

---

[53] In Oxford, Bodleian Library MS Eng. poet. e.I; Greene 1977: no. 175A. *IMEV* no. 1914.
[54] Oxford, Balliol College MS 354, Greene 1977: no. 175B. The poem has eight stanzas and describes five branches.
[55] London, BL MS Sloane 2593; Greene 1977: no. 175C. This poem comprises seven stanzas.

> The ferste braunch is ful of might,
> That sprong on Crystemesse nyght;
> The sterre schon ouer Bedlem bright,    [Bethlehem]
>    That is bothe brod and long.
>
> The secunde braunche sprong to helle
> The fendys power doun to felle;    [fiend's power]
> Therin might non sowle dwelle;    [no soul]
>    Blyssid be the tyme the rose sprong.
>
> The thredde branche is good and swote;    [sweet]
> It sprang to heuene, crop and rote,
> Therin to dwellyn and ben our bote;    [our remedy]
>    Euery day it schewit in prystes hond.    [priest's hand]

The rose now has only three branches, and they are distributed in space rather than in sacred history, so that the effect is of a kind of cosmic axis stretching from hell to heaven and passing through the star over Bethlehem. This kind of textual simplification is what we might expect if the poem had been subject to the transformative pressures of the oral tradition. The references to the Five Joys in the first version are not so obvious that they would be self-evident to an unlearned audience, and they might thus easily be modified in the more familiar direction of traditional diction, where three is the significant number.

One reason for keeping a songbook seems to have been to have a collection of songs for different occasions, and not all of these occasions were religious. While songs for religious feast days and poems suitable for private devotions make up a large portion of the carol collections, there are also plenty of songs to be sung at convivial social gatherings; singing games, drinking songs and bawdy carols were apparently quite as popular in the Middle Ages as later. Among the most genuinely traditional are the songs about Holly and Ivy (*Holvyr and Heyvy*):[56]

> Holvyr and Heyvy mad a gret party,    [great argument]
> Ho xuld haue the maystre    [who should have the mastery]
>    In londes qwer thei goo.    [where]
> Than spake Holuyr: 'I am frece and joly    [fresh]
> I wol haue the maystre
>    In londes qwer thei goo.'
> Than spake Heyvy: 'I am lowd and prowd,    [loud and proud]
> And I wyl haue the maystre
>    In londes qwer thei goo.'
> Than spak Holvyr, and set hym downe on his kne:
> 'I prey the, jentyl Heyvy, sey me no veleny,    [don't speak uncourteously]
>    In londes qwer we goo.'

The contention between Holly and Ivy, where holly stands for the male and ivy for the female, appears in traditional English Christmas customs documented by Greene from as far back as the seventeenth century (1977: cxxiii–cxxvii). He feels this poem may be a genuine folksong.

---

[56] Oxford, Bodleian Library MS Eng. poet. e. I. *IMEV* no. 1225.

One of the earliest of the carol collections is London, BL MS Sloane 2593. Greene (1977: 306) writes that it comes from Bury St. Edmunds, 'almost certainly from the great Benedictine monastery there', and most of the poems in this manuscript are religious or didactic carols. But there are also seven pieces written in a distinctive form, in slightly irregular long couplets with a caesura. Two of them, 'Saint Steven and Herod' and 'Robyn and Gandeleyn', are narrative poems closely related to the ballad. The rest are copied close together in the manuscript.[57] Three are something like riddle poems, with fairly clear sexual innuendoes.[58] One is 'I have a gentil cok', about a splendidly noble rooster who perches every night in my lady's chamber. Another poem of the same kind is 'I have a newe gardyn':[59]

> I have a newe gardyn    and newe is begunne;
> Swych another gardyn    know I not under sunne.  [such]
>
> In the myddis of my garden    is a peryr set    [middle] [pear-tree]
> And it wele non pere bern    but a pere jenet.    [jonette][60]
>
> The fairest mayde of this toun    preyid me
> For to gryffyn here a gryf    of myn pery tre;    [to graft her a graft]
>
> Quan I hadde het gryffid    alle at here wille,    [as she wanted it]
> The wyn and the ale    che did in fille.    [she]
>
> And I gryffid here a gryf    ryht up in here honde,
> And be that day xx wowkes    it was qwyk in here wombe. [weeks]
>
> That day twelfve monith    that mayde I mette.
> Che seyd it was a pere robert    but non pere jonet.

Both of these poems depend for their effect on a sexual double-entendre. They also, for this reader at least, have echoes of well-known nursery rhymes that have been recorded repeatedly in oral circulation.[61] Another song from this group is even more strongly linked to oral tradition:[62]

> I have a yong suster    fer beyondyn the se,
> Many be the drowryis    that che sente me.    [love-gifts that she sent to me]
>
> Che sente me the cherye    withoutyn ony ston;    [she]
> And so che dede the dowe    withoutyn ony bon;    [dove] [bone]
>
> Sche sente me the brere    withoutyn ony rynde;    [briar] [bark]
> Sche bad me love my lemman    withoute longgyng.    [lover]
>
> How xuld ony cherye    be withoute ston?    [should]
> And how xuld ony dowe    ben withoute bon?
>
> How xuld ony brere    ben withoute rynde?
> How xuld y love myn lemman    without longyng?

---

[57] Numbers 25, 26, 28, 29, and 31 in Wright's 1856 edition.
[58] See also Duncan 1995: xxxvii.
[59] Wright 1856: no. 31. *IMEV* no. 1302.
[60] A *jonet* is a fruit-tree ripening early. In the last line, however, *pere jonet* is to be read as 'pear John' (opposed to 'pear Robert').
[61] 'Goosey, Goosey Gander' (Opie and Opie 1951: 190–93, no. 189) and 'I Have a Little Nut Tree' (Opie and Opie 1951: 330–31, no. 381).
[62] Wright 1856: no. 29. *IMEV* no. 1303.

| | | |
|---|---|---|
| Quan the cherye was a flour, | than hadde it non ston; | [when] [flower] |
| Quan the dowe was an eye, | than hadde it non bon; | [egg] |
| Quan the brere was on bred, | than hadde it non rynd; | [was a bud] |
| Quan the maydyn hath that che lovit | che is without longyng. | |

Modern parallels to this song include a ballad and a nursery rhyme from the north of England repeatedly recorded in oral circulation.[63] Riddles and their answers are very ancient elements of popular tradition. But even if we had no such evidence, we would still tend to see this poem as a product of an oral poetic tradition, given its triple parallelism of construction (riddle, repetition of riddle, answer to riddle), its use of incremental repetition not so much to reveal information as to delay the discovery of it, and the light sexual double-entendre delicately revealed in the last line. The riddles themselves rely on nature imagery of a profoundly traditional kind: fruits, berries, flowers, birds as the setting for a young couple in love. All the answers to the riddles – cherry blossoms, birds' eggs, budding briars – are phenomena of spring and early summer, the traditional (and medieval) season of love, and all are natural elements which grow and ripen with the passage of time; the implication is, as it was a century earlier in the Rawlinson lyrics, that the human world, by being aligned with the natural world, will be fruitful and multiply.

There are also two religious lyrics in the same long couplet form in the Sloane manuscript. One is *Adam lay i-bowndyn*:[64]

| | | |
|---|---|---|
| Adam lay i-bowndyn | bowndyn in a bond, | |
| Fowre thowsand winter | thowt he not to long; | [Four] [thought] [too] |
| And al was for an appil, | an appil that he tok, | |
| As clerkes fyndyn wretyn | wretyn in here book. | [written] |
| Ne hadde the appil take ben, | the appil taken ben, | |
| Ne hadde never our lady | a ben hevene quen. | |
| Blyssid be the tyme | that appil take was! | |
| Therfore we mown syngyn | *Deo gracias*. | [we should sing] |

The theology of the *felix culpa* behind this little poem is of learned origin, but the poem itself is formally very reminiscent of folksong. The reference to what 'clerkes fyndyn wretyn ... in here book' does not betray any personal familiarity with either clerks or books, and the Latin phrase at the end is a standard response from the mass. The repetitions, while they have an incremental function, are also closely linked to the rhythm of the poem, so closely that they seem to be due to the effects of the melody, especially when a repetition links two half-lines across the caesura, as in lines 1, 3, and 5. Whether written or oral composition, this lyric is very close to the oral tradition in style and diction.

The final example from the Sloane manuscript that I want to discuss is also the most baffling. This is 'I syng of a mayden', arguably the most elegant of all Middle English lyrics:[65]

---

[63] Wright 1856: 109–15, cites both. See Child 1882–98: no. 46.
[64] Wright 1856: no. 28; I reproduce the emendation in line 4 proposed by Duncan (1995; 2005b: 28). *IMEV* no. 117.
[65] Wright 1856: no. 25. *IMEV* no. 1367.

> I syng of a mayden that is makeles      [matchless]
> Kyng of alle kynges to her sone che ches.      [she chose]
>
> He can also stylle ther his moder was,      [to where his mother was]
> As dew in Aprylle that fallyt on the gras.
>
> He can also style to his moderes bowr,      [bower]
> As dew in Aprille that fallyt on the flour.      [flower]
>
> He cam also stylle ther his moder lay
> As dew in Aprille that fallyt on the spray.
>
> Moder and mayden was never non but che:
> Wel may swych a lady Godes moder be.

W. W. Greg (1909–10: 21–23) noted that this poem bears some relationship to a much older text from Cambridge, Trinity College MS 323, 'Nu þis fules singet hand maket hure blisse'. This is a rather typical written religious lyric of the thirteenth century. The opening lines borrow from the popular convention of the spring-song, but instead of singing of worldly love, the poet announces he will sing of the Virgin. The second stanza stresses Mary's sinlessness and her descent from the royal line of David, and the two central stanzas contain a brief narrative of the Annunciation, with Gabriel's words to Mary and her reply, leading up to a celebration of her miraculous virginity in the fifth stanza and ending in the sixth with a blessing on Mary and her child. The focus of the poem is didactic, stressing the doctrinal points involved in the Annunciation and ending with a pious devotional sentiment.

The poem in the Sloane manuscript is quite different. It has borrowed four lines (the first and last stanzas, slightly reworked) from the earlier poem, but it replaces the narrative of the central section with a triple metaphor for the Incarnation in absolute parallelism of construction, conveying in its elegant form some of the 'stillness' that the metaphor wishes to express. Barbara Raw (1960) has shown that this metaphor derives from Old Testament *figurae* of the Incarnation which had been included in various parts of the liturgy, especially the antiphons for the Advent and Christmas season (though the dew in this poem does not materialize on Gideon's fleece but on the grass and flowering boughs of an English meadow in spring).[66] The source of the central metaphor of the poem is thus learned and ecclesiastical; in fact, the kind of intimate familiarity with the liturgical texts that is needed to make the use of the Latin imagery as effortless and natural as it is in this poem would argue strongly for a clerical author. But the techniques that the poet has used in reworking the earlier text are not those of the re-writing of a written lyric, but point rather to a process of re-composition with a memory of the earlier poem somewhere in the back of his mind. The poem shows precisely those formal characteristics that would result from expert use of the compositional techniques of the oral tradition: apparent simplicity, great economy of phrasing, heavy reliance on traditional imagery and implied meaning, lyrical focusing through parallel construction and incremental repetition, and avoidance of any obviously learned vocabulary, complex syntax, or direct scholarly references. It was also, apparently, meant to be sung.[67]

---

[66] See Woolf 1968: 286–87.
[67] Fletcher (2005: 208–209) points out that in a sermon of the late fourteenth or early fifteenth century, the poem is referred to as *canitur*, 'sung'.

We recall that in the Rawlinson lyrics and the fragments of popular songs from the sermons, the poets often use nature imagery in a manner designed to bring the human world into harmony with the natural world through a sexual encounter between a man and a woman. Interestingly, the changes that the Sloane poet has introduced in comparison to the older poem have the effect of reinterpreting the Incarnation in terms of this kind of encounter: the lady chooses her son (instead of being chosen), he comes to her as a lover comes to his mistress, and the result will indeed be to bring the human world into harmony, not only with nature, but with God.[68] I am not suggesting that 'I syng of a mayden' is a folksong, but it may well be the result of the activities of a learned poet who was also capable of composing within the oral tradition.

There is not much continuity between the fifteenth-century carol collections and the popular dance songs of the thirteenth and fourteenth centuries. If we judge by the manuscripts, it would seem that the semi-literate popular culture of the towns is replacing the oral culture of earlier centuries. This may, of course, simply be a result of the fact that book ownership has become more common among the middle class. But whatever the reason, the effect is to foreground certain kinds of lyrics at the expense of other material. The ability to write seems to have been much more common among men than among women; one side effect is that the carol collections reflect male tastes and singing traditions. There are many songs about shrewish wives and the dangers of marriage; there are fewer carols in praise of women. There are songs about young women seduced and abandoned, but the situation is depicted as comic and the girl as silly and frivolous; there are no more women's dance songs or complaints about bad husbands. Even among the Holly-and-Ivy carols, which seem to have been part of a traditional Christmas game, the songs about holly are more common than the corresponding songs about ivy.

This male perspective is very evident in the commonplace book that Richard Hill, grocer of London, kept in the early years of the sixteenth century (Oxford, Balliol College MS 354). Among the very great variety of material that he copied into this volume are over a hundred lyrics, most of them religious carols, but also several carols of antifeminist satire. There are, however, very few pieces that seem to have any relation to an oral tradition. Hill seems to have gotten his religious carols, and many of the convivial songs as well, from written copies; his selection includes Latin verses and poems by Gower, Lydgate, and Dunbar (Greene 1977: cxxxiv–cxxxv).

Of the two or three items in Richard Hill's book that could perhaps come from the oral tradition, the 'Corpus Christi Carol' is undoubtedly the best documented:[69]

> *Lulley, lulley; lully, lulley;*
> *The fawcon hath born my mak away.*   [falcon] [mate]
>
> He bare hym vp, he bare hym down;
> He bare hym in to an orchard brown.
>
> In that orchard ther was an hall,
> That was hangid with purpil and pall.

---

[68] The poet's use of the traditional diction of the love song has been pointed out by, among others, Speirs 1957: 67–69, and Gray 1972: 102–6. Sarah Stanbury (2005: 231) writes that 'it celebrates desire, even in its sexual form, as a powerfully transformative force.'

[69] Greene 1977: no. 322. *IMEV* no. 1132.

> And in that hall ther was a bede;    [bed]
> Hit was hangid with gold so rede.
>
> And yn that bed ther lythe a knight,    [lies]
> His wowndes bledyng day and nyght.
>
> By that bedes side ther kneleth a may,
> And she wepeth both night and day.
>
> And by that beddes side ther stondith a ston,
> 'Corpus Christi' wretyn theron.    [written]

This poem has actually survived up to modern times as a folksong in oral circulation. It poses several problems of interpretation and has been the subject of much debate (Gray 1972: 164–67). The interpretation offered by the last stanza, that the poem is about the dead Christ and the Virgin, is not entirely convincing; it seems to be an attempt to disambiguate the poem by turning it into a devotional lyric. If this is so, it must have struck a chord, for later versions of the song continue the process of revision in the same direction, replacing the burden with unambiguously religious references (Greene 1977: no. 322, versions B, C and E).

But in Richard Hill's version, there are no religious references at all in the first five stanzas or in the burden. The imagery is one of loss, separation, and mourning: the singer has lost her mate, the orchard is withered, the maiden weeps for a wounded knight.[70] There is a gradual loss of movement, of confinement to ever narrower spaces: from the flying falcon to the orchard, to the hall, to the motionless knight on the bed and the kneeling maid, and finally to a stone. Rather like *Maiden in the moor lay*, this poem is ambiguous and suggestive, without giving us clear answers to the questions that it raises. Indeed, its ambiguity has continued to inspire singers and audiences for close to five centuries. It is perhaps not too far-fetched to suggest that this haunting suggestiveness is one reason why the lyric poetry of the medieval oral tradition still appeals to us today.

# References

Axton, Richard. 1974. *European Drama of the Early Middle Ages*. London: Hutchinson.
Bäuml, Franz. 1984. 'Medieval Texts and the Two Theories of Oral-Formulaic Composition: A Proposal for a Third Theory.' *New Literary History* 16: 31–49.
Boklund-Lagopoulou, Karin. 2002. *'I have a yong suster': Popular Song and the Middle English Lyric*. Dublin: Four Courts P.
Boffey, Julia. 2005. 'Middle English Lyrics and Manuscripts.' In Duncan 2005a: 1–18.
Brook, G. L., ed. 1968. *The Harley Lyrics: The Middle English Lyrics of MS Harley 2253*. 4th ed. Manchester: Manchester UP.
Brown, Carleton, ed. 1932. *English Lyrics of the XIIIth Century*. Oxford: Clarendon.
Burke, Peter. 1978. *Popular Culture in Early Modern Europe*. London: Maurice Temple Smith.
Burrow, John, ed. 1977. *English Verse 1300–1500*. London: Longman.
Child, Francis James, ed. 1882–98. *The English and Scottish Popular Ballads*. 5 vols. New York.

---

[70] Interestingly, the nineteenth-century version from Scotland (Greene 1977: no. 322D) disambiguates the poem in this direction, presenting the knight and the maiden as lovers.

Crane, Susan. 1999.'Anglo-Norman Cultures in England, 1066–1460.' In *The Cambridge History of Medieval English Literature*. Ed. David Wallace. Cambridge: CUP. 35–60.
Crocker, Richard. 1990. 'Polyphony in England in the Thirteenth Century.' In *The New Oxford History of Music. II. The Early Middle Ages to 1300*. Ed. Richard Crocker and David Hiley. Oxford: OUP. 679–720.
Dronke, Peter. 1961.'The Rawlinson Lyrics.' *Notes and Queries* N. S. 8: 245–46.
–. 1965.'The Beginnings of the Sequence.' In *Beiträge zur Geschichte der deutschen Sprache und Literatur* (Tübingen) 87: 43–73.
–. 1990. 'On the Continuity of Medieval English Love-Lyric.' In *England and the Continental Renaissance: Essays in Honour of J. B. Trapp*. Ed. Edward Chaney and Peter Mack. Woodbridge, Suffolk: Boydell and Brewer. 7–21.
–. 1996. *The Medieval Lyric*. 3rd ed. Cambridge: Brewer.
Duncan, Thomas, ed. 1995. *Medieval English Lyrics 1200–1400*. Harmondsworth: Penguin.
–, ed. 2005a. *A Companion to the Middle English Lyric*. Cambridge: Brewer.
–. 2005b.'Middle English Lyrics: Metre and Editorial Practice.' In Duncan 2005a: 19–38.
Fein, Susanna, ed. 2000. *Studies in the Harley Manuscript: The Scribes, Contexts, and Social Contexts of British Library MS Harley 2253*. Kalamazoo: Medieval Institute, Western Michigan U.
Finnegan, Ruth. 1977. *Oral Poetry: Its Nature, Significance, and Social Context*. Cambridge: CUP. [Rpt. Bloomington: Indiana UP, 1992.]
–. 1988. *Literacy and Orality*. Oxford: Blackwell.
Fletcher, Alan J. 2005.'The Lyric in the Sermon.' In Duncan 2005a: 189–209.
Gillespie, Vincent. 2005.'Moral and Penitential Lyrics.' In Duncan 2005a: 68–95.
Gray, Douglas. 1972. *Themes and Images in the Medieval English Religious Lyric*. London: Routledge and Kegan Paul.
–. 2005.'Middle English Courtly Lyrics: Chaucer to Henry VIII.' In Duncan 2005a: 120–49.
Greene, Richard Leighton, ed. 1974. *The Lyrics of the Red Book of Ossory*. Medium Aevum Monographs, N. S. 5. Oxford: Blackwell.
–, ed. 1977. *The Early English Carols*. 2nd ed. Oxford: Clarendon.
Greg, W. W. 1909–10.'"I sing of a maiden that is makeless".' *Modern Philology* 7: 21–23.
Gummere, Francis B. 1907. *The Popular Ballad*. New York: Houghton Mifflin.
*IMEV*: Carleton Brown and Rossell Hope Robbins. *The Index of Middle English Verse*. New York: Columbia UP, 1943. / Rossell Hope Robbins and John L. Cutler. *supplement to the Index of Middle English Verse*. Lexington, KY: U of Kentucky P, 1965. / Julia Boffey and A. S. G. Edwards. *A New Index of Middle English Verse*. London: The British Library, 2005.
Jeffrey, David L. 1984.'James Ryman and the Fifteenth-Century Carol.' In *Fifteenth-Century Studies*. Ed. Robert Yeager. Hamden, CT: Archon. 303–20.
–, and Brian J. Levy, eds. 1990. *The Anglo-Norman Lyric: An Anthology*. Studies and Texts 93. Toronto: Pontifical Institute of Mediaeval Studies.
Lord, Albert Bates. 1960. *The Singer of Tales*. Cambridge, MA: Harvard UP. [Re-edition with a CD and a new introduction by Stephen Mitchell and Gregory Nagy, 2000.]
Oliver, Raymond. 1970. *Poems Without Names: The English Lyric, 1200–1500*. Berkeley: U of California P.
Ong, Walter. 1982. *Orality and Literacy: The Technologizing of the Word*. London: Methuen.
Opie, Iona, and Peter Opie, eds. 1951. *The Oxford Dictionary of Nursery Rhymes*. Oxford: Clarendon.
Owst, G. R. 1961. *Literature and Pulpit in Medieval England*. 2nd ed. Oxford: Blackwell.
Raw, Barbara. 1960.'"As Dew in Aprille".' *Modern Language Review* 55: 411–14.
Reichl, Karl. 1973. *Religiöse Dichtung im englischen Hochmittelalter: Untersuchungen und Edition der Handschrift B.14.39 des Trinity College in Cambridge*. Texte u. Unters. zur engl. Phil. 1. Munich: Fink.

–. 2005a. *Die Anfänge der mittelenglischen weltlichen Lyrik: Text, Musik, Kontext.* Nordrhein-Westfälische AW, Vorträge, G404. Paderborn: Schöningh.
–. 2005b. 'The Middle English Carol.' In Duncan 2005a: 150–70.
Renwick, Roger deV. 1980. *English Folk Poetry: Structure and Meaning.* London: Batsford.
Reward, Carter. 2000. 'Scribe and Provenance.' In Fein 2000: 21–109.
Richter, Michael. 1995. 'Muttersprache und Literatursprache. Methodisches zur Situation in England im 12. Jahrhundert.' In his *Studies in Medieval Language and Culture.* Dublin: Four Courts P. 175–86.
Robbins, Rossell Hope, ed. 1952. *Secular Lyrics of the XIVth and XVth Centuries.* Oxford: Clarendon.
Salter, Elizabeth. 1983. *Fourteenth-Century English Poetry: Contexts and Readings.* Oxford: Clarendon.
Scattergood, John. 2005. 'The Love Lyric Before Chaucer.' In Duncan 2005a: 39–67.
Speirs, John. 1957. *Medieval English Poetry: The Non-Chaucerian Tradition.* London: Faber and Faber.
Stanbury, Sarah. 2005. 'Gender and Voice in Middle English Religious Lyrics.' In Duncan 2005a: 227–41.
Stevens, John. 1961. *Music and Poetry in the Early Tudor Court.* London: Methuen.
–. 1982. 'Medieval Lyrics and Music.' In *Medieval Literature: Chaucer and the Alliterative Tradition.* Pelican Guide to English Literature, vol 1, part 1. Ed. Boris Ford. Harmondsworth: Penguin. 248–76.
–. 1986. *Words and Music in the Middle Ages: Song, Narrative, Dance and Drama 1050–1350.* Cambridge: CUP.
Tristram, Hildegard.1992. *Medialität und mittelalterliche insulare Literatur.* ScriptOralia 43. Tübingen: Narr.
Wenzel, Siegfried. 1974. 'Unrecorded Middle-English Verses.' *Anglia* 92: 55–78.
–. 1986. *Preachers, Poets, and the Early English Lyric.* Princeton: Princeton UP.
Whitehead, Christiania. 2005. 'Middle English Religious Lyrics.' Duncan 2005a: 96–119.
Wilshere, A. D., ed. 1982. *Edmundus Aberdonensis Miroir de Seinte Eglyse (Saint Edmund of Abingdon's Speculum Ecclesiae).* London: Anglo-Norman Text Society.
Wilson, A. M. 1970. *The Lost Literature of Medieval England.* 2nd ed. London: Methuen.
Woolf, Rosemary. 1968. *The English Religious Lyric in the Middle Ages.* Oxford: OUP.
Wright, Thomas, ed. 1856. *Songs and Carols from a Manuscript in the British Museum of the Fifteenth Century.* London.

## 22   The Pastourelle as a Popular Genre

*Lucilla Spetia*

Orality is the salient characteristic of the medieval lyric, in particular from the Gallo-Romance tradition, not only because it was destined for oral performance and hence aural reception, but mainly because from the beginning it had a musical dimension inseparable from the words. The musical dimension is underlined, among many others by statements of two of the oldest troubadours. Marcabru (fl. 1130–1150) asserts in his poem 'Pax in Nomine Domini': 'Fez Marcabruns los moz e·l so' (Marcabru composed the words and the melody), and Jaufre Rudel (fl. 1130–1170) maintains: 'Non sap chantar qui so non di,/ ni vers trobar qui motz no fa' (He who does not compose the melody does not know how to sing,/ nor does he compose a poem who does not create the words).[1]

If one uses the idealized categories proposed by Paul Zumthor, one can speak of 'secondary orality' with reference to medieval lyric. This means not only that orality coexisted with literacy, but that these poems had as their starting-point a written composition, or rather re-composition in cases where it is possible to invoke pre-existing folklore traditions, where the poems can be traced back to 'primary orality' (1983: 21–43). In this respect, the pastourelle, perhaps more than any other lyric genre, can serve as an example of this type of orality. It has figures from the pastoral world who have been incorporated into poetry from a courtly milieu, not by chance, but rather so as to allude, at least in the original intentions of its inventor Marcabru, to a poetic tradition that belongs to the pastoral world and has a long history behind it. In fact, even in ancient Greece we already have evidence for the existence of pastoral songs, a tradition so firmly rooted that it lasted for centuries; this is curiously witnessed by the testimony reported by Zumthor about the prohibition imposed by Louis XIV on the Swiss regiments, who were forbidden to carry out the *Ranz des vaches* on the grounds that such pastoral laments might lead to desertion (1983: 264).

Although there are no direct testimonies for the existence of pastoral songs in the medieval period and especially no evidence of the genesis of a lyric genre like the pastourelle, cultivated by poets belonging to the clerical and aristocratic world (in particular Walter of Châtillon and Thibaut de Champagne, King of Navarre), we can nevertheless avail ourselves of significant indications which are defined by Zumthor as signs of orality. The most important of these are formal indications connected to the use of the voice:

---

[1]   Marcabru: Gaunt, Harvey and Paterson 2000: 438; Pillet and Carstens 1933 (abbreviated as PC): no. 293.35 (l. 2); Jaufré Rudel: Chiarini 1985: 57; PC 262.3, ll. 1–2.

more specifically the dialogue between shepherdess and knight. The presence of this dialogue is more relevant than the strophic-thematic interconnections in the oldest extant example of the genre, Marcabru's 'L'autrer jost' una sebissa' (which will be discussed below)[2] and it is an important structural characteristic of the Occitan representatives of the genre.

There are, furthermore, two allusions to the uncouth song of the shepherds, which, despite being isolated and also fairly ancient with regard to the period in which the genre flourished (namely, the first half of the thirteenth century), can be assigned to two of the most sophisticated troubadours and clearly reveal their polemic character. The first was identified by Maria Dumitrescu (1966) in the poem 'Pro ai del chan essenhadors' (I have many masters of song) by Jaufre Rudel. In ll. 9–12 the poet is said to allude to the song of the shepherds, which is considered rustic and childish – an allusion in other words to the pastourelle of unambiguously popular origin, with its extremely banal sentiments, in contrast to the refined love celebrated by Jaufré Rudel:

> Las pimpas sian als pastors
> et als enfanz burdens petitz,
> e mias sion tals amors
> don ieu sia jauzens jauzitz![3]

Let the shawms be the property of shepherds/ and of little frolicking children,/ and let my property be the love/ that gives joy and happiness to me!

The reference to shepherds is also found in the poem 'Chantarai d'aquestz trobadors' (I will sing of those troubadours) by Peire d'Alvernha (fl. 1149–1168), an orthodox follower of Marcabru's, at least in the first phase of his poetic activity. In the very first stanza Peire gives a warning to professional poets (troubadours), in particular to those who with their lack of technical awareness can be ranged with shepherds (ll. 1–6) :

> Chantarai d'aquestz trobadors
> que chantan de manhtas colors
> e·l pieier cuyda dir mout gen;
> mas a chantar lor er alhors,
> qu'entremetre·n vei cen pastors,
> q'us no sap que·s monta o·s dissen.[4]

I will sing of those troubadours/ who sing in different styles [rhetorical colours]/ and of whom the worst thinks that he expresses himself very elegantly;/ but they have to sing elsewhere [or: in another manner],/ because I see a hundred shepherds mix with them,/ none of whom knows whether to rise or to descend [melodically].

The connection between the two passages has not escaped the notice of Aurelio Roncaglia, who has not only suggested that they be considered in the discussion of the origins of the pastourelle, but who has above all interpreted the confrontation of *trobadors* and *pastors* as the translation into medieval terms of the modern distinction between *poesia d'arte* and *poesia popolare* (even if, in Roncaglia's opinion, the poem refers primarily to

---

[2] PC 293.30. For text and translation, see the appendix to this chapter.
[3] Chiarini 1985:66; PC 262. 4, ll. 9–12.
[4] Fratta 1996:52; PC 323.11, ll. 1–6.

music [1968:74]). In this sense then, despite the incontestable predominance of art poetry in the troubadour tradition, the fairly restricted number of Occitan pastourelles (about forty) can serve as a confirmation *e contrario* of the popular origin of the pastourelle. In the French lyric tradition the pastourelle is far more prominent, with more than 150 poems; it is also more open to lower forms of poetry, as shown by the various typologies of the *chansons de femme* (from the *chansons de toile* to the *chansons de mal-mariée*).[5]

Finally, the presence of *refrains* in French lyric alone (but, as will be seen, with notable exceptions in Occitan) can be interpreted as an indication of orality; relevant in this context are not so much *refrains* that are apparently fragments of other texts (for which a written origin can in fact not be excluded) as rather the simple musical *vocalises*, meaningless syllables such as *tra la la*, *vaduvaduvaduri*, *dorenlot* etc. Gaston Paris had already traced these *refrains* back to the dance songs performed by shepherds and shepherdesses, in particular on the feasts of May, and the sound of their musical instruments.[6]

Some of the elements identified here as indications of orality were already used by older scholars with the intention of attributing a popular origin to the pastourelle. In particular the *contrasto* or the *débat amoureux* between knight and shepherdess, in which the knight attempts to seduce the girl, generally with success, has been recognized by Alfred Jeanroy as originally a variant of the alternating song, an elementary form of popular poetry, which is not restricted to Romance literature and in which two opponents compete in poetic virtuosity by improvising on one or more topics. According to Jeanroy, another topic of popular poetry has by its natural proximity been associated with the *contrasto* (from which also the *tenzone* originated), namely the *oaristys*, the meeting and union of lovers.[7] With its reception in art poetry, the pastourelle has acquired a narrative character on account of the identification of the knight with the author, who in conformity with the age-old predilection of the *gab* – which is for instance present in the famous poem 'Farai un vers, pos mi sonelh' (I will compose a *vers*, since I am asleep) by the first troubadour, Guillaume IX, Duc d'Aquitaine (1071– 1127)[8] – delights in telling the circumstances of his encounter with a shepherdess and its erotic conclusion.

Later scholars, however, have progressively limited the importance of the *contrasto* in favour of the *oaristys*, in light of the considerable number of French examples in which the narrative component and pastoral milieu are prevalent, basing the search for the origin of the genre on a quantitative criterion.

---

[5] [On these genres see ch. 20 by A. L. Klinck in this volume.] The corpus of French pastourelles is conveniently collected in the three volumes of Rivière 1974–76. For a representative collection of medieval pastourelles with English translations, see Paden 1987. The pastourelles in Occitan are collected in Audiau 1923 and in Franchi 2006b.

[6] See Paris 1891–92. For a collection of French *refrains*, see van den Boogaard 1969; for a discussion of their music and popular character, see Stevens 1986:171–77, Butterfield 2002:75–86.

[7] On Jeanroy's view of the development of the pastourelle, see his *Les origines de la poésie lyrique en France au Moyen Âge* (1925:1–44).

[8] For Guillaume's poem (PC 183.12), see Pasero 1973:113–55; D'Agostino 2005. – Provençal and French *gab* or *gap* means 'mockery'; see Kraemer 1967. Italian *contrasto* means 'strife, discord'; on the best-known example of the Italian genre of *contrasto*, the 'Contrasto' of Cielo d'Alcamo (first half of the thirteenth century), see Spampinato Beretta 2008. Greek *oaristys* means 'intimate dialogue'; the term is used by Theocritus in his *Idylls*; see Kirstein 2007.

The presence of a woman has, on the one hand, led to the derivation of the pastourelle from archaic woman's songs (Gaston Paris), also in the form of a girl's complaint (Erich Köhler); or, in the attempt to recapture a connection with a primordial pastoral world and its figures, the shepherdess has been made into a representative of the 'wild woman' of demonic character and irresistible erotic impulses associated with the spring festivals (Michel Zink).[9] On the other hand, there has been an emphasis on the narrative structure of the pastourelle: while Alfred Pillet (1902) saw the *oaristys* as a short tale of popular origin, Maurice Delbouille (1926) affirmed that the *chansons de rencontre* of Medieval Latin clerical poetry lie at the basis of the genre. The latter interpretation, rather than that proposed by Edmond Faral (1923), who had instead talked of a Virgilian influence, was favourably accepted by scholarship in the time between the Wars, when popular culture had fallen into disgrace in the wake of Bédier's ideas.

The clearest formulation of this stance is found in the work of Edgar Piguet of 1927, who in his study of the evolution of the genre in France saw in the folkloristic pastourelle no more than a survival of the classical and medieval pastourelle. This position could not be shaken by William Powell Jones' attempt, some years later (1931), to recover the popular matrix of the pastourelle with the help of the methodology of the Finnish School, according to which there is a constant change of the story in an oral tradition, with the addition or influence of elements that had no connection to the original circumstances.

As to the *refrains*, which, according to Paris, point to the popular origin of the pastourelle, Pillet's study brought to light the notion that they are also present in 'L'autrer jost' una sebissa'. The proof is found in the structure of the strophe, composed of heptasyllabic lines rhyming in aaaBaaB, with a feminine cadence, where the fourth line always has the rhyme-word *vilaina* (obviously chosen for reasons of content), while in the seventh line different rhyme-words are found, all ending in –a(i)na; hence right from the beginning a final (or primary) refrain must have corresponded to the internal (or secondary) refrain, which later became incorporated into the end of the stanza. Furthermore, another pastourelle by Marcabru, 'L'autrier, a l'issuda d'abriu' (The other day, at the end of April), also has a similar rhyme-structure (octosyllabic lines, rhyming aaabab). Pillet derived from these the existence of an *Ur*-type of the pastourelle, with mono-rhyme stanzas of four or five octosyllabic lines with a masculine cadence and a final refrain, and later an internal refrain, a structure, in other words, analogous to that of the *chansons de toile*.

For Pillet, Marcabru's pastourelles, despite their archaic traits, represent the genre in its decadence on account of their original and capricious character (predominance of the dialogue, absence of an erotic conclusion, and especially no identification of the knight with the poet, who speaks rather through the mouth of the *tozeta* in the first and of the *mancipa* in the second pastourelle). Curiously, after Marcabru there was a pause in the composition of pastourelles in the south of France until Guiraut de Bornelh takes the genre up again in the last part of the twelfth century.

Pillet's opinion was vigorously opposed by Ada Biella (1965), who stressed the powerful poetic personality of Marcabru and attributed to him (although not explicitly)

---

[9] See Paris 1891–92; Köhler 1952; Zink 1972.

the role of the inventor of the genre. Biella instead sees in the later Occitan poems a degeneration of 'L'autrer jost' una sebissa', which is characterized by such elements as anti-courtly polemics and the search for paradox, underlined by realistic and incisive language and embedded in a structurally perfect composition, thematically focused on a love debate. Despite this position, Biella follows the line of thought initiated by Delbouille in her belief in a continuity with the Medieval Latin tradition, which she showed to have been particularly precocious and receptive in comparison with the Romance examples of the genre, as is seen in the Medieval Latin pastourelles, especially in those of a sophisticated cleric like Walter of Châtillon.

Ada Biella's argumentation seems to have been decisive for critical reflection about the origin of the genre, because Marcabru's poem has rightfully regained the centre of the scene, and it is precisely from this text that we must start in order to give the pastourelle back to the popular world to which it originally belonged. Nicolò Pasero has identified the polemical target of the pastourelle in some poems by Guillaume IX, in particular in the *gab* 'Farai un vers, pos mi sonelh', which is placed within the antinomy of *clerc* vs. *chevalier*, an opposition well known in the medieval Romance and Latin *débats*.[10] Pasero's analysis has shown the closeness of the *gab* to the pastourelle in its dramatic structure and the situation depicted, with historical identification of the protagonists (the knight is to be identified with Guillaume IX, while the shepherdess is Marcabru's mouthpiece). Other scholars have sought to clarify the appearance of a shepherdess on the scene, asking why Marcabru has chosen a shepherdess out of all women of a lowly station.

Maria Luisa Meneghetti, noting textual elements relative to the place in which the *débat* of Marcabru's long pastourelle unfolds as well as important lexical traces (especially *mancipa* 'girl' in his second, fragmentary pastourelle 'L'autrier, a l'issuda d'abriu' as a vestige of Iberian Vulgar Latin), has put forth the hypothesis of a trans-Pyrenean invention of the genre by Marcabru, who lived between 1134 and 1143 at the court of Alfonso VII of Castille and León.[11] Furthermore, Meneghetti sees the similarity between the metrical schema of 'L'autrer jost' una sebissa' and a fragmentary *zajal* of the Arabic-Andalusian poet Abū Isḥāq ad-Duwainī (aax aax bbx bbx etc.) as no accident. She interprets this in the light of testimonies that show that at least some *zajal*s were inspired by the coarser songs of country people, possibly songs of Iberian origin in which the female protagonist impudently takes the erotic initiative and of which traces can be found in the legends concerning *foeminas maias* or *agrestes* (May women, pastoral women), in clerical allusions of the early Middle Ages, even in a Middle Latin *chanson de rencontre*, the 'De somnio' of Anónim Enamorat de Ripoll (end of the twelfth century), which Delbouille had already suggested as an antecedent of the pastourelle.[12] Finally, Meneghetti suggests that the adjective *mestissa* 'of humble origin', by which the girl of 'L'autrer jost' una sebissa' is characterized, is to be interpreted in the light of a gloss by Jerome on

---

[10] See Pasero 1983. In Guillaume's poem the narrator, disguised as a pilgrim (evidently an allusion to the clerical world) boasts of an erotic adventure with two noble ladies.

[11] See Meneghetti 1993. Marcabru's pastourelle 'L'autrier a l'issuda d'abriu' (PC 293.29) is edited with English translation in Gaunt, Harvey and Paterson 2000: 369–73.

[12] See Meneghetti 2002. The 'wild women' have also been discussed by Zink 1972: 86–96. The 'De somnio' is edited in Moralejo 1986: 202–13; for text and English translation, see also Paden 1987: I, 52–55. [On the *zajal*, see ch. 23 by J. Monroe in this volume.]

ll. 17–18 of chapter 3 of the prophet Nahum, in which the expression *pastores misticii* in the sense of 'shepherds of different origin' occurs. The *tozeta mestissa* is therefore seen as a stranger or – if we think of Spain – as an Arab girl, whose ethnicity underlines the socio-ideological contrast to the *segner*.

While on the one hand remote folkloristic origins of the pastourelle can therefore be discerned (in particular with respect to its contents), there are on the other hand also antecedents that are educated and inspired by Christianity. The latter are emphasized by Lucia Lazzerini, for whom behind the *vilana* there appears the image of the spouse of the *Song of Songs*, Shulalmith *nigra sed formosa*, of Arabian origin and pastoral provenience (1993: 362 n. 323).

Vincent Pollina has highlighted the structural folkloric element that can be traced back to primary orality in his analysis of the extant melodies of Marcabru's poems.[13] The melody of 'L'autrer jost' una sebissa' is characterized by a rigorous structural regularity (which is not found in the other examples); three out of four verse melodies are repeated. The musical pattern AB AB CCD with the classic bipartition in *pedes* with alternate rhyme(s) (ll. 1–4) and *cauda* in a free form (ll. 5–7) is, however, on the whole independent of the rhyme scheme (heptasyllabic lines, rhyming aaabaab). Even more relevant is the observation that the musical style seems to be based on that of a traditional dance, with numerous melodic traits functioning as choreographic signals. Pollina established a strong contrast between the popularizing melodic structure and the content of the song, which was destined for an aristocratic audience.

Despite intensive research, the origin of the pastourelle is still not entirely clear, because scholars tend to neglect the fact that in the oldest realization of the genre there is no more than a dialogue between a man and a woman. This blindness is all the more surprising in a period such as the present, in which the schematic rigidity of the positivistic period, which only admitted a descent 'from above to below', has been replaced by the more realistic idea of osmosis, i. e. of communication that works in two directions. This idea is more appropriate for the Middle Ages, for the beginnings of vernacular languages and literatures, for a society marked by its cultural multilingualism and by a continuous meeting of impulses and different aims, learned and popular, clerical and lay, which both run parallel to one another and cross over.

The existence of an expressive pattern analogous to that adopted by Marcabru and the identical way in which the poem is also set in the pastoral world in the Greek and later Latin traditions invite further reflection and the extension of our study in a diachronic and diatopic direction in order to track down the cultural and social conditions that are common to the two different historical realities. Thus, at the height of the Hellenistic era (fourth century BC), one witnesses a division into the culture of the ruling classes, linked to literacy, and the culture of the lower classes, linked to orality, that is analogous to the medieval situation when the vernacular languages assert themselves in opposition to the Latin language of the clerics and the educated classes. There is, however, no space here for a detailed discussion (see Spetia 2010). The antecedents of the pastourelle as a genre of pastoral poetry in Greek bucolic poetry, in particular in the

---

[13] See Pollina 1993; Marcabru's melodies are also edited in Fernandez de la Cuesta and Lafont 1979: 58–69; the melody of 'L'autrer jost' una sebissa' is found on p. 65.

*Idylls* of Theocritus, have been noted by a number of scholars, and Classicists have found popular parallels to Greek bucolic poetry in improvised contest songs of various traditions.[14] In particular, the rules that regulated the real contests among shepherds have been worked out: an opposition of the masculine and feminine genders, made explicit in the motifs treated, unfolds by a perfect structural mechanism, which proceeds by association and opposition in a horizontal sense (between proposal and reply), in a vertical sense (between proposals and replies within the same group) or finally in an oblique sense (in each group every reply provokes in turn the proposal of the succeeding pair). In Classical Latin poetry the Greek bucolic tradition underwent some changes. The centre of attention has shifted to the poem's contents, with successive re-interpretations in Latin literature and an admixture of non-traditional elements (political vicissitudes, religious anxieties or literary tendencies). The realistic scenery of Greek bucolic poetry has given way to an ideal landscape with *pastores otiosi*, who sing songs instead of engaging in argument. In the medieval world we find a convergence in bucolic poetry between the Virgilian and the Christian shepherd, a convergence that began with Endelechius and his *De more boum* of the fourth century.[15] A Christianization of the pastourelle is found in the *Ecloga Theoduli* of the ninth century, describing a contest between the shepherdess Alithia from the lineage of David, who represents the Old Testament, and Pseustis, a shepherd from Athens, who advocates the position of paganism, with Fronesis, also a shepherdess, as judge (Mosetti Casaretto 1997).

The case is different in 'L'autrer jost' una sebissa', where we witness a verbal duel between a *toza* and a *segner*, a girl and a gentleman. This encounter progresses effectively by the association and opposition of motifs like those found in Theocritus' *Idylls* and hence confirms the existence of a secular oral tradition, diffused in a pastoral milieu.[16] The binary development of the encounter is ultimately consolidated by the connection of the stanzas as *coblas doblas* 'parallel stanzas'. After a very short narrative introduction in the first stanza, essentially devoted to the description of the girl, the dialogue begins in the second stanza. The commences, but he is given only two lines, while the woman has four. From the third stanza onwards the alternation of the dialogue is perfect, with a whole stanza of attack and counterattack allocated to each interlocutor. This alternation is underlined by the repetition of *toza/bella* and *segner/don* at the beginning of a stanza. The *segner* begins by expressing his concern for the cold that torments the girl, but she answers that she is happy and healthy despite the wind (stanza II). When the *toza* invokes God in l. 12, a connection to the following stanza is established, as the man characterizes her as *douc' e pia* (literally 'sweet and pious') and proposes a type of special companionship, the *pareil-paria* 'equal companionship', the very nucleus of the *contrasto* (st. III). She refuses this companionship, however, since it is only seemingly equal (st. IV). The *segner*, evidently with reference to the *noirissa* 'nurse' whom the girl had invoked in l. 12, now attempts to flatter her and presumes that she must be of noble

---

[14] See Sbardella 2006: 94–95; see especially Merkelbach 1956; Serrao 1981; Pretagostini 1992; Kirstein 2007.
[15] In this poem three shepherds enter into a dialogue and become Christians after having observed God's workings on earth; see Walsh 1977.
[16] The only scholar, after Jeanroy, who has approached the dialogic mechanism of the pastourelle in the amoebean manner appropriate to the poetic pastoral contest is Charles Fantazzi (1974: 391).

descent, at least on her father's side, being the daughter of a knight who sired her with a *corteza vilaina* 'courtly peasant woman' (st. V). She promptly turns the argument around and affirms that while she is certain of her modest origin, going back to the 'sickle and plough', the same cannot be said of him, thus insulting the would-be knight in his pride in his descent (st. VI). The *segner* does not admit defeat and maintains that her beauty derives from a fairy, in this way characterizing her, like her mother earlier on, as a *corteza vilaina*: brutish mating (with him on top and her underneath) is said to paradoxically increase her worth (st. VII). At this point she rebuts him by disappointing his expectations with a shock (st. VIII). The *tozeta*'s low birth claimed by herself in stanza VI is now recognized by him, but he nevertheless proposes to keep good company *ab amistat de paratge* 'with noble affection' (st. IX). The *toza* repeats what was said about the stupidity of the man who promises recompense and she repels the homage offered to her, unwilling to exchange her virginity for the name of a whore (st. X). But this is precisely what she is in the view of the *segner*, who actually reminds her: 'Bella, tota criatura revertei' a ssa natura' (My pretty one, every creature reverts to its nature) and proposes again to make love in a little get-together (*pareillar pareillatura*, with alliteration, harking back to ll. 19 and 24) (st. XI). Taking up the topic of folly again, the *toza* insists that everybody must keep his own place: everybody must mate according to his or her nature in the name of *mezura* 'good measure', just as the ancients have prescribed (st. XII).[17] As the man has come to his wits' end in the dialogue, he calls her the most perfidious woman in Christendom (st. XIII). To this she answers that while he, *insensatus*, is enchanted by a merely painted object, she expects the manna (*maina*) of just retribution: metaphors that seem to point to scriptural passages (st. XIV).

Marcabru's openness toward the world of folklore and the reception of folkloristic elements in his poem is not surprising when one thinks not only of the use he makes in his lyrics of a vocabulary with strong popular connotations, but also of the incorporation of the motif of the *turlù* in his poem 'L'iverns vai e·l temps s'aizina' (Winter is going and the weather is becoming pleasant), an onomatopoetic refrain with remote folkloristic connections.[18]

But this is not all. If one takes account of Pillet's insight into the particular structure of the pastourelle stanza and furthermore of Pollina's comments on the musical character of the poem, it emerges clearly that Marcabru has inserted the mechanism of the dialogue among shepherds into the strophic structure of an ancient Romance folkloristic tradition, connected to song and dance, the *zajal* strophe, which consists of three mono-rhyme lines and a refrain (a pattern which, it has to be stressed, is also found in the *gab* of Guillaume IX).[19]

---

[17] In l. 84 the edition by Gaunt, Harvey and Paterson 2000 (see appendix) has *la genz cristiana*, but I prefer the reading *genz ansiaina*, transmitted in the manuscripts C, R and T. This gives a better sense and also avoids the repetition of the rhyme with l. 87.
[18] Text and English translation in Gaunt, Harvey and Paterson 2000: 390–95; PC 293.31. See Avalle 1985: 1–53 and Lazzerini 1990: 83–85.
[19] See Beltrán 1984. In this context Roncaglia's suggestion to choose the reading *ab sol una tropellada* (1978: 212) is preferable to other readings as it alludes ultimately to a kind of dance (this is the reading also found in the edition of poem by Gaunt, Harvey and Paterson 2000; see appendix).

22 – Beginning of Marcabru's 'L'autrer jost' una sebissa', BnF MS fr. 22543, fol. 5ra (13th c.)

Marcabru's choice must have seemed astonishing, with the presence of a shepherdess, who, although an expression of the popular world, showed an exemplary moral authority when thanks to the mechanism of the alternating song she talked on equal terms with the knight.

It did not take long for the clerical reaction to set in, as is attested by the oldest pastourelle in Medieval Latin, number 89 of the *Carmina Burana*, 'Nos duo boni'.[20] This is a difficult text, with lacunae and corruptions in some places, and is generally not listed among Medieval Latin pastourelles.[21] This poem is metrically built like a sequence with a double *cursus*, in which every stanza comprises six lines. It figures as its protagonists two shepherds, who are identified in the Virgilian style (*Nos duo boni* 'We two good fellows'), and a shepherdess, who is clothed in poor garments and characterized as a *nigra puella*. The poem is basically an altercation between shepherds and shepherdess; erotic motifs are absent. What is interesting is the violent invective with which the two shepherds, claiming the prerogative of song only for themselves, intend to strike down the act of pride of the shepherdess, who has dared to reproach their love of doing nothing and their desire for gain, and by silencing her, to push her back to the limits of her inferior condition as a woman even more than as a shepherdess. Interpretations of the poem vary. Pillet, who first pointed out its significance for the origin of the pastourelle, saw it as a religious parody of the genre. Hans Spanke, however, interpreted the poem as the first Medieval Latin pastourelle and dated it to the period around 1150, which makes it the Medieval Latin equivalent of 'L'autrer jost' una sebissa'.[22]

---

[20] Edited with German translation in Hilka et al. 1974: 296–300; for textual criticism, see Hilka and Schumann 1941: 83–85.

[21] Two texts by Walter of Châtillon ('Sole regente lora' and 'Declinante frigore') and the numbers 79, 90, 157 and 158 of the *Carmina Burana* are generally considered to be pastourelles in Medieval Latin. All these texts are edited and translated in Paden 1987. There is, however, disagreement among scholars about the distinction between *chansons de rencontre* and poems in which the female protagonist is a shepherdess.

[22] See Spanke 1942. The characterization of the shepherdess as *nigra puella*, while on the one hand confirming the interpretation of *tozeta mestissa* proposed by Meneghetti, on the other places a heavy

In the Benediktbeuren manuscript this poem is followed by a short poem of three four-line stanzas, 'Exiit diluculo' (There went out at dawn).[23] In it a situation is sketched that is the very opposite of that in 'L'autrer jost' una sebissa': the girl goes out in the morning with her small flock, sees a youth in the grass and, without preamble, proposes an erotic encounter.[24] The close connection between this poem and the preceding one is expressed by textual parallels (in both poems the girl is characterized as a *rustica puella*, and their herds are similarly composed of various animals) and perhaps also by the use of a melody for two voices, an infrequent use for secular melodies. We can therefore suppose a contemporary composition and a similarly inspired intention for both texts.

As to the pastourelle 'L'autrer jost' una sebissa', it is possible that Marcabru's stay in Spain was responsible for its composition, as was suggested by Maria Luisa Meneghetti. He could, however, have been familiar with the modality of alternating song even from the shepherds in Poitou, when he was in the service of Guillaume VIII (the son of the 'first troubadour') at the beginning of his career. To this region lead perhaps the observations of William Powell Jones about the prevalence of the pastoral world, certainly also the word *chalmissa* of l. 8 (in the sense of 'mountain heath' or 'plateau', where the encounter takes place), which is also attested in Poitou.[25] Marcabru's other two pastourelles, 'L'autrier, a l'issuda d'abriu' and 'A la fontana del vergier', datable to around 1147,[26] must be seen as posterior to 'L'autrer jost' una sebissa' on account of their repeated use of the dialogue structure (not in any way more perfect), of the metrical patterns (octosyllabic six-line stanzas rhyming aaabab in the first and aaabaac in the second poem) and of the depicted scene, with the treatment of themes of stricter troubadour observance (in the first pastourelle a shepherd is introduced who sings with a *mancipa*, who laments the decadence of *pretz, jovens e jois* 'worth, youth and joy') or of a political nature (in the second pastourelle the scene is set in an orchard and the girl, *filha d'un senhor de castelh* 'daughter of the lord of the castle', bemoans the departure of her friend for the Second Crusade, which was proclaimed by Louis VII, against whom she is inveighing). In all probability they represent an attempt on the part of Marcabru to correct the orientation of the poems and to try in this way to avoid clerical censure, which is responsible for the long silence in the composition of pastourelles.

'L'autrer jost' una sebissa' must have had success perhaps on the level of oral tradition,[27] so much so that between 1170 and 1180 a cleric of the North began to explore the genre, imposing on it, however, substantial modifications in order to limit its sub-

---

burden on the choice of an Arab girl as female protagonist of Marcabru's main pastourelle, in connection with the verses in Arabic incorporated by Guillaume IX into 'Farai un vers pos mi sonelh' and transmitted only in manuscript C (ll. 10–12); see Spetia 2010.

[23] *Carmen Buranum* no. 90; edited and translated in Paden 1987: I, 146–47. Some scholars have contested the integrity of the poem; not so Dronke 1975: 118–21.

[24] See Liver 1988: 322. The girl has a *baculus*, a typical piece of equipment of the shepherds of the Virgilian tradition and a woollen dress; furthermore she alone is without a companion, while her animals have their mates. This underlines her brutish condition in proposing a love-play to the youth.

[25] See Jones 1931: 192, and Roncaglia 1978: 211–12.

[26] Both are edited and translated in Gaunt, Harvey and Paterson 2000: 40–45 ('A la fontana del vergier'; PC 293.1) and 369–73 ('L'autrier, a l'issuda d'abriu').

[27] For an analysis of Marcabru's poem in the light of its probable performative realization, see Pulega 1992–93.

versive power. Recent studies have confirmed that the two pastourelles of Walter of Châtillon as well as the pastourelles among the *Carmina Burana* take as their point of departure Marcabru's 'L'autrer jost' una sebissa', which is parodied both on the level of form and of content.[28] In 'Declinante frigore' (When the cold decreases), however, Walter takes the pastourelle back to the schema of the *invitatio amicae* of clerical tradition, with the prevalence of descriptive and narrative stanzas and the presence of a single male voice; in 'Sole regente lora' (As the sun guided its reins) we find the love debate with two voices distributed over five stanzas with alternating repartees, somewhat weakened, however, by their insertion in a context of classical allusions. The protagonists are different: in the first poem, a cleric, seated under a tree in a *locus amoenus*, talks to the lady, who is seen as a supernatural being, and refers to reading and writing, activities that are appropriate to him; in the second poem appear a knight, who is getting down (from a horse?) and who is satirically presented by the author, and a *virguncula*, who is guarding her flock. Both texts agree with one another in devoting plenty of space to the narrative (in the manner of the *chansons de rencontre*) and above all in having the same conclusion: the girl is forced to yield.

The road for the transplantation of the pastourelle to the North is now open. Although in the French pastourelles the violent seduction of the girl is not found in the majority of texts, the narration of an erotic conclusion, to which the poem tends, is nevertheless the defining characteristic of the genre in the North and distinctive with respect to the Occitan representatives of the genre.[29] Also where the embrace is gladly accepted by the shepherdess, often in exchange for gifts – a motif of clerical origin and absent in Marcabru – the prevalent result is a restructuring of the hierarchic relationship between the sexes with a competent and smart, but usually not particularly virtuous, shepherdess and a male protagonist who is also an object of irony and once and for all identified as a knight.

It is no accident that the transplantation of the genre to the North was effected by the activity of clerics like Walter of Châtillon and also others who were criticized by Gautier de Coinci,[30] as well as especially under the auspices of Artesian society: a society dominated by bourgeois economy, a social class on the rise, critical in its confrontation with the courtly world and eager to distance itself from its humble origins.

---

[28] See Moleta 1970:228–31; Bate 1983:21–26; Liver 1988:319–20. Walter's pastourelles are edited with English translations in Paden 1987: I, 48–53.

[29] On the French pastourelle, see Bec 1977–78: I, 119–36, and the texts in II, 47–58; on the corpus, see Spetia 2001.

[30] See his religious pastourelle 'Hui matin a l'ajornee' in the *Miracles de Nostre Dame*: *Chant Robins des robardeles, / Chant li sos des sotes / Mais tu, clers, qui chantez d'eles, / Certes tu rasotes! / Laissons ces viés pastoreles, / Ces vielles riotes, / Si chantons chancons noveles, / Biax dis, beles notes / De la fleur / Dont sanz sejor / Chantent angele nuit et jour* ( ll. 26–35) (Robin sings *robardeles* (dances), the silly person sings silly things, but you, cleric, who are singing these, are certainly becoming silly! Let us leave these old pastourelles, these old *riotes*, and let us sing new song, beautiful words and beautiful notes, of the flower (the Virgin Mary) of whom the angels sing without intermission). The music and text are edited in Chailley 1959:138–42, 179–81. Is it due to the Latin world that the introduction of the term *pastorella* (which appears in *Carmen Buranum* no. 79 'Estivali sub fervore') is reserved for the girl and then by metonymy to the genre from the very moment that in French *s* generally becomes mute before consonants? I will come back to this question in a detailed study of the pastourelle genre.

In Arras, Jean Bodel belonged to this world; Bodel was active for somewhat more than a decade (between ca. 1187 and the very first years of the thirteenth century) and was considered a great innovator of French literature in composing the first narratives in the form of the *fabliau* and the first miracle story in the vernacular, but also in his invention of the lyrical genre of the *congés*, or 'good-bye to the world'.[31] It is acknowledged today that the five pastourelles transmitted under his name or attributed to him and which cover the entire spectrum of the genre's possibilities of realization are among the earliest. His compositions straddle the expressive world of the jongleur tradition and of clerical culture, each often in opposition to the other. This is shown, as Luciano Rossi (1991) has pointed out, by the pastourelle 'L'autrier me chevalchoie' (The other day when I was riding along), which uses the same intrigue and even the same expressions as the poem 'Lucis orto sidere' (At sunrise) from the *Carmina Burana* (no. 157), but differs in its conclusion by insisting on the considerable brutality of the knight, in whom, however, traces of a satire on the violence of clerics can also be detected.[32] The pastourelle becomes a mouthpiece, at least in its initial phase, of bourgeois resentment against the knights and, to a smaller degree, the clerics; on the other hand, the contact of the poets with the popular source itself, which is embodied in the figure of the shepherdess, explains the modes of realization of the French poems, through the revalorization of folkloric elements (Wolfzettel 1992: 558), in the midst of all the *refrains* with their representation of the singing that accompanies the dancing.

Once the pastourelle was collected in the courtly lyric codex, it became the focus for the discussion of topics developed in the *chanson* in the North as well as in the South, where, however, the neutralization of the subversive intention of the first pastourelle passes through the break-down or negation of Marcabru's fundamental assumptions. On the one hand, the assumption of the point of view of the author/poet on the part of the knight (and no longer that of the shepherdess), which can be observed in the later pastourelles, must have seemed to the author of the *vida* of the troubadour Cercamon – who, active in the first third of the twelfth century, 'trobet vers e pastoretas a la uzanza antiga' (composed *vers* and pastourelles in the ancient manner) – as the break-down of the constitutive element of the genre, as has been proposed by Pietro Beltrami (2001). If Cercamon composed pastourelles – which have not been preserved (because of censorship?) – then these certainly followed Marcabru's œuvre chronologically. Furthermore, the negation of the role played by Marcabru's *tozeta* and her ethnic identity can be clearly seen in Guiraut de Bornelh's pastourelle 'L'altrer, lo primer jorn d'aost' (The other day, on the first day of August), in which the knight, who is accosted by the shepherdess wearing a *gonela* (a kind of dress) and turning out to be somewhat loquacious, declines her advances for the sake of his courtly love to a lady and puts her in her place by reestablishing the distance between them with the words: 'mas vos ab la tencha nieira / non crezatz que plus vos quieira' (but you with the black colour, / don't you believe that I desire you any more).[33]

---

[31] On Jean Bodel see Rossi 1991 and Jacob-Hugon 1998.
[32] 'L'autrier me chevalchoie' is edited and translated in Paden 1987: I, 70–73; 'Lucis orto sidere' *ibid.*: I, 150–52.
[33] PC 242.44, ll. 44–45. For text and translation (into French viz. Italian), see Audiau 1923: 10–15, and Franchi 2006b: 64–73. Instead of *tencha* 'ink, colour' Audiau has *senha*, translated by him as

From this moment onwards and following this negation of the original intent of the genre, the pastourelle is cultivated in Provence – in modest numbers – only within the bedrock of the troubadour tradition and it is in time considerably influenced by the French poetic experience.

Marcabru's experiment of opening the genre to folklore has nevertheless been powerful enough to be effective in different periods and places and to overcome censorship and criticism, in the infinite variations of form and content that distinguish them. The pastourelle has also become a popular genre in the medieval literatures of other Romance countries as well as in Middle English and Middle High Germany poetry.[34]

For the modern resurgence of the genre, two recent Italian examples can be cited, which are closely linked to the world of the troubadours and hark back, certainly involuntarily, to Marcabru's poetry. In the 1940s Pier Paolo Pasolini, inspired by the formal rigour of the troubadours, composed *contrafacta* of the Occitan pastourelles in the Friulian dialect, a dialect (in north-east Italy) deprived of a written and literary tradition and therefore associated with rustic language, returning in this way to his own roots (his mother came from Friuli) (Gérard-Zai 1998). As to the second example, it has been correctly observed that the poem *Carlo Martello ritorna della battaglia di Poitiers* (Charles Martel returns from the Battle of Poitiers) composed in 1963 by the singer-poet Fabrizio De André and the comedian Paolo Villaggio (both from Genua) has all the characteristics of a pastourelle: an erotic adventure is narrated of the king on his return from the famous battle with a country woman and his flight after she has made her material demands on him (Franchi 2006a: 198 n. 79). It should be stressed that on the one hand the authors were fined on account of the content of the poem, which was considered too permissive, and that on the other Villaggio has recently explained that he modelled the figure of Charles Martel after De André had made him listen to the melody, which he characterized as 'troubadouresque'.[35] In the light of the present discussion on the origin of Marcabru's pastourelle, the choice, even if unconscious, of Charles Martel, who defeated the Arabs at Poitiers, as protagonist of this folk pastourelle turns out to be a fairly happy one.

---

*visage*, and Franchi *sencha* 'belt'. While *tencha* is not found in the manuscripts but goes back to an error in the first edition of the poem, it can nevertheless be justified in the light of our discussion of Marcabru's pastourelle 'L'autrer jost' una sebissa'.

[34] On the pastourelle on the Iberian Peninsula, see Lorenzo Gradín 1991 and Ferrari 1999. On the Middle High German pastourelle, see Brinkmann 1985; on the Middle English pastourelle, see Reichl 1987 and Sichert 1991.

[35] In an interview with Paolo Villaggio in the programme *La storia siamo noi*, dedicated to De André and broadcast on January 11, 2008, on Rai Tre.

## Appendix: Marcabru's 'L'autrer jost' una sebissa'[36]

I    L'autrer jost' una sebissa
trobei tozeta mestissa,
de joi e de sen masissa:
si con fillia de vilaina;
chap'e gonel'e pellissa    5
viest, e camiza traslissa,
sotlars e caussas de laina.

The other day, beside a hedge, I found a common little wench brimming with joy and wisdom: just like the daughter of a peasant woman, she wears a cape, a tunic lined with a pelt, a coarsely woven blouse, shoes and woollen stockings.

II    A leis vinc per la chalmissa.
'Bela,'[37] fiz m'ieu, 'res faitissa,
dol ai car lo fregz vos fissa.'    10
'Segner,'[38] so·m ditz la vilaina,
'merce Dieu e ma noirissa,
pauc o prez si·l venz m'erissa
c'alegreta·n soi e sana.'

I came to her across the heath. 'My pretty one', said I, 'you lovely thing, I am so sorry that you are stung by the cold.' 'Sir', said the peasant girl to me, 'thanks to God and my nurse, I care little that the wind dishevels me, for I am happy about it and healthy.'

III    'Bella', fiz m'ieu, 'douc'e pia,    15
destortz me soi de la via
per far ab vos compagnia,
c'anc aitals toza vilaina
non dec ses pareil-paria
gardar aitanta bestia    20
en aital terra soldaina.'

'My sweet, dear pretty one', said I, 'I turned off the road to keep you company, for such a peasant wench as you ought never to have been looking after so many beasts without a suitable companion in such an isolated place as this.'

IV    'Don', fetz ela, 'qi qe·m sia,
ben conosc sen o folia.
La vostra pareillaria,
segner', so·m diz la vilaina,    25
'lai on s'estai, si s'estia,
car tals la cuid'en bailia
tener, no·n a mas l'ufaina.'

'My lord', she said, 'whoever I may be, I know wisdom or folly when I see it. Let your "companionhood", sir', thus said the peasant woman to me, 'remain where it is fitting, for she who thinks she is the mistress of it has nothing more than the vain illusion of it.'

---

[36] The poem is transmitted in nine manuscripts with a number of variant readings, some affecting the sense. Here text and translation are taken from Gaunt, Harvey and Paterson 2000: 378–83.
[37] Instead of *bel(l)a* some manuscripts have *toza*.
[38] Instead of *segner* the spelling *senher* is also found in the manuscripts.

V    'Bella, per lo mieu veiaire,
     cavalers fo vostre paire         30
     qe·us engenrec en la maire,
     car fon corteza vilaina.
     On plus vos gart m'es bellaire,
     et ieu per lo joi m'esclaire –
     si·m fossetz un pauc umana.'     35

'My pretty one, to my way of thinking your father, who sired you in your mother, was a knight, for she was a courtly peasant woman. The more I look at you the more it pleases me and I brighten up with joy – if only you were a little kind to me.'

VI   'Don, tot mon ling e mon aire
     vei revertir e retraire
     al vezoig et a l'araire,
     segner', so·m diz la vilaina,
     'qe tals si fai cavalgaire       40
     qe deuri' atretal faire
     los seis jorns en la setmana.'

'My lord, I can see all my lineage and family going back and returning to the sickle and plough, sir', thus said the peasant woman to me, 'whereas a man may act like a knight who should do the same six days a week.'

VII  'Bella', fiz m'ieu, 'gentils fada
     vos faizonec cant fos nada:
     fina beutat esmerad' a           45
     e vos, corteza vilaina,
     e seria·us ben doblada,
     ab sol un' atropellada,
     mi sobra e vos sotraina.'

'My pretty one', said I, 'a noble fairy fashioned you when you were born: there is in you a pure and rarified beauty, and it would be easily doubled with just one union, me on top and you underneath.'

VIII 'Segner, tan m'avetz lauzada     50
     qe tota·n soi enoiada.
     Pos em pretz m'avetz levada,
     segner', so·m ditz la vilaina,
     'per so m'auretz per soudada
     al partir: bada fols bada,       55
     en la muz' a meliaina!'

'Sir, you have praised me so much that I am very angry about this. Since you have exalted my reputation so much', thus said the peasant woman to me, 'because of this you shall have me as your reward when you leave: gape fool, gape in your mid-day siesta!'

IX   'Toz' estraing cor e salvatge
     adomesz' om per usatge.
     Ben conosc al trespassatge
     d'aital tozeta vilaina           60
     pot hom far ric companjatge,
     ab amistat de paratge,

se l'us l'autre non engana.'

'Wench, one tames a cruel and savage heart with practice. I well know that a man can have a mighty good time when he has a chance encounter with such a little peasant wench, with noble affection, as long as one does not cheat the other.'

> X  'Don, om cuitatz de folatge
> jur' e pliu e promet gatge.    65
> Tant fariatz omenatge,
> segner', so·m diz la vilaina,
> 'mais ieu per un pauc d'intratge
> non voil jes mon pieuzelatge
> chamjar per nom de putana.'    70

'My lord, a man excited by the heat of folly swears and makes pledges and guarantees. You would pay such homage sir', thus said the peasant woman, 'but I, for a small entrance fee, do not wish to exchange my maidenhood for the title of whore.'

> XI  'Bella, tota criatura
> revertei' a ssa natura.
> Pareillar pareillatura
> devem, eu et vos, vilaina,
> a l'ombra lonc la pastura    75
> car plus n'estaretz segura
> per far pareilla dousaina.'

'My pretty one, every creature reverts to its nature. We should get together a little get-together you and I, peasant girl, in the shade beside the pasture, for you'll feel safer there to have sweet togetherness.'

> XII  'Don, hoc, mas segon drechura
> encalz fols sa folatura,
> cortes cortez' aventura,    80
> e·l vilas ab sa vilaina,
> qu'en tal luec fa senz frachura,
> don om non garda mezura:
> so ditz la genz cristiana.'

'Yes my lord, but according to what is right, let the fool pursue his folly, the courtly man his courtly adventure and the peasant [his adventure] with his peasant woman, for wisdom is lacking in the place where one does not observe restraint: thus say Christian people.'

> XIII  'Toz', anc de vostra figura    85
> non vi una plus tafura
> en tota gent christiana.'

'Wench, never have I seen among the likes of you a more perfidious woman in all of Christendom.'

> XIV  'Don, lo chavetz nos aüra
> qe tals bad' a la penchura
> c'autre n'espera la maina.'    90

'My lord, the owl predicts for us that a man gapes at an image when another expects the sustenance.'

# References

Audiau, Jean, ed. 1923. *La pastourelle dans la poésie occitane du Moyen-Âge*. Paris: De Boccard.
Avalle, D'Arco Silvio. 1985. *La commedia degli inganni. Strutture e motivi etnici nella poesia italiana delle origini*. Turin: Giappichelli.
Bate, Keith. 1983.'Ovid, Medieval Latin and the Pastourelle.' *Reading Medieval Studies* 9: 16-33.
Bec, Pierre. 1977-1978. *La lyrique française au Moyen Âge (XII$^{ème}$-XIII$^{ème}$ siècles). Contribution à une typologie des genres poétiques médiévaux. Études et textes*. 2 vols. Paris: Picard.
Beltrami, Pietro G. 2001.'Giraut de Borneil, la pastorella "alla provenzale" e il moralismo cortese.' *Zs. für französische Sprache und Literatur* 111: 138-64.
Beltrán, Vicente. 1984.'De zéjeles y *dansas*: origines y formación de la estrofa con vuelta.' *Revista de Filología Española* 64: 239-66.
Biella, Ada. 1965.'Considerazioni sull'origine e sulla diffusione della "pastorella".' *Cultura Neolatina* 25: 236-57.
Brinkmann, Sabine Christiane. 1985. *Die deutschsprachige Pastourelle, 13.-16. Jahrhundert*. Göppinger Arbeiten zur Germanistik 307. Göppingen: Kümmerle.
Butterfield, Ardis. 2002. *Poetry and Music in Medieval France: From Jean Renart to Guillaume de Machaut*. Cambridge: CUP.
Chiarini, Giorgio, ed. 1985. *Il Canzoniere di Jaufre Rudel*. Romanica Vulgaria 5. L'Aquila: Japadre.
Chailley, Jacques, ed. 1959. *Les chansons à la Vierge de Gautier de Coinci (1177[78]-1236)*. Publications de la Société Française de Musicologie. Paris: Heugel et C$^{ie}$.
D'Agostino, Alfonso. 2005.'*Farai un vèrs, pòs mi sonelh*. Materiali per un'edizione plurima.' *La parola del testo* 9: 29-78.
Delbouille, Maurice. 1926. *Les origines de la pastourelle*. Mémoires de l'Académie Royale de Belgique, Classe des Lettres 20, fasc. 2. Brussels: Hayez.
Dronke, Peter. 1975.'Poetic Meaning in the *Carmina Burana*.' *Mittellateinisches Jahrbuch* 10: 116-37.
Dumitrescu, Maria. 1966.'Les premiers troubadours connus et les origines de la poésie provençale. Contribution à l'étude du problème.' *Cahiers de Civilisation Médiévale* 9: 345-54.
Fantazzi, Charles. 1974.'Marcabru's Pastourelle: Courtly Love Decoded.' *Studies in Philology* 71: 385-403.
Faral, Edmond. 1923.'La pastourelle.' *Romania* 49: 204-59.
Fernandez de la Cuesta, Ismael, and Robert Lafont, eds. 1979. *Las cançons des trobadors*. Toulouse: Institut d'Estudis Occitans.
Ferrari, Anna. 1999.'Marcabru, Pedr'Amigo de Sevilha e la pastorella galego-portoghese.' In *Studi Provenzali 98/99. Romanica Vulgaria. Quaderni 16/17*. L'Aquila: Japadre. 107-31.
Franchi, Claudio. 2006a. *'Trobei pastora'. Studio sulle pastorelle occitane*. Alessandria: dell'Orso.
-, ed. 2006b. *Pastorelle occitane*. Alessandria: dell'Orso.
Fratta, Aniello, ed. 1996. Peire d'Alvernhe. *Poesie*. Manziana: Vecchiarelli.
Gaunt, Simon, Ruth Harvey, and Linda Paterson, eds. 2000. *Marcabru: A Critical Edition*. Cambridge: Brewer.
Gérard-Zai, Marie-Claire. 1998.'Résurgence de la pastourelle.' In *Miscellanea Mediaevalia. Mélanges offerts à Philippe Menard*. Ed. Claude Faucon, Alain Labbé and Danielle Quéreul. 2 vols. Paris: Champion. I, 547-59.
Hilka, Alfons, and Otto Schumann, eds. 1941. *Carmina Burana*. I.2 *Die Liebeslieder*. Heidelberg: Winter.
-, Otto Schumann, Bernhard Bischoff, eds., Hugo Kuhn, trans. 1974. *Carmina Burana. Die Lieder der Benediktbeurer Handschrift. Zweisprachige Ausgabe*. Munich: Artemis.
Jacob-Hugon, Christine. 1998. *L'œuvre jongleresque de Jean Bodel. L'art de séduire un public*. Brussels: De Boeck Université.

Jeanroy, Alfred. 1925. *Les origines de la poésie lyrique en France au Moyen Âge. Études de littérature française et comparée suivies de textes inédits*. 3rd ed. Paris: Champion.
Jones, William Powell. 1931. *The Pastourelle: A Study of the Origins and Tradition of a Lyric Type*. Cambridge, MA: Harvard UP.
Kirstein, Robert. 2007. *Junge Hirten und alte Fischer. Die Gedichte 27, 20 und 21 des Corpus Theocriteum*. Berlin: de Gruyter.
Köhler, Erich. 1952. 'Marcabrus *L'autrier jost' una sebissa* und das Problem der Pastourelle.' *Romanistisches Jahrbuch* 5: 256–68.
Kraemer, Erik von. 1967. 'Sémantique de l'ancien français *gab* et *gaber* comparée à celle des termes correspondants dans d'autres langues romanes.' In *Mélanges de philologie et de linguistique offerts à Tauno Nurmela*. Turku: University of Turku. 73–90.
Lazzerini, Lucia. 1990. 'Marcabru, *A l'alena del vent doussa* (BdT 293, 2) : proposte testuali e interpretative.' *Messana* 4: 47–87.
–. 1993. 'La trasmutazione insensibile. Intertestualità e metamorfismi nella lirica trobadorica dalle origini alla codificazione cortese.' *Medioevo Romanzo* 18: 154–205, 310–69.
Liver, Ricarda. 1988. 'Mittellateinische und romanische Pastourellen.' In *Festschrift für Paul Klopsch*. Ed. Udo Kindermann, Wolfgang Maaz, and Fritz Wagner. Göppingen: Kümmerle: 308–23.
Lorenzo Gradín, Pilar. 1991. 'A pastorela peninsular: cronoloxía e tradición manuscrita.' In *Homenaxe ó profesor Constantino García*. Ed. Mercedes Brea. 2 vols. Santiago de Compostela: Universidade de Santiago de Compostela. II, 351–59.
Meneghetti, Maria Luisa. 1993. 'Una *serrana* per Marcabru?' In *O cantar dos trobadores. Actas do Congreso celebrado en Santiago de Compostela (26–29 abril 1993)*. Santiago de Compostela: Xunta de Galicia. 187–98.
–. 2002. 'Marcabru e le origini iberiche della pastorella.' In *Das Schöne im Wirklichen – Das Wirkliche im Schönen. Festschrift für Dietmar Rieger*. Ed. Anne Amend-Söchting, Kirsten Dickhaut, Walburga Hülk, Klaudia Knabel, Gabriele Vickermann. Heidelberg: Winter. 135–42.
Merkelbach, Reinhold. 1956. 'ΒΟΥΚΟΛΙΑΣΤΑΙ. (Der Wettgesang der Hirten).' *Rheinisches Museum für Philologie* 99: 97–133.
Moleta, Vincent. 1970. 'Style and Meaning in Three Pastourelles.' *Arcadia* 5: 225–41.
Moralejo, José-Luis, ed. and trans. 1986. *Cancionero de Ripoll (Anónimo): Carmina Rivipullensia (Ms. 74 Rivipullensis)*. Barcelona: Bosch.
Mosetti Casaretto, Francesco, ed. 1997. Teodulo. *Ecloga. Il canto della verità e della menzogna*. Florence: SISMEL ediz. del Galluzzo.
Paden, William, ed. and trans. 1987. *The Medieval Pastourelle*. 2 vols. New York: Garland.
Paris, Gaston. 1891–92. 'Les origines de la poésie lyrique en France.' *Journal des Savants*: (1891) 674–88, 729–42; (1892) 155–67, 407–30. [Review of A. Jeanroy, *Les origines de la poésie lyrique en France au Moyen Âge*, 1st. ed., Paris, 1889.]
Pasero, Nicolò, ed. 1973. Guglielmo IX d'Aquitania. *Poesie*. Modena: STEM Mucchi.
–. 1983. 'Pastora contro cavaliere, Marcabruno contro Guglielmo IX. Fenomeni di intertestualità in *L'autrier jost' una sebissa* (BdT 293,30).' *Cultura Neolatina* 43: 9–25.
PC: see Pillet and Carstens 1933.
Piguet, Edgar. 1927. *L'évolution de la pastourelle du XII$^e$ siècle à nos jours*. Bâle: Helbing & Lichtenhahn.
Pillet, Alfred. 1902. 'Studien zur Pastourelle.' In *Festschrift zum X. deutschen Neuphilologentage*. Breslau. 87–142.
–, and Henry Carstens 1933. *Bibliographie der Troubadours*. Schriften der Königsberger gelehrten Gesellschaft, Sonderreihe 3. Halle: Niemeyer. [Rpt. New York: Burt Franklin, 1968.]
Pollina, Vincent. 1993. 'Les mélodies du troubadour Marcabru: questions de style et de genre.' In *Atti del Secondo Congresso Internazionale della 'Association Internationale d'Etudes Occitanes'*

*(Torino, 31 agosto–5 settembre 1987).* Ed. Giuliano Gasca Queirazza. 2 vols. Turin: Dipartimento di Scienze Letterarie e Filologiche, Università di Torino. I, 289–306.
Pretagostini, Roberto. 1992. 'Tracce di poesia orale nei carmi di Teocrito.' *Aevum Antiquum* 5: 67–87.
Pulega, Andrea. 1992–93. 'Il pubblico di Marcabruno e la pastorella.' *Quaderni del Dipartimento di Lingue e Letterature Neolatine dell' Università di Bergamo* 7: 7–41.
Reichl, Karl. 1987. 'Popular Poetry and Courtly Lyric: The Middle English Pastourelle.' *REAL. The Yearbook of Research in English and American Literature* 5: 33–61.
Rivière, Jean-Claude, ed. 1974–76. *Pastourelles*. Textes littéraires français 213, 220, 232. 3 vols. Geneva: Droz.
Roncaglia, Aurelio. 1968. *La generazione trobadorica del 1170*. Testi e appunti del corso di Filologia romanza, per l'anno accademico 1967–68. Rome: De Santis.
–. 1978. 'La critique textuelle et les troubadours (quelques considérations).' *Cultura Neolatina* 38: 207–14.
Rossi, Luciano. 1991. 'L'œuvre de Jean Bodel et le renouveau des littératures romanes.' *Romania* 112: 312–60.
Sbardella, Livio. 2006. *Oralità. Da Omero ai mass media*. Rome: Carocci.
Serrao, Gregorio. 1981. 'La poesia bucolica: realtà campestre e stilizzazione letteraria.' In *Storia e civiltà dei greci*. Ed. Roberto Bianchi Bandinelli. Vol. IX: *La cultura ellenistica*. 2nd ed. Milan: Bompiani. 180–99.
Sichert, Margit. 1991. *Die mittelenglische Pastourelle*. Studien zur engl. Philologie, NF 27. Tübingen: Niemeyer.
Spampinato Beretta, Margherita. 2008. 'Cielo d'Alcamo.' In *I poeti della scuola siciliana*. Edizione promossa dal Centro di studi filologici e linguistici siciliani. Vol. 2: *Poeti della corte di Federico II*. Ed. Costanzo Di Girolamo. Milan: Mondadori. 513–56.
Spanke, Hans. 1942. 'Die älteste lateinische Pastourelle.' *Romanische Forschungen* 56: 257–65.
Spetia, Lucilla. 2001. 'Il *corpus* delle pastorelle francesi: una questione ancora aperta.' In *Convergences médiévales. Épopée, lyrique, roman. Mélanges offerts à Madeleine Tyssens*. Ed. Nadine Henrard, Paola Moreno and Martine Thiry-Stassin. Brussels: De Boeck Université. 475–86.
–. 2010 'Alle origini della pastorella, un genere popolare.' *Studi mediolatini e volgari* 56: 167–216.
Stevens, John. 1986. *Words and Music in the Middle Ages: Song, Narrative, Dance and Drama, 1050–1350*. Cambridge: CUP.
van den Boogaard, Nico H. J., ed. 1969. *Rondeaux et refrains du XII$^e$ siècle au début du XIV$^e$*. Paris: Klincksieck.
Walsh, P. G. 1977. '*Pastor* and Pastoral in Medieval Latin Poetry.' In *Papers of the Liverpool Latin Seminar 1976. Classical Latin Poetry / Medieval Latin Poetry / Greek Poetry*. Ed. Francis Cairns. Liverpool: University of Liverpool. 157–69.
Wolfzettel, Friedrich. 1992. 'Überlegungen zum Stellenwert der (nord-) französischen Pastourelle des Mittelalters : Gattungsfunktion – Gesellschaftlicher Ort – Mythische Struktur.' In *Beiträge zur sprachlichen, literarischen und kulturellen Vielfalt in den Philologien. Festschrift für Rupprecht Rohr zum 70. Geburtstag mit einem Vorwort*. Ed. Gabriele Birken-Silverman and Gerda Rössler. Stuttgart: Steiner. 552–67.
Zink, Michel. 1972. *La pastourelle. Poésie et folklore au Moyen Âge*. Paris: Bordas.
Zumthor, Paul. 1983. *Introduction à la poésie orale*. Paris: Seuil.

# 23 Andalusī-Arabic Strophic Poetry as an Example of Literary Hybridization: Ibn Quzmān's 'Zajal 147' (The Poet's Reluctant Repentance)

*James T. Monroe*

## 1 Preliminary Remarks

Américo Castro once argued that the foundation myth accounting for the origin of the shrine of Santiago de Compostela, according to which the body of Saint James the Apostle had been brought from the Holy Land, in a miraculously unsinkable stone boat, to be buried in Galicia was, in fact, a brilliant fabrication, devised in order to provide the Christians in the north of the Medieval Iberian Peninsula with an equivalent to the Islamic ritual of pilgrimage to Mecca.[1] By means of this argument, Castro was able to show that the Christian north of the Peninsula, far from adhering to any orthodox version of the faith of Jesus had, instead, borrowed a basic religious idea from Islam, the better to resist the latter's further expansion. Santiago was, according to Castro, a Christian response to the challenge posed by the forces of the Prophet Muḥammad. To this interpretation, let us add that, whenever Santiago came down from the heavens, mounted upon a horse, to aid the beleaguered Christians in their battles against Muslims, thereby earning for himself the epithet of Matamoros, ('Moor-Slayer') the holy Apostle was, in all likelihood, following the brilliant example of the Archangel Gabriel who, in the year 15/624, swooped down from heaven, mounted on his horse Ḥayzūm, to rescue the Prophet Muḥammad and his outnumbered Muslim army from a vastly superior force of disbelievers belonging to the tribe of Quraysh, during the battle of Badr, a town southwest of the holy city of Medina, in the Arabian Peninsula.[2]

Secondly, Castro pointed out that the Arabs were the first people in recorded history to combine the use of religion and language into a single instrument of imperial expansion.[3] That is to say, their method in empire-building was to conquer new lands

---

[1] See Castro 1954: 130–201 (chapter 6, 'Christianity Faces Islam: The Belief in Saint James of Galicia').
[2] See Wüstenfeld 1858: I, 427–34, II, 666; Guillaume n. d.: 300, 303–4.
[3] See Castro 1962: xxvii–xxviii. 'Sin musulmanes y judíos, el Imperio cristiano de los españoles no hubiera sido posible. El conquistar para cristianizar estuvo precedido del conquistar para islamizar.' (Without Muslims and Jews the Christian empire of the Spaniards would not have been possible. Conquering in order to Christianize was preceded by conquering in order to Islamize.) See too the discussion of this passage in Monroe 1976: 75–76.

with their armies, settle down in those lands, take wives from among the native population, and gradually proceed to convert the latter, largely by persuasion and tax incentives rather than by force. Once a convert was won over, he or she would have no alternative but to learn Arabic, since Islamic ritual prayers, which are obligatory, are only valid when conducted in that language. In this way, and from Andalus to Iraq, masses of conquered peoples were gradually turned into Arabs and absorbed into the cultural sphere of the latter. The vast majority of them, however, were of native, non-Arab descent on the maternal side. From the Arabs, the Spanish and Portuguese learned the unique method of using language and religion as a means of spreading and maintaining their own empires, which is why Spanish is spoken from California to Patagonia, and Portuguese from Brazil to Macao while, at the same time, all these areas are predominantly Christian lands. In this instance, Castro was showing how the methods of imperial expansion used by Iberian Christians were borrowed from techniques used by the Arabs, who had been the first to devise them, in the process of establishing their own empire.

Thirdly, on the micro-level of language, Castro drew attention to the many loan translations from Arabic that may be found in Spanish and Portuguese.[4] To illustrate this point, let me offer one specific example of what is otherwise a well-known linguistic phenomenon. The royal epithet 'el Sabio', normally applied to the Castilian king Alfonso X (r. 1252–1284), is often mistranslated into English as 'the Wise', when in fact, it means 'the Learned'. In this instance English has two words that allow it to distinguish a person who is 'wise' from one who is 'learned', as does French (*sage* and *savant*), and Italian (*savio* and *sapiente*). In contrast, Spanish uses the same word (*sabio*) to designate both concepts, as does Portuguese (*sábio*). In this instance, Alfonso X 'el Sabio', should be rendered as 'the Learned' because here, both Spanish and Portuguese are reproducing the meaning of the Arabic word *ḥakīm*, which may mean either 'wise' or 'learned', as the case may be,[5] while Alfonso X, a notoriously unwise politician, was a scholar renowned for his learning. Thus, a Spanish and Portuguese word of Latin derivation (*sapiens*) has acquired a new meaning and function derived from Arabic. In this type of hybridization, therefore, the linguistic *form* of the word is Romance, whereas the *meaning* is Arabic.

Castro thus identified three key areas, relevant to the following discussion, in which Ibero-Romance peoples had borrowed from the Arabs and Islam, specifically those of (1) Religion (Saint James), (2) Politics (imperial expansion), and (3) Language (loan translations) respectively. This allowed him to argue that Spaniards were not, culturally speaking, identical to their Iberian, Roman, and Visigothic genetic ancestors, contrary to how certain historians would have it. They were instead, the outcome of a subtle and complex process of cultural hybridization that had nothing to do with genes, but that had taken place between Christian and Islamic, Romance and Arabic, cultural elements; that is to say, they were a *mudéjar* phenomenon in every sense of the word.

---

[4] See Castro, 1954: 100 (in chapter 4 on 'Islam and Hispania', pp. 81–129).

[5] See Lane 1863: II, 618, col. a: '*Ḥakim* – *Possessing knowledge* or *science*; [in its most usual sense,] possessing *ḥikma* [as meaning *wisdom*] [...] [*wise*; *a sage*: and in the modern language, *a philosopher*: and particularly *a physician*:] one *who performs*, or *executes*, *affairs firmly, solidly, soundly, thoroughly, skillfully, judiciously,* or *well* [...] *al-ḥakim* [as meaning *The All-wise*] is one of the names of God.'

What these three areas of hybridization all have in common is that, in all three, a native, Ibero-Romance system that I shall call a *structure*, be it religious, political, or linguistic, incorporated within itself foreign, Arab elements that I shall call *materials*, in order to produce a very specific form of cultural admixture. In order to clarify this phenomenon, let us consider the following analogy: The fertile imagination of the Ancients has left us with a certain number of mythological creatures such as satyrs, centaurs, sirens, and sphinxes, which are, respectively, goat, horse, fish, or lion from the waist down, and human from the waist up. To these one might add the Minotaur, who conversely, sports the head of a bull on the body of a man, or even that famous contemporary Mexican painting depicting the body of a deer bearing the head of Frida Kahlo.[6] In all these examples, members of two incompatible species are hybridized so as to produce offspring that are neither fish nor fowl, *ni chicha ni limonada, ni viande ni poisson*, if one may be allowed to use a multicultural hybrid metaphor. The resultant combination is not a harmonious blending of two parents' bodies, but rather, a grotesque juxtaposition of their individual body halves.

In contrast, where other forms of hybridization are concerned, it sometimes happens that one culture provides the form or structure, and another, the content or materials for the finished product. Consider, for example, a *mudéjar* church:[7] Its structure is essentially that of a Christian temple of worship and, as such, it contains an altar that bears a cross; it normally has three naves, since the number three is of special significance to Christianity, and it is oriented toward Jerusalem, not Mecca. And yet, many of the elements that enter into its composition are borrowed from Islamic art: It exhibits Arabesque designs and decorations on its walls; it has geometrically-patterned coffered ceilings, its belltowers are decorated with elaborate brick-work designs inspired by those of minarets, and so on. Nevertheless, and despite the many Arab elements that enter into its structure, it remains unmistakably a church, for unlike the Spanish Christians, the Spanish Muslims built mosques, not churches, while these faced Mecca, not Jerusalem, they exhibited no crosses since, according to Islamic tradition, Jesus was not crucified, and they had multiple naves, not three, since the Trinity, in Islam's strictly monotheistic view, stood for the polytheistic worship of three gods, namely the Father, the Son, and the Virgin Mary (*sic!*).[8] In contrast to the kind of hybridization exemplified by the Minotaur and his like, in the realm of architecture we are thus dealing with a phenomenon in which the conquering Christians have introduced new *structural* principles, whereas the vanquished Muslims have provided local *materials* that are destined to be restructured in a new way.

---

[6] 'The Little Deer', 1946. See Herrera 1991:189.

[7] The bibliography on *mudéjar* art is vast. Among many other works, see especially, Bevan 1938:104–14 (chap. 12, 'Mudéjar'); Pavón Maldonado 1973. For an overview of *mudéjar* history, see Chalmeta 1993. To the bibliography provided in that article, add the more recent, and extremely valuable contribution by Catlos 2004. For hybridization as a cultural concept, see the remarks and useful bibliography in Stewart 1999.

[8] The Islamic denial of the crucifixion, along with its belief that Christians worship a Trinity that includes the Virgin Mary are, interestingly enough, two doctrines central to Gnosticism, from which Islam possibly got some of its views about Christianity. For the Islamic denial of the crucifixion, see Qur'ān, 4:157; for Mary as a member of the Trinity, see Wensinck and Johnson 1991; for these two doctrines as characteristic of certain Gnostic beliefs, see Pagels 1979, especially chap. 3, 'God the Father/God the Mother', pp. 48–69; chap. 4, 'The Passion of Christ', pp. 70–101.

The same phenomenon is true of literature and, moreover, it works both ways for, in the case of the medieval Iberian Peninsula, the Arabs had also incorporated native, Romance materials, into their own Arab and Islamic structures (their mothers were, after all, predominantly of Ibero-Romance descent). I would, therefore, like to examine one literary example that exhibits this latter form of hybridization, namely the strophic genre of Arabic poetry known as *zajal*, in which a native, Romance poetic form served to house the thematic content of those two Arabic genres known as *qaṣīda* and *maqāma*.

## 2 The *zajal* and the Romance Tradition

Since the *zajal* and its derivative, the *muwashshaḥa*, were the two major genres of post-Classical poetry cultivated in Andalus, let us pause a moment to consider several key aspects of their nature and origin.

To begin, the two genres of Andalusī strophic poetry we are considering were primarily songs, rather than poems intended only for recitation. On this point, abundant evidence exists both from the medieval and from the modern periods. In any tradition such as that of the medieval Arabs, in which musicians lacked a system of notation, melodies were transmitted orally, from teacher to student. Another means by which melodies could be transmitted, was by quoting, in the body of the poem, an easily remembered line, or group of lines (especially the oft-repeated and thus highly memorable refrain) of an earlier song, whose melody was well known. This is the technique used in the *muwashshaḥa*, in which the *kharja*, quoted from another poem, usually from the latter's initial refrain, and often from that of a previously known *zajal*, had the function of reminding the singers of the melody to which the poem was intended to be sung.[9] The *muwashshaḥa* is, therefore, primarily a case of musical *contrafactura*. This way of proceeding stands in sharp contrast to that of Classical Arabic poetry, in which poems were composed mainly for recitation, although there is no reason why they could not be set to music later, as they often were. In sum, in the case of the *muwashshaḥa* and *zajal*, the melody came first, and the words were written for it, whereas in Classical Arabic poems, the words were composed first, for the purpose of recitation, and could either be set to music or not, at the discretion of musicians (Monroe 1982). Moreover, the very fact that *muwashshaḥa*s often quote refrains from earlier *zajal*s as their *kharja*s (in contrast to which, *zajal*s normally do not quote refrains from earlier *muwashshaḥa*s), strongly suggests that the *muwashshaḥa* is based upon the *zajal* both metrically and musically and, ultimately, that the *zajal* genre antedates that of the *muwashshaḥa*. It also goes without saying that, if a *muwashshaḥa* quotes a refrain from a *zajal*, as its *kharja*, in order to indicate the melody to which that *muwashshaḥa* should be sung, it naturally follows that the quoted *zajal* must also have been sung, an inference that is confirmed by Ibn Quzmān (d. 555/1160), that major exponent of the genre, who, on several occasions, specifically refers to the singing of his *zajal*s.[10]

---

[9] See Monroe 1984. The *kharja*s themselves, when in Romance, betray evidence of remarkable archaism in their usage of formulaic diction. See Monroe 1975; Hernández 1989.
[10] See *zajal*s 2:10, 10:1, 19:13, 37:7, 42:5, 54:8, 71:7, 74:7, 94:31, 182:5.

What was the metrical system employed in these poems? As far as the *muwashshaḥa* is concerned, it is composed in Classical Arabic, which is a quantitative language. It is thus not surprising that all the (surviving) examples of the genre exhibit regular quantitative patterns. These patterns, however, do not always coincide with those of the Khalīlian system of prosody that is employed in Classical Arabic poetry, so that many poems depart from that system entirely, exhibiting new metres unknown to the Classical tradition. On other occasions, they exhibit Classical metres that have been shortened or otherwise modified by the suppression and/or inversion of entire feet. Indeed, these erratic metres seem to have been superimposed on, and made to harmonize with, an underlying Ibero-Romance syllabic system that constitutes the tail wagging the dog.[11] In the *muwashshaḥa*, as in medieval Spanish popular poetry, there are usually no lines longer than twelve syllables, and the only regular stress in each line falls on the accented syllable of its rhyme-word. In this sense, it would seem to be a hybrid system in which Arabic quantitative patterns are being adjusted to fit the mold of an underlying Romance syllabic system. In the case of the *zajal*, matters are seemingly more complicated. Since the *zajal* is in Colloquial Andalusī Arabic, and that dialect lacked quantity (Harvey 1971), we might expect its metrical system to be purely syllabic. Instead, it appears to manipulate orthography in order to provide the illusion of long and short syllables, on the level of spelling,[12] and thus, to offer the appearance of a regular quantitative metre when, in fact, all the syllables are linguistically and phonetically of equal duration. In the *zajal*, as in the *muwashshaḥa*, not to speak of popular Ibero-Romance poetry, the only regular stress also falls on the accented syllable of the rhyme-word. Hence, the *orthographically* quantitative system that has been superimposed on a non-quantitative language seems to be an Arabic way of making sense of what is, in essence, a non-Arabic metrical system for, as in the case of the *muwashshaḥa*, and of medieval Spanish popular poetry, in the *zajal* too, there are rarely any lines longer than twelve syllables. Here then, we seem to have an extraordinary case of hybridization on the metrical level.[13] Furthermore, there are overwhelmingly obvious arguments to suggest that the underlying reason why Arabic prosody is being adjusted to fit Romance metres has much to do with the originally Romance melodies to which the Arabic songs were sung.

What is the nature of the relationship between *zajal* and *muwashshaḥa*, and which of the two first appeared on the historical scene? On this point, medieval sources inform us that the *zajal* was already in existence as early as *c.* 319/931, yet no specific individual is singled out by name, in those sources, as being the inventor of the genre. Instead, the *zajal* was already there, according to one early text, being sung in the streets (Monroe 1989). Since the *zajal* is couched in Colloquial rather than in Classical Arabic, this circumstance would tend to suggest that the genre was originally popular and oral; that it

---

[11] In a recent and very important article, it has been shown that Classical, mono-rhymed poems were also composed in Andalus with non-Khalīlian quantitative metres, and that there were even poems in Classsical Arabic with no discernibly regular quantitative patterns whatsoever. See Garulo 2005.

[12] The Arabic script is of such a nature that one can immediately differentiate long from short vowels and syllables written in that script.

[13] See Monroe 1994. It should also be remembered that the Andalusī anthologist Ibn Bassām (d. 543/ 1147) states specifically that, in the vast majority of *muwashshaḥa*s, no regular, quantitative, metre can be identified. See Monroe 1990 and Harvey 1971.

flourished among minstrels, and that it was sung before a popular audience. Such a tradition must have existed, in a 'latent state', since time immemorial (Monroe 1989). In contrast, we are informed that the *muwashshaha* (which, with the exception of its Colloquial *kharja*, is entirely in Classical Arabic), was invented by a known poet at the court of the Cordovan Amīr 'Abdullāh (r. 275/888–300/912) and, therefore, around the end of the ninth or the beginning of the tenth centuries (Monroe 1990). That same source informs us that, in those cases where the poems had internal, blank, or unrhymed caesuras, either in the *vueltas/simṭ*s or *mudanzas/ghuṣn*s, a series of later poets introduced the innovation of adding internal rhymes, first in the *vueltas/simṭ*s and then in the *mudanzas/ghuṣn*s. The earliest poems to have survived, however, are from the late tenth century, after these innovations had already been incorporated into the genre. Therefore, we have no examples of *muwashshaha*s with internal blank caesuras. Such forms have, however, survived in the *zajal*, which did not experience the process of assimilating internal rhymes to the extent that occurred in the case of the *muwashshaha*. This circumstance, by itself, would tend to suggest that the learned *muwashshaha* is a derivative of the popular *zajal*, and not the reverse (Monroe 1989).

A major problem is whether the *zajal* and *muwashshaha* were of native, Ibero-Romance, or of Eastern, Arabic origin. On this point, attempts have been made to derive the Andalusī strophic forms from the Classical Arabic strophic *musammaṭ*, but here we are faced with two major problems: (1) The individual lines of the strophic *musammaṭ* never contain internal caesuras, while its *maṭla'* or initial refrain[14] normally contains four times (aaaa, bbba, ccca, etc) rather than twice the number of lines normally found in the *vuelta/simṭ* of the *zajal* (AA, bbba, ccca, etc. [the structure of the *muwashshaha* is AA, bbb*aa*, ccc*aa*, etc.]). (2) The *musammaṭ* is a very rare form, both in the Arab East and in its West, of which hardly a dozen examples are known to exist, all of which are extremely learned compositions. It is, therefore, highly unlikely that a rare form, composed in Classical Arabic, such as the strophic *musammaṭ*, could have given rise to an extremely popular genre of poetry. (3) The oldest reliably dated *musammaṭ* in Arabic (and it is not strophic) is from the early ninth century, and is attributed to the Eastern poet Abū Nuwās (d. 200/815).[15]

In all fairness, it may be conceded that the previous conclusions are reasonable, if not incontrovertible assumptions and, therefore, subject to challenge. Nevertheless, no one can question the fact that the colloquial *zajal* coincides remarkably in its form, if not in its content, with the medieval *rondeau*, the *virelai*, the *dansa*, the *cantiga*, the *villancico*, the *laude*, and the *ballata*, all of which surface beginning around the thirteenth century, in Northern France, Provence, Galicia, Castile, and Italy respectively. Since the Arabic *zajal* is documented earlier, in the late eleventh century, while references to its existence go back as far as the early tenth, the basic question is whether the

---

[14] If what is, in fact, the first strophe of the poem may be called a refrain, for which there is no evidence whatsoever, in contrast to which, the *maṭla'* of the *muwashshaha* and *zajal* is unambiguously described as a refrain by medieval contemporaries, a fact that is borne out both by Arab musical practice, and by that of the *zajal*'s putative Romance congeners. See Liu and Monroe 1989.

[15] See Schoeler 1993, whose general view of the problem is otherwise contrary to the one I have outlined above.

*zajal* was the source of its putative European strophic congeners, or whether the reverse was the case.[16]

On this point, a text previously known to Celtic and Romance specialists,[17] but that has, as yet, been ignored or overlooked by Arabists, is that of a poem, partially in the *zajal* form, included in the Old Irish epic known as the *Táin Bó Cúalnge* (Cattle-Raid of Cooley). It is a lament by a hero named Cuchulainn (The hound of Culann), over the death of his close friend, the hero Ferdiad (The man [warrior, *vīraḥ*] of the pair).[18] According to Myles Dillon, the *Táin* 'is a conflation of two recensions and dates probably from the ninth century [...]. It is believed that the story was committed to writing in the middle of the seventh century by a *fili* who was acquainted with the Latin learning of the monasteries and wished to record the native heroic tradition in a worthy form.'[19] The poem begins as follows:

| | | |
|---|---|---|
| 0 | Cluchi cách, gaíne cách<br>co roich Fer ṅDiad issin n-áth. | *Play was each, pleasure each,*<br>*Till Ferdiad faced the beach;* |
| 1 | Inund foglaim fríth dúinn,<br>innund rograim ráth,<br>inund mummi máeth<br>ras slainni sech cách. | *One had been our student life,*<br>*One in strife of school our place,*<br>*One our gentle teacher's grace*<br>*Loved o'er all and each.* |
| | 'Cluchi cách, gaíne cách<br>go roich Fer Diad issin n-áth. | *Play was each, pleasure each,*<br>*Till Ferdiad faced the beach;* |
| 2 | Inund aisti arúath dúinn,<br>inund gasced gnáth.<br>Scáthach tuc dá scíath<br>dam-sa is Fer Diad tráth | *One had been our wonted ways,*<br>*One the praise for feat of fields,*<br>*Scatach gave two victor shields*<br>*Equal prize to each.* |
| | 'Cluchi cách, gaíne cách<br>go roich Fer Diad issin n-áth. | *Play was each, pleasure each,*<br>*Till Ferdiad faced the beach;* |

The first four strophes of the poem exhibit a remarkably *zajal*esque structure, including an initial refrain, *mudanzas/ghuṣn*s with rhymes that differ from the refrain, and *vueltas/simṭ*s with rhymes that coincide with the latter, the only exception being that of the fourth strophe, which, due to a *lacuna*, lacks a *vuelta/simṭ*. The last four strophes, in contrast, exhibit a different structure. If the poem is datable to the seventh century, then it is obviously earlier than the Arab conquest of the Iberian Peninsula, which took place in AD 711. If it is from the ninth, its date is still earlier than that of the earliest Arabic reference to the *zajal* in Andalus. Either way (and Dillon is not specific on this point) the existence of the Old Irish lament indicates that the *zajal* form was widespread in Western Europe at a date early enough to make it highly improbable that it was a genre

---

[16] See Monroe 1988a; 1990.
[17] See Roolvink 1975; Morrás 1988.
[18] This is the etymology given by Hamp 1982.
[19] Dillon 1948: 3. For the complete poem, see the appendix below. For the verse adaptation of the first five strophes, see Sigerson 1925: 119–20. In matters having to do with Old Irish poetry, I wish to thank my colleague, Professor Daniel F. Melia, for his expert and illuminating guidance.

imported from the Near East.[20] Instead, it seems far more likely that it was a European form adopted by Arabic-speaking minstrels from their Romance-speaking colleagues at an early period, when Ibero-Romance was still the predominant language spoken in the Iberian Peninsula.

All roads, therefore, seem to lead, if not to Rome itself, at very least, to the westernmost outposts of its former Empire, while this circumstance strongly supports the view that the *zajal*, and its daughter, the *muwashshaha*, were Arabic poetic forms borrowed from the Romance tradition, and inspired by popular Ibero-Romance songs, of which the only surviving fragments are the Romance *kharjas*. As far as the content of these strophic forms is concerned, however, that is another matter, for a significant body of these poems exhibits a remarkable form of hybridization in which the Romance, *zajal*-esque structure is used to house thematic materials borrowed from the Classical Arabic panegyric *qaṣīda* or 'ode'. Let us then, turn to one such *zajal*, by that prince of the genre, Abū Bakr ibn Quzmān, for further understanding of the problem of literary hybridization.

## 3 Ibn Quzmān and his Literary Profile

All we know, for certain, about Ibn Quzmān is that he flourished in Córdoba under Almoravid rule, and died in 555/1160. Since such a biography is sketchy, to say the least, allow me, instead, to introduce his literary *persona*, through three typical examples borrowed from his poetry: (1) In 'Zajal 20', the poet portrays himself as an accomplished seducer: One night, while his wife is away (possibly in bed with his next-door neighbour), he succeeds in sneaking that very neighbour's wife into his own home for a night of lovemaking that fails to take place because of the poet's ineptness as a lover. (2) In 'Zajal 87', Ibn Quzmān finds himself loitering at the door of his house, when a beautiful lady walks by. When he makes a pass at her, she invites him to visit her by night, while her husband is away. As soon as he shows up at her doorstep, however, all the neighbours come out of their houses to jeer at him, whereupon he realizes that he, the would-be trickster, has had the tables turned on him by the lady. (3) In 'Zajal 90', Ibn Quzmān beds a prostitute in a brothel. Next morning, when it becomes apparent that he has no money to pay for her services, he is ejected and soundly thrashed by the establishment's personnel. The ensuing scandal causes him a serious loss of reputation. Such erotic misadventures immediately remind us of those undergone by Juan Ruiz, Archpriest of Hita, and reputed author of the fourteenth-century Spanish *Libro de buen amor*, to whom I shall return, below.

In view of this general tendency to cast himself in the light of a fool, Ibn Quzmān's 'Zajal 147', which I would like to discuss here, is, indeed, extremely unusual.

---

[20] For other Old Irish examples of strophic poetry exhibiting a *vuelta/simṭ*, see Meyer 1909: 25, parag. 72; Murphy 1961: 70–73.

## 4 Ibn Quzmān's 'Zajal 147'

| | | | |
|---|---|---|---|
| 0 | | dār al-ḥabīb mudh bān | Since he went away, the hall |
| | | mahdūma la-l-qāʿ | Of the beloved's dwelling has collapsed. |
| | | ʿalà ḥafīr ad-dār | Toward the drainage-channel of his house |
| | | li-waddu narjāʿ | Do I repair, for love of him. |
| A | 1 | raḥal ʿan al-mawṭan | He whose moment of departure had arrived, |
| | | man hān raḥīlu | Left his dwelling-place behind, |
| | | wa-d-dār qāʿan ṣafṣaf | His abode is now 'a smooth and level plain,'[21] |
| | | ka-dhā faṣīlu | Along with its enclosing wall. |
| | | yarthī fīh al-qumrī | Inside, the ringdove mourns, |
| | | ʿalà hadīlu | And coos with gentle voice. |
| | | man fāraq al-khillān | He who loses those he loves, |
| | | f-ay khayra yaṭmaʿ | What good may he expect to find? |
| | | bal yandub al-ʾathār | Alas, he'll weep at the abandoned ruins, |
| | | mawḍaʿ fī mawḍaʿ | Place after place. |
| B | 2 | qad ḥirtu fī buʿdu | I'm left bewildered by his absence |
| | | wa-ʾinqiṭāʿu | And by my separation from him; |
| | | mass an-nujūm aqrab | To reach the stars would be far easier |
| | | min irtijāʿu | Than witness his return. |
| | | tarà fī-hā l-qumrī | Among them you will see the ringdove, |
| | | kamā ṭibāʿu | As is its wont. |
| | | ... aban quzmān | ... Ibn Quzmān |
| | | ......... aʿ | .......... |
| | | man dār [ʿalayh mā dār | Whoever's suffered [what he's suffered |
| | | kān] ba-l-lāh [yawjaʿ] | Will], by God, [be pained]. |
| C | 3 | ayn darb aban zaydūn | Where's the Lane of Ben Zaydūn,[22] |
| | | w-ayn iḥtifālu | And those who used to cruise it? |
| | | w-ayn ḥawmat al-jāmiʿ | Where's the quarter of the Mosque; |
| | | wa-ʾayn jamālu | Ah, where's its beauty gone? |
| | | ḥummil min al-makrūh | It's suffered more misfortunes |
| | | fawqa ḥtimālu | Than can be borne. |
| | | aqrub tarāh faddān | Look close: it's now an empty field |
| | | yuḥrath wa-yuzraʿ | For plowing and for sowing; |

---

[21] Qurʾān, 20:106. In this context, it is revealed that, on the Day of Judgment, God will level the mountains, scattering their dust, and turning them into a 'level plain'.

[22] Known as a place of assignation for sodomites. See Corriente 1995:419, n. 2, who refers to Bencherifa 1975: I, 256–57. Here, az-Zajjālī is referring specifically to catamites (Arabic, *qaṭīm*, pl. *quṭamāʾ*, *qaṭama*; Latin, *catamitus*, from the Greek name of Ganymede, Zeus's cupbearer), and cites a source according to which 'There is not to be found in all of Andalus a town as notorious for its abundance of catamites, as Córdoba and, in particular, its Lane of Ibn Zaydūn, so that by way of hinting, they say: "He is from the Lane of Ibn Zaydūn".' Bencherifa adds: 'Perhaps the Lane of Ibn Zaydūn was named after the well-known poet, who was accused by Wallāda of having had that inclination, while proverbs and anecdotes indicate that the Cordovans used to avail themselves of black slaves for the purpose of sodomy.' On the famous Cordovan poet Ibn Zaydūn (394/1003–463/1070), and his stormy love affair with the Umayyad poet-princess Wallāda (d. 484/1091), daughter of the last Umayyad caliph, al-Mustakfī (who briefly reigned from 414/1024–416/1025), see Lecomte 1979. For the poet-princess herself, see Ben Abdesselem 2002.

|     |                          |                                      |
| --- | ------------------------ | ------------------------------------ |
|     | wa-l-bāqī ESHTEPĀR       | *The rest's a wilderness of rockrose* |
|     | la-l-qāma yaqṭaʿ         | *Rising to the height of man.*       |
| C' 4 | kaʾannī lam nakhḍur     | *It seems as if I never had attended* |
|     | dhīk al-majālis          | *Those festive gatherings,*          |
|     | maʿ kulli mustaẓraf      | *With elegant sophisticates,*        |
|     | malīḥ muʾānis            | *Good-looking, very friendly,*       |
|     | yā fī ḥusna z-zaynah     | *And oh, how handsomely attired,*    |
|     | min al-malābis           | *In the finery they wore.*           |
|     | wa-n-naqri ba-l-ʿīdān    | *All the while, the plucking of the lute-strings* |
|     | yafʿal wa-yaṣnaʿ         | *Was in progress,*                   |
|     | wa-ṣawlat al-mizmār      | *And the shrillness of the oboe*     |
|     | min barra tusmaʿ         | *Could be heard from well without.*  |
| B' 5 | qad tāb aban quzmān     | Ben Quzmān has now repented –        |
|     | ṭūbā lu 'in dām          | Blessings be upon him (if it lasts)! |
|     | qad kānat ayyāmu         | All his days once used to be         |
|     | ʾaʿyād fā–l-ayyām        | Holidays, among the days.            |
|     | baʿd aṭ-ṭabal wa-d-duff  | But after beating drum and tambourine, |
|     | wa-fatl al-akmām         | And rolling up his sleeves to dance, |
|     | min ṣumʿat al-ʾādhān     | *He now climbs up and down*          |
|     | yahbaṭ wa-yaṭlaʿ         | *The minaret, announcing prayer:*    |
|     | ʾimām fī masjid ṣār      | *He's become a mosque's imām,*       |
|     | yasjud wa-yarkaʿ         | *Who kneels and bows his head.*      |
| A' 6 | ṣawt al-ghurāb makrūh   | The raven's voice is hateful         |
|     | min ajli qubḥu           | Because it is so ugly.               |
|     | mā ʾawḥashu miskīn       | How dreary is that wretched bird;    |
|     | mā qalli milḥu           | How lacking in attractiveness.       |
|     | dāyim narà ḥuznu         | I always see it mourning;            |
|     | matà hu farḥu            | Whenever is it happy?                |
|     | f-alʾan-hum min ghirbān  | Accursèd are all ravens              |
|     | manẓar wa-masmaʿ         | To look at and to hear!              |
|     | yā ʾaswadan miṭyār       | O black, ill-omened bird,            |
|     | kam dhā tarawwaʿ         | What dread you do inspire![23]       |

Echoing the Pre-Islamic poetic tradition, the poet informs us, in the refrain of this *zajal* that, after his beloved's departure, the latter's house has collapsed, adding that the poet has visited its ruins, to mourn over its drainage-channel (*ḥafīr*). He thus finds himself mourning over an urban dwelling-place built of solid materials, and not over an ephemeral Bedouin tent, thereby breaking a fundamental rule formulated by the medieval Arabic rhetoricians.[24] Furthermore, the traditional trench dug around the Bedouin tent to

---

[23] See Corriente 1995: 418–20 (translation mine).

[24] In the largely prescriptive manner that characterizes Ancient and Medieval rhetoricians, as opposed to the descriptive approach adopted by our own, contemporary literary critics, Ibn Qutayba (213/828–276/889) provides the following guidelines for any budding poets among his contemporaries: 'A Modern poet should not abandon the custom of the Ancients, with regard to the various sections of the *qaṣīda*, and halt at an inhabited dwelling, or weep over lofty buildings plastered with gypsum, for the Ancients halted at the abandoned ruins and erased traces of Bedouin encampments; neither should he travel on a donkey or a mule, nor describe either of these, for the Ancients traveled on female or male camels; nor should he water them at fresh, running streams, for the Ancients watered their camels at tainted, stagnant wells; nor should he cross fields of narcissi, myr-

prevent rainwater from entering it (*nu'y*),²⁵ has been replaced here by a drainage system (*ḥafīr*) taking waste out into the street. The poet is, therefore, updating the old motifs, but in so doing, he is violating established literary precepts, while this very fact should arouse our suspicions, and suggest to us that not everything in this poem will turn out to be as traditional as it appears to be at first sight. In strophe (2), the poet continues his lament over the absence of the beloved, whereas in strophes (3–4), he muses over the good old days, during which he had devoted himself fully to a life of pleasure. This entire section (strophes 1–4), in traditional terms, would be equivalent to the *nasīb* or 'amatory prelude' of the old Arabic *qaṣīda* or 'ode'. The second section (strophe 5) is one in which the poet declares his repentance from sin, gives up his pursuit of music and dance, along with certain illicit sexual activities, and declares that he has become the *imām* of a mosque, and now spends his days either climbing up and down the minaret calling the faithful to prayer, or bowing to the ground and kneeling in oration. This section corresponds to the traditional *raḥīl* or 'journey' section of the *qaṣīda*. Here, however, and by way of parody, the poet has replaced the traditional, horizontal motion involved in travel across the desert on a camel, that is typical of the old *qaṣīda*, with the vertical motion involved in climbing up the minaret and bowing down to the ground. Ibn Quzmān's is, in sum, an absurdly *vertical*, rather than a *horizontal raḥīl*. Finally, in the third section of his *zajal* (strophe 6), the poet provides a satire (*hijā'*) of the raven, the traditional, evil-omened harbinger of separation so often mentioned in pre-Islamic poems. Here too, the poet is taking liberties with the genre, since the appropriate object of satire would normally be a human being, not a bird. From this thematic perspective, the poem is a parody of the tri-partite *qaṣīda*; in this case, a parody that satirizes the raven that has brought about the poet's separation from his beloved. Furthermore, this parody is grotesquely disproportionate, in that four strophes are devoted to the *nasīb*, and only one each to the *raḥīl* and *hijā'*.

In strophe (1) we are told more explicitly that the beloved has departed; that his house, using a Qur'ānic phrase, has become a 'smooth and level plain' (*qā'an ṣafṣaf*), and that the ringdove mourns among its ruins. As will be shown, this poem, like others by Ibn Quzmān, is structured according to the principles of ring composition,²⁶ as follows:

---

tle, and roses on his way to the patron he is eulogizing, for the Ancients crossed fields of broom-plant, basil, and ox-eye.' Ibn Qutayba 1964: I, 22 (my translation). For a summary of the views of medieval Arabic rhetoricians on the pre-Islamic *qaṣīda*, see Trabulsi 1956.

²⁵ See the 'Mu'allaqa' by the famous poet Zuhayr ibn Abī Sulmà, in which he refers to the *nu'y*:
athāfiyya suf'an fī mu'arrasi mirjalin       wa-nu'yan ka-jidhmi l-ḥawḍi lam yatathallami
*I recognized* the three stones blackened *by fire* at the place where the kettle used to be placed at night, and the trench *round the encampment*, which had not burst, like the source of a pool.
Johnson 1893: 68–69, l. 5. For more on the poet himself (fl. 7th c.?), see Bettini 2002.

²⁶ For ring composition as a universally used literary technique, see the bibliography listed in Niles 1970. The validity of this critical approach to reading literary texts was discussed by Peterson (1976). For a recent and most welcome study, see Douglas 2007. That distinguished anthropologist states: 'Ring composition is found all over the world, not just in a few places stemming from the Middle East, so it is a worldwide method of writing. It is a construction of parallelisms that must open a theme, develop it, and round it off by bringing the conclusion back to the beginning. It sounds simple, but, paradoxically, ring composition is extremely difficult for Westerners to recognize. To me this is mysterious. Apparently, when Western scholars perceive the texts to be muddled

## 5 The Chiastic Structure of 'Zajal 147'

0   Present: Beloved's house has collapsed after his departure. Poet weeps next to its drain.

A 1   Present: Former abode is now a 'level plain' (Qur'ānic simile). Ringdove mourns in it. It announces union. Poet weeps over ruins.

B 2   Present: Poet is bewildered by separation. Stars are unreachable. Ringdove is up among the stars. Separation from beloved may be permanent. Name of poet is invoked. Name of God is invoked.

C 3   Present: Where is Ibn Zaydūn Lane? Where is neighbourhood of Great Mosque? They are now an empty field plus a wild growth of rockrose. Outdoors. Urban area gone wild, Silence. Emptiness.

C' 4   Past: Parties with well-dressed, friendly, good-looking sophisticates. Noise of musical instruments. Indoors, Urban area full of people. Noise. Fullness.

B' 5   Present: Poet has repented. Adherence to God may not last. Poet used to make music and dance. Today he is a muezzin and *imām*, rising up and down. Name of poet is invoked. Name of God is silently implied.

A' 6   Present: Raven is a hateful bird. It always mourns. It is evil-omened (Pagan motif). It announces separation. It inspires dread.

0   Present: Beloved's house has collapsed after his departure. Poet weeps next to its drain.

Since the study of any given poem's structure can help us to identify its individual nuances of meaning, thereby allowing us to distinguish it from other specimens within the genre (this being something that other critical methods and approaches cannot do), let us now turn from the first strophe of our *zajal*, to its sixth and last, which I have designated as (A'). In the latter, the poet expresses his intense dislike of the raven, whose voice he declares to be ugly, who is always mourning, who is a bird of evil portent, and who arouses dread among those who see and hear it. In sum, the poem opens and closes with the images of two birds, namely the ringdove and the raven, in that order.

The renowned anthropologist Claude Lévi-Strauss has pointed out a circumstance that is of some importance for our understanding of the pre-Islamic *qaṣīda*: According to that author, in Mediterranean latitudes, the constellation of the Raven or Crow (Latin *corvus*, Greek *kórax*, Arabic *ghurāb*) makes its first yearly appearance above the horizon at the beginning of the dry season.[27] Lévi-Strauss further invokes a Greek legend, according to which the God Apollo (to whom the raven was sacred [Rose

---

and class the authors as simpletons, it is because they do not recognize the unfamiliar method of construction' (p. X). Although Professor Douglas does not include Arabic literature in her study, the last sentence of the above quotation from it, accurately reflects much that has been misunderstood about Arabic poetry by several generations of Western scholars. For individual Quzmānī *zajal*s previously analyzed by me, in which ring composition has been identified and used as a tool of interpretation, see (1) Monroe 1979 (On *Zajal 12*); (2) 1985–86 (On *Zajal 137*); (3) 1987 (On *Zajal 10*); (4) 1988b (On *Zajal 148*); (5) 1996 (On *Zajal 84*); (6) 1997 (On *Zajal 133*); (7) (with Mark F. Pettigrew) 2003 (On *Zajal 90*); (8) 2005 (On *Zajal 87*); (9) 2006 (On *Zajal 20*); (10) 2007 (On *Zajal 88*); (11) (forthcoming) (On *Zajal 118*). See too Hernández 1991; Farrin 2004 (On *Zajals 8* and *48*). For further bibliography on the Andalusī *zajal*, see Heijkoop and Zwartjes 2004. See especially, the groundbreaking study by Raymond K. Farrin (2006).

[27] The subject is discussed repeatedly by Claude Lévi-Strauss, throughout his *Introduction to a Science of Mythology* (1973–81).

1956: 138]) ordered that bird to fetch some water for him. The raven, however, succumbed to temptation at the sight of a field of green wheat, which it entered, in order to wait all summer long, until the grain was ripe enough to eat, thereby forgetting the mission on which it had been sent by the god. In his anger at such neglect on the part of the raven, Apollo punished it by condemning it to suffer from a raging thirst that was to last throughout the summer.[28] This legend was used by the Greeks to explain, on the one hand, why the sound of the raven's cawing was so raucous and, on the other, why the heavenly constellation of Corvus was a harbinger of forthcoming drought, thirst, and misfortune.

In contrast, but also in Mediterranean latitudes, the constellation of the Pleiades first appears over the horizon at the beginning of the rainy season. In Classical Mythology, the Pleiades were seven daughters of Atlas and a nymph, who were turned into doves (*peleiádes*), and placed among the stars to save them from the pursuit of Orion.[29] Their appearance, among the Ancients, signaled the arrival of the spring rains and, consequently, of associated concepts such as prosperity, fertility, and love. Let us also note that doves, which were sacred to Aphrodite, and were considered to be the lovebirds of Antiquity, are monogamous, and mate for life. Thus, when a dove loses its mate, it mourns disconsolately.[30] We should note, then, that doves are, simultaneously, symbols of hope and of despair. As such, they have an ambiguous function in literature.

Now, in the pre-Islamic, Arabic *qaṣīda*, the stock figure of the 'raven of separation' (*ghurāb al-bayn*) commonly appears toward the beginning of the poem, in its *nasīb*. Typically, the poet recalls a time when he hears the ominous cawing of the raven, after which his beloved departs with her tribe, leaving him behind to mourn her loss, in his own tribe (Pellat 1983). The explanation for this motif lies in the fact that groupings of different Bedouin tribes often pastured their camels collectively during the rainy season, when desert vegetation was at its most verdant, and could thus support a more intensive degree of grazing. With the appearance of the constellation of Corvus, however, it would

---

[28] 'Although the details of the story vary, it is mainly about the crow that was asked by Apollo to fetch water but stopped in a field of green wheat or near a fig tree and waited for the corn or the fruit to ripen before carrying out its mission. Apollo punished it by condemning it to remain thirsty throughout the summer [...]. The Crow of the Greek myth, and the prototype of the constellation that was to take its name, is afflicted with *thirst* [...]. Because of the dry season, on the other hand, the voice of the crow was to become raucous, and its throat parched.' Lévi-Strauss 1973–81: I, 237–39. The raven was originally white, and was turned black by Apollo as a further punishment for its disobedience. For more on the raven in Arabic folklore, see Westermarck 1926: II, 331–33. See too, Marzluff and Angell 2005, especially chap. 4, 'Inspiration for Legend, Literature, Art, and Language' (108–51).
[29] On the Pleiades, the seven daughters of Atlas and Pleïone according to Greek mythology, see Hard 2004: 517–19. For more on the dove in Arabic folklore, see Westermarck 1926: II, 337–38.
[30] The Greek cult of Aphrodite was borrowed from earlier, Semitic religions, in which she was not only a love goddess, but also a goddess of war. She is equivalent to the Phoenician Ashtoreth (Astarte), the Syrian Atargatis (Derpeto), the Babylonian Belit (Mylitta), and the Arabian Ilāt (al-lāt), and was introduced to the Hellenic world via Cyprus, Cythera, and Crete, by Phoenician colonists; one of her sacred birds is the dove. See Hard 2004: 194–203. On the theme of the dove as a messenger of love, peace, and good fortune in Arabic poetry, see Vajda 1979: 110. See too, Pérès 1953: 506, s. v. *colombe*; 512, s. v. *pigeon*; 514, s. v. *tourterelle*, for specific examples in Andalusī poetry of doves either announcing the forthcoming joy of love, or mourning over its loss.

become clear to them that the arrival of the dry season was approaching, during which time, less vegetation would be available. At this crucial moment, the different tribes would thus part company from one another, while their poets, if the ladies they loved were from another tribe, would be forced to endure the loss of such ladies, who would normally be required to leave with the tribe to which they belonged, according to the endogamous system of marriage that prevailed among the desert Arabs.[31] Such is the anthropological explanation for the reason why the raven came to be viewed by pre-Islamic Arabs as a harbinger of separation, drought, and misfortune.

As we have mentioned, the first appearance of the constellation of the Pleiades over the horizon announced the beginning of the rainy season. At that time, those same tribes that had wandered apart during the dry season, would get together once again, in order to pasture their camels communally, so that their poets could expect, either to encounter their former ladies once more, or to make the acquaintance of new ones. As a result, the dove came to represent the concepts of rain, fertility, love, and general prosperity. In many *qaṣīda*s, the ominous cawing of the raven announces the separation that, soon thereafter, takes place between the poet and his beloved. In contrast, in the 'Mu'allaqa' of Imru' al-Qays, to cite but one famous example, the Pleiades are said to be shining in the sky on a night when the poet is leaving his own camp, and stealthily approaching the nearby, and well-guarded abode of his beloved, in her own camp, in order to spend the night in her arms.[32]

Viewed from this perspective, let us note that not everything is as we might expect it to be in 'Zajal 147': In the initial refrain of the poem (0) the poet describes the now dilapidated state of his beloved's house. Then, in its first strophe, which I have designated thematically as (A), the poet, in his despair, begins his ritual lament over the abandoned ruins. On the one hand, this situation has not been preceded by an invocation of the image of the raven (a symbol of loss and despair), as would normally be expected in a Pre-Islamic poem. Instead, the poet alludes to the dove, a symbol of despair, but also of love and hope (since it can fly, it can follow after, and seek out, its departed mate, which the poet cannot do). In strophe (2) the poet further links the dove to its corresponding heavenly constellation ('Among them [i. e. "the stars"] you will see the ringdove / as is its

---

[31] Thus, when two individuals from different tribes fell in love, their marriage was often difficult, if not impossible, to arrange. See Smith 1963. The pattern of seasonal separations and regroupings is not restricted exclusively to the Bedouins of Arabia, but is a feature of nomadic, pastoral life in general. See Shahrani 1979. It is an unusual pleasure to thank the distinguished archaeologist, J. Cameron Monroe, for the above reference.

[32] idhā mā *th-thurayyā* fī s-samā'i ta'arraḍat    ta'arruḍa 'athnā'i l-wishāḥi l-mufaṣṣalī
[...] at a time, when the Pleiades appeared in the heavens, *as the appearance of the gems* in the spaces in the ornamented girdle, set with pearls and gems.
Johnson 1893: 11, l. 27. For more on Imru' l-Qays (d. *c.* AD 550?), see Boustany 1979. In Arabic, the Pleiades are called *ath-thurayyā*, a diminutive related to the roots *th-r-w* and *th-r-y* (said of people or cattle: 'to become many'; said of persons: 'to become abundant in cattle'; said of the earth: 'to become moist and soft, after drought and dryness; to become watered by rain that penetrated its moistness'). Lane 1863: I, 335–36. The Arabic name of the Pleiades, which is more familiar to Western readers as the woman's name Zoraya, in its Persianized form, thus clearly suggests the ideas of prosperity, abundance, fecundity and, particularly, of rain-induced moisture leading to overwhelming fertility in the fields.

wont'). Thus, all is not hopeless, where the dove is concerned, in strict contrast to which, in the final strophe (A'), where one would expect to encounter renewed hope, the poet presents us with the hateful image of the raven of separation, loss, and despair. In the case of this *zajal*, we should, therefore, note that the poet seems to have put the right birds in the wrong places. We should also note that, whereas in (A) the abandoned ruins of the beloved's house are described in Qur'ānic, that is to say, Islamic terms, (they are 'a smooth and level plain'), in (A') the raven is described as being of evil portent. As such, strophe (A') strongly suggests that the stars, rather than God, are in control of man's Fate, this being a clearly Pagan belief. We thus find that there are two incompatible belief systems in conflict with one another, namely the Islamic and the Pagan, in the first and last strophes of the poem.

Strophe 2, which I have designated as (B), corresponds to the penultimate one (5), which I have designated as (B'). In (B), the poet turns from the previous objective description of the abandoned abode of the beloved, to his own subjective feelings over their separation, adding that it would be easier to reach the stars (where the ringdove is to be found) than to witness the beloved's return. In the textually corrupt *vuelta/simṭ* that follows, the poet's own name has been identified by the editor, while the poet also utters a statement that is not entirely clear in the MS, but that invokes God's name in support of its validity. In the corresponding strophe (B'), the poet further invokes his own name, adding that he has repented from sin, which claim is quickly followed by a curious statement to the effect that the poet will deserve blessings or congratulations should his repentance last. In contrast to former times, when he loudly beat his drums and rolled up his sleeves to dance, he has now become the *imām* of a mosque, and spends all his time either climbing up the minaret to call the faithful to prayer, or bowing down to earth before God. In sum, in (B) his separation from the beloved may be permanent (since, unlike the ringdove, he cannot reach the stars, i. e., he cannot fly off to be reunited with her), whereas in (B') his recent adherence to God, as a result of his repentance, may not be permanent. In this respect it is suggestive to note that, in the initial refrain (*maṭlaʿ*) of the very next *zajal* of the only extant MS of Ibn Quzmān's poetry (i. e. 'Zajal 148'), the poet quotes the words of a jurist who orders him to repent.[33] The poem goes on to describe an orgy in which the poet participates, which is broken up by the police, and in which he is arrested for disorderly conduct and indecent behaviour.[34] 'Zajal 148' thus tends to suggest that the poet's moments of repentance were

---

[33] 'asmaʿ ash qāl lī l-faqī tūb 'inna dhā fuḍūlī 'aḥmaq
kif nutūb wa-r-rawḍa ḍāḥikah wa-n-nasīm ka-l-miski yaʿbaq
Hear what the jurist said to me: 'Repent!' – What an impertinent fool!
How can I repent, when the garden is smiling, and the breeze is fragrant as musk?
See Corriente 1995: 420 (translation mine).

[34] Corriente 1995: 420–22. For an analysis of the poem, see Monroe 1988b. While scholars, to the best of my knowledge, have yet to come up with an explanation for the order of the poems as they appear in the only extant MS of Ibn Quzmān's *Dīwān*, there is no evidence whatsoever that such an order is either alphabetical or chronological. The poet does, however, explain to us in his 'Introduction', that he himself collected his poems, and gathered them into a *dīwān* on his own: 'The reason that had prevented me from collecting and recording my *zajal*s; and had restrained me from perfecting and setting them down, was that I had been seeking a generous patron with whose name to embroider them and with whose stamp to adorn them.' He goes on to say that he eventually found

normally followed by serious lapses from virtue. It is also obvious that, from the very fact that the poet questions the permanence of his repentance, he is raising serious doubts in our minds about that permanence. The dubious nature of the poet's repentance may be confirmed from another angle: In Islam, the public confession of one's former sins is, in itself, a sin leading to hellfire. Thus, when the poet boasts of his previous life of debauchery, he is committing a further, mortal sin (*kabīr*). On this point, there is a specific *ḥadīth*, according to which, one should never reveal one's past sins, on pain of eternal damnation.[35]

Strophe (3) corresponds thematically to (4). From the point of view of ring composition the two have been designated as (C) and (C') respectively. In these two strophes, the poet first introduces and then develops the theme of *ubi sunt*. In (C) he asks what has become of Ibn Zaydūn Lane. This was a notorious place of assignation for sodomites, evidently much frequented by him. He then asks what has become of the neighbourhood of the Great Mosque of Córdoba, where he appears to have attended many and frequent revelries of a less than pious nature. These locations have now been reduced, partly to an open field that is ploughed and sowed, and partly to a wasteland overgrown with rockrose, i. e. to an area that is partly wild, and partly cultivated, but that is entirely empty of humankind. The location of so many former illicit pleasures has thus been reduced to an open, empty space in which silence prevails. Not only is the poet weeping over the disappearance of an urban area, thereby violating the rules of poetic composition formulated by the medieval Arabic rhetoricians,[36] but it should also be noted that the entire scene is an outdoor one.

In sharp contrast to the present, ruinous and abandoned state of the area, in (C') the poet describes past revelries, in the company of fashionably dressed dandies, held indoors, in which there was a full house, and in which musical instruments were played so loudly that they could be heard from outside. The overall contrast between (C) and

---

such a patron, namely an otherwise unidentified individual named Abū Isḥāq Ibrāhīm ibn Aḥmad al-Washkī, and adds: 'I found nothing better with which I could endear myself to him, nor any token of respect to offer him, aside from collecting my *zajal*s for him, both the old and the new.' See Corriente 1995:21. Put differently, the poet assumes all responsibility for collecting his own poems and, presumably, for arranging them according to a principle that has, as yet, to be fathomed. Normally, in *dīwān*s of Classical Arabic poetry (which is mono-rhymed), the poems are arranged alphabetically, according to the order of the rhyme consonant. In this case, however, in which the poetry is strophic and poly-rhymed, such a criterion is not being followed. Perhaps his organizational criteria were thematic. If so, 'Zajal 148' might indicate, if not strictly chronologically, then at very least thematically that, in the case of our poet, repentance was often followed by renewed sinful behaviour.

[35] 'My entire religious community will be forgiven their sins on the Day of Judgment *save for those who disclose those sins*. Such disclosure includes the case of that believer who commits a sinful deed by night, then gets up in the morning and, despite the fact that his Lord has provided a cover for that sinful deed, proceeds to declare: "O So-and-So, I committed such and such a sin last night!" Such a person spent the night protected from disgrace by his Lord, and would have continued to remain so protected by Him, had he not gotten up in the morning, and deliberately removed God's cover from himself.' Imām an-Nawawī n. d.: no. 2990, pp. 329–30 (my translation). See the perceptive commentary on this passage by Zargar 2006:64 and n. 94. It is a pleasure to thank Cyrus Zargar for pointing out this *ḥadīth* to me.

[36] See n. 24, above.

(C') is, therefore, one between present and past, emptiness and fullness, outdoors and indoors, silence and noise. Both strophes coincide, however, in enumerating the delectable pleasures of the past, while simultaneously expressing regret over their absence in the present. Just as the beloved's personal dwelling-place had fallen into ruin in (A) and (B), the entire neighbourhood has now vanished in (C) and (C'). The licentious poet, now turned pious *imām* (and these two professions are, in themselves, grossly incompatible with one another) is, furthermore, violating Islamic precepts by publicly revealing his past sins. Neither should we overlook the fact that the scenario of past and delectable sins, encompassing two strophes, constitutes the very centre, architecturally speaking, of this poem and, therefore, must be of paramount importance within the poet's axiological system. Add to this, the fact that the bitter hatred expressed by the poet for the raven, which was instrumental in his separation from his beloved, along with the poet's subsequent repentance from sin, have not resulted in a happy life for him as an *imām*. Otherwise, we should have expected the poet to be singing the raven's praise for having delivered him from evil and steered him toward the path of eternal salvation. This he does not do.

It was pointed out earlier, that the image of the raven, which, in the Pre-Islamic *qaṣīda*, is normally invoked at the beginning of the poem, appears at the end of this *zajal*, whereas the ringdove, which, as a symbol of hope, love, and fertility, might have been expected to appear at the end of a *qaṣīda*, appears here at the beginning. In this respect, our Quzmānī *zajal* would seem, upon our first reading of it, to be anomalous, with the right birds, as we have said, in the wrong places. Let us not forget, however, that the dove is also a monogamous bird that mates for life: When it loses its partner, it goes into mourning for the latter. In this respect, the image of the dove has an ambivalent function in this poem: On the one hand, as one mourning for its lost mate, it is analogous to the grieving poet; on the other, its cooing is also a hint of new rains, fertility, and love yet to come. Furthermore, its position in the heavens allows it to do what the poet cannot do, namely to fly off in pursuit of its mate. Thus, the depth of despair expressed by the mourning of the dove may simultaneously be read as a declaration of hope for a renewal of love in the future. If so, such a reading undercuts the hopelessness of the entire first part of the poem, and adds little to support the permanence of the poet's repentance: He may soon find a new love, and thus revert to his old record of misdeeds, in short order.

As we read the poem, we are also struck, as mentioned earlier, by the fact that the raven is invoked at its end rather than at its beginning. In this sense, the raven is also out of place in the poem. Furthermore, coming after the announcement of the poet's repentance, the raven also represents the poet's firm belief in a Pagan force that is in full control of his fate. Such a belief is totally at odds with his belief in the all-controlling God of Islam, to whom he has just previously offered his repentance. As a result, the poet's belief system is a contradiction in terms, insofar as he may be described, from the perspective of religion, as a Pagan/Muslim. That is to say, in matters of faith, he is trying to have things both ways. This circumstance, in turn, further undercuts the sincerity of the entire second half of the poem, including the sincerity of the poet's loudly trumpeted repentance.

Such a conclusion is, however, the direct result of treating the poem as a text to be read, rather than as a song to be sung, the latter being what *zajal*s really were. Here, we should keep in mind that, in the act of musical performance, the initial refrain of a *zajal* was normally repeated chorally, after a soloist had sung each strophe. As a result, the song ends, vocally if not textually, with the same refrain with which it begins. Thus, after strophe (6), in which both the raven, along with the misfortune it portends, are invoked, the chorus would repeat the refrain (0), mentioning the departure of the beloved and the collapse of his house. As a result, the normal Pre-Islamic sequence of events: (1) Cawing of the raven, followed by (2) Separation of the poet from his beloved, is restored, as the song/text ends with exactly the same words with which it begins, thereby constituting an unending cycle. This being so, the conflict between the Islamic belief that God's Providence ('foresight') is in total control of this world, on the one hand, and the Pagan belief in the blindness of Fate, on the other, is radicalized even further in the *zajal* under scrutiny. In turn, this casts even greater doubt upon the validity and sincerity of Ibn Quzmān's repentance.[37]

We may thus conclude that, in what constitutes a remarkable case of hybridization, Ibn Quzmān has adopted the Ibero-Romance literary form or *structure* of the *zajal*, and used it to reconfigure a whole series of literary motifs or *materials* taken from the poetic tradition of the Arabic *qaṣīda*.

In Classical Arabic literary fiction, the theme of repentance from sin is a major concern of the *maqāma* genre, to be found, not only in the work of Badī' az-Zamān al-Hamadhānī (358/969–398/1008),[38] the reputed inventor of the genre, but also in that of al-Ḥarīrī of Basra (445/1054–515/1122)[39] and the Andalusī writer as-Saraqusṭī (d. 538/1143).[40] Whereas Ibn Quzmān (d. 555/1160) is very likely to have known the work of the last two authors, he does not specifically mention them in his extant poetry.[41] In contrast, he certainly was aware of Badī' az-Zamān, the inventor of the genre, for, in his 'Zajal 95:7', dedicated to an unknown vizier and man of letters, to whom he introduces himself, he specifically mentions that author by name.[42]

---

[37] Alternatively, should one be inclined to argue that the raven is a mere instrument of God, whose function it is to foretell the vicissitudes of a Fate determined by God, then one would have to conclude that the satire of the raven contained in this *zajal* is ultimately, a satire, albeit indirect, of God Himself. Either way, the piety of the poet is seriously in question.

[38] See the discussion in Monroe 1983:77–85 (chap. 6).

[39] See Monroe 1983 (chap. 6).

[40] See Monroe 2002:490–501.

[41] Al-Ḥarīrī's work was introduced to al-Andalus soon after the year 504/1111. See Monroe 2002:2, whereas as-Saraqusṭī's imitation of it appears to have been written between the years 519/1126 and 532/1138 (Monroe 2002:44). Therefore, it is entirely possible for Ibn Quzmān to have been familiar with their works. Both authors wrote respective *maqāma*s in which they also dealt with the theme of false repentance, which seems to have become a required *topos* of the *maqāma* genre.

[42] qīl lī 'an-k fa-stama'tu shayyan 'ajīb
wa-dakhal f-udhnī kulli shayyan gharīb
fa-shtahà fummī 'an yakallam ḥabīb
wa-'aradt an narà *badī' az-zamān*
I have been told, and I have heard, such marvelous things about you,
While such rare accounts have reached my ear,

In his 'Maqāma 26' ('The Exhortation') Badīʿ az-Zamān has his protagonist appear in a street of the Iraqi city of Baṣra, when he is an old man, and where he is preaching a sermon in which he exhorts his listeners to repent before it is too late to do so.[43] The sermon, however, is based upon principles maintained, and authorities revered, by the theological school of the Muʿtazila, according to which a deathbed repentance is a futile act, insofar as it will not lead to Divine forgiveness.[44] Since the speaker is now old, it becomes clear that, according to the Muʿtazilī doctrine he is espousing, and which provides the intellectual and moral underpinnings for his sermon, his words, moving though they may seem, are hardly applicable to his own situation: After a lifetime of dishonesty, it is too late, from the Muʿtazilī perspective, for an old man to repent and expect to be pardoned in the Hereafter. Therefore, it becomes clear that the preacher is being portrayed as a man who does not practice what he preaches. Put differently, he is a hypocrite, and his sermon is no more than a ruse designed to extract monetary donations from a crowd of gullible sympathizers. The text is also, by implication, a Muʿtazilī critique of that well-known doctrine espoused by the theological school of the Ashʿariyya, according to whom, a deathbed repentance can lead to Divine forgiveness. We may, therefore, conclude that Ibn Quzmān, in offering us the example of his own dubious repentance, has also been inspired by the *maqāma* genre, to which he has contributed by inverting it: Whereas the *maqāma* is composed in a form of Classical Arabic prose that is extremely ornate and rarified in nature, Ibn Quzmān has adopted a (deceptively) simple register of Colloquial, poetic diction that (appears) to be easily accessible; whereas the protagonist of the *maqāma* is a rogue who normally succeeds in tricking his first-person narrator, Ibn Quzmān presents himself, simultaneously, as a first-person narrator and would-be rogue, who systematically fails to trick his potential victims; whereas the trickery in the *maqāma* normally involves money, the failed trickery in the Quzmānī *zajal* more often than not involves forms of sex that are either illicit, unobtainable or, as in the case of this poem, no longer available.

At this point in our reading of 'Zajal 147', we may finally confirm our suspicions that it too, deals with far more serious problems than its surface level initially suggests. The poet, who has sinned in the past, has now lost his beloved, and has consequently repented, only to become a prayer-leading *imām*. The announcement of that repentance is, however, followed by the curious statement to the effect that it is hoped that the repentance will last, which is clearly calculated to raise serious doubts in our minds concerning its permanence. Add to this, the fact that the repentance is placed within a Pagan scenario in which old loves will vanish, while new ones will appear, according to a cyclical pattern governed, not by the will of God, but by the influence of the stars, specifically, the constellations of Corvus and the Pleiades, symbolized by the raven and the ringdove. The cyclical nature of this pattern is further reinforced by the circular

---

That, in you, my mouth would like to converse with Ḥabīb,
And, in you, my eyes would like to see Badīʿ az-Zamān.
See Corriente 1995:306 (translation mine). Ḥabīb is the great ʿAbbāsid panegyrist Ḥabīb ibn Aws Abū Tammām (188/804–c.231/845), on whom, see Ritter 1979. For an inspiring study of Abū Tammām's poetry, see Stetkevych 1991. On the inventor of the *maqāma* genre, see Blachère 1979.

[43] See the discussion in Monroe 1983:77–83 (chap. 6).
[44] See Monroe 1983:47–63 (chap. 4).

structure of the poem which, by beginning and ending with the same refrain, implies that the cycle of sin, followed by loss of love, and declaration of repentance, in that order, will be followed by future cycles of sin, further losses of love, and further declarations of repentance. Thus, a cyclically structured poem suggests the strong possibility that the poet will spend the rest of his life first loudly lamenting a series of lost loves, and then loudly proclaiming a series of newly adopted acts of repentance. The poem's very circularity thus constitutes a critique of insincere repentances.

A further detail is worthy of notice: In this poem, the rhymes of the initial refrain and subsequent *vueltas/simṭ*s are *-ān, -aʻ, -ār, -aʻ*, in which the first and third *ā* of the (internal) monosyllabic rhyme-syllables evoke a prolonged sound of lamentation (the weeping of the poet; the mourning of the ringdove?), whereas the second and fourth *aʻ*, of the (final) rhyme-syllables, which are closed by the constrictive velar consonant *ʻayn*, evoke a choking sound (the sobbing of the poet; the raucous cawing of the raven?). In contrast, the rhymes of the intercalated *mudanzas/ghuṣn*s tend to be bi-syllabic and, as such, they suggest a more rapid, tripping, and therefore, joyful tempo.[45] Thus, the alternation between joy and sorrow suggested by the alternating sets of rhymes in this skillfully constructed poem, coincides with its motifs as well as its larger, thematic structure, in order to convey the same underlying message, in an extraordinary example of what the Romantics once most aptly termed 'organic unity'.[46]

Let me also point out that 'Zajal 147' is a remarkable example of literary hybridization: From the native, Ibero-Romance tradition, it has borrowed the *zajal* structure, whereas the materials out of which the poem is constructed have been provided by the imported Arabic *qaṣīda* and *maqāma*. Put differently, the form is Western, whereas the content is Eastern.

## 6 Concluding Remarks

At the beginning of this exposition, it was pointed out that *mudéjar* churches were hybrid monuments, the *structure* of which was provided by the imported, *dominant*, Ibero-Romance culture, whereas their *materials* were borrowed from the local, *dominated* Arabic civilization. Exactly the opposite occurs in the case of architectural monuments such as the Mosque of Córdoba, whose structure is essentially that of a mosque, whereas many of the elements out of which it is built are borrowed from non-Islamic civilizations. Thus, its columns are Roman, its horseshoe arches are Visigothic, the alternating bands of stone and brick out of which those arches are built are Byzantine, its

---

[45] This is generally so, with the notable exception of the mournful rhymes in strophe 5, which are in *-ām*. This is the very strophe in which the poet tells of his repentance. If that strophe's rhymes are any accurate indication of his feelings, then he seems less than overjoyed at his new calling as muezzin and *imām*.

[46] See Brennan 1953; 2002: 859, where the concept is defined as follows: 'Most generally the notion of organic unity indicates a unity comprising different systems that function independently of, and yet which are coterminous with one another.' Thus, in the case of 'Zajal 147', both the poem's system of rhymes and its system of literary commonplaces, along with their structure, are contiguous and, therefore, support and reinforce one another.

23 – Bayāḍ singing to the lute, Bibl. Vaticana MS Ar. 368 (13th c.)

rows of superimposed arches were inspired by Roman aqueducts, while the mosaics decorating its *miḥrāb* were the gift of a Byzantine emperor to a Cordovan Caliph. And yet, despite the many foreign elements out of which this remarkable structure is built, it is unmistakably a mosque for, unlike the Muslim Arabs, the (Christian) Romans, the Byzantines, and the Visigoths built churches, rather than mosques.[47]

Let me briefly end this exposition by indicating that the famous fourteenth-century Spanish literary masterpiece known as the *Libro de buen amor*, attributed to a certain Juan Ruiz, Archpriest of Hita, and written two centuries after Ibn Quzmān, is also a hybrid work. In what way are the *Libro de buen amor* and the Quzmānī *zajal* related to one another?

From a comparative perspective, the structure of the *Libro de buen amor* is Arabic and Islamic. By this, I mean that its structure, as was long ago argued by Francisco Fernández y González and María Rosa Lida de Malkiel, is a derivative of the Arabic *maqā-*

---

[47] On the structure of the original Arabian mosque at Medina, see Sauvaget 2002. For this Arabian structure's hybridization with local Iberian elements in the specific instance of the Mosque of Córdoba, see Dodds 1992. Andalus was hardly the only place where the Islamic Mosque imposed its distinctive organizational structure on local materials. The Umayyad Mosque of Damascus, built on the site of a former church of Saint John the Baptist, made use of Byzantine mosaics and the square-based minaret typical of Christian churches in the region (see Flood 2001), while the portico of the twelfth-century Maghak-i Attari Mosque in Bukhara contains elements typical of Zoroastrian fire-temples (see Knobloch 2001: 125). See too Hillenbrand et al. 1991.

*ma* genre,[48] to which I would add that this structure has been modified by the technique of inserting 'enframed' tales within its various picaresque episodes. This technique was, in turn, borrowed from Oriental works such as the *Book of Kalīla wa-Dimna*, which was translated directly from the Arabic into Spanish, *c.* AD 1251, at the command of Alfonso X, the Learned. The original Arabic *maqāma* genre has been further modified by an inversion of perspective, after the fashion of the Quzmānī *zajal*: In the Classical *maqāma* a *victim* narrates how he was *successfully* deceived by a *trickster*, whereas in the *Libro de buen amor*, a *would-be trickster* narrates how he was *unsuccessful* in his attempts at deceiving a potential *victim*, exactly as occurs, all too often, in the Quzmānī *zajal*. The structure of the *Libro de buen amor* is, therefore, in itself, a hybrid of the *maqāma*, the frametale, and the *zajal* genres, all three of which either came to the Iberian Peninsula via the Arab East (as is the case of the *maqāma* and frametale), or were adopted and developed in the Iberian Peninsula by Arab poets (as is the case of the *zajal*). In contrast, the *Libro*'s materials are largely Graeco-Latin and Christian. This is so, in the sense that the work recounts the numerous attempts, made by a Christian Archpriest, to seduce various and sundry women, all of whom (with the exception of two nuns, who are as desperate for sex as he is) reject his advances. The work further includes characters adopted from Classical Antiquity, such as the Pagan divinities Lady Venus and Lord Eros. As in the case of the Quzmānī *zajal*, sex is, therefore, one of the major, obsessive concerns of the *Libro de buen amor*.

Ultimately, the *Libro de buen amor* is subversive, insofar as it attempts to criticize the rule of priestly celibacy that had been imposed upon the Western Christian clergy by the Roman Church only a century before the *Libro* was written. In this respect, Juan Ruiz was an early precursor of Martin Luther. Years ago, the *Libro de buen amor* was characterized by Américo Castro, as being a *mudéjar* work.[49] To his keenly perceptive suggestion, let me add the following nuance: In both the *Libro de buen amor* and the Quzmānī *zajal*, the literary structure is borrowed from the *dominated* culture (the structure of the Spanish *Libro de buen amor* is Arabic and Eastern, whereas that of the Arabic *zajal* is Romance and Western), in contrast to which, the literary materials used in both works are largely borrowed from the *dominant* culture (the Arabic *zajal*'s materials are Arabic, insofar as they are borrowed from the *qaṣīda* and the *maqāma*, whereas those of the Spanish *Libro de buen amor* are Graeco-Latin and Romance). This feature appears to coincide with the fact that both these works are subversive, insofar as they both offer a critique of certain social norms and customs prevalent in the two authors' respective societies: Ibn Quzmān views the deathbed repentance of sinners as insincere and, consequently, as hollow. He is thus critical of the Ashʿarī theological doctrine of repentance that prevailed in the Andalus of his day. Similarly, Juan Ruiz views the Western Christian rule of priestly celibacy as inhumane. It should be further pointed out that, if these two literary examples are any indication of the validity of a rule with wider implications, we might suggest that, when a hybrid work is subversive, it tends to abandon the norms that are usually expected of the formal, high culture and to adopt, in their stead, literary

---

[48] See Fernández y González 1894:52; Lida de Malkiel 1961:1–50.
[49] See Castro 1954:392–465 (chap. 12, 'The Archpriest of Hita and His "Libro de Buen Amor"') and, specifically, p. 403.

strategies borrowed from the popular rank and file (the Quzmānī *zajal* is couched in Colloquial Arabic diction even though Ibn Quzmān was a learned poet conversant with Classical Arabic, at the same time that Juan Ruiz, who obviously read Latin, and was a man of some learning, conceals his true nature behind the *persona* of a popular minstrel; he writes in Castilian, rather than Latin, and he goes out of his way to stress his lack of theological expertise). On this basis, we could postulate the following set of correspondences:

(1) When the *structure* of a work is provided by the *dominant* culture, whereas its *materials* are borrowed from the *dominated* culture (Islamic mosques, Christian *mudéjar* churches), then a *Classical* medium of expression is adopted, in order to *uphold* official values.

(2) When the *structure* of a work is borrowed from the *dominated* culture, whereas its *materials* are provided by the *dominant* culture (Arabic *zajal*; Spanish *Libro de buen amor*), then a *Colloquial* medium of expression is adopted, in order to *subvert* official values.

If these two principles are acceptable, let us note that literary works such as the Quzmānī *zajal* and the *Libro de buen amor* correspond with one another, insofar as they both belong to the second category identified above. Therefore, the *Libro de buen amor* is not a 'straightforward' *mudéjar* work, as Américo Castro brilliantly postulated, but rather, it is what one might call an 'inverted' *mudéjar* work. In a similar, but parallel fashion, the Quzmānī *zajal* represents an 'inversion' of those principles of hybridization that characterize the Mosque of Córdoba, insofar as its materials are Arabic and, therefore, *dominant*, whereas its structure is Romance and, therefore, *dominated*. Both the *Libro de buen amor* and the Quzmānī *zajal* are, thus, structurally parallel, if culturally opposite, expressions of that extraordinary, multicultural society that was medieval Iberia.[50] Finally, let me suggest that, when a literary work is subversive, that is to say, when it is critical of certain social practices prevalent in the dominant culture, its author may prefer to adopt a literary structure borrowed from the often oppressed social stratum of the underdog, as a convenient, psychological vantage point from which to lash out with impunity at abuse and corruption in the high places of his own dominant culture. In so doing, the author is deliberately adopting the Bakhtinian critical perspective of what Claudio Guillén, in his masterly study of Spanish picaresque literature, brilliantly identified as the societal 'half-outsider'.[51]

### Appendix: Verse Passage from the *Táin Bó Cúalnge*[52]

'Cluchi cách, gaine cách   'Play was each, pleasure each,
0 co roich Fer ńDiad issin n-áth.  Till Ferdiad faced the beach;

---

[50] On the multicultural nature of those medieval Iberian literatures written in Arabic, Hebrew, and Spanish, see two recent and most welcome books: Hamilton 2007; Wacks, 2007.
[51] On the concept of the 'half-outsider' in Spanish picaresque literature, see Guillén 1971: 80.
[52] The verse-translation of the first five strophes is taken from Sigerson 1925: 119–20, who does not provide a rhymed, verse adaptation of the last three strophes (6–8), which I have, therefore, left untranslated. The text is found in O'Rahilly 1967: 99–100. The more literal, prose translation, provided by O'Rahilly (p. 234) does, in contrast, include a complete translation of the entire poem and is here added to the text.

| | | |
|---|---|---|
| 1 | Inund foglaim fríth dúinn, | One had been our student life, |
| | innund rograim ráth, | One in strife of school our place, |
| | inund mummi máeth | One our gentle teacher's grace |
| | *ras slainni sech cách* | *Loved o'er all and each.* |
| | *Cluchi cách, gaíne cách* | *Play was each, pleasure each,* |
| | *go roich Fer Diad issin n-áth.* | *Till Ferdiad faced the beach;* |
| 2 | Inund aisti arúath dúinn, | One had been our wonted ways, |
| | inund gasced gnáth. | One the praise for feat of fields, |
| | Scáthach tuc dá scíath | Scathach gave two victor shields |
| | *dam-sa is Fer Diad tráth* | *Equal prize to each.* |
| | *Cluchi cách, gaíne cách* | *Play was each, pleasure each,* |
| | *go roich Fer Diad issin n-áth.* | *Till Ferdiad faced the beach;* |
| 3 | Inmain úatni óir | Dear that pillar of pure gold |
| | ra furmius ar áth. | Who fell cold beside the ford. |
| | A tarbga na túath | Hosts of heroes felt his sword |
| | *ba calma ná cách.* | *First in battle's breach.* |
| | *Cluchi cách, gaíne cách* | *Play was each, pleasure each,* |
| | *go roich Fer Diad issin n-áth.* | *Till Ferdiad faced the beach;* |
| 4 | In leóman lassamain lond, | Lion fiery, fierce, and bright, |
| | in tond báeth borr immar bráth. | Wave whose might no thing withstands, |
| | [. . . . . . . . . . . . . . . . . . . . . . | Sweeping, with the shrinking sands, |
| | . . . . . . . . . . . . . . . . . . . . . . .] | *Horror o'er the beach.* |
| | *Cluchi cách, gaíne cách* | *Play was each, pleasure each,* |
| | *go roich Fer Diad issin n-áth.* | *Till Ferdiad faced the beach;* |
| 5 | Indar lim-sa Fer dil Diad | Loved Ferdiad, dear to me: |
| | is am díaid ra bíad go bráth. | I shall dree his death for aye |
| | Indé ba métithir slíab, | Yesterday a mountain he, – |
| | indiu ní fuil de acht a scáth. | But a Shade to-day.' |
| 6 | Trí díríme na Tána | |
| | darochratar dom láma, | |
| | formna bó, fer 7 ech | |
| | roda slaidius ar cech leth. | |
| 7 | Girbat línmara na slúaig | |
| | táncatar ón Chrúachain chrúaid, | |
| | mó trín is lugu lethi | |
| | ro marbus dom garbchluchi. | |
| 8 | Nocho tarla co cath cró | |
| | níra alt Banba dá brú, | |
| | níra chind de muir ná thír | |
| | de maccaib ríg bud ferr clú.' | |

'Game was all and sport was all until it came to my meeting with Fer Diad on the ford. The same instruction we had, the same power of guarantee (?). The same tender foster-mother we had whose name is beyond all others.

All was play and sport compared with my meeting with Fer Diad on the ford. The same nature we had, the same fearsomeness, the same weapons we used to wield. Scáthach once gave two shields to me and to Fer Diad.

All was play and sport compared with my meeting with Fer Diad on the ford. Beloved was he, the golden pillar, whom I laid low on the ford. O strong one of the tribes, you were more valiant than all others.

All was play and sport compared with my meeting with Fer Diad on the ford, the furious, fiery lion, the wave, wild and swelling, like the day of doom.

All was play and sport compared with my meeting with Fer Diad at the ford. I thought that beloved Fer Diad would live after me for ever. Yesterday he was huge as a mountain, today only his shadow remains.

Three uncountable bands there fell by my hand on the Foray. The finest men, the finest cattle and horses I slaughtered on very side.

Though numerous the army which came from stout Crúachu, yet I slew more than a third of them and less than half with the rough plying of my weapons.

There has not come into the centre of battle, nor has Banba ever nurtured, nor has there travelled over land or sea any king's son more famous than Fer Diad.'

# References

Ben Abdesselem, A. 2002.'Wallāda.' *Encyclopaedia of Islam*, XI, 133.
Bencherifa, Mohamed, ed. 1975. *Proverbes andalous de Abū Yaḥyà az-Zajjālī (1220–1294)*. 2 vols. Fez: Maṭbaʿa Muḥammad al-Khāmis.
Bettini, Lidia. 2002.'Zuhayr.' *Encyclopaedia of Islam*, XI, 556–58.
Bevan, Bernard. 1938. *History of Spanish Architecture*. London: Batsford.
Blachère, R. 1979.'al-Hamadhānī.' *Encyclopaedia of Islam*, III, 106–7.
Boustany, S. 1979.'Imru' al-Kays b. Ḥudjr.' *Encyclopaedia of Islam*, III, 1177–78.
Brennan, Maynard J. 1953.'Organic Unity: The Principle and its Application in the Criticism of Coleridge.' Ph.D. Thesis, University of Michigan.
–. 2002.'Organic Unity.' In *The Continuum Encyclopedia of Modern Criticism and Theory*. Ed. Julia Wolfreys. New York: Continuum.
Catlos, Brian. A. 2004. *The Victors and the Vanquished: Christians and Muslims of Catalonia and Aragon*. Cambridge: CUP.
Castro, Américo. 1954. *The Structure of Spanish History*. Trans. Edmund L. King. Princeton: Princeton UP.
–. 1962. *La realidad historica de España*. Rev. edition. Mexico City: Porrua.
Chalmeta, Pedro. 1993.'Mudéjar.' *Encyclopaedia of Islam*, VII, 286–89.
Corriente, Federico, ed. 1995. *El cancionero hispanoárabe de Aban Quzmán de Córdoba (m. 555/ 1160): 'Iṣābat al-aghrāḍ fī dhikr al-aʿrāḍ'*. Cairo: Majlis al-'Aʿlà li-th-Thaqāfa.
Dillon, Myles. 1948. *Early Irish Literature*. Chicago: U of Chicago P.
Dodds, Jerrilynn D. 1992.'The Great Mosque of Córdoba.' In *Al-Andalus: The Art of Islamic Spain*. Ed. Jerrilynn D. Dodds. New York: The Metropolitan Museum of Art. 11–25.
Douglas, Mary. 2007. *Thinking in Circles: An Essay on Ring Composition*. New Haven: Yale UP.
*Encyclopaedia of Islam*. Ed. B. Lewis, C. E. Bosworth, P. J. Bearman et al. New edition. 12 vols. Leiden: Brill, 1960–2004.
Farrin, Raymon K. 2004.'Season's Greetings: Two 'Īd Poems by Ibn Quzmān.' *Journal of Arabic Literature* 35:247–69.

—. 2006. 'Reading Beyond the Line: Organic Unity in Classical Arabic Poetry.' Ph.D. Thesis in Near Eastern Studies, University of California, Berkeley.
Fernández y González, Francisco. 1894. 'Influencia de las lenguas y letras orientales en la cultura de los pueblos de la península Ibérica.' *Discursos leídos ante la Real Academia Española*. Madrid.
Flood, Finbarr Barry. 2001. *The Great Mosque of Damascus: Studies on the Makings of an Umayyad Visual Culture*. Leiden: Brill.
Garulo, Teresa. 2005. '*Wa-huwa wazn lam yarid 'an al-'arab*. Métrica no jaliliana en al-Andalus.' *Al-Qanṭara* 26: 263–67.
Guillaume, Alfred, trans. n. d. *The Life of Muhammad: A Translation of Ibn Ishaq's 'Sirat Rasul Allah'*. Oxford: OUP.
Guillén, Claudio. 1971. *Literature as System: Essays Toward the Theory of Literary History*. Princeton: Princeton UP.
Hamilton, Michelle M. 2007. *Representing Others in Medieval Iberian Literature*. New York: Palgrave Macmillan.
Hamp, Eric P. 1982. 'Fer Diad.' *Ériu* 33: 178.
Hard, Robin. 2004. *The Routledge Handbook of Greek Mythology. Based on H. J. Roses's 'Handbook of Greek Mythology'*. London: Routledge.
Harvey, Leonard Patrick. 1971. 'The Arabic Dialect of Valencia in 1595.' *Al-Andalus* 36: 81–115.
Heijkoop, Henk, and Otto Zwartjes. 2004. *Muwaššaḥ, Zajal, Kharja: Bibliography of Strophic Poetry and Music from al-Andalus and their Influence in East and West*. Leiden: Brill.
Hernández, Guillermo E. 1989. 'Jarcha Antecedents in Latin Inscriptions.' *Hispanic Review* 57: 189–202.
—. 1991. 'El arte satírico de Ibn Quzmān: Zéjel núm. 20.' In *Actas del Congreso Romancero-Cancionero*. Ed. Enrique Rodríguez Cepeda. 2 vols. Madrid: Gredos. II, 383–408.
Herrera, Hayden. 1991. *Frida Kahlo: The Paintings*. New York: HarperCollins.
Hillenbrand, R., et al. 1991. 'Masdjid.' *Encyclopedia of Islam*, VI, 644–707.
Ibn Qutayba. 1964. *Kitāb al-shi'r wa-sh-shu'arā*. 2 vols. Beirut: Dār ath-Thaqāfa.
Johnson, F. E., Captain of the Royal Artillery, ed. and trans. 1893. *Al-Sab' al-Mu'allaqāt: The Seven Poems Suspended in the Temple at Mecca*. Bombay.
Knobloch, Edgar. 2001. *Monuments of Central Asia: A Guide to the Archaeology, Art and Architecture of Turkestan*. London: Tauris.
Lane, Edward William. 1863. *An Arabic-English Lexicon*. 8 vols. London.
Lecomte, G. 1979. 'Ibn Zaydūn.' *Encyclopaedia of Islam*, III, 973–74.
Lévi-Strauss, Claude. 1973–81. *Introduction to a Science of Mythology: 1 The Raw and the Cooked; 2 From Honey to Ashes; 3 The Origins of Table Manners; 4 The Naked Man*. Trans. John and Doreen Weightman. New York: Harper & Row.
Lida de Malkiel, María Rosa. 1961. *Two Spanish Masterpieces: The 'Book of Good Love' and 'The Celestina'*. Illinois Studies in Language and Literature 49. Urbana: U of Illinois P.
Liu, Benjamin M., and James T. Monroe. 1989. *Ten Hispano-Arabic Songs in the Modern Oral Tradition: Music and Texts*. University of California Publications in Modern Philology 125. Berkeley: U of California P.
Marzluff, John M., and Tony Angell. 2005. *In the Company of Crows and Ravens*. New Haven: Yale UP.
Meyer, Kuno. 1909. *A Primer of Irish Metrics*. Dublin: Hodges and Figgis.
Monroe, James T. 1975. 'Formulaic Diction and the Common Origins of Romance Lyric Traditions.' *Hispanic Review* 43: 341–50.
—. 1976. 'The Hispanic-Arabic World.' In *Américo Castro and the Meaning of Spanish Civilization*. Ed. José Rubia Barcia and Selma Margaretten. Berkeley: U of California P. 69–90.
—. 1979. 'Prolegomena to the Study of Ibn Quzmān: The Poet As Jongleur.' In *El Romancero hoy: historia, comparatismo, bibliografía crítica*. Ed. Samuel G. Armistead, Diego Catalán, and Antonio Sánchez Romeralo. Madrid: Gredos. 78–128.

-. 1982. 'The Tune or the Words? (Singing Hispano-Arabic Strophic Poetry).' *Al-Qanṭara* 8: 265–317.
-. 1983. *The Art of Badīʿ az-Zamān al-Hamadhānī as Picaresque Narrative*. Beirut: Center for Arab and Middle East Studies, American University of Beirut.
-. 1984. 'Poetic Quotation in the *Muwaššaḥa* and its Implications.' *La Corónica* 12: 230–50.
-. 1985–86. 'Prolegómenos al estudio de Ibn Quzmān: el poeta como bufón.' *Nueva Revista de Filología Hispánica* 34: 769–99.
-. 1987. 'Wanton Poets and Would-be Paleographers (Prolegomena to Ibn Quzmān's *Zajal No. 10*.' *La Corónica* 16: 1–42.
-. 1988a. 'Ibn Quzmān on *I'rāb*: A *"zéjel de juglaría"* in Arab Spain?' In *Hispanic Studies in Honor of Joseph H. Silverman*. Ed. Joseph V. Ricapito. Newark, DE: Juan de la Cuesta. 45–56.
-. 1988b. 'Salmà, el toro abigarrado, la doncella medrosa, Kaʿb al-Aḥbār y el conocimiento del árabe de don Juan Manuel: Prolegómenos al *Zéjel Núm. 148* de Ibn Quzmān.' *Nueva Revista de Filología Hispánica* 36: 853–78.
-. 1989. 'Which Came First, the *Zajal* or the *Muwashshaha*? Some Evidence for the Oral Origins of Hispano-Arabic Strophic Poetry.' *Oral Tradition* 4: 38–64.
-. 1990. 'On Re-reading Ibn Bassám: "Lírica Rómanica" After the Arab Conquest.' In *Actas del Congreso Romancero-Cancionero, UCLA (1984)*. Ed. Enrique Rodríguez Cepeda and Samuel G. Armistead. 2 vols. Madrid: Porrúa. II, 409–46.
-. 1994. 'Elements of Romance Prosody in the Poetry of Ibn Quzmān.' In *Perspectives on Arabic Linguistics*, vol 6. Ed. Mushira Eid et al. Current Issues in Linguistic Theory 115. Amsterdam: Benjamins. 63–87.
-. 1996. 'The Underside of Arabic Panegyric: Ibn Quzmān's (Unfinished?) *Zajal No. 84*.' *Al-Qanṭara* 17: 79–115.
-. 1997. 'The Striptease That Was Blamed on Abū Bakr's Naughty Son: Was Father Being Shamed, or Was the Poet Having Fun? (Ibn Quzmān's *Zajal No. 133*).' In *Homoeroticism in Classical Arabic Literature*. Ed. J. W. Wright Jr. and Everett K. Rowson. New York: Columbia UP. 94–139.
-, trans. 2002. *Al-Maqāmāt al-luzūmīyah by Abū l-Ṭāhir Muḥammad ibn Yūsuf al-Tamīmī al-Saraquṣṭī, ibn al-Aštarkūwī (d. 538/1143)*. Studies in Arabic Literature 22. Leiden: Brill.
-. 2005. 'Improvised Invective in Hispano-Arabic Poetry and Ibn Quzmān's *"Zajal 87"* (When Blond Meets Blonde).' In *Voicing the Moment: Improvised Oral Poetry and Basque Tradition*. Ed. Samuel G. Armistead and Joseba Zulaika. Center for Basque Studies 3. Reno: U of Nevada. 135–59.
-. 2006. 'The Mystery of the Missing Mantle: The Poet as Wittol? (Ibn Quzmān's *Zajal 20*).' *Journal of Arabic Literature* 35: 1–45.
-. 2007. 'Literary Hybridization in the *Zajal*: Ibn Quzmān's *"Zajal 88"* (The Visit of Sir Gold).' *Journal of Arabic Literature* 38: 324–51.
-. Forthcoming. 'Ibn Quzmān's *"Zajal 118"*: An Andalusī "Ode to the Onion".' In *Proceedings: 'Los quilates de su Oriente': La pluralidad de culturas en la Península Ibérica durante la Edad Media y en los albores de la Modernidad: A Conference in Honor of Francisco Márquez Villanueva*. Ed. Ángel Sáenz-Badillos, Luis Girón Negrón, and Mary Gaylord.
-, and Mark F. Pettigrew. 2003. 'The Decline of Courtly Patronage and the Appearance of New Genres in Arabic Literature: The Case of the *Zajal*, the *Maqāma*, and the Shadow Play.' *Journal of Arabic Literature* 34: 138–77.
Morrás, María. 1988. '¿Zéjeles o formas zejelescas? Observaciones para el estudio de un problema de historia literaria.' *La Corónica* 17: 52–75.
Murphy, Gerard. 1961. *Early Irish Metrics*. Dublin: Royal Irish Academy.
al-Nawawī, Imām. n. d. *Sharḥ Ṣaḥīḥ Muslim*. 19 vols. Beirut: Dār al-Qalamī.
Niles, John D. 1979. 'Ring Composition and the Structure of *Beowulf*.' *PMLA* 94: 924–35.

O'Rahilly, Cecile, ed. and trans. 1967. *Táin Bó Cúalnge from the Book of Leinster*. Irish Texts Society 49. Dublin: Dublin Institute for Advanced Studies.
Pagels, Elaine H. 1979. *The Gnostic Gospels*. New York: Random House.
Pavón Maldonado, Basilio. 1973. *Arte toledano islámico y mudéjar*. Madrid: Instituto Hispano-Árabe de Cultura.
Pellat, Ch. 1983. 'Ghurāb.' *Encyclopaedia of Islam*, II, 1096-97.
Pérès, Henri. 1953. *La poésie andalouse en arabe classique au XI$^e$ siècle: ses aspects généraux, ses principaux thèmes, et sa valeur documentaire*. 2nd ed. Paris: Adrien-Maisonneuve.
Peterson, R. G. 1976. 'Critical Calculation: Measure and Symmetry in Literature.' *PMLA* 91: 367-75.
Ritter, H. 1979. 'Abū Tammām.' *Encyclopaedia of Islam*, I, 153-55.
Roolvink, Hednig. 1975. 'El origen céltico en la poesía rimada medieval, sobre todo en relación con el zéjel español.' *Neophilologus* 59: 1-13.
Rose, H. J. 1956. *A Handbook of Greek Mythology (Including its Extension to Rome)*. 6th ed. London: Methuen.
Sauvaget, Jean. 2002. 'The Mosque and the Palace.' In *Early Islamic Art and Architecture*. Ed. Jonathan M. Bloom. Vol. 23 of *The Formation of the Classical Islamic World*. Ed. Laurence I. Conrad. Burlington, VT: Ashgate. 108-47.
Schoeler, Gregor. 1993. 'Musammaṭ.' *Encyclopaedia of Islam*, VIII, 660-62.
Shahrani, M. N. 1979. *The Kirghiz and Wakhi of Afghanistan: Adaptation to Closed Frontiers*. Seattle: U of Washington P.
Sigerson, George. 1925. *Bards of the Gael and Gall: Examples of the Poetic Literature of Erinn Done Into English After the Meters and Modes of the Gael*. 3rd ed. Dublin: Talbot P.
Smith, William Robertson. 1963. *Kinship and Marriage in Early Arabia (with Additional Notes by the Author and by Ignaz Goldziher)*. Ed. Stanley A. Cook. Boston: Beacon P.
Stetkevych, Suzanne Pinckney. 1991. *Abū Tammām and the Poetics of the 'Abbāsid Age*. Studies in Arabic Literature 13. Leiden: Brill.
Stewart, Charles. 1999. 'Syncretism and its Synonyms: Reflections on Cultural Mixture.' *Diacritics: A Review of Contemporary Criticism* 29: 40-62.
Trabulsi, Amjad. 1956. *La critique poétique des arabes jusqu'au V$^e$ siècle de l'Hégire (XI$^e$ siècle de J. C.)*. Damascus: Institut Français de Damas.
Vajda, G. 1979. 'Ḥamām.' *Encyclopaedia of Islam*, III, 108-10.
Wacks, David A. 2007. *Framing Iberia: 'Maqāmāt' and Frametale Narratives in Medieval Spain*. The Medieval and Early Modern Iberian World 33. Leiden: Brill.
Wensinck, A. J., and Penelope Johnson. 1991. 'Maryam.' *Encyclopaedia of Islam*, VI, 628-29.
Westermarck, Edward. 1926. *Ritual and Belief in Morocco*. 2 vols. London: Macmillan.
Wüstenfeld, Ferdinand, ed. 1858. *Das Leben Muhammed's nach Muhammed Ibn Ishâk Bearbeitet von Abd el-Malik Ibn Hischâm*. 2 vols. Göttingen.
Zargar, Cyrus Ali. 2006. 'The Satiric Method of Ibn Dāniyāl: Morality and Anti-Morality in *Ṭayf al-Khayāl*.' *Journal of Arabic Literature* 37: 68-108.

# 24 Orality and the Tradition of Arabic Epic Storytelling

*Thomas Herzog*

Arab culture is an originally oral culture in which the spoken word occupies a central position. All important foundation texts of Arab culture are orally performed and transmitted texts: pre-Islamic poetry and prose, the Qur'ān – which according to Islamic tradition was finally written down more than three decades after the first revelations – and tales about the 'heroic age' of the Muslims, the conquest of the Prophet and the early Muslims. This original orality explains why oral performance and transmission play an important role alongside literacy in Arab-Islamic culture to this day. In this chapter the most important stages of oral epic narration will be traced from the *jāhilīya*, the pre-Islamic period (lit. 'the time of ignorance'), to the heyday of the cultivation of popular oral narratives from the twelfth to the nineteenth centuries. The writing down of the Qur'ānic revelation, marking the beginning of an era of parallel orality and literacy, and, from the third Islamic century onward, the existence of diglossia – the dichotomy of a learned standard language, in which 'true' texts are composed, and a vernacular of the unlettered, whose verbal productions cannot claim any truth – explain why Arab culture has not developed any narratives that are openly designated as epics, while it nevertheless possesses a genre that might be termed 'epic'.

If epic is understood in its widest sense as a narration of events that are of importance to a society and provide a grounding in its (primordial) past, as a narration that creates and consolidates identities and provides an orientation in the presence of the narrative,[1] then the art of oral epic composition and narration was known to the Arabs from earliest times. For the pre-Islamic Arabs, who led the life of nomads in a desolate expanse of desert, filled by the whiteness of glaring heat, poetry played a prominent role and was even the centre of their cultural creativity. In the pre-Islamic era, practically each of the nomadic groups (tribes, clans) on the Arabian Peninsula counted among its ranks a *shāʿir* or poet. The *shāʿir* was endowed with a special power of speech and was believed to be inspired through the world of spirits; his speech was both prophecy and spellbinding magic word. His main function, however, was that of a mouthpiece of his clan; he went to battle with his tribesmen, derided their enemies (*hijāʾ* 'satire') and countered their poets' attacks, praised his clan's past deeds of prowess and exalted their heroes (*fakhr*); he was the living memory and historian of his clan.[2] Poets have repeatedly con-

---

[1] See Assmann 1997 and Halbwachs 1925.
[2] The second caliph ʿUmar b. al-Khaṭṭāb (r. 13–23/634–644) is reported to have said that poetry is the *dīwān* (register, memory) of the Arabs.

tributed to victory by their presence in the front-line and have given consolation to the survivors of a battle by their poetic exaltation of the slain. Clans and tribes gathered habitually for poetic contests, frequently in connection with pilgrimages to the deities of pre-Islamic Arabia.³ To no small degree the weal and woe of a clan depended on the poetic talent of their *shāʿir*; a clan or tribe without a renowned poet counted for nothing.⁴ The *shāʿir* often had as associates one or more *rāwī*s, 'rhapsodes', transmitters of the clan's traditions in poetry and prose.⁵ We owe to them the preservation of (probably only a small part of) pre-Islamic poetry⁶ and at least partially also the transmission of mostly short prose narratives, some with inserted poems, about the so-called 'days of battle' of the Arabs before they united under the banner of Islam.⁷

These tales about pre-Islamic tribal feuds⁸ are recollections of small skirmishes, individual cattle-raids (*ghazwa*) or murders,⁹ but also of great wars between mighty tribal federations, which lasted for decades, and they are told again and again in the evening

---

³ In this way the famous *muʿallaqāt*, the 'suspended (verses)', came about; they were the verses of the best poets that were attached to the Kaʿaba in Mecca, which was a sanctuary already in the pre-Islamic era. Every pupil in the Arab world even today can quote by heart the 'suspended verses' of Imruʾ l-Qays and of ʿAntara b. Shaddād, to mention only the most famous of these poets. For the *muʿalaqāt*, see Lecomte 1993.

⁴ For the pre-Islamic tribal poets, see Blachère 1952–66: II, 383 ff. See also Fahd 1997. The tradition of oral poetry is still alive on the Arabian Peninsula today; see Sowayan 1985 and 1992; Kurpershoek 1994–99; Caton 1990.

⁵ For the *rāwī*, see Jacobi 1995. [See further ch. 5 on performance and performers by J. Harris and K. Reichl in this volume.]

⁶ The debate about the purely oral character of this tradition (see Zwettler 1978: 85–88) and the early use of writing, at least as a mnemotechnic help (see Sezgin 1967–2007: 53 ff.; Brockelmann 1943–49: II, 14 ff.; 22–33), has not yet been settled. Fuat Sezgin, who transfers insights from research on the Prophet's sayings and deeds (*ḥadīth*) to the transmission of poetry, conjectures with good reason that written poetry collections existed already in the early Islamic period. According to Jacobi (1987: 21) there are no unequivocal proofs for a written transmission as early as the sixth century. J. T. Monroe (1972) and M. Zwettler (1978) apply Parry's and Lord's oral theory (Lord 1960) to Old Arabic poetry and reach the conclusion that the Old Arabic *qaṣīda* is basically an orally composed genre in Parry's and Lord's sense. They have, however, expressed reservations about the uncritical application of the oral theory, formulated with regard to long anonymous South Slavic epics, to the Old Arabic poems, which are neither consistently narrative nor anonymous and are in addition relatively short. Hence, as Jacobi notes, 'their theories are in the end not as revolutionary [...] as it a first seemed' (1987: 22). It can nevertheless be supposed that pre-Islamic poetry was composed orally and probably for long periods of its early history was also transmitted orally. [See further ch. 2 on the oral-formulaic theory by J. M. Foley and P. Ramey in this volume.]

⁷ For the *ayyām al-ʿarab* see the authoritative work by Caskel 1931. Tribal feuds did not, of course, disappear after the introduction of Islam, but only few of them have been incorporated into the corpus of the *ayyām al-ʿarab*, which was put together in writing in the third Islamic century (ninth century). The reason for this is on the one hand the interest especially in the pre-Islamic 'pagan period' from a cultural and historical point of view, on the other that the acceptance of Islam meant the entry into a principally inner-Islamic peaceful society (*umma*).

⁸ The technical term for an *ayyām* report is *ḥadīth*, the same word which was later used for the accounts of the sayings and deeds of the Prophet Muḥammad.

⁹ 'Tribes among which there was no contract *muwādaʿa*, *ʿahd* [...], are in a state of war, i. e. they try to raid each other's herds in armed raids. [...] Even an assault on a family, a murder, counts as a "day"' (Caskel 1931: 2).

tribal meetings (*majālis*).¹⁰ In the second Islamic century (8th c.) the traditions of the *ayyām al-'arab* (as well as pre-Islamic poetry¹¹) were collected and written down by Arab philologists and preservers of documents about the pagan prehistory of the Arabs.¹² With reference to the preserved traditional layers of the Old Arabic epic material, Caskel has clearly demonstrated how extended epics can arise from even the smallest single narratives. He has convincingly shown how, the more remote the historical 'day of battle', the more these narratives developed from brief reports to voluminous 'chains of legends', in which several 'days' are woven into a narrative unity. Similarly, we can observe 'the predilection for romantic¹³ instead of realistic motifs and, instead of concise accounts, the preference for elaborately constructed tales' (1931:76). The 'battle days' of some clans which occurred shortly before unification under Islam (at least ideally) have been transmitted as brief single tales; the long wars that were presented as having lasted for decades and were thought to have been the feuds of whole tribes, ¹⁴ such as the wars of Basūs and Dāḥis, were placed several generations before the Prophet Muḥammad. Caskel writes that 'these wars were not real. They are the product of a tradition, in the course of which several "days" coalesced and were put into a frame. [...] The process of giving theses stories a frame was still fluid when the texts were written down [...]. There were certainly no wars of Dāḥis and Basūs, just as there was no war between the Bakr and the Tamīm, about which we could possibly read if the unsettling of the Old Arabic tradition by Islam had happened fifty years later.'¹⁵

The revelation of the Qur'ān, the 'collection of the texts recited by the Prophet Muḥammad between *c*. 610 and 632 as divine revelations issued to him' continues the cultural tradition, i. e. the tradition of the oral recitation of poetic and aesthetically

---

¹⁰ Caskel notes (1931): In the *majālis* 'even today the "days" of the present time are told.' As evidence Caskel quotes Leachmann's report from the military camp of Ibn Rashīd in 1910 [*The Geographic Journal*, March 1911, 271]: 'At night the conversation in the diwans is of a most enlightened character, chiefly consisting of battle stories or family history [...].' Caskel continues: 'As the heroes of these tales one might think of men like, in the present time, Ḥuwayṭāṭ–Shāikh 'Awda Abū Ṭayah, "the greatest fighting man in Northern Arabia", of whom Lawrence [of Arabia] writes: "He saw life as a saga. All the events in it were significant: all personages in contact with him heroic. His mind was stored with poems of old raids and epic tales of fights [...]'"' (1927:94).
¹¹ The hypothesis that the largest part of pre-Islamic poetry was faked, advanced simultaneously by the Egyptian Ṭāhā Ḥusain (1926) and by D. S. Margoliouth (1925), is meanwhile considered to have been proved wrong.
¹² Famous transmitters are al-Aṣmā'ī (d. 213/828) and Abū 'Ubaida (d. 210/825), as well as Ibn al-Kalbī (d. 204 or 206/819 or 821). The old *ayyām* books of these authors have been lost. Remnants have, however, been preserved in the works of later authors, as for instance in the *Kitāb al-Aghānī* of Abū l-Faraj al-Isfahānī (d. 356/967) and especially in the *'Iqd al-Farīd* of Ibn 'Abd ar-Rabbih (d. 328/940), both of whom tried to harmonize diverging sources, an effort that has not always led to a smooth result without contradictions. In the Abbasid era (2nd/8th – 7th/13th c.) knowledge of the 'days' of the pagan Arabs was part of 'humanistic education' (Caskel). Great universal historians and encyclopaedists of the post-classic period like Ibn al-Athīr (d. 630/1224) and an-Nuwairī (d. 732/1332) used the reports about the *ayyām al-'arab* for the section on the pre-Islamic history of Arabia.
¹³ Such as giving shelter, vendetta, heroic deeds.
¹⁴ This is unhistorical, as Caskel says, 'because these tribes form no political, but an ideal and genealogical unity' (Caskel 1931:76).
¹⁵ Caskel 1931:76–77. The 'war of the Bakr and Tamīm' could have been the title of the collection of many 'days' of these two tribal federations shortly before the advent of Islam.

pleasing texts; from a literary point of view, the Qur'ān certainly has such poetic and aesthetic qualities. Although the Qur'ān is not composed in a poetic metre, it nevertheless contains frequent passages in rhymed prose (*saj'*), and it was probably recited by the Prophet in an expressive and aesthetically impressive manner, not unlike the poetry of the pre-Islamic era. The poetic as well as the oral character of the Prophet's revelations is underlined by the words which 'a figure clothed in light' – the Archangel Gabriel according to Islamic tradition – spoke in the Prophet's first revelation in a cave near Mecca around the year 610:

> 'Iqra' bi-smi rabbika / alladhī khalaq /khalaqa l-insāna min 'alaq / iqra' wa-rabbuka l-akram / alladhī 'allama bi-l-qalam / 'allama l-insāna mā lam ya'lam [...]'[16]
>
> Recite: In the Name of thy Lord who created, created Man of a blood-clot. Recite: And thy Lord is the Most Generous, who taught by the Pen, taught Man that he knew not.

Orality is implied by the imperative *iqra'* of the verb *qara'a*, which means primarily 'to recite' and has taken on the meaning 'to read' only in the course of a later semantic development.[17] While the Qur'ānic revelation continues oral tradition, it also marks the beginning of the era of writing. For, in the early period of preaching Islam, the Qur'ān's recitator, the Prophet, found himself in a precarious competitive relationship to the adherents of Old Arabian polytheism and their preachings. The Prophet was repeatedly blamed for being no more than another of these poets (*shā'ir*) or magicians who tell invented tales.[18] Modern Qur'ān scholarship is of the opinion that the Qur'ān was written down very early on, an event which gave the Arabs a written 'book' (like earlier the Jews and the Christians with whom they were in contact);[19] this opinion is founded on the fact that it was vital for the survival of the young religion to distance itself from the reproach of poetry and magic. According to the Qur'ān scholar Angelika Neuwirth it is precisely this (dangerous) closeness to the modes of poetic reciting that makes it probable that even in the earliest period the Qur'ān was in fact not entirely recited and memorized without some help of writing.[20] At the latest, with the writing down of the Qur'ān in its canonical form under the third caliph 'Uthmān (r. 23/644–35/656), the

---

[16] Sura 96 Sūrat al-'Alaq/The Blood-Clot [i. e. the embryo], 1–5. English translations are taken from Arberry 1964 (here, p. 651).

[17] According to Muslim tradition, the Prophet was illiterate. The word Qur'ān comes from the same root as *qara'a*; it is a text to be recited. See also below n. 20.

[18] These reproaches have found their way into the Qur'ān in the form of vehement rejections; see, e. g., sura 21, 3; 5 (Sūrat al-Anbiyā'/The Prophets). According to unanimous opinion, this sura was revealed in Mecca; it therefore belongs to the suras of the early period, in which Muḥammad met with much hostility and was in the end forced into emigration (*hijra*) from Mecca to the oasis of Yathrib, the later Medina.'The evildoers whisper one to another, "Is this aught but a mortal like to yourselves? What, will you take to sorcery with your eyes open?" [...] Nay, but they say: "A hotchpotch of nightmares! Nay, he has forged it; nay, he is a poet [*shā'ir*]! Now therefore let him bring us a sign, even as the ancient ones were sent as Messengers"' (Arberry 1964: 323).

[19] The Qur'ān calls itself a 'book' (*kitāb*) in sura 2, 2 (al-Baqara/ The Cow), which was revealed at a relatively late date: 'That is the Book, wherein is no doubt, a guidance to the godfearing' (Arberry 1964: 2).

[20] See Neuwirth 1987: 102. Neuwirth argues from a philological point of view with reference to Syriac *qeryānā* that the Qur'ān, at least for a certain period of its genesis, was a lectionary or a collection of texts for liturgical recitation.

Qur'ān changed from the realm of primary orality to that of secondary orality, i. e. oral recitation on the basis of a fixed written text. The written text, which came about through the necessity to distance the Prophet from the poets and seers of the pre-Islamic period, to preserve the divine revelation verbatim,[21] to eliminate competing versions and to be on a par with Jewish and Christian 'possessors of the book', also marks a mental change: the transition to an era in which written texts are seen as composed by cultural authorities and hence endowed with a claim to being true, while oral works, especially those in the vernacular, in colloquial Arabic, which have not been put down in writing by authorities, are assigned an inferior status. From this we may understand how the writing down of the Qur'ān and the rise of a class of literate religious scholars, who have the monopoly of interpretation and who, following the Prophet, have defended the Qur'ān against all assimilation with poetry or legend (usṭūra),[22] have determined the attitude of Arabic-Islamic culture vis-à-vis oral fiction and in consequence oral epic as well. Nevertheless the Islamic scholarly world is until today characterized by the co-existence of orality and literacy. Central texts of religion, philosophy and all kinds of science were transmitted by word of mouth, side by side with their recording in writing; in fact, listening to the Prophet's tradition from the mouth of an authorized transmitter has always had a higher value than simply reading it in a manuscript.[23] The Arabic poetry which was cultivated in the courts during the first five Islamic centuries was always orally recited and partially also orally transmitted. The Qur'ān itself is memorized to this day and comes fully alive only in oral recitation (as a text intended for aural reception), while the written book of the Qur'ān often only serves as a prop for memory and a guarantor of the correct recitation of God's word (with the exception of blind recitators, who of course have no written props).

With the unprecedented victorious spread of Islam within only a few years over a huge territory with a non-Muslim and often non-Arab population, which was slowly but steadily Islamized, attacks of the Prophet's enemies on him and on the Qur'ān were pushed into the background. The definition of what is truth and what is lies, of what is history and what is legend was now in the hands of a cultivated class of specialists that belonged to the ruling Muslim minority. In that early period the narrative Jewish, Christian and South-Arabian traditions, which had probably circulated orally before, were writ-

---

[21] According to Islamic doctrine, the Qur'ān is the direct word of God: in his revelations, extending over more than twenty years, God is believed to have communicated the text to the Prophet Muḥammad with exactly these words and sounds. On the various schools of Qur'ānic interpretation, see Goldziher 1920.

[22] This reproach, in the form of a vehement rejection, has also found repeated expression in the Qur'ān, as, for instance, in sura 6 (al-An'ām/Cattle), 25; 28–29: 'And some of them there are that listen to thee [the Prophet], and We lay veils upon their hearts lest they understand it, and in their ears heaviness; and if they see any sign whatever, they do not believe in it, so that when they come to thee they dispute with thee, the unbelievers saying, "This is naught but the fairy-tales of the ancient ones [asāṭīr (pl. of usṭūra) al-awwalīn]." [...] they are truly liars. And they say, "There is only our present life; we shall not be raised."' (Arberry 1964: 123–24).

[23] This is the reason why Islamic scholars, in their early years and often during their entire life-time, travelled to search for knowledge (ar-riḥla fī ṭalab al-'ilm), to hear as many traditions about the Prophet and scholarly works directly from the mouth of an authorized transmitter (samā'a) and to receive from him a licence (ijāza) for (oral) transmission. See also Berkey 1992: 24.

ten down. According to Franz Rosenthal, these 'historical novels', as he calls them, 'became a part of historical literature which was no longer transmitted by storytellers, but by the ordinary process of written or oral scholarly transmission, and the novelistic origin of which was no longer realized' (1952:164). The wish to collect and write down these South-Arabian legends and tales about the Jewish prophets (called *isrā'īliyāt*) stems from the fact that the Qur'ān repeatedly either talks about or alludes to events of South-Arabian history and Jewish religious history, on the presupposition that those listening to the Qur'ān preached by the Prophet would already be familiar with these stories.[24] These stories, however, are never told consecutively from beginning to end as in the Hebrew Bible.[25]

As the knowledge of South-Arabian history or of the Hebrew Scriptures could not be expected of the newly converted Muslims in the conquered territories, and was often lacking also in native Muslim families, it had to be supplied in order to provide an understanding of the Qur'ān. These narrative traditions were therefore collected and written down, in particular by converted Jews and/or Yemenites, the most famous of whom was the Yemenite Wahb b. al-Munabbih (d. 110/728 or 114/732).[26] It can be assumed that these narratives, in addition to their place in Muslim exegesis and historiography, were soon also transmitted in the milieu of oral popular narratives, in particular at a period when an increasing number of people became Islamized; no traces of this have, however, been preserved from the early Islamic era.[27]

In the time of Wahb b. al-Munabbih, the second Islamic century (8th c.), the prose narratives about the life and deeds of the Prophet and the conquests during and after his life-time were written down. Summary descriptions of the Prophet's military expeditions (his 'battle days', *ayyām*), which are called *maghāzī*, arose as early as the first half of the second/eighth century, also from the pen of Wahb b. al-Munabbih, and, at a somewhat later date, the best-known older work of this genre, the *Kitāb al-Maghāzī* by 'Umar al-Wāqidī (d. 207/822) was composed (Leder 2005). Together with other sources, these tales furnished the building blocks of the Prophet's biography, the *Sīrat an-Nabbīy* or *Sīrat Rasūl Allāh*.[28] The natural continuation of the *maghāzī* and *sīra* literature were the so-called *futūḥ* (conquest) books, at first works about the conquest of individual countries, as for instance the *Kitāb futūḥ ash-Shām* (Book of the conquest of Syria) and the *Kitāb futūḥ al-'Irāq* (Book of the conquest of Mesopotamia) by Wahb b. al-Munabbih, both lost today.[29] Later on comprehensive descriptions were written, such as the

---

[24] How many of the Meccan listeners to the Qur'ān actually knew these events and stories is difficult to assess. It is nevertheless clear that the Qur'ān presupposes such a knowledge.

[25] In this the Qur'ān resembles pre-Islamic poetry, which also merely alludes to events that could be supposed to be known to the poet's audience. Here the Qur'ān is decidedly different from the consecutive narratives of the Bible.

[26] Important collectors in addition to Wahb b. al-Munabbih were Ka'b al-Aḥbār, (d. 32/652–653), a Yemenite Jew before his conversion to Islam and an authority on Biblical history and the South-Arabian tradition; 'Abdallāh b. Salām (d. 43/663–664), a Jew from Medina, who was converted to Islam by the Prophet himself; and Ibn Sharya, whose historicity is disputed.

[27] See below, p. 635, on the so-called *qiṣaṣ al-anbiyā'*.

[28] The most important *sīra* author is Ibn Isḥāq (d. 151/768). The original is lost; his work is preserved only in Ibn Hishām's (d. 215/830) revision. See further Busse 1987:264–68.

[29] To Ibn 'Abd al-Ḥakam (d. 257/871) is due a book on the conquest of Egypt and Northern Africa (*Kitāb futūḥ miṣr wa-l-maghrib*); Ibn Qūṭīya (son of a Gothic mother) (d. 367/977) wrote a work on the conquest of Spain, etc.

famous *Kitāb futūḥ al-buldān* (Book of the conquest of the countries) by al-Balādhurī (d. 279/892).

It is highly likely that in addition to the *sīra*, *maghāzī* and *futūḥ* literature composed by learned authors there circulated unauthorized, orally performed and transmitted popular *sīra*, *maghāzī* and *futūḥ* narratives from the earliest Islamic period onward.[30] Already from this period we have reports about spontaneous preachers and orators who told events from the life of the Prophet and his companions (*sīra*), from his and his successors' conquests (*maghāzī* and *futūḥ*) to their audience in the mosques or the bazaars in an attempt to familiarize them with the teachings of Islam. These popular preachers, generally called *qāṣṣ* (plural *quṣṣāṣ*; also *mudhakkir* or *wāʿiz*) (Pellat 1978), inserted into their sermons not only canonical South-Arabian legends and the *isrāʾīlīyāt* (Jewish Biblical tales), but also inauthentic narratives about the Prophet, tales from Iranian tradition and fantastical legends of all kinds of provenance, which resulted in their being forbidden to preach in the mosques. If one believes the criticism of the religious scholars, who were concerned about their monopoly of interpretation, then these preachers of religious 'truths' have to be seen in the vicinity of mountebanks and popular entertainers. It is said that already ʿAlī b. Abī Ṭālib, the Prophet's son-in-law, had expelled the *quṣṣāṣ* from the mosque of Baṣra. Many more interdictions followed, but apparently failed, since these narrators, while they did not preach any more in the mosques, had considerable success outside the mosques among the gullible masses. From this early period no texts of the popular *maghāzī* have been preserved; the extant texts come predominantly from the seventeenth century, some also from the fifteenth century.[31] The popular *maghāzī* of these late manuscripts are in part based on 'historic' events, but they are also in part creations of pure imagination. Their main hero, apart from Muḥammad, is especially his cousin and son-in-law ʿAlī b. Abī Ṭālib. From the twelfth century onward we have numerous learned, but also popular, often romance-like elaborated manuscript texts of the genre *qiṣaṣ al-anbiyāʾ*, stories about the pre-Islamic prophets, in which Islamic as well as extraneous narrative traditions about the prophets before Muḥammad (Qurʾān, South-Arabian legends, *isrāʾīlīyāt*) were woven into consistent narratives.[32] According to Rudi Paret the popular *futūḥ* tales were composed in the period between the ninth and eleventh centuries (possibly earlier in oral form) (1970:746). These 'romance-like enlarged legendary accounts' of the great Islamic conquests after Muḥammad's death – of ash-Shām (Syria), al-ʿIrāq (Mesopotamia), Miṣr (Egypt) – have generally been attributed to al-Wāqidī, the author of canonical *futūḥ* books, but cannot come from his pen on account of their style and contents; they are

---

[30] It can be inferred from the 'novellistic style of the accounts of some early Islamic historiographers such as Saif b. ʿUmar [who lived at the end of the second/eighth century] that in that period the process of popular fictionalization was already in full swing' (Heath 1990:428).

[31] About half of these texts name an enigmatic (Abū l-) Ḥasan al-Bakrī as *rāwī* (transmitter/ redactor/ author – the various nuances of this word are fluid), who is placed by Paret in the end of the thirteenth/ beginning of the fourteenth century. Paret bases his chronology on the traditional philological method, which, however, is not fully adequate to this type of literature. See Paret 1930:155–56.

[32] See Nagel 1967, 1986a and 1986b; Rippin 2002.

most probably anonymous, popular works, which were 'widely disseminated particularly during the Crusades as an incitement to the warriors for the faith'.[33]

The fact that, beginning with the ninth century, an increasing number of manuscripts of popular narratives concerning the legendary life of the prophets (*qiṣaṣ al-anbiyā'*) and the Islamic conquests (*maghāzī* and *futūḥ*) have come down to us, is an indication of a fundamental change in the Arabic language and culture of this time. While in the first two Islamic centuries (7th–8th c.) Arabic was the living language of the dominant minority in the conquered territories and underwent a process of standardization and adaptation in the works of Arab lexicographers and grammarians,[34] in the course of Islamization and Arabization there arose a situation of diglossia, in which a grammatically and lexically standardized, highly nuanced and complex written language was confronted by grammatically simpler, lexically reduced and regionally varying vernacular Arabic dialects. At the same time as this freezing of Classical Arabic into a pure language of writing and of the elite, starting roughly in the beginning of the fourth Islamic century (10th c.) (Fück 1950:86), and the powerful rise of spoken dialects, the political unity of Islam under a universal Islamic-Arab caliphate began to succumb to a spreading process of erosion. The old Arab elite was to a growing degree supplanted by a formerly unfree, at any rate non-Arab military class, which alone could guarantee the safety of the Arab Empire – at one time united and centrally administrated, but now broken up into single dominions – against the inroads of the Turks and Mongols from the East and the European Crusaders from the West. At the end of this development we have the Mongol conquest of Bagdad, the seat of the caliph, the murder of the last Abbasid caliph in Bagdad in 1258 and the definitive assumption of power by the Mamluks, a dynasty of originally military slaves, in the person of Sultan Baybars I in Egypt and Syria in 1260. While in the first three Islamic centuries (7th–9th c.) the elite was Arab or at least thoroughly Arabicized and the people accepted Arabic only slowly and for a long time still continued to compose, narrate and communicate in the old 'pre-Islamic' languages, the situation changed fundamentally from the tenth century onward. Now the ruling class often had an insufficient command of Arabic, and occasionally needed an interpreter to communicate with their administration, while the people became predominantly Arabicized from the twelfth century onward. In view of the lack of interest and also the linguistic incompetence of the elite, who often belonged to the military class, literature in Classical Arabic, which had flourished in the previous centuries, lost an important economic and cultural basis in the courts. At the same time the creative power of Arabic popular literature was greatly boosted. The time of Islamic synthesis had arrived (Heath 1990:424).

From the ninth and tenth centuries onward, in addition to the popular legends of the prophets and the tales of conquests, there flourished various types of folktales like the *Arabian Nights*, a collection of tales that gained world-fame in Europe but was long looked down upon in the Arab world on account of its popular nature.[35] We also find

---

[33] Brockelmann 1943–49: I, 142 (margin no. 136).
[34] This process of standardization also comprises lexical and syntactic changes which the Bedouin poetic language underwent when it developed to become the cultural and administrative language of an empire in the first/seventh and second/eighth centuries.
[35] See Littmann 1960; Gerhardt 1963; Miquel 1977 and 1981; Mahdī 1984–94 and 1995.

popular poetry that freed itself, at least partially, from the metrical rules of Classical Arabic poetry (Heath 1990:434). In the period beginning with the eleventh/twelfth century, on the stage of popular narrative a predominant role was played by the genre of the oral *sīra* (plural *siyar*), a popular pseudo-historical heroic tale about the biography of the main protagonist.[36] This exceedingly productive genre can with some justification be seen as a synthesis of (mostly) Arabic narrative material with a form that was imported from the Iranian area, an area that had once again become linguistically and politically independent of the Arab world. Both before and after Islamization, Iran had a flourishing tradition of popular heroic narratives,[37] of which some are also known in Arabic versions – such as *Sīrat Fīrūz Shāh* (The history of Fīrūz Shāh)[38] and *Qiṣṣat Bahrām* (The tale of Bahrām).[39] Apart from the synthesis of form, these popular *siyar* also represented a synthesis of content with regard to Islamic and Islamized cultures; they provided a kind of survey of almost the entire Islamic and pre-Islamic culture, which was now common to all Muslims. At times they engaged in a process of sorting out the transmitted heritage, of ordering and evaluating it anew, and of mentally separating the traditions worthy of preservation from those that did not conform to the Islamic order. The popular *siyar* at first creatively continued the form and spirit of their predecessors; later, however, the newly composed *siyar* themselves became models for new tales about the more recent past, for which there were no exemplars in Old Arabian or non-Arab history. The *ayyām al-ʿarab* and *futūḥ* narratives were thus continued (with the addition of the originally Iranian episodic, often cyclically expanded heroic biography) in the *Sīrat az-Zīr Sālim*, the *Sīrat ʿAntara b. Shaddād* and the *Sīrat Dhāt al-Himma*. The *Sīrat az-Zīr Sālim* and the *Sīrat ʿAntara b. Shaddād* are continuations of the *ayyām al-ʿarab* narratives about the so-called Basūs war between the tribes of the Bakr and the Taghlib.[40] The historical ʿAntara of the *Sīrat ʿAntara b. Shaddād* was one of the authors of the poems that were suspended on the Kaʿba on account of their poetic qualities (*muʿallaqāt*, see above); elements of pre-Islamic history were hence preserved in this character. The *Sīrat Dhāt al-Himma* (*wa-Baṭṭāl*), on the other hand, treats of tribal feuds and the *jihād* on the border of Syria/Mesopotamia and the Byzantine Empire at the time of the Umayyads (7th–8th c.) and the Abbasids (8th–13th c.).[41] It continues in an entirely pseudo-historical way the genre of the *futūḥ* in the form of the popular

---

[36] Surveys of scholarship on the *siyar* are found in Canova 1977; Heath 1984; Canova 2003b; and Herzog 2006:5–10. Easy access to the contents of the most important *siyar* is provided by Lyons 1995.

[37] On Iranian epic, see Rypka 1968:44–45, 151–166 and 617–648. See also Hanaway 1970. [See also ch. 25 on medieval Persian epic and narrative by J. Rubanovich in this volume.]

[38] This tale deals with early Iranian history; its main hero is the son of the Achaemenid king Darius II. See Grant 2003

[39] Also called *Qiṣṣat Bahrām Gūr*. The action takes place in the time of the Sassanian dynasty. See Hanaway 1974; Pantke 1974. The *Sīrat Iskandar*, the popular romance of Alexander the Great, does likewise not orignate in an Arabic milieu. See Doufikar-Aerts 2003 [and also in ch. 25 (J. Rubanovich) pp. 661 ff.].

[40] On the *Sīrat az-Zīr*, see Oliverius 1965 and 1971; Gavillet-Matar 2005. On the *Sīrat ʿAntara b. Shaddād*, see Norris 1980; Heath 1996; Herzog 2005; see also Cherkaoui 201a and 2001b.

[41] On the *Sīrat Dhāt al-Himma*, see Steinbach 1972 and Ott 2003. The text has been edited in seventy parts in Cairo (see *Sīrat Dhāt al-Himma*).

heroic legend.⁴² One of the other conquest *siyar* that have their basis in an Arab tribal milieu is the decidedly popular *Sīrat Banī Hilāl* (or *Sīra hilālīya*). The *Sīrat az-Zīr Sālim*, mentioned already, serves as its 'prologue'; here, as in the *ayyām al-'arab* narratives, we find the formation of legendary cycles, into which several, originally independent traditions are woven to form one great narrative. This narrative has as its subject the forced emigration of the Banū Hilāl from the Arabian Peninsula and their move to the west to Morocco (which took place in the eleventh century).⁴³ Although the *Sīrat Saif b. Dhī Yazan* does not have its origin in history, it does use South-Arabian legendary traditions as they were collected by men like Wahb b. al-Munabbih as a background to its colourful tale, packed with demons and witchcraft (Paret 1924). One of the reasons for seeing an 'Islamic synthesis' in these popular Arabian *siyar* is that some of their pre-Islamic, in reality pagan Arab heroes – such as 'Antara b. Shaddād and Saif b. Dhī Yazan – are reinterpreted as forerunners of the Prophet Muḥammad (Paret 1927: 12–13). The figure of 'Antara b. Shaddād – the son of an Abyssinian slave-girl and an Arabian sheikh, who has fallen in love with his cousin 'Abla and has to fight for a long time to be acknowledged as a free warrior – illustrates the process of sifting and re-arranging the inherited traditions. The *Sīrat 'Antar* begins with a long auctorial passage in which the contrast between 'Antar, who has paved the way for Islam, and his enemies, who persist in their pagan vices, is underlined:

> [We are told of] the courageous bedouins of pre-Islamic times (*'urban al-jāhilīya ash-shuj'ān*), how they adored false gods and how they retreated full of veneration to idols and oracle shafts. The Devil (*ash-shaiṭān*) had led them astray [...]. Every one of them wanted to be esteemed alone of all the world – the brave among them were fervently hated. They did not fear God and did not seek his nearness; they had no awe of him and did not hold him in respect. When God, however, wants to destroy a people he lets pride and arrogance enter their hearts. Then he humiliates them, subdues them with the help of the lowliest and despises them. This is easy for him. This he did with the help of the slave [...] 'Antar b. Shaddād, who in his time was like a spark that sprang from kindling wood. Through him God subdued the tyrants at the time of ignorance (*al-jabābira fī zaman al-jāhilīya*), so that he ['Antar] might pave the way for the coming of your lord Muḥammad, the noblest of men. (*Sīrat 'Antara*: I, 3–4)

This contrast is repeatedly mentioned throughout the epic. 'Antar and his friends are shining examples of the Bedouin ideals; he is the protector of the poor, the weak and the women; he is generous, brave and lofty, filled by a true sense of honour. His enemies, however, accord to the negative stereotype of the pre-Islamic bedouin: they are selfish tyrants, who hate the courageous and the noble and again and again resort to treacherous tricks in battle. The words, too, which the narrator puts in the mouths of 'Antar's enemies are meant to show that they have fully submitted to the spirit of paganism. They repeatedly swear by the pre-Islamic deities, something that 'Antar never does; even

---

⁴² On the parallels in *Digenis Akritis*, see Grégoire and Goossens 1934. [See also ch. 17 on medieval Greek epic poetry by E. Jeffreys in this volume.] The *Sīrat Ḥamza* is also a *jihād* narrative; it tells the story of Hamza b. 'Abd al-Muṭallib, the Prophet's uncle (see *Qiṣṣat Ḥamza*; Meredith-Owens 1986).

⁴³ The *Sīrat Banī Hilāl* has been well researched; see, *inter alia*, Pantůček 1970; Saada 1985; Connelly 1986; Slyomovics 1987; Galley and Ayyub 1983; Nacib 1994; Reynolds 1995.

his mother swears by 'the one and only [God], by him who has ordered dawn to light up in the sky'.[44] In addition, a certain parallelism between 'Antar and the Prophet is developed. Like the Prophet, 'Antar causes offence to his tribe by his conduct and is rejected by some of the influential members of his tribe. 'Antar, too, questions the pre-Islamic order, not by preaching a new religion which introduces new social norms, but by his demand to be recognized as a fully free Arab, even if he is the fruit of a union that is not legitimized through the marriage of freeborn partners and although the colour of his skin is black. Like the Prophet, 'Antar emigrates from his tribe and temporarily fights against it until he is finally recognized and can return. When one thinks of the enormous impact of the Prophet's biography on the Islamic world, this parallel is not surprising; it underscores once again the Islamic character of the narrative material and of the tale itself. A further development of the *siyar* genre, the 'urban' *siyar*, which were composed shortly before and during the Mamluk period, leave the Arab tribal milieu: the *Sīrat al-Ḥākim bi-Amrillāh*, whose plot is centred on the Fatimid caliph Ḥākim bi-Amrillāh (r. 386/996–411/1021); the *Sīrat al-Malik aẓ-Ẓāhir Baybars*, which until recently was extremely popular;[45] and smaller cycles on Aḥmad ad-Danaf and 'Alī az-Zaibaq, two clearly untypical protagonists.

In the Arabic East (Egypt, Palestine, Syria, Iraq), the places where the popular *siyar* were performed prior to the Ottoman period (before the sixteenth century) were in all probability the same as those where the *quṣṣāṣ* had recited their works at an earlier time: in front of the mosque, in the *ḥammām* (public bath), on public squares and streets and at the men's social gatherings in the evening. Al-Maqrīzī (d. 845/1442) reports that at the end of the twelfth century groups were to be found in the evenings on Cairo's most-frequented thorough-fare of the time, the Khaṭṭ Baina al-Qaṣrāin, in which the *siyar* und *akhbār* were recited and other kinds of entertainment provided:

> When the days of the Fāṭimids were coming to an end [...] this place turned into a bazaar [...], a promenade where the nobles and their like walked on foot in the evening to see the enormous multitude of candles and lanterns and everything that men long for and that delights their eyes and gladdens their senses. There used to sit a number of groups, where *siyar*, *akhbār* and poems were recited and where all kinds of games and pastimes were indulged in. There was such a crowd in this place, whose number cannot be calculated and which can be neither related nor described. (Maqrīzī: 1853–54: II, 28, lines 18 ff.)

From the sixteenth/seventeenth centuries onward, the *siyar* were probably recited more and more in the simple coffee-houses of the common people. For the eighteenth and nineteenth centuries, at any rate, we have, from the descriptions of European travellers and from Arabic sources, ample evidence of the style of these coffee-house narrators, who performed the *siyar* into the 1960s in Syria and Egypt. The 'Encyclopedia of the Trades of Damascus', the German Carsten Niebuhr, who travelled in the service of the king of Denmark, the authors of the *Description de l'Égypte* and the Englishman E. W.

---

[44] *Sīrat 'Antar b. Shaddād*, Paris, BnF MS arabe 3790, fol. 113b, line 1.
[45] On the *Sīrat Baybars*, which has been well researched, see Wangelin 1936; French translation by Bohas and Guillaume 1985 ff., as well as a number of articles by Bohas, Guillaume, and Herzog (see the bibliography in Herzog 2006); Vidal Luengo 2000; Garcin 2003; Zakharia 2004; and the detailed monograph Herzog 2006.

Lane give us an essentially identical picture:[46] the popular narrators patronize the coffee-houses in order to recite the popular *siyar* to the guests from a raised seat, with or without the *rabāba*, a one-stringed fiddle. As Lane writes:

> Reciters of romances frequent the principal kahwehs (or coffee-shops) of Cairo and other towns, particularly on the evenings of religious festivals, and afford attractive and rational entertainments. The reciter generally seats himself upon a small stool on the maṣṭabah, or raised seat, which is built against the front of the coffee-shop: some of his auditors occupy the rest of that seat, others arrange themselves upon the maṣṭabahs of the houses on the opposite side of the narrow street, and the rest sit upon stools or benches made of palmsticks; most of them with the pipe in hand; some sipping their coffee; and all highly amused, not only with the story, but also with the lively and dramatic manner of the narrator. The reciter receives a trifling sum of money from the keeper of the coffee-shop, for attracting customers: his hearers are not obliged to contribute anything for remuneration: many of them give nothing; and few give more than five or ten faḍḍahs.[47]

24 – 'A Shá'er, with his accompanying Violist, and part of his Audience' (Lane, p. 393)

---

[46] See Qāsimī 1960, 112–14; Niebuhr 1772: 106–7; Panckoucke 1826: 161–62.
[47] Lane 1860: 391. Compare Kremer 1863: II, 305–6.

The performance sometimes assumed theatrical traits. According to the information of the late owner of the Damascus coffee-house an-Nawfara, Aḥmad ar-Ribāṭ/Abū Ṣāliḥ, some narrators ran up and down in the coffee-house and, with a helmet on their heads and a wooden sword in their hands, imitated the actions of the heroes (Aswad 1990:59). The *ḥakawātī* (narrator) Abū Aḥmad al-Munʻish is said to have recited the *Sīrat al-Malik az-Ẓāhir Baybars* by heart and in dialect and to have imitated the protagonists' way of speaking, while walking from one end of the coffee-house to the other. Despite his great age, Abū Aḥmad al-Munʻish rushed on the imaginary enemies of his hero and 'destroyed' them with his wooden sword.[48] Often the coffee-house narrators would recite their texts freely or use a manuscript merely as a memory aid.[49] Only the *Sīrat ʻAntar*, which is predominantly composed in Classical Arabic and therefore occupies a special position, was apparently regularly read from manuscripts. There was no lack of coffee-houses in which narrators were active, although perhaps not all coffee-houses have narrators, as the 'Encyclopedia of the Trades of Damascus' maintains (Qāsimī 1960:112). According to Johann Gottfried Wetzstein, the Prussian consul in Damascus, in the 1860s the *Sīrat Baybars* alone was recited every evening in three dozen coffee-houses; Seetzen speaks of thirty narrators in Cairo in 1809, while Lane assumes the existence of about one hundred narrators in the Cairo of the 1820s and 1830s.[50] Lane distinguishes three groups of narrators, decreasing in number: about fifty narrators of the *Sīrat Banī Hilāl*, called *shuʻarā* (poets), who are accompanied by the *rabāba* and chant the verses from memory (1860:392); about thirty *muḥaddithīn* (storytellers), who recite the *Sīrat Baybars* – a work 'written in the most vulgar style of modern Egyptian Arabic' – from memory and without instrumental accompaniment (400); finally about six *ʻantarīya*, who recite the *Sīrat ʻAntar* from a book. Lane adds that the inserted verse passages were chanted, while the prose was read 'in the popular manner'. In addition to the *Sīrat ʻAntar*, which was only imperfectly understood by their audience, the *ʻantarīya* also performed the *Sīrat Dhāt al-Himma*, the *Sīrat Saif b. Dhī Yazan* and sometimes too *Alf Laila wa-Laila*, the *Arabian Nights* (414). According to Niebuhr, who travelled in Syria and Egypt during the second half of the eighteenth century, the adventures of Rustām Zāl, a Persian hero from the *Shāh-nāma*, the history of the Ayyūbids and the tale of Baḥlūl-dāne, a clown at the court of Hārūn ar-Rashīd, were also told in the coffee-houses (1772:106–7). There is no reason to doubt that the repertoire of these narrators comprised also the Romance of Alexander, other *siyar shaʻbīya* (popular *siyar*) and all kinds of tales. Niebuhr calls the narrators 'poor scholars (Mullâs)', which indicates their social origin (107). Some of the Syrian narrators of the late nineteenth and the twentieth centuries, whose traces I have followed in an earlier study, come from both a poor

---

[48] Aswad 1990:61. The term *ḥakawātī* (pl. *ḥakawātīya*) is used for popular narrators in Syria.
[49] Such a memory aid is, e. g., the manuscript Ahlwardt 1896, no. 9164 (Spr 1355) of the *Sīrat Baybars*; see Herzog 2006:33, 432 and 437. In al-Budayrī's local chronicle *Ḥawādith Dimashq al-yaumīya* from the eighteenth century we read about the *ḥakawātī* Sulaimān al-Ḥashīsh, who told the *Sīrat az-Ẓāhir*, the *Sīrat ʻAntara*, the *Sīrat Saif* and curious anecdotes from Turkish and Arabic (*nawādir gharība min at-turkī wa-l-ʻarabī*), although he was illiterate. Budayrī 1959:43.
[50] Wolff 1864. – Seetzen is said to have been informed by the sheikh of narrators in 1809 that 'in Kahira there are thirty public narrators under him' (Wangelin 1936:307–8, where unfortunately no sources are given).

and an uneducated background (Herzog 1994:19–21). Abū l-Ḥann, a *ḥakawātī* from Aleppo, was a demobilized soldier of the Ottoman Empire, who earned his living as a narrator after his return to his home town in 1920, an occupation that he followed until 1960.[51] Abū ʿAlī Shāhīn, who was active in Damascus coffee-houses from 1890 until 1920, worked in the sericulture trade and his colleague Abū Aḥmad al-Munʿish was a sweets vendor during the day. By their performances in the evening they supplemented their income (Aswad 1990:57, 61).

The *siyar* were not only publicly performed in the coffee-houses, they were also read privately; people would frequently borrow a written version from a scribe or manuscript lender (*warrāq*) either to read the *sīra* on their own or to read it out aloud in a circle of family, friends and acquaintances. These private readers were persons who were unable to assist the narrators' recitals in popular coffee-houses on account of their social position or their sex, or who were living away from the towns and had no coffee-houses with *siyar* performances in their vicinity. In my study of the manuscripts of *Sīrat Baybars* in the possession of Abū Aḥmad, I was able to show on the basis of readers' annotations in the manuscripts that a number of them were used for reading and reciting in the villages around Damascus in the first half of the twentieth century (Herzog 1995:66–80).

Like the popular *maghāzī* and *futūḥ* narratives, the popular *siyar* were put into writing at a very early time. On the one hand this was done to preserve an exceptionally successful version as a model for future narrators.[52] Having a *siyar* in written form made it possible, on the other hand, to enjoy the stories as a private reader. From as early as the twelfth century we have two accounts by doctors who in their youth read (and also copied) stories (*aḥādīth*) about ʿAntara b. Shaddād. Thus the physician and minor poet Abū al-Muʾayyad Ibn aṣ-Ṣāʾigh, who lived in the middle of the sixth/twelfth century, earned his bread in his younger years by copying *aḥādīth* of ʿAntar.[53] In the same period, the Bagdad physician and mathematician as-Samawʾal Ibn Yaḥya al-Maghribī (d. c. 575–76/1180) mentions in his autobiography that between the ages of ten to thirteen he loved to read stories and tales of past centuries, long poems and legends, like the tales about ʿAntar, Dhāt al-Himma wa-l-Baṭṭāl, Alexander the Great, al-ʿAnqāʾ, aṭ-Ṭaraf b. Lūdhān and others (Schreiner 1898:127). The fifteenth-century writer as-Sakhāwī (830(1427–902/1497) tells a story about the miller Khalīl from near the Bāb al-Qarāfa in Cairo who possessed a number of notebooks (*kurrāsa*) of the *Sīrat ʿAntar* and the *Sīrat Dhāt al-Himma* as well as tales about the great Arab hero ʿAmr b. al-ʿĀṣ and about the Prophet's companions. Khalil, as-Sakhāwī writes, gave these notebooks to Sheikh Badr ad-Dīn Sharabdār, a famous popular preacher, to be recited to a paying audience, which the latter, however, declined for unknown reasons. This story about a miller shows that the popular *siyar*, *maghāzī* and *futūḥ* also

---

[51] Interview with Muḥammad Yaḥyā Ḥamawī, Aleppo, 5 February 1994 (by Thomas Herzog).
[52] Nevertheless the transmission of the *siyar* basically takes place orally. The manuscripts of the *Sīrat az-Zīr Sālim* and the *Sīrat Baybars*, for instance, document that orality frequently played a role in the transmission of these *siyar*. It can be shown that some of these texts are dictated texts; M. Gavillet Matar (2005:70) has identified cases of phonetic orthography that have arisen thanks to dictation in a Berlin manuscript of the *Sīrat az-Zīr Sālim*. Some texts have clearly been written down from memory, probably going back to an oral performance; see Herzog 2006:147.
[53] *Yaktubu:* probably in the sense of 'copy'. Ibn Abī Uṣaybiʿa 1884: II, 290–97.

circulated among tradesmen.⁵⁴ Most of the extant manuscripts of the popular *siyar* date from the seventeenth, eighteenth and nineteenth centuries;⁵⁵ some *siyar* have been preserved in manuscripts from the twelfth century.

All popular *siyar* share a number of characteristics. They are generally anonymous productions, with no known author, despite their attribution to famous authors, as with the popular *futūḥ* narratives. They are composed in a kind of *kunstsprache*, an idiom, in which elements of Classical Arabic are combined with traits of colloquial Arabic.⁵⁶ Although the perfomance of the *siyar* is situated in a popular milieu, they contain often intertextual references, not only to other popular *maghāzī*, *futūḥ* and *siyar*, but also to scholarly works, for instance in the field of historiography.

This shows that men of a certain level of education were also involved in the composition and transmission of these *siyar*, a fact that contradicts the widely held thesis of the purely popular character of this type of literature.⁵⁷ The authors/ redactors/ narrators of the popular *siyar* often rely greatly on a limited number of narrative patterns and motifs, which they combine ever anew with the plots and figures of the narratives.⁵⁸ As a rule, the *siyar* are divided into episodes; these sometimes have a title in the manuscripts, and form self-contained units.⁵⁹ As is true of most anonymous popular epic tales, there are as many versions of a *sīra* as there were performances. Even in the frequent case when a *sīra* was not fully recited from memory, the recital from manuscripts nevertheless left room for free invention. The *siyar* finally developed into extended narratives with a tendency to form cycles of tales. Many *siyar* are characterized by a large number of stereotypical expressions; furthermore, the language of the passages in rhymed prose (*saj'*) is highly formulaic.⁶⁰

The formulaic nature of the passages in rhymed prose in the popular *siyar* points to the hybrid oral-written character of the *siyar* transmitted in manuscripts. As Claudia Ott has shown in connection with the *Sīrat Dhāt al-Himma*, the medium of these texts is, of course, writing, while their conceptualization is mostly due to orality, but also to literacy.⁶¹ The oral theory developed by Parry and Lord in connection with the Homeric

---

⁵⁴ See Sakhāwī 1934–36: VII, 224–25 (quoted from Shoshan 1993: 350).
⁵⁵ They have often found their way into the archives of European libraries. For the *Sīrat Baybars*, see Herzog 2006: 31 ff.
⁵⁶ This variety of Arabic is often termed 'Middle Arabic'; see Fück 1950: 57–62; Blau 1966–67: *passim*. I try to avoid this term, because it suggests a developmental stage in the history of Arabic (as with Middle High German, Middle English etc.), which does not apply, however, to the diglossic situation of Arabic.
⁵⁷ On the intertextuality of the *Sīrat Baybars* and learned Arabic historiography, see Herzog 2006: 358–92.
⁵⁸ This trait is typical of popular improvised tales, in which within the framework of a basic plot, the narrator builds new episodic adventures for his heroes from a limited number of linguistic and narrative units.
⁵⁹ The episodes in the popular *siyar* can be compared to the episodes of a television serial; on the whole they form complete stories which can be understood even by an infrequent listener who knows only the basic plot and the main characters of the narrative.
⁶⁰ On the formulaic character of the passages in rhymed prose in the manuscript of the *Sīrat Dhāt al-Himma*, see Ott 2003: 141 ff. On the *Sīrat Baybars*, see Herzog 1994 and Guillaume 2004.
⁶¹ On the difference between the conceptual and medial aspects of orality, see Raible 1994 and Koch and Oesterreicher 1994.

epics and South Slavic heroic poetry cannot be applied mechanically to the Arabic *siyar*: the texts have not been composed purely orally, but rather in an interplay of orality and literacy, both in creation and transmission; and almost all *siyar*, with the notable exception of the *Sīrat Banī Hilāl*,[62] are in prose or rhymed prose rather than in verse.[63] There is nevertheless a justification for applying the oral theory to the Arabic popular *siyar*. The passages in rhymed prose in the *siyar* are characterized by a high incidence of formulas, as shown by Ott in the *Sīrat Dhāt al-Himma* and by Guillaume in the *Sīrat Baybars*, which leads to the conclusion that the written text reflects an original orality. These formulas do not usually advance the action, but are rather found in descriptions or at turning-points of the narrative. Ott has pointed out the presence of formulas in the *Sīrat Dhāt al-Himma* at places where the times of the day are indicated, where landscapes or the beauty of a man, woman or horse are described, where the sudden arousal of fear, surprise, anger or joy is expressed and where battles and fights are depicted. The descriptions of battles are in their entirety formulaic to such a degree that they can be called 'themes' in the terminology of the oral theory (2003: 145). A brief example is the depiction of dawn, which is identically expressed in the *Sīrat Dhāt al-Himma* studied by Ott and in the *Sīrat 'Antara b. Shaddād*, in the *Sīrat Baybars* and without doubt also in other popular *siyar*:

> fa-lamma aṣbaḥa ṣ–ṣabāḥ
> wa-aḍā'a bi-nūrihi wa-lāḥ [...]

and as morning dawned/ and shone and gleamed with its light [...][64]

With reference to four *siyar* (*Sīrat 'Antara*, *Sīrat Dhāt al-Himma*, *Sīrat az-Zīr Sālim* and *Sīrat Banī Hilāl*), Madeyska was able to show that in addition to fixed formulas there are more often variable formulas which consist of keywords and variable words for which synonyms can be substituted. For the concept 'to be killed', for examples, the following variable formula is found:[65]

> *saqā/asqā/shariba*
> <u>*ka's*</u>
> *al-ḥimām/ar-radāl/al-'aṭab/al-mahālik/al-maniyyāt/at-talaf/al-ajal*

The keyword is *ka's* 'cup' (underlined in the middle), the formula is 'to drink the cup of death', where 'to drink' can be replaced by 'to give to drink' (*saqā*) or 'to sip' (*asqā, shariba*) and 'death' (*al-ḥimām*) by synonyms such as 'destruction', 'doom' etc. (*ar-radāl* etc.).

---

[62] Until the recent past and partly until today, wandering bards (called *shā'ir*) recited the *Sīrat Banī Hilāl* from memory in the villages of Upper and Lower Egypt. Although their performance is based on a memorized text, every performance creates a new text with the help of previously acquired formulas, themes, and narrative patterns. On the performance of the *Sīrat Banī Hilāl* in Egypt, see, *inter alia*, Connelly 1986; Slyomovics 1987; Reynolds 1995; on Algeria, see Nacib 1994. See also the 'Sirat Bani Hilal Digital Archive' (edited by D. Reynolds) at <http://www.siratbanihilal.ucsb.edu/>.

[63] See Guillaume 2004: 56–58, and Ott 2003: 144. On the question of whether the *siyar* can be called 'epics' comparable to the texts that formed the basis of Parry's and Lord's theory, see below, p. 645.

[64] See Ott 2003: 145, and Guillaume 204: 59.

[65] Madeyska 1993: 52 (quoted in Ott 2003: 149).

The beginning of a new episode is also stereotypically formulaic. In the *Sīrat Baybars*, the new episode, after mentioning the calm and stability at the end of the previous episode, almost always starts with the words:

> ilā an kāna yawm min al-ayyām / kāna l-malik jālis / fī ṣadr al-majālis / yaqẓān ghair nā'is [...] (Guillaume 2004: 60)
>
> Until one of these days / the king was sitting / at the head of the council, / fully awake and not sleepy [...]

Also formulaic are the passages that describe the orally conceived rituals of the coffeehouse performance in the manuscript texts (Ott 2003: 155–60). They comprise the naming of the narrator, the *qāla r-rāwī* formula (the narrator said), which occurs at the narrative's intersection points (*qāla r-rāwī/qāla n-nāqil, yā sāda ya kirām*); calls to prayer with the so-called *ṣallū* formula, a blessing of the Prophet (*ṣallā llāhu 'alā nabīyyinā Muḥammad, ṣallā llāhu 'alaihi wa-sallama*), with variants; appeals to the audience to *listen* (*ayyuhā s-sāmi'* [...], 'O listeners [...]'); the *basmalla* formula, the ritual expression *bismillāh* (in the name of God); finally the night formula, which refers back to the narrative situation and which is always used when the recital is interrupted, generally at a particularly dramatic point in the narrative: *wa-l-lail amsā wa-tamām al-ḥadīth fī-l-juz' illī (alladhī) warā'uhu*, 'Night has come on and the continuation follows in the next part.' Finally, all *siyar* passages containing direct speech are lexically, morphologically and syntactically very close to dialect and colloquial speech. Here the attempt to transfer oral speech into the written medium is most noticeable (Ott 2003: 151).

So much for the dominance of conceptual orality in the manuscripts of the *siyar*. The *siyar* in manuscripts (and, from the end of the nineteenth century, in numerous printed editions) also exhibit the opposite phenomenon, i. e. conceptual literacy: the endeavour, in terms of style and self-presentation, to approach as closely as possible the model of learned historiography, written in Classical Arabic. Examples of this are the frequent hypercorrect passages, which demonstrate the (failed) effort to employ an erudite manner of writing, and above all the choice of words, which are meant to prove that the *sīra* in question is a text that has been collected, compiled, transmitted, written down and copied according to the established scholarly norms.[66] All the *siyar* with which I am familiar contain an attribution to a learned transmitter, redactor or author. The *Sīrat 'Antara b. Shaddād*, for instance, states at its very beginning that the famous polygrapher al-Aṣma'ī (d. 213/828) was one of the *rāwīs* of this *sīra*. The text underlines its trustworthiness by identifying him as one of the transmitters of the *ḥadīth*s of the Prophet Muḥammad.[67] After citing several other canonical *ḥadīth*-transmitters and claiming them to be authors of the *sīra*, the text affirms that each of them transmitted (*rawā*) what he saw (*mā shahida*) [...] and what he had heard from trustworthy people who were present at the (pre-Islamic) Bedouins' battles.[68] The text of the Cairo edition of *Sīrat Baybars* claims in a very similar way to be based on the eye-witness report (*mā*

---

[66] See the examples in Ott 2003: 163–68.
[67] *Wa-huwa min jumlati man rawā l-ḥadīth 'an rasūli l-lāh. Qiṣṣat 'Antara*: 5.
[68] *Wa-sami'a 'amman yūthaqu bihi mimman ḥaḍara waqā'ia al-'urbān. Qiṣṣat 'Antara*: 5–6.

*shāhadūhu wa-mā 'āyanūhu*) of the 'renowned noble scholars' ad-Dīnārī and ad-Duwaidārī and on what they learned from other trustworthy sources.[69]

This attribution to a learned authorship brings us back to the break which had occurred with the writing down of the Qur'ān and with the formation of a written, educated literature in the Classical language by an elite that had the monopoly of defining what was to be counted as truth and what as a lie. The criticism of the Prophet's adversaries that his preaching was nothing but poetry, led pre-modern Arab scholars to postulate a contrast between learned, serious, allegedly factual and popular, allegedly non-factual narratives and to characterize the latter as lies.[70] Learned scholars in Arab-Islamic culture often vigorously denounced the imaginary world of storytelling, especially when it touched on the field of history. These scholars often characterized such stories as mere inventions or dangerous lies which do not serve God and waste the time of the believers,[71] and then juxtaposed them with trustworthy accounts in the official *hadith* and historiographical traditions.[72] In order not to be condemned in this way, the composers of the *siyar* passed their works off as the texts of great scholars, as historiographical scientific accounts rather than fictional epic narratives. Unlike listening to popular fairytales or texts like the *Arabian Nights*, pre-modern Arab listeners and readers of *siyar* simply could not understand these texts as works of imagination, since they were trapped by the implicit prohibition on invention or the propagation of fictional events and persons, especially if they were meant to relate closely to the history of the *umma*, the Muslim nation. Arab pre-modern audiences had to perceive the narratives either as more or less *true* accounts about the past or as more or less sophisticated *lies*, or as an intricate mixture of both. Even if some audiences may have more or less consciously experienced the storyteller's historical narration as a moment of playful imagination situated in the forbidden no-man's-land where truth and lies cohabit, pre-modern Arabic society could not overtly articulate their pleasure, but had to conceal it and pretend that they were listening to serious, truthfully transmitted, educational accounts of history. In a typically elitist stance, Rudi Paret denied the popular *futūḥ* narratives their qualification as epics, precisely because of their guise as historiographical accounts and their 'low artistic level' (an appraisal basically also applicable to the *siyar*).[73] With this opinion he

---

[69] *As-sādāt al-kirām al-mashhūrīn bi-l-'ilm wa-'ulwi l-maqām ad-Dīnārī wa-d-Duwaidārī wa-mā naqalūhu min as-sāda min ikhwānihim al-ladhīna ya'timidūna min kalāmi ṣ-ṣidq 'alaihim. Sīrat al-Malik al-Ẓāhir*: 10–11; practically identical to Paris, BnF MS arabe 4981, fol. 1b–2a.

[70] The following remarks on fiction and Arabic *siyar* are taken from Herzog 2010.

[71] The famous Tāj ad-Dīn as-Subkī (d. 771/1370) wrote: 'The copyists have the duty to keep away from copying books that do not serve God, such as the *Sīrat 'Antar* and various other works of imagination, which waste your time and which are of no use to religion.' *'Al-kutub al-latī lā–yanfa' allāh bihā ka-Sīrat 'Antar'* (Myhrman 1908: 186).

[72] At the end of the fifteenth century, the *faqīh* al-Wansharīsī (d. 1508) cites the *fatwa* of one of his colleagues, Ibn Qaddāḥ, who stated that it was forbidden to sell the popular *siyar* and other narratives of notoriously untruthful character. A reader of the *Sīrat 'Antar* could neither be an *imām*, nor a witness in court, because he was incapable of distinguishing truth from lies. A person believing lies of that kind, should be considered a liar himself or herself. Grunebaum 1963: 573, note 73. Grunebaum cites Pérès 1958: 33.

[73] 'An sich würde manches für eine positive Antwort [auf die zuvor gestellte Frage: "Kann die legendäre *futūḥ*-Literatur als arabisches Volksepos bezeichnet werden?" T. H.] sprechen. Der Gegenstand, die arabisch-islamischen Eroberungen, bietet sich als Stoff zu einem Epos sozusagen von selber an.

misses the peculiar Arabic tension between orality and literacy and between official, learned, 'true' narration in the standard language and unofficial, fictional, 'lying' narration in the colloquial vernacular. In a culture of parallel orality and literacy, it is essential that, in order to effectively defend in learned circles the claim of truth for its canonical texts (which are of ultimately oral origin), all competitive storytelling about one's own history must be looked down upon, and even, if possible, forbidden and nipped in the bud. Next to the Qur'ān and the official *maghāzī, futūḥ* and *qiṣaṣ al-anbiyā'* narratives therefore no epic, explicitly so named, could be tolerated. If epic, however, is understood as defined above (p. 629), then the Arabs have known oral epic compositions and narratives belonging to the genre of epic from the earliest period onward.

## References

Ahlwardt, W. 1896. *Die Handschriften-Verzeichnisse der Königlichen Bibliothek zu Berlin. Verzeichniss der arabischen Handschriften*. Vol. 8. Berlin. 1896.
Arberry, Arthur J., trans. 1964. *The Koran Interpreted*. London: OUP.
Assman, Jan. 1997. *Das kulturelle Gedächtnis. Schrift, Erinnerung und politische Identität in frühen Hochkulturen*. Munich: Beck.
Aswad, Nizār al-. 1990. 'Al-ḥakawātī fī Dimashq.' *Al-Ma'thūrāt ash-sha'bīya* 18: 56–63.
Berkey, Jonathan Porter. 1992. *The Transmission of Knowledge in Medieval Cairo: A Social History of Islamic Education*. Princeton: Princeton UP.
Blachère, Régis. 1952–66. *Histoire de la littérature arabe des origines à la fin du XV$^e$ siècle de J.-C.* 3 vols. Paris: Adrien-Maisonneuve.
Blau, Joshua. 1966–67. *A Grammar of Christian Arabic, Based mainly on South-Palestinian Texts from the First Millenium*. Corpus Scriptorum Christianorum Orientalium 267, 276, 279. 3 vols. Louvain: Secrétariat du Corpus SCO.

---

[...] Dazu kamen die Möglichkeiten im sprachlichen Ausdruck. Wie ich schon in anderem Zusammenhang bemerkt habe, wäre im Arabischen ein Epos denkbar, das in sinnvollem Wechsel von den Sprachformen der Prosa und der Reimprosa Gebrauch macht und durch Liedeinlagen in seiner inneren Struktur aufgelockert und akzentuiert wird.
Aber Stoff und sprachliche Mittel allein reichen nicht aus, um ein literarisches Kunstwerk herzustellen. Dazu bedarf es vor allem der Genialität eines Künstlers. Und daran fehlte es. Die arabischsprachige Welt hat keinen Firdausi hervorgebracht. Die Literaten, die sich mit der Futūḥ-Literatur abgaben und sie vor allem der breiten Masse mundgerecht und schmackhaft zu machen suchten, waren – sagen wir es unverblümt – kleine Geister. Mit ihrer Schwarzweißmalerei vertraten sie ein primitives Lebensgefühl, zu primitiv, um großartig zu sein, gradlinig und ungebrochen, aber eben deshalb auch ohne innere Spannung. Von Tragik fehlt in der Darstellung jede Spur. Alles Geschehen verläuft an der Oberfläche. Die mangelnde Tiefe wird durch Quantität und Hypertrophie ersetzt.
Dazu kommt ein Weiteres. Der Verfasser oder Überlieferer hatte gar nicht die Absicht, die Geschichte der arabisch-islamischen Eroberungen nur als Stoff zu benützen, um daraus ein literarisches Kunstwerk zu schaffen. [...] im Grunde genommen wollte er Historiker sein und als solcher ernst genommen werden. Das beweisen die vielen in den Text eingestreuten Isnāde [Überliefererketten zur Bezeugung der Wahrhaftigkeit des Überlieferten – analog zu den Prophetentraditionen: *ḥadīth*; T. H.]. Unter diesen Umständen konnte sich die legendäre Futūḥ-Literatur nicht zum Epos entwickeln. [...] Sie ist weder Fisch noch Fleisch: einerseits Pseudohistorie, die als echte Historie gelten möchte, andererseits Dichtung, die sich selber nicht wahrhaben will und deshalb im Ansatz zur Entwicklung einer eigenen literarischen Gattung steckengeblieben ist.' (Paret 1970: 746–47) – Compare also Guillaume 1996.

Bohas, Georges, and Jean-Patrick Guillaume, trans. 1985 ff. *Le Roman de Baïbars*. 10 vols. to date. Paris: Sindbad.
Brockelmann, Carl. 1943–49. *Geschichte der arabischen Litteratur*. 2nd ed. 3 vols. Leiden: Brill. [2 vols. supplement, 1937–42.]
Budayrī, Aḥmad ash-shaikh Aḥmad al-Budairī al-Ḥallāq. 1959. *Ḥawādith Dimashq al-yawmīya*. Cairo.
Busse, Heribert. 1987. 'Arabische Historiographie und Geographie.' In Gätje 1987: 264–97.
Canova, Giovanni. 1977. 'Gli studi sull' epica popolare araba.' *Oriente Moderno* 57: 211–26.
–, ed. 2003a. 'Studies on Arabic Epics.' *Oriente Moderno* n. s. 22 (83): v–xxi, 255–574 (second issue).
–. 2003b. 'Twenty Years of Studies on Arabic Epics.' In Canova 2003a: v–xxi.
Caskel, Werner. 1931. 'Aijām al-'Arab. Studien zur altarabischen Epik.' *Islamica* 4: 1–99.
Caton, Steven C. 1990. *'Peaks of Yemen I Summon': Poetry as Cultural Practice in a North Yemeni Tribe*. Berkeley: U of California P.
Cherkaoui, Driss. 2001a. *Le Roman de 'Antar. Une perspective littéraire et historique*. Paris: Présence Africaine. 2000.
–. 2001b. 'The Pyramidal Structure in Arabic *siyar*: The Example of *Sirat "Antar*.'' *Al-'Uṣūr al-Wustaa* 13: 6–9.
Connelly, Bridget. 1986. *Arab Folk Epic and Identity*. Berkeley: U of California P.
Doufikar-Aerts, Faustina. 2003. '*Sīrat al-Iskandar*: An Arabic Popular Romance of Alexander.' In Canova 2003a: 505–20.
*Encyclopaedia of Islam*. Ed. B. Lewis, C. E. Bosworth, P. J. Bearman et al. New edition. 12 vols. Leiden: Brill, 1960–2004.
Fahd, T. 1997. 'Shā'ir. 1. In the Arab World. A. Pre-Isalmic and Ummayyad Periods.' *Encyclopaedia of Islam*, IX, 225.
Fück, Johann. 1950. *'Arabīya. Untersuchungen zur arabischen Sprach- und Stilgeschichte*. Abhandlungen der Sächsischen AW zu Leipzig, Philologisch-Historische Klasse 45,1. Berlin: Akademieverlag.
Galley, Micheline, and Abderrahman Ayoub, eds. and trans. 1983. *Histoire des Beni Hilal et de ce qui leur advint dans leur marche vers l'ouest. Versions tunisiennes de la Geste hilalienne*. Paris: Colin.
Garcin, Jean-Claude, ed. 2003. *Lectures du 'Roman de Baybars'.* Marseille: Parenthèses.
Gätje, Helmut, ed. 1987. *Grundriß der Arabischen Philologie. II. Literaturwissenschaft*. Wiesbaden: Reichert.
Gavillet Matar, Marghérite, ed. and trans. 2005. *La geste de Zīr Sâlim d'après un manuscrit syrien*. 2 vols. Damascus: Institut Français du Proche-Orient.
Gerhardt, Mia I. 1963. *The Art of Storytelling: A Literary Study of the 1001 Nights*. Leiden: Brill.
Goldziher, Ignaz. 1920. *Die Richtungen der islamischen Koranauslegung. An der Universität Upsala gehaltene Olaus-Petri-Vorlesungen*. Veröffentlichungen der 'De Goeje-Stiftung' 6. Leiden: Brill.
Grant, Kenneth. 2003. '*Sīrat Fīrūzśāh* and the Middle Eastern Epic Tradition.' In Canova 2003a: 521–28.
Grégoire, Henri, Roger Goossens. 1934. 'Byzantinisches Epos und arabischer Ritterroman.' *ZDMG* 88: 213–32.
Grunebaum, G. E. von. 1963. *Der Islam im Mittelalter*. Zürich: Artemis. [Rev. translation of *Medieval Islam: A Study in Cultural Orientation*, 2nd ed. Chicago: U of Chicago P, 1953.]
Guillaume, Jean-Patrick. 1996. 'Y-a-t-il une littérature épique en arabe?' In *L'épopée: mythe, histoire, société*. Ed. J.-P. Martin and F. Suard. Littérales 19. Nanterre: Centre des sciences de la littérature. 91–107.
–. 2004. 'Les scènes de bataille dans le *Roman de Baybars*. Considérations sur le "style formulaire" dans la tradition épique arabe.' In Zakharia 2004: 55–76.

Günther, Hartmut, Otto Ludwig et al., eds. 1994. *Schrift und Schriftlichkeit/ Writing and Its Use. Ein interdisziplinäres Handbuch internationaler Forschung/ An Interdisciplinary Handbook of International Research*. Handbücher zur Sprach- und Kommunikationswissenschaft 10. Berlin: de Gruyter.
Halbwachs, Maurice. 1925. *Les cadres sociaux de la mémoire*. Paris: Alcan.
Hanaway, William L., Jr. 1970. 'Persian Popular Romances before the Safavid Period.' Ph.D. Thesis. Columbia University, New York.
–, trans. 1974. *Love and War: Adventures from the Fīrūz Shāh Nāma of Sheikh Bīghamī*. Persian Heritage Series 19. New York: Scholars Facsimiles and Reprints.
Heath, Peter. 1984. 'A Critical Review of Modern Scholarship on *Sīrat ʿAntar ibn Shaddād* and the Popular *Sīra*.' *Journal of Arabic Literature* 15: 19–44.
–. 1990. 'Arabische Volksliteratur im Mittelalter.' In *Neues Handbuch der Literaturwissenschaft*. Vol. 5. *Orientalisches Mittelalter*. Ed. Wolfhart Heinrich. Wiesbaden: AULA. 423–39.
–. 1996.: *The Thirsty Sword: Sīrat ʿAntar and the Arabic Popular Epic*. Salt Lake City: U of Utah P.
Herzog, Thomas. 1994. 'Présentation de deux séances de ḥakawātī et de deux manuscrits de la Sīrat Baybars recueillis en Syrie en 1994.' Maîtrise d'arabe, sous la direction de Claude Audebert et de Jean-Paul-Pascual. Université de Provence, Aix-en-Provence.
–. 1995. 'Présentation, classification et analyse linguistique d'une collection de manuscrits de la Sīrat Baybars.' DEA d'arabe, sous la direction de Claude Audebert et de Albert-Louis de Prémare. Université de Provence, Aix-en-Provence.
–. 2005. 'Wild Ancestors – Bedouins in Mediaeval Arabic Popular Literature.' In *Shifts and Drifts in Nomad-Sedentary Relations*. Ed. Stefan Leder and Bernhard Streck. Nomaden und Sesshafte 2. Wiesbaden: Reichert. 421–41.
–. 2006. *Geschichte und Imaginaire. Entstehung, Überlieferung und Bedeutung der Sīrat Baibars in ihrem sozio-politischen Kontext*. Wiesbaden: Harrassowitz.
–. 2010. '"What they saw with their own eyes..." – Fictionalisation and "Narrativisation" of History in Arab Popular Epics and Learned Historiography.' In *Fictionalizing the Past: Historical Characters in Arabic Popular Epics*. Ed. Sabine Dorpmüller. Cairo: American U of Cairo P. 25–43.
Ḥusain, Ṭāhā. 1926. *Fī-š-ši'r al-ǧāhilī*. Cairo.
Ibn Abī Uṣaybiʿa. 1884. *ʿUyūn al-anbāʾ fī ṭabaqāt al-aṭibāʾ*. Ed. A. Müller. 2 vols. Königsberg.
Jacobi, Renate. 1987. 'Die altarabische Dichtung (6.–7. Jahrhundert).' In Gätje 1987: 20–31.
–. 1995. 'Rāwī.' *Encyclopaedia of Islam*, VIII, 466.
Koch, Peter, and Wulf Oesterreicher. 1994. 'Schriftlichkeit und Sprache.' In Günther, Ludwig et al. 1994: 587–604.
Kremer, Alfred von. 1863. *Ägypten. Forschungen über Land und Volk während eines zehnjährigen Aufenthalts*. 2 vols. Leipzig.
Kurpershoek, P. Marcel, ed. and trans. 1994–99. *Oral Poetry and Narratives from Central Arabia. I. The Poetry of Ad-Dindan. II. The Story of a Desert Knight. III. Bedouin Poets of the Dawāsir Tribe*. 3 vols. Leiden 1999.
Lane, Edward William. 1860. *An Account of the Manners and Customs of the Modern Egyptians*. 5th ed. London. [Rpt. with an introduction by Jason Thompson, Cairo and New York, 2003.]
Lawrence, Thomas Edward. 1927. *Revolt in the Desert*. London: Jonathan Cape.
Leder, Stefan. 2005. 'Al-Wāḳidī, Muḥammad b. ʿUmar b. Wāḳidī.' *Encyclopaedia of Islam*, XI, 101.
Lecomte, G. 1993. 'Muʿallaḳāt.' *Encyclopaedia of Islam*, VII, 254.
Littmann, Enno. 1960. 'Alf Layla wa-Layla.' *Encyclopaedia of Islam*, I, 358.
Lord, Albert Bates. 1960. *The Singer of Tales*. Cambridge, MA: Harvard UP. [Re-edition with a CD and a new introduction by Stephen Mitchell and Gregory Nagy, 2000.]
Lyons, M. C. 1995. *The Arabian Epic: Heroic and Oral Story-Telling*. 3 vols. Cambridge: CUP.

Madeyska, Danuta. 1993. *Poetyka Siratu. Studium o arabskim romansie rycerskim*. Warsaw: Wydawnictwa Uniwersytetu Warszawskiego.
Mahdī, Muḥsin, ed. 1984–94. *The Thousand and One Nights (Alf Layla wa-Layla)*. 3 vols. Leiden: Brill.
Mahdī, Muḥsin. 1995. *The Thousand and One Nights*. Leiden: Brill.
Maqrīzī, Taqī ad-Dīn: Taqī ad-Dīn Aḥmad. 1270/1853–54. *al-Mawāʿiẓ wa-l-iʿtibār fī dhkr al-khiṭaṭ wa-l-āthār*. II. Boulaq.
Margoliouth, D. S. 1925. 'The Origins of Arabic Poetry.' *JRAS* 3: 417–49.
Meredith-Owens, G. M. 1986. 'Hamza b. ʿAbd al-Muṭṭalib.' *Encyclopaedia of Islam*, III, 152.
Miquel, André, trans. 1977. *Un conte des 'Mille et Une Nuits', 'Ajīb et Gharîb'*. Paris: Flammarion.
–. 1981. *Sept contes des 'Mille et Une Nuits' ou il n'y a pas de contes innocents*. Paris: Sindbad.
Monroe, James T. 1972. 'Oral Composition in Pre-Islamic Poetry.' *Journal of Arabic Literature* 3: 1–53.
Myhrman, David W., ed. and trans. 1908. *Tāj ad-Dīn as-Subkī. Kitāb muʿīd an-niʿam wa-mubīd an-niqam*. Luzac's Semitic Text and Translation Series 18. Leiden: Brill; London: Luzac.
Nacib, Youssef. 1994. *Une geste en fragments. Contribution à l'étude de la légende hilalienne des Hauts-Plateaux algériens*. Paris: Publisud.
Nagel, Tilman. 1967. *Die Qiṣaṣ al-anbiyāʾ. Ein Beitrag zur arabischen Literaturgeschichte*. Ph.D. Thesis. University of Bonn.
–. 1986a. 'Ḳiṣaṣ al-Anbiyāʾ.' *Encyclopaedia of Islam*, V, 180.
–. 1986b. 'Al-Kisāʾī.' *Encyclopaedia of Islam*, V, 176.
Niebuhr, Carsten. 1772. *Beschreibung von Arabien. Aus eigenen Beobachtungen und im Lande selbst gesammelten Nachrichten*. Copenhagen.
Neuwirth, Angelika. 1987. 'Koran.' In Gätje 1987: 96–135.
Norris, H. T., trans. 1980. *The Adventures of Antar*. Warminster: Aris & Phillips.
Ott, Claudia. 2003. *Metamorphosen des Epos. Sīrat al-Muğāhidīn (Sīrat al-Amīra Ḏāt al-Himma) zwischen Mündlichkeit und Schriftlichkeit*. Leiden: Research School of Asian, African, and Amerindian Studies, Universiteit Leiden.
Oliverius, Jaroslav. 1965. 'Aufzeichnungen über den Basūs-Krieg in der Kunstliteratur und deren Weiterentwicklung im arabischen Volksbuch über Zīr Sālim.' *Archiv Orientální* 33: 44–64.
–. 1971. 'Themen und Motive im arabischen Volksbuch Zīr Sālim.' *Archiv Orientální* 34: 129–45.
Panckoucke, Charles Louis Fleury, ed. 1826. *Description de l'Égypte ou recueil des observations et des recherches qui ont été faites en Égypte pendant l'expédition de l'armée française*. 2nd ed. Vol. 18 *État moderne*. Paris.
Pantke, Mechthil. 1974. *Der arabisch Bahrām-Roman. Untersuchungen zur Quellen- und Stoffgeschichte*. Studien zur Sprache, Geschichte und Kultur des Islamischen Orients 6. Berlin: de Gruyter.
Pantůček, Svetozár. 1970. *Das Epos über den Westzug der Banū Hilāl*. Prag: Academia.
Paret, Rudi. 1924. *Sīrat ibn Dhī Jazan. Ein arabischer Volksroman*. Hannover: Lafaire.
–. 1927. *Die Geschichte des Islams im Spiegel der arabischen Volksliteratur*. Philosophie und Geschichte 13. Tübingen: Mohr.
–. 1930. *Die legendäre Maghāzi-Literatur. Arabische Dichtungen über die muslimischen Kriegszüge zu Mohammeds Zeit*. Tübingen: Mohr.
–. 1970. 'Die legendäre futūḥ–Literatur, ein arabisches Volksepos?' In *Atti del Convegno internazionale sul tema: La poesie epica e la sua formazione*. Accademia Nazionale dei Lincei 367, quaderno 139. Rome: Accademia Nazionale dei Lincei. 735–47.
Pellat, Charles. 1990. 'Ḳāṣṣ.' *Encyclopaedia of Islam*, IV, 733.
Pérès, Henri. 1958. 'Le roman dans la littérature arabe des origines à la fin du Moyen Age.' *Annales de l'Institut d'Études Orientales, Université d'Alger* 16: 5–40.

Qāsimī, Muḥammad Saʿīd, and Jamāl ad-Dīn al-Qāsimī. 1960. *Qāmūs aṣ-ṣināʿāt ash-Shāmīya. Dictionnaire des métier damascains*. Monde d'outre-mer, passé et présent 3. Paris: Mouton. [Rpt.]
*Qiṣṣat ʾAntāra*: *Qiṣṣat ʾAntara b. Shaddād al-ʾAbsī*. 6 vols., 59 *ajzāʾ* [parts]. Cairo: M. Bābī al- Ḥalabī, 1961.
*Qiṣṣat Ḥamza*: *Qiṣṣat al-Amīr Ḥamza al-Bahlwān*. 4 vols. Cairo, n. d.
Raible, Wolfgang. 1994. 'Orality and Literacy.' In Günter, Ludwig et al. 1994: 1–17.
Reynolds, Dwight Fletcher. 1995. *Heroic Poets, Poetic Heroes: The Ethnography of Performance in an Arabic Oral Epic Tradition*. Ithaca, NY: Cornell UP.
Rippin, A. 2002. 'Al-Thaʿlabī.' *Encyclopaedia of Islam*, X, 434.
Rypka, Jan. 1968 *History of Iranian Literature*. Written in collaboration with Otakar Klíma, ed. Karl Jahn. Dordrecht: Reidel.
Rosenthal, Franz. 1952. *A History of Muslim Historiography*. Leiden: Brill.
Saada, Lucienne, ed. and trans. 1985. *La Geste hilalienne. Version de Bou Thadi (Tunisie). Récitation de Mohammed Hsini*. Paris: Gallimard.
Sakhāwī, Shams ad-Dīn Muḥammad. 1934–36. *Aḍ-Ḍauʾ al-lāmiʿ*. 12 vols. Cairo: Maktabat al-Qudsī.
Sezgin, Fuat. 1967–2007. *Geschichte des arabischen Schrifttums*. 13 vols. Leiden: Brill; Frankfurt a. M.: Institut für Geschichte der Arabisch-Islamische Wissenschaften.
Schreiner, Martin 1898. 'Samauʾal b. Jahjâ al-Maġribî und seine Schrift "Ifḥâm al-Jahûd".' *Monatsschrift für Geschichte und Wissenschaft des Judenthums* 42 (N. F. 6): 123–33.
Shoshan, Boaz. 1993. 'On Popular Literature in Medieval Cairo.' *Poetics Today* 14: 349–65.
*Sīrat al-amīr ʾAntara*: *Sīrat [...] al-amīr ʾAntara b. Šaddād*. 8 vols., 32 *aǧzāʾ* [parts]. Cairo: Maṭbaʿa al-ʿāmira aš–šarīfa, 1306–11 H.
*Sīrat al-Malik aẓ-Ẓāhir*: *Sīrat al-Malik aẓ-Ẓāhir Baybars*. Ed. Jamāl al-Ghītānī. Cairo: Al-Hayʾa al-miṣrīya al-ʿāmma li-l-kitāb, 1996.
*Sīrat Dhāt al-Himma*: *Sīrat al-Amīra Dhāt al-Himma*. 70 *ajzāʾ* [parts]. Cairo, n. d.
Slyomovics, Susan. 1987. *The Merchant of Art: An Egyptian Hilali Oral Epic Poet in Performance*. University of California Publications in Modern Philology 120. Berkeley: U of California P.
Sowayan, Saad Abdullah. 1985. *Nabaṭi Poetry: The Oral Poetry of Arabia*. Berkeley: U of California P.
–. 1992. *The Arabian Oral Historical Narrative: An Ethnographic and Linguistic Analysis*. Semitica Viva 6. Wiesbaden: Harrassowitz. 1992
Steinbach, Udo. 1972. *Ḏāt al-Himma. Kulturgeschichtliche Untersuchung zu einem arabischen Volksroman*. Wiesbaden: Steiner.
Vidal Luengo, Ana Ruth. 2000. *La dimensión mediadora en el mito árabe islámico: la Sirat Baybars*. Granada: Universidad de Granada.
Wangelin, Helmut. 1936. *Das arabische Volksbuch vom König Aẓẓāhir Baibars*. Bonner Orientalische Studien 17. Stuttgart: Kohlhammer.
Wolff, Ph. 1864. 'An junge Arabisten.' *ZDMG* 18: 631.
Zakharia, Katia, ed. 2004. '*Sīrat al-Malik al-Ẓāhir Baybars*. De l'oral à l'écrit. From Performance to Script.' *Arabica* 51, issues 1 and 2.
Zwettler, Michael. 1978. *The Oral Tradition of Classical Arabic Poetry: Its Character and Implications*. Columbus: Ohio State UP.

## 25 Orality in Medieval Persian Literature

*Julia Rubanovich*

The issue of orality and the interplay between the oral and the written have long been an 'academic backwater' in the study of medieval Persian literature.[1] There were mainly two reasons for this: (1) the choice of subject-matter for scholarly research has all too often been guided by evaluative aesthetic criteria, restricting it to the study of acknowledged masterpieces and leaving out whole layers of medieval literary production which might offer themselves most opportunely to inquiry from the viewpoint of orality, such as, for example, folk prose literature; (2) there has been a reluctance to make use of theoretical tools and approaches developed on the basis of inquiry into similar issues in Western literatures. In the last two decades, however, the problem of the interdependence of oral and written traditions has received growing attention, first of all in the context of *Shāh-nāma* studies. The *Shāh-nāma* (The Book of Kings) of Abū al-Qāsim Firdausī (d. *c.* 1020) is a vast epic poem, whose current standard edition includes over 50,000 rhymed couplets (Khāliqī–Muṭlaq 1988–2008). The epic spans Iranian history from the mythical Gayōmart, the First Man, to the fall of the historical Sasanian dynasty as a result of the Arab conquest in the seventh century, and is thus considered the national epos of Iran.[2]

The other focal point for studying orality in medieval Persian literature has become the Persian *dāstān*. *Dāstān*s are capacious fictional prose narratives with branching plots, which relate the heroic-romantic adventures of their eponymous heroes, often with a religious, Islamic emphasis. Their composition and transmission are connected with the institution of professional or semiprofessional storytellers, who at different historical periods were known as *muḥaddithūn*, *qiṣṣa-khʷānān*, and, more recently, since about the Safavid period (sixteenth century onwards), as *naqqālān*.[3] Lacking a strict genre definition, *dāstān*s were variously referred to by their authors as 'tale, story' (*dāstān, rivāyat, ḥikāyat* or *qiṣṣa*) or 'book' (*kitāb*). In research literature they are defined as folk stories (*dāstān-hā-yi 'āmmiyāna*),[4] as *narodnye dastany* (Borshevskiy 1963: 10–11), popular romances (Hanaway 1970: 7, and 1971), or as heroic novels (*romanhāi pahlavānī*) (Salimov 1971: 14–15). The writing down of the *dāstān*s most probably began in the eleventh century; the tradition of their composition survived till the second half of the

---

[1] The expression is borrowed from Mukerji 1991:1.
[2] For a synopsis of the epic's contents, see de Fouchécour 1976. On the poet, see Khāliqī–Muṭlaq [Khaleghi-Motlagh] 1999.
[3] See Hanaway 1996; Lisān 1975.
[4] See, e. g., Maḥjūb 2003a: 125–27; Bayḥaqī 1988: 44–45, 49, 53–54; Marzolph 1999: 279, 281–83.

nineteenth, while their dissemination in lithographic and in typographic print as 'popular booklets' continued well into the twentieth century.[5]

## 1 The *Shāh-nāma* and the Quest for Orality: Sources and their Provenance; Patterns of Composition and Transmission

The relationship of the *Shāh-nāma* to oral tradition and in particular to pre-Islamic Iranian oral poetics proves to be a knotty issue, owing to the disappearance of Firdausī's sources and to our very partial, mostly conjectural, knowledge of the state of the art of Middle Persian epic poetry which might have influenced his work.[6] Following the conclusions of fundamental studies on the Iranian national epic, notably by Theodor Nöldeke (Nöldeke 1896–1904; 1890), it has come to be generally believed that Firdausī relied on written sources, first and foremost a recension, probably in New Persian, of a lost Middle Persian *X^w adāy-nāmag* (Book of Kings), a prose collection of legendary and historical materials pertaining to the Iranian past and compiled in the late Sasanian period.[7] Even if some oral material was added to this, it was reworked with firm adherence to contemporary written literary poetic patterns, including the use of quantitative meter (*mutaqārib* in the case of the *Shāh-nāma*), unknown in Middle Persian poetry and shaped under the influence of Arabic poetics.[8]

At the same time, attempts were made to trace a more immediate connection of the *Shāh-nāma* with oral traditional poetic forms and themes. Thus, Olga M. Davidson argued for the oral sources of Firdausī's epic and its close connection with the Indo-European epic heritage (drawing mostly on George Dumézil), and suggested that the *Shāh-nāma* should be considered as an 'authoritative corpus of Iranian oral poetic traditions'.[9] Davidson interpreted the expressions of speaking and listening, as well as references current in the epic to *mūbad*s (Zoroastrian priests), *dihqān*s (courtly landed gentry) and *sarāyandagān* (singers, narrators), who in Iranian tradition were credited as bearers and guardians of the mytho-heroic past, as indicative of Firdausī's use of oral,

---

[5]  See Marzolph 1994:1–4. Extant works comprise *Samak-i 'Ayyār, Iskandar-nāma, Dārāb-nāma, Abū Muslim-nāma, Junayd-nāma, Fīrūzshāh-nāma* (the work was originally published under the mistaken title *Dārāb-nāma*, and later emended by the same editor to *Fīrūzshāh-nāma*; see Ṣafā 1960–63: II, 765–66); the so-called Safavid *Iskandar-nāma* that came down in several disparate versions, some of which are attributed to Manūchihr Khān Ḥakīm; *Ḥamza-nāma; Ḥusayn-i Kurd-i Shabistarī; Amīr Arsalān; Salīm-i Javāhirī* and some others.

[6]  On the only surviving specimen of ancient Iranian epic poetry in Pahlavi, *Ayādgār ī Zarērān* (Memorial of Zarēr), see Boyce 1989. For the possible role of Parthian minstrels (*gōsān*s) in the dissemination of the epic tradition in Sasanian Iran, see Boyce 1957 and 2003; see, however, the critical comments by M. Omidsalar on the limited value of this evidence for our knowledge of the development of the epic in New Persian (Omidsalar 1995:451–52, and 1996:239–40). A survey of the controversy around the issue of Middle Iranian metrics, as well as hypotheses as to their nature, appears in Shaked 1970.

[7]  For a summary of the contention concerning Firdausī's sources, see de Blois 1994:120–24, and Yamamoto 2003:3–6.

[8]  For a succinct survey of transitions in the metrical system from Middle Persian to Neo-Persian poetry, see de Blois 1994:42–53.

[9]  Davidson 1994:169; see also Davidson 1985; 1988; 1998; 2000.

performative (as against textual) sources, thus dismissing the prevalent view of his mediated reliance upon the Middle Persian chronicle mentioned above. In addition, she made an attempt to apply to the *Shāh-nāma* the concepts of the oral-formulaic theory of M. Parry and A. B. Lord, suggesting that the building-blocks of the epic were functional formulas.[10]

The endeavour to prove that the composition of the *Shāh-nāma* was based on the rules of oral poetry has generated an intense discussion of pros and cons among scholars.[11] In fact, the use of 'oral' verbs, especially in medieval texts, has only limited corroborative value for their oral provenance, while references to the figures conventionally associated with oral tradition and transmission, might have entered Firdausī's work from his written sources and functioned as *topoi* or rhetorical means.[12] Rather than reflecting the mentality of an oral poetic tradition or a myth-made stylization of oral poetry, as Davidson believes (1994: 48–53, esp. 48; 2000: 44–58), the claim that a written source has been followed suggests that the author no longer justifies his work from within oral tradition (Green 1994: 162). Moreover, the formulaic language – provided its existence gets proved beyond the limited selection analysed by Davidson – is not necessarily indicative of the oral composition of the epic.[13]

The Oral-Formulaic Theory being of limited value in dealing with the *Shāh-nāma*, an alternative Oral Performance Model (abbreviated as OPM) was further proposed to appraise the extent to which the oral tradition might have affected Firdausī's work, as well as later epics which emulated the *Shāh-nāma* in metre, themes and motifs (Yamamoto 2003: esp. 51–52). The OPM suggests examining samples from the *Shāh-nāma* in light of structural and thematic features of the practice of *naqqālī* performance, a form of Persian professional storytelling that evolved since the Safavid period (sixteenth century) onwards. The *Shāh-nāma* figured prominently in the *naqqālī* repertoire, albeit in prose retelling, having been amplified and blended with the material of the so-called 'secondary' epics comprising the Persian 'Epic Cycle'.[14]

According to the OPM, some formal and thematic criteria typical of storytellers' *ṭūmār*s, i. e., 'scrolls' containing the written basic story-line of an orally performed prose narrative, are found in Firdausī's work as well.[15] On a formal level these include the

---

[10] See Davidson 1988; 1994: 171–81; 1998; 2000: 1–8. [On the 'Oral Theory', see also ch. 2 by J. M. Foley and P. Ramey in this volume.]

[11] See de Blois 1994: 53–58, and 1998a; Davis 1996; Omidsalar 1995; 1996; 2002; 2009; Meisami 1996.

[12] K. Yamamoto has painstakingly recorded all the instances of Firdausī's allusions to his sources, showing that their interpretation as oral and/or written is essentially ambiguous and ambivalent (2003: 60–80). She concluded that Firdausī was '[...] manifestly conscious of the "literary-written" nature of his undertaking' (80). See further de Blois 1994: 54–55; Omidsalar 1995: 442–49, and 1996: 240–41; Khāliqī–Muṭlaq 2009: 1–7.

[13] See Finnegan 1977; Yamamoto 2003: 12–15.

[14] On the Persian 'Epic Cycle' and on 'secondary' epics and their characteristics see de Blois 1998b; 1994: 562–76; Molé 1953; Hanaway 1978; on the influence of the *Shāh-nāma* on the *naqqālī* tradition, see Rubanovich 2010b.

[15] On *ṭūmār*s see Page 1979: 198–212; Rubanovich 2010b. The materials on the basis of which the OPM was elaborated and tested by its author, comprised the *ṭūmār* containing the story of Rustam and his son Suhrāb by the storyteller Murshid 'Abbās-i Zarīrī (see Dūstkhᵛāh 1991) and the part on the reign of King Kay Khusrau from the *Shāh-nāma* (Khāliqī–Muṭlaq 1988–2008, vols. 3 and 4).

punctuation of episode boundaries by narrative markers (e. g., 'on this/that side') and temporal markers (e. g., 'when', 'then', descriptions of sunrise/sunset), the variety of which, however, is much narrower than in storytellers' *ṭūmārs*, perhaps due to metric constraints (Yamamoto 2003:85–93). On a thematic plane, in conformity with the OPM, similarly to a *naqqāl*, Firdausī appears to have used such narrative techniques as interlacing, i. e., weaving two story-lines together; introducing irony and suspense and changing narrative speed; using structural repetition and false signals.[16] At the same time, although Yamamoto's sample meets the thematic criteria characteristic of oral performance in the sense that the story is constructed around a key motif accentuated by the narrative techniques indicated above, it nevertheless does not demonstrate the full array of formal characteristics typical of oral *naqqālī* performance as embodied in the *ṭūmār* studied (2003:107–9, 141–42). Whereas the *ṭūmār* text is structured in a serial way by means of instalments and episodes of more or less equal length, to satisfy the performing *naqqāl*'s pragmatic audience-oriented need for a similar duration of storytelling sessions, no such regularity is observed in the *Shāh-nāma*.[17] Viewed pragmatically from the standpoint of transmission and reception, this finding means that Firdausī could hardly have intended his work for oral serial performance. Another observation emerging from the application of the OPM to the text of the *Shāh-nāma* concerns the virtual lack of immediate interaction of the narrator with his audience, of the kind that A. Dundes has pertinently termed 'raconteur's asides', be they of explanatory, evaluative, amusing, didactic or other nature (1966:511). This is not to say that the *Shāh-nāma* is devoid of meta-narrative comments, quite the opposite; in the epic, however, the narrator's digressions follow the logic of the literary text, which, contrary to oral performance, is meant to be read and pondered upon, and the narrator's commentaries are therefore mostly patterned as prologue or epilogue to entire stories.[18]

The general conclusion drawn by Kumiko Yamamoto as regards oral influence on the characteristics and structure of the *Shāh-nāma* as they emerge from her application of the OPM to a concrete sample story is that Firdausī 'modelled this particular story [...] intuitively on oral performance' due to his personal experience with oral performances as a listener. At the same time, according to Yamamoto, Firdausī broke with the oral tradition in that he revised the orally-based story in view of the written medium 'to enhance its "readability"' by altering the length of instalments and episodes, varying the number of episodes in each instalment and modifying the dramatic intensity of the instalments (2003:141).

As for the *Shāh-nāma*'s distribution, a view has often been expressed in favour of parallel oral and written transmission. This notion rests largely on two unsubstantiated premises: the fluid manuscript tradition of Firdausī's work and the epic's broad popularity in Iranian folk oral tradition since its composition (tenth and early eleventh centuries) up to the present. Thus, drawing on Paul Zumthor's model of *mouvance*, Davidson argues that 'patterns of variation' in the text of the *Shāh-nāma* attest to its performativ-

---

[16] For the examination of these narrative techniques in the *ṭūmār*, see Yamamoto 2003:42–45; in the section from the *Shāh-nāma*, Yamamoto 2003:97–107.

[17] See Yamamoto 2003:31, 96–97; Page 1979:197–98.

[18] For examples and detailed examination, see Sarrāmī 1989:111–53; see also Yamamoto 2003:93, 108.

ity and an ongoing recomposition-in-performance.[19] Statistical sampling, however, shows that textual variants in the *Shāh-nāma* manuscripts can largely be explained in standard paleographic terms rather than as representing different performances.[20] Regarding the epic's popularity, in support of which the activities of *naqqāl*s are anachronistically evoked, the ready dissemination of the *Shāh-nāma* in folk culture is not to be taken for granted. Prior to the Safavid period there is little historical evidence of any significant oral performative ways of transmitting Firdausī's poetry.[21] Although since early medieval times there existed an institution of *shāh-nāma-khʷān*s (*Shāh-nāma* readers/narrators), who specialized in the recitation of epic-heroic stories, including that of Firdausī, they seem to have practiced mostly prose retelling, sporadically interspersing their epic material with poetic passages.[22] Furthermore, as I have shown elsewhere, until the fifteenth century the reception of the *Shāh-nāma* may have been restricted to learned circles of courtly makers of lyric and epic poetry and historical writings, while its infiltration into folk literature spanned a longer period (Rubanovich 2010a). The absorption of the *Shāh-nāma* into the medieval folk milieu appears to have succeeded the canonization of the epic in 'high', courtly literature, in which it provided, among other things, a useful tool for conferring legitimacy on non-Iranian, Turco-Mongol rulers.[23]

Although in Persian culture the improvised composition and recitation of poetry *(badīha-sarāʾī)* were widespread and much praised throughout the centuries, it was nevertheless first and foremost an elaborate and erudite art based on the poet's mastering of the contemporaneous poetic canon and his minute acquaintance with poetic metrics and rhetorical figures.[24] In the twelfth and thirteenth centuries Firdausī's *Shāh-nāma* constituted a recommended text to be read and studied by courtly writers of both prose and poetry in order to attain perfection in eloquence and versification.[25] Extemporized performances were presented at court or during learned gatherings *(majālis)*; they were largely limited to 'small' poetic genres – *ghazal* (lyric poem), *qaṣīda* (ode), *muʿammā*

---

[19] Davidson 1994: 54–72; 2000: 1–8; see Zumthor 1972: 64 ff.
[20] See Omidsalar 2002: 269–77; Khāliqī–Muṭlaq 2009: 12–13.
[21] See Davidson 1994: 56–60. – Besides the scarcity of evidence, our knowledge of transmission patterns in medieval Persian culture is further impeded by the polysemanticity of the Persian verb *khʷāndan*, which can be interpreted as 'to read', 'to sing', 'to recite', or 'to study'.
[22] Firdausī's *Shāh-nāma* is only one version of the Iranian national epic generally known as the *Xʷadāy-nāmag* (Book of the Kings) tradition. The *Shāh-nāma* was preceded by a number of works in prose and verse, now lost (for a recent detailed analysis of the relationship of various early medieval Arabic and Persian sources for the 'Books of the Kings', see Khāliqī–Muṭlaq 2009: 24–42, and the stemma on p. 48. Hence, the references to the *Shāh-nāma* in Persian sources of the tenth and eleventh centuries for the most part concern epic works other than Firdausī's. See Lisān 1975: 7–8; see also Afshārī and Madāyinī 1998: Introduction, 27.
[23] See Melikian-Chirvani 1997 and 1988. On a theoretical level, the historical reception of the *Shāh-nāma* finely reflects the dynamic nature of the literary system as viewed in the Polysystem Theory, when a device, a product, a model of writing etc., after having been canonized, is transferred in the course of time to the periphery of the literary system and is adapted by its non-canonical stratum. See Even-Zohar 1990: 13–17; Sheffy 1990.
[24] See Bagley 1989. Examples of the extemporized composition of poems by courtly poets, which demonstrate the importance of this technique in classical Persian poetry, can be found in Niẓāmī ʿArūḍī's *Chahār maqāla* (see Muʿīn 2001: 57, 68, 74, 85).
[25] See Muʿīn 2001: 22; Iqbāl 1921: 57.

25 – Rustam defeats one of Afrāsiyāb's warriors, from an early 15th-c. *Shāh-nāma* MS

(riddle) and others, – and were guided by conventions which had nothing in common with the oral composition-in-performance of folk bards, except for the shared media, i. e., oral and aural channels of transmission and reception. It seems, moreover, that in Iranian oral popular poetic tradition as such, both medieval and modern, the component of rote memorization with the subsequent reproducing of a text exercised a significant role, downplaying the element of improvisation.

Thus, while enumerating the six rules of poetry recitation (*naẓm-khʷānī*) in his chapter on popular entertainers, Mullā Ḥusayn Vāʿiẓ-i Kāshifī (d. 1504/5) urges the reciter to explain to the audience the meaning of a difficult verse.[26] In addition, the reciter is adjured to pay homage to the composer of the poem (*ṣāḥib-i ān naẓm*) he recites, either at the beginning of the performance or at the end, by citing the author's name and sending him blessings. Beside dependence on a fixed text – whether memorized from the writing or by ear – such prescriptions imply the foregrounding of the author and of his authority at the expense of the performer, who is perceived as a transmitter and a proficient commentator, rather than as a (co-)creator. In such a case, the oral performer's skilfulness, instead of recomposition, would be expressed in his ability to impress and move his listeners and avoid tedium and incomprehensibility.

The importance of the text in the transmission and distribution of the *Shāh-nāma*, either by means of silent, private reading or through reading aloud, can be glimpsed from occasional references in an anonymous *dāstān*, the *Iskandar-nāma* (The Book of

---

[26] Maḥjūb 1971:305; the full translation of the passage is in Omidsalar 1984:207–8.

Alexander [the Great]), written down approximately in the twelfth century and reworked probably in the fourteenth century. Thus, the narrator comments on the popularity of the tales of Siyāvush, Kay Khusrau and Afrāsyāb, all three being characters of Firdausī's epic, saying: 'These tales are in the mind of most of the people who have read the *Shāh-nāma*.'[27] In another instance the reference is entwined in the characters' dialogue; Alexander, having heard the tale of Kay Khusrau's disappearance in a snowstorm recounted to him by his vizier Aristotle, asks the latter: 'Did you read all this from the written (*az nivishta khʷāndī*)?' – 'Yes', – was the answer.[28]

It appears that starting from the end of the eleventh/ beginning of the twelfth century the common way to familiarize oneself with the *Shāh-nāma*, perhaps due to its sheer bulk, was by means of mediatory works which included selected fragments (Rubanovich 2006: 256–58, and 2010a). With regard to folk literature, we know of collections which were compiled by professional storytellers and comprised an inventory of ready-made poetic examples to be memorized and then recited in relevant narrative contexts during performance.[29] The study of *dāstān*s which show a substantial affinity to oral traditional patterns, demonstrates that from the fifteenth century onwards verses from the *Shāh-nāma* used to be inserted in set narrative contexts, such as exhortations on the vicissitudes of fate, depictions of battle scenes, descriptions of the alternation of day and night and the like, probably extracted from such collections. The fragmentary reception of the *Shāh-nāma* accounts for various modifications that the verses underwent on their insertion into prose narratives. These include de-contextualization, substitution for the sake of plot adjustment, and inventive augmentation, where the verses are freely diluted by stylized lines of the storytellers' own making (Rubanovich 2006: 253–54, 258, and 2010a). The *Shāh-nāma* is thus perceived by folk storytellers as an ample reservoir of materials to be reworked in accordance with the traditional aesthetics of the *dāstān* genre, i. e., its profound narrativity, formulaity, and aural mode of reception.

Theories of oral composition thus appear to be hardly effective in dealing with the *Shāh-nāma*, whose author conceived of his work as a book to endure through the centuries and become a monument (*yādgār*) to his name – an aspiration in line with the established written literary tradition of Firdausī's time.[30] In view of the absence of

---

[27] Afshār 1964: 201; the translations are mine if not otherwise stated.
[28] Afshār 1964: 208. For a similar reference, see Ṣafā 1965–68: I, 509 ('Everybody who read the *Shāh-nāma*, knows [the tales of Gaudarz]'). It cannot be ruled out, however, that here some other collection of heroic legends, generically known as *Shāh-nāma,* is meant. See n. 22 above.
[29] Rubanovich 2006: 250–51. See Mary E. Page's observations as regards the training of *naqqāl*s in modern Iran. Each day an apprentice (*shāgird*) is apportioned by his teacher (*ustād*, 'master'), himself a professional storyteller, a segment from the *Shāh-nāma* to be memorized line by line. The material learned is then checked the next day (Page 1979: 198). Thus a *naqqāl* gets acquainted with the story-line of the epic and stocks in his memory a sufficient amount of verse citations from the *Shāh-nāma* to recite them occasionally at relevant points of prose narration in the course of his performance.
[30] Most manifestly the concept of *yādgār* is expressed in Firdausī's invocation to Sultan Maḥmūd of Ghazna: 'O King, I rendered a service / in order that the memory of me would remain in the world.// The inhabited buildings will decay / by rains and the heat of the sun. // [However] I laid down a lofty palace out of [my] verse / which will not be destroyed by gusts and rainfalls. // Years shall pass over this book / those possessing wisdom shall keep reading it' (*yak-ī bandagī kardam ay shahriyār / kih mānad zi-man dar jahān yādʾgār // banā–hā–yi ābād gardad kharāb / zi-bārān-u az*

knowledge about Firdausī's sources and their provenance, as well as the uncertainty concerning the problem of continuity between the Middle Persian poetic tradition and its Neo-Persian post-Islamic counterpart, the quest for orality in the *Shāh-nāma* is a hazardous undertaking. To draw inferences about the oral traits and modalities of performance in the *Shāh-nāma* by means of projecting the data obtained in the study of the relatively modern practice of *naqqālī* without attending to possible structural differences conditioned by the changing media (poetry *versus* prose) of the material, can hardly be considered methodologically sound. Tenable in the orality context is the examination of the impact exercised by Firdausī's epic on medieval popular literature, such as *dāstān*s in the domain of subject-matter, motif transformation, poetic interpolations and the like.

## 2 The *dāstān* Genre in Medieval Persian Literature: Aspects of Production

From the point of view of their making, *dāstān*s do not represent the product of oral composition-in-performance: they do not constitute transcriptions of concrete storytelling events or or the outcome of dictation, as has sometimes been suggested with regard to some of them.[31] As I shall make clear below, the *dāstān*s were composed in writing by authors who were part and parcel of the world of medieval literacy. In contrast to a work composed in a purely oral manner without recourse to writing, the production of *dāstān*s was therefore removed in time and space from the phase of transmission and reception.

Oral antecedents must have played a considerable part in the evolution of *dāstān*s. It is highly probable that thematically and structurally the *dāstān*s are based on cycles of folktales or legends which had crystallized around the eponymous heroes and had been transmitted orally in the course of multiple storytelling events.[32] At a certain point these fragmentary narrative traditions were unified into a coherent narrative framework;[33]

---

*tābish-i āftāb // pay afgandam az naẓm kākh-ī buland / kih az bād-u bārān nayābad gazand // barīn nāma bar 'umr-hā bugzarad / hamī khʷānad-ash har kih dārad khirad*; Khāliqī-Muṭlaq 1988–2008: IV, 173–74, ll. 65–68). See also the elaborate reflection on the instrumental role of writing down tales (original as well as translated) in immortalizing one's (mostly, a ruler's) name in the older preface to the so-called Abū Manṣūr prose *Shāh-nāma* (c. 957–958) (Riyāḥī 1993: 171–72 and n. 7 above). See the statement of Niẓāmī 'Arūḍī-yi Samarqandī in his *Chahār maqāla* (Four Discourses; compiled in 1156–1157): 'The richest portion and most excellent part of poetry are to immortalize one's name (*baqāʾ-i ism-ast*)' (Muʿīn 2001: 47). For additional references, emphasizing the centrality of the notion of *yādgār* in medieval Persian literature, see Rubanovich 2009: 133, n. 32.

[31] Throughout the chapter I use the phrase 'storytelling event' in a terminological sense according to the model proposed by Robert Georges (1969). – For the suggestion that some of the *dāstān*s are dictated texts, see Sarvar-Maulāʾī 1974: 1129–30; Bayhaqī 1988: 45; Salimov 1971: 115; Ṣafā 1960–63 : I, Introduction, 12; II, 768; Hanaway 1990.

[32] See Salimov 1971: 115, 150; Ismāʿīlī 2001: I, Introduction, 33–38.

[33] The majority of the medieval *dāstān*s appears to have been written down between the end of the eleventh and the beginning of the thirteenth centuries (e. g., the anonymous *Iskandar-nāma* is dated to the end of the twelfth/ beginning of the thirteenth c.; see Maḥjūb 1967: 454–55; *Dārāb-nāma* very cautiously to the eleventh – twelfth c.; see Salimov 1971: 36–37; or to the end of the twelfth

hence the conventional self-identification of the authors of *dāstāns* as 'compilers/gatherers' (*jam'-āvaranda, jam'-kunanda*) and the description of their activity as 'compiling/gathering' (*jam' kardan*). Farāmarz b. Khudādād al-Arrajānī, the author of *Samak-i 'Ayyār*, affords a rare glimpse into how he composed his book: having heard a great many tales from the masters delighting the heart (*ustādān-i dil-shād*), he found them all 'incomplete' (*nā–tamām*), not covering every subject. Therefore, on the insistence of his friends (*dūstān*), he 'arranged, combined and put in proper order' (*biyārāstam-u darham afkandam-u tartīb kardam*) an account that would comprise adventures, experiences and feelings of all kinds.[34]

While piecing the parts into the whole, the authors of *dāstāns* used to expand their narratives with miscellaneous extraneous materials borrowed from books of a popular variety, such as hagiographical collections of 'Stories of the Prophets' (*qiṣaṣ al-anbiyā*), Qur'ānic commentaries (*tafsīrs*), compendiums of *mirabilia* (*'ajā'ib*), historical works, epic poems, as well as from oral folk tradition. The sources of the borrowed subject-matter are almost never mentioned; the material itself is largely reworked in conformity with the conventions of folk tradition, in the spirit of what Lauri Honko termed 'geographical-morphological' and 'traditional-morphological' adaptation.[35] Some of the *dāstāns*, namely the anonymous *Iskandar-nāma* and *Samak-i 'Ayyār*, were further subject to redaction at the hands of medieval redactors, the former most probably in the fourteenth, the latter in the sixteenth century. The anonymous redactors' tampering with the original text betrays their learned, scholarly stance, presenting a sharp contrast to the traditional folk patterns characteristic of the work of the original compilers and thus creating a peculiar interplay between popular folk culture and the learned, 'high' counterpart.[36]

Just as the authors of *dāstāns* barely offer information on the manner of their work, likewise they do not supply any details about themselves or elaborate on the reasons for

---

c.; see Piemontese 2000a: 98–99, 106–7, and 2000b: 137; *Abū Muslim-nāma* is dated to the second half of the eleventh/ early twelfth c.; see Bartol'd 1909:134–35; *Samak-i 'Ayyār* is rather broadly placed at the beginning of the twelfth/ end of the thirteenth c.; see Gaillard 1987:12). The intensive process of writing down *dāstāns* corresponded in time to the active composing of 'secondary' epic poems (see above, p. 655 and n. 14; for a summarizing table of the poems and their dating, see Yamamoto 2003:112, Table 9). The interrelationship between the two genres, although not yet properly studied, must have contributed to their evolution, that is, epic poems could have functioned as source and reservoir of themes for *dāstān* authors (see Borshevskiy 1963:22); at the same time, the opposite possibility of versifying prose *dāstāns* cannot be ruled out.

[34] Khānlarī 1959–67: IV, 3–5. A similar line of development is typical of the Arabic folk *sīra* (*sīra sha'biyya*) and the Turkish *dāstān* in prose, two genres homologous to the Persian *dāstān*. Thus, for example, it follows from the account of the anonymous author of the *sīra Qiṣṣat Fīrūzshāh* that he recorded the tales about Fīrūzshāh which had circulated orally, putting them in proper order and supplementing them with poems of renowned poets (Ṣafā 1960–63: II, 766). Likewise, Abū al-Khayr Rūmī, the author/compiler of the Turkish *Salṭuq-nāme*, intimates that whenever he heard a legend about Sarī Salṭuq, the eponymous hero of the *dāstān*, he wrote it down and then arranged the material he had recorded in the form of a book (İz 1974–84: fols. 617r–v; see also Dedes 1996: I, 43). [See also ch. 24 on the Arabic *siyar* by T. Herzog and ch. 26 on Turkish medieval oral epic and romance by K. Reichl in this volume.]

[35] For discussion, see Rubanovich 2004:131–35, and 2010b.

[36] For a detailed discussion of the compiler-redactor relationship as reflected in the *Iskandar-nāma*, see Rubanovich 1996:72–78; 1998:235–37.

undertaking the compilation.[37] The author might as well be an external observer who, having watched the storytellers, sets about writing down the materials he has heard, in a new narrative framework. He might do this either at the order of a patron or on his own initiative, striving to present the tales in a fresh form to an audience which would differ from that of storytellers, such as a court circle.[38] Curiously, the particular situation of recording stories at a behest 'from above' is reflected in the plot of the anonymous *Iskandar-nāma*; there the king, Alexander, orders his vizier Aristotle to write down the tales related to him by various storytellers who themselves function as secondary characters in the narrative (e. g., Afshār 1964: 279, 286, 434). Aristotle thus acts as an educated agent, an outsider to the world of the storytellers, who is authoritatively commissioned by his master to keep a written record of the orally transmitted accounts. This procedure could have been interpreted as a conventional motif found in abundance, for example, in the *Arabian Nights* (Elisséeff 1949: 102–3), if it were not for the fact that it is the *Iskandar-nāma* proper into which the tales are inserted. Furthermore, not only the tales recounted to Alexander, but all his adventures during his circumnavigation of the world are put down in writing. He bids Aristotle: 'We have completed [our travels] in the West, and all the marvels were written down. Now, start a new volume, where the adventures and the marvels of the East will be registered [...]' (Afshār 1964: 220). It is as if the book is being simultaneously composed on two levels – on the fictional level of the plot on Alexander's orders and in the meta-textual reality by the actual author of the *dāstān*. Self-reflexivity, *mise-en-abîme*, is thus created: the work reflects itself, possibly replicating in the plot the mode of its own production.[39] The case of the anonymous *Iskandar-nāma*, however, remains idiosyncratic. Neither this *dāstān* nor other *dāstān*s contain the name of a benefactor or a dedication of some kind which might confirm the possibility of their compilation on the initiative of some patron.[40]

---

[37] Contrary to other genres of medieval Persian prose, *dāstān*s are generally devoid of the authorial prefaces and/or epilogues which are conventional *loci* for meta-narrative statements. On the absence of paratextual units in *dāstān*s as conditioned by the high degree of their orality, see below, pp. 671–72.

[38] See M. Gaillard's suggestion with regard to *Samak-i 'Ayyār*; Gaillard 1987: 166–67.

[39] One wonders whether keeping a record of Alexander's travels in the *Iskandar-nāma* could be a vestige of a vague tradition that ascribes to Alexander himself the chronicling of his journeys. See Carra de Vaux 1896: 263–64, and more explicitly the Ethiopian version of the Alexander Romance (composed between the 14th and 17th centuries): 'He (i. e., Alexander) reached the heights of heaven and explored them. And he saw the east and the west thereof, and the beauties and the terrible things thereof, and the stations of the rising stars and their courses. And he described fully all these things in a large book which he called, "The Book of the Works of the whole World"' (Budge 1933: 167).

[40] Compare in this respect the case of the Turkish *Salṭuq-nāma*, compiled on the order of an Ottoman prince Jim Sultan (d. 1494) (İz 1974–84: fols. 617r-v; also Dedes 1996: I, 43), as well as the Turkish translation of the *Sīrat 'Antar* made at the behest of Sultan Mehmet (Heath 1996: 241). The request 'from above' to compile a *dāstān* should be distinguished from ordering a copy of a manuscript, which indeed occurs time and again with regard to the MSS of some Persian *dāstān*s. Thus, for example, the sixteenth-century MS of the *Dārāb-nāma* was copied by a certain Kay Qubād ibn Mahyār-i Pārsī for Nūshīravān ibn Bahmanshāh-i Pārsī, the latter probably being a nobleman of Nausārī in the Indian Gujarat. It is noteworthy that according to the scribe's post-note to the text, the MS he copied had been borrowed from the Royal Library of the Emperor Akbar due to the unavailability and rarity of the MSS of the *Dārāb-nāma* during the scribe's time-period (Ṣafā 1965–

To pursue further the possibility of *dāstān* compilation by external observers, one might think of an individual with a strong literary mindset who, disapproving of the multiformity of orally transmitted stories, sets them down in writing in order to preserve them from 'distortion' and 'aberration'. Such was the motive, for instance, of the Arabic compiler of the *Qiṣṣat Fīrūzshāh* (The Story of Fīrūzshāh); he objected to the proliferating circulation of accounts about this hero, to the original version of which 'one added and the other deleted as they wished'.[41] Among the Persian *dāstān*s, however, no indications of such a way of production can be traced.

Whereas these scenarios of production imply a strict dichotomy between the literate/learned/written and the illiterate/uneducated/oral, the latter being identified with the world of the storytellers, the reality appears both more dynamic and more subtle. Muḥammad-i Bīghamī, the fifteenth-century author of the *Fīrūzshāh-nāma* (The Book of Fīrūzshāh), explains his motives for compiling the *dāstān* as follows: 'The aim of putting this tale together is that the name of the humble one (i. e., Bīghamī himself) would endure amongst the people of speech (*ahl-i sukhan*), and, God willing, [the story] will be received [favourably] by the brothers (*barādarān*); and if there is any flaw in it (i. e., in the story), they shall generously correct it and magnanimously pardon the humble one. Verse:[42] When this renowned book comes to an end / the world will become full of praise of me;// From now on I will not die, I will endure, / for I have spread the seeds of speech;// Everyone in possession of understanding, good sense and knowledge / will exalt me after my death' (Ṣafā 1960-63: II, 372-73). Muḥammad-i Bīghamī therefore compiled the work on his own initiative with the purpose of gaining a certain position among 'the people of speech' and 'the brothers'. Although he does not specify who these two groups are, we learn from the *Futuvvat-nāma-yi Sulṭānī* of the above-mentioned Mullā Ḥusayn Vā'iẓ-i Kāshifī, Bīghamī's near contemporary, that the expression 'people of speech' denotes popular performers whose occupation is connected with verbal activity, as opposed to the display of physical prowess by 'the people of strength' (*ahl-i zūr*) and of tricks by 'the people of play' (*ahl-i bāzī*) (Maḥjūb 1971:279). According to Vā'iẓ-i Kāshifī the 'people of speech' are divided – in a diminishing order of importance – into the extollers of the Prophet Muhammad and his family (*maddāḥān va gharrā-khᵛānān*), the soothsayers (*khᵛāṣṣ-gūyān va bisāṭ-andāzān*) and the tellers of stories and legends (*qiṣṣa-khᵛānān va afsāna-gūyān*) (Maḥjūb 1971:280). Bīghamī must have belonged to the third category.[43] In the same section of the *Futuvvat-nāma-yi Sulṭānī* the expression 'the brothers of the path' (*barādarān-i ṭarīq*) is used to designate fellow-professionals, i. e., performers (*ma'raka-gīrān*), who by the fifteenth century may have been organized in a guild of some sort, to which 'the people of speech' also belonged (Maḥjūb 1971:279).

---

68: II, 598). Another example is the copy of the third volume of the *Fīrūzshāh-nāma*, which the scribe prepared with the intention of presenting it to a local prince, hoping for reward (Maḥjūb 1991:43).

[41] *Qiṣṣat Fīrūzshāh* 1946: I, 2. Compare similar lamentations of the Turkish translator of the *Sīrat 'Antar* (Heath 1996:242-43).

[42] The lines that follow are borrowed with modifications from Firdausī's *Shāh-nāma*; see n.30 above.

[43] See Ṣafā 1960-63: I, Introduction, 12; Hanaway 1990.

The professional storyteller Muḥammad-i Bīghamī, who probably specialized in the tale of Fīrūzshāh, thus intended his work for distribution first and foremost among his colleagues, either to enrich their repertoire or to provide a manual which could be used in the professional training of apprentices.[44] The possibility of 'inner consumption' of the *Fīrūzshāh-nāma* has further support in a specific terminology employed by the author in the storytelling formula that punctuates the text.[45] There the addressees are mostly defined as 'friends, fellows' (*dūstān*), once as 'young and clever' (*javānān-u ʿāqilān*) and once as 'experts of speech' (*dānandagān-i sukhan*), the two latter expressions apparently indicating various levels of skill in Bīghamī's fellow storytellers.[46] The same designation – 'friends, fellows' – as referring to the intended audience is also given by the author of *Samak-i ʿAyyār* (see above, p. 661), a fact that bespeaks a certain consistency corroborating the possibility of the *dāstān*s' 'inner consumption'. In fact, apprentices used to acquire the necessary knowledge of the story while listening to the performances of experienced storytellers, or by learning the text by heart, either independently or under the guidance of a master. However, whereas the former way of learning presupposed exceptional memorizing abilities and could not suit every one, the utilization at the stage of apprenticeship of a full textual version of the story prepared by an experienced storyteller like Maulānā–yi aʿẓam (the great master) Bīghamī or some other authoritative storyteller in case of another *dāstān*s, was a more accessible way of mastering the profession.

However, besides the need to satisfy the professional demands of their fellow storytellers, *dāstān* compilers were motivated by a strong belief in the power of the written word which they saw as the most appropriate means to immortalize their name. The author of *Samak-i ʿAyyār* expresses the hope that thanks to his work he will deserve being prayed for after his death (Khānlarī 1959–67: IV, 5); Bīghamī emphasizes the same view, with the help of the almost clichéd verses of Firdausī on the subject, cited above, while the author of the *Iskandar-nāma*, again through the voice of his hero, Alexander, sees the act of recording as the only way to gain a good name in this world and secure God's mercy in the next. The expressiveness and clarity with which the matter is stated in the *Iskandar-nāma* are apparent in two passages which fully display the apologetic stance of the author, camouflaged in Alexander's words: 'This chronicle of mine (i. e., *Iskandar-nāma*) will become renowned in the world, it will be copied and studied; when kings of the world will hear my life story, they will rejoice; they will read, copy and learn my history till the Day of Judgment [...]. But my life, alas! Were it loyal to me, I would have extracted from the world so many marvels that a mule would be needed to

---

[44] Bīghamī's work was already copied in his life-time by a certain Maḥmūd Daftar-khʷān, 'the reciter of booklets'; *daftar-khʷān*s specialized in reciting books at courts (Dihkhudā 1994; Ṣafā 1960–63: II, 768).

[45] On the storytelling formula as one of the oral features of the *dāstān* genre see below, pp. 667–68.

[46] For *dūstān* see, e. g., Ṣafā 1960–63: I, 430, 579, 592, 663; II, 304, 755; *javānān-u ʿāqilān*: Ṣafā 1960–63: I, 204; *dānandagān-i sukhan*: Ṣafā 1960–63: I, 674. – Compare one of the fundamental rules prescribed to storytellers (*ādāb-i ḥikāyat-gūyān*) by Vāʿiẓ-i Kāshifī: 'If [the storyteller] is a novice, he has to read/recite the story that he wishes to perform to his master; whereas if he is experienced, he must repeat [the story] to himself in order not to get stuck [in the course of a performance]' (Maḥjūb 1971:304).

carry the *Iskandar-nāma* (Afshār 1964: 164). And again: 'I hope that the redemption of my many sins will be in that when I depart from this world and the *Iskandar-nāma* shall remain and will be read, one of the slaves of Allah, be He extolled, will hear some of my chronicles, will shed a tear and his heart will rejoice; then God, be He extolled, on his entreaty will pardon and in His generosity take compassion [upon] me, for God is forgiving and merciful' (Afshār 1964: 185).

In their work of writing down the *dāstān*s, professional storytellers were thus guided by their firm belief in the immortalizing and absolving power of the written word in general and the book in particular as imbued with the potential to arouse empathy in the addressee and afford an emotional-aesthetic pleasure bordering on catharsis. This approach did not differ from the ethic-pragmatic view on the value of writing as the basis of cultural activity that permeated the state of mind of medieval learned Perso-Arabic litterateurs.[47] The authors of *dāstān*s were conscious of creating an independent entity, a book, quite unlike the purely oral singer/storyteller who could not detach himself from his creation.

At the same time, although influenced by the rhetoric of the written word, *dāstān* authors were not affected by the idea of textual fixity and did not cherish individual authorship. Thus, instead of claiming propriety rights to the written version of the *Fīrūzshāh-nāma* to obviate any likelihood of tampering with his text, Muḥammad-i Bīghamī, for example, encourages his colleagues to introduce changes and improvements into it, if they find it necessary. This approach clearly contradicts the attitude of a purely literary author towards his text, who would strongly resist any interference with his original work.[48] Thus, although the arranging in writing of scattered, orally-transmitted tales into unified narratives was an effort on the part of professional storytellers to bring forth a model for future performances, regulating to a certain extent the framework for prospective storytelling events, they by no means meant to produce fixed authoritative and canonical textual versions. They continued to consider the text in terms of oral poetics as multiform and open to addition and change, as one that is not given to the exceptional authority of the author/compiler, but constitutes an integral part of the storytelling tradition.

The inquiry into the aspects of *dāstān* production has shown an interplay between the literate and oral traditional patterns of text production. Functioning on the interface between the written and the oral, the creators of *dāstān*s made use of the technology of writing with its possibilities for the linear organization of the text; they displayed

---

[47] See, e. g., Arazi 1997: 377–78, 398–401; Rosenthal 1974: 6–7; Heck 2002: 107–10. It should be noted that the attitude of literary circles to the written word as described here was opposed to the views upheld by the Muslim religious milieu of *ḥadīth* scholars, who claimed priority for oral discourse in the transmission of knowledge and perceived writing as corrupting the quality of transmission, but in practice could not renounce its usage completely; see Cook 1997; Heck 2002.

[48] To cite two examples illustrating the difference: the Arab historian al-Masʿūdī, the author of a voluminous *Murūj al-dhahab*, rigorously prohibits the slightest modification or distortion of his original text, threatening the trespassers with God's wrath (Barbier de Meynard and Courteille 1861–77: I, 22–23; IX, 78–80). Likewise, the Persian historian Muḥammad-i Rāvandī in his *Rāḥat aṣ-ṣudūr va āyat as-surūr* hurls one hundred thousand curses at those who would dare add a letter or a word to his work, to abridge it or interfere with it in some other manner (Iqbāl 1921: 64). See also Zhukovsky 1926: Persian text, 2; Rosenthal 1974: 46.

acquaintance with certain cognitive patterns characteristic of the literary mindset, e. g., belief in the superiority of the written word as authoritative and immortalizing. But they remained true to the aesthetics of folk oral tradition, which conditioned their flexible approach to a text and dictated quite specific ways of the textualization of traditional materials, to be discussed below.

## 3 Modalities of Communication

On the basis of indirect historical evidence, it is generally believed that *dāstāns* were transmitted in performance, performative situations ranging from re-enacting a memorized text with varying degrees of improvisation to reading aloud.[49] The basic orientation of *dāstāns* towards interaction with the addressee determines the discourse mode of 'involvement', as opposed to 'detachment' in the case of silent reading.[50] On the level of discourse structure, the mode of involvement implies the wide use of meta-communicative markers which function as pragmatic devices intended to sustain interrelation between the narrator and his audience. They also facilitate the addressee's aural reception of the text by means of punctuating shifts in the story-line.[51] Meta-communicative markers in Persian *dāstāns* include:

(a) *Expressions indicating speaking and listening*, such as the verbs 'say, tell, relate' (*guftan*), 'retell' (*bāz guftan*), 'listen' (*shanīdan*) and a participial noun 'listener(s)' (*shanavanda(gān)*). Examples are: 'God willing, we (i. e., the narrator) shall tell [the story] in its proper place' (*Iskandar-nāma*); 'Their tale will also be told' (*bi-khidmat gufta khᵛāhad shudan*) (*Fīrūzshāh-nāma*); 'This is an extraordinary story, listen [to it]! (*bishinau!*)' (*Fīrūzshāh-nāma*); 'And you, listen to the command of God, be He extolled, so that you realize that nothing is in your hands' (*Fīrūzshāh-nāma*); 'There is no doubt that God, be He praised and extolled, sliced him (i. e., the vicious enemy) in two by means of Alexander's sword, in order that it would be a lesson to the listeners' ([...] *tā 'ibrat-i shanavandagān bāshad*) (*Dārāb-nāma*).[52]

(b) *Deictic references*, represented by deictic phrases and adverbial expressions, which assist the addressee to follow the narration, at the same time providing anaphoric and cataphoric cross-references. Theoretically, these can be divided into two broad categories, namely, deictic references pertaining to time and those denoting space, their choice being conditioned by two different cognitive systems of conceptualizing the discourse in temporal or spatial terms. The 'metaphor' of time entails a dynamic process that takes shape during reading aloud/listening and is thus associated first and foremost with oral medium and oral/aural discourse. By contrast, the 'metaphor' of space verbalizes the two-dimensionality of a written text, having evolved with the appearance of the concept of the book.[53]

---

[49] See Maḥjūb 2003a: 127–32; Maḥjūb 2003b; Ṣafā 1989: 463; Rubanovich 2004: 223–28, 238–239.
[50] In Chafe's terminology (1982: 45).
[51] See Georgakopoulou and Goutsos 1997: 114.
[52] Afshār 1964: 93; Ṣafā 1960–63: II, 35; I, 915; II, 117; Ṣafā 1965–68: II, 17. For additional examples and a more detailed discussion, see Rubanovich 2004: 229–33.
[53] See Fleischman 1991: 291, 293–94. The findings in the field of medieval French prose demonstrate

In the *dāstān*s temporal meta-narrative markers, such as 'now' (*aknūn*) and 'then, that time' (*āngāh*) prevail. Examples from the *Dārāb-nāma*: 'We (i. e., the narrator) have now reached the story of Ṭamrūsiya's mother'; 'Now we shall tell what happened to Hamārpāl'; 'And we shall resume storytelling about them when it will be the turn [to relate] about Alexander. When Alexander comes to them, then (*āngāh*) we shall tell what happens with the ascetic and the merchant' (Ṣafā 1965–68: I, 268; II, 211; I, 131). The last example, in which the temporal aspect is reinforced by the syntactic means of a temporal clause, corroborates the ambient relation between the 'metaphor' of space and the high degree of orality of a discourse. In it the difference between the discourse time and the event time of the narration is annulled, as if the narrator experiences the events in the plot as actually taking place during the storytelling. The blending of the real time of storytelling with the fictional time of the plot echoes the conception of time typical of the ritual-mythological thinking of oral culture, when the performer identifies himself with the myth, whose pattern is being reconstructed in the performance ritual.

(c) *Discourse markers facilitating the segmentation of discourse.* In texts of the *dāstān* type which are communicated orally and received aurally, the segmentation of discourse bears a pragmatic function of prime significance. The oral/aural mode discards the conventional graphic division of a lengthy text into chapters with headings as of no use to listeners, privileging instead more scrupulously detailed structural means of holding the listener's attention throughout the lengthy narrative. The reservoir of discourse markers employed in the *dāstān*s is too vast and various both morphologically and syntactically to be listed here in full; I shall concentrate therefore on the most typical and representative ones:

(1) *A storytelling formula.*[54] This is a characteristic feature of *dāstān*s and is paradigmatic in the sense that it possesses a fixed syntactical structure (noun phrase + complex predicate in the present tense) and a shared phraseology, indicative of oral narration. For instance, 'The possessor of the story thus relates that [...]' *(khudāvand-i ḥadīth chunān rivāyat mīkunad kih)* or 'The teller of the tale thus says [...]' *(rāvī-yi dāstān chunīn gūyad).*[55] Functionally, the storytelling formula provides a structuring device that organizes the narrative.[56] It appears at points of switching from one episode to another, indicates shifts in theme, marks the retrieving of the story-line after a descriptive passage, a poetic insertion or the like. W. Hanaway draws an apt comparison between the storytelling formula in *dāstān*s and a typographical device of indentation (1970:250); in fact, the storytelling formula loses its semantic significance, becoming a discourse marker meant to articulate structural relations within

---

that the shift from predominantly aural text reception to silent reading in the thirteenth century was accompanied by adopting the meta-language characteristic of the spatial concept of discourse: thus, the adverb *or* (now) came to be gradually replaced by *ci* (here); Fleischman 1991:303–4.

[54] Hanaway (1970:148) refers to the device as 'conventional opening phrase', which however misidentifies its function, since it appears in different segments of the text and not only at beginnings. In addition, it is necessary to distinguish between the storytelling formula treated here and formulas as units of oral composition in Parry's and Lord's sense.

[55] For more variants of the storytelling formula, see Rubanovich 2004:248–49.

[56] See Hanaway 1970:250–51; Salimov 1971:115–18; Gaillard 1987:85.

the text for both performer and addressee. Indeed, it guides the performer in the pacing of his performance, signalling the eye-voice span and preparing him for a change in the narrative subject or for placing the correct logical-intonational emphases at relevant points.[57] Such functioning explains the frequent interpolation of the storytelling formula by copyists on the margins of manuscripts, as well as the use in red ink in some manuscripts to distinguish the formula from the rest of the text.[58] As for the audience, the storytelling formula punctuates narrative segments, such as episodes, for instance, drawing the listener's attention to a forthcoming change and thus facilitating the processing of the orally-transmitted text.

(2) *Connectors.* The common use of connectors – such as *pas* (then), *va* (and), *aknūn* (now), *al-qiṣṣa* (so) – has frequently been referred to by scholars who have studied or translated Persian *dāstān*s. The usual approach is to consider them as 'weed-words' and to dismiss them in translation and even in scholarly editions.[59] The connectors, however, have an important pragmatic function in structuring segments of discourse, losing their conventional lexical meaning and turning instead into discourse markers. One example will suffice to illustrate the phenomenon: '[King Alexander] travelled till he reached a town. Then[1] (*pas*), when they arrived two stations from the town, there was a despotic and heathen ruler in the town, who spent his days and nights bothering girls and established this bad habit in the town. Then[2] (*pas*), when King Alexander arrived in the town, a rumour [about his arrival] spread out [...]'.[60] The first 'then[1]' introduces expositional information on the despotic king, while the second 'then[2]' signals a return to the plot-line after the orientation segment, both 'then's being deprived of their temporal meaning and narrative function. Notwithstanding the typicality of the discourse segmentation in the *dāstān* genre, not every change or digression from the plot-line is signalled by discourse markers. Their use therefore does not seem obligatory or systematic and no strict conventions of segmentation can be established.

(d) *Manifestations of interaction 'storyteller → audience'.* These include:

(1) *Direct address of the narrator to the addressee* to attract attention to structural changes in the narrative or to a didactic message. Examples: 'Keep them (i. e., the heroes) here and listen from the other side (i. e., a parallel plot-line)' (*Abū Muslim-nāma*); 'Leave them (i. e., the heroes) till we (i. e., the narrator) reach their story' (*Abū Muslim-nāma*); 'But this is a marvellous story, listen!' (*Fīrūzshāh-nāma*); 'Now, look well at the account of Alexander and take example from this just king'

---

[57] See Levin 1979: 1. Compare in this regard the conclusions of D. Pinault concerning the pragmatic role of the storytelling formulas *qāla ar-rāwī* (The narrator said) and *qāla ṣāḥib al-ḥadīth* (The possessor of the story said) in *A Thousand and One Nights*. These formulas mostly conclude secondary stories framed by the main narrative or else follow verse passages, thus conveying to the professional reciter of the written text an alteration in narrative tempo or voice (Pinault 1992: 13–14, 171–72, 174).

[58] See, e. g., the *Dārāb-nāma* MS, London, India Office Library MS 980, fols. 11a, 12b, 19a, 20a, 72b etc.; Ṣafā 1960–63: I, Introduction, 14–15. Compare the same phenomenon in Arabic MSS of *A Thousand and One Nights* (Pinault 1992: 14, 174).

[59] See Southgate 1978: 4; Ismāʿīlī 2001: I, 188–89.

[60] Afshār 1964: 128–29. For more examples and discussion, see Rubanovich 2004: 269–71.

(*Dārāb-nāma*); 'I related [the story] so that you may know that there was no injustice (in what had happened)' (*Samak-i ʿAyyār*).⁶¹

(2) *Rhetorical questions* meant to invoke the addressee's interest in the continuation of the story. Examples: 'What was the washerman's story?' (*Dārāb-nāma*); 'Who was that mounted warrior and where did he take the queen of the fair ones?' (*Fīrūzshāh-nāma*); 'What happened to them?' (*Fīrūzshāh-nāma*); 'What kind of horse is it?' (*Samak-i ʿAyyār*).⁶²

(3) *Reconstruction of the storytelling event or some of its components.* The phenomenon is most prominently expressed in the anonymous *Iskandar-nāma*, occurring in connection with the tales – thirty-seven in number – inserted into the main narrative by the original compiler of the *dāstān* and later abridged and/or deleted by the medieval redactor (see above, pp. 661–62). Since the subject has been dealt with in detail elsewhere, here I shall briefly present the principal findings (Rubanovich 1996: 71–100; 2004: 135–43). The insertion of tales into the main narrative reproduces the general scheme characteristic of setting up a story session by a storyteller. This comprises a number of stages. During the preparatory stage the storyteller signals his addressee (King Alexander in the case of the *Iskandar-nāma*) that the storytelling event is about to begin by asking the king's permission to relate the story and announcing the story's theme. The choice of the theme is conditioned by a number of factors, such as the contextual circumstances of the main narrative. Examples: Alexander's misadventures with women are illustrated by a series of misogynic tales with a didactic and therapeutic purport, communicated to Alexander by various storytellers (Afshār 1964: 260–62, 279–86); the physical location of Alexander (e. g., when going to Turkestan, Alexander asks a storyteller to tell him tales of Iranian heroes whose exploits are linked to this area) (Afshār 1964: 201, also 129); as well as the ethnic or religious adherence of the internal storyteller (e. g., the headman of Egypt recounts to Alexander the story of the Arab king's daughter; an aged ascetic 'from among the descendants' of the Prophet David is asked by Alexander to narrate accounts of the Prophets David and Solomon) (Afshār 1964: 157–62, 259, also 251–52). The choice of theme is often accompanied by a ceremonial negotiation between the storyteller and his addressee, with the potential to evolve further into an active interaction between the two, during the storytelling proper and in its aftermath (e. g., Afshār 1964: 345–46; 250–51).

The interaction in the course of the storytelling comprises addresses to Alexander on the part of storytellers, including the conventional phrase of salutation 'Long live the King of Kings!'; Alexander intervenes in the process in order to request an explanation or clarification of certain points or to express solidarity with the story, drawing on his personal experience (Afshār 1964: 293, 346, 158). The identification of the listener with the message of the story is also characteristic of the last stage of the storytelling, as it is reconstructed in the *Iskandar-nāma*. At times Alexander parallels the situation to the state of his own affairs, trying to extract a lesson from the story or else he authoritatively

---

⁶¹ Ismāʿīlī 2001: I, 231; II, 191; Ṣafā 1960–63: I, 915; Ṣafā 1965–68: II, 597; Khānlarī 1959–67: V, 475. For additional examples and a more detailed discussion, see Rubanovich 2004: 235–36.

⁶² Ṣafā 1965–68: I, 62; Ṣafā 1960–63: II, 239; 437; Khānlarī 1959–67: II, 101.

confirms the storyteller's account; in other cases, he reacts in an emotional way, expressing satisfaction, delight, empathy 'moistening his robes with tears', or anger.[63] Besides the verbal and sensorial responses which are common to every audience whatever its social status, Alexander's reactions are further conditioned by the doubling of his function as a listener with his social role as king. Hence the rewarding of favoured storytellers with 'the robe of honour' (khal'at) in line with the medieval courtly tradition prevalent at the time when the Iskandar-nāma was committed to writing (Afshār 1964:189, 130, 263). Yet another manifestation of the royal benevolence is Alexander's encouragement of specific storytellers to continue their storytelling in consecutive evening sessions, or his order to write down the most rare and instructive tales, to be stored in the royal repository (Afshār 1964:154–55, 162–63, 348, 279, 434).

Besides the Iskandar-nāma, some components of the storytelling event are reconstructed in Samak-i 'Ayyār. In this dāstān one encounters the narrator's/ storyteller's asides, when he halts his narration creating suspense, and asks his audience for remuneration, otherwise he will stop telling the story. For example:

> Shirvān Bashan approached Farrukh-rūz and said something into his ear. Farrukh-rūz wept, then laughed. 'Ālam-afrūz was so astonished: 'What had been said that he (i. e., Farrukh-rūz) wept and laughed?' However hard he thought, he could not figure out [...]. You (i. e., listeners) also will not figure it out, unless you give [me] ten sugar candies [to prepare] rose-water, for my throat sores. If not, then pronounce one al-ḥamd prayer for the sake of the book's compiler in order that God, be He extolled, will spare him. We shall resume our talk and relate what Shirvān Bashan said into Farrukh-rūz's ear, why Farrukh-rūz [first] wept and then laughed. Thus relates the possessor of the story and the storyteller [...] (Khānlarī 1959–67: IV, 295)

On other occasions the storyteller requires monetary reward from his listeners to buy sherbet or a tray of sugared halva; in some cases he contents himself with asking for prayers for the sake of the compiler or the copyist (Khānlarī 1959–67: III, 244; IV, 101, 286, 295; V, 15–16).

A peculiar instance of such meta-narrative asides occurs when the link of the fictional world of the narrative with the extra-narrative reality becomes most conspicuous. This involves the characters' intercession for the storyteller, as in the following example:

> 'Ālam-afrūz said: 'O, woman, who are you after all?' Saman-rukh answered: 'If you want me to tell you who I am, then request that this audience (i. e., the extra-narrative listeners to the story) should give one thousand golden dīnārs to the compiler of this book, for he has experienced much hardship and expended much time to compile the story. I mentioned [the sum] which I myself find proper. If they do not have and cannot give [it], let them give according to their own capacity, but not less than five dīnārs. Now, each and every one should pronounce an al-ḥamd prayer for the sake of the lives of the book's maker (sāzanda-yi kitāb) and of the book's copyist and entreat God Almighty to pardon him [sic], so that God, be He exalted and extolled, will pardon and spare them in His mercy and grace.' 'Ālam-afrūz said: 'Everything has been fulfilled, so who are you? [...]'[64]

---

[63] Afshār 1964:162; 129–30; 201 (see also 156, 191, 207, 297); 199.
[64] Khānlarī 1959–67: V, 609. For additional examples, see Khānlarī 1959–67: IV, 198; V, 531–32. The examples are cited also in Khānlarī 1985:66–67, and Gaillard 1987:165–66.

In general, this kind of aside reflects a traditional storytelling practice, as can be seen from a brief remark of the Turkish translator of *Samak-i 'Ayyār*, who, rendering one of the storyteller's requests for remuneration, glosses it as 'the habit of the masters' (*qā'ida-yi ustādān*); the practice was still very much alive in the 1920s in Iran, documented, for example, for performances of the puppet theatre (*khayma-shab-bāzī*) (Galunov 1929: 3).

Whether the vestiges of storytelling events preserved in these *dāstān*s testify to the actual history of these texts or, alternatively, function as a stylized device, is difficult to determine with any certainty (see also above, p. 662). It is apparent, however, that in itself such a reconstruction is indicative of the profound anchoring of the *dāstān*s' producers in the oral storytelling tradition, the patterns and frames of which they continued to perpetuate.

## 4 Oral Traditional Aesthetics

In addition to aspects of production and communication, the impact of orality in *dāstān*s is manifest in the feature of traditional referentiality that to a large extent determines the decoding of their meaning.[65] The meaning in an oral tradition-oriented text can be successfully inferred only if one takes into account, – i. e., 'refers' to – motifs, narrative patterns, protagonists, characters and other background information which has been accumulating for many generations and is stored in the reservoir of a particular oral narrative tradition, each performance echoing earlier ones and thus validated by the tradition itself. In the following I will demonstrate the mechanisms of traditional referentiality in the *dāstān*s, inquiring into three of their most characteristic facets, namely the lack of paratextual apparatus, the phenomenon of lacunas in the plot, and the chronological inconsistency in the narrative.[66]

*(a) The absence of a paratextual apparatus.* Theoretically, the paratext in general and particularly the preface are meant to mediate between the author (and his work) and the addressee, imposing on the latter a certain interpretative approach towards the text, as well as claiming the author's ownership of his work (Genette 1997: 197–98; 209–29). It implies physical distance and emotional detachment between the author and the community of readers, at the same time signifying a rather crystallized concept of individual authorship. Persian *dāstān*s usually start and end *ex abrupto*, the only paratextual unit being, as a rule, a colophon. Although in some cases, the lack of preface and postface can be explained by the physical incompleteness of certain manuscripts, this will not apply to the majority of the *dāstān*s which have been preserved in full.[67] Although mostly written down in the twelfth and thirteenth centuries or later, i. e., during the period when in 'courtly' prose the authorial preface and postface had assumed a firm canonical status ushering in the formation of the authorial personal voice, *dāstān*s lack

---

[65] For the definition and elaboration of the concept of traditional referentiality, see Foley 1991: 6–8.
[66] For the term 'paratext' and its definition, see Genette 1997.
[67] Thus, for instance, the only extant MS of the *Iskandar-nāma*, on which the scholarly edition is based, lacks a couple of folios at the beginning and a large part at the end. The *Fīrūzshāh-nāma* supposedly possessed additional volumes (on one of these, probably the third, copied in 1787, see Maḥjūb 1991). But see also n. 68.

any contextual framework which might offer the author's statement of intent and his status vis-à-vis the tradition, and define his target-audience, thus serving as an instrument of authorial control (Rubanovich 2009: esp. 128).

The transmission of *dāstān*s in an unmediated interaction with the listener seems to weaken or even eliminate altogether the necessity for any preliminary contextual information, as well as for explanations regarding the preferred way of reception. Indeed, due to its variable nature, each and every performance sets up a new context as far as performer, audience, and temporal and local circumstances are concerned. Prefacing a text intended for multiple performances implies the fixation of a specific context out of a variety of potential performative situations, thus going counter to the rationale of this type of communication. In addition, unlike an author targeting addressees distanced from him in time and place, an oral storyteller possesses a range of linguistic, para-linguistic (intonation, rhythm), and non-linguistic (facial expressions, body movements) means enabling him to control and channel the audience's response at every point of the performance. The addressee thus activates various semiotic codes and situational contexts to complete the textual message (Oesterreicher 1997:209–10). What is more: the common reservoir of themes, motifs, allusions etc., shared by a storyteller and his audience, obviates the need for some sorts of contextual information; recourse to conventional devices anchored in the oral tradition, such as the storytelling formula, is sufficient for a performer to inform the addressee that the traditional framework of performance is being set in motion, thus activating pre-knowledge regarding the oncoming event and its contents (for details, see pp. 672–74 below).

At the same time, since the concept of individual authorship appears to have been alien to the creators of *dāstān*s, who conceived a text in terms of oral poetics as multi-variant and receptive of changes and additions (see above, pp. 663, 665), they did not feel a need to have recourse to a preface for stating their ownership of the work.[68]

(b) *Filling up lacunae and deciphering allusions.* The narrative texture of Persian *dāstān*s reveals a dense web of lacunae, elliptic passages, dim allusions, and obscure motifs which could have been filled out and made comprehensible by reference to extra-narrative reality, namely, the tradition shared by the storyteller and his addressee. Although some parts of the tradition, being oral, have been irreversibly lost to research, in certain cases the gaps can still be reconstructed by mining extant written materials, mostly of epic character. As an example, let us look at the following passage from the *Dārāb-nāma*, alluding to certain events from Iranian epic-heroic history: 'Gushtāsp put his son [= Isfandiyār] in chains, so that they captured and killed Luhrāsp and took his (i. e., Gushtāsp's) daughters to Turkistān, till with the help of a thousand tricks he (i. e., Gushtāsp) came back, and removed Isfandiyār's chains, so that he (i. e., Isfandiyār) went

---

[68] The irrelevance of prefatory writing to the very essence of the *dāstān* genre is pertinently reflected in the curious case of *Samak-i 'Ayyār*. There we encounter an addition, a kind of preface, in which the author/compiler describes his work and elaborates on various themes the *dāstān* is going to deal with (Khānlarī 1959–67: IV, 3–5). However, the addition is awkwardly located at the beginning of the third volume of the MS, equivalent to the beginning of the fourth volume of the printed edition, i. e., at the very core of the narration. Provided the addition is authentic and not a later interpolation (Mīnuvī 1958:335), it loses its structural function of text delimitation as well as its import as a means for the author to secure a certain interpretive approach on the part of his addressee.

and brought his sisters back [...]' (Ṣafā 1965–68: I, 448). The passage features a highly compressed style, implying the addressee's acquaintance with the *dramatis personae* mentioned. The conciseness is coupled with the constant switching of the referents for personal pronouns (supplied in brackets in the above passage), creating an ambiguity which can be removed only by recourse to the traditional reservoir of epic themes, as they appear, for instance, in the *Shāh-nāma*.[69]

Another type of filling gaps with the help of traditional knowledge is associated with the deciphering of allusions. For example, while experiencing hardships and arduous toil, the future king Darius consoles himself by pondering: 'I am not nobler than my grandfather Gushtāsp. The same happened to him. Now, I shall suffer adversities, in order not to get conceited [about being a king]' (Ṣafā 1965–68: I, 289). The allusion refers to epic stories of King Gushtāsp who, in disguise, was a manual labourer in Rūm before ascending the throne of Iran (Khāliqī–Muṭlaq 1988–2008: V, 14–18). The addressee's acquaintance with the epic tradition allows him not only to restore the elliptic passage on the surface level, but to retrace the 'deep' meaning of the whole episode in the *Dārāb-nāma* as well. Indeed, by way of traditional referentiality, the allusion to Gushtāsp's tale seems to evoke the archetypical paradigm of a hero undergoing ordeals before attaining power, an initiation motif, well-known in world as well as in Iranian folklore. The tale of Darius' trials, rather than representing an autonomous and individual plot, is joined to parallel plots and motifs in the epic tradition and thus metonymically anticipates the development of the narrative (namely, Darius' forthcoming ascent to the throne), which at the same time agrees with the listener's expectations.

To illustrate the mechanism of traditional referentiality working in the case of a more obscure motif, I shall adduce the motif of Alexander covering his hair when going in the guise of an ambassador to various rulers (Afshār 1964: 59, 108). The explanation for the curious act is not given in the narrative; it can be understood, however, due to the traditional knowledge of Alexander as 'Two-Horned' (*Dhū al-Qarnayn*), that is having two plaits in the form of horns which should be concealed lest the king be recognized. The decoded motif in turn activates a deeper meaning that entails the concept of Alexander in the Arabo-Persian tradition as the champion of Islam conquering the world and converting peoples to the true faith.[70]

*(c) Chronological inconsistency in the narrative*. The phenomenon is manifested in deviations from the logical temporal development of the plot, when an episode, an event or a character trait are mentioned in the narration as if already occurred and known, before they have actually been reported. Thus, for example, Būrāndukht, the female protagonist of the *Dārāb-nāma*, laments the absence of a weapon which would have enabled her to engage the foe as she had done on Maḥkūy Island (Ṣafā 1965–68: II, 257); this combat, however, is described only much later in the plot (Ṣafā 1965–68: II, 416–19). In another case the same heroine is being warned by the Indian sage not to attack the enemy army on account of 'that (*ān*) dream' which she had had and which foretold calamities,

---

[69] Khāliqī–Muṭlaq 1988–2008: V, 146–69; 178–85; 188–98; 264–66. Instructive in this respect is the translation of the *Dārāb-nāma* into Russian (Kondyreva 2000), where imperfect knowledge of the epic tradition significantly obstructed the correct comprehension of the text, leading to blunders on the part of the translator (see Rubanovich 2002).

[70] For more examples, see Rubanovich 2004: 249–54.

but her dreaming and the contents of the dream actually follow the warning, instead of preceding it (Ṣafā 1965–68: II, 157–58). Similarly, in the *dāstān*s devoted to his adventures, from the very beginning of the narrative Alexander is represented as 'the King of the Universe' (*shāh-jahān*) (Ṣafā 1965–68: I, 551); 'the King of the East and the West' (*pādshāh-i mashriq-u maghrib*) (Afshār 1964: 165, 433, 510 etc.); 'the King of Seven Climes' (*pādshāh-i haft iqlīm*), these qualifiers coming much earlier than Alexander's factual conquest of the world.[71] The recurrent descriptions of Alexander as the Ruler of the Universe while ignoring the chronological consistency of the narrative are designed not so much to portray the hero as to set off the theme which is central to the traditional perception of Alexander and thus echoic of the Alexander tale as a whole.[72]

It is a peculiarity of *dāstān*s that traditional knowledge does not seem to be restricted to the storyteller and his addressee, but is shared by the characters in the plot; hence, for example, the description of Alexander by various personages as 'King of the East and the West', or Darius' allusion to his ancestor Gushtāsp, carry the same referential import for the extra-narrative storyteller and his listeners as they do for the fictional characters. This, as well as the utterances of the *dramatis personae* supporting the storyteller's claim to reward from his real audience in *Samak-i ʿAyyār*, or the *Iskandar-nāma*'s parallel composition within the plot and in the extra-textual reality (see above, pp. 669–71 and 662, respectively), evince the blurring of boundaries between the fictional world of the plot and the extra-narrative world of actual storytellers and their listeners. Indeed, in the course of performance, the storyteller can enact roles, minimizing the narrative distance between himself and the characters. At the same time, by means of direct addresses to the listeners, both by storyteller and by characters within the plot, the audience gets involved – emotionally and sometimes even physically – in the fictional narrative world. A model of dynamic relationships between all the actors is established which implies considerable involvement (versus detachment) and maximum cooperation of all the sides in the communicative act and essentially contradicts the unidirectional relation of 'text → addressee'.

The impact of orality is palpable in all aspects of *dāstān* production, transmission, reception, and subject-matter. Considered from the point of view of medial orality, the delivery and reception of *dāstān*s were distinguished by medium shift, i. e., switches between graphic signs (silent reading/reading aloud) and phonetic signs (speaking/hearing).[73] In delivery the oral mode of transmission (and aural reception) prevailed, actual-

---

[71] Ṣafā 1965–68: II, 29. For additional examples in the same vein, see Ṣafā 1965–68: I, 547, 551; II, 29, 410; Afshār 1964: 46.

[72] Compare the description of Odysseus in the *Iliad* as 'much-suffering' before he was subjected to any sufferings in the narrative time of the epic; see Nagy 1990: 23.

[73] See Oesterreicher 1997: 190–93; Koch 1997. – It should be noted that in medieval Persian literature the medium shift could have accompanied other types of text as well, such as epistolary compositions, which in addition to being read silently might have been transmitted by reading aloud (see Luther 1990: 94). However, oral/aural transmission and reception did not serve as a primary medium of such texts; they were designed to be received by a private reader and structured accordingly. In fact, their 'vocality' dimension – or *vocalité*, to use the term coined by P. Zumthor (1987: 21 ff.) – functioned in a purely rhetoric way, as a ritual discourse of sorts, a good example being the formal ceremonial recitation of epistles in an assembly. For a related situation in medieval Arabic *adab* literature, see Sadan 1998: 4.

ized in a gamut of performative situations: from reading aloud to utilizing a written text as a prop to performing a text memorized by rote with various degrees of improvisation. The performance-oriented character of *dāstān*s was one of the factors determining their high degree of 'conceptional orality' (Oesterreicher 1997: 193–95), and introducing the pragmatic constraints that shaped the narrative. These include the patterning of narration by means of the storytelling formula; a substantial 'narrator-addressee' interactivity; the reconstruction of the oral storytelling mode within the narrative; and lingual-stylistic features typical of oral discourse. Besides the modalities of performance, *dāstān*s' high degree of conceptional orality ensues from their essentially traditional nature, when the knowledge of the narrative epic tradition common to the storyteller and his audience becomes a prerequisite for successful communication and comprehension. *Dāstān*s are context-embedded; their seeming chronological inconsistency and excess of ellipticity, the significance of which eludes the outsider, appear perfectly coherent to the insider steeped in the tradition.

## References

Afshār, Īraj, ed. 1964. *Iskandar-nāma*. Teheran: Bungāh-i tarjuma va nashr-i kitāb.
Afshārī, Mihrān, and M. Madāyinī, eds. 1998. *Haft lashkar (ṭūmār-i jāmiʿ-i naqqālān) az Kayūmarth tā Bahman*. Teheran: Pazhūhishgāh-i 'ulūm-i insānī va muṭāliʿāt-i farhangī.
Arazi, Albert. 1997.'De la voix au calame et la naissance du classicisme en poésie.' *Arabica* 44: 377–406.
Bagley, F. R. C. 1989.'Badīha-sarāʾī.' *Encyclopaedia Iranica*, III, 379–80.
Barbier de Meynard, C., and P. Courteille, eds. and trans. 1861–77. *Maçoudi. Les Prairies d'or*. 9 vols. Paris.
Bartol'd, V. V. 1909.'K istorii Merva.' *Zapiski Vostochnogo obshchestva Rossiyskoy AN* 19: 115–38.
Bayhaqī, Ḥusayn ʿAlī. 1988. *Pazhūhish-u barrasī-yi farhang-i ʿāmma-yi Īrān*. [Mashhad:] Idāra-yi mūza-hā-yi āstān-i quds-i Raḍavī.
Borshchevskiy, Yuri. 1963. 'Persidskaya narodnaya literatura.' In *Plutovka iz Bagdaga*. Ed. N. N. Tumanovich. Moscow: Izd. Vostochnoy Literatury. 5–26.
Boyce, Mary. 1957.'The Parthian *gōsān* and Iranian Minstrel Tradition.' *JRAS* 1957: 10–45.
–. 1989.'Ayādgār ī Zarērān.' *Encyclopaedia Iranica*, III, 128–29.
–. 2003.'Gōsān.' *Encyclopaedia Iranica*, XI, 167–70.
Budge, E. A. W., trans. 1933. *The Alexander Book in Ethiopia*. London: OUP.
Carra de Vaux, Bernard, trans. 1896. *Maçoudi. Le Livre de l'Avertissement et de la Revision*. Paris.
Chafe, Wallace L. 1982.'Integration and Involvement in Speaking, Writing, and Oral Literature.' In *Spoken and Written Language: Exploring Orality and Literacy*. Ed. Deborah Tannen. Norwood, NJ: ABLEX. 35–53.
Cook, Michael. 1997. 'The Opponents of the Writing of Tradition in Early Islam.' *Arabica* 44: 437–530.
Davidson, Olga M. 1985.'The Crown-Bestower in the Iranian Book of Kings.' In *Papers in Honour of Professor Mary Boyce*. Ed. H. W. Bailey et al. 2 vols. Acta Iranica 24, 25. Leiden: Brill. I, 61–148.
–. 1988.'A Formulaic Analysis of Samples Taken from the *Shahnāma* of Firdowsi.' *Oral Tradition* 3: 88–105.
–. 1994. *Poet and Hero in the Persian Book of Kings*. Ithaca, NY: Cornell UP.
–. 1998.'The Text of Ferdowsi's *Shāhnāma* and the Burden of the Past.' *JAOS* 118: 63–68.

—. 2000. *Comparative Literature and Classical Persian Poetics: Seven Essays*. Costa Mesa, CA: Mazda Publishers.
Davis, Dick. 1996. 'The Problems of Ferdowsi's Sources.' *JAOS* 116: 48–57.
de Blois, François. 1994. *Persian Literature. A Bio-bibliographical Survey. V. Poetry of the Pre-Mongol Period*. London: The Royal Asiatic Society.
—. 1998a. 'Review of Davidson 1994.' *JRAS*, Third Series 8: 269–70.
—. 1998b. 'Epics.' *Encyclopaedia Iranica*, VIII, 474–77.
de Fouchécour, Charles-Henri. 1976. 'Une lecture du *Livre des Rois* de Ferdowsi.' *Studia Iranica* 5: 171–202.
Dedes, Yorgos, ed. and trans. 1996. *Battalname*. 2 vols. Sources of Oriental Languages and Literatures, Turkic Sources 31. Cambridge, MA: Department of Near Eastern Languages and Civilizations, Harvard U.
Dihkhudā, ʿAlī Akbar. 1994. 'Daftar-khʷān.' *Lughat-nāma-yi Dihkhudā*. Ed. Muḥammad Muʿīn and S. J. Shahīdī. Teheran: Muʾssasa-yi intishārāt va chāp-i dānishgāh-i Tihrān. VII, 9627.
Dundes, Alan. 1966. 'Metafolklore and Oral Literary Criticism.' *The Monist* 50: 509–12.
Dūstkhʷāh, Jalīl, ed. 1991. *Dāstān-i Rustam-u Suhrāb. Rivāyat-i naqqālān*. Naqd va nigārish-i Murshid ʿAbbās-i Zarīrī. Teheran: Intishārāt-i Tūs.
Elisséeff, Nikita. 1949. *Thèmes et motifs des 'Mille et Une Nuits'. Essai de Classification*. Beyrouth: Institut Français de Damas.
*Encyclopaedia Iranica*. Ed. Ehsan Yarshater. Vol. 1 ff. London: Routledge and Kegan Paul. Also available online at <www.iranica.com>.
Even-Zohar, Itamar. 1990. 'Polysystem Studies.' *Poetics Today* 11: 1–268.
Finnegan, Ruth. 1977. *Oral Poetry: Its Nature, Significance and Social Context*. Cambridge: CUP.
Fleischman, Suzanne. 1991. 'Discourse as Space/ Discourse as Time: Reflections on the Metalanguage of Spoken and Written Discourse.' *Journal of Pragmatics* 16: 291–306.
Foley, John M. 1991. *Immanent Art: From Structure to Meaning in Traditional Oral Epic*. Bloomington: Indiana UP.
Gaillard, Marina. 1987. *Le Livre de Samak-e ʿAyyâr. Structure et idéologie du roman persan médiéval*. Paris: Institut d'études iraniennes, Université de la Sorbonne Nouvelle.
Galunov, R. A. 1929. 'Khéymé shab bāzi – teatr marionetok.' *Iran III*. Ed. V. V. Bartol'd. Leningrad: AN. 1–50.
Genette, Gérard. 1997. *Paratexts: Thresholds of Interpretation*. Trans. Jane E. Lewin. Cambridge: CUP. [Or. Paris, 1987.]
Georgakopoulou, Alexandra, and D. Goutsos. 1997. *Discourse Analysis: An Introduction*. Edinburgh: Edinburgh UP.
Georges, Robert A. 1969. 'Toward an Understanding of Storytelling Events.' *JAF* 82: 313–28.
Green, D. H. 1994. *Medieval Listening and Reading: The Primary Reception of German Literature 800–1300*. Cambridge: CUP.
Hanaway, William L., Jr. 1970. 'Persian Popular Romances Before the Safavid Period.' Ph.D. Thesis, Columbia University.
—. 1971. 'Formal Elements in the Persian Popular Romances.' *Review of National Literatures. Iran* 2: 139–60.
—. 1978. 'The Iranian Epics.' In *Heroic Epic and Saga: An Introduction to the World's Great Folk Epics*. Ed. Felix J. Oinas. Bloomington: Indiana UP. 76–98.
—. 1990. 'Bīǧamī.' *Encyclopaedia Iranica*, IV, 249.
—. 1996. 'Dāstān-sarāʾī.' *Encyclopaedia Iranica*, VII, 102–3.
Heath, Peter. 1996. *The Thirsty Sword. 'Sīrat ʿAntar' and the Arabic Popular Epic*. Salt Lake City: U of Utah P.
Heck, Paul L. 2002. 'The Epistemological Problem of Writing in Islamic Civilization: al-Ḥaṭīb al-Baġdādī's (d. 463/1071) *Taqyīd al-ʿilm*.' *Studia Islamica* 94: 85–114.

Iqbāl, Muḥammad, ed. 1921. Muḥammad ibn 'Alī Rāvandī. *Rāḥat aṣ-ṣudūr va āyat as-surūr*. London: Luzac.
Ismā'īlī, Ḥusayn, ed. 2001. Abū Ṭāhir-i Ṭarṭūsī. *Abū Muslim-nāma*. 4 vols. Teheran: Intishārāt-i Mu'īn; Nashr-i Qaṭra; Anjuman-i Īrānshināsī-yi Farānsa dar Īrān.
İz, Fahir, ed. 1974–84. *Ṣaltuḳ–nāmē, the Legend of Sarı Ṣaltuḳ, Collected from Oral Tradition by Ebū'l-Ḫayr Rūmī*. 5 vols. Sources of Oriental Languages and Literatures, Turkic Sources 4. Cambridge, MA: Department of Near Eastern Languages and Civilizations, Harvard U.
Khāliqī–Muṭlaq, Jalāl, gen. ed. 1988–2008. Abū al-Qāsim Firdausī. *Shāh-nāma*. 8 vols. Persian Text Series, N. S. 1. New York: Bibliotheca Persica.
– [Khaleghi-Motlagh, Djalal]. 1999. 'Ferdowsī, Abu'l-Qāsem. i. Life.' *Encyclopaedia Iranica*, IX, 514–23.
–. 2009. 'Az *Khudāy-nāma* tā *Shāh-nāma*. Justār-ī dar bāra-yi ma'ākhiz-i mustaqīm va ghayr-i mustaqīm-i *Shāh-nāma*.' *Tār-numā–yi nūf*. January. <http://www.noufe.com/persish/Khaleghi/pdf/azshahnametakhodayname.pdf>
Khānlarī, Parvīz Nātil, ed. 1959–67. Farāmarz b. Khudādād b. 'Abd Allāh al-Kātib al-Arrajānī. *Samak-i 'Ayyār*. 5 vols. Teheran: Sukhan; Intishārāt-i dānishgāh-i Tihrān.
–. 1985. *Shahr-i Samak. Tamaddun-u farhang, āyīn-i 'ayyārī, lughāt, amthāl va ḥikam*. Teheran: Mu'assasa-yi intishārāt-i āgāh.
Koch, Peter. 1997. 'Orality in Literate Cultures.' In *Writing Development: An Interdisciplinary View*. Ed. Clotilde Pontecorvo. Amsterdam: Benjamins. 149–71.
Kondyreva, N. B., trans. 2000. Abū Ṭāhir Ṭarsūsī. *Dārāb-nāme, ili Kniga o Darabe*. Moscow: Ladomir, Nauka.
Levin, Harry. 1979. *The Eye-Voice Span*. Cambridge, MA: MIT P.
Lisān, Ḥusayn. 1975. 'Shāh-nāma-khānī.' *Hunar va mardum* 159–60: 2–16.
Luther, Kenneth A. 1990. 'Islamic Rhetoric and the Persian Historians.' In *Studies in Near Eastern Culture and History in Memory of Ernest T. Abdel-Massih*. Ed. James A. Bellamy. Ann Arbor: The U of Michigan Center for Near Eastern and North African Studies. 90–98.
Maḥjūb, Muḥammad Ja'far. 1967. 'Iskandar-nāma.' *Sukhan* 17: 447–57.
–. 1991. 'Jild-i sivvum-i dāstān-i Fīrūzshāh.' *Īrānshināsī* 3/1: 41–54.
–, ed. 1971. Maulānā Ḥusayn Vā'iẓ-i Kāshifī-yi Sabzivārī. *Futuvvat-nāma-yi Sulṭānī*. Teheran: Intishārāt-i bunyād-i farhang-i Īrān.
–. 2003a. 'Muṭāla'a dar dāstan-hā–yi āmmiyyāna-yi fārsī.' In his *Adabiyyāt-i āmmiyyāna-yi Īrān. Majmū'a-yi maqālāt dar-bāra-yi afsāna-hā va ādāb-u rusūm-i mardum-i Īrān*. Ed. by Ḥasan Dhu 'l-Faqārī. 2 vols. Teheran: Nashr-i chashma. I, 121–60.
–. 2003b. 'Taḥavvul-i naqqālī va qiṣṣakhānī, tarbiyyat-i qiṣṣakhānān va ṭūmār-hā–yi naqqālī.' In his *Adabiyyāt-i āmmiyyāna-yi Īrān. Majmū'a-yi maqālāt dar-bāra-yi afsāna-hā va ādāb-u rusūm-i mardum-i Īrān*. 2 vols. Ed. by Ḥasan Dhu 'l-Faqārī. Teheran: Nashr-i chashma. II, 1079–113.
Marzolph, Ulrich. 1994. *Dāstānhā-ye šīrīn. Fünfzig persische Volksbüchlein aus der zweiten Hälfte des zwanzigsten Jahrhunderts*. Stuttgart: Steiner.
–. 1999. 'A Treasury of Formulaic Narrative: The Persian Popular Romance *Hosein-e Kord*.' *Oral Tradition* 14: 279–303.
Meisami, Julie S. 1995. 'The *Šāh-Nāme* as Mirror for Princes. A Study in Reception.' In *Pand-o sokhan. Mélanges offerts à Charles-Henri de Fouchécour*. Ed. C. Balaÿ, C. Kappler and Ž. Vesel. Teheran: Institut français de recherche en Iran. 265–73.
–. 1996. 'Review of Davidson 1994.' *Journal of Islamic Studies* 7: 85–90.
Melikian-Chirvani, Assadullah Souren. 1988. 'Le Livre des Rois, Miroir du Destin.' *Studia Iranica* 17: 7–46.
–. 1997. 'Conscience du passé et résistance culturelle dans l'Iran Mongol.' In *L'Iran face à la domination mongole. Études réunies et prés. par Denise Aigle*. Teheran: Institut français de recherche en Iran. 136–77.

Mīnuvī, Mujtabā. 1958. 'Yād-dāsht-ī dar-bāra-yi Samak-i 'Ayyār.' *Sukhan* 9: 333–36.
Molé, Marian. 1953. 'L'épopée iranienne après Firdōsī.' *La Nouvelle Clio* 5: 377–93.
Mu'īn, Muḥammad, ed. 2001. Niẓāmī-yi 'Arūḍī-yi Samarqandī. *Chahār maqāla*. Teheran: Amīr Kabīr.
Mukerji, Chandra. 1991. 'Introduction.' In *Rethinking Popular Culture: Contemporary Perspectives in Cultural Studies*. Ed. Chandra Mukerji and M. Schudson. Berkeley: U of California P. 1–61.
Nagy, Gregory. 1990. *Greek Mythology and Poetics*. Ithaca, NY: Cornell UP.
Nöldeke, Theodor. 1890. 'Beiträge zur Geschichte des Alexanderromans.' *Denkschriften der Kaiserlichen AW in Wien, Philosophisch-historische Classe*, 38, 5. Vienna.
–. 1896–1904. 'Das iranische Nationalepos.' In *Grundriß der iranischen Philologie*. Ed. Wilhelm Geiger and Ernst Kuhn. 2 vols. Strassburg. II, 130–211.
Oesterreicher, Wulf. 1997. 'Types of Orality in Text.' In *Written Voices, Spoken Signs: Tradition, Performance, and the Epic Text*. Ed. Egbert Bakker and A. Kahane. Cambridge, MA: Harvard UP. 190–214.
Omidsalar, Mahmoud. 1984. 'Storytellers in Classical Persian Texts.' *JAF* 97: 204–12.
–. 1995. 'Review of Davidson 1994.' *Īrānshināsī* 7: 436–57.
–. 1996. 'Unburdening Ferdowsi.' *JAOS* 116: 235–42.
–. 2002. 'Orality, Mouvance, and Editorial Theory in Shāhnāma Studies.' *Jerusalem Studies of Arabic and Islam* 27 *(Studies in Honour of Shaul Shaked)*: 245–82.
–. 2009. 'Mutūn-i sharqī, shīva-hā-yi gharbī. *Shāhnāma* va ab'ād-i īdiūlūjīk-i Shāhnāma-shināsī dar maghrib-zamīn.' *Āīna-yi mīrāth* 7/17: 19–67.
Page, Mary E. 1979. 'Professional Storytelling in Iran: Transmission and Practice.' *Iranian Studies* 12: 195–215.
Piemontese, Angelo M. 2000a. 'Alexandre le "circumnavigateur" dans le Roman Persan de Tarsusi.' *Mélanges de l'école française de Rome. Moyen Âges* 112: 97–112.
–. 2000b. 'Anciens monuments sur l'eau, selon Tarsusi.' In *Trails to the East: Essays in Memory of Paolo Cuneo*. Ed. Marisa Calia et al. *Environmental Design: Journal of the Islamic Environmental Design Research Centre* 1 (1997-98-99): 137–43.
Pinault, David. 1992. *Story-Telling Techniques in the Arabian Nights*. Leiden: Brill.
*Qiṣṣat Fīrūzshāh* 1946: *Qiṣṣat Fīrūzshāh ibn al-malik Ḍārāb*. 4 vols. Cairo: 'Abd al-Ḥamīd Aḥmad Ḥanafī.
Riyāḥī, Muḥammad Amīn. 1993. *Sar-chashma-hā-yi Firdausī–shināsī. Majmū'a-yi nivishta-hā-yi kuhan dar-bāra-yi Firdausī va 'Shāh-nāma' va naqd-i ānhā*. Teheran: Mū'ssasa-yi muṭāla'āt va taḥqīqāt-i farhangī.
Rosenthal, Frantz. 1974. 'The Technique and Approach of Muslim Scholarship.' *Analecta Orientalia* 24: 1–74.
Rubanovich, Julia. 1996. 'Storytelling and Meta-narration in Medieval Persian Folk Romance.' *Jerusalem Studies in Jewish Folklore* 18: 63–103 (in Hebrew).
–. 1998. 'The Reconstruction of a Storytelling Event in Medieval Persian Prose Romance: The Case of the *Iskandarnāma*.' *Edebiyât* 9: 215–247.
–. 2002. 'Review of Kondyreva 2000.' *Jerusalem Studies in Arabic and Islam* 27: 602–9.
–. 2004. 'Beyond the Literary Canon: Medieval Persian Alexander-Romances in Prose.' Ph.D. Thesis, The Hebrew University of Jerusalem (in Hebrew; publication in English in preparation).
–. 2006. 'Aspects of Medieval Intertextuality: Verse Insertions in Persian Prose *dāstāns*.' *Jerusalem Studies in Arabic and Islam* 32: 247–68.
–. 2009. 'Metaphors of Authorship in Medieval Persian Prose: A Preliminary Study.' *Middle Eastern Literatures incorporating Edebiyât* 12: 127–35.
–. 2010a. 'Tracing the *Shahnama* Tradition in Medieval Persian Folk Prose.' In *Shahnama Studies II*. Ed. Charles Melville and G. R. van den Berg. Leiden: Brill.

—. 2010b. 'Shāh-nāma as a Source for Popular Narratives.' *Encyclopaedia Iranica*. (forthcoming)
Sadan, Joseph. 1998. 'Hārūn al-Rashīd and the Brewer: Preliminary Remarks on the *Adab* of the Elite Versus Ḥikāyāt.' In *Studies in Canonical and Popular Arabic Literature*. Ed. Shimon Ballas and R. Snir. Toronto: York P. 1–22.
Ṣafā, Dhabīḥ Allāh, ed. 1960–63. Muḥammad Bīghamī. *Dārāb-nāma*. 2 vols. Majmūʿa-yi mutūn-i fārsī 4, 14. Teheran: Bungāh-i tarjuma va nashr-i kitāb. [= *Fīrūzshāh-nāma*.]
—, ed. 1965–68. Abū Ṭāhir Muḥammad b. Ḥasan b. ʿAlī b. Mūsā al-Ṭarsūsī. *Dārāb-nāma-yi Ṭarsūsī*. 2 vols. Teheran: Bungāh-i tarjuma va nashr-i kitāb.
—. 1989. 'Ishāra-yī kūtāh bi-dāstāngudhārī va dāstāngudhārān tā daurān-i ṣafavī.' *Īrānshināsī* 1/3: 463–471.
Salimov, Yuriy. 1971. *Nasri rivojatii forsu tojik*. Dushanbe: Donesh.
Sarrāmī, Qadam ʿAlī. 1989. *Az rang-i gul tā ranj-i khār. Shikl-shināsī-yi qiṣṣa-hā-yi ʿShāh-Nāmaʾ*. Teheran: Shirkat-i intishārāt-i ʿilmī va farhangī.
Sarvar-Maulāʾī, Muḥammad. 1974. 'Baḥth-ī dar-bāra-yi dāstān-i Samak-i ʿAyyār.' *Sukhan* 23: 1122–34; 1247–56.
Shaked, Shaul. 1970. 'Specimens of Middle Persian Verse.' In *W. B. Henning Memorial Volume*. Ed. Mary Boyce and Ilya Gershevitch. London: Lund Humphries. 395–405.
Sheffy, Rakefet. 1990. 'The Concept of Canonicity in Polysystem Theory.' *Poetics Today* 11: 511–22.
Southgate, Minoo. S., trans. 1978. *Iskandarnamah: A Persian Medieval Alexander Romance*. New York: Columbia UP.
Yamamoto, Kumiko. 2003. *The Oral Background of Persian Epics: Storytelling and Poetry*. Brill Studies in Middle Eastern Literatures 26. Leiden: Brill.
Zhukovsky, V. A., ed. 1926. *Raskrytie skrytogo za zavesoy, ʿKyashf-al'-Maxdzhub.*' Leningrad: Nauchno-Issledovatel'skiy Institut sravnitel'nogo izucheniya literatury i yazykov Zapada i Vostoka, Leningrad U. [= Abū Ḥasan al-Hujvīrī, *Kashf al-maḥjūb*.]
Zumthor, Paul. 1972. *Essai de poétique médiévale*. Paris: Seuil.
—. 1987. *La lettre et la voix de la 'littérature' médiévale*. Paris: Seuil.

# 26 Medieval Turkish Epic and Popular Narrative

## Karl Reichl

In his *Canterbury Tales*, Geoffrey Chaucer (*c*. 1340 – 1400) introduces as the first narrator a knight who is joining the group of pilgrims on their way to Canterbury straight from one of the many military expeditions in which he has taken part. He has been active in Eastern Europe, in Spain and in the Middle East, generally on the side of the Christians, but occasionally also in the service of non-Christians:

> This ilke worthy knyght hadde been also
> Somtyme with the lord of Palatye
> Again another hethen in Turkye [...][1]

This same worthy night had also been/ at some time with the lord of Palatye/ (in his war) against another heathen in Turkey [...]

Palatye is modern Balat (ancient Miletus) on the Aegean coast of Turkey. In the fourteenth century, the 'lord of Palatye' was a Turkish emir who had kept his independence from the rising Ottoman empire and was involved in numerous feuds with the neighbouring emirates (Jones 1980: 86–88). Two hundred years earlier the Turkish Seljuks made their first inroads into Asia Minor; under their sultan Alp Arslan they took Caesarea (modern Kayseri in central Anatolia) in 1067. In 1071 they defeated a Byzantine army in Manzikert (Manāzgird) north of Lake Van, a victory that marked the beginning of the Turkish conquest of Anatolia, to be completed by the fall of Constantinople in 1453.

When the Seljuks invaded Anatolia in the eleventh century they had already established their rule in Iran. The Seljuks belong to the large family of Turkic-speaking peoples, which today stretches from the Yakuts of north-eastern Siberia to the Turks of Turkey. More specifically, they belong to the Oghuz tribal group, which, by the tenth century, was found in the area of the lower Jaxartes (Syr Darya), in the vicinity of the Aral Sea. From there they moved further west, into Iran and into Asia Minor. At the end of the eleventh century, the Great Seljuk Empire was at its zenith, reaching from the Oxus to the Persian Gulf in the south and the Aegean in the west. The reign of the Seljuks of Asia Minor, the Rum Seljuks, lasted until the beginning of the fourteenth century; in 1299 Osman I, leader of a Turkish warrior group in the service of the Rum Seljuks, declared himself sultan and founded the Ottoman dynasty. By the end of the fifteenth

---

[1] Fragment A, ll. 64–66. Quoted from Benson 1987: 24. –Unless indicated otherwise, all translations of quotations from primary and secondary sources are mine.

century, the Ottomans had become the dominant Turkish power in Anatolia and had established an empire which would rule over a large part of the Middle East and southeastern Europe until its final collapse after the end of World War I.[2]

From Central Asia the Turks brought their language, their way of life and their culture, and hence also their poetry and music. At its roots their culture was that of a nomadic tribal society, and their poetry that of an oral society. This nomadic culture continued in some areas of Central Asia into the present age, and oral poetry has played an important role in Turkey too, as will be discussed below. Towards the end of the tenth century the Seljuks converted to Islam; both through their adoption of Islam and their conquests of ancient civilizations such as that of Iran they came into contact with writing and literacy. Niẓām al-Mulk (1018–1092), the vizier of Alp Arslan, who had defeated the Byzantines at Manzikert, and of his son and successor Malikshāh, was one of the ablest statesmen of his time. He is the author of the *Siyāsat-nāma*, a book of government and mirror for princes, which is one of the classics of medieval Islamic literature.[3] Niẓām al-Mulk wrote his 'advice for rulers' in Persian, the language of administration and literature in the Sultanate of the Great Seljuks. Persian was also the language of the greatest mystic poet of the Seljuk era in Asia Minor, Jalāl ad-Dīn Rūmī (1207–1273), who spent the greater part of his life in Konya, where he founded the mystical brotherhood of the 'dancing dervishes'.[4]

While Persian and Arabic were the languages of government, law, theology, philosophy, science, and literature, Turkish was also cultivated as a literary language in the pre-Ottoman and medieval Ottoman period. In Jalāl ad-Dīn Rūmī's poetry there is only the occasional verse in Turkish, but at the end of the thirteenth/ beginning of the fourteenth century another mystical poet of Anatolia, Yūnus Emre, composed his poems entirely in Turkish. For his poetry Yūnus Emre used the Turkish syllabic metre, rather than the quantitative metres of Arabic and Persian poetry. This is certainly one of the reasons why his poems became popular and have retained their popularity until today.[5] With the ascendancy of the Ottoman Empire Turkish gained an ever increasing importance in literature, although Arabic and Persian works retained their place in Ottoman culture and were often the models and sources of Turkish imitations and translations.[6]

As in other medieval literatures, Turkish oral poetry from the Middle Ages is only indirectly accessible. Although we know about the cultivation of oral poetry from contemporary descriptions and allusions, the works themselves are, of course, only preserved if they were written down. There is, however, a difference from the medieval European literary traditions in that medieval orality is still alive in Turkey, both in song and in epic or romance. The oral epic traditions, it is true, are gradually becoming extinct, but can

---

[2] On the historical background, see Cahen 1968 (pre-Ottoman Turkey) and Inalcık 1973 (Ottomans, 1300–1600).
[3] For an English translation, see Darke 1960.
[4] For a perceptive introduction, see Schimmel 1993.
[5] His biography as well as his dates of birth and death are uncertain; 1320 is generally thought to have been the year of his death. For an introduction to his poetry and an English translation of some of his poems, see Smith 1993.
[6] For surveys of early Turkish (Seljukid and Ottoman) literature, see Bombaci 1968, esp. pp. 175–199, 223–307; Björkman 1964a and 1964b.

nevertheless still be studied. I will return to the modern descendants of medieval epic and romance at the end of this chapter.

## 1 Popular 'Romance'

'Epic' and 'romance' are two terms which cannot be sharply differentiated in the case of Turkish oral literature. In this, the Turkish situation is similar to that found in medieval European literature, where, as I have discussed above, the two genres overlap and intersect. There is some consensus, however, in seeing epic as being primarily heroic in outlook and romance as being focused on love adventures (see ch. 1, section 5.3). The distinction between epic and romance is riddled with additional problems in the case of Turkish medieval oral or popular narrative poetry.[7] The first problem concerns form. While there are narrative *poems* in Turkish, i. e. narratives in verse, the predominant form of popular narrative is the mixture of verse and prose, a genre also known under the medieval Latin term *prosimetrum*.[8] 'Narrative poetry' in most cases means prose narratives with verse insertions. In some cases the narratives are entirely in prose, occasionally with passages in rhymed prose (*saj'*). Another problem concerns narrative structure. All narratives can be loosely characterized as 'tales of adventure', in which heroic deeds are in the foreground. In many narratives these adventures are linked to build a larger narrative or narrative cycle; their structure is additive, and the succession of adventures resembles the ever-continuing quests and *aventures* of the medieval Arthurian knight, even if the objects of the quests are quite different. Love stories form a minority, and they are not focused on the ideals of courtly love as formulated in the *roman courtois* – which is not to say that ideals as well as idealized love are absent from popular Turkish narratives. The closest analogues in occidental medieval literature are the late medieval Spanish *libros de caballería*, the chivalresque romances satirized in Cervantes' *Don Quixote*.

There are nevertheless generic differences between the various types of medieval Turkish 'epics and romances'. In her edition of one of these narratives, Irène Mélikoff draws a basic distinction between 'the epic that was created spontaneously on the ancestral soil in pre-Islamic times and the epic that developed among the Islamized Turks, transplanted into foreign countries' (1960b: I, 41). The former is represented in an epic cycle commonly entitled 'The Book of Dede Korkut' (see below). The latter comprises a number of different subtypes. Here a symbiosis of foreign models and native creative spirit has taken place: 'From their new home [the Turks] have the epic elements and the plots with which they have amalgamated their own; they have adapted them to their tastes and their mentality and, by transforming the foreign elements in this way, they have created a new Turkish epic literature' (1960b: I, 41–42). Two areas of foreign influ-

---

[7] Similar problems are encountered in Arabic and Persian oral literature; see ch. 24 by T. Herzog on Arabic and ch. 25 by J. Rubanovich on Persian in this volume; for a discussion of some of the tales of the *Arabian Nights* under the generic term 'romance', see Heath 1987–88.
[8] For a survey of narratives in a mixture of verse and prose in world literature, see Harris and Reichl 1997.

ence can be distinguished, the Iranian and the Arabian. The Persian epic tradition, centred on Firdausī's *Shah-nāma* and its popularization, has led to the composition of imitations and continuations in Turkish which, according to Mélikoff, are characterized by their 'extrême naïveté' (1960b: I, 42). From the Persians the genre of the historical romance was also borrowed and adapted, such as the romance of *Abū Muslim*, a historical figure from the first half of the eighth century. He fought against the Umayyads to help install the 'Abbāsids, but was treacherously killed by the second 'Abbāsid Caliph, al-Manṣūr, in 755.[9]

From a Persian source is also derived the Turkish romance of Ḥamza, the *Ḥamza-nāme*.[10] Ḥamza b. 'Abd al-Muṭṭalib was the Prophet's paternal uncle, who has become the hero of a popular romance, of which versions are found not only in Persian and Turkish, but also in Arabic, Urdu and other languages, generally differing significantly from one another.[11] The earliest Ottoman version extant was composed around 1400 by Ḥamzevī, a lengthy narrative, which in Alessio Bombaci's words, has become proverbially synonymous with a fabulous tale.[12] The *Ḥamza-nāme* was extremely popular in the Ottoman Empire, well beyond the Middle Ages. Evliya Çelebi (Chelebi), the seventeenth-century traveller, gives in his *Seyahat-nāme* (Book of Travels) a vivid description of Erzurum, then (in 1645) an 'international' town with Persian, Indian and Chinese merchants and a Turkish, Armenian and Georgian population. He found the Muslim women enchanting, was impressed by the longevity of the men and is full of praise for their oratorical skills:

> [...] the Musselmán women wear pointed caps of gold and silver stuff, velvet trowsers [sic] and yellow boots: they are extremely pretty, their teeth as well arranged as their words; with their beautiful hair, dragging a thousand lovers after them as slaves. The men are long-lived, in society may be found many men past seventy years of age, with full use of all their faculties. They generally speak a peculiar dialect, but their divines and poets speak with great eloquence, and their storytellers delight intelligent people by their tales of Hamza, and by Chinese shades. (Hammer[-Purgstall] 1834: II, 114)

Evliya Çelebi does not elaborate on the art of the storytellers. As far as we have texts of the *Ḥamza-nāme*, the bearers of tradition are named in an introductory phrase which has become formulaic and is found in this type of popular narrative as far afield as Uzbekistan. In a manuscript from 1200 H/AD 1785/86 the 69th part of the romance begins with the phrase:

---

[9] See Moscati 1960 and the study by Irène Mélikoff 1962.
[10] In Turkish the titles of these popular romances are generally compounds with Persian *nāma* 'book' as second element. In modern Turkish orthography the spelling of this word is *nâme* (or just *name*); the emphatic sounds in Arabic names and loan-words (symbolized by a dot under the letter in Latin transliteration) are simply spelled as *h, t, s* etc. in Modern Turkish.
[11] See Meredith-Owens 1986; Hanaway and Pritchett 2003; for the Arabic *Sīrat Ḥamza* see the paraphrase and analysis in Lyons 1995: II, 223–38; III, 534–85. See also ch. 24 by T. Herzog in this volume.
[12] 'Vers 1400, Ḥamzevī, frère de Aḥmedī, dédiait à l'histoire de Ḥamza, oncle du Prophète, tombé dans la bataille de Uḥud, un prolixe *Ḥamza-nāme*, devenu proverbialement synonyme de récit fabuleux.' Bombaci 1968: 260.

Râviyân-ı ahbâr u nâkilân-ı âsâr ve muhaddisân-ı rûzi-gâr revîler öyle rivâyet iderler ki [...][13]

The narrators of stories and the transmitters of traditions and the storytellers of the world, the narrators tell a story thus [...]

An Uzbek version of *Abū Muslim* has a similar opening phrase:

Ammo roviyoni axbor va noqiloni osoru muhaddisoni shiriniguftor andog' rivoyat qilibdurlarki [...][14]

Now, the narrators of stories and the transmitters of traditions and the sweet-spoken storytellers tell a story thus [...]

All the words for 'narrator' in this formula are Arabic: Turkish *râvi* and Uzbek *roviy* come from Arabic *rāwin* 'narrator, storyteller, transmitter'; from the same Arabic root *rivayat/rivoyat* 'narrative' is also formed; T. *nâkil*/ Uzb. *noqil* come from Ar. *nāqil* 'bearer, transmitter' (as well as *naqqāl* used in Persian), and T./Uzb. *muhaddis* comes from Ar. *muḥaddith* 'speaker, storyteller, transmitter of tradition', related to *ḥadīth* 'talk, story, tradition' and, of course, *ḥadith*, the words and deeds of the Prophet according to Islamic tradition. A similar formula is found in the Arabic popular epic narratives, the *siyar*, whose narrators are generally called *rāwī*.[15]

There is indeed a close connection between the Arabic popular *sīra*, *maghāzī* and *futuḥ* narratives and the Turkish popular romances.[16] One of the most popular Turkish romances, the *Baṭṭāl-nāme*, is inspired by Arabic models. It is an epic narrative on Seyyid Baṭṭāl, a *ghāzī* or warrior for the faith of Islam, active in the wars of the Umayyads and early 'Abbāsids against the Byzantines in the eighth century.[17] The Turkish popular romance probably goes back to the beginning of the thirteenth century (Mélikoff 1960b: I, 47). In the *Baṭṭāl-nāme*, Seyyid Baṭṭāl, the 'battle-hero,'[18] fights as general of the pashalik of Malatia against the Byzantines, of course victoriously, and in the course of his extraordinary military campaigns crosses the Seven Seas and reaches, not unlike Alexander, distant and fabulous lands. H. L. Fleischer has aptly characterized the hero:

Conforming to the ideals of his people, Baṭṭāl is the union and model of all chivalrous virtues and clerical perfections; he is the flower of *aventure* – Achilles, Ulysses, Roland, Abellino, all in one person. On his expeditions to most parts of the world, in various disguises, often for a long time unrecognized even by his friends, he overcomes the most dangerous adventures with the help of his singular audacity, presence of mind, cunning and craftiness and performs

---

[13] Sezen 1991: 91. The form *revîler* is somewhat unusual; compare the formula in the 'Tale of Gül and Ali Şir' (*Gül ile Ali Şir Hikâyesi*) edited by Boratav (1946: 230): *Râviyan-ı ahbâr, nakılân-ı asâr, muhaddisân-ı ruzigâr şöyle rivayet ederler ki* [...]

[14] This is the beginning of the second part; the beginning of the first is somewhat more involved. Sarimsoqov 1992–93: II, 3. Uzbek is here written in present-day orthography.

[15] See Jacobi 1995; Ott 2003: 42.

[16] The topic of the *sīra* (pl. *siyar*) is the lives and heroic deeds of legendary or historical persons, of the *maghāzī* the wars of the warriors for Islam and of the *futuḥ* the Muslim conquests; see further ch. 24 by T. Herzog in this volume.

[17] See Mélikoff 1960a; for a detailed discussion, see Fleischer 1888; for a German translation, Ethé 1871; for an analysis, in particular of the tale's characters and motifs, see Köksal 1984.

[18] Arabic *seyyid* 'lord' denotes also a descendant of the Prophet; Ar. *baṭṭāl* means 'brave man, hero'.

unheard-of deeds of prowess so that his appearance alone, even the mere sound of his name puts great numbers to flight.[19]

The *Baṭṭāl-nāme* is in prose; a verse version dates from the middle of the eighteenth century.[20] The prose is simple; 'there are no traces of Ottoman literary prose with its endless chains of complex sentences, of Arabic and Persian rhetoric, of parallelism in the structuring of speech and of inserted proverbs and verses' (Fleischer 1888: 239). Its relationship to the Arabic *siyar* is more one of style and spirit than of textual dependence. Irène Mélikoff makes this point in her discussion of the epic genre in Turkish literature:

> On a supposé l'existence d'une geste arabe dont le Baṭṭālnāme serait la traduction. A l'époque où la littérature populaire turque était surtout orale, on ne peut guère parler de traduction. [...] Le Roman de Seyyid Baṭṭāl a eu pour point de départ des récits épiques arabes racontés dans des milieux de Gāzis; mais, transformés par l'adjonction d'éléments turcs et de motifs iraniens turquisés, ces récits ont donné naissance à une épopée anatolienne à partir de laquelle s'est formée une littérature épique ayant pour sujet la conquête de l'Anatolie.[21]

One of the works of this newly created 'Turkish epic literature' is the *Dānişmend-nāme* edited by Mélikoff. The Dānishmendids were *ghāzis* of Turkmen origin, who rose to power in eastern Anatolia at the end of the eleventh century. For their military campaigns against the Byzantines they were awarded the title *malik*, 'king'. Their kingdom ended when their territories came under Seljukid dominion in *c.* 1180.[22] As Mélikoff has shown, the oral legends about the founder of the Dānishmendids were first put down in writing in the first half of the thirteenth century; in the middle of the fourteenth century a second version was composed by a chronicler by the name of 'Ālī 'Ārif. His version is in prose with intercalated verse passages; the earliest manuscript of this version dates to the sixteenth century.[23] The romance as it is transmitted in manuscript form has clearly had a written textual history. The variations in the manuscripts, to judge from the examples given, show a certain latitude in phrasing, but, considering that the extracts are in prose, the different manuscript texts resemble one another sufficiently to suggest a basically written transmission (Mélikoff 1960b: I, 175–76). Scribes of popular works felt free to change, add or omit, in the West as much as in the East. When Ethé compared the manuscripts of the *Baṭṭāl-nāme*, he noticed that 'in almost no single place do they agree with one another – as is not surprising in popular romances of this kind – and manifold insertions, here and there, make it very difficult to find the correct reading of what was probably the original text.'[24]

---

[19] Fleischer 1888: 236. – Abellino was the Venetian bandit hero of a novel and a drama by Heinrich Zschokke (1771–1848), which was very popular in Fleischer's time.
[20] For a survey of manuscripts and versions (including modern ones), see Köksal 1984: 17–23.
[21] Mélikoff 1960b: I, 46–47. 'The existence of an Arabic romance of which the *Baṭṭālnāme* is a translation has been postulated. At a time when Turkish popular literature was mainly oral one can hardly speak of a translation. [...] The romance of Seyyid Baṭṭāl had as its point of departure Arabic epic narratives which were told in the circles of the *ġāzis*, but, transformed by the addition of Turkish elements and Turkicized Iranian motifs, these narratives have brought about an Anatolian epic which resulted in the creation of epic works about the conquest of Anatolia.'
[22] For the historical background, see Cahen 1968: 91–106; Mélikoff 1960b: I, 71–101.
[23] See Mélikoff 1960b: I, 53–70 (composition) and 171–76 (manuscripts).
[24] Ethé 1871: I, vi. The German term for my translation 'popular romances' is *Volksbücher*. German *Volksbuch* 'popular book' generally denotes printed popular novels and romances (chapbooks), a

Not all variations are due to the activity of scribes, however. These works were generally recited and read aloud to an audience, and in the process of their performance changes were introduced which reflect both the skill of the narrator and the taste of his audience. Before turning to performance and the various types of Turkish 'minstrels' and epic singers, I would like to discuss what Mélikoff called 'the epic that was created spontaneously on the ancestral soil in pre-Islamic times'.

## 2 The Book of Dede Korkut

This work is extant in two manuscripts from the sixteenth century, one in the Vatican Library, the other in the Saxonian State and University Library in Dresden.[25] In addition to an introductory chapter, the Dresden MS contains twelve narratives, while the Vatican MS contains only six of them. According to linguistic and historical criteria, the text in its present form goes back to the fourteenth or fourteenth/fifteenth century. The composition of the narratives in their original form, however, is certainly earlier. Here opinions differ, and not all tales in the *Book of Dede Korkut* need be of the same age. As the narratives treat of the deeds of the Oghuz, it can be assumed that the oldest among them go back to the period before some of the Oghuz tribes moved westward into Anatolia. This is supported by additional evidence (see below).[26]

The personage after whom this work is named is alternatively called 'Dede Korkut', 'Korkut Ata' (both 'Grandfather Korkut') and 'Dedem Korkut' (my Grandfather Korkut). *Dede* and *ata* mean 'grandfather', but are also terms of respect, especially when referring to saintly persons.[27] In the Dresden MS the text is preceded by the heading *Kitāb-i Dedem Qorqud ʿalā lisān-i ṭāʾifa-i oghūzān*, 'The Book of my Grandfather Korkut according to the language of the tribe of the Oghuz.' Dede Korkut, however, is not the main hero of the epic cycle but rather its 'chronicler'. He makes his appearance in the narratives as a wise counsellor of the Oghuz khan, but also as the person who composed the tales of the adventures narrated. At the end of the first tale, for instance, we find in the Vatican MS the words:

form (originally as lithographic editions) in which a number of these Turkish popular romances have circulated.

[25] Vatican Library, MS Turco 102, and Dresden, Sächsische Staats- und Universitätsbibliothek, MS Ea.86. Photographs of the Dresden MS are available at <http://digital.slub-dresden.de/sammlungen/werkansicht/280873166/0/>. See Illustration 26.

[26] The *Book of Dede Korkut* is considered to be a central text not only for the Turks of Turkey and Azerbaijan, but also of Central Asia; there is consequently a huge literature on this work, of which only a few important items can be referred to here. For English translations, see Sümer, Uysal, and Walker 1972 and Lewis 1974; for a critical edition of both manuscripts, see Ergin 1958–63, and of the Vatican MS (with an Italian translation) Rossi 1952. For studies of the *Book of Dede Korkut* see Zhirmunsky 1974 and Korogly 1976; a useful comparative analysis of the motifs found in the tale-cycle is given by Ruben 1944: 193–283. An encyclopaedic collection of texts and studies was published in Kazakhstan in 1999 (Nysanbaev 1999, in Russian and Kazakh). For a short characterization, see also Reichl 1992: 43–55.

[27] The transliteration *Qorqut* (on account of the velar character of the *k*-sounds) and *Qorqud* are also found; Ergin's critical text has *k* with a dot beneath to symbolize velarity. When quoting from the original text, I will use *q* instead for velar *k*.

26 – Beginning of *The Book of Dede Korkut* in the Dresden MS

Dedem Qorqut boy boyladı, soy soyladı, bu Oğuz-nāmeyi söyledi.[28]

My Grandfather Korkut composed a tale, made verses, told this *Oghuz-nāme*.

Dede Korkut narrates and composes poetry, he also plays the *qopuz*, a lute, and presumably sings. At the end of the eleventh tale (only found in the Dresden MS) we read:

---

[28] Ergin 1958–63: I, 94; facsimile in Rossi 1952, fol. 19v.; see also his translation on p. 111 ('Dede Qorqut narrò il racconto, parlò in poesia e disse questo *Oğuznāme*').

Dedem Qorqut geldi, kopuz çaldı, ğāzi erenler başına ne geldügin söyledi. (Ergin 1958–63: I, 243)

My Grandfather Korkut came, played the *qopuz* and told what had happened to the brave warriors for the faith (*ghāzi*).

In the preface to the cycle of narratives, Dede Korkut is introduced as a man from the Bayat tribe who lived close to the time of the Prophet and was a 'consummate soothsayer' (*tamam biliçisi*).²⁹ There follow a number of maxims and proverbial sayings, among them:

Qolça qopuz götürüp ilden ile, bigden bige ozan gezer.
Er cömerdin, er nākesin ozan bilür.
İleyüñüzde çalup aydan ozan olsun.
Azup gelen qazayı Tañrı savsun, hanum hey. (Ergin 1958–63: I, 75)

The singer (*ozan*) goes with his *qolça qopuz* from land to land, from *beg* to *beg*.³⁰
The singer recognizes a generous man, a stingy man.
May the singer play and speak in your presence.
May God chase away ominous bad fortune, oh my khan.

Dede Korkut is such a singer (*ozan*); this is explicitly stated when it is said that 'the *ozan* speaks from the tongue of Dede Korkut'.³¹ He is a bard, but a bard of special importance and capability. In the *Pedigree of the Turkmens* of Abū 'l-Ghāzī, khan of Khiva in the first half of the seventeenth century, it is written about Dede Korkut: 'Korkut Ata performed many unusual deeds (*karāmatlar*). He lived to an age of 295 years and served as vizier under three rulers.'³² Among these rulers Salur Kazan is mentioned; for him Dede Korkut composed a praise-poem, which Abū 'l-Ghāzī inserts into his *Pedigree*.³³ Salur Kazan appears also in the narratives of the *Book of Dede Korkut*.

Dede Korkut is not only a vizier or counsellor, possibly with some basis in history, nor just a bard and oral chronicler. He is an exceptional figure. There are a great number of legends about him in Central Asia, in particular in Kazakh oral tradition. In one of them he sees someone digging a grave and when he asks for whom the grave is being dug, he is told that it is for him. Dede Korkut tries to flee from death, but wherever he rides on his camel, someone is digging his grave. In the end he realizes that there is no escape and returns to the banks of the river Syr-Darya, where he dies and where his mausoleum is found in the vicinity of Kazalinsk.³⁴ As early as 1852 Chokan Valikhanov, the Kazakh scholar and ethnographer, pointed out that the flight from death as told in this legend is a shamanistic trait, and he calls Korkut 'the first shaman, who taught (the

---

²⁹ Lewis' translation (1974: 190).
³⁰ The *qolça qopuz* is lit. an 'arm *qopuz*'; Lewis translates 'arm-long lute' (1974: 192). A *beg* is a nobleman.
³¹ *Dede Qorqut dilinden ozan aydur.* Ergin 1958–63: I, 76. On the *ozan*, see Köprülü 1966.
³² Kononov 1958: 57 (Russian translation), 42–43 (Arabic page numbers) (text); Ar. *karāmāt* means 'miracles (performed by saints)'.
³³ Kononov 1958: 71–72 (Russian translation), 66–67 (Arabic page numbers) (text).
³⁴ See the texts in Nysanbaev 1999: 34–122 (where the Kazakh *küy* (melodies) on Dede Korkut are also discussed). The Central Asian *qobuz* is not a plucked lute like the *qopuz* mentioned in the *Book of Dede Korkut*, but a bowed viol-type instrument; it is the instrument that the Kazakh *baqsï* (shaman, faith-healer) and the Karakalpak *jïrau* (epic singer) use.

Kazakh shamans) to play the *qobuz* and to sing *saryn* (a type of melody)' (Valikhanov 1985:65). There can be no doubt that Dede Korkut is a complex figure – both shaman and primeval bard – who harks back to the pre-Islamic world of the Central Asian Turks.³⁵

In all twelve narratives in the *Book of Dede Korkut* war-like deeds are related. They are legendary stories, but have, at least in part, some basis in history. The Oghuz are already mentioned in the earliest writings in a Turkic language, in the runic inscriptions in the Orkhon valley from the eighth century. They are also the subject of genealogical, legendary and historical literature, such as the *Pedigree of the Turkmens*, mentioned already, the *Jamiʿ at-tawārīkh* (Universal History) of the Persian historian Rashīd ad-Dīn (d. 1318) and a legendary history of Oghuz Khan (Oghuz Qaghan), the ancestor of the tribe, which is preserved in a manuscript in Old Uighur script from the fifteenth century, thought to be considerably older.³⁶ The various historical elements in the *Book of Dede Korkut* have been the subject of scholarly debate; in the context of this chapter there is no space for further pursuing this question.³⁷

Various groups can, however, be distinguished according to plot. In six of the tales a rescue from captivity is narrated.³⁸ The beginning of 'The Tale of the Pillage of Salur Kazan's House' sets the scene for the ensuing adventures in epic grandeur:

> Bir gün Ulaş oğlı,
> tülü quşuñ yavrısı,
> beze miskin umudı,
> Amıt suyınuñ aslanı,
> Qaraçuğuñ qaplanı,
> qoñur atuñ iyesi,
> Han Uruzuñ ağası,
> Bayındır Hanuñ güyegüsi,
> Qalın Oğuzuñ develti,
> qalmış yigit arhası Salur Qazan yirinden turmuş–idi.
> Toqsan başlu ban iverlin qara yirüñ üzerine dikdürmiş–idi.
> Toqsan yirde ala qalı ipek döşemiş–idi.
> Seksen yirde badyalar qurılmış–idi.
> Altun ayaq surāhiler düzilmiş–idi.
> Toquz qara gözlü,
> hub yüzlü,

---

³⁵ See Basilov 1970: 40–54; see also Rossi 1952: 21–25.
³⁶ On the relevant parts of the *Jamiʿ at-tawārīkh*, see Jahn 1969 and Shukyurova 1987; on the legend of Oghuz Qaghan, see Bang and Rachmati 1932 and Shcherbak 1959: 13–110; see also the discussion in Reichl 1992: 33–39.
³⁷ On the historical elements in the *Book of Dede Korkut*, see, among others, Zhirmunsky 1951 and 1962, as well as Zhirmunsky 1974; see also Rossi 1952: 31–35 and Boratav 1983. In appearance at least, the most historically oriented of the tales is the last one, 'The Tale of the Rebellion of the Outer Oghuz against the Inner Oghuz and the Death of Beyrek'.
³⁸ (1) The Tale of Dirse Khan's Son Buğaç Khan; (2) The Tale of the Pillage of Salur Kazan's House; (4) The Tale of How Kazan Bey's Son Uruz Bey was Taken Prisoner; (7) The Tale of Kazılık Koca's Son Yigenek; (10) The Tale of Uşun Koca's Son Segrek; (11) The Tale of How Salur Kazan was Taken Prisoner and his Son Uruz Freed him. – Numbering according to the order of the tales in the Dresden MS.

saçı ardına örilü,
göksi qızıl dügmelü,
elleri bileginden qınalu,
parmaqları nigarlu,
mahbub käfir qızları kalın Oğuz biglerine sağraq sürüp içerlerler-idi.[39]

One day the son of Ulaş,
the young of the feathered bird,
the hope of the wretched and miserable,
the lion of the Amıt river,
the tiger of Karaçuk mountain,
the master of the chestnut horse,
the father of Khan Uruz,
the son-in-law of Bayındır Khan,
the good fortune of the numerous Oghuz,
the support of the young warriors left behind: Salur Kazan rose up from his place.
He had his ninety rich tents with golden tops put up on the black earth.
On ninety places he had spread multicoloured silk carpets.
On eighty places jars were placed.
Golden cups were lined up.
Nine black-eyed infidel girls, pretty-faced,
beautiful infidel girls,
their hair plaited behind,
their breast red-buttoned,
their hands from the wrist dyed with henna,
their fingers ornamented,
filled the cups of the *beg*s of the numerous Oghuz and they drank.

Salur Kazan decides to go hunting, but leaves the encampment without sufficient protection. The infidels under the Georgian king Şökli attack the encampment and lead the women into captivity. When they also want to take ten thousand sheep along with their plunder, the shepherd Karaçuk opposes them together with his brothers. Meanwhile Salur Kazan has been warned in a dream and returns with his warriors. He hears from Karaçuk what had happened, but is at first unwilling to take him along on his expedition against King Şökli. Karaçuk, however, succeeds in persuading Salur Kazan by his determination and loyalty. Salur Kazan and his companion arrive just at the moment when King Şökli is about to have Salur Kazan's wife and son killed. After a heroic battle, the captives are freed and the infidels defeated. At the end we read that 'My Grandfather Korkut came, composed a tale, made verses, told this *Oghuz-nāme*.'[40] Before the tale ends, Dede Korkut speaks a poem on the transience of human life and gives a blessing.

This tale is like the others composed in a mixture of prose and verse. There are eighteen verse passages in Ergin's edition, ranging from two lines to seventeen. They are found in different situations and express different moods. One example will have to suffice. When Salur Kazan at first refuses to take Karaçuk along, the brave shepherd insists and demands to be apparelled for the campaign:

---

[39] Ergin 1958–63: I, 95. I have printed the text so that the parallelism of the prose comes out more clearly. For syntactic reasons, *mahbub kāfir qızları* in the last line had to be moved further forward in the translation.
[40] *Dedem Qorqut gelüben boy boyladı, soy soyladı, bu Oğuz-nāmeyi düzdi qoşdı*; Ergin 1958–63: I, 115.

>     Qoñur atuñ virgil maña
>     Altmış tutam gönderüñi virgil maña
>     Ap alaca qalqanuñı virgil maña
>     Qara polat öz qılıcuñ virgil maña
>  5  Sadağuñda seksen oquñ virgil maña
>     Ağ tozluça qatı yayuñ virgil maña
>     Kāfire men varayın
>     Yeñiden toğanın öldüreyin
>     Yiñüm-ile alnum qanın ben sileyin
> 10  Ölür-isem senüñ uğruña ben öleyim
>     Allah Taʿāla qor-ise ivüñi ben qurtarayın (Ergin 1958–63: I, 104)

>     Give me your chestnut horse,
>     Give me your spear of sixty spans,
>     Give me your multicoloured shield,
>     Give me your sword of black steel,
>  5  Give me your quiver with eighty arrows,
>     Give me your strong bow with the white grip,
>     I will go to the infidel,
>     I will kill the newly born,
>     I will wipe the blood off my forehead with my sleeve,
> 10  If I die, I will die for your sake,
>     If God Almighty protects me, I will save your house (family).

The poetic form of this verse passage is typical of all verse portions in the epic cycle. Lines rhyme in irregular groups (here ll. 1–6 and 7–11). Sometimes a rhyme pattern might be interrupted by non-rhyming lines. Also, the rhyme might consist of a constant rhyming word, as in lines 1 to 6 (where actually the two last words of the line rhyme). The rhyming vowels are dependent on vowel harmony, which can result in slightly differing rhymes (*öldüreyin*, *sileyin* with front vowels vs. *varayın*, *qurtarayın* with back vowels). Morphological variants can also rhyme (the first person singular optative form *öleyim* rhymes with *öldüreyin* etc.). The metre is syllabic, but irregular. The verse lines in this passage comprise between seven and sixteen syllables, with a predominance of twelve syllables. In modern popular epic poetry verse passages in lines of 7/8 and 11/12 syllables are the rule.[41]

When comparing these verse lines with the prose passage given above, it can be seen how a strongly patterned parallelistic prose can, as it were, merge into verse. In the Turkic languages the verb comes at the end of the sentence; furthermore the structure of Turkic morphology is agglutinative. This means that various grammatical categories (tense, person, mood, number etc.) are expressed by distinct suffixes, 'glued' to the verb stem. The form *öldüreyin* (I may/will kill) consists of the morphemes *öl-* (die), *-dür-* (causative), *-e-* (optative) and *–(y)in* (1st person singular), lit. 'may I cause to die'. From this it follows that parallelistic lines will almost automatically have 'grammatical rhyme', i. e. the same verbal suffixes at the end of a sentence or clause. This extends to other sentence parts, as in the various nominal appositions in the introductory sentence of this

---

[41] See Boratav 1964: 11–14. On the form of the *Book of Dede Korkut*, see also Rossi 1952: 87–91 and Zhirmunsky 1974: 615–29.

tale. Viktor Zhirmunsky (1985) has suggested that the verse of Turkic oral epic poetry has its origin in parallelism, a suggestion which is supported by the style of both prose and verse of the *Book of Dede Korkut*.

The tale in the *Book* that has aroused most scholarly interest outside Turcology is the 'Tale of How Basat killed Tepegöz' (no. 8). In 1815 Heinrich Friedrich von Diez published a study with the title *Der neuentdeckte oghuzische Cyklop verglichen mit dem Homerischen* (The newly-discovered Oghuz Cyclops compared with the Homeric [Cyclops]). Diez, who owned the Dresden MS, edited and translated the text of this tale and discussed its relationship to the Cyclops of the *Odyssey*. 'Tepegöz' or 'Depe Göz' is compounded of *tepe/ depe* 'top, crown of the head' and *göz* 'eye'; this describes Tepegöz, who, like Polyphemus, is an ogre with only one eye on his forehead. The hero of this narrative is Basat, the son of Uruz Koca. Basat was brought up by a lion and has traces of a ferocious animal in his character. Tepegöz, the Cyclops, is the son of a shepherd and a *peri* (fairy). He harrasses the Oghuz with his forays and demands a tribute of sixty-six men per day, a number that Dede Korkut manages to bring down to two. When Basat's help is sought and he hears that his brother had lost his life through the ogre, he goes to fight the ogre. Tepegöz puts Basat, who is unable to wound him with the arrows he shoots at him, into his boot. At night Basat frees himself and blinds the ogre with a spit heated in the fire. Basat escapes from the ogre's den by a ruse similar to that employed by Odysseus (he kills a ram and leaves the ogre's cave in the ram's skin) and in the end kills the giant. The Polyphemus motif is widely diffused in folklore and also in folktales of the Turkic peoples. The similarity to the Polyphemus story is striking, but the precise relationship of this folklore motif to the Homeric epic remains unclear.[42]

Folkloristic motifs are also found in other tales of the *Book of Dede Korkut*. One is the central motif of the 'Tale of Deli Dumrul' (no. 5). It is motif D1855.2 in Stith Thompson's *Motif-Index of Folk-Literature*, 'Death postponed if substitute can be found'. In the Turkish narrative, Deli Dumrul, a dare-devil Oghuz hero and also something of a simpleton (*deli* means both 'crazy' and 'brave') is one day a witness to how a man dies in the flush of youth. In his naïveté Deli Dumrul asks how this can be and is told that 'Azrā'īl, the Angel of Death, has taken the young man. Deli Dumrul challenges 'Azrā'īl, but has to admit defeat in the end. He is given a reprieve if he can find someone to sacrifice his or her life for him. Neither Deli Dumrul's father nor his mother are willing to give their life for their son. His wife, however, is ready to make the sacrifice, but Deli Dumrul is not in agreement and would rather die with her. As a reward God grants Deli Dumrul and his wife a long life, but carries off his parents. This motif is best known from Greek myth: Admetus has to die but will be granted life if someone else dies for him. His aged parents refuse, but his young wife Alcestis descends for him into Hades. According to Euripides' drama, Alcestis was, however, saved in the end and brought back to earth by Heracles.[43] This motif with variations is also found in the Greek ballads

---

[42] On the 'Polyphemus motif' in *Dede Korkut*, see Grimm 1857; Ruben 1944: 244–53; Mundy 1956. For this motif in folklore, see Hackman 1904; for Turkish folktales with this motif, see Eberhard and Boratav 1953: 159–60 (Type 146).

[43] See Thompson 1955–58; Ruben 1944: 230–38

(*tragoudia*) about Digenis Akritis, the Byzantine border warrior against the Muslims; a mutual influence is not unlikely.[44] Deli Dumrul, who is ready to wrestle with the Angel of Death on account of an unknown youth, clearly embodies the heroic ideal of these tales.

Two of the narratives are bridal quests, 'The Tale of Kam Püre's Son Bamsı Beyerek' (no. 3) and 'The Tale of Kañlı Koca's son Kan Turalı' (no. 6). 'The Tale of Bamsı Beyrek' is perhaps the more interesting of the two, because elements of its plot show a close resemblance to the return of Odysseus in Homer's *Odyssey*, but also because the tale in the *Book of Dede Korkut* is the earliest version of a widely diffused heroic oral epic from Central Asia, the epic of *Alpamysh*. The narrative opens with a common motif of Turkish and Turkic epic and popular romance, the childlessness of a couple, which is remedied through divine intervention. Bay Büre Beg and Bay Bican Beg are at first childless, and when they have children – Bay Büre a son and Bay Bican a daughter – they promise to marry them to one another. After Bay Büre's son Beyrek has shown his valour, he is ceremonially named Bamsı Beyrek of the Grey Stallion by Dede Korkut. Bamsı Beyrek sees Banu Çiçek, his betrothed, for the first time when he is out hunting. He falls in love with her, but is challenged by her to a bow-shooting contest, a horse-race, and a wrestling match. Although Bamsı Beyrek wins these contests, marriage is delayed until Banu Çiçek's brother Deli Karçar is satisfied with the bride-price. Dede Korkut manages to collect the demanded animals, including one thousand huge fleas, and gets Deli Karçar to give his consent to the marriage. At the night of the wedding feast the infidels attack the Oghuz and Bamsı Beyrek is led into captivity together with thirty-nine of his companions. Sixteen years pass without news from Bamsı Beyrek, who is the ruler of Bayburt's prisoner. Yartaçuk, who was once given a shirt by Beyrek, dips this in blood and 'proves' in this way that Beyrek has died. He asks for Banu Çiçek's hand and is promised to be married to her. When Beyrek hears of this, he breaks out of prison with the help of the king of Bayburt's daughter, who had fallen in love with him. On his return he exchanges clothes with a minstrel (*ozan*) and meets first with his shepherds, who have remained loyal to him, and then with his sisters, who lament their brother's death. At the wedding feast Beyrek is given his own bow and shoots an arrow through the mark, the bridegroom's ring. He addresses songs to the khan and his court and exchanges songs with his wife, who, it becomes clear, had been tricked into marrying Yartaçuk, but who has remained faithful to her husband. Beyrek finally reveals his identity and miraculously heals his father's blindness. In the end Beyrek's companions are freed, Bayburt is destroyed, Beyrek's seven sisters are married to his companions, and the king of Bayburt's daughter becomes Beyrek's second wife.

This is clearly also the plot of the epic of *Alpamysh*, an epic which is found in Uzbek, Kazakh, Karakalpak and other Central Asian Turkic traditions; there are even versions in non-Turkic languages.[45] All of these versions exhibit the same structure: the combination of a bridal quest including suitor contests that consist of bow-shooting, horse races, wrestling and others, and a return story, with the motifs of the disguise of

---

[44] See Deter-Grohmann 1968: 27; Politis 1909. On *Digenis Akritis*, see also ch. 17 by E. Jeffreys in this volume.
[45] For a detailed study, see Zhirmunsky 1960; see also Reichl 1992: 160–70, 333–53, and 2000: 21–36.

the returning husband, the testing of retainers, family and wife, and the recognition of the hero through skills such as the ability to wield a mighty bow.[46] In some traditions the legend of *Alpamysh* is preserved in the form of a folktale (Tatar), in others in the form of the archaic heroic tale (Altaian). In Uzbek, Kazakh and Karakalpak the poetic form of the legend of *Alpamysh* must be called heroic epic, even if in most of these traditions the epic is in a mixture of verse and prose. It should be stressed, however, that in many of these works it is not verse that is inserted into prose, but rather prose that connects the sometimes very extensive verse passages.[47] Interestingly, the enemies in the *Book of Dede Korkut* are the Christians and their king, while in the Central Asian epics the hero's adversaries are the Buddhist Kalmucks (both qualified as infidels). In both cases, adjustments of the story to later historical circumstances have been made, to the wars of the Seljuks and other Oghuz tribes with their Christian neighbours in the west, and in Central Asia, to the bloody clashes between Turks and Oirats (Kalmucks) in the seventeenth and eighteenth centuries. These are later adaptations of a legend whose origin in all probability antedates the move of the Seljuks south-west from Central Asia, from where it must have been carried to Anatolia.[48]

A final remark on this tale in the *Book of Dede Korkut* concerns the relationship of the last part of the narrative to the homecoming of Odysseus. V. Zhirmunsky (1967) has pointed out the striking similarities between *Alpamysh* and the *Odyssey*. How these similarities can be explained, is an intriguing problem which has not been solved. For the present discussion it is one further indication of the firm rooting of at least some of the narrative material in *Dede Korkut* in a more ancient world of oral poetry, whether this world reaches back to antiquity or not.

## 3 Epic Singers, Minstrels, Public Entertainers

In the Dresden MS the cycle of epic tales is entitled *Kitāb-i Dedem Korkut*, 'the Book of my Grandfather Korkut'. In the Vatican MS it has the title *Ḥikāyat-i Oghuz-nāma*, where both the Persian *nāma*, meaning 'book' like Arabic *kitāb*, and the Arabic word *ḥikāya* 'tale' indicate the genre. The tales of the Oghuz are a book in the sense that they have been written down, but it is uncontroversial that they were not composed as written literature, as a 'book'. The term *ḥikāya* (Modern Turkish *hikâye*) is used in Turkish for the tales of the Turkish minstrel, the *âşık*. The word *âşık* (an Arabic loan-word) means 'lover' and underlines the important role that love (divine and worldly) plays in their poetry; it has been used for the Turkish minstrel since the fifteenth century. The *âşık*s perform lyric poetry, both of their own composition and of poets like Yūnus Emre, mentioned at the beginning of this chapter, and they traditionally also recited narratives,

---

[46] The names *Bamsı* and *Alpamysh* can be interpreted as being related if one derives *Alpamysh* from *Alp Bamysh/Mamysh* (Hero Mamysh); *Mamysh/Bamysh* and *Bamsı* are most likely variants of the same name. See Zhirmunsky 1960: 71.
[47] For a more detailed discussion of prosimetrum in Turkic oral epics, see Reichl 1997.
[48] The history of this legend/ epic is difficult to retrace; see the discussion in Zhirmunsky 1960: 145–55. For a German translation of an Uzbek version of *Alpamysh*, see Reichl 2001.

both romances and epics. They accompany themselves on the *saz*, the Turkish long-necked lute. The generic differentiation, as was said above, is difficult; many of these tales are love-romances, but some, like the tales of the *Köroğlu*-cycle, are heroic tales, close to the heroic epic. As with other traditional art forms, the reciter of *hikâye*s is fast disappearing. One of the last Turkish traditional minstrels is Âşık Şeref Taşlıova (b. 1938), whose repertoire of *hikâye*s has recently been published.[49] In Central Asia, the oral epics performed by the 'singers of tales' are generally called *destan* (or *dāstān*, a Persian loan-word). This word is also used in Turkish as a genre term, where it can either mean, as in the Central Asian Turkic languages, a traditional epic (with generic variations), or a type of traditional poem on a heroic or historical topic (Elçin 1967).

Book epics in Turkish are composed in rhymed couplets; on account of their metrical form, they are designated by the Arabic term *mathnawī* (Modern Turkish *mesnevi*).[50] One of these is the tale of *Varqa and Gülşâh*, a love romance from the fourteenth century, the first of its kind in Anatolian Turkish.[51] The author of this work is called Yūsuf-i Meddāḥ, Yūsuf the *meddāḥ*. The *meddāḥ* – an Arabic word meaning 'panegyrist' – is a public storyteller and reader of popular narratives, similar to the storyteller of the Arabian coffee-house.[52] In Central Asia this type of entertainer is generally called *qiṣṣa-khʷān*, 'reader of *qiṣṣa*s (stories)'.[53] What is noteworthy is that this type of narrator and popular entertainer clearly depends on written texts, but often uses these written texts fairly loosely, to say the least. In other words, literacy and orality are intimately intertwined in the performance of a *meddāḥ* or *qiṣṣa-khʷān*, the predominance of one or the other depending both on the skill of the entertainer and on his willingness to adapt to the wishes and interests of his audience. In the quotation from Evliya Çelebi's *Seyahat-nāme* above, the word 'storyteller' translates *meddāḥ*; at other places in his travel book, Çelebi also uses the word *qiṣṣa-khʷān*. Georg Jacob, in an early study of the Turkish *meddāḥ*, characterizes this type of public entertainer as follows:

> The *meddāḥ*s, the professional narrators, are masters of oratory. They enact mostly comical situations from the everyday life of the lower strata of society, which on the basis of astute observation they copy and caricature. They represent these situations with humour and liveliness, favouring the form of the dialogue and imitating various dialects and voices in it. They emphasize their gestures through the use of a stick and a cloth.[54]

These are the *meddāḥ*s whom Jacob has studied and some of whose texts he has translated. Some were not only, or perhaps not even primarily, actors and mimes, but also

---

[49] On the Turkish *hikâye* as a genre, see Spies 1929; Boratav 1946; Eberhard 1955; Çobanoğlu 2000; Başgöz 2008. On the Turkish *aşık*, see also Moyle 1990; on Âşık Şeref Taşlıova's *hikâye*s, see Türkmen, Taşlıova, and Tan 2008. For a general survey of Turkish and Turkic epic and *hikâye*, see Boratav 1964.

[50] See Flemming 1990a. The Arabic term, derived from the root *thanā* 'to fold', refers to the metrical form of these poems.

[51] Modelled on a Persian source; for an introduction, edition and translation, see Smith 1976.

[52] See ch. 24 by T. Herzog in this volume.

[53] On these and other terms for the 'singer of tales' in the Turkic languages, see Reichl 1992: 57–91. – In Modern Turkish orthography, these terms are spelled *meddah* and *kıssahan*; *-han* is derived from Persian *khʷāndan* 'to read'.

[54] Jacob 1904: 6. On the Turkish *meddah*, see also Nutku 1976; Boratav 1986.

readers of popular romances, as too was the entertainer whom Evliya Çelebi saw and heard in Erzurum. Here, too, the *meddāḥ*'s performance is marked by a dramatic enlivening of the narrative, a recital which, in the case of a gifted *meddāḥ*, uses the manuscript or printed text as a prop rather than as a text to be followed faithfully word for word.

The *meddāḥ* and *qiṣṣa-khʷān* was also a familiar figure in Central Asia. H. Vámbéry noted that in Bukhara in 1863 in front of the Divanbegi mosque (madrassa) there were some trees 'where the dervishes and meddah (narrators), employing strenuous mimics, narrate in verse and prose the heroic deeds of warriors and prophets and are always listened to by a curious audience' (1865: 142). H. Zarif and V. Zhirmunsky, in their study of Uzbek oral epic poetry, stress the importance of this type of narrator/entertainer for the meeting of orality and literacy, written and oral tradition:

> In the towns and the villages around towns there were also professional readers (the so-called *qissa-xon*), who read popular books aloud to an illiterate audience, performing in the bazaars or, by invitation, in private homes. On these occasions an experienced reader could re-tell a text from memory, with corresponding individual deviations. The folk singers (*ashulachi*) had in their musical-poetic repertory works of Classical Uzbek poetry and music. Through these routes the influence of written literature has long since penetrated into Uzbek oral epic poetry. (1947: 28–29)

It is incontestable that works like the *Book of Dede Korkut* have their roots in oral poetry, and it is equally incontestable that, with the *âşık*, the art of the oral poet has continued in Turkey into the present time. On the other hand, from an early period onward, this oral art has been in close contact with literacy, both as a tool for putting orally performed narratives into writing and as a form of literature, in the narrow sense of the word, that has helped mould and shape oral poetry.[55] Narrators like the *meddāḥ* stand, as it were, at the cross-roads of orality and literacy, reading, reciting, performing from memory and even 'composing in performance', as the skill of the narrators allows or the performance situation might demand. In the modern world an entirely new situation has arisen, at first with the spread of oral poetry in the form of audiotapes and later in the form of video-clips. YouTube offers performances by Turkish *âşık*s, and there are, of course, film and television adaptations of the Dede Korkut narratives as well as of the *Baṭṭāl-nāme* and popular epics like *Köroğlu*. This is a new orality, but in a fixed, re-playable form, and in this way not unlike the fixed written text. The transformations entailed by these new media is a fascinating story, but well beyond the limits of this chapter.

# References

Bang, W., and G. R. Rachmati, eds. and trans. 1932. 'Die Legende von Oghuz Qaghan.' In *SB der Preußischen AW, Phil.-hist. Klasse* 25: 683–724.
Başgöz, İlhan. 2008. *Hikâye: Turkish Folk Romance as Performance Art*. Bloomington: Indiana UP.
Basilov, V. N. 1970. *Kul't svyatykh v islame*. Moscow: Izd. Mysl'.
Benson, Larry D., gen. ed. 1987. *The Riverside Chaucer*. 3rd ed. Boston: Houghton Mifflin.
Björkman, Walther. 1964a. 'Die altosmanische Literatur.' In Deny et al. 1964: 403–26.

---

[55] See also Flemming 1990b, and for the Arabic *rāwī*, Ott 2003: 138–89.

—. 1964b.'Die klassisch-osmanische Literatur.' In Deny et al. 1964: 427–65.
Bombaci, Alessio. 1968. *Histoire de la littérature turque*. Trans. I. Mélikoff. Paris: Klincksieck.
Boratav, Pertev Naili. 1946. *Halk Hikâyeleri ve Halk Hikâyeciliği*. Ankara: Millî Eğitim Basımevi.
—. 1964.'L'épopée et la "ḥikâye".' In Deny et al. 1964: 11–44.
—. 1983.'Dede Korkut Hikâyelerindeki Tarihi Olaylar ve Kitabın Telif Tarihi.' In his *Folklor ve Edebiyat (1982). II*. Istanbul: Ada Yayıcılık. 109–40. [Or. 1958.]
—. 1986.'Maddāḥ.' In *Encyclopaedia of Islam*, V, 951–53.
Cahen, Claude. 1968. *Pre-Ottoman Turkey: A General Survey of the Material and Spiritual Culture and History c. 1071–1330*. Trans. J. Jones-Williams. London: Sidgwick and Jackson.
Çobanoğlu, Özkul. 2000. *Âşık Tarzı Kültür Geleneği ve Destan Türü*. Ankara: Akçağ.
Darke, Hubert, trans. 1960. *The Book of Government, or Rules for Kings: The Siyāsat-nāma or Siyar al-Mulūk of Niẓām al-Mulk*. London: Routledge and Kegan Paul.
Deny, Jean, Pertev Naili Boratav et al., eds. 1964. *Philologiae Turcicae Fundamenta*, Vol. 2. Wiesbaden: Steiner.
Deter-Grohmann, Isemene. 1968. *Das neugriechische Volkslied, dargestellt am Beispiel ausgewählter Gattungen*. Munich: Heimeran.
Diez, Heinrich Friedrich von. 1815. *Der neuentdeckte oghuzische Cyklop verglichen mit dem Homerischen*. Halle.
Eberhard, Wolfram. 1955. *Minstrel Tales from Southeastern Turkey*. Folklore Studies 5. Berkeley: U of California P.
—, and Pertev Naili Boratav. 1953. *Typen türkischer Volksmärchen*. Wiesbaden: Steiner.
Elçin, Şükrü. 1967.'Wort und Begriff *destan* im Türkischen.' In *Der Orient in der Forschung. Festschrift für Otto Spies*. Ed. Wilhelm Hoenerbach. Wiesbaden: Harrassowitz. 147–57.
*Encyclopaedia of Islam*. Ed. B. Lewis, C. E. Bosworth, P. J. Bearman et al. New edition. 12 vols. Leiden: Brill, 1960–2004.
Ergin, Muharrem, ed. 1958–63. *Dede Korkut Kitabı*. 2 vols. Türk Dil Kurumu Yayınları, 169, 219. Ankara: Türk Dil Kurumu.
Ethé, Hermann, trans. 1871. *Die Fahrten des Sajjid Batthâl. Ein alttürkischer Volks- und Sittenroman*. 2 vols. Leipzig.
Fleischer, Heinrich Leberecht. 1888.'Ueber den türkischen Volksroman Sîreti Seijid Baṭṭâl.' In his *Kleinere Schriften*. Vol. 3. Leipzig. 226–54.
Flemming, Barbara.1990a.'Türkische Epik.' In Heinrichs 1990: 319–25.
—. 1990b. 'Das Verhältnis von Hoch- und Volksliteratur im Türkischen.' In Heinrichs 1990: 475–81.
Grimm, Wilhelm. 1857.'Die Sage von Polyphem.' *Abhandlungen der Königl. AW zu Berlin, Phil.-hist. Klasse* 1857: 1–30.
Hackman, Oskar. 1904. *Die Polyphemsage in der Volksüberlieferung*. Akademische Abhandlung. Helsingfors.
Hammer[-Purgstall], Joseph von, trans. 1834. *Narratives of Travel in Europe, Asia, and Africa, in the Seventeenth Century by Evliyâ Efendî*. 2 vols. London.
Hanaway, William L., Jr., and Frances W. Pritchett. 2003.'Ḥamza-nāma.' *Encyclopaedia Iranica*. Ed. Ehsan Yarshater. London: Routledge. XI, 649–51. Also available online at 'www.iranica.com'.
Harris, Joseph, and Karl Reichl, eds. 1997. *Prosimetrum: Crosscultural Perspectives on Narrative in Prose and Verse*. Cambridge: Brewer.
Heath, Peter. 1987–88. 'Romance as Genre in *The Thousand and One Nights*.' *Journal of Arabic Literature* 18: 1–21; 19: 1–26.
Heinrichs, Wolfhart, ed. 1990. *Orientalisches Mittelalter*. Neues Handbuch der Literaturwissenschaft 5. Wiesbaden: AULA.
Inalcık, Halil. 1973. *The Ottoman Empire: The Classical Age 1300–1600*. Trans. Norman Itzkowitz and Colin Imber. London: Weidenfeld & Nicolson.

Jacob, Georg. 1904. *Vorträge türkischer Meddâh's (mimischer Erzählkünstler)*. Berlin: Mayer & Müller.
Jacobi, Renate. 1995.'Rāwī.' *Encyclopaedia of Islam*, VIII, 466.
Jahn, Karl, trans. 1969. *Die Geschichte der Oğuzen des Rašîd ad-Dîn. Mit 25 Miniaturen und 26 Facsimiles*. Forschungen zur islamischen Philologie u. Kulturgeschichte, 4; Österr. AW, Philos.-hist. Kl., Denkschriften 100. Wien: Österreichische AW.
Jones, Terry. 1980. *Chaucer's Knight: The Portrait of a Medieval Mercenary*. London: Weidenfeld & Nicolson.
Köksal, Hasan.1984. *Battalnâmelerde Tip ve Motif Yapısı*. Kültür ve Turizm Bakanlığı, Millî Folklor Araştırma dairesi yayınları 59, Halk Edebiyatı Dizisi 10. Ankara: Başbakanlık Basımevi.
Kononov, A. N., ed. and trans. 1958. *Rodoslovnaya Turkmen. Sochinenie Abu-l-Gazi, khana khivinskogo*. Moscow, Leningrad: Izd. Akademii Nauk SSSR.
Köprülü, Fuat. 1966.'Ozan.' In his *Edebiyat Araştırmaları. 1.* Türk Tarih Kurumu Yayınları, Seri 7, 47a. Ankara: Türk Tarih Kurumu. 131–44. [Or. 1934.]
Korogly, Kh. 1976., *Oguzskiy geroichskiy èpos*. Moscow: Glavnaya Redaktsiya Vostochnoy Literatury.
Lewis, Geoffrey, trans. 1974. *The Book of Dede Korkut*. Harmondsworth: Penguin.
Lyons, M. C. 1995. *The Arabian Epic: Heroic and Oral Story-Telling*. 3 vols. Cambridge: CUP.
Mélikoff, Irène. 1960a.'al-Baṭṭāl (Sayyid Baṭṭāl Ghāzī).' *Encyclopaedia of Islam*, I, 1103–4.
–, ed. and trans. 1960b. *La Geste de Melik Dânişmend. Étude critique du Dânişmendnâme*. Bibliothèque Archéologique et Historique de L'Institut Français d'Archéologie d'Istanbul 10, 11. 2 vols. Paris: Adrien Maisonneuve.
–. 1962. *Abû Muslim. Le 'porte-hache' du Khorassan dans la tradition épique turco-iranienne*. Paris: Adrien Maisonneuve.
Meredith-Owens, G. M. 1986.'Hamza b.'Abd al-Muṭṭalib.' *Encyclopaedia of Islam*, III, 152.
Moscati, S. 1960.'Abû Muslim.' *Encyclopaedia of Islam* I, 141.
Moyle, Natalie Kononenko. 1990. *The Turkish Minstrel Tale Tradition*. New York: Garland.
Mundy, C. S. 1956.'Polyphemus and Tepegöz.' *Bulletin of the School of Oriental and African Studies* 18: 279–302.
Nutku, Özdemir. 1976, *Meddahlık ve Meddah Hikâyeleri*. Ankara: Atatürk Kültür Merkezi.
Nysanbaev, Abdimalik, ed. 1999. *Korkut Ata. Èntsiklopedicheskiy sbornik/ Qorqut Ata. Entsiklopediyalyq zhyynaq*. Alma-Ata: Qazaq èntsiklopediyasy.
Ott, Claudia. 2003. *Metamorphosen des Epos. Sīrat al-Muǧāhidīn (Sīrat al-Amīra Ḏāt al-Himma) zwischen Mündlichkeit und Schriftlichkeit*. Leiden: Research School of Asian, African, and Amerindian Studies, Universiteit Leiden.
Politis, N. G. 1909.'Akritika asmata: O thanatos tou Digeni.' *Laographia* 1: 169–275.
Reichl, Karl. 1992. *Turkic Oral Epic Poetry: Traditions, Forms, Poetic Structure*. New York: Garland.
–. 1997. 'The Mixture of Verse and Prose in Turkic Oral Epic Poetry.' In Harris and Reichl 1997: 321–48.
–. 2000. *Singing the Past: Turkic and Medieval Heroic Poetry*. Ithaca, NY: Cornell UP.
–, ed. and trans. 2001 *Das usbekische Heldenepos Alpomish. Einführung, Text, Übersetzung*. Turcologica 48. Wiesbaden: Harrassowitz.
Rossi, Ettore, ed. and trans. 1952. *Il 'Kitāb-i Dede Qorqut'. Racconti epico-cavallereschi dei Turchi Oğuz tradotti e annotati con 'facsimile' del MS. Vat. Turco 102*. Studi i Testi 159. Città del Vaticano: Biblioteca Apostolica Vaticana.
Ruben, Walter. 1944. *Ozean der Märchenströme. I. Die 25 Erzählungen des Dämons (Vetālapancavimśati). Mit einem Anhang über die 12 Erzählungen des Dede Korkut*. FF Communications 133. Helsinki: Academia Scientiarum Fennica.
Sarimsoqov, Bahodir, ed. 1992–93. *Abu Muslim jangnomasi. Dostoni Abu Muslim Sahibqiron*. 2 vols. Tashkent: Yozuvchi.

Schimmel, Annemarie. 1993. *The Triumphal Sun: A Study of the Works of Jalāloddin Rumi*. Rev. ed. Albany, NY: SUNY P.
Sezen, Lütfi. 1991. *Halk Edebiyatında Hamzanâmeler*. Kültür Bakanlığı Yayınları 1287, Gençlik ve Halk Kitapları Dizisi 59. Ankara: Kültür Bakanlığı.
Shcherbak, A. M. 1959. *Oguz-nāme. Mukhabbat-nāme. Pamyatniki drevneuygurskoy i starouzbekskoy pis'menosti*. Moscow: Izd. Vostochnoy Literatury.
Shukyurova, R. M., trans. 1987. *Fazlallakh Rashid ad-Din: Oguz-Name*. Baku: AN Az. SSR, Inst. Vostokovedeniya.
Smith, Grace Martin. 1976. Yūsuf-i Meddāḥ. *Varqa ve Gülşāh. A Fourteenth Century Anatolian Turkish Mesnevī*. Leiden: Brill.
–. 1993. *The Poetry of Yūnus Emre, a Turkish Sufi Poet*. University of California Publications in Modern Philology 127. Berkeley: U of California P.
Spies, Otto. 1929. *Türkische Volksbücher. Ein Beitrag zur vergleichenden Märchenkunde*. Form und Geist 12. Leipzig: Eichblatt.
Sümer, Faruk, Ahmet Edip Uysal, and Warren S. Walker, trans. 1972. *The Book of Dede Korkut: A Turkish Epic*. Austin: U of Texas P.
Thompson, Stith. 1955–58. *Motif-Index of Folk-Literature*. 6 vols. Rev. ed. Bloomington: Indiana UP.
Türkmen, Fikret, Mete Taşlıova, and Nail Tan, eds. 2008. *Âşık Şeref Taşlıova'dan Derlenen Halk Hikâyeleri*. Türk Dil Kurumu Yayınları 931. Ankara: Türk Dil Kurumu.
Valikhanov, Ch. Ch. 1985. 'Sledy shamanstva u Kirgizov.' In *Sobranie sochineniy v pyati tomakh*. Vol. 4. Alma-Ata: Glavnaya Redaktsiya Kazakhskoy Sovetskoy Èntsiklopedii. 48–70. [Or. 1852.]
Vámbéry, Hermann. 1865. *Reise in Mittelasien*. Leipzig.
Zhirmunsky, V. M. 1951. 'Sledy oguzov v nizov'yakh Syr-Dar'yi.' In *Tyurkologicheskiy Sbornik* 1. Moscow, Leningrad: Izd. AN SSSR. 93–102.
–. 1960. *Skazanie ob Alpamyshe i bogatyrskaya skazka*. Moscow: Izd. Vostochnoy Literatury.
–. 1962. 'Istoricheskie istochniki skazaniya o razgrablenii doma Salor-Kazana.' In *Drevniy mir. Sbornik statey Akademiku Vasiliyu Vasilevichu Struve*. Leningrad: Izd. Vostochnoy Literatury. 377–85.
–. 1967. 'The Epic of "Alpamysh" and the Return of Odysseus.' In *Proceedings of the British Academy* 52 (1966): 267–86.
–. 1974. 'Oguzskiy geroicheskiy èpos i "Kniga Korkuta".' In his *Tyurkskiy geroicheskiy èpos*. Leningrad: Nauka. 517–631. [Or. 1962.]
–. 1985. 'Rhythmico-Syntactic Parallelism as the Basis of Old Turkic Folk Epic Verse.' In his *Selected Writings: Linguistics, Poetics*. Trans. Sergei Ess. Moscow: Progress. 320–52. [Or. 1964.]
–, and Kh. T. Zarifov. 1947. *Uzbekskiy narodny geroicheskiy èpos*. Moscow: Gosudarstvennoe Izd. Khudozhestvennoy Literatury.

# 27 Dramatic Pastime, Custom and Entertainment

*Thomas Pettitt*

As a distinct and unified cultural system whose definitive aim was the achievement of dramatic performances, theatre was unknown in the Middle Ages. Some late-medieval dramatic traditions may indeed be antecedents of some aspects of the fully fledged theatre which emerged, in several countries, in the sixteenth century, but those traditions themselves effectively belonged to several different theatres (George Kernodle [1960] made it seven), each with its own, distinct, history. Or, rather, there were several late-medieval cultural systems involving dramatic performances, but the latter were an integral part of those other activities rather than an end in themselves. This chapter will accordingly deal with the significance of oral tradition for late-medieval dramatic activities which also (or rather) qualify as customs (the observation of secular or ecclesiastical festivals), or pastimes (games in which almost anyone can participate), or entertainment (with a clear demarcation between audience and performers with particular and perhaps professional talents). A unilinear, developmental view of theatre history has distorted the picture both in seeing them as primitive forms of theatre rather than as sometimes sophisticated forms of other cultural activities, and in attempting to assign them places in an evolutionary line from the most 'primitive' (Christian liturgy or pagan ritual) to the most theatrical (Pettitt 2005b).

There has been a corresponding distortion more particularly relevant to present purposes in the similarly evolutionary notion that medieval drama must have been more 'oral' than later phases, say more given to improvisation, or to performance independent of the written texts characteristic of a less primitive stage:

> Improvisation and adaptation caused by changes in cast or local events were probably very common and while the basic plot remained the same the dialogue would have varied considerably. Parts would have been learnt and passed on, principally orally, and this too would have led to variations. (Richardson and Johnston 1991:24)

The reviewer of a significant collection of essays on improvisation in the arts of the medieval and Renaissance periods (McGee 2003) has similarly remarked on 'the astonishing extent to which improvisation could permeate the dramatic strategies of the late medieval stage' (Karitzky 2006: 150), but in his authoritative survey of 'Improvisation in Medieval Drama' contributed to that collection, Clifford Davidson (2003) struggles hard for a meagre harvest of documented instances, particularly if the improvisation is also to encompass dialogue as well as action or music. *Verbal* instability and improvisation – indeed oral tradition altogether – may actually have been more typical of Renaissance drama than of late-medieval, or, in the terms just urged, more characteristic of dramatic entertainment (which came to dominate Renaissance theatre) than of dramatic custom and pastime (which dominated in the late-medieval period).

## 1 Textual Imperatives

While drama is by definition performance, any written texts involved being essentially auxiliary, rather than an alternative medium of communication, as might have been true of medieval narrative, or as may later have become the case for drama itself with the emergence of printed plays and the dramatic 'works' of particular playwrights (Peters 2000), dramatic performance, to a greater degree than others, is other than oral. All oral traditions are of course corporal (pun intended), what is uttered by the voice supplemented by whatever the body from which it emerges can contribute by way of facial expression, gesture and movement.[1] But although a medieval canonist could claim (in his own intended pun) that storytellers, *ystoriones*, were scarcely to be distinguished from *ystriones*, actors, this 'inherent corporality' (Baldwin 1997: 630) of the entertainment profession is true of drama to a special degree. And the greater the visual element the less the relative significance of the oral, with a zero option, unique to drama, in which there is no oral element at all, be it the miming of civic pageantry or the mumming of winter customs.[2]

Wordless drama will by definition fall outside the scope of this study, and that includes forms which are oral but not verbal, like traditional semi-dramatic games in which figures guised as beasts engage in improvised violent interaction with each other or with human figures, the shouting and laughing of the latter probably no more coherent than the grunting and squealing of the former.[3]

But there will have been other traditions a little further along the spectrum in which the subordination of the oral to the corporal was emphatic rather than absolute, for example 'folk' traditions like the late-medieval English Robin Hood plays, of which a few texts, miraculously, survive, but whose dialogue seems largely designed to provide links between action involving single combats, mêlées, or sporting contests (archery, wrestling, stone-throwing). 'In all these texts speech is subordinated to action', notes Bruce Smith, who goes on to cite Stephen Knight's perception that in these performances the essence is actually what happens when there is no text: 'What seems to be textual silence may indeed be the high point of performance: the dramatic character of the plays can itself be suggested by lack of words' (1999: 152). Clifford Davidson suggests rather that the silence of these texts was filled by oral improvisation, but it will have been purely auxiliary to the action (2003: 195–96). Similar points might be made about

---

[1] See Zumthor 1983: 195; Dobozy 2005.
[2] At the other extreme the medieval period did have an exclusively oral form of drama with no visual aspect, in the highly idiosyncratic form of indoor entertainments, documented for both Spain (Richards and Richards 1990: 24–25) and England (Pettitt 2000: 467), in which a single performer, hidden behind a door or curtain, impersonated different characters by speaking in different voices and represented their interaction with appropriate sound effects.
[3] See Fletcher 1986; Pettitt 2003b: 72–74.

the late-medieval German folk plays dramatizing the Neidhart figure's invariably violent encounters with peasant-figures.[4]

The dominance of the visual aspect was not restricted to dramatic customs and pastimes, and could also characterize – if for different reasons – ostensibly more sophisticated community drama. Religious plays were designed to prompt pious meditation, to which end visual signals were recognized by the Church as more potent than verbal (Plesch 1994–95: 475). On the basis of extensive financial and administrative records generated by a massive Passion Play performed at Châteaudun, France, in 1510, Graham Runnalls was able to pin down the cost of manuscripts as amounting to barely ten percent of the total expenditure (1994: 34).

On the other hand that ten percent actually represents quite a lot of written material: Runnalls estimates that this production deployed, in scripts directly related to performance, something like sixty folio sheets per day (1994: 28). The paucity of surviving texts often lamented in English scholarship, and sometimes echoed elsewhere,[5] seems due more to the loss of texts than to any essentially oral quality in medieval drama which had no need for them: texts of the major dramatic genres – mystery plays, saints' plays, farces, moralities, Shrovetide interludes and the like – survive by the score or even by the hundred from one or other language area (French, German, Flemish) in continental Europe. Late-medieval drama was less oral than might be expected not merely through being other than oral, but by being significantly more textual than other forms of medieval performance culture, more given to deploying written texts in connection with performance, in response to both internal and external factors.

Drama normally involves collective performance, in which characters (who in narrative speak through the voice of the single narrator) are represented by different actors. To be successful, this mode, distinguished in medieval French commentary as performance *par personnages* (Frank 1936: 382), requires that the participants stick closely to a fixed order of speeches and a fairly fixed order of words within those speeches:

> Improvisation – by which I mean merely the freedom to depart from the text briefly, to change the emphasis in certain scenes, and vary the 'business' – is a dangerous undertaking unless the actors have worked together a long time and know each other's strengths and weaknesses. (Oreglia 1968: xiv)

This would not normally have been the case with the local amateurs in the festival performances dominating medieval drama, the kind who, according to the rubrics of the thirteenth-century *Cyprus Passion Cycle*, are to be warned precisely to 'take heed not to interrupt each other or cut in so that confusion follows [...]' (Muir 2001: 175). And in a culture where functional literacy (the ability to read vernacular texts) was relatively widespread, the best way to ensure a known and stable order between and within speeches was a written text: a script.

External factors include the concern of the authorities, secular and ecclesiastical, that this essentially public activity should be in accordance with officially approved ideologies, typically manifested in the requirement that the performance be based on a

---

[4] See E. Simon 1969. [See also ch. 10 by J.-D. Müller in this volume, section 3.4.]
[5] For Spain see Stern 1973: 187.

fixed script which should be submitted for scrutiny prior to performance.⁶ A particularly illuminating case of the importance of written texts, even in a semi-literate environment, concerns a performance at Dijon in 1447 comprising a saint's play performed by the local Carmelites, intermixed, as often in late-medieval France, with a farce performed by artisans of the city. During the latter members of the audience were alarmed that passages could be deemed insulting to the royal family, and the city magistrate (*procureur*) instigated an enquiry. In addition to interrogating the actors, he demanded to see the script to check if it had been performed as written – by implication to determine whether blame attached to the author or the actors. One of the latter explained that he had been provided only with the text of his own part, and could not answer for the rest. The artisan who had actually acquired the script explained that he had seen and enjoyed the farce during a visit to another town, and had paid the performers there to have the script copied, for use in Dijon should opportunity arise: as far as he knew only one word had been changed, but couldn't be certain as he himself was illiterate (Bouhaïk-Girones 2003: 118–19, 127).

As this suggests, 'transmission' from one place to another typically took the form of borrowing and copying texts from other communities (and paying for the privilege) (Meredith and Tailby 1983: 47), rather than oral transmission. The incident is also a reminder that textual material took several forms for any one production.⁷ In addition to one or more full scripts for the whole play (and of individual plays making up a cycle, if their production was devolved to particular groups), the more elaborate plays required a director's scenario which reproduced and elaborated on the stage directions, listed properties and noted the opening line of each speech. More importantly each performer was provided with a copy of his role literally in the form of a roll, a narrow strip of paper, up to several metres long, wound around a stick. It contained his own speeches, each preceded by his cue, that is the last line of the preceding speech by another character. Quite a number of such actors' rolls survive from medieval France (Runnalls 1986–87; 1988), and the practice is widely attested in the financial or administrative documents associated with community theatre, from Spain and Italy, via France and Germany, to England and the Netherlands. They bring us very close to the performance itself, and indeed it is quite possible that in some cases a performer spoke his role *from* his roll, which was conveniently designed to literally unroll as the play progressed.⁸

Verbal instability in performance would also be checked by the presence of a prompter, sufficiently well documented for the medieval period, and this too could literally bring the script on stage. While the rules for the dramatic competitions staged by the relatively sophisticated Dutch Chambers of Rhetoric specified that the audience should not be able to see the prompter (Strietman 2007: 14), an exasperated sixteenth-century order from the organizers of the Lucerne Passion Play suggests very strongly that he would probably need to intervene quite forcibly:

'People are to be henceforth more industrious in learning their parts and not leave everything to the Director [...]. [They] should make an effort to note when in the play they have to

---

⁶ See Petit de Julleville 1885: 137, 310, 319, 433–34; 1880: 358–59, 383,
⁷ See Neumann 1987: I, 38–42; Runnalls 1990.
⁸ See Runnalls 1990: 98; E. Simon 2000: 149.

speak or do something or when it is their turn, so that they get used to it themselves and on the acting area do not first have to be told or shown. Also with regard to the gestures and speaking.' (Tailby 1987:88)

It is presumably such a figure who looms large with his book and baton in one of the most celebrated late-medieval illustrations of religious drama, Jean Fouquet's 'The Martyrdom of St Apolonia' (*The Hours of Étienne Chevalier, c.* 1460), where he seems to be imperiously both prompting and directing the multifarious performers in a complex scaffolds-and-place acting area (see Illustration 27).[9] Fouquet's qualifications, and the documentary value of the illustration for medieval performance conditions, have been the subject of vigorous discussion,[10] but in a series of studies – reinforced by practical experiments – Philip Butterworth (1999; 2001; 2007b) has juxtaposed this illustration with other evidence of similar practices, not least Richard Carew's 1602 account of the performance of mystery plays in Cornwall, in which 'the players conne not their parts without booke, but are prompted by one called the Ordinary, who followeth at their back with the booke in his hand, and telleth them softly what they must pronounce aloud' (1999:231).

This emphatic textuality is shared by the best documented dramatic or semi-dramatic seasonal custom of the later Middle Ages, the Shrovetide interludes – *Fastnachtspiele* (DuBruck 2004), closely analogous to modern traditions of folk drama (Pettitt 1982). In Nuremberg they were performed by groups of journeymen on visits to the carnival feasts of the craft guilds, and administrative records indicate that by the second half of the fifteenth century their visual display – say a group of performers 'disguised as old women'; or 'a morris dance and others dressed as peasants' – was being supplemented by a verbal element in the form of 'rhymes' (Tailby 2001:404–6). The texts of no less than 110 Nuremberg Shrovetide interludes survive from the fifteenth century (G. Simon 1970:9), many of them in the most elementary dramaturgy – a *Reihenspiel* comprising a sequence of short speeches by a series of characters who engage in little or no interaction with each other – making it difficult to postulate a yet more primitive, antecedent, 'oral' tradition of 'short improvised sketches [...] not worthy of permanent record'.[11]

Their sheer number suggests very strongly that a new script was written and performed each year, rather than the same play reproduced from memory (or passed on in oral tradition) year after year, and this was certainly the situation in medieval Lübeck, where Shrovetide interludes were performed by members of local guilds on wagons moved from venue to venue through the streets. Only one play survives, but the guild records are very informative on procedures: each year a small committee of guildsmen was appointed to produce the plays, and their duties included writing or commissioning a new play (E. Simon 1993; 2000:144).

The same seems to apply to the very different but equally traditional pastime of 'mock sermons', *sermons joyeux*, performed under festive auspices such as wedding feasts, clerical revels and guild banquets. The context is suitable for oral transmission and

---

[9] See also Tydeman 1978:136, illustration 10.
[10] See Rey-Flaud 1973:113–17; Kipling 1997a and 1997b; Runnalls 1997.
[11] E. Simon 2000:164; see van Abbé 1960:38.

27 – Detail from Jean Fouquet's 'The Martyrdom of St Apolonia' (c. 1460)

improvisation (Koopmans 1988a: 459), but they were evidently quite skilled, parodying the content, style and devices of regular sermons (Koopmans 1988b: 31–46). A number of complete texts survive, and in an unusually well-documented English case (if from 1601) it is evident both that the sermon was composed in writing and that in performance it was read from a text (Jones 1997: 98).

## 2 The Role of Oral Tradition

The endemic textual dependence of late-medieval drama does not completely exclude the potential significance of oral tradition in one sense or the other, but its presence must evidently be demonstrated rather than taken for granted, and the 'oral' element in dramatic tradition will more likely relate to a given player's reproduction of the verbal material from memory, than to transmission by word of mouth from one performer to another.

The situation will of course have varied over time, and there will also have been differences between the customary, amateur drama of communities, institutions and households, and the dramatic entertainment proffered by professionals. It is also fairly clear that whatever the overall situation with regard to community drama, a degree of verbal licence was extended to specific character types, whose unscripted contributions (most of the time) were tolerated and even expected.

These will have included the improvised *diablerie* in religious plays, perhaps because anything the devils might say was by definition erroneous. It appears very early, in the thirteenth-century Anglo-Norman *Adam*, in which:

> the demons are always full of energy and hilarity, dancing with glee at the imprisonment of Adam and Eve, 'shouting to one another in their joy' – apparently *extempore*. In contrast to

the historical personae, the devils can improvise both words and gestures [...] (Axton 1974:116)

A perhaps natural extension into the human sphere is the 'raging' of the many wicked tyrants of medieval biblical drama. Most are supplied with scripted harangues, but they are extremely formulaic, and the celebrated stage direction in the Coventry mystery plays, *Here Erode ragis in the pagond and in the strete also*, usually invoked in connection with staging, is followed by another indicating that this 'raging' was separate from speaking the scripted speech: *Here Erode ragis ageyne and then seyth thus* [...].[12] It has been suggested that such ad libbing may explain the 'roughness' and formulaic quality of the rantings of the many tyrants in the English saint's play, *Mary Magdalen* (Baker et al. 1982: xxxiv–xxxv).

Also tolerated, at least at times, was the ubiquitous Fool. In many French mystery plays his role is fully scripted, but an interesting clash of opinions is reflected in a fifteenth-century manuscript of a play on St Sebastian performed in the Duchy of Savoy, in which the role of the Fool is added in a different hand from the rest, in accordance with an annotation from the ducal censor that he could not finally approve the script until it included the Fool's lines (McCrary 1976: 122). A different balance of power may be reflected in the 1490 manuscript of a mystery play from Troyes, lasting several days. In the script for the first day the Fool's role is written out in full (but in the margin, and in a different hand); thereafter it is merely indicated when he is to speak, not what he says, implying that he improvised something (McCrary 1976: 103). At the opposite extreme is a fifteenth-century five-day play on St Barbara which throughout indicates only when the Fool is to speak (*Stultus loquitur*), not what he is to say, again presumably indicating improvisation (McCrary 1976: 115–16). On the other hand it might be queried to what degree any such improvisation qualifies as 'dramatic' in involving action as well as words, and significant interaction with other characters as opposed to direct address to the audience (Longtin 2007: 205).

It might also be claimed that oral performance is anticipated, and so reflected, in some aspects of the texts as composed. Most medieval drama is in verse, presumably to aid memorization and oral reproduction from memory, and a more specific mnemonic aid is the way plays in French invariably open a new speech with a line completing a rhyming couplet which began as the last line of the preceding speech.[13] The strong alliterative beat in some of the northern English mystery cycles will similarly have been a help to both delivery and reception, notes Meg Twycross, and:

> Even the apparently otiose tags and repetitions of the 'minstrel' style – 'When I am dead *and laid in clay*', 'Till God's Son come, *The sooth to say*' [...] – gives the audience a chance to assimilate the information they are being given which a more condensed form of dialogue would not under the circumstances allow. (1994: 44)

Alexandra Johnston likewise sees performance-orientation as explaining 'the poetic paucity of the Chester text with its line fillers and formulaic rhymes' (1993: 23), and of York Richard Beadle reckons that the basically auditory nature of the experience, 'condi-

---

[12] Craig 1902: 27 (stage direction after l. 783) and 28 (stage direction after l. 801).
[13] See van Dijk 1985: 241; Roy 1977: 80.

tioned by habits of hearing rather than seeing words', has determined that cycle's deployment of 'a range of internally cohesive "significatory words"' occurring with some frequency: 'In every play the dialogue will thus foreground this basic range of vocabulary, often expressed in repeated formulae, which it is guaranteed to share with both its immediate and distant neighbours in the Cycle as a whole' (2000: 169, 173).

As this suggests some of the verbal features of medieval drama, not least the deployment of verbal formulas, which elsewhere would be attributed to oral tradition, seem to occur under circumstances which suggest to drama historians that they are generated rather in composition, and with this we approach the central conundrum of oral tradition in connection with medieval drama: the relationship between actual performance and the surviving texts.

If Glynne Wickham was right when he claimed that 'no text in the theatre can ever be more than shorthand notes for actors' (cited in Kahrl 1993:132), it was only with regard to what might be designated dramatic *pre-texts*, the scripts on which performance was based, and from which performance may have deviated to greater or lesser degree. While preferred for the production of conventional editions, they will by definition reveal nothing about the impact of oral tradition; but this will not apply to *post-texts*, documents which in some way record what was actually spoken in performance (and anything that might have happened between performances).

Post-texts can have been achieved in various ways. If community drama did 'evolve' from a more primitive, oral and improvised, initial phase, in due course committed to writing, as envisaged by Martin Stevens for the York Mystery Cycle (1987:88), then the text thus established, whether dictated by the actors or recorded by a spectator, would have the status of a recording of the play as performed at that time. More plausibly, the same would apply to any text which resulted from a systematic updating of the script of a given play, be it for practical or administrative reasons, to bring it into line with performance.

And it is evident that despite the efforts of the authorities to control what was said in the plays of community theatre, performance did not always conform to the original script, be the change deliberate or unconscious, pre-meditated or in the heat of performance. Of deliberate, premeditated change there is a fictional but illuminating example in the intervention of the German trickster-figure, Till Eulenspiegel, in the performance of a Resurrection play, as narrated in a 1515 printed collection of his comic exploits. At a time when he was a parish sexton, Eulenspiegel was instructed by the priest to produce and direct the church's annual Easter Play, which would be performed in Latin by the priest (as Christ), the priest's elderly maidservant, who was also his mistress (as the angel guarding the tomb), Eulenspiegel himself (as one of the three Maries) and two farmers (as the other two Maries). Eulenspiegel coached these last two in their lines, but could not resist the chance of some mischief, so come the performance, when the maidservant in her role of angel asked the Maries 'Whom do you seek?', one of the farmers, as First Mary, replied as he had been instructed, not with the expected 'Jesus of Nazareth [...]', but: 'We seek the priest's old, one-eyed whore', provoking a show-stopping fracas.[14]

---

[14] See Walsh 1992:43–45, for full German text and translation.

This change was oral, in the sense of at no point being reflected in a text, but Clifford Davidson is over-optimistic in classifying it as an example of 'subversive improvisation' (2003:204): indeed its success depended precisely on performers who could be depended on to reproduce in performance exactly what they had been told to say. As Martin Walsh notes in a careful study of the incident in relation to the realities of latermedieval religious drama in the region concerned, 'There is nothing inherently implausible about peasants ignorantly learning their lines by rote for an annual parish play' (1992:49), and the hapless maidservant opted for the role of angel precisely because *sie kund den Reimen usswendig* (she knew the rhyme by heart).

An equally notorious but historical instance of subversive revision occurred in Suffolk, in the performance of what was evidently an allegorical morality play in the context of a May Day festival in 1537. As the Duke of Suffolk reported to the government of Henry VIII, the play

> was of a kinge how he shuld Rulle his Realm And Amonges other thynges there came in oon & Playde hussbandry which said many thyngs Agaynst gentillmenn *myche more thenn was in the boke of the playe*. (Ingram 1992:77; my emphasis)

Clearly unscripted, one wonders how deliberate or spontaneous the outburst was. It also proves that organizers of community drama were right to warn their performers against the practice, as at Lucerne in 1597: 'Nobody is to change the text of his role, either add to it or subtract from it, without express instruction from the Committee, but is to speak it as is written in the rehearsal text' (Meredith and Tailby 1983:60).

For scholarly purposes it is of course vital to know whether such possibly oral changes ever come to be reflected in the text of the play. Attitudes clearly varied: a grumpy comment in the manuscript of a French play staged in 1456, notes that

> Rejected and not included in this manuscript are any unusual additions which some of the players of this *mystère* thought fit to add at will, in that they were irrelevant to the subject and were censured by masters of theology. (Tydeman 1978:214)

while by contrast at Châteaudun in 1510, the master-copy of a mystery play was revised by the prompter's assistant 'according to the views of the actors', including the insertion of 'several additions offered by the said actors' (Muir 2001:300).

Over the longer term, in those local traditions (actually not all that typical) where the same play was performed over a number of years, the script may also have been updated to keep pace with the play's evolution, effectively oscillating between pre-text and post-text. German examples are the Corpus Christi plays from Künzelsau, the manuscript of which has many appendices, pasted-in slips and annotations, and Freiburg im Breisgau, whose several manuscripts also clearly reflect revision over time (Wainwright 1974). It has similarly been asserted that the texts of secular plays collected in the Tyrol by Vigil Raber in the early sixteenth century reflect both adjustments to local conditions and extemporized changes in performance (Bauer 1982:562). The English mystery play manuscripts all date between 50 and 200 years after the plays' first composition, and so comprise, Ian Lancashire suggests, 'Layers upon layers of accretions, alterations, and excisions by revisers, actors, or scribes from various regions and periods' which leave 'even relatively homogeneous cycles like Chester and York looking like patchwork quilts' (Lancashire 1977:65).

Deliberated revisions will have been supplemented by those more or less conscious changes occurring in the process of reproducing verbal material under the pressure of performance conditions. Imperfect memories were a recurrent concern of the communities producing much medieval drama, whose regulations insist on the selection of suitably talented performers and their due diligence in committing their parts to memory (Petit de Julleville 1880:362). And due effort was certainly needed, not least in continental European community plays lasting a day or several days in which amateur performers will have reproduced from memory parts of over a thousand lines (Petit de Julleville 1885:281), or even up to four thousand for the part of Christ (Petit de Julleville 1880:375). Not all will have had the insufferable school-girlish competence of the young lady playing St Catherine in Metz in the mid-sixteenth century, who according to a contemporary account 'had 2300 lines of dialogue; and nevertheless, she had every line at the tip of her tongue' (Enders 2002:17, 204).

Verbal change, some of it influenced by oral tradition, is therefore likely in late-medieval community drama, and some of it may get into the documentary record, but as with other traditions in order to discern its presence, we need either a (post-)text which we know is a transcript of performance, or, preferably, multiple versions of a given play, say a pre-text showing the text as written or at least as readied for performance, and a post-text showing what became of it in performance or over several performances, or perhaps two post-texts representing different stages in the play's trajectory through a tradition of performances.

For instance a Passion play was performed by the Gonfalone Confraternity on a stage in the Roman Coliseum between 1490 and 1539 (Newbigin 1999). Its evolution can be charted partly by a series of early printings between 1496 and *c.* 1515 claiming to give the play 'as it is recited and performed word for word' (*secondo che recita e representa de parola a parola*), and a cluster of early manuscripts, both full texts and part rolls for single characters. Changes are particularly discernible in the speeches of Judas, for whom several part roles survive. In a fascinating analysis Nerida Newbigin identifies as particularly informative one copy from the 1520's which contains only the first lines of Judas's speeches, together with specification of the characters who have speeches in between, and brief stage directions (1999:27–32; 2007:99). Newbigin concludes that the role was performed several years in a row by a performer who got to know the lines so well he needed only these hints to prepare himself ahead of a new acting season. A somewhat personal document, in other words, which may therefore reflect this performer's individual interventions. It has not merely lines which are not in other versions – which might equally well be a result of deliberate revision – but variants which may reflect the effect of memorisation and recall, e. g. 'Ah false Judas, full of avarice' rather than 'Ah Judas, traitor false and treacherous'; 'From the day I was born' for 'From the dark day I came into this world'.

Particularly intriguing insights are provided by the York Corpus Christi Play, a full cycle of mystery plays covering redemption history from the Creation to Doomsday, performed on pageant wagons at multiple stations in the streets of York – the whole documented by extensive contemporary administrative records, a single text of one of the constituent plays, and a full text of the complete cycle. The central document is this last, a 'Register', compiled – evidently on the basis of the contemporary scripts of the constituent plays – between 1463 and 1477. Very much in accordance with the official monitoring of dramatic performances mentioned above, administrative records indicate that from 1501 onwards a city clerk observed the performance of each play at the first station, and checked it against the manuscript.[15] In the early sixteenth century a particular official, John Clerke, took this task to include – over several years – noting in the Register where the words actually spoken in performance differed from the script, in many cases correcting the text to bring it into line with performance or adding material or comments in the margin.[16] It accordingly offers instances of variation which may in some cases be due to oral tradition in one or other sense.

A striking example of memory lapse on the part of an actor is registered in a marginal annotation explicated in a brilliant piece of textual detective work by Peter Meredith (1983:23). At a moment in 'Abraham and Isaac' (Play X), when Isaac's suspicions about his father's intentions with regard to the burnt offering are first aroused, he asks cautiously:

> Fadir, I see here wood and fyre,
> Bot wherof sall oure offerand be? (ll. 162–63)

to which Abraham replies:

> Sertis son, gude God oure suffraynd syre            [certainly] [sovereign]
> Sall ordayne it in goode degré. (ll. 164–65)

But while the text in the York Register has Abraham's speech continue for another sixteen lines, John Clerke notes in the margin that Isaac interrupts here with the question:

> father wold God I shuld be slayne[?]

He should not have done so, and Clerke has later crossed out the note. The York boy playing Isaac has manifestly come in too soon, anticipating a very similar exchange twenty or so lines later in which his fate is made explicit:

> Isaac    But fadir, nowe wolde I frayne full fayne
>          Wharof oure offerand shuld be grathid?            [prepared]
> Abraham  Sertis sone, I may no lengar layne:               [conceal]
>          Thyselfe shulde bide þat bittir brayde.
> Isaac    Why fadir, will God þat I be slayne? (ll. 185–89)

One might also speculate that his *wold* in the anticipation adjusts the proper line's *will* under the influence of the *wolde* and *shulde* in preceding lines.

Opportunities of a different kind are provided by the play of 'Cain and Abel' (Play VII) in which two leaves of the original manuscript were missing, and the loss is partly made up for by twenty-nine lines supplied by Clerke, presumably based on performance. Some of these (e. g. ll. 86–100) display a concentration of verbal repetition possibly

---

[15] See Beadle 1982:11–12. – On the documentary evidence (for England, Ireland and Wales) see Tydeman 2001b.
[16] See Meredith 1981:255–60; Meredith 1983; Beadle and Meredith 1983: xxi-xxiii.

reflecting the impact of oral transmission. That the York plays could over time develop such repetition patterns through internal contamination is indicated by some smaller but clearer examples where we have both the original and the performed formulations. Thus in Play XVI, 'Herod and the Magi' (as performed by the Goldsmiths) the First King according to the script is to say to Herod (concerning Christ): 'Sir, he shall be kyng / Of Jewes and of Judé' (ll. 175–76), but Clerke has crossed out *Judé* and substituted *all Jury*, in saying which the actor was in all likelihood influenced by Herod's 'And I am juge of all Jury' six lines later (183) – which he will have heard in however many rehearsals there were this year and over thirty performances a year every year he had performed the role.

This document may also show the deployment of a 'dramatic' formula which involves interaction between characters as well as purely verbal aspects. In Play XXIX, 'Christ before Annas and Caiaphas', the Register has Caiaphas instruct his soldiers to go out and arrest Christ:

> And therefore sir knyghtis –
> I charge you chalange youre rightis [...] (ll. 23–24)

but Clerke notes that in performance the soldiers respond to his first line before he goes on to the second:

> And therefore sir knyghtis –
> *Tunc dicunt* Lorde
> I charge you chalange youre rightis [...]

They evidently respond with the medieval equivalent of a 'Yes sir!' as he addresses them for the first time following his opening harangue to the audience. Peter Meredith rightly includes this among the 'momentary impressions of staging' which 'come through [...] in the marginal additions' (1983:23), and plausibly suggests the soldiers may have caught this 'heel-clicking' from their comrades in Play XXX, 'Christ before Pilate', who respond similarly (this time as scripted in the register) when Pilate turns to them with similar instructions:

> *Pilatus*   And þerfore sir knyghtis –
> *Milites*                           Lorde.
> *Pilatus*   Sir knyghtis þat are cruell and kene,
>             That warlowe ye warrok and wraste (ll. 525–26).

But this is also a dramatic formula: on three occasions in the very 'bad' quarto of Marlowe's *Massacre at Paris*, when a superior is to give a subordinate instructions to deal with another character (ll. 80 ff. the Guise and an Apothecary; 98 ff. the Guise and a Soldier; 111 ff. Navarre and Pleshe), the subordinate is addressed by name, acknowledges with 'My Lord', receives his instructions, and then (like both sets of York soldiers) acknowledges with affirmation of his readiness to carry them out.[17] Shakespeare deploys this dramatic formula in *Richard III* (IV.ii.32 ff.) when he has Richard instruct the 'Boy' to find someone to murder the princes in the Tower (Evans 1997).

---

[17] Edited in Greg and Chambers 1928; for discussion Pettitt 2005a.

An alternative, but less immediate approach to observing verbal change over time involves juxtaposing a later version of a speech with an earlier, although more often than not the status of the texts and their relationship have first to be established, and may not be entirely suitable for the purpose. The classic instance in England relates to the circumstance that the 'Towneley' mystery cycle, which may have been associated with Wakefield, has evidently taken over a lot of material from that of nearby York. In the case of the five plays containing long passages closely derived from York the Towneley author/compiler probably had access to York texts, but in other instances oral tradition may have been involved in one way or another (Stevens and Cawley 1994: xxviii). Peter Happé suggests for example that some of the more sporadic echoes 'may have occurred through odd flashes of memory' on the part of someone who had seen performances of the York Cycle (2007:35), perhaps particularly in the case of 'idiomatic phrases' from 'demotic speech' (50). As instances of an intermediate degree of indebtedness he cites the close reproduction of three speeches from York's 'The Incredulity of Thomas' in the Towneley play on 'Thomas of India'.[18] But two of the York speeches are rather similar to each other, and the way they are handled in the Towneley derivative merits closer, comparative, inspection. In the first speech, Christ invites the other apostles to ascertain by direct touching that he indeed has risen in the body:

| York 41.56–60 | Towneley 28.133–36 |
|---|---|
| Felys me grathely euerilkone, | |
| And se þat I haue flessh and bone. | Grope and fele flesh and bone |
| Gropes me nowe, | And fourme of man well-wroght; |
| For so ne has sperite none [...] | Sich thyng has goost none, |
| þat schall ȝe trowe. | Loke wheder ye knaw me oght. |

A little later, when Thomas arrives and expresses doubts, one of the apostles refers back to this experience:

| York 41.152–56 | Towneley 28.379–84 |
|---|---|
| Forwhy he bad vs euerilkon | |
| To grope hym grathely, bloode and bone, | Man has both fleshe and bone, |
| And flesh to feele. | Hu, hyde, and hore thertill; |
| Such thyngis, Thomas, has sperite none, | Sich thyng has goost none. |
| þat wote thou wele. | Thomas, lo, here thi skyll. |
| | Goddys son toke of Mary flesh and bone |
| | What nede were els thertill? |

The similarities between the two York passages have evidently provoked some internal contamination between them, very much in the manner documented in the oral tradition of ballads, and indeed Elizabethan drama, with the result that the verbal parallels are more extensive in the Towneley version (Pettitt 2005a). It is also typical of oral transmission that a change at one end of a repetition pattern provokes an analogous change at the other end, as here when the phrase *has spirit none* in the two York passages becomes *has ghost none* in both of the Towneley passages. Given the adjustment of verse-

---

[18] See Happé 2007:34; 'The Incredulity of Thomas' is Play 41 in Beadle 1982; 'Thomas of India' is Play 28 in Stevens and Cawley 1994.

form, it would seem more likely that this process occurred in the transmission of the Towneley play after composition than in that of the York play on its way to Wakefield.

Similar opportunities may be offered by analogous instances of derivation, for example of the Abraham play in the Chester Mystery Cycle (No. IV), part of which reproduces equivalent moments from the 'Brome' play of 'Abraham and Isaac':[19] In his influential study pinning down the direction of the influence, J. Burke Severs (1945) speculated that oral transmission may have been a factor. Similarly one of the Cornish Mystery Plays, the *Creation of the World*, includes almost two hundred lines reproduced near verbatim from an earlier Cornish play, the *Origo Mundi*, if with some changes in spelling and the replacement of Cornish words with their English equivalents (in the context qualifying as a modernisation). Most of them are speeches by God or speeches by others in the same scenes, prompting speculation that the later dramatist was using, or himself undertaking, a memorial reconstruction of the earlier play, somewhat in the manner postulated for some Elizabethan bad quartos.[20]

## 3 Elements of Improvisation

The players in these customary dramatic performances under the auspices of institutions, associations and communities differ from the 'singer of tales' of other oral traditions in that at any given moment an individual performer's active repertoire probably encompasses only one role in one play. However large the role, and however familiar he may become with other roles in that play, his performance is not part of an intertextual matrix of the kind we associate with performers whose active repertoires comprise many epics, romances, ballads or wondertales, constituting the 'enabling referent' for the word-power of oral tradition.

But this contrast between the narrator with many narratives frequently performed and the actor with one play performed only once or at intervals breaks down in the case of professional dramatic entertainment, whose practitioners are more likely to have commanded a repertoire with more numerous dramatic items, each with a substantially higher incidence of performance. Glynne Wickham accordingly sees the emergence of what look very much like 'oral' elements as precisely a symptom of the late- or post-medieval professionalization of dramatic activity:

> If a device worked – that is, if it provoked laughter as desired or some notable effect – then it was retained, repeated and reworked from one play to the next. In this way the repertoire of stage business expanded and developed in parallel with the stock of plots and characters at the disposal of the playmakers. A particular physical game or routine became an item of dramaturgy on which a variety of verbal patterns could be superimposed, just as a particular confrontation of characters or juxtaposition of arguments could be used as a basis for varied physical interpretations. (1987: 189)

The concept of the formula is indeed readily applicable to Elizabethan and Jacobean drama, both in the form of purely verbal formulas, of the same kind encountered in

---

[19] See Davis 1970; see Lumiansky and Mills 1983:91.
[20] See Neuss 1971 and 1983:241–45; Murdoch 1994:225.

narrative tradition, and dramatic formulas, of the kind postulated by Wickham, in which the verbal element – if there is any – is auxiliary to the action (Pettitt 1988).

The conditions of professional entertainment, particularly at its down-market end 'on the road', may generally be more conducive to oral tradition than medieval community or household auspices, even in more recent, emphatically literate, times. Speaking of his days with a travelling company in the North of England in the 1930's, actor Cyril Luckham (1983) recalled that they had no scripts, and newcomers had to learn their parts from established members. Improvisation was also an option (or a necessity): a stroller performing in English provincial fairground theatres in the nineteenth century reported that he had more than once been 'told what character he's to take, and what he's to do, and he's supposed to be able to find words capable of illustrating the character' (Rosenfeld 1960: 149).

Nonetheless such instability in professional performance is seen in relation to a 'play' which is conceived of essentially as a text. The view of the medieval authorities that drama was scripted, and that scripts should be controlled, applied to professional groups as well (Petit de Julleville 1885: 330, 343, 345), and in a fifteenth-century French *sottie* which is actually about a company of players, one of them is so celebrated for a particular role that when he dies his fellows plan to bury him wrapped in the script (Hindley 1999b: 92). On the basis of English evidence from the sixteenth century during the consolidation of professional theatre, William Ingram concludes that 'it seems to have been an unstated assumption throughout the period that plays required books, that they were not simply unwritten improvisations or skits' (1992: 77).

The late-medieval exception effectively proving the rule is provided by the period's most notorious incident of dramatic improvisation, when the young Thomas More, in service in the household of Cardinal Morton (*c.* 1490):

> thoughe he was younge of yeares, yeat wold he at Christmas tyde sodenly sometimes steppe in among the players, and neuer studyeng for the matter, make a parte of his owne there presently among them, which made the lookers on more sporte then all the plaiers beside. (Hitchcock 1935: 5)

It is not reported what the players, probably a semi-professional household company, made of this 'sport', but there is a fascinating response to the incident from people close to the Elizabethan popular theatre in connection with its incorporation into the plot of *Sir Thomas More*, a collaborative work by five or more playwrights: that some of them were also players is more important than whether one of them was Shakespeare (Gabrielli and Melchiori 1990: III.ii.260–77). Like other Elizabethan plays within plays, this one is likely to be a comment on the theatrical arts, and the authors seem agreed not to be impressed by More's achievement: he contributes only two brief speeches, with a response by another character in between, the order of speaking clearly directed by the leader of the troupe. They are commonplace moralizings (More takes on the role of 'Good Counsel' in a moral interlude), and insofar as they are meet for the purpose it is made very clear that More was already familiar with the play (III.ii.65–66). The *fictional* players are duly impressed, but their criterion of success is precisely how well the performance approximated to a script-based one: 'did ye marke how extempirically he fell to the matter, and spake Lugginses parte, almost as it is in the very booke set downe' (III. ii.293–96).

There may be a further metatheatrical comment in Sir Thomas's own assessment, 'Thus fools oft times do help to mar the play' (III.ii.289), for the Elizabethan stage clown was notorious for his improvisations, which were not always for the good of the performance as a whole. As with all the improvisations discussed here, it is only under special circumstances that those of the stage clown are recorded, but as it happens the manuscript of *Sir Thomas More*, which survives, and which has been subject to extensive revision, may indeed provide instances where this has happened (Rasmussen 1991).

Of such improvised clownery within the confines of an otherwise scripted play, there is a direct and relatively well-documented late-medieval antecedent, as David Klausner has noted (2003), in the antics of the Vice figure of the late-medieval morality plays and the Tudor moral interludes (mostly performed by household players who were the direct antecedents of the Elizabethan companies). While symbolizing or exemplifying the sinful behaviour that would ultimately lead to damnation, the Vice operated under homiletic auspices which acknowledged that sin was attractive, and he was consequently the great entertainer of the play. That this duty to entertain also encompassed licence to improvise is indicated in the surviving texts by instructions which tell him what to do but not what he is to say (Happé 1981:24), or by speeches which leave him to his own devices with an encouraging 'etc.'.[21]

An alternative opportunity for historical extrapolation lies in the recognition that the improvisatory aspect of the stage clown's competences was also in part inherited from the pre-theatrical, extra-theatrical, and so possibly medieval, Fool. There are anecdotes of England's Henry VIII and his court jester, Will Sommers, improvising rhymes together and capping one another's verses, with Cardinal Wolsey sometimes joining in (Billington 1984:34). This competence was regularly deployed by the Elizabethan stage clowns (Billington 1984:35), but of course is exclusively verbal and essentially non-dramatic: indeed it was most often exercised in a solo performance by the clown after the main play was over.

Many French farces, probably performed under professional auspices, included a *fol* or *badin*, and we have the authority of Rabelais' Pantagruel to the effect that the role was always assigned by the jongleurs to the best player of their accompany, which may, as Judith McCrary suggests, imply that the role would be to a large degree ad-libbed. On the other hand, when the Fool's role is reflected in the surviving script, it tends to be outside the plot, in solo intermezzos of which the other characters do not take cognizance (1976:166–67).

The most 'oral' tradition of early European drama is of course the Italian *commedia dell'arte*, in which largely improvised performance independent of a fixed script is a characteristic feature, rendering it suitable for treatment (with due allowance for its collective aspect and visual dimension) under the auspices of the oral-formulaic theory (Fitzpatrick 1995). But as noted earlier the skills it requires are emphatically restricted to the cultural system of professional entertainment, and there is much to suggest this is an idiosyncratic local tradition which it may not be legitimate to extrapolate geographically into

---

[21] See Happé 1981:20; Klausner 2003:276.

other countries (other than as visits by Italian touring companies). In the sixteenth century England could fully match the Italians in the development of professional dramatic skills, but with the balance tipped significantly more in favour of the playwright than the performer (Felver 1963): the Italians' way of doing things was unfamiliar enough to merit comment. But there were, as might be predicted from the above, compatibilities from an oral perspective between the clowns of the respective traditions (Henke 1996).

There is also the chronological question. The characteristic *commedia dell'arte* performance is not documented prior to the mid-sixteenth century (Lea 1934:224), and historical extrapolation depends very much on the nature of its relationship to the conventional, text-based traditions of drama, which were equally strong in contemporary Italy, notably in the form of the academic *commedia erudita*. So is *commedia dell'arte* a continuation and consolidation of antecedent oral-improvisational traditions, to which it therefore bears indirect witness, or rather a recent 'oralization' of a textual tradition, perhaps even dependent on trained memories and performance techniques essentially the product of Renaissance academic rhetoric? In the latter case it can tell us nothing about oral tradition in medieval drama.[22]

The truth is probably a particular permutation of the options noted, with the main characters and plot-bearing scenes of *commedia dell'arte* deriving from a *commedia erudita* firmly within Renaissance textual culture, but to a degree deploying improvisational techniques stemming – predictably – from the clown (*zanni*) routines packaging and linking them, which in turn probably have roots in popular oral tradition, not least the buffoons of the Venetian carnival (Henke 2002:74–75). As such they usefully supplement the substantial but largely external documentation in the early-modern and late-medieval period, throughout much of Europe, for vigorous traditions of popular entertainment, offered to a wide variety of audiences, from palaces, through city halls and piazzas to village greens and farmyards, by professionals operating as individuals or in groups of varying sizes, and with repertoires encompassing varying permutations of acrobatics, juggling, animal acts, prestidigitation, music, song, and drama.

Here too a perhaps romantic trend in historical research would like to explain the absence of early texts by the essentially oral nature of the tradition:

> Comic plays were perhaps handed down through generations of jongleurs as part of an essentially oral tradition, to be given permanent form only by the printers and publishers of the fifteenth century. (Hindley 1980:101)

For evidence is emerging that they too used scripts, including part-rolls, so the textual silence may rather be because 'most texts were used for a specific performance and often discarded otherwise' (Hindley 1980:101).

The record is confused by the sustained and close association linking these clowns, buffoons, minstrels and players with travelling quacksalvers hawking patent medicines or undertaking tooth extractions, commonly designated mountebanks (with reference to performance on raised benches) and charlatans (with reference to their persuasive speech). The entertainers put on a side-show to attract an audience for the mountebank,

---

[22] See Schmitt 2004:55–63; Erenstein 1989:122–23.

whose harangue in favour of his medicines, not to mention his diagnoses and healing practices, were themselves pretty theatrical.[23]

Both the mountebank's performance and the side show undoubtedly had significantly oral qualities, in the sense of being unscripted and deploying a good deal of improvisation. The harangue indeed was evidently an improvisational tradition of vernacular rhetoric involving considerable skill. As Thomas Coryat observed of Venetian charlatans in 1611: 'Truly I often wondred at many of these naturall Orators. For they would tell their tales with such admirable volubility and plausible grace, even extempore', prompting (together with a remark by Erasmus) Carol Cark's conclusion that it was probably passed on from one practitioner to another, and certainly 'learned on the job'(1979:541). And as Robert Henke, who also quotes Coryat, notes, the mountebank:

> [...] created his improvisatory harangues from a mental repertoire of words, phrases, tales, set speeches, jokes, dialogues, proverbs, curses, riddles, insults, blessings, and songs that could be patched together in ever-new combinations. (1997:7)

An authentic oral tradition, in other words, worthy to be placed alongside others covered in this volume, but as Clark also notes, never recorded verbatim until the nineteenth century, and not for the first time here of limited value in being almost purely verbal.

This buffoon, *commedia*, mountebank complex opens up another possible route to a late-medieval tradition of professional, dramatic entertainment with a strong oral-improvisational element, and suggests that the repertoire is likely to have involved dramatic items which were not merely shorter, but involved fewer performers, than either medieval community drama or later professional theatre. Indeed more typical will have been the opposite extreme, the single performer offering a one-man show which qualifies as dramatic in that he impersonates someone else, or indeed assumes several roles in the course of the performance, known in French tradition respectively as the *monologue dramatique* and the *mime dialogué* (Faral 1910a: 235–38). In relation to discussion above it would be proper to note that a well-documented medieval one-man routine is precisely an imitation of the mountebank, or rather his close cousin, the apothecary, extolling his drugs and the cures they have achieved (Faral 1910b: 55–79), a tradition continued (to confuse matters further) by those same buffoons who might also accompany the real mountebank (Katritzky 2001: 135–36). It is natural to suppose that these performances were improvised, but of course as we have them they are texts, and the main thrust of research has been rather to determine that the texts were indeed designed for (or in some way recorded) performance, rather than purely literary compositions (Freeman 1981: 282–85).

Improvisation may also be implied (but it may not be verbal) in the very early record of the mimicking of monastic depravity by marketplace entertainers (*mimi*), complained of by the Anglo-Saxon King Edward in the tenth century, hailed by J. D. A. Olgivy as one of the period's clearest indications of dramatic presentation (1963: 613–14). On the other hand a major piece of evidence, the Carolingian mock epitaph of one

---

[23] See Burke 1978:94–100. [On the entertainers of the High and Late Middle Ages, see also ch. 5 by J. Harris and K. Reichl in this volume, section 3.]

such, Vitalis, explicitly includes a verbal element, but the performances concerned are evidently solo turns:

> I used to mimic the face, manner and words (*ac verba loquentum*) of those talking, so that you would think many people spoke (*plures* [...] *loqui*) from one mouth (*uno* [...] *ore*). (Axton 1974: 17)

It is hard to pin down evidence for anything more conventionally dramatic, although in his useful analysis of the available evidence Richard Axton suggests this may be precisely because they were non-textual: 'no doubt unscripted improvisation upon routine outlines was common' (1974: 19). The examples he refers to (routines with a performing dog, cruel tricks plaid on a blind man), are turns which could certainly be improvised, but in the texts he invokes they are fully scripted, and external evidence is not always cooperative.

There is however an interesting account of 'an improvised diversion occasioned at a feast by a weeping dog' in the eleventh-century Latin romance, *Ruodlieb* (Axton 1974: 22). The actual performers are the minstrel-entertainer and his trained dog, the entertainment comprising a display of the tricks it can do on command, such as not eating food it is told was 'cooked by an evil person', but a series of these involve 'dramatic' interaction with the spectators, and are ordered into a sequence which might well be 'improvised' to suit the immediate circumstances (as would be the exact formulation of the instructions): in this case, barking at a servant who has stolen an object, identifying the rightful owner and giving it back to him, attacking the thief, then expressing regret (the weeping alluded to) and making friends (Zaydel 1959: 106–7, ll. 71–104).

## 4 Conclusion

This remains a meagre harvest, and that it should be so hard to document or even argue for the significance of oral tradition in so manifestly an oral performance art as medieval drama is frankly surprising. As will have been noted, under virtually every heading touched on above it is possible to find authoritative statements postulating an oral or improvisational phase of tradition just behind the phase actually represented by the available documents. It has proved thus far, an ungraspable illusion, and it is quite possible that for the reasons explored – the practicalities of collective performance; the requirements of control and censorship; the absence of fully-fledged professional traditions – there was no medieval drama that was fully oral, or no medieval oral tradition that was fully dramatic. But it is equally clear that those many assumptions about the oral, improvisational nature of medieval drama have not been matched by the direct and systematic explorations characterizing scholarly attention devoted to medieval narratives.

The field evidently awaits exploration, and the current situation may be auspicious. The number of available texts is increasing, as more continental plays are discovered and more achieve publication; in England it seems more likely that the increase will take the form of more medieval texts being recognized as inherently dramatic (Symes 2002). Historical, contextual documentation of performance is becoming increasingly available, thanks to the efforts both of collective projects such as 'Records of Early English Drama', and of highly productive individuals (Neumann 1987). And as with other traditions, much may by achieved by juxtaposing this medieval material with the insights gained from the study of living or more recently living traditions of customary drama (like the mummers' plays) or professional performance culture (say the itinerant mountebank or the puppet show) which if not direct continuations, are at least useful analogues, of late-medieval custom, pastime and entertainment.

## References

Axton, Richard. 1974. *European Drama of the Early Middle Ages*. London: Hutchinson.
Baker, Donald C., et al., eds. 1982. *The Late Medieval Religious Plays of Bodleian MSS Digby 133 and E Museo 160*. EETS 283. Oxford: OUP.
Baldwin, John W. 1997. 'The Image of the Jongleur in Northern France around 1200.' *Speculum* 72: 635–63
Bauer, Werner M., ed. 1982. *Die weltlichen Spiele des Sterzinger Spielarchivs nach den Original-handschriften (1510 – 1535) von Vigil Raber und nach der Ausgabe Oswald Zingerle (1886)*. Wiener Neudrucke 6. Vienna: Österreichischer Bundesverlag.
Beadle, Richard, ed. 1982. *The York Plays*. London: Edward Arnold.
–, ed. 1994. *The Cambridge Companion to Medieval English Theatre*. Cambridge: CUP.
–. 2000. 'Verbal Texture and Wordplay in the York Cycle.' *Early Theatre* 3: 167–84.
–, and Peter Meredith, eds. 1983. *The York Play: A Facsimile of British Library Ms Additional 35290*. Leeds Texts and Monographs. Medieval Drama Facsimiles 7. Leeds: School of English.
Billington, Sandra. 1984. *A Social History of the Fool*. Brighton: Harvester.
Bouhaïk-Girones, Marie. 2003. 'Le procès des farceurs de Dijon.' *European Medieval Drama* 7: 117–34.
Burke, Peter. 1978. *Popular Culture in Early Modern Europe*. London: Temple Smith.
Butterworth, Philip. 1999. 'Prompting in full view of the audience: a medieval staging convention.' In Hindley 1999a: 231–47
–. 2001. 'Prompting in Full View of the Audience: The Groningen Experiment.' *Medieval English Theatre* 23: 122–71.
–, ed. 2007a. *The Narrator, the Expositor, and the Prompter in European Medieval Theatre*. Turnhout: Brepols.
–. 2007b. 'Richard Carew's "Ordinary": The First English Director.' In Butterworth 2007a: 327–42.
Clark, Carol. 1979. '"The onely languag'd-men of all the word": Rabelais and the Art of the Mountebank.' *Modern Language Review*. 74: 538–52.
Craig, Hardin, ed. 1902. *Two Coventry Corpus Christi Plays*. EETS ES 87. London: Kegan Paul, Trench, Trübner.
Davidson, Clifford. 2003. 'Improvisation in Medieval Drama.' In McGee 2003: 193–221.
Davis, Norman, ed. 1970. *Non-Cycle Plays and Fragments*. EETS SS 1. London: OUP.
Dobozy, Maria. 2005. *Re-Membering the Present: The Medieval German Poet-Minstrel in Cultural Context*. Turnhout: Brepols.
DuBruck, Edelgard E. 2004. 'German Carnival Comedies: Strategies of Entertainment.' In *New Approaches to European Theater of the Middle Ages*. Ed. Barbara I. Gusick and Edelgard E. Dubruck. New York: Peter Lang.
Enders, Jody. 2002. *Death by Drama and Other Medieval Urban Legends*. Chicago: U of Chicago P.

Erenstein, Robert L. 1989. 'The Humour of Commedia dell'Arte.' In *The Commedia dell'Arte from the Renaissance to Dario Fo*. Ed. Christopher Cairns. Lewiston: Edwin Mellen P. 118–40.
Evans, G. Blakemore, ed. 1997. *The Riverside Shakespeare*. 2nd ed. Boston: Houghton Mifflin.
Faral, Edmond. 1910a. *Les jongleurs en France au moyen âge*. Paris: Champion.
–, ed. 1910b. *Mimes français du XIIIe siècle*. Paris: Champion.
Felver, Charles S. 1963. 'The *Commedia dell'Arte* and English Drama in the Sixteenth and Early Seventeenth Centuries.' *Research Opportunities in Renaissance Drama* 6: 24–34.
Fitzpatrick, Tim. 1995. *The Relationship of Oral and Literate Processes in the Commedia dell'Arte: Beyond the Improvisation/Memorisation Divide*. Lewiston: Edwin Mellen P.
Fletcher, Alan J. 1986. '"Farte Prycke in Cule": A Late-Elizabethan Analogue from Ireland.' *Medieval English Theatre* 8: 134–39
Frank, Grace. 1936. 'The Beginnings of Comedy in France.' *Modern Language Review* 31: 377–84.
Freeman, Michael J. 1981. 'Aspects du théâtre comique français des XVe et XVI siècles: la sottie, le monologue dramatique et le sermon joyeux.' In *Le Théâtre au moyen âge*. Ed. Gari R. Muller. Montreal: Aurore/Univers. 279–98.
Gabrielli, Vittorio, and Giorgio Melchiori, eds. 1990. *Sir Thomas More*. Revels Plays. Manchester: Manchester UP.
Greg, W. W., and E. K. Chambers, eds. 1928. Christopher Marlowe. *The Massacre at Paris*. Malone Society Reprints 65. London: The Malone Society. [Rpt. New York: AMS, 1985.]
Happé, Peter. 1981. '"The Vice" and the Popular Theatre, 1547–80.' In *Poetry and Drama 1570 – 1700: Essays in Honor of Harold F. Brooks*. Ed. Antony Coleman and Antony Hammond. London: Methuen. 13–31.
–. 2007. *The Towneley Cycle: Unity and Diversity*. Cardiff: U of Wales P.
Henke, Robert. 1996. 'Orality and Literacy in the *Commedia dell'Arte* and the Shakespearean Clown.' *Oral Tradition* 11: 222–48.
–. 1997. 'The Italian Mountebank and the *Commedia dell'Arte*.' *Theatre Survey* 38.2: 1–29.
–. 2002. *Performance and Literature in the Commedia dell'Arte*. Cambridge: CUP.
Hindley, Alan. 1980. 'Medieval French Drama: A Review of Recent Scholarship. Part II: Comic Drama.' *Research Opportunities in Renaissance Drama* 23: 93–226.
–, ed. 1999a. *Drama and Community: People and Plays in Medieval Europe*. Turnhout: Brepols.
–. 1999b. 'Acting Companies in Late Medieval France: Triboulet and his Troupe.' In Hindley 1999a: 78–98.
Hitchcock, Elsie Vaughan, ed. 1935. William Roper. *The Life of Sir Thomas Moore, Knighte*. Ed. Elsie Vaughan Hitchcock. EETS 197. London: OUP.
Ingram, William. 1992. *The Business of Playing: The Beginnings of the Adult Professional Theater in Elizabethan England*. Ithaca, NY: Cornell UP.
Johnston, Alexandra F. 1993. 'The *York Cycle* and the *Chester Cycle*: What do the Records Tell Us?' In *The Chester Mystery Cycle: A Casebook*. Ed. J. Harty. New York: Garland. 18–35.
Jones, Malcolm. 1997. 'The Parodic Sermon in Medieval and Early Modern England.' *Medium Ævum* 66: 94–114.
Kahrl, Stanley J. 1993. 'The Staging of Medieval English Plays.' In *The Theatre of Medieval Europe: New Research in Early Drama*. Ed. Eckehard Simon. Cambridge: CUP. 130–48.
Katritzky, M. A. 2001. 'Marketing Medicine: The Image of the Early Modern Mountebank.' *Renaissance Studies* 15: 121–53.
–. 2006. 'Review of McGee 2003.' *Early Theatre* 9: 149–52.
Kernodle, George R. 1960. 'Seven Medieval Theatres in One Social Structure.' *Theatre Research* 2: 26–36.
Kipling, Gordon. 1997a. 'Theatre as Subject and Object in Fouquet's "Martyrdom of St Apollonia".' *Medieval English Theatre* 19: 26–80.
–. 1997b. 'Fouquet, St Apollonia, and the Motives of the Miniaturist's Art: A Reply to Graham Runnalls.' *Medieval English Theatre* 19: 101–20.

Klausner, David. 2003. 'The Improvising Vice in Renaissance England.' In McGee 2003: 273–85.
Koopmans, Jelle. 1988a. 'Folklore, tradition et révolte: Le fonctionnement social des Sermons Joyeux Français de la Fin du Moyen Age.' In *Le théatre et la cité dans l'Europe médiévale: Actes du V$^{ème}$ colloque international de la Société Internationale pour l'Étude du Théatre Médiéval*. Ed. Jean-Claude Aubailly and Edelgard E. DuBruck. Stuttgart: Heinz. 457–70.
–, ed. 1988b. *Recueil de Sermons Joyeux*. Geneva: Droz.
Lancashire, Ian. 1977. 'Medieval Drama.' In *Editing Medieval Texts*. Ed. A. G. Rigg. New York: Garland. 58–85.
Lea, K. M. 1934. *Italian Popular Comedy: A Study in the Commedia dell'Arte 1560 – 1620*. 2 vols. Oxford: Clarendon.
Longtin, Mario. 2007. 'Prompting the Action: The Prologue, the Messenger, and the Fool.' In Butterworth 2007a: 191–210.
Luckham, Cyril. 1983. 'Memories of a Strolling Player.' BBC Radio 4. 7 August, 4.45–5.00p. m.
Lumiansky, R. M., and David Mills. 1983. *The Chester Mystery Cycle: Essays and Documents*. Chapel Hill: U of North Carolina P.
McCrary, Judith. 1976. 'The Fool in French Medieval Drama.' Ph.D. Thesis, University of Missouri.
McGee, Timothy J., ed. 2003. *Improvisation in the Arts of the Middle Ages and Renaissance*. EDAM Monograph Series 30. Kalamazoo: Medieval Institute, Western Michigan University.
Meredith, Peter. 1981. 'John Clerk's Hand in the York Register.' *Leeds Studies in English* N. S. 12: 245–71.
–. 1983. 'Scribes, Texts and Performance.' In *Aspects of Early English Drama*. Ed. Paula Neuss. Cambridge: Brewer. 13–29.
–, and John E. Tailby, eds. 1983. *The Staging of Religious Drama in Europe in the Later Middle Ages: Texts and Documents in English Translation*. EDAM Monographs 4. Kalamazoo: Medieval Institute, Western Michigan University.
Muir, Lynette R. 2001. 'Extra-liturgical Latin and Early Vernacular Drama.' In Tydeman et al. 2001a: 137–204.
Murdoch, Brian O. 1994. 'The Cornish Medieval Drama.' In Beadle 1994: 211–39.
Neumann, Bernd. 1987. *Geistliches Schauspiel im Zeugnis der Zeit. Zur Aufführungen mittelalterlicher religiöser Dramen im deutschen Sprachgebiet*. 2 vols. Munich: Artemis.
Neuss, Paula. 1971. 'Memorial Reconstruction in a Cornish Miracle Play.' *Comparative Drama* 5: 129–37.
–, ed. and trans. 1983. *The Creacion of the World*. New York: Garland.
Newbigin, Nerida. 1999. 'Judas and the Jews in the Easter Plays of the Roman Confraternity of the Gonfalone.' *European Medieval Drama* 3: 19–39.
–. 2007. 'Directing the Gaze: Expository Modes in Late Medieval Italian Plays.' In Butterworth 2007a: 69–92.
Ogilvy, J. D. A. 1963. '*Mimi, Scurrae, Histriones*: Entertainers of the Early Middle Ages.' *Speculum* 38: 603–19.
Oreglia, Giacomo. 1968. *The Commedia dell'Arte*. Trans. L. F. Edwards. London: Methuen.
Peters, Julie Stone. 2000. *The Theatre of the Book 1480 – 1880: Print, Text and Performance in Europe*. Oxford: OUP.
Petit de Julleville, Louis. 1880. *Les Mystères*. 2 vols. Paris.[Rpt. Geneva: Slatkine, 1968.]
–. 1885. *Les Comédiens en France au moyen age*. Paris. [Rpt. Geneva: Slatkine, 1968.]
Pettitt, Thomas. 1982. 'English Folk Drama and the Early German *Fastnachtspiele*.' *Renaissance Drama* N. S. 13: 1–34.
–. 1988. 'Formulaic Dramaturgy in Doctor Faustus.' In *A Poet and a Filthy Play-Maker: New Essays on Christopher Marlowe*. Ed. Kenneth Friedenreich, Roma Gill, and Constance B. Kuriyama. New York: AMS P. 167–91.

—. 2000.'Local and "Customary" Drama.' In *A Companion to English Renaissance Literature and Culture.* Ed. Michael Hattaway. Oxford: Blackwell. 464–76.

—. 2003b.'The Folk Interlude: Dramatic Aspects of Traditional Games, Gambols and Songs.' In *Folk Drama Studies Today: Papers Given at the International Traditional Drama Conference 19–21 July 2002, University of Sheffield, England.* Ed. E. Cass and P. Millington. Sheffield: Traditional Drama Research Group. 67–88.

—. 2005a.'Marlowe's Texts and Oral Transmission: Towards the *Zielform*.' *Comparative Drama* 39: 213–42.

—. 2005b.'When the Golden Bough Breaks: Folk Drama and the Theatre Historian.' *Nordic Journal of English Studies* 4.2: 1–40.

Plesch, Véronique. 1994–95.'"Étalage complaisant"? The Torments of Christ in French Passion Plays.' *Comparative Drama.* 28: 458–85.

Rasmussen, Eric. 1991.'Setting Down what the Clown Spoke: Improvisation, Hand B, and *The Book of Sir Thomas More*.' *The Library* 13: 126–36.

Rey-Flaud, Henri. 1973. *Le cercle magique. Essai sur le théâtre en rond à la fin du Moyen Age.* Paris: Gallimard.

Richards, Kenneth, and Laura Richards. 1990. *The Commedia dell'Arte: A Documentary History.* Oxford: Blackwell.

Richardson, Christine, and Jackie Johnston. 1991. *Medieval Drama.* London: Macmillan.

Rosenfeld, Sybil. 1960. *The Theatre of the London Fairs in the Eighteenth Century.* Cambridge: CUP.

Roy, Jean, ed. 1977. *Le Jeu de la Feuillée.* Paris: Bordas.

Runnalls, Graham. 1986–87.'The Medieval Actors Rôles Found in the Fribourg Archives.' *Pluteus* 4–5: 5–67.

—. 1990.'Towards a Typology of Medieval French Play Manuscripts.' In *The Editor and the Text.* Ed. P. E. Bennett and G. A. Runnalls. Edinburgh: Edinburgh UP. 96–113.

—. 1994.'Were They Listening or Watching? Text and Spectacle at the 1510 Châteaudun *Passion Play*.' *Medieval English Theatre* 16: 25–36.

—. 1997.'Jean Fouquet's "Martyrdom of St Apollonia" and the Medieval French Stage.' *Medieval English Theatre* 19: 81–100

Schmitt, Natalie Crohn. 2004.'*Commedia dell'Arte*: Characters, Scenarios, and Rhetoric.' *Text and Performance Quarterly* 24: 55–73.

Severs, J. Burke. 1945.'The Relationship between the Brome and Chester Plays of Abraham and Isaac.' *Modern Philology* 42: 137–51.

Simon, Eckehard. 1969.'The Staging of the Neidhart Plays with Notes on Six Documented Performances.' *Germanic Review* 44: 5–20

—. 1993.'Organizing and Staging Carnival Plays in Late Medieval Lübeck: A New Look at the Archival Record.' *JEGP* 92: 57–72.

—. 2000.'Manuscript Production in Medieval Theatre: The German Carnival Plays.' In *New Directions in Manuscript Studies.* Ed. Derek Pearsall. York: York Medieval P: 143–65.

Simon, Gerd. 1970. *Die erste deutsche Fastnachtsspieltradition: Textkritik und Chronologie der Nürnberger Fastnachtspiele des 15. Jahrhunderts (mit kurzen Einführungen in Verfahren der quantitativen Linguistik).* Germanische Studien 240. Lübeck: Matthiesen.

Smith, Bruce R. 1999. *The Acoustic World of Early Modern England.* Chicago: U of Chicago P.

Stern, Charlotte. 1973. 'The Early Spanish Drama: From Medieval Ritual to Renaissance Art.' *Renaissance Drama* N. S. 6: 177–201.

Stevens, Martin. 1987. *Four Middle English Mystery Cycles: Textual, Contextual, and Critical Interpretations.* Princeton: Princeton UP.

—, and A. C. Cawley, eds. 1994. *The Towneley Plays.* EETS ss 13. London: OUP.

Strietman, Elsa. 2007.'"Every Man, I wyll go with thee and be thy gyde": Narrators, Expositors and Prompters in the Drama of the Low Countries.' In Butterworth 2007: 11–44.

Symes, Carol. 2002. 'The Appearance of Early Vernacular Plays: Forms, Functions, and the Future of Medieval Theater.' *Speculum* 77:778–831.
Tailby, John E. 1987. 'The Role of Director in the Lucerne Passion Play.' *Medieval English Theatre* 9:80–92.
–, ed. 2001. 'The German-Speaking Area.' In Tydeman et al. 2001a: 353–420.
Twycross, Meg. 1994. 'The Theatricality of Medieval English Plays.' In Beadle 1994:37–84.
Tydeman, William. 1978. *The Theatre in the Middle Ages*. Cambridge: CUP.
–, et al. eds. 2001a. *The Medieval European Stage, 500 – 1550*. Theatre in Europe: A Documentary History. Cambridge: CUP.
–. 2001b. 'England, Ireland, Scotland and Wales.' In Tydeman et al. 2001a: 205–78.
van Abbé, Derek M. 1960. 'What is Fastnachtspiel?' *Journal of the Australasian Universities Language and Literature Association.* 12:36–44
van Dijk, Hans. 1985. 'The Structure of the "Sotternieën" in the Hulthem Manuscript.' In *The Theatre in the Middle Ages*. Ed. Herman Braet et al. Leuven: Leuven UP. 238–50.
Wainwright, Elizabeth. 1974. *Studien zum deutschen Prozessionsspiel. Die Tradition der Fronleichnamspiele in Künzelsau und Freiburg und ihre textliche Entwicklung*. Munich: Arbeo-Gesellschaft.
Walsh, Martin. 1992. 'Eulenspiegel (Episode 13) as a Theater-Historical Document.' *Early Drama, Art and Music Review* 14:43–52.
Wickham, Glynne. 1987. *The Medieval Theatre*. Cambridge: CUP.
Zaydel, Edwin H., ed. and trans. 1959. *Ruodlieb. The Earliest Courtly Novel (after 1050)*. Chapel Hill: U of North Carolina P.
Zumthor, Paul. 1983. *Introduction à la poésie orale*. Paris: Seuil.

# Notes on the Illustrations

The illustrations are reproduced with the permission of the libraries and museums (Archäologisches Landesmuseum, Konstanz, Archaeological Museum of Ancient Corinth, Staatliches Museum für Völkerkunde, Munich) holding the originals; their permission is gratefully acknowledged. In the following notes the location of the originals is indicated and information provided on facsimile editions and library websites.

1 (p. 19) – Beginning of *La Prise de Cordres et de Sebille*, chanson de geste of the 12th/13th c. Paris, BnF MS fr. 1448, f. 164r. Reproduction in Hermann Suchier and Adolf Birch-Hirschfeld, *Geschichte der Französischen Litteratur von der ältesten Zeit bis zur Gegenwart* (Leipzig and Vienna: Bibliographisches Institut, 1900), plate opposite p. 34.

2 (p. 76) – Avdo Medjedović, a South Slavic *guslar*. The photo is no. 29 in Albert B. Lord's photo album (Milman Parry Collection, Harvard University). See <http://chs119.chs.harvard.edu/mpc/index.html>. Avdo's version of the *Wedding of Smailagić Meho* is translated in volume 3 of the *Serbo-Croation Heroic Songs* (Cambridge, MA: Harvard UP, 1974).

3 (p. 113) – Beginning of the *Gododdin*. In *The Book of Aneirin* (*Llyfr Aneirin*), c. 1265. Cardiff Central Library, MS 2.81, p. 1. Reproduction in J. Gwenogvryn Evans, ed., *Facsimile and Text of the Book of Aneirin* (Pwllheli, 1908). See <http://www.gtj.org.uk/en/small/item/GTJ10900/>.

4 (p. 125) – Caedmon's Hymn. Cambridge University Library, MS Kk.4.1b, fol. 128v (Moore Bede). Reproduction in Peter Hunter Blair, ed., *The Moore Bede: Cambridge University Library Kk. 5. 16*, with a contribution by R. A. B. Mynors, Early English Manuscripts in Facsimile 9 (Copenhagen: Rosenkilde & Bagger, 1959).

5 (p. 165) – Lyre, from Trossingen (6th c.), restored original (top) and reconstruction (below). Reproduction in Barbara Theune-Großkopf, 'Die vollständig erhaltene Leier des 6. Jahrhunderts aus Grab 58 von Trossingen, Ldkr. Tuttlingen, Baden-Württemberg: Ein Vorbericht', *Germania* 84 (2006): 93–142, at 111 and 139. See also <http://www.konstanz.alm-bw.de/>.

6 (p. 169) – Two musicians, from the *Cantigas de Santa Maria*. The illumination is found in MS j. b. 2 (also known as b. I .2) of the Real Monasterio de El Escorial (13th c.). Reproduction in Ramón Menéndez Pidal, *Poesía juglaresca y origenes de la literaturas romanicas. Problemas de historia literaria y cultural*, 6th ed. (Madrid: Instituto de Estudios Politicos, 1957), plate opposite p. 96.

7 (p. 211) – *Branwen Uerch Lyr* in the White Book of Rhydderch (14th c.). Aberystwyth, National Lib. of Wales MS Peniarth 4, fol. 10va. See <http://www.llgc.org.uk/index.php?id=whitebookofrhydderchpeniart>.

8 (p. 264) – *Frá dauða Sigurðar* in the *Poetic Edda*. Codex Regius (MS GKS 2365 4to), p. 66 (now in the Árni Magnússon Institute of Icelandic Studies, Reykjavik). Reproduction in Ludv. F. A. Wimmer and Finnur Jónsson, eds., *Håndskriftet nr. 2365 4to gl. kgl. sammling på det store Kgl. bibliothek i København (Codex regius af den ældre Edda) i fototypisk og diplomatisk gengivelse* (Copenhagen, 1891).

9 (p. 282) – *Acallam na Senórach*. Bodl. Library, MS Laud Misc. 610, fol. 124rb. Reproduction in Brian Ó Cuív, ed., *Catalogue of Irish Language Manuscripts in the Bodeleian Library Oxford and Oxford College Libraries*, Part 2: Plates and Indexes (Dublin: School of Celtic Studies Dublin Institue for Advances Studies, 2003), plate 8.

10 (p. 316) – Beginning of the Old High German *Hildebrandslied*. University Library Kassel, MS Theol. 54, fol. 1r. Reproduction in Georg Baesecke, ed., *Das Hildebrandlied. Eine geschichtliche*

*Einleitung für Laien, mit Lichtbildern der Handschrift, alt- und neuhochdeutschen Texten* (Halle: Niemeyer, 1945), Plate I.
11 (p. 344) – Beginning of *Sir Tristrem*. Edinburgh, Nat. Lib. of Scotland MS Advovates 19.2.1 (Auchinleck MS), fol. 281ra. Reproduction in *The Auchinleck Manuscript, National Library of Scotland Advocates' MS. 19.2.1*, with an introduction by Derek Pearsall and I. C. Cunningham (London: Scolar Press, 1977). See also <http://digital.nls.uk/auchinleck/>.
12 (p. 356) – Beginning of the *Chanson de Roland*. Oxford, Bodl. Lib. MS Digby 23, fol. 1r. Reproduction in Charles Samaran, ed., *La Chanson de Roland. Reproduction phototypique du ms. Digby 23 de la Bodleian Library d'Oxford* (Paris: SATF, 1933). See also <http://image.ox.ac.uk/show?collection=bodleian&manuscript=msdigby23b>.
13 (p. 372) – *Cantastorie* (with vièle), from a popular print (16th c.) in the Biblioteca Nazionale Marciana of Venice (Misc. 2213.9). Reproduced with permission of the Ministerio dei Beni e delle Attività Culturali e del Turismo – Biblioteca Nazionale Marciana.
14 (p. 407) – *Taraf* of Dumitrache Ochialbi. Painting by Carol Popp de Szathmáry, 1812–1888 in the National Museum of Art/ Muzeul Naţional de Artă in Bucharest. Reproduction in Viorel Cosma, *Lăutarii de ieri şi de azi*, 2nd ed. (Bucharest: Editura du Style, 1996), p. 120.
15 (p. 413) – *El libro de los cincuenta romances* (The Book of Fifty *romances*), 1550–1551, title page. Reproduction in Antonio Rodríguez Moñino, *Silva de Romances (Zaragoza 1550–1551). Estudio, bibliografía e índices* (Zaragoza, 1970), title page.
16 (p. 452) – The Ballad of Judas. Cambridge, Trinity College MS B 14. 39, fol. 34r.
17 (p. 464) – Digenis and a Princess. Byzantine glazed plate (12th c.) in the Archaeological Museum of Ancient Corinth. See <http://www.ancientcorinth.net/museum.aspx>.
18 (p. 488) – Battle on the Kulikovo Pole, from a manuscript of *The Mighty Battle of Mamay* (17th c.). Reproduced in E. A. Mishina, *Russkaya gravyura na dereve, XVII–XVIII vv.* (St. Petersburg: D. Bulanin, 1998), p. 42.
19 (p. 503) – Seder Table, Second Nuremberg Haggadah (15th c.). See the website of the Jewish National and University Library, Jerusalem, at <http://jnul.huji.ac.il/dl/mss-pr/mss_d_0076/index.html.> 'The "Second Nuremberg Haggada" is an illuminated manuscript haggada, apparently from the mid-15th century. It's name derives from its being held by the Stadtbibliothek of Nuremberg from the mid-19th century until 1957. Its previous provenance is not known. In 1957 the Haggada was acquired by the Schocken Collection in Jerusalem and in 2004 was purchased by Mr. David Sofer of London.' (Website)
20 (p. 523) – Woman Dancer, from Paris, BnF MS lat. 1118, fol. 114r (first half of 11th c.). Reproduction in Leonardo Olschki, *Die romanischen Literaturen des Mittelalters* (Potsdam: Athenaion, 1928), p. 194. See the website 'Mandragore' of the Bibliothèque nationale de France at <http://mandragore.bnf.fr/html/accueil.html>.
21 (p. 567) – 'Svmer is icumen in', BL MS Harley 978, fol. 11v. Reproduction in Richard Wülker, *Geschichte der Englischen Literatur von den ältesten Zeiten bis zur Gegenwart*. 2 vols. (Leipzig and Vienna: Bibliographisches Institut, 1906), I, 95. See the website of the British Library 'Catalogue of Digital Manuscripts' at <http://prodigi.bl.uk/illcat/welcome.htm>.
22 (p. 589) – Beginning of Marcabru's 'L'autrer jost' una sebissa', BnF MS fr. 22543, fol. 5ra (13th c.). See the website 'Mandragore' of the Bibliothèque nationale de France at <http://mandragore.bnf.fr/html/accueil.html>. The manuscript is manuscript R of the troubadour manuscripts. The figure at the bottom of the MS page is not related to the poem.
23 (p. 621) – Bayāḍ singing to the lute. Bibl. Vaticana, MS Ar. 368 (13th c.). Reproduction in A. R. Nykl, ed. and trans., *Historia de los Amores de Bayāḍ y Riyāḍ. Una 'Chantefable' Oriental en Estilo Persa (Vat. Ar. 368)* (New York: Hispanic Society of America, 1941), p. 16.
24 (p. 640) – 'A Shá'er, with his accompanying Violist, and part of his Audience'. Illustration in Edward William Lane, *An Account of the Manners and Customs of the Modern Egyptians*, 5th ed. (London, 1860), p. 393.

25 (p. 658) – Rustam defeats one of Afrāsiyāb's warrior. From an early 15th-c. *Shāh-nāma* MS. Reproduced in Andreas Lommel, ed., *Persische Kunst. Katalog zur Ausstellung des Staatlichen Museums für Völkerkunde, München, Maximilianstraße 42* (Munich: Staatliches Museum für Völkerkunde, 1963), p. 57. The manuscript comes from the Preetorius Collection (L I 284).

26 (p. 688) – Beginning of *The Book of Dede Korkut* in the Dresden MS (Sächsische Staats- und Universitätsbibliothek Dresden, MS Ea. 86). Reproduction in Muharrem Ergin, ed., *Dede Korkut Kitabı.* 2 vols. Türk Dil Kurumu Yayınları, 169, 219 (Ankara: Türk Dil Kurumu, 1958–63), vol. 1. See also <http://www.slub-dresden.de/en/about-us/ausstellungen-veranstaltungen/museum-of-books/virtual-treasury/>.

27 (p. 706) – Detail from Jean Fouquet's 'The Martyrdom of St Apolonia' (c. 1460). Reproduction in André Lagarde and Laurent Michard, *Moyen-Age. Les grands auteurs français du programme, I* (Paris: Bordas, 1964), plate 30 opposite p. 162. See also <http://expositions.bnf.fr/fouquet/grand/f112.htm>. The illumination is found in the *Heures d'Estienne Chevalier* (Musée Condé, Chantilly).

# Index

See also the Detailed Chapter Contents on pp. IX–XIV above. In the Index the language of medieval works not written in Latin has been indicated; in addition to the language abbreviations listed on pp. XIX–XX the following abbreviations have been used: Ar (Arabic), Da (Danish), Gr (Greek), Heb (Hebrew), Ir (Irish), It (Italian), MHG (Middle High German), MLG (Middle Low German), OF (Old French, including Anglo-Norman), OHG (Old High German), P (Persian), Po (Portuguese), Pr (Provençal), Rom (Romanian), Ru (Russian), SC (Serbian and Croatian), Sp (Spanish), T (Turkish), W (Welsh).

*Abenámar* (Sp)   414
*Abraham and Isaac* (ME) ('Brome' play)   711, 714
*Abrogans* (OHG)   302
Abū al-Khayr Rūmī   661
– *Salṭuq-nāme* (T)   661
Abū Isḥāq ad-Duwainī   585
Abū 'l-Ghāzī   689
– *Pedigree of the Turkmens* (Chaghatay)   689, 690
Abū Muslim (P, T)   654, 660, 668, 684, 685
Abū Nuwās   606
*Acallam na Senórach* (Ir)   281–87, 290, 291, 529
Achilles Tatius   462, 466, 468
*Adam* (OF)   706
Adam de la Halle   354, 534, 535
Ælfric Bata   136
– *Colloquies*   136
Ælfric of Eynsham   136, 162
– *Colloquy* (OE)   136
aesthetics see oral aesthetics
*Aga Bălăceanu* (Rom)   398
Ahimaaz ben Paltiel   514–16
– *The Chronicle of Ahimaaz* (Heb)   514, 515
Airas Nunez   542
Alain Chartier   46
*alba*   532, 533, 535, 539, 541, 542
al-Balādhurī   635
– *Kitāb futūḥ al-buldān* (Ar)   635

*alborada*   541, 543
Albrecht von Kemnaten   307
– *Goldemar* (OHG)   307, 317, 318
al-Budayrī   641
Aldhelm   81, 172
– *De virginitate*   172
Alecsandri, Vasile   387, 402–5
– *Poesii populare ale românilor* (Rom)   387
Alegret   180
*Alësha Popovich* (Ru)   37
Alexander (ME) (*King Alisaunder*)   22, 342
*Alexander and Semiramis* (Gr) (*A&S*)   465, 469, 470, 473, 475
*Alexanderlied* (MHG)   306
*Alf Laila wa-Laila* (Ar)   636, 641, 646
Alfonso X of Castille, King   51, 169, 183, 602, 622
– *Cantigas de Santa Maria* (Po)   169
Alfred, King   93
al-Masʿūdī   662, 665
*Álora* (Sp)   416
*Alpamysh* (Uzbek)   694, 695
*Alpharts Tod* (MHG)   315, 318
*Ältere Not* (MHG)   312
al-Wāqidī   634, 635
*Amīr Arsalān* (P)   654
*Amis and Amiloun* (ME)   82
Anacreon   525
*Ancroia* (It)   379
*Andreas* (OE)   91, 95, 96
Aneirin   112

*Annales Cambriae* 111
*Annals of Quedlinburg* 305
*Annolied* (OHG) 304, 307
an-Nuwairī 631
*Anseïs de Metz* (F) 179
*aoidos* 27
Apollonius Rhodius 378
*Arabian Nights* see *Alf Laila wa-Laila*
Ariosto, Ludovico 190, 237, 376, 378–83
– *Orlando Furioso* 190, 237, 371, 378–80
*Aristander and Kallithea* (Gr) (*A&K*) 462
Aristophanes 524
– *The Wasps* 524
Aristotle 304
*Arnaldos* (Sp) 423
Arnaut de Mareuil 180
Arnim, Achim von 43
*Arte de Trovar* (Po) 527
*aşık* 30, 696
as-Sakhāwī 642
as-Saraqusṭī 618
Asser 93, 127–34, 136
– *Life of Alfred* 93
*Atharvaveda* 268
*Atlakviða* (ON) 264
*Atlamál* (ON) 158
*aube* 533
*Aucassin et Nicolette* (OF) 21, 187
Auchinleck MS see Manuscripts
*Audigier* (OF) 354
*Aufreihlied* 267
Augustine, St 112
*Auraicept na n-Éces* (Ir) 24
aural / aurality 15, 17, 18, 20–22, 85, 93, 234, 238, 262, 323, 430, 431, 581, 633, 658, 659, 666, 667, 674
*ayyām al ʿarab* (Ar) 630, 631, 634, 637, 638
az-Zamā 618, 619

*Badiul cârciumarul* (Rom) 398
*bakhshi* 24
*balada* 32, 532
*ballata* 606
*Bänkelsänger* 174
Barbour, John
– *Bruce* (ME) 343
*barcarola* 544
*Baṭṭāl-nāme* (T) 685, 686, 697
Baude de la Quarière 45, 46

*Baudouin de Sebourc* (OF) 354
Bede (Beda Venerabilis) 31, 89, 112, 122–27, 134, 136, 221, 222
– *Historia ecclesiastica gentis Anglorum* 89, 112, 122–27, 221
*Bel Gherardino* (It) 373, 381, 383
*Bele Aelis* (OF) 44
Benjamin of Tudela 505, 511, 513, 516
Benoît de Ste Maure 469, 470
– *Roman de Troie* (OF) 469, 470, 475
*Beowulf* (OE) 3, 8, 9, 10, 13, 39, 53, 81, 83, 84, 90–92, 95, 96, 231, 243, 260, 266–70
Béroul 281
– *Tristan* (OF) 281
*Bestiary* (ME) 342
*Beues of Hamtoun* (ME) 340
*Beuve de Hantone* (OF) 357
Bible 8, 11, 16, 105, 111, 117, 177, 231, 302, 377, 382, 507–11, 516, 524, 537, 586, 587
*Biblos Basileion* (Gr) 467
*Biterolf and Dietleib* (MHG) 17, 18, 317
*Bjarkamál* (ON) 156, 157
Boccaccio, Giovanni 373–77
– *Filostrato* (It) 376
– *Ninfale fiesolano* (It) 376
– *Teseida* (It) 376, 377
*Boèce* (Pr) 360
Boethius 304
Boiardo, Matteo-Maria 376, 379, 381, 383
Boniface, St 82
*Bonny Baby Livingston* (Child 223) 447, 448
book-epic / *Buchepos* 10, 164, 314, 315
*Book of Memories* (Heb) 514
*Boyhood Deeds of Finn* (Ir) 287
*Branwen Uerch Lyr* (W) 209–11, 218
Brentano, Clemens 43
broadsides 429, 430–32, 435, 440–42, 445, 449–51
*Brot af Sigurðarkviðu* (ON) 263
*Brown Adam* (Child 98) 447
*Brunanburh* (OE) 269
*Buch von Bern* (MHG) 301, 307, 315, 317, 318
Bucharest Bible (Rom) 394
bucolic poetry 586, 587
buffoon 172, 174, 183, 718
*bufos* 183

*bylina*  6, 22, 24, 28, 30, 34–37, 174, 187, 485, 486, 488–91, 494, 496
Byzantine Iliad (Gr) (*ByzIl*)  469

Caedmon  31, 122–127, 136, 221–23
– *Caedmon's Hymn* (OE)  122–27
Caesar  279, 280, 290
*Cambridge Songs*  536, 537
Cancioneiro da Ajuda see Manuscripts
Cancioneiro da Biblioteca Nacional see Manuscripts
*canso*  32, 176, 177, 532, 533
*Cantar (Poema) de Mio Cid* (Sp)  16, 206, 209, 416–23, 425
*Cantar de Roncesvalles* (Sp)  417
*Cantare dei cantari* (It)  177, 179, 185, 188, 190, 377, 378
*Cantare di Florio e Biancifiore* (It)  382
*Cantare di Florio e Platzia flore* (It)  469
*Cantari di Carduino* (It)  379
*Cantari di Griselda* (It)  382
*cantastorie*  173, 190
*cântece bătrânești*  387
*Cântecul nașului* (Rom)  398
Cantemir, Dimitrie  397, 400, 401
*canterino*  173, 190, 372, 377, 378, 380–84
*cantiga de amigo*  50, 51, 526, 527, 534, 541, 543
*cantiga de amor*  526, 527
*cantiga de loor*  51
*cantus gestualis*  186, 366
*Canu Heledd* (W)  528
Carducci, Giosue  375
*Carmen Campi Doctoris*  420
*Carmina Burana*  536, 537, 589, 591, 592
carnival  15, 327, 328, 705, 717
carol  40, 45, 48, 337, 544, 559, 570–77
*carole*  45, 560
Cassiodorus  107
– *Variae*  107
Cercamon  31, 180, 182, 190
Cervantes  683
– *Don Quixote*  683
*Chanson d'Aspremont* (OF)  17, 18, 20
*chanson d'aventure*  430, 534, 544, 571
*chanson de croisade*  534
*chanson de délaissée*  534, 536, 544
*chanson de femme*  521, 524, 532, 533, 534, 541, 583
*Chanson de Guillaume* (OF)  354, 362

*chanson de mal-mariée*  532, 534, 583
*chanson de rencontre*  584, 589, 591
*Chanson de Roland* (OF)  16, 53, 84, 205–9, 211, 354–56, 358, 359, 363, 365–67, 516
*chanson de toile*  430, 534, 583, 584
*chantefable*  21, 187
*Charidemos* (Gr)  462
Charles d'Orléans  45, 46
charms  15, 33, 51, 92, 240, 241, 243, 258, 268, 302, 545
*Charroi de Nîmes* (OF)  354
charters  4, 14, 106, 111, 395
Chartier: see Alain Chartier
Chaucer, Geoffrey  4, 19, 20, 88, 92, 341, 348, 681
– *Astrolabe* (ME)  4
– *Book of the Duchess* (ME)  341
– *Canterbury Tales* (ME)  88, 681
– *Sir Thopas* (ME)  88, 348
– *Troilus and Criseyde* (ME)  20, 88, 341
*chelidonismata*  230, 233
*Chester Mystery Cycle* (ME)  707, 710, 714
*Child Waters* (Child 63)  447, 448
*Chira Chiralina* (Rom)  398
Chrétien de Troyes  16, 306
– *Erec et Enide* (OF)  177, 306
*Christ and the Samaritan Woman* (OHG)  303
*Christ before Annas and Caiaphas* (ME)  712
Christine de Pisan  46
Christoph Egenolf  310
*Christos Paschon* (Gr)  462
*Chronicle of the Morea* (Gr) (*CoM*)  469, 470, 471, 473, 475, 476
*Chronicle of Tocco* (Gr) (*ChTocco*)  469, 476
Cicero  108
– *De Oratore*  108
Cielo d'Alcamo  583
*Clerk Colvill* (Child 42)  35
*coblas doblas*  587
Codex Buranus see Manuscripts
Codex Regius see Manuscripts
*Codrean* (Rom)  402
Colin Muset  181, 182
Collection of Kirsha Danilov (Ru)  485
Columba, St  110, 286, 288–90
*commedia dell'arte*  384, 717

Commonplace book of Richard Hill see Manuscripts
communicative event   32, 188, 225
composition in performance   17, 25, 29, 30, 31, 53, 78, 95, 186, 697
Comtessa de Dia   532, 538
*Conde Claros* (Sp)   422
Constantin Brâncoveanu (Rom)   400
contest poetry   30, 115, 116, 128, 129, 228, 244, 587, 694
*contrafacta*   559, 566, 593
*contrasto*   583, 587
*Corbea* (Rom)   398
Cornish Mystery Plays   714
*Corpus Christi Carol* (ME)   577
*corridos*   412
*Couronnement de Louis* (OF)   354, 355
Coventry Mystery Plays (ME)   707
*Creation of the World* (ME)   714
Croce, Benedetto   40, 379
*Cycle de Doon de Mayence* (OF)   367
*Cycle de Guillaume* (OF)   367
*Cycle du roi* (OF)   367

Dallán   288, 289
– *Amrae Coluim Chille* (Ir)   288, 289
dance song   32, 43, 44, 45, 532–34, 559–62, 565, 571, 572, 577, 583
*Dānişmend-nāme* (T)   686
Dante Alighieri   150, 237, 372, 375, 376, 382, 385, 512
– *De vulgari eloquentia*   372
– *Divina Commedia* (It)   237, 372, 376, 382
*Dārāb-nāma* (P)   654, 660, 662, 666, 667, 668, 669, 672, 673
*Darmstädter Aventiurenverzeichnis* (MHG)   315
*dāstān*   653, 658–65, 667–70, 672, 674, 696
*Daurel e Beton* (Pr)   181
dawn songs   322, 532, 539
*De Heinrico*   303, 313
*Dede Korkut* (T)   683, 687–95, 697
*Delgadina* (Sp)   411
*Deor* (OE)   157–59
Der Marner   188, 317, 320
Der von Kürenberg   538, 540
Der Wunderer (MHG)   317
*Des Knaben Wunderhorn*   310

Deschamps see Eustache Deschamps
*descort*   176, 177
*despedida*   541, 544
*Deux bordeors ribauz* (OF)   178
*Dietrichs Flucht* (MHG)   317
*Digenis Akritis* (Gr) (*DA*)   232, 243, 460–66, 470–77, 694
Diodorus Siculus   280
*disour*   173
*Dobrişan* (Rom)   398
*Dobrynya Nikitich* (Ru)   37
*Doicin bolnavul* (Rom)   398
*doina*   52
Dom Denis   51
Domenico da Prato   374
Donatus   110
*drápa*   152, 222
*Dresdner Laurin* (MHG)   318
*Dresdner Wolfdietrich* (MHG)   318
*Dresdner Wunderer* (MHG)   318
*drótt*   151, 153
*dróttkvætt*   215
*Dukus Horant* see Manuscripts
*duma*   34, 489, 490

*Earl Crawford* (Child 229)   443
*Eckenlied* (MHG)   317, 318, 319
*Ecloga Theoduli*   587
*Edda, Poetic* (ON)   260, 263, 264, 268, 529
*Edige* (Karakalpak)   84
*Edmund of Abingdon*, St   569
– *Speculum Ecclesie*   569
*Edward* (Child 13)   435, 446
*Eger and Grime* (ME)   335, 346–49
Egill Skalla-Grímsson   154
*Egils saga* (ON)   215, 221
Eilhart von Oberg   281
– *Tristan* (MHG)   281
Einarr Skúlason   154
*Einfache Formen* see simple forms
Einhard   10, 114, 116, 303
– *Vita Caroli Magni*   10, 303, 374
*eisteddfod*   30, 116
elegy   81, 149, 159, 163, 270
*El libro de los cincuenta romances* (Sp)   413
*Elveskud* (Da)   444
Endelechius   587
*Enfances Guillaume* (OF)   367
*ensenhamen*   24, 31, 32, 181, 184

*envoi* 46, 180
*erfikvæði* 154
*Espinelo* (Sp) 423
*estribillo* 48, 49, 543
*estribot* 32
ethnopoetics 79, 85, 91, 93, 142, 217, 218, 237
eulogy 150, 151, 157, 159, 163, 164, 269, 271
Euripides 526
Eustache Deschamps 46
Eustathios 231
- *Commentarii ad Homeri Odysseam* 231
Evliya Çelebi 684, 696, 697
- *Seyahat-nāme* (T) 684, 696
*exemplum* 159, 383, 507, 509, 511, 566
Exeter Book (OE) see Manuscripts

*fabliau* 33, 168, 178, 182, 184, 361, 362, 592
*Fáeth Fiada* (Ir) 290
*Fáfnismál* (ON) 157
Farāmarz b. Khudādād al-Arrajānī 661
farce 319, 703, 704, 716
Felice Tancredi da Massa 380
*Femina* (OF) 346
Fernández, Diego 49, 50
*Fierabras* (OF) 343, 360
*fili* 23, 24, 115, 607
Firdausī 39, 653–60, 663, 664, 684
- *Shāh-nāma* 24, 39, 641, 653–60, 663, 673, 684
*First Lay of Guthrun* (ON) 529
*Fīrūzshāh-nāma* (P) 654, 662–68, 669, 671
*Five Joys of Mary* (ME) 572, 573
fixed text 23, 28, 160, 237, 314, 658
*Flamenca* (Pr) 176, 177, 181, 184
Flavius Josephus 72
*flokkr* 152
*Florindo e Chiarastella* (It) 381
*flyting* 158, 257, 269
*folkeviser* 146, 429, 430, 449
folksong 8, 9, 40–43, 46, 50–52, 55, 146, 229, 235, 236, 241, 325, 440, 446, 449, 503, 557, 560, 562, 563, 569, 573, 575, 577, 578
folktale 34, 39, 207, 208, 222, 240, 266, 268, 390, 415, 490, 494, 505, 507, 509, 510, 512, 516, 636, 660, 693, 695

Folquet de Marseille 180
*forme fixe* 44, 45
*Fonte Frida* (Sp) 415
Foscolo, Ugo 380
*Frá dauða Sigurðar* (ON) 263, 264
*Fragment de La Haye* (OF) 367
Franco Sacchetti 372
*Frauendienst* (MHG) 322, 324
*Frauenlied* 521, 522, 524
Froissart see Jean Froissart
Frutolf von Michelsberg 305
*futūḥ* narratives 634, 635, 637, 642, 643, 646, 685
*Futuvvat-nāma* (P) 663

*gab* 583, 585, 588
*Gallarda* (Sp) 416
*Galluslied* (OHG) 302
García Lorca, Federico 49, 50
- *Romancero gitano* 49
Gautier de Coinci 591
- *Miracles de Nostre Dame* (OF) 591
*Gaydon* (OF) 360
*Geißlerlieder* 52
*Genesis* (OE) (OS) 8
*Georgslied* (OHG) 313
*Gerbert de Metz* (OF) 179
*Gerineldos* (Sp) 422
*gestour* 173, 337
gestures 14, 108, 133, 171, 189, 238, 319, 323, 381, 696, 702, 705, 707
*Geta e Birria* (It) 374
*ghazal* 657
Ghigo Brunelleschi 374
Gildas 111
Gilgamesh 390
*Ginevra degli Almieri* (It) 373, 377, 382
*Girart de Roussillon* (OF) 361
Gislebert of Mons
- *Chronicon Hanoniense* 171
*giullare* 173, 177, 178, 183, 185, 188
*gleman / glēoman* 173
*glosa* 543
Goethe, Johann Wolfgang 34
*Gospel Harmony* (OHG) 302
Gottfried von Strassburg 188, 279, 281
- *Tristan* (MHG) 279, 281
Gregory I, Pope 112, 114
- *Moralia in Iob* 114
Gregory of Tours 109

Grimm, Jacob and Wilhelm   34, 263, 264, 267, 310, 317
- *Fairy Tales* (*Kinder- und Hausmärchen*)   263, 264, 310
- *German Legends* (*Deutsche Sagen*)   264
- *Teutonic Mythology* (*Deutsche Mythologie*)   264
*griot*   25, 366
*Guerra dell'Aquila* (It)   381
*Gui de Nanteuil* (OF)   177
*Gui de Warewic* (OF)   348
Guilhalmi   31
*Guillaume d'Orange* (OF)   185
*Guillaume de Dole* (OF)   44, 45, 46
Guillaume de Machaut   40, 45, 46
Guillaume IX of Aquitaine   583, 585, 588, 589
Guiraut de Bornelh   180
Guiraut de Calanso   180, 181, 184
Guiraut Riquier   183
*Gül ile Ali Şir Hikâyesi* (T)   685
*gusan*   175
*guslar*   74, 75, 77, 78, 85, 89, 391, 392
Guthlac, St   122, 123
*Guy and Colebrand* (ME)   348, 349
Guy of Amiens   367
- *Carmen de Hastingae proelio*   367
*Guy of Warwick* (ME)   19, 187, 340, 346, 348

Ḥabīb ibn Aws Abū Tammām   619
*ḥadīth*   23, 616, 630, 645, 647, 665, 667, 668, 685
*Haggadah* (Heb)   502, 503, 504, 516
haiduc songs   389, 401, 402
*ḥakawātī*   641, 642
Hakenstil   259
*Ḥamza-nāma* (P)   654
*Ḥamza-nāme* (T)   684
harper   170, 284, 285, 337, 338, 344, 345
Hartmann von Aue   306
- *Der arme Heinrich* (MHG)   306
- *Erec* (MHG)   306
- *Iwein* (MHG)   306
*Havelok* (ME)   17, 18, 20, 88, 336, 342, 345
Ḥawādith Dimashq al-yaumīya   641
Heaney, Seamus   3
Hegel, Georg Wilhelm Friedrich   38
Heinrich von München   317

- *Weltchronik* (MHG)   317
Heinrich von Mügeln   321
Heinrich von Ofterdingen   307
Heinrich von Veldeke   189
- *Eneas* (MHG)   189
Hektorović, Petar   38
- *Ribanje* (SC)   38
*Heldenbuchprosa*   315, 319
*Heliand* (OHG)   117, 260, 262, 270, 303
Heliodorus   462
- *Aithiopika* (Gr)   462
Herder, Johann Gottfried   43
- *Stimmen der Völker in ihren Liedern*   43
*Herod and the Magi* (ME)   712
*Herzog Ernst* (MHG)   173
Hesiod   390
*Hildebrandslied* (OHG)   10, 53, 116, 262, 300, 303, 313, 316
Hippolytus   526
*Historia Roderici*   418, 420, 425
historical poem / historical song   34, 37, 388, 486, 494, 496
*histrio*   171, 172, 173, 702
*Ḥofuðlausn* (ON)   222
*Holly and Ivy* (ME)   573
holster books   185
Homer   14, 27, 38, 53, 72, 73, 74, 75, 76, 77, 79, 85, 95, 390, 694
- *Iliad*   72, 73, 75, 85, 674
- *Odyssey*   9, 72, 73, 75, 77, 83, 85, 693, 694, 695
Homeric Question   71, 72, 75, 94
*Horn* (OF)   23
*Horn Childe* (ME)   340
*Hughes Capet* (OF)   361
Hugo von Trimberg   317
- *Der Renner* (MHG)   317
*Huon de Bordeaux* (OF)   354
*Hürnen Seifried* (MHG)   315
Ḥusayn-i Kurd-i Shabistarī   654

*Iancu Jianu* (Rom)   402
Ibn al-Athīr   631
Ibn al-Kalbī   631
Ibn Bassām   605
Ibn Hishām   634
Ibn Isḥāq   634
Ibn Qutayba   610
Ibn Qūṭīya   634
Ibn Quzmān   601, 604, 608–23

Ibn Zaydūn   529
*igric*   175
*Il'ya Muromets* (Ru)   37
*Ilincuţa Şandrului* (Rom)   398
*Imberios and Margarona* (Gr) (*I&M*)   469, 470, 475
Imru' l-Qays   614, 630
incremental repetition   432, 451, 541, 563, 569, 575, 576
*ioculator*   117, 167, 171, 173, 175, 183, 187, 348
*ioculatrices*   171
*Iovan Iorgovan* (Rom)   390
*Ipomadon* (ME)   336
Isaac ben R. Eleazar of Worms, Rabbi   511
- *Sefer ha-Gan* (Heb) (attrib.)   510, 511
Isidore of Seville   109
- *Etymologiae*   56
*Iskandar-nāma* (P)   654, 658, 660–62, 664–66, 669, 670, 671, 674
Ives, Charles   40

Jacob ben Nathaniel   513
Jaufre Rudel   32, 581, 582
Jean Bodel   182, 189, 361
- *Chanson des Saisnes* (OF)   182, 361
- *Le Congés d'Arras* (OF)   182
- *Jeu de saint Nicolas* (OF)   361
Jean de Joinville   175
- *Histoire de Saint Louis* (OF)   175
Jean Froissart   19, 46
Jean Renart   44
*Jehan de Lanson* (OF)   355, 357, 359, 361, 362
Jehan de Lescurel   46
Jelāl ad-Dīn Rūmī   682
Jerome   105, 585
*jogelour*   172, 173
*joglar*   23, 24, 31, 32, 173, 180, 181, 182, 183, 189
*jogral*   51, 173, 183
*jongleur*   16, 20, 22, 23, 31, 117, 166–90, 306, 353–68, 391, 392, 592, 716, 717
Johan Zorro   542, 543
Johannes de Grocheio   186, 353, 366
- *De musica*   186
John Chrysostom   525, 531, 534
John Dygoun   563
Joinville see Jean de Joinville

Jordanes   269
*Jovan i divski starješina* (SC)   390
Juan Ruiz, Arcipreste de Hita   608, 621–23
- *Libro de buen amor* (Sp)   90, 608, 621–23
Judah he-Ḥasid, Rabbi   510–13
- *Sefer Ḥasidim* (Heb)   510
juggler   167, 168, 169
*juglar*   173, 176, 178
*jugleor*   167
*Judas* (ME) (Child 23)   450–52
*junačke pjesme*   34, 38
*Junayd-nāma* (P)   654
*Jüngeres Hildebrandslied* (MHG)   313
Juvenal   523

*Kallimachos and Chrysorrhoe* (Gr) (*K&Ch*)   469–71, 473
*Kaiserchronik* (MHG)   305, 307
*Kalevala* (Finnish)   12, 85, 237, 244
*Kalīla wa-Dimna* (Ar)   622
*kaliki*   174
*Katomyomachia* (Gr)   462
*Katzipori* (MHG)   310
Kennedy, Walter
- *Passioun of Crist* (ME)   341
kennings   3, 215, 219
*kharja*   7, 46, 47, 530, 531, 547, 604, 606, 608
*King Ermanaric's Death* (MLG)   313
*Kitāb al-Aghānī* (Ar)   631
*Kitāb al-Maghāzī* (Ar)   634
*Kitāb futūḥ al-'Irāq* (Ar)   634
*Kitāb futūḥ miṣr* (Ar)   634
Komnene, Anna   231
- *Alexias* (Gr)   231
*König Rother* (MHG)   173, 188, 317
Koran see Qur'ān
*Köroğlu* (T)   696, 697
Krist see Otfrid von Weissenburg *Evangelienbuch*
*Kudrun* (MHG)   317, 318, 322
*Kunstsprache*   73, 91, 214
*kveđa*   166

*La Bella Camilla* (It)   379
*La Chevalerie Ogier* (OF)   367
*La Compiuta Donzella* (It)   540, 541
*La Prise d'Orange* (OF)   22

*La Prise de Cordres* (OF)   19
*lai*   23, 33,115, 166, 167, 176, 177, 188, 285
lament   37, 85, 222, 226–8, 241, 342, 405, 521, 527, 528, 531, 535, 540, 541, 543, 547, 563, 564, 568, 569, 607, 611, 614, 694
Langland, William   338, 339
– *Piers Plowman* (ME)   338, 340
Langton , Stephen   44
*lauda*   52, 606
*Laurin* (MHG)   307, 317–19
*lausavísur*   269
*läutar*   174, 388, 389, 390, 391, 392, 394, 395, 396, 397, 398, 399, 400, 401, 402, 403, 404, 405, 406, 407
Lay of Hildebrand see *Hildebrandslied*
Layamon   86, 87
– *Brut* (ME)   86, 87
*Le Couronnement de Louis* (OF)   354
*Leggenda di Vergogna* (It)   383
*Les Narbonnais* (OF)   368
Lewis, C. S.   203, 204, 223
– *Chronicles of Narnia*   203
*Leys d'Amors* (Pr)   32
*Libro de Alexandre* (Sp)   523
*Libro de Apolonio* (Sp)   523
Life of Æthelberht   158, 159
*Liombruno* (It)   373, 377, 378, 381
*Livistros and Rhodamne* (Gr) (*L&R*)   469–73, 475, 477
*ljóðaháttr*   157
Llyfr Aneirin see Manucripts
Llywarch Hen   528
Lönnrot, Elias   85
*Lord Randal* (Child 12)   435
Lucian   280, 462
– *Heracles*   280
*Ludwigslied* (OHG)   269, 300, 303, 313

*Mabinogi* see *Branwen Uerch Lyr*
macaronic poems   313, 536, 570
Machaut see Guillaume de Machaut
Macpherson, James   37
– *Ossian*   37
*Mädchenlied*   539
*Madonna Eléna* (It)   381, 382
*maghāzī* narratives   634, 635, 636, 642, 643, 647
Maid in Sorrow   442

Maimonides   507
Makrembolites   462
– *Hysmene and Hysmenias* (Gr) (*H&H*)   462, 466, 473
*Manas* (Kirghiz)   27
Manūchihr Khān Ḥakīm   654
Manuscripts:
– Aberystwyth, National Lib. of Wales MS Peniarth 4 (White Book of Rhydderch)   209, 211
– Brussels, Royal Library MS 1650   172
– Cambrai, Bibl. Municipale MS 619   106
– Cambridge, Jesus College MS 13   565
– Cambridge, Trinity College MS B.1.45   558
– Cambridge, Trinity College B. 14. 39 (James 323)   452, 565, 576
– Cambridge, Trinity College MS O.2.1   558
– Cambridge, University Lib. MS Ff.1.17   564
– Cambridge, University Lib. MS Ii.3.8   559, 564
– Cambridge, University Lib. MS T-S 10. K.22 (*Dukus Horant*)   175
– Cardiff, Central Libr. MS 2.81 (Llyfr Aneirin)   113
– Dresden, Sächsische Staats- und Universitätsbibliothek, MS Ea.86   687, 688, 690, 693, 695
– Dublin, Trinity College MS 347   565
– Edinburgh, Nat. Lib. of Scotland MS Advocates 19.2.1 (Auchinleck MS)   21, 185, 340, 341, 343
– El Escorial, Real Monasterio, MS j. b. 2   169
– Exeter, Cathedral Library MS 3501   33, 81
– Kassel, University Lib. MS Theol. 54   316
– Kilkenny, Episcopal Palace, Liber Rubeus (Red Book of Ossory)   559–61, 563
– Lisbon, Biblioteca Nacional MS Colocci-Brancuti, Cod. 10991 (*Cancioneiro da Biblioteca Nacional*)   527
– Lisbon, Biblioteca da Ajuda, MS Pert. Col. Nobres/ Comp. Jesus (*Cancioneiro da Ajuda*)   523
– London, BL MS Add. 11579   566

- London, BL MS Add. 27879 (Percy Folio)   335, 346–49
- London, BL MS Arundel 57   570
- London, BL MS Arundel 292   44
- London, BL MS Cotton Faustina A.v   564
- London, BL MS Harley 505   564
- London, BL MS Harley 978   566, 567
- London, BL MS Royal 20 D XI   185, 367
- London, BL MS Royal Appendix 58   571
- London, BL MS Sloane 2593   572, 574–76, 577
- London, Lincoln's Inn MS Hale 135   571
- Madrid, Biblioteca Nacional MS Vitr. 7-17 (*Cid* MS)   206
- Madrid, Palacio Real, Biblioteca, MS 1335 (*Cancionero de Palacio*)   48, 50
- Montpellier, Bib. de l'École de Médicine MS H 196   46
- Montpellier, Bib. de l'École de Médicine MS H 247   367
- Munich, Bayerische Staatsbibliothek Clm. 4660   317, 590
- Munich, Staatliches Museum für Völkerkunde, Preetorius Collection MS L I 284   658
- Oxford, Balliol College MS 354 (Commonplace book of Richard Hill)   572, 577, 578
- Oxford, Bodl. Lib. MS Ashmole 61   338
- Oxford, Bodl. Lib. MS Digby 23   206, 356, 364, 366
- Oxford, Bodl. Lib. MS Eng. poet. e. I   572, 573
- Oxford, Bodl. Lib. MS Laud Misc. 610   282
- Oxford, Bodl. Lib. MS Or. 135   500
- Oxford, Bodl. Lib. MS Rawlinson D. 913   560
- Oxford, Jesus College MS 111 (Red Book of Hergest)   116, 209
- Oxford, Magdalen College MS 60   563
- Oxford, New College MS 88   564
- Paris, BnF MS arabe 3790   639
- Paris, BnF MS fr. 1448   19, 22
- Paris, BnF MS fr. 12615 (Chansonnier de Noailles)   45
- Paris, BnF MS fr. 22543   589
- Paris, BnF MS lat. 1118   169, 523
- Reykjavik, Árni Magnússon Institute of Icelandic Studies, Codex Regius (*olim* MS GKS 2365   4to)   263, 264
- Stuttgart, Württembergische Landesbibliothek, MS HB XIII 1 (Weingartner Liederhandschrift)   324
- Vatican, Bibl. Vaticana MS Ar. 368   621
- Vatican, Bibl. Vaticana MS Reg. 1725   44
- Vatican, Bibl. Vaticana MS Turco 102   687, 695
- Venice, Biblioteca Nazionale Maricana, Misc. 2213.9 (Print)   372
- Vercelli, Biblioteca capitolare, MS CXVII (Vercelli Book)   162
- Worcester, Cathedral Library MS F. 126   560

maqāma   504, 604, 618–20, 622
Marcabru   32, 50, 581–93
*Märendichtung*   319
Marie de France   167, 177
- *Chevrefoil* (OF)   177
- *Les Deus Amanz* (OF)   177
marinha   542, 544
Marino, Giovan-Battista   376
*Marko Kraljević i brat mu Andrijaš* (SC)   38
Marlowe, Christopher   712
- *Massacre at Paris*   712
Maroie de Diergnau   535
Martial   523
Martianus Capella   304
Martin Codax   50, 51, 542, 544
Martin Ginzo   542
Master Thomas   23
maṭla'   606, 615
Matthew Paris   171
- *Chronica maiora*   171
Mayor Arias   544
maxims   14, 310, 689
meddaḥ   52, 696, 697
Meistersinger   190, 320
*Memoirs of the Marquis of Clanricarde*   222
memorization   17, 23, 25–29, 30, 31, 74, 123, 135, 136, 176, 186, 214, 226, 360, 362, 380, 434, 658, 664, 707

Menachem ben Peretz ha-Hevroni   500, 513
Mendinho   542
*menestrel*   170, 173, 178, 179, 181
*menestrier*   175
*Merkdichtung*   33
Michael Glykas   462
– *Eisiterioi* (Gr)   462
– *Spaneas* (Gr)   462
Michael Psellos   232, 233
– *Chronographia*   233
Michel Beheim   321
*Midrash of the Ten Commandments* (Heb)   507, 509, 512, 513
*Midrash Vayikra Raba* (Heb)   508
*mīmos*   174
*mimus*   116, 167, 171–73, 269, 718
*Minnesang*   40, 307, 320–25, 537
minstrel manuscripts   185, 186, 367
mixture of verse and prose see *prosimetrum*
mnemonic   15, 29, 214, 215, 219, 220, 221, 299, 307, 356, 378, 568, 707
*Mocedades de Rodrigo* (Sp)   417
modes of performance   91, 141, 157, 167, 168, 177, 205, 380
*Möðruvallabók* (ON)   215
*Moniage Guillaume* (OF)   354
*Moraima* (Sp)   416
*Moriskentanz*   328
*Morte Arthure* (ME)   257
*Moşneagul* (Rom)   398
mountebank   174, 717, 718, 720
*mouvance*   22, 50, 234, 656
*muʿallaqāt*   614, 630, 637
*mudanza*   48, 49, 606, 607, 620
*mudéjar*   602, 603, 620, 622, 623
*muḥaddithūn*   653
Muḥammad-i Bīghamī   663–65
Muḥammad-i Rāvandī   665
Murūj al-dhahab   665
*musammaṭ*   606
*Muspilli* (OHG)   303
*muwashshaḥ(a)*   46, 47, 530, 604–6, 608

Na Castelloza   532
Nabokov, Vladimir   36
*Nachtbüchlein* (MHG)   319
*naqqāl*   653, 656, 659, 685
Neidhart   703
Nennius   111

neotraditionalism   16, 145
Neri Pagliaresi   380, 384
*Nibelungenklage* (MHG)   314, 315, 317
*Nibelungenlied* (MHG)   231, 516
Niccolò Cicerchia   380
Nikephoros Gregoras   232
– *Byzantina Historia* (Gr)   232
Niketas Eugeneianos   233
– *Drosilla and Charikles* (Gr) (D&Ch)   233, 462
Nissim ben Jacob ibn Shahin, Rabbi   506, 508
– *An Elegant Composition Concerning Relief after Adversity* (Heb)   506, 510, 513
Niẓām al-Mulk   682
– *Siyāsat-nāma* (P)   682
Niẓāmī ʿArūḍī   657, 659
– *Chahār maqāla* (P)   657, 659
Njegoš, Petar Petrović   85
*Norna-Gests þáttr* (ON)   155
*Nota Emilianense*   367
Notker Balbulus   15
– *Liber Hymnorum*   15
Notker of St. Gall   230, 304
– *Gesta Karoli*   230
*Novac and Gruia* (SC)   398
*Nuremberg Haggadah*   503
nursery rhymes   574, 575

*oaristys*   583, 584
*Oghuz Qaghan* (T)   690
*On Good and Bad Fortune* (Gr) (*Peri E&D*)   469, 472, 473
oral aesthetics   13, 79, 80, 81, 94, 95, 204, 208, 229, 353, 357, 363–66, 659, 666
oral composition   29–31, 42, 73, 90, 186, 223, 226, 261, 286, 360, 366, 417, 420, 438, 451, 470, 471, 476, 556–58, 569, 575, 655, 658–60, 667
*Ormulum* (ME)   87
*Ortnit* (MHG)   37, 317, 318
*Ossian* see Macpherson
Otfrid von Weissenburg
– *Evangelienbuch* (OHG)   299, 300, 303
*ottava rima*   177, 374, 375, 376, 380, 381, 383
Ovid   367, 378, 474, 535
– *Amores*   535
– *Ars Amatoria*   535

- *Heroides* 474, 535
- *Remedia Amoris* 535

*Pābūjī* (Rajasthani) 28
Palladius 110
parallelism 21, 48, 50, 143, 217, 218, 219, 362, 521, 541, 575, 576, 639, 686, 691, 692, 693
Paris Glosses 302
*Partenoble de Blois* (OF) 179
Patrick, St 109, 110, 115, 282–88, 290, 291
- *Confessio* 110, 115
Peire Cardenal 180
Peire d'Alvernha 582
*Pèlerinage de Charlemagne* (OF) 354
*Perceval le Galais* (OF) 179
Percy, Thomas 335, 346–49, 439
- *Reliques of Ancient Poetry* 335
Percy Folio see Manuscripts
Pero Meogo 542
Pethachiah of Regensburg, Rabbi 513
Peter of Blois 189
- *Liber de Confessione Sacramentali* 189
Petrarca, Francesco 380, 382
- *Canzoniere* 380, 382
*Petruslied* (OHG) 302
Pfaffe Konrad 306
- *Rolandslied* (MHG) 305
*Phlorios and Platzia-flora* (Gr) (*Ph&P*) 469, 470, 473
*Pierre de Provence et la belle Maguelonne* (OF) 469
*planctus* 317, 355, 358
Plato 459, 525
- *Phaedo* 459
Plautus 374
- *Amphitruo* 374
*pliegos sueltos* 412
Pliny 523
*Poema de Fernán González* (Sp) 417
*poesia popolare* 40, 582
Poggio Bracciolini 371, 372
*Ponzella Gaia* (It) 377, 379
popular culture 15, 85, 229, 231, 232, 233, 384, 429, 506, 555, 577, 584
popular song 41, 42, 46, 49, 52, 231, 235, 237, 402, 450, 545, 555, 559, 560, 562, 566, 568, 570–72, 577
Posidonius 162

Pound, Ezra 180
*Preislied* 269, 270
primary orality 8, 28, 122, 209, 254, 297, 308, 581, 586, 633
Priscus 150, 151, 159, 269
*Prise d'Orange* (OF) 354, 360
Procopius 149
- *Vandalic War* 149
Prodromos, Theodore 462, 466
- *Ptochoprodromika* (Gr) 462, 466, 468
- *Rhodanthe and Dosikles* (Gr) (*R&D*) 462, 466
professional readers (see also *qiṣṣa-khʷān*) 19, 133, 697
*Promptorium Parvulorum* (ME) 172
*prosimetrum* 39, 92, 187, 683, 695
Prosper of Aquitaine 110, 134
- *Chronicle* 110
- *Epigrammata* 134
proverbs 33, 55, 85, 88, 92, 214, 219, 226, 227, 229, 310, 319, 543, 558, 568, 609, 686, 689, 718
Psalms 123, 129, 130, 131, 136, 531
public reading 19, 30, 93, 309, 336, 340, 344
Pucci, Antonio 380
Pulci, Luigi 190, 379, 383
- *Morgante* (It) 190
puppet theatre 52, 181, 183, 184, 671, 720
Püterich von Reichertshausen 318
- *Ehrenbrief* (MHG) 318
*puy* 190

*qaṣīda* 604, 608, 610–13, 617, 618, 620, 622, 630, 657
*qiṣṣa-khʷān* 653, 663, 696, 697
*Qiṣṣat Bahrām Gūr* (P) 637
*Qiṣṣat Fīrūzshāh* (P) 661, 663
*Qiṣṣat Ḥamza* (P) 638
*Queen Dagmar in Denmark* (Da) 444
Qur'ān 23, 499, 629, 631–35, 646, 647

*Rabenschlacht* (MHG) 315, 317, 318
Radloff, Wilhelm 74
*Radu Calomfirescu* (Rom) 398, 399
*Raoul de Cambrai* (OF) 355
Rashīd ad-Dīn 690
- *Jami' at-tawārīkh* (Ar) 690
*Rastbüchlein* (MHG) 310

*rāwī* 630, 635, 645, 668, 685, 697
Rawlinson lyrics 560, 562, 567, 575, 577
*reacaire* 222
reading aloud 18–20, 22,108, 121, 129, 133, 160, 185, 310, 346, 658, 666, 674, 675
*Reali di Francia* (It) 52
Red Book of Hergest see Manuscripts
Red Book of Ossory see Manuscripts
*refrains* 40, 44–46, 48, 49–52, 151, 152, 159, 167, 451, 452, 521, 525, 528, 532–36, 539, 541–45, 558, 562, 570, 583, 584, 588, 592, 604, 606, 607, 610, 614, 615, 618, 620
*regös* 175
*Reinbrun* (ME) 340
Reinmar der Alte 320, 321, 324, 538
Reinmar von Zweter 320
*remendadors* 183
Richard de Ledrede 559
riddles 33, 55, 82, 204, 226, 227, 229, 268, 468, 489, 565, 574, 575, 658, 718
Rilke, Rainer Maria 36
*rímur* 166
Rinaldo d'Aquino 534, 540
ritual dirges 242
ritual *drômenon* 236
ritual song 227, 228, 233, 240, 243
Robert Mannyng 342
– *Chronicle* (ME) 342
*Robert of Cisyle* (ME) 89
*Robin Hood* (ME) 242
*Robin Hood and Little John* (Child 125) 439
*Robin Hood and the Tanner* (Child 126) 440
*Rollwagenbüchlein* (MHG) 319
*Roman de Thèbes* (OF) 32
*Romance de Virgilios* (Sp) 423
*Romance del Prisionero* (Sp) 423
*romances fronterizos* 414
*romaria* 541–43
*Roncesvalles* (OF) 185
*rondeau* 44–46, 534, 535, 606
*Ropstvo Jankovića Stojana* (SC) 398
*rotrouenge* 32, 167
*Ruodlieb* (MHG) 719
Sacchetti, Franco 372, 384, 385
*Sachsenspiegel* (MLG) 307
*Sächsische Weltchronik* (MLG) 170

*saga* 4, 53, 141, 147, 148, 151–56,159, 160, 215, 220–22, 231, 263, 265, 271–73, 283, 305, 313, 631
*Saga of Erik the Red* (ON) 147
Sage 265, 538
*saj'* 632, 643, 683
Salīm-i Javāhirī 654
*saltimbanco* 174
*Samak-i 'Ayyār* (P) 654, 660–62, 664, 669–72, 674
Samuel bar Samson 513
*Sangspruchdichtung* 304, 307, 319–21
*sarāyandagān* 654
Sargado, Rabbi 499–501
*Şarpele* (Rom) 390
Saxo Grammaticus 156, 157
*Scéla mucce Meic Dathó* (Ir) 220
*Schnaderhüpfel* 30, 31
*scholae mimorum* 24
*scop* 3, 92, 96, 146, 159, 163, 164, 298
*scurra* 171, 173
Sebastian Franck 310
*Sefer ha-Kabbala* (Heb) 514
*segrel / segriers* 51, 173, 183, 184
semi-orality 9, 295 ff.
sermon 44, 106, 161, 162, 309, 311, 451, 558, 559, 560, 564, 565, 576, 619, 706
Sestini, Bartolomeo 376
*shā'ir* 31, 629, 630, 632, 641, 644
Shakespeare, William 4, 521, 712, 715
– *Richard III* 712
– *Twelfth Night* 521, 547
*Shalshelet ha-Kabbala* (Heb) 514
Sidney, Sir Philip
– *Defence of Poetry* 190
*Sigenot* (MHG) 317, 318, 319
Simone Prodenzani 375
– *Solazzo* (It) 375
simple forms 33, 227, 268
*Sir Cleges* (ME) 338, 339
*Sir Degre* (ME) 335
*Sir Eglamour* (ME) 335
*Sir Gawain and the Green Knight* (ME) 39, 337
*Sir Generydes* (ME) 185
*Sir Lambewell* (ME) 335
*Sir Lionel* (ME) 439
*Sir Thomas More* (ME) 715, 716
*Sir Triamore* (ME) 335
*Sir Tristrem* (ME) 340, 343–45

*Sīrat al-Ḥākim* (Ar)   639
*Sīrat az-Zīr Sālim* (Ar)   637, 638, 642, 644
*Sīrat Banī Hilāl* (*Sīra hilālīya*) (Ar)   638, 641, 644
*Sīrat Baybars* (*Sīrat al-Malik aẓ-ẓāhir Baybars*) (Ar)   639, 641–45
*Sīrat 'Antar* (*Sīrat 'Antara b. Shaddād*) (Ar)   637–39, 641, 642, 644–46
*Sīrat Dhāt al-Himma* (*wa Baṭṭal* ) (Ar)   637, 641–44
*Sīrat Fīrūz Shāh* (Ar)   637
*Sīrat Ḥamza* (Ar)   684
*Sīrat Iskandar* (Ar)   637
*Sīrat Rasūl Allāh* (Ar)   634
*Sīrat Saif b. Dhī Yazan* (Ar)   638, 641
sirventes   32, 181, 525
skald   146, 151, 155, 156, 158, 163, 298
*Skaldatal* (ON)   151
skaldic poetry   151, 153–57, 164, 166, 219, 256, 257, 262, 269, 495
*Skírnismál* (ON)   157
skomorokh   174, 189
slam poetry   85
Snorri   263
– *Prose Edda* (ON)   263
*Soarele și luna* (Rom)   390
Sofoniy   490
Solomon ibn Verga   515, 516
– *Shevet Yehudah* (Heb)   515
*Son of Armouris* (Gr)   468
*Sonatorrek* (ON)   154
*Song of Bagdad* (SC)   11, 25
*Song of Igor* (Ru) (*Slovo o polku Igoreve*)   36, 37, 55, 485–95
*Song of Songs*   44, 537, 543, 586
songere   163
sottie   715
*Spielmann* / *spilman*   20, 173–75, 189, 393, 523
*Spielmannsepen*   173, 184, 188
*Spielmannsidiom*   214
spilwîf   523
*St Stephen and Herod* (ME)   450
Statius   378, 523
*Storia del calonaco di Siena* (It)   377, 382
Strabo   280
*Sturlu þáttr* (ON)   153
*Sturlunga saga* (ON)   153

Tacitus   254, 257, 269
– *Germania*   254
*Tagelied*   539
tail-rhyme   29, 188, 336, 348
*Táin Bó Cúailnge* (Ir)   290, 607, 623
*Tale of Achilles* (Gr) (*Ach*)   465, 469–72, 474, 475
Taliesin   112
Talmud   499, 505, 506
Tancredi da Massa   380
*Tănislav* (Rom)   398
*taraf*   388, 406, 407
Tasso, Torquato   376
Tatian   302
*tenson* / *tenzone*   30, 31, 32, 583
textualization   8–10, 54, 77, 88, 91, 254, 666
*The Battle of Maldon* (OE)   160, 212
*The Chronicle of Yerachme'el* (Heb)   514
*The Death of Queen Jane* (Child 170)   439
*The Knight in a Deerskin* (Da)   451
*The Lass of Roch Royal* (Child 76)   447, 448
*The Maid Freed from the Gallows* (Child 95)   435
*The Mighty Battle of Mamay* (Ru) (*Skazaniya o Mamaevom poboishche*)   487–90, 492, 493, 496
*The Old Riverside*   446
*The Owl and the Nightingale* (ME)   87
*The Saga of Erik the Red* (ON)   164
*The Seege of Troye* (ME)   336
*The Tale of the Destruction of the Russian Land* (Ru) (*Slovo o pogibeli Russkoy zemli*)   491
*The Unfaithful Husband* (Norwegian)   443
*The Unquiet Grave* (Child 78)   571
*The Wedding of Mustajbey's Son Bećirbey* (SC)   78, 97
*The Wedding of Smailagić Meho* (SC)   16
*The Wife's Lament* (OE)   527, 528, 545
Thegan   116, 117
Theocritus   583, 587
– *Idylls*   583, 587
Theodore Meliteniotes   473
– *To Chastity* (Gr) (attrib.)   473
Thibaut de Champagne   581
*Thidrekssaga* (ON)   37, 313
Thomas of Bayeux   559
Thomas of Chobham   171, 172

– *Summa de penitentia* 171, 176
Thomas of Ely 558
*Three Brothers in Fair Warwickshire* 446
Till Eulenspiegel 708
*Timarion* (Gr) 462
*Toma Alimoş* (Rom) 402
'Towneley' Mystery Cycle (ME) 713, 714
training (of performers) 23–25, 28, 41, 135, 162, 221, 222, 261, 287, 296, 298, 461, 555, 557, 659, 664
*tresgiteor* 167
*Tristan de Nanteuil* (OF) 368
*trobairitz* 526, 532, 535, 544, 546
troubadour 23, 24, 31, 40, 51–53, 176–78, 180–82, 321, 526, 532, 540, 583, 590, 592, 593
trouvère 40, 45, 51, 52, 181, 182, 522, 527, 533
*trovador* 184
*Tryggðamál* (ON) 268
type-scene/ typical scene/ theme 25, 27, 28, 53, 74, 80, 83, 86–88, 94–96, 208, 212, 213, 236, 260, 362, 365, 436
*þáttr* 153, 155, 156
*þulr* 163
*þyle* 163

Uhland, Ludwig 43, 44
Ulfilas 11, 105
Ulrich Fuetrer 318
– *Buch der Abenteuer* (MHG) 318
Ulrich von Liechtenstein 322, 324
*Ultime imprese e morte di Tristano* (It) 381, 382
'Umar al-Wāqidī 634
*Uraicecht na ríar* (Ir) 115

*Vafþrúðnismál* (ON) 157
*Vanto dei paladini* (It) 381
*Vartici* (Rom) 398, 399
vates 117, 306
*Velthandros and Chrysantza* (Gr) (*V&Ch*) 469–71
Venantius Fortunatus 269
verbatim recall 28, 29, 81, 83, 204, 405, 434, 633, 714, 718
Vercelli Book see Manuscripts
*vida* 49, 180, 324, 592
*villancico* 45, 48, 52, 606
Vintsentzos Kornaros 235

– *Erotokritos* (Gr) 235–237, 242
*virelai* 45, 48, 52, 606
Virgil 16, 367, 378
– *Aeneid* 8, 10, 23, 376
*Virginal* (MHG) 317–19
Vital de Blois 374
vocality / *vocalité* 9, 18, 54, 93, 121, 153, 233–35, 237, 255, 363, 364, 674
*Volkslied* 41, 449
*vuelta* 48, 49, 606, 607, 608, 615, 620
Vuk Stefanović Karadžić 34, 38, 390, 398, 402, 405

Wace 166–68, 172, 177
– *Roman de Brut* (OF) 166
Wagner, Richard 365
– *Tristan* 365, 368
Wahb b. al-Munabbih 634
Wallāda 529, 530, 533
Walter of Châtillon 581, 585, 589, 591
*Waltharius* 8, 9
Walther von der Vogelweide 320, 321, 538
*War of Troy* (Gr) (*WoT*) 469, 470, 472, 475, 477
*Wegkürtzer* (MHG) 310
Weingartner Liederhandschrift see Manuscripts
White Book of Rhydderch see Manuscripts
*Widsith* (OE) 268, 269
William of Malmesbury 367, 559
– *Gesta regum Anglorum* 367
Williram von Ebersberg 304
*winileodas* 527, 528, 537
Wolf, F. A. 72, 73
– *Prolegomena ad Homerum* 72
*Wolfdietrich* (MHG) 305, 317, 318
Wolfram von Eschenbach 305, 306, 318, 539
– *Parzival* (MHG) 305, 306
– *Titurel* (MHG) 318
– *Willehalm* (MHG) 306
*Wormser Rosengarten* (MHG) 317, 318
*Wulf and Eadwacer* (OE) 527, 543
Wulfstan 81, 82, 90, 162
*Würzburg Chronicle* 305

*X"adāy-nāmag* (Middle P) 654, 657
*Y Gododdin* (W) 112
*Yon de Metz* (OF) 179

*York Mystery Cycle* (ME)   707, 708, 710–14
*Yosippon* (Heb)   514
Yūnus Emre   682
Yūsuf-i Meddāḥ   696
– *Varqa and Gülşāh* (T)   696

*Zadonshchina* (Ru)   489–96
zajal   46, 48, 52, 55, 529, 585, 588, 604–8, 610–12, 615, 617–23

*Zeitgedicht*   269, 270
*Ženidba kneza Lazara* (SC)   399
zersingen   50, 433
*Zidanje Ravanice* (SC)   399
*zinger un ferleyener*   175
*Zmija mladoženja* (SC)   390
Zuhayr ibn Abī Sulmà   611